Politics in
Europe

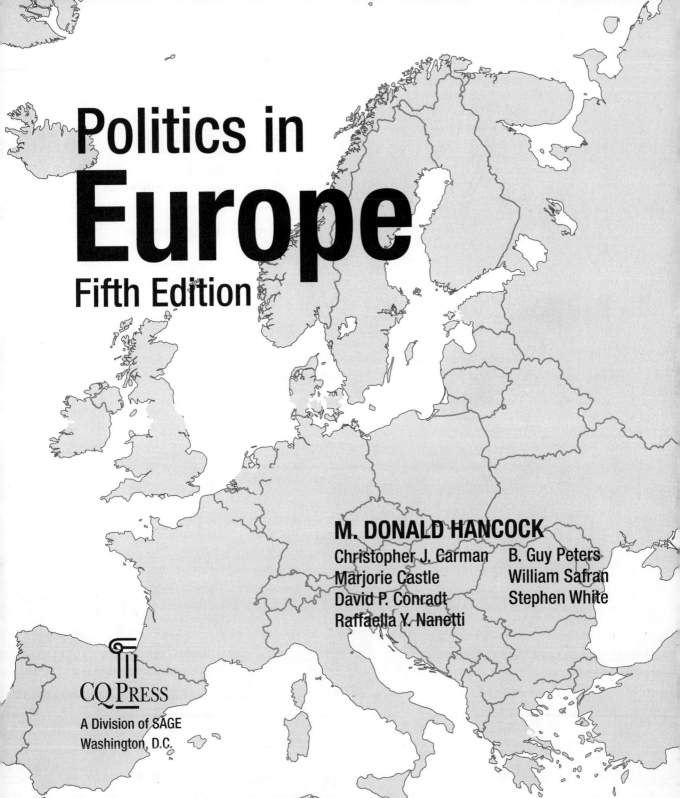

Politics in
Europe
Fifth Edition

M. DONALD HANCOCK

Christopher J. Carman   B. Guy Peters

Marjorie Castle   William Safran

David P. Conradt   Stephen White

Raffaella Y. Nanetti

CQ PRESS

A Division of SAGE

Washington, D.C.

CQ Press
2300 N Street, NW, Suite 800
Washington, DC 20037

Phone: 202-729-1900; toll-free, 1-866-4CQ-PRESS (1-866-427-7737)

Web: www.cqpress.com

Cover design: M Design & Print
Cover photo: iStockphoto/© Nikada
Maps: International Mapping Associates
Composition: C&M Digitals (P) Ltd.

♾ The paper used in this publication exceeds the requirements of the American National Standard for Information Sciences—Permanence of Paper for Printed Library Materials, ANSI Z39.48-1992.

Printed and bound in the United States of America

15   14   13   12   11   1   2   3   4   5

Library of Congress Cataloging-in-Publication Data

Politics in Europe / M. Donald Hancock … [et al.]. — 5th ed.
    p. cm.
  Includes bibliographical references and index.
  ISBN 978-1-60426-611-5 (alk. paper)
  1. Europe—Politics and government—1945- I. Hancock, M. Donald.

JN94.A91P63 2012
940.56'1—dc22   2010051858

Contents

Part 2. France

William Safran

Part 3. Germany

David P. Conradt

Part 5. Sweden

M. Donald Hancock

Part 6. Russia

Stephen White

Part 7. Poland

Marjorie Castle

Part 8. European Union

M. Donald Hancock and B. Guy Peters

8.1 The Context of European Union Politics   623

8.2 Where Is the Power?   639

8.3 Who Has the Power?   657

8.4 How Is Power Used?   666

Tables, Figures, Boxes, and Maps

Tables

Figure

Boxes

Maps

Preface

T HE FIFTH EDITION OF *POLITICS IN EUROPE* CONSTITUTES A comprehensive and timely revision. National elections have been held in all of the case study countries, as well as for members of the European Parliament. New coalition governments have been formed in the United Kingdom, Germany, Italy, Sweden, and Poland, and new presidents exercise power in Russia, Poland, and the European Union. Shifts in executive leadership have been accompanied by varying degrees of policy innovation, ranging from what the *Economist* has proclaimed "the West's most daring government" in Britain to more nuanced attempts to fine-tune public expenditures and tax policies in Germany, Italy, Sweden, and elsewhere. The onset of a severe international economic and financial crisis in 2008 led to plummeting national growth rates, growing budgetary deficits, rising unemployment, electoral volatility, street-level citizen protests, and intensified public debate about immigration. European politics remains, in short, a constantly moving target requiring continuous reexamination and updated prognoses.

Globalization and democratization are central themes of both European history and contemporary politics. As noted in the introduction, globalization has deep historical antecedents rooted in the growth of international trade and commerce. In recent decades globalization has assumed new dimensions, some of them salutary—such as the diffusion of cultural norms affirming greater equality and individual choice—and many of them deeply disruptive—including virulent forms of international terrorism, renewed religious and social conflicts, and increased electoral support for radical right political parties.

A special variant of globalization is the increased salience of Europeanization, as measured by the territorial expansion of the European Union and increased trade and investments by member states both within its boundaries and with nonmember countries. Europe also offers a compelling universe of diverse forms of democratization distinguished by differences in historical sequence, institutional arrangements, and domestic politics.

This edition of *Politics in Europe* addresses these overarching phenomena in various ways. Each of the contributors explores domestic consequences of globalization, as appropriate to his or her analysis, and national paths of democratization. The introduction has been expanded to include a broader treatment of multiple facets of globalization and a comparative assessment of democratization as both process and contrasting system outcomes. The empirical scope of this assessment extends beyond the seven country case studies to the thirty-four European nations (plus the United States and Canada for comparative purposes). Several significant patterns stand out: the contrast between relatively stable democratic transitions in Britain and Sweden and the more tumultuous historical developments in France, Germany, and Italy; older waves of democratization in Western Europe and more recent democratic transformations throughout postcommunist Central and Eastern Europe (including, with qualifications, the Russian Federation); and institutional and political variations encompassing federal versus unitary political systems, parliamentary versus mixed presidential-parliamentary forms of government, and different types of national party systems. Democracy, like capitalism, clearly does not conform to a uniform model.

Part 8 has been substantially revised to take into account sweeping changes affecting the European Union through the implementation of the Lisbon Treaty in December 2009. Drafted in response to the rejection of a more ambitious blueprint for a European constitution by a majority of voters in France and the Netherlands in May 2005, the Lisbon Treaty streamlines and strengthens the EU's legal and institutional foundations. Important revisions include the creation of a presidential office, whose incumbent is chosen by leaders of the twenty-seven member states of the Community; new executive responsibilities accorded the High Representative for Foreign Affairs and Security Policy (the EU's de facto foreign minister); and an expansion of legislative powers exercised by the directly elected European Parliament. Elections to the European Parliament in June 2009 provided the legislative basis for the formation of a new executive-level European Commission, made up of representatives of each of the member states, which exercises an array of refined powers under the Lisbon Treaty.

The international economic and financial crisis that began in 2008 severely strained the political fabric of the Union, especially relations between more affluent member states in the north and laggard performers in the south. Nevertheless, measured in terms of aggregate economic performance, the EU remains one of the world's most powerful economic actors. It is eminently worthy of systematic study.

Features of this Volume

The fifth edition of *Politics in Europe* retains the central emphasis on the forms, instruments, and uses of political power that distinguished previous editions. The volume is organized to facilitate both single-country analysis and cross-national comparisons. Each part is made up of five chapters and structured so that authors address the same set of overarching questions, thereby enabling students to make cross-national comparisons of actors, institutions, and policies. The first chapter in each part introduces the context of case-study politics, including historical patterns of development, democratization, and political culture. The second chapter addresses the institutional and legal basis of power, and the third assesses who exercises power, with a particular emphasis on political parties and organized interest groups. The fourth chapter examines the procedural and substantive uses of power. The fifth and concluding chapter considers the future of national (and in Part 8, EU) politics.

Pedagogical aids include improved country maps, photographs, a set of "At a Glance" boxes profiling the governments and political systems of each country and the EU, the extensive use of tables offering important data, and a comprehensive "For Further Reading" resource at the end of each part. In addition, this edition includes a reference list of political parties in the front matter and an appendix of comparative tables and figures containing relevant demographic, political, economic, and social data on the case studies as well as the United States and Canada. These data are intended to encourage instructors and students to make systematic comparisons among the various countries over time. They also serve as a potential basis for generating hypotheses and initiating research on topics such as electoral behavior, political parties and party systems, and comparative socioeconomic performance. The tables, figures, and maps from the entire book are available to students and instructors at www.cqpress.com/cs/europe. For use in lectures, discussion sections, or student reference, they are easily downloadable in both PowerPoint and PDF form.

Acknowledgements

As with previous editions, my fellow contributors and I dedicate this volume to students of comparative and international politics who are seeking to acquire enhanced knowledge of the European democracies—both old and new—and their responses to ongoing processes of domestic, regional, and global transformation. On a personal note, I would like to thank colleagues on both sides of the Atlantic for sharing their knowledge and wisdom over the years—among them Russell Dalton, Mary Hampton, Henry Krisch, Peter H. Merkl, Bernt Schiller, Helga Welsh, and the late John Logue. A special acknowledgement is due Irek Kusmiserczyk, Ellie Durham, and Matthew McGrath, who contributed important insights into contemporary European politics as analytically diligent and intellectually demanding Vanderbilt students. For their research and editorial assistance, I am grateful to Larry Romans, Brian Boling, and Frank Lester at the Heard Library at Vanderbilt University, and to Victor Supyan at the Institute for the Study of the United States and Canada of the Russian Academy of Science in Moscow. I also gratefully acknowledge the unstinting encouragement and professional assistance of the editors at CQ Press: Elise Frasier, acquisitions editor for international relations and comparative politics; Joan Gossett, senior production editor; Carolyn Goldinger, copy editor; and others who helped keep the project moving forward. Thanks, too, to the reviewers who offered useful suggestions to improve the content and scope of the volume: James L. Newell, University of Salford; William J. Parente, University of Scranton; Martin Rhodes, University of Denver; and Mitchell P. Smith, University of Oklahoma.

—M. Donald Hancock
Vanderbilt University

About the Authors

Christopher J. Carman is John Anderson Senior Research Lecturer in politics at the University of Strathclyde. He previously taught at Glasgow, Pittsburgh, and Rice Universities. His research specializes in the behavioral and institutional aspects of political representation. Carman is coauthor of the forthcoming books *Elections and Voters in Britain* (2011), with David Denver and Robert Johns, and *Of Conscience and Constituents: Religiosity and the Political Psychology of Representation in America* (2011) with David Barker. He has also published a variety of articles on British, Scottish, and American politics and conducted evaluations of Scotland's Public Petitions System for the Scottish Parliament.

Marjorie Castle is author of two books on Polish politics: *Triggering Communism's Collapse: Perceptions and Power in Poland's Transition* (2003) and *Democracy in Poland* (2002), coauthored with Ray Taras. She teaches political science at the University of Utah.

David P. Conradt is professor of political science at East Carolina University. He has also held joint appointments at universities in Konstanz, Cologne, and Dresden in Germany. Among his publications are *The German Polity* (2009), *A Precarious Victory: Schröder and the German Elections of 2002* (2005), and *Power Shift in Germany: The 1998 Election and the End of the Kohl Era* (2000). Conradt has also published a variety of articles and monographs on German political culture, parties, and elections, including "The Shrinking Elephants: The 2009 Election and the Changing Party System" (*German Politics and Society,* 2010).

M. Donald Hancock is professor emeritus of political science at Vanderbilt University. He previously taught at Columbia University, the University of Texas (UT) at Austin, and the Universities of Bielefeld and Mannheim in Germany. Hancock is the founding director of two centers for European Studies—the first at UT Austin and the second, founded in 1981, at Vanderbilt. The latter is now designated the Max Kade Center for European and German Studies (at which Hancock has also served as associate director for outreach activities). He is coauthor with Henry Krisch of *Politics in Germany* (2009), and coeditor and coauthor of *Transitions to Capitalism and Democracy in Russia and Central Europe* (2000), *German Unification: Process and Outcomes* (1994), and *Managing Modern Capitalism: Industrial Renewal and Workplace Democracy in the United States and Western Europe* (1991). Hancock has served as cochair of the Council for European Studies and as president of the Society for the Advancement of Scandinavian Studies and the Conference Group on German Politics. He is currently working on a collaborative study of energy, societal, and military security in the Baltic region.

Raffaella Y. Nanetti is professor of urban planning and policy (UPP) in the College of Urban Planning and Public Affairs, University of Illinois at Chicago, having served as the UPP director in the 1990s at the time of the creation of the new College. She was a member, with Robert D. Putnam and Robert Leonardi, of the study team that carried out the twenty-year longitudinal study of Italian regional and local institutions from which the concept of "social capital" was empirically derived (*Making Democracy Work: Civic Traditions in Modern Italy*, 1992). Since the mid-1990s she has worked on the application of the concept of social capital to the field of urban planning, focusing on social capital–building strategies to improve institutional performance and to promote and sustain local and regional development.

B. Guy Peters is Maurice Falk Professor of American Government at the University of Pittsburgh and also professor of comparative governance at Zeppelin University (Germany). He has held numerous visiting and honorary teaching positions at institutions across the United States and around the world. His recent books include *The Coordination of Public Sector Organizations* (with Geert Bouckaert and Koen Verhoest, 2010) and *Tradition and Public Administration* (coedited with Martin Painter, 2010). He is also coeditor of the *European Political Science Review*.

William Safran is professor emeritus of political science at the University of Colorado, Boulder. He also taught at City University of New York and at the Universities of Grenoble and Bordeaux in France. He has written numerous articles on French and European politics. His recent books include *The French Polity*, 7th ed. (2009); *Language, Ethnic Identity, and the State* (2005); and *The Secular and the Sacred: Nation, Religion, and Politics* (2002). He is the founding editor of the journal *Nationalism and Ethnic Politics*.

Stephen White is James Bryce Professor of Politics at the University of Glasgow, and also adjunct professor of European studies at the Johns Hopkins University Bologna Center and visiting professor at the Institute of Applied Politics in Moscow. He was president of the British Association for Slavonic and East European Studies from 1994 to 1997 and is chief editor of the *Journal of Communist Studies and Transition Politics*. His recent publications include *Understanding Russian Politics* (2011), *Developments in Russian Politics 7* (coedited, 2010), and *Putin's Russia and the Enlarged Europe* (with Roy Allison and Margot Light, 2006). He is currently working on the implications of EU and NATO enlargement for Russia, Ukraine, and Belarus, and on changes in the political elite over the Putin and Medvedev presidencies.

Contemporary European Political Parties

Parties are listed alphabetically by country; bold-face type denotes the most important parties in terms of governance and/or electoral strength.

United Kingdom

Alliance Party, Northern Ireland
British National Party (BNP)
Conservatives
Democratic Unionist Party (DUP), Northern Ireland
Green Party of England and Wales
Labour Party
Liberal Democrats
Plaid Cymru, Wales
Sinn Féin, Northern Ireland
Scottish Green Party
Scottish National Party (SNP)
Social Democratic and Labour Party (SDLP), Northern Ireland
Ulster Unionist Party (UUP), Northern Ireland
United Kingdom Independence Party (UKIP)

France

Communist Party of France (PCF)
Democratic Movement (MoDem), previously the Union for French
   Democracy (UDF)
Greens
Left Radical Party (RPG), formed from a merger of the Radical Socialist Party
   (PRS) and the Left Radical Movement (MRG)
Movement for France (*Mouvement pour la France*), founded by Philippe de Villiers
National Front (NF), radical right
New Anticapitalist Party (NPA)
New Center (*Nouveau Centre*)—rump of the former UDF outside of MoDem, and
   allied to UMP
Republican and Citizens' Movement (*Mouvement Républicain et Citoyen*)
Socialist Party (PS), democratic socialist
Union for a Popular Movement (UMP), formerly the Union for the New
   Republic, UNR; later renamed the Democratic Union for the Republic, UDR;
   later the Union for the Defense of the Republic, UDR

Germany

Christian Democratic Union/Christian Social Union (CDU/CSU)
Free Democratic Party (FDP), neo-liberal
Greens (die Grünen)
Left Party (postcommunist/radical social democratic), a merger of the former Party of Democratic Socialism (PDS) and the Electoral Alternative Social Justice Wahl (WASG)
Social Democratic Party (SPD)

Italy

Christian Democracy (DC), of postwar historical significance; dissolved in 1994
Democratic Party (PD), formed from a merger of the former Democrats of the Left (DS) and Italian Popular Party (PPI) in 2008
Federation of the Greens (*Verdi*)
Forza Italia (FI), merged into the People of Freedom (PL) in 2008
Italian Socialist Party (PSI), of postwar historical significance; dissolved in 1994
Liberal Democrats (LD)
National Alliance (AN), postfascist; merged into the People of Freedom (PL) in 2008
Northern League (LN), allied with the People of Freedom (PL) in 2008
People of Freedom (PDL), formed from a merger of the former Forza Italia (FI) and the National Alliance (AN) in 2008
Party of Communist Refoundation (PRC)
Union of Christian and Center Democrats (UDC), formed from a merger of the Christian Democratic Center (CCD), the United Christian Democrats (CDU), and European Democracy (DE)

Sweden

Center Party (C), formerly the Agrarian Party
Christian Democratic Union (KDS)
Environmentalist Party—The Greens (MP)
Left Party (V), postcommunist
Liberals (People's Party, FP)
Moderate Unity Party (M), liberal conservative
Swedish Social Democratic Workers' Party (SAP)
Sweden Democrats (SD), anti-immigrant

Russia

A Just Russia, social democratic–centrist; pro-Kremlin
Communist Party of the Russian Federation (CPRF)
Liberal Democratic Party of Russia (LDPR), right-wing nationalist
Party of Russian Unity and Concord (PRUC)
Right Cause, formed from a merger of the Union of Right Forces, Civic Force, and the Democratic Party of Russia (DPR)

United Russia (UR), formed from a merger of the pro-Kremlin Unity Party and
  Fatherland—All Russia; pro-Putin
Yabloko Party, liberal-centrist

Poland

Civic Platform (PO)
Democratic Party (PD)
Democratic Left Alliance (SLD)
Law and Justice Party (PiS)
League of Polish Families (LPR)
Polish Peasant Party (PSL)
Self-Defense
Social Democracy of Poland (SdPl)

European Union

Alliance of Liberals and Democrats for Europe (ALDE)
Europe of Freedom and Democracy (EFD), right-wing Euroskeptics
European Conservatives and Reformists (ECR), anti-federalist Euroskeptics
European People's Party (EPP), Christian Democrats
European United Left Nordic Green Left (GUE/NGL)
Greens/European Free Alliance (Greens/EFA)
Socialists and Democrats (S&D)

Introduction: The Why, What, and How of Comparative Politics

COMPARATIVE POLITICS CLAIMS A VENERABLE INTELLECTUAL TRADITION dating from Aristotle's classification of Greek city-states according to the number of their rulers and the quality of their rule.[1] Throughout its evolution out of successive eras of classical and modern political philosophy into modern social science, comparative politics has served to promote a better understanding of diverse forms of politics. Comparative politics approximates laboratory conditions of systematic observation of political systems and subsystems across space and time by facilitating empirical, normative, and theoretical analysis of their similarities and differences. As Robert Dahl explains, empirical analysis focuses on descriptive data and typologies; normative study deals with the analysis of social values and preferences; and theoretical analysis seeks to formulate and test scientific propositions to promote better understanding of social phenomena and to predict behavioral consequences.[2]

Comparative politics emerged as a recognized subfield within the fledgling discipline of political science in the early part of the twentieth century.[3] Early Anglo-American practitioners concentrated on constitutional norms, institutional arrangements, and largely atheoretical descriptive studies of the established democratic systems of the United Kingdom, the United States, France, and, for a time, Weimar Germany. Their European counterparts, in contrast, were more preoccupied with the critical analysis of social classes, elites, and ideologies as products of industrial and political development and their accompanying political conflicts.[4] A crisis of democracy and the rise of authoritarian-totalitarian regimes throughout much of Europe during the interwar period prompted the exodus of many continental scholars to Great Britain and the United States and the beginning of a synthesis of the Anglo-American and European approaches to social science.

As a result, post–World War II comparative scholarship became increasingly diverse and dynamic. The field was broadened to encompass the study of political parties, interest groups, citizen attitudes, and electoral behavior. Many of the most creative scholars focused their attention on problems of modernization, political leadership, and revolution in the developing countries of Asia, Latin America, the Middle East, and Africa in an effort to devise more rigorous concepts and methods of comparative analysis.[5] Among the important innovations was Gabriel Almond, James Coleman, and G. Bingham Powell's formulation of structural functionalism, a concept based on David Easton's earlier work on general systems theory.[6] Others were Almond and Sidney Verba's path-breaking study of political culture in the United States, Mexico, and three European countries[7] and the rapid growth of survey research as a powerful instrument of political inquiry. A behavioral revolution swept social science and all its subfields, bringing with it new methodologies and a greater emphasis on theoretical analysis.[8]

A central feature of the postwar transformation of comparative politics was the burgeoning growth of area studies programs.[9] New centers for research and teaching were established throughout North America—and at a somewhat laggard pace in Europe—to promote greater academic and practical knowledge of Latin America, the communist bloc, Western Europe, Asia, the Middle East, and Africa. External funding for the centers was partially motivated by cold war largesse on the part of governments, but much support was generated by independent research institutions such as the Ford Foundation, the Social Science Research Council, the Rockefeller Foundation, and the German Marshall Fund. Area studies programs produced generations of scholars as well as young professionals training to enter public service.

European Relevance to Comparative Politics

Throughout the transformation of political science and related disciplines, European studies has remained a core component of comparative politics. A traditional rationale for the relevance of the European experience is the contributions of France, Germany, Great Britain, Italy, Sweden, and other European countries to the basic philosophical, cultural, and institutional tenets of Western civilization. Immigrants from throughout Europe, including Russia and Central Europe, helped to create new nations in the United States, Canada, Israel, Australia, and elsewhere. On a personal intellectual level, many of their descendants understandably look to Europe to comprehend the significance of their national origins and the European roots of their own countries' constitutional and political development.

Europe also provides important insights into the comparative study of what Robert Dahl calls different "paths to modernity."[10] The striking contrast between the success of Great Britain and Sweden in sustaining an evolutionary pattern of political change and the far more tumultuous trajectories of France, Germany, Italy, Poland, and Russia during the nineteenth and twentieth centuries provides crucial knowledge about underlying factors of system change and political performance.[11] During the postwar era, these historical differences have largely yielded to a series of "most similar cases" of political stability that are broadly comparable to other advanced industrial democracies in North America, parts of Asia, and most of the British Commonwealth—thereby providing additional rich comparative data.

Historical and postcommunist patterns of democratization constitute another compelling justification for the study of European politics. Transitions to democracy have assumed many different forms, in Europe and elsewhere.[12] A minimal empirical definition is that democratization is a process by which a political system institutes effective procedures for the selection of leaders on the basis of free competitive elections.[13] Normatively, democratization also entails the institutionalization of constitutional norms embodying the rule of law, respect for minority rights, the peaceful resolution of conflict, institutional transparency, and executive-legislative-administrative accountability. To be effective and reasonably stable, a democracy must embrace elite-mass consensus on these basic principles. European countries provide both positive models and cautionary tales of the democratization process in comparative perspective.

Globalization constitutes an additional compelling reason to focus attention on Europe. Within the world of nations, economic forms of globalization have deep roots. As the authors of a survey by the International Monetary Fund have observed: "Economic integration among nations is not a new phenomenon. Indeed, the increasing integration of the world economy in recent decades can in many ways be seen as a resumption of the intensive integration that began in the mid-1880s and ended with World War I."[14] During the postwar era, globalization accelerated at an exponential rate, propelled not only by an expansion of international trade and the internationalization of labor but also by the integration of world financial, investment, and energy markets.

A significant subset of economic and financial integration is the European Union (EU), whose twenty-seven member states have progressively eliminated tariffs and most other discriminatory barriers to the free movement of goods, services, and people among themselves. In the process, much of Europe has achieved unprecedented levels of material prosperity and regional peace under the authority of the EU as a new center of international (primarily economic) power. Socially, Europeanization has been accompanied by national efforts to promote greater gender and sexual equality among citizens through reform legislation sponsored primarily by moderate left parties and abetted by European court decisions. Among the countries at the forefront of equalization reforms are Great Britain, Portugal, Spain, and Sweden.

At the same time, globalization has myriad debilitating consequences. Many of its critics have publicly protested against globalization's discriminatory economic practices against developing countries and their citizens through oftentimes unruly street-level demonstrations during summit meetings of government leaders from the richer nations. A much more virulent form of deadly assault is the systematic use of international terrorism against public authorities, institutions, and citizens by nongovernmental actors intent on conducting religious and ethnic warfare against Western dominance. The September 11, 2001, attacks in New York City and at the Pentagon and subsequent bombings in Madrid in 2004, London in 2005, and Stockholm in 2010 are territorial extensions of what Samuel P. Huntington has depicted as an epic "clash of civilizations" between the democratic West and religious/ethnic insurgents in the Middle East and Asia.[15]

Increased economic interdependence has also made nations highly vulnerable to recurrent cycles of fluctuations in investments, the viability of financial institutions, market performance, and employment. A devastating example is the international economic crisis that began in 2008 and engulfed the United States, most of Europe, and many parts of the developing world. The average annual growth rate had declined precipitously in virtually all advanced nations by 2009, accompanied by a general increase in unemployment and a surge in public indebtedness triggered by government actions to mitigate the effects of the worst international economic crisis since the Great Depression in the 1930s. (See the tables on comparative economic performance in the Appendix and the CQ Press Web site for this volume, www.cqpress.com/cs/europe).

The Universe of European Democracies

The Political Handbook of the World classifies thirty-four European countries as democracies as defined above. Of this total, three countries are characterized as semi-democracies (Russia, Ukraine, and Georgia); *The Political Handbook* lists one state as a non-democracy (Belarus). Table I-1 provides a cursory overview of basic similarities and differences among the thirty-four cases.[16] They are grouped, from top to bottom, in three categories: (1) West

European countries that joined the European Community between 1951 and 2004; (2) newer members of the European Union (since 2004); and (3) nonmember nations. The United States and Canada are included in the third category for comparative purposes.

Table I-1 reveals a significant distinction among European nations with respect to the timing of their democratic transitions. Seven countries achieved democratization during the latter decades of the nineteenth century or the early part of the twentieth century. All

Table I-1 Typologies of European and North American Democracies

Country	Unitary/federal	Type of government	Contemporary party system	Democratization
Europe of 15, 1951–2004				
Austria	Federal	Parliamentary	Multiparty/limited competition	Interwar/postwar
Belgium	Federal	Parliamentary + constitutional monarchy	Multiparty/hyper competitive	Interwar/postwar
Denmark	Unitary	Parliamentary + constitutional monarchy	Multiparty/hyper competitive	Older
Finland	Unitary	Presidential-parliamentary	Multiparty/highly competitive	Interwar
France	Unitary	Presidential- parliamentary	Multiparty/limited competition	Older/postwar
Germany	Federal	Parliamentary	Multiparty/hyper competitive	Interwar/postwar
Greece	Unitary	Parliamentary	Multiparty/limited competition	Postwar
Ireland	Unitary	Parliamentary	Multiparty/limited competition	Interwar
Italy	Federal	Parliamentary	Multiparty/highly competitive	Interwar/postwar
Luxembourg	Unitary	Parliamentary + constitutional monarchy	Multiparty/limited competition	Interwar/postwar
Netherlands	Federal	Parliamentary + constitutional monarchy	Multiparty/highly competitive	Interwar/postwar
Portugal	Federal	Parliamentary	Multiparty/limited competition	Postwar
Spain	Federal	Parliamentary + constitutional monarchy	Multiparty/limited competition	Interwar/postwar
Sweden	Unitary	Parliamentary + constitutional monarchy	Multiparty/highly competitive	Older
United Kingdom	Quasi federal	Parliamentary + constitutional monarchy	Multiparty/highly competitive	Older

New Member States, 2004–2007

Bulgaria	Unitary	Parliamentary	Multiparty/limited competition	Post-communist
Cyprus	Unitary	Parliamentary	Multiparty/limited competition	Postwar
Czech Republic	Unitary	Presidential/parliamentary	Multiparty/limited competition	Post-communist
Estonia	Unitary	Parliamentary	Multiparty/highly competitive	Post-communist
Hungary	Unitary	Parliamentary	Multiparty/hyper competitive	Post-communist
Latvia	Unitary	Parliamentary	Multiparty/highly competitive	Post-communist
Lithuania	Unitary	Parliamentary	Multiparty/limited competition	Post-communist
Malta	Unitary	Parliamentary	Two-party	Postwar
Poland	Unitary	Presidential-parliamentary	Multiparty/limited competition	Post-communist
Romania	Unitary	Presidential/parliamentary	Multiparty/highly competitive	Post-communist
Slovakia	Unitary	Parliamentary	Multiparty/highly competitive	Post-communist
Slovenia	Quasi federal	Parliamentary	Multiparty	Post-communist

Non-EU Member States

Russia	Federal	Presidential/parliamentary	Multiparty/highly competitive	Post-communist
Ukraine	Federal	Presidential/parliamentary	Multiparty/highly competitive	Post-communist
Georgia	Federal	Presidential/parliamentary	Multiparty/limited cooperation	Post-communist
Switzerland	Federal	Council form/rotating presidency	Multiparty/highly competitive	Older
Iceland	Unitary	Parliamentary	Multiparty/limited competition	Older
Norway	Unitary	Parliamentary	Multiparty/highly competitive	Older
Turkey	Unitary	Presidential/ parliamentary	Multiparty/limited competition	Interwar/postwar
United States	Federal	Presidential	Two-party	Older
Canada	Federal	Parliamentary	Multiparty	Older

Source: Compiled from *Political Handbook of the World* (electronic version: cqpress.com, 2009).

of them are situated in Western Europe: France (except for the interregnum of German occupation and the authoritarian Vichy regime from 1941 to 1944), Great Britain, and four of the Scandinavian countries (Norway, Denmark, Iceland, and Sweden). Fourteen other West European nations experienced stable democratization either during the interwar period (Finland) or after World War II: Austria, Belgium, Cyprus, Greece, Ireland, Italy, Luxembourg, Malta, the Netherlands, Portugal, Spain, Turkey, and West Germany. Eight Central and East European countries have undergone postcommunist democratic transitions. The most successful cases are the Czech Republic, Hungary, Poland, Slovakia, Slovenia, and the three Baltic republics (Estonia, Latvia, and Lithuania). Georgia, Russia, and Ukraine manifest less institutionalized forms of democracy because of irregularities in their electoral processes and a weaker elite-mass democratic consensus.

The historical timing of democratic transitions has important consequences for the development of national political parties and electoral competition. As Richard Rose has pointed out in his comparative study of Europe's new democracies, the formation of modern political parties preceded full democratization in Great Britain and Scandinavia, whereas the emergence of democratic opposition movements to communism coincided with abrupt transitions to democracy in Russia and Central and Eastern Europe.[17] This contrast has yielded sharply different kinds of party systems in the two aggregates: class-based parties drawn at an early stage into democratic electoral competition in the former case, more fragmented party systems based on conflicting national memories, ethnicity, and more exclusive ideological appeals in the latter. These differences are partially reflected in the column on "contemporary party systems" in Table I-1, which contains *The Political Handbook*'s summary distinction between different types of electoral competition: limited competition, highly competitive, and two-party. Much deeper political analysis is required in each case to elicit adequate levels of information and understanding of the effects of these different types.

Two other salient features of European democracies include the constitutional distinction between unitary and federal political systems and between parliamentary and "mixed" presidential-parliamentary systems. As shown in Table I-1, twenty-one of the thirty-four European countries have unitary political systems (that is, political power is concentrated in the hands of national executives and legislatures), and twelve are federal systems (with power shared by national and regional or state governments). The United Kingdom and Slovenia can be considered "quasi-federal" because in both cases significant political powers have been "devolved" from the national level of government to regional assemblies. A second majority norm is the prevalence of parliamentary systems of government throughout Europe: twenty-four countries are parliamentary democracies, and nine are mixed systems with presidents exercising varying degrees of executive power alongside prime ministers who are accountable to parliament. France and Russia are notable examples. Switzerland has a unique council form of national government characterized by a rotating presidency.

The European Union constitutes a thirty-fifth case of European democracy. The EU's equivalent of a constitution takes the form of a succession of treaties among its member-states—most recently the Lisbon Treaty, which entered into effect in December 2009. Politically, the EU is a confederal political system whose division of power between central community institutions and national governments resembles the historical precedent of the United States under the Articles of Confederation (1781–1789). The EU has a distinctive form of executive authority consisting of an indirectly elected president of the European Council (which is made up of the heads of government and/or state of its twenty-seven member states) and a rotating presidency of the Council of Ministers (composed of cabinet officials representing the member states). It also has a directly elected European Parliament that shares legislative powers with the various councils. Earlier criticisms of the EU's "democratic deficit" have yielded to greater accountability and transparency in its decision-making processes and use of power.

Contrasting System Types

Transcending descriptive indicators of democratization and formal legal-institutional norms are three basic types of democratic polities that mediate national decision-making processes and their outcomes: (1) pluralist (Great Britain, Italy, Poland, and the European Union), (2) étatist (France and Russia), and (3) democratic corporatist (Sweden and, to a lesser extent, Germany).[18]

Pluralist Systems

Pluralist democracies are characterized by dispersed political authority and a multiplicity of autonomous organized interest groups representing employers, farmers, labor, and other special interests in relation to the state. In such systems, competitive economic and electoral relations dominate intergroup relations, with most groups oriented more toward short-term material and social gains than intermediate or long-term goals of system transformation. A dominant feature of pluralist systems is political reliance on coalition formation, often with respect to specific policy issues, as a means of maximizing a group's economic or political influence. British examples include historical patterns of close cooperation between the Labour Party and unions and between the Conservative Party and the Confederation of British Industry.

Majoritarian pluralism characterizes political systems dominated by a majority party in parliament, such as during alternative periods of Conservative and Labour governance in the United Kingdom. (This dominant pattern was superseded, at least temporarily, by the formation of a Conservative–Liberal Democratic coalition government in 2010.) *Fragmented pluralism,* by contrast, characterizes systems in which power is dispersed among a multiplicity of parties, none of which is able to command a sustained legislative majority in its own right. Policymaking in majoritarian pluralist systems can yield decisive policy outcomes, whereas political outcomes tend to be incremental and often tentative in fragmented pluralist regimes, with successful outcomes dependent on the strength (or fragility) of winning coalitions. Examples of decisive outcomes in Great Britain are the privatization of most state-owned firms and services under Prime Minister Margaret Thatcher in the 1980s and the more recent constitutional reforms under "New Labour" such as the devolution of degrees of political power to regional assemblies (notably in Scotland). By contrast, the rapid succession of postwar governments in Italy until Silvio Berlusconi's rise to power in 2002 reveals a much more fragile pattern of coalition formation and maintenance. Fragmented pluralism also characterizes the European Union, where neither the large countries nor the smaller ones can consistently dominate ordinary legislation.[19] Fragmented pluralism has also tended to dominate non-European polities such as the United States and Canada.

Étatist Systems

In contrast to pluralist systems, étatist systems are political regimes that embody more centralized authority structures and policymaking processes. A chief feature of étatist regimes is the concentration of bureaucratic power at the apex of the political system, such as in France and Russia. If accompanied by a parallel concentration of executive power, such as in the Fifth Republic of France and in Russia under Vladimir Putin, the former president and now prime minister, the likely result is a high degree of institutional efficacy in the political process. An example was Putin's initiative while he was president to strengthen the political center in Moscow at the expense of regional governments, demonstrating that forceful policies can be more efficiently decided and implemented in étatist regimes than is typically true in pluralist systems. And yet for that very reason these policies can be more readily reversed by an incumbent or a successor government. This reversal was aptly demonstrated during the 1980s and 1990s in France during successive phases of nationalization and privatization in which the government even under the Socialists began returning some firms and services to private hands. Such policies also may be subject to less legislative control than in pluralist systems, because the legislature is not as effective in checking the power of the executive.

Corporatist Systems

Democratic corporatist systems encompass institutionalized arrangements whereby government officials, business groups, and organized labor jointly participate in making economic and social policies. Such decisions are subsequently enacted through executive decrees, legislative endorsement, or both.[20] A Swedish example is institutionalized cooperation among government officials, private industry, and trade unions in implementing an active labor market policy designed to maximize employment opportunities. Democratic corporatist arrangements were introduced in Germany in the late 1960s to stimulate economic growth and price and wage stability in response to sluggish economic performance.[21] By facilitating institutionalized participation by organized interest groups in the political process, democratic corporatism encourages a "partnership" approach to problem solving in specified policy areas, such as economic reconstruction in eastern Germany. Critics, however, fault corporatist arrangements because they tend to bypass legislative channels of representation, impede leadership accountability, and discourage democratic participation by rank-and-file members of trade unions and other mass organizations.[22]

These different system types are relevant for explaining contrasting patterns of socioeconomic and political performance by modern democracies. Without question, many aspects of system performance—including those measured by basic indicators such as annual rates of economic growth, inflation, and unemployment levels—are influenced by external economic and other factors beyond the direct control of national policy actors. A sobering instance was the onset of an international economic and financial crisis in 2008. Nevertheless, national policymaking institutions and processes mediate the domestic economic and social consequences of exogenous trends and events. As political scientist Hugh Heclo has observed in commenting on different national responses to the international crisis of stagflation during the 1970s and early 1980s: "Each nation . . . embarked on a search for innovations in economic policymaking, although each [did] so in its own way.

This recent agitation for economic policy innovation in the midst of constraints provides a good example of what [has been] termed 'structured variation' in public policy."[23] "Structured variation" remains an important feature of European politics, but it has been partially eclipsed by economic and monetary harmonization under the aegis of the European Union and a policy shift toward market-oriented neoliberalism throughout the region.

Choice of Cases

Contributors to this volume concentrate their efforts on a sample of eight case studies from the larger universe of European politics. Their choice is based on a variety of considerations. The first is the traditional inclusion of France and the United Kingdom in most comparative courses on European politics. Both countries have made major contributions to the emergence of Western democracy and continue to play important political and economic roles in regional and world affairs. A second consideration is the significance of Germany as a compelling instance of fundamental system transformation over time. Theoretically and empirically, the German case offers crucial insights into the processes of socioeconomic and political development under successive historical conditions of regime discontinuity, postwar stability in the West, the failure of communism in the former German Democratic Republic, and unification in 1990. Third, the inclusion of Italy and Sweden provides important systemic contrasts with the more familiar case studies because of their distinctive patterns of alternating periods of earlier long-term political dominance by the Christian Democrats and the Social Democrats, respectively. Finally, Poland and Russia's transitions to democracy and a market economy pose fundamental questions about system transformation and performance.

The eighth section of this volume deals with the European Union. Since the early 1950s, institutionalized economic and political cooperation has transformed the European Community into an increasingly important regional and global actor. This transformation is manifest in the completion of an integrated Single Market and the attainment of the Economic and Monetary Union (EMU) accompanied by the introduction of a common currency (the euro). A majority of EU member states have joined the euro zone since its inception in January 1999. The addition of the twelve new member states in Central and Eastern Europe and the Mediterranean since 2004 further enforces the EU's international economic status as both a partner of and competitor to the United States and its other principal trading partners, China and Russia.

A Common Analytical Framework

A major issue in comparative political analysis concerns the most appropriate methodology for addressing interactive themes of economic, social, and political change. One approach, which is largely quantitative, utilizes as many case studies as possible to analyze such themes. Important examples of "large N" studies include Ronald Inglehart's global surveys of the "cultural shift" from predominantly materialist values emphasizing survival and economic security to postmaterialist values embracing a greater appreciation of environmentalism and human rights.[24] An alternative methodology is the utilization of "small N" studies to allow for greater in-depth analysis of particular cases. The authors in this volume have chosen the latter approach, emphasizing the use of political power in eight political systems on the basis of a common analytical framework designed to facilitate both single-case and cross-national analysis. These country and regional specialists have divided their analysis of seven important European nations and the EU along the following lines:

- The Context of _____ Politics. These chapters describe the basic geographic and demographic factors, historical development, democratization, and political culture of each political system studied. The contextual chapters are intended to introduce students to each case study in turn.

- Where Is the Power? In these chapters, readers are introduced to the formal decision-making institutions and implementation structures, including national executives, parliaments, and the civil service. Fundamental differences distinguish the parliamentary systems of Germany, Great Britain, Italy, Poland, and Sweden; the mixed presidential-parliamentary systems of France and Russia; and the unique system of governance in the European Union. Other differences include unitary political systems in France, Poland, and Sweden; federalism in Germany and Russia; and "quasi-federalism" in Italy and the United Kingdom, both of which have devolved power to their regions. Because of its complicated institutions and decision-making processes, the EU also can be classified as "quasi-federal."

- Who Has the Power? These chapters describe the central roles played by political parties, organized interest groups, and electoral behavior in the political process.

- How Is Power Used? Policy processes and policy outcomes are highlighted in these chapters, with an emphasis on the distinctive features of both. Process and outcomes are closely related, but specific political decisions reflect a distinctive range of value preferences produced by historical patterns of development, dominant ideologies, and whichever leaders, institutions, parties, interest groups, and citizen coalitions happen to be most influential in the policy process.

- What Is the Future of _____ Politics? These chapters address the pending effects of changing domestic, regional, and international conditions in each of the cases.

The emphasis on political power will enable students to more easily compare the seven countries and the EU as they "travel" through their comparative course. Accompanying the country sections are photographs as well as tables and boxed features. Taken together, the eight case studies contained in this volume address the most relevant questions of comparative political analysis: who governs, on behalf of what values, with the collaboration of what groups, in the face of what kind of opposition, and with what socioeconomic and political consequences? The European experience reveals illuminating answers to these questions.

NOTES

1. Aristotle, who lived from 384 to 322 BCE, compiled and studied the constitutions of more than 150 Greek city-states in his work *Politics,* which became a classical cornerstone of modern social and political science. For a modern translation, see Stephen Everson, ed., *Aristotle, The Politics* (Cambridge and New York: Cambridge University Press, 1988).

2. Robert Dahl, *Modern Political Analysis,* 4th ed. (Englewood Cliffs, N.J.: Prentice Hall, 1984).

3. Gabriel Almond provides a useful historical account of the emergence of political science in *Ventures in Political Science: Narratives and Reflections* (Boulder, and London: Lynne Rienner, 2002). See also Bernard Brown, "Introduction," in Bernard E. Brown, ed., *Comparative Politics: Notes and Readings,* 10th ed. (Belmont, Calif.: Thompson/Wadsworth, 2006), 1–18.

4. Classical European contributions to comparative politics include Émile Durkheim, *The Division of Labor in Society* (New York: Free Press, 1984; originally published in 1892 as *De la division du travail social*); Karl Mannheim, *Ideology and Utopia: An Introduction to the Sociology of Knowledge* (New York: Harcourt, Brace, 1936, and London: K. Paul, Trench, Trubner, 1936; reprinted in 1985, San Diego: Harcourt Brace Jovanovich; originally published in 1929 as *Ideologie und Utopie*); and Max Weber, a prolific German scholar of bureaucracy, different forms of authority, the role of religion in political development, and numerous other topics. For a sample of his work, see H. H. Gerth and C. Wright Mills, eds., *From Max Weber* (New York: Oxford University Press, 1946). Bernard E. Brown provides an informative and thoughtful overview of historical and contemporary approaches to comparative politics in "Introduction: On Comparing Nations," in his edited volume *Comparative Politics: Notes and Readings.*

5. For a summary overview of innovation in postwar approaches to comparative political analysis, see Ronald H. Chilcote, *Theories of Comparative Politics: The Search for a Paradigm* (Boulder: Westview Press, 1981). Standard sources on the methodology of comparative research include Mattei Dogan and Dominique Pelassy, *How to Compare Nations: Strategies in Comparative Politics,* 2nd ed. (Chatham, N.J.: Chatham House, 1990); Adam Przeworski and Henry Teune, *The Logic of Comparative Social Inquiry* (New York: Wiley-Interscience, 1970); and Robert Holt and John Turner, eds., *The Methodology of Comparative Research* (New York: Free Press, 1970).

6. Gabriel A. Almond and James S. Coleman, eds., *The Politics of the Developing Areas* (Princeton: Princeton University Press, 1960); David Easton, *A Framework for Political Analysis* (Englewood Cliffs, N.J.: Prentice Hall, 1965), and Easton, *A Systems Analysis of Political Life* (New York: John Wiley and Sons, 1965).

7. Gabriel A. Almond and Sidney Verba, *The Civic Culture: Political Attitudes and Democracy in Five Nations, An Analytic Study* (Boston: Little, Brown, 1965). See also its sequel collection of essays by various contributors, Almond and Verba, eds., *The Civil Culture Revisited: An Analytic Study* (Boston: Little, Brown, 1980).

8. A critical assessment of the failure of the behavioral revolution to live up to many of its promises can be found in Lawrence C. Mayer, *Redefining Comparative Politics: Promise versus Performance* (Newbury Park, Calif.: Sage Library of Social Research, 1989).

9. For a more extensive discussion of the role of area studies programs in comparative research, see Almond, *Ventures in Political Science.*

10. Dahl, *Modern Political Analysis.*

11. See Barrington Moore Jr., *Social Origins of Dictatorship and Democracy* (Boston: Beacon Press, 1966); and Charles Tilly, ed., *The Formation of National States in Western Europe* (Princeton: Princeton University Press, 1975).

12. See Arend Lijphart, *Patterns of Democracy: Government Forms and Performance in Thirty-Six Countries* (New Haven: Yale University Press, 1999).

13. This definition of democratization and democracy characterizes a number of texts in political science, especially in American politics. It is derived from Joseph Schumpeter's *Capitalism, Socialism, and Democracy,* which was originally published in 1942. It has been

republished many times, including by Harper and Row (New York, 1976). Schumpeter was one of many European scholars who emigrated from Europe to the United States in the 1930s to escape National Socialism.

14. International Monetary Fund, *World Economic Outlook* (Washington, D.C.: IMF, 1997), 45.

15. Samuel P. Huntington, *The Clash of Civilizations and the Remaking of World Order* (New York: Touchstone, 1997).

16. Table I-1 does not include systems such as Liechtenstein, Morocco, or Vatican City.

17. Richard Rose and Neil Munro, *Elections and Parties in New European Democracies* (Washington, D.C.: CQ Press, 2003).

18. The distinctions among étatist, pluralist, and democratic corporatist regimes are utilized to help explain contrasting patterns of economic policy management in M. Donald Hancock, John Logue, and Bernt Schiller, eds., *Managing Modern Capitalism: Industrial Renewal and Workplace Democracy in the United States and Western Europe* (Westport, Conn.: Greenwood-Praeger, 1991).

19. The reason is the introduction in 1986 of qualified majority voting in many Council of Ministers decisions, which places a premium on bargaining and compromise.

20. Excellent compilations of reprinted articles and original research on varieties of democratic corporatism can be found in Philippe Schmitter and Gerhard Lehmbruch, eds., *Trends toward Corporatist Intermediation* (Beverly Hills, Calif.: Sage Publications, 1979); and in Gerhard Lehmbruch and Philippe Schmitter, eds., *Patterns of Corporatist Policy-Making* (Beverly Hills, Calif.: Sage Publications, 1982). Also see Reginald J. Harrison, *Pluralism and Corporatism: The Political Evolution of Modern Democracies* (Boston: Allen and Unwin, 1980).

21. Democratic corporatism was most fully institutionalized in former West Germany in the form of "concerted action," which involved high-level consultations focusing on economic policy among government officials and representatives of employer associations and trade unions from 1967 to 1977. Since then, formal trilateral policy sessions have been replaced by more informal policy discussions among influential economic actors who are periodically convened at the behest of the federal chancellor. See M. Donald Hancock, *West Germany: The Politics of Democratic Corporatism* (Chatham, N.J.: Chatham House, 1989).

22. From a critical ideological perspective, Leo Panitch argues that corporatism in liberal democracies promotes the "co-optation" of workers into the capitalist economic order and thus impedes efforts to achieve greater industrial and economic democracy. Panitch, "The Development of Corporatism in Liberal Democracies," *Comparative Political Studies* 10 (1977): 61–90.

23. Arnold J. Heidenheimer, Hugh Heclo, and Carolyn Teich Adams, *Comparative Public Policy: The Politics of Social Choice in America, Europe, and Japan,* 3d ed. (New York: St. Martin's Press, 1990), 136.

24. Ronald Inglehart, *Modernization and Postmodernization: Cultural, Economic, and Political Change in 43 Countries* (Princeton: Princeton University Press, 1997); Inglehart, *Culture Shift in Advanced Industrial Society* (Princeton: Princeton University Press, 1990); Inglehart, *Human Values and Beliefs: A Cross-National Sourcebook: Political, Religious, Sexual, and Economic Norms in 43 Societies: Findings from the 1990–1993 World Values Survey* (Ann Arbor: University of Michigan Press, 1998). For a discussion of methodological issues related to large N studies, see Robert W. Jackman, "Cross-National Statistical Research and the Study of Comparative Politics," *American Journal of Political Science* 29 (1985): 161–182.

Part 1

United Kingdom

**B. Guy Peters and
Christopher J. Carman**

The Context of British Politics

1.1

BRITISH SOCIETY AND BRITISH POLITICS ARE OFTEN DISCUSSED IN terms of their tradition, homogeneity, and integration. Some authors have written of the absence of significant social cleavages other than social class and of the presence of a uniform set of political and social values. Others have argued that a consensus exists on the nature of the political system and on the general policies of government. The impression commonly given, then, is one of homogeneity, stability, and indeed of a rather boring locale in which to study politics. The impression of stability was reinforced by the ability of two political leaders—Margaret Thatcher and Tony Blair—to each remain in power for more than a decade. Further, even after the election of Blair's "New Labour" government to a third term in 2005, many Conservative policies remained in effect—enough, in fact, to prompt traditional supporters of Labour to argue that there has been too much continuity in British politics.

In reality, the social and political systems of the United Kingdom are substantially more diverse than they are frequently portrayed, and many of the factors that divide other democracies politically also divide the citizens of the United Kingdom. There are differences in religion, language, regional interests, and perceptions of issues that both mitigate and reinforce the traditionally dominant class divisions in British politics. Those divisive factors have become even more important, because immigration, Europeanization, continuing economic change, and the "war on terror" have tended to increase the salience of the existing social divisions and create new ones. The scandal over expenses claimed by members of Parliament that erupted in 2009 highlighted traditional social class and elite-mass cleavages that simmer below the surface of British politics. Further, the coalition government formed after the 2010 general election adds an interesting dimension to governance in the United Kingdom.

Not only is there diversity, but also the setting of British politics has some seemingly contradictory elements that make the management of government much more of a balancing act than might be thought at first glance. In fact, the genius of British politics in maintaining a stable political system over several centuries is not the good fortune of operating in a homogeneous society but the development of a set of institutions, values, and customs that permit the pragmatic acceptance of diversity and an effective accommodation to change. Historically, these changes were rather gradual, but the pace of transformation accelerated in the late twentieth century. This chapter explores several contradictory elements within the environment of British politics and their relationship to the functioning of the political system.

A United Kingdom of Four Countries

The diversity in British politics stems in part from the fact that the United Kingdom is a multinational state composed of four parts. This section begins, therefore, by introducing some nomenclature with real political importance. The proper name of the nation usually referred to as Great Britain is the United Kingdom of Great Britain and Northern Ireland. Great Britain, in turn, is composed of England, Wales, and Scotland. All are constituent parts of the United Kingdom, albeit rather unequal partners in terms of population and economic productivity. More than 84 percent of the total population of the United Kingdom lives in England, 9 percent in Scotland, 5 percent in Wales, and the remainder in Northern Ireland. More than 90 percent of total wages and salaries in the economy are paid in England, with only 1 percent going to residents of Northern Ireland.

The three non-English components of the United Kingdom, sometimes called the Celtic Fringe, joined with England at various times and various ways.[1] Wales was added first, by conquest, in the early fourteenth century. The English and Scottish crowns were united in 1603 when the Scottish king, James VI, also became King James I of England. The parliaments of the two countries were joined by the Act of Union in 1707. This unification did not, however, terminate the conflict between the northern and southern portions of Great Britain. Scottish uprisings in 1715 and again in 1745 resulted in English occupation of Scotland and the outlawing of some Scottish customs such as the kilt and bagpipes. But these restrictions were removed, at least informally, by 1822, and manifestations of Scottish nationalism have been substantially less violent since that time.

The desire of some Scots (and substantially fewer Welsh) for greater autonomy or even independence did not, however, disappear entirely. A nationalist party began to run some candidates in Scottish elections during the 1880s and gained one seat in a by-election in 1945. Since 1967 the Scottish National Party (SNP) has been able to secure representation in Parliament in every election. During the 1970s the pressure for independence was sufficiently strong to force a nationalist referendum on the issue of home rule. That referendum failed, but the issues of self-determination and autonomy did not go away.[2] As the United Kingdom continued to elect Conservative national governments through the 1980s and early 1990s, the push for home rule among the mostly Labour-voting Scots grew in intensity. Another referendum in 1997 approved the devolution of some powers to a Scottish parliament, which formally took office in July 1999. Although its relationship with the British national Parliament at Westminster is complicated at best, the Scottish Parliament exercises primary legislative authority over most domestic policy areas within Scotland. The relationship between the parliaments and the devolution agreement is far from settled as the SNP minority government, elected in Scotland in 2007, has continued to press for expanded powers and has said it will hold a public referendum on Scottish independence. Wales also received its own assembly in 1997, although that body, being limited to the exercise of secondary legislative authority, has substantially fewer powers than the Scottish Parliament. Devolution in the UK has to some extent been connected with the European Union and its interest in promoting regionalism and the rights of subnational territories in all European countries.

The involvement of the British government in Ireland has had a long and tortuous history. English armies began invading Ireland in 1170; the island was finally conquered in 1603 and was formally joined with Great Britain to form the United Kingdom in 1800. The unity created was more legal than actual, and Irish home rule was a persistent political issue during the second half of the nineteenth century. Political arguments were accompanied by increasing violence and then by armed uprisings against British rule. The most famous of these was the Easter Uprising of 1916, which marked the onset of years of serious violence. After a long period of negotiation, the twenty-six southern counties of Ireland were granted independence in 1922 as the Irish Free State (later the Republic of Ireland), and six northern counties in Ulster remained part of the United Kingdom. But this partition did not solve the "Irish Question." The ongoing tensions and outbreaks of violence in Northern Ireland between Catholics seeking to join with the rest of Ireland and Protestants desiring to maintain their unity with the United Kingdom have been a problem for British government since the beginning of the "troubles." The London government did try in various ways to establish a political settlement, all in the general context of Ulster remaining within the United Kingdom. For a short time, it devolved substantial rule to Belfast and experimented with arrangements for power sharing with Catholic groups. But none of the plans was successful, and they were followed by a return to direct rule and the large-scale use of British troops in Ulster.

After years of mutual distrust, the United Kingdom and the Irish Republic entered into negotiations over the future of Ulster. The Anglo-Irish Agreement signed in 1985 by the United Kingdom and the Republic of Ireland was meant to foster a spirit of compromise, but by itself it could not put an end to the troubles in Northern Ireland. Most of the violence was not officially sanctioned, and therefore formal agreements among governments were unlikely to produce real results. During 1994 the violence was finally voluntarily put on hold, if not ended permanently, first by the Irish Republican Army (IRA) and then by the Protestant paramilitary organizations.

In February 1995 Prime Minister John Major and John Bruton, the *Taoiseach* (prime minister) of Ireland, reached an agreement establishing the conditions for initial negotiations for an enduring settlement.[3] Of this agreement's points, the most important was a democratic means of negotiating a more enduring solution to the ongoing dispute. More immediately, the agreement meant that after several decades of doing so, British soldiers stopped patrolling the streets of Belfast. If nothing else, this halt removed a symbol of the troubles and a continuing irritant for the Roman Catholic population.

Moving beyond the initial cease-fire agreement to more meaningful negotiations proved to be more difficult. Progress toward talks was repeatedly stalled by the British government's insistence that the IRA decommission all its weapons before talks began to demonstrate its commitment to peace and a political settlement. For the IRA, however, decommissioning was equivalent to surrender, because there was no reciprocal demand for decommissioning weapons held by the Protestant paramilitary forces.[4]

A highly significant step toward resolving the question of Northern Ireland was the "Good Friday" agreement of 1998, signed by Prime Minister Blair, the Irish prime minister, the leaders of Sinn Fein (the political arm of the IRA), and the Ulster Unionists. The agreement called for electing a new assembly for Northern Ireland, establishing institutions formed from both the nationalist and Unionist communities, and creating a joint consultative body between Dublin and Belfast to address issues that affect all of the island of Ireland. The most fundamental point was that a greater measure of self-government was to be returned to the province. A referendum on the agreement passed overwhelmingly in Northern Ireland and even more so in a simultaneous vote in the Republic of Ireland.

Peace seemed to be returning to Northern Ireland. Elections were held for the Assembly in the spring of 1999, and in July the executive assumed office, with David Trimble, an

Ulster Unionist, as first minister. The executive also included members of several important parties in the province, including Sinn Fein. Initial optimism over the government proved short-lived, however, when the peace process stalled over the question of decommissioning weapons held by the IRA and the Protestant paramilitaries. In response, London restored direct rule over the province. The political impasse was tentatively resolved when Sinn Fein, in an unprecedented move, called on the IRA in October 2001 to begin decommissioning its weapons. Trimble, who had resigned in July, was reelected first minister in November. After these steps, there was little movement in the peace process until July 2005 when the IRA announced that it was officially ending its "armed campaign" and ordered its units to "dump" their weapons.[5] The Protestant paramilitaries then followed suit.[6] The peace and reconciliation process again moved ahead in 2007 when a power-sharing government was established in Belfast between Ian Paisley, hardcore Protestant unionist and leader of the Democratic Unionist Party, and Martin McGuinness, avowed Catholic republican and leader of Sinn Fein, respectively serving as leader and deputy leader of the Northern Ireland executive.[7] These once sworn adversaries became the face of a more unified and conciliatory Northern Ireland government. Several nights of rioting in Belfast in July 2010, however, reveal that Northern Ireland still has a long way to go before it can resolve the sectarian and political tensions that have driven the conflict.

Preserving the unity of the United Kingdom does not prevent the expression of differences among its constituent parts, and to some degree those differences are enshrined in law and the political structure. Before devolution, each of the three non-English components of the United Kingdom had a cabinet department responsible for its affairs. Most laws were passed by Parliament with separate acts for England and Wales, for Scotland, and for Northern Ireland. This differentiation stems, in part, from the fact that both the Scottish and Ulster legal systems are substantially different from the English (and Welsh) systems, and legislation had to be tailored to conform to those differences. In addition, Scottish and Welsh legislation was treated somewhat differently in Parliament; committees composed of the members of Parliament (MPs) of each of the two regions reviewed the legislation while it was being considered by other parliamentary committees.[8]

With the devolution of many issues to the new legislative bodies in Wales and Scotland, and perhaps Northern Ireland, this system was amended, although not simplified. Most domestic matters—such as agriculture, education, criminal law, social welfare, health care, and the environment—are now handled by the Scottish Parliament, while the British Parliament at Westminster retains the right and responsibility to regulate all policy areas that have national and international implications. The fact that the Scottish "domestic" and UK "national and international" policy areas are not strictly mutually exclusive areas of authority has caused several disputes within and between the Parliaments.[9] Relations between Westminster and the National Assembly for Wales (Cynulliad Cenedlaethol Cymru) in Cardiff are somewhat less strained, because the Welsh Assembly does not hold primary legislative authority, although a referendum on devolving further powers to Wales may pave the way for expanding the Assembly's powers.

Prior to the imposition of direct rule in Northern Ireland in 1972, Stormont, the Northern Ireland Assembly, had a major role in policymaking for that province, and a separate Northern Ireland civil service continues to implement the policies of the government in London. After direct rule, the role of Stormont was virtually eliminated, but one part of the proposed settlement with the Roman Catholic groups was the restoration of some powers to a legislature in Northern Ireland. Northern Ireland's experiences with some of the areas of self-government have, however, revealed cracks in the power-sharing arrangements put in place by the Good Friday agreement. With almost all of the parties in Stormont having ministers in the Northern Irish government, there are few parliamentarians to fill out the role of the "loyal opposition" and question the actions of the executive.[10]

Law, language, and religion differ in the four parts of the United Kingdom. Scottish law is derived in part from French and Roman law, as well as from common law, and various legal procedures and offices differ between English and Scottish practice. Language is also different in various parts of the United Kingdom. Welsh is recognized as a second language for Wales (and all official government documents in Wales must be published in both English and Welsh), although only about 20 percent of the population can speak Welsh and a mere 1 percent speak it as their only language. Some people in Scotland and Northern Ireland speak forms of Gaelic, but it has not been accorded formal legal status, perhaps because only just over 1 percent of the population speaks fluent Gaelic. The Scottish Parliament does, however, allow its members (MSPs) to address the Parliament in Gaelic or Scots (providing they give the presiding officer prior notice) and publishes most of its official documentation in both English and Gaelic.

The established religions of the parts of the nation vary as well: the Church of England (Anglican) in England and the Church of Scotland (Presbyterian) in Scotland. Wales and Northern Ireland do not have established churches because of their religious diversity. The diversity in Wales between Anglicans and various "chapel religions" (Methodism in particular) has not produced the dire consequences of the differences between Protestants and Catholics in Northern Ireland, but it has been a source of political diversity and somewhat different patterns of voting in the principality than in England.[11] These traditional religious divisions are becoming less important as church membership declines, but they are being replaced by differences with non-Christian religions, especially Islam.

Finally, the four components of the United Kingdom differ economically. This difference is less true of their economic structures than of their economic success. Unemployment levels are on average higher in the non-English parts of the United Kingdom (especially Northern Ireland) than in England. Another measure of economic success, average personal income, is lower in all three parts of the Celtic Fringe than in England, and by a large margin for Northern Ireland. Differences in the proportion of the working population employed in manual jobs, or even in the proportion employed in agriculture, are relatively slight between England and the Celtic Fringe. The major difference in employment patterns is the substantially higher rates of public employment in the Celtic Fringe, especially in Northern Ireland. Finally, in economic terms the divide in the United Kingdom is as much between the south of England and the rest of the country as it is between England and the non-English nations. Unemployment rates in some parts of northern England are as high as or even higher than in Scotland or Wales, whereas the southwest and southeast have at times in the recent past experienced shortages of workers (see Table 1-1). London is a special case, having boroughs with some of the lowest (2.5 percent) and highest (11.3 percent) unemployment rates in the country. All these economic differences have political importance, because they create a sense of deprivation among non-English groups within the United Kingdom, as well as among some residents

Table 1-1 Unemployment Rates by Region: United Kingdom, 2009 (percent)

England	
Northeast	8.6
Northwest	7.7
Yorkshire and Humberside	7.1
West Midlands	7.9
Southeast	4.8
East Midlands	6.4
Southwest	5.1
East Anglia	5.5
London	7.5
Northern Ireland	5.7
Scotland	5.1
Wales	7.6
United Kingdom	6.5

Source: Adapted from "Labour Market Statistics, March 2009," *National Statistics,* March 18, 2009, www.statistics.gov.uk/pdfdir/lmsuk 0309.pdf (accessed September 2, 2009).

of northern England. Not surprisingly, these areas have tended to vote heavily for the Labour Party.

Although the differences among the four nations of the United Kingdom are manifested politically, fortunately it is seldom with the violence of Ulster politics. Scottish nationalism did not die entirely after the Act of Union, but has experienced cyclical declines and surges. Votes for the Scottish National Party surged from 1959 to 1974: the SNP at least doubled its vote in every election during that period. In the 1970s and 1980s the SNP's growth rate slowed, however. The party received more than 6 percent of the Scottish vote in the October 1974 Westminster election, but only 14 percent in 1987, some thirteen years and three elections later. In the Westminster elections of 1992, 1997, and 2001, the SNP held steady with slightly more than 20 percent of the Scottish vote (1992, 21.5 percent; 1997, 22.04 percent; 2001, 20.06 percent). With the redrawing of the constituency boundaries in Scotland for the 2005 elections (and Scotland's drop from seventy-two MPs to fifty-nine MPs), the SNP garnered almost 18 percent of the Scottish vote. Although this figure seems to be a drop for the SNP, because of the new constituency boundaries and the fewer number of Scots being sent to Westminster it actually represents a net gain of two seats for the SNP. In 2010 the SNP held this result with 20 percent of the vote and six seats in Westminster. In short, the SNP seems to have secured a position as one of the leading opposition parties in Scotland.

Although Welsh nationalism has been less successful than Scottish nationalism as a political force, Plaid Cymru, the Welsh national party, did win over 13 percent of the Welsh vote in the October 1974 Westminster election. Nationalist voting declined after 1974 but remained a significant factor in these Celtic portions of the United Kingdom. In the 1997 election, Plaid Cymru won 10 percent of the vote and continued to push for the referendum that eventually approved setting up the National Assembly for Wales. The party received 14.3 percent in 2001, but slipped to 12.6 percent in 2005 and dropped again to 11.3 percent in 2010.

Party politics in Northern Ireland, which has been based as much on cleavages of the seventeenth century as those of the twenty-first century, bears little resemblance to politics in the rest of the United Kingdom. Two parties represent the Roman Catholic population, and one is allied with the IRA. Two parties also represent the Protestant majority, varying primarily in the intensity with which they express allegiance to the United Kingdom and distrust of Roman Catholics, especially the IRA. Finally, one party attempts to be a catch-all for the two confessional groups. Some elements of economics and class are in the political party equation—one of the Roman Catholic parties also has a moderate socialist agenda—but the fundamental basis of politics has been religion.

Thus the first feature of the context of contemporary politics in the United Kingdom is that it is a single state composed of separate parts. Unlike the states of the United States, these elements of the union possess no reserved powers—only the powers delegated to them by the central government. This delegation of powers is true even for the Scottish Parliament and the Welsh National Assembly. Although these institutions were created in response to regional referenda, they exert only the authority delegated to them by Westminster. The political system, therefore, remains unitary, while allowing an increasing degree of latitude for the Scottish and Welsh governments and the potential for a greater role for an executive in Northern Ireland. Although the 1997 referendums on the devolution of additional powers to governments in Scotland and Wales appear to have made the unity of the United Kingdom even less problematic, some—especially the current SNP minority government in Scotland—have argued that devolution is merely a step on the path to an eventual Scottish independent state. Indeed, the SNP promised in its 2007 manifesto to hold a referendum on independence before the 2011 Scottish Parliament elections.

Stability and Change

A second feature of the context of contemporary politics in the United Kingdom is the continuity of social and political institutions, combined with a significant degree of change. If a subject of Queen Victoria were to return during the reign of the present monarch, Elizabeth II, he or she would find very little changed, at least on the surface. Most of the same political institutions would be operational, including the monarchy, which has vanished in some other European nations. Laws are still made by the House of Commons and the House of Lords, and a prime minister continues to link Crown and Parliament. Most of the procedures and the vestigial offices involved in making law are also almost entirely unchanged, including the anachronistic outfit worn by the Speaker of the House of Commons (although recently worn by a woman). Political parties, though some new since Queen Victoria's reign, command the important positions in partisan politics. Finally, the majority of the subjects of the queen are still loyal to and supportive of the basic structures and policies of the government.

Yet there is a great sense of change in the UK. The political system has been greatly democratized since Victorian times. When Queen Victoria came to the throne in 1837, only about 3 percent of the adult population was eligible to vote, despite the Great Reform Act of 1832. During the reign of Elizabeth II, almost all adults have been entitled to vote.

Before 1911, the House of Lords was almost an equal partner in making legislation; since then, the House of Lords has exercised far less influence over policy. A Victorian prime minister was definitely *primus inter pares* (first among equals), whereas in the twentieth century collegial patterns of decision making changed to create something approaching a presidential role for the prime minister. The monarchy in Victoria's day still had substantial influence over policy, but today it has been constitutionally reduced to virtual impotence. Finally, but not least important, the United Kingdom has evolved from perhaps the strongest nation on earth and the imperial master of a far-flung empire to a second-class power—economically and militarily—in a nuclear age.

Social and economic trends have paralleled political trends. Just as the monarchy has been preserved, so, too, has a relatively stratified social system that includes hereditary (as well as life) peerages. Meanwhile, working-class organizations such as trade unions have tended to lessen the domination of the upper classes and to generate some democratization of the society as well as the political system. The economic structure of the United Kingdom is still primarily based on free enterprise, but government ownership and regulation have had a significant, if declining, impact. The decade and a half of Conservative Party domination of politics that ended in 1997 weakened the unions and enhanced the power of business interests, and "New Labour" governments under Tony Blair and Gordon Brown did little to strengthen the influence of the unions. One strategy of the Conservatives in their conscious attempts to reinforce capitalism was the spread of wealth in the society through selling off public housing and privatizing public corporations. The Labour government first elected in 1997 continued to follow many of the same policies, albeit for different ideological reasons. It is likely that the Conservative–Liberal Democrat coalition with David Cameron serving as prime minister will continue to pursue moderate, right-of-center policies.

Compared with those of many other industrialized nations, the British economy is no longer the great engine of production it once was. The relative poverty of the United Kingdom, when it is compared with its European and North American counterparts, has severely restricted the policy options available to British government. This is especially true following the global banking and economic crisis of 2009. The government invested a great deal to prop up the financial industry in the UK, sending the public treasury deeply into debt. The coalition government elected in 2010 will have to further restrain public spending if the UK is to bring down the country's massive public debt.

The evolutionary change so characteristic of British political life has been facilitated by the absence of a written constitution. Or perhaps it would be more accurate to say the absence of a single written document serving as a constitution, because many documents—the Magna Carta, the Bill of Rights, the Petition of Right, the 1911 Parliament Act, and the Statute of Westminster—have constitutional status. In addition, the Parliament of the day, expressing the political will of the British people, is able to do virtually anything it deems necessary without the limitations of judicial review that exist in the United States. For example, the Scotland Act and the Government of Wales Act create a quasi-constitutional form of intergovernmental relations that would have been alien to a centralized regime. But such constitutionally unlimited powers have the potential for great tyranny, inasmuch as only other politicians, the threat of elections, and their own good sense restrain governments.

The Blair government undertook to make major changes in the constitution through acts of Parliament. These acts included those devolving powers to Scotland and to Wales and attempts to do the same for Northern Ireland. There were also further reductions in the powers of the House of Lords, or at least a reduction in the number and powers of hereditary peers sitting in that body. And, not least, a limited freedom of information bill that ended decades of secrecy in the government.

Although many aspects of the monarchy and Parliament have changed little, the executive branch of government underwent a revolution during the Thatcher government (1979–1990), and the pace of change lessened little during Major's tenure (1990–1997). Among other changes, large cabinet departments were broken up into "executive agencies" headed by chief executives who could be recruited from outside the civil service or other government organizations. In addition, in major policy areas, such as those covering the National Health Service, market-based instruments were introduced in an attempt to increase the efficiency of those services. Procedural changes also were introduced to improve the efficiency and economy of the public sector. The Blair government embraced many of these changes, with some retreat from the internal markets in health, but with a continuing interest in corporatization and privatization. In mid-1999 the Blair government converted the Post Office into a corporation, a move not dared even by Margaret Thatcher.

Traditional and Modern: The Political Culture of the United Kingdom

In the United Kingdom, much of the ability to accommodate political change while maintaining older political institutions may be explained by its political culture—that is, the values and beliefs that political elites and ordinary citizens have about politics and government. One way of describing this culture is "traditionally modern."[12] Specifically, traditional views are combined with modern elements to produce a blend that, if apparently internally contradictory, appears to produce effective government. This culture has not been static; rather, it has permitted relatively gradual change based on pragmatic acceptance of changing national needs and changing social values. The traditional elements of the political culture are best known, with deference, trust, and pragmatism still important to understanding how the British political system functions.

As for *deference,* the British population is generally deferential to authority. Authority implies citizens' lack of opposition to the actions of their government, or perhaps even positive acceptance of those actions. The British government has, by all accounts, a large reservoir of authority, for few citizens question the correctness of the current political arrangements or the right of the government to make and enforce laws. Because the populace gives *diffuse support* (or trust in the institutions of government) to the political system and is willing to obey laws and accept the authoritative decrees of government, the United Kingdom is a much easier nation to govern than most.

Over the years, the authority of elected governments in the United Kingdom has encountered only a few major challenges, aside from the peculiar politics of Ulster. The trade unions attempted to bring down Conservative governments and their economic and industrial policies, succeeding against the government of Edward Heath in 1974, but not against Thatcher in the mid-1980s. In both attempts, the miners union was central. The miners were able to bring about the changes they desired with the fall of Heath, but a year-long strike against mine closings and working conditions under Thatcher resulted merely in a reassertion of the power of government to make law. Finally, during the early 1990s the Thatcher government's attempt to change the system of local government finance from property taxes (rates) to a per capita community charge (poll tax) provoked political violence and significant tax evasion.

The obverse of the public's trust is the responsible behavior of elected leaders. Government has generally conducted itself responsibly, even benevolently, and, for the most part, has not violated existing political norms. When those norms have been violated, such as when elections were suspended during the two world wars, it has been by broad agreement among the political parties. Responsibility has also meant that parties and governments are expected to deliver more of what they promised in election campaigns than would be expected of American parties. Yet despite relatively broad, diffuse support, specific support for governments and institutions in the United Kingdom has been declining over the last two decades. In response to this decline and to public scandals during the Thatcher decade, Major announced in 1994 the establishment of the Committee on Standards in Public Life.[13] This committee was tasked with monitoring the ethical environment in Westminster and researching and reporting on public attitudes toward government and governance.

Scandals have, however, continued to undermine specific support of elected politicians and civil servants. Many in Britain questioned the Blair government's motivations in invading Iraq, going so far as to call the prime minister "George [W.] Bush's poodle."[14] Further, the 2009 scandal over expenses claims submitted by MPs, with daily revelations in the *Telegraph* newspaper, seems to have further eroded public support for politicians. Certainly the revelations that among some of the MP expense claims were the costs of a "duck island" in a private pond, repairing a tennis court, and moat cleaning caused voters and taxpayers to question the politicians' honesty.[15] Indeed, somewhat over a month after the scandal first broke, the British Election Study's Continuous Monitoring Survey found that 59 percent of survey respondents said that the expenses scandal *proved* that *most* MPs are corrupt.[16]

Events such as the expenses scandals may serve to undermine the traditional British norm of deference over time, but another feature of the political culture that remains secure is *pragmatism*. Although ideologies are frequently spouted during campaigns or in speeches delivered for mass consumption, British politics is extremely practical. Indeed, an empirical, pragmatic mode of political thought has so dominated British political life that the preservation of traditional political institutions such as the monarchy is justified not on grounds that they are right and just but on grounds that they have worked. Even in the more ideological Thatcher government, there were enough turnarounds and changes in policy to illustrate the pragmatic mode of thinking about government at work. This pragmatism certainly infused the Blair and Brown Labour governments in their support of privatization in the public sector, and the political compromises struck to secure the Conservative–Liberal Democrat coalition government all but enshrined the idea of practical, pragmatic politics. Obviously, such a political epistemology will be associated with continual adjustment to changing conditions, thereby helping the system to modify all but its essential features to accommodate a modern world.

The traditional values of deference, trust, and pragmatism exist even in the context of a modern, or even postindustrial, political system. The policies pursued, the presence of mass democracy and mass political parties, a very high level of public revenues and expenditures, and some increasingly close linkages between state and society are evidence of the modernity of the political system. Yet with all that, political leaders are allowed the latitude to discuss and decide political issues without directly involving the public or press. This is a modern democracy, but a democracy that allows an elite to govern and exercises latent democratic power only at agreed-upon times.

Class Politics, But . . .

Social class (meaning primarily levels and sources of income) has been the principal basis of social differentiation and political mobilization in the United Kingdom, although education and ancestry still matter as well. Traditionally, the major partisan alignments in politics are along class lines, with the Labour Party representing the interests of the working classes and the Conservative Party (and to a lesser extent the Liberal Democrats) reflecting the interests of the middle and upper classes. The correspondence between class and party may be less than perfect and has been declining over time, but the generalization remains a useful one.

Social class is both an objective and a subjective phenomenon. Objectively, the United Kingdom has significant inequalities of income, even after the effects of redistribution of taxes and government expenditures are taken into account. According to the World Bank, income inequality rose "dramatically" in the United Kingdom from 1980 to 1990, when it began to level off (but not go down).[17] Yet despite the prominence given to class politics in Great Britain, the inequalities are in general no greater than in many other industrialized democracies. In the United Kingdom, the bottom one-tenth of income earners receive 2.6 percent of total income, whereas in the United States the same proportion of income earners receive only 1.8 percent of total income. The highest decile in the United Kingdom earns 27.3 percent of total income, compared with 30.5 percent in the United States and 23.7 percent in Germany.[18] Great Britain is more class-based, however, in that a larger proportion of British income earners are still employed in industrial working-class occupations (meaning primarily manual labor), whereas the largest single category of employment in most other European and North American nations is now service jobs. Finally, according to some of the most recent evidence, in the United Kingdom intergenerational mobility is, at best, "limited," signifying that younger generations generally do not dramatically improve their class standing relative to their parents' position in their own generation. This limited mobility is, however, not markedly different from that in other European countries, and intergenerational mobility has been declining in the United States as well.

Access to other goods and services is also affected by class considerations, although again, perhaps, not to the extent as in other European nations. In particular, education is class-related, both in the small, elite private sector and in the larger state sector. Access to postsecondary education retains a pronounced upper-class bias, although again less so than in many European nations.

Subjectively, people in the United Kingdom are generally more willing to identify themselves as members of a particular social class than are Americans, who overwhelmingly identify themselves as members of the economic middle class. Issues of all kinds may become polarized on a class basis. Any policy that preserves or extends the privileges and power of the more affluent is immediately held suspect by the Labour Party and the trade unions, even when the policy (such as selling council houses to their current tenants) may have benefits for working-class families as well as the government.

Several caveats must be raised about a simple class model of British politics. The first is that it is changing. The rise of the working classes into the middle class, so obvious in many European nations, is occurring in Great Britain as well. Manual labor is a declining share of the labor force, even though it remains a larger share in the United Kingdom than in many Western European countries. Also, the wages paid to manual workers now often approach or even surpass wages and salaries paid to many nonmanual workers, and manual workers find some of their economic interests served by the Liberal Democrats and even the Conservatives. These changes within the occupational and economic structure may mitigate the impact of class on politics, making class a less resolute predictor of voting behavior across the country.

Other factors also have reduced the dominance of class. The ethnic and regional cleavages based on the national constituent elements of the United Kingdom were noted earlier. Within those cleavages, nationalism in Scotland and Wales has tended to cut broadly across class lines. Also, in 2001 an estimated 3.4 million people of New Commonwealth and Pakistani origin lived in Great Britain, comprising almost 6 percent of the population.[19] These ethnic minorities now dominate many of the older industrial towns such as Birmingham, Manchester, and Nottingham, and in some inner-city schools English is taught as a second language. Because these groups are also multiplying more rapidly than white Britons, the specter of nonwhite domination and the loss of jobs by whites is a powerful weapon for some political groups, especially the British Nationalist Party, which won two UK European Parliament seats in the 2009 elections. Pressure by minorities for representation has already begun to affect the local and national political systems, with the main political parties attempting to court the ethnic minority vote.

Religion also plays a role in British politics. The monarch is required to be a Protestant, which, in practice, has meant a member of the Church of England, though prominent politicians have suggested that the ban on Catholic monarchs instituted in the 1701 Act of Settlement should be repealed.[20] The Anglican monarch (Presbyterian while in Scotland) rules a population that is only about three-quarters Christian and contains a significant Roman Catholic minority. This characteristic has been most visible in Northern Ireland, but cities such as Liverpool and Glasgow also have large and politically relevant Roman Catholic populations. Overall, however, Christianity in Great Britain is, with the exception of Northern Ireland, of decreasing relevance, because only a small and declining proportion of the population actually practices its nominal religion. For many, "Christianity" is a cultural—not religious—identification.

Perhaps even more important, the fastest-growing religions in Great Britain are not Christian of any denomination, but rather are Muslim, Hindu, and Buddhist. As well as affecting political behavior, these new religions raise questions about civil liberties and tolerance in a country without a formal bill of rights. The tensions created by the growing ethnic diversity are not as great as in France or Germany, but they are present nevertheless, and racial tensions are becoming of increasing concern to the police and civil libertarians alike. Ethnic and religious tensions have increased since the July 7, 2005, bombings in London that killed fifty-six people (including the four suspected bombers) and injured

Caroline Lucas, the first Green Party member of Parliament, poses after casting her ballot in Brighton. The May 2010 election was the closest since 1992, with no party winning an outright majority of seats in Parliament.

Source: Luke MacGregor/Reuters/ Corbis

seven hundred people. This was the worst terrorist attack in the United Kingdom since the 1988 bombing of a Pan Am jet over Scotland. The July 7 attacks were followed two weeks later by another incident in which four bombs placed in the London Underground fortunately failed to detonate. The terrorist group al Qaeda claimed responsibility for the attacks, and a video released later showed one of the suspected bombers from the July 7 attacks, all of whom were raised in the United Kingdom, claiming to be a "soldier" waging a religious war to protect Islam. Although these attacks were not as severe as those that brought down the towers of the World Trade Center in New York City on September 11, 2001, they shocked Britons and were the catalyst that dramatically increased religious and racial tensions across the country.

In summary, politics in Great Britain is not entirely about class, but social class is still relevant for politics. The importance of other cleavages varies with the region of the nation (with the Celtic Fringe being the most influenced by other cleavages) and with the time and circumstances of the controversy. That said, politics in Great Britain also may revolve around substantive issues. For example, the green (environmental) movement has not been as powerful in Great Britain as in most of the rest of Europe, but its influence is growing. The Green Party enjoyed some success in the 2003 Scottish Parliament elections (when it won seven seats) but has since seen its electoral fortunes wane, winning just two seats in the 2007 Scottish Parliament elections and 8.6 percent of the vote (and two seats) in the 2009 European Parliament elections. In the 2010 general elections, the Green Party elected its first MP to Westminster (Caroline Lucas, Green Party chair, received 31.3 percent of the vote in the Brighton Pavilion constituency). The nature of the electoral system prevents new parties or social movements from gaining representation in the British Parliament rapidly, but there does appear to be a real interest in issues that go beyond simple class politics.

Conservatively Liberal Policy Ideas

Another apparent paradox about British political life is the "conservatively liberal" nature of many UK policies and policy ideas. For much of the postwar period, members of the Labour Party regularly spoke about the virtues of socialism, and they often sang the "Red Flag" at their party congresses. Members of the Conservative Party regularly spoke about restoring laissez-faire economics, dismantling a good deal of the welfare state, and returning Great Britain to its more significant role in the world.

In practice, however, during the postwar period most of the policies adopted by most of the governments bore a remarkable resemblance. The Labour Party accepted the fact that most of the British economy would be privately owned, and at the same time it pressed for the nationalization of certain large industries and the extension of social services to the disadvantaged. The Conservative Party, while in office, generally accepted the virtual entirety of the welfare state, as well as government ownership of industries such as coal, steel, and the railways. The major deviation from this pattern was Thatcher's Conservative government, which began to sell off government stock in nationalized industries such as British Gas, British Telecom, British Steel, and British Airways and began to encourage local authorities to sell off their council housing to sitting tenants. There also was talk of ending the Post Office's monopoly over the delivery of mail. Meanwhile, some social programs were cut or more stringent requirements for recipients were introduced.

These Thatcherite policies, largely continued by the Major government that followed, represented a significantly more ideological approach to policymaking than has been true for most postwar governments in the United Kingdom. The public water supply system was sold off to the private sector, and some local government services such as garbage collection were contracted out to the private sector under a system of "compulsory competitive tendering."[21]

In something of a return to the traditional British consensual style, the Blair government continued many of the programs of the previous governments. "New Labour" was much less interested in talking seriously about socialism than was old Labour. Instead, there was a good deal of discussion about how to use the private sector to provide many public services and the need to make government more like the private sector. The Blair government pursued the "third way," by seeking to inject "competition" in the system through programs such as quasi-privatization schemes within the National Health Service.[22] Following the 2010 election, the coalition government headed by David Cameron is a clear expression of consensual politics.

Despite the episodic intrusions of ideology, there is broad support for a mixed-economy welfare state. All major political parties favor the principal programs of the welfare state such as pensions, other social insurance programs such as unemployment protection, and the National Health Service. At the same time, the majority of the population accepts private ownership and management as the primary form of economic organization, despite the presence of a (declining) number of nationalized industries. What the parties and politicians appear to disagree about is the proper mix of a mixed economy and just how much welfare there should be in the welfare state.

Isolated but European

One of the standard points made about the history of Great Britain is that its insular position in relation to the European continent isolated the country from various influences and allowed it to develop its own particular political institutions and political culture. The mental separation from Europe was to some degree greater than the geographic separation, and so Great Britain may have looked European from North America, but Britons did not always feel European. The separation of Great Britain from the Continent and from the world can, however, be overstated; as John Major said, "We are only an island geographically." The country has not been invaded successfully since 1066, but it has been deeply involved in European politics and warfare. Also, Great Britain has by no means been insular when dealing with the rest of the world, managing a far-flung empire and even more far-flung trade routes from its little islands.

One of the major changes in the political environment of the United Kingdom has been its entry into the European Union (EU) three and a half decades ago. After two denials of admittance, largely at the instigation of France and Charles de Gaulle, Great Britain joined the EU in 1973, followed by the first advisory public referendum in its history. Joining the EU not only has brought Great Britain closer to its continental counterparts but also has had important domestic consequences, including the introduction of a whole new level of government—some of the previously exclusive rights of Parliament to legislate for British subjects now actually reside in Brussels. In addition, in keeping with the EU's move toward closer integration of the Europe market, some economic decision-making power has been transferred to Brussels. Meanwhile, the move toward greater political integration arising from the Maastricht Treaty of 1992 and the adoption of the euro as a common currency by most EU member states (but not the UK) placed even more pressure on the British government to bring its policies in line with those of the continental countries. The Blair government pressed, if gingerly, for greater involvement in the EU, but it faced stiff opposition from Conservatives and from a largely "Euro-skeptic" population.[23] The British people, more than those of any other nation in Europe, are reluctant to accept any greater economic and political unification by the EU. Great Britain may be a part of Europe, but it maintains some distance (psychological as well as geographic) from its EU partners. In fact, the closer integration with Europe has caused a great deal of controversy, with the Euro-skeptics charging that the Labour government ceded virtually all British parliamentary sovereignty to the European government. As an overt demonstration of this skepticism, 16.5 percent of those who voted in the 2009 European Parliament elections (turnout was only 34 percent of the voting population) voted for UKIP, the UK Independence Party, which advocates separation from the EU.

Great Britain's involvement with Europe has become an important issue in domestic politics. Thatcher lost her office in no small part because of her European policies, but she continued to oppose deeper involvement from the back benches. Prime Minister Major sought to follow the more moderate path of a greater political role for European institutions, but without supporting a more complete political union. Nevertheless, divisions within his party over Europe hastened the downfall of his government. Under the Blair and Brown Labour governments the UK moved more in alignment with the EU, although skepticism remained high.

The UK's position with regard to the European Union is likely to be a major issue of controversy and disagreement within the Conservative–Liberal Democrat coalition. Prime Minister Cameron, while being right of center on most issues, has given Euro-skeptics voice in the cabinet. William Hague, the Conservative foreign secretary, has spoken of "repatriating" powers from Brussels and keeping Europe at arm's length. At the same time, Deputy Prime Minister Nick Clegg, a Liberal Democrat, is an avowed advocate of closer ties to Europe, being a former member of the European Parliament and campaigner for the adoption of the euro in the UK. Of the several points of disagreement between the coalition partners, their relative positions on the relationship between the UK and the European Union may offer the greatest potential for fissures to develop in the coalition.

NOTES

1. See, for example, Richard Rose, *The Territorial Dimension of Government: Understanding the United Kingdom* (Chatham, N.J.: Chatham House, 1982).
2. In some ways, the referendum was designed to fail. Passage required approval by a majority of all eligible voters, not just those actually voting.
3. "A Knock at Number Ten," *Economist,* February 4, 1995.
4. "Peace Comes Dropping Slow," *Economist,* March 18, 1995.
5. "Now IRA Stands for I Renounce Arms," *Economist,* July 28, 2005.
6. Unfortunately, in early 2006 riots once again broke out in Belfast and across Northern Ireland, marking the worst violence seen in the province in seven years. The sectarian riots began in response to a government directive rerouting an Orange Order (Unionist) parade away from a Catholic neighborhood.
7. Alan Cowell and Eamon Quinn, "Two Former Enemies are Sworn to Lead in Northern Ireland's Government," *New York Times,* May 8, 2007, http://www.nytimes.com/2007/05/09/world/europe/09nireland.html.
8. For example, the Scottish Grand Committee deals with the second reading of all Scottish bills. It is composed of all seventy-one Scottish MPs, along with enough other members to preserve the partisan balance found in the entire House. There is a similar structure for Welsh legislation.
9. Although there are agreements about which policy areas have devolved, it will be difficult at times to separate UK law and Scottish law cleanly. For example, education has devolved, but research and science support have not.
10. Mark Devenport, "Stormont's power-sharing flaws," BBC News, September 4, 2009, http://news.bbc.co.uk/1/hi/uk_politics/northern_ireland/8237962.stm.
11. Kenneth Wald, *Crosses on Ballots* (Princeton: Princeton University Press, 1983).
12. Richard Rose, "England: A Traditionally Modern Political Culture," in *Political Culture and Political Development,* ed. Lucian Pye and Sidney Verba (Princeton: Princeton University Press, 1965).
13. The scandals include disinformation about the sinking of the *General Belgrano* during the Falklands War and suspect dealings about the purchase of helicopters from Westland Corporation. See Magnus Linklater and David Leigh, *Not with Honour* (London: Sphere, 1986).
14. Nick Asinder, "Blair battles 'poodle' jibes," BBC News, February 3, 2003, http://news.bbc.co.uk/1/hi/uk_politics/2721513.stm.
15. See the *Telegraph*'s dedicated Web page on the expenses scandal at http://parliament.telegraph.co.uk/mpsexpenses/home.

16. Harold Clarke, Savid Sanders, Marianne Stewart, and Paul Whiteley, "Public Reactions to the MPs' Expenses Claims Scandal: Evidence from the BES-CMS," paper presented at the annual meeting of Elections, Public Opinion, and Parties, August 29–31, 2009, University of Strathclyde, Glasgow, Scotland.

17. World Bank, *World Development Report, 2006* (New York: Oxford University Press, 2006), 45–46.

18. World Bank, *World Development Report, 2002* (New York: Oxford University Press, 2002), 234–235. Country data span the years 1991–1997 and therefore are not wholly comparable.

19. Office for National Statistics, UK, "Census 2001," http://www.statistics.gov.uk.

20. Mark Macaskill, "Gordon Brown aims to end royal ban on Catholics," *TimesOnline,* November 16, 2008, http://www.timesonline.co.uk/tol/news/uk/scotland/article5162693 .ece.

21. Kieron Walsh, *Public Services and Market Mechanisms: Competition, Contracting and the New Public Management* (Basingstoke, UK: Macmillan, 1995).

22. See Anthony Giddens, *The Third Way and Its Critics* (Cambridge, UK: Polity Press, 2000).

23. See David Baker, "Islands of the Mind: New Labour's Defensive Engagement with the European Union," *Political Quarterly* 76 (2005): 22–36.

Where Is the Power?

T HE GOVERNMENT OF THE UNITED KINGDOM IS PARLIAMENTARY, and in such a government executive powers are linked directly to legislative powers. The executive of a parliamentary government is not elected directly by the people but by the legislature. Therefore, voters know that when they vote for a party that achieves a majority in the legislature, the leader of that party is likely to serve as the country's next executive, or prime minister in the case of the United Kingdom. The British people did not elect David Cameron as prime minister in May 2010. Instead, enough citizens voted for Cameron's Conservative Party in their constituencies to make it the largest party in Parliament, but not to control an overall majority of the Parliament's seats. On the night of May 6, 2010, a situation confronted the United Kingdom that had not occurred since 1974—a "hung parliament" with no party having majority control. When the Conservative Party negotiated a coalition agreement with the Liberal Democratic Party, David Cameron succeeded Gordon Brown as prime minister.

The government of the United Kingdom is a parliamentary government of a particular type, described by Arend Lijphart as "majoritarian." [1] The operative tradition is that at least a majority of members of the lower house must at all times support the government. Failing that, a government can remain in power if a majority of the members of Parliament (MPs) do not disavow it in a vote of no confidence. There is little acceptance of minority governments, which have been successful in many other European countries, although this option was considered after the 2010 election. For most of the modern era, the British government has been in essence a two-party system so that governments have generally been composed of members of a single political party. Yet since the 1970s the growing popular support for the Liberal Democratic Party has threatened to produce the need to create a true coalition government. Tacit coalitions have emerged in the past (for example, the "Lib-Lab" agreement during the late 1970s), but since the wartime government of 1940–1945 no true coalition had surfaced until 2010.[2]

If at any time a majority of the members of Parliament decide they no longer want the current government to continue in office, they can remove that government by a vote of no confidence or by defeating a major government legislative proposal. Because the 2005 election produced a large majority of Labour deputies in Parliament, Gordon Brown's removal would have required the defection of members of his own party, an uncommon but not unheard-of occurrence.[3] The possibilities of defection are much higher in a coalition, especially one made up of parties with some fundamentally different policy ideas. Such is the case with the coalition formed in May 2010. The potential of defections is likely to serve as a constant subtext to the coalition government as commentators watch for signs of cracks between the coalition partners.

Remaining the "queen's first minister" requires the continual support of Parliament. If that support is lost, the prime minister and the other ministers must, by convention, either reorganize themselves or go to the people for a new election.[4] Gordon Brown became prime minister through a reshuffle of the cabinet when Tony Blair resigned, but this turn of events is not the norm. Usually, under the doctrine of collective responsibility the government as a whole must resign and a general election held.[5] Individual ministers may be forced out of office by the prime minister for their own particular failures—whether policy, administrative, or personal—but when a government falls, all ministers leave. If a new government of the same party were formed, however, many would soon be back in office.

Another implication of collective responsibility is that government decisions must be made collectively and be supported by the entire cabinet. Ministers are expected to argue for their positions in cabinet, but once the collectivity has made its decision, they must all support that decision publicly. If a member of the government cannot support the decision, then he or she should resign, which Robin Cook, leader of the House of Commons, did over the Iraq war in 2003. Furthermore, ministers are expected to respect the secrecy of the Cabinet Room and not reveal who was on which side in the discussion (a significant amount of leaking and briefing occurs in practice, however). The government is expected to present a united front to Parliament and to the public.[6] Although still the norm, collective responsibility appears to be anachronistic, because policymaking in British government has become dominated increasingly by the prime minister as the government looks more "presidential."[7] The principle of collective responsibility does, however, become more interesting in a coalition government.

One virtue of a parliamentary government, especially a majoritarian one, is that it allows an executive, once elected to office, to govern. In presidential governments—even "semi-presidential" regimes such as that in France—the legislative and executive branches frequently disagree over which body should control a policy issue, but such disagreements rarely occur so overtly in a parliamentary regime.[8] A political executive that cannot command the acquiescence of the legislature will soon cease to be the executive. This unity of the two institutional forces enables a strong prime minister such as Margaret Thatcher to push through policies, such as the poll tax, that are unpopular even within her own party in Parliament.[9] Even less powerful British prime ministers such as John Major or Gordon Brown are able to exert much stronger policy leadership than would be possible in more consensual parliamentary regimes, much less in presidential regimes. And when a prime minister such as Tony Blair has a substantial majority of his or her party in Parliament (355 of 646 seats in the House of Commons elected in 2005), there is an almost unlimited capacity to implement a desired program of legislation, provided the prime minister does not stray too far from that party's traditions and programs.

British Parliamentary Government

Although many political systems practice parliamentary government, each practices it differently. Several features characterize parliamentary government as practiced in the United Kingdom. The first is the principle of government and opposition. With rare exceptions (such as policy affecting Northern Ireland), bipartisanship has little place in this form of parliamentary government; instead, it is the role of the opposition to oppose the government. Even if the opposition agrees with the basic tenets of the government's

United Kingdom at a Glance

Type of Government
Constitutional monarchy and parliamentary democracy, Commonwealth realm

Capital
London

Administrative Divisions
England: twenty-seven two-tier counties, thirty-two London boroughs, one City of London (Greater London), thirty-six metropolitan districts, fifty-six unitary authorities (including four single-tier counties)
Scotland: thirty-two council areas
Northern Ireland: twenty-six district councils
Wales: twenty-two unitary authorities
Dependent areas: Anguilla, Bermuda, British Indian Ocean Territory, British Virgin Islands, Cayman Islands, Falkland Islands, Gibraltar, Guernsey, Isles of Man, Jersey, Montserrat, Pitcairn Islands, Saint Helena and Ascension, South Georgia and the South Sandwich Islands, Turks and Caicos Islands

Independence
England has existed as a unified entity since the tenth century. The union between England and Wales, begun in 1284 with the Statute of Rhuddlan, was not formalized until 1536 with an Act of Union. In another Act of Union in 1707, England and Scotland agreed to permanently join as Great Britain. The legislative union of Great Britain and Ireland was implemented in 1801, with the adoption of the name the United Kingdom of Great Britain and Ireland. The Anglo-Irish Treaty of 1921 formalized a partition of Ireland; six northern Irish counties remained part of the United Kingdom as Northern Ireland. The current name of the country, the United Kingdom of Great Britain and Northern Ireland, was adopted in 1927.

Constitution
Unwritten; partly legislative statutes, partly common law and practice, European law

Legal System
Common law tradition with early Roman and modern continental influences. Has nonbinding judicial review of Acts of Parliament under the Human Rights Act of 1998. Accepts compulsory international Court of Justice jurisdiction, with reservations.

Suffrage
Eighteen years of age, universal

Executive Branch
Chief of state: reigning monarch
Head of government: prime minister
Cabinet: Cabinet of Ministers appointed by the prime minister
Elections: The monarchy is hereditary. National elections to the House of Commons are held at five-year intervals, unless an early election is called at the behest of the incumbent prime minister. After legislative elections, the leader of the majority party or the leader of the majority coalition is usually chosen the prime minister. He or she is formally appointed by the monarch.

Legislative Branch

Bicameral parliament: House of Lords and House of Commons. House of Lords: 740 members, including 622 life peers, 92 hereditary peers, and 26 clergy. In 1999, as provided by the House of Lords Act, elections were held in the House of Lords to determine the 92 hereditary peers who would remain members. Pending further reforms, elections are held only as vacancies in the hereditary peerage arise. House of Commons: 650 seats since the 2010 election. Members are elected by popular vote to serve five-year terms unless the House is dissolved earlier.

Note: In 1998 elections were held for a Northern Ireland Assembly. Because of unresolved disputes among the major parties, the transfer of power from London to Northern Ireland came only at the end of 1999. Recurrent sectarian violence prompted the national government in London to suspend powers of the Northern Ireland Assembly; the latest instance was from 2002 to May 2007. Following elections in March 2007, the Northern Irish Assembly once again assumed full legislative power. In 2007 elections were held for a new Scottish Parliament and a new Welsh National Assembly.

Judicial Branch

Supreme Court of the United Kingdom, established by the Constitutional Reform Act of 2005, began serving in October 2009. The Supreme Court has assumed powers of appellate jurisdiction previously exercised by the Lords of Appeal in Ordinary, which had consisted of members of the House of Lords appointed by the monarch. Other courts include the Senior Courts of England and Wales, the High Court of Justiciary in Scotland, and the Court of Judicature in Northern Ireland.

Major Political Parties

Conservative and Unionist Party; Democratic Union Party (Northern Ireland); Labour Party; Liberal Democrats; Party of Wales (Plaid Cymru); Scottish National Party (SNP); Sinn Fein (Northern Ireland); Social Democrats and Labor Party (SDLP, Northern Ireland); Ulster Unionist Party (Northern Ireland); Greens.

Source: U.S. Central Intelligence Agency, *The World Factbook,* https://www.cia.gov/library/publications/the-world-factbook/.

policy, it still must present constructive alternatives to that policy if it is to do its job appropriately. It is assumed that through this adversarial process better policies will emerge and that the voters will be given alternative conceptions of the common good from which to choose at the next election. The major exception to this principle is in times of war or crisis, but even then the opposition is expected to question the means by which goals are pursued.[10]

British parliamentary government is also party government. Although there are certainly barriers to the effective implementation of party government, the idea that political parties are extremely important for governing pervades the system. Parliament is now conceived of, to some degree, as an institution in itself, but also as an arena where the political parties clash. Parties are expected to be responsible, to stand for certain policies and programs, and to attempt to carry out those programs if elected. Once a party is elected to office, some compromises are always necessary, but parties are expected to attempt to implement their programs or to have a reasonable justification for failure to do so.

Finally, British parliamentary government is sovereign. There are, strictly speaking, no legal limitations on the powers of Parliament, and there is virtually no means by which a citizen can challenge an act of Parliament as unconstitutional, although some actions may be found to go beyond the powers of a particular minister. That said, limitations on the discretion of Parliament have come into play through Great Britain's membership in the European Union and the Council of Europe (for example, it must adhere to the European Convention on Human Rights), but these are appeals to external standards rather than strictly British constitutional rules.[11] There are, of course, very real political limitations on the activities of Parliament, but its actions, once taken, are law until Parliament acts again.

These features of Great Britain's parliamentary government provide the context for the rest of this chapter, which briefly describes and discusses the six major institutions of British national government: the monarch, the prime minister, the cabinet and government, Parliament, the courts, and the civil service. More specifically, it describes the features most salient for understanding the manner in which the British system converts proposals into law. The final section describes some important actors that do not fit conveniently into those six major structures.

The Monarch

The United Kingdom is a constitutional monarchy in which the powers of the monarch are constrained by both law and convention. Britons grumble frequently about the cost of maintaining the royal household and about the wealth of the queen and the royal family. At times critics of the monarchy call for an end of the monarchy in favor of a republic.[12] The role of the royal family became even more contentious after Diana, Princess of Wales, was killed in an automobile accident in 1997. And her divorce from Prince Charles and other widely publicized family problems had already brought the monarchy into some disrepute. The current sentiment leans toward reducing the power and influence of the monarchy, although this sentiment waxes and wanes with specific events.

The powers of the monarchy are very closely circumscribed. Although many acts are performed by the monarch or in the monarch's name, the prime minister or the cabinet makes the actual decisions. Declaring war, making treaties, granting peerages, and granting clemency to prisoners are all royal prerogatives, but, in fact, all are exercised only on the advice of the prime minister and other ministers, or even by those ministers alone in the case of Orders in Council (described later in this chapter). Similarly, royal assent is needed for legislation to become law, but it has not been refused since Queen Anne in 1707.

One point at which the monarch could wield a major influence over policy and politics is in the selection of the prime minister. If one major party wins a clear majority in Parliament, as Labour did in the 1997, 2001 and 2005 elections, there is little or no possibility that the monarch can exercise independent judgment. But if there is no clear winner, the monarch might be able to do so, albeit with the advice of the outgoing prime minister and senior civil servants. The conventions governing such an eventuality only began to be clearly articulated in the early 1990s, and the monarch would have to be extremely careful not to overstep the tacit boundaries in a society increasingly doubtful about the efficacy of continuing the monarchy.[13] With predictions of a hung parliament leading up to the election in 2010, the monarch's authority to participate in selecting the prime minister was again heavily scrutinized and debated, highlighting that even among well-respected legal scholars, some provisions of the UK's constitution are less than clear.

The monarch also is empowered to dissolve a sitting Parliament, and the decision to do so could (in theory at least) be made independently if the government did not resign and call for elections after a vote of no confidence or if it lost on a major issue. Because governments since the 1970s have appeared unwilling to resign in the face of policy defeats, this potential power of the monarch to force a government to go to the people may become important in government policymaking. Likewise, a monarch could refuse to dissolve a Parliament when asked by the prime minister if he or she believes it is not in the national interest to do so. Any monarch would, however, exercise these powers at some peril, because any such direct intervention into the political life of the country might threaten the legitimacy of the institution of the monarchy.

In the late 1860s the great commentator on British politics Walter Bagehot described the monarch as a real part of the policymaking system in Britain, though concealed in a cloak of dignity and ceremony.[14] Indeed, much of the impact of the monarch on policy and politics remains hidden and subtle. The monarch's influence is exercised through frequent meetings and consultations with the prime minister, preceded by thorough ministerial briefings. The power of the monarch, then, may be as personal as the power of any other political actor, or even more so. But to be effective, the monarch must not only perform the extensive ceremonial functions of the office but also be an effective politician in his or her own right. The most important function of the monarch, however, is to serve as a symbol of the nation as a whole and to rise above the partisan strife. The monarch must be a unifying force when much else in the political system tends to be centrifugal, divisive, and adversarial.

The Prime Minister

The monarch is head of state—that is, the representative of the nation as a whole and the symbolic head of the entire governing system. The prime minister is head of the government of the day and its chief executive officer. In the United States, the two roles are merged in the president, who is at once head of state and head of government. Because the two roles are separated in Great Britain, a citizen or a politician can more readily criticize the prime minister without being seen as attacking the legitimacy of the entire system of government.

The office of prime minister has evolved slowly since the beginning of the eighteenth century. The prime minister is at once just another minister of the Crown and above the other ministers. Concerns are emerging, however, that the role of the prime minister is becoming presidential, because more power appears to be flowing into 10 Downing Street (the prime minister's official residence in London).[15] This alleged "presidentialization" of the prime minister stems from several factors. The first is that parliamentary campaigns have become directed more toward electing a particular prime minister than toward selecting a political party to govern. The personalization of British politics increased substantially while Thatcher was prime minister, but some earlier campaigns were oriented toward the appeal and personality of individuals as well. The Labour government of Tony Blair placed an even greater emphasis on personal loyalty than the Thatcher government.[16] It remains to be seen how coalition government, with David Cameron as prime minister and

Following the May 2010 elections, the new Conservative Prime Minister David Cameron (left) and Liberal Democrat Deputy Prime Minister Nick Clegg, pictured outside Number 10 Downing Street, formed the first coalition government in the UK since the wartime government under Winston Churchill (May 1940–July 1945).

Source: Andy Rain/epa/Corbis

Nick Clegg as deputy prime minister, will influence and be influenced by presidentialization and personalization. The introduction of televised debates among the party leaders in the 2010 election emphasized the importance of personality in the choice of prime minister.[17] Party remains important in the voting decision, but so, too, is the prospective leader of the nation.

Other aspects of the presidentialization of the office of prime minister are the staffing and organization of the office. Thatcher placed several special assistants in departments, especially in the Treasury, thereby making an early move toward extending the authority of the prime minister substantially beyond its traditional role of *primus inter pares* ("first among equals"). Blair intensified this process through administrative and organizational innovations. Among other things, he appointed special assistants to the prime minister's Private Office for presentation and planning, significantly expanded the prime minister's Policy Unit, and created a new Strategic Communications Office with a staff of six. Following the American precedent, Blair also appointed a chief of staff "to pull together the work of the Prime Minister's Office and to co-ordinate it with that of the Cabinet Office."[18] In addition to the chief of staff, prime ministers now appoint a number of special advisors and "czars" to help them place their personal stamp on a range of policies. The Prime Minister's Office also created the Office of Public Service Reform and several task forces to address major cross-cutting policy issues such as the social exclusion of individuals and groups from intended policy benefits.

Another innovation under Blair was the integration of the formerly separate Cabinet Secretariat and Office of Public Service into a single cabinet office under the management of a cabinet secretary. This move was accompanied by the creation of a Constitution Secretariat in 1997, whose chief purpose is to oversee Labour's constitutional reform program, and a Central Secretariat in 1998 charged with advising on ministerial responsibilities and accountability.[19]

The cumulative effect of these moves, dating from the Thatcher years onward, has been the evolution of the Prime Minister's Office in the direction of the Executive Office of the President in the United States and the Bundeskanzlersamt in Germany, although on a much smaller scale.[20] There is every indication that Cameron's coalition government will continue this trend. Although there is a great deal of discussion of devolving power to the people through greater control in local schools and expanded public involvement in policymaking, it is likely that the Cameron government will continue developing the executive aspects of the office.

Certain characteristics and powers of and limitations on the prime minister are important for understanding the office. First, the prime minister is the leader of the majority party in the House of Commons. (Until 1902 prime ministers frequently came from the House of Lords, but by convention the prime minister is now a member of Commons. For that reason, in 1963 Sir Alec Douglas-Home renounced his hereditary title to sit in the House of Commons and eventually become prime minister.) The political party first makes the selection of a potential prime minister. Therefore whoever would be prime minister must first win an election within the party. Even sitting prime ministers may have to be reelected leader by their party, because sometimes they lose the confidence of their party, as Thatcher did in 1990. This aspect of the office is but one of many ways in which the customs and conventions of the British political system reinforce the cohesiveness and integration of political parties. The prime minister must be able to command the apparatus both of a political party and of government.

In addition to being the leader of a political party, by convention the prime minister is the political leader within the House of Commons. Becoming prime minister may indeed say more about an individual's abilities in Parliament than about the skills necessary to run a government. The prime minister is expected to lead parliamentary debates, and the ability to win in verbal jousts in the House of Commons frequently appears more important to success as prime minister than winning less visible policy and administrative battles. Prime Minister's Question Time, which now occurs only once a week, is watched widely and is a test of the verbal and political skills of the prime minister.

Although technically the prime minister is only *primus inter pares,* the powers of the prime minister are actually substantial. First, that official is the formal link between the Crown and the rest of government. After the monarch invites a prospective prime minister to form a new government, the relationships between the monarch and Parliament are channeled through the prime minister. In like manner, the prime minister serves as chief political adviser to the monarch, especially on major issues such as the dissolution of Parliament. The monarch and the prime minister routinely meet on a weekly basis, especially if important political issues are on the agenda.

The prime minister also "dispenses office." Once the monarch has invited a prospective prime minister to form a government, it is the prime minister who assembles the government team. This role may be weakened somewhat in a coalition government involving negotiations with the other party, but it remains important. Certainly, members of the team selected will have political followings of their own, and others may have to be included to placate certain segments of the party, but the office held by each cabinet member will be the decision of the prime minister. The power to fill offices also extends to the increasing number of lucrative positions in the "quangos" (quasi–nongovernmental organizations to which the government has devolved tasks and power).[21] The prime minister also can decide on life peerages, which nominally are appointed by the Crown but in actuality are in the gift of the prime minister. Opposition parties can nominate life peers as well. In all cases, the nominees are subject to scrutiny to ensure their eligibility.

Once in office, the prime minister has considerable personal power over policy and the activities of the cabinet. As the organizer, leader, and summarizer of the business of the cabinet, the prime minister is also in a position to enforce his or her views over nominal equals. As the head of government, the prime minister has substantial public visibility and influence over society. This public influence has increased with the growing power of the media—a situation noted particularly by the Blair government.[22] As prime minister, Blair deftly used the media to influence public opinion as one strategy to push forward the peace process in Northern Ireland. That said, the media can also undermine a prime minister as happened to Gordon Brown on issues such as managing the recession and the war in Afghanistan. Finally, in times of emergency the powers of a prime minister are not limited by a constitution, as are those of the U.S. president.

The leader of the opposition, who as head of the largest minority party in the House of Commons would probably be prime minister if the sitting government were defeated in an election, is able to wield influence and powers as well. Although lacking the official powers of office, the role of the leader of the opposition is not unlike that of the prime minister: leader of a political party, a leader in Parliament, and the leader of a cabinet, albeit one out of office (the "shadow cabinet"). The adversarial style of British politics obliges the leader of the opposition to oppose the government's programs and to propose alternatives to government programs in preparation for the day when the opposition becomes the government and must introduce its own policy proposals. As the alternative prime minister, the leader of the opposition receives a salary in addition to that of an MP and is kept briefed on important policy issues and matters of national security, because this member must be ready to become prime minister on very short notice.

Cabinet and Government

Working under—or with—the prime minister are the cabinet and the government. Although these terms are often used interchangeably, they actually designate somewhat different entities. The *cabinet* is composed of the individuals—nineteen men and four women in the 2010 coalition government—who meet with the prime minister as a collectivity called the cabinet and who make collective policy decisions. The term *government* is more encompassing, including all ministers regardless of their seniority or degree of responsibility. In 2010 more than ninety ministers, junior ministers, and parliamentary private secretaries made up the government. The cabinet is technically a committee of the government selected by the prime minister to provide advice in private meetings and to share in the responsibility for policy. Although the prime minister is certainly primarily responsible for government policies, the cabinet is also collectively responsible to Parliament, and cabinet members generally rise and fall as a unit rather than as individuals.

There are several varieties of ministers—secretaries of state, ministers, and junior ministers—and, to some degree, parliamentary private secretaries have some ministerial functions. The distinction between secretaries of state and ministers is rather vague. Each tends to head a department of government, such as the Department of Defence, the Department for Work and Pensions, or the Department for Environment, Food and Rural Affairs. Although all major departments are now headed by secretaries of state, some members of the cabinet may carry titles other than minister: chancellor of the exchequer, the chief Treasury minister, is one example. The government, and in some instances the cabinet, also includes posts without departmental responsibilities, either ministers without portfolios or holders of titles such as the Lord Keeper of the Privy Seal. These officials are included in the government as general or political advisers, or in the leadership of the House of Commons or the House of Lords.

Junior ministers are attached to a department minister to provide political and policy assistance in the management of the department, and these positions serve as stepping-stones for persons on the way up in government.[23] Ministers of state are junior ministers, placed between parliamentary undersecretaries of state and parliamentary private secretaries. Each department has one minister to deal with Lords business, who may be of any rank. Finally, parliamentary private secretaries are unpaid (aside from their normal salaries as members of Parliament) assistants to ministers and are responsible primarily for liaison between the government and the rest of Parliament.

The job of minister is a demanding one. Unlike U.S. political executives, a British minister remains a member of the legislature and an active representative of a constituency and must fulfill various positions and responsibilities simultaneously. The first of these multiple tasks is to run the department—not only its day-to-day management but also its policies. Because few politicians have experience with the management of such large organizations, most are at some disadvantage in running a department effectively. As for managing the policies of the department, the minister must develop policies appropriate to the department's responsibilities and in keeping with the overall priorities of the government. In this task, ministers are generally hindered by their lack of expertise. Ministers are seldom chosen for their expertise in a policy area; more often, they are appointed for their general political skills and voter support. It is estimated that only five of the fifty-one ministerial appointees in the Harold Wilson government of 1964–1970 had any prior experience in the area of their departments' responsibilities, and there is evidence that the knowledge base of ministers has not improved substantially.[24] The consequences of their lack of expertise are exacerbated by the tendency to shift ministers from one department to another, even during the lifetime of a government. The Labour government reshuffled its ministers in the summer of 1999, at the halfway point in its five-year (maximum) term of office, and in that shuffle some ministers who had gained substantial expertise in an area were moved, even in the important economics area.[25] Furthermore, in their departments ministers are faced with experienced and relatively expert civil servants who tend to have views of their own about proper departmental policies. Inexperienced and inexpert ministers must then fight very hard just to manage their own departments. The tensions between ministers and top civil servants were even the subject of the British sitcoms *Yes Minister* and, more recently, *The Thick of It*.

Related to their policy work, ministers are likely to have some personal policy advisers, whether paid by public money or by party funds. The Thatcher government, more than previous governments, sought more partisan and ideological policy advice than it was likely to receive from civil servants. The Blair government continued that practice and to some extent expanded its use, so that the role of these advisers has now become more clearly defined, and in the process has devalued the role of the civil service.

Ministers who are also members of the cabinet encounter additional demands on their time. Traditionally, the cabinet has met five to six hours a week, and preparation for those meetings requires even more time. Membership in the cabinet also requires that each minister be briefed on all current political issues. And ministers must serve on the cabinet committees needed to coordinate policies and deal with issues requiring consideration prior to their determination by the cabinet.[26] Ministers cannot afford to take cabinet work lightly, even though they may be only a part of a collectivity often dominated by the prime minister. In the cabinet, as in Commons, political reputations are made, and in both bodies the interests of the minister's department must be protected and advanced.

Because ministers are also active members of Parliament, they must appear in Parliament for a substantial amount of time each day, especially when the government has only a small majority. Ministers also must be prepared to speak in Parliament on the policies of their departments or for the government as a whole. A minister must as well be prepared to respond to questions during Question Time, and may have to spend hours being briefed and coached on the answers to anticipated questions. The constitutional responsibility of the executive to the legislature places a great burden on ministers in a parliamentary government.

Finally, ministers must serve their constituents in the districts from which they were elected. This service involves spending weekends in the "surgery" (that is, the constituency office or other locations in the district) and receiving delegations from local organizations when in London. Unlike politicians in other countries, members of the British Parliament may not reside in the constituencies from which they were elected, and therefore they may have to learn about the local issues. Moreover, because there is no fixed term for a Parliament other than that an election must occur within five years, British politicians, even more than American politicians, must always be preparing for the next election.

The cabinet is supported in its work by the Cabinet Office. In fact, one of the important innovations in British politics has been the development and expansion of this office, which grew out of the Committee of Imperial Defense in World War I. In recent years, the Cabinet Office has undertaken other important policy functions, including managing British policy toward the European Union (EU).[27] Responsibility for the management of EU relations is shared with the Foreign Office, which runs the Permanent Representation in Brussels. Currently, the Cabinet Office is composed of a senior civil servant and a small number of associates. The secretary to the cabinet is quite influential in shaping cabinet decisions, although not by any obvious means. The secretary creates the cabinet agenda and distributes cabinet papers to the appropriate individuals. By so doing, the secretary determines which ministers will be heard quickly and which will have to wait for their day in cabinet. Although the prime minister summarizes cabinet meetings orally, it is the secretary to the cabinet who, based on the meetings, drafts written communications to the departments for action and prepares the formal written records of the meetings. These records are not subject to change, even by the prime minister. Although there is little or no evidence of these powers being abused, the position of secretary to the cabinet is extremely influential.

The prime minister's small but growing staff of political and personal advisers also provides the government with support. This group is far smaller than the White House staff in the United States or even the staff of the Bundeskanzlersamt in Germany, but its growth is viewed as just one more bit of evidence that policymaking powers are becoming concentrated in the cabinet rather than in Parliament as a whole.

Parliament

Despite the nominally strong position of Parliament in the constitutional arrangements of the United Kingdom, serious questions have arisen about the real, effective powers of Parliament. As the political executive grows in strength and political parties become more disciplined, Parliament as an institution grows less capable of exercising control over policies. In response, it has been attempting to create a more powerful position in the political process, especially in the oversight of the executive, but the evidence suggests that these efforts have met little success. The significant majority enjoyed by Labour governments between 1997 and 2010 made Parliament's attempts to serve as a counterweight to the executive all the more difficult. With the closely split Parliament elected in 2010 and a somewhat fragile coalition between the Conservatives and Liberal Democrats in government, it remains to be seen if the Parliament will be able to use the political environment to exert more control over the government.

Members of Parliament

The Parliament elected in 2010 has 650 members, each elected from a single constituency. The average member of Parliament (MP) represents approximately 90,000 people, compared with the approximately 700,000 people represented by members of the U.S. House of Representatives. Compared with members of most other legislative bodies, MPs have few advantages. Their annual pay, even with continuing raises, is £64,766 (or about $94,000 at 2010 exchange rates), compared with $174,000 for rank-and-file U.S. representatives and senators. In previous parliaments, MPs received about the same amount for personal expenses, including weekend travel to their districts and rent for a second residence in London. In 2009 the use of these allowances became a public scandal and produced a political firestorm over the apparent abuse of position by MPs. Some of the more egregious cases were using parliamentary allowances to clean a moat and to build a house for ducks on an estate.

Some members of Parliament have sponsoring organizations that either help members with their expenses in office or provide some direct remuneration. For Labour politicians, these organizations are commonly trade unions; for Conservatives and a few Liberal Democrats, they are industrial groups or large corporations, or perhaps other types of interest groups. The appearance of corruption, however, is prompting parties to rethink the place of sponsorship. The Labour Party has begun to restrict union sponsorship of its members.[28] Moreover, the many scandals about the finances of the political parties have tended to make the parties more circumspect in their financial relationships.

In return for relatively modest rewards, MPs work long hours and receive relatively little staff support. Unlike American legislators who can have several dozen staff members, the average MP receives funding for only a part-time assistant or secretary, unless the member is paying personally for the assistance or is receiving assistance from a sponsor. Historically, many MPs lacked private offices, unless they were in the government or the shadow government, and so they were forced to share small offices with other MPs. Today, most have offices of their own in a new building near the Houses of Parliament, but even there, accommodations remain cramped. The truth is, the job of member of Parliament was designed for a person of independent means, and the rewards of office have not changed sufficiently to match the demands of modern legislative bodies.

Organization

Both the House of Commons and the House of Lords are involved in making policy, but Commons is crucial to the process of forming governments and setting the public budget. Because the House of Lords has become relatively less important in the policymaking process, it is described only briefly in this section, and a fuller discussion is devoted to the House of Commons.

The House of Lords is composed of the lords spiritual (representing the hierarchy of the Church of England) and the lords temporal. The lords temporal comprise hereditary and life peers. Hereditary peers, who once made up an overwhelming majority of members in the House of Lords, claim their seats based on inherited titles; life peers are appointed by the monarch, on the advice of the government, only for their lifetime. Dating from 1958, the concept of life peers was designed in part to rectify the partisan and ideological bias of the hereditary peers against the Labour Party. In 1999 the Labour majority in the House of Commons voted to abolish the privileged status of the hereditary peers in the House of Lords in favor of a chamber dominated by life peers. As a result of the 1999 constitutional reform, all but ninety-two hereditary peers were removed from the House of Lords, most elected by their own political party group within Lords.

As of November 2009 the House of Lords had some 739 members, of whom all but 118 were life peers.[29] Conservatives, with 190 peers, no longer constituted the largest group in the chamber (compared with 212 Labour peers and 71 Liberal Democrats). About a quarter of members of Lords were nonparty, "cross-bench" peers. This shift from Conservative domination of the House of Lords significantly facilitated Labour-sponsored legislation. Until enactment of the constitutional reform, even the Blair government with its solid majority in Commons faced recurrent problems with the House of Lords.

The impetus for limiting the powers of the House of Lords began with David Lloyd George's "people's budget" of 1909. This budget introduced a progressive income tax (the first since the Napoleonic wars) and a rudimentary public health insurance program. The Conservative Lords balked at this Liberal proposal and refused to pass the budget. Parliament was then dissolved, but when the Liberals were returned with a (reduced) majority, the House of Lords accepted the budget. After a second election in 1910, in which the Liberals were again returned with a majority, the House of Lords accepted the Parliament Bill of 1911, which greatly limited its powers.

Today, the House of Lords may not delay money bills longer than one month—nor can it vote them down and prevent their implementation—and any legislation passed by the House of Commons in two successive sessions of Parliament, provided one calendar year has passed, goes into effect without approval by Lords. Lords does still occasionally delay or even vote down legislation (as it did recently on an animal health bill). Mainly, however, it serves as a debating society and as a locus for government acceptance of amendments to its proposals that it would be less willing to accept in the more politicized House of Commons. This said, the House of Lords actually serves a useful function in British policy-making despite its diminished role, because its attention results in many useful modifications to legislation. Furthermore, Lords has chosen to become specialized in some areas of policy, such as science and technology, where its committee reports must be considered carefully. The Blair government even used the House of Lords to initiate legislation when its legislative calendar became clogged in its first year.

Despite its numerous uses, the House of Lords is still the target of reform efforts. In votes in 2007 the House of Commons expressed strong sentiment for an elected House of Lords, just as there was sentiment in the House of Lords to retain an all-appointive body. This voting registered the opinions of the members but did not move forward toward adoption of real reform. The coalition government formed in 2010 has proposed reconsidering the reform of the House of Lords, although few specific proposals were forthcoming.

The structure and functions of the House of Commons have evolved over centuries and to some degree still reflect their medieval roots. Much of the ceremony and procedure derives from the past, but despite complaints about the vestigial aspects of the procedures, they do not appear to inhibit in any significant way the functioning of a modern legislative body. To the extent that other institutions of British government seriously overshadow the House, the fault resides more with the other structural and cultural characteristics of British government than with the quaint trappings of power within the House of Commons.

British politics is conducted in an adversarial style, and even the design of the House of Commons emphasizes that fact. Most legislatures sit in semicircles, and the individual members sit at desks and go to a central rostrum to address the body. The House of Commons is arranged as two opposing ranks of benches, placed very close together in a small chamber. Speakers generally face their political opponents, and although the form of address is to the Speaker, the words are clearly intended for the opponents. Because the proceedings of the House of Commons are now broadcast, statements by members are also directed at the voting public and the media. The cabinet and other members of the government populate the front benches on one side of the aisle, while their opposition counterparts are arrayed on the other side. From these two front-row trenches, the two major belligerents conduct the verbal warfare that is parliamentary debate. Behind the front benches are the foot soldiers of the back benches, ready to vote to their party's call, and perhaps little else. The style of debate in the House of Commons, as well as being contentious and rather witty, is very informal, and the MP addressing that body enjoys few protections against heckling.

The House of Commons is both a partisan body and a national institution. Ideas of cabinet government and collective responsibility are closely allied with ideas of party government, and there is a strong sense that political parties, whether in or out of government, should present clear and consistent positions on policy issues that the electorate can then judge when voting in the next election. The dependence of the executive on the ability to command a majority of the House also requires that parties vote together. Political parties in the House of Commons are organized so they can deliver votes when required. Members know that voting against their party on an important issue can be tantamount to political suicide (although it sometimes serves as a springboard to future political success), and each party has a whip whose job it is to ensure that the needed votes are present. The British system of government does not allow much latitude for individual MPs to have policy ideas of their own, although the parties generally do allow their members free votes on issues of a moral nature, such as abortion or capital punishment.

From the partisan organization and behavior of the House of Commons, it follows that it is a national institution. The U.S. House of Representatives is usually conceptualized as a group of ambassadors from their constituencies, and European legislatures are perhaps even more national because of proportional representation and the absence of any real connection to geography. The House of Commons is somewhere between those two extremes, although the British generally acknowledge that MPs are more responsible to the party and its national goals and priorities than to the individual interests of their constituencies. This party allegiance is signaled by the fact that MPs are not required to live in their constituencies, and many do not. Naturally, MPs do try to satisfy their constituencies whenever possible, but it is generally assumed that members owe their offices to their respective parties and the national policies advanced in the election campaigns rather than to any geographically narrow interests of their constituencies. Nevertheless, like the free votes on moral issues, MPs are often allowed to abstain from voting for, and in rare cases voting against, party proposals that clearly would be inimical to the interests of their constituencies.

Perched above this sea of adversarial and partisan politics on a throne between the two front benches is the Speaker of the House, an impartial figure who traditionally has dressed in the style of the eighteenth century.[30] The Speaker is elected from the membership of the Commons, not for having been a vociferous partisan, but for being someone who can be elected unanimously rather than produced by a partisan confrontation. Competitive elections for Speaker have occurred in the Commons only five times since the beginning of the twentieth century, most recently in June 2009 when ten MPs were nominated. Conservative John Bercow was elected. This election was particularly contentious because the previous Speaker, Michael Martin, had been forced out of office because of mismanaging the parliamentary expenses scandal (see above).

Once elected, a Speaker may remain in the office as long as he or she wishes. The Speaker's parliamentary seat is rarely contested, and another member discharges his or her constituency duties. The Speaker votes only in the case of a tie, but by convention the Speaker's vote is cast to preserve the status quo. The Speaker is not without real influence over decisions, however; one example is the Speaker's use of the "kangaroo," the standing order that allows the Speaker to determine which amendments to legislation will be debated and which will not, and the Speaker's acceptance of a motion of closure ends debate—but only after the Speaker believes all relevant positions have been heard. Likewise, the Speaker enforces the rules of the Commons, not only in debate but also for matters such as suspending members who have violated financial disclosure rules.[31]

Although the House of Commons does have committees, they are by no means as central to the legislative process as the committees in the U.S. Congress or the German Bundestag. Instead, they are miniature legislatures in which bills are discussed and improved, and the government can accept amendments without jeopardizing a bill's political stature in the Commons. An indication of this more limited capacity is that a bill enters the committee stage after the principal political debate on the bill rather than before its primary consideration. Therefore, the major battles over legislation occur before the committee sees it. The committee's task is to refine legislation rather than significantly influence its basic nature and purpose. The eight general committees in the House of Commons are composed of from sixteen to fifty members. Unlike congressional committees, only the core of the committee is permanent; other members are added to the committee depending on the nature of the bill being considered. The composition of the committees reflects not only the expertise of Commons members but also the partisan composition of the Commons as a whole.

Special committee provisions governed legislation affecting Scotland until the convening of the Scottish Parliament in 1999. Because most legislation until then was passed with a separate Scottish bill—in part a result of special features of Scottish law—a separate committee system existed for Scottish bills. But with the devolution of legislative power from London to Edinburgh in 1997, the Scottish Parliament now exercises autonomous authority over Scottish affairs except for economic policy and foreign affairs. The Scottish Parliament exercises limited rights of taxation and receives an annual block grant of around £15 billion (about $22.5 billion), which it can allocate as it wishes. Skirmishes between England and Scotland over road tolls and student fees, however, reveal that lawmakers have yet to agree on important details of the constitutional division of power between the national and regional capitals. Persistent political conflicts also raise what has come to be called the "West Lothian Question"—whether Scottish MPs in Westminster should be barred from taking part in votes on legislation that affects only England, in the same way that English MPs no longer have a vote on most Scottish matters.[32]

By contrast, Wales remains much more subordinate to London. The separate Welsh committees in Parliament never exercised as much influence as the previous Scottish committees, because no separate Welsh assembly or body of Welsh law was in place before the union with England. Consequently, much Welsh legislation is joined with English. The Welsh National Assembly exercises only "persuasive powers" in relation to London and the right of secondary rulemaking within Wales itself, although a referendum, scheduled for 2011, on whether to extend the Welsh Assembly's powers may shift more authority to the Assembly.

In addition to the standing committees, several select committees function within the House of Commons. The most important of these are the Statutory Instruments Committee and the Public Accounts Committee. The first of these committees monitors the issuing of statutory instruments, or delegated legislation, by government departments. Like all governments of industrialized societies, the British government has found that its workload has increased to the point that Parliament cannot make all the needed laws. Instead, it delegates the authority to decide many legislative matters to the relevant executive departments, with the provision that this delegated legislation be subject to review by the Statutory Instruments Committee and potentially (if rarely) by the entire House of Commons.

The Public Accounts Committee is a modern manifestation of the traditional parliamentary function of oversight of expenditures; it monitors the government's expenditure plans, especially through the postaudit of the final expenditures. It has also at times become engaged in more analytic exercises, such as value-for-money audits, and has gained a reputation as an authoritative body whose reports require some sort of government response. By tradition, this committee is chaired by an MP from the opposition. Its work is now greatly aided by the National Audit Office, which, like most other government accounting offices, has become increasingly concerned with value for money in addition to judging the probity of public expenditures.

One of the most interesting developments in the committee structure of Parliament has been the creation of select committees to follow the activities of government departments. This development is an attempt to establish the legislative oversight by committee so familiar to American political executives, although a similar suggestion was made by Richard Crossman in 1963, and even earlier by the Haldane Commission on the structure of government (1918).[33] Each of the fourteen select committees monitors a functional area of government policy and holds hearings on and independent investigations into policy. Although their success has varied, they have provided Parliament with more institutionalized mechanisms for investigation, and some of them have had a substantial impact on the direction of policy. For example, the Treasury and Civil Service Select Committee monitored and evaluated the major administrative reforms of the Conservative government such as Next Steps (described later in this chapter). Augmenting the work of the departmental select committees are seventeen nondepartmental select committees, which were appointed after Labour's electoral victory in 1997. Most of them deal with domestic matters cutting across traditional departmental boundaries. Examples include a catering committee, a standing orders committee, and a committee on standards and privileges. Other nondepartmental committees have been charged with powers of investigative oversight over matters such as the environment, public administration, and EU legislation.

As indicated by the activities of the select committees, an important function of Parliament is the scrutiny of the political executive and its policies. Perhaps the most famous mechanism through which this takes place is Question Time. On four out of five sitting days during the week, the House of Commons opens its legislative day with an hour of questions for the government from members of the House. Questions are submitted in writing at least forty-eight hours in advance, so that a minister has the opportunity to prepare an answer. In recent years, however, the practice has been to ask a vague question in writing and then follow it orally with more probing supplemental questions. A seemingly innocuous question about whether the prime minister intends to visit Finland during the year may be an introduction to more important questions about foreign policy. All members of the government may be subjected to questioning, but the prime minister answers questions on only one of the four days. Question Time places an additional burden on already overburdened ministers, but in a political system in which secrecy is the norm, this institution serves as one mechanism for Parliament, and for the people as a whole, to find out what is happening in government and to exercise some control through the ventilation of possible malfeasance.

As an institution, Parliament is threatened. It has had difficulty maintaining its independent powers in the face of the growing powers of the prime minister and cabinet. Most of the important weapons in the struggle are in the hands of the executive. These assets include information, access to staff, and, more important, party discipline. Parliament now rarely exercises free and thorough scrutiny of the activities of the government; the outcomes of votes are known in advance, and it is the rare politician who will risk his or her political career on the basis of principle. That said, there are instances in which Parliament does have a more open and influential debate on policy, as it did over European policy in the summer of 1991, and there are still revolts by backbenchers—approximately sixty Labour MPs voted against a government social policy reform in the summer of 1999, and backbench dissent has continued to rise since over issues such as the Iraq war and restraints on terrorism. Yet even with those exceptions, parliamentary government has, in effect, become cabinet or party government. These venerable institutions, however, are sometimes thought to be threatened by the increased power of the next actor in the political process to be discussed, the civil service.

The Civil Service

The civil service has changed perhaps more than any other institution of British government. The traditional pattern of a nonpolitical, career civil service with substantial influence over policy has been one of the great paradoxes of British government. On the face of it, the British civil service has appeared unprepared to perform the expert role expected of it in the policymaking process. The recruitment of civil servants has been less on the basis of expert knowledge in a substantive policy area than on the basis of general intellectual abilities. Also, for a large proportion of their careers, civil servants are moved frequently from job to job (although many remain within a single department throughout their careers), gaining permanent appointments only rather late in their careers. The cult of the "talented amateur" and the generalist has dominated thinking about the selection and training of civil servants, despite attempts at reform following the 1968 findings of the Fulton Committee, which expressed concern about the absence of specialized education in the backgrounds of persons selected for the civil service.[34]

For several decades after the Fulton report, the pattern of recruitment changed relatively little, with more humanities graduates than scientists or social scientists entering the civil service.[35] One of the changes introduced during the Thatcher government and continued in subsequent governments was an emphasis on management, rather than policy advice, in the role of senior public servants—political appointees were to gradually fill the role of policy adviser. This change also involved opening recruitment for many senior positions to noncareer appointees and in general breaking down the monopoly over these positions that career public servants had enjoyed. This pattern of recruitment has been especially evident in filling the chief executive positions of agencies created to implement public policies. In general, then, the civil service has been somewhat deinstitutionalized, with greater competition and less protection from political influence.

Despite these changes, the civil service continues to have a substantial influence over policy. Several factors seem to be related to this influence. The first is that although its members may lack formal training in a policy area, the senior civil service is composed of a talented group of individuals who have the intellectual ability to grasp readily the subject matter it must administer. Second, despite their lack of specialized training compared with civil servants in other countries, British civil servants are generally more knowledgeable than their political masters about departmental policy.[36] They learn a great deal on the job, whereas their ministers are not on the job very long themselves. Civil servants have a much longer time perspective than politicians, and they are able to wait out and delay any particular minister with whom they disagree. Furthermore, their ministries have an even longer collective memory than any single civil servant, and so the accumulation of expertise and experience can easily counteract the legitimacy of the political master.

The relationship between civil servants and their political masters is important for defining and understanding the role of the civil service in policymaking. The prevailing ethos of the civil service is that it can serve any political master it may be called on to serve. But ministers may interpret this service—and sometimes rightly so—as an attempt to impose the "departmental view," or the particular policy ideas of the department, on the minister. Any number of reasons can be advanced to explain why the ideas of the minister are not feasible and why only the proposals made by the department itself will ever work.

The minister's task of countering a departmental view is further burdened by the fact that the department may appear to speak with one voice. American executive departments tend to be fragmented, with the independent bureaus advancing their own policy ideas. Executive departments in Great Britain have had few such independent organizations. Policy ideas arising in departments are channeled upward through the hierarchical structure to the permanent secretary, who is the primary link between the political world and the civil service. The permanent secretary is the senior civil servant in a department (several departments now have two or more civil servants of this rank) and serves as the personal adviser to the minister.

The creation of numerous executive agencies has fragmented British cabinet departments, thereby diminishing the power exercised by permanent secretaries and senior public servants. The principal effect, however, has been to separate implementation from policymaking. Indeed, the British central government looks increasingly like Scandinavian governments, with small, policy-oriented departments supervising the larger agencies that implement policies.[37] But that separation is not as easy to make in reality as it is in theory, and indeed the quasi-autonomous agencies are beginning to link their managerial problems with substantive policy changes.

Because ministers lack any substantial personal staff, they have had to rely heavily on the permanent secretaries both for policy advice and for management of the departments. This dependence, in turn, has given the civil service, through the permanent secretary, significant influence over policy. It is not argued here that the civil service has abused this position. In fact, in general the evidence is that its members have been responsible and scrupulous in the exercise of their duties. Nevertheless, the structural position in which the civil service is placed as the repository of information and of a departmental perspective, and the lack of alternative views presented to most ministers, place the civil service in a powerful position. Thus the cozy world of the civil service is now facing a considerable challenge, complicated no doubt by the politicization of the civil service instigated by the Thatcher and Major governments.[38]

A second major challenge to the traditional role and functions of the civil service is that many individual civil servants question whether they have obligations to Parliament and to the public that transcend their loyalty to ministers. Several civil servants have chosen to blow the whistle on malfeasance in government, and in some cases the courts have supported their actions. But actions of this sort are uncomfortable and difficult in a system built on secrecy and ministerial responsibility, and so the need for greater openness in government has become a political question. In 1994 the Major government adopted rules removing some of the secrecy in the public sector, but achieving the openness found in most other European governments is still a distant goal. In 1999 the Blair government introduced its own legislation to create greater openness in government, but advocates of freedom of information have argued that it is excessively weak.[39] Again the coalition elected in 2010 has made a major commitment to increased transparency, although the initial proposals have been in relation to local rather than to national government.

The third challenge facing the civil service are the reforms implemented by the Thatcher and Major governments and designed to minimize the policy advice role of the civil service and emphasize its managerial role. The most important of these reforms is Next Steps, which has created several hundred semiautonomous agencies (including local National Health Service trusts) to implement most government policies.[40] The policy and planning functions are being retained within relatively small ministries that are also responsible for supervising the operations of the agencies and are a mechanism for enforcing parliamentary accountability. The heads of the new agencies are not necessarily civil servants, and even where they have been, they are hired on fixed-term contracts with performance standards.

This administrative change also means that ministers may be less responsible for activities that appear to be under their supervision and that some of the traditional mechanisms for accountability in the system of government will be less viable. For example, in October 1995 the head of the Prison Service—a Next Steps agency—was fired because of a scathing report on the way the service handled escapes, even though the total number of escapes was down. He chose to contest his dismissal in court, arguing that he was held responsible for failures in government penal policy.[41] Overall, few things about the role and status of the civil service in the United Kingdom can now be taken for granted, as the internal machinery of government, and even some constitutional principles, undergo some very fundamental changes.

Finally, the growing use of patronage for government positions is threatening to undermine the tradition of apolitical public servants. As already noted, some of the policy advice traditionally offered by senior civil servants is now provided by personal advisers selected on partisan grounds. Likewise, the leadership of executive agencies and the boards of the numerous quasi-governmental organizations are all appointed, if nominally on merit grounds.

The Judiciary

Courts in the United Kingdom are by no means as central to the political process as courts in the United States. In large part, this absence of centrality is the result of the doctrine of parliamentary supremacy and the consequent inability of the courts to exercise judicial review of legislation. In short, there is little or no way that British courts can declare an act of Parliament unconstitutional. As British jurist A. V. Dicey put it many years ago, if Parliament decided that all blue-eyed babies should be murdered, the preservation of blue-eyed babies would be illegal.[42]

Yet in recent years, several things have acted to expand the powers and activities of the British judiciary. The most significant change in the role of the courts has stemmed from Great Britain's membership in the European Union. The European Court of Justice has declared some activities of the British government to be out of conformity with the Treaty of Rome. For some conservatives (both small and large "c"), the European Court has had too much influence on British policy, as well as policies affecting Great Britain. Furthermore, British courts must now participate in deciding whether British government policies are in accordance with the European Convention on Human Rights. Decisions to the contrary have angered many British political leaders and have raised more questions about the desirability of continued membership.

The Labour victory in 1997 ushered in a period of substantial constitutional change in the UK. Under Tony Blair, Britain saw the devolution of powers to Scotland and (to a lesser extent) Wales, the creation of the Greater London Assembly and an elected mayor for London, the adoption of the Freedom of Information Act, reform of the House of Lords, the adoption of the Human Rights Act of 1998, and the creation of the Supreme Court.[43]

To establish separation between the upper chamber of Parliament and the senior judges in the judiciary, the Constitutional Reform Act of 2005 considerably altered the top-level judicial institutions in the UK, moving the highest civil law court, the Appellate Committee of the House of Lords, out of Lords to create an independent Supreme Court. The Supreme Court sat for the first time in October 2009. The Court serves as the final court of appeal in all civil cases in the UK, and it is the final appellate court for criminal cases in England, Wales, and Northern Ireland (Scotland retains its own unique criminal high court). The focus of the Court is to be on cases that deal with points of law of interest to the public at large (much like the U.S. Supreme Court) and will also consider "devolution" issues, settling legal disputes relating to the powers of the devolved institutions.

The head of the judiciary shifted from the Lord Chancellor to the new Lord Chief Justice of the Supreme Court, though the Lord Chancellor retains many important duties and roles such as the statutory obligation to ensure an independent judiciary and the power to appoint justices to the Supreme Court. To ensure some degree of separation of powers, an independent Judicial Appointments Commission was created to propose judicial nominees to the Lord Chancellor. The commission puts forward one nominee at a time to fill a vacancy on the Court, and the Lord Chancellor has the right to either accept the recommendation or ask the commission to reconsider and put forward another nominee.[44]

The newly established Supreme Court has not gained expanded judicial review. That said, under the Human Rights Act of 1998, the Court does have the right to issue a "declaration of incompatibility," stating that an act of Parliament is at odds with the Human Rights Act of 1998. Although this declaration does not have formal influence on the legitimacy of the statute and does not overturn the offending act (it remains the case that only Parliament may strike down an act of Parliament), it is a clear signal that Parliament should revisit the act to bring it into compliance with the Human Rights Act and the European Convention on Human Rights.

The Rest of Government

British government is unitary, but local governments have a substantial impact on the ultimate shape of public policies in the United Kingdom. In a similar manner, many public activities are carried out through public corporations, quasi-public bodies, and formerly government (but now largely regulated) industries rather than directly by a government department. This choice of institutions for service delivery has consequences for the ability of government to control these functions, as well as for the nature of the services being delivered.

Local Government

British local government is not an independent set of institutions with its own constitutional base of authority such as that found for states or provinces in a federal system. Instead, British local government is the creation and the creature of the central government. Local government is organized in different formats in Scotland and Wales, and in England. In Scotland and Wales, there is now a single level of local government, the product of a reform that abolished the previous two-tier system.[45] In England, a disparate system of counties, and districts under those counties, serves much of the country, although an increasing number of unified authorities are exercising the responsibilities of both levels. Meanwhile, London has its own integrated government structure.[46]

The reorganization that created the current system of local government has been the subject of much criticism of both the inefficiency of the arrangements created and the loss of political accountability and involvement. The latter critique is based on the large number of voters for each councillor in the large local government units that have been created. This apparent loss of local democracy has been offset to some extent by the creation of elected mayors in London and other cities, such as Lewisham (a district of London),[47] but British local government is not the locus of grassroots democracy as it is in many other countries.

The loss of democratic control is even more evident when considering the creation of unelected bodies to perform many services that were once either provided by local governments or governed by boards named by local governments. Services such as housing, some aspects of health care, education, and training have all been turned over to a variety of local quangos or to other self-governing organizations.[48] The Blair government reversed this trend toward quasi-governmental service provision only slightly, in part because the existence of these organizations provides a convenient source of patronage positions to the government. Therefore, unlike most other developed democracies, the British government has been centralizing over the past several decades (in relation to local government but not regional), leaving local governments with little autonomy and fewer functions to perform. An important example of this centralization is the reduction in the number of local police forces in Great Britain, in part in response to terrorist threats.

Unlike U.S. state and local governments, local governments in the United Kingdom are closely supervised by the central government. Since May 2002 the Office of the Deputy Prime Minister has been responsible for supervising local governments in England and for determining their range of activity, funding, and political structures. Even after devolution, the Scotland Office and the Wales Office continue to exercise some (limited) supervision over local governments in their respective portions of the United Kingdom. After home rule was revoked in Northern Ireland in early 2000, supervision of local government in that province was returned to Whitehall. (Home rule was restored in late 2001 and then revoked again, continuing the erratic course of home rule for the province.) Because in the

United Kingdom a much larger proportion of the expenditures of local governments is funded through grants from the central government than is true in the United States (48 percent as opposed to 20 percent in 2002), British local authorities are more dependent on the center. These factors do not preclude conflict between central government and local authorities, especially when the two authorities happen to be governed by different political parties. In the early 1990s, major conflicts erupted between the central government and local governments over finance, especially the implementation of the poll tax. The council tax levied on property continues to be a point of contention for local governments that lack other sources of revenue.

London has been an especially important locus for issues concerning local government and local democracy. In part because it was headed by Ken Livingstone, a member of the left wing of the Labour Party, the Thatcher government abolished the Greater London Council, an umbrella government for the city's thirty-three boroughs, and required the boroughs to deliver services themselves. Some common functions, such as London Transport, remained, but the notion of London as a political and governmental entity was largely abandoned. The Labour government re-created a unified government for London, and Livingstone was elected mayor in May 2000. The current mayor is Boris Johnson, a Conservative. Having an elected mayor distinguishes London from most other local authorities in Great Britain, but in the end Westminster can always withdraw the relative autonomy given to the capital.

Public Corporations and Regulatory Bodies

Public corporations have been an important part of the total governmental sector in the United Kingdom even though they are, at least in theory, distinct from the government itself. The Labour government elected at the end of World War II nationalized many of the major British industries, including the railways, steel, coal, telecommunications, electricity, and gas. Government also was heavily involved in other industries such as petroleum.

The central government appointed members to the boards of the public corporations that ran these industries and made broad policy decisions, including about finance. The day-to-day decisions about these industries were made independently, although this independence was constrained by the industries' reliance on government funds to cover operating deficits and to provide capital for new ventures. Also, decisions by a nationalized industry often provoked political discontent with a government, such as in 1979 when the decision by the National Coal Board to close several less productive Welsh pits prompted a strong outcry, and again in the mid-1980s when more pit closings led to a bitter year-long strike.

When the Thatcher government took office in 1979, nationalized industries made up a significant share of economic activity in the United Kingdom. Such a large share of industry in public hands gave the government a great, albeit indirect, influence over the economy, especially in a period of high inflation when wage settlements in the nationalized industries were frequently used as guidelines for settlements in the private sector and when the pressures to keep wage settlements down produced labor unrest.

The Thatcher government was anxious to reduce the role of the public sector in the economy and to strengthen the private economy. This desire led Conservatives to privatize some nationalized industries, including gas, telecommunications, road transportation, and

British Airways. The government also sold off much of a major local industry, its council (public) housing, to the occupying tenants (about 80 percent of tenants in London took advantage of this opportunity, but only about 30 percent in the Glasgow region did so). These sales helped to balance the budget and helped to fulfill ideological dreams and campaign promises on behalf of free enterprise. The process of privatization continued with other public assets, including some public utilities such as electricity and water. The British government was becoming much less of a direct economic actor.

Government has not been able to get out of the economy entirely, however. Moreover, almost every privatization has required greater regulatory authority to control the new industries. For example, privatizing gas led to the creation of the Office of Gas Regulation, or OFGAS, which is now merged with the electricity regulator, and privatizing telecommunications produced OFTEL, the Office of Telecommunications Regulation. The principal task of these independent offices was to set the rates that the newly created private monopolies, or oligopolies, could charge and also to set standards of service.[49] Unlike most American regulators, in setting the rates these offices focused more on the retail price index than on return on capital, attempting to drive consumer prices downward and efficiency up. The rate-setting role of the regulators has diminished, however, as competition for services has increased.

Government may have privatized industries and created nominally independent regulators, but it cannot escape the political fallout from the privatized industries. The public still remembers that these enterprises were once public and still thinks of them as public utilities that should be operated with some concern for the common good. Poor service, higher fares, and several major accidents have produced a hue and cry over the profits being earned by the firms that now provide railway services. One consequence is that the government has taken back ownership of rails and switches, although the railroads themselves remain in private hands.

Once installed in 1997, the Labour government maintained much the same policy toward industry as the previous Conservative governments, placing more emphasis on economic growth and job creation than on redistributive issues. Some of the reduced direct public involvement in the economy reflects changes in the economic structure, such as the significant job losses in heavy industry and rapidly rising employment in service industries. Although employment and growth have been high, the loss of well-paying manufacturing jobs has tended, as in many other industrialized countries, to raise new issues about economic and social inequality.

The Quasi-Governmental Sector

The quasi-governmental sector is one of the biggest areas of activity in the public sector, representing up to one-third of public spending. A principal example is the National Health Service, which is the largest organization in Western Europe, either public or private. Although government-funded and government-controlled through the Department of Health, it represents an attempt to maintain some independence for the practice of medicine. The same attempt to maintain independence has been directed at the universities, some of which no longer rely on public funds for the majority of their income, and also at some research organizations funded more or less directly by the public sector.

Other parts of the quasi-governmental sector are kept under somewhat closer control by the government, although the control is indirect through appointments as much as it is through direct accountability mechanisms. Indeed, one of the most important critiques of the quasi-governmental sector is that it is less accountable than the more traditional means of delivering public services. The Thatcher government launched an offensive against quangos early in its time in office, in part to impose greater control over government and public expenditure. By the end of its period in office, however, it had created hundreds of new quasi-governmental organizations. These new organizations helped to make the public sector appear even smaller and also provided ways to diminish Labour Party control over local service delivery activities. The coalition elected in 2010 has also pledged to reduce the size and cost of the quasi-governmental sector.

NOTES

1. Arend Lijphart, "Democratic Political Systems: Types, Cases, Causes, and Consequences," *Journal of Theoretical Politics* 1 (1991): 33–48.
2. The Scottish Parliament elected in 1999 adopted the basic Westminster form of government, but the Labour and Liberal Democratic Parties formed a coalition in order to have a majority, something of a precursor to the Westminster coalition in 2010. In 2007 the Scottish National Party (the largest in Scotland) formed a minority government.
3. Philip Cowley, *Revolts and Rebellions: Parliamentary Voting under Blair* (London: Politico's, 2002).
4. Ivor Jennings, *Cabinet Government,* 2nd ed. (Cambridge: Cambridge University Press, 1969), 277–289.
5. Charles Polidano, "The Bureaucrats Who Almost Fell Under a Bus: The Reassertion of Ministerial Responsibility," *Political Quarterly* 71 (April-June 2000): 177–183.
6. An eighteenth-century prime minister, Lord Melbourne, is responsible for the aphorism "It matters not what we say, so long as we all say the same thing."
7. The characterization of the British system as increasingly "presidential" belies the fact that U.S. presidents and those in much of Latin America face a separated legislature.
8. Roy Pierce, "The Executive Divided against Itself: Cohabitation in France, 1986–1988," *Governance* 4 (1991): 270–294.
9. David Butler, Andrew Adonis, and Tony Travers, *Failure in British Government: The Politics of the Poll Tax* (Oxford: Oxford University Press, 1994).
10. For example, immediately after the Kosovo crisis in 1999 the opposition called for a review of the policy and conduct of the war.
11. R. Blackburn, *European Convention on Human Rights: The Impact of the European Convention on Human Rights in the Legal and Political Systems of Member States* (London: Cassell Academic, 1997).
12. Peter Fearon, *Behind the Palace Walls: The Rise and Fall of Britain's Royal Family* (London: Citadel Press, 1999).
13. Peter Hennessy, "The Throne Behind the Power," *Economist,* December 24, 1994, 77–79.
14. Walter Bagehot, *The English Constitution* (London: Fontana, 1963).
15. Michael Foley, "Presidential Attribution as an Agency of Prime Ministerial Critique in a Parliamentary Democracy: The Case of Tony Blair," *British Journal of Politics and International Relations* 6 (2004): 292–311.

16. Peter Hennessy, "Rulers and Servants of the State: The Blair Style of Government, 1997–2004," *Parliamentary Affairs* 58 (2005): 6–16.

17. That said, Nick Clegg as leader of the Liberal Democrats was generally considered to have won these debates, but it did him and his party little good in the elections.

18. David Coates and Peter Lawler, eds., *New Labour in Power* (Manchester and New York: Manchester University Press, 2000), 68.

19. Ibid., 70.

20. Chris Clifford, "The Prime Minister's Office in Britain," in *Administering the Summit*, ed. B. G. Peters, R. A. W. Rhodes, and V. Wright (London: Macmillan, 2000).

21. "Quangos: Under the Carpet," *Economist*, February 11, 1995; Chris Skelcher, *The Appointed State* (Buckingham, UK: Open University Press, 1998).

22. Nicholas Jones, *Sultans of Spin: The Media and the New Labour Government* (London: Victor Gollancz, 1999).

23. Kevin Theakston, *Junior Ministers in British Government* (Oxford, UK: Blackwell, 1987).

24. Bruce Headey, *British Cabinet Ministers* (London: Allen and Unwin, 1975); Martin Burch and Ian Holliday, *The British Cabinet System* (London: Harvester Wheatsheaf, 1998).

25. George Parker, "Reshuffle: Bill Affecting the City May Be Disrupted," *Financial Times*, July 31, 1999; David Wighton, "Reshuffle: Blair's New Faces Lack Business Background," *Financial Times*, July 30, 1999.

26. Brian W. Hogwood and Thomas T. Mackie, "The United Kingdom: Decision Sifting in a Secret Garden," in *Unlocking the Cabinet: Cabinet Structures in Comparative Perspective*, ed. Mackie and Hogwood (London: Sage, 1985). Also see Simon James, "The Cabinet System since 1945: Fragmentation and Integration," *Parliamentary Affairs* 47 (1994): 613–629.

27. Hussein Kassim, "The United Kingdom," in *Coordinating European Policy: The National Dimension*, ed. H. Kassim, B. Guy Peters, and V. Wright (Oxford: Oxford University Press, 2000).

28. These restrictions are intended to improve the image of Parliament as well as to distance the Labour Party from the unions. See "Blair Set to Axe Trade Union Sponsorship of Labour MPs," *Sunday Times*, June 11, 1995.

29. Prior to the 1999 constitutional reform, some one thousand peers were nominal members of the House of Lords. In practice, however, fewer than a third of that number participated in legislative activities. The hereditary peers elected among themselves the ninety-two hereditary peers who remain in the House of Lords. An analysis of the composition of the House of Lords is available at http://www.parliament.uk/directories/house_of_lords_infor mation_office/analysis_by_composition.cfm.

30. The incumbent in 2005–2006, a Labour MP from Scotland, wore a business suit for normal meetings of the House. That Speaker's immediate predecessor was the first woman to hold the position.

31. The Speaker generally follows the advice of the Commons' Committee on Privileges.

32. This question is so called because Tam Dalyell, who represents the West Lothian constituency in Westminster, first raised it.

33. Gavin Drewry, *The New Select Committees*, rev. ed. (Oxford: Oxford University Press, 1989).

34. John Garrett, *Managing the Civil Service* (London: Heinemann, 1980); Colin Campbell and Graham K. Wilson, *The End of Whitehall: Death of a Paradigm?* (Oxford, UK: Blackwell, 1995).

35. Gavin Drewry and Tony Butcher, *The Civil Service Today* (Oxford, UK: Blackwell, 1989).

36. See Edward C. Page and Bill Jenkins, *Policy and Bureaucracy* (Oxford: Oxford University Press, 2004).

37. See Oliver James, *The Executive Agency Revolution in Whitehall* (Basingstoke, UK: Palgrave Macmillan, 2006).

38. Campbell and Wilson, *End of Whitehall.*

39. K. G. Robertson, *Secrecy and Open Government* (London: Macmillan, 1999).

40. Brian W. Hogwood, "Restructuring Central Government: The 'Next Steps' Initiative," in *Managing Public Organizations,* 2nd ed., ed. K. Eliassen and J. Kooiman (London: Sage Publications, 1993); Patricia Greer, *Transforming the Civil Service: The Next Steps Initiative* (Buckingham, UK: Open University Press, 1993).

41. "A Riot over Prisons," *Economist,* October 21, 1995, 61–62.

42. A. V. Dicey, *Introduction to the Study of the Law of the Constitution,* 10th ed. (New York: St. Martin's Press, 1959), 74.

43. Jack Straw, "New Labour, Constitutional Change and Representative Democracy," *Parliamentary Affairs* 63 (April 2010): 356–368.

44. Robert Hazell, "The Continuing Dynamism of Constitutional Reform," *Parliamentary Affairs* (January 2007): 3–25.

45. See John McCarthy and David Newlands, eds., *Governing Scotland: Problems and Prospects* (Avesbury, UK: Ashgate, 1999).

46. Michael Chisholm, *Structural Reform of British Local Government* (Manchester, UK: University of Manchester Press, 2000).

47. For a personal account, see Ken Livingstone, *Livingstone's London* (London: Victor Gollancz, 2000). Also see "The Dangers of Devolution," *Economist,* February 26, 2000.

48. See Skelcher, *Appointed State.*

49. Because effective competition is difficult in many of these industries, the market is not an efficient price-setting institution.

Who Has the Power?

A DEMOCRATIC POLITICAL SYSTEM REQUIRES MECHANISMS THAT allow the public to influence the decisions of its political leaders. This influence may be exercised only intermittently, such as during elections, but in most democratic systems it is exercised almost continually through mechanisms such as political parties, interest groups, and increasingly public opinion polls and the media. The government of the United Kingdom is no different. Although some commentators have said that the United Kingdom is a democracy only once every five years (the statutory maximum term for a sitting Parliament), the day-to-day decisions of the British government are in fact influenced by popular demands and pressures, including through partisan institutions (the majoritarian style of UK politics tends to give substantial power to a single majority party until it is thrown out of office) and pressure groups. Furthermore, the government is attempting to provide more opportunities for participation at times other than elections. That said, the relative secrecy favored by the British government may protect it from the degree of external pressure on policy encountered by some other European countries, such as Sweden.

Political Parties

Although British political parties do have discernible policy stances, even if sometimes these are adopted merely to oppose the stated policies of the other party, they are primarily "catchall parties," and so any one party includes a relatively wide range of opinion. In this way, they differ from the more ideological parties found in most other European countries. The catchall feature is applicable to the parties even though Conservatives had an ideological bent during the 1980s and 1990s. After a series of electoral failures during that period, the Labour Party attempted to enhance its image as a broad, nonideological party by purging its more confrontational elements on the left and then revoking its commitment to public ownership. Labour's appeal to the middle class helped to produce three consecutive electoral victories in 1997, 2001 and 2005, making Blair and Thatcher the only two postwar leaders to win three consecutive parliamentary majorities. The Labour Party's policy changes, however, have alienated some of its traditional supporters in the working class, who still want a party that advocates socialism and vehemently defends the interests of the industrial working class.

Perhaps the major difference between British and continental political parties is that the majoritarian style of the British parliamentary system means that the government is most likely to be formed by a single party—though the current Conservative–Liberal Democrat coalition government shows that a "hung parliament," in which no party controls a clear majority of seats, is a real possibility. More than in other countries, British elections tend to be about the performance of the party currently in government and the capacity of another (clearly identifiable) party to assume the role of government—the rare coalition government is the exception to the rule.[1] Because of this characteristic, which, again, arises from the majoritarian nature of British parliamentary government, the responsibility for policies and performance is clearer in the British parliamentary system than in many others. One of the clear public concerns with the formation of the coalition government in 2010 was that the coalition partners negotiated a series of policy agreements and, therefore, the public did not "vote for" the policies the coalition agreed.

The Party and Electoral Systems

The British party system has been described variously as a two-party system and as a two-and-one-half-party system. Historically, the dominant parties were the Tories (antecedents of today's Conservatives) and the Liberals, both of which emerged out of legislative factions dating from the seventeenth century. The Tories, who were identified with the more privileged sectors of society, committed themselves to the defense of existing institutions and policies, including the Crown and church at home and imperialism abroad. They also affirmed the need for a strong state, the primacy of "law and order," the sanctity of private property, and an evolutionary program of social change. The Liberals, by contrast, represented primarily the middle classes and positioned themselves ideologically as a party advocating free trade, home rule in Ireland, and social reform. The failure of the Liberals to accommodate the political and economic demands of Great Britain's rapidly growing class of industrial workers during the latter part of the nineteenth century prompted a coalition of trade union leaders, socialists, and more idealistic Fabians to form the Labour Party in 1900 as an extraparliamentary organization dedicated to a more radical course of reform. By the 1920s the Labour Party had displaced the Liberals as Great Britain's other large party.

Since that time, the United Kingdom has retained a predominantly two-party system in which ideological and regional "third parties" play an important indirect role in the political process. Today, the two major parties in the United Kingdom remain the Labour Party and the Conservative (Tory) Party. They are national parties in every sense of the term and almost always run candidates in virtually every parliamentary constituency in Great Britain, except the Speaker's.

The Liberals, now known as the Liberal Democrats, constitute a "half" party on the national level and are the current coalition partners in the Conservative-led government. The Liberal Democrats were formed out of two parties, the original Liberals and the Social Democrats, a moderate faction that broke away from the Labour Party in the early 1980s. The two parties formed the Liberal-Social Democratic Alliance based on their joint opposition to the radicalization of both Labour and the Conservatives, and they pledged not to nominate candidates against each other in national elections.[2] In 1987 the Alliance won twenty-two seats scattered from the Shetlands to Cornwall, with most of its support concentrated in Scotland and Wales. After that election, the party divided again, eliminating, at least in the short run, any real potential this centrist grouping had of presenting an electoral alternative to the free-market neoliberalism of the Conservatives and the collectivism of the Labour Party. In 1988 the parties again merged as the Liberal Democrats and, despite a few years of troubled consolidation, have performed well in elections since 1992. In 1997 they won 17.2 percent of the popular vote and forty-six seats (an increase of twenty-six from the previous election), and in 2001 they increased their share to

18.8 percent of the vote and fifty-two seats. In 2005 the Liberal Democrats won sixty-two seats by increasing their share of the vote by about 3 percent.[3] The 2010 election cata-pulted the Liberal Democrats into a coalition government with just 23 percent of the vote and fifty-seven seats—a *loss* of five seats.

As for the bigger picture, election results during the 1970s, party realignments during the 1980s, and the coalition government formed in 2010 reveal the emergence of a more complex multiparty system. Although the House of Commons continues to be dominated by the two largest parties, within the electorate the parties that constitute the additions to the two- (or two-and-a-half) party system have had some difficulty organizing themselves and presenting viable alternatives for forming a government. Yet there has been some real change in the system. In some parts of the United Kingdom, one of the two major parties may actually be the third party in the electorate. This situation appears increasingly true for Conservatives in Scotland. In the 2001, 2005, and 2010 Westminster elections, Con-servatives won just one seat in Scotland, whereas in the Scottish Parliament Conservatives are the third party, holding just seventeen seats after the 2007 elections. Indeed, even Scot-tish Labour is in opposition in the Scottish Parliament. After the 2007 elections the Scot-tish National Party formed a minority government (with 47 out of 129 seats), winning one more seat than did Scottish Labour.

The Scottish National Party (SNP) and Plaid Cymru, the Welsh national party, are the two main nationalist parties in United Kingdom that regularly win parliamentary seats (a third nationalist party, Sinn Fein, is discussed later in this section). These parties expe-rienced a marked decline in their electoral fortunes in 1979, after defeat of devolution referendums in 1978. They made a minor comeback in the 1987 election, increasing their total from four to five seats, and then moved up to seven seats (four from Plaid Cymru) in 1992. The vote of the nationalist parties as a percentage of the vote in their regions also increased—to almost 14 percent for the SNP in Scotland in 1987, to 21.5 percent in 1992, and then to more than 22 percent in 1997. Electoral support declined 2001 to 20.1 percent and again in 2005 to 17.7 percent, but given the electoral system, the SNP actually gained two seats in Westminster. In the 2010 election in Scotland the number of seats held by the SNP did not change, but the vote of 2.3 percent was a slight uptick. In Wales, Plaid Cymru increased its vote in 1987 (to 8 percent), 1992 (to almost 9 percent), 1997 (to almost 10 percent), and 2001 (to 14.3 percent), only to have it slip somewhat in 2005 to 12.6 percent and again in 2010 to 11.3 percent and three seats in Parliament.

Within their own regions, there is substantial variation in the vote for the nationalist parties. Often this variation is a function of factors such as the degree of urbanization (generally the nationalist parties do better outside the large urban areas) and industrializa-tion of the constituency. Plaid Cymru received a high of 44.3 percent and a low of just 2.1 percent in Welsh constituencies in 2010. Overall, in 2010 Plaid Cymru commanded less than 10 percent of the vote in two-thirds of the Welsh constituencies. Before the establish-ment of the Scottish Parliament, the SNP vote ranged between 55.7 percent and 8.8 percent in Scottish constituencies in 1992, with only two constituencies returning less than 10 percent SNP votes. After the establishment of the Scottish Parliament, however, the SNP saw its share of the Westminster vote slip. In the 2010 Westminster elections, the SNP constituency vote ranged from a high of 45.7 percent to a low of just 7.7 percent. More to the point, the SNP vote was below 10 percent in five constituencies, but this represents a slight improvement on the 2005 election result. Home rule has been a help to the nationalist parties, with the SNP in the Scottish Parliament forming a minority Scottish government and Plaid Cymru forming a coalition Welsh government (with Labour) following the national elections of 2007. Yet critics of the nationalist parties argue that now that Scotland and Wales have their own deliberative bodies, these parties are less relevant in the British Parliament, and in 2010 the SNP again found itself struggling to explain its relevance in Westminster.

The partisan politics of Northern Ireland reflect the troubled history of that province and the religious and nationalist cleavages that divide the population. In 2010 four political parties and one independent won Westminster seats. The Democratic Unionist Party (DUP) is a Protestant party with an intense dedication to the continuing union of Northern Ireland and the United Kingdom. Two of the other parties winning seats in Northern Ireland are primarily Roman Catholic, and they would like to unite Northern Ireland with the Republic of Ireland to its south. The Social Democratic and Labour Party (SDLP) is overwhelmingly Catholic and would like to unite all of Ireland as a single, socialist society. Despite its sectarian appeal, the SDLP is a secular (constitutional nationalist) organization. The other Catholic party is Sinn Fein, once regarded as the political arm of the Irish Republican Army (IRA). Sinn Fein, led by Gerry Adams, is committed to the unification of Ireland. The big winner in the 2010 general election in Northern Ireland was the DUP, with eight seats. Sinn Fein held its five seats, and the SDLP also broke even (together, the nationalists hold eight seats). The Alliance Party, a nonsectarian party seeking to "heal the divisions" in Northern Ireland by having the nationalists and unionists find common ground, won one seat in Westminster as did a unionist independent.

General elections in the United Kingdom are held under a single-member district, plurality system. Each constituency elects a single representative (member of Parliament), and all that is required for election is a plurality—that is, the individual with the most votes wins whether receiving a majority or not. Such a system has the advantage of usually producing majorities for Parliament, and although no British party since 1945 has won a majority of the popular votes, parliamentary majorities have been produced by each election except those in February 1974 and May 2010. Although some are popular with the broad national electorate, the smaller parties are severely disadvantaged by this electoral system. For that reason, the Liberal Democrats have advocated proportional representation (PR) as a more equitable means of selecting members of Parliament. Because the Liberal Democrat vote is spread widely across Great Britain, that party is more disadvantaged by the current system than are the nationalist parties whose votes are more concentrated. In 2005 the Liberal Democrats received just 9.5 percent of the seats with 22.1 percent of the vote, and in 2010 they received 8.8 percent of the seats with 23 percent of the vote. In contrast, in 2010 the Conservatives won 47 percent of the seats with 36 percent of the vote, and Labour won about 40 percent of the seats in Westminster with just 29 percent of the popular vote. As part of the coalition agreement struck between the Conservatives and the Liberal Democrats, the Conservatives agreed to put forward a referendum on switching to the nonproportional alternative vote system. The Liberal Democrats see this compromise as a move toward adopting the proportional single transferable vote electoral system.[4]

In other elections the United Kingdom is beginning to experiment with proportional representation. Elections for the European Parliament are run on a closed-list PR basis. Elsewhere, members of the Scottish Parliament and the Welsh National Assembly are elected using a mixed-member proportional system that elects a portion of the parliamentarians using single-member districts and the rest through a closed-list proportional system. The Northern Ireland Assembly that sprang from the Good Friday agreement is elected entirely by means of the single transferable vote system, the same complex system used in the Republic of Ireland. The single transferable vote is now used for Scottish local council elections as well. Finally, the mayor of London is elected using a supplementary vote system. These are interesting experiments, but as long as the existing Westminster electoral system continues to benefit the parties in power, it is unlikely to be changed.

One clear change in the British system of parliamentary representation is the reduction in the number of Westminster constituencies in Scotland that took effect with the 2005 elections. Historically, Scotland and Wales were overrepresented, with more parliamentary seats than might be expected on the basis of population, in part because both regions have more rural areas. Meanwhile, Northern Ireland was significantly underrepresented until 1980. The justification for this misdistribution of parliamentary seats was that Scotland and Wales, because of their national identity and history, were deemed to have special interests requiring greater representation. By contrast, Northern Ireland was underrepresented because, until 1972, it had substantially greater self-government, with its own parliament sitting at Stormont, than did other parts of the United Kingdom. With the imposition of direct rule from Westminster, that justification was no longer valid. And with subsequent changes in the distribution of seats, Northern Ireland's representation began to resemble that in Great Britain, albeit still lower than that in Scotland and Wales (see Table 1-2).

The Scotland Act, the law passed by the British Parliament that created the Scottish Parliament in 1997, called for the number of Westminster seats in Scotland to be reduced after the creation of the Scottish Parliament. This partial equalization in the apportionment of seats across regions of the United Kingdom was one of the compromises made during the negotiations establishing the parliament in Scotland. Because the Scottish Parliament now exercises legislative authority over matters of "domestic" policy within Scotland, it was agreed that a "fairer" distribution of Westminster seats was in order. But because only limited authority devolved to the National Assembly for Wales in the Wales Act (1997), no changes were made to the size of the Welsh Westminster delegation.

One aspect of the British electoral system that differentiates it from the U.S. system and most European systems is the importance of by-elections. If a seat becomes vacant during the life of a Parliament, an interim election (by-election) is held to fill the seat. As well as ensuring full membership of the House of Commons, by-elections are seen as something of an ongoing vote of confidence by the people, and poor electoral performance can be

Table 1-2 Citizens per Parliamentary Seat: United Kingdom, 1995 and 2005

	England	Wales	Scotland	Northern Ireland
1995				
Seats	529	40	72	18
Citizens per seat	89,600	73,900	71,500	92,900
2005				
Seats	529	40	59	18
Citizens per seat	92,890	72,577	85,797	93,626

Note: Citizens per seat calculated using 1991 and 2001 UK Census data available at http://www.statistics.gov.uk.

quite embarrassing for a sitting government. Gordon Brown's government, for example, was plagued by a series of by-election defeats in Norwich North, Glenrothes, and Glasgow East, among others. By-elections were also used as gauges of Margaret Thatcher's electoral strength, as well as that of the Liberal-Social Democratic Party Alliance, and they became one component of the evidence used in deciding when to call the 1987 election. By-elections also can lead to the loss of a parliamentary majority, as occurred in Parliaments sitting between October 1974 and 1979 and 1992 to 1997.

Elections to the European Parliament and local council elections are similar barometers of public opinion toward the government in power. The 2004 European Parliament election was widely regarded as a referendum on the Blair government's support of the Iraq war. Turnout for this election (at 38.2 percent) was up from the 1999 election (at 24 percent).[5] And the Labour Party received its lowest vote share in any election since 1918. The outspoken UK Independence Party, by contrast, increased its number of members of the European Parliament (MEPs) from three to twelve, pushing it to third place in the UK's European delegation. Similarly, the anti-immigrant, anti-Europe British National Party won two seats in the European Parliament elections of 2009. This election, along with a similarly poor showing in the English local council elections, threatened to topple an already destabilized Brown government.

The Two Major Parties

Although many voters may choose other parties, only two parties—Labour and Conservative—can usually be expected to form a UK government. But these governments may depend on the explicit or implicit support of smaller parties, as did the Conservative Party in May 2010. When it became clear on the evening of the election count that the Conservatives would not win an outright majority, speculation ensued that either Brown's sitting Labour government would attempt to cobble together a coalition of all the small parties or that the Conservatives might try to form a minority government. Instead, David Cameron and Nick Clegg agreed to a power-sharing coalition government with the Liberal Democrats having a significant, but clearly junior, role in the government. Although John Major and the Ulster Unionists did not reach a specific coalition agreement, Major depended on the Ulster Unionists to stave off defeat toward the end of his government in 1997.

A great deal divides the two major parties in Great Britain, but in many ways they are similar. Both are essentially elite, or caucus, parties in that, compared with their electoral strength, they have a relatively small mass membership. The parties are also aggregative—both cover a range of social and political opinion and consequently have internal ideological divisions as well as disagreements with the other party. Finally, compared with decentralized American parties, both are relatively centralized and disciplined, although not so easy to discipline as some continental parties in which parliament members lack direct links with constituencies.

The Labour Party

The roots of the British Labour Party lie in the Industrial Revolution. The Labour Party is the principal representative of the working class in British politics, although its support is broader than just industrial labor. Indeed, the 1997, 2001, and 2005 elections demonstrated that the Labour Party has substantial appeal among almost all segments of society. Historically, the Labour Party professed socialism as a major portion of its program, but it is an aggregative party that includes many adherents who do not accept socialism as the goal of the party or society. "New Labour," for example, is very muted in speaking about socialism and has given up public ownership of the major means of production as a significant policy goal.

Ideological cleavages within the Labour Party are highly visible and intense. For much of the 1980s, intraparty factionalism prevented the party from being a viable competitor to the Conservatives. In response, party leader Neil Kinnock sought to create a more moderate image and heal some of the strife within the party. In the early 1990s the Labour Party dropped its campaign pledge of unilateral nuclear disarmament so it might appear stronger in foreign affairs, and it moderated its stances on the renationalization of privatized industries, as well as its earlier criticism of the European Union (EU). In other words, it has behaved like a party in a two-party system should—seeking the electoral center—but it has found that center farther to the right than it had been. Tony Blair, the Labour Party's leader from 1994 to 2007, moved the party even more to the right on traditional class issues. Following his urging, in 1995 the party dropped its commitment to Clause Four of the party's constitution of 1918 and with that a commitment to government ownership of principal means of production and distribution.[6] Blair also has sought to broaden the appeal of the party to women and minorities. The party pledged to nominate female candidates for half of the safe Labour and winnable marginal seats in the 1997 election.[7] Gordon Brown, Blair's successor as prime minister, did not, despite initial hopes of party members on the left, significantly move Labour away from the political center.

The organization of the Labour Party outside Parliament becomes clearer once one understands the role that labor unions have traditionally played in the party. The British Labour Party originally was an alliance of trade unions and socialist organizations, with unions traditionally the dominant element in that coalition. Currently, many party members and the majority of the party's financial base come from the labor movement. Therefore, when one speaks of the membership of the Labour Party, one is really speaking of the unions, although the voting strength of the unions in the annual conference of the party has been reduced by changes in the party constitution. Moreover, individual party members, through socialist organizations and constituency parties, now have influence that is much greater than their numerical strength. Their power was increased by a change in the party's constitution in 1980 involving the election of the party leader through an electoral college that has a disproportionate share of constituency party members, albeit still dominated by the parliamentary party.

The National Executive Committee (NEC) of the Labour Party supervises party operations outside Parliament and, to an increasing extent, manages the whole party. Of the thirty-three members of this committee, twelve are direct representatives of labor unions and six represent the constituency parties. The remaining members are the leader and deputy leader of the party, the treasurer (who is elected by the annual party conference), three members of the Labour parliamentary party, three government representatives, two Labour councillors, the leader of Labour members of the European Parliament, a Young Labour representative, and two representatives of the Socialist Societies in Britain. Fifteen of these members are women. Because of major voices in the NEC and the annual conference that belong to those other than elective politicians, the actions of the Labour NEC are less predictable and manageable than those of the Conservative Party's executive committee. This instability is especially true when the Labour Party is the opposition party and the leader lacks the power of office. The bureaucratic arm of the party is the Labour Party secretary and his or her staff. As noted, the party bureaucracy is closely controlled by the National Executive Committee. This control extends to having subcommittees of the NEC supervise various sections of the party organization such as research, press and publicity, and finance.

The Labour Party has regional organizations, but these organizations do not have the degree of importance of their equivalents in the Conservative Party. Until the 1980 changes in the party's structure, Labour's constituency parties lacked even the autonomy granted to their equivalents in the Conservative Party. These constituency parties now have the right to reselect their candidates before each election, removing that power from the central party. This power has led to the selection of some extreme left-wing candidates and some further division within the party. For example, in a 1991 Liverpool by-election the moderate Labour candidate was opposed by a "real Labour" candidate from Militant Tendency, the extreme left of the party. Since 1997, however, control over candidate selection has shifted in an awkward start-and-stop fashion toward the central party. In 1997 Labour adopted the all-women short list for candidates and gave some constituencies only lists of approved female candidates. This policy was stopped after a legal challenge on the basis of ("positive") sex discrimination. In 2002, however, the Labour-controlled Parliament passed the Sex Discrimination (Election Candidates) Act, once again making all-women short lists possible.

The power of the unions in the Labour Party's annual conference has markedly declined. Of the approximately four thousand participants in these autumn affairs, more delegates represent constituency parties than unions. Voting is not based on the number of delegates present, however, but on the number of dues-paying party members represented by those present. Unions formerly held the balance of power, controlling approximately five-sixths of all votes, but presently their members cast about one-half of the votes.

At times, the annual conference has attempted to force its views on the Parliamentary Labour Party (PLP). The formal statements of the party do, in fact, indicate that the annual conference has the right to make binding policy decisions for the PLP, but party leaders from the inception of the party have been unwilling to be controlled by policy pronouncements of those out of office, especially when there is a Labour government. The tension arises from the fact that Labour began as a movement that created a parliamentary party to serve its interests, so there is a greater tradition of mass party control than in the Conservative Party, which began as a faction in Parliament.

The conflict over the Commission of Inquiry mandated by the 1979 annual conference illustrates the tensions, both institutional and ideological, between segments of the Labour Party. This commission was charged with investigating the structure and constitution of the Labour Party, especially questions of the authorship of the party manifesto, the reselection of parliamentary candidates in each constituency prior to each general election, and the election of the party leader by a more broadly constituted body than the PLP. All these issues pitted the ideological left of the party, based in constituency organizations, against the ideological right in the PLP, especially the leadership of the PLP (then most prominently James Callaghan and Denis Healey). These issues came to a head after the 1980 annual conference accepted the commission's report, which favored the stand of the left, whereupon Callaghan resigned as party leader. The provisions of the new constitutional arrangement for electing a party leader were now finally decided, and Michael Foot—a representative of the left, although a less divisive one than most—was elected leader. These changes in the Labour Party led to the defection of what became the Social

Democrats from the party, and they seemed to be pushing the Labour Party further left than had been true in the past.

Several disastrous electoral defeats under the left-leaning leadership gave the right and center an opportunity to reassert their case for a more centrist Labour Party dedicated to winning elections, not ideological wrangles. Even the modernized party could not win the 1992 election, however, and Neil Kinnock resigned and was replaced by John Smith. Smith's untimely death soon after his selection led to the selection of Tony Blair, a young, energetic, and reformist leader for the Labour Party.[8] Blair's subsequent success in transforming Labour into a more centrist "New Labour" party embracing neoliberal economic and social policies while distancing itself from organized labor was a principal factor contributing to Labour's landslide electoral victories in 1997 and 2001. With 44.4 percent of the popular vote in 1997 (compared with 34.4 percent five years earlier), Labour won 419 seats to displace the Conservatives as Britain's governing party for the first time since 1979. Popular support declined marginally in the June 2001 election to 42.2 percent, largely because of a low voter turnout, but with 413 MPs the Labour Party easily won reelection for a second full term. Prime Minister Blair promptly affirmed his determination to act on the party's campaign promises to improve public services, including education and health care, while cautiously exploring the prospect of Great Britain eventually joining the European Union's Euro Area, the group of European countries that use the euro as their common currency. Blair's electoral successes in 1997 and 2001 then fell victim to the Labour government's decision to join the U.S.-led campaign that invaded Iraq in 2003. This issue deeply divided the country and Blair's party. The election of 2005 returned a weakened Labour government to power with a majority of sixty-six seats (the previous winning Labour majorities were 179 in 1997 and 167 in 2001). Labour lost forty-seven seats and won only 35.3 percent of the vote. With the electoral success of high-profile antiwar activists such as George Galloway, who won a constituency in London, it appeared that Labour and Blair were being widely chastised. After the election, Blair acknowledged that Iraq had been a "deeply divisive" issue and that the public had sent a message to which, he said, "I have listened and I have learned." [9] Despite the importance attributed by the media and prominent politicians to Iraq in influencing the 2005 British vote, postmortem analyses of the election indicate that the Blair government's economic performance and public service delivery, as well as evaluations of the party leaders, were the most significant factors leading to the election outcome.[10] Apparently, the influence of the Iraq war on the election of 2005 was indirect, operating through leadership evaluations.

Blair lasted as prime minister until June 2007, when his public support had so eroded that he stepped down, turning over the keys to Number 10 Downing Street to Gordon Brown. Brown had been the longest serving chancellor of the exchequer, in office from 1997 until becoming prime minister in 2007. Given the nature of parliamentary democracy in the UK, where the majority party selects the prime minister, Blair's relinquishing the premiership to Brown did not require a national election. In some ways, however, Brown's "coronation" as prime minister, without a national electoral mandate, served to undermine his credibility and political capital and set the stage for Labour's defeat in 2010.

The Conservative Party

The Conservative Party has its roots in the political conflicts of the eighteenth century, and to some degree those roots produce conflicts within the emerging character of the

Conservative Party today. In the late 1980s, the majority of adherents to the Conservative Party felt akin to conservative parties in Europe and North America, resisting government encroachments into the affairs of individuals. Traditionally, however, the Conservative Party advocated a strong central government, in part because of an elitist perception that the poor and less educated cannot be counted on to make proper decisions on their own and need guidance by their "betters." "Old Tories" therefore want significant government control over the private sector, albeit control used to preserve the interests of the upper classes, or at least to preserve the existing social order.[11]

"New Tories," or Thatcherite Conservatives, tend to advocate greater freedom for individual and business activities, and consequently they advocate a diminished role for government in economic and social life. Today, long after Thatcher's time in office, there are conflicts within the party over the meaning of conservatism. The leader of the party in 2000, William Hague, appeared closer to the Thatcherite wing than to the Old Tories, and he faced a formidable challenge in attempting to balance views within the party to win elections with a public that had grown skeptical of the perceived extremism of the party during the Thatcher and Major years. David Cameron, however, who became leader of the Conservatives in 2005, shifted the party to the middle, seeking to rebrand the party as one concerned with green issues and social mobility.

The Conservative Party is an elite party, both in terms of the socioeconomic characteristics of the bulk of its adherents and in terms of the relationship between party members and the party's voting strength. The number of British citizens voting for the Conservative Party is many times greater than its formal membership. The party is now thought to have some 290,000 members, down from more than 1 million not too many years ago.[12] Still, it remains a relatively small mass organization compared with its ability to organize voters and to manage national campaigns. The elitism of the party is further typified by the domination of the party by the parliamentary party, and perhaps even more by the leader. The party does have some democratic structures, but in practice a small leadership group tends to be dominant.

The Conservative Party outside Parliament has two major components. The first is a mass organization headed by the National Union of Conservative and Unionist Associations in England and Wales; there are similar bodies in Scotland and Northern Ireland. The governing body of the National Union is its Party Board, which has seventeen members. Subordinate bodies include forty-two area councils.

The territorial organization of the Conservative Party is similar to the national organization. Within each of the twelve provincial area councils, the party is organized by constituencies, each with a leadership structure similar to that of the national party. The constituencies are also served by agents responsible for the administrative functions of the party (this is also true of the Labour Party). The constituency parties are important, because it is at this level that most funds are raised and local campaigning is managed. Also, the constituency must decide to accept candidates offered to them by the national party or to develop candidates of their own who will be acceptable to the national party. Over time, constituency parties have grown more assertive and are now willing to deselect even sitting MPs as their candidates, or to retain candidates opposed by the party leadership. The Conservative Party is centralized for many important activities, such as writing the party platform (manifesto), but for other critical functions the party is becoming more decentralized to its constituency parties.

Assisting the local and national officers is the Central Office, the second major component of the Conservative Party outside Parliament. This office, which is directed by the chair of the party organization, employs various professional workers, including those in the Conservative Research Department. The major officials in the Central Office are appointed by the party leader, and it is from this direct connection with the party leadership that the Central Office derives most of its authority. Indeed, this connection highlights the overriding fact that the Conservative Party is largely a party based on Parliament. Certainly, the annual conference of the party has become more assertive than it once was, and a leader must pay attention to the mass members of the party, but the real control over a leader is exercised by the party in Parliament, not the mass membership.

The basis of Conservative Party organization in the House of Commons is the 1922 Committee, composed of all Conservative members of the Commons other than ministers when the party is in government. The 1922 Committee has exercised considerable power over Conservative leaders, and that power appeared to be increasing before Thatcher became prime minister. The leader of the Conservative Party does not have to stand for annual election, but can be challenged every year. Five of the sixteen leaders of the party since 1902 have been forced out of the leadership by backbenchers, either by direct vote or by their obvious disapproval. Serving as prime minister for more than a decade and having molded the party in her own image did not prevent Thatcher from being removed from office when a majority of Conservatives in the House of Commons considered her policies to be poorly conceived and to be leading them toward electoral problems.

In addition to exercising control over the leadership, another function of the party in Parliament is to maintain the voting discipline of the party members. The Conservative Party leadership can "deny the whip" (expel a member), but it does so only rarely. The eight Tory MPs who abstained on an important vote on European Union policy in late 1994 were disciplined. Michael Howard, who was party leader from 2003 to 2005, denied the whip to MP Howard Flight in 2005 (and removed him from his constituency's Conservative ticket just forty-two days before the election) for saying at a private dinner that the Conservatives would dramatically cut government spending if elected. Flight initially attempted to fight off Howard, saying that his constituency would put him forward as an independent Conservative, but the constituency party quickly announced that it would accept the leader's decision. By contrast, over the last fifteen years some Conservative members have resigned the whip, and one conservative MP "crossed the aisle" to Labour in 1995, protesting the social policies of the Conservative government. Until the 1990s, the Conservative Party was not beset with the deep internal splits that have plagued the Labour Party, and the Conservatives have found it less necessary to employ the available sanctions, although conflicts over European Union policy, in particular, have raised internal tensions. Also important for conflict management within the Conservative Party are certain genteel traditions, such as not taking votes in the 1922 Committee but instead reading the sense of the meeting.

Selection of party leader was traditionally left almost entirely to the parliamentary party, although there were provisions for constituency parties and other concerned groups within the party to make their views known. This method entailed a ballot of all Conservative MPs, with provisions for runoff elections among the leading candidates. The party broadened the selection process in 1998 by establishing a two-stage process. First, the parliamentary MPs taking the Conservative whip use a series of ballots to select their top two candidates for the leader position. Then an electoral college consisting of all party members elects the party leader from these two candidates. In September 2001 a majority of 61 percent of the party's 318,000 eligible members utilized the new procedure to elect Iain Duncan Smith—an erstwhile skeptic of European integration—over Kenneth Clarke, a former chancellor of the exchequer who had advocated closer ties with the European Union. Duncan Smith succeeded William Hague, who had announced his resignation after the party's loss in the June 2001 election. By 2003 a lack of confidence in Duncan Smith's leadership had led to his ouster through a ballot of Conservative MPs. To avoid a split in the party, only one candidate, Michael Howard, was nominated to replace Duncan Smith. After the parliamentary elections in 2005, Howard announced that he would step down as leader, thereby sparking a contest between the moderate and "Euro-skeptic" wings of the party for the leadership position. A hard-fought four-way contest ensued, with David Cameron, the self-described "modern compassionate conservative," the clear winner.

Crucial divisions within the party over domestic social and economic policy and, even deeper, Europe's and Great Britain's role in an expanding and ever more powerful European Union were an important factor in the disastrous showing of the Conservatives in the 1997 election, when the party's share of the vote plummeted to 31.4 percent from 41.9 percent in 1992, and the number of Conservative MPs fell from 336 to 165. The Conservatives gained one seat in the June 2001 election, but popular support for the party was the second lowest since 1880, and the number of its supporters at the lowest level since the introduction of universal suffrage in 1929. Despite using the hot-button issues of immigration, asylum seekers, and the proposed European constitution to chip away at Labour's parliamentary majority in 2005, the Conservatives barely increased their share of the vote (32.3 percent) over the previous two contests. The 1997, 2001, and 2005 defeats prompted a change of party leadership and intense internal debates over fundamental policy issues. Cameron's approach has been to remake the Conservative "brand," emphasizing more moderate social policies and promoting green issues and a more "compassionate conservatism" to attract younger, more socially moderate voters. Although this approach has garnered (significant) criticism from traditional Conservatives, the party, at the end of 2009, was substantially ahead of Labour in public opinion polls. Perhaps more telling, most polls in September 2009 showed Cameron to be a far more popular leader than Gordon Brown.

The 2010 election demonstrated that Cameron's strategy of policy moderation resonated with the British electorate, if not with the more conservative members of his party. In May 2010 the Conservative Party gained ninety-seven seats to make it, with 307 seats, the largest single party in the House of Commons, but not large enough to constitute a majority. As has been said elsewhere in these chapters, in the wake of the "hung parliament," the Conservatives joined in coalition with the Liberal Democrats to form the government. The coalition agreement was announced with a great deal of enthusiasm by both parties, but it remains to be seen how well this government will function and the extent to which the coalition will be able to strike a balance between the policy commitments in the agreement and real-world, unexpected events.

Voting and Elections

Elections are a crucial driving force of democratic politics. Or are they? Certainly, all conventional analyses of British politics assume that government policies are decided by the clash of political parties over issues. In like manner, voters are assumed to be both interested in politics and to make their choices among parties on the basis of issues. These assumptions, however, may be largely unsubstantiated by evidence. This section looks at the evidence about voter turnout and the reasons for voting choices, and then asks a few pertinent questions about the role of elections in policy choice in the United Kingdom.

But first a look at several salient features of British elections is in order. Elections for the House of Commons are national in character, but they are national elections conducted in individual constituencies. Although it is clear who will be prime minister should one party or the other win, only one constituency actually votes for the prospective prime minister—the constituency he or she will represent. Also, British constituencies are quite small compared with electoral districts in most Western countries. As of the 2005 election, the average English MP represented almost 93,000 people, the average Scottish MP roughly 86,000 people, and the average Welsh MP about 73,000 people. By way of contrast, the average member of the National Assembly in France represents more than 100,000 people and the average legislator in the United States about 600,000 people.

In addition to size differences, the expenses of constituency campaigning in Great Britain are regulated, so that a candidate in 2005 could not spend more than £7,150 ($12,456) plus 5 pence (about 9 U.S. cents) per voter in urban districts and 7 pence per voter in rural districts.[13] Under the new spending limits that went into effect with the 2001 election, parties are limited to spending no more than £30,000 ($56,262) per contested constituency. These spending restrictions, combined with the short campaign period (usually six weeks or less) and the difficulty encountered in purchasing electronic media time other than for the limited party political broadcasts provided free on all networks, ensure that British campaigns are very different from those in the United States. An average major-party candidate contesting an election in an urban constituency of 93,000 people would be limited to spending no more than £11,800 ($20,556) for the duration of the election campaign. When the expenditure allowed the parties is added, the total on average that could be spent per candidate contesting an urban constituency of 93,000 is £41,800 ($72,819). The average U.S. House candidate spends about $890,000, and the average Senate candidate spends around $4.8 million.[14] These figures do not even include what the parties and other interests spend to support House and Senate candidates. Despite the concerns about the escalating party spending in British election campaigns, they remain relatively inexpensive.

A final difference is that in Great Britain the parties control the selection of candidates more centrally than American parties do, although this control has been softening over time. Partially in response to the expenses scandal and partly to fulfill Cameron's desire to attract new voters to the Conservative Party, in August 2009 the Conservatives held Britain's first open primary to select one constituency's parliamentary candidate. Voters in the Totnes constituency selected a physician with no political experience to replace the incumbent, Anthony Steen, who, at the outbreak of the expenses scandal, infamously accused voters of jealousy over his "very, very large" house.[15] Despite this innovation, it is unclear how widely primaries may be used in future candidate selection contests. Traditionally, new prospective candidates would have to be accepted by the constituency party, with the Central Office exercising a largely advisory role. Candidates already sitting for a seat in Parliament, or who stood for a seat in the constituency in the previous election, have not needed to be reselected in the Conservative Party, whereas now they must be reselected in the Labour Party.

Voter Turnout

British citizens tend to vote more readily than American citizens, although not so readily as citizens in most other Western democracies. Turnout is also relatively evenly distributed across the country. As is true for most other countries, the abstainers are concentrated in the working class, although it is unclear exactly what impact this "differential turnout" between the social classes has on British election outcomes. In their foundational work on British electoral behavior, David Butler and Donald Stokes asserted that the difference in turnout among members of different social classes could influence election outcomes.[16] Survey analysts, however, have noted more recently that the individual-level data seem to indicate that sources of differential turnout between members of different social classes may vary with the context of each election. Therefore, it is difficult to come up with any definitive statement of how working-class or middle-class abstainers may influence electoral outcomes in general and over time.[17]

Much was made over the drop in turnout in the 2001 election. From 1945 to 1997, the average British voter turnout was 76.3 percent, with a high of 83.9 percent in 1950 and a low of 71.4 percent in 1997. In 2001 voter turnout fell to 59.4 percent. A slight bounce occurred in 2005, with turnout reaching 61.3 percent, and in 2010 turnout went up to 65 percent. Why the drop in 2001? Political pundits claimed that either voter apathy or distrust of elected officials was the likely explanation. But the survey evidence reveals a somewhat different story. Evidence from the British Election Study shows that people were dissatisfied enough with the performance of Labour to stay home, but not enough to feel inclined to vote (heavily) for the opposition. Further, the general impression seemed to be that the election was a foregone conclusion, so interest in the election was somewhat lower than in previous years. These factors, along with growing generational gaps in feelings of civic duty led to voters staying away from the polls in 2001.[18]

Partisan Choice by Voters

As well as deciding whether to vote, a voter must decide for whom to vote. From the substantial research devoted to determinants of the partisan choice of voters, four interacting factors have emerged: social class, regional patterns of residence, demography, and issues. Members of the social classes are not evenly spread across the country; more working-class voters live in Scotland, Wales, and the industrial north and Midlands of England, and more middle- and upper-class voters live in the southeast or southwest of England.[19] The issues to which citizens are assumed to respond also have different impacts on members of different social classes, on different ethnic and age groups, and on residents of different regions of the country.

Social Class The pioneering studies of Butler and Stokes identified social class as an important factor in explaining voting in Great Britain. As noted earlier, much of British politics has been conceptualized in class terms. And although there is strong evidence that class remains a predictor of voting decisions, there is also evidence that it is no longer as overwhelming as often believed.[20] Labour still has an advantage in working-class support, but the Conservative Party no longer has the clear advantage in middle- and professional-class support. In the 2001 election, 61 percent of manual workers voted for the Labour Party, and 20 percent voted Conservative. By contrast, the Conservatives slumped to four percentage points behind Labour in middle- and professional-class support (34 percent voted Conservative, and 38 percent voted Labour).[21] Social class remains a general predictor of party preference, but its importance has declined in recent elections as voters have become more attuned to particular issues and personalities.

In general, members of labor unions are substantially more likely to vote Labour than are members of the working class as a whole. In 1997, 60 percent of union members voted Labour, while only 44 percent of working-class voters who were not union members voted Labour. This was the case even though many of those not voting for Labour were in objectively worse socioeconomic conditions than the union members. Overall, the impact of union membership on voting has declined, in part because many union members who have jobs have begun to make middle-class incomes and have begun to behave politically more like the middle class. Moreover, aggregate trade union membership has fallen to approximately 26 percent of the workforce.

Despite its past dominance, social class has declined as a predictor of voting intention in the UK. Analysts argue that lifestyle factors have become more important in explaining patterns of voting behavior than simple membership in a social class. Indeed, Harold Clarke and his colleagues have recently demonstrated that the relationship between social class and voting behavior has weakened over time to the extent that "at the end of the twentieth century, class had come to play a very limited role in determining the voting preferences of the British electorate."[22]

Religiosity and religious affiliation also tend to affect voting behavior. Adherents of the Church of England tend to vote Conservative more often than do members of other churches. To characterize the Church of England as the Tory Party at prayer may be to overstate the identity of church and party, but church membership appears to have a significant influence. Catholic members of the working class tend to vote Labour more consistently than do workers as a whole. Even leaving aside the influence of Northern Irish politics on voting, Catholic voters in cities such as Glasgow and Liverpool are among the most consistent Labour supporters.

Finally, certain lifestyle characteristics are important in explaining why members of the working or middle classes tend to vote for or against the nominal interests of their class. Working-class voters living in council (public) housing, which varies considerably by region, are much more likely to vote Labour than are members of the working class living in other accommodations. Similarly, members of the middle class who own homes and enjoy middle-class amenities such as automobiles (in 2002, 70 percent of UK households owned one or more vehicles) are more likely to vote Conservative than are their less-well-off colleagues. Finally, the receipt of social benefits appears to have some influence on voting, with those receiving benefits more likely to vote Labour.

Patterns of Residence Where people live seems to affect their voting behavior. First, living in the Celtic Fringe tends to affect voting. Leaving aside opportunities and motivations to vote for national or third-party candidates, the division of votes between the two major parties differs in different parts of the country. Wales and Scotland are the most heavily Labour portion of the United Kingdom. Indeed, were it not for Wales and Scotland, the Conservatives' strength in England would overwhelm Labour, making it highly unlikely Labour would ever control the House of Commons. The north of England has become more similar to the Celtic Fringe, with the partisan divide (as well as the economic divide) in Great Britain now appearing to lie on a line from the Wash to Bristol Channel. Traditional

Post–2010 Election Constituency in the United Kingdom

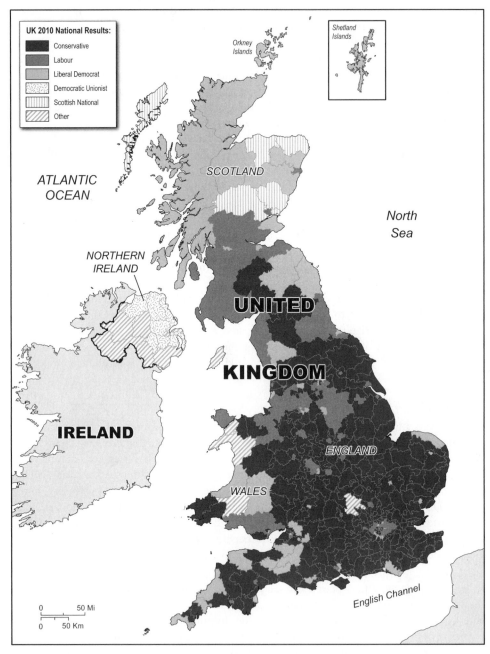

UK 2010 National Results:
- Conservative
- Labour
- Liberal Democrat
- Democratic Unionist
- Scottish National
- Other

ATLANTIC
OCEAN

SCOTLAND

North
Sea

NORTHERN
IRELAND

UNITED

KINGDOM

IRELAND

ENGLAND

WALES

English Channel

Orkney
Islands

Shetland
Islands

0   50 Mi

0   50 Km

Source: "Election 2010," BBC News, http://news.bbc.co.uk/2/shared/election2010/results.

class differences have persisted north of this divide, but those cleavages tend to have eroded south of that line.[23]

Second, rural voters tend to vote Conservative in greater proportions than urban voters. This difference is in part a function of the concentration of workers in urban industrial areas. In addition, the constituency within which a voter lives influences voting. This is especially true of prospective Labour voters, who tend to vote Labour in much greater proportions in safe Labour constituencies than in competitive, or safe Conservative, constituencies. This tendency is a function of the reinforcing effects of interactions with other Labour voters and of union efforts to mobilize the vote.

Demography   Voters also appear to behave differently based on fundamental demographic characteristics. Women have traditionally tended to support the Conservative Party more than men, although in recent years this gender gap seems to have dissipated (or even, according to some survey analyses, flipped).[24] In addition, the effect of gender appears to be less strong in Great Britain than in other European democracies, in part because voters have come to view the Conservative Party as somewhat moderate. The evidence of voting by age group is even less comforting to the Conservative Party. The relationship between age and voting Conservative is clear—the older the voter, the more likely he or she is to vote Conservative, which helps to explain David Cameron's attempt to rebrand the Conservative Party to make it more appealing to younger voters.[25]

Race and ethnicity are increasingly important issues for voting in Great Britain, where the minority population is approaching 3.4 million out of a total of some 59.8 million. Because this population is also relatively young, its importance as a voting group will grow. Labour tends to do very well among minority voters, especially in the industrial cities where they are generally concentrated. Moreover, a growing number of Labour politicians are from ethnic minority groups. Although the 2005 election saw the first black elected as a Conservative to the House of Commons, the Conservative Party's emphasis in that election on curtailing immigration and the number of asylum seekers allowed into Britain did not likely help to win it many voters from the ethnic minority community.

Issues   One assumption of democracy is that voters respond to candidates on the basis of the issues. British parties are at once centrifugal and centripetal. They express class differences more clearly than do U.S. parties, but, as Labour did in the run-up to the 1997 election and the Conservatives seem to be doing under Cameron's leadership, they also move close enough to the political center to disguise some of their potential policy differences in order to gain votes. Although some issues divide voters, in Great Britain the majority of voters of both parties tend to be on the same side of most major political issues, with conflicts often being over how best to reach the common goals.

Within the parties, however, disagreement on the issues can be substantial. Labour supporters have split over the issue of education reform in England, and Conservatives are divided over the UK's place in the EU. The level of agreement within parties has not always been higher than the level of agreement across parties. For example, the New Labour–Old Labour split over whether to enter the Iraq war was more significant than the split between Blair's New Labour faction and its Conservative opposition across the aisle. But perhaps more than any other ongoing issue, the role of the European Union in British public life and its implications for British sovereignty have tended to create cleavages both within and across the parties.

Despite the pressures toward greater ideological thinking by Conservatives and Labour's attempts to call its faithful back to the fold after years of defection, partisan identification has been declining in Great Britain. Strong identifiers with parties have decreased by more than 50 percent since the 1960s. A similar popular dealignment is also found in most other Western countries. It appears that voters are indeed more willing to think for themselves and to make decisions in each election based on issues, candidates, performance in government, or whatever. Such a development makes the task of political leaders that much more difficult, because they are less able to count on a solid base of party identifiers when they begin their election campaigns.

Overall, there is no neat way to summarize Britons' voting behavior. The class model does not seem to fit the growing complexity of the situation as well as is often assumed, and yet no other model adequately describes the complexity of the situation either. More important, some question whether elections and the choice of parties really have much consequence for government policies. Political scientist Richard Rose has conducted a detailed analysis of whether parties in Great Britain make a difference in policy terms. He concluded that the differences that do result are more matters of emphasis and the timing of policies than absolute differences in the content of policies.[26] Clearly, parties do make a difference, but the differences are subtle and not much based on a simple class model of politics.

Pressure Groups and Corporatism

One factor that has contributed to the homogenization of policies between the two parties is the growing influence of interest groups in British politics. From the 1960s through the 1970s, there was in Great Britain, like in most industrialized countries, a movement toward "corporatism" in which interest groups were granted something approaching official status as generators of demands for policies and implementers of them once adopted. The role of interest groups in British policy is rarely acknowledged officially—the doctrine of parliamentary supremacy is still invoked—but in practice much public policy is influenced, or even determined, by such groups.[27] One consequence of Thatcherism, as confirmed by the succeeding governments, has been a move away from corporatism.[28] But, no matter which party is in office, there are pressures for continuity of policies rather than change from one government to the next.

The policies made in conjunction with pressure groups tend to be made through stable patterns of interaction between civil servants and pressure group leaders and through institutionalized processes of advice for the ministries. Changes in government, therefore, would not substantially influence the basic dynamics of policymaking. In Great Britain, interest groups may not be as closely linked to policymaking as in Germany or Sweden, but the connections between government and groups are close and enduring.

Major Interest Groups

The various interest groups that affect British policymaking range from small pressure groups with narrow and largely noneconomic concerns, such as ecological groups and peace activists, to large, influential interest groups that seek to have their economic interests served through the policy process. The most obvious example of an economic group is the labor unions, although business and agriculture are also highly organized and politically effective. The clout exercised by the large economic groups is substantial, but small pressure groups also have been known to exercise substantial influence over policy.

Labor Unions The largest and probably still the most influential of the interest groups are the unions, which represent 26 percent of the total labor force. Most of the unions are organized into one national federation, the Trades Union Congress (TUC). The Labour Party is directly linked to the TUC, which gained a reputation as one of the world's most vociferous labor movements because of the large number of strikes called in Great Britain in the 1960s and 1970s. Unions were once a major counterforce to the power of government, and British elections were fought over whether the unions or the government actually ran the country, with ambiguous results. Indeed, the political power of the unions, combined with the threat of industrial action by their members, made them a formidable political influence until their decline in membership in the 1980s and 1990s and their loss of political influence under Blair.

Several factors help to explain the TUC's loss of some of its power. First, a declining proportion of the labor force belongs to unions. This decline in union membership has a generational component: 33 percent of people over the age of thirty-five are union members, but only 25 percent of men and women aged twenty-five to thirty-four are union members. Second is the shift from blue-collar to white-collar union membership. Although some white-collar unions have shown a willingness to use the strike weapon (for example, those in the public sector), most are less militant than blue-collar workers. Third, the TUC has not been able to enforce any discipline on its own members. When the miners struck in 1985–1986, the TUC, after some negotiations with the government, urged them to return to work, but they refused. The failure of the miners to win concessions from the government weakened the trade union movement. Union militancy can still produce widespread and disruptive strikes (for example, the transportation strikes), but a good deal of the power appears to be gone. This loss of power was also evident in the willingness of the Labour government under Blair to almost ignore the unions when making policy.

Business and Management Unlike the single large labor movement, business and management groups are divided into several groups. The Confederation of British Industry (CBI) is the major management organization, but other general and specialized industrial groups speak for management as well. The linkage between management groups and the Conservative Party is not as close as that between the unions and the Labour Party, and yet it certainly does exist. The Institute of Directors is another important group speaking for business. Although not really management per se, financial interests in the City of London also have a substantial influence over economic policy. These became especially apparent when financial deregulation during the Thatcher government helped the London Stock Exchange and other financial markets to prosper. During the 1990s, several scandals and a general slowing of the economy reduced the influence of the City, and in 2009 the government had to take over failing banks to help prop up the economy in the face of the global economic problems.

Agriculture Relatively few workers are employed in agriculture in the United Kingdom, but farmers and their colleagues in fishing are well organized and very effective. Even though the most important organization is the National Farmers Union (NFU), commodity groups ranging from beekeepers to dairy farmers are actively engaged in lobbying and other political activity. Agricultural groups traditionally have been successful in obtaining subsidies for their crops, and they were especially advantaged by Great Britain's entry into the European Community. They may have shifted a good deal of their lobbying focus to the

European level in Brussels, but they are still effective in extracting subsidies and benefits from the Department for Environment, Food and Rural Affairs in London and the Scottish Environment and Rural Affairs Department in Edinburgh. Similarly, the beleaguered fishing industry, concentrated mainly in Scotland, has shown a willingness to organize in an attempt to influence both the Scottish and British government responses to European Commission threats to impose a cod fishing ban in the North Sea.

Professional Organizations The large number of professional organizations in the United Kingdom include groups such as the British Medical Association, Royal College of Nursing (a trade union affiliated with the TUC), and the British Association of Social Workers. These groups tend to be politically unaffiliated and traditionally more concerned with maintaining professional standards of practice than protecting the political and economic interests of their members. In the former role, professional groups frequently serve in a public capacity as the source and implementers of standards and as accrediting agencies for practitioners. Nevertheless, because the major employer of health care professionals and social service professionals is the government, these associations do press their own political interests. These interests are related to economic issues such as pay and working conditions, as well as social concerns such as the overall level of funding for and service in the National Health Service. The changes in the National Health Service imposed by both the Conservative and Labour governments provoked a good deal of opposition from these groups, including industrial action.

Education is another service area dominated by the public sector. The major education associations in the United Kingdom are at once professional associations and unions. The National Union of Teachers (NUT) and the Association of University Teachers (AUT) are both affiliated with the TUC, and both have struck or threatened to strike. They are also vitally concerned with professional issues such as academic freedom and job security. The AUT was especially active during the Thatcher and Major years, attempting to ward off the effects of resource starvation and the higher student numbers produced by the government's higher education policy.

Pressure Groups The huge number of pressure groups important to British politics almost covers the gamut of social issues. Three sets of groups have been particularly important: the peace movement groups, nature and environmental groups, and human rights groups.

The Campaign for Nuclear Disarmament (CND) is the longest-lived of the peace movement groups; its first protests were in the 1950s against British nuclear weapons and U.S. weapons on British soil. The CND has been joined by other peace and antinuclear groups in establishing a permanent protest of the UK's Trident nuclear missile system outside the submarine base at Faslane, Scotland.

With the Royal Society for the Prevention of Cruelty to Animals at one end of a spectrum of tactics and radical antivivisection groups at the other, the nature and environmental movement has sought to protect wildlife in Great Britain and has been involved with similar issues throughout the European Union.

Among the groups promoting human rights are Amnesty International, Oxfam, Save the Children, Shelter, and a host of other social service and international aid organizations. Partially in preparation for a large-scale human rights demonstration targeting the 2005 G8 meeting at Gleneagles, Scotland, a grand coalition of these groups launched the Make

Poverty History campaign calling for trade justice and forgiveness of developing country debt. The highlight of the campaign was the "Live 8" concerts held in ten countries across the globe.

Patterns of Influence

Like pressure groups in virtually all democratic systems, those in the United Kingdom have access to many different means of influencing government policies. Government in the United Kingdom is formally less receptive to interest groups than many other governments. It lacks institutionalized means of legitimating interest group involvement, and therefore the routes of exerting that influence may be somewhat more circuitous. The four major methods for pressure group influence in the United Kingdom are lobbying, direct sponsorship of MPs, direct representation on government bodies, and consultation with ministries.

Lobbying Lobbying lawmakers is perhaps less common in the United Kingdom than in the United States, in part because party discipline makes it less likely to influence an MP's vote. Lobbying does occur, however, with the purpose of getting a voice in Parliament, more than a vote. MPs receive delegations from their constituencies and from nationally based organizations. Such delegations are particularly influential when a constituency has a single major economic interest. Facing upcoming elections in the spring of 2005, the Labour government scrambled to propitiate workers at MG-Rover's Longbridge production facility when the plant's closure was projected. Some pressure groups are sufficiently well organized to hire parliamentary agents or correspondents to maintain contact with members, attempting to influence the few potential crossover MPs and feeding friendly MPs with ideas and information. In turn, the lobbies receive attention for their interests during those parliamentary intervals when even backbench MPs have to interject themselves into parliamentary business such as Question Time or adjournment debates.

Interest groups have increased their lobbying activities since the 1970s. This increase to some degree reflects the greater contact between the public and private sectors initiated by the Thatcher government. It also reflects the growth in communications opportunities and activities in contemporary society, as well as society's greater demands for participation and involvement. British government has always been subject to political pressure, but the lobbying is now more overt. Despite living in a democracy of long standing, the British population has been relatively quiescent, but that cultural pattern is rapidly changing.

Direct Sponsorship of MPs In the United Kingdom, interest groups are allowed to sponsor prospective MPs. Groups do not contribute a majority of an MP's electoral and other expenses, but some do pay MPs to represent particular causes in Parliament such as American tobacco interests. A group may even keep an MP on a regular retainer as long as that relationship is registered with the Register of Members' Interests. Sponsorship historically has been especially important in the Labour Party as a means of permitting manual laborers to go to Parliament. Naturally, sponsorship involves some degree of control by the sponsor, although in cases such as union and working-class MPs, it is unlikely that the sponsor would ask the MP to do anything he or she would not otherwise have done. Occasionally, however, scandals over sponsorship and lobbying erupt, raising questions about the relationships between parliamentarians and their outside business relationships. For example, in early 2009 it was learned that a few members of the House of Lords were accepting substantial fees (up to £120,000) to introduce specific amendments to laws on behalf of clients. Such behavior is subjecting sponsorship to questioning and reconsideration.

Direct Representation In a comparative sense, the British government has experienced less of the corporatist pattern of interest intermediation that has characterized many other European countries.[29] Nevertheless, interest groups have had direct and official links with government in several ways. In some instances, interest groups have been directly represented in the advisory committees attached to ministries. In others, pressure groups have actually composed the majority of public organizations, such as the former National Economic Development Council ("Neddy"), which was established under Conservative aegis in the early 1960s to promote economic growth through the cooperation of business, labor, and government. This experiment with corporatism was abolished in the late 1980s because of Thatcher's aversion to programs of this type. Finally, interest groups may actually administer programs for government, which the Law Society does with Legal Aid and agricultural groups do for some farm programs. In all of these cases, it is clear, first, that governments cannot readily ignore interest groups so closely tied to the public sector, and second, that many of the traditional ideas about the separation of state and society in Western democracies make little sense in the light of the greater use of private organizations for public purposes.

Consultation Less formally, government organizations frequently consult with interest groups. Interest groups have expert knowledge of their particular areas, and they are able to predict the reactions of their members to proposed policy changes. From such consultations, a government agency might not only improve the technical quality of its proposals but also gain legitimacy for them prior to enactment. In an era in which delegated legislation is increasingly important, a substantial amount of policy will be determined by consultations between civil servants and interest group members, with a consequent decline in the relative influence of political parties and elective politicians.

NOTES

1. Peter Hennessy and Anthony Seldon, eds., *Ruling Performance: British Governments from Atlee to Thatcher* (Oxford, UK: Blackwell, 1987).
2. David Denver, "The Centre," in *Britain at the Polls, 1992,* ed. Anthony King (Chatham, N.J.: Chatham House, 1993).
3. Despite this improvement in their electoral fortunes, the Liberal Democrats were thrown into a state of disarray in early 2006 when their leader, Charles Kennedy, was forced to step down after admitting that he had long suffered from alcoholism.
4. The alternative vote (AV) system is referred to as instant runoff voting (IRV) in the United States. In practice, the main difference between AV (or IRV) and the single transferable vote (STV) is that STV makes use of multimember constituencies. Both systems ask voters to rank candidates in their order of preference.
5. BBC News, "European Election: United Kingdom Result," updated June 14, 2004, http://news.bbc.co.uk.
6. Nyta Mann, "Blair Set for Clause Four Victory," *New Statesman and Society,* March 10, 1995, 7–8.
7. Patricia Wynn Davies, "Labour to Impose All-Women Shortlists," *Independent,* September 27, 1995.

8. See Paul Anderson and Nyta Mann, *Safety First: The Making of New Labour* (London: Granta Books, 1999).

9. BBC Online, "Blair: I've Listened and Learned," May 6, 2005, http://news.bbc.co.uk/1/hi/uk_politics/vote_2005.

10. See Paul Whiteley, Marianne Stewart, David Sanders, and Harold Clarke, "The Issue Agenda and Voting in 2005," *Parliamentary Affairs* 9 (2005): 802–817.

11. The term *Old Tories* comes from Samuel H. Beer, *British Politics in a Collectivist Era* (New York: Knopf, 1965). For a useful discussion of the contemporary Conservative Party, see Paul Whiteley, Jeremy J. Richardson, and Patrick Seyd, *True Blues: The Politics of Conservative Party Membership* (Oxford, UK: Clarendon Press, 1994).

12. These figures are estimates; no definitive figures are available for Conservative Party membership.

13. U.S. dollar equivalents in this section are based on an exchange rate of £1 = $1.74210.

14. U.S. campaign spending figures from the Center for Responsive Politics, http://www.opensecrets.org.

15. James Kirkup, "GP becomes Tory candidate in first 'open primary' election," *Telegraph*, August 5, 2009 (available online at http://www.telegraph.co.uk/news/newstopics/politics/conservative/5972954/GP-becomes-Tory-candidate-in-first-open-primary-election.html).

16. David Butler and Donald Stokes, *Political Change in Britain* (London: Macmillan, 1969).

17. See, for example, the discussion of turnout of Labour, Conservative, and Liberal Democrat supporters in Charles Pattie and Ron Johnston, "Voter Turnout at the British General Election of 1992: Rational Choice, Social Standing or Political Efficacy?" *European Journal of Political Research* 33 (1998): 263–283. Also see David Denver, *Elections and Voters in Britain* (Basingstoke, UK: Palgrave Macmillan, 2003).

18. Harold Clarke, David Sanders, Marianne Stewart, and Paul Whiteley, "Britain (Not) at the Polls, 2001," *PS: Political Science and Politics* 1 (2003): 59–64.

19. See J. Mohan, *The Political Geography of Contemporary Britain* (London: Macmillan, 1989).

20. Mark N. Franklin, *The Decline of Class Voting in Britain* (Oxford, UK: Clarendon Press, 1985); Anthony Heath et al., *Understanding Political Change: Britain Votes 1964–87* (Oxford, UK: Pergamon, 1988); Ivor Crewe, "Labor Force Changes, Working Class Decline and the Labour Vote," in *Labor Parties in Postindustrial Societies,* ed. Frances Fox Piven (Oxford, UK: Polity Press, 1991).

21. See Harold Clarke, David Sanders, Marianne Stewart, and Paul Whiteley, *Political Choice in Britain* (Oxford: Oxford University Press, 2004), 42.

22. Ibid., 50.

23. In the south of England, unemployment appears more important as a predictor of voting than does the nominal occupation of an individual.

24. For an extensive discussion of voting behavior in the 2001 election, see Clarke et al., *Political Choice in Britain.*

25. There is some evidence that voters tend to behave somewhat more conservatively as they age, so these data do not mean that the same patterns necessarily will persist.

26. Richard Rose, *Do Parties Make a Difference?* (Chatham, N.J.: Chatham House, 1980).

27. Some scholars argue that groups are in many ways more central to policy than parties. See Jeremy Richardson and A. Grant Jordan, *Government under Pressure* (Oxford, UK: Martin Robertson, 1979). For a critique of British pluralism, see Samuel H. Beer, *Britain against Itself* (London: Faber, 1982).

28. See especially Table 5 in Alan Siaroff, "Corporatism in 24 Industrial Democracies: Meaning and Measurement," *European Journal of Political Research* 36 (1999): 175–205.

29. Ibid.

How Is Power Used?

T HIS CHAPTER ATTEMPTS TO BRING THESE STRUCTURES TO LIFE AND to explain how actors and institutions produce public policies. It also demonstrates how the distinctive character of British government institutions affects the policies produced and how policies may differ from those emanating from other political systems, even those faced with similar policymaking problems. In particular, the majoritarian nature of British parliamentary democracy tends to produce somewhat stronger swings in policy than might be found in the consensual democracies, such as Germany, the Netherlands, and Sweden.

This discussion considers two broad kinds of policymaking that must go on in any government. The first is making new policies, which occurs when government institutions decide to pursue new activities in the public sector or undertake their current activities in significantly different ways. This type of policymaking typically takes the form of a legislative process, although administrative actors are certainly involved in the propagation of new policy ideas and again during their implementation. Meanwhile, the making of new policies tends to be more overtly politicized, with parties and interest groups directly involved in the process. Another possibility, however, might be for government institutions to take no action at all on an issue. This too may be highly politicized.

The second major form of policymaking is simply maintaining the existing government policies and programs. This kind of policymaking is frequently less political in a strictly partisan sense. Instead, discussions regarding existing programs may involve bargaining among ministers and the managers with their financial overseers (in Great Britain, primarily the Treasury), as well as overt or covert competition among the existing programs. For the most part, therefore, this policymaking activity is not legislative but involves executive and administrative actors. Furthermore, government does not have an opportunity to exercise very much discretion in most decisions in this category of policymaking, because the existing commitments of government to citizens and organizations must be honored. This chapter will look at the British political system as it processes both kinds of policy decisions.

One important departure from the typical pattern of policymaking has been the greater emphasis given to reducing the size of the public sector. This emphasis means that very few programs are able to escape serious scrutiny when they come up for funding or reconsideration. The economic crisis that began in 2007[1] emphasized the need for such scrutiny, and the 2010 "emergency budget" produced by the Conservative–Liberal Democrat coalition imposed stringent reconsideration of public expenditure. Although the coalition has promised to maintain support for services such as the National Health Service, international aid, and some aspects of education, the reductions in public expenditures and increases in taxation are dramatic.

The Parliamentary Process and New Policies

To illustrate how new policies are made and then put into operation, this section follows a typical piece of legislation through the lawmaking process—from its birth as an issue placed on the agenda for consideration through its implementation. In reality, no piece of legislation is typical. Some bills are enacted in a matter of days (or even hours in an emergency) the first time they are proposed, but others must wait for years before being passed. In the summer of 1999, legislation implementing the Northern Ireland agreements was expected to pass through Parliament in one or two days. There were some delays, but still it passed in less than a week. Some policy ideas may never evolve into law, or they may have their intentions almost totally altered through implementation. Despite these differences, an underlying policymaking process is common to all proposals.

Agenda Setting and Policy Formulation

The first step in the adoption of legislation is its placement on the policymaking agenda, both in an informal sense in that the policy must be considered sufficiently important for the government to act on and in the more formal sense in that it must be placed before Parliament for consideration and possible adoption.[2] In an even more fundamental way, societal problems must be identified before they can be placed on a government agenda in the form of legislation. For example, it has taken some time for race to be recognized as an important issue in the increasingly heterogeneous country that is now the United Kingdom.[3]

Deciding which issues are public and require the consideration of government is a very diffuse and uncertain process in Great Britain, as it is in almost all countries. Political parties and the governments they form are the principal agents in placing issues on the agenda, but other actors are also involved. Individual members of Parliament may have special interests and may strive—sometimes for years—to have an issue considered. Interest groups may attempt to dramatize the needs and desires of their members. For their part, the media are actively inserting issues into the consciousness of citizens and that of governing institutions. Finally, with membership in the European Union (EU), issues arising in Brussels show up on the British government's agenda, if only to implement EU decisions.

In a formal sense, the easiest way for an issue to come before Parliament is its inclusion in the government's legislative program. Parliament's legislative time is limited, and the government must select those issues and bills it believes are most important. To make this selection, the government must make some difficult choices, because it introduces relatively few bills in any one year. During the Thatcher and Major years, governments introduced an average of just under fifty bills per session. The Blair and Brown governments, though more active, still introduced fewer than ninety bills each year. Because several of the bills involved annual budget and financial considerations and a large number of the remaining bills involved consolidation and clarification of existing legislation, few significant policy bills were introduced during each parliamentary session.[4] In almost all cases, the policy bills that were passed were a part of the government's program, and the government can if it wishes (and it usually does) control the parliamentary agenda.

Bills and issues not part of the government's program may also come before Parliament. Backbenchers can introduce legislation, but it has little chance of being passed—only about 7 percent of all legislation passed in Parliament comes from MPs with no governmental responsibilities, or "private members." To introduce legislation, a backbencher must first win a lottery to have the opportunity to actually introduce a bill, but even then consideration of the bill is limited to one of the ten to twelve Fridays—the only day on which private members' bills are debated—during a session. Bills also can be introduced under the ten-minute rule, which allows ten minutes of debate, pro and con, followed immediately by a vote. Both kinds of legislation can lead to consideration of issues the government may prefer to forget or issues of a moral nature on which the government does not wish to take a stand. Indeed, sometimes private members' bills are submitted as a favor to a government that does not want to have to take a stand on a difficult issue such as divorce or abortion. Most private members' bills are not, however, likely to generate political controversy. One restraint on this form of legislation is that backbenchers cannot introduce legislation involving the expenditure of public funds—only ministers can make those proposals.[5]

It is far easier for the nongovernmental parties and backbenchers in the majority party to bring issues up for discussion in Parliament than to achieve the passage of legislation. Question Time is an obvious opportunity for generating that discussion. Adjournment debates and early day motions[6] by private members also allow individual members of Parliament (MPs) to air grievances; the last thirty minutes of each daily session are devoted to an adjournment debate on matters raised by backbenchers. On one day in October 2005, the issues raised ranged from the serious—European sugar subsidies—to the trivial—lauding the success of the Harry Potter books—and the same would be true for most days. On average, backbenchers receive approximately 15 percent of all parliamentary time, an allocation made by the government, and much of that time is spent discussing specific constituency grievances rather than general issues. Because this allocation permits the average member relatively little opportunity to have an impact on major policy issues, MPs may decide to counteract some of this imbalance of power by specializing in particular policy topics, a strategy made easier by the creation of the select committees.[7] Expanded use of the electronic media gives members of Parliament yet another chance to air their opinions and to have at least an indirect influence over policy.

The opposition receives parliamentary time to present its alternatives to the government program, largely during the extended debate on the Queen's Speech (actually written for her by the government as a statement of its policy objectives for the session), which opens each session of Parliament, and the twenty "opposition days" scattered throughout the parliamentary session, which allow the leaders of the opposition parties to criticize the government by selecting the topics for debate. Again, however, although this debate may be useful for ventilating opinions, it usually has little real effect on policy choices, in part because the government has already established the agenda and all the opposition can do is to react to its propositions. Furthermore, if the government maintains its party discipline, the opposition can do little to prevent the government's legislation from being adopted.

In addition to controlling the agenda and timetable, the government is heavily involved in formulating legislation. Most of the broad ideas for policy formulation come from the party's election manifesto, but ministers also have their own ideas about good policy. The ministers receive advice on policy initiatives from their civil servants and from political advisers in their departments. Within the cabinet, legislation is typically first considered by a cabinet committee composed of interested ministers (usually with some Treasury representation) before being considered by the entire cabinet.[8] The shape of legislation to be introduced generally is decided by the full cabinet prior to formal proposal of the legislation to Parliament. In the full cabinet, the prime minister plays a significant role, not least because he or she summarizes the debate and says finally what was decided.

Parties and political leaders are not the only source of policy intentions and policy formulation—many policy ideas come from the departments themselves and their civil servants.[9] And, as is true in many industrialized democracies, the balance of power between elective and nonelective officials may have swung in favor of the unelected.[10]

No matter which set of actors is most powerful, the process of formulating policy is complex, involving the interaction of ministers with their civil servants and, in turn, consultation with the affected interests in society. The increased emphasis on managerialism in the British civil service has weakened its policy capacity, although the separation of many implementation functions from policymaking through the creation of agencies provides the remaining civil servants in departments with more time to deal exclusively with policy.

Policy Legitimation

Once the cabinet has agreed on a policy proposal, it is introduced into Parliament as a bill. All politically controversial legislation, by convention, goes first to the House of Commons. For a bill to become law, it must pass the House of Commons, pass the House of Lords (unless it is passed by three successive sessions of the Houses of Commons or is a money bill), and gain royal assent. But there are ways of short-cutting this process, and therefore a significant amount of lawmaking in Great Britain is done by the government itself, using orders in council and statutory instruments that do not require the approval of Parliament.[11]

When a bill is introduced into the House of Commons, it is given a formal first reading and then printed for distribution. After two or three weeks, the second reading takes place, which is the major political debate on the principles of the legislation. For noncontroversial legislation, however, the second reading may occur in committee. After the second reading, a bill typically goes to committee for detailed consideration and possible amendment—that is, after the Commons has agreed to the legislation in principle. Although committees are organized to mirror the partisan composition of Parliament, the government is generally more willing to accept amendments in committee than on the floor of the Commons, where acceptance might be taken as an admission of defeat. Finally, the bill is reported out of committee with any amendments, receives a third reading, and then is usually passed.

After passage in the Commons, a bill goes to the House of Lords for consideration and possible amendment. Any amendments made in the Lords must be later considered by the Commons. In the adversarial political system of the United Kingdom, the House of Lords can be an extremely useful institution. There, the government can accept amendments and negotiate improvements in legislation without appearing to back away from its policy proposals. The House of Lords also has chosen to specialize in several areas such as science policy that are less partisan than many others but for which some longer-term considerations are paramount. A government can even accept defeat in Lords without serious damage to its prospects of retaining office. Although deadlocks between the two houses are possible, they are infrequent, and yet Lords can delay legislation for up to three years. In recent years, Lords was able to delay the passage of legislation banning fox hunting with dogs, as well as a bill establishing the Supreme Court for the United Kingdom.

After agreement is reached between the two houses, the bill is given to the monarch for royal assent, which is virtually automatic.

In reality, legislation does not necessarily move so easily through the policymaking system, and therefore some way is needed to regulate the flow and, particularly, to prevent the delay of important legislation. At the report stage, amendments may be reported out of committee, and the Speaker is given the power to decide which amendments should be debated and which would be repetitious of debates in committee. The government can also attempt to impose closure and the "guillotine" (allocation of time order). Closure, a motion to end debate made by one hundred or more MPs, is accepted only if the Speaker believes all relevant positions have been heard. When different points of dissent emerge and closure is ineffective, the guillotine is employed. An allocation of time order is voted by the House of Commons, and the government determines how much debate time will be devoted to each section of the bill. Once that time is exhausted, the Speaker must move the section to a vote. The use of the guillotine is often cited as contradictory to the interests of the House as a deliberative body, especially when it is imposed on major constitutional issues, such as the devolution debates during the Callaghan government in the 1970s. But the guillotine may be necessary if Parliament is to process the amount of legislation a contemporary democracy requires.

Although the factor of party discipline seems to foreordain much of the legislative activity of Parliament, that activity is still important. First, the legal and constitutional requirements for the passage of legislation must be fulfilled. Second, amendments must be considered and the amended legislation must be approved, both at the committee stage in Commons and in Lords. Finally, some legislation that seems perfectly reasonable to the majority of the cabinet may not appear so reasonable to backbenchers in the party, and therefore the legislation may never be passed. On average, about 10 percent of all government bills introduced in Parliament do not become law; few are defeated, but others may be withdrawn. Although the presence of disciplined majorities in the House of Commons is important, legislative action is never certain and may become even less certain with a coalition government in office.

The Scottish Parliament and Welsh Assembly have adopted many of the same types of procedure used in Westminster. They have, however, attempted to loosen some of the domination of the majority party over the proceedings. The Scottish Parliament has created cross-party committees to consider legislation and to make suggestions without having to abide by strictly partisan considerations.

British democracy has long been representative democracy, but since the 1970s there have been several interesting uses of direct democracy as a means of legitimating policies. Of particular significance are two referendums on policy issues—in 1975 on whether Great Britain should remain in the Common Market and in 1979 on the devolution proposals in Scotland and Wales. The latter proposals were voted on only in Scotland and Wales, but the principle was the same: the government and Parliament to some degree abdicated their decision-making powers to the people in an election. Although these referendums were not legally binding, they were declared binding by the major parties. Referendums in 1997 approved devolution for Scotland and Wales and were followed by the Scotland Act and Wales Act in 1998. Referendums represent a major departure from the traditional means of decision making in British government and have potential importance for major policy decisions, including questions of British membership in the Economic and Monetary Union and adoption of a European constitution.[12]

Policy Implementation

Perhaps the most difficult portion of the process of changing society through government action occurs after a bill is passed by Parliament. The implementation process involves taking the bare bones of parliamentary legislation and putting some meat on them by formulating both substantive policy declarations and the organizational structure to carry out the intent of Parliament, or, at times, to thwart that intent. Most legislation passed by Parliament is passed in a broad form, allowing a great deal of room for interpretation as the laws are put into effect.

Public policies may be implemented several ways. Probably the most common is through departments of the central government. Most legislation coming from Parliament contains a broad mandate of power, but Parliament leaves it up to the ministry to make the regulations and engage in the activities needed for the intent of the legislation to come into being. A principal means by which the departments do this is through statutory instruments developed pursuant to acts of Parliament. Statutory instruments, which contain more detailed regulations than do acts, allow the executive to have a major impact on the nature of the policy actually implemented. Parliament exercises scrutiny over these instruments, but it cannot hope to master completely the volume or technical content of all such regulations. Even when the issuance of a statutory instrument is not required, the departments are heavily involved in shaping the meaning of policy and in making it work. Yet the departments also can serve as barriers to effective implementation, especially when the policy enacted by Parliament appears to run counter to their usual practices. In like manner, the regional and local offices of a ministry are frequently associated with varying patterns of implementation and, at times, great variations from the original intentions of Parliament in some parts of the country.

Policies of the central government are also implemented through local authorities. Unlike in a federal system, local authorities are creatures of the central government in Great Britain. The result is less differentiation between national and local policy than in the United States.[13] Although the major policy decisions in areas such as education, health, social services, and law enforcement are made by the central government, these services are actually delivered by local authorities, or by local units of national organizations such as the National Health Service. But these public services are not delivered uniformly; local authorities provide different quantities and qualities of service, albeit within centrally determined parameters and subject to inspection and control by the central government. This relationship between central policymaking and local administration does not, however, work without friction, especially when local and central governments are controlled by different parties. During its first term, Blair's Labour government placed greater pressures on local authorities to improve the quality of service provision, thereby producing some conflicts even with Labour local councils that had their own views about how policies should be designed and implemented.[14]

In September 2003 Prime Minister Tony Blair greeted a patient at King's College Hospital in London as part of his tour of the hosptial's new Golden Jubilee Wing, a 60 million pound ($99 million) Private Finance Initiative (PFI) project funded by Hospital Partnership's Consortium.

Source: Peter Macdiarmid/AFP/Getty Images

In return for the administration of national policies, the local authorities receive the majority of their revenues from the central government. Some of the grants to local authorities are tied to the provision of specific services such as law enforcement, but the largest single grant—the rate support grant—is a general grant. (The formula for computing the rate support grant does, however, include weightings for the levels of service provided by a local authority.) If a local authority wishes to provide services not funded directly by the rate support grant or the categorical grants from central government, it must be willing to raise funds from local revenues, generally through the council tax system.

Finally, policies may be implemented by private organizations. Although interest groups are often regarded as barriers to effective implementation, such groups may be important to effective implementation. At a minimum, an interest group can function as a watchdog on the implementation of a policy, replacing the army of public inspectors that might otherwise be required. Environmental groups have been particularly active in this monitoring role. In addition, a group may actually implement a policy for government, such as in agriculture when the Royal Society for the Prevention of Cruelty to Animals (RSPCA) applies general policies in enforcing animal welfare legislation. These activities would otherwise require huge amounts of time and public money and might not be performed as well. Finally, at times the government subsidizes an organization to provide a service that government supports as a matter of policy and that would have to be provided at public expense if the private organization were not willing to provide it. One example of such a service is the legal assistance the Law Society provides to the indigent.

The Blair government undertook an even more extreme version of involving private businesses in implementation. The Private Finance Initiative enables firms to build and operate what might normally be a public facility, such as a toll road, and to receive the revenues as the return on its investment. After that return has been achieved, the facility may become public.[15] The coalition government formed in 2010 is expected to continue and perhaps expand the activities of the private sector in delivering public services—that is, if the coalition partners can work through their disagreements.

Policy Evaluation

The last stage of policymaking—formal policy evaluation—occurs some time after the policy has been adopted or even implemented (informal evaluation begins almost at the time of passage). Policy evaluation is also closely related to policy continuation, the next major topic, because the annual decisions made during the budgetary process to continue policies and programs to some degree involve evaluation of the effectiveness and efficiency of those policies.

Parliament is assumed to conduct ongoing oversight of government policies, and some instruments for policy evaluation are housed within the government itself. The now-defunct Programme Analysis and Review (PAR) and the diminished Public Expenditure Survey Committee linked program evaluation directly with financial management. The select committees of the House of Commons are increasingly active in evaluating existing programs, and the few committees in the House of Lords are engaged in limited oversight. A growing staff in the Prime Minister's Office also monitors policies on behalf of the executive, especially major programs such as health and education. Through the parliamentary commissioner, or ombudsman, Parliament maintains additional evaluative control over policy administration. This official can, if only at the request of an MP, investigate alleged malfeasance of public administration. Finally, the comptroller, auditor general, and the National Audit Office have become important watchdogs. Like auditing organizations in other industrialized nations, these offices have added policy evaluation to their former duties as financial auditors. They monitor policy developments in both the central government and the local authorities.

Some mechanisms for policy evaluation exist outside the government. One of the most commonly used devices is the appointment of parliamentary or royal commissions to investigate particular fundamental policy concerns that merit outside advice. These commissions and their reports often constitute milestones in the evolution of policy and program management. Examples are the Fulton report on the civil service, the Plowden report on public expenditure control, and the Kilbrandon report on devolution. The commissions have no formal powers, however, and even excellent reports often go unheeded. In part because of her reliance on her own advisers and on a more ideological style of government, almost no royal commissions were convened during the Thatcher years. Since then, various public inquiries have been held on specific policy questions, some with substantial policy and political relevance such as nuclear power and the fire in the London

Underground, and after some thirty-eight years the Saville Inquiry Report on violence in Northern Ireland was issued in 2010. Of the several commissions appointed by the Blair government, the most important was the Jenkins Commission on electoral reform.

In addition are the less official mechanisms for generating policy evaluation. One such mechanism is the news media, which exercise a considerable degree of self-censorship in their assessments of policy. The restrictions imposed by the Official Secrets Act and the public's lack of access to important information limit the capacity of public involvement in policy assessment. Passage of Great Britain's Freedom of Information Act in 2000 has opened up government to some degree, even though the law is more limited than similar acts in most other democracies. The number of policy think tanks also continues to increase, some of them representing clearly defined ideological positions, while others strive toward greater objectivity, and they use the information generated to help shape policy through their contacts with parties and through the media. Finally, research units of political parties and pressure groups also evaluate existing policies. Overall, then, a great deal of official and unofficial policy evaluation occurs, but tight government control of the parliamentary agenda ensures that many policy changes will likely not be scrutinized, unless it suits the purposes of the incumbent government.

Although policy evaluation ends one cycle of policymaking, it often begins the next.[16] Governments rarely make perfect policies the first time they try, but often they know so little about the dynamics of the problem area into which they intervene that trial-and-error learning may be the only means available for improving conditions. Therefore, governments often have to modify existing policies based on their experience with those policies—that is, experience frequently reflected in the evaluation process. The social and economic conditions that are the objects of a particular policy may change as well, and government will have to modify its programs to meet those changing conditions. Although policymaking is depicted here as a delimited process, the end of the process may be just the start of another cycle. At times, the messages from the consumers of policies are very clear signals that change is needed, as they were for the poll tax in 1991 and for railway safety in the 1990s and after.

Policy Continuation: Budgeting

Most policymaking is not about making new policies; rather, it is about reaffirming old policies or making marginal adjustments in those policies. In many ways, this form of policymaking is politically more sensitive than making new policies, because existing programs have existing employees, clients, and organizations, whereas new policies have no inertia pushing existing commitments forward. Although there may be some modifications or even threatened terminations, in most years the most important decisions for continuing policies are made in the budgetary process. That process involves financing the huge number of existing policy commitments, with their relative priorities determined in pounds and pence. (Here the reference to the budgetary process is in the U.S. sense; in Great Britain the term *budget* usually refers to the government's revenue, not expenditure, proposals.)

Historically, control of the public purse has been central to the powers of the British Parliament, but the existence of disciplined partisan majorities, and the general uncertainty about economic growth, has transformed substantially the locus of effective budgetary powers. Even now, however, the British government appears to spend more time trying to get the machinery of financial allocation "right," when compared with most other parliamentary systems, and it has developed elaborate machinery for budget and financial management. Budgeting is best thought of as taking place in two stages. The first is an executive stage during which the spending ministries negotiate with the Treasury and with their colleagues in the cabinet over expenditure commitments. The second is the parliamentary stage during which these decisions are legitimated, and only occasionally changed.

The Executive Stage

The Treasury is the central actor at the executive stage of budgeting. It is charged not only with making recommendations on macroeconomic policy but also with formulating detailed expenditure plans that fall within those economic constraints. Traditionally, the Treasury has been the most prestigious appointment for a civil servant, and those in the Treasury have adopted the "Treasury view" about the proper amount of public spending and who should spend the money. Since at least the days of William Gladstone, holders of that view have been skeptical about expenditures and concerned with saving "candle ends" as well as billions of pounds. This view does not always prevail, but it must always be considered.

The first round of bargaining over expenditures is typically at the level of civil servants—those from spending departments and those from the Treasury. This bargaining takes place with the knowledge of the relevant ministers, but it can be conducted more easily by officials who know both one another and the facts of the programs. Interpersonal trust and respect are important components of the success of any bargainer, especially when the spending departments must have their requests reviewed annually.[17] Because the same Treasury civil servants may see the same departmental civil servants year after year, any attempts to manipulate or deceive may gain in the short run, but will surely lose in the long run. Also, civil servants tend to understand the technical aspects of their programs better than ministers do. In addition to bargaining annually (or at times more frequently) for expenditures, departments must bargain for deviations from expenditure plans during the year, thereby giving the Treasury several opportunities to monitor and intervene in departmental policies.

The second stage of executive bargaining occurs among the spending ministers, the Treasury, and the cabinet as a whole. Budget decisions are manifestly political, and, if nothing else, they reflect the relative political powers and skills of the ministers involved. The task of the spending ministers is to fight for their programs and to try to get as much money as they can. The Treasury ministers (the chancellor of the exchequer and the chief secretary of the Treasury) are the guardians of the public purse and play the role of skeptic. They perform an important function in budgetary politics and are responsible for much of the nitty-gritty in day-to-day allocations and oversight. The prime minister must moderate any conflicts that arise, but knows that he or she can rarely go against the Treasury ministers if the government is to function smoothly. Also, in today's more conservative period, there is some political advantage to opposing expenditure increases.

The fight over the budget occurs on a one-to-one basis between spending ministers and the Treasury ministers in cabinet committees and finally in full cabinet meetings. Under the Thatcher government, a special cabinet committee (called the "Star Chamber") was formed to review disputes between the Treasury and spending departments, and it usually sided with the Treasury. Faced with an immense public debt, the 2010 coalition government is reinstating this procedure.

The position of Treasury was enhanced after 1992, with the chancellor of the exchequer heading the cabinet committee reviewing expenditures. The Treasury is in a powerful position politically and enjoys the right of making the first presentation of expenditure figures in cabinet meetings, but after that the spending ministers tend to gang up against the Treasury. Because this process is political, a coalition can usually be formed to increase expenditures that enable all spending ministers to make their constituents happy and make them look good in the eyes of their departments. It takes a very strong chancellor, backed by an equally strong prime minister, to oppose that type of coalition.

Opposition to spending in government was very successful under Margaret Thatcher, but it appeared less cohesive under the less assertive and somewhat less conservative John Major. In keeping with his strategy to promote long-term fiscal policy and to loosen the supply side (which no longer was considered a demand management tool), Major introduced three-year expenditure plans to be discussed in the context of setting monetary policy. Major also introduced an "escalation clause" on fiscal taxes (that is, taxes were to rise in percentage terms faster than inflation) and funding rulings for the National Health Service (that is, spending was to rise to about 6 percent above inflation). After it formed a government in 1997, Labour stuck with the idea that current expenditures should not rise faster than growth, but investment expenditures were allowed to go beyond that. The idea was that current expenditures should not cause a deficit on the fiscal account, but investment expenditures could do so. Tony Blair and his chancellor, Gordon Brown, were not always in agreement on these policy issues, Brown being somewhat more willing than Blair to spend on social issues.[18] Despite any internal conflicts within government, in recent years the British public sector was closer to balance than most others in Europe, and the economy has enjoyed a period of steady growth.[19] This all ended during the financial crisis beginning in 2008, so that the public debt has risen to be one of the highest in Europe.

The British government has made a great deal of effort to control the costs of government through analytic programs such as PAR and the Public Expenditure Survey Committee (PESC). The PESC projects the expenditure implications of existing programs—that is, what the expenditure level would be if programs were to provide the same level of services in the year being budgeted as in previous years. PAR was intended to be a comprehensive evaluation of specific programs, with the objective of making those programs more efficient or perhaps eliminating them. But PAR obviously ran counter to the established norms of government and budgeting and was quietly phased out by the Thatcher government. In addition to rationalist methods of expenditure control, the British government has used blunter instruments, such as cash limits. A program is assigned a maximum expenditure level and is not allowed for any reason to spend any more money.

The Parliamentary Phase

After the civil servants and the cabinet prepare their expenditure plans (estimates), the plans are presented to Parliament for adoption. Although the emphasis on control and on techniques for budgeting such as the PESC have significantly modernized the budgeting process, much of the terminology and procedure used by Parliament when considering public expenditures dates from earlier periods in which the monarch and Parliament were engaged in more intense conflicts over power. The major debates on expenditures occur during the twenty-six "supply days" each session, although the topics selected by the opposition for debate on these days range far beyond expenditures. The civil estimates are introduced into Parliament by the chief secretary of the Treasury in February, and the minister of defense introduces defense estimates at about the same time. Parliament then has until July or early August to pass the Consolidated Fund Bill (Appropriations), authorizing the expenditure of funds. Because of the difficulties in forecasting expenditures, especially in uncertain economic circumstances, the government usually must also introduce supplemental estimates in December and March.

The budget is an important locus for parliamentary control over the executive. By standing order, Parliament cannot increase expenditures on its own; any increases must be recommended by a minister. Parliament can, however, recommend decreases. One means of expressing displeasure with the management of a ministry is to move for the reduction of the salary of the minister, frequently by a trivial amount such as £100. This gesture signals a debate not so much about the £100 as about the policies of the department in question. Members of Parliament may move for less trivial changes in expenditure plans as well, but all these are likely to be defeated by the majority party, lest it be seen to be losing confidence in the Commons.

Even if it is not able to alter expenditure plans directly, Parliament has become more effective at monitoring the spending decisions of government. Parliament as a whole is perhaps too large and disorganized to scrutinize expenditure programs effectively, and so it has developed a pair of committees to more closely examine the government estimates. The first is the Treasury and Civil Service Select Committee, a rather small committee composed of members of the House of Commons who are well versed in issues of public spending. Despite its expertise, this committee cannot cover the total range of the budget each year (it has almost no professional staff support), and so it concentrates on particularly important spending issues. This committee has influenced the development of policy in Great Britain and aired important issues, sometimes to the discomfort of the government.

One government institution that occasionally experiences discomfort is the Expenditure Committee, the successor to the Estimates Committee. The Expenditure Committee does its work in subcommittees, but unlike the Appropriations Committee in the U.S. Congress, it does not presume to cover the entire range of public expenditures each year. Instead, each subcommittee focuses on one or a few particular topics for a more detailed analysis. Because the government is usually able to secure passage of whatever it desires by Parliament, the Expenditure Committee has been unable to alter much public policy directly, although it has been effective in airing ideas and opinions about the expenditure of funds. The committee also is important in restoring some parliamentary control over expenditures.

The second important parliamentary committee for controlling public expenditures is the Public Accounts Committee (PAC). Unlike most committees in Parliament, PAC is headed by a member of the opposition; it has the task of monitoring public expenditures after they have been made and after they have been audited by the National Audit Office. Out of the mass of public expenditures, PAC selects certain topics for consideration each year and has the power to call civil servants before it to account for their actions. Other than calling attention to mismanagement or outright deception, however, PAC has few powers to improve the expenditure of funds.

In addition to the two principal committees examining expenditures, the select committees created during the late 1970s for monitoring activities of the executive departments may be a useful device for parliamentary control of expenditures. Indeed, it appears that these committees have been more successful than had been anticipated in exercising oversight. They have attracted the interest of many MPs and have demonstrated their ability to keep track of the huge volume of paper and decisions produced by the ministries. These committees primarily publicize any failures in the executive to the public and to Parliament, and that publicity can function as a useful restraint on the power of ministers and civil servants.[20]

To this point, this section has focused on the expenditure side of budgeting. On the revenue side, there is the same balance of power in favor of the cabinet and the Treasury. If anything, the balance of power resides even more in the hands of the executive, because Parliament has yet to develop a committee structure for monitoring revenue proposals. A small subcommittee of the Treasury and Civil Service Select Committee does examine revenue issues, but this is a minor role compared with the scrutiny of public expenditures. And within the executive, the balance appears to favor executive officials, because ministers do not push for increased taxation, only for increased expenditures. This is not to say that there are no political influences on taxation, and part of the debate on how to deal with the deficit in 2010 involves discussion of tax options. Those political influences were all too evident in the shift from direct taxation (income taxes) to indirect taxation (value-added tax, VAT) in the first Thatcher budget and the launching of the poll tax in her third term.

Revenue recommendations are introduced each year around the first of April in the chancellor's budget message. Commons rapidly passes the necessary budget resolutions, allowing for the immediate collection of some or all of the proposed taxes. This immediate action is taken to prevent the legal avoidance of taxes by purchasing large quantities of alcoholic beverages, selling assets, paying off debts, and so on, under the preexisting tax laws. That action is followed by a period of debate leading to the formal introduction of the Finance Bill, which is usually passed sometime before Parliament takes its summer recess in August. Rarely has Parliament voted down new taxes or increased government expenditures. In 2000 a VAT increase on fuel was rescinded only after massive public protests and a complete stoppage of the economy in the fall of that year. In fact, because of hostility to taxes in and out of Parliament, until 2002 Parliament pursued few increases in visible taxes. Instead, it enacted many "stealth taxes" such as those on insurance premiums, air tickets, and most obviously on pension funds.

One of the common criticisms of the British budgetary process is similar to one leveled at the budgetary processes in many other nations: that there is little or no integration of revenue and expenditure decisions. Citizens and politicians alike tend to like expenditures and loathe taxation, which commonly results in the government's failure to collect enough revenues to meet expenditures, thereby creating a deficit budget. Changes to coordinate taxation with expenditures would require changing many historic procedures, but it might well improve the management of public sector finances. The Blair government promised to address some of these issues in its "Green Paper" on planning reforms published in December 2001. Despite these institutional problems, the British government (unlike that of the United States) has not run substantial deficits since the early 1980s, apparently because of the political will of the prime ministers and their fiscal advisers. Even though the British economy has not been as productive as many other economies, this commitment to fiscal probity has persevered.

Policymaking in Great Britain

Policymaking in Great Britain involves the interaction of cabinet, Parliament, and the civil service, to mention only the primary actors. In this interaction, the formal location of power and the actual location of decision making may be markedly different. The formal powers of decision making reside in Parliament, but the effect of strong party discipline has, in practice, made the cabinet the primary decision-making institution. Backed by a government majority, once the cabinet decides on a policy the dutiful members of the party will almost certainly ratify it on the floor of the House of Commons. In those few instances in which the backbenchers overtly or covertly oppose government policy, the cabinet rarely tries to run roughshod over its own party members. Policy toward the European Union is the one area in contemporary British politics in which this may happen. In most policy areas, however, if it is willing to push, the cabinet does have the ability to get most of what it wants passed into law without much real internal party opposition.

The powers of the cabinet are, however, restrained in other ways. First, ministers must contend with skillful and permanent civil servants. Especially within the budgetary process, the Treasury and its "mandarins" dominate decision making. Even in nonfinancial decisions, the expert knowledge of civil servants, when compared with the relative dearth of expertise held by their nominal political masters, places the permanent civil service in a powerful position to influence outcomes. The reforms of the structure of British government to separate executive agencies from policy advisers in the departments are designed to improve political control over implementation, but the civil service still holds power at the formulation stage.

Finally, some interests and organizations other than the cabinet, Parliament, and the civil service influence policy decisions. Interest groups not only attempt to influence policy as it is being formulated but also may directly implement policies for the government. The increased use in Great Britain of "quangos" and private sector organizations for policy formulation and implementation also reduces the degree of direct control over policy implementation by government. Because local governments administer and implement a significant share of the central government programs, the central government must attempt to co-opt and encourage local governments to implement the policy as it was intended. Local governments also are effective lobbyists for their interests and may help to shape as well as merely implement public policy.

NOTES

1. BBC News Online, "Timeline: Credit Crunch to Downturn," at http://news.bbc.co.uk/2/hi/business/7521250.stm.
2. On agenda setting in British government, see Simon James, *British Government: A Reader in Policy-Making* (London: Routledge, 1997), 60–88.
3. S. Saggar, *Race and Politics in Britain* (Hemel Hempstead, UK: Harvester, 1992); Saggar, "Racial Politics," *Parliamentary Affairs* 50 (1997): 691–707.

4. These figures are drawn from Ivor Burton and Gavin Drewry, "Public Legislation," *Parliamentary Affairs,* various years.

5. See House of Commons Information Office, "Factsheet L2 Legislation Series: Private Members' Bills Procedure," http://www.parliament.uk/documents/commons-information-office/l02.pdf, revised June 2010.

6. According to the House of Commons Information Office, "Early day motion (EDM) is a colloquial term for a notice of motion given by a Member for which no date has been fixed for debate. EDMs exist to allow Members to put on record their opinion on a subject and canvass support for it from fellow Members. In effect, the primary function of an EDM is to form a kind of petition that MPs can sign and there is very little prospect of these motions being debated on the floor of the House." See House of Commons Information Office, "Factsheet P3 Procedure Series: Early Day Motions," http://www.parliament.uk/documents/commons-information-office/p03.pdf, revised June 2010.

7. David Judge, *Backbench Specialization in the House of Commons* (London: Heinemann, 1989).

8. C. Hood and O. James, "The Central Executive," in *Developments in British Politics,* vol. 5, ed. P. Dunleavy et al. (Basingstoke, UK: Macmillan, 1997).

9. See Edward C. Page and Bill Jenkins, *Policy Bureaucracy: Government with a Cast of Thousands* (Oxford: Oxford University Press, 2005)

10. Martin Smith, *The Core Executive in Britain* (Basingstoke, UK: Macmillan, 1999), 106–142.

11. See R. Baldwin, *Rules and Government* (Oxford: Oxford University Press, 1995). Parliament does, however, review the content of these instruments through a select committee.

12. With the defeat of this constitution in France and the Netherlands in referenda in 2005, any referendum in the UK is uncertain.

13. R. A. W. Rhodes, *Beyond Westminster and Whitehall: The Sub-Central Governments of Britain* (London: Unwin Hyman, 1988).

14. G. Boyne, "External Regulation and Best Value in Local Government," *Public Money and Management* 24 (2000): 11–18.

15. Stephen Glaister, "Past Abuses and Future Use of Private Finance and Public Private Partnerships," *Public Money and Management* 19 (1999): 29–36.

16. Brian W. Hogwood and B. Guy Peters, *Policy Dynamics* (Brighton, UK: Wheatsheaf, 1983).

17. Hugh Heclo and Aaron Wildavsky, *The Private Government of Public Money* (Berkeley: University of California Press, 1974), 76–128.

18. But see the comments from an "Old Labour" politician: Roy Hattersely, "The Secret Socialist at Number 11," *Guardian,* March 13, 2000.

19. HM Treasury, *Prudence for a Purpose: A Britain of Stability and Strength* (London: HM Treasury, 2004).

20. Keith Krehbiel, *Information and Legislative Organization* (Ann Arbor: University of Michigan Press, 1991).

What Is the Future of British Politics?

Every government must constantly deal with crises and make difficult decisions, even those with the most prosperous and well-managed political systems. Despite significant improvements in its economy and society, Great Britain has been neither the most prosperous nor the best-managed nation on earth, and it must sustain itself in the face of a significant number of challenges to its political and economic systems. Many of these challenges arise from the international economic and political environment within which Great Britain operates. Globalization and Europeanization continue to alter that environment and perhaps lessen the capacity of governments to control their economies. Some of the challenges also arise from the changing character of the political system itself, because constitutional reform alters many traditional ways of doing things in government.

This chapter examines the variety of challenges that continue to confront the government of the United Kingdom. Some are economic and social, and some are more clearly in the public sector itself, but all will require effective responses from British government.

The Economy

Although the economy had proved a serious problem for both Conservative and Labour governments throughout much of the postwar period, the British economy outperformed those of most of its European neighbors during the early years of the twenty-first century. Britain's annual growth rate, which had averaged 2.5 percent from 1985 to 1995, grew from 3.3 percent in 1997 to 3.9 percent in 2000—compared to an annual average of 2.7 percent among the Euro Area countries during the same five-year period.[1] Just as previous governments had taken the blame for poor economic performance, Labour under Tony Blair sought to take credit for the improved economy on its watch. In particular, by adopting some aspects of Thatcherite economic policy (such as deregulation, privatization, and somewhat lower tax rates) and adding some features of its own (such as granting greater autonomy to the Bank of England to set monetary policy), the Labour Party indeed helped orchestrate a short period of rapid growth. Fortuna then intervened to conspire against Labour's record. Annual economic growth began a slow decline during the early years of the decade—and abruptly plummeted to 0.6 percent with the onset of the international economic and financial crisis in 2008. By the next year the growth rate had fallen still further to an abysmal -4.7 percent.[2] By March 2010 the nation's budget deficit reached a peacetime high of 11 percent of GDP.[3] This negative trajectory severely eroded the authority of the newly appointed prime minister, Gordon Brown, and contributed in no small measure to Labour's debilitating electoral defeat in May.

In one of its first major policy initiatives, the Conservative–Liberal Democratic coalition government unveiled an emergency budget in June 2010 that combined draconian budget cuts—up to 25 percent in many departments—with an increase in the national value-added tax (VAT) from 17.5 percent to 20 percent. The budget plan also called for a two-year wage freeze for most public sector employees, a three-year freeze on children's benefits paid to parents, and more stringent medical screenings for persons on disability. With this move, the coalition partners repudiated the previous Labour government's economic stimulus measures in favor of "a historic gamble: that austerity measures will help balance the government's books without pitching the country into a double-dip recession." [4] Events during the run-up to Britain's next general election (scheduled at the latest in 2015) will determine whether the Conservative–Liberal Democratic policy expectations are valid.

Other issues present challenges, now and in the future. One is the problem of regional disparity in economic performance and standards of living. Northern Ireland, the north of England, and to some extent Scotland and Wales have not grown at the same rate as the south of the United Kingdom, especially the London area. In addition, economic globalization is creating a group of people in Britain and other industrialized nations who appear to be faced with permanent unemployment or underemployment. This situation creates a serious political problem for any contemporary government, and it has been exacerbated by the effects of the international financial-economic crisis that began in 2008. Furthermore, globalization is generating economic forces that widen income disparities within the population, and the life chances for anyone left behind in this economic transformation are less favorable than they would have been in times of expanding welfare state benefits.

The underlying uncertainty about the economic future of Great Britain has become even greater as a result of the accelerated movement toward greater economic (and political) integration within the European Union (EU). The member nations of the EU now constitute more of a single economic area than ever before, despite difficulties inherent in the expansion of the community since 2004 to include ten post-communist countries in Central and Eastern Europe plus Malta and Cyprus in the Mediterranean. Even more important, successive EU treaties—beginning with the Maastricht Treaty of 1992 and culminating in the Treaty of Lisbon, which was implemented in December 2009—constitute the legal and institutional basis for further economic integration. Both Conservative and Labour governments have resisted relinquishing the British pound in favor of adopting the euro, which a majority of EU member states now use as a common currency. Yet greater international economic openness has placed British industries in direct competition with continental industries, many of which are considered more efficient. In the long run, then, the United Kingdom may not be able to avoid competitiveness problems posed by continental Europe, the rest of the world economy, and a usually strong British pound that makes British exports expensive. Continuing to be the "Euro-skeptic" may not serve the long-term economic goals of Great Britain well.

The Public Sector

The nature of the British public sector is linked with economic changes in Great Britain. Despite the efforts of the Thatcher and Major governments to reduce the size of government, public expenditures as a percentage of the gross national product (GNP) were little reduced by the end of the more than eighteen years of Conservative government.[5] The amount of deficit public borrowing was finally under control, but Great Britain continued to spend a great deal of money through the public sector. Although the Labour government might have been expected to return to even higher levels of public expenditure, the opposite proved true; the public sector remained stable or even declined, with the exception of increased spending on the National Health Service (NHS). Likewise, the 1997–2010 Labour government did not try to return to the high levels of public ownership of industry that was a central policy of most previous Labour governments.

Privatization did, however, shift the terms of the debate on the size and nature of the public sector in British political life. The postwar consensus on the mixed economy welfare state has been broken, perhaps for good, and governments now have the capacity to make their own choices about the social and economic future of the nation. Yet such choices run the risk of accentuating economic divisions in the country and therefore raising the political stakes in any policy discussion. What may be happening, however, is that a new consensus is emerging across much of the population—a consensus that calls for a smaller and less intrusive public sector, even if that change leaves some portions of the population behind.

By the time Prime Minister John Major left office in 1997, there was relatively little industry left to privatize, but the nature of the state continues to change significantly. Instead of shedding activities to the market, Labour's reforms tended to impose market-type mechanisms within government. On the one hand, many of the industries that have been privatized require regulation because they are monopolies, and so the British government has developed effective means of controlling rates and quality. On the other hand, the level of support for, and the quality of service provided by, the NHS continues to be a major political issue in Great Britain. Over a period of ten years, the Labour government was not able to return the NHS to its former state of respect by the population.[6] The coalition government has said it will protect the NHS budget, but it remains to be seen whether significant reforms will be put in place.

The coalition government, in part to cut expenditures and reduce the size of the government debt and in part to pursue the Conservative Party's ideological commitment to smaller government, announced that it would implement a strategy aimed at reducing the size of the civil service and quangos. Immediately upon this announcement the trade unions vowed to fight the public sector cuts. Given the pressures on the public budget it seems all but inevitable that the coalition government will have some measure of success in reducing the size of the civil service. How much success it will have and how much public support it will cost is unknown.

In addition, the United Kingdom, like all industrialized democracies, has an aging population, and the commitments of the public sector to providing pensions and medical care for this segment of the population are beginning to represent a major challenge to both the public sector and the economy. Will there be enough workers to support the growing elderly population without large increases in taxes or significant reductions in the value of pensions? Because pensions in the United Kingdom are among the least generous in Europe, there seems to be little opportunity to reduce benefits, so the taxing and spending question is even more salient.

Who Rules Great Britain?

One of the major outcomes of successive long-serving Conservative and Labour governments has been a reassertion of the primacy of cabinet, if not always parliamentary, government in Great Britain. This may sound like an odd statement given that the existence of democracy has not been challenged in the United Kingdom in the same way that it has been in other countries, even in other European countries. In Great Britain, the central question during the period of Conservative and Labour rule was about the extent of influence exerted by trade unions and business interests in the policy process.

The power of the trade unions was broken during the Thatcher government. The miners attempted several times to exert their control over government policy with mixed results, and in the summer of 1989 the railway workers tried their hand. Somewhat later, the public sector unions challenged the capacity of the Thatcher government to rule when the government proposed reducing the size of the public sector and eliminating the recognition of unions at the Government Communications Headquarters, a major intelligence installation. In the end, the unions lost all these battles against a determined Conservative government. Later, "New Labour" moved to reduce the power of the unions within its ranks, and certainly the Labour government succeeded in being less beholden to the labor movement than were previous governments from that party.

The influence of business interests in policymaking has received a good deal of attention following the "cash for questions" scandal in the House of Lords. Although it has long been recognized that sitting parliamentarians may represent different interests, the closeness of these relationships causes some unease in the public and among media watchdogs. Additionally, various party funding scandals, from Labour's "cash for honours" scandal to Conservative's problems associated with Lord Ashcroft's (the major financier of the party's 2010 election campaign) nonresident tax status, have raised concerns about connections between the parties and large financial interests.

It is not the parties' ties to outside interests that has dampened public support for the Conservatives and Labour (and boosted the Liberal Democrats, the national parties, and the smaller parties); rather, it is also concerns that the two main parties have converged too closely on the ideological middle. To win the 1997 election and retain control of parliament, New Labour migrated away from traditional leftist policies to the ideological center. Likewise, David Cameron's Conservatives shifted to the center on environmental and social issues for the 2010 election. Although some may see the parties' ideological convergence as a signal of agreement that could be reflected in more consensual politics, many in the "chattering classes" take the view that the public is actually being denied policy choices and alternatives. Additionally, the ideological gap may have somewhat narrowed between the main parties, but both the Conservatives and Labour still actively engage in what in the UK is called "Punch and Judy-style politics," with members taking political shots at each other, rather than focusing on substantive policy.

Who Rules in Government?

Usually in the UK there is no question about which party is generating policy and which parties are in opposition. At the center of the UK's strong party system is the belief that parties put forward competing manifestos during election campaigns and that through the electoral process the public selects which slate of policies the majority would like to see adopted. With a coalition government, however, this certainty of policy adoption is obscured. The Conservatives and Liberal Democrats negotiated a rather specific set of policies that they, together, would attempt to enact. Both parties had to compromise and both had to agree to not pursue certain parts of their manifesto promises. It will take some time to see how well these bargains hold up. A bigger problem, however, could be how the coalition partners will handle unforeseen events. Advance negotiation can settle the known issues, but unexpected problems will test the partners and raise questions about the final location of power within the government.

In addition to the questions about how a coalition government will be able to effectively and efficiently respond to events, it would be helpful to know which institutions are most influential in policymaking. The problem here is also one of democratic governance. Voters in the United Kingdom go to the polls every few years and make choices about the party they wish to govern them for a period of up to five years. And Parliament, to which the members of that victorious party are elected (along with the opposition parties), nominally has the power to govern. Rather than the MPs, however, the cabinet and the prime minister within the partisan institutions of government and the civil service within government as a whole have become more important in policymaking, and the voting choices of millions of citizens may be negated or ignored in the policy-making process. This sense of exclusion, whether justified or not, is a serious problem for all democratic political systems, because citizens may start to believe that their government institutions are no longer responsive to their wishes and are overly bureaucratic and technocratic rather than democratic. This alienation appears weaker in the United Kingdom than in several other industrialized countries, but it is still an important threat to the legitimacy of the system of government.[7]

In the 1980s the Conservative government addressed at least one component of the problem of democratic governance. Rightly or wrongly, that government did not consider many members of the civil service sufficiently committed to the party program to implement it faithfully. Therefore, the Conservatives, and perhaps especially Prime Minister Margaret Thatcher, sought to reduce the influence of the civil service over policy by using more personal policy advisers in government and ignoring advice from senior civil servants. Several structural reforms were also undertaken to make the civil service more managerial and less a source of policy advice. In short, the structure of government was changed, apparently permanently, to provide the party in power with even greater control over policy. Such changes may make the system more "democratic," but perhaps at the price of reducing the overall quality of policymaking by government. Once in office, the Blair government maintained, and even extended, the influence of partisan members of government over the civil service and over the noncareer officials now appointed as heads of executive agencies, and it institutionalized the role of special advisers to ministers. And if the initial appointments made by the coalition government are an indication, it seems that Cameron's government will continue this practice.

Another question about who rules in government is whether Great Britain is a cabinet government (or perhaps a parliamentary government) or whether it is becoming more a government dominated by the prime minister. This issue was raised about Thatcher, but it was at least as applicable to Tony Blair. The Blair government strengthened the policy machinery in the Prime Minister's Office and, along with the party leaders who are very loyal to the prime minister, attempted to exert rather close control over what Labour members of Parliament could say and do in their public life. Party discipline is a part of political life in a parliamentary regime, but under the coalition government it may become even more important. It is possible that "rebels" in the parties could demand more input in exchange for their loyalty. If this were to happen, it could weaken the Prime Minister's Office and cause difficulties for the coalition government.

It also could be argued that the most important problem for government in the United Kingdom is its ability to make and implement unpopular policies with little effective restraint, thereby reducing the legitimacy of government with the population. The clearest manifestation of this possibility was the poll tax debacle at the end of the Thatcher government. The continuing failures to increase funding for the National Health Service had much the same impact, as did some elements of Labour education and transportation policies. The adversarial and majoritarian nature of British politics enables the party in government to push through policies that ultimately will undermine government—raising yet more problems for a coalition government that could have a difficult time responding to attacks in a unified way. This remains a conundrum for the present coalition government.

The electoral system of the United Kingdom also raises some questions about the democratic nature of the system. The single-member district, simple plurality system of choosing members of Parliament has (generally) been an effective means of generating parliamentary majorities from what has become effectively a multiparty system. Although this electoral system is beneficial in a parliamentary system with a majoritarian tradition, it is also increasingly regarded by people as undemocratic. The Liberal Democrats, including their earlier manifestations, have campaigned for many years for a move to proportional representation (PR) and pushed for a referendum on PR as part of the coalition agreement. The Conservatives, however, oppose adopting PR for Westminster elections. The negotiated agreement calls for a referendum to be held on adopting an Alternative Vote (AV) system. AV is not a PR system, but Liberal Democrat leaders have argued that it is a step in that direction. Many Conservatives, despite the coalition agreement, are likely to oppose the referendum, possibly risking increased tensions within the cabinet room.

Another institution with an unclear future is the House of Lords. In 1999 the Blair government abolished the right of all but ninety-two hereditary peers to sit in the House of Lords and established an appointments committee to grant peerages. Controversies remain, however, over further reforms. The Labour government did not deliver substantial House of Lords reform because Blair did not like the idea of an elected second chamber. It is true that an elected Lords would greatly complicate the legislative process in the United Kingdom, because the House of Commons is presently the only chamber that can claim a popular mandate for its actions. That said, with a push from Deputy Prime Minister Nick Clegg, the coalition government has expressed support for an elected second chamber, although the government has not determined which of the many options it will pursue.

Finally, beyond the question of which institution within British government is dominant is the broader question of the role of the emerging EU government in Brussels. The ideas of parliamentary sovereignty and cabinet government are being challenged from abroad just as they are at home. Many British politicians and citizens also consider some EU actions undemocratic and intrusive, but extricating themselves from Europe does not appear a desirable option for most officials. That said, according to most polls, had there been a referendum in 2005 in the United Kingdom on the proposed European constitution, it would almost certainly have failed as it did in France and the Netherlands.[8]

The nature of Britain's part in an ever-expanding Europe is not yet known, but it is likely to be different from that existing today. The United Kingdom must decide what to do about the monetary union with the rest of the EU; remaining outside the Euro Area, while perhaps profitable in the short term, may have serious long-term economic consequences. As mentioned previously, although the settled policy of the coalition government is to keep Europe "at arms length," the Liberal Democrats have long favored closer ties to the European Union, setting the stage for potential disagreements between the coalition partners. In short, the coalition forged between the Conservatives and Liberal Democrats is a marriage of convenience, not one of ideological love.

Continued Devolution, Breakup, or What?

Will there continue to be a United Kingdom? Indications are strong that this question can be answered in the affirmative, at least for the time being, although devolutionary pressures certainly put the long-term situation in greater doubt. By the time of the referendums in September 1997, a large majority of Scots and a smaller proportion of Welsh voters favored devolution. The success of these two referendums resulted in new governments being established in Edinburgh and Cardiff and, especially for the Scottish government, a transfer of substantial powers to those new loci of governing. The process of moving toward greater autonomy in Northern Ireland has been more complicated, but a devolved government has emerged in Belfast, and London and Dublin agreed about self-government in what remained a part of the United Kingdom.

In the nation as a whole, there appears to be relatively little interest in devolution or other substantial changes from the current constitutional arrangements. As for local government in England, the Conservative governments in the 1980s and into the 1990s centralized control over policy and local government finances. If anything, the Labour government that followed them extended and tightened that control and used its regulatory and inspection organizations to attempt to make the local authorities conform to the wishes of central government. One enduring question is whether the British government will find ways to accommodate these interests within a governing framework that is historically unitary and centralized. One option that has been explored is to allow regional assemblies in England modeled on the Welsh National Assembly and having only secondary legislative authority.[9] But this proposal has not received support of any significance in the English regions. In a referendum held on November 4, 2004, voters in northeast England decisively rejected a proposed regional assembly by a vote of 696,519 to 197,310. Slightly less than half of the electorate turned out to vote.

Perhaps the only issue that has much real resonance in England as a whole is the "West Lothian Question"—that is, following devolution of Scottish domestic matters to the Scottish Parliament, whether Scottish members of Parliament in Westminster should be barred from taking part in votes on legislation that affects only England, in the same way that English members of Parliament no longer have a vote on most Scottish matters.

This asymmetry strikes some observers as undesirable and unsustainable. The reduction in the number of Scottish MPs in Westminster after the 2005 elections temporarily relieved a bit of the tension surrounding the West Lothian Question, but it has not resolved the issue.

British policymakers are much like other policymakers, although they have their own particular processes, problems, and potential. The conduct of contemporary democratic government requires the British government to balance traditional norms and procedures that legitimate decisions against the more modern techniques for analysis and control. Today's more technically sophisticated and professionally qualified officials are challenging the older institutions for control over policymaking. And the underlying social divisions in society refuse to be homogenized, despite the pressures of the mass media, industrialization, and urbanization. Whether in the United Kingdom or elsewhere, modern government is a balancing act between the new and the old—those things that unite and those that divide.

NOTES

1. See Table A-2 in the Appendix and the CQ Press Web site for this volume.
2. That the British economy is more closely linked with the U.S. economy than with those of the other European countries also may contribute to this performance level.
3. "Britain's emergency budget. The meaning of austerity," *Economist,* June 24, 2010.
4. "Britain Unveils Emergency Budget," *New York Times,* June 22, 2010.
5. In fact, during the early years of the Thatcher government, public expenditures increased as a proportion of the GNP, in large part because the GNP was stable or declining.
6. For example, the quality of services provided to cancer patients has been found to be much lower than that provided in other European countries.
7. See Max Kaase and Kenneth Newton, *Beliefs in Government* (Oxford: Oxford University Press, 1996).
8. Alan Cowell, "Britain Suspends Referendum on European Constitution," *New York Times,* June 7, 2005.
9. The European "government of the regions" provides opportunities for regional governments and may make this change in England more desirable.

FOR FURTHER READING

Bale, Tim. *The Conservative Party: From Thatcher to Cameron.* London: Polity, 2010.

Bartle, John, and Anthony King, eds. *Britain at the Polls 2005.* Washington, D.C.: CQ Press, 2006.

Blair, Tony. *A Journey: My Political Life.* New York: Knopf, 2010.

Bogdanor, Vernon. *Politics and the Constitution: Essays on British Government.* Aldershot, Hants, UK: Dartmouth, 1996.

Butler, David, and Dennis Kavanagh. *The British General Election of 1997.* Basingstoke, UK: Macmillan; New York: St. Martin's Press, 1997.

Clarke, Harold, et al. *Political Choice in Britain.* Oxford: Oxford University Press, 2004.

Coates, David, and Peter Lawler, eds. *New Labour in Power.* Manchester and New York: Manchester University Press, 2000.

Cowley, Philip. *The Rebels: How Blair Mislaid his Majority.* London: Politicos, 2005.

Denver, David. *Elections and Voters in Britain,* 2nd ed. London: Palgrave, 2006.

Drewry, Gavin, and Tony Butcher. *The Civil Service Today.* 2nd ed. Oxford, UK: Basil Blackwell, 1989.

Faucher-King, Florence, and Patrick Le Galès. *The New Labour Experiment: Change and Reform under Blair and Brown.* Palo Alto, Calif.: Stanford University Press, 2010.

Foley, Michael. *The Rise of the British Presidency.* Manchester: University of Manchester Press, 1993.

George, Stephen. *Britain and the European Community: The Politics of Semi-detachment.* Oxford, UK: Clarendon Press, 1992.

Heath, Anthony, et al. *Understanding Political Change in Britain: The British Voter, 1964–1987.* Oxford, UK: Pergamon Press, 1991.

Hennessy, Peter. *The Hidden Writing: Unearthing the British Constitution.* London: Gollancz, 1996.

———. *Whitehall.* New York: Free Press, 1989.

Hogwood, Brian. *From Crisis to Complacency? Shaping Public Policy in Britain.* Oxford, UK: Clarendon Press, 1987.

Jones, Tudor. *Remaking the Labour Party: From Gaitskell to Blair.* London and New York: Routledge, 1996.

Judge, David. *Representation: Theory and Practice in Britain.* London: Routledge, 1999.

Kavanagh, Dennis. *Thatcherism and British Politics: The End of Consensus?* Oxford: Oxford University Press, 1990.

Kellas, James G. *The Scottish Political System.* 4th ed. New York: Cambridge University Press, 1989.

King, Anthony, et al. *Britain at the Polls, 1992.* Chatham, N.J.: Chatham House, 1993.

———. *Britain at the Polls, 2001.* New York: Chatham House, 2002.

———. *New Labour Triumphs: Britain at the Polls.* Chatham, N.J.: Chatham House, 1998.

King, Desmond, and Gerry Stoker. *Rethinking Local Democracy.* Basingstoke, UK: Macmillan, 1996.

Marsh, David. *The New Politics of British Trade Unionism: Union Power and the Thatcher Legacy.* Ithaca, N.Y.: ILR Press, 1992.

Marsh, David, and R.A.W. Rhodes. *Implementing "Thatcherism": A Policy Perspective.* Buckingham, UK: Open University Press, 1989.

———, eds. *Policy Networks in British Government.* Oxford, UK: Clarendon Press, 1992.

McIlroy, John. *Trade Unions in Britain Today.* 2nd ed. Manchester and New York: Manchester University Press, 1995.

Miller, William L., et al. *Political Culture in Contemporary Britain: People and Politicians, Principles and Practice.* Oxford and New York: Oxford University Press, 1996.

Norton, Bruce. *Politics in Britain.* Washington, D.C.: CQ Press, 2007.

Norton, Philip. *Does Parliament Matter?* New York and London: Harvester Wheatsheaf, 1993.

———. *Parliament in British Politics.* Basingstoke, UK: Palgrave Macmillan, 2005.

Parry, Geraint, George Moyser, and Neil Day. *Political Participation and Democracy in Britain.* Cambridge, UK: Cambridge University Press, 1993.

Pattie, Charles, Patrick Seyd, and Paul Whiteley. *Citizenship in Britain: Values, Participation and Democracy.* Cambridge, UK: Cambridge University Press, 2004.

Rogers, Robert, and Rhodri Walters. *How Parliament Works.* 6th ed. Harlow, UK: Pearson Longman, 2006.

Studlar, Donley T. *Great Britain: Decline or Renewal?* Boulder: Westview Press, 1996.

Thain, Colin, and Maurice Wright. *The Treasury and Whitehall.* Oxford, UK: Clarendon Press, 1995.

Thatcher, Margaret. *The Downing Street Years.* New York: HarperCollins, 1993.

Webb, Paul D. *The Modern British Party System.* London: Sage Publications, 2000.

Whiteley, Paul, Patrick Seyd, and Antony Billinghurst. *Third Force Politics: Liberal Democrats at the Grassroots.* Oxford, UK: Oxford University Press, 2006.

Whiteley, Paul, Patrick Seyd, and Jeremy Richardson. *True Blues: The Politics of Conservative Party Membership.* Oxford, UK: Clarendon Press, 1994.

Part 2

France

William Safran

The Context of French Politics

2.1

FRANCE IS WIDELY CONSIDERED TO BE THE FIRST MODERN NATION-state. It is also one of the oldest and most important countries in Europe. The culture, architecture, and cuisine of France have been much admired and copied. Its language once served as the chief medium of diplomacy, and its political philosophies and institutional patterns have exerted influences far beyond the country's borders. Until the end of World War II, France had the second-greatest colonial empire, with possessions in Southeast Asia, the Caribbean, and North and West Africa.

The third-largest country in Europe (after Russia and Ukraine), France is more than twice the size of Great Britain, 60 percent larger than Germany, and four-fifths the size of Texas. Except in the north and northeast, France has natural frontiers: the Atlantic Ocean on the west, the Pyrenees in the south, and the Alps and Jura mountains in the east. Its wide variations in landscape—the northern flatlands of Flanders, the forests of Normandy, the mountainous east and center, the beaches of the Vendée in the west, and the subtropical Riviera coast in the south—are accompanied by regional trends in cuisine, dress, speech, and attitude.

Ever since the country's early efforts at unification under centralized auspices, Paris has been the locus of national political power, as well as France's cultural and economic center. Paris contains the biggest university complex, three-fourths of the nation's theaters, and the majority of its museums and art galleries, and it is the hub from which most of the railroad lines radiate. The Paris region constitutes about 2 percent of the nation's land area, but it boasts its largest factories and accounts for a third of its industrial production. It also contains more than 20 percent of its total population, which in 2009 reached 65 million.[1]

In recent years, however, differences between north and south and between Paris and the rest of the country have been narrowing because of advancements in national transportation and communications and the growing geographic mobility of the population.

For many generations, the French referred to "our ancestors the Gauls"; they prided themselves on their descent from Gallo-Roman tribes that had fused over centuries into a homogeneous nation. In fact, however, France is the most ethnically and racially diverse country in Europe, with 20 percent of its population having a foreign-born parent or grandparent. The Italians, Germans, Poles, and others who settled in France over the course of several generations blended easily into the melting pot of Celtic, Latin, and other elements, and the more recent immigrants from Africa and Asia have made the population truly multiethnic. At the same time, the French acquired a deep sense of national identity from living in one of the first large European countries to have its boundaries more or less permanently fixed. Several decades ago, however, the collective consciousness of minorities began to reawaken. Alsatians, Bretons, Corsicans, and other ethnic groups—and more recently the Jewish, Muslim, and other ethnoreligious communities—have demanded that their cultural uniqueness be recognized. The retention of a monolithic national identity has become more difficult in view of the changed nature of immigration. In 2009 more than 3 million foreigners lived in France, making up 5 percent of the population. This figure is smaller than the number of immigrants, because many of the latter have been naturalized, a process that traditionally has been relatively easy.[2] A large proportion of the newcomers since the 1960s came from non-European countries and adhered to non-Christian religions. This development led to an extensive debate about the future of national identity, a debate that Nicolas Sarkozy encouraged when he campaigned for the presidency and that was officially launched in 2009 by Eric Besson, the newly appointed minister for immigration, integration, national identity, and solidarity. The government has floated new proposals under which immigrants would be admitted on a quota system based on their economic utility and naturalization would no longer be automatic—applicants would have to demonstrate knowledge of the French language and political system.[3] Moreover, illegal immigrants would not be candidates for naturalization; instead, they would be deported in larger numbers, and those aiding them would be punished.

For many years, foreigners and natives widely believed that, apart from Paris, France was essentially a peasant country. The Industrial Revolution did not proceed so early and so thoroughly in France as it did in Great Britain and Germany; by the end of World War II an estimated one-third of the French labor force was still employed in agriculture. Most of the farms were and still are small, as the consolidation of landholdings was impeded by the traditional division of a family's acreage among several descendants. Industrial development was long delayed by the lack of private investment capital and the limited need for industrial manpower in the cities. In the past sixty years, however, agricultural modernization has been impressive. As a consequence, employment in agriculture has declined from more than 30 percent of the active population in 1946 to less than 5 percent today. In 1946 a little over half the population (then 40.5 million) lived in cities; today, more than 85 percent do so.[4] As the number of farms and rural villages declined steadily and the number of urban agglomerations continued to grow, the French began to speak of a "terminal peasantry." In a parallel development, an extensive national superhighway system, high-speed rail transport, and a modern telecommunications network tied the provinces more closely to Paris, and the sense of separation between the small towns and the capital diminished.

Yet despite urbanization, many French men and women continue to share the belief that life in the country is more satisfying than an urban existence, which may account for the tendency of middle-class, big-city dwellers to acquire second homes in the country. Indeed, the "peasant romanticism" long fortified by the patterns of family loyalty, parsimony, and conservative moral values carefully nurtured by the Catholic Church has been rediscovered today as an ideal by those disenchanted with the economic insecurities, overcrowding, unemployment, and growing social disorganization and crime in the cities, and it has become a component of the ideology of extreme-right movements. There is no doubt that urbanization has contributed to a rapid increase in crime and in the prison population, which increased from 48,000 in 1992 to nearly 60,000 in 2009.

Religion and Social Class

For a long time, most of the population of France embraced Roman Catholicism; indeed, France was considered the "most Catholic" of countries. Once the Protestant Reformation spread to France in the sixteenth century, the country became riven by bitter struggles between Catholics, who were supported by the ruling elite, and Protestant Huguenots (mainly Calvinists), many of whom were massacred. After a period of toleration, the privileges of the Protestants (such as the right to live in certain fortified towns) were revoked in the seventeenth century, and many Protestants left the country. With the consolidation of absolute rule under the Bourbon kings, the position of Catholicism as the state religion was firmly established. Dissatisfaction with monarchism implied a questioning of the church and its privileges, and revolutionary sentiments were accompanied by anticlerical attitudes.

Anticlericalism and republicanism, then, are closely intertwined. The revolutionary commitment to *laïcité* (secularism), associated with a "religion of reason," made considerable headway during the Third Republic (1870–1940), when, under the leadership of left-wing parties, a national school system was created from which religion was entirely absent. Meanwhile, the hold of Catholicism gradually weakened as a consequence of industrialization, the rise of a new working class, and demographic and social changes. In 1905 the Catholic Church was formally "disestablished." France became, like the United States, a secular country, at least in constitutional terms (except in the province of Alsace where, for historic reasons, the clergy continues to be supported by public funds).[5] According to recent surveys, the majority of the French population is nominally Roman Catholic, but fewer than a third of Catholics attend church regularly.[6] Many inhabitants of the larger cities, and the great majority of industrial workers, are "de-Christianized" except in the most formal sense.

Yet Catholicism cannot be divorced from French culture and political consciousness. The cathedral remains the heart of small towns, most legal holidays are Catholic, and many political movements and interest groups are still influenced by Catholic teachings. (When Pope John Paul II died in April 2005, flags in France were flown at half-staff, and in Marseilles civil service workers received a half-day off work so that they could go to church.) Furthermore, public policy attitudes have often been inspired by Catholic social doctrine: aid to large families, the notion of class collaboration (instead of conflict) and the "association" of employers and workers in factories, the long-held opposition to the legalization of birth control and abortion, and the legal dominance—until well into the 1960s—of the male head of the family. Today, between 15 percent and 20 percent of parents opt to send their children to Catholic parochial schools, which benefit from governmental financial support.[7]

Of the 1.5 million French Protestants, many are prominent in business, the so-called free professions (such as lawyers, physicians, and architects), and, more recently, politics and administration. The current Fifth Republic had three Protestant prime ministers (Maurice Couve de Murville, Michel Rocard, and Lionel Jospin) and numerous Protestant cabinet ministers and presidential candidates.

Jews have lived in France since before the Middle Ages, and today they number about 700,000. During the Dreyfus Affair in the 1890s, antirepublican feelings were accompanied by a campaign to vilify Jews and to eliminate them from public life. During the Nazi occupation of France (1940–1944), persecutions and deportations of Jews ravaged the Jewish community and reduced it by a third. Since the early 1960s, the number of Jews has been augmented by repatriates from North Africa. Much like Protestants, Jews have tended to support republican regimes and have decidedly preferred left-of-center parties identified with anticlericalism. Although Jews are fully integrated into French life, anti-Semitism has not been eliminated and tends to be perpetuated by extreme-right political parties and, more recently, by Muslim immigrants.

Since the mid-1960s, France has experienced a significant influx of Muslims, primarily from North Africa. Many of them perform the most menial work in industrial cities. Estimated at about 6 million, the Muslim population constitutes the second-largest religious group. Many French people, especially the lower-middle and working classes, feel that the growing presence of these "exotic" immigrants has contributed heavily to the growth of unemployment and criminality in France and will sooner or later transform the very nature of French society. Moreover, practicing Muslims, unlike other minorities, are said to adhere to a "fundamentalist" religion that rejects the primacy of French civil law, secular education, gender equality, and religious pluralism and therefore poses a challenge to the values of the republic. Other observers are more optimistic: they argue that Islam comes in many forms, and that a large number of Muslims have become acculturated to French values and way of life.[8]

The growing racial, ethnic, and religious diversity in France, which has generated conflict and violence against minorities, has been met with a variety of responses. On the one hand, the National Assembly has passed both antidiscrimination laws and legislation penalizing the dissemination of ethnic, racial, and religious hatred, and the government and others have made efforts to acculturate minorities and integrate them into the mainstream. On the other hand, the French people have been hesitant to accept cultural pluralism.[9] They have been uneasy about *communautarisme,* the maintenance of cultures and subcommunities based on ethnicity or religion.

The growth of the Muslim population and the continuing decline of Christianity have led to a renewal of the debate about the place of religion in a republic committed to the principle of *laïcité.* In an attempt to "westernize" Islam, the government established the French Council of the Muslim Faith (Conseil Français du Culte Musulman [CFCM]) with branches at the regional level. The CFCM represents a variety of Muslim organizations and functions as official interlocutor with the public authorities.[10] To dilute religious influence in education, the government successfully sponsored legislation to ban the wearing of the Islamic headscarf (*hijab*) by Muslim schoolgirls as well as the wearing of ostentatious Christian and Jewish accoutrements in public schools.

Superficially, the French social system is typical of that found in other European countries. The medieval divisions of society into nobility, clergy, townspeople, and peasants gradually gave way to a more complex social structure. The traditional, land-based aristocracy declined as a result of the use of the guillotine and the diminishing economic value of agriculture, and today the aristocracy has a certain vestigial importance only in the military officer corps and the diplomatic service.

Members of the modern upper class or *haute bourgeoisie*—a status derived from graduation from a prestigious university or the inheritance of wealth or both—generally make up the higher echelons of the civil service and serve as the directors of large business firms and as bankers. The next social group is the *grande bourgeoisie,* which includes university professors, high school teachers, engineers, members of the free professions, middle-echelon government functionaries, and the proprietors of medium-size family firms. The middle and lower-middle class, today the largest social category, comprises elementary school teachers, white-collar employees, small shopkeepers, and lower-echelon civil servants. The lower classes (*classes populaires*) include most of the industrial workers, small farmers, and possibly artisans.

These class divisions have been important insofar as they have influenced a person's political ideology, general expectations from the system, lifestyle, place of residence, and choice of political party. A typical member of the free professions has tended to adhere to a liberal party (that is, one oriented toward individualism), a businessman to a conservative (or moderate) party, and an industrial worker to a socialist party. The class system and interclass relationships have been constantly changing, however. These changes have taken place with particular rapidity since the dramatic events of May–June 1968, when masses of students and workers joined in a general strike and almost brought down the government. Nor is the correlation between class membership and adherence to a specific political party as predictable as it once was. In recent years, there has been a growing underclass consisting of uprooted farmers and redundant artisans, industrial workers now jobless because of the decline of traditional manufacturing and the growth of the high-technology sector, and immigrants who cannot be precisely categorized and whose relationship to the political system is fluid, if not marginal. Moreover, distinctions between classes have been partially obscured by the redistributive impact of a highly developed system of social legislation and the progressive democratization of the educational system. Table 2-1 reveals some of the changes that have taken place over sixty years.

Table 2-1 France: Some Changes over Sixty Years

	1946	1975	1985	1990	1995	2000	2005	2009 (est.)
Total population (millions)	40.5	52.6	55.0	56.56	58.3	59.8	60.7	65.4
Number of adolescents over age fourteen enrolled in schools (thousands)	650	4,000	4,200	5,400	5,600	6,400	7,700	6,644
Average annual duration of full-time work (hours)	2,100	1,875	1,763[a]	n.a.	1,500	1,355	1,450[b]	—
Infant mortality per thousand live births	84.4	13.8	10.1	7.5[c]	4.9	4.4	4.3	3.33
Number of private cars in circulation (thousands)	1,000	15,300	20,800	22,750[c]	n.a.	27,500	n.a.	
Longevity of males (years)	61.9	69.1	71[d]	73.3	73.8	75.2	76.0	77.8
Longevity of females (years)	67.4	77.0	79[d]	80.6	81.9	82.7	84.5	

Sources: Based on Jean Fourastié, *Les Trente glorieuses ou la révolution invisible* (Paris: Fayard, 1979), 36; *Quid* 1988, 1992, 1996, 2001, 2006 (Paris: Robert Laffont); Dominique Borne, *Histoire de la société française depuis 1945* (Paris: Armand Colin, 1988), 95; Gérard Mermet, *Francoscopie 2001* (Paris: Larousse, 2000), 195, 301–302; INSEE estimates for 2009.

[a] 1986.
[b] 2004.
[c] 1989.
[d] 1982.

Education

The centralized national school system established at the end of the nineteenth century was based on uniform curriculums stressing national, secular, and republican values and theoretically creating opportunities of upward mobility on the basis of talent, not wealth. Traditionally, the Ministry of Education controlled the educational curriculums, from public elementary school in small villages to lycées in large cities, and was the major voice in the administration of universities. In practice, the system (at least until the late 1950s) fortified existing social inequalities, because most children of the working and peasant classes were not steered toward the lycées, the academic secondary schools whose diplomas were required for admission to university, and therefore were condemned to perpetual lower-class status. Since the early 1960s, a spate of reform legislation has been aimed at the "comprehensivization" of schooling, at least up to the age of sixteen. Curricula are now more practical, more technological, and less classical-humanistic. Under new laws, universities have become more flexible and less hierarchical, and they allow students to participate in decision making (but there are complaints that the pace of implementation has occasionally been impeded by insufficient funds and the resistance of the academic establishment). As a consequence, most lycée students now get the *baccalauréat*, the *lycée* diploma, and with it, the right to enroll at a university. University enrollments have exploded, rising from 1 million in 1985 to nearly 2.3 million in 2008/2009.[11] But the inability of many university graduates to find jobs has acted as a brake to further significant increases. Moreover, a large proportion of students drop out after one or two years at a university.[12] Although tuition fees are minimal, many students from families in straitened circumstances complain that state scholarship aid (*bourses*) covering registration and other fees as well as living expenses and books is inadequate. Since the election of Nicolas Sarkozy, many French universities have been granted more autonomy (often against their will) to decide on budgets, curricula, student admissions, and contracts with the private sector.

Among the major beneficiaries of educational reforms, and of social changes in general, are women. Before World War II, women could not vote. Although they obtained that right in 1945, they gained complete equality only gradually. In 2000 the constitution was amended—followed by legislation—to institute a system of gender "parity" in the nominations for elective office, but only 12.3 percent of the members of the National Assembly elected in 2002 were women (compared with 10 percent in the previous Assembly). In 2007 the representation of women in the Assembly had risen to 18.5 percent, but was still far short of parity. But women have done well in the regional councils, where they make up 47.6 percent of the membership.[13] The place of women was greatly enhanced in 2007, when President Sarkozy appointed several women to important ministerial positions in Prime Minister François Fillon's cabinet. Women have also made considerable headway in the private sector and in associational politics. The French Democratic Confederation of Labor (Confédération Française Démocratique du Travail [CFDT]), one of the three largest trade unions, was headed by a woman president in the 1990s, and in 2005 the Association of French Entrepreneurs (Mouvement des Entreprises de France [MEDEF]), with 700,000 member firms, elected a woman as president.

The attitudes of the French toward politics have been shaped by their education and social condition. Scholars have suggested that the French are more critical of their regime

Table 2-2 France: Political Cycles and Regimes

Moderate monarchy	Liberalization	Conservative reaction
Constitutional monarchy of 1791 Restoration of 1815 Early Third Republic (1870–1879)	Republic of 1792 "July Monarchy" of 1830 Later Third Republic (1879–1940) Fourth Republic (1947–1958) Fifth Republic (since 1981)	Dictatorial government of 1795 Second Empire (1852–1870) Vichy regime (1940–1944) Early Fifth Republic (1958–1981)

Source: Adapted from Dorothy Pickles, *The Fifth French Republic,* 3rd ed. (New York: Praeger, 1965), 3–5.

than are Americans or Englishmen, and there are periodic studies of what is wrong with their country.[14] French citizens have frequently participated in uprisings and revolutions, and they have exhibited "anticivic" behavior patterns such as tax evasion, draft-dodging, and alcoholism. They also have often shown contempt for law (and the police), and members of the working class, in particular, have been convinced that the legal system favors the "established" classes. Finally, a large segment of the population has adhered to political ideologies and parties oriented to replacement of the existing political order.

This insufficient acceptance of the existing regime—a phenomenon called "crisis of legitimacy"—was produced by, and in turn reflected in, the apparent inability of the French to create a political formula that would resolve satisfactorily the conflict between the state and the individual, centralism and localism, the executive and the legislature, and representative and "direct" democracy. Since the abolition of the old regime of royal absolutism, there has been a dizzying succession of governments—republics, monarchies, empires, and republics again—most of them embodying drastically different conceptions of the proper division of governmental authority (see Table 2-2).

Revolutions, Regime Changes, and Legitimacy Crises

Many regimes created institutional solutions that were too extreme and therefore could not last. The Revolution of 1789, which led to the abdication of King Louis XVI in 1792, was followed by a series of experiments that, collectively, has been termed the First Republic. It was characterized by the abolition of the old provinces and the restructuring of administrative divisions, a reduction in the power of the church and the inauguration of a "rule of reason," a proclamation of universal human rights, and the passing of power from the landed aristocracy to the bourgeoisie. It was also marked by assassinations and mass executions—the "Reign of Terror"—which ended when order was established under Napoleon Bonaparte. At first leader of a dictatorial Consulate (1799) and then president (1802) of what was still, formally, a "republic," Napoleon had himself proclaimed emperor in 1804. In 1814 Napoleon's empire collapsed after a military defeat, but the emperor left behind a great heritage of reforms: the abolition of feudal tax obligations, a body of codified laws, the notion of a merit-based professional bureaucracy (much of it trained in specialized national schools), and a system of relationships (or rather, a theory about such relationships) under which the chief executive derived his legitimacy directly from the people through popular elections or referendums. The chief executive's rule was unimpeded by a strong parliament, subnational government units, or other "intermediary" institutions or groups. At once heroic and popular, the "Bonaparte's" approach to politics had a strong impact on segments of the French nation; much of what came to characterize Gaullism was heavily influenced by that approach.

The power of the clergy and nobility was revived in 1815 when the Bourbon monarchy was restored, but that was to be a constitutional regime patterned on the English model and guaranteeing certain individual liberties and limited participation of the parliament. In 1830 the Bourbon dynasty, having become arbitrary and corrupt, was replaced by another regime, that of Louis-Philippe of the House of Orleans. In 1848 the French rebelled once more and inaugurated what came to be known as the Second Republic. They elected Louis Napoleon (a nephew of Napoleon I) president for a ten-year term, but in 1852 he too proclaimed himself emperor. The "Second Empire" was a "republican" empire insofar as a weak legislative chamber continued to exist and, more important, because Louis Napoleon derived his power from the people rather than from God.

The Second Empire was noted for many achievements: industrial progress, a stable currency, and the rebuilding and modernization of Paris. But popular disenchantment with what had become a dictatorial regime and France's military defeat at the hands of the Prussians in 1870 brought it down.

The Third Republic, the regime that followed, was inaugurated in bloodshed: the Paris Commune of 1871, in which thousands of "proletarians" rebelled and were brutally suppressed by bourgeois leaders. Most of these leaders did not, in fact, want a republic. The National Assembly (then called the Chamber of Deputies) was elected to make peace with Prussia. It was dominated by monarchists, but they disagreed on which of the competing pretenders—Bourbon, Orléans, or Bonaparte—should be given the throne. Consequently, the Assembly adopted a skeletal constitution that provided, on a temporary basis, for an executive and a legislative branch and outlined the relationship between them. This constitution, which contained no bill of rights, lasted nearly seventy years and set the pattern for subsequent republican regimes.

In the beginning, the president, who was elected by parliament for seven years, tried to govern while ignoring that body, and he even tried to dissolve the National Assembly, whose political composition he did not like. In 1877 parliament rebelled and forced the president to resign. Henceforth, presidents became figureheads, and prime ministers and their cabinets were transformed into obedient tools of powerful parliaments and were replaced or reshuffled about once every eight months. Many observers viewed this instability as endemic to republican systems as such and encouraged romantic monarchists to attempt to subvert the republic. Yet this republic had many achievements to its credit, not the least of which was that it emerged victorious and intact from World War I. It might have lasted even longer had France not been invaded and occupied by the Germans in 1940.

After the German defeat of France, the "unoccupied" southern half of the country was transformed into the "French State," which took the form of an authoritarian puppet regime led from Vichy, a provincial resort town, by Marshal Philippe Pétain, an aging hero of World War I. The behavior of the French during this period, both in the Vichy state and in the occupied part of the country, was complex and ambivalent, and the debate about who collaborated with the Nazis and who resisted them continues.[15]

The Fourth Republic, which was instituted in late 1946, two years after France was liberated, essentially followed the pattern established during the Third Republic. Although its highly detailed and democratic constitution included an impressive bill of rights, it

Gen. Charles de Gaulle (center) walks through the streets of Bayeux, France, after its liberation in June 1944. The same year he became the provisional civilian leader of liberated France, presiding over a government coalition composed of Christian Democrats, Socialists, and Communists.

Source: AP/Images

made for a system even less stable than that of the Third Republic. There were twenty governments (and seventeen prime ministers) over a twelve-year period; the National Assembly, though theoretically supreme, could not provide effective leadership. Ambitious deputies, seeking a chance to assume ministerial office, easily managed to topple cabinets, and a large proportion of the legislators—notably the Communists on the left and the Gaullists on the right—were not interested in maintaining the regime.

Yet the Fourth Republic was not without accomplishments. It inaugurated a system of long-term capitalist planning under which France rebuilt and modernized its industrial and transport structures. It put in place an extensive network of welfare state provisions, including comprehensive statutory medical insurance. And it took the first steps toward decolonization—relinquishing control of Indochina, Morocco, and Tunisia—and paved the way for intra-European collaboration in the context of the European Coal and Steel Community and, later, the Common Market. Some of the failures of the Fourth Republic— for example, its inability to institute meaningful local democracy and its foot-dragging on tax reform—were also failures of the political system that replaced it.

The Fourth Republic probably would have continued had it not been for the problem of Algeria and the convenient presence of a war hero, Gen. Charles de Gaulle. France was unable to decolonize Algeria easily, or grant it independence, because more than 2 million French men and women, many of them able to trace their roots in that territory several generations back, considered it not only their home but also an integral component of France. A succession of Fourth Republic politicians lacked the will or the stature to impose a solution to the problem. Meanwhile, the war that had broken out in Algeria in the mid-1950s threatened to spill over into mainland France and helped to discredit the regime.

Under the pressure of the Algerian events (and the threat of a military coup in continental France and North Africa), the Fourth Republic leadership decided in mid-1958 to call on de Gaulle. De Gaulle had been a professional soldier, a member of the general staff, and, several months after the outbreak of World War II, deputy minister of war. After France's capitulation in June 1940, de Gaulle refused to accept the permanence of surrender and the legitimacy of the Pétain regime. Instead, he fled to London, where he established a "government in exile" and organized the "Free French" forces, which were joined by many of the Frenchmen who had escaped in time from the Continent. In 1944 de Gaulle became the provisional civilian leader of liberated France, presiding over a government coalition composed of Christian Democrats, Socialists, and Communists. In 1946 he retired from the political scene, having failed to prevent the ratification of the Fourth Republic constitution (a document he opposed because it granted excessive powers to the parliament). In retirement, de Gaulle continued to be a political force: more precisely, a force of inspiration to a political movement, the Rally of the French People (Rassemblement du Peuple Français [RPF]). These original "Gaullists" wanted to replace the Fourth Republic with a new regime that would be led by a strong executive.

The Fifth Republic, established in 1958, is an institutional mixture of a powerful executive and a weak legislature. The institutional relationships common to this republic are described in Chapter 2.2; what follows here is a description of the French political culture—that is, political attitudes that are widely held and behavior patterns that cut across specific social classes and party ideologies.

Aspects of French Political Culture

Except for parts of the industrial working class, most French people have shared the universal ambitions of French civilization and have not seemed to consider the often exaggerated chauvinism of their intellectual elite to be inconsistent with such ambitions. They have taken pride in France's international prestige, cultural patrimony, and intellectual accomplishments, although these may have borne little relationship to objective reality, may not have benefited all citizens equally, and may not have compensated for the more immediate economic needs of the underprivileged. In recent years, some members of the intellectual elite have been worried about the excessive influence of mass culture and the "pollution" of the French language by Americanisms.

The French have had a tendency toward hero worship that has led them, on several occasions, to accept "men on horseback": the two Napoleons, Marshal MacMahon (in the 1870s), Marshal Pétain, and General de Gaulle. This tendency has been balanced by one of rebelling against authority. Moreover, although the French have often opted for leftist or revolutionary ideologies and politicians, such leftist thinking and speaking have sometimes been meaningless exercises because there was little expectation that they would (or ought to) translate into leftist government policies. Public opinion polls conducted from the 1950s to the 1990s typically showed that the proportion of French voters preferring Socialist Party candidates was consistently higher than the proportion of those who favored the nationalization of enterprises or the equalization of incomes—both traditional components of socialist ideology.

The French have often held their politicians in contempt; indeed, according to a recent survey, 69 percent of respondents thought that they are little or not at all concerned with what the citizens think.[16] At the same time, the French have allowed politicians greater leeway than have Americans with respect to tax evasion, collusion with business, or (personal) behavioral departures from bourgeois moral norms. Only in the past few years has such toleration been replaced by popular impatience with, and the electoral punishment of, corrupt politicians. A manifestation of that impatience, reflected in an increasingly independent judiciary, has been the indictment—and in some cases, conviction—of nearly a hundred elected officials of both the right and the left for the misappropriation of public funds and a variety of other legal violations.[17] The disillusionment with the "political class" has also manifested itself in negative voting behavior: about half of adults do not vote, and most of those who do tend to vote against the government, as they did in the presidential elections of 2002, the regional elections of 2004 and 2010 (see Chapter 2.3), and the referendum on the European constitution in 2005.

At the same time, the French have a widespread desire to enter public service, and much prestige is attached to it. Traditionally, the French have been sharply critical of the regime, but they have had a highly developed sense of belonging to the nation and great expectations from the "state" in terms of what it should do for them. Some examples include the strikes in the fall of 1995 by public transport workers, who were protesting threatened cuts in social security protections and demanding a lowering of the retirement age; the strikes a year later, for similar aims, of drivers in the private trucking industry; and the massive strikes in 2006 against a government bill to make it easier for employers to lay off young entrants into the labor force. Although greatly inconvenienced by these events, the general public supported the strikers—both to express their social solidarity and to avoid having traditional welfare state entitlements for any part of the population called into question.

Ideology is now far less important than it was at the beginning of the Industrial Revolution, and a growing number of French men and women have become market-oriented. Such a change, however, is a far cry from an unqualified embrace of classic liberalism. France's traditional nationalism has been moderated, and most of its citizens are more open to Europe and the world at large. Yet at the same time they are not quite willing to accept the consequences of globalization.

Other important changes have emerged as well, especially over the past two decades. For example, there is now little question about the legitimacy of the political system: more than 90 percent of the French people accept the institutions of the Fifth Republic, a consensus signaled by the gradual convergence of the parties of the right and left and, indeed, in a growing impatience with ideological labels.

Conversely, the state has been desanctified in the eyes of many French citizens, and the role of the market has become more widely accepted. At the same time, the state retains at once its role as protector, insofar as 4 million French citizens work for it and several million more depend on it. A poll conducted by SOFRES at the end of 2004 found that 75 percent of respondents believed it was up to individuals more than the state to move society forward. Yet 74 percent opposed the privatization of hospitals; 85 percent opposed an increase in cost sharing by patients for medical care; 78 percent opposed raising the retirement age to sixty; and 81 percent opposed easing protection against layoffs by employers.[18] Although the French still have an "instrumental" view of the state in the sense that it is expected to continue to be important in economic, social, and cultural affairs, their expectations have become somewhat more realistic. This development is reflected in the fact that in recent years the French have been attaching greater value to liberty than to equality. A poll taken a decade ago revealed that for 63 percent of respondents French national identity was essentially symbolized by a commitment to human rights—roughly the same percentage for whom that identity is symbolized by French cuisine.[19] Even though the French have become more ego-oriented, they have also come to attach increasing importance to "civil society" and its component parts. For example, in addition to placing greater reliance on the market, the French have participated in the rapid growth of voluntary associations on the national and local levels. These developments have served to reduce the social distrust and lessen the "fear of face-to-face relations" that was once considered a major aspect of French political culture.[20] They also tended to foster a greater openness to "out-groups," both within France and outside it. One manifestation of that change is the widespread public support of fairer treatment of immigrants (which compensates for pockets of intolerance) and a higher appreciation of aspects of non-French culture. The massive riots by Muslim and African immigrants and their descendants—the "immigrants of the second generation"—in October and November 2005 challenged France's position on ethnic and racial minorities. Many of the rioters were unemployed, lived in suburban ghettos, and felt politically, socially, and economically marginalized. They saw no way out of their isolation and neglect. These events introduced considerable doubt about the efficacy and seriousness of government efforts to integrate immigrants into a monocultural French society and even called into question the relevance of the Jacobin monocultural ideal itself.

NOTES

1. Population growth is indicated by the following comparative figures (in thousands): 1950, 41,647; 1970, 50,528; 1990, 56,577; 2004, 60,200. Laurent Toulemon, "Population, grand tendances," in *L'Etat de la France 2005–2006* (Paris: La Découverte, 2005), 24. The demographic surge, which represented the second-highest fertility rate in Europe (after Ireland), was the result of natalist policies, such as generous income supplements for families with children, free nursery schools maintained by cities, and paid leaves of absence for nursing mothers.
2. Naturalization has been based on the principle of *jus soli* (law of the soil), the criterion of birth or residence in the country. Immigrants may seek naturalization after a minimum residence of five years, and foreigners born in France may opt for French citizenship upon reaching majority (age eighteen).
3. Jacky Durand, "En France, bientôt un examen civique," *Libération*, August 13, 2005.
4. Updated from Antoine Haumont, "Cadre de vie: Grandes tendances," in *L'État de la France 2005–2006* (Paris: La Découverte, 2005), 55.
5. Alsace and the department of Moselle (Lorraine) were annexed by Germany in 1870 after the Franco-Prussian war. When these areas were returned to France in 1918, the government

continued the system of support of the "official" religions (Catholicism, Protestantism, and Judaism) that had been in force in Germany.

6. According to a January 2007 Harris poll, 51 percent described themselves as Catholics, 31 percent as atheists, 4 percent as Muslims, 3 percent as Protestants, and 1 percent as Jews. (*Daily Telegraph,* January 10, 2007). These figures must be used with caution, however, because the figure for Muslims is much higher. Note also that many who are nominally Catholic do not believe in God.

7. On the place of Catholicism and other religions in French public life, see Jean-Paul Willaime, "Religion et Politique en France dans le Contexte de la Construction Euro-péenne," *French Politics, Culture & Society,* 25 (Winter 2007): 36–61.

8. See Jonathan Laurence and Justin Vaisse, *Integrating Islam: Political and Religious Challenges in Contemporary France* (Washington, D.C.: Brookings Institution, 2006); and John R. Bowen, *Can Islam Be French?* (Princeton, N.J.: Princeton University Press, 2009).

9. See Edouard Balladur, *La fin de l'illusion jacobine* (Paris: Fayard, 2004); and Pierre-André Taguieff, *La République enlisée: Pluralisme, communautarisme, citoyenneté* (Paris: Editions des Syrtes, 2004).

10. See special issue on "Le Conseil Français du Culte Musulman," *French Politics, Culture & Society* 23 (2005).

11. Ministère d'Education Nationale, de l'Enseignement Supérieur et de la Recherche, and INSEE, *La France en Chiffres, 2005–2006* (Paris, 2006, updated).

12. See Stéphane Beaud, "L'echec à l'université des enfants de la démocratisation," *Cosmopolitiques* 10 (2005): 13–14.

13. For these and other statistics, see Anne Chemin, "Une nouvelle génération de femmes s'est lancée en politique," *Le Monde,* March 8, 2005.

14. Somewhat older exercises of this sort are Michel Crozier, *La société bloquée* (Paris: Seuil, 1970); and Alain Peyrefitte, *The Trouble with France* (New York: Knopf, 1981). Among the more recent studies in "declinology" are Nicolas Baverez, *La France qui tombe* (Paris: Perrin, 2004); and Alain Lefebvre and Dominique Méda, *Faut-il brûler le modèle social français?* (Paris: Seuil, 2006). Also see Sophie Meunier, "Free-Falling France or Free-Trading France?" *French Politics, Culture & Society* 22 (Spring 2004): 98–107.

15. The debate even involved President François Mitterrand. In 1994 many details began to surface about his involvement with the Vichy regime and his earlier identification with right-wing movements and personalities. See Pierre Péan, *Une jeunesse française, 1934–1947* (Paris: Fayard, 1994); and Emmanuel Faux, Thomas Legrand, and Gilles Perez, *La main droite de dieu* (Paris: Seuil, 1994).

16. SOFRES poll of March 2006, reported in "La défiance des Français vis-à-vis des hommes politiques s'accroît," *Le Monde,* March 26–27, 2006.

17. The list of those convicted includes Jean Tibéri, the mayor of Paris, Alain Juppé, former deputy major of Paris and current mayor of Bordeaux, Charles Pasqua, former minister of the interior, and Jean-Christophe Mitterrand, the eldest son of the former president. See Jérôme Dupuis, Jean-Marie Pontaut, and Jean-Loup Reverier, "100 élus dans le collimateur: Le Who's Who des mis en examen," *Le Point,* June 10, 1995, 36–45.

18. Sylvie Pierre-Brossolette, "La fin des tabous?" *Figaro-Magazine,* January 17, 2004, 41–50. A poll conducted in 2005 confirms such figures. See Emmanuel Rivière, "Valeurs idéologiques: La France à la recherche d'elle-même," in *L'État de l'opinion 2006,* ed. Olivier Duhamel and Brice Tenturier (Paris: Seuil, 2006), 35–36.

19. See Claudius Brosse, *L'Etat dinosaure* (Paris: Albin Michel, 2000).

20. See Michel Crozier, *The Bureaucratic Phenomenon* (Chicago: University of Chicago Press, 1969), 220–221.

Where Is the Power?

T HE CONSTITUTION OF THE FIFTH REPUBLIC WAS DRAWN UP SEVERAL weeks after Gen. Charles de Gaulle was invested as the (last) prime minister of the Fourth Republic. The new constitution, which was adopted by an 80 percent vote in a popular referendum held in September 1958, was tailor-made for de Gaulle. It contained many features found in previous French republics: a president, a prime minister, and a parliament composed of two chambers—a National Assembly and a Senate. Institutional relationships were rearranged, however, to reflect the political ideas that the famous general and his advisers had often articulated—that is, the ideology of Gaullism.

The President and the Government

De Gaulle and his advisers—foremost among them Michel Debré, the principal draftsman of the constitution, who was to become the Fifth Republic's first prime minister—wanted to have a strong government. It would be capable of making decisions and conducting an assertive foreign policy without having to worry about excessive parliamentary interference or premature ouster.

The president is clearly the central feature of the Fifth Republic system. The constitution originally provided for presidential election by an electoral college composed of some eighty thousand national, regional, and local legislators, but since the approval by referendum of a constitutional amendment in 1962, presidents have been elected by popular vote. Because many political leaders, including aspirants to the presidency and former presidents, found the seven-year presidential term of office too long, the term was reduced to five years by referendum in 2000.

The president is invested with near-monarchical powers, which were expanded through interpretation by the first three of the six incumbents of the office so far: Charles de Gaulle (1959–1969); Georges Pompidou (1969–1974); Valéry Giscard d'Estaing (1974–1981); François Mitterrand (1981–1995); Jacques Chirac (1995–2007); and Nicolas Sarkozy (since May 2007). Under the constitution of the Fifth Republic, the president appoints the prime minister, who then supposedly selects the rest of the cabinet. De Gaulle and Pompidou took an interest in many of these appointments, and Giscard d'Estaing and Nicolas Sarkozy decided the composition of the entire cabinet on a rather personal basis. The composition of these cabinets was endorsed almost automatically by the National Assembly, which was controlled by politicians more or less in the same (conservative) ideological camp as the respective presidents.

Under President Mitterrand, a Socialist, the situation became more complicated. For five years after his election in 1981 and the election immediately thereafter of a Socialist-controlled Assembly, the composition of governments reflected the president's wishes to a large extent. But after the parliamentary elections of 1986, and again in 1993, when the

Gaullists and their allies recaptured control of the Assembly, the president was forced to appoint a prime minister and cabinet to the Assembly's liking rather than his own. The "cohabitation" of a Socialist president with a Gaullist government—a situation not clearly envisaged by the drafters of the Fifth Republic constitution—led to a restructuring of the relationship between the two: a delicate form of power sharing in which the prime minister took responsibility for most domestic policies and the president retained a measure of authority in foreign affairs and national defense as well as a vaguely defined influence in internal affairs.

After Mitterrand's reelection as president in 1988 and the recapture of control of the Assembly by the Socialists immediately thereafter, the situation returned to "normal"— that is, the president's preeminence was reestablished. Mitterrand, however, decided not to exercise his restored powers fully but to share them with his prime minister, Michel Rocard, and, to a lesser extent, with parliament—not only because the cohabitation experience had chastened him but also because he had, in a sense, become an elder statesman who transcended politics.

A "normal" situation of presidential supremacy was restored again in 1995 with the election of Jacques Chirac, a Gaullist, as president and the appointment of Gaullist Alain Juppé as prime minister. Two years later, however, France was subjected to a third experiment with cohabitation as a consequence of a premature parliamentary election. Although the Assembly elected in 1993 was supposed to remain in place until 1998, Chirac decided in 1997 to dissolve it and call for early elections (see Chapter 2.3). This move was prompted by the pressure on France to make drastic cuts in public expenditures in preparation for participating in the common European currency, which was scheduled to be inaugurated in January 1999. The requirement to reduce the government deficit to a maximum of 3 percent of the gross domestic product would force the parliament to make unpopular cuts in the welfare state budget. Although the Assembly had an overwhelming Gaullist and center-conservative majority, the retrenchment measures required under the European Union's common monetary policy could not be completely enacted before the expiration of the normal life of the Assembly, and it was feared that the public would take revenge on that legislative chamber at the next regular election. The early election was, therefore, seen as a preventive step. Although the president expected the Gaullists and their allies to lose some votes, he was confident that they would still retain comfortable control of the Assembly.

The victory of the Socialist Party and its left-wing allies in the parliamentary elections of 1997 was as dramatic as it was unexpected. Because it was an unnecessary election, its outcome, a consequence of Chirac's miscalculations, served to undermine his presidential authority. He had no choice but to appoint Lionel Jospin, the Socialist leader who had run as a presidential candidate only two years earlier, as prime minister. In this new cohabitation, Jospin asserted himself strongly as a decision maker, so that he came to rival, and even eclipse, the authority of the president not only in domestic affairs but also in foreign policy. Sarkozy's election to the presidency in 2007 was followed in short order by legislative elections, which resulted in continuing control of the National Assembly by the Union for a Popular Movement (Union pour un Mouvement Populaire [UMP]), the party of the president. This outcome gave Sarkozy virtually complete control over the decision-making apparatus, which he used to structure a (more or less nonideological) government to his liking and promote far-reaching policy innovations and institutional reforms (see below).

Under normal as well as cohabitation situations, the president has a variety of appointive powers that can be exercised without interruption over military officers, political advisers, and some of the members of several judicial organs (on the advice, to be sure, of the prime minister). In addition, the president retains the powers traditionally associated with chiefs of state: to appoint ambassadors and other high civilian personnel, to receive foreign dignitaries, to sign bills and promulgate laws and decrees, to issue pardons, and to preside over cabinet sessions and to send messages to parliament. The president cannot veto bills, but he may ask parliament to reexamine all or a part of any bill he does not like. The president also has the right to dissolve the Assembly before the expiration of its maximum term of five years and to call for new elections. The only two constraints are rather mild: the requirement that the president "consult" with the prime minister and the Speakers of the two chambers and the stipulation that the Assembly not be dissolved less than a year after its election. So far, presidents have made use of the dissolution power on five occasions: in 1962, 1968, 1981, 1988, and 1997.

France at a Glance

Type of Government
Republic

Capital
Paris

Administrative Divisions
Twenty-two regions, subdivided into ninety-six departments. Overseas departments are French Guiana, Guadeloupe, Martinique, and Réunion, and overseas territorial collectivities are Mayotte and Saint Pierre and Miquelon.
Regions: Alsace, Aquitaine, Auvergne, Basse-Normandie, Bourgogne, Bretagne, Centre, Champagne-Ardenne, Corse, Franche-Comté, Haute-Normandie, Ile-de-France, Languedoc-Roussillon, Limousin, Lorraine, Midi-Pyrénées, Nord-Pas-de-Calais, Pays de la Loire, Picardie, Poitou-Charentes, Provence–Alpes–Côte d'Azur, Rhône-Alpes
Dependent areas: Bassas da India, Clipperton Island, Europa Island, French Polynesia, French Southern and Antarctic Lands, Glorioso Islands, Juan de Nova Island, New Caledonia, Tromelin Island, Wallis and Futuna

Independence
486 (unified by Clovis)

Constitution
Adopted by referendum September 28, 1958; became effective October 4, 1958; amended many times

Legal System
Civil law system with indigenous concepts; review of administrative but not legislative acts

Suffrage
Eighteen years of age; universal

Executive Branch

Chief of state: president

Head of government: prime minister

Cabinet: Council of Ministers appointed by the president on the suggestion of the prime minister

Elections: president elected by popular vote for a five-year term (changed from seven-year term in October 2000); prime minister appointed by the president

Legislative Branch

Bicameral parliament: Senate and National Assembly. Senate: 321 seats—296, metropolitan France; 13, overseas departments and territories; 12, French nationals abroad. Between 2006 and 2010, 25 new seats were to be added to the Senate for a total of 346 seats: 326, metropolitan France and overseas departments; 2, New Caledonia; 2, Mayotte; 1, Saint-Pierre and Miquelon; 3, overseas territories; 12, French nationals abroad. Members are to be indirectly elected by an electoral college, with one-half the seats being renewed every three years. Term: six years. National Assembly: 577 seats. Members are elected by popular vote under a single-member majority system and serve five-year terms.

Judicial Branch

Supreme Court of Appeals: judges appointed by the president from nominations of the High Council of the Judiciary; Constitutional Council: three members appointed by president, three appointed by president of National Assembly, and three appointed by president of Senate; Council of State

Major Political Parties

Citizen and Republican Movement (MCR); Democratic and European Social Rally (RDSE); Democratic Movement (MoDem), formerly Union for French Democracy (UDF); French Communist Party (PCF); Greens; Hunters' Party (CPNT); Left Radical Party (PRG), previously Radical-Socialist Party and Left Radicals Movement; Movement for France (MPF); National Front (NF); New Anticapitalist Party (NPA); Socialist Party (PS); Union for a Popular Movement (UMP)

Source: U.S. Central Intelligence Agency, *The World Factbook: 2005,* updated. http://www.cia.gov/cia/publications/factbook/geos/fr.html.

The president is involved in the political process in a variety of ways. He may submit to the Constitutional Council an act of parliament or a treaty of doubtful constitutionality, and he may submit to a popular referendum any organic bill (that is, one relating to the organization of public powers) or any treaty requiring ratification. The constitution stipulates that the president may resort to a referendum only on the proposal of the government (while parliament is in session) or after a joint motion by the two parliamentary chambers (which meet in congress in Versailles for formal ratification). President de Gaulle ignored this stipulation, however, when he called for a referendum in 1962. Since the founding of the Fifth Republic, there have been nine referendums (after the popular ratification of the constitution itself): in January 1961 on self-determination for Algeria; in April 1962 on the Evian agreement on independence for Algeria; in October 1962 on the method of electing the president; in April 1969 on the reform of the Senate; in April 1972 on approving Great Britain's entry into the European Common Market; in November 1988 on proposals for autonomy for New Caledonia, a French dependency in the

Pacific; in September 1992 on the ratification of the Maastricht Treaty on European Union (EU); in November 2000 on the reduction of the presidential term of office; and in May 2005 on the constitution of the EU.

The president also conducts the nation's diplomacy. He negotiates and signs (or "ratifies") treaties, and he must be alerted to the progress of all international negotiations conducted in the name of France.

One of the most interesting and significant constitutional provisions relating to presidential power is Article 16, which reads in part: "When the institutions of the Republic, the independence of the nation, the integrity of its territory or the fulfillment of its international commitments are threatened in a grave and immediate manner and when the regular functioning of the constitutional governmental authorities is interrupted, the president of the Republic shall take the measures commanded by these circumstances, after official consultation with the prime minister, the chairs (Speakers) of the assemblies and the Constitutional Council." Such emergency powers, which exist in various Western democracies, are intended for use during civil wars, general strikes, and similar public disorders that presumably cannot be handled through the normal, and often time-consuming, deliberative parliamentary processes. De Gaulle invoked the provisions once, during a failed plot organized in 1961 by generals opposing his Algeria policy. Although Article 16 is not likely to be used again soon, and although there is a stipulation that parliament must be in session when this emergency power is exercised, its very existence has been a source of disquiet to many who fear that a future president might use it for dictatorial purposes. Others view Article 16 more liberally—that is, as a weapon of the president in his role as a constitutional watchdog, mediator, and umpire.

The constitution makes a clear distinction in its wording between the chief of state and the head of government. The prime minister, not the president, "directs the action of the government," "ensures the execution of the laws," "exercises regulatory powers," and "proposes constitutional amendments to the president." Unfortunately, some doubt whether the prime minister and the government can be functionally separated from any president who wishes to be more than a figurehead. Indeed, the constitutional text is not without ambiguity. For example, one article specifies that the prime minister is in charge of national defense, and another makes the president commander in chief of the armed forces. Similarly, the prime minister's power to "determine the policy of the nation" may conflict with, and be subordinated to, the president's responsibility for "guaranteeing national independence."

In fact, except during the first two periods of cohabitation, prime ministers have had little independence and little discretion in relation to the president in all areas in which the latter has taken a personal interest. Furthermore—here again, except under "abnormal" conditions when the Assembly and the president are on different sides of the political divide—the prime minister may be dismissed not only by parliament but also (though the constitution does not stipulate this) by the president. Indeed, twelve of the eighteen prime ministers preceding François Fillon were replaced for a variety of reasons while still enjoying the confidence of the Assembly. Although their appointment does not need to be officially approved by parliament, most prime ministers have, in fact, gone before the Assembly to be "invested" (formally confirmed for office). Prime ministers do not, in principle, have to reflect the party composition of the Assembly, and they do not have to belong to any party at all, although in practice it is clear that they cannot function, or even remain in office, without the support of a majority of deputies.

Michel Debré, who became prime minister in 1959, had been a loyal Gaullist even during the Fourth Republic, but he was replaced in 1962 by Georges Pompidou, a former lycée professor and banker (but not party politician) who had once worked intimately with de Gaulle and led his presidential staff. In 1968, when it became necessary to deflect from the president the mishandling of problems that had given rise to the mass rebellions in May and June of that year, Pompidou was replaced by Maurice Couve de Murville, a professional diplomat.

When Pompidou was elected to the presidency in 1969, he chose Jacques Chaban-Delmas, a former Radical-Socialist and hero of the wartime Resistance, to serve as prime minister. Pompidou wanted to cultivate a more progressive image and entice centrist parties to join the government majority forces in parliament. But in 1972 Chaban-Delmas was ousted, in part because his popularity threatened to eclipse the president's own, and he was replaced by Pierre Messmer, a Gaullist.

In 1974 Jacques Chirac was chosen as prime minister of the first government under Valéry Giscard d'Estaing's presidency as a reward for having bolted the Gaullist party—temporarily, as it turned out—and having supported Giscard d'Estaing's candidacy. Because of disagreements over economic policy and Chirac's insistence on a more significant decision-making role, he was replaced in 1976 by Raymond Barre, a "nonpolitical" professor of economics.

Pierre Mauroy, the first Socialist prime minister of the Fifth Republic, was selected in 1981 by President Mitterrand because of Mauroy's nearly ideal background. Scion of a working-class family and trained as a teacher, he had served as the mayor of a large industrial city. He also had been prominent in the old Socialist Party of the Fourth Republic and managed to get along well with the leaders of the party factions.

Mauroy was succeeded by Laurent Fabius in 1984 when Mitterrand decided to change direction from a progressive, redistributive policy to a program of austerity and economic restraint. Then, in 1986, Mitterrand had little choice but to reappoint Chirac as prime minister because the Gaullist party that Chirac led had gained dominance of the National Assembly.

Michel Rocard was chosen to head the government in 1988, in part because he had an important following within the ranks of the Socialist Party and among the population at large. An ambitious politician and an undogmatic and technocratic Socialist, he had in late 1980 been a rival of Mitterrand for nomination as a candidate for the presidency and had served in various ministerial posts under Mauroy.

In 1991 Rocard was replaced by Edith Cresson. It is unclear whether this change constituted an abrupt firing or an "amicable divorce" of two politicians whose political marriage had been one of convenience. In any case, it had become necessary because the public image of the government—and, by derivation, that of Mitterrand himself—had been tarnished by the ongoing unemployment, growing delinquency, immigrant riots, and scandals involving campaign funding of Socialist politicians. Cresson, the first woman prime minister in French history, had headed a succession of ministries. She had a reputation both as a loyal follower of Mitterrand and his brand of socialism, which was to the left of Rocard's, and as a proponent of government policies favoring business and industry.[1]

In 1992 Mitterrand asked Cresson to resign as prime minister. This decision followed on the regional and cantonal elections a month earlier in which the Socialist Party had incurred heavy losses. Cresson's successor, Pierre Bérégovoy, had served as Mitterrand's presidential chief of staff, as minister of social affairs, and (before and after the first cohabitation period) as minister of finance. In that last position, Bérégovoy developed a reputation for fiscal responsibility.

After the parliamentary elections of March 1993, the time for a change had come again. Because the Rally for the Republic (Rassemblement pour la République [RPR]) and the Union for French Democracy (Union pour la Démocratie Française [UDF]) won over-whelming control of the National Assembly, Mitterrand had to appoint a Gaullist, Edouard Balladur, to head a new government, which was the second experiment with cohabitation. Balladur had closely collaborated with Prime Minister Pompidou, served as the general secretary of the presidential office when Pompidou became president, and later became minister of finance in the cohabitation government of Chirac.

The first prime minister appointed by Chirac after he was elected president in 1995 was his close friend and political ally Alain Juppé. Juppé had begun his career in the higher civil service as an inspector of finance. He developed close links with Chirac when he served as the deputy mayor of Paris and later as minister of the budget in Chirac's cohabitation cabinet and then as his official government spokesman. As foreign minister in the Balladur government, Juppé was an early and consistent supporter of Chirac's presidential candidacy.

A change of prime ministers occurred in June 1997 after the premature parliamentary elections. The new prime minister, Lionel Jospin, had been a member of the diplomatic service, a professor of economics, a secretary-general of the Socialist Party, and a minister of education. In the presidential elections of 1995, he had captured nearly half of the popular vote as the Socialist candidate. Chirac had little choice in appointing Jospin, who had become the unchallenged leader of the democratic left and was widely considered the architect of the victory of the Socialists and their left-wing allies.

With the election of Chirac to a second presidential term in 2002 and the gain of a solid majority of the National Assembly by the UMP, the neo-Gaullist party, Chirac regained a free hand and appointed Jean-Pierre Raffarin as prime minister. Raffarin had been an unassuming regional politician—he was a member of the Senate—and was unlikely to upstage the president. But this government gradually became unpopular because of its policy shortcomings, among them the failure to tackle the unemployment problem, and its inadequate response to an unexpected heat wave in August 2003 that resulted in the death of nearly fifteen thousand people. When the UMP was soundly defeated in the regional elections of 2004, Chirac reshuffled the cabinet, replacing the embattled ministers of health and education.

Raffarin was replaced at the end of May 2005 after the referendum on a treaty to put in place a constitution for the European Union. Chirac had called for the referendum instead of letting the parliament decide, and he campaigned strongly for a "yes" vote. The victory of the "no" vote—the public rejection of the EU constitution—was attributed to the campaign waged against it by the trade unions and leftist parties, whose leaders believed that the constitutional draft posed a threat to prevailing wage structures, labor protections, and farm price supports, and by those on the extreme right, who feared a further erosion of national sovereignty. The referendum also was used to express dissatisfaction with Chirac and his government, and the vote represented a humiliating defeat for him. Yet he refused to resign, as did de Gaulle in 1969 when a referendum on a reform of the Senate failed.[2] Instead, he replaced the government.

Dominique de Villepin, who became prime minister in 2005, had impressive credentials. A career diplomat, he had been a major adviser to Chirac on foreign policy, and he had served as foreign minister under Prime Ministers Balladur and Raffarin. He also directed Chirac's 1995 presidential campaign and served as secretary-general of the presidential palace. Although Villepin was regarded as completely loyal to Chirac, as were most of the members of the cabinet after Chirac's authority was seriously undermined by the results of the referendum on the EU, Villepin emerged as the major decision maker. His relationship with Parliament, however, was tenuous, in part because he had never been elected to it (nor to any other national or subnational office) and he often ignored it. He lost support when he introduced an employment bill that was hotly contested and not backed by Chirac.

François Fillon, the current prime minister, whom Sarkozy appointed immediately after his election, had been by turns a National Assembly deputy and a member of various cabinets, most recently as minister of education. Fillon also managed Sarkozy's presidential election campaign.

Cabinet stability has been much greater under the Fifth Republic than under the Fourth Republic, with only eighteen prime ministers—one of them, Chirac, serving on two separate occasions—over a forty-eight-year period, 1959–2007 (see Tables 2-3, 2-4, and 2-5). But there were more than thirty cabinet rearrangements during that time. Such rearrangements were made for a variety of reasons: deaths, changes in domestic or foreign policy orientations, voluntary resignations (often prompted by disagreements over government policy), and changes in the political party composition of the Assembly. During ordinary periods, most of these "reshuffles" were made at the behest of the president; during cohabitation, they tended to be decided by the prime minister, often to rearrange the partisan makeup of the cabinet or to "freshen up" the image of the government.

Under the constitution, the chief of state presides over cabinet sessions. Similar provisions existed in earlier regimes, but, especially in the Third and Fourth Republics, they meant little, because "working" sessions of the cabinet were, in effect, led by the prime minister. In the Fifth Republic, the president—except, again, during cohabitation interludes—has effectively led most cabinet meetings and determined their agendas. Moreover, he has had a major voice in determining the size of the government, which has ranged from twenty-four to forty-nine full and junior ministers, and in deciding which of the full ministers—usually between sixteen and twenty-eight—are "cabinet" ministers—that is, they participate in the weekly cabinet sessions. Such liberty will be limited in the future, because under a constitutional amendment of 2008, the size of the cabinet will be subject to legislation by parliament.

The role of the prime ministers has not been negligible. They have been political personalities in their own right, and most have had experience in elective office.[3] They have

Table 2-3 Political Composition of Selected French Fifth Republic Governments before 1981

President:	de Gaulle				Pompidou		Giscard d'Estaing		
Prime minister:	Debré	Pompidou		Couve de Murville	Chaban-Delmas	Messmer	Chirac	Barre	
Political party	January 1959	April 1962	April 1967	July 1968	June 1969	July 1972	June 1974	August 1976	July 1979
Gaullists	6	9	21	26	29	22	12	9	12
Republicans	—	3	3	4	7	5	8	10	11[a]
Centrists	3[b]	5[b]	—	—	3[c]	3[c]	2	2[d]	4[d]
Radicals	1	1	—	—	—	—	6[e]	5	1[f]
Left Radicals	—	—	—	—	—	—	—	—	—
Socialists	—	—	—	—	—	—	—	—	—
Communists	—	—	—	—	—	—	—	—	—
Miscellaneous	7[g]	—	—	—	—	—	—	—	3[h]
Nonparty	10	11	5	1	—	—	8	10[i]	10[i]
Total (including prime minister)	27	29	29	31	39	30	36	36	41

Source: Compiled by the author.

[a] Known until 1977 as Independent Republicans.
[b] Popular Republican Movement (MRP).
[c] Center for Democracy and Progress (CDP).
[d] Center of Social Democrats (CDS).
[e] Reformers.
[f] "Democratic Left."
[g] Includes five independents.
[h] Includes one Social Democrat, one member of the National Center of Independents and Peasants (CNIP), and the prime minister, attached to the Union for French Democracy (UDF).
[i] Collectively designated as the "presidential majority."

accepted the prime ministership for reasons of ambition, more than half viewing it as a stepping-stone to the presidency. Nevertheless, they have played a distinctly subordinate role in policymaking except during periods of cohabitation; they have rarely been given credit for the achievements of their governments; and they have been used as "fall guys," to be replaced when the president loses popularity. Yet as government leaders, prime ministers have presided over important interministerial committees, counseled presidents on policy, and promoted and defended legislation in parliament and before public opinion. But the association between president and prime minister does not necessarily constitute a genuine policy-making partnership; in fact, all presidents thus far have clearly rejected the notion that there is a two-headed executive and have affirmed presidential supremacy, except during the cohabitation periods 1986–1988, 1993–1995, and 1997–2002, when the executive was temporarily "depresidentialized." [4]

The complex and ambiguous relationship between the president and prime minister has given rise to a debate about which of the two has been the more important decision maker. Chirac has been quoted as saying, "I decide, the minister[s] execute." [5] Sarkozy has made similar statements; he has asserted that he was elected to act and that he intended to

Table 2-4 Political Composition of Selected French Fifth Republic Governments, 1981–1988

President:	Mitterrand					
Prime minister:	Mauroy		Fabius[a]	Chirac[b]	Rocard	
Political party	May 1981	June 1981	July 1984	March 1986	May 1988[c]	June 1988[d]
Gaullists	—	—	—	20	—	—
Republicans	—	—	—	7	—	1
Centrists	—	—	—	7[e]	—	1
Radicals	—	—	—	2	1	1
Left Radicals	3	2	3	—	2	3
Socialists	39	37	36	—	26	25
Communists	—	4	—	—	—	—
Miscellaneous	1[f]	1[f]	1[g]	—	2[h]	3[h]
Nonparty	—	—	3	6	11	15
Total (including prime minister)	43	44	43	42	42	49

Source: Compiled by the author.

[a] Cabinet: eighteen ministers (including fourteen Socialists).

[b] Cabinet: fifteen ministers (including seven Gaullists, five various Union for French Democracy [UDF], three nonparty).

[c] Cabinet: nineteen ministers (including fourteen Socialists).

[d] Cabinet: twenty-two ministers (including fourteen Socialists, one Left Socialist, four UDF, three nonparty).

[e] Center of Social Democrats (CDS).

[f] Movement of Democrats, an ex-Gaullist group supporting Mitterrand in the presidential elections of 1981.

[g] Unified Socialist Party (PSU).

[h] Direct (nondifferentiated) members of UDF.

do so. Prime Minister Fillon accepted the primacy of the president; as he put it, "it is the president who governs." [6] In practice, this statement means that the president may make decisions that contravene the policies preferred by the prime minister.[7] The majority view is that the president is the real power, but, according to some, it is the prime minister who makes the concrete *domestic* policy decisions that count.[8] Still others take a more balanced view.[9] In fact, the relative power of each depends on the political composition of the National Assembly. If, on the one hand, that body is controlled by the president's party, the president's authority is virtually unchallenged. If, on the other hand, the Assembly is controlled by a different party, the prime minister, whose tenure depends on support by the Assembly, plays the dominant executive role and the president's position is more or less reduced to that of a figurehead. The president may be weakened for other reasons as well. After the failed referendum of 2005, Chirac, although continuing to have the nominal support of the parliament, was discredited both at home and abroad and considered a political dinosaur.[10]

In contrast, Sarkozy's position was strengthened when the parliamentary election that followed soon after his accession to the presidency produced an Assembly dominated by his own party. As a result, he was able to get major pieces of legislation enacted, including a number of institutional reforms embodied in constitutional amendments.

Table 2-5 Political Composition of Selected French Republic Governments since 1991

President:	Mitterrand		Chirac					Sarkozy
Prime minister:	Cresson[a]	Bérégovoy	Balladur	Juppé	Jospin	Raffarin	Villepin	Fillon
Political party	May 1991	April 1992	March 1993	May 1995	June 1997	May 2002	May 2005	June 2007
Gaullists	—	—	14	19	—	16	30	21
Republicans	—	—	7	8	—	6[n]	1[n]	—
Centrists	2[b]	—	5[c]	6[c]	—	8[o]	1[o]	—
Radicals	—	—	1	1	—	1	1	—
Left Radicals	2[d]	2	—	—	3	—	—	—
Socialists	32	31	—	—	18	—	—	5
Communists	—	—	—	—	3	—	—	—
Miscellaneous	1[e]	—	2[f]	2[g]	2[h]	—	—	3
Nonparty	9	9	1[i]	6	1	8	—	3
Total (including prime minister)	46	42[j]	30[k]	42[l]	27[m]	39[p]	33[q]	32[r]

Source: Compiled by the author.

[a] Cabinet: twenty ministers, including sixteen Socialists, one centrist (France United), one Ecologist, two nonparty. The government included six women, two in the cabinet. Cresson was replaced by Pierre Bérégovoy in April 1992.

[b] France United—a coalition formed in the Assembly in 1990 of left radicals and centrists to enlarge the presidential majority toward the center and support Michel Rocard.

[c] Center of Social Democrats (CDS).

[d] Movement of Left Radicals (MRG). These two ministers also belonged to France United.

[e] Ecologist movement.

[f] Two "direct" adherents of Union for French Democracy (UDF).

[g] Direct (nondifferentiated) members of UDF.

[h] One from the Greens and one from the Citizens' Movement (MDC).

[i] Simone Veil, a centrist close to Giscard d'Estaing.

[j] Cabinet: twenty-one ministers.

[k] Cabinet: twenty-four ministers.

[l] Cabinet: twenty-seven ministers.

[m] Cabinet: fifteen ministers.

[n] Liberal Democracy.

[o] UDF.

[p] Cabinet: sixteen ministers.

[q] Cabinet: seventeen ministers.

[r] Cabinet: sixteen ministers.

The Parliament

In terms of its bicameral structure and internal organization, the legislature of the Fifth Republic bears a clear resemblance to that of earlier republics. The National Assembly is composed of 555 deputies from metropolitan France and 22 from overseas departments and territories. All are elected for a five-year term by direct popular vote on the basis of a single-member constituency. Until recently, members of the Senate were chosen for nine-year terms by an electoral college composed of National Assembly deputies, department councillors, and delegates of city councils. One-third of the membership was renewed every three years. The number of senators has been increased periodically—from 295 in

1979 to 305 in 1981, 319 in 1987, and 321 in 1991. In July 2003 the parliament approved an organic law that reduced the term of senators from nine to six years and called for renewal of half of its membership every three years and an increase in its membership from 331 in 2004 to 341 in 2007 and 346 in 2010. The new law also reduced the age of eligibility for election to the Senate from thirty-five to thirty years.

The organization of the parliament follows traditional patterns. Each chamber is chaired by a president (Speaker), who is elected in the Assembly for five years and in the Senate for three years. The Speaker is assisted by vice presidents (or Deputy Speakers), six in the Assembly and four in the Senate, reflecting roughly the number of major party groupings in each chamber. These officers, who collectively constitute the "conference of presidents" in each chamber, formally determine the allocation of committee seats and the organization of parliamentary debates.

To participate meaningfully in legislative affairs, deputies must belong to a parliamentary party (*groupe parlementaire*). In the Fourth Republic, a minimum of fourteen deputies constituted a parliamentary party. With the establishment of the Fifth Republic, the required number was raised to thirty. This change forced small contingents of deputies to align (*s'apparenter*) with larger ones, thereby reducing the number of parties in the legislature. After the parliamentary elections of 1988, the number was reduced to twenty in order to reward the twenty-seven Communist deputies for their selective support of the government and, in particular, for supporting Laurent Fabius, the former Socialist prime minister, as Speaker of the Assembly.

The maximum duration of ordinary sessions of parliament used to be five-and-a-half months a year: eighty days in the fall (from early October) and ninety days in the spring (from early April). In 1995 the constitution was amended to provide for a single ordinary session of nine months, from October through June, totaling 120 days. Special sessions may be convened at the request of the prime minister or a majority of the deputies, but such sessions must have a clearly defined agenda. Since 1981 many special sessions have been called, largely to deal with budgetary matters.[11]

In theory, both chambers have equal powers with the following exceptions: budget bills must always be submitted first to the Assembly, and only the Assembly may oust the government on a vote of censure (described later in this section). The decision-making role of parliament as a whole, however, is limited, particularly in comparison with the legislature's role in earlier French republics and in other Western European democracies. The areas in which parliament may pass legislation are clearly enumerated in the constitution (Art. 34). They include, notably, budget and tax matters; civil liberties; penal and personal-status laws; organization of judicial bodies; education; social security; jurisdiction of local communities; establishment of public institutions, including nationalized industries; and rules governing elections (where not spelled out in the constitutional text). Matters not stipulated fall in the domain of decrees, ordinances, and regulations, which are promulgated directly by the government. The distinction between laws and decrees is not a clear-cut one. In some areas—for example, local government, education, or labor and social policy—the parliament often does little more than establish general principles and leaves it to the government to fill in the details by decree or executive order. In addition, the government may ask the parliament (under Art. 38) to delegate to the government the power to issue decrees in areas normally under parliamentary jurisdiction. This procedure was used frequently during de Gaulle's presidency. This "fast-track" approach was used most recently in July 2005 by Prime Minister Villepin for an emergency employment bill. This procedure has a limited duration—six months—and the action taken must be validated by a formal government bill.

As is the custom in all parliamentary democracies, a distinction is made in France between a government bill (*projet de loi*) and a private member's bill (*proposition de loi*). The former has priority; in fact, since the founding of the Fifth Republic less than 15 percent of all bills passed by parliament have originated with private members (or backbenchers), and most of these passed because the government raised no objections or because it encouraged such bills. Finance bills can be introduced only by the government, and backbenchers' amendments to such bills are permissible only if they do not reduce revenues or increase expenditures. Furthermore, if parliament fails to vote on (in practice, to approve) a budget bill within seventy days of its submission, the government may enact the budget by decree.

The government has the deciding voice on what bills are to be discussed in parliament and how much time shall be allocated to debate on parts of a bill. It can also prevent amendments to a bill by resorting to the "blocked-vote" procedure—that is, demanding that the legislative body vote on the text of the bill as a whole. This procedure has been used well over 140 times in the Assembly, with more than 90 percent of such bills passing. In the Senate, about a third of the bills introduced in the blocked-vote fashion have been rejected.

Enactment of a bill requires passage in both the Assembly and the Senate. Should the two chambers disagree on any aspect of a bill, a variety of procedures can be used to achieve agreement. The bill in question may be shuttled back and forth between the chambers until a common text is agreed on. Alternatively, the government may call for the appointment of a conference committee, or it may ask each chamber for a "second reading." [12] If disagreement persists, the Assembly may be asked to decide by a simple majority vote, thereby enacting the bill in question. Neither chamber allows members to filibuster.

Constitutional amendments are subject to a special procedure. The initiative belongs both to the president (after consulting with the prime minister) and to parliament. Once an amendment bill has passed both chambers in identical form, it is submitted to the people for ratification. A referendum may be avoided if parliament, in a joint session convoked for this purpose by the president, ratifies the amendment by a three-fifths majority. [13]

Checks on the Executive

Although the constitution grants the legislature jurisdiction in areas broad enough to embrace the most important domestic policy matters, in the Fifth Republic the parliament has been in a poor position to exercise this power. In the Fourth Republic, more than two dozen Assembly standing committees contributed much to the legislative process. Indeed, these committees, because of the expertise of their members, became quasi-independent centers of power. Although they produced high-quality legislative proposals, they sometimes offered counterproposals to government bills, designed to embarrass the government and bring it down. By contrast, in the Fifth Republic only six standing committees (usually consisting of 61–121 deputies each) are permitted under the constitution. They do their work within carefully limited time periods and are forbidden to produce substitute bills.

In theory, the parliament can do more than just register and ratify what has been proposed to it by the government. During the first decade of the Fifth Republic, parliament, and above all the Assembly, was relatively docile. Especially since the mid-1970s, however, parliament has been more actively engaged in lawmaking (see Chapter 2.4). Evidence of this more active role is the growing number of successful amendments to government bills introduced both by legislative committees and backbenchers.

During the weekly question periods in the National Assembly, deputies pose questions (in written or oral form) to individual ministers. Answers, which are not immediately forthcoming, may be provided by a minister or by a person deputized by him, such as a higher civil servant. Such question-and-answer sessions are sometimes followed by a very brief debate, or sometimes by no debate at all. These sessions cannot be followed by a vote of censure, which would prompt resignation of the government.

Motions of censure must be introduced by a unique and specific procedure and separately from the Assembly's routine business. These motions require the signatures of at least one-tenth of all the deputies, who may cosponsor only one such motion during each parliamentary session. A "cooling-off" period of forty-eight hours also must precede the vote on such a motion. A motion of censure carries only if an absolute majority of the entire membership of the Assembly supports the censure. The government may also challenge or provoke the Assembly to consider a motion of censure simply by making a specific bill or a general policy declaration a matter of confidence (Art. 49, sec. 3). If no successful censure motion is approved, the bill in question is considered to have passed, and the government remains in place. In the fifty years between 1959 and 2008, the government resorted successfully to this "provocation" method more than sixty times. Among the more recent instances were an electoral reform bill in 2003, a decentralization bill in 2004, and the labor relations bill of February 2006 that provoked massive demonstrations and strikes. During the same period, more than forty motions of censure were introduced by deputies, but only one, in October 1962, obtained the requisite majority vote. In that particular instance, President de Gaulle was required to accept the parliamentary dismissal of his prime minister (then Pompidou). But de Gaulle nullified the effect of the censure vote by dissolving parliament and, after the elections that followed, simply reappointing Pompidou to head a "new" government. The constitutional reforms ratified on July 23, 2008, restricted the use of Article 49: it can henceforth be used only for finance bills or bills on the funding of social security, and no more than once during each parliamentary session.[14] The 2008 reforms provided for many other measures aimed at strengthening the role of parliament. Among them are the following:

the right of the Conférence des Présidents (a committee of parliamentary leaders including the chairs of each parliamentary party) of the Assembly to lengthen the time allotted for debate on a bill;

the reduction of the amount of time allotted to the government to answer written parliamentary questions;

an increase in the maximum number of standing committees raised from six to eight;

the requirement that certain nominations made by the president be confirmed by a joint committee of the two chambers of parliament; and

the obligation of government to seek parliamentary authorization for the use of armed forces outside the country for more than six months.

The reforms also expanded the rights of the opposition by increasing its role in proposing the parliamentary agenda and in calling for the appointment of committees of inquiry.

Many of these constitutional changes, which are based substantially on the recommendations of the "Balladur Committee on Executive-Legislative Equilibrium," an ad hoc body chosen by Sarkozy,[15] still required follow-up organic laws to be passed by parliament. They constitute the first major restructuring of executive-legislative relations since 1958 and serve to democratize political life. They were ratified in joint session on July 23, 2008 by 539 votes to 537, one vote more than needed.[16] Yet it is not clear how they will affect the dominance of the executive over the legislative process.

Another weapon that parliament can use against the executive is the Constitutional Council. This body consists of nine members—one-third each chosen by the president, the Speaker of the Assembly, and the Speaker of the Senate—appointed for nine-year terms, with one third renewed every three years. Originally, the council was viewed as largely advisory. But under the constitution it must be consulted on the constitutionality of an organic bill before it becomes law and on the constitutionality of treaties before they are considered ratified. It also pronounces on the legality of parliamentary regulations and the propriety of referendum procedures and watches over presidential and legislative elections and confirms the results. It must also be consulted if the president invokes the emergency clause (Art. 16) of the constitution. In addition, the president, the prime minister, the Speaker of either chamber, and, since the passage of a constitutional amendment in 1974, sixty deputies or sixty senators may submit any bills, before they become law, to the council for a judgment. Under the original text of the constitution, the validity of a bill could be challenged only before it became law, a challenge used most often by members of the opposition. Under a constitutional amendment ratified in 2008, ordinary citizens may appeal to the Constitutional Council to challenge an action based on legislation (*after* it has been passed, as in the United States and Germany) in violation of fundamental liberties (Art. 61–1). Such challenges must go through the "filter" of the highest administrative courts and civil/criminal courts, the Council of State or the Court of Cassation, respectively.

The Constitutional Council's decisions have had a significant impact on legislation, as recent cases show. In 2009 it invalidated a bill creating the High Authority for the Diffusion of Art Works and the Protection of Copyright on the Internet (HADOPI), which aimed at the regulation of the Internet, on the grounds that it infringed on freedom of expression, As a result, the bill, which parliament had adopted in special session, had to be revised. In the same year, the council voided a government "carbon tax" bill that applied to the use of oil, gas, and coal by households and businesses. The council argued that it contained too many exemptions for polluters. This decision was welcomed as a rebuke to Sarkozy, whose government was forced to revise the bill, but it was criticized by his supporters as judicial overreach. Critics also argued that the council had been excessively politicized: several of its members, notably its president, had been appointed by lame-duck presidents of the republic.[17]

Incompatibilities and Cumulations

Under the Fourth Republic, deputies were often too willing to unseat a government in the hope that there would be a portfolio for them in a subsequent cabinet. If they should, in turn, be ousted from the cabinet, they would still retain their parliamentary seats. The constitution of the Fifth Republic, however, purposely changed all that. Under Article 23, a position in the cabinet is incompatible with simultaneously occupying a seat in parliament. Consequently, any deputy (or senator) who ascends to the cabinet must resign his or her parliamentary seat—which is immediately filled, without special election, by that person's "alternate" or replacement (*suppléant*), whose name was listed on the ballot alongside that of the deputy during the preceding Assembly elections. If the alternate resigns or dies, a by-election must be held.[18] Deputies appointed by the government for special tasks (as *chargés de mission*) may retain their parliamentary seats if the appointment is for less than six months.

The spirit of the incompatibility clause has been violated repeatedly. Cabinet ministers have run for parliamentary seats they do not intend to occupy, and presidents have encouraged that practice to test popular support for the government. Constituents vote for such candidates because they are better able to secure "pork-barrel" appropriations when their representative sits in the cabinet rather than in the parliament.

The incompatibility rule has not affected the traditional accumulation of concurrently held elected offices (*cumul des mandats*). For many years, most deputies were concurrently mayors or members of regional, departmental, and municipal councils, and a sizable number were serving as members of the European Parliament as well. Of the 577 deputies elected to the Assembly in 2007, 80 percent were *cumulards,* holding at least one supplementary office, half of them as mayors. A typical combination of members of parliament has been mayor and/or president of an urban agglomeration. In 2009, 80 Socialist deputies out of 185 concurrently held a local elective office: 64 as mayors, 12 as presidents of general (departmental) councils, and 4 as presidents of regions. About 20 hold only a parliamentary position. Of 99 Socialist senators, 43 also hold a subnational executive office: 25 as mayors, 14 as presidents of a conseil général, and 4 as presidents of a region. In the UMP, 160 out of 308 deputies and 82 out of 151 senators hold a local executive position. Others combine their parliamentary mandates with an executive position in intercommunal organizations or "mixed" (public-private) agencies.[19]

The concurrent holding of subnational elective positions, while multiplying the deputies' incomes, has cut deeply into the time available to the deputies or senators to devote themselves to their parliamentary work or to oppose the government. To rectify this situation, and perhaps to increase the attention span of parliamentarians, parliament passed a law in 1985 to limit the accumulation of elective offices to no more than two.[20] Such a limitation, let alone abolition of the *cumul,* is not enthusiastically accepted by many politicians, nor has it been completely effective. Since enactment of this reform, about half of deputies have opted to retain their positions as mayors as well as their parliamentary seats.[21] The problem also extends to cabinet ministers, even though from 1997 to 2002 Prime Minister Jospin required all his cabinet appointees to relinquish their positions as mayors of large cities as a precondition for taking office—a practice not followed by his successors. President Sarkozy himself is an example of "cumulation" by a cabinet minister.

In 2005 he was minister of the interior, president of the UMP, and president of the general council of the department of Hauts-de-Seine, his local political base. In 2004 President Chirac had imposed his own idea of incompatibility when he forced Sarkozy to choose between remaining minister of the interior and becoming president of a major political party, the UMP. Sarkozy then resigned his ministerial post, but a year later Chirac reappointed him to that post while allowing him to retain his party leadership as well.

The limitations on the power of deputies have not served to improve their public images or, indeed, their self-images. Still, there is no proof that individual legislators in France are substantially less powerful or less rewarded than their counterparts in Great Britain. In 2009 the gross annual salary of French deputies and senators was about €80,000 after taxes (roughly corresponding to that of higher civil servants and senior university professors), a sum that included base pay plus rental subsidy. In addition, the typical deputy received reimbursements for administrative assistance (partly paid for by the Assembly), as well as travel allowances and tax concessions. For many deputies, such compensation is insufficient to cover the cost of maintaining two residences and traveling to and from their constituencies, and some are forced to pursue their "normal" professions as best they can.

In fact, most deputies are not wealthy, and in terms of social background, age, and occupation they are reasonably representative of the population. The National Assemblies produced in the seven elections held from 1981 to 2007 included a large number of government officials, educators (especially among the Socialists), white-collar employees, and a fair number of physicians. The number of blue-collar workers and farmers has been insignificant, however.

Parliament continues to be a major pool for recruits to ministerial positions, although in recent years it has faced some competition from the civil service and occasionally from the corporate world.[22] It may no longer be as powerful in the legislative process as it was in the Fourth Republic, but parliament is still important as forum for the debate and processing of government-initiated bills.

The Administrative State

One feature of the French polity that has changed little, and is not likely to do so in the near future, is the administrative system. Since the time of the Old Regime and Napoleon, this system has been highly centralized; the various echelons below the national government—departments (*départements*), districts (*arrondissements*), and communes—continue to be administrative rather than decision-making entities, whose responsibilities can be defined, expanded, or contracted at will by the national government.

At the pinnacle of the system is the permanent civil service. Defined in its broadest sense, it is the corpus of more than 3 million government employees and constitutes about 15 percent of France's total labor force. In addition to the ordinary national civil servants, it includes military officers, teachers (public elementary school through university), employees of local government bodies, and employees of the railroads, civil aviation, electric power companies, and other nationalized sectors. Denationalization (or privatization) policies, pursued at a steady pace for the past several years, will undoubtedly result in a reduction in the number of state employees.

The civil service proper (*la fonction publique*) numbers about 1 million. It is subdivided into several categories, ranging from custodial and manual workers to high administrative functionaries who are directly responsible to cabinet ministers. The civil service is functionally divided into "sectoral" categories. The most prestigious of these are the General Inspectorate of Finance, Court of Accounts, Foreign Ministry, and Council of State (the pinnacle of the national administrative court system)—collectively labeled the *grand corps.* This body also includes the prefectoral corps, whose members, the prefects, are the chief agents of the government at the departmental and regional levels and are under the authority of the minister of the interior.

Since the time of Napoleon, recruitment to the higher civil service has been tied to the educational system. A variety of national schools, the likes of which are not found in other countries, train specialized civil servants. These *grandes écoles,* which are maintained alongside the regular universities, have highly competitive entry and graduation requirements. The best known are the Ecole Polytechnique, which trains civil engineers and scientists; the Ecole Normale Supérieure, whose graduates become professors in prestigious lycées and universities; and the Ecole Nationale d'Administration (ENA). The ENA, which opened its doors only in 1946, has trained the majority of higher administrative personnel for the *grand corps* and the prefectoral corps. It numbers among its graduates two presidents (Chirac and Giscard d'Estaing), several prime ministers (Fabius, Chirac, Rocard, Balladur, Juppé, Jospin, and Villepin), and many cabinet ministers.[23]

The French have often criticized the independent stature and self-assured behavior of the higher civil service. They have argued that although it makes for stability, it tends to undermine democracy. This criticism has been based on the upper- and upper-middle-class origins of most of the higher functionaries, on the fact that they are subject to neither popular elections nor adequate controls, and on the belief that they have tended to serve not the citizen but an abstraction called "the state."

Nevertheless, the higher civil service has not been monolithic or dictatorial, nor has it been immune from internal conflicts and external pressures. Although the ENA has recruited only a minuscule portion of its student body from the working class and the peasantry—despite a number of half-hearted attempts to broaden the method of recruitment[24]—its graduates, the *Enarques,* have been as likely to be progressives (even leftists) as they are conservatives or reactionaries.

Sometimes, conflicts erupt between the civil servants who work for the Ministries of Finance and Industry and who often have close personal and ideological ties with big-business managers, and those who work in the Ministries of Health and Education and who tend to have affinities with their clientele and therefore have a social reform outlook. Differences of opinion also often occur between the civil servants in the Ministry of Justice, who are concerned with procedural propriety, and those in the Ministry of the Interior, who tend to be sympathetic with the police's preoccupation with public order. There is also a certain tension between the traditional bureaucrats who serve in the standard ministries and have a legalistic orientation and the technocrats who have been trained in economics, statistics, and management methods. Despite periodic commitments to rationalize operations, the size of the civil service has grown steadily. While the number of national civil service positions, especially in education, has been reduced since 2007, others, such as in social administration, increased substantially in 2009.

The number of independent administrative authorities has grown steadily. At this writing there are about forty of them, including the following: Commission nationale de l'informatique et des libertés [CNIL]), created in 1978 to guard against abuse of government files on citizens; the Conseil supérieur de l'audiovisuel (1989); the Commission nationale de contrôle des interceptions de sécurité, dealing with the bugging of telephones (1991) and created in response to criticisms by the European Court of Human Rights; the High Authority in the Fight against Discrimination and for Equality (Haute autorité de lutte contre les discriminations et pour l'égalité, 1999); and the Nuclear Safety Authority (Autorité de sûreté nucléaire, 2006).[25] Like the independent regulatory commissions, their U.S. counterpart, these agencies are supposed to be immune to partisan intrusions, but charges of partisan political interference persist.

Public Corporations

A component of the administrative system that is difficult to categorize, and yet is of great importance, is the nationalized sector. The state's involvement in the management of economic matters has resulted in special approaches to recruitment, job classification, and political control. On occasion, positions of responsibility in nationalized, or "public," enterprises are given to individuals co-opted from the private sector or are handed over as political "plums" to politicians who have proved their loyalty to the president.[26] Because of the complexity of the management problems, parliamentary oversight of nationalized enterprises has been difficult. Yet at the same time, their very existence can be a useful weapon in the hands of a government interested in long-term economic policymaking or at least in influencing the behavior of the private economic sector in its production and pricing policies.

From the beginning of the postwar period to the early 1980s, about 15 percent of the French economy was in government hands, including mass transport, gas, electricity, nuclear energy, the postal service, civil aviation, the procurement and distribution of fuel, a large proportion of banking and insurance, and one automobile manufacturing firm (Renault). In 1981–1982, the Socialist government (in conformity with its preelection platform) introduced bills to bring additional sectors under public control, among them a dozen industrial conglomerates (manufacturing metals, chemicals, electronics, machine tools) and most of the remaining private banks. Such a policy proved to be ill-advised, however, and soon after coming to power in 1986 the Gaullist Chirac government proceeded to denationalize most of these sectors, as well as most of the government-owned television networks. When the Socialists returned to power in 1988, they continued the privatization policy, but at a slower pace. The pace sped up considerably, however, after the installation of the Gaullist governments of Balladur and Juppé. For them, privatization, in addition to conforming with the Gaullists' recently emerging neoliberal (market-oriented) ideology, served to bring a quick infusion of funds into the public treasury. Not all the privatization projects had smooth sailing, however: Juppé's proposal to privatize the Thomson firm, France's largest industrial-military production conglomerate, was shelved because of widespread opposition. For similar reasons, the Socialist government of Jospin, which took office in 1997, had to scale back the privatization of the country's civilian airline and the telecommunications monopoly. Later, the Villepin government, spurred on by both EU rules as well as the need for cash, resumed attempts at privatization, notably of the network of superhighways and civilian maritime lines, in the face of fierce opposition by the trade unions and leftist political parties. The Fillon government continued this policy, as it prepared to transform the postal service from a government department to a mixed enterprise.

Control and Redress

One institution that has played a significant role as a watchdog over administrative activities is the Council of State (Conseil d'Etat). Originally created in 1799 by Napoleon to resolve intrabureaucratic disputes, it has gradually assumed additional functions. It advises the government on the language of draft bills; it reviews the legality of decrees and regulations issuing from the executive; and, most important, it acts as a court of appeal for suits brought by citizens against the administration. Such suits, involving charges of bureaucratic arbitrariness, illegalities, or abuse of power, are initiated in department (prefectoral) administrative tribunals. Unfortunately, several years may elapse before such cases come before the Council of State.

A 1973 innovation was the "mediator," the French equivalent of the ombudsman or citizens' complaint commissioner. This official, appointed by the president for a six-year term on the recommendation of parliament, may examine a variety of complaints involving, for example, social security agencies, prisons, nationalized industries, and administrative and judicial malfunctions. The mediator may request from any public agency information considered pertinent to the investigation, initiate judicial proceedings against misbehaving bureaucrats, and suggest improvements in the laws to the government. Appeal to the mediator, which is free of charge, is not direct; rather, it comes through a deputy or senator. In 2009, following a constitutional amendment ratified a year earlier, parliament enacted a law creating a new position: defender of the rights and liberties of citizens. This official, to be appointed by the president for a nonrenewable six-year term, will replace the mediator in 2011. Citizens will be able to appeal directly to this office.

Subnational Government and Administration

The extent to which national decisions can be, or should be, influenced by officials at the local level has been intensely debated in France over the past two decades. Questions have also arisen about whether the existing subdivisions are the proper size, whether they are adequately financed, and whether they provide a meaningful arena for the political participation of citizens.

Metropolitan France consists of ninety-six departments (*départements*), which are the basic subnational administrative units into which the country was divided during the Revolution of 1789. In addition, there are four overseas departments.[27]

Each department is both self-administering *and* an administrative subunit of the national government. Whatever autonomy the departments possess is reflected by its general council, which votes a budget, decides on local taxes and loans, and passes laws on housing, roads, welfare services, cultural programs, and educational services (supplementary to those made mandatory by the national government). Members of the general council are popularly elected by single-member constituencies—the cantons—for six-year terms; half of the membership is renewable every three years. The council, in turn, elects a president, or chair. Traditionally, however, the executive officer of the department was the prefect, an agent of the national government who used to be charged with administering the department on behalf of the Ministry of the Interior and other national ministries.

Therefore, the prefect was involved in maintaining public order, together with the mayor of a town. The local police force, however, was an instrument of national administration and, as such, was directly under the authority of the minister of the interior in Paris.

In 1982 the prefects were renamed commissioners of the republic. They still functioned as agents of the national government, but they left budgetary and many other policy decisions to the general councils, except for services and expenditures mandated by national legislation. In 1987 the title of commissioner was changed back to prefect. The prefect is assisted by a cabinet composed of specialists in public works, agriculture, housing, and other services.

On the level beneath the departments are the 325 arrondissements, the basic single-member constituencies for parliamentary elections. Some heavily populated arrondissements are subdivided into two or more constituencies. A further subdivision is the canton, which contains agencies such as units of the national gendarmerie, tax offices, and highway services.

Since 1972 the departments have been grouped into twenty-two regions. The regions have their own assemblies, elected by popular vote on the basis of proportional representation for six-year terms. The regional assemblies and their presiding officers all serve to coordinate the activities of several departments.

The lowest, but most significant, administrative unit is the commune. The more than 36,000 communes range in size from villages of fewer than one hundred inhabitants to the national capital. Communes have varied responsibilities, including fire protection, upkeep of elementary school buildings, provision of selected social services, imposition of certain taxes, and maintenance of public order.[28] When some communes have become too small to provide a full range of services, they have been either administratively merged with neighboring communes or compelled to associate with them functionally. Under provisions put into effect in the early 1970s, certain services, such as water supply and fire protection, may be performed jointly by several communes. Conversely, some communes are so large that special regimes have been invented for them: Paris and Lyons are themselves subdivided into arrondissements.

Paris has always been a special case. Between 1871 and 1977, Paris did not have a mayor but was ruled by two prefects directly on behalf of the national government: a prefect of the Seine (the former name of the department in which the capital is located) and a prefect of police. Each of the twenty arrondissements had its own mayor, whose functions were generally limited to maintaining civil registers, performing marriages, changing street names, and the like. Since the reinstitution of the mayor for all of Paris, the twenty district mayors have been replaced by "civil administrators." The prefect of the Paris department and the prefect of police, however, remain in place.

The relationship between the national government and the subnational units has been rendered confusing by the functional units that overlap geographic boundaries. In addition to the departments and regions, there are twenty-five educational districts (*académies*), which administer the educational system from elementary school through university; sixteen social security regions; and six military districts. All of these functional units have been, in the final analysis, administrative conveniences put in place by the national government, and they have provided little in the way of local decision-making opportunities.

The subject of subnational government has not escaped Sarkozy's attention. Among the reforms proposed by him—based on another ad-hoc committee headed by Balladur[29]—is the restructuring of departments and regions and their administrative responsibilities, and the creation of new "metropolitan regions." One of them would be a special regime for a "Greater Paris," which would include the city as well as a number of surrounding departments.[30]

Decentralization: Processes, Consequences, and Problems

The competences of the various subnational authorities and the relationship between them began to change dramatically with the decentralization policies inaugurated during the presidency of Mitterrand in the early 1980s. These policies, which continue to this day, have provided for greater autonomy of the prefect in relation to the national government, greater decision-making competence in selected domains such as education, welfare, and housing for local, departmental, and regional units, and increased revenue-gathering authority.[31] Such changes have been made not by constitutional revision but by acts of parliament and therefore can be rescinded, at least in theory. In March 2003 a constitutional amendment ratified by parliament in joint session formally stipulated that France was a republic whose organization was "decentralized," although it is not entirely clear what this amendment and the ensuing legislation empower local units to do. In any case, decentralization is not federalism, because national government tutelage (*tutelle*) remains. The local units can, however, resort to local referenda and organize mergers of communes. And they have greater fiscal responsibility, which was delegated to them under the slogan of "financial autonomy." In return, these units are receiving less and less money from the national government. This buck passing has meant, among other things, that the departments have greater responsibility for funding recipients of monthly minimum income support,[32] of whom there were more than a million in 2004, and for maintaining the network of national roads, which has been transferred to the departments. Some communes, especially the less affluent, complain that although the national government imposes mandatory services upon them, it does not provide adequate financial resources for these services. Indeed, local and regional politicians complain that the national government, instead of permitting greater latitude in revenue gathering, has actually imposed limits on local taxes.[33] The most recent instance has involved the *taxe professionnelle,* a tax imposed locally on investments in business. In 2009 the government proposed to abolish it and replace it with a tax on energy consumption (*taxe carbone*), but the move was opposed by mayors (and by many senators who also happened to be mayors) because the *taxe professionnelle* provided about €22.6 billion annually to local communities and constituted a significant part of their revenue.[34]

Complaints have also been heard from the presidents of the regional assemblies, especially Socialist presidents, who have refused to sign proposals for the "transfer of competences."[35] These proposals, or conventions, were based on a law of 2004 on "local responsibilities and liberties." Buck passing has affected Paris as well, especially since control of that city has passed into the hands of the Socialists. The decentralization reforms have made possible a degree of policy experimentation on various subnational levels, brought government closer to the people, and spawned a variety of approaches to "participatory democracy," but they also have introduced confusion, exacerbated inequalities, and sharpened rivalries among regional, departmental, and local authorities. Although the mayors of the larger towns welcomed decentralization, many have refrained from seeking reelection or have given up their parliamentary mandates because of the increased pressures associated with decentralization. For many small communes, decentralization also has been a handicap, as they are too poor to manage by themselves some of the services that were the responsibility of the national government.[36]

A more complex problem is that of the island of Corsica, which became part of France in the eighteenth century and differs from the mainland in its language, unique social patterns, and growing separatist sentiments. Since the mid-1980s, the island has been given greater autonomy, especially with respect to education and culture, but for many Corsicans such changes have not been enough. A minority of French politicians would like to grant the island complete independence, but because it was Napoleon Bonaparte's birthplace and, more important, because large numbers of mainland French people have settled there, many argue against such an outcome.

A major purpose of subnational units is to serve as arenas for citizen involvement in politics and the recruitment of politicians for both national and subnational offices. This is particularly true of communes: the outcome of municipal elections, which occur every six years and produce nearly 500,000 councillors, ultimately affects the composition of the Senate, because the councils are part of the electoral college that chooses senators. Municipal elections also enable the citizens to express their midterm feelings about the performance of the national government and, more specifically, that of the party in power.

NOTES

1. Cresson, however, developed a reputation for outspokenness and lack of tact, and within a few weeks of her assumption of office the popularity of her government plummeted, as did Mitterrand's.
2. Chirac used as precedent Mitterrand's announcement, just before the Maastricht referendum, that he would serve out his term regardless of the outcome.
3. Only three had never been elected to any office before becoming prime minister: Pompidou, Barre, and Villepin. Raffarin had been a member of the Senate, and therefore was not the product of direct popular election.
4. For a detailed statement of the legal-constitutional position of the prime minister, see Philippe Ardant, *Le Premier Ministre en France* (Paris: Montchrestien, 1992). For a discussion of the evolution of the prime ministers' actual relationship with presidents, see Robert Elgie, *The Role of the Prime Minister in France, 1981–91* (New York: St. Martin's Press, 1993).
5. TV channel France 2, July 14, 2004.
6. Interview, France 2, July 3, 2007. See also Alain Auffray and Antoine Guiral, "A quoi sert Fillon? Le premier ministre cherche à exister au côté d'an président hyperactif," *Libération,* June 28, 2007.
7. For example, in April 2004 Chirac decided to promote a more socially progressive orientation and contravened the decisions of Prime Minister Raffarin. Béatrice Gurrey, "M. Chirac impose un virage social au nouveau gouvernement," *Le Monde,* April 3, 2004. In 2009 Sarkozy was in favor of giving noncitizens the right to vote in local elections, while Fillon opposed it.

8. See interview with Dominique Chagnollaud by Alain Auffray, "Matignon reste le coeur de l'État," *Libération*, February 7, 2005.

9. Robert Elgie, "Semi-Presidentialism: Concepts, Consequences and Contesting Explanations," *Political Studies Review* 2 (2004): 314–330.

10. Marc Semo et al., "Chirac, serial-loser vu de l'étranger," *Libération*, May 29, 2005.

11. Seventeen special sessions were held between 1981 and 1986, four between 1986 and 1988, four in 1989, and eleven between 1990 and 1992.

12. Typically, more than half of the bills passed have not required the use of conference committees.

13. The most recent constitutional amendments adopted by such a joint session—a "congress" assembled in Versailles—were passed in June 1999 (providing for the domestic applicability of decisions handed down by the International Penal Court and for gender equality in putting up candidates for elective office); in January 2000 (ratifying the Treaty of Amsterdam of 1997, which empowered the European Union to determine supranational immigration and asylum policies); and in March 2003 (specifying the "decentralized organization" of the Republic).

14. Assemblée Nationale, 13e Législature, No. 820, *Projet de loi constitutionnelle de modernization des institutions de le Ve République,* April 23, 2008. See also Pascal Jan, "Un parlement modernisé et renforcé," *Regards sur l'Actualité* 354 (October 2009): 78–89.

15. Dominique Chagnollaud, "Les propositions du comité Balladur pour une Ve République plus démocratique," *Regards sur l'Actualité* 339 (March 2008): 15–25.

16. Some of these changes had been demanded for some time by the Socialists, but only one Socialist deputy (Jack Lang) voted for the constitutional amendments, thus providing the extra vote.

17. For example, Robert Badinter, Mitterrand's minister of justice, appointed in 1995; and Jean-Louis Debré, an ardent supporter of Chirac, who had been Speaker of the Assembly, appointed in 2007.

18. As soon as Raffarin left his post as prime minister in 2005, his *suppléant* in the Senate resigned that seat so that Raffarin could regain it in that chamber. Not all *suppléants* have been so accommodating. In the mid-1990s, the attempt by Catherine Trautmann to regain her post as mayor of Strasbourg when she was replaced as a cabinet minister met with the successful opposition of her *suppléant*.

19. See Raphaëlle Bacqué, "Cumul des mandats: pourquoi les élus résistent," *Le Monde*, September 1, 2009. A perhaps extreme example of multiple office holding was Sen. Jean Lecanuet, who, in addition to holding the leadership of the UDF in the 1970s, concurrently served as mayor of the sizable town of Rouen, president of a general departmental council, member of a regional council, and member of the European Parliament.

20. See Albert Mabileau, "Le cumul des mandats," *Regards sur l'Actualité* 169 (March 1991): 17–29.

21. One of the rare exceptions to this development was the decision of Alain Carignon in 1988 to resign his position as deputy and retain those of mayor of Grenoble and member of the general council of his department. In 1995, however, he was forced to resign from these offices in the wake of his conviction for the misuse of public funds.

22. For example, Thierry Breton, who was appointed minister of economics and finance early in 2005, had been the chief executive officer of France Télécom.

23. Another specialized school, the Ecole Nationale de la Magistrature, which was established in 1958 and is located in Bordeaux, trains state attorneys, investigating magistrates, and judges.

24. In 1983 the Socialist government attempted to reduce the ENA's bias in favor of Parisians, graduates of the better universities, and children of higher civil servants by allowing local politicians and middle-echelon officials of public agencies to enter the ENA by means of special examinations. The Chirac government, however, later suspended that method. In a related move, the Cresson government in 1991 initiated a policy of "delocalizing" the ENA by moving it from Paris to the provincial city of Strasbourg. Although subsequent governments committed themselves to this move, some classes were retained in Paris or returned to it. The definitive move was completed only in 2005.

25. Martin Collet, "La creation des autorités administratives indépendantes: symptôme ou remède d'un Etat en crise?" *Regards sur l'Actualité* 330 (April 2007): 5–14.

26. Patronage of this sort may cause conflicts of interest, as in the case of Henri Proglio, who remained president of a private corporation after his appointment as chief executive officer of a public electricity company in 2009 and for a time received a double salary.

27. In January 2010 Martinique, one of the overseas departments in the Caribbean, was given the option of greater autonomy from Paris, but (largely for economic reason) voted against it.

28. Since the mid-1980s, a series of laws have been passed to permit localities to appoint their own municipal police to supplement the national gendarmerie. The size of such police forces, appointed by mayors and approved by prefects, and their relationships to the national police, vary widely. See Marie Vogel, "La loi sur les polices municipales," *Regards sur l'Actualité* 253 (July-August 1999): 43–52.

29. The Comité pour la réforme des collectivités locales. See Eduard Balladur, "Pourquoi réformer les collectivités locales?" *Regards sur l'Actualité* 351 (May 2009): 5–8.

30. If these recommendations, which have been submitted to parliament, are enacted, the regional councilors, to be elected in 2010, and the general (departmental) councilors, to be elected in 2011, would end their mandates in 2014.

31. "Le réforme de l'Etat territorial," special issue of *Regards sur l'Actualité* (August-September 2005): 5–51.

32. This support, labeled *revenue minimum d'insertion* (RMI), was first instituted by the Rocard government in 1988.

33. See Thomas Lebegue, "Villepin unit élus locaux de gauche et de droite contre lui," *Libération,* September 30, 2005.

34. *Les finances publiques et la réforme budgétaire* (5th ed.), Collection Découverte de la vie politique (Paris: Documentation Française, 2009), 104–105.

35. Olivier Pognon, "Les régions présidés par le PS et le gouvernement amorcent un dégel," *Figaro,* June 27, 2005.

36. The relative poverty of small towns and the low salaries of elected municipal officials have impelled many mayors, especially those who hold well-paid parliamentary seats, not to seek reelection to that office. Cécile Chambraud, "Les nouveaux paramètres des élections municipales de 2001," *Le Monde,* February 29, 2000. On the confusing (and constantly changing) fiscal situation of local communities, see "Fiscalité locale: Pourquoi rien ne va plus?" *Pouvoirs locaux: Les cahiers de la décentralisation,* trimestriel no. 64 (March 2005).

Who Has the Power?

IN REPRESENTATIVE DEMOCRACIES, THE COLLECTIVE POLITICAL WILL IS expressed by a variety of institutions, foremost among them political parties and interest groups. They formulate specific demands that reflect both the existing social cleavages and the conflicting conceptions of the role of the state and its relationship to civil society.

Political Parties: Traditional 'Political Families'

France has a complex political party system that, some observers claim, is symptomatic of disorder and confusion. At any given time, and especially during elections, more than a dozen parties may be active. Some of these parties can be traced back several generations and have been of national importance; others are of passing interest because of their ephemeral or purely local nature or weak organization; and still others are mere political clubs, composed of small clusters of people more anxious to have a forum for expressing their political views than to achieve power.

The Third and Fourth Republics were marked by a multiplicity of parties ranging from right to left that embraced the following divisions, or "political families," based for the most part on ideology: conservatism, Catholicism, classic liberalism, socialism, and communism. The ideologies were often associated with class.

These political families, which can be grouped into the left, the center, and the right, still exist. Each of these families—or "political chapels," as they have been called—has tried to represent different electoral camps or different views on economic policy, executive–legislative relations, and the place of religion in politics. Their positions, however, have not always been consistent; their traditional ideologies have often not been adjusted in line with changing socioeconomic realities, including the structure of the electorate; politicians elected under the label of one party have sometimes shifted to another; and tactical considerations have often forced parliamentary deputies to vote on issues in such a way as to ignore their party platforms.

The Right

Historically, the political right was characterized by its identification with the status quo. It favored monarchism and deplored the Revolutions of 1789 and 1848. Inclined toward authoritarian rule, the right evolved from support of Bourbon kings to that of Napoleon Bonaparte and other "heroic" leaders. It favored an elitist social structure, defined society in "organic" and hierarchical terms, had contempt for the masses, and invested the "state" with an aura of sanctity. Traditionally, the right was supported by the established classes: the aristocracy, the landed gentry, the clergy, and the military, and, as the economy developed, big business. At the end of World War II, fascism was discredited, and in the waning years of the Fourth Republic monarchism was almost extinct, but a new extreme-right party, the Poujadist movement, made its appearance. That movement, named after its founder, Pierre Poujade, appealed to small shopkeepers, farmers, and others who suffered from the consequences of modernization. It had a significant antiparliamentary and anti-Semitic component.[1]

The dominance of the political right gradually faded during the 1950s with the transformation of the French economy and society—specifically, the decline of those sectors that had been its main electoral base. Furthermore, by the beginning of the Fourth Republic much of that ideological family had become unpopular because many of its adherents had been collaborators of the Germans during the war, while the "respectable" right had converted to republicanism. The main political expression of the postwar right was the National Center of Independents and Peasants (Centre National des Indépendants et Paysans [CNIP]), a group of politicians sometimes also known as moderates. The CNIP (later known simply as the CNI) was weakly represented in the National Assembly, in part because it reflected two conflicting positions: a liberal one—a belief in laissez-faire economics—and a conservative one—a continued commitment to the values of elitism, religion, authority, and family. Another reason for the weakness of the traditional right was that it had to compete with the center parties for voters. And yet another, and the most important, reason was the rise of Gaullism, a political movement that drained off many of the right's old supporters, notably the nationalist and populist-authoritarian elements.

Gaullism is a unique phenomenon. Many Frenchmen shared Gen. Charles de Gaulle's dislike of the Fourth Republic. They objected to its central feature: a parliament that was, in theory, all-powerful but, in practice, was immobilized because it was faction-ridden. They favored a regime with a strong leader who would not be hampered by political parties and interest groups; both were considered particularistic and destructive interpositions between the national leadership and the citizenry. Above all, Gaullists wanted France to reassert its global role and rediscover its grandeur. Many of the early supporters of Gaullism were identified with the general as former members of his Free French entourage in London or former members of the Resistance. Others had worked with him when he headed the first provisional government after the Liberation, and still others saw in him the embodiment of the hero-savior. Gaullism therefore can be described as nationalistic as well as "Caesarist" or "Bonapartist" in the sense that the legitimacy of the national leader was to be based on popular appeal.

Gaullists never put forth a clear domestic policy program, and, at least in the beginning, they did not seem to show great interest in economic reform or social justice and therefore failed to receive significant support from the working-class electorate. Yet Gaullists would vehemently reject the label of "rightist," because, they argued, nationalism is not incompatible with social reform, and because the first Gaullist party, the Rally of the French People (Rassemblement du Peuple Français [RPF]), established in 1947, was intended to be a movement that would appeal to all social classes. The RPF, however, did not become a mass party until the collapse of the Fourth Republic.

The Left

Leftism and socialism have been particularly important in modern French political history because they have stood for progress, equality, and democratic government—themes associated with the Revolution of 1789. In response to the gradual democratization of the franchise and the growing electoral importance of the working class, many parties appropriated the label "socialist." Socialist parties have been inspired by different traditions—utopian, revolutionary, and reformist—some of them dating to the eighteenth century, but these parties have shared a preoccupation with the systematic explanation of social phenomena: an emphasis on the importance (and the claims) of society as a whole and a belief that economic, political, and social structures are intimately related.

The major party of the left is the Socialist Party (Parti Socialiste [PS]). Originally formed in 1905 out of small and disparate leftist groups and known until 1969 as the Section Française de l'Internationale Ouvrière (SFIO), the Socialist Party was inspired by revolutionary Marxism and appealed to the industrial working class. In response to increased parliamentary representation, participation in bourgeois governments, and the takeover of leadership positions by intellectuals and other middle-class elements, the Socialist Party lost its revolutionary dynamism and accepted the idea of gradual, nonviolent reform. The party gradually attached as much value to maintaining democratic processes as to supporting redistributive policies. In 1936 Léon Blum, the party's leader, headed a government that, with the support of some of the other leftist parties, instituted far-reaching social reforms. When the party was reconstituted in the Fourth Republic, it continued to promote progressive legislation. But the Socialist Party was hampered in its growth by competition from the Communist Party.

Established in 1920, the French Communist Party (Parti Communiste Français [PCF]) took much of the Socialists' working-class electorate from them. The two parties of the left collaborated on many bills in the legislature, but while the Communists wanted to bring down the Fourth Republic, the Socialists were committed to maintaining it. In 1958 most Socialists voted in favor of the investiture of de Gaulle as prime minister, but the Communists opposed it. Later that year, a large number of Socialist leaders endorsed the Fifth Republic constitution, and the Communists expressed opposition to it. Finally, in the 1960s the Socialists lost much of their membership, but the Communists were able to retain most of their hard-core adherents. Both leftist parties were eventually consigned to opposition status from which they emerged only in 1981.

The Center

For at least a century, one political family has represented the broad interests of the *petite bourgeoisie*—the shopkeepers, artisans, and certain farmers—as well as portions of the intellectual and free professional classes. It has occupied the "center" position in French politics insofar as it has rejected both the elitism and static orientation of conservatives and the egalitarianism of the left. It has favored selective social reforms, but it has rejected collectivism. It has been committed to republicanism and to a progressive democratization of political institutions, which has meant, among other things, extension of the franchise and greater power for parliament. The political center has always been difficult to pin down with precision, because many centrists have pretended to adhere to a more fashionable "leftism" and have provided themselves with misleading labels, and because the center has been fragmented.

There are two basic kinds of centrism: Radical-Socialist and Catholic. Officially founded in 1901, the origins of he Radical-Socialist Party can be traced to the beginning of the Third Republic and, as some would insist, to the French Revolution. During the Third and Fourth Republics—that is, between the 1870s and 1950s—the party, which backed a strongly centralized republic, was consistently led by local notables. It was "radical" in the sense that it favored—and helped to achieve—elimination of the Catholic Church's participation in politics and promotion of a secular school system. The party viewed the state as the enemy and argued strongly for civil rights, especially property rights. But this stand did not prevent the Radicals from asking the state to protect that segment of their electorate that felt its livelihood was being threatened by economic consolidation at home and competition from abroad.

Such attitudes were "leftist" enough as long as the *petite bourgeoisie* constituted the bulk of the politically underprivileged masses. But with industrialization, a new class became important: that of factory workers. The Socialist ideology—a belief in the class struggle and opposition to private productive property—that this new class embraced rendered the Radicals' leftism increasingly illusory and pushed them into a defensive posture. Nevertheless, the tactical position of the Radical-Socialist Party often made it an indispensable partner in government coalitions and allowed it to play a dominant role in the Third and Fourth Republics and to provide both regimes with numerous prime ministers.

Another orientation that must be classified as centrist is that of Christian (or Catholic) democracy. Originally, Catholicism could not be equated easily with either republicanism or social progress; the Popular Party founded toward the end of the Third Republic, which supported the parliamentary system, was insignificant. But political Catholicism gained a new respectability during World War II. After Liberation, devout Catholics who had been active in the Resistance established the Popular Republican Movement (Mouvement Républicain Populaire [MRP]), which, although clericalist in orientation, was committed to civil liberties and social reform in a republican context. In the beginning of the Fourth Republic, the MRP's position was leftist enough, and its parliamentary representation strong enough, to make it a coalition partner with the Socialists and Communists. Moreover, the party competed with the Radicals in its adaptability. Toward the end of the Fourth Republic, the MRP weakened for the same reason as the Radicals. Some of the party's leftist adherents turned with interest to the Socialists, while its conservative ones, who were far more numerous, embraced Gaullism. In 1958 a large proportion of the MRP politicians joined the Gaullist bandwagon (and the pitiful remnant of the MRP dissolved in 1966).

Under the system of proportional representation in use in the Fourth Republic, all these parties were represented in parliament. But no party achieved a majority of seats in the national legislature, leaving unstable government coalitions made up of several parties. With the inauguration of the Fifth Republic, the number of parties was sharply reduced, largely because of changes in the electoral system and the overpowering personality of General de Gaulle. In due course, the number of parties with national significance was further reduced by an evolving consensus about the constitutional system and a growing programmatic convergence between the mainstream right and left. Since the 1980s the number of parties having realistic prospects of participating in governance has not changed much except for their labels.

Parties and Elections in the Fifth Republic

The return of de Gaulle to power produced a temporary eclipse of all political parties that the public associated with the discredited Fourth Republic. The virtual guarantee of representation under proportional representation enabled most of the mainstream parties, in particular those located in the center of the spectrum, to turn toward the right or left, or to switch from support of the government to opposition status. The system of Assembly elections instituted in 1958, however, forced parties to make the kind of clear choice they were often unprepared to make. Under that system, which is based on the single-member district, a candidate for the National Assembly must obtain an absolute majority of all votes cast in his or her district. If no candidate obtains such a majority, a runoff is held one week later, and the winning candidate needs only a plurality of the votes cast. (Only those candidates who received the support of at least 12.5 percent of the registered voters in the first round may run in the second.) The system of presidential elections is quite similar: if an absolute majority is not obtained in the first round, a runoff is held two weeks later between the two candidates who received the largest number of first-round votes.

The membership of the Senate is determined not by direct popular vote, but by an electoral college composed of delegates of the municipal councils. To what extent these reforms strengthen local political influence is open to question. As has been the case for many years, the Senate has a right-of-center majority, but in 2004 the Gaullists lost so many seats that the majority could be maintained only with the support of the Union for French Democracy (Union pour la Démocratie Française [UDF]).

The methods of election in subnational races are even more complicated. Members of the general councils, the representative bodies of each of the ninety-six departments, are chosen for six-year terms by the cantons, which are subdivisions of the departments,. Half of the membership of the general councils is renewed every three years. Each canton elects a councillor on the basis of the single-member constituency system in two rounds. If no candidate receives an absolute majority in the first round, the candidate receiving the most votes in the second round is elected. The general councils select their presidents for three-year terms. Members of regional councils are also elected for six-year terms. These councils, in turn, elect their respective presidents for six-year terms.

In France, the details of the electoral system are not fixed by the constitution; rather, they are changed periodically by an organic law, usually based on partisan considerations. In 1986 proportional representation was reintroduced by the Socialists for elections to the National Assembly to minimize the representation of Gaullists and their allies. When the Gaullists captured control of that chamber, they promptly passed a law returning the country to the former single-member constituency system. The most recent changes were related to the method of regional elections: it provided for the mixed use of proportional representation and the single-member constituency system with two rounds, the mixture depending on the size of departments.[2] Under reforms enacted in 2003 and used in 2004, election is on the basis of party lists (scrutin de liste) in two rounds. In the first round, a party list receiving an absolute majority of the votes receives a quarter of all seats. The other seats are distributed on the basis of proportionality among all the lists receiving at least 5 percent of the votes. If no party achieves an absolute majority, a second round of voting is held a week later in which all parties that received at least 10 percent of the first-round votes can participate. In the second round, these parties can join those that failed to receive 5 percent of the first-round votes. In this round, the party list receiving a plurality of the votes gains a quarter of all seats; the other seats are distributed among the parties that received at least 5 percent of the votes.

Parliament also changed the dates of elections. Because the presidential and National Assembly elections were scheduled for April and May 2007, respectively, the government introduced a bill to move the dates of senatorial, municipal, and cantonal elections from 2007 to 2008 in order not to overcrowd the electoral calendar. It did so on the advice of the Council of State and the Constitutional Council. Moreover, the bill extended the terms of the members of general councils elected in 2004 to 2011 to preserve the triennial cycle of renewal of half of the membership of the general councils.[3]

How have France's political parties responded to changes in the electoral system over the course of the Fifth Republic? The French are fond of saying that "on the first ballot one votes, and on the second, one eliminates." Electoral realism has dictated that to maximize its chances a political party must join forces with another party by means of preelectoral deals and second-round withdrawal, or mutual support, agreements. But such activities have produced polarizing tendencies: fewer political parties and their rearrangement into two opposing camps, much as in the United States and Great Britain (see Table 2-6).

Reduction and Rearrangement

The Gaullist party emerged as the major beneficiary of the electoral system introduced at the outset of the Fifth Republic. Relabeled the Union for the New Republic (Union pour la Nouvelle République [UNR]) and later renamed the Democratic Union for the Republic (Union Démocratique pour la République [UDR]), it achieved a dominant position in the Assembly and became relatively institutionalized. Gaullist machines were set up in many localities, and many local notables, drawn by the magnet of power, associated with them. Most of the old centrist formations remained in the opposition, although a large proportion of centrist voters had flocked to the banner of de Gaulle while not necessarily embracing Gaullist ideology. One of the collecting points of the anti-Gaullists was the Democratic Center (Centre Démocrate), which included some of the old MRP politicians who distrusted or detested the general.

Meanwhile, both major parties of the left were reduced to impotence. The Communist Party could count on the support of about 20 percent of the electorate, but it could not win without allies, and the only one possible was the Socialist Party [PS]. The Socialists had, theoretically, two options: an alliance with the Communist Party or with the opposition centrists. In the presidential elections of 1965, a "united left" tactic was preferred, but one that implied the co-optation of part of the center. Both major parties of the left agreed on a single presidential candidate, François Mitterrand. The position of Mitterrand was considerably strengthened when he succeeded in forming the Federation of the Democratic and Socialist Left (Fédération de la Gauche Démocratique et Socialiste [FGDS]), which grouped around the PS a variety of small leftist clubs as well as the Radical-Socialist Party, which had begun its decline into insignificance. But after various electoral failures, and because of the continued disunity between the Socialists and Communists, this alliance disintegrated, and in 1969 each party fielded its own presidential candidate.

The Socialists then decided to restructure their organization, rejuvenate their leadership, alter their platform, and project an image of dynamism. One idea they advocated for years was *autogestion,* a form of self-management of industrial firms by workers. At the same time, the party enrolled many members of the bourgeoisie: shopkeepers, white-collar employees, technicians, and even devout Catholics. Encouraged by its new position of

Table 2-6 Parliamentary and Presidential Elections: France, 1958–2007 (percent of total votes cast)

Elections		Communists	Socialists	Radicals and Left Radicals	MRP	Democratic Center	Independents & Moderates	Gaullists	National Front	Others
Parliamentary	Presidential									
1958 (1)		18.9	15.5	11.5	11.6		19.9	17.6		5.0
(2)		20.7	13.7	7.7	7.5		23.6	26.4		0.4
1962 (1)		21.7	12.6	7.5	8.9	9.6	4.4	31.9		0.4
(2)		21.3	15.2	7.0	5.3	7.8	1.6	40.5		1.3
	1965 (1)		32.2[a]			15.8[b]		43.7[c]		8.3
	(2)		45.5[a]					54.5[c]		—
1967 (1)		22.5	18.8[d]			17.9	37.8			3.0
(2)		21.4	24.1[d]			10.8	42.6			1.1
1968 (1)		20.0	16.5[d]			10.3	43.7			9.5
(2)		20.1	21.3[d]			7.8	46.4			4.4
	1969 (1)	21.5[e]	5.1[f]			23.4[g]	43.8[h]			6.1
	(2)					42.4[g]	57.6[h]			—
1973 (1)		21.5	21.2		13.1[i]		36.4			7.8
(2)		20.6	25.1		6.1[i]		46.2			2.0
	1974 (1)		43.2[a]			32.6[j]		15.1		10.1
	(2)		49.2[a]			50.8[j]				—
1978 (1)		20.5	22.5	2.3[k]		23.9[j]		22.6		8.2
(2)		18.6	28.3	2.3[k]		24.8[j]		26.1		—
	1981 (1)	15.3[m]	25.8[a]	2.2[n]		28.3[j]		17.9[o]		10.3[p]
	(2)		51.8[a]			48.2[j]				—
1981 (1)		16.2	37.5[q]					20.8		6.3
(2)		6.9	49.3[q]					22.4		2.7
1986		9.8	31.0	0.4[k]			21.5[r]	11.2	9.7	0.9
	1988 (1)	6.7[s]	34.1[a]	8.3[l]		16.6[t]		19.9[o]	14.4[u]	8.2[v]
	(2)		54.0[a]	16.6[t]				45.9[o]		—
1988 (1)		11.3	37.5[w]			19.2[l]	40.4[x]		9.7	0.9
(2)		3.4	48.7[w]			18.6[l]	46.8[x]		1.1	2.6
1993 (1)		9.2	19.2[w]				39.7[y]		12.4	19.5[z]
(2)		4.6	31.3[aa]				55.0[ab]		5.7	3.3[ac]
	1995 (1)	8.6[ad]	23.3[ae]				18.6[af]	20.8[o]	15.0[u]	
	(2)		47.4[ae]					52.5[o]		
1997 (1)		9.8	25.7[q]	6.7[ag]			14.9[ah]	16.5	15.2	11.2
(2)		3.6	39.1[q]	5.6[ag]			21.2[ah]	23.6	5.7	1.2

(Continued)

Table 2-6 (Continued)

Parliamentary	Presidential	Communists	Socialists	Radicals and Left Radicals	MRP	Democratic Center	Independents & Moderates	Gaullists	National Front	Others
	2002 (1)	3.4[ai]	16.2[aj]	2.3[n]		6.8[ak]	3.9[al]	19.9[o]	16.9[u]	33.0
	(2)							82.2[o]	17.8[u]	
2002 (1)		4.8	24.1	8.3[am]		4.8[ah]	0.4[an]	33.3[ao]	11.3	
(2)		3.3	35.3	6.7[am]			3.9[ah]	47.3[ao]	1.9	
	2007(1)	1.9[ap]	25.8[aq]			18.6[ar]		31.1[as]	10.0	
	(2)		46.9[aq]					53.1[as]		
2007(1)		4.3	24.3	6.5[at]		7.6[au]		39.5	4.3	13.0
(2)		2.3	42.2			0.5		46.3		4.0

Source: Compiled by the author.

Note: (1) = first ballot; (2) = second ballot; horizontal arrows (←———→, ———→) = extent of support; MRP = Popular Republican Movement. Occasionally columns do not align to indicate instances in which parties moved further left or right.

[a] François Mitterrand.
[b] Jean Lecanuet.
[c] Charles de Gaulle.
[d] Federation of Democratic and Socialist Left.
[e] Jacques Duclos.
[f] Gaston Defferre.
[g] Alain Poher, Christian-Democratic Centrist.
[h] Georges Pompidou.
[i] "Reformers."
[j] Valéry Giscard d'Estaing.
[k] Left Radicals (MRG).
[l] Union for French Democracy (UDF) and "presidential majority."
[m] Georges Marchais.
[n] Michel Crépeau, a Left Radical.
[o] Jacques Chirac.
[p] Including 3.9 percent for Brice Lalonde, the environmentalist candidate.
[q] Including Left Radicals (MRG).
[r] Gaullist-UDF combined list.
[s] André Lajoinie.

[t] Raymond Barre, UDF.
[u] Jean-Marie Le Pen.
[v] Including 3.8 percent for ecologists (Greens) and 4.4 percent for miscellaneous left.
[w] Including Left Radicals (MRG) and other allies.
[x] Union of the Rally and of the Center (URC), an electoral alliance of the Rally for the Republic (RPR) and UDF.
[y] Union for France (UPF) and alliance of RPR (19.83 percent), UDF (18.64 percent), and smaller groups.
[z] Of these, three are environmental parties, accounting for 10.7 percent, subdivided among the Greens, 4.02 percent; Ecology Generation, 3.61 percent; and New Ecologists, 2.5 percent.
[aa] Socialist Party, 29.79 percent, Left Radicals and other allies, 1.54 percent.
[ab] UPF, of which the RPR accounts for 27.84 percent and the UDF for 25.11 percent.
[ac] Ecologist groups, 0.18 percent, and miscellaneous right-wing parties, 2.85 percent.
[ad] Robert Hue.
[ae] Lionel Jospin.

[af] Edouard Balladur.
[ag] Includes Greens and other democratic left candidates.
[ah] UDF.
[ai] Robert Hue.
[aj] Lionel Jospin.
[ak] François Bayrou (UDF).
[al] Alain Madelin, Liberal Democracy.
[am] Includes Greens, Citizens' Movement, and other democratic-left parties.
[an] Liberal Democracy.
[ao] Union for a Popular Movement (UMP).
[ap] Marie-Georges Buffet.
[aq] Ségolène Royal.
[ar] François Bayrou.
[as] Nicolas Sarkozy.
[at] Radical Left, Greens, other Left.
[au] MoDem.

strength, the PS rebuilt its alliance with the Communists. In 1972 the two parties signed a joint platform, the "Common Program of the Left," and agreed to support each other in subsequent national elections.

The centrists, meanwhile, remained weak. Some politicians of the Democratic Center, already starved for power, used Georges Pompidou's election in 1969 as an excuse to join the conservative majority. They reasoned that the new president was more inclined to accommodate himself to centrist thinking than de Gaulle had been. Specifically, they hoped that Pompidou would support European unification and more power for parliament.

Those centrists who were still unwilling to make peace with Gaullism embraced another option: an electoral alignment with the Radical-Socialists known as the Reformers' Movement. The creation of that movement marked a turning point in French politics, because it implied that the Catholic anticlerical discord had been reduced to a manageable scale. But the movement rested on too narrow an electoral base. Moreover, the left wing of the Radical-Socialist Party was offended by this open collaboration with "clericalist" forces and wanted no part of the Reformers' experiment. Instead, they formed a distinct party, the Left Radicals Movement (Mouvement des Radicaux de Gauche [MRG]), and joined the Socialists and Communists in the Common Program alliance.

Bipolarization and Fragmentation

By the early 1970s the French party system appeared to have become permanently bipolarized into a right-wing majority and a left-wing opposition. But the presidential elections of 1974, into which France was propelled by the sudden death of Pompidou, began as a three-way race. Mitterrand was again the candidate of a united left. The Gaullist party candidate was Jacques Chaban-Delmas, whose background as a faithful follower of the late general and as a former Radical-Socialist was intended to appeal to a good portion of the heretofore oppositionist centrist electorate. Valéry Giscard d'Estaing's candidacy complicated the presidential race. Giscard d'Estaing, a prominent politician since the beginning of the Fifth Republic, had supported de Gaulle's presidency and had served as minister of finance for several years but never joined any Gaullist party. Originally, he had been associated with the conservative CNIP, which had remained a component of the majority. But in the early 1960s he formed his own political organization with the help of other CNIP parliamentarians.

This group, the Independent Republicans, articulated a pragmatic approach to a policy of industrial modernization and a reorientation toward free-market economics as distinct from the Gaullist emphasis on the directing hand of the state. Giscard d'Estaing also differed from the Gaullists in taking a stronger stand in favor of an enlarged role for parliament. Finally, Giscard d'Estaing opposed the Gaullist-sponsored referendum of 1969 for the restructuring of the Senate, and he was instrumental in its defeat, thereby bringing about de Gaulle's resignation. Giscard d'Estaing's background, his youthful image (he was born in 1926), his selective non-Gaullist policy positions, his promises of social reform, and his apparent sympathy for close intra-European cooperation—all these factors secured for him the support of most Democratic Centrists and most Radicals. They were persuaded that Giscard d'Estaing was a centrist himself and that he would pursue policies that would be neither Gaullist nor collectivist.

Giscard d'Estaing's election to the presidency in 1974 (with the support of the Gaullists in the second round) raised the questions of whether the old polarization of French politics was ending and whether France was in the process of becoming "post-Gaullist." A year before the parliamentary elections of 1978, it appeared that bipolar confrontation would continue. On the left, the parties adhering to the Common Program pledged to support each other electorally. On the right, a similar alliance, known as "the presidential majority," was formed; it included many Gaullists, the Independent Republicans (now known as the Parti Républicain), the Radicals, and the Democratic Center, restructured since 1976 and relabeled the Center of Social Democrats (Centre des Démocrates Sociaux [CDS]).

Unfortunately, the internal cohesion within both camps was short-lived. Within the left, a bitter quarrel had broken out between the Communists and the Socialists over the meaning of the Common Program, particularly the extent to which industries would be nationalized, wages would be equalized, and cabinet seats would be allocated in the event of a victory of the left. The Communist Party accused the Socialist Party of not really wanting a genuine restructuring of the economy and of using the Communists to gain power. The Socialists, now the senior partner of the left alliance, accused the Communists of not having "de-Stalinized" themselves sufficiently and of hoping to destroy democratic institutions. In the end, the left failed, by a few percentage points, to gain a parliamentary majority—a result widely attributed to the refusal of the left-wing parties in many constituencies to support each other in the second round.

Within the majority there were similar problems. Upon assuming the presidency, Giscard d'Estaing had co-opted the Gaullists—they had no place else to go—by giving them a few cabinet posts and by retaining the essentials of Gaullist foreign policy: hostility to the North Atlantic Treaty Organization (NATO), the development of an independent nuclear strike force, and a show of independence in relation to the United States. Giscard d'Estaing's first prime minister, Jacques Chirac, was a Gaullist, but he resigned his post in 1976 after disagreements with Giscard d'Estaing. Later, Chirac became the leader of the Gaullist party—by then renamed Rally for the Republic (Rassemblement pour la République [RPR])—as well as mayor of Paris, and he made no secret of his ambition to run for the presidency in 1981. Giscard d'Estaing, who intended to run for a second term, still needed the support of the Gaullists, the largest party in the National Assembly, but he wanted to reduce this dependence. Shortly before the 1978 legislative elections, he encouraged the creation of the Union for French Democracy (Union pour la Démocratie Française [UDF]), an electoral federation of all non-Gaullist elements of the presidential majority: the Republicans, the CDS, the Radicals, and a few smaller groups. The UDF decided to put up single first-round candidates in many districts and to support Gaullist candidates only if necessary in the second round. One result of this tactic was a realignment within the majority: an impressive expansion of the number of Giscardist deputies at the expense of the Gaullist parliamentary party.

The Elections of 1981

Early in 1981, as the presidential election approached, the Common Program had been shelved, the unity of the left was near collapse, and the Socialist and Communist Parties each ran its own candidate, Mitterrand and Georges Marchais, respectively. Before the first round of balloting in April, Marchais was almost as critical of Mitterrand as of Giscard d'Estaing, but after obtaining only 15 percent of the popular vote (the lowest for the Communist Party since the end of World War II) compared with Mitterrand's more than 26 percent, Marchais endorsed Mitterrand in the second round, thereby permitting himself to claim the victory of the Socialist candidate as that of his own supporters. The mutual support agreement between the Socialist and Communist candidates also held in the second round of the parliamentary elections that followed Mitterrand's accession to the presidency, and Socialist parliamentary candidates were the principal beneficiaries.

After these elections, it was clear that although the Socialist Party had emerged with an absolute Assembly majority for the first time since 1936, the Communist Party, with barely 9 percent of the seats, had been reduced to a marginal status. Reasons for this decline were the excessive Stalinism of its leadership; the deteriorating public image of Georges Marchais, its general secretary; the party's refusal to condemn Soviet aggression in Afghanistan and elsewhere; the widespread blame placed on the party for the defeat of the left in 1978; and the lack of internal democracy. In any case, the Communist Party had become a supplicant; in exchange for several lower-level ministerial posts, the party accepted the conditions imposed on it by Mitterrand: condemnation of Soviet actions in Afghanistan and Poland, commitment to the Western alliance, respect for public liberties, and adherence to a policy of gradually transforming the economy by means of democratic methods.

Within the camp of the Gaullist and centrist-conservative alliance, the complications were far greater. In the first round of presidential balloting, both Giscard d'Estaing and Chirac found themselves competing for the same bourgeois and right-of-center electorate. While criticizing each other's personalities and policy preferences, both candidates stressed the disastrous consequences for France of a victory for the left. During the runoff between Giscard d'Estaing and Mitterrand, Chirac gave only a halfhearted endorsement of Giscard d'Estaing. In the end, Giscard d'Estaing believed that his reelection was sabotaged by Chirac's refusal to issue a clear call to his Gaullist supporters to vote for him.

During the parliamentary elections, the erstwhile majority of Gaullists (RPR) and Giscardists (UDF) reestablished an uneasy electoral alliance. The optimistically named Union for the New Majority (Union pour la Nouvelle Majorité [UNM]) decided to support common first-round candidates in more than three hundred constituencies and made the usual mutual support agreements for the second round. The alliance was virtually buried by a Socialist landslide, which significantly altered the complexion of the parliament and, indeed, of the whole political party system for the first time since the founding of the Fifth Republic.

Of the various reasons for the defeat of the Gaullist-Giscardist forces, the first was the lack of unity: the incessant infighting between Giscard d'Estaing's friends and the "Chiraquists" had sapped the strength of both. Second was the widespread conviction that Giscard d'Estaing's policies were inadequate for dealing with the growing inflation and unemployment. Third, several scandals had erupted involving some ministers and, in fact, Giscard d'Estaing himself. The feeling that Giscard d'Estaing had been corrupted by power was exacerbated by his increasingly "monarchical" behavior: his contempt for parliament; his unsatisfactory press conferences, which in terms of their stage-managed nature began to resemble those of de Gaulle; the tightening of presidential control over the news media; and what many considered to be an unscrupulous use of presidential patronage.

Many French voters were uneasy about the prospect of having Giscard d'Estaing as president for another term. But the Gaullists and Giscardists had argued that a transfer of power to the left would be too dangerous because the Socialists would be "hostages" to the Communists. But such an argument proved less convincing as the PS strengthened its position in relation to the PCF, and it lost most of its scare value after the first round of the presidential elections in which the Socialists received nearly twice as much support as the Communists.

After the parliamentary elections of 1981, the now leaderless UDF was reduced to a demoralized vestige of some sixty deputies, or about half of its previous strength. Some of the UDF politicians were hoping that at some time in the future Giscard d'Estaing would come out of retirement, as de Gaulle had once done, and revive their party. Several leaders of the CDS, the Christian Democratic component of the UDF, were examining the possibility of autonomous measures, including, perhaps, a rapprochement with the new majority. The Radical-Socialist Party, however, had been so decimated that it seemed to have no credible options left. Chirac now prepared to assume leadership of the combined centrist-conservative (or Giscardist-Gaullist) opposition forces. Although he finally achieved his ambition of eclipsing Giscard d'Estaing, it was a hollow victory, because the Gaullist contingent in the Assembly had itself been cut in half.

The Socialist majority in the 1981 Assembly was so overwhelming that Mitterrand and his government were able to use it to put into effect an ambitious program of reforms. Among the most important reforms were enhancement of civil liberties, an expanded budget for education, liberalization of the penal code, and an ambitious program of administrative decentralization. In addition, the government nationalized some industries and undertook a redistribution of income by means of more steeply progressive taxation, higher minimum wages, and expanded social benefits. These policies corresponded to elements of the Common Program, and, by and large, the Communists supported them. By 1983, however, the Socialists' reforming zeal had begun to cool. As the budget deficit grew, the cost of nationalizing proved too high and its benefits doubtful. Production slumped and unemployment, higher than 10 percent, persisted. In response to these developments, the government abruptly changed course and embraced an austerity program aimed at rationalizing industry, keeping wages under control, and encouraging economic growth.

The new strategy alienated the Communist Party, whose ministers opted out of the government. A more serious consequence was the Socialists' slippage in public support in response to the government's failure to solve the problems of unemployment, a rising crime rate, and the presence of masses of North African immigrants—all three phenomena widely believed to be interrelated. One symptom of the growing public concern with these problems was the sudden rise of the National Front (Front National), an extreme-right party led by Jean-Marie Le Pen.

At the same time, the popularity of the RPR and UDF was growing, and public opinion polls predicted that in the next parliamentary elections the Socialists would lose their majority. To limit the damage, the Socialist government reintroduced a variant of the old (Fourth Republic) system of proportional representation. It was thought that under such a system the National Front would get enough votes to gain representation in the Assembly, but in so doing would take enough electoral support away from the Gaullists to make the victory of the latter less certain and less crushing.

The Rise of Marginal Parties: The National Front and the Greens

Founded in 1972, the National Front is a conglomerate of fascists, Pétainists, right-wing Catholics, ultranationalists, erstwhile supporters of Algérie Française, antiparliamentarists, former Poujadists, anti-Semites, and racists. It burst onto the French political scene in the municipal elections of 1983, when it captured 17 percent of the vote in an industrial town near Paris heavily settled by immigrants, and in the elections to the European Parliament a year later, when it won 10.5 percent of the popular vote.

The rise of the National Front was balanced to some extent by that of another political grouping, the ecologists, especially the Green Party (Verts). That party grew out of environmentalist interest groups, which made their appearance in the 1970s. But their attempts to sponsor environmentalist candidates at the national level were unsuccessful for several reasons: the public was paying little attention to environmental problems; the mainstream parties—notably the Socialists—had the requisite environmentalist planks in their program; and the electoral system did not favor small parties. In the presidential elections of 1981, the Green Party received only 3.9 percent of the first-round votes, and in the parliamentary elections that followed, it obtained even less support and failed to get any seats in the National Assembly.

The First 'Cohabitation' Interlude

The results of the legislative elections of March 1986 proved the wisdom of the Socialists' electoral stratagem. The RPR and UDF together obtained a bare majority (291 out of 577 seats) in the National Assembly, not enough to enable them to undertake policy changes without the support of the National Front, which managed to seat thirty-two deputies. But it was enough to enable them to insist on the appointment of a politically compatible (that is, Gaullist-Giscardist) government. The new government embarked on an unprecedented experiment in power sharing, as described earlier. Its head, Gaullist leader Chirac, was forced to cohabit with a Socialist president. During the early phases of cohabitation, France appeared to undergo a process of "de-presidentialization" as Prime Minister Chirac asserted his (and the government's) leadership in the formulation and execution of internal policies, particularly those related to privatizing public enterprises. President Mitterrand confined himself largely to foreign policy pronouncements and, intermittently, to selective criticism of Chirac's domestic measures.

But Chirac's power to govern turned out to be less than absolute. It was limited by the need of the Gaullists to cohabit with the Giscardists, who were not always in a cooperative mood. They were unhappy not only about some of Chirac's policy choices but also about an inadequate sharing of political patronage. Furthermore, there were rivalries between the leaders of the RPR and UDF, as well as disagreements between them—and within the RPR itself—about the posture to be adopted toward the National Front. The liberals wanted to have nothing to do with Le Pen, whom they regarded as a danger to democracy, but the hard-liners—notably among the Gaullists—advocated a selective embrace of the National Front's positions, especially on immigrants, in order to strengthen their base of support within the Assembly and, more important, to retrieve the support of former Gaullist voters who had crossed over to the National Front and to prevent further attrition. Because of these conflicts, Chirac's leadership suffered, and he became the major target of popular discontent. Mitterrand, by contrast, looked like a conciliatory, unifying statesman.

Consensus and Convergence: The Elections of 1988

The presidential elections of April and May 1988 pitted Mitterrand against three major rivals on the right: Chirac (RPR), Raymond Barre (UDF), and Le Pen (National Front). Several months before the elections, cohabitation, at first welcomed by most French citizens, appeared to be of dubious worth as the president and the prime minister sought to draw electoral advantage by discrediting each other. The reelection of Mitterrand suggested that he had succeeded better than his rival. But his impressive margin of victory must also be attributed to the disunity among the right. The outcome of the first round reflected that disunity as Barre and Chirac publicly criticized one another. In addition, Le Pen, the leader of the National Front, drew votes from the "respectable" right, especially from the RPR, and made a surprisingly strong showing.

Mitterrand's decision just after the presidential election to dissolve the National Assembly and to call for new elections was made in the hope that the delicate power-sharing pattern of the previous two years would be replaced by a more normal relationship between president and parliament. The result of the Assembly elections, however, was ambiguous. Although the RPR and UDF, which put up joint candidates in most constituencies, lost control of the Assembly, the Socialists failed to get the absolute majority the pollsters had predicted. Several explanations account for the outcome of that election in which the abstention rate (more than 34 percent) was the highest since 1962. Some traditional Socialist voters had abstained because Mitterrand, running as a statesman above parties rather than as a Socialist, had not made great efforts to appeal to them or even to mobilize the party activists. Others had been so sure of a Socialist victory that they believed their votes to be unnecessary. And still others were tired of voting so often. In addition, there were those who had supported Mitterrand but did not want a clearly Socialist regime, hoping instead that Michel Rocard, the new prime minister, would construct a pragmatic center-left government.

Rocard did not disappoint them. His government, as reconstituted after the legislative elections, included twenty-five Socialists and twenty-four non-Socialists, among them six centrists of the UDF. Moreover, in an attempt to show that he paid as much attention to "civil society" as to the political establishment, he also included fourteen nonparty people.

Rocard's overture toward the political center was a reflection of the changes in France's party system, in which some parties had lost their traditional supporters, others their credibility, still others their ideological coherence, and all of them many of their dues-paying members.[4] Just as the victory of Mitterrand was not quite a victory for the Socialist Party, the reestablished dominance of the party in the political arena and in the National Assembly was not quite a victory for socialism. Under the pressures of electoral reality and, later, of government responsibility, the PS had given up most of its Marxism and had transformed itself into a moderate party resembling the social democratic parties of Scandinavia or Germany. During the 1988 election campaigns, it presented a minimum platform whose planks—social justice, productivity, solidarity among various segments of French society, and the construction of Europe—did not differ sharply from the equally vague generalities of the RPR/UDF about liberty, economic progress, and patriotism. This platform was designed to paper over continuing disagreements among the major party personalities, including Mitterrand, Rocard, and former prime ministers Pierre Mauroy and

Laurent Fabius. These disagreements were not only matters of personal ambition but also related to the tactical and long-term orientations of the Socialists. While Rocard sought to distance himself as much as possible from the Communists, Mitterrand continued to advocate keeping the left as united as possible and keeping the door open to traditional Communist voters.

These disagreements were echoed at the Socialist Party congress in Rennes in 1990. There, the nationalists were pitted against the Europeanists; the Jacobins—the believers in a France "one and indivisible"—against the pluralists and decentralizers; the statists against the liberals; and the growth-oriented productivists against those favoring redistribution and socioeconomic equality. This war of party factions was hardly resolved by a document that aimed at a synthesis of these diverse positions.[5] The internal divisions were aggravated during the 1990–1991 Persian Gulf crisis, which set Mitterrand and his loyalists, who supported the U.S. war effort, against a faction led by Jean-Pierre Chevènement that favored a foreign policy that combined Gaullist independence-mindedness with hysterical anti-Americanism. These divisions and the conflict between tactical and programmatic orientations were reflected in the government of Prime Minister Edith Cresson, who was accused of "conducting a policy of the right while positioning herself on the left."[6] Specifically, she prepared a rapprochement with the Communists and alienated the centrists, while abandoning the Socialists' traditional infatuation with developing countries and even appearing to adopt the kind of hard-nosed stance toward immigrants that previously had been associated with the right. Nevertheless, the various factions decided to suspend their disputes until the National Assembly elections of 1993.

The Communist Party, too, was divided. In 1987 the Communists who rejected the rigid Stalinism of the party and held that outlook—and its leader, Georges Marchais—responsible for its steep electoral decline set up a rival party of "Renovators," and in 1988 they put up their own presidential candidate. After the elections, the Communist Party alternated between a desire to remain in opposition and a readiness to support the government on specific issues. How much the Communist leadership would be influenced by perestroika and glasnost in the Soviet Union remained to be seen. The twenty-seventh congress of the Communist Party in 1990 saw an expression of interest in a pluralistic communism instead of a bureaucratic and authoritarian one, a more open discussion than ever before, and even the submission of a minority report.[7] Yet Marchais's autocratic leadership was reconfirmed.

The RPR was torn between the nationalism and populist statism of the disciples of de Gaulle, on the one hand, and a pro-European neoliberalism, on the other. Moreover, although some Gaullist politicians were still considering rapprochement with the National Front, most of the Gaullist leadership had come to reject collaboration with that party on any level. The UDF (from which the RPR had copied much of its neoliberalism) was divided between the elitism of the Republican Party, its largest component, and the moderate progressivism of some Christian Democratic (CDS) and Radical-Socialist politicians. In a confusion of strategies, some Giscardists wanted to align themselves closely with the RPR and harden their opposition to the new government; others, including Giscard d'Estaing himself, who had become the official leader of the UDF, wanted to signal that party's centrist views by a "constructive opposition." Still others, including Barre, even held out the possibility of an eventual cohabitation with the Socialist-led government.

Meanwhile, the CDS, which had increased its National Assembly representation from thirty-five to fifty in the 1988 elections, reconstituted itself as a separate parliamentary party while formally remaining a component of the UDF. Finally, while the RPR and UDF were preparing their lists of candidates for the elections to the European Parliament in 1989, younger politicians in both parties made abortive attempts to oust Giscard d'Estaing and other veterans from leadership positions.

To maintain the integrity and influence of their respective organizations while achieving a measure of unity—and, incidentally, to be better equipped to face Le Pen and his National Front—in 1990 the RPR and UDF founded a confederation called the Union for France (Union pour la France [UPF]). The UPF began issuing joint communiqués and discussing the adoption of a system of primaries for designating a common candidate for the presidential election of 1995. This common approach would, it was hoped, be used for future legislative elections as well.

The National Front, which was responsible for some of the problems of the RPR and UDF, was itself torn; it alternated between the bourgeois and respectable behavior of some of its politicians and the provocative pronouncements of others. One was reflected in an emphasis on the neoliberal segments of the party's platform such as the free market and individual rights, the other in the promotion of nationalist and racist themes. Some regarded the National Front as a genuine alternative to the "gang of four"—the PCF, PS, UDF, and RPR—but many more voters were turned off from the party by Le Pen's irrepressible penchant for demagogy and came to consider him a danger to democracy.

As the National Front's credibility as a democratic alternative party weakened, that of another party, the Greens, assumed increased importance. Formed in the early 1980s out of a number of environmental associations, the Greens opposed the construction of nuclear reactors. Although officially aligned with neither the right nor the left, the Greens advocated policies often associated with the left, such as reducing the workweek, strengthening local government, and creating a foreign policy more sympathetic to developing countries. The Greens did surprisingly well in the first round of the presidential elections, but achieved insignificant scores in the parliamentary elections.

By the early 1990s, the popularity of the Socialists was beginning to decline. This decline was manifested in the regional and cantonal elections of March 1992, in which less than 20 percent of the electorate voted for that party. The Socialist Party was held responsible for various problems and failures: persistent unemployment, crime and urban violence, financial scandals involving Socialist politicians, the revelation that the government allowed the use of blood products contaminated with the AIDS virus, and the Habbash affair, in which a Palestinian terrorist leader was secretly flown to France for medical treatment and after a public outcry was spirited out of the country. The Socialist Party was not helped by its continuing internal divisions—between the radical egalitarians and the pragmatists, between those favoring development of European integration and those against it, and between those advocating closer collaboration with the Communist Party and those opposed to it.

The other major parties did not fare much better; the RPR and UDF together gained only 33 percent of the votes in the 1992 cantonal elections. The two right-wing parties suffered from internal divisions and a lack of credibility. The major gainers were the National Front and the environmentalist parties, which made significant inroads into regional councils. But the ecologists were hurt by a division of this movement into two parties, the Greens and the Ecology Generation (Génération Écologie), whose leaders sniped at one another while proclaiming a desire for unity.

Punishing the Incumbents: National Elections in the 1990s

The results of the elections just described signaled, above all, a disenchantment with the political class. This disenchantment was reflected in the steeply falling approval ratings not only of Prime Ministers Edith Cresson and Pierre Bérégovoy but also of President Mitterrand. The public's impatience with the government was starkly reflected in the results of the 1993 parliamentary elections. These results constituted a virtual rout of the Socialist Party and its allies, the Left Radicals. Gaining only 57 seats, compared with the 472 seats obtained by the RPR and UDF combined, the Socialists were left with the lowest National Assembly representation since 1968. The outcome threatened to fragment, if not destroy, the party as a whole, and it reduced the role of Mitterrand, already a lame-duck president, to a marginal and symbolic one. The new government of Prime Minister Edouard Balladur began with high popular opinion ratings and a parliamentary majority of more than 80 percent—the largest majority enjoyed by any group in more than a century. These ratings, which held for several months, reflected the public's perception of Balladur as a calm and reasonable political leader, and they improved as Balladur's government chalked up some policy successes, among them the international trade negotiations of 1994.

In preparing for the presidential election of 1995, the Socialist Party was in a much weaker position than the right-wing parties. The party, which had been in power too long, had to bear the brunt of attacks for policy shortcomings and for scandals involving a significant number of Socialist politicians. Because Mitterrand had been president for nearly fourteen years, many French voters decided it was time for a change. Still, there were indications that the Socialists might win the presidential race if Jacques Delors, the outgoing president of the European Commission, became the Socialist candidate. But he declined to run, and so the Socialists hurriedly chose Lionel Jospin, a former minister of education, as the alternative candidate. Jospin did not have the enthusiastic support of all Socialist politicians, and Mitterrand gave him only a perfunctory endorsement.

These developments would normally have guaranteed the election of a Gaullist candidate. The RPR and its ally, the UDF, were reasonably united. The disagreement over the Maastricht Treaty on the European Union, which had split the two conservative formations and divided the RPR internally, seemed to have been resolved. Meanwhile, there was an informal understanding that Chirac, the mayor of Paris and the president of the RPR, would be that party's candidate again, as he had been in 1981 and 1988. But public opinion polls throughout 1993 and 1994 were so favorable to Balladur that he decided to run for the presidency himself. The Gaullists, then, had two presidential candidates. As late as January 1995, polls showed Balladur considerably ahead of Chirac, and it was widely assumed that Balladur would easily be elected president. But suddenly the French electorate's enthusiasm for him began to sour. He was held responsible for mishandling several problems, among them education and employment, and his patrician demeanor suggested an inability to identify with the problems of ordinary people.

As the election approached, voters had reservations about both major formations. In previous years, they had tended to opt for one or another of these formations on the basis of where they usually placed themselves along the right-left continuum. But the distinctions between right and left had gradually been moderated by a growing programmatic convergence on several issues such as decentralization, the need to check the growth of welfare state expenditures, and, above all, the institutions of the Fifth Republic. On other issues, such as education, tax policy, and the development of the European Union, there was an overlap of opinions.

This confusion of opinions explains why 20 percent of the electorate was still undecided just two weeks before the first round. Compounding the problem was the voters' difficulty in detecting differences among Jospin, Chirac, and Balladur. All three seemed to favor measures to reduce unemployment, improve the system of justice, and further European integration, among other issues. If there was a difference, it revolved around the presidency. Jospin advocated reducing the presidential term of office to five years; Balladur favored the existing seven-year term but wanted to eliminate the possibility of reelection; and Chirac preferred the status quo. In addition, Jospin favored reducing the workweek from thirty-nine to thirty-seven hours, and Chirac and Balladur wanted to leave that matter to the marketplace and to collective contract negotiations.

In the end, more than 35 percent of voters cast ballots for candidates of minor or marginal parties. In doing so, they had a wide choice among nine candidates: two Gaullists, a Socialist, a Communist, a "Trotskyist" radical, the leader of the Green Party, a right-wing nationalist running under the label of the Movement for France (Mouvement pour la France [MPF]), an extreme-rightist (Le Pen), and a right-wing political newcomer, Jacques Cheminade.

The second round produced a kind of electoral recomposition: Jospin secured the support of most of the left-of-center to extreme-left electorate, while Chirac reassembled most of the right-of-center electorate. Exit polls, however, indicated that more than 40 percent of the 4.6 million citizens who had voted for extreme-rightist Le Pen in the first round abstained or cast blank ballots in the second round.

Chirac's second-round victory could not be interpreted as a victory for the Gaullist Party (the Socialist Party did almost equally well in terms of popular votes), but rather as the victory of a person who had not been a national decision maker for several years and therefore could not be blamed directly for recent policy failings.

The election results indicated that the right-left distinction in French politics retained some meaning and that more than 50 percent of the working-class electorate had opted for one of the parties of the left. Nevertheless, about a third of the various parts of the population classified as underprivileged had voted for Le Pen in the first round. The results also showed that Chirac had transcended the limitations of previous Gaullist presidential candidates by broadening his electoral base. In the second round, Chirac captured the votes of 43 percent of workers, 54 percent of students, 60 percent of the retired, and half of eighteen- to twenty-one-year-olds. According to an exit poll, 68 percent of voters interpreted the election of Chirac as the electorate's desire for change and reform, and only 26 percent saw it as a victory of the left over the right.[8]

The election results also suggested that the National Front had achieved sufficient respectability to be seen by many as having entered the mainstream of French politics. It had attracted members of the urban working class who had traditionally supported left-wing parties and had increased its appeal to the educated electorate. Conversely, as a result of the collapse of the Soviet Union and a change in the party leadership, the Communist Party, although not able to widen its appeal beyond the working class, was no longer feared as the tool of a foreign power.

Chirac's victory proved to be short-lived, however; it was abruptly undermined by the unexpected victory of the Socialists and their left-wing allies in the National Assembly elections of 1997.[9] As noted earlier, that election was a needless miscalculation. It discredited not only Prime Minister Alain Juppé but President Chirac as well, and it weakened the authority of both within the Gaullist Party. That party was thrown into disarray as internecine conflicts broke out, not only about the leadership but also about the party's future direction and its relationship with other right-wing parties. Some Gaullists favored a more rapid evolution toward the market and a more positive stance toward European integration, including a common European currency. Others, reacting to the victory of the left, were pressing their party to return to its traditional statism (and a concern with the protection of national sovereignty) and to adopt a more "social" orientation. Some Gaullists argued for a merger with the UDF; others favored a rapprochement with the National Front, or at least a more systematic effort to capture that party's electorate. Still others argued for a change of name to give the party a new image. And others again—notably former prime minister Balladur—favored a fusion of all right-of-center formations into a single party, with the RPR as the nucleus. This last outcome remained an unlikely prospect, largely because of the rival personal ambitions of the leaders of these factions. Some of the RPR politicians, including Chirac himself, were no longer Gaullists in the traditional sense. Other politicians were still nostalgic for the old nationalist rhetoric that made little sense in an age of transnationalism and globalization. This group included Gaullist nationalists who opposed the surrender of sovereignty to the European Union—among them, Charles Pasqua, who, together with Philippe de Villiers, formed a new party, the Rally for France, which incorporated de Villiers's Movement for France. De Villiers soon abandoned that party, however, claiming that Pasqua wanted to dominate it.[10]

The UDF was particularly disoriented. Valéry Giscard d'Estaing, its former leader and the original *raison d'être* of that electoral umbrella organization, had aged and become politically marginalized. At the same time, the major component parts of the UDF, especially the Republican Party, now relabeled Liberal Democracy (Démocratie Libérale [DL]) and the CDS, henceforth known as the Democratic Force (Force Démocrate), maintained their respective individualities. In 1998 the DL left the UDF altogether.[11]

The Socialist Party, by contrast, conveyed the impression of being more united than ever, because the authority of Jospin had silenced its traditional internal factions. Moreover, Jospin had succeeded in reestablishing an alliance with most of the other left-wing formations, including the Communist Party, and they were rewarded for their cooperative attitudes with cabinet positions. In the afterglow of the left's election victory, there seemed to be considerable coherence in government policy as most left-wing politicians rallied around Jospin's leadership, but it remained to be seen how long this cohesion would last in the face of the controversial economic policy decisions that would have to be made.

As the parliamentary and presidential elections of 2002 loomed on the horizon and Jospin began to lay the groundwork for a second attempt to gain the presidency, the Socialist Party maintained its unity. To be sure, factionalism was not entirely eliminated.[12] It was, however, moderated by the readmission of the party's "old elephants," including followers of Mitterrand, into leading government positions; a reduction of policy options; and the need to present a solid front in face of Socialist Party relations with other parties in the "pluralist left" government: the Citizens' Movement (Mouvement des Citoyens [MDC]), the Greens, and the Communist Party.[13] The Communist Party had become more moderate, except for a small group among the rank and file that retained its radicalism, but the Greens were increasingly articulating policy differences.

The parties outside the mainstream had their own problems. In 1998 the National Front split into two rival factions because of personal conflicts between Le Pen and Bruno Mégret, leader of the National Republican Movement (Mouvement National Républicain [MNR]). Le Pen, the more charismatic figure, appealed largely to the electorate, while Mégret's support came from the party apparatus.

The Elections of 2002: A Political Earthquake

A stark illustration of the bipolarization that had overtaken elections was provided by the 2002 national elections. The two rounds of the presidential election were scheduled for April 21 and May 5, to be followed in June by two rounds of parliamentary elections. Sixteen candidates competed in the presidential election, more than in any previous presidential election in the Fifth Republic. They ranged from the National Front's Le Pen on the extreme right to nominees of three different extreme-left (Trotskyist) parties—the Workers' Struggle (Lutte Ouvrière), the Communist Revolutionary League (Ligue Communiste Révolutionnaire), and the Workers' Party (Parti des Travailleurs). During the campaign, it was widely assumed (and predicted by public opinion polls) that Chirac, the incumbent president, and Jospin, the incumbent prime minister, would emerge as the two top vote-getters and would confront each other in the second round.[14]

The first-round result, however, was an unexpected upset: Chirac came in first and Le Pen came in second after edging out Jospin by less than one percentage point. There were several explanations for this shocking outcome. Only three months before the election, the polls had shown Jospin clearly ahead of Chirac, who was considered to be a politician without a clear program and more interested in political power for its own sake. Moreover, Chirac had been accused of corruption both as mayor of Paris and as president, and he might have been indicted but for the fact that the incumbent presidency gave him immunity. By contrast, Jospin was regarded as one of the best prime ministers of the Fifth Republic. Unfortunately, he lacked the charisma of Chirac, who was an excellent campaigner.

More important, the government of the "pluralist left" led by Jospin was riven by disagreements between the Socialist Party and its coalition partners as well as by rivalries within the party. Traditional leftist voters criticized Jospin both for abandoning the working class—in midcampaign he had asserted that his program was not socialist—and for minimizing the importance of a rapidly growing crime rate. Many of these voters therefore opted for candidates of the smaller leftist parties—the PCF, the MDC, and the Trotskyist parties—and even for the National Front. They did so not to help these candidates to win, but to warn Jospin. As it turned out, these parties ended up as spoilers; they prevented Jospin from figuring in the second-round runoff. The dissatisfaction with both major candidates was attested by the low voter turnout, in the electoral indecision—more than 40 percent of the electorate remained undecided as late as two weeks before the election—and by both Chirac and Jospin garnering fewer popular votes than they had received in 1995, as did Le Pen.

The unusually high vote for marginal parties as well as the high abstention rate reflected a widespread belief that the mainstream parties were not responding to the needs of the people.[15] Moreover, the poor performance of the Socialist Party and that all the left-wing parties together got only 43 percent of the working-class vote in the first round (compared with 63 percent in the presidential elections of 1988) seemed to confirm the thesis that "the privileged relationship of a century between the world of the worker and the parties of the left" had ended.[16]

Most of the supporters of leftist and left-of-center parties found it unpleasant to have to choose between Chirac and Le Pen in the second round. To voters, Le Pen represented too great a risk; because of his reputation and program, his election could endanger democracy. Therefore, against a backdrop of slogans such as "Vote for the crook, not the fascist," Chirac won the runoff easily. He had the overwhelming support of the left, who voted for him not because they endorsed him or his program but because they rejected Le Pen in the name of "republican defense."

In the ensuing National Assembly elections, voters provided Chirac with a clear majority (see Table 2-7). Most voters were pressing for legislative action and did not want to continue the power sharing between a president belonging to one party and an Assembly controlled by an opposing party. The victory of the political right in this election was also due to the fact that it had capitalized on Chirac's victory. Several months before the presidential elections, Chirac had created the Union in Movement (Union en Mouvement [UEM]), an electoral alliance of various right-of-center formations, led by the RPR, that would support him. Immediately after the first round, the UEM was transformed into the Union for the Presidential Majority (Union pour la Majorité Présidentielle [UMP]), an umbrella party that soon swallowed up both the RPR and several smaller parties, including Liberal Democracy (Démocratie Libérale) and most of the UDF. Just before the parliamentary elections, the acronym UMP was retained, but it now stood for Union for a Popular Movement (Union pour un Mouvement Populaire). A rump of the UDF, led by François Bayrou, held out for independence, but because the UMP had gained an absolute majority of seats in the National Assembly, UDF influence in that chamber would amount to little if anything. Yet, even though it distanced itself from the UMP—and voted with the opposition against the budget bill in 2005—the UDF refused to join any alliance with the left.

The political left was in a state of disorganization and demoralization. The Communist Party was near collapse—it obtained its lowest vote in national elections since the end of World War II—but it still managed (barely) to win enough Assembly seats to constitute itself as a parliamentary group. The Greens lost most of their support, ending up with only three seats. The Trotskyists won no seats. The MDC, which was rebaptized during the election campaign as the Republican Pole (Pôle Républicain), was finished, as was, so it seemed, the political career of Chevènement. The Socialist Party survived as the largest formation of the left, but it was beset with confusion and uncertainty about its leadership and its future orientations. There was a tug-of-war between the more ideological leftists, who wanted to return to the traditional redistributive policies of the Socialist Party and retrieve the lost working-class support, and the pragmatic moderates, who wanted to embrace the market more fully and widen the party's appeal to the bourgeoisie.

The election of President Nicholas Sarkozy, shown here addressing the Paris Bar Association on June 24, 2010, represented something of a break with the past in French elections.

Source: Reuters/Philippe Wojazer

Both the National Front and its extreme-left rival, the National Republican Movement, were left out in the cold, gaining no seats at all. Although it appeared that about a third of the French electorate shared many of the National Front's ideas—for example, on immigrants, on law and order issues, and on Europe—its future prospects did not seem promising because of the age of its leader (Le Pen was nearly seventy-four) and the bipolarizing effect of the national electoral system.

The Elections of 2007: A Post-Gaullist Rupture?

In many respects, the presidential election of 2007 resembled earlier contests between the right and the left. It revolved around the issues of the cost of living, unemployment, taxation, and education, and it engaged the usual contestants on both sides of the political spectrum. A dozen candidates competed in the first round, and the second round was a runoff between Nicolas Sarkozy, the candidate of the UMP, and Socialist Ségolène Royal. Both candidates had been chosen in primary elections in which active members of their respective parties had taken part. As the leader of his party, Sarkozy was certain to be the nominee. The only credible rival was Dominique de Villepin, Chirac's last prime minister, but he had lost popularity as a result of his haughty behavior toward parliament and his mishandling of an employment bill. The choice of a Socialist candidate was more problematic. There were three major contenders for the nomination: Laurent Fabius, a former prime minister; Dominique Strauss-Kahn, a former finance minister; and Ségolène Royal, a former minister for the environment who had held other minor ministerial posts. Fabius presented himself as a leftist, but he was distrusted in this role because as minister of economics under Mitterrand he had pursued rather moderate policies, and Strauss-Kahn was distrusted by the more leftist politicians for his "social-democratic" (in other words, insufficiently leftist) orientation. Royal emerged as a compromise choice, and for the first several weeks of the campaign she was comfortably ahead in the polls.[17] Her candidacy, however, was beset with numerous problems. Her campaign was poorly organized, and her own performance was inept; many of her public statements were ill-informed and contradictory; and she received only half-hearted support from the party leadership.[18]

Moreover, the PS was marked by internal division and programmatic incoherence.[19] Sarkozy waged an aggressive campaign in which he portrayed himself as both a loyal Gaullist and an innovator who was prepared to "rupture" the status quo in order to achieve much-needed reforms.[20] In several respects, Sarkozy's presidential nomination was a break with the past: he had originally not been considered suitable for the presidency because he was not a graduate of ENA or any of the other grandes écoles; he was the son and grandson of immigrants; and he was short of stature. But he had held important cabinet posts; and as minister of the interior, he had developed a reputation as being tough on criminals. His hard-line position on the rioting of October–November 2005 sharply increased his popularity within the party, which had gained many new adherents, in part because it was seen as a credible alternative to the National Front on issues of law and order.

A complicating factor was the candidacy of François Bayrou, the president of the UDF, who had served as a minister in the conservative governments of Juppé and Balladur. But during the second term of the Chirac presidency, he had selectively distanced himself from the UMP and in 2007 announced that he would be the UDF candidate for president. Bayrou hoped to profit from the electorate's dissatisfaction with both the UMP and the PS, and for a while he appeared to be a serious alternative. But in the end, the bipolar tradition asserted itself: Bayrou came in third in the first round, and in the second round, Sarkozy won the presidency with a score of 53 to 47. Bayrou used his strong first-round performance to create a new party, the Democratic Movement (Mouvement Démocrate [MoDem]),[21] which would field "centrist" candidates in the forthcoming parliamentary elections.

The parliamentary elections of June 2007 produced a solid majority for the UMP. At the same time, they confirmed the bipolar thrust of French electoral politics. The dominance of the two major mainstream parties and the continuance of the traditional right-left division have also been confirmed in a number of subnational elections, although local issues often prevailed, and many parties fielded candidates.

Bipolarity and Multiplicity in Subnational Elections

The bipolar tendencies of electoral outcomes in the National Assembly and the presidency do not necessarily apply to other elective bodies in France: the regional, departmental, and municipal councils, nor to the Senate, which reflects subnational partisan realities. The use of proportional representation in subnational and supranational elections, such as for regional councils, the Senate, and the European Parliament, explains why there are many more parties in the game, including those of purely local interest, and why alliances are more diverse and unpredictable.[22]

Subnational systems of election are frequently subjected to reforms by ordinary acts of parliament. Normally, such reforms are designed to favor the party in power and reduce the chances of the opposition. Partisanship, however, does not usually enter into the redrawing of Assembly electoral constituency boundaries, as this is done by bipartisan committees that take into account population shifts. In the most recent redrawing, which took place in 2009, the main loser in the suppression of thirty-three seats in France's metropolitan areas was the PS, while in the reduction of Assembly constituencies of Paris from twenty-one to eighteen the UMP lost two seats.

As Tables 2-8 and 2-9 indicate, multipolarity—specifically, a significant representation of the left, the center, Gaullists, and the traditional right—can still be seen in the Senate, the general (departmental) councils chosen in cantonal elections, and the regional councils. In

Table 2-7 Composition of the National Assembly: France, 1956–2007

Parliamentary elections	Communists	Socialists and allies	Radicals and allies	MRP and center	Conservatives, Moderates, Independents	Gaullists	Miscellaneous and unaffiliated	Total seats
1956	150	99	94	84	97	22	50	596
1958	10	47	40	56	129	206	64	552
1962	41	66	43	55		268[a]	9	482
1967	73	121[b]		41[c]		242[a]	10	487
1968	34	57[b]		34[c]	344[d]		18	487
1973	73	100[e]	34[f]		270[d]		13	490
1978	86	105	10[g]	123[h]	9[j]	153	5	491
1981	44	286[e]		62[h]		88	11	491
1986	35	214[e]		132[h]		158	38[l]	577
1988	27	277[e]		130[h]	129	14[m]		577
1993	23	70[e]		213[k]		247	24[n]	577
1997	36	250	33[o]	113[k]		140	5[p]	577
2002	22	141[q]		29[h]		365[r]	20[s]	577
2007	24[t]	204[u]		23[v]		320[r]	6[w]	577

Source: Compiled by the author.

Note: MRP = Popular Republican Movement. Occasionally columns do not align to indicate instances in which parties moved further left or right.

[a] Gaullists and Independent Republicans.
[b] Socialist and Radical alliance.
[c] Progress and Modern Democracy.
[d] Gaullists, Independent Republicans, and pro-government centrists.
[e] Socialist and Left Radicals (MRG).
[f] Reformers (moderate radicals and opposition centrists).
[g] MRG.
[h] Union for French Democracy (UDF).
[i] National Center of Independents and Peasants.
[j] Identified only (and directly) with UDF rather than one of its components.
[k] UDF (Republicans, CDS, and moderate Radical-Socialists).
[l] Including thirty-two National Front and six unaffiliated.
[m] Including thirteen miscellaneous right and one National Front (who has since left the party).
[n] National Center of Independents and Peasants (CNIP) and others affiliated with center-right coalition.
[o] Including thirteen Left Radicals, eight ecologists, and seven from Citizens' Movement.
[p] Including one National Front and one Movement for France.
[q] Including one apparenté.
[r] Union for a Popular Movement (UMP).
[s] Including Left Radical, miscellaneous left, Greens, and miscellaneous right.
[t] Including fifteen Communists, four Greens, and five miscellaneous left.
[u] Including eighteen apparenté (among them Left Radicals and Citizens' Movement).
[v] Including twenty Nouveau Centre.
[w] Including three MoDem.

the municipal elections that followed the presidential contest in June 1995, there was no Chiraquist carryover for Gaullist candidates: most of the mayors belonging to left-wing parties were reelected, and the National Front secured control over one fairly large city (Toulon) and three smaller towns. Regional and local elections correspond to parliamentary elections neither in form nor alliance-building. In the Senate elections of 2004, prominent leftist politicians were elected or reelected.

Table 2-8 Regional Elections, 2010 (percent of total vote)

	First round (March 14)	Second round (March 21)
Extreme left	3.40	
Communists and allies	5.84	0.26
Socialists	23.52	3.11
Miscellaneous left	3.06	3.30
Greens	12.18	0.98
Union of the Left	5.62	46.40
Other lists	1.88	
Regionalists	0.75	0.56
Center-MoDem	4.20	0.84
UMP and allies	26.02	35.38
Miscellaneous right	1.24	
National Front	11.42	9.18
Other extreme right	0.89	
Registered voters	43,642,325	43,350,204
Voters	20,219,958	22,201,265
	(46.33%)	(51.21%)
Abstentions	23,422,367	21,148,939
	(53.67%)	(48.79%)

Sources: Ministry of Interior, *Le Monde*, various issues, and Anne Muxel, "Les élections régionales de 2010," *Regards sur l'Actualité* 362, June-July 2010, 63–64.

The behavior of voters in subnational elections often reflects their general political mood and their views of presidential and governmental performance. The outcome of the municipal elections of 1983, in which many Socialist and Communist councillors (and, indirectly, mayors) were replaced by Gaullist or Giscardo-centrist ones, was viewed as an expression of voters' impatience with the record of the Mitterrand presidency and the Socialist government after two years in office. Conversely, the outcome of the municipal elections of 1989, in which many Gaullists were ousted, was interpreted as a reflection of a relative satisfaction with the performance of the Socialist government led by Rocard.

In the municipal elections of 2001, local issues predominated. At the same time, these elections had national significance, insofar as the outcome reflected the national image of the major political parties and served as a political "weather vane" for their prospects in the national—that is, presidential and parliamentary—elections scheduled for 2002. On the one hand, the victories of right-wing parties in many of the provincial towns were encouraging to the Gaullists and their right-of-center allies. On the other hand, the victories of the left in two of the three largest cities—Paris and Lyons—were good news to Prime Minister Jospin and the Socialist leadership. The election of a Socialist, Bertrand Delanoë, as mayor of Paris for the first time in a century, however, stemmed less from ideology or policy than from the fact that the outgoing Gaullist mayor, Jean Tibéri, had been charged with acts of corruption that dated back to the time when Chirac was the mayor. These acts included the appointment of phantom municipal employees whose

Table 2-9 Composition of the Senate: France, 1959–2010 (selected years)

	Communists	Socialists	Democratic Left[a]	Democratic Center	MRP/ Indepen-dents	Gaullists	Unaffil-iated	Total
1959	14	51	64	34	92	41	11	307
1965	14	52	50	38	79	30	11	274
1968	17	54	50	40	80	29	13	283
1981	23	63	38[b]	67[c]	51[d]	41	15	305
1989	16	66	23[e]	68[c]	52[d]	91	5	321
1992	15	70	23[e]	66[c]	47[d]	90	10	321
1998	16	78	22[e]	52	47	99	7	321
2004	23	97[f]	15[e]	33[g]	0	156[h]	7	331
2010	23[i]	116	17[e]	29[g]	0	151[h]	7	343

Sources: *L'Année politique, 1959–2004; Le Monde,* various issues; and *Regards sur l'Actualité,* various issues.
Note: MRP—Popular Republican Movement. Figures for each party include affiliated *apparentés.*
[a] Mainly Radical-Socialists.
[b] Includes Movement of Left Radicals (MRG).
[c] Center Union.
[d] Republicans and independents.
[e] Democratic and European Social Rally.
[f] Including Greens.
[g] Union for French Democracy (UDF).
[h] Union for a Popular Movement (UMP).
[i] Communist, Republican and Citizen Group (CRC).

salaries went into the coffers of the Gaullist party, as well as the maintenance of electoral registers that included nonexistent voters. In the regional and cantonal elections of 2004, the tables were turned: the victory of left-wing parties over the right-of-center parties represented a loss of credibility of the Raffarin government. The municipal elections of 2008 revolved around local issues as well, but they also allowed citizens to express their views of the Sarkozy presidency. As it turned out, the right and left gained approximately equal numbers of votes; but it was a setback for Sarkozy, because the Socialist mayors were reelected in Paris and Lille and the PS captured the mayor's offices in Toulouse, Strasbourg, and a dozen midsize cities. The overall turnout of two-thirds of the electorate was fairly typical.

The regional elections of 2010 reflected a further decline in Sarkozy's popularity on the national level. In those elections, the Socialists, in alliance with the Communists, Left Radicals, and Greens, received 46 percent of the vote in the second round—compared with 35 percent received by the right (the UMP and UDF combined)—and won control of twenty-two of France's twenty-five regions. As suggested above, subnational elections usually serve as indicators of public reaction to the performance of the national parties as well as a hint on preparing for the next national elections. The Socialist Party, whose problems continued after the elections of 2007, was particularly concerned. The PS was so demoralized and disorganized after being defeated in three successive presidential elections that some observers argued that it was exhausted; others suggested that its members should permit the party to die and start a new one; and still others wondered whether it was already dead.[23] To be sure, the PS remains the largest party of the left and continues to constitute the nucleus of the opposition, but it is beset with a number of problems. It does not have a coherent program; nor does it have a credible left or left-center alliance strategy. It has no new ideas to convince voters that the PS is a useful alternative to the UMP. It has no unchallenged leader, and there are too many rivals for leadership. The only position that seems to unite the "elephants," the younger politicians, and the various factions (courants) is anti-Sarkozysm.[24] In pursuit of their own presidential ambitions, various Socialist politicians have been trying to construct rival parties[25] or create possible electoral alliances by appealing to a variety of small parties, both on the right and the left. These efforts are often incompatible and alienate one or another group. Since her electoral defeat in 2007 and the disintegration of her support network, Royal has toyed with a number of mutually incompatible alliance strategies in her solitary pursuit of a rematch in the 2012 presidential elections without the backing of the PS or Martine Aubry, the party's general secretary. Royal proposed a broad coalition ranging from Olivier Besancenot, the leader of the New Anticapitalist Party (Nouveau Parti Anticapitaliste [NPA][26] to Bayrou's MoDem—in other words, from the extreme left to the center—and led by her. The PS would have none of it, preferring instead an enlarged and more unified Left, but the NPA preferred to go it alone, as did the PCF, which planned to do the same.[27]

Subsequently, Royal proposed an alliance with MoDem, to begin with the first round of the regional elections of 2010 (for which she promised to guarantee five places to that party on her candidate list of Poitou-Charentes, the region she presides over), but Bayrou's poor performance in the EU Parliament elections of 2009—his fourth defeat[28]—raised doubts about whether an alliance with him was worth making. Bayrou's options, too, were limited. He burned his bridges to the UMP, but he cannot easily turn to the Left; and what alternative there is tends to be occupied increasingly by the European Ecology (Europe Ecologie [EE]) coalition. That coalition, whose position is that environmentalism is incompatible with capitalism, is an alliance led by Daniel Cohn-Bendit of the Green Party and José Bové, a leader of the radical-left Federation of Peasants (Fédération Paysanne), who opposes the cultivation of genetically altered food and has been a voice against globalization. It is a strange alliance because Bové was against the EU in 2005, and Cohn-Bendit in favor. But the alliance ran neck and neck with the PS in the EU elections in June 2009, in part by taking votes away from traditional supporters of the PS.

The UMP seemed to be much better placed for the foreseeable future. It was reasonably united, and its electoral prospects promising enough to attract parties to its right. For example, the Hunters' Party (Chasse, Pêche, Nature et Traditions [CPNT]), despite its narrow electoral support, has had considerable clout in southwestern France, and it has been able to pressure the government into altering its environmental policies.[29] For reasons of institutional self-preservation, the CPNT decided to ally with the UMP for the regional elections of 2010, as did DeVilliers's Movement for France (Mouvement pour la France [MPF]), even though the anti-EU attitudes of these parties must surely conflict with Sarkozy's pro-Europeanism.

Even if they cannot influence the policies of the mainstream parties, some of these marginal groupings may act as spoilers. This has been true of Jean-Pierre Chevènement's Citizens' Movement (MDC)[30] and of the National Front, both of which prevented Jospin from competing with Chirac in the runoff round of the 2002 presidential elections.

The National Front has been the most important of the marginal parties. But it, too, has problems of internal cohesion. With the virtual collapse in 2004 of Bruno Mégret's National Republican Movement, the National Front has lost its most important rival on the extreme right; but the fight over the succession to the aging Le Pen is not fully settled, and there is a conflict between the relatively moderate position of Le Pen's daughter, Marine, and the adamant xenophobia of others in the party leadership. One indication that the National Front could not be discounted was the invitation of one of its representatives to the office of a prime minister (Villepin) in 2005 for the first time since the party's founding, thereby giving it unaccustomed respectability and causing Socialist leader François Hollande to boycott the invitation. The riots of November 2005 increased the appeal of the National Front.

The rising fortunes of Europe Ecologie and the mere existence of MoDem raise the question whether the traditional ideological divide between right and left is still relevant. By and large, traditional distinctions continue to have meaning—the left favoring equality and the collectivity, the right favoring liberty and the individual—but they are often eclipsed by issues on which there is an overlap, such as Europe, decentralization, multiculturalism, and the reform of the electoral system. In addition, there are new divisions, such as community versus the individual, environmentalism versus productivity, and protectionism versus globalization.[31] Equally important, policy issues are often eclipsed by personal ambitions of politicians, who shift from one party to another.

Other problems cause disagreements within both major parties and reach across the right-left divide. Within the UMP, there are differences of opinion about European integration, immigration, law and order, and, most recently, about the policies regarding ethnoreligious minorities who are unemployed, inhabit suburban slums, and are involved in street violence. Within the PS, there were sharp divisions in 2005 between those favoring the European constitution and those opposed.

Some of these challenges have manifested themselves at the various congresses of the Socialist Party since the early 1980s. Instead of facing them, the PS took up a variety of clashing propositions introduced by competing factions (courants) with names such as Ségolène Royal's "Désirs d'avenir" and Bertrand Delanoë's "Clarté, courage, créativité" and ended up with seeming "syntheses" and vague and sometimes contradictory slogans, such as "collective values," "renaissance of the individual," and "facing up to the challenges of the twenty-first century." Apart from the conflicts of orientation, there were disagreements about a more practical question: whether to have primaries for PS presidential candidates, and when, at what level and location, and how.

Debates within and between political parties have often been informed by ideological rigidities as well as personal ambitions and rivalries, which have resulted in recombinations, scissions, and changes of party label. In contrast to political parties in other countries, parties in France frequently change their names, as if in so doing they can improve their images and electoral fortunes. But another reason is to suggest that the party has expanded its base, as in the case of the transformation of the SFIO into the PS and the successive name changes of the Gaullist and post-Gaullist parties from RPF to UNR, UDR, RPR, UNM, and UMP. In the past half-century, all parties have changed their names, with the single exception of the PCF. Moreover, there has been a tendency to use a designation other than *parti*, such as *mouvement, rassemblement, force, union*—each with its own factions, slogans, program, and, more recently, Web sites. Some of these formations are microparties within existing larger parties; they are created to obtain separate funding and to serve as instruments of ambitious politicians. In some cases, a political party may reflect a purely personal agenda—as, for example, La France Solidaire, which was created by Dominique de Villepin to fill a space between a weakening MoDem and an UMP made vulnerable by a growing criticism of Sarkozy's presidency.[32]

Labels, however, have meanings and evoke associations. MoDem was created by François Bayrou out of the old UDF as his personal vehicle toward the presidency. Similarly, a rump of the UDF reorganized as Nouveau Centre to support Sarkozy in the 2007 elections; but at end of 2009, its few politicians spoke of reclaiming the label UDF—a challenge to the historical legitimacy of MoDem to it—and even envisaged running a separate candidate in the presidential elections of 2012.

In summary, right and left divisions still roughly define the French political party system, but the nature of the bipolar arrangement has changed, especially since 1974, when the Gaullist dominance that began in 1958 came to an end. For about twenty years—from the election of Valéry Giscard d'Estaing in 1974 to that of Jacques Chirac in 1995—there was a sort of "bipolar quadrille," with the Gaullists and the UDF on one side and the Socialists and the Communists on the other. Since 1995 bipolarity has been simplified in the sense that each side is clearly dominated by a single party—the UMP on the right and the Socialist Party on the left, with each party maintaining a solid membership base.

The cleavages between these two parties have been moderated by a growing convergence on a number of issues: reducing the gap between rich and poor, retaining the welfare state, reforming the judiciary, and promoting a greater role for civil society and the market. Sarkozy, in pursuit of making the UMP more inclusive, has called upon it to embrace "social liberalism."[33] For her part, Martine Aubry, who became general secretary of the PS in 2008, has declared that "[the party] must invent postmaterialism."[34]

In view of this convergence, *alternance*—the electoral rotation between the right and the left—has been less about clear policy alternatives than about punishing the incumbents for perceived poor performance, at least since the early 1980s. The 2007 presidential election was an exception, for it constituted the Socialists' third defeat in a row; but the reasons for that were not programmatic. Since the mid-1980s, electoral changes have not led to abrupt changes of policy. Mitterrand's presidency had begun with socioeconomic policies in a redistributive direction, but they were gradually adjusted toward market liberalism; Chirac's presidency was noted for its tactical and nonideological opportunism; and Sarkozy has veered considerably from orthodox Gaullism and co-opted politicians and policies from the left—all in the interest of reform, sometimes pursued impulsively. This activity has led some to wonder whether Sarkozy was a closet leftist.[35] But it has also been a manifestation of his "catch-all" strategy: to co-opt as many sectors of the electorate to fortify his party and buttress his presidency.[36]

Sarkozy's steep fall from grace two years after his election seemed to put the PS in a good position to regain the presidency in 2012. Indeed, opinion polls suggested that any of several "elephants" of the party would defeat Sarkozy, but that possibility revived the contest among them and weakened the party's unity, at a time when it has not yet resolved its ideological ambiguities or produced a clear program of government.

Interest Groups

French citizens who become disillusioned with political parties, finding them confusing or doubting their effectiveness, can voice their demands more directly through interest groups. Originally, French political thinkers with centralizing perspectives were as suspicious of economic and professional associations as of political parties. After the Revolution of 1789, organized groups were banned for nearly a century. A law enacted in 1901 permitted the creation of interest groups without prior official authorization; nevertheless, a tradition of distrust of interest groups persisted, and lobbying was seen as incompatible with the public interest. In recent years, lobbying has come to be regarded as "normal" as the work of political parties.[37] Today, France's many interest groups are freely organized, and they play a significant role in the country's political life. On a national level, groups represent every conceivable sector and interest: labor, business, agriculture, the free professions, teachers, and proponents of diverse outlooks or policies such as Catholicism, antiracism, women's rights, and environmental protection. Interest groups in France participate in the political process in much the same way they do in the United States. They lobby with the executive, the leadership of political parties, and (to a limited extent) individual members of parliament;[38] they participate in electoral campaigns, and they seek to influence the higher civil service. They engage in collective bargaining, in tripartite negotiations at the national level, in social administration and adjudication, and in numerous permanent as well as ad hoc consultative committees, appointed both by the government and parliament. These activities have focused on a variety of subjects, among them the media, retired persons, highway safety, and pollution. In 2009 there were more than seven hundred such committees. Some are quite important, but many others have outlived their usefulness and rarely meet.[39] Some are periodically abolished; others live on. After his election, Sarkozy appointed a number of ad hoc consultative committees, whose recommendations led to a number of innovative policies. The foremost example is that of the Balladur committee, whose proposals formed the basis of the constitutional reforms of 2008 and 2009.

The number of national, regional, and local voluntary associations has grown incessantly, reaching more than thirty thousand and attesting to the growth of pluralism rather than to a decline of state authority.[40] The state is involved in regulating, legitimating, and sometimes subsidizing interest groups, and delegating public-administrative tasks to them.[41]

Two of the more important characteristics of French interest groups are their ideological fragmentation and their linkage to political parties. These characteristics are clearly evident in the several competing organizations that represent labor. The oldest, and once the largest, is the General Federation of Labor (Confédération Générale du Travail [CGT]). Essentially a federation of constituent unions such as the automobile, chemical, metal, and transport workers' unions, it has had a revolutionary ideology—that is, the conviction that the interests of the working class can best be promoted through direct political action. In its belief in the class struggle and its opposition to the capitalist system, the CGT has shown a clear affinity for the Communist Party. Many of the CGT's members, which today number about 900,000, in the past voted Communist, and a significant proportion of its leaders were prominent in the Communist Party hierarchy. Indeed, the relationship between the CGT and the Communist Party was sometimes so close that the union was described as a "transmission belt" of the party. In that role, the CGT frequently engaged in strikes and other political action for the Communists' political purposes, such as opposition to NATO, to French policy in Algeria, to German rearmament, and, more recently, to the Socialist government's overall socioeconomic policies. With the disintegration of the Soviet Union in 1991 and the dramatic weakening of the Communist Party, the CGT began to assume a more autonomous and somewhat more moderate stance.[42]

Another labor union is the French Confederation of Labor (Confédération Française Démocratique de Travail [CFDT]), which has about 800,000 members. Originally inspired by Catholicism, it split in the mid-1960s from the French Confederation of Christian Workers (Confédération Française des Travailleurs Chrétiens [CFTC]), which continues to exist, and "deconfessionalized" itself. One of the most dynamic trade unions, it is closely related to, though not formally affiliated with, the Socialist Party. An important idea of the CFDT, the promotion of self-management (autogestion), was incorporated into the Socialist platform in the 1970s.

The Workers' Force (Force Ouvrière [FO]) and the General Confederation of "Cadres" (Confédération Générale des Cadres [CGC]) are two other unions of some importance. The FO, with its about 1.1 million members, is an industrial workers' federation noted for its preference for union autonomy in relation to political parties, for its staunch anticommunism, and for its emphasis on U.S.-style collective bargaining. The CGC, which has about 450,000 members, is not very ideological in orientation; it represents supervisory, middle-echelon technical and other white-collar employees. Finally, there are several teachers' unions, which are fragmented by professional level or ideology.[43]

This fragmentation, coupled with the relatively feeble extent of unionization—fewer than 8 percent of French workers are unionized today—has added to the predicament of organized labor. Traditionally, unions have been at a disadvantage whenever their "patron" parties, notably the Communists and Socialists, were in the opposition. To overcome that disadvantage, unions learned to cooperate in practical matters. They often present common demands to employers and the government and join in demonstrations and strikes. During the Socialist government of 1981–1986, trade unions gained important concessions under legislation (the Auroux laws) that strengthened their right to organize and bargain collectively at plant levels. But these concessions have in part been nullified by developments that weakened the position of unions: the "scab" effect of immigrant workers; the growth of the tertiary sector in which unionization has been weak; and the decline of traditional "smokestack" industries and the concomitant reduction in total union membership. Finally, the bargaining power of unions has been dramatically reduced by the privatization of industries, mandated by European Union rules, and delocalization, a consequence of globalization. Yet unions are able to disrupt economic life by short nationwide strikes, especially in large cities.

Divisions among trade unions persist, although the ideologies that differentiated them have become less relevant and their former linkages to political parties have loosened. Various unions have evolved ideologically: the FO has become more radical, and the CGT has become more moderate and has even accepted capitalism, although with reservations. The CGT's once close relationship with the PCF has largely disappeared. In particular, Bernard Thibault, head of the CGT, has had a fairly reasonable approach to economic policy, and his relationship with Sarkozy has been friendly.[44] For that reason, Thibault has been criticized by the more radical rank-and-file who remain committed to the class struggle and who have challenged his leadership. Nevertheless, in 2009 he was reelected to another term. Despite the reduced relevance of ideological divisions between trade unions, they compete with one another for representation on enterprise and national levels.

Organized business is much more unified than organized labor. The major business association is the Movement of French Enterprises (Mouvement des Entreprises de France [MEDEF]), which was known until 1998 as the National Council of French Employers (Conseil National du Patronat Français [CNPF]). This umbrella organization of more than eighty manufacturing, banking, and commercial associations represents more than 800,000 firms. In its lobbying efforts, this employers' group has been fairly effective. Many of its leaders have old-school ties with the government's administrative elite; it is well-heeled financially; it has provided ideas and other kinds of assistance to the right-of-center parties that have ruled France intermittently since 1958; and it has been an important partner of the government in the push toward economic modernization. At the same time, there are internal disagreements among leaders of business regarding wage structures, government subsidies, and, more recently, the size of bankers' bonuses.

Shopkeepers, artisans, and small- and medium-size manufacturing firms have their own organizations, such as the General Federation of Small and Medium Enterprises (Confédération Générale des Petites et Moyennes Entreprises [CGPME]), which represents 1.5 million firms. These groups have lobbied separately to fight economic consolidation policies that have posed a threat to them, including the growth of supermarkets, but their success has been mixed.

The greatest organizational complexity is found in agriculture, where associations speak for different kinds of farms, product specialization, ideology, and even relationships to the government. There are associations of beet growers, wine producers, cattle raisers, young farmers, Catholic farmers, agricultural laborers, and so on. The most important of them in terms of inclusiveness and access to decision makers has been the National Federation of Agricultural Enterprises (Fédération Nationale des Syndicats d'Expoitants Agricoles [FNSEA]), an umbrella organization with about 400,000 members. In the past, farmers' interests were well represented by centrist and conservative parties, but the decline of these parties has been associated with the decline in the number of farmers and the diminishing importance of agriculture in the French economy because of industrialization and urbanization.

Farmers once constituted an important source of political power, but with the constraints of the EU and the decline of the agricultural sector to less than 4 percent of the active population in 2007 and to 2.3 percent of the electorate, farmers have continued to lose their political clout. Yet they retain a measure of support in the Senate, and they periodically call attention to their plight by mass demonstrations in Paris and the provinces.

Farmers cannot be totally neglected, if only for social reasons, and they often find a receptive ear in the government. In recent years, farmers' associations have collaborated with the government in shaping policies that encourage land consolidation, mechanization, retraining of redundant farmers, and promotion of agricultural exports, especially in the context of the European Union and its supranational Common Agricultural Policy.

One of the important features of French interest group politics is the fairly institutionalized relationship that most groups have with government authorities. Numerous advisory councils—on education, immigration, the environment, highway safety, and so on—are attached to ministries. These councils, composed largely of representatives of interest groups, furnish data that may influence policy suggestions and regulations that emanate from ministries. Similarly composed councils are attached to the highly differentiated national and regional social security organisms that administer statutory health care, unemployment insurance, pension schemes, and family subsidy programs. The implementation of pricing policies takes place with the participation of farmers' groups (within the limits imposed by EU rules); the application of rules on apprenticeships involves employers' associations; and the adjudication of labor disputes takes place in specialized tribunals (*conseils de prud'hommes*), which include the major "social partners"—that is, trade union and business representatives. Interest group delegates to these bodies and to regional professional, agricultural, and commercial chambers, factory councils, and similar institutions are elected by the groups' rank-and-file members without the mediation of political parties. On occasion, interest groups "colonize" parliament in the sense of having their officials elected (via a sympathetic party) to the National Assembly. Finally, interest group leaders may be co-opted into official positions in a ministry with which they have "clientelistic" relations.

Such institutional involvement has given rise to a debate over pluralism and corporatism. If corporatism suggests that the state ultimately prevails in contests with the private sector, and especially interest groups, then why does the state often capitulate in the face of strong action by organized interest groups or anomic groups such as transport workers, teachers' unions, farmers, and truckers, who organize social movements (*mouvements sociaux*) such as strikes and other forms of protest?[45] In the end, pluralism prevails, especially when freedom of group action or rivalry between interest groups is the issue. Still, the government is involved in legitimating specific interest groups that seek consultations with the government and participation in elections to social security boards and labor relations tribunals.[46]

Whether the institutionalization of relations enhances or reduces the power of groups is a matter of controversy. In the first place, not all interests are sufficiently important or well enough organized to benefit from reliable patterns of relationships with the government—for example, foreign workers, ethnic minorities, domestics, and certain categories of small business owners. Second, although a formalized network of involvement, sometimes labeled "neocorporatism," guarantees group access to public authorities, such access does not by itself ensure that the views of a particular group will prevail. Furthermore, highly formalized relationships with the government may weaken the will of a group to bargain collectively or to resort to more traditional means of pressure such as strikes.

To many observers, the events of May–June 1968 suggested that the access of interest groups to the authorities was too underdeveloped and inadequate to influence political decisions. Students and workers, in a rare display of unity, engaged in a massive general strike that paralyzed the country for two weeks and threatened to bring down the government and endanger the republic itself. These events had several causes: for workers, dissatisfaction with de Gaulle's economic and social policy that seemed to favor big business and permitted wages to lag woefully behind prices; for students, disgruntlement over the government's failure to modernize, with sufficient speed and thoroughness, a university system whose curriculum was antiquated and not relevant to the labor market, whose physical facilities were cramped, and whose administration was too rigid. The general strike, an example of anomic political behavior, achieved certain reforms that formalized interest group relations with the government had failed to achieve: the partial democratization of university governance, enormous wage increases for workers, improved trade union rights, and a loosening of relations between social classes. In the process, however, de Gaulle's leadership was discredited and his image severely tarnished. Similarly, the massive strikes of public transport workers in 1995 and of the private truckers in 1996, while not directly bringing down the government, succeeded in derailing Prime Minister Juppé's attempts to reform the social security system and ultimately weakened his authority. Recent examples of the effectiveness of mass action, and of the power of labor unions despite their numerical weakness, were the teachers' strikes in 2004 that forced the government to abandon its educational reform proposals; the maritime workers' strike in 2005 that resulted in modification of the proposals to privatize passenger and shipping connections between the mainland and Corsica; and the repeated strikes of railroad workers in 2004 and 2005 that prompted President Chirac to promise that the national railway system would never be privatized. Examples of mass action sponsored by trade unions and student organizations were the countrywide demonstrations and strikes early in 2006 to force Prime Minister Villepin to withdraw a bill that would make it easier for employers to lay off young entrants into the labor force. These successes must be attributed in part to the support of many other sectors of the general public, which, although inconvenienced, expressed solidarity with the strikers because they feared that their own welfare, state entitlements, might be endangered.

Most interest groups have been complaining about loss of power, a loss they attribute to globalization and the growth of transnational controls over economic processes, especially those of the EU. This is especially true of the trade unions, whose memberships account for less than 10 percent of the labor force and whose influence over political parties has weakened. Nevertheless, interest groups, and in particular labor unions and employers' associations, have continued to play important roles in social administration and the adjudication of labor disputes. Such disputes are addressed in the *conseils de prud'hommes*, the labor tribunals, in which they are formally represented. In 2007 alone, the 210 councils took up nearly twenty thousand cases. The tribunals have not been as effective as expected, and there are discussions within the government about abolishing them.[47]

One of the most important arenas for a formal presence of interest groups is the Economic, Social, and Environmental Council (Conseil economique, social, et environnemental [CESE]),[48] which must be consulted on all pending socioeconomic legislation. Under reform proposals presented to the cabinet in 2009, its size of 233 members will remain the same as before, but the minimum age will be reduced from twenty-five to eighteen and their mandate limited to two terms of five years each. The representation of labor, business, agriculture, and other interests will be internally redistributed around three "poles" or domains—economic and social dialogue (including workers, white-collar, private enterprise, artisans, and free professions), 140; environment (including associations and foundations), 33; and "social and territorial cohesion" and miscellaneous associational groups (mutual societies, family association, youth and students, and overseas interests), 60. The representation is to include 40 "qualified individuals" distributed among the three poles (among them 15 who are particularly competent in environmental matters.[49]

The role of a host of noneconomic interests or sectors, such as women, ethnic minorities, and environmentalists must not be neglected. France has several national women's associations. These groups may not be as large or as well organized as their U.S. counterparts, but since the mid- to late 1960s they have successfully pressured the authorities to abolish legal disabilities based on gender (such as inheritance, adoption, and property ownership), to legalize birth control and abortion, and to make the initiation of divorce easier for women. A major and more recent political victory for women has been legislation providing for gender parity: the requirement that 50 percent of the candidates in legislative elections be women.[50] Environmental groups have grown rapidly during the same period. In all parliamentary elections since 1978, and in the presidential elections of 1981, 1988, 2002, and 2007, ecologists running under various labels have fielded their own candidates. Indeed, today the Green Party has several deputies in the National Assembly, and its former leader was an important member of Jospin's leftist coalition government. Antiracist groups such as SOS-Racisme have developed rapidly since the early 1980s to fight for the rights of ethnic minorities, particularly immigrants. At the same time, the government has made it legal for (and sometimes encouraged) immigrants to form their own associations. These associations have become increasingly important lobbies, as have ethnoreligious organizations such as those of Muslims and Jews.[51] Recent strikes by nurses, teachers, physicians, investigating magistrates, and municipal bus and tram drivers, some of them spontaneous in nature rather than organized by their respective associations, have taken place largely to promote economic as well as noneconomic demands—for example, for more staff or better protection against violence. One development of increasing importance, and a cause of increasing violence, has been the anomic street action of poorly organized categories, such as undocumented immigrants, the homeless, and the unemployed.[52]

NOTES

1. Pierre Poujade was a bookseller and stationer whose party began as the Union for the Protection of Shopkeepers and Craftsmen (Union pour la Défense des Commerçants et Artisans) in 1953. Three years later, Poujade ran successfully for election to the National Assembly under the label French Union and Fraternity (Union et Fraternité Française).
2. Proportional representation is to be used in departments electing four (instead of three) or more senators, and the single-member constituency (majority) system is to be used in departments electing three (instead of two) or fewer senators.
3. For an analysis of the laws passed since 1966 postponing the dates of elections, see Jean-Marie Pontier, "Le report des élections locales et sénatoriales," *Revue Administrative* (January 2006): 70–78. See also Pierre Martin, "Les modes de scrutin aux élections en France et leurs conséquences politiques," *Regards sur l'Actualité* 329 (March 2007): 17–26.
4. As of 2005, the membership of the various parties was estimated as follows: Union for a Popular Movement (Union pour un Mouvement Populaire, or UMP), 190,000; Socialist Party, 130,000; Communist Party, 120,000; National Front, 100,000+; UDF, 40,000. These figures are approximate and based on a number of often conflicting sources. Typical annual membership dues are about $30. In the past few years, all political parties have lost dues-paying members. The sharpest decline was experienced by the Socialist Party, whose membership fell from about 700,000 in 1979 to 275,000 in 1996 and to less than 140,000 by 2005.

5. On these cleavages, see Pascal Perrineau, "Les cadres du Parti Socialiste," in SOFRES, *L'Etat de l'opinion 1991*, ed. Olivier Duhamel and Jérôme Jaffré (Paris: Seuil, 1991).

6. Jean-Pierre Soisson, "Les grands mots," *Le Point*, July 13, 1991, 16.

7. Alain Rollat, "M. Leroy se réfère au communisme . . . balsacien!" *Le Monde*, September 25, 1990.

8. Specifically, the electorate voted for Chirac because they had confidence that he would address seriously the following issues, in descending order: unemployment, the construction of Europe, immigration, and the fight against social exclusion. Thomas Ferenczi, "Les Français attendent de M. Chirac qu'il mette en oeuvre le changement," *Le Monde*, May 11, 1995, 9.

9. See Pascal Perrineau and Colette Ysmal, eds., *Le vote surprise: Les élections législatives des 25 Mai et 1er Juin 1997* (Paris: Presses de Sciences-Po, 1997); and Michael S. Lewis-Beck, ed., *How France Votes* (New York: Chatham House, 2000).

10. Pasqua often acted like a loose cannon. In the municipal elections of March 2001, he supported the reelection of Jean Tibéri, the mayor of Paris. Tibéri, after being disavowed by the Gaullist leadership because of corruption and prevented from leading the right-of-center ticket for the Paris mayoralty, ran as an independent candidate.

11. One of the signs of the incoherence of the UDF was the rapprochement, especially within the parliament, of its moderate component, the Radical-Socialist Party, with the left-wing Radicals, which continued its alliance with the Socialists.

12. For example, differences remained between traditional leftists, such as Minister of Labor Martine Aubry and former Assembly Speaker Henri Emmanuelli, both of whom favored reducing the workweek to thirty-five hours, and pragmatists, such as Minister of Economics Dominique Strauss-Kahn and his successor Laurent Fabius, both of whom were more reserved about such a policy.

13. William Safran, "The Socialists, Jospin, and the Mitterrand Legacy," in *How France Votes*, ed. Michael S. Lewis-Beck (New York: Chatham House, 2000), 14–41.

14. Preelection polls are taken frequently, but their results cannot be made public later than 48 hours before voting.

15. See Frédérique Matonti, ed., *La démobilisation politique* (Paris: La Dispute, 2005).

16. Bruno Cautrès and Nonna Mayer, "Les métamorphoses du 'vote de classe,'" in *Le nouveau désordre électoral: Les leçons du 21 avril 2002*, ed. Cautrès and Mayer (Paris: Presses de Sciences-Po, 2004), 145.

17. David Revault d'Allonnes, "Ségolène Royal incarne une forme de virginité partisane," *Libération*, September 16, 2006.

18. See "Les cent propositions du 'pacte présidentiel' de Ségolène Royal," *Le Monde*, February 12, 2007. The program was published on "Désirs d'avenir," Royal's Internet site.

19. According to a CSA/*Le Monde* poll of November 2005, 60 percent of respondents believed that the PS would not be ready to govern in 2007. See Isabel Mandraud, "Le regard très critique des Français sur le PS," *Le Monde*, November 15, 2005.

20. See "Je revendique la rupture," interview of Sarkozy by Sylvie Pierre-Brossolette and Michel Schifres, *Figaro-Magazine*, September 2, 2006, 40–45.

21. This new party included most of the former UDF politicians. The group of holdovers of that party renamed itself the New Center (Nouveau Centre [NC]) and continued its alliance with the UMP.

22. For example, the UDF and the Gaullists have made selective deals with the National Front in regional elections, despite opposition from the national leadership of these mainstream parties.

23. Pascal Lamy, "La mort du PS? C'est possible," *Le Monde*, August 26, 2009.

24. François Fressoz, "L'effet boomerang de l'antisarkozysme," *Le Monde,* June 8, 2009.

25. In 2002 Arnaud Montebourg, a "young Turk," formed the Nouveau Parti Socialiste (NPS) to promote his own presidential ambitions, but it got nowhere.

26. The NPA was formed in February 2009 from the Trotskyist Communist Revolutionary League (Ligue Communiste Révolutionnaire [LCR]) and other extreme-left groups and claimed nine thousand members.

27. In preparation for the regional elections of 2010, the PCF formed its own alliance, the Unified Left (Gauche Unitaire) together with other leftist groups, including leftist Socialists who had separated earlier from the PS. This alliance seemed to surpass that of Besancenot in popularity.

28. The other defeats were in the presidential and parliamentary elections of 2007 and the municipal elections of 2008.

29. As a result of the Hunters' pressure, in August 2005 the Gaullist minister of the environment suspended EU rules for hunting birds and lengthened the duck hunting season, but he was overruled by the Council of State.

30. Known since 2005 as Citizen and Republic Movement (Mouvement Républicain et Citoyen, or MCR).

31. Pierre Martin, "Comment analyser les changements dans les systèmes partisans d'Europe occidentale depuis 1945?" *Revue Internationale de Politique Comparée* 14 (2008): 1–21.

32. Samuel Laurent, "Villepin lance son mouvement, 'libre et indépendant' de l'UMP," *Le Monde,* March 25, 2010.

33. Rémi Barroux and Claire Guélaud, "L'UMP cherche une synthèse dans le social-libéralisme," *Le Monde,* June 15, 2008.

34. Jean-Pierre Sueur, "Le postmatérialisme selon Martine Aubry," *Le Monde,* August 18, 2009.

35. Saïd Mahrane, "Sarkozy est-il de gauche?" *Le Point,* August 20, 2009, 16–19.

36. For municipal elections of March 2008, the UMP supported several hundred candidates of the left and the center—in part, in order to prevent the FN and the PS to win seats. In these elections, more candidates than ever before were women and people representing "diversity"—in other words, racial and ethnic minorities. On Sarkozy's "catch-all" behavior in 2007, see Georges-Marc Benhamou, "Un Mitterrandisme de droite," *Le Point,* May 10, 2007.

37. See Florence Autret and Bernard Wallon, "Le lobbying dans tous ses états," *Après-Demain* (January-March 2004): 5–6.

38. On interest-groups' access to deputies, see Hélène Constanty and Vincent Nouzille, *Députés sous influences* (Paris: Fayard 2006). Lobbying with individual deputies or senators is difficult, due to party discipline and the limited role of individual deputies and senators in initiating bills.

39. Patrick Roger, "Les 719 'comités' plus ou moins utiles de la République," *Le Monde,* November 6, 2009.

40. See Cornelia Woll, "The Demise of Statism? Associations and the Transformation of Interest Intermediation in France," in *The French Republic at Fifty,* ed. Sylvain Brouard, Andrew M. Appleton, and Amy G. Mazur (New York: Palgrave-Macmillan, 2009), 226–244.

41. Michel Chauvière, "Les associations d'action sociale: quelle légitimité dans un contexte en mutation?" *Regards sur l'Actualité* 333 (August-September 2007): 25–40.

42. Hervé Nathan and Pascal Virot, "La CGT lache le PCF en rase campagne," *Libération,* October 8, 1999.

43. Among the most important of them are the Federation of National Education (Fédération d'Education Nationale [FEN]), oriented toward socialism and secularism (*laïcité*), and the

Unitary Union Federation of Teaching, Education, Research and Culture (Fédération Syndicale Unitaire de l'Enseignement, de l'Education, de la Recherche et de la Culture [FSU]), with a more eclectic membership. Each of the two unions has about 180,000 members.

44. See Christophe Soulard, *Syndicats* (Paris: Gnos, 2006), 153–170.

45. *Mouvements sociaux* refers both to strikes and to (often spontaneous) mass action on the street and must not be confused with the "social movements" that, to Anglo-American political scientists, denote more or less organized groups similar to interest groups.

46. In 2004 the Council of State was asked to rule on the "representativeness" of a rival trade union, the National Union of Autonomous Syndicates (Union Nationale des Syndicats Autonomes), established in 1993. Rémi Barroux, "Le Conseil d'Etat peut modifier le paysage syndical français," *Le Monde,* October 22, 2004.

47. The participation in elections of these councils by workers and white-collar employees, which take place every five years, has steadily declined. Abstention rates were 41.3 percent in 1982 and 74.5 percent in December 2008, the most recent elections.

48. Until 2008 known as Economic and Social Council.

49. "La réforme du CESE ménage les susceptibilités," *Les Echos,* August 26, 2009.

50. See Béatrice Manjoni d'Intignano, *Égalité entre femmes et hommes: Aspects économiques* (Paris: Documentation Française, 1999).

51. See William Safran, "Ethnoreligious Politics in France: Jews and Muslims," *West European Politics* 27 (May 2004): 423–451.

52. See Johanna Siméant, *La cause des sans-papiers* (Paris: Presses de Sciences-Po, 1998). For a comprehensive listing of marginal, extremist, and "postmaterialist" organizations, see Xavier Crettiez and Isabelle Sommier, *La France rebelle: Tous les foyers, mouvements et acteurs de la contestation* (Paris: Editions Michelon, 2002).

How Is Power Used?

A MERE OUTLINE OF THE POWERS OF THE PRINCIPAL INSTITUTIONS— the executive, the legislature, and the civil service—enumerated in the constitution and the laws cannot adequately convey how policies in France are decided and implemented. The distinction between what the French have called "the legal country" and "the real country" are evident in the tendency of Fifth Republic presidents to interpret the constitution in such a way as to increase their power at the expense of that of their prime ministers. This tendency has applied not only to cabinet appointments, in which most presidents have had an almost free hand (except during "cohabitation" episodes), but also, and most important, to the content of policy decisions. President Charles de Gaulle, who took little interest in economics, and President Georges Pompidou allowed their prime ministers a great deal of discretion except in the areas of foreign and defense policies, but President Valéry Giscard d'Estaing, an *Enarque* (graduate of the National School of Administration [Ecole Nationale d'Administration, or ENA]) who specialized in economic matters, took an active lead in almost all aspects of domestic policy even while his government was headed by Raymond Barre, a professor of economics. Giscard d'Estaing even "meddled" in the drafting of the language of government bills.

In short, the president's domain, as distinct from that of the government, has been stretched almost at will. Under de Gaulle, presidential decisions included blackballing Great Britain's entry into the Common Market, raising the minimum wage of industrial workers, and vetoing an appointment to the prestigious Académie Française. Pompidou devalued the franc, lowered the value-added taxes on foodstuffs, and modified the rules on the maximum height of buildings in Paris. Giscard d'Estaing oversaw hundreds of intrusions into matters affecting taxes, wages, social security, and interest rates. François Mitterrand (before and after the cohabitation interludes) personally decided on the construction of a series of grandiose public buildings and even interfered in the appointment of the director of an opera house.

In promoting his policies, the president uses his ministers to transform his ideas into concrete legislative proposals, to defend them in parliament, and to take the blame for them when they prove unpopular or unsuccessful. The distance the president thereby establishes in the public mind between himself and his ministers is a political convenience. For example, although the austerity policies adopted between 1976 and 1980 were largely inspired by Giscard d'Estaing, public opinion surveys showed that the president was less unpopular than Prime Minister Barre. Even during the cohabitation period of 1986–1988, President Mitterrand was able to veto Prime Minister Jacques Chirac's original choices for several cabinet posts, including that of foreign minister. Moreover, although Mitterrand could not interfere effectively in the government's domestic policy decisions, he was able to prevent some measures from being enacted by decree. Yet the president was sufficiently

President Jacques Chirac answers questions during a live televised debate with young people about the forthcoming referendum on the European Union constitution in Paris in April 2005. The constitution was not approved by the electorate, and Chirac saw his public standing and authority falter.

Source: Reuters/Patrick Kovarik

removed from the daily operations of government that his popularity rose while that of Chirac declined. During the second cohabitation period, Mitterrand left virtually all aspects of domestic policy to the discretion of Prime Minister Edouard Balladur, because the control of the National Assembly by the Rally for the Republic (Rassemblement pour la République [RPR]) and the Union for French Democracy (Union pour la Démocratie Française [UDF]) was so overwhelming and the degree of cohesion between these parties so significant that Mitterrand was unable to exploit internal political differences. Furthermore, Mitterrand had a terminal illness (he died in 1996), and he wished to devote his remaining energies to symbolic acts and safeguarding his positive leadership image for future historians.[1] Whatever the reason, his withdrawal from an active decision-making role contributed to his relatively amicable relationship with his prime minister.

Some observers suggest that in calling for an early and unnecessary parliamentary election in 1997 in which his party was defeated, Chirac so undermined his presidential authority that he transformed himself into a lame-duck president even though five years remained in his presidential term. Others, however, argue that Chirac retained significant presidential power, including the power to dissolve the National Assembly again should Lionel Jospin's government become unpopular. The relationship between Chirac and Jospin was tense, oscillating between cooperation on selective policy issues, such as expanding the membership of the European Union, reducing the presidential term to five years—a change realized by constitutional referendum in 2000—and reforming the judiciary, and competition in appealing to public opinion. In this contest, Jospin initially seemed to have the advantage; his popularity rating was uncharacteristically high for a prime minister after nearly four years in office. He used this situation to his advantage. He had a fairly free hand in reshuffling his cabinet, and he increasingly concerned himself with foreign policy, a matter that was hitherto considered an almost exclusively presidential domain. Conversely, Chirac had difficulty recovering from his ill-advised dissolution of the National Assembly, and his relationships with his own Gaullist party and with other right-of-center forces were frequently less than cordial. Chirac again miscalculated in 2005 when he put his authority on the line in campaigning publicly in favor of the European Union (EU) constitution. But when he lost on that issue and replaced the prime minister, he did not regain authority; rather, that authority was shifted to the new prime minister.

Normally, and to a limited extent even during cohabitation, presidents make use of the cabinet, but they do not rely on it alone. They appoint, and preside over, "restricted" committees composed of selected ministers, higher civil servants, and whatever additional personalities they may co-opt. Furthermore, there is a growing staff of presidential experts, who, like the White House staff in the United States, often function as a supplementary cabinet.

Deputies, Senators, and Decisions

In a formal sense, the French parliament has been weakened by the constitution as well as by the legislature's own standing orders. Nevertheless, that institution is not intrinsically so weak as to be dismissed. Although for most domestic policy decisions—and certainly in all budget matters—the initiative belongs to the government, deputies have succeeded in significantly modifying government bills through amendments on matters such as abortion, unemployment, farm credits, education, the reorganization of the television networks, and the reform of local fiscal administration.

Sometimes, the government abandons a legislative project to which it is ostensibly committed if support for the project is insufficient among deputies belonging to the majority. This situation occurred in 1976 for capital gains taxation and in 1993 and 1994 for Balladur's proposals related to the employment of young people at wages below the minimum and a variety of educational reforms. In other cases, the government permits, or encourages, leaders of a parliamentary group belonging to the majority to introduce legislation. In 1980 the Gaullists sponsored a bill on "participation"—the distribution of industrial shares to workers in given companies. The government itself lacked enthusiasm for the policy, but it did not wish to needlessly antagonize the Gaullist party, whose support would be needed for other matters. In still other cases, public opposition to a project may be strong enough to pose political risks for its supporters, thereby inciting deputies to abandon their endorsement of it and the government to abandon it. This situation arose in 1983 for a bill to bring private schools under greater control of the Ministry of National Education and for a bill introduced in 1986 to reform the citizenship and naturalization laws. Yet government bills affecting labor, social security, and the naturalization of immigrants have been significantly modified by parliamentary input. One of the most recent government proposals, intended to legalize the cohabitation of same-sex couples, was extensively altered by the parliament, especially the Senate.[2]

A lack of evidence of open conflict over policy between majority deputies and the government does not necessarily mean that deputies have resigned themselves to inaction. Instead, it may indicate that they made their influence felt during the drafting phase of the bill through backstage negotiations with ministers or higher civil servants. Frequently, too, a government bill reflects the pressures of interest groups. Watered-down tax bills, softer price controls, and the government's failure to institute the genuine participation of workers in industrial decisions within firms have all stemmed largely from the successful lobbying of business associations. Similarly, the government's acquiescence on wage demands and retirement benefits must be attributed to the pressure of labor unions, especially those representing transport workers. Such pressure is not U.S.-style lobbying by means of appearances before legislative committees; instead, lobbying is carried out through frequent contacts between leaders of big business and higher civil servants. In this respect, trade unions have been at a disadvantage because the personal links of their leaders to upper-echelon bureaucrats are weak. In the past, unions compensated for this weakness by threatening strikes and unrest, and they succeeded in pushing the government into making periodic wage adjustments in their favor, particularly during election years. But in view of the continuing moderation and the increasingly "centrist" orientation of the Socialist leadership under Prime Minister Jospin, such methods were likely to bear less fruit than they had in previous years, even when the Socialist Party was in power. When the right controls the government, as it did from 1993 to 1997, the unions are in an even weaker position. The Jospin government, which took office thereafter, was so dependent on the support of Communist and other leftist deputies, some of them close to the unions, that it had to initiate various policies favored by organized labor, including reducing the workweek to thirty-five hours, raising corporate taxes, and modifying some privatization attempts.

Parliamentarians who are unhappy with government bills have a juridical weapon at their disposal: the Constitutional Council. That body is not a judicial review organ in the sense of the U.S. Supreme Court; it is not a court of appeals to which citizens' complaints about constitutional violations may be brought; and it does not have the authority to nullify laws already in effect. Its major legislative function used to be simply examining organic bills (which could also include the budget) *before* they were passed by parliament and before they were signed into law. (For these reasons, many observers have regarded the council as a supplementary branch of the legislature rather than a court.) In recent years, however, the council has widened its scope considerably, beginning with a ruling in 1971 by which it forced the government to withdraw a bill that would have given prefects the power to forbid or cancel public meetings. In this case, the council acted on the grounds that the bill violated freedom of association.[3] In 1977 the council nullified a bill that would have allowed the police, without a warrant, to search parked cars, because the bill violated a constitutional provision (Art. 66) on judicial safeguards of individual liberties. In 1980 the council nullified a bill aimed at special surveillance of foreign workers on the grounds that it violated the principle of equality before the law. Then in 1982 the council voided parts of the Socialist government's nationalization legislation dealing with compensation to private shareholders on the grounds that it amounted to an unconstitutional deprivation of property. Earlier in the Fifth Republic, during the tenures of Presidents de Gaulle and Pompidou, the council, which was heavily Gaullist in composition, tended not to take issue with decisions by the executive. Since then, and in large part because it has been increasingly called on by opposition deputies, it has taken a very independent position.

If parliament's contributions to the legislative process have amounted to less than many had hoped, it reflects not only the "rationalized" legislative process but also the condition and behavior of the deputies themselves. Parliamentarians have often lacked the expertise of the administrative professionals who draft government bills. Furthermore, deputies' absenteeism has made it difficult for them to acquire mastery over a subject or to participate in parliamentary debates with consistency. Absenteeism has continued to be a problem despite the recent limitation of the number of additional elective offices a deputy might hold.

Even if such problems were overcome completely, deputies would still be unable to make their wills prevail as individuals. Under Gaullist presidents and under Giscard d'Estaing, the deputies belonging to parties of the left lacked unity and voting strength, and the Gaullist or Giscardo-centrist deputies hesitated to confront the government in open parliamentary sessions, for they, too, were divided between enthusiastic and reluctant supporters of the government.

After the elections of 1981, the tables were turned: the right-of-center parties were too small and fragmented to fight the executive, whereas the Socialist deputies became part of an obedient machine for endorsing presidential wishes. After the parliamentary elections of 1993, the tables were turned again. The conservative control of the National Assembly and the internal cohesion of the RPR and UDF strengthened the position of the prime minister in relation to the president, but it also strengthened the position of the conservative parliamentary parties in relation to the prime minister. Following these elections, the position of these parties, and of the Assembly as a whole, was strengthened not only because Prime Minister Balladur disliked confrontation and was inclined to share the burden of delicate policies with parliament, but also because the new Speaker, Philippe Séguin (1993–1997), worked hard to upgrade the level of participation of the Assembly. He did so by taking an active role in the articulation of policy alternatives, encouraging legislative amendments, inviting foreign dignitaries to the Assembly, and controlling absenteeism by attempting to do away with "proxy" voting. He also held numerous hearings with government officials. Laurent Fabius, who succeeded Séguin as Speaker, thereby resuming the position he had held from 1988 to 1991, continued efforts to upgrade the role of the Assembly in the shaping of domestic policy until he moved to a cabinet position in 2000. Further changes were made by Jean-Louis Debré, who became Speaker in 2002. Debré asserted that he "act[ed] neither [in behalf of] the right or the left, but for this chamber." [4] He increased the number of parliamentary committees and expressed his desire to have some of them chaired by the opposition as well as to have commissions of inquiry co-chaired by majority and opposition. Yet he was torn between his desire to project the power of parliament and his firm loyalty to Chirac.

Among the additional constraints on the actions of parliament are the occasionally strained relations between the National Assembly and the Senate, which are not always in agreement. Party discipline is a factor as well. Moreover, majority deputies do not wish to endanger their prospects for political advancement (such as appointment to ministerial posts) or their pork-barrel favors to their constituents. Overall, the lack of seriousness with which deputies have often viewed their own efforts can be attributed in part to their realization that much of the work carried out in parliament does not necessarily have permanent value: the decisions that count are made elsewhere, including by the bureaucracy.

Bureaucratic Politics

In theory, civil servants do not make policy; they only carry out the research and prepare the groundwork for policy and then implement it at various levels. But, in effect, career administrators are co–decision makers. During the Fourth Republic, the political executive was subject to such frequent change and was therefore so unstable and weak that the French government depended on the permanent, professional civil service for decisional continuity and even initiative. In the Fifth Republic, the distinction between the political decision-making elite and the higher bureaucracy has been obscured by the tendency of presidents to recruit (or to persuade the prime minister to recruit) a large portion of their cabinets from the administrative corps. In addition, civil servants frequently dominate interministerial committees as well as the *cabinets ministériels,* the staffs of collaborators appointed by each minister. In principle, the members of these cabinets are responsible to the minister whom they serve, but because they understand the technicalities of a dossier better than the minister, they often act according to their own discretion, sometimes in concert with the staffs of other ministries.

During the Fifth Republic, the size of the staffs of the individual ministers has grown steadily, from an average of about 10 per minister, or about 300 for the ministries collectively, during the 1960s and 1970s, to 12.5 per minister, for a total of 580 under Prime Minister Chirac (1987) and more than 600 under his successor, Prime Minister Michel Rocard. This growth of what has been called a "parallel administration"[5] reflects in part the growth in the number of ministries, but it is also a manifestation of a spoils system in which jobs are given to more people. Yet money is saved because a smaller proportion of the appointees (for example, 22 percent under Rocard as compared with 36 percent under Chirac) are the more highly paid professional civil servants who graduated from the ENA. More recently, this growth has been kept under control. The staff of the ministers in Fillon's cabinet numbered 517 when he took office in 2007, but subsequently increased to 626.

The position of the *Enarchie* in the French political system can be appreciated from the fact that during the Fifth Republic, two presidents, seven prime ministers, and five of the twelve candidates in the 2002 presidential election were graduates of that institution. But some important politicians such as Nicolas Sarkozy and Jean-Pierre Raffarin have not been part of this "old boy" network. In recent years, there has been a spate of arguments about the continued utility of the ENA, as well as suggestions about rethinking the structure and recruitment basis of that institution.

As for the size of the national bureaucracy (*fonction publique*), the government periodically proposes some pruning, in part because a growing number of sectors that were once part of the state have been privatized. Yet the national bureaucracy, with its nearly 2.4 million employees in 2005, continues to be important. At its pinnacle is the Council of State (*Conseil d'Etat*), which is heavily involved in the drafting of government bills and is the ultimate source of appeal by citizens for administrative malfeasance.

Other participants in the decision-making process are the study commissions, *comités de sages,* whose appointment is from time to time encouraged by the president, the prime minister, or individual ministers. These commissions, which are roughly comparable to the Royal Commissions in Great Britain, may include academicians, managers of public enterprises, military officers, and politicians, but they have tended to be dominated by civil servants. Examples of some of the many study commissions convened during the Fifth Republic are the Toutée Commission on wage negotiations in nationalized industries (1967), the Sudreau Commission on workers' participation in industrial management (1974), the Nora Commission on the impact of computer technology (1978), the Giraudet Commission on the reduction of the workweek (1980), the Long Commission on the reform of citizenship and naturalization laws (1987), the Stasi Commission on secularism in the republic (2003), and the Camdessus Commission on the reform of labor laws (2004). The commissions' reports to the government, which reflect the input of interest group representatives and miscellaneous experts, may be used by the government as a basis for legislative proposals, or, if the government does not agree with the reports' conclusions, they may be ignored. Several reasons explain the proliferation of commissions: the need to circumvent a parliament that might make proposals that would be unwelcome to the government or, conversely, to supplant a parliament that has been unwilling to make decisions (and failed to use the power to set up its own special study or investigation committees); the desire of the government to "pass the buck" for politically risky policies; and—on a more positive note—the quest for a policy based on a broad consensus.

Once the parliamentarians have passed a bill, it gains substance only when it is enforced. But governments (and higher civil servants) may demonstrate their reservations about a bill by failing to produce the necessary implementing regulations or ordinances. The government has "denatured" acts of parliament by delaying, or omitting, follow-up regulations on bills dealing with educational reforms, birth control, prison reform, and the financing of local government. Occasionally, the administrative bureaucracy may, at the behest of a minister, produce regulations that contravene the intent of the law passed by parliament. In the 1980s, after parliament passed a bill requiring equal treatment of immigrant workers, administrative regulations subjected them to special restrictions. Similarly, an act of parliament forbidding discrimination on the basis of religion or race aimed at businesses engaged in international trade was followed by a government regulation permitting such discrimination. The Council of State may nullify such regulations after a legal challenge, but litigation is selective and may take several years.

The interplay between bureaucratic and legislative actions illustrates the complexity and pluralism of the decision-making process. In this pluralism, the public at large plays a role inside as well as outside the formal institutional framework. Indeed, it was "the street" that incited the government to abandon bills on educational reform,[6] agriculture, and social security reform. During massive public demonstrations to keep the thirty-five-hour workweek, one demonstrator declared, "If the government doesn't give in to these public demonstrations, it isn't a democracy."[7] Such an attitude reflects widely prevailing doubts about the efficacy of "normal" political institutions.

Delegating Responsibility for Decisions

At times, the executive and its administrators may resort to various forms of buck-passing to weaken the effects of long-established legislation. To avoid using public monies to keep the government-controlled health insurance funds solvent, the government has occasionally permitted the funds to raise the social security contributions of the insured. Similarly, the autonomous public corporation that runs the Paris transport system has contracted with private firms to clean the metro stations instead of employing its own workers and paying them the minimum wage generally granted by legislation to public employees. Finally, although all subnational administrative activities are ultimately subject to the supervision or "guardianship" (*tutelle*) of the national government, the latter has saved itself trouble and money by permitting considerable local variations in the implementation of primary school curriculums and vacation policies, public health standards, and social services for the aged. The decentralization measures begun in 1982–1983 institutionalized that approach and at the same time provided for greater local autonomy and grassroots participation.

Since the early days of the Fourth Republic, governments have been committed to a form of capitalist national planning. Four-year economic modernization plans were prepared through complex procedures involving the cabinet (notably the Ministry of Finance), government statistics offices, and several hundred technocrats working in a National Planning Commission and tripartite subcommittees (*groupes de projet*) dealing with themes such as growth, employment, and regional development, and composed of representatives of the government, the "social partners," and independent experts. This harmonizing of conflicting class interests was supposed to result in a fair macroeconomic plan that represented a fine balance between a productivity orientation and a social one. The plan therefore was invested with a certain moral authority, and, with that in mind, the government and parliament processed specific pieces of legislation that were consistent with the plan, such as bills on public works investments, social welfare, wages, employment, and housing. For both President de Gaulle and President Pompidou, the plan was an "ardent obligation." Under President Giscard d'Estaing and his prime ministers, the planning institutions were retained, but planners did little more than prepare position papers and statistical forecasts, and the government ignored many of their policy recommendations.

After the election of Mitterrand to the presidency in 1981 (and the appointment of Rocard as minister of planning), the economic plan was to be not only revived, geared to the production of social goods, and made more redistributive in orientation, but also given extra weaponry with a larger number of nationalized industries and a plethora of economic regulations. Yet the Ninth Development Plan, theoretically in effect in 1983, became in practice a dead letter, because it was "displaced" by an interim plan conforming to the austerity policy to which the government had committed itself. Moreover, part of the plan was replaced by piecemeal economic policy contracts with individual regions (*contrats Etat-région*). Under the Chirac government that began in 1986, not much remained of the plan except its name and its institutions. Whatever economic policy there was to be was confined to the cabinet and, more specifically, to the Ministry of Finance. Indeed, in view of its program of reprivatizing a variety of industries and banks, its commitment to deregulation and "degovernmentalization," and its reliance on market forces, the government would have little if any room for planning. With the installation of the Rocard government in 1988, the Tenth Development Plan (1989–1992) was adopted, but only a junior minister was in charge of it, and planning in a meaningful sense was not revived. Under Rocard's successors, planning has fared no better: plans are still made, but because of the increasing role of the market and the relocation of certain aspects of economic decision making and monetary policy to the transnational levels of the European Union, the policy impacts of plans are open to question. In 2005 Villepin fired the national planning commissioner who had been appointed by Raffarin, Villepin's predecessor; he abolished the Planning Commission; and he replaced it with data-gathering agencies under the direct authority of the prime minister.[8] Villepin finished the job by dismissing the last of France's planning commissioners and abolishing the position.

Conflicts within the System

The analysis presented above suggests that the government's attitudes are not monolithic. Occasionally, the national administration is hampered by internal conflicts as well as conflicts with parliamentary and local politicians. For example, the ministers in charge of labor (especially unskilled labor) and social affairs have sought to raise minimum wages and upgrade working conditions, but the ministers of finance have interfered with such policies to save money both for the Treasury and for the influential business sector whose profits are maximized by cheap labor. The minister of the interior, who is in charge of the police, has been concerned with internal order and security, whereas the minister of justice has sought to protect the rights of citizens.

Some of these conflicts are resolved in response to political considerations rather than merely administrative ones. Administrative institutions are not immune to political influence; moreover, National Assembly deputies may serve on the boards of nationalized industries, on regional bodies, and in agencies involved in economic policymaking. Such deputies may be trained technocrats or civil servants and therefore professionally concerned with "objective" approaches to problem solving. Yet at the same time they are politicians responsive to local electorates.

The conflict between administration and politics is seen most clearly in the relationship between the mayor and the prefect. The prefect, who is legally responsible to the national government, has the power to nullify acts of a city council, to veto the budget adopted by the general council, and even, under certain circumstances, to depose a mayor. A prefect takes such action rarely, however, because a mayor may be more powerful than a prefect, especially if the mayor heads a large city and is simultaneously a member of parliament or, even better, is a cabinet minister. A large number of ministers, including most of the prime ministers, continued to function as mayors of towns while exercising their national functions. In fact, shortly after becoming prime minister after the presidential elections of 1995, Alain Juppé was elected mayor of Bordeaux in the municipal elections that followed. When Jospin became prime minister in 1997, however, he required his cabinet members to relinquish their posts as mayors, so that they would be able to devote their full attention to their national tasks. This innovation may serve as a precedent.

Sometimes, a mayor may be too political and too powerful to suit the taste of the national government. In 1978 Chirac, the mayor of Paris, was "punished" for his presidential ambitions and his unreliable support of President Valéry Giscard D'Estaing. Chirac, at the president's instigation, failed to obtain a national financial supplement for maintenance of the municipal police force—a situation that forced Chirac to increase local tax assessments and threatened to reduce his popularity.

This description of the French political system is not intended to suggest that France has a mixed system in which various institutions and individuals filling a variety of different political positions play equally significant roles. Still, the fact that the constitution has given presidents vast powers to make decisions and that they have added to these powers by one-sided interpretation does not mean that they always make use of these powers. Under Giscard d'Estaing, the distinction between president and prime minister was made more obscure than before. Giscard d'Estaing did not, in reality, freely decide all policies.

He sometimes avoided tough decisions for electoral reasons, contenting himself with making a good impression on television and otherwise "playing at being president." During the election campaign of 1988, Mitterrand, in a "Letter to all the French," [9] outlined his ideas about the constitution, economic policy, education and research, social security, citizenship, and foreign and defense policies, but after he retrieved his presidential powers he gave only general direction to Prime Minister Rocard. The latter, in turn, produced his own "circular" in which he articulated his ideas of government. [10] In a television debate with Jospin during the presidential election campaign of 1995, Chirac deplored the "monarchical drift" of French decision-making patterns and contended that presidents were increasingly behaving like "super prime ministers" instead of confining themselves to articulating grand visions and providing general "impulses" to political actions. He argued that the French regime was basically parliamentary rather than presidential, and he called for an increase in the power of the parliament to legislate and control the actions of the government. [11] But during his second term, Chirac became an active decision maker and in 2005–2006, as his presidency was nearing its end, he behaved in an increasingly irresponsible manner. [12]

Almost immediately after he assumed the presidency and appointed his ministers, Sarkozy announced that he was "the decider," that he was given a mandate to act, and that he would make every effort to promote the policies to which he had committed himself during the election campaign. As president he proved true to his promises. His style of leadership has been that of a "hyper-president," engaged in what his critics regarded as a solitary exercise of power: he has made all decisions, and Prime Minister François Fillon, a personal friend, has played a clearly secondary role. The composition of the government, which was entirely determined by Sarkozy, has been the most diverse of the Fifth Republic: it included women, several of them Muslim, in important cabinet posts; and he also named a number of Socialists to official positions in an attempt to show that he was not bound by traditional ideological constraints. Although he was considered by many as impulsive and even vulgar, his reform agenda has been impressive (see Chapter 2.5), and he has had little difficulty getting the support of a UMP-dominated parliament. Yet Sarkozy's domination is not absolute: Prime Minister Fillon does not always agree with him; for instance, Sarkozy favors resident foreigners' right to vote in municipal elections (as do most Socialists), but Fillon opposes it (as do many UMP deputies). There are occasional disagreements within the cabinet, and challenges to some of Sarkozy's policies within his own parliamentary majority, especially in the Senate. He is also constrained by public opinion and by external pressures.

NOTES

1. Mitterrand failed in that effort because some unpleasant aspects of his past were revealed, including his extreme-right connections before World War II, his involvement with the Vichy regime, and his continuing friendships with fascist collaborators after the war.
2. As noted, one example of this mode concerned the government bill (Civil Solidarity Pacts) intended to legalize the status of unmarried and same-sex couples. The Senate watered the bill down by exempting incestuous cohabitation. See Suzanne Daley, "France Gives Legal Status to Unmarried Couples," *New York Times*, October 14, 1999.

3. The actual provisions of the 1958 constitution do not include a bill of rights. Nevertheless, the preamble of that document includes references to the Declaration of the Rights of Man and Citizen of 1789 and to the preamble of the Fourth Republic constitution, both of which have extensive listings of rights and liberties, including freedom of association. In its decisions, the Constitutional Council has "inserted" these references into the constitution by according them operational validity.

4. Didier Hassoux, "Debré, incontrôlable, fait grincer à l'UMP," *Libération*, December 23, 2004.

5. Jean-François Doumic, "L'administration parallèle," *Le Monde*, February 2, 1989.

6. Public demonstrations forced the government to shelve a proposal to nationalize the private schools in the 1980s and to reform secondary education in 2005.

7. France 2 broadcast, March 10, 2005. Nevertheless, the thirty-five-hour workweek, enacted in 2000, was made more flexible in 2005 by enabling employers to offer more hours with overtime pay.

8. "Villepin limoge Etchegoyen, commissaire général du Plan," *Le Figaro*, October 28, 2005.

9. "Lettre à tous les Français," *Le Monde*, April 8, 1988.

10. "Gouverner autrement," dated May 25, 1988, in *Regards sur l'Actualité* 143 (July-August 1988): 15–18.

11. "Le débat télévisé entre les deux candidats," *Le Monde, Dossiers et Documents, L'Election Présidentielle*, 1995, 55.

12. In March 2006, in the face of massive public protest and growing parliamentary opposition, Chirac signed and promulgated the *Contrat première embauche*, the controversial legislation to facilitate layoffs of young workers, but suggested that the law not be enforced. See Antoine Guiral and Vanessa Schneider, "Chirac à tort et à travers," *Libération*, April 1, 2006.

What Is the Future of French Politics?

IF INSTITUTIONAL STABILITY AND ECONOMIC PROGRESS ARE USED AS the principal criteria for judging a political system, the Fifth Republic is a success. Five decades after its inauguration, the regime has amply reflected the themes of "change within continuity" articulated by Presidents Georges Pompidou and Valéry Giscard d'Estaing. A remarkable balance has been achieved between French traditionalism and the spirit of innovation; the old institutions have been retained, but their functional relationships have been rationalized. The executive has sufficient unity and power to make decisions, and it has used this power fairly effectively.

Stability, Modernization, and Democracy

In the Fifth Republic, the political party system has been simplified, and political conflicts have been reduced, in part by the manipulation of the system of elections, but more important, by socioeconomic changes and a clear popular consensus about the legitimacy of the constitutional system. As a result of the decentralization reforms that began in the early 1980s and are still continuing, subnational (that is, regional, district, and municipal) administration has been adapted to respond to new realities, and local communities have been given significantly greater powers of decision and revenue gathering. The voting age has been lowered to eighteen, and great progress has been made toward legal equality for women, minorities, homosexuals, and children born out of wedlock. Institutions have been created to make the bureaucracy more accountable. Apart from occasional lapses, freedom of association, including the rights of workers to organize in factories, has been made more secure. Meanwhile, continuing experimentation is aimed at modernizing and democratizing the educational system and adapting it to the requirements of the job market, despite budgetary constraints and the opposition of part of the traditional academic establishment. The networks of national and urban mass transport have been modernized and are among the finest in existence. The social security system has responded fairly well to the needs of the majority, and it is holding its own despite the pressures imposed by the European Union and by globalization to hold the line in welfare state expenditures. In short, France has become a prosperous country oriented to mass consumption, and the living standard of its people corresponds to that of Americans.

On the international front, during the 1950s and 1960s, France achieved decolonization without undue bloodshed (except for Indochina and, later, Algeria) and without tearing French society apart, and the North African "repatriates" have, for the most part, been successfully integrated. The French economy has adapted with remarkable success to the challenges of the European Union, and France has reached the status of the world's fifth-largest industrial power and fifth-largest exporter.

Administration and Justice: Developments and Reforms

To many of the French, especially Gaullists, the "administrative state" has been preferable to the "regime of parties" because civil servants have been viewed as more professional, less ideology-ridden, and less particularistic than party politicians. Being less influenced by electoral pressures, the administrative bureaucracy is supposed to be better at making long-term policy in the public interest.

It is true that most upper-echelon civil servants are highly cultivated and public-spirited; moreover, the social esteem and excellent pay they have received have made them, by and large, immune to corruption (at least in comparison with elected politicians). But because of their bourgeois or upper-class origins, they also have tended to be elitist and paternalistic. They are often too far removed from the people, and their actions are not subjected to adequate parliamentary surveillance. Citizens' means of redress against bureaucratic misbehavior are unreliable, despite institutions such as the administrative courts, topped by the Council of State and newer institutions such as the mediator.

The judicial system, whose essential features date to Napoleon Bonaparte's rule, needs liberalization. The network of courts is large; the appeals echelons are well distributed geographically; and most Western-type due process criteria are followed. Although Anglo-American–style habeas corpus provisions are omitted in the constitution, they have been introduced gradually by means of ordinary legislation. Yet elements of class justice persist; preventive (pretrial) detention is often still too long, especially for suspects belonging to the working class and the peasantry. The police, the prosecuting attorneys, and the courts have dealt particularly harshly with immigrants from developing countries. For many years, the government hesitated to liberalize the penal code, a hesitancy attributed in part to continued fear (shared by large segments of the population) of disorder and violence. This fear had (until 1981) prevented governments from sponsoring legislation to abolish the death penalty; it also explained the retention of the State Security Court, which dealt with cases of sedition. That court had been set up in 1963 in the wake of a series of violent acts by opponents of Charles de Gaulle and his policies. Under François Mitterrand, the State Security Court was abolished.

In spring 1980 the government introduced and the Assembly passed a bill to reform the penal code. This bill, labeled "Security and Liberty," aimed at making the punishment for crimes of violence more severe and at reducing the discretion of judges in the imposition of sentences. At the same time, the bill reduced the maximum period of pretrial detention. During the first term of Mitterrand's presidency, the government initiated numerous measures aimed at reforming the legal system. The illiberal features of the Security and Liberty law were rescinded; prison conditions were improved; the indigent were guaranteed the right to counsel; the rights of immigrant aliens were more or less aligned with those of citizens, and aliens were given greater protection against harassment by public officials; and the power of the police was curbed—but not without opposition from the minister of the interior.[1]

Even though much remains to be done to deal with the problems of understaffed courts, underpaid police officers, overcrowded prisons, and the (still) inadequate protection of the rights of citizens against the state, the process of reforming the judicial system is continuing. In mid-1997 a blue-ribbon commission appointed earlier by President Jacques Chirac recommended measures to modernize the judiciary and make it more independent. The rights of those detained for criminal investigation were enlarged, and legislation was adopted to make firmer the presumption of innocence of the accused.[2] Finally, to better protect human rights, Mitterrand favored a constitutional amendment that would permit the Constitutional Council to examine bills at its own initiative and that would grant ordinary citizens the right to bring the issue of the constitutionality of a law before the council.

In recent decades, the judicial system has become overloaded because of increasing lawlessness, which has been reflected in the overcrowding of prisons.[3] Among the responses have been premature releases, suspended sentences, and the appointment of volunteer *juges de proximité* to judge petty infractions and small claims of less than €4,000.[4] There also have been changes in due process, and, to lighten the load of the courts, steps have been taken toward simplifying penalties for traffic offenses.

The reform agenda of President Nicolas Sarkozy has been particularly ambitious. Based on the recommendation of the Léger commission, he has supported the introduction of plea bargaining (as in the United States) to lighten the dockets of criminal courts. The Jean-Michel Darrois commission recommended a common training for various magistrates, trial lawyers, and notaries public, at least in the first year of the Ecole Nationale de la Magistrature. Another reform would be the abolition of the office of *juge d'instruction,* who is independent of the ministry of justice. Among the most contested proposals was the reduction of the number of local courts in the name of efficiency, which has met with citizen opposition. The majority of the members of the legal profession, however, have opposed all these reforms.

Some of the impetus for improvement has come from the European Union. The constitutional amendment to grant alien residents the right to vote in municipal elections, passed in 2001, brought France in line with a supranational European standard. The same is true of gender equality with respect to working conditions.[5] Other pressures have come from the Council of Europe. In 1999 the European Court of Human Rights censured France for the use of torture.[6] Finally, France continues to be under pressure to conform to European norms on the legitimation of minority languages.

On occasion, governments have intervened in judicial matters, thereby degrading political democracy. Such intervention was sometimes inspired by foreign policy considerations. Examples include in 1977 the release, without trial, of an Arab suspected of terrorist action; in 1980 the physical interference by the (nationally controlled) Paris police in a peaceful demonstration in front of the Soviet embassy; and in 1987 the (unsuccessful) attempt by the Chirac government to interfere in the trial of another Arab implicated in the assassination of diplomats in Paris. Conversely, the judicial establishment has been more lenient in prosecuting and convicting members of the political elite, especially high government officials. Chirac was not subject to prosecution during the exercise of his presidency for corrupt behavior while he was mayor of Paris. Former prime minister Alain Juppé, while mayor of Bordeaux, was convicted for corrupt acts he had committed as

In November 2005 riot police stand guard outside the National Assembly while Prime Minister Dominique de Villepin addresses the deputies. The violence by young slum dwellers of Arab and African origin that prompted Villepin's address spread to many cities in France, spurring the government to declare a state of emergency.

Source: AP/Images/Michel Euler

deputy mayor of Paris, but he was handed an unusually lenient sentence, which would permit him to seek candidacy for political office after only a year's interruption. More recently, however, the judiciary has behaved in a more independent manner, even vis-à-vis prominent politicians. In 2009 Jean Tibéri, a former mayor of Paris, was convicted for the creation of phantom jobs at City Hall used to finance the Gaullist political party; and even Chirac, after the expiration of his presidential term, was asked to testify for the same malfeasance. That same year, Charles Pasqua, a former minister of the interior, was sentenced to a year in prison for arms trafficking ("Angolagate"), and in 2010 Dominique de Villepin faced charges of attempting to frame Sarkozy by implicating him in illegal transactions with a foreign country.[7]

The greatest challenge to due process and to public liberties has come from the threat of terrorism and domestic disorder. In the 1990s the government instituted the so-called *vigipirate* program, which has given the police greater leeway to make identity checks, often based on racial profiling, and Sarkozy, who was minister of the interior, proposed increasing surveillance of telephones and e-mail. These and other approaches have met with a reserved reaction on the part of the Commission Nationale de l'Informatique et des Libertés (CNIL), the major civil liberties watchdog. In response to massive violence by young slum dwellers of Arab and African origin in November 2005 that spread to many cities in France, the government, invoking a law passed in 1955, declared a "state of emergency," which permitted departments and communes to institute curfews, conduct searches, ban open rallies, and detain suspects.[8]

Under the presidencies of de Gaulle, Pompidou, and Giscard d'Estaing, some constraints were placed on the expression of opinion in the mass media. Before the 1980s the television networks and most radio stations, which were public monopolies, were often used by the government to distort the news. The press was free and pluralistic, but governments would occasionally confiscate issues of periodicals that had published articles critical of the president, and in one case (under Giscard d'Estaing) even instituted legal proceedings against a newspaper. Under Mitterrand, such practices ceased; moreover, private radio stations were permitted, and the television networks were put under autonomous management and very often privatized. The content of news, especially that related to international issues, continues to be heavily influenced by the government (especially the Foreign Office) via Agence France-Presse, the major semigovernmental news agency. But in the electronic mass media, there is now competition not only from private channels within France but also from abroad. Yet freedom of speech and press are not unlimited. A series of laws enacted between the 1970s and 2004 provide penalties for public speech disseminating ethnic, religious, or race hatred, or denying the historicity of the Holocaust.

Problems and Prospects for France

The problems that lie ahead for France are likely to fall into three areas. The first concerns the economic challenges of dealing with the welfare state that has been evolving since the Third Republic and the "neoliberalism" that took root in the 1980s. The second is foreign policy, which continues to center on Europe. The third relates to societal and systemic issues, among which the presence of several million immigrants and their impact on French society ranks high.

The Economic Challenge: Welfare Statism and 'Neoliberalism'

For many years, most French citizens accepted their country's version of the "mixed economy" under which a large and pluralistic private sector coexisted with a significant array of nationalized industries. In addition, France has had a highly developed welfare state, reflected in a complex of redistributive policies that evolved gradually from the end of the Third Republic through the first years of the Mitterrand presidency. These policies include a progressive income tax; income supplements to families with several children; low- and moderate-rent housing; state-subsidized (and virtually tuition-free) higher education; and (compared with the United States) generous retirement, unemployment, maternity, and medical benefits and paid vacations (of five weeks) financed in large part by employers. In addition, there are government-imposed minimum wages (which are higher than in the United States), complemented, until recently, by a system of semiautomatic wage increases pegged to the cost-of-living index.

Although most citizens accepted these features as almost inalienable rights, they were not regarded as solutions to some persistent problems such as the inequality of incomes, housing shortages, unemployment, and large-scale tax fraud—compensated only in part by the more or less automatic (but regressive) system of value-added taxes required for all members of the European Union. Moreover, the government's heavy involvement in social and economic matters was thought to have a stifling effect on private initiative in general and industrial (and employment-creating) investment in particular; and the existence of a large nationalized sector was held responsible for impeding productivity and competition. Responding to the pressures of the international and the European market, and inspired to some extent by the presumably successful examples of the United States (under Reagan) and Germany, French governments—especially under the prime ministerships of Raymond Barre, Laurent Fabius, and Jacques Chirac—discovered the virtues of the marketplace and promoted policies of selective denationalization and deregulation. Such "neoliberal" policies continued under the Gaullist governments of Edouard Balladur and Alain Juppé, but they were subjected to modification under electoral pressures and the threat of massive strikes, and they were partially reversed when Lionel Jospin became prime minister, only to be resumed under Jean-Pierre Raffarin and Dominique de Villepin.

Today, many of these problems persist. The annual growth rate between 2002 and 2005 was only about 1 percent, bankruptcies are averaging about forty thousand a year, and unemployment is hovering around 9 percent. Despite the introduction of measures to promote greater labor market flexibility, job creation is being impeded by the mandatory costs of layoffs to the employer and a relatively short workweek.[9]

In part because of France's aging population, both its medical insurance funds and retirement pension funds are threatened with depletion—indeed, the medical insurance funds are running a deficit of more than €10 billion—but it is not certain that the government measures[10] will be sufficient. The pension funds are in even worse shape because the average retirement age is only sixty. But raising that age is difficult because of general public resistance and particular opposition by civil servants and trade unions, all of whom believe that such measures would spell the end of the French social model.[11]

That model was being called into question by an increasing number of observers.[12] Yet despite a budget deficit of €138 billion (or 7.9 percent of the gross domestic product) in mid-2009 and a national debt of €1.4 trillion, governments found it difficult to tamper with the status quo.[13] The only short-term way to stabilize this debt was an infusion of capital from massive privatizations. Among such proposals were the privatization of the national superhighway network and the maritime ferry between the mainland and Corsica.

The global financial meltdown, which began in 2008, posed a challenge to President Sarkozy, who had campaigned on a platform of liberalizing the market and revalorizing the work ethic. His policies have turned out to be a mixture of welfare-state and market-oriented policies—what has been called "buttressed liberalization"[14]—the groundwork for which had been laid a decade earlier. It included tax concessions to small business and the gradual abandonment of the thirty-five-hour workweek, which would allow greater flexibility to enterprises and unions in collective contract negotiations. It would enable more individuals to work overtime, in conformity of Sarkozy's call to individuals to "work harder to earn more." Like his predecessors, he tried to raise the age of retirement, which, at age sixty for public service workers, and even earlier for workers in the national railroad system, is the lowest in Europe, but that effort continued to be resisted, especially by public-service employees. He used government funds to bail out a number of large banks, and helped to save the French auto industry by subsidizing the purchase of French cars. He continued the privatization policy by proposing that the post office be turned into a publicly owned corporation (*société anonyme*), which would permit it to modernize operations and raise its own capital (and would also conform to EU rules). This idea is opposed by the CGT and the Left, which fear that it will lead to complete privatization and loss of jobs. Furthermore, Sarkozy's government introduced various environmental measures aimed at reducing energy consumption (by 20 percent over a ten-year period) and increasing the use of renewable energy sources, measures adopted almost unanimously in special session of parliament in 2009.

At the same time, the Sarkozy government introduced legislation to curb bankers' profits and raise taxes steeply on bonuses of corporate executives, especially those who benefited from the government bailout. He continued the policy of raising the minimum wage (SMIC) in line with the rise in the cost of living and supplemented it with the Active Solidarity Income (Revenu de Solidarité Active [RSA]), to be funded by a special tax on capital.[15] This policy, and especially its extension to youth under twenty-five, was criticized by organized business and part of his own majority, but welcomed by the Left.[16] Sarkozy's critique of "finance capitalism"[17] and his insistence that the financial crisis proved the soundness of the French model of social protection and that the state must continue to play a major role raised the question among some whether he was really a leftist after all.[18]

Foreign Policy: Europe and Beyond

Under Charles de Gaulle, France's foreign policy was inspired by dreams of grandeur. Because of the limitations of the country's economic and military power, however, these dreams could not be realized. Unable to be influential in the international system, de Gaulle instead pursued a policy of symbolism and rhetoric that expressed itself in hostility to the two superpowers, in opposition to the institutional development of a supranational Europe, in futile attempts to interfere in regional disputes outside Europe such as in the Middle East, and in efforts to mediate relationships between industrialized Europe and the developing countries, notably in Africa. An important element of de Gaulle's policy was his resentment of the "Anglo-Americans," reflected in his hostility to the North Atlantic Treaty Organization (NATO). Such attitudes were in part determined by fears of U.S. economic domination and of U.S. cultural hegemony and by doubts about the reliability of the U.S. commitment to defend Europe in the face of Soviet aggression.

Responding to the pressures of the Gaullist party and reflecting the outlook of much of the French intellectual elite, Pompidou and (to a lesser extent) Giscard d'Estaing continued the main lines of de Gaulle's foreign policy, but with considerably less hostility to the United States or to the development of European unity. Under Mitterrand, France continued to develop its national nuclear deterrent and, on a cultural level, to foster as much as was still possible cultivation of the French language abroad. At the same time, the country abandoned the Gaullist illusions about its international power and became more favorably inclined toward NATO. Henceforth, France's foreign policy was increasingly marked by concern with its economic aspect, such as global and regional competitiveness. This aspect, however, could not be separated from France's role in Europe. As of the early 1970s, it had become clear that Germany was the economic powerhouse of Europe. As long as Germany was divided, however, France retained a degree of political dominance on the continent. With the reunification of Germany, French fears of that country were revived, mixed with resentment and admiration. To compensate for their reduced weight in Europe, the French have utilized various opportunities for asserting their role in world affairs, whether military (such as peacekeeping in Bosnia and elsewhere), economic (aid to Russia and developing countries), humanitarian (such as French medical missions around the globe), and symbolic (such as participation in the Gulf War). Furthermore, France has continued to maintain a presence in francophone sub-Saharan Africa, especially in its former colonies, which are considered by many as the country's "backyard." It has exercised its influence by means of banking connections, technical assistance, a military presence in selected countries, and occasional political interference.

Some of France's foreign policy moves have been indicative of a hard-nosed realism tinged with cynicism. These moves have included, in particular, the country's dealings with tin-pot dictators and an almost automatic pro-Arab position, especially with respect to the Arab-Israeli conflict. Other moves have been little more than efforts to maintain France's presence on the diplomatic stage and shore up its cultural influence—efforts manifested in President Jacques Chirac's frequent (and often maladroit and futile) travels to the Middle East, China, Africa, and Russia. A more recent policy, France's participation in the creation of a sixty thousand–member European rapid intervention force, is designed both to retain the country's military "parity" with a reunited Germany and to assure its autonomy in relation to NATO.

The major focus of French policy beyond its borders continues to be Europe. France had been a major proponent of European integration, from the Coal and Steel Community in the early 1950s to the adoption of the Treaty of Maastricht in 1992, which established the European Union (EU). It is under EU auspices, and, more specifically, the Common Agricultural Policy (CAP), that France has enjoyed a strong system of protection and subsidy for its farm products. In 2005 CAP accounted for 43 percent of total EU expenditures, and in 2005 France received 22 percent of them. Nevertheless, between 1992 and 2002, France paid € 300 million to fruit and vegetable farmers in aid, supplementary to what the EU gave them. In 2009 the EU demanded reimbursement of € 500 million, including interest, a sum the government of France hoped to extract from its farmers.

France has played an important role in EU institutions, such as the European Commission, the European Bank for Reconstruction and Development, and the European Parliament. Although there is no binding European institution to decide on a common foreign policy, French pressure has been crucial in shaping a "European" policy for the Middle East, sub-Saharan Africa, and, via the World Trade Organization, international trade, including limits on Chinese imports. Most recently, France has used its position in the EU to promote a policy of global-level "cultural pluralism"—that is, the protection of the French language and culture against American "cultural imperialism" by means of controls on imports such as movies and television programs.

France had been one of the major promoters of a common currency, and it replaced the franc with the euro without problems. But soon thereafter, France, like Germany, ignored the mandatory limit of 3 percent on deficit spending. Moreover, French governments have had difficulties in adhering to EU rules providing for cross-border competition in transport, telecommunication, and other sectors. The transnationalization, privatization, and delocalization of industries associated with these rules have been opposed especially by the trade unions, which fear competition from cheap labor.[19] This fear, as well as a widespread worry about a threat to the French model of social protection, was one reason for the rejection of the EU constitution in the May 2005 referendum.[20] That rejection, however, served to reduce France's influence within the EU institutions, a fact that will weaken its position in its fight with Great Britain over the EU budget and with Germany over the admission of Turkey to EU membership.[21] Europe continues to have an important place in the consciousness of the French, even as their faith in it declines: in 1987, 74 percent thought that EU membership was a good idea, but only 47 percent in 2008.

One of the first foreign policy measures under Sarkozy's presidency was the adoption of the Treaty of Lisbon, accompanied by the appropriate constitutional amendments. Like his predecessors, he hoped to promote a united EU foreign policy (preferably under French leadership), including a common energy policy and a united approach to fighting terrorism. But the EU was not united enough, except in the area of international trade.

Sarkozy has reduced France's presence in sub-Saharan Africa, but not abandoned it. He has been attempting to set up a corollary relationship by creating a Mediterranean Union, which would promote collaborative projects among European, North African, and Near Eastern countries; but little if anything is likely to come of it, largely due to the unwillingness of Arab countries to collaborate on common projects with Israel.

An important change was the improved relationship with the United States, especially since the departure of President George W. Bush and the election of Barack Obama. One of the first steps in this direction was France's decision to rejoin the integrated command of NATO and to contribute more soldiers to the war in Afghanistan. There is also considerable agreement on imposing sanctions on Iran. Conversely, disagreements persist with respect to global warming and the Middle East conflict; and there is a continuing rivalry between the two countries over the sale of arms and civilian aircraft.

Societal and Systemic Issues

The problems that preoccupy the majority of the residents of France are domestic in nature. Chief among them is the presence of several million immigrants and their impact on French society. Progressive elements, led by Mitterrand and other moderate Socialists, attempted to fight racism and speed the process of legal integration and cultural assimilation of immigrants, and to that end they promoted a liberal approach to naturalization. But opponents expressed the fear that easy acquisition of French citizenship would actually hamper the assimilation process and that ultimately French society would be changed beyond recognition. A related problem is how to meet the needs and desires of regional and nonterritorial ethnic minorities such as Bretons, Alsatians, Basques, Arab Muslims, and Southeast Asian immigrants. A growing sensitivity to these minorities has been evinced in the Socialists' decentralization policies, a greater tolerance of cultural diversity, and the grants of autonomy to Corsica, a particularly violent and troublesome region, and some overseas territories, including New Caledonia. Some measures have been symbolic, such as Raffarin's and Villepin's appointment of descendants of North African immigrants to minor ministerial posts, but other measures are being seriously entertained, such as limited affirmative action. Several years ago, the prestigious Institut d'Etudes Politiques began to admit some young people from ghetto neighborhoods on a special basis, and in 2004 thirty-five major private firms signed a "charter of diversity" committing themselves to hiring members of ethnic and racial minorities.[22] In 2008 President Sarkozy established the Commission on Diversity and appointed an Algerian-born businessman to head it. Nevertheless, some observers fear that excessive attention to the claims of minorities might weaken France's cultural and political unity and undermine its "national identity." [23]

Governmental and public responses to the problem of national identity have been ambiguous, in particular to the question of how it relates to racial, religious, and ethnic minorities. In the early 1980s Socialist governments accorded de facto legitimation of ethnoregional languages by subsidizing their teaching, but this policy was followed in 1992 by a constitutional amendment inserting the statement that "the language of the Republic shall be French," and the continued refusal to ratify the European Charter on minority languages. In 2008, however, a constitutional amendment specifically acknowledged that regional languages are part of "the patrimony of France." Laws exist to protect minorities against discrimination in employment and housing, but they are difficult to enforce.[24] Political leaders have made numerous commitments to reduce continuing inequalities between "visible minorities," such as Beurs (North African Muslims) and blacks, and the rest of the population, but no precise statistical data have been gathered on these groups for more than a century. Some have suggested listing questions on race, religion, and ethnicity in the census, but the Council of State has opposed this idea on the grounds that it would violate the principle of equality of individuals, and others (especially Socialists) have argued against it for fear that it would "ethnify" social policy.[25]

National identity became an important issue during Sarkozy's campaign for the presidency, in part because he wanted to appeal to the xenophobic elements of the electorate, in particular the traditional supporters of the National Front. The public debate on the issue (see page 110) was undertaken at the end of 2009 in part to divert the electorate's attention from growing economic problems as well as from Sarkozy's declining popularity. The debate has spread to political parties, parliamentary deputies, and academics. It was part of the reaction to public concern about the large number of immigrants, especially "visible" minorities, whose presence attested to the increasingly multiethnic, multiracial, and multicultural texture of French society. It was probably also motivated by a desire to prevent the growth of extreme-right organizations, which have profited from the spread of urban violence, much of which has been attributed to immigrants. The debate went hand-in-hand with the continuing campaign against *"communautarisme"* and with a parliamentary inquiry into the wearing in public of the *burqa*, a cloak that covers strictly observant Muslim women from head to toe, with only slits for eyes. Sarkozy favored banning it, arguing that it was not an expression of religious liberty but of women's subservience, and parliament enacted the ban.

The growing sensitivity toward minorities and provincial aspirations constitutes evidence that the traditional Jacobin ideology of republican regimes—the idea of France as a culturally homogeneous and centralized nation-state—which has been an important aspect of French "exceptionalism," is being called into question and that pluralisms of all kinds are developing. This development is seen not only in the existing rivalries between political parties and interest groups, and more specifically between the various trade unions, but also in the more assertive behavior of parliament; in the growing acceptance of power sharing between president and prime minister; in the greater government readiness to grant a degree of legitimacy to regional ethnic languages; and in the competition between private and public educational systems and mass media, between national and subnational centers of decision making (albeit stopping short of federalism), and between the state and the market.[26]

The social and economic problems are plentiful: overcrowded and often unsafe secondary schools and an insufficient number of teachers, environmental pollution, the persistence of unemployment and its corollary, the risk of depleted social security funds. Finally, there is widespread recognition of the need for strong measures to curb delinquency, urban violence, and terrorism and to protect society from the spread of AIDS, but without infringing on civil liberties in taking those measures.

In recent years, citizens' loss of interest in traditional forms of political participation has raised concerns. Greater numbers of citizens are abstaining from voting. The abstention rates were 35.6 percent in the first round and 39.7 percent in the second round of the 2002 National Assembly elections, compared with abstention rates of 22.8 percent in the first round and 25.2 percent in the second round of the Assembly elections of 1958. In the crucial referendum of 2000 to reduce the president's term of office, the abstention rate was nearly 70 percent.[27] Furthermore, citizens' identification with political parties has declined steadily, as reflected in the loss of dues-paying members in all the major parties. This situation is only partly compensated by the growing memberships of interest groups, especially on the local level.

These phenomena are indicative of an impatience with mainstream political parties and a distrust of politicians. The fact that in recent national elections marginal parties, including the National Front, garnered more than a third of the vote does not, however, mean that the French want to replace the existing democratic system with another one. On the contrary, there is a widespread consensus about the regime itself. To be sure, disagreements continue on the best ways to reduce the social security deficit and to administer the welfare state, about how to reform the educational system, about how to stem the delocalization of industries, and about which policies should be adopted to deal with immigration. There continue to be disagreements about specific institutional questions as well: whether there should be a full or partial return to proportional representation for National Assembly elections; whether the practice of holding more than one elective office simultaneously should be maintained or abolished; whether the government should resort to the referendum more often or less often; and to what extent the relationship between the judiciary and the executive should be redefined. Moreover, proposals continue to be advanced about reforming the relationship between the legislature and the executive, reconfiguring the relationship between the president and the prime minister, and restructuring the distribution of power between the central government and the regional and local authorities.[28] There are even proposals to replace the existing constitutional system with a new one, a Sixth Republic.[29] But there is little doubt that the political system as a whole is sound and well enough designed to meet France's future challenges.

NOTES

1. See William Safran, "Rights and Liberties under the Mitterrand Presidency: Socialist Innovations and Post-Socialist Revisions," *Contemporary French Civilization* 12 (Winter/Spring 1988): 1–35.

2. At the end of 2000, members of the judiciary, while fully supporting such a policy, went on strike to obtain an addition to the panels of investigating magistrates needed to deal with the added caseload required to implement it.

3. In 2008 nearly 65,000 men and women were in prisons, but those prisons had places for only 50,000.

4. Professional judges have complained about the lack of training of these volunteers, who numbered more than three thousand in 2003.

5. In order to provide such equality, the French government has introduced a bill to change the labor code, under which "women may not be employed in any job that requires night work." Clarisse Fabre, "Le travail de nuit des femmes divise la majorité," *Le Monde*, November 23, 2000.

6. Services France et Société, "La condamnation de la France pour 'torture' embarrasse le gouvernement," *Le Monde*, July 30, 1999. After the mandatory limit of twelve days as an executive order, the measure was extended by legislative action for three months.

7. The "Clearstream" affair reflected an intense rivalry between the two verging on mutual hatred. In 2010 the charges were dismissed for insufficient evidence.

8. After the mandatory limit of twelve days as an executive order, the measure was extended by legislative action for three months.

9. These measures include taking a more flexible approach to the thirty-five-hour workweek; introducing rules that make layoffs of workers easier, especially for small enterprises; encouraging businesses by giving them subsidies to hire unemployed workers for a two-year period; and reducing benefits for unemployed workers who refuse to accept jobs offered them by the national employment office. Rémi Barroux, "Des sanctions renforcés pour les demandeurs d'emploi," *Le Monde*, July 23, 2005.

10. Among them, the mandatory use of generic drugs, increased copayments, and the end of reimbursement of more than two hundred medications by the social security funds.

11. According to a poll conducted by SOFRES at the end of 2004, 75 percent of the respondents believed that it was up to individuals more than the state to move society forward. At the same time, however, they opposed the privatization of hospitals (74 percent); an increase in cost sharing by patients for medical care (85 percent); the raising of the retirement age to sixty-five (78 percent); and an easing of protection against layoffs by employers (81 percent). Reported by Sylvie Pierre-Brossolette, "La fin des tabous?" *Figaro-Magazine*, January 17, 2004, 41–50.

12. See Roger Fauroux and Bernard Spitz, *Etat d'urgence: Réformer ou abdiquer, Le choix français* (Paris: Laffont, 2004); and Nicolas Baverez, *La France qui tombe* (Paris: Perrin, 2004).

13. On the contrary, the government increased the income supplements for families having more than two children—both in order to appease the electorate and to promote a natalist policy.

14. Mark Vail, "Rethinking Social Protection in the Fifth Republic: 'Buttressed Liberalization' in an Age of Austerity," in *The French Fifth Republic at Fifty*, ed. Sylvain Brouard et al. (New York: Palgrave-Macmillan, 2009), 192f.

15. The RSA replaced the Minimum Insertion Income (RMI), a minimum monthly income guarantee introduced by the Rocard government in 1988.

16. Claire Guélaud, "M. Sarkozy taxe les revenus du capital pour financer le RSA," *Le Monde*, August 28, 2008; and Michel Delberghe, Christophe Jakobyszyn, and Patrick Roger, "Malgré les protestations, Nicolas Sarkozy assume la nouvelle taxation du capital," *Le Monde*, August 29, 2008.

17. At an international meeting in Davos, Switzerland, in January 2010.

18. Saïd Mahrane, "Sarkozy: est-il de gauche?" *Le Point*, August 20, 2009, 16–21.

19. The partial privatization of Air France, maritime transport, and the electricity supply has provoked particularly sharp opposition.

20. One of the contributors to this fear was the Bolkestein directive issued by the European Commission early in 2005, which proposed that an EU member country having a plant in another country could apply its own rules on wages and social protections in that country.

21. An example of France's reduced influence in European institutions was the summary rejection by the European Commission of Chirac's demand in 2005 that it bail out those French workers being laid off by the American company Hewlett-Packard.

22. See *Discrimination positive: Donner ses chances à l'égalité*, special issue of *Le Monde de l'Education*, February 2004. Affirmative action had been advocated by Sarkozy when he was minister of the interior but firmly opposed by President Chirac and Prime Minister Villepin.

23. See William Safran, "State, Nation, National Identity, and Citizenship: France as a Test Case," *International Political Science Review* 12 (July 1991): 220–239.

24. For example, racial profiling of blacks and Arabs is illegal, but it is practiced regularly by police.

25. Bariza Khiari, "Statistiques ethniques: contre l'ethnicisation de la question sociale," *Regards sur l'Actualité* 327 (January 2007): 65–70.

26. See Vivien A. Schmidt, "The Changing Dynamics of State-Society Relations in the Fifth Republic," in *The Changing French Political System*, ed. Robert Elgie (London: Frank Cass, 2000), 141–165; and William Safran, "Institutional Pluralism and Multiculturalism in France: Post-Jacobin Transformations," *Political Science Quarterly* 118 (Fall 2003): 437–465.

27. Rates of abstention in other recent elections are 37.9 percent in the first round of the 2004 regional elections, 39.1 percent in the first round of the cantonal elections that year, and 57.2 percent in the 2004 elections for the European Parliament. In the 2007 presidential elections, the abstention rate was only about 16 percent in both rounds, but in the ensuing parliamentary elections it went up to 40 percent.

28. See, for example, Jack Lang, *Changer* (Paris: Plon, 2005); and Jérôme Chartier, *Le lifting de Marianne* (Paris: L'Archipel, 2005).

29. See Olivier Duhamel, *Vive la VIe République* (Paris: Seuil, 2002); and Bastien François and Arnaud Montebourg, *La constitution de la VIe République* (Paris: Odile Jacob, 2005).

FOR FURTHER READING

Aldrich, Robert, and John Connell, eds. *France in World Politics*. London and New York: Routledge, 1989.

Andrews, William G., and Stanley Hoffmann, eds. *The Fifth Republic at Twenty*. Albany: State University of New York Press, 1980.

Ardagh, John. *France Today*. New York and London: Penguin, 1987.

Baumgartner, Frank R. *Conflict and Rhetoric in French Policy Making*. Pittsburgh: University of Pittsburgh Press, 1989.

Boy, Daniel, and Nonna Mayer, eds. *The French Voter Decides*. Ann Arbor: University of Michigan Press, 1993.

Brouard, Sylvain, Andrew Appleton, and Amy G. Mazur, eds. *The French Republic at Fifty*. New York: Palgrave-Macmillan, 2009.

Christofferson, Thomas R. *The French Socialists in Power, 1981–1986*. Newark: University of Delaware Press, 1991.

Cole, Alistair, Patrick le Galés, and Jonah Levy, eds. *Developments in French Politics*. London: Palgrave-Macmillan, 2005.

Converse, Philip E., and Roy Pierce. *Political Representation in France.* Cambridge: Harvard University Press, 1986.

de Gaulle, Charles. *The Complete War Memoirs.* 3 vols. New York: Simon and Schuster, 1972.

Elgie, Robert. *The Changing French Political System.* London: Frank Cass, 2000.

———, ed. *The Role of the Prime Minister in France, 1981–91.* New York: St. Martin's Press, 1993.

Elgie, Robert, and Steven Griggs. *French Politics: Debates and Controversies.* London and New York: Routledge, 2000.

Evans, Jocelyn, ed. *The French Party System.* Manchester and New York: Manchester University Press, 2003.

Feldblum, Miriam. *Reconstructing Citizenship: The Politics of Nationality Reform and Immigration in Contemporary France.* Albany: State University of New York Press, 1999.

Fenby, Jonathan. *France on the Brink.* New York: Arcade Publishing, 1999.

Flynn, Gregory, ed. *Remaking the Hexagon: The New France in the New Europe.* Boulder: Westview Press, 1995.

Friend, Julius W. *Seven Years in France: François Mitterrand and the Unintended Revolution, 1981–1988.* Boulder: Westview Press, 1989.

Godt, Paul, ed. *Policy-Making in France from de Gaulle to Mitterrand.* London: Pinter, 1989.

Gourevitch, Peter A. *Paris and the Provinces.* Berkeley: University of California Press, 1980.

Guyomarch, Alain, Howard Machin, and Ella Ritchie, eds. *France in the European Union.* London: Macmillan, 1998.

Hauss, Charles. *Politics in Gaullist France: Coping with Chaos.* New York: Praeger, 1991.

Hazareesingh, Sudhir. *Political Traditions in Modern France.* New York: Oxford University Press, 1994.

Hollifield, James F., and George Ross, eds. *Searching for the New France.* New York and London: Routledge, 1991.

Judt, Tony. *The Burden of Responsibility: Blum, Camus, Aron, and the French Twentieth Century.* Chicago and London: University of Chicago Press, 1999.

Keeler, John T. S. *The Politics of Neocorporatism in France.* New York: Oxford University Press, 1987.

Keeler, John T. S., and Martin A. Schain, eds. *Chirac's Challenge: Liberalization, Europeanization and Malaise in France.* New York: St. Martin's Press, 1996.

Knapp, Andrew. *Parties and the Party System in France.* Basingstoke, UK, and New York: Palgrave-Macmillan, 2004.

Lewis-Beck, Michael. *The French Voter: Before and After the 2002 Elections.* New York and London: Palgrave-Macmillan, 2004.

———. *How France Votes.* New York and London: Chatham House, 2000.

Northcott, Wayne. *Mitterrand: A Political Biography.* New York: Holmes and Meier, 1992.

Raymond, Gino G., ed. *Structures of Power in Modern France.* New York: St. Martin's Press, 2000.

Rohr, John A. *Founding Republics in France and America.* Lawrence: University Press of Kansas, 1995.

Ross, George, Stanley Hoffmann, and Sylvia Malzacher, eds. *The Mitterrand Experiment.* New York: Oxford University Press, 1987.

Saadah, Anne. *Contemporary France: A Democratic Education.* Lanham, Md.: Rowman and Littlefield, 2003.

Safran, William. *The French Polity.* 7th ed. New York: Longman, 2009.

Schmidt, Vivien A. *From State to Market? The Transformation of French Business and Government.* New York: Cambridge University Press, 1996.

Smith, Paul. *The Senate of the Fifth French Republic.* New York: Palgrave-Macmillan, 2009.

Stone, Alec. *The Birth of Judicial Politics in France: The Constitutional Council in Comparative Perspective*. New York: Oxford University Press, 1992.

Suleiman, Ezra. *Elites in French Society: The Politics of Survival*. Princeton, N.J.: Princeton University Press, 1978.

Thody, Philip. *The Fifth French Republic: Presidents, Politics, and Personalities*. London and New York: Routledge, 1998.

Tiersky, Ronald. *France in the New Europe: Changing Yet Steadfast*. Belmond, Calif.: Wadsworth, 1994.

Weber, Eugen. *Peasants into Frenchmen: The Modernization of Rural France, 1870–1914*. Stanford, Calif.: Stanford University Press, 1976.

Wilson, Frank L. *Interest-Group Politics in France*. Cambridge: Cambridge University Press, 1988.

Part 3

Germany

David P. Conradt

The Context of German Politics 3.1

O N MAY 23, 2009, THE FEDERAL REPUBLIC OF GERMANY commemorated its sixtieth anniversary. As in past anniversaries, celebrations were low-key: no parades, long speeches, or the dedication of new monuments. The highlight of the day was the election by the Federal Assembly of the president of the republic, a largely ceremonial post. After the results were announced, flower bouquets were given to the winner (the incumbent) and the other candidates, a small orchestra played the national anthem, and by 2:30 in the afternoon everyone went home. One of the participants, the chief executive of the state of Lower Saxony, was delighted that the vote took only one ballot because he and others did not want to miss the big soccer match later that day.

The few speeches that were given emphasized the success of the constitution ratified sixty years earlier and the political stability it had brought to the country. Some even cited polls in which a majority of Germans stated that they were proud of and even loved their constitution. This was a constitution that works and would continue to structure political activity through good times and hard times.

Indeed, at the sixty-year mark of its postwar history, Germany—like its European and North American allies—finds itself in hard times. The worldwide economic crisis, which began in the United States in 2008, spread to Germany and other developed countries in Europe, Asia, and Latin America with remarkable speed. By the second quarter of 2008 the economy began to contract, and by the end of the year Germany was officially in recession.

This crisis was the worst since the Great Depression of the 1930s, which ushered in the twelve-year nightmare of Adolf Hitler's Third Reich. In the republic's early years from 1949 until about the early 1970s, many analysts considered democracy to be on a very fragile footing and highly susceptible to an economic downturn. It was considered by many a "fair weather democracy." Today, after sixty years of democratic stability, there is no doubt as to the legitimacy of the political process we examine in the following chapters. Indeed, few societies have greater resources to deal with these problems than the Federal Republic.

The current economic slowdown and Germany's postwar history illustrate why in any study of modern European politics an examination of Germany must occupy a prominent place. From 1949 to 1990 Germany was divided into two states: the Federal Republic of Germany (FRG), or West Germany, and the German Democratic Republic (GDR), or East Germany. The unified Federal Republic, formed in 1989–1990, is—unlike France, Great Britain, Italy, or Sweden—one of Europe's newer states, even though Germans certainly rank among Europe's oldest people and are the most numerous people in Western and Central Europe. Unified Germany is also Europe's largest *federal* state. As Europe strives for an ever closer union, Germany's experience with federalism gives added weight to its importance in the councils of the European Union.

The collapse of the East German state in 1989–1990 and its incorporation into the Federal Republic is just one more example of the frequent changes that have characterized Germany's history. Indeed, the study of modern German politics offers an exceptional opportunity to examine the problems associated with political change and development. Few societies have experienced such drastic changes in their political system. In little more than a century, Germany has assumed the form of an empire (1871–1918), an unstable democratic republic (1919–1933), a totalitarian dictatorship (1933–1945), a military occupation (1945–1949), two separate states (1949–1990), and, since 1990, a single federal state. Germany and the Germans have therefore experienced most of the major political and ideological movements in modern history. The development of the Federal Republic since 1949 illustrates the extent to which a country can largely overcome its political heritage and change its political culture. In fact, few modern democracies have been as stable and legitimate as the one examined in the following chapters. The success of West Germany and its attraction to East Germans was an important factor in the deterioration of the East German communist regime. West Germany's record as a model democracy and peaceful neighbor since 1945 enabled the 1989–1990 unification to take place with the support of the European and international communities.

How can all these changes be explained? Not only is the Federal Republic a stable democracy, but also in recent decades it has emerged out of the shadows of the Third Reich to become an important and assertive actor in European and international politics. It is one of the world's largest trading nations, and it has Europe's biggest economy. Its army is the major national contingent in the North Atlantic Treaty Organization (NATO). Yet the Federal Republic is firmly committed to deepening its relations with Eastern Europe and the states of the former Soviet Union and has become the leading advocate in the West of a new era of East-West cooperation. With the collapse of communism in Eastern Europe and the Soviet Union along with the breakup of the Soviet empire, Germany has assumed a greater leadership role in Central and Eastern Europe. The country's increased confidence in international affairs was also demonstrated in 2002–2003 when it refused to join the United States and Great Britain in their military action in Iraq. The worldwide economic and finance crisis that began in the United States has also resulted in policy differences between Germany and its Anglo-American partners.[1] Clearly, much is to be learned from an examination of Germany's politics.

Historical Context

Europe has known German-speaking people and German political units for almost a thousand years. Nevertheless, the Federal Republic is only sixty years old—a time span hardly comparable to that of most of its European neighbors. Although a relatively young state, the Federal Republic claims to be the legitimate successor to the Bismarckian Second Reich, the Weimar Republic, and the Third Reich. This claim also makes the Federal Republic heir to the German political tradition, a tradition characterized by national division and frequent change. Before there were "Germans," Europe was populated by numerous Germanic tribes: Saxons, Franks, Bavarians, Swabians, Silesians, and Thuringians, to name a few. But no single state has ever united all of Europe's ethnic Germans. The 1949–1990 division between West Germany, East Germany, and the "eastern territories" now part of Poland and the Russian Federation, was only one more variation in an ongoing theme in German and European history. The political division of the German nation has been the rule rather than the exception.

The Empire (1871–1918)

Until 1871 Europe's German-speaking people were divided into many small principalities, a few moderate-size kingdoms, and two large, yet divided, major powers: Austria in the southeast and Prussia in the north. The German Reich, or Empire, proclaimed in 1871 was a Prussian-dominated structure that did not include Austria. Nevertheless, it was by far the most successful unification effort in German history. This empire was largely the work of Otto von Bismarck, the Prussian prime minister and first imperial chancellor, or head of government, and was brought about through classical European power politics. Prussia, under Bismarck, fought successful wars against Denmark (1864), Austria (1866), and France (1870) to become the dominant power in northern and western Germany.

National unification did not, however, represent any success for German liberalism. Nationalism, which historically has been closely associated with liberalism in countries such as France and the United States, has been an illiberal force in the German political experience. The empire was established through the fabled "blood and iron" policies of Bismarck and not by Germany's parliamentary liberals. After 1871, most of them, in fact, deferred to the "Iron Chancellor" and became more national than liberal.

During the imperial period, Germany became one of the world's great powers. Industrialization and urbanization advanced rapidly, as did the Reich's military power. Yet the industrialists and other members of the expanding middle class did not challenge the political authority of the traditional Prussian ruling elites: the military, the bureaucracy, and the landed nobility. Germany had become a modern society ruled by a premodern, traditional elite. The empire was an authoritarian political structure with some democratic features. Although the kaiser (emperor), the hereditary head of the Hohenzollern dynasty, appointed the chancellor and his government, a freely elected parliament held the power of appropriations and could exert some influence and control over the executive. The upper house, however, which represented the states and could block most lower-house initiatives, was effectively dominated by Prussia. And in Prussia the voting system still gave a disproportionate influence to the upper-middle and upper classes. Military and foreign policy as well as internal security remained very much the province of the traditional Prussian elite. Parliament could not, for example, prevent Bismarck's campaigns of suppression against Catholics and socialists.

None of Bismarck's successors was able to maintain the delicate foreign and domestic equilibrium that characterized Germany from 1871 to 1890. In creating the Reich, Bismarck and the Prussians made many enemies in Europe, especially France, which lost the provinces of Alsace and Lorraine after the 1870 Franco-Prussian War. To the east, Russia feared German power. Bismarck was able to avoid a Franco-Russian alliance, but his successors were not. With Kaiser Wilhelm—a romantic nationalist—on the throne, Germany after Bismarck sought to acquire overseas colonies and, through the expansion of the fleet, to challenge British naval superiority. By the turn of the century, this aggressive post-Bismarck foreign policy had managed to provoke France, Great Britain, and Russia to ally against the Reich.

Internally, the paradox of a rapidly modernizing society controlled by premodern political elites continued to produce socioeconomic and political tensions. The expanding working class provided a solid electoral base for the Social Democratic Party (SPD), but the party was unable to achieve political influence commensurate with its growing numerical strength. The middle-class parties that also grew throughout the empire were unable and probably unwilling to oppose the militarist and imperialist policies of the kaiser and his chancellor. Indeed, Germany's middle-class parties often deferred to the traditional Prussian elites and supported measures such as the naval arms race with Great Britain. Unlike their counterparts in Great Britain and France, the German middle classes did not exert a moderating influence on policy. Militant nationalism was one means by which the traditional elite could unify a divided society and maintain its power position.

The empire so carefully constructed by Bismarck did not survive World War I. As the war dragged on after the failure of the initial German offensive, the many tensions and contradictions in the socioeconomic and political structures of the empire became apparent. Socialists, liberals, and Catholics began to question a conflict that pitted Germany against countries such as Great Britain and the United States, whose democratic values and constitution they hoped to achieve someday in Germany. A victory on the battlefield would strengthen a regime these groups had opposed in peacetime.

As the war went on, severe rationing caused by the Allied blockade, mounting casualty lists, and the pressures of wartime production began to take their toll on civilian morale, especially among factory workers. When the army's 1918 spring offensive failed, the military, which in the final years of the war actually made most important economic and political decisions, advised the kaiser to abdicate and the parliamentary leadership to proclaim a republic and negotiate a peace with the Western powers.

The Weimar Republic (1919–1933)

In January 1919 Germans elected delegates to a constituent assembly that met in the city of Weimar to formulate a new constitution for the postwar republic. The delegates, many of whom were distinguished legal scholars, produced a model democratic constitution, one of the most advanced in the world. It contained an extensive catalogue of human rights and provided numerous opportunities for popular participation through referendums, petitions, and the direct election of a strong president.

The republic, however, began under very unfavorable circumstances. After the departure of the kaiser, some German Marxists attempted to duplicate the Bolsheviks' success in Russia. Workers' and soldiers' councils were established in several cities, and Bavaria experienced a short-lived socialist republic. Eventually, a coalition of moderate social democrats, liberals, and conservative nationalists crushed these abortive efforts at a communist revolution. As a consequence, the working class remained divided throughout the Weimar Republic between the Social Democratic Party, which supported the parliamentary system, and the Communist Party, which sought its overthrow. These events also established a pattern of political violence that was to continue throughout the period. In addition, the republic was identified from the beginning with defeat, national humiliation, and ineffectiveness.

Meanwhile, the conservative nationalists, urged on by the military, propagated the myth that Germany had not really lost World War I, but had been "stabbed in the back" by the

"November criminals," identified as socialists, communists, liberals, and Jews. Large segments of the bureaucracy and the judiciary also were more attached to the authoritarian values of the empire than to those of the republic, and they acted accordingly.

The republic's brief history was characterized by a steady polarization of politics between left and right. In the early elections of the 1920s, pro-Republican parties—Social Democrats, the Center (Catholic) Party, and the Democratic Party (Liberals)—had a solid majority of seats. By the early 1930s, the pro-Republican share of the vote had dropped from about 65 percent to only 30 percent. The Nazis on the right and the Communists on the left together held more than half of the parliamentary delegates. With most voters supporting parties opposed to the republic, it became impossible to build a stable governing coalition. Policymaking became increasingly the responsibility of the president, who made extensive use of his power to issue executive decrees without regard for the wishes of the fragmented parliament.

The worldwide depression of 1929 dealt the republic a blow from which it could not recover. By 1932 more than a third of the workforce was unemployed, and the Nazis became the largest party in the parliament. The public wanted an effective government that would "do something." The democratic parties and their leaders could not meet this demand.

The Third Reich and World War II (1933–1945)

The only party that thrived on this crisis was the Nazi Party, under its leader, Adolf Hitler. The National Socialist German Workers Party (NSDAP) was one of many nationalist and *völkisch* (racialist) movements that had emerged after World War I. Hitler's leadership ability set the Nazis apart from the others. A powerful orator, Hitler was able to appeal to a wide variety of voters and interests. He denounced the Versailles treaty that had imposed harsh terms on Germany after World War I and the "criminals" who signed it for Germany. To the unemployed, he promised jobs in the rebuilding of the nation (rearmament and public works). To business interests, he represented a bulwark against communism. To farmers and small businessmen, caught between big labor and business, he promised recognition of their proper position in German society and protection against Marxist labor and "Jewish plutocrats."

In January 1933 President Paul von Hindenburg asked Hitler to form a government. The conservatives around the president believed they could easily control and "handle" Hitler once he had responsibility. Two months later, the Nazis pushed an Enabling Act through the parliament that essentially gave Hitler total power; the parliament, constitution, and civil liberties were suspended. The will of the *Führer* (leader) became the supreme law and authority. By 1934 almost all areas of life had become "synchronized" (*gleichgeschaltet*) to the Nazi pattern.

There is little doubt that most Germans, at least until the start of World War II, supported Hitler. A survey conducted in 1951, six years after the war, found that a majority of citizens under forty-five years of age still believed that the prewar years of the Third Reich (1933–1939) were the "best" that Germany had experienced in that century.[2] Those years were ones of economic growth and at least a surface prosperity: unemployment was virtually eliminated; inflation was checked; and the economy, fueled by expenditures for rearmament and public works, boomed. That during these "good years" thousands were imprisoned, tortured, and murdered in concentration camps and hundreds of thousands of German Jews were systematically persecuted was apparently of minor importance to most citizens in comparison with the economic and policy successes of the regime. Indeed, most Germans, at least between 1933 and 1939, were willing to give up the democratic political order and the liberal society and accept the regime's racism and persecution of political opponents in exchange for economic prosperity, social stability, and a resurgence of national pride.

As for World War II in Europe, it was, in the words of Helmut Schmidt, a former chancellor of the Federal Republic, "totally started, led, and lost by Adolf Hitler acting in the name of the German people." [3] The world paid for this war with a total of about 60 million dead, including 8 million Jews and other political and racial victims murdered in concentration camps. The most ruthless and inhuman Nazi actions were directed against European Jewry. From the beginning of the Nazi movement, the Jews were regarded as the prime cause of all the misfortune, unhappiness, and disappointments endured by the German people. Hitler in his autobiography, *Mein Kampf,* written in the early 1920s, repeated in print his oft-spoken conviction that Jews were not humans, nor even subhumans, but rather "disease-causing bacilli" in the body of the nation that must be exterminated. Unfortunately, at the time few Germans took his ranting seriously, and yet Hitler and the Nazis remained committed to this policy after they came to power. From 1933 on, first in Germany and then throughout the conquered lands of Europe, the Nazis systematically began a process that denied the Jews their dignity, economic livelihood, humanity, and finally, by the early 1940s, their right to physically exist.

The "final solution" to the "Jewish problem" was the murder of millions of Jewish men, women, and children, first by special SS (*Schutzstaffel)* killing units, German military personnel, and militarized police detachments and later at extermination camps especially constructed for this purpose in isolated sections of Europe. Hitler and other leading Nazis were able to carry out this Holocaust in part because of deeply rooted traditions of anti-Semitism in Germany and other parts of Europe. As recent research has shown, many "ordinary" Germans who were neither Nazis nor members of the SS willingly participated in the torture and murder of innocent Jews. They believed, as did Hitler, that Jews were a mortal threat that had to be eliminated. [4]

Only the total military defeat of the Third Reich in May 1945 by France, Great Britain, the Soviet Union, the United States, and forces from other allied nations prevented the Nazis from totally exterminating European Jewry. The remnant that remained amounted to less than 10 percent of the prewar Jewish population of Europe. The Federal Republic has accepted legal and moral responsibility for the crimes of the Nazi era. Even though it is, of course, impossible to atone for the Holocaust, since the early 1950s the Federal Republic has paid almost $90 billion in reparations to the state of Israel and Jewish victims of Nazism. [5]

For many Germans, the real distress began after the war. During the war, the Nazis, mindful of the effects of Allied blockades during World War I, had gone to great lengths to ensure a relatively well-fed, housed, and clothed population. But military defeat ended this supply of foodstuffs, raw materials, and labor from the occupied territories, which had been ruthlessly exploited by the German armies. After 1945 the Germans found themselves in the same position as the populations in other European countries. In 1945 and

1946, the average caloric intake was set at only a third of the daily requirement. In large cities such as Berlin and Düsseldorf, 80 percent to 90 percent of all houses and apartments were uninhabitable; in Cologne, a city with a population of 750,000 before the war, only 40,000 people remained during the winter of 1945–1946. Heating fuel was also in critically short supply. Before the war, the coal mines of the Ruhr produced an average of 400,000 tons a day; in 1945–1946, they produced only 25,000 tons a day.

The end of World War II meant the end of Germany as a political entity. The victorious Allies returned some of the territory conquered by the Nazis to its prewar owners (Austria, Czechoslovakia, France, Poland, and Yugoslavia,) and divided the remainder into zones of military occupation. But by the late 1940s, the onset of the cold war had dashed any hopes that the wartime coalition could agree on a single postwar German state. In 1949 the U.S., British, and French zones of occupation became the Federal Republic of Germany, or West Germany, with its capital in the small city of Bonn on the Rhine River. In the same year, the Soviet zone of occupation became the German Democratic Republic, or East Germany, with the Russian sector of Berlin as its capital.

The Federal Republic

During the past six decades, the Federal Republic has developed into a strong, dynamic democracy. Unlike the Weimar Republic, the Federal Republic has, since its earliest days, been identified with economic prosperity and foreign and domestic policy successes. There is also considerable evidence that a consensus on democratic values and norms has developed during this period. The vast majority of the population supports this system and believes in its fundamental norms: individual freedom, the rule of law, civil liberties, free political competition, and representative institutions. In this sense, Germany and the Germans have changed.

The history of the Federal Republic can be divided into four rather distinct phases. The first is the *formative period* (1949–1961), which was characterized by an emphasis on economic reconstruction and the stabilization of the new political system both internally and externally through German participation in the European Community and the Atlantic Alliance (NATO). This stabilization occurred within the context of the cold war. The Christian Democratic Union (CDU) and the republic's first chancellor, Konrad Adenauer, dominated politics during this period.

The second phase, from 1966 to 1982, was an *era of reform* dominated by the Social Democrats and their first two chancellors, Willy Brandt and Helmut Schmidt. Here the emphasis was on change, internal and external. Internally, a variety of economic, social, and cultural innovations were enacted. The welfare state was expanded to become one of the most generous in Europe—it was time for the workers to get their share of the wealth created during the booming 1950s and 1960s. This period also witnessed the launch of the greater mass political participation that continued throughout the 1970s. The student protest movement, the "extra parliamentary opposition" spawned by dissatisfaction with the 1966 "Grand Coalition" between the Christian Democratic Union–Christian Social Union (CSU) and the Social Democratic Party, and the beginnings of a grassroots citizens' action group movement (*Bürgerinitiativen*) were all expressions of this growing politicization. In foreign policy, the Social Democrats initiated a new approach of reconciliation with its communist neighbors in Eastern Europe and the Soviet Union.

219

The third phase, the *unification* or *Kohl era,* covers the period 1982–1998. Helmut Kohl, together with his Free Democratic partners, promised a *Wende,* or fundamental change, especially in the republic's domestic policies. Social programs were cut; incentives to business were increased; and government budget deficits declined. This approach was a modest German version of the supply-side economics practiced by Prime Minister Margaret Thatcher in Great Britain and President Ronald Reagan in the United States. But the new government also attempted to turn the country away from what it regarded as the excessive permissiveness and liberalism of the social-liberal era. Traditional values of family, country, thrift, work, and duty were emphasized, at least by Kohl. Yet the trends toward increased politicization and mass protest evident since the late 1960s continued. In 1983 the first new political party in almost thirty years, the Greens, entered the national parliament. Its success was attributable above all to the "new politics" of environmental protection, women's rights, and disarmament. During this phase the Federal Republic also assumed a higher profile in international relations. In 1989 West Germany strongly opposed the policies of the United States on the modernization and deployment of new short-range missiles in West Germany. After 1990 unification or "putting Germany back together again" became the focus of politics.[6] By 1998 almost a trillion dollars had been poured into the economic and social reconstruction of the five new eastern states that joined the Federal Republic.

The final and present phase is one of *economic crisis.* The international credit and financial meltdown that began in the United States in September 2008 had by early 2009 spread to Germany and much of Europe—Germany is not alone. But prior to the American recession the German economy was Europe's problem. The trouble began in 1998 with the return to power of the Social Democrats, whose partner, the Greens, assumed national political responsibility for the first time. As described earlier, Germany by 2005 was at the bottom of the European economic leaderboard. Between 1995 and 2005, it had the lowest growth rate in Western and Central Europe.[7] By 2005 unemployment and public debt had reached record levels. In this period the unstable economic situation was also reflected in increasing voter volatility. In 2005 voters compelled the two major parties, now reduced to less than 40 percent of the vote each, to form a Grand Coalition, the first such alignment since 1966. The Grand Coalition, which took office in November actually presided over an impressive economic recovery from 2006 to late 2008, which was cut short by the above-mentioned international credit, financial, and economic crisis. Under the Grand Coalition real economic growth jumped from only 0.8 percent in 2005 to 3.0 percent in 2006 and 2.5 percent in 2007. From 2005 to September 2008 over 1.5 million new jobs were created. But in 2009 voters decided to keep one of the coalition partners, the Christian Democrats, in power and reduced the support of the other, the Social Democrats, to their lowest level in the history of the Federal Republic. The Social Democrats then went into opposition, and the Free Democrats became the coalition partner of the Christian Democrats.

Federalism

Germany, unlike France, Great Britain, Italy, or Sweden, is a federal state in which certain government functions are reserved to the constituent *Länder* (states), each of which has a constitution and parliament. The sixteen states have fundamental responsibility for education, the mass media, and internal security and order (police power). In addition, the bureaucracies of the *Länder* administer most laws passed at the national level.

German states vary widely in area, population, and socioeconomic structure (see Tables 3-1, 3-2, and 3-3). The three "city-states" of Hamburg, Berlin, and Bremen are largely Protestant and industrial commercial areas. They have generally been strongholds of the Social Democrats throughout most of the postwar period. The two other northern Protestant states are Schleswig-Holstein, which is relatively rural and small town, and Lower Saxony, which is more balanced between urban-industrial and rural-agrarian activity. Both states have had competitive politics for most of the postwar period with alternations between Christian Democratic–and Social Democratic–controlled governments.

The most populous state in the Federal Republic is North Rhine-Westphalia, which contains more than 20 percent of the Federal Republic's 82.2 million inhabitants. A heavily industrialized and urbanized state, North Rhine-Westphalia has a relative balance between Catholics and Protestants. Although its politics has been largely controlled by the Social Democrats during the past twenty years, in 2005 the Christian Democrats became the largest party. But in May 2010 the Social Democrats returned to power in a coalition with the Greens. Hesse, another very industrialized, religiously balanced, western *Land,* was ruled as well by Social Democrats for most of the postwar period, but it has been governed by the Christian Democrats since 1999.

Table 3-1 States of the Federal Republic of Germany: Area and Population

	Capital	2008 Population (millions)	Area (thousands of km^2)	Population per km^2
North Rhine–Westphalia	Düsseldorf	18	34.1	528
Bavaria	Munich	12.5	70.6	177
Baden-Württemberg	Stuttgart	10.8	35.8	301
Lower Saxony	Hannover	8	47.6	167
Hesse	Wiesbaden	6.1	21.1	288
Saxony	Dresden	4.2	18.4	229
Berlin	—	3.4	0.9	3,834
Rhineland-Palatinate	Mainz	4	19.8	204
Saxony-Anhalt	Magdeburg	2.4	20.4	118
Schleswig-Holstein	Kiel	2.8	15.8	180
Brandenburg	Potsdam	2.5	29.5	86
Thuringia	Erfurt	2.3	16.2	142
Mecklenburg–West Pomerania	Schwerin	1.7	23.2	72
Hamburg	—	1.8	0.8	2,344
Saarland	Saarbrücken	1	2.6	404
Bremen	—	0.7	0.4	1,640
Total or average		82.2	357.2	230

Source: Federal Statistical Office (Wiesbaden).

Table 3-2 States of the Federal Republic of Germany: Gross National Product, 2008

	Total (€ billions)	Percentage of total	Per capita (€)
North Rhine–Westphalia	541.1	21.7	30,113
Bavaria	444.8	17.8	35,530
Baden-Württemberg	364.3	14.6	33,876
Lower Saxony	214.4	8.6	26,902
Hesse	220.8	8.9	36,382
Saxony	95.1	3.8	22,620
Berlin	87.5	3.5	25,554
Rhineland-Palatinate	107.5	4.3	25,777
Saxony-Anhalt	53.8	2.2	22,427
Schleswig-Holstein	73.6	3	25,945
Brandenburg	54.9	2.2	21,721
Thuringia	49.8	2	21,875
Mecklenburg–West Pomerania	35.9	1.4	21,439
Hamburg	89.6	3.6	50,640
Saarland	32.2	1.3	30,168
Bremen	27.7	1.1	41,918
Total or average	2,492.0	100	30,343

Source: Federal Statistical Office (Wiesbaden).

Two other western states—Rhineland-Palatinate and the Saarland—have large Catholic populations. Rhineland-Palatinate is less industrialized than the much smaller Saarland, which has had an extensive, but now declining, steel industry. In the Saarland, the Social Democrats were in the minority until 1985, when they won their first state election since 1945. In 1999 they returned to the opposition. After the 2009 state election, the first-ever "Jamaica" coalition (named after the colors of the Jamaican flag) composed of Christian Democrats (Black), Free Democrats (Yellow), and Greens was formed in this state. Rhineland-Palatinate, until 1991, had been governed continuously by Christian Democratic–led coalitions. In 2006 the Social Democrats won an absolute majority of legislative seats and now govern this state alone for the first time in its history.

Western Germany's "sunbelt" is composed of the two states of Bavaria and Baden-Württemberg. Bavaria is largely Catholic. It is the only large *Land* whose borders were restored intact after the war. It calls itself a "free state" with its own strong historical traditions. Indeed, separatism in various forms has at times been a significant force in Bavarian politics. Bavaria has been governed without interruption since 1957 by the Christian Social Union, the sister party of the Christian Democratic Union—that is, the CDU does not contest elections in Bavaria. Historically rural and small town in character, Bavaria has over the past half-century become an urbanized state and a center of high-tech industry.

Over the past twenty years, Baden-Württemberg has had the most dynamic economy of any state. It is home to Germany's computer, robotics, and other high-tech industries. Many marquee firms such as Daimler-Benz and Porsche are located here. Its high rate of economic growth contrasts with those of the more sluggish economies of many northern areas. The Christian Democrats have been the dominant party.

Table 3-3 States of the Federal Republic of Germany: Workforce, Religion, and Politics

	Foreign Residents (Percent)	Workforce in agriculture (2008, percent)	Unemployment (2008, percent)	Roman Catholics (percent)	2010 governing party or coalition
North Rhine–Westphalia	11	2	8.5	47	SPD–Greens
Bavaria	10	4	4.2	62	CSU-FDP
Baden-Württemberg	12	3	4.1	41	CDU-FDP
Lower Saxony	7	4	7.7	20	CDU-FDP
Hesse	12	2	6.6	24	CDU-FDP
Saxony	3	3	12.8	5	CDU-FDP
Berlin	13	—	13.9	8	SPD–The Left
Rhineland-Palatinate	8	3	5.6	47	SPD
Saxony-Anhalt	2	4	14	5	CDU-SPD
Schleswig-Holstein	5	3	7.6	6	CDU-FDP
Brandenburg	3	4	13	5	SPD–The Left
Thuringia	2	4	11.3	9	CDU-SPD
Mecklenburg–West Pomerania	2	5	14.1	4	SPD-CDU
Hamburg	15	—	8.1	11	CDU-Greens
Saarland	9	—	7.3	74	CDU-FDP-Greens
Bremen	13	—	11.4	11	SPD-Greens
Total or average	9	3	7.8	33	

Source: Federal Statistical Office (Wiesbaden).

Note: CDU= Christian Democratic Union; CSU =Christian Social Union; FDP= Free Democratic Party; SPD= Social Democratic Party.

The five eastern states that joined the Federal Republic in 1990 are all relatively small. The largest, Saxony, with about 4 million residents, is only the sixth largest of the sixteen states. Saxony is also the major industrial center of the former East Germany, accounting for about 35 percent of the area's gross national product. Before 1933 Saxony was a stronghold of the Social Democrats, but the Christian Democrats won an absolute majority at the state's first free election in 1990 and have been reelected at all subsequent elections. The strip mining of lignite, an outmoded chemical industry, and decades of neglect left the state with major environmental problems.

The remaining four states are all smaller and less industrialized than Saxony. Its neighbor, Saxony-Anhalt, has the shortest history as an independent political entity. The state, which contains some of Germany's most fertile farmland, is currently governed by a coalition of Christian Democrats and Social Democrats. Thuringia, with 2.3 million inhabitants, has a more mixed economy than Saxony or Saxony-Anhalt. It was the center of the former East Germany's high-tech microelectronics industry. The Christian Democrats are the major governing party in this state. Brandenburg, once the core province of Prussia, is a sparsely populated state in the northeast. Until 1920 Berlin was a province of Brandenburg; the city lies within its borders, and the two states have been discussing a merger. Brandenburg's politics have been dominated by the Social Democrats. The smallest of the new states, with less than 2 million residents, is the coastal state of Mecklenburg-West Pomerania. This region is primarily agricultural, but it has a shipping industry that could become competitive in the international marketplace. In 1998 the Social Democrats, in a controversial decision, formed a governing coalition with the Party of Democratic Social-ism (PDS), the former Communist Party, marking the first time since unification that the PDS, which merged in 2005 with a western left movement, the Electoral Alternative Jobs and Social Justice and later became the Left Party, had assumed power at the state level. This government fell in 2006 and was replaced by a coalition of Social Democrats and Christian Democrats.

Finally, Berlin, the capital, is also a state. Like the country, it was unified in 1990. The four victorious World War II powers, the United States, the Soviet Union, Great Britain, and France, who technically controlled the city since 1945, ended their occupation. Divided since 1961 by a wall, East Berlin was the capital of the German Democratic Republic while West Berlin had a special status as a city under the official control of the United States, Great Britain, and France, but administered by a freely elected government. Since the double uni-fication of 1990, the two parts of the city also lost their special status and the abundant sub-sidies they received as a consequence of their "show case" position in the cold war. The city must now fend for itself, and that has been difficult. Currently, it is one of the most indebted of all the states. After unification, unemployment doubled, almost 20 percent of its popula-tion is on welfare, and 400,000 industrial jobs (mainly in the eastern section) have been lost.

Since 2001 it has been governed by a "Red-Red" coalition of Social Democrats and the Left Party. It continues to seek special status and economic relief from the national govern-ment. Currently, the city and the national government are attempting, with considerable difficulty, to negotiate a "treaty" that would determine the extent of this support.

Geographic and Demographic Context

Unified Germany comprises about three-fourths of the pre–World War II territory of the Reich. The remainder is now part of Poland or the Russian Federation. With a total area of about 138,000 square miles, the Federal Republic is roughly half the size of Texas. Its population of about 82.2 million, however, makes Germany one of Europe's largest and most densely populated states. Since 1945 the population has grown through (1) the influx between 1945 and 1961 of 14 million refugees and expellees from Germany's for-mer eastern territories and East Germany; (2) the in-migration of foreign workers, which began in the late 1950s and reached a high point of about 3 million workers in 1973; and (3) the addition of 16 million East Germans by unification. Since the late 1980s, almost 1 million ethnic Germans, largely from Poland, the former Soviet Union, and other areas in Eastern Europe, have resettled in Germany.

Most Germans live in towns and cities with populations greater than twenty thousand; and more than half of the 82 million inhabitants live on less than 10 percent of the land. The population of nine major urban areas exceed 1 million: the Rhine-Ruhr region between the cities of Düsseldorf and Dortmund; the Rhine-Main, or Frankfurt, area; Ber-lin; Stuttgart; Hamburg; Munich; the Rhine-Neckar region; and in the east the Leipzig and Dresden regions.

As for the makeup of the population, since 1970 the Federal Republic has experienced a demographic decline; it has had one of Europe's and the world's lowest birthrates. Indeed, over these forty years deaths have outnumbered births, and whatever growth in population western Germany has experienced has stemmed from the much higher birthrates associated with foreign workers. Between 1970 and 1987 the native German population actually declined by 1.3 million, while the number of foreign residents increased by 1.7 million. By 2005 the native population had declined to about 75 million. Also by 2005, one-fourth of German women were childless, one of the highest rates in the world. The 2005 birthrate of about 1.3 children per female of child-bearing age was half of what it was in 1965. Among females with university degrees, more than 40 percent are childless.[8]

After unification, the birthrate in eastern Germany dropped by almost 60 percent. Uncertainty about the future, the massive loss of jobs, and the end of special state subsidies for children and child-care programs were the major factors in the decline. The drop has been most pronounced among well-educated easterners in the under forty age group, many of whom have immigrated to the western states in search of better jobs. One eastern state, Thuringia, has adopted a policy once popular in the GDR. Upon the birth of the first child, the new parents are eligible for a low-interest (1.5 percent) loan of €5,000, parts of which are forgiven with each succeeding child. A second child reduces the principal to €4,000; the third child brings a further reduction to €2,500, and if the couple has a fourth child, the entire loan is forgiven. The loan is conditional upon a favorable credit rating. In the absence of a good rating, the couple is still eligible for a one-time grant of €500, which does not have to be repaid. Thuringia's program began in July 2008.[9] Another eastern state, Brandenburg, even offered a €500 grant to the parents of each newborn child. Nevertheless, since the fall of the Berlin Wall the eastern states have had a net population loss of about 2 million (13 percent). Of even greater concern is the type of people who are moving to the west: they are overwhelmingly young and well educated—the population groups critical to economic growth.[10]

These low birthrates, coupled with longer life expectancy, have made Germany, like many of its European neighbors, an older society. Between 1955 and 2002 the proportion of the population under twenty years of age dropped from 30 percent to 21 percent, and the size of the over-sixty age group increased from 16 percent to 24 percent. The young dependency ratio—that is, the ratio of those under twenty to those in the twenty- to fifty-nine-year-old group—has dropped from 56 percent to 38 percent. The elderly dependency ratio—the ratio of those over sixty to those in the twenty- to fifty-nine-year-old group, has increased from 29 percent to 44 percent. These changes mean that fewer younger people are now entering the productive period of their life cycle, and the number leaving the productive period and entering into the elderly group has increased. Put another way, fewer and fewer people are now working, but more people are dependent on this smaller productive segment of the population. This "demographic decline" is a major factor in the current financial problems affecting the pension and health insurance systems.

Religion

Most Germans are "born" into one of two churches: the Roman Catholic or the Evangelical Protestant (Lutheran).[11] Since the Reformation, Protestants and Catholics have been divided along regional lines. The east and north are predominantly Protestant; in the south and west, adherents of Roman Catholicism are in the majority. Historically, the respective secular rulers (princes) in these areas acted as "protectors" of the faith in their kingdoms, thereby making the churches dependent on state authority for their survival. The close, dependent relationship with the state meant that both churches, but especially the Protestant, which has no international ties comparable to those of the Roman Catholic, were conservative, status quo–oriented institutions. The separation of church and state, fundamental in the political tradition of the United States, is alien to the German political tradition; both churches occupy a privileged position in society and politics.

Lutheran and Catholic churches are largely financed through a church tax, a surcharge of about 8 percent on the individual income tax. The tax is collected by the state via withholding and is transferred at minimal cost to the churches' treasuries, which are thereby assured of a generous, inflation-proof income. Perhaps for that reason, the Cologne archdiocese of the Roman Catholic Church is the richest in the world. An individual can escape the church tax only by formally leaving the church, a procedure that most West Germans have declined to follow. Yet between 1970 and 2005, the proportion of members electing to contract out of the church tax increased from 8 percent to more than 20 percent. In recent years, both denominations have had to close and sell church property. And the Catholic Church has a severe shortage of priests.[12]

Although formal affiliation with the established churches is generally automatic and therefore high, most West Germans and especially Protestants are not very active religiously. Yet the political position and influence of the churches have been strong. The postwar occupation authorities viewed the churches as relatively untainted by Nazism and gave them preferential treatment. In addition, the Christian Democratic Union, the dominant political party from 1949 to 1969, was generally successful in projecting an image of a movement that would govern under Christian principles. Cynics and political opponents strongly disputed this CDU claim that it was more concerned with religion and morality than were other parties, but the CDU has definitely enjoyed the favor of, especially, the Catholic Church. This close CDU/CSU–Catholic Church relationship also compelled the Social Democrats by the late 1950s to seek at least a normalized, less conflictual relationship with the church. Both churches retain a privileged status. One example is that religious instruction in public schools by teachers acceptable to the churches is underwritten by public funds, and the state also pays the salaries of some church officials.

Historically, the regions that constituted East Germany were predominantly (about 90 percent) Protestant. The communist regime imposed after 1945 at first tried to eliminate the churches as independent social institutions. Funds for the upkeep of church buildings, seminaries, and publications, as well as the salaries of pastors, were steadily reduced. Religious instruction was banned from the schools and replaced by courses on scientific atheism. As a substitute for the traditional confirmation, the Communist Party instituted a *Jugendweihe* ceremony in which young people pledged fidelity to socialism and eternal friendship with the Soviet Union. Failure to participate usually meant that the young person would be denied admission to a university-track secondary school program. This antireligious policy of the regime had some success. In 1991 only 21 percent of East Germans, compared with 61 percent of West Germans, reported believing there was a God, and belief in a life after death was held by 14 percent in the east and 51 percent in the west.[13] About 75 percent of East Germans reported no religious affiliation, compared with 17 percent of West Germans.[14] Today, about 20 percent of East Germans remain affiliated with the Protestant Church, which throughout all the turmoil of the communist era still maintained close ties with its West German counterpart; about 3 percent are practicing Catholics.

Socioeconomic Structure

Germany has one of the most exposed and open economies of any major advanced industrial society. Although not immune to the ups and downs of the business cycle and the world economy, West Germany's economic record from 1949 to 2000 could not be matched by that of any other large, advanced industrial society, with the possible exception of Japan. In 2008 more than a third of Germany's gross domestic product (GDP) was from exports, which totaled almost $1.4 trillion. In 2007 and 2008 it was the world's largest exporter of goods, surpassing China, Japan, and the United States.

From 2000 to 2005, however, Germany's economic performance was among the poorest in Europe. Indeed, the economy hardly grew over the four-year period from 2001 to 2005 (see Table 3-4). Unemployment by 2005 reached nearly 5 million or about 11 percent of the workforce. And the budget has been in deficit since 2001. These deficits, which have exceeded 3 percent of GDP, have put the country in violation of the requirements of the Economic and Monetary Union (EMU) that countries in "Euroland" keep their public debt below that level. Only the inflation level has remained low over this period.

In spite of its recent economic record, Germany is still one of the world's major economic powers. Its per capita income, industrial production, and currency reserves are among the worlds highest. The economic system is mixed, with private property and free enterprise coexisting with substantial state involvement. It is also a social market economy in which an elaborate social welfare system is supported by both management and labor, as well as by all the significant political parties. But this generous welfare system, once lauded as a model for the world, is sometimes cited as a factor in the country's slow growth and high unemployment.

The well-educated work force is technically proficient; 84 percent of all business firms use computers, and more than half of all employees work daily with information and communication technologies. From 1991 to 2008 the number of employees with college and university degrees grew by 40 percent, and the number of workers without any vocational training dropped by 5 percent. About 70 percent of the workforce therefore is in

Table 3-4 The German Economy, 2000–2010

	2001	2001	2002	2003	2004	2005	2006	2009	2010[a]
Real gross domestic product increase	3.0	1.3	0.1	2.2	1.6	0.8	3.2	−5.0	3.4
Unemployment (millions)	3.9	3.8	4.1	4.4	4.4	4.9	4.5	3.4	3.1
Percent unemployed	9.1	8.9	9.4	10.2	10.1	10.8	9.8	7.8	7.7
Inflation (percent)	1.9	2.0	1.4	1.1	1.6	1.6	1.6	0.4	1.5
Budget (deficits)/ surplus (billion euros)	23.9	−58.6	−77.4	−86.6	−81.2	−74.2	−38.1	−105.5	100.0

Sources: Deutsches Institut für Wirtschaftsforschung (DIW-Berlin), Wochenbericht, no. 26-27, Summer 2004, 412; and no. 42, October 12, 2009; and no. 39, October 4, 2010; Ifo Institute, "Konjunkturprognose," Munich, December 19, 2005; Federal Statistical Office, "Öffentliches Finanzierungsdefizit auf 105.5 Milliarden Euro gestiegen," press release, March 31, 2010.

Note: The budget deficits from 2002 to 2005 and in 2009 all exceeded the Maastricht 3 percent criteria.

[a] The figures for 2010 are estimates.

knowledge-intensive occupations, and only 24 percent is in the traditional industrial jobs of manufacturing.[15] Industrial production is, however, still the largest single contributor to the country's GDP. The dominant industrial enterprises are concentrated in the electronics, motor vehicle, machine tool, chemical, and energy sectors. The remainder of the workforce is composed of those in independent nonmanual occupations (small businessowners, shopkeepers), independent professionals (physicians, lawyers), and those who work in agriculture, forestry, and fishing.

The fruits of the economic system have enabled the great majority of Germans to achieve a high standard of living. In spite of inflation, the disposable income of all occupational groups, including industrial workers, has steadily risen during the past sixty years. Foreign vacations, automobiles, television sets, and modern appliances and gadgets are now commonplace in most families.

Nevertheless, inequality is very much a characteristic of this society. The same manual workers who are satiated with consumer goods are much less likely to own a home or apartment in their lifetimes, and their children in all likelihood will not receive a university education. Whereas only 17 percent of western white-collar employees had net monthly incomes in 2002 of less than $1,900, 30 percent of manual workers were in this category. Among various occupations in the eastern and western states of Germany, at the top of the income ladder are independent nonmanual workers, owners and proprietors of businesses, free professionals (doctors, lawyers), and civil servants (see Table 3-5). Most earn net monthly incomes of well over $3,000. Indeed, the net household income of independents averages $8,500 nationally and that of civil servants $4,000. Manual workers average $2,900 (these data are not shown in Table 3-5).[16] Between 1992 and 2006 the income of the top 10 percent increased by 31 percent, while that of the lowest 10 percent declined by 13 percent. The overall income increase during this period was 10 percent.[17]

In the eastern states, income differences were substantially less than in the western states; independents and white-collar employees had similar net monthly incomes. About 37 percent of manual workers in the eastern states had monthly incomes of less than $1,900, compared with about 25 percent of the white-collar and independent groups. The

Table 3-5 Income by Occupation: East and West German States, 2006 (percent)

	Net monthly income[a]							
	Less than $1,100[b]		More than $1,100–$1,900		$1,900–$3,000		More than $3,000	
Occupational group	West	East	West	East	West	East	West	East
Independents (owners, directors of enterprises, free professionals, farmers)	7	12	12	19	26	34	56	32
White-collar, civil servants	4	8	13	17	31	41	52	24
Manual workers	7	12	23	25	47	45	23	17

Source: Federal Statistical Office, *Datenreport 2008* (Bonn: Federal Center for Political Education, 2009), 146.

[a] After deductions for taxes and social insurance contributions, approximately 40–50 percent.

[b] Calculated at $1.00 = €1.15.

incomes of independents and white-collar employees in the eastern states were actually closer to those of manual workers in the western states than to their nonmanual colleagues in the west. As economic development proceeds in the former East Germany, these regional differences should decline (see Chapter 3.5).

There is even greater inequality in the ownership of capital resources: land, stocks, bonds, securities, savings, and life insurance. The richest 10 percent of the population has about 60 percent of the country's wealth (stocks, bonds, real estate, savings accounts, and other capital). And the top 1 percent owns 20 percent of the wealth. More than two-thirds of the population has little or no capital resources.[18] This general pattern has changed little over the past twenty years, an indication that governments, including those led by the Social Democrats, have not pursued policies designed to redistribute the country's capital resources.

According to the data, then, beneath the surface prosperity of the Federal Republic are substantial differences in personal wealth. This distribution of capital reflects in part the postwar decision of German and Allied occupation elites to take the free-market route to economic recovery. West German political leaders of all the major parties, even the Social Democrats, have generally sought to create a favorable climate for investment capital through low tax rates on profits and dividends, as well as subsidies and tax benefits for new plants and equipment. The currency reform of 1948 clearly favored capital-holding groups: Germans with savings accounts or cash in old reichsmarks received only about one new deutsche mark for every fourteen old marks. Millions of lower- and lower-middle-class citizens saw their savings largely wiped out, but those with stocks, securities, and land lost nothing.

Education

The educational system has generally reflected and reinforced this socioeconomic inequality. Traditionally, this system was designed to give a basic general education to all and advanced academic training to only a few. Most education is still structured along three tracks. At about the age of six, all children enter a four-year primary school. Then in most states, after the fourth year when most children are about age ten, the tracking process begins:

- About 20 percent of all children will attend a general secondary school for an additional six years. Then, at about the age of sixteen or seventeen, they will enter the workforce, in most cases as apprentices, and attend vocational school part time for about three years.

- A second group, making up about 30 percent of a given age group, will attend an intermediate school (*Realschule*) for six to eight years. The *Realschule* combines academic and job-oriented training. Medium-level careers in business and administration usually require a middle-school educational background.

- The remaining school-age children will pursue an academic or university-level educational program. Attendance at an academic high school (*Gymnasium*) or comprehensive school (*Gesamtschule*) for up to nine years yields an *Abitur* (a degree roughly comparable to a U.S. junior college diploma) and the right to attend a university.

It is possible for children to change tracks, especially during the first two or three years, which are considered an orientation period. Many students, however, do not switch, and the decisions made by their parents and teachers after four to six years of school usually determine their educational and occupational futures.

The entire system has had a class bias. The *Gymnasium* and the university are still largely preserves of the middle and upper-middle classes, and the majority of children in the general vocational track have working-class backgrounds. In spite of decades of attempted reform, little progress has been made toward providing more equality of opportunity. As one study concludes, "The educational chances of young people depend largely on their social background." [19] Although there has been an enormous expansion of enrollments at gymnasiums and universities, the social bias remains: about 30 percent of the workforce is in manual or blue-collar occupations, but only 13 percent of university students come from such a social background. [20] Children of middle- and upper-class parents are far more likely to have participated in the recent educational expansion. The proportion of young people attending universities whose parents are civil servants, for example, increased from 46 percent in 1982 to 73 percent in 2000. [21]

German education has no lack of critics. Reformers emphasize, in addition to the class bias, the system's inflexibility: children encounter great difficulty in changing tracks as their interests and values change. In the 1960s the principal element in plans for reforming and restructuring education was the consolidation of the three-track secondary system into a single comprehensive school (*Gesamtschule*). Instead of being tracked after the fourth grade, all children would remain in the same school for an additional six years, or until about the age of sixteen. At that point, the tracking process would begin. The purpose of the comprehensive school plan was to provide more equality of educational opportunity and social mobility. Comprehensive schools were introduced in all states, but more extensively in those governed by social democratic or liberal political parties. Conservatives generally opposed comprehensive schools, citing their concerns about a decline in educational standards and their support for the traditional gymnasium. By 2008 only about 10 percent of secondary school students were still attending these schools. [22] Many of them have become reestablished as gymnasiums or general secondary schools.

Politics has a lot to do with access to the various types of schools. In Bavaria, where the traditional structure supported by the conservative Christian Social Union is still dominant, less than 33 percent of children attended a gymnasium in 2008, compared with 46 percent of the children in Brandenburg, a Social Democratic state. [23] The idea of delayed tracking, however, has not been abandoned. The poor performance of German schools and students in recent international student assessment programs has sparked a renewed interest in creating more equality of opportunity for students from less privileged socioeconomic backgrounds. [24]

Since unification, the eastern states have largely restructured their educational systems to fit the pattern in the western states. This massive task has involved the establishment of new schools, curriculums, textbooks, and teacher retraining. The communist system, in addition to the standard academic subjects, included extensive programs designed to indoctrinate young people with Marxist-Leninist ideology and produce the "new Socialist man." The influence of the Communist Party was pervasive. Most teachers and almost all school administrators were in the party. Communist youth organizations, modeled on their counterparts in the former Soviet Union, were present in all schools.

Upon initiating the restructuring, the eastern states placed most teachers on probationary status for as long as five years. Many administrators—principals and assistant principals—were dismissed or demoted. By 2000 about 40,000 of the 185,000 East German teachers had been either replaced or retired. Many of these teachers, however, were let go for financial and not political reasons. The East German schools, like many other sectors of the state administration, were overstaffed.

The population decline in the eastern states since unification has forced the closing of schools. In one eastern state, Saxony, the number of children in primary and secondary schools dropped from about 800,000 in 1990 to 570,000 in 2004, and by 2011 this number will have declined further, to about 400,000. By 2005 about a third of all elementary schools in Saxony were closed, with middle schools and high schools scheduled to follow. Not only do school closings mean longer commutes for children and parents, but they also affect parents' decisions about where to live. For many easterners, a school closing finalizes their decision to leave for the west.[25]

Political Attitudes

In 1949 few if any observers in Germany or elsewhere gave the Federal Republic of Germany much of a chance to survive, much less prosper. The decision to establish a West German state was made by neither the German political leadership nor the German electorate in any referendum; it was the decision of the three victorious Western powers in World War II—France, Great Britain, and the United States. The Federal Republic was a product of the foreign policies of these countries, which sought to counter what they perceived to be a growing Soviet threat in Central and Western Europe. The Germans living in the American, British, and French occupation zones therefore had imposed on them by their conquerors a new political system, which they were to regard as their own. Moreover, the new state was to be a liberal parliamentary democracy, a form of government that Germany had tried between 1919 and 1933 with disastrous consequences. Even the committed democrats had few fond memories of that first democratic experience—the Weimar Republic. In addition, some citizens perceived the establishment of a West German state as a move that would result in the permanent division of the country. The regional and state leaders in the western zones, who were asked to begin the process of drafting a constitution for the new state, were reluctant to make the republic appear as a permanent entity. The constitution that was drafted was not even called such, but rather the Basic Law.

Although the Germans were not consulted about their new state, many of them in 1949 did not really care. The great majority of the population was fed up with "politics," "parties," and "ideals." After the mobilization of the Nazi years, the incessant propaganda, the endless calls for sacrifice, and the demands of total war, they wanted above all to put their private lives back together again. They had been badly burned by politics and were quite willing to let someone else, even foreigners, make political decisions for them as long as they were more or less left alone to pursue their private concerns: family, making a living, catching up on all that was missed during the war years. In short, Germans were willing to follow the orders of their occupiers and become citizens of a democracy, even though most had had little if any experience with a successful, functioning democratic political order.

Thus, the institutions of democracy preceded the development of an attitudinal consensus on democracy. For that reason, Western and especially American occupation authorities and some Germans recognized that they needed to educate the postwar population and change political attitudes.

But one did not have to be an enthusiastic supporter of political democracy to oppose any sort of return to a Nazi-style dictatorship after 1945. Apart from any personal predilection for a one-party state, the *performance* of the Third Reich made it distinctly unattractive as an alternative to most Germans in the postwar period. Although there has been a consistent relationship between a positive attitude toward the Third Reich and opposition to the values and institutions of the Bonn Republic after 1945, it should not be overlooked that a sizable proportion of respondents with little sympathy for liberal democracy still rejected a return to some form of dictatorship. This was hardly a firm foundation on which to build a stable and effective political democracy, and yet it did provide postwar elites and the consciously democratic segments of the larger population with breathing space in which the republic was given an opportunity to perform and socialize postwar generations to its values and norms.

The early years of the republic were characterized by widespread ambivalence about political democracy. Surveys revealed that significant proportions of the population retained the traditional authoritarian if not antidemocratic attitudes acquired during earlier regimes. In 1949 about half the population still agreed with the statement: "National Socialism was a good idea, which was only badly carried out." When asked to choose between a hypothetical government that guaranteed economic success and security and one that guaranteed political freedom, Germans in the late 1940s preferred the former by a two-to-one margin.[26]

In the early 1950s about a fourth of the adult population still preferred a one-party state; in 1951 almost half of the electorate stated it would be "indifferent" to an attempt by a new Nazi party to take power; and one of every three adults had positive attitudes toward a restoration of the monarchy. Moreover, although the turnout at elections was high, most voters went to the polls out of a sense of duty and not because they believed they were participating in important political decisions. Only about a fourth of the population in the early 1950s expressed any interest in political questions, and most Germans reported that they rarely talked about politics with family or friends. They had, in short, largely withdrawn from political involvement beyond the simple act of going to the polls.

This pattern of mass political attitudes and behavior was not conducive to the long-term viability of the new Federal Republic should it have encountered a major economic or social crisis. Most citizens in the 1950s, even those with fascist or authoritarian dispositions, were quite willing to support political democracy as embodied in the Federal Republic as long as it "worked," but they could not be counted on if the system encountered major problems. The Germans were "fair weather" and not "rain or shine" democrats, but they were willing to give democracy a chance.

Today, after sixty years of experience with democratic government, this pattern of political attitudes has changed.[27] There is now a solid consensus on the basic values, institutions, and processes of parliamentary democracy. Support for values such as political competition, freedom of speech, civil liberties, and the rule of law ranges from a minimum of about 75 percent to more than 95 percent for a principle such as political competition. Similar proportions of West German citizens had by the 1980s a positive orientation

Table 3-6 Satisfaction with Democracy: Germany, Great Britain, France, Italy, European Union (percent)

	Germany[a]	Great Britain	France	Italy	European Union[b]
Satisfied[c]	61	63	57	44	57
Not satisfied[d]	38	33	39	52	40
Undecided or no response	1	4	4	4	3

Source: European Commission, *Euro-Barometer 62* (Brussels: European Commission, 2005), 18.
[a] German percentages include the former East Germany.
[b] Twenty-five nation average.
[c] Percentages of "very satisfied" and "fairly satisfied."
[d] Percentages of "not very satisfied" and "not at all satisfied."

toward the parliament, the constitution itself, and the federal structure of the state. Consistent with this consensus on the present political system is the level of satisfaction with the way democracy is functioning. Germans are among the most satisfied of the citizens of the major European countries in which this question was asked (see Table 3-6). This satisfaction is an important cultural resource as the country now confronts its serious economic and social problems.

That said, what effect is unification having on the political attitudes of the 16 million East Germans who joined the Federal Republic in 1990 after living for forty years in a political, economic, social, and cultural setting vastly different from West Germans? Will the postwar consensus on liberal democratic values, institutions, and processes change because of those attitudes? Will the Federal Republic move to the left as East Germans demand the social and economic programs—a guaranteed job, low rents, subsidized food, low-cost day care—that some in the old German Democratic Republic considered the successes of the former communist regime?

The evidence so far is mixed. On the one hand, there is little doubt about the commitment to democratic values among the East German revolutionaries who brought down the communist regime. The great majority of voters in a series of free elections in 1990 supported democratic parties. On the other hand, there is also evidence that forty years of authoritarian rule have left their mark on the East German political psyche. Some studies have found that East Germans are more authoritarian and alienated than West Germans. They are more supportive of the "old" German values of discipline, order, and hard work than of the "new values" of individualism, self-realization, and tolerance. East Germans have less trust in the institutions of liberal democracy such as the parliament and courts than West Germans do. Their acceptance of foreign residents is also lower than that of West Germans. And many East Germans have a more simplistic, either/or conception of democracy than do West Germans. They see democracy either as a very elitist system—the chancellor or state must take care of them—or as a very participatory system—they must demonstrate to secure their demands. Democracy as a system in which intermediate organizations such as parties, interest groups, and parliament play major roles of channeling citizen demands into policies is still not fully understood in the former East Germany.[28]

These findings are not surprising. Although they have been able to watch democracy in the West through television, East Germans are new at participation in democratic politics.

As in West Germany during the 1950s and 1960s, the *performance* of the democratic order will be a major factor in the political integration of East Germany.

The stability and performance of German democracy during the past sixty years do not mean, however, that the Federal Republic is a political system without problems or that it has become an ideal democracy. As noted earlier in this chapter, Germany is a society with many problems—unemployment, sluggish economic growth, a soaring public debt, low birthrates, an aging population, and the formidable costs of unification, "putting Germany back together again." The Federal Republic also has Europe's largest number of foreign residents and is a major target country for immigrants. The integration of these foreign residents and new arrivals is a critical social problem. Germany must continue to deal as well with the legacy of its Nazi past, its national identity, and its new role in international politics. The stability and performance of German democracy also do not mean that there are no individuals and groups calling for basic changes in the country's social, economic, and political structures. What the data signify, however, is that these problems will be debated within a consensual framework. In short, the question is no longer whether Germany will remain a liberal democracy, but what kind of and how much democracy Germany will have. This is a question that other European democracies also face.

NOTES

1. In 2009 the Merkel government was critical of the "easy money" (low interest) policies of the American Federal Reserve and its chairman, Ben Bernanke. For the Germans, the Fed seemed indifferent to the problem of debt. Germany and some of its neighbors would also prefer stronger government regulation of financial markets than practiced in Washington.

2. Most respondents over age forty-five in 1951 considered the imperial years, 1900–1914, to be the best Germany had experienced in that century. Institut für Demoskopie Survey No. 0044, October 1951.

3. Helmut Schmidt, "Erklärung der Bundesregierung zur Lage der Nation vor dem deutschen Bundestag," May 17, 1979, printed in *Bulletin* (Bonn), May 18, 1979, 596.

4. See Christopher R. Browning, *Ordinary Men: Reserve Police Battalion 101 and the Final Solution in Poland* (New York: HarperCollins, 1992); and Daniel Jonah Goldhagen, *Hitler's Willing Executioners* (New York: Knopf, 1996).

5. In 1990 the first and last freely elected government in the German Democratic Republic acknowledged East Germany's responsibility for the Holocaust and apologized to the world Jewish community and the state of Israel for the refusal of the communist regime to deal with this issue. In May 2005, sixty years after the collapse of the Third Reich, a memorial to the murdered Jews of Europe was opened in Berlin. It stands in the heart of the capital between the Brandenburg Gate and Potsdam Square, in view of the Reichstag (parliament building) on the same ground once occupied by Joseph Goebbels's propaganda ministry.

6. East Germany was established in 1949. It comprised the Soviet zone of military occupation; its capital was Soviet-controlled East Berlin. East Germany was an early casualty of the end of communism. Unlike Czechoslovakia, Hungary, or Poland, East Germany was not a nation. Indeed, its only source of identity and legitimacy was its claim to be the only "socialist" German state. East German leaders believed that if this commitment to the ideology of Marxism-Leninism were to be diluted or abandoned, as Soviet leader Mikhail Gorbachev seemed to be proposing, it would eventually lead to demands for unification and the end of the East German state.

They were right. In the summer and fall of 1989, East Germans on "vacation" used the newly opened border between Hungary and Austria to escape to the West. Later, the "Great Escape" would also take place via Czechoslovakia and even Poland. Between May and September 1989, more than ninety thousand East Germans fled, the largest number since the construction of the Berlin Wall in 1961. Meanwhile, those who stayed behind began to demonstrate and organize new, but illegal, opposition political parties. By October 1989, when Gorbachev arrived in East Berlin to commemorate the fortieth anniversary of the regime, an additional sixty thousand East Germans had departed. Gorbachev told the aging and ailing East German leader, Erich Honecker, that the time for reform had come and that "life punishes those who arrive too late." But his warning fell on deaf ears. The demonstrations continued as hundreds of thousands took to the streets in Leipzig, East Berlin, and other cities, chanting "Wir sind das Volk!" ("We are the people!") and demanding reform. For the first time in German history, a grassroots democratic revolution was under way. By mid-October, Honecker had been forced to resign. On November 9, in a desperate attempt to acquire some popular support, the new communist leadership opened the country's borders to West Germany, including the Berlin Wall. As the world watched, millions of East Germans flooded into Berlin and West Germany. But the vast majority returned and now called for a unified Germany—"Wir sind ein Volk!" ("We are one people!") was added to their demands.

By the end of 1989, the East German state was on the verge of collapse. The country's first (and last) free elections were set for March 1990. West German parties moved quickly to organize the East German electorate. At the election, about 80 percent of the voters supported parties advocating a speedy unification. In May 1990 the two German states concluded a treaty that unified their monetary, economic, and social security systems. On July 1 the West German mark (DM) became the sole legal currency for all of Germany. Two days later, on October 3, less than a year after the fall of the Berlin Wall, East Germany ceased to exist and, reconstituted as five states (*Länder*), joined the Federal Republic. Europe's 82 million Germans were once again united in a single state. But unlike the Bismarckian Reich or Hitler's Third Reich, German unity in 1990 was achieved without violence and with the full support of its neighbors in Eastern and Western Europe.

7. Hans-Werner Sinn, "Lösen Sie mit am deutschen Rätsel," *Frankfurter Allgemeine Zeitung,* April 9, 2005, 42.
8. Kate Connolly, "German Women Told: We Need More Babies," News Telegraph, January 28, 2006, http://www.telegraph.co.uk/news/worldnews/europe/germany/1509056/German-women-told-we-need-more-babies.html; also see Julia Bonstein et al., "Generation Kinderlos," *Der Spiegel,* September 12, 2005, 62–72.
9. *Frankfurter Allgemeine Zeitung,* November 15, 2007, 17.
10. Ulrich Blum, "Perspektiven für den Osten," *Frankfurter Allgemeine Zeitung,* November 8, 2008, 15; Nicholas Kulish, "In East Germany, a Decline as Stark as a Wall," *New York Times,* June 19, 2009, 3.
11. Almost 300,000 Jews live in the Federal Republic. Seventy-three Jewish congregations receive state financial support. The largest (more than five thousand members) Jewish communities are in Berlin and Frankfurt. After the collapse of the Soviet Union in 1991, Germany offered Jews from the former Soviet bloc the right to settle in the country. By the end of 2003, about 190,000 Jews had accepted the offer, which more than tripled the size of the German Jewish community. In 2004 the Schröder government decided to reassess its policy, because the number of Soviet Jews coming to Germany was now higher than the

number immigrating to Israel. In 2004, 9,400 Russian Jews immigrated to Germany, and only about 8,000 went to Israel. About 2.5 million Muslims also live in the Federal Republic, most of whom are Turkish nationals. The some sixteen hundred Muslim organizations, including mosques, that have been established generally do not receive state financial support. In a growing number of western states, however, the public schools offer Islamic religious instruction, and the teachers, approved by the local Islamic religious authorities and school officials, are paid with public funds. These classes are generally taught in German, and most instructors were educated at German universities.

12. In 2003 only 1,128 men were preparing for the priesthood, compared with 3,627 in 1990. Data cited in Daniel Deckers, "Klasse statt Masse?" *Frankfurter Allgemeine Zeitung,* June 18, 2004, 4.

13. *Der Spiegel,* Special No. 1, 1991, 73–74.

14. General Social Survey (ALLBUS), 2008, Variable 521.

15. Hans-Peter Klös and Benjamin Schnarnagel, "Arbeitsmarktpolitik seit 2003: Reformbilanz und Handlungsbedarf," *Aus Politik und Zeitgeschichte* 27 (June 2009), 21–22.

16. Federal Statistical Office, *Datenreport 2004,* 2nd ed. (Bonn: Federal Center for Political Education, 2005), 125.

17. DIW figures cited in *Der Spiegel,* December 17, 2007, 22–23.

18. Deutsches Institut für Wirtschaftsforschung, *Wochenbericht,* November 7, 2007, 668. The top 10 percent had an average net worth of about $750,000. The bottom 10 percent has no capital resources, but rather an average debt of about $9,500. *Armutsbericht der Bundesregierung* (Berlin: Social Welfare Ministry, 2005), 36.

19. Federal Statistical Office, *Datenreport 2004,* 492.

20. Federal Labor Ministry, *Lebenslage in Deutschland* (Berlin: Federal Labor Ministry, 2001), 157.

21. Federal Statistical Office, *Datenreport 2005* (Bonn: Federal Center for Political Education, 2006), 497.

22. *Frankfurter Allgemeine Zeitung,* December 15, 2008, 6; "Waiting for a Wunder," *Economist,* German Survey, February 11, 2006, 6.

23. *Frankfurter Allegemeine Zeitung,* December 15, 2008, 6.

24. In the 2001 Europewide Program for International Student Assessment, Germany ranked twenty-first in reading and twentieth in mathematics and science among the thirty-one countries tested. The 2005 results were better, but they also showed a strong class bias in student performance. Student test scores in Germany were more dependent on socioeconomic background than in any other country. "Waiting for a Wunder," 7.

25. Reiner Burger, "Die halbierte Generation," *Frankfurter Allgemeine Zeitung,* January 14, 2005, 3.

26. Max Kaase, "Bewusstseinslagen und Leitbilder in der Bundesrepublik Deutschland," in *Deutschland-Handbuch. Eine doppelte Bilanz, 1949–1989,* ed. Werner Weidenfeld and Hartmut Zimmermann (Bonn: Bundeszentrale für politische Bildung, 1989), 205.

27. For an analysis of these changes, see David P. Conradt, "Changing German Political Culture," in *The Civic Culture Revisited,* ed. Gabriel Almond and Sidney Verba (Boston: Little, Brown, 1980), 312–372; and "Political Culture in Unified Germany: Will the Bonn Republic Survive and Thrive in Berlin?" *German Studies Review* 21 (February 1998): 83–104.

28. Ursula Feist, "Zur politischen Akkulturation der vereinten Deutschen. Eine Analyse aus Anlaß der ersten gesamtdeutschen Bundestagswahl," *Aus Politik und Zeitgeschichte* 11–12 (March 1991): 21–32. For additional data, see David P. Conradt, "Political Culture and Identity: The Post-Unification Search for 'Inner Unity,' " in *Developments in German Politics 3,* eds. Stephen Padgett et al. (New York: Palgrave Macmillan, 2003), 269–287.

Where Is the Power?

POLITICAL POWER IN THE FEDERAL REPUBLIC OF GERMANY IS FRAGMENTED and dispersed among a wide variety of institutions and elites. There is no single locus of power.

Policymaking Institutions

At the national level, Germany has three major policymaking structures: (1) the Federal Parliament (Bundestag), the lower house of parliament; (2) the Federal Council (Bundesrat), which represents the states and is the German equivalent of an upper house; and (3) the federal government, or executive (the chancellor and cabinet). In addition, the sixteen states that constitute the Federal Republic are important in decision making, especially in education and internal security. The states also have a direct influence on national policymaking through the Bundesrat, which is composed of delegates from each of the states. The Federal Constitutional Court, which has the power of judicial review, is an important actor as well in the policy process. At the national level the federal president, indirectly elected but with little independent responsibility for policy, serves as the ceremonial head of state and is expected to be a unifying or integrating figure, above the partisan political struggle.[1]

The Federal Republic, like other members of the European Union (EU), has transferred some policymaking power and responsibility to European-wide institutions. Monetary policy is now largely the province of the European Central Bank in Frankfurt; and the European Commission, the Council of Ministers, and the European Parliament (which divides its sessions between Strasbourg, France, and Brussels) make most agricultural policy. In recent years, the European Court of Justice (Luxembourg) has also issued rulings that have been accepted as binding on German courts. National political institutions, however, still hold veto power over many of the decisions of EU bodies.

Formal power is vested in these institutions, but their integration and effectiveness are also very much functions of the party system that has emerged in the postwar period and the well-organized, concentrated system of interest groups (see Chapter 3.3).

The Federal Parliament (Bundestag)

Constitutionally, the center of the policymaking process is the Bundestag, a legislative assembly currently consisting of 622 deputies, who are elected at least every four years. They are the only political officials in the national constitutional structure directly elected by the people. The constitution assigns to the Bundestag the primary responsibility for (1) legislation, (2) the election and control of the government, (3) the supervision of the bureaucracy and military, and (4) the selection of judges to the Federal Constitutional Court.

Plenary chamber of the remodeled Reichstag building. Visitors can walk up and around the transparent dome and look down on their representatives at work. The redesigned parliament was the work of British architect Sir Norman Foster.

Source: Bernd Settnik/EPA/Landov.

Parliamentary government has a weak tradition and a poor record of performance in German political history. During the empire, or Bismarckian Second Reich (1871–1918), effective control over important areas such as defense and foreign affairs and the supervision of the civil service was in the hands of a chancellor appointed by the monarch. In addition, because Prussians controlled the upper house, important legislative proposals of the parliament could be blocked at the will of the Prussian ruling elite. Parliament had the influential power of the purse, but it could not initiate any major policy programs. Its position toward the executive, bureaucracy, and military was therefore defensive and reactive. While parliament "debated," the government "acted."

Under the constitution of the Weimar Republic (1919–1933), the powers of parliament were expanded. The chancellor and his cabinet were directly responsible to it and could be removed by a vote of no confidence. But the framers of the constitution made a major error when they also provided for a strong, directly elected president independent of parliament, who could in "emergency situations" (that is, when the government lost its parliamentary majority) rule by decree. The Weimar parliament, especially in its later years, was also fragmented into many different, ideologically oriented parties, which made effective lawmaking difficult. The institution became immobile—there were frequent majorities against governments, but rarely majorities in favor of new governments. In the last elections of the republic, most voters elected parties (Nazi, Nationalist, and Communist) that were in one way or another committed to abolishing the institution. The parliament then became identified in the public mind as weak and ineffective. By approving the Nazi Enabling Act in 1933, it ceased to function as a legislative institution.

In the postwar parliament, this pattern of legislative immobility has not been repeated. Although important initiatives remain the province of the restructured executive, the parliament's status as an instrument of supervision and control has grown.

The Bundestag, similar to other parliaments, has responsibility for electing and controlling the government. After each national election, a new parliament is convened, and its first order of business is the election of the federal chancellor.[2] The control function, however, is much more complex and occupies a larger share of the chamber's time. Through the Question Hour, a procedure adopted from English parliamentary practice, a member may make direct inquiries of the government either orally or in writing about a particular problem. A further control procedure is the parliament's right to investigate government activities and to demand the appearance of any cabinet or state official.

The main organizational unit of the Bundestag is the *Fraktion,* the parliamentary caucus of each political party. Committee assignments, debating time, and even office space and clerical assistance are allocated to the *Fraktionen* and not directly to individual deputies. The leadership of these parliamentary parties effectively controls the work of the Bundestag. Freshman deputies soon discover that a successful and influential parliamentary career is largely dependent on the support of the leadership of their parliamentary *Fraktionen.*

The committee system of the Bundestag is more important to lawmaking than those in Great Britain and France, yet less powerful than the committees in the U.S. Congress. The twenty-three standing committees, like their U.S. counterparts, mirror the partisan composition of the Bundestag, but committee chairmanships are allotted proportionately, according to party strength. Therefore, the minority opposition party or parties chair several of the standing committees. These committees have become more significant in recent years because of the introduction of U.S.-style hearings and the greater use of committee meetings as forums by the opposition. But German committees, like those in other parliamentary systems, are still reluctant to engage in the full-blown criticism of the executive associated with presidential systems. This reluctance reflects the generally higher level of party discipline in the German system and the government's dependence on a parliamentary majority for continuance. Committee criticism, if comprehensive enough, could be interpreted as an attempt to bring down the chancellor. This is a major problem with strong committee systems in parliamentary governments.

Because many committee members specialize in various subject areas, the day-to-day committee sessions tend to concentrate on the details of proposed legislation and rarely produce any major news. As for reporting out bills, committees cannot pigeonhole them—all must be reported out. About four of every five bills submitted by the government are reported out with a favorable recommendation, albeit with a variety of suggested revisions and amendments. Outright rejections are rare. When the government discovers a bill is in trouble, the bill is usually withdrawn for "further study" before a formal committee vote.

Germany at a Glance

Type of Government
Federal republic

Capital
Berlin

Administrative Divisions
Thirteen states and three "free" states*: Baden-Württemberg, Bavaria*, Berlin, Brandenburg, Bremen, Hamburg, Hesse, Lower Saxony, Mecklenburg–West Pomerania, North Rhine–Westphalia, Rhineland-Palatinate, Saarland, Saxony*, Saxony-Anhalt, Schleswig-Holstein, Thuringia*

Independence
January 18, 1871 (German Empire unification). Divided into four zones of occupation (British, U.S., Soviet, and later French) in 1945, after World War II. Federal Republic of Germany (FRG or West Germany) proclaimed on May 23, 1949, and included the former British, U.S., and French zones; German Democratic Republic (GDR or East Germany) proclaimed on October 7, 1949, and included the former Soviet zone. West Germany and East Germany were unified on October 3, 1990; all four powers formally relinquished rights on March 15, 1991.

Constitution
Adopted on May 23, 1949, and known as Basic Law; became constitution of the united German people on October 3, 1990

Legal System
Civil law system with indigenous concepts; judicial review of legislative acts undertaken in the Federal Constitutional Court. Has not accepted compulsory International Court of Justice jurisdiction.

Suffrage
Eighteen years of age; universal

Executive Branch
Chief of state: president
Head of government: chancellor
Cabinet: cabinet or *Bundesminister* (federal ministers) appointed by the president on the recommendation of the chancellor
Elections: president elected for a five-year term by a Federal Assembly including all members of the Bundestag and an equal number of delegates elected by the state parliaments; chancellor elected by an absolute majority of the Bundestag for a four-year term

Legislative Branch
Bicameral parliament: Federal Parliament and Federal Council. Federal Parliament (Bundestag): 622 seats. Members elected by popular vote under a system combining direct and proportional representation; a party must win 5 percent of the national vote or three direct mandates to gain representation. Term: four years. Federal Council (Bundesrat): sixty-nine votes. State governments are directly represented by votes; each has three to six votes, depending on population, and is required to vote as a bloc.

Note: There are no elections for the Bundesrat—composition is determined by the composition of the state-level governments. Composition of the Bundesrat has the potential to change any time one of the sixteen states holds an election.

Judicial Branch

Federal Constitutional Court (Bundesverfassungsgericht): half the judges elected by the Bundestag and half by the Bundesrat

Major Political Parties

Greens; Christian Democratic Union (CDU); Christian Social Union (CSU); Free Democratic Party (FDP); Left Party; Social Democratic Party (SPD)

Source: U.S. Central Intelligence Agency, *The World Factbook: 2010,* https://www.cia.gov/library/publications/the-world-factbook/geos/gm.html.

The Federal Council (Bundesrat)

The Bundesrat, or Federal Council, represents the interests of the states in the national policymaking process. It is composed of sixty-nine members drawn from the sixteen state governments. Each state, depending on the size of its population, is entitled to three to six members. Most Bundesrat sessions are attended by delegates from the state governments and not the actual formal members, who are state-level cabinet ministers.

The framers of the Basic Law envisioned the Bundesrat as an administrative watchdog over the political process in the Bundestag. It was not intended to become a politicized institution, but rather was to "protect the country from excessive partisanship."[3] Indeed, the Bundesrat rarely initiates legislative proposals. Because the states implement most national legislation, the Bundesrat has tended to examine proposed programs from the standpoint of how they can be best administered at the state level.

Since 1969, when, alas, the Bundesrat lost its political innocence, Germany has frequently had a form of "divided government"—that is, the party in power in the Bundestag has not had a majority in the Bundesrat. When the chambers are not controlled by the same party or coalition, the party or coalition controlling the Bundesrat can cause many problems for the government. From 1969 to 1982 the Christian Democrats were the majority party in the Bundesrat. During this period, the frequency of Bundesrat objections to government legislation increased to the point that the leaders of the government accused it of becoming an "extended arm" of the Bundestag opposition. It was even suggested that the Christian Democratic Union (CDU)/Christian Social Union (CSU) was seeking to obstruct the government's electoral majority by turning its majority in the Bundesrat into a politicized countergovernment. The Bundesrat blocked or forced compromises on the government on issues such as divorce law reform, speed limits on autobahns, higher education reform, tax policy, and a controversial "radicals" in public employment law.

In 1991 the Social Democratic Party (SPD), now the opposition party, gained control of the Bundesrat after a series of victories in state elections. The party promptly used its majority to force the government to change some provisions of a new tax law designed to finance the costs of unification. The 1993 Solidarity Pact, which restructured the financing of unification, was passed only after SPD objections were met. In 1997 the SPD Bundesrat majority blocked a major tax reform proposal of the Kohl government. This SPD veto became an issue in the 1998 federal election.

In 1999, less than a year after their victory in Bundestag elections, the governing SPD-Green coalition lost its majority in the Bundesrat, and Germany once again had divided government. Before passage of landmark citizenship legislation in 1999, the government, headed by Gerhard Schröder, had to make concessions to the Bundesrat or the legislation would have failed. In 2000 the government's tax reform program passed only after Schröder made a host of last-minute "concessions"—that is, promises of extra money to several states. The Schröder government's Agenda 2010 reform program was passed in 2004 only with the consent of the Christian Democratic majority in the Bundesrat.

To become a genuine second chamber, however, the Bundesrat's delegations, still controlled by state leaders, must be willing to accept direction from the opposition party's national leadership in the lower house. So far, support for the opposition has emerged on only some issues. Generally, the more remote an issue supported by the opposition is from the concerns of state leaders, the more likely they are to go along with the national leadership in the lower house and try to block the bill in the Bundesrat. Conversely, state leaders can quickly forget their party loyalty if the issue directly affects their region.

A Bundesrat veto of a proposed bill by a majority of two-thirds or more can be overridden in the Bundestag only by a two-thirds majority of the *members present and voting*. Therefore, if a minority party in the Bundestag controls forty-six or more delegates in the Bundesrat, it can, because a two-thirds majority in the Bundestag is very rare, bring the legislative process to a halt and force new elections. Such a development, however, would run counter to the intentions of the framers of the Basic Law, who did not envision the Bundesrat as a party-political body. Yet because the respective state governments determine the composition of the Bundesrat, political and electoral developments at the state level can have direct national political consequences. State elections have indeed become Germany's version of "midterm" elections at which national issues and personalities dominate the campaign.

This national role for state elections was demonstrated dramatically in 2005. After elections in Schleswig-Holstein and North Rhine–Westphalia, the ruling SPD-Green coalition no longer had any corresponding support in the states—that is, none of the sixteen states had an SPD-Green government. The opposition CDU/CSU and Free Democratic Party (FDP) had a lop-sided majority in the Bundesrat and probably could have vetoed any legislative proposal of the government. In response to this unprecedented case of "divided government," Chancellor Schröder announced he would ask for new elections before the end of the normal legislative period. A few months later, Germany had a new national government headed by a new chancellor, Angela Merkel.

The Chancellor and the Cabinet

The chief executive of the Federal Republic is the chancellor. The powers of this office place it somewhere between those of a strong president in the United States and the prime minister in the British parliamentary system. Constitutionally, the German chancellor is less powerful than a U.S. president, yet a chancellor has more authority and is more difficult to remove than a prime minister in the British model.

The Weimar constitution provided for a dual executive: a directly elected president and a chancellor chosen by the parliament. The president, who was head of state and commander in chief of the armed forces, could in an emergency dismiss the chancellor and his cabinet and rule by decree. The president during the final years of the Weimar Republic, former field marshal Paul von Hindenburg, misused especially this latter power and helped to undermine public support for democratic institutions. During 1932, the last year before the Nazi seizure of power, the parliament passed only five laws, but the president issued sixty-six decrees. The framers of the Basic Law sought to avoid a repetition of this problem by concentrating executive authority in the chancellor.

The power of the chancellor in the Federal Republic derives largely from the following sources: the constitution, the party system, and the precedents established by the first chancellor, Konrad Adenauer. With the chronic instability of Weimar governments in mind, the framers of the postwar constitution made it difficult to remove an incumbent government before the end of the normal four-year legislative term. In contrast to most parliamentary systems, a government cannot be brought down by a majority of opposition votes. This "negative majority" must also represent a "positive majority" for a new chancellor. In the absence of a positive majority, the incumbent government remains in office. If a new majority cannot be mobilized within twenty-one days, the incumbent chancellor can ask the federal president to order the dissolution of parliament and new elections. This positive or *constructive vote of no confidence* increases the power of the executive at the expense of the parliament.

Under the constitution, the chancellor is also responsible for determining the main guidelines of the government's policies. This responsibility places chancellors above their ministers, although the ministers are, in turn, responsible for policy within their specific areas. In selecting cabinet members, chancellors must consider the demands of their coalition partners as well as the various factions and wings of their own party. The qualifications and expertise of potential members also play a role in selection, but they are not as important as political considerations. For example, in 2005 in the Merkel government the first minister of agriculture really wanted to be the minister of health, but that position was already claimed by the other party in the coalition. The new minister of agriculture readily admitted that he had little expertise or interest in agricultural questions. The current Merkel cabinet has sixteen members; eleven from the CDU/CSU and five from the Free Democrats. Once in office, an individual cabinet member can be removed only by the chancellor. If the parliament wants a particular cabinet member dismissed, it must vote no confidence in the whole government, including the chancellor.

The constructive vote of no confidence has been tried only twice—in April 1972 when the CDU/CSU opposition attempted (unsuccessfully) to bring down the Brandt government and in October 1982 when Helmut Kohl replaced Helmut Schmidt as chancellor. The rare use of this procedure has reflected the strength of the new party system. Chancellors in the Federal Republic, unlike their Weimar predecessors, can usually count on the firm support of a majority of the parliament throughout the four-year session. Because there are fewer but larger parties in the Federal Republic than in the Weimar Republic, the political ties between government and parliament are much stronger. The concentration of electoral support in two large, disciplined parties and three smaller parties has assured most chancellors of firm parliamentary majorities.

Article 68 of the constitution also allows the chancellor to ask the parliament for a vote of confidence. Unlike the "constructive vote of no confidence" (Article 67) that can be initiated by the opposition in order to replace the chancellor with its own candidate, this vote enables chancellors to strengthen their position by stabilizing the governing majority—that is, compelling dissidents in the chancellor's party and perhaps the coalition partners to support the government or risk new elections. The vote can, however, also be used to trigger new elections. If the chancellor loses the confidence vote, whether deliberately or not, he or she can resign, ask the president to dissolve the parliament, and then remain in office as the head of a minority government until the end of the legislative term or be removed through a constructive vote of no confidence. A few months after the successful use of the constructive no-confidence vote in 1982, Chancellor Kohl, in an effort to legitimate his government and quell criticism of a power grab, deliberately lost a confidence vote. With the help of the CDU federal president, he was then able to secure the dissolution of parliament, and new elections were held in March 1983. Chancellor Gerhard Schröder invoked the same procedure in 2005, but he, unlike Kohl, wanted new elections. Schröder was faced with a large opposition majority in the Bundesrat, and his own party seemed unwilling to support further cuts in social programs.

'Chancellor Democracy'

The first chancellor of the Federal Republic, Konrad Adenauer, set the standards by which future chancellors would be evaluated. His performance in the office and the substance he gave to its constitutional provisions influenced all of his successors. Indeed, Adenauer's presidential-like control over the cabinet, bureaucracy, and even parliament soon became known as "chancellor democracy," a parliamentary system with a strong, quasi-presidential executive. Since Adenauer's departure, the Federal Republic has had sixteen governments headed by only seven chancellors, a record of stability that compares well with that of other European democracies.

From Adenauer to Kiesinger

Konrad Adenauer assumed the office of chancellor in 1949 at the remarkable age of seventy-three, and he remained in power until 1963. Before the Third Reich, he had been lord mayor of Cologne, but he held no national political office during the Weimar Republic. Shortly after the Nazis seized power in 1933, he was removed and allowed to retire. Although he had some contact with anti-Nazi resistance groups and was arrested, imprisoned, and nearly executed in 1944, he essentially sat out the Third Reich.

From the beginning, Adenauer's chancellorship was characterized by a wide variety of domestic and foreign political successes: the postwar "economic miracle," the integration of 10 million refugees from the eastern territories, membership in the European Community, and the alliance with the United States.

He used to the fullest extent the powers inherent in the chancellor's office. In firm control of his party, he was out front on all major foreign and domestic policies and usually presented decisions to his cabinet and the parliament as accomplished facts. Under Adenauer, there was no extensive consultation within either the cabinet or the parliament before important decisions were made. The chancellor *led:* he initiated policy proposals, made the decisions, and then submitted them to the cabinet and parliament essentially for ratification. He did not always succeed in this approach, but on most issues, such as rearmament and membership in the North Atlantic Treaty Organization (NATO) and the Common Market, his views prevailed. During his tenure, the office of the chancellor clearly became the center of the policymaking process. Since then, all his successors have benefited from the power Adenauer gave to the office.

In governing, Chancellor Adenauer was pessimistic about the capacities of the average German to measure up to the demands of democratic citizenship. Through his authoritarian-paternalistic style, he encouraged Germans to go about rebuilding their private lives and leave politics to the "old man," as he was often termed. Most citizens probably agreed with this approach, but it meant that his successors would encounter a host of unfinished business, particularly in the area of citizen involvement in public affairs. In retrospect, Adenauer's major contribution was to demonstrate to many Germans, who were indifferent if not ignorant of democratic norms and values, that a liberal republic could be efficient and successful in Germany.

Adenauer's first two CDU/CSU successors, Ludwig Erhard (1963–1966) and Kurt Georg Kiesinger (1966–1969), assumed the office at a time when support for the CDU/CSU was on the decline. Erhard, a successful economics minister, never had control of his party. As long as conditions remained favorable, he could attract voters and was tolerated by the Christian Democrats. But when the Federal Republic suffered its first economic recession in 1966–1967, he was promptly dropped, with his own party taking the lead in urging his departure. Kiesinger then became chancellor of the "Grand Coalition" government with the SPD, a novel arrangement that called for a leader adept at compromise and mediation with a record of good relations with the Social Democrats. Because no one in Bonn had met these requirements, the CDU/CSU had to look farther afield, recruiting Kiesinger from Stuttgart, where he had been chief executive of Baden-Württemberg. When the CDU/CSU failed to gain enough votes in the 1969 election to form another government, Kiesinger passed from the national scene.

The First Social Democratic Chancellors: Brandt and Schmidt

The first two Social Democratic chancellors, Willy Brandt (1969–1974) and Helmut Schmidt (1974–1982), offer a contrast in personality, political style, and policy emphasis. Willy Brandt's two governments were characterized by the introduction of a new foreign policy of reconciliation with Germany's eastern neighbors and the acceptance of the permanence of postwar boundaries in Eastern Europe. This *Ostpolitik* (eastern policy) involved negotiating and ratifying treaties with the Soviet Union (1970), Poland (1970), East Germany (1972), and Czechoslovakia (1973). This policy put West Germany at the forefront of the worldwide trend toward détente and made Brandt one of the world's most respected political leaders. For this policy of reconciliation, he was awarded the Nobel Peace Prize in 1971, only the fourth German ever so honored. For many—as a man of peace and goodwill accepting moral responsibility for the acts committed in Germany's name by the Nazis–he personified the "other Germany." As the first chancellor with a record of uncompromising opposition to Nazism, he contributed greatly to the republic's image abroad as a society that had finally overcome its totalitarian past. For many Germans, especially the young, he became a symbol of a political system that was now democratic in content as well as form.

The fifth chancellor, Helmut Schmidt, assumed the office with more successful national-level experience than any of his four predecessors. An academically trained economist, he had been the leader of the SPD parliamentary party (1966–1969), defense minister (1969–1972), and finance minister (1972–1974). In these posts, Schmidt acquired the reputation as a very capable political decision maker. But he also was criticized for what some regarded as an overbearing, arrogant, "cold" personal style. Although he clearly lacked Brandt's emotional, "warm" image, Schmidt is given higher marks for his concrete performance.

Schmidt became chancellor in the midst of the worldwide economic recession that followed the 1973 Arab oil embargo and subsequent astronomical rise in oil prices. His expertise and experience in national and international economic affairs and his ability to take charge in crisis situations, such as a 1977 terrorist hijacking and commando raid, soon became apparent. Within two years, inflation was brought under control and unemployment was reduced, although unemployment would remain well above pre-1973 figures. In addition, the Schmidt governments continued, albeit at a lower key, the *Ostpolitik* of their predecessors.

Unlike Brandt, Schmidt had little patience with the left wing of his party. He was a strong supporter of a mixed economy, and he maintained a close relationship with the Federal Republic's economic and industrial elite. Indeed, even many CDU voters saw him as more capable than their own party's candidates. Schmidt's policy successes, however, were not matched by his performance as the leader of the Social Democrats. He was unable to overcome and integrate the opposition of the SPD left to many of his policies, especially the 1979 NATO decision, which Schmidt initiated, to station a new generation of mid-range nuclear missiles in the Federal Republic should negotiations with the Soviet Union fail. He also overestimated the intensity of opposition within his own party and in the country as a whole to nuclear power as an energy source.

Germany was unable to avoid the worldwide recession that followed the second oil price shock in 1979. By 1981 unemployment had risen to 7.5 percent, up from less than 4 percent in 1979. The worsening economy coupled with increasing conflict within the Schmidt government over budget cuts for social programs took their toll, and in September 1982 Helmut Schmidt lost his parliamentary majority when the Free Democrats, the junior partner in the coalition with the SPD, left the government. Shortly thereafter, the leader of the CDU, Helmut Kohl, became the republic's sixth chancellor, heading a new coalition composed of the Christian Democratic Union and the Free Democrats.

Helmut Kohl and German Unity

Helmut Kohl (1982–1998) was the dominant figure in German politics for almost two decades. He first attracted national attention in 1973, when he assumed the leadership of a badly divided and weakened CDU. He is credited with initiating a thorough modernization and revitalization of the party's organization. In 1976, as the chancellor candidate, he conducted a well-planned and well-executed campaign, which almost toppled the SPD–FDP government.

More than any of his predecessors, Kohl, as the first chancellor who did not experience the Third Reich as an adult, attempted to appeal to patriotic symbols and national pride. The evocation of national themes remains a very sensitive subject in the political culture. Terms such as *Vaterland* (fatherland) and nation and an emphasis on post-1945 German history as an object of pride were frequent themes in his speeches. While not denying Germany's responsibility for the Third Reich and World War II, Kohl, together with some conservative intellectuals, urged Germans in general and postwar generations in particular to develop a positive sense of German history.

The collapse of the East German communist regime in 1989–1990 and the desire of most East Germans for unity with West Germany provided Kohl with the greatest opportunity and challenge of his political career. Seizing the initiative in late November 1989, just weeks after the opening of the Berlin Wall, Kohl outlined a ten-point plan for unity within five years. But when faced with the continuing exodus of East Germans to the West, the government had to accelerate this timetable. Kohl's personal intervention in East Germany's first free election in March 1990 was a major factor in the victory of the "Alliance for Germany," a coalition of three center-right parties put together by Kohl only a month earlier. A few months after this vote, the two states completed a treaty that unified their currencies, economies, and social welfare systems. The opposition parties and some foreign governments, especially Britain and France, criticized Kohl's "rush to unity," but he continued to press for the complete unification of the two states, including all-German elections and the end of all four-power (France, Great Britain, the Soviet Union, and the United States) rights in Germany and Berlin, by the end of 1990. When his governing coalition dominated the December 1990 election, the first free vote in all of Germany since 1932, Kohl became Germany's "Unity Chancellor."

The breakneck pace of the unification process was prompted by both political and policy factors. Kohl was, in fact, more popular among East German voters than those in the West. His promises of rapid economic prosperity corresponded with East German desires to catch up with their cousins as soon as possible. The drive for unification, however, also reflected the fear that any delay could prompt millions of East Germans to stage a massive exodus to the West, resulting in the collapse of the East German state and an unbearable burden for the West German political, economic, and social system.

In 1994 Kohl became the first chancellor since Adenauer to win four straight elections. His government's majority in the parliament, however, fell from 134 seats to only 10. The slow pace of economic and social unification in the east, coupled with an economic recession and voter discontent in the west over the higher taxes needed to finance unification, took their toll on the chancellor's majority. In short, after profiting from the upside of unification in the heady days that followed the 1990 unification, Kohl experienced in the early 1990s the downside of this issue as Germans struggled with the day-to-day frustrations of putting their country back together.

The elder statesman among Europe's major political leaders, Kohl became in 1997 the longest-serving chancellor since the legendary Otto von Bismarck. Looking ahead to his last major task—the successful completion of the European Monetary Union (EMU), Kohl decided to run in 1998 for an unprecedented fifth term. But it was to be his last hurrah. After a record sixteen years in power, Kohl and his Christian Democrats were told by the voters that it was time to go. The government was soundly defeated by the

Social Democrats and Greens led by Gerhard Schröder and Joschka Fischer. A weak economy, high unemployment, and continued discontent in the east with the slow pace of unification were major factors contributing to Kohl's defeat.

About a year after Kohl left office, his legacy as the unifier of Germany and a champion of European unity was tarnished when he was implicated in a major scandal involving the finances of the Christian Democratic Union. Kohl admitted that he had indeed kept secret bank accounts outside of regular party channels to reward favored CDU regional organizers and leaders. He vehemently denied, however, that the funds had come from illegal kickbacks. In the end, Kohl was not charged with any crime, and a few years later he was once again a revered elder statesman.

Gerhard Schröder: First Chancellor of the 'Berlin Republic'

Gerhard Schröder, Germany's chancellor from 1998 to 2005, succeeded where five previous SPD candidates had failed. His 1998 victory marked the first time in German history that an entire incumbent government—that is, all parties in the coalition—was replaced. Schröder differed from his unsuccessful predecessors in his single-minded determination to win the election by changing his party's reputation for favoring big government tax and spend programs. A strong "Kohl must go" sentiment also helped.

Schröder's childhood spanned the end of World War II, the Allied occupation, and the formative years of the Federal Republic. Born in Lower Saxony, Schröder left school early to work as an apprentice salesclerk. He later earned a law degree at the University of Göttingen and joined the SPD shortly after the completion of his degree. Schröder rose quickly in party ranks and was first elected to the Bundestag in 1980. A leader of the Young Socialists during his early political career, Schröder gradually abandoned his leftist sympathies in favor of ideological moderation and a probusiness orientation. In 1986 he was elected head of the Lower Saxony SPD and a member of the party's national executive.

The May 1990 election in Lower Saxony catapulted Schröder into the national political spotlight. The SPD defeated the incumbent CDU and joined with the Green Party in forming a coalition government with Schröder as minister-president. He utilized his executive status to develop a political profile that distinguished him from most traditional Social Democrats—above all, a reputation for toughness tempered by pragmatism and a savvy sense of public relations. Schröder's effectiveness in office helped the SPD to win a narrow majority in its own right in 1994 and then sweep to an even more convincing victory in 1998. Party leaders honored the latter triumph by choosing Schröder over his chief rival, Oskar Lafontaine, minister-president of the Saarland, to oppose Chancellor Kohl in the fall national election.

Borrowing image and tactics from British prime minister Tony Blair, Schröder presented himself during the campaign as a centrist "modernizer" in a calculated effort to mobilize crucial swing voters while retaining the loyalty of the SPD's core supporters. Schröder shrewdly kept his options open about the choice of a potential coalition partner after the election, leaving it to political pundits to speculate whether the SPD might enter into a Grand Coalition with the Christian Democrats or form a "Red-Green" government with the Greens. In the end, Schröder opted for the Green Party.

The SPD-Green cabinet got off to a slow start during its first year in office, in part because of the inexperience of its members in holding national office, but also because of the intense rivalry between Schröder and the more leftist Lafontaine, who had joined the cabinet as minister of finance. Lafontaine's abrupt resignation in March 1999 freed Schröder to concentrate executive power within the party in his own hands and to focus his energies as chancellor on a major tax reform in 2000.

Narrowly reelected in 2002, Schröder could not deliver on his pledge to reduce unemployment and stimulate economic growth. By early 2005 Germany had more than 1 million more unemployed than when Schröder took office in 2002. Although his personal popularity remained high, support for his party plummeted. In the 2005 election, his government fell well short of the votes needed for reelection. Most analysts give him credit for beginning the reform process that the Merkel Grand Coalition after 2005 largely continued. He is also credited with keeping Germany out of the Iraq war in 2003 and establishing a more independent posture toward the United States and especially the administration of President George W. Bush.

Angela Merkel: Chancellor for 'Hard Times'?

In November 2005 Angela Merkel became the Federal Republic's eighth chancellor and the first woman to lead Germany. She was also the first chancellor from the eastern region that joined the Federal Republic in 1990. Before 1990 Merkel had not participated in politics; rather, she had pursued a career as a physicist, a field relatively free of communist political influence. But the fall of the Berlin Wall changed her life, as it did those of many other East Germans. Merkel was appointed secretary-general of the Christian Democratic Union in 1998, and her outsider status proved to be a major plus when the 1999 finance scandal threatened the party. In a newspaper op-ed article, she distanced the party from Kohl and called for a thorough reform of the organization.

Under Merkel's leadership (she became party chair in 2000), the CDU recovered from the scandal, and as the 2002 election approached it appeared that she could become the CDU/CSU's candidate for chancellor. But the minister-president of Bavaria and longtime leader of the CSU, Edmund Stoiber, also wanted to run, and Merkel, with no executive experience, was eventually persuaded to defer to Stoiber. It was a wise decision. Stoiber lost a close race, and Merkel, as a loyal supporter, found herself well positioned to be the next candidate.

When Schröder called for early elections in 2005, Merkel was named the CDU standard-bearer. Despite squandering a fifteen-point advantage during the campaign, the CDU/CSU received slightly more votes than Schröder's SPD. The CDU/CSU rallied behind Merkel and insisted that in any coalition with the SPD, the CDU/CSU, as the largest party, should provide the chancellor. Battered but not bowed, Merkel finally prevailed. She assumed leadership of a coalition in which half of her ministers belonged to the Social Democrats. Indeed, her foreign minister was Schröder's former chief of staff.

Like her predecessor, Merkel and her government had to deal with the country's pressing economic problems. She promised cuts in social programs, tax subsidies, and in 2007 a big hike in the country's national sales tax (value-added tax), all in an effort to create jobs and reduce the country's soaring national debt. In large part because of the reforms introduced by the Schröder government, Merkel's Grand Coalition from 2006 to 2008 presided over a significant economic recovery.

As chancellor of this coalition, Merkel attempted to mediate and conciliate between the two roughly equal partners rather than get involved in partisan political conflict; that she left to others. This strategy together with a personal style emphasizing calm deliberation rather than dramatic bold initiatives earned her a high popularity level. Critics, however, charge her with a lack of political courage and conviction.

During the Grand Coalition (2005–2009) Merkel had to balance her preferences with that of the coalition partner. She personally wanted freer markets, less welfare spending, and lower taxes to spur economic development, but she had to reinvent herself as a consensus builder. This style was rewarded at the 2009 elections. She let surrogates do the hard, partisan campaigning, while she stayed above the fray. Although the CDU/CSU vote declined, its total number of seats increased due to some peculiarities in the electoral system. Merkel now leads a government in which her party is the dominant partner. She can no longer blame the demands of a Grand Coalition for her tendency to avoid the big issues. Her foremost task will be to lead Germany out of the current recession. She must also deal with the demands of her new coalition partner, the probusiness Free Democrats, who want major cuts in taxes and social programs.

Merkel's new government got off to a rocky start. The Free Democrats, coming off the biggest win in their history, felt they had received a mandate and had to make up for the eleven years they spent in the opposition. Merkel and the Christian Democrats, however, saw the coalition as largely an opportunity to continue the work they began in 2005, only this time with a smaller and more compliant partner. Merkel was therefore caught in the middle, and the intergovernmental bickering took its toll on her popularity. By early 2010 her approval ratings had dropped from almost 80 percent to just over 50 percent. When both governing parties lost at an important state election in May 2010, she had to reassess her government's priorities. Citing high deficits, she took any tax cuts off the table. Job creation, health care reform, and the stability of the European monetary system moved up on her policy agenda.

Formal Policymaking Procedures

How do the legislative bodies and the executive come together to produce policy? Most legislation is drafted in the ministries of the national government and submitted to the parliament for action. Two additional, but relatively minor, sources of legislative proposals are the state governments and both houses of the parliament itself. State governments may submit national legislation via the Bundesrat, but at least nine states (a majority) must support the bill. If at least 5 percent of the Bundestag deputies cosponsor a bill, it also enters the legislative process.

Administrative regulations and legal ordinances that deal largely with the technical, procedural aspects of existing programs are introduced and enacted by the government and do not require the consent of parliament. If regulations and ordinances affect the states, however, they must be approved by the Bundesrat. They also can be challenged in the courts. The president may, in some cases, refuse to sign the regulation or ordinance.

Before a draft bill is submitted to the parliament, it is discussed and approved by the cabinet (government). If the legislation affects several ministries, the Chancellor's Office coordinates the drafting process and attempts to resolve any interministerial conflicts. At the cabinet level, the states, through the Bundesrat, are asked to submit their reactions to the legislation. Because cabinet approval is needed for all draft legislation coming out of the ministries, a minister will usually have the legislation put on the cabinet agenda only if approval is very likely. Indeed, because the chancellor directs this entire process, most cabinet meetings dealing with legislation already in draft form tend to formalize decisions already taken informally between the chancellor and the relevant ministers.

After government approval, the proposed bill is presented to the Bundesrat for its first reading. The Bundesrat usually assigns it to a committee, which issues a report and recommends acceptance, rejection, or, in most cases, amendment of the legislation. Because the Bundestag can override a Bundesrat veto, it considers the bill regardless of Bundesrat action.

In the Bundestag, the bill is given a first reading and assigned to the relevant committee. Because the government has a majority in each committee, a bill is rarely returned to the floor with a negative report. When the committee report comes before the whole chamber, the second reading is held and any amendments to the proposed legislation are considered. If after the debate on the second reading the bill is approved without amendment, the third and final reading follows immediately. In the Bundestag, a simple majority or plurality (a majority of those present and voting) is needed to pass legislation. For votes in the Bundesrat, however, an absolute majority is required. Constitutional amendments require an absolute two-thirds majority of both the Bundestag and the Bundesrat.

After adoption by the Bundestag, the bill goes back to the Bundesrat for a second reading. If approved there without amendment, the legislation goes directly to the president for a signature and promulgation. If the policy area requires Bundesrat approval and it vetoes the bill, it is dead. At times, however, the Bundesrat proposes amendments to the lower-house version, and the two houses form a conference committee to resolve the differences.

The Judiciary

Germany is a law- and court-minded society. In addition to local, regional, and state courts for civil and criminal cases, corresponding court systems specialize in labor, administrative, tax, and social security cases. On a per capita basis, there are about nine times as many judges in the Federal Republic as in the United States. The German legal system, like that of most of its Western European neighbors, is based on code law rather than case, judge-made, or common law. These German legal codes, influenced by the original Roman codes and the French Napoleonic Code, were reorganized and in some cases rewritten after the founding of the empire in 1871.

In a codified legal system, the judge only administers and applies the codes, fitting the particular cases to the existing body of law. A judge, in theory at least, may not set precedents and thereby make law, but must be a neutral administrator of these codes. Counsel for the plaintiff and defendant assist the judge in this search for justice. The assumption behind this system, which is common to other Western European societies, is that a right and just answer exists for every case. The problem is to find it in the codes. The judge is expected to take an active role in this process and not be merely a disinterested referee or umpire of court proceedings. Court observers accustomed to the Anglo-American system would be surprised by the active posture assumed by the judge. Indeed, at times both judge and prosecution seem to be working against the defendant. Unlike the Anglo-American system, the process is not one of *advocacy,* with both sides presenting their positions as forcefully and persuasively as possible and with the judge or jury making the final decision; it is more *inquisitorial,* with all participants, defense attorneys, the prosecution, and judge expected to join together in a search for the "truth."

This approach to law has been termed "legal positivism" or "analytical jurisprudence." Some critics of the legal system consider positivism to be a basic cause of the scandalous behavior of judges during the Third Reich, when most judges disclaimed any responsibility for judging the content of laws they were to administer.

The independence of judges, protected by law, is limited by their status as civil servants. All judges, with the exception of those on the Federal Constitutional Court, are under state or national ministers of justice. Moving up in the judicial hierarchy, then, requires that judges perform their duties in a manner consistent with the standards set by their superiors. This bureaucratization of the judiciary, common to all continental European societies, discourages the type of independence associated with judges in Anglo-American systems. Judges are also a tightly knit, largely middle- and upper-class group. Hardly radicals, their attitudes and values (as determined in a number of studies) are quite conventional and conservative. Some critics have charged that many judges dispense "class justice," because they know little about the problems or lifestyles of the working-class and lower-middle-class defendants who come to their courts.

Justice in East Germany

During the forty-year reign of the Communist Party in East Germany, the rule of law was generally subordinate to the ideology and demands of the party. All East German judges were members either of the Communist Party or of the puppet parties associated with it in a pseudo-democratic "National Front." They were instructed to consider, above all, the interests of the "working class" and its party, the Communists. Once again, then, Germany had to deal with judges who administered political justice for offenses such as "fleeing the republic" and "behavior damaging to the state," which resulted in numerous political prisoners and questionable legal judgments.

In the years after unification, most of the fifteen hundred East German judges and prosecutors either retired or were dismissed, with West German judges and recent graduates of West German law schools filling the gap. But eastern law schools are now producing graduates, and the differences between the two regions are diminishing.

The Federal Constitutional Court

The practice of judicial review—the right of courts to examine and strike down legislation emanating from popularly elected legislatures if it is considered contrary to the constitution—is alien to a codified legal system. Nevertheless, influenced by the American occupation authorities and the tragic record of the courts during the Third Reich, the framers of the postwar constitution created a Federal Constitutional Court and empowered it to consider any alleged violations of the constitution, including legislative acts. Similar courts also were established at the state level.

This court, located in the southwestern city of Karlsruhe, has in its first fifty years built an impressive record of constitutional interpretation. In doing so, it has also become an increasingly powerful political institution. Unlike other courts, it is independent of any justice ministry. Both houses of parliament select its members, and its budget and other administrative matters are dealt with in direct negotiations with the parliament's judiciary committees. The court achieved this independence only after several years, however; the government and others had to first recognize that it was an indispensable prerequisite for the performance of the court's constitutional responsibilities.

The Federal Constitutional Court has rendered decisions on various controversial political cases such as the *Ostpolitik* treaties, abortion reform, university governance, the powers of the Bundesrat, the employment of "radicals" in the civil service, codetermination in industry[4], the deployment of German military forces in non-NATO areas, the right of Bavarian school authorities to display a crucifix in public school classrooms, the constitutionality of same-sex unions, and major European Union treaties. As the importance of European Union law increases in policymaking, the Court has emphasized that EU treaties and laws must conform to the German Constitution. In 2009 it approved the Lisbon Treaty only on the condition that the parliament pass supplementary legislation affirming the inviolability of Germany's federal structure and the civil liberties and rights contained in the first twenty articles of the Basic Law.

Like the U.S. Supreme Court, the Federal Constitutional Court has also been criticized for becoming "too political," for usurping the legislative and policymaking prerogatives of parliament and the government, and for not exercising sufficient "judicial restraint." To students of judicial review, this is a familiar charge and reflects the extent to which the court since its founding has become a legitimate component of the political system. Most important, both winners and losers in these various cases have accepted and complied with the court's decisions.

NOTES

1. In 2009 Horst Köhler, the former head of the International Monetary Fund, was elected to a second term. (See Chapter 3.1.) A year later he abruptly resigned over media reaction to comments he had made about the Federal Republic's military action in Afghanistan. In a radio interview he had linked Germany's involvement to its position as a leading economic and trading power. He was roundly criticized in the media for overstepping the boundaries of the office by making such blatant political statements. Offended by the reaction, he simply quit.

   According to the constitution, a successor had to be elected by the Federal Assembly within thirty days. The Assembly met on June 30, 2010. The CDU-FDP candidate, Christian Wulff, the minister-president of the state of Lower Saxony, had a solid majority of the seats. But the SPD and the Greens went "outside the box" and nominated an easterner, Joachim Gauck, a Protestant clergyman and former director of the office investigating Stasi crimes and abuses. Gauck projected a nonpartisan appeal that attracted a solid majority in public opinion polls. The Gauck nomination also appealed to many eastern delegates, regardless of party. Therefore, this usually pro forma vote had become highly political and was viewed as a challenge to the Merkel government. If the CDU-FDP majority in the Assembly broke down and Gauck was elected, it would probably have meant the end of her governing coalition—a stunning vote of no-confidence from both state-level officials and from her own national parliamentary caucus. Indeed, in the first two rounds of voting, Wulff failed to secure an absolute majority. But in the third round, which required only a simple majority, he prevailed and was elected as the tenth federal president.

2. Although the chancellor is elected by the parliament, he or she does not have to be a member of the parliament or affiliated with any political party. However, only one of the Federal Republic's eight chancellors, Kurt Kiesinger (1966–1969), has not had a Bundestag seat, and all have clearly been identified with a political party (CDU or SPD).

3. *Der Spiegel,* December 12, 2005, 64.

4. Codetermination is the practice of giving workers' representatives, usually trade union officials, in large firms up to half the seats on a firm's supervisory board (roughly equivalent to a board of directors).

Who Has the Power?

SINCE ITS FOUNDING, THE STABILITY OF THE FEDERAL REPUBLIC'S major political institutions has been based largely on a strong political party system and an effective structure of interest representation. This chapter first examines this party and interest group structure before turning to the ultimate power holders, the German voters. As described in this chapter, these voters are increasingly disenchanted with both the parties and the interest groups that have functioned so well since 1949, but are now associated with the major economic and social problems facing the country.

Political Parties

One of the most striking changes in postwar Germany has been the emergence of a system of political parties that has effectively organized and controlled the political process. Traditionally, parties were marginal factors in political life. Their home was the legislature, and the executive and the bureaucracy dominated politics; the parties had little influence in these institutions. This pattern was also dominant during most of the Weimar Republic (1919–1933), when the party system was fragmented and stable parliamentary majorities became impossible to form. By the end of the Weimar Republic, the democratic political parties were unable to defend the new democracy against the Nazi onslaught.

This system of weak, unstable, fragmented parties did not reemerge after 1949. Indeed, democratic political parties began to assert themselves early in the occupation period, and they assumed major leadership roles in the parliamentary council that drafted the Basic Law establishing the West German state. Never before in German history have democratic political parties been as important and powerful as they are in the Federal Republic today.

Related to the expanding power of political parties was the decline from 1949 to 1980 in the number of parties seriously contending for power. During the Weimar Republic, up to a hundred parties contested elections, and as many as twenty-five gained parliamentary representation, with no single party able to secure a majority of seats. Coalition governments consisting of several parties were the rule. Because these governments were, for the most part, unstable, they had to expend their resources on surviving instead of planning and implementing policy programs. During the fourteen-year Weimar Republic, there were twenty different governments.

By contrast, the postwar party system has been characterized by a concentration of electoral support in two large parties, the Christian Democratic Union (CDU) and the Social Democratic Party (SPD), together with the smaller Free Democratic Party (FDP). Another political party, the Greens, entered parliament in 1983 and then joined the Social Democrats in a national coalition government in 1998. Unification in 1990 also brought the Party of Democratic Socialism (PDS), East Germany's communist party, into the parliament.

In 1949 seventeen different parties contested the first national election, and nine succeeded in entering the first parliament. Since 1961 no parliament has had more than five parties, and only four—the Christian Democrats, the Social Democrats, the Free Democrats, and the Greens—have been in government. These parties, especially the two largest, have dominated the selection and control of government personnel and have had a major influence on setting the country's policy agenda.

The postwar democratic parties had several advantages over their Weimar predecessors. First, the parties' competitors in previous regimes—the state bureaucracy, the army, the landed nobility, and even big business—were discredited through their association with the Third Reich. Second, from the outset the parties enjoyed the support of the occupation powers, and they accrued numerous material and political benefits that put them in a strong starting position when the decision was made by the Allies in 1948 to launch a West German state. Third, the parties largely organized and controlled the proceedings of the parliamentary council. Under the constitution, the parties were quasi-state institutions with fundamental responsibility for "shaping the political will of the people." This provision has also been used to justify the extensive public financing of the parties both for their normal day-to-day activities and during election campaigns. Fourth, these same parties, exploiting their strong constitutional and political positions, made certain that their supporters staffed the local, state, and national postwar bureaucracies, at least at the upper levels. In contrast to the Weimar bureaucracy, the civil service in the Federal Republic has not been a center of antirepublican sentiment, but has been firmly integrated into the republican consensus.

This system of strong political parties has, however, had a downside: all too frequently parties have manipulated the laws governing their financing. They have voted themselves generous subsidies for election campaigns and have not been fully accountable for the funds they have received. In recent years, several major investigations have surrounded the payment of large kickbacks to party officials in exchange for favorable political decisions. Meanwhile, such scandals and the poor policy performance of recent governments have taken their toll on public support for the parties. Party membership is down, and a generalized sense that the parties have lost touch with the public is clearly evident in recent polls. In a 2004 survey, more than 80 percent of Germans said they "tended not to trust" the political parties.[1] In a more recent survey, almost two-thirds of respondents stated that the parties offered them no real alternatives, and only 20 percent felt that the parties encouraged political activity.[2] Since 1990 the SPD has lost 40 percent of its members, and the CDU/CSU 25 percent.

In the 2009 national election, the two largest parties, the Christian Democrats and the Social Democrats, saw their combined share of the vote drop to its lowest level in the history of the Federal Republic. The three opposition parties secured the highest totals in their histories. This party system, so successful in the first six decades of the Federal Republic's history, may be on the verge of a major transformation that will see the further decline of the once-large parties and the emergence of a more fragmented multiparty system.

The Christian Democrats

The Christian Democratic Union, together with its Bavarian partner, the Christian Social Union (CSU), is a postwar political movement. Like the Gaullists in France, the

CDU/CSU developed largely as a vehicle to facilitate the election and reelection of a single political personality, Konrad Adenauer. The CDU did not even have its first national convention until after it became the major governing party in 1949. From the outset in 1945, the CDU was a broad-based movement that sought to unite Protestants and Catholics in a political organization that would apply the general principles and values of Christianity to politics. (The religious division between Protestants and Catholics was regarded as one factor in the rise of Nazism.) The CDU also stressed that it was open to all social classes and regions. The CDU/CSU became a prototype for the new "catchall" parties that emerged in postwar Europe—that is, parties that sought through a pragmatic, nonideological image to attract as broad an electoral base as possible. The CDU wanted voters, not necessarily believers, and it refused to place itself in one of the traditional liberal, conservative, socialist, or communist ideological categories. To more traditionally minded politicians and some intellectuals, such an approach was nothing more than opportunism. How could a party not have a clearly articulated ideology and program? The CDU/CSU represented a new development in politics.

In the 1950s the CDU, benefiting from the remarkable success of Chancellor Adenauer in foreign policy and the free-market policies of his economics minister, Ludwig Erhard, became Germany's dominant party. In the 1957 election, it became the first, and to that point the only, democratic party in German history to secure an absolute majority of the popular vote. The CDU/CSU's program was very general: free-market economic policies at home, alliance with the United States and other countries of the North Atlantic Treaty Organization (NATO), and staunch anticommunism abroad; otherwise, "no experiments" (the party's main slogan in the 1957 election).

This approach worked well throughout the 1950s, but the construction of the Berlin Wall in 1961 and the 1966–1967 economic recession revealed the weaknesses in the CDU/CSU's policies. Anticommunism and a refusal to recognize the legitimacy of postwar boundaries in Eastern Europe had not brought Germany any closer to unification. Moreover, the weak U.S. response to the Berlin Wall was for many a sign that the Federal Republic could not rely entirely on the United States to run its foreign policy. On the economic front, the recession, although mild in comparison with past economic declines and with those experienced by other industrial societies, indicated that the postwar boom was over and that the economy was in need of more management and planning. Within the party, it had become obvious that almost two decades of governing had taken their toll on the party leadership. Erhard, who succeeded Adenauer as chancellor, lacked the political skill of the "old man." Also, the Social Democrats had, since the late 1950s, begun to revamp their program, organization, and leadership. The collapse of the Erhard government in 1966 was followed by a "Grand Coalition" between the CDU and the SPD. By sharing power with its chief adversary, the CDU enabled the SPD to show middle-class voters that it could indeed be entrusted with national political responsibility.

After the 1969 election, the SPD and FDP formed a coalition that ended twenty years of CDU/CSU government. Lacking a programmatic focus, the party went through four different chancellor candidates in search of a winner who could bring it back to power. In opposition, it expended much of its time in internal conflicts revolving around this leadership question.

The Christian Democrats returned to power in 1982, after thirteen years in opposition. Although the party did not receive any direct electoral mandate that year, the state elections and national public opinion polls revealed that the CDU/CSU enjoyed a sizable advantage over the Social Democrats. This advantage was confirmed in the March 1983 election when the CDU scored a solid victory over the SPD.

But the late 1980s, just prior to the opening of the Berlin Wall in 1989 and the collapse of the East German regime in 1990, found the fortunes of the Christian Democrats at low ebb. In public opinion polls throughout the first ten months of 1989, the party's level of support ranged from 33 percent to 38 percent. In June, Chancellor Helmut Kohl's leadership of the party was challenged by several intraparty dissidents. The prospects for the CDU in the upcoming national election were not good.[3] The unity issue, however, gave the party new political life. Led by Chancellor Kohl, the CDU received 43.8 percent of the vote in the December 1990 all-German election and, together with the Free Democrats, enjoyed a commanding majority of 134 seats in the parliament.

After the 1990 election, however, taxpayers began to get the bills for unification. In spite of its campaign pledge of "no new taxes," the CDU-led government announced in 1991 that Germany's contribution to the Gulf War and the unexpectedly high costs of unification necessitated a temporary tax increase. The voters were not amused, and the CDU's performance in state elections declined sharply. Only an improving economy, the popularity of Chancellor Kohl, and the mistakes of the rival Social Democrats enabled the party to stay in power after the 1994 election, albeit with a majority of only ten seats.

In 1998, after sixteen years in power, the party suffered one of the worst defeats in its history. "Kohl fatigue" and a poor economy, especially in the eastern regions, were the major factors in the electoral debacle. The CDU now had to prepare for life after Helmut Kohl. In 1999 the Kohl legacy took a new and ominous turn for the CDU. The party was hit by a major scandal when the former chancellor admitted that he had kept secret bank accounts outside of regular party channels to reward favored CDU regional organizers and leaders, and several other party figures were accused of accepting illegal kickbacks for favorable government decisions. In 2000 the scandal spread to Kohl's successor as party leader, Wolfgang Schäuble, who admitted that he also had received campaign contributions from the same people under investigation in the Kohl case. Schäuble then resigned under heavy pressure from the CDU members of parliament.

Hoping to turn the party's fortunes around, the CDU selected Angela Merkel as its new leader in 2000. She became the first female to lead any major political party. But in her two-year tenure as party leader, Merkel was unable to unite the party or develop any convincing electoral strategy to defeat Chancellor Gerhard Schröder, who was running for reelection under the SPD banner. In seeking a chancellor candidate for the 2002 election, the party turned for the second time in its history to Bavaria. Many Christian Democrats believed that the economy would be the main issue in the election, and Edmund Stoiber, Bavaria's minister-president, was presiding over a strong economy. Stoiber, however, lost in a very close election. Two issues that arose late in the campaign—Schröder's opposition to the Iraq war and his efficient handling of a major flood in the eastern states—gave his government a narrow advantage.

Despite the close outcome, Stoiber was not given a second chance in the 2005 election. Instead, the CDU selected Merkel, the first female candidate for chancellor in German history. Entering the campaign, the Christian Democrats held a large lead in public opinion polls and appeared to be a sure winner. But a poor campaign strategy featuring a promise to increase taxes and reduce subsidies for home buyers and commuters enabled the Social Democrats to portray Merkel and the CDU/CSU as indifferent to the plight of the average voter. In truth, Merkel was unable to present the need for reform. As a result, the party received only 35 percent of the vote and was unable to form a coalition with the Free Democrats, its preferred partner. Yet it did receive about 440,000 more votes and four more parliamentary seats than the Social Democrats. After three weeks of negotiations, the Christian Democrats formed a Grand Coalition with the Social Democrats, and Merkel became the first woman chancellor in German history.

During the 2005–2009 Grand Coalition the CDU/CSU veered away from many of the pro-business policies it had advocated during the campaign. The near-loss in 2005 with this neoliberal program had a sobering effect on the party and especially on Chancellor Merkel. The demands of its nearly equal coalition partner, the Social Democrats, also played a role. But as the 2009 election approached, the party was determined to end the Grand Coalition and form a coalition with the Free Democrats, as it had intended to do in 2005.

In spite of Merkel's high popularity, the CDU/CSU's vote in 2009 actually dropped from 35.2 percent to 33.8 percent. But its major competitor, the Social Democrats, did much worse with a record low of only 23 percent. The CDU was able to form a coalition with the Free Democrats, who received a record high of almost 15 percent of the party vote. Nonetheless, it was a muted victory for the CDU; its Bavarian cousin, the CSU, dropped to its poorest performance since 1949.

The Social Democrats

The Social Democratic Party is Germany's oldest political party and the only one to emerge virtually intact after the collapse of the Third Reich. The heir to Germany's rich Marxist tradition, the SPD was outlawed and persecuted by Chancellor Otto von Bismarck and the kaiser during the nineteenth century and by the Nazis in the twentieth century. In 1945 it appeared that the SPD's hour had finally come. Unlike other Weimar parties, its record of opposition to Nazism was uncompromising—in 1933 it was the only political party to vote against Adolf Hitler's Enabling Act. Its commitment to socialism had long been tempered by its even greater support for the principles and values of political democracy. Even during the Weimar Republic, the party's interest in the class struggle and the realization of the revolutionary vision had given way to a policy of reformist gradualism designed to change the society and economy by peaceful political means.

During the Third Reich, the SPD retained a skeletal organization in exile and a small underground movement in Germany. Although many Socialists did not survive the war and the concentration camps, the party was still able to regroup in a relatively short time after 1945—its loyal members emerged literally from the ruins of Germany's cities to begin the task of reconstruction. Yet the outcome of the first parliamentary election in 1949 did not elevate the SPD to the position of largest party, and so it found itself in opposition. After the landslide CDU/CSU victories of 1953 and 1957, the SPD could claim the support of only about 30 percent of the electorate.

The SPD's first postwar leader, Kurt Schumacher, was unable to convert the party's opposition to Nazism and its resultant moral authority into electoral success. Although he made a substantial contribution to postwar democracy by preventing a merger of the SPD and the German communists and by shaping the SPD into a viable opposition party, his overall political strategy was unsuccessful. Specifically, Schumacher failed to recognize that the post-1948 success of free-market (capitalist) economic policies left the bulk of the electorate with little interest in socialism, with its connotation of government ownership of means of production, of centralized economic planning, and of class struggle. He also overestimated the interest of the average German in an independent "nationalist" foreign policy designed to secure reunification of the country. Most West Germans, at least by the early 1950s, were willing to accept the division of the old Reich in exchange for the economic prosperity, individual freedom, and security they received from German integration into the U.S.-led Atlantic Alliance. Finally, Schumacher's political style, with its emphasis on conflict, polarization, and ideology, simply reminded too many voters of the Weimar Republic. Postwar Germany and Western Europe had tired of this approach to politics—this was the heyday of the "end of ideology," and most voters were supporting consensual, middle-of-the-road parties and leaders.[4]

During the 1950s an increasing number of SPD leaders in *Länder* such as Hamburg, Frankfurt, and West Berlin responded to the party's woes by advocating major changes in the party's program, organization, and leadership. The reformers wanted the party to accept the pro-Western foreign policy course of Adenauer and abandon its opposition to the free-market economic policies of the CDU/CSU.

This reform movement culminated in the party's 1959 program, which was adopted at its convention in Bad Godesberg. In the program, the SPD dropped its advocacy of nationalization of means of production and compulsory economic planning, and it stressed its opposition to communism and its support of NATO and the Western alliance. Shortly thereafter, the party sought to broaden its membership base to include more white-collar employees and even independent business owners. It also asked the young, politically attractive mayor of Berlin, Willy Brandt, to serve as its national chair and as its 1961 candidate for chancellor. But the national political responsibility that accompanied the party's eventual electoral success in 1969 brought with it new problems, especially from the SPD's old left—the trade unions and traditional Marxists—and the new left—students, counter-culture groups, and environmentalists. The old left, made up of socialists who had always opposed the reforms, and the new left, mainly in the party's youth organization, argued that the party had sold out its ideological and revolutionary heritage and its commitment to social and economic change for political power.

Conflicts within the party peaked during the latter years of Helmut Schmidt's chancellorship (1974–1982) and were a major factor in the party's return to the opposition after the 1983 election. In opposition, the SPD was unable to make significant progress toward resolving its internal divisions until 1985, when it won decisive victories in two state elections. In the 1987 national election, however, the question of how to deal with the Greens again divided the party, and its vote dropped to 37 percent, its lowest level since 1961.

The 1989–1990 unification both surprised and divided the SPD. For years, the party had sought to improve the living conditions of East Germans by negotiating with the communist regime. This contact with the East German leadership, however, also gave the communists a certain legitimacy and status in the view of many Germans. Therefore, when the revolution began, the SPD was ill prepared. Although the party had good contacts with the now-beleaguered East German "elite," it had few if any with the "street"—that is, the fledgling democratic opposition, including the churches. The "rush to unity" that followed the opening of the Berlin Wall also divided the party. Many members under the age of forty-five had no living memories of a united Germany. They had accepted at least tacitly the permanence of Germany's division, or believed that it could be overcome only within a united Eastern and Western Europe.

In the 1990 election, these SPD activists, including the party's 1990 chancellor candidate, Oskar Lafontaine, were unable to comprehend the broad appeal that unity had in the west and its fundamental importance for the new voters in the east. Older Social Democrats, such as former chancellors Willy Brandt and Helmut Schmidt, enthusiastically supported unification and had few problems with the euphoria this issue generated. Lafontaine's lukewarm approach to this issue hurt the SPD in the 1990 election, especially in the east, where the SPD received only 24.5 percent of the vote. Overall, its total of 33.5 percent represented the party's worst performance since 1957.

In 1994 the party had high hopes of finally returning to power. It had gained control of the Bundesrat in 1991 through its numerous victories in state elections, and its internal divisions appeared to be resolved as Björn Engholm, the party's leader from 1991 to 1993, and Rudolf Scharping, the SPD's chancellor candidate for 1994, moved toward the center of the political spectrum. A weak economy throughout 1993 further enhanced the SPD's electoral fortunes.

But in early 1994, the economy began to improve, and the Kohl government was able to eke out a narrow victory in October for the Christian Democrats. Although the SPD's proportion of the vote increased to its highest level since 1987, it still lost its fourth straight election.

Not long after the vote, internal conflicts flared up again among the SPD's leadership. The aggressive minister-president of Lower Saxony, Gerhard Schröder, who narrowly lost out to Rudolf Scharping in the vote for party leader in 1993, attacked Scharping and the national leadership for their continued advocacy of classic Social Democratic nostrums such as increased spending for public works, welfare programs, and a reduced workweek. In November 1995 at the SPD convention, Lafontaine successfully challenged Scharping for the leadership. After the leadership change, the SPD went on the offensive and focused on the high unemployment and sluggish economic growth record of the Kohl government. Although Lafontaine had unified the party, the SPD still needed a candidate to challenge Kohl in 1998. Lafontaine yearned for another chance at Kohl, but Schröder was convinced that he was the only Social Democrat who could defeat the chancellor. Indeed, Schröder's victory in a state election in early 1998 and his standing in public opinion polls compelled even his opponents in the party to concede that he had the best chance of dethroning Kohl. In the end, then, even though the SPD's heart wanted Lafontaine, its brain said Schröder could win.

In 1998, after sixteen years in the political wilderness, the Social Democrats finally regained national political power. The party presented a united front in 1998 and positioned itself at the center of the electorate. Like the Democratic Party in the United States under Bill Clinton and the British Labour Party of Tony Blair, it advocated a "third way" between unfettered capitalism and traditional social democracy with its emphasis on big government and high taxation. But it took one more intraparty struggle between the traditionalists, led by Lafontaine, and the modernizers, led by Schröder, before this new course was set. After a stormy cabinet meeting in early 1999, Lafontaine left the new government, but not before he denounced Schröder's probusiness policies. He would return to the political stage a few years later as the founder of a new political movement.

The new SPD-led government got off to a bad start in 1998. It was slow to react to the country's pressing economic problems and the need to reform the welfare state and the labor market. Throughout most of the government's first term, the SPD languished in the polls and continued to hemorrhage voters at state elections. Although it did pass a new liberalized citizenship law in 1999, it was not until 2000 that major tax reform legislation was finally approved. The party's narrow victory in the 2002 election was largely a tribute to Schröder's popularity and his strong opposition to the Iraq war, but not to any policy achievements of his government.

After the 2002 election, the party had little time to enjoy its come-from-behind victory. The harsh realities of a poor economy and increasing public debt did not disappear during the campaign. Schröder's Agenda 2010 reform package, designed to create jobs and economic growth through cuts in social spending, deeply divided the SPD and led to the defection of thousands of members and the formation of a new Left Party led by Lafontaine.

With few prospects for the rest of his legislative program, Schröder called for new elections in September 2005. Because neither large party was able to form a government with the smaller parties after the election, the SPD entered into a Grand Coalition with the Christian Democrats. In the Grand Coalition (2005–2009) the party's contingent, especially the ministers of finance and foreign affairs, performed well. The larger party, however, remained divided. The party chairmanship merry-go-round continued as four different chairmen led the party over the four-year Grand Coalition: in 2006 the architect of the Grand Coalition resigned over disputes with the left, his replacement quit after a few months, allegedly for health reasons; his successor lasted until September 2008 when he resigned after a mini-putsch by party pragmatists who doubted his ability to lead the SPD during the 2009 campaign. Frank-Walter Steinmeier, the foreign minister under Merkel, became the party's standard-bearer for the 2009 election.

At this election the SPD suffered its worst defeat since the founding of the Federal Republic. In fact, its total of only 23.0 percent was the lowest for the party since 1893. The impact of the deep divisions within the party over the Agenda 2010 reform program had taken its toll. It was small comfort for the SPD that voter support for Merkel and the CDU also declined, albeit slightly; neither partner seems to have been rewarded for the achievements of their Grand Coalition. Now in opposition, the party has the opportunity to address its internal problems of leadership, program, and organization. It must also define its relationship to the Left Party. The SPD left wing would like to make peace with the Left Party, which in the western regions contains many SPD prodigal sons and daughters.

The Free Democrats

The Free Democratic Party is the only small party to survive the postwar emergence of a concentrated and simplified party system. Ideologically and programmatically, it is somewhere between the two large parties. On economic issues, it is closer to the

CDU/CSU than to the SPD, but on matters such as education, civil liberties, and foreign and defense policies, the FDP has had more in common with the Social Democrats and the Greens.

The FDP, like the two newer smaller parties, the Greens and the Left, owes its continued existence and relative success to the electoral system, which gives the party a proportionate share of the parliamentary mandates as long as it secures at least 5 percent of the vote. From 1961 to 1994 the FDP held the balance of power in national elections. Both major parties tended to prefer coming to terms with the Free Democrats in a small coalition to forming a Grand Coalition with the other major party. Between 1949 and 1957, and again from 1961 to 1965, the Free Democrats were the junior coalition partner in CDU/CSU governments. From 1969 to 1982 they were in coalition with the Social Democrats. In 1982 the FDP changed partners once again and returned to the Christian Democrats. This last move sharply divided the party, but it was still able to surmount the 5 percent barrier in the 1983 and 1987 elections.

With 11 percent of the vote in the 1990 all-German election, the FDP achieved the third-best result in its history. This success was largely a tribute to the role that the party's titular leader, longtime foreign minister and vice chancellor Hans-Dietrich Genscher, played in the unification process. As FDP campaign speakers never tired of reminding the voters, "Bismarck unified Germany with blood and iron. Helmut Kohl did it with Hans-Dietrich Genscher!" The FDP also benefited from its "no new taxes" pledge and did especially well in East Germany, from which Genscher had fled in the 1950s.

In 1998 the party went down with Helmut Kohl. For the first time in almost thirty years, the Free Democrats were not in the national government. Although the party was able to surmount the 5 percent barrier, it ran a lackluster campaign devoid of popular leaders or an attractive program. But many saw the defeat as an opportunity to rejuvenate the party. Freed from its ties to Kohl and the Christian Democrats, the FDP could now move in new directions.

In 2002 the FDP did not campaign on any promise of forming a government with the Christian Democrats; instead, it claimed to be open to both major parties as a partner. The same year, the FDP also attempted to project itself as an up-and-coming major party with the goal of securing 18 percent of the vote. This strategy failed, however, and it remained in the opposition. In the 2005 election, the FDP returned to its role as a potential partner of the CDU and secured almost 10 percent of the vote. But much of its support came from Christian Democratic voters splitting their ballots, and so the FDP's gains meant losses for its potential partner. When the combined CDU/CSU-FDP total fell well short of the majority needed to form a government, the Free Democrats once again found themselves in the opposition.

As the 2009 election approached, the FDP felt the wind at its back. Merkel's move to the center enabled the party to gain votes from the free-market wing of the Christian Democrats. The cornerstone of the FDP program was tax reform. In fact, that issue was just about all the party talked about; its program, in the words of one observer, "reads like a tax consultant's handbook." [5] The party proposed a more "simple," "just," three-tiered system with rates at 10 percent, 15 percent, and 28 percent. The reduced revenues would be compensated by cuts in subsidies and social programs together with expected added revenue through increased investments by the private sector and a decline in tax avoidance;

in other words, the party's hope was that lower and fairer taxes would reduce tax fraud. After taxes, the Liberals emphasized their traditional commitment to civil liberties and the rule of law. They strongly oppose any efforts to increase electronic surveillance of Internet communications.

The FDP's 2009 election strategy earned the party 14.6 percent of the vote, the best result in its history. The FDP also achieved its goal of forming a coalition government with the Christian Democrats under Chancellor Merkel. Guido Westerwelle, the party's leader and architect of the 2009 victory, became vice chancellor and foreign minister. Reflecting its vote total, the party also received a record five ministries in the new cabinet. It must now deliver on its campaign promises of lower taxes; less government spending, especially on social welfare markets; and a more probusiness approach to economic and finance questions. Whether it can prevail against the moderate, social wing of the Christian Democrats remains an open question.

The Greens

In the late 1970s a variety of environmentalist groups opposed to the government's plans to expand nuclear energy plants banded together to create the Federal League of Citizen Groups for the Protection of the Environment, or more simply the "Environmentalists" or "Greens." The Greens were a new face on the political scene. Their antiestablishment, grassroots, idealistic image had an appeal that was especially strong among younger voters. In October 1979 the Green Party gained entrance into the parliament of the city-state of Bremen, and in March 1980 it surmounted the 5 percent hurdle in the relatively large state of Baden-Württemberg.

In the early 1980s the Greens were, above all, a protest movement with a single issue—the environment. Their opposition to placing U.S. medium-range missiles in West Germany gave them the additional issue they needed to gain representation in the Bundestag in 1983. In doing so, they were the first new party to enter the parliament since the 1950s.

In spite of its successes, the party in the late 1980s was divided on what to do next. Should it seek power through a coalition with the SPD, or should it remain a protest movement unsullied by any association with the established parties? Most Green voters preferred an alignment with the SPD. The party's activists and leaders, however, were divided. One group, the fundamentalists, rejected any cooperation with the SPD, whereas a second wing, the realists, were willing to form coalitions with the Social Democrats at the state and national levels to achieve Green goals, if only in piecemeal fashion. At the 1987 election the party was able to increase its share of the vote from 5.6 percent to 8.3 percent, and the party was also now represented in most state parliaments. The Greens had clearly become accepted by most voters as a legitimate political force.

In 1990 the Greens were ill prepared for the unification issue. Their predominantly young electorate had little interest in a unified Germany, having known only the reality of two German states. Most Greens wanted the indigenous East German revolutionary groups to have more time to find a "third way" between the Stalinism of the old East German regime and what they considered the antienvironmentalist capitalism of the West. But with only 3.9 percent of the vote, down from 8.3 percent in 1987, the party failed to return to parliament. The Greens in the former East Germany, however, did surmount the 5 percent barrier in their region and entered the parliament.

After the 1990 election, the Greens rebounded in public opinion polls and in state elections. With the euphoria over unification past, the Greens in 1994 became the first party ever to return to the Bundestag after a failure to clear the 5 percent hurdle in a prior election.

By 1998 the realist faction had control of the party. The Greens were determined to finally assume national political power as a junior coalition partner of the Social Democrats, and with the 1998 election they succeeded. Fischer became foreign minister, and other Greens took over the environment and health ministries. The party had become part of the establishment it once so strongly condemned.

Led by Fischer, who quickly became one of the country's most popular leaders, the Greens were spared many of the criticisms of the Schröder government. During the first term (1998–2002), several important Green policies such as the gradual closing of all nuclear power plants, an energy tax, liberalized citizenship laws, and same-sex marriage were passed. But Fischer's honeymoon with the voters ended abruptly in early 2005 with a controversy over the granting of visas at the embassy in Kiev. Under Green pressure, it was charged, Fischer's Foreign Ministry developed a very liberal and careless visa policy that allowed Ukrainians to have practically uncontrolled entry into Germany. Moreover, after policy and security officials alerted the Foreign Ministry to this large influx of Ukrainians, some of whom were involved in the drug trade, prostitution, and other illegal activities, Fischer loyalists did nothing or sought to downplay the problem.

Schröder did not consult the Greens before his 2005 decision to seek new elections. The once close relationship then deteriorated rapidly, and the Greens had to campaign on their own. Although they were able to hold their vote share at about 8 percent, they refused to enter into any coalition with the CDU and the FDP—the so-called "Jamaica" coalition, named for the colors of the Jamaican flag: black (CDU), yellow (FDP), and green. Such a government would have had a numerical majority, but there was little or no agreement on policy among the three such divergent parties.

In 2005 therefore the Greens were not in any government at either the state or the national level for the first time since 1987. After the election, the party also lost Fischer, who retired from political life. In opposition, the Greens found themselves forced to compete with both the Free Democrats and the new Left Party for media and voter attention. Public interest in environmental questions is waning. Among younger voters, once the core of Green support, the environment is an "uncool" topic. With their environmental concerns now the common property of all the parties, the Greens have to redefine themselves if they are to remain a viable component of the party system.

As the 2009 election approached, the Greens made solid gains, largely at the expense of the Social Democrats, in state elections and the June European Parliament election. The Green Party also made major revisions of their program and electoral themes. It attempted to link its established ecological identity to economic growth, jobs, international competitiveness, and technological innovation. The Greens promised a "Green New Deal" that included 1 million new "green" jobs within four years; and the strategy was successful. With 10.7 percent of the party vote, the Greens achieved the best result in their history, but it was not enough to return them to national political responsibility, as the collapse of the Social Democrats made any coalition impossible. Nevertheless, the Greens remain an important component of Germany's complex party system.

The Left Party

The newest addition to the party system is the Left Party, PDS, which at its first election in 2005 secured almost 9 percent of the vote and increased its vote in 2009 to a record 11.9 percent. The party is a curious union of the eastern Party of Democratic Socialism, the successor to the ruling Communist Party in the former East Germany; western Social Democrats; and other assorted far-left groups dissatisfied with the course the Schröder government took after 2002. This western component was founded in early 2005 and called Labor and Social Justice—The Electoral Alternative (WASG). The Electoral Alternative was led by Oskar Lafontaine, the former SPD leader and 1990 chancellor candidate, who left the Schröder government in 1999. Lafontaine then went into self-imposed exile and was content to attack Schröder from the sidelines by means of books and media appearances. Agenda 2010 was the last straw for Lafontaine; he left the SPD and launched the Electoral Alternative.

Meanwhile, the PDS looked lost in unified Germany. It had no foothold in the western states and was struggling on its eastern home turf. It failed to clear the 5 percent hurdle in 2002 and was left with only two members in the parliament, representing the only two districts in which it won a plurality of votes. The PDS also suffered in 2002 when its most popular figure, Gregor Gysi, resigned from the party leadership and, like Lafontaine, retreated to the sidelines. Both men, however, saw Schröder's troubles as an opportunity for their own political comeback.

It was a perfect campaign marriage. The PDS badly needed western support, and the Electoral Alternative had few voters in the eastern states. The PDS also had more funds and a much stronger organization than the newly founded Electoral Alternative. In early 2005 Lafontaine and Gysi decided to merge and run a common campaign.

So far the Left Party.PDS is a protest party. Its program in 2005, which it frankly admitted had no chance of being implemented, contained the usual left-wing panaceas: "soak the rich" tax plans, a massive and very expensive public works campaign for the unemployed, and a repeal of all the "antilabor" policies of Agenda 2010. The Left also wanted the immediate withdrawal of all foreign troops from Afghanistan. Germany's NATO membership is another target of the party; it wants Germany to leave NATO. There were, however, some areas where the Left's positions were similar to those of the mainstream Social Democrats. Both parties want a national minimum wage and stringent regulations of international capital markets.

With fifty-four seats and the leadership of two of the most talented political speakers in the country, the Left Party was poised after 2005 to make a lot of noise in the parliament. But mutual suspicions abound in this alliance, with the PDS fearing a western takeover by Lafontaine and the westerners wary of the former communists whose organizational strength is far greater than that of the western component. Many in the PDS also fear that Lafontaine is merely using the PDS to make a comeback in his old party, the Social Democrats.

Nevertheless, led by Lafontaine, the Left Party by 2009 was represented in five western state parliaments, and in August 2009, just weeks before the national election, the Left secured more than 20 percent of the vote in the Saarland, Lafontaine's home state. At the September national election, the Left vote jumped to 11.9 percent. It is now the fourth-largest party with seventy-six parliamentary seats; after the 2002 election, the party had only 2 parliamentary seats. Returned to the opposition, the Left must deal with the question of whether it will remain a protest party at the national level or seek a new relationship with its opposition "partner" the Social Democrats, the party whose policies were a major factor in the Left's formation.

Interest Groups

In the Federal Republic, like in other Western European societies, a wide variety of groups, associations, and movements play significant political roles. The major interest groups—business, labor, agriculture, religious, and professional—are well organized at the local, state, and national levels and work closely with the political parties and state bureaucracy. They have been joined in the past two decades by less structured but widely based "new social movements"—environmentalists, peace and disarmament activists, women's rights groups, as well as movements for various social minorities. Less established than the traditional interest alignments, the new social movements, nevertheless, have had a growing influence on the political process.

The hierarchical structure of the established interest associations allows their top officials to speak authoritatively for the membership and ensures them access to state and party elites. Indeed, it is standard operating procedure in German ministries to consult with the leading representatives of interest groups when drafting legislation that relates to a group's area of concern. Unlike in the United States, where the terms *interest groups, pressure groups,* and *lobbyists* have negative connotations, Germany treats such groups as legitimate and necessary participants in the policy process. Each major interest group alignment also maintains contact with all the major parties, although not uniformly. For example, the labor unions have closer ties to the Social Democratic Party than to the Christian Democrats or the Free Democrats. Yet there is also a labor wing within the CDU, and the FDP, at least while it was in a coalition with the Social Democrats, that maintained contacts with trade union leaders. Business and industrial interests enjoy a warmer relationship with the center-right CDU/CSU than the SPD, but again, there are supporters of the SPD among the ranks of Germany's business-industrial elite.

This pattern of strong government/interest group/political party integration has at times become somewhat institutionalized. In 1998 newly elected chancellor Gerhard Schröder made his "Alliance for Jobs" the cornerstone of his plan to reduce unemployment. The alliance consisted of representatives from business, labor, and government, who met periodically to propose job programs. Alas, it eventually disbanded as business and labor representatives were unable to reach any viable agreement on job creation.

The Alliance for Jobs and the other less formal interest group/government contacts have prompted some analysts to call Germany a "neocorporatist" state.[6] *Corporatism,* an old term in social and political thought, refers to the organization of interests into a limited number of compulsory, hierarchically structured associations recognized by the state and given a monopoly of representation within their respective areas. These associations become in effect quasi-governmental groups with state approval, training, and licensing, and they may even exercise discipline over members. The power of these associations is not determined by a group's numerical size alone, but also by the importance of its function for the state and community.

Business and Industrial Interests

Three organizations speak for business and industry in the Federal Republic: the League of German Industry, which represents large industrial and business interests; the National Association of German Employers, which essentially represents small and medium-size firms; and the German Industrial and Trade Chamber, composed of smaller, independent businesses (shopkeepers, artisans).

The impressive accomplishments of the economy and the importance of economic conditions to the political health of any government assure these associations easy access to the political elite. Business interests in Germany, as elsewhere in Europe, advocate cuts in government spending on and business contributions to social programs, usually citing their negative effect on Germany's competitive position in the world market. Reducing nonwage labor costs—that is, payments for health insurance, pensions, unemployment compensation, and sick leave—is a current top priority.

The ability of business interests to influence government policy even under the Red-Green coalition that governed from 1998 to 2005 (see Chapter 3.2) was on view in the 2000 tax package, which substantially cut business taxes, as well as in the Agenda 2010 program, which reduced union influence at the plant level. The program also encouraged the development of a low-wage job sector—something long advocated by business interests.

Labor Groups

The labor movement, like the political parties, has changed extensively in the postwar period. During the Weimar Republic, labor was divided along politico-ideological lines into socialist, communist, Catholic, and even liberal trade unions. These unions, especially the socialist and communist groups, were concerned with more than wages, hours, and working conditions. They sought to mobilize their members to support and implement a comprehensive ideology of social, economic, cultural, and political change. Indeed, many of their resources were spent on developing and refining this ideology and the accompanying tactics, which included confronting fellow workers in competing unions. The labor movement was therefore fragmented and relatively ineffectual in securing solid economic gains for its members and in preventing the Nazis' seizure of power in 1933.

The postwar Western occupation authorities and many prewar German trade union leaders sought to restructure and reform the unions. The result of their work is the German Trade Union Federation (*Deutscher Gewerkschaftsbund*—DGB), an organization composed of eight different unions with a total membership of more than 7 million in western Germany and about 1 million in the former East Germany.[7]

The DGB has become labor's chief political spokesperson and has essentially pursued a policy of "business unionism," concentrating on wages and working conditions. Labor leaders as well as economic policymakers within the Social Democratic Party advocate a pragmatic position on the market economy best summed up by the adage "Do not kill the cow we want to milk."

The trade unions have been successful in securing steady and solid economic gains for workers. The unions have also shared in this prosperity. One factor behind the low strike rate is the economic strength of organized labor, which induces business to take union proposals seriously and seek compromises. Business knows that labor has the financial resources to sustain an extensive strike action. The unions' ties to all parties, especially to the Social Democrats, give them direct access to the government. This political power is an additional factor in close worker-management cooperation.

That said, trade unions throughout the country have experienced a steady decline in membership. By 2008 total membership had dropped to about 8 million from 13.7 million in 1991.[8] The proportion of wage earners organized into unions declined from 41 percent in 1991 to 22 percent in 2006. Many of the losses have come from the east, where trade union membership was artificially high in the first years of unification. But in the west, membership has also declined, mainly because of the loss of blue-collar jobs.[9] Only among white-collar, service, and government workers have unions been able to grow.

After the 2002 election, the Schröder government's cuts in social programs such as unemployment compensation and sick leave as well as proposals to loosen the job protection many employees enjoy drew the intense opposition of the trade union movement. Many trade union leaders who had strongly supported the Schröder government felt betrayed by its postelection policies. In 2005 some of them supported Lafontaine and his Left Party. During the Grand Coalition labor continued to oppose any further cuts in social programs, especially the decision to increase the retirement age to sixty-seven from sixty-five. At the 2009 election most unions were officially neutral, but generally supported the Social Democrats, albeit with little enthusiasm. Among union members the SPD vote dropped from 47 percent in 2005 to only 24 percent in 2009, a decline that far exceeded the national average. Many trade union leaders would now like to see the SPD return to its commitment to social justice and the comprehensive welfare state and form an eventual coalition with the Left Party.

Agricultural Groups

Few interest groups in the Federal Republic have been as successful in securing government policies beneficial to their members as the various organizations representing farmers. Farmers constitute less than 5 percent of the workforce, and agriculture's contribution to the gross national product is less than 3 percent. Yet no occupational group is as protected and as well subsidized by the government as farmers. They receive guaranteed prices for most of their products, and they are given subsidies and tax benefits for new equipment, construction, and the modernization of their holdings. The increase in the value of farmland has led some observers to call farmers Germany's "secret rich." [10]

Even though a succession of "green plans" has consolidated many small farms into larger, more efficient units, German agriculture would not be able to compete with other Western societies were it not for the strong European Union protective tariff system for farm products and additional subsidies from Berlin. These benefits to farmers add an estimated 10 percent to 15 percent to the food bill of consumers, but all governments since 1949, regardless of their party configuration, have essentially continued these policies.

Agriculture in the former East Germany has been transformed. Under the communists, almost all farmers were forced to join collective farms. Since unification, some have reclaimed their land and become independent, and others have reorganized the former collectives into cooperatives. Many of these new cooperatives are run by the managers of the former collective farms. These "Red Barons" acquired a controlling interest in the cooperatives by buying out former members at cut-rate prices. They then modernized the operations through investments in new equipment and personnel cuts. The result is that many farms in eastern Germany are twenty to thirty times larger than their counterparts in western Germany. The large size of agricultural holdings makes them more efficient. Indeed, agriculture is one of the most productive sectors of the eastern economy.[11]

Citizens and Elections

Elections in the Federal Republic offer citizens their chief opportunity to influence the political process. Convinced that Adolf Hitler and the Nazi regime were supported by the German rank and file during most of the Third Reich, the founders of the Federal Republic essentially limited popular involvement at the national level to participation in periodic elections.[12] Therefore, Germany's Basic Law does not provide for the direct election of the president or the chancellor, referendums, the recall of public officials, or direct primaries to ensure more popular involvement at the national level.[13]

As in other Western European parliamentary systems, national elections do not directly determine who holds the top-level positions in government. The chancellor and cabinet are elected by the parliament after the parliament has been elected by the voters. Elections must be held at least once every four years, but can take place more frequently if a government loses its majority and parliament is dissolved. The Federal Republic has automatic registration and universal suffrage for all citizens over eighteen years of age.

Electoral System

Generally, Western democracies use one of two basic procedures for converting votes into legislative seats: a proportional system, in which a party's share of legislative mandates is proportional to its popular vote, and a plurality, or "winner-take-all," system, under which "losing" parties and candidates (and their voters) receive no representation. Proportional systems are usually favored by smaller parties, because under "pure" proportionality a party with even a fraction of a percentage of the vote would receive parliamentary representation.

Conversely, plurality systems are usually favored by the large parties, which have both the resources and candidates to secure pluralities in electoral districts. Some political scientists have hypothesized that a causal relationship exists between the electoral law and the number of political parties, with a proportional law producing a multiparty pattern and a plurality system producing a concentration of electoral support in two parties.

German electoral law has elements of both plurality and proportionality, but it is essentially a proportional representation system. Half of the delegates to parliament are elected on a plurality basis from 299 districts; the other half are chosen under the proportional representation principle from state (*Land*) lists. The voter receives two ballots—one listing district candidates, the other listing parties. The second ballot is by far the more important. The proportion of the vote a party receives on the second ballot ultimately determines how many seats it will have in parliament, because the number of district contests won by the party's candidates is deducted from the total due it on the basis of the second-ballot vote.

There are three exceptions to the proportional character of this system. First, to participate in the proportional distribution of seats, a party must receive a minimum of 5 percent of the second-ballot vote. If it does not, these now "wasted" votes go proportionally to the parties that did clear the 5 percent barrier. Second, if a party receives more district victories than it is entitled to under proportional representation, it can keep these extra or "excess" seats, and the total number of deputies in the parliament is increased.[14] In 2009 there was a record number (24) of such excess mandates, and the size of the parliament grew from 598 to 622.

Third, if a party wins in at least three districts, the 5 percent clause is waived and it participates in the proportional distribution based on the second-ballot vote. These latter two provisions of the system, until recently, rarely affected elections. But in 1994 the Party of Democratic Socialism (the old Communist Party) failed to clear the 5 percent mark, but it did win four district seats and therefore participated in the proportional payout.

Not surprisingly, many citizens do not fully understand this complicated system.[15] An example from the 2009 election may then make the system clearer (see Table 3-7). In 2009 the CDU/CSU received 33.8 percent of the second-ballot vote (proportional list) and was entitled to 202 seats in the Bundestag. But because it won 218 district victories on the first ballot, it received no seats from the proportional list. Its final total of 239 seats included the original 202 seats plus 13 seats from the "wasted" votes of the small parties and 24 of the "extra" seats it won at the district level. The Social Democrats' total of 146 came from 64 district victories, 74 list mandates and 8 from the small parties. Although the FDP won no district seats, it did receive a record 14.6 percent of the party-list vote. It therefore received 87 party-list seats plus 6 from the wasted vote pool of the small parties. The Left Party won in 16 districts, another record, and received 55 list seats and 5 from the small party share for a total of 76. The Green total of 68 seats included 1 district victory and the remainder from the list and the small parties. The 6 percent that went to the (very) small parties produced a pool of 36 seats that were distributed to the parties that cleared the 5 percent mark.

Table 3-7 Seat Distribution, 2009 German Election

Party	Percent on first ballot	Percent on second ballot	No. of seats earned[a]	No. of district seats won[b]	No. of list candidates elected[c]	Total
CDU/CSU	39.4	33.8	202	218	21	239
SPD	27.9	23.0	138	64	82	146
FDP	9.4	14.6	87	0	93	93
Left.PDS	11.1	11.9	71	16	60	76
Green	9.2	10.7	64	1	67	68
Minor parties	3.0	6.0	36	0	0	0
Total	100	100	598	299	323	622

Source: Federal Statistical Office.

Note: SPD = Social Democratic Party; CDU/CSU = Christian Democratic Union/Christian Social Union; FDP = Free Democratic Party; PDS = Party of Democratic Socialism.

[a] Under proportional representation.

[b] In first ballot.

[c] Includes twenty-four excess mandates for the CDU/CSU. The CDU/CSU received thirteen seats from the "other parties," the SPD eight, the FDP six, the Left five, and the Greens four.

The electoral system was intended to combine the best features of the plurality and proportional representation systems. The district contests were meant to introduce a "personalized" component into elections and give voters a means of identifying with "their" parliamentary deputy. The party-list allocations were meant to ensure the presence of a programmatic or policy dimension to elections. The 5 percent clause was designed to prevent small, antisystem splinter parties from gaining representation and making coalition building in parliament difficult.

In spite of the basically proportional electoral system, between 1949 and 1976 the party system became very concentrated—that is, the two-party (CDU/CSU-SPD) share of the vote grew from 60 percent in 1949 to 91 percent in 1976. During the past thirty years, however, the system has become more diffuse. The two largest parties in 2009 received only 56.8 percent of the vote. The three smaller parties now in the parliament—FDP, Green, and Left Party—still owe their existence largely to this system. Naturally, these parties are opposed to any shift toward an Anglo-American plurality electoral system. There will, however, have to be some change before the 2013 election (see note 14, p. 280).

Candidate Selection

Candidates for the party lists are selected at state-level party conventions held several months before the general election. Composing a list involves considerable bargaining both within the party and between the party and its major interest clientele. Generally, the very top positions on the list are reserved for the party's notables in the state, followed by representatives of factions and interest groups. Most of the candidates in safe districts are also given a "seat on the life boat"—a good list position—as a backup. In some instances, a candidate assigned a relatively weak district will be compensated by a promising list position. All participants in this procedure have a rough idea of how many list positions will be allotted to the party—that is, how many candidates will actually be elected. As the assumed cutoff point is approached, the intensity of the bargaining increases.

District candidates are nominated at local meetings of party organizations. These meetings are intended to give all party members an opportunity to screen prospective candidates. But, in fact, the district leadership of the party dominates the proceedings, and state and national party leaders have relatively little influence on the district-level nominating process.

Because most candidates are incumbents, the most obvious qualification for nomination to the parliament is previous job experience. A successful local- or state-level legislative background, long service in a local party organization, and close association with an interest group important to the party are other major qualifications. For a list nomination, expertise in a particular policy area also can be an important factor.

The West German Voter, 1949–1987

The results of the seventeen national elections held between 1949 and 2009 (see Figure 3-1) reveal several major electoral trends:

- A generally high rate of turnout, which by the 1970s exceeded 90 percent, the highest figure of any major Western democracy without legal penalties for nonvoting. This high turnout not only reflects the strong emphasis that the political culture places on voting as a duty, but also indicates a tendency to perceive elections as a way in which citizens can influence the policymaking process.

- The increasing concentration of support in two large parties from 1949 to 1976, as well as two small but strategically important third parties from 1983 to 1990, all of which support the basic democratic structure of the system.

- The hegemonic position of the CDU/CSU between 1953 and 1969 and from 1983 to 1998. During these periods, the CDU was the largest political party and the major partner in all coalition governments.

- The steady rise of the SPD between 1953 and 1972 from the "30 percent ghetto" to relative parity with the Christian Democrats.

- The decline in support for the two major parties since 1976. Since 2002 no major party has been able to secure 40 percent of the vote.

In 1949 nine political parties entered the parliament, but by 1957 most of them were absorbed into the Christian Democrats led by Konrad Adenauer. Extremist parties such as the Communist Party and several radical right-wing groups also disappeared by

Figure 3-1 Federal Elections, 1949–2009

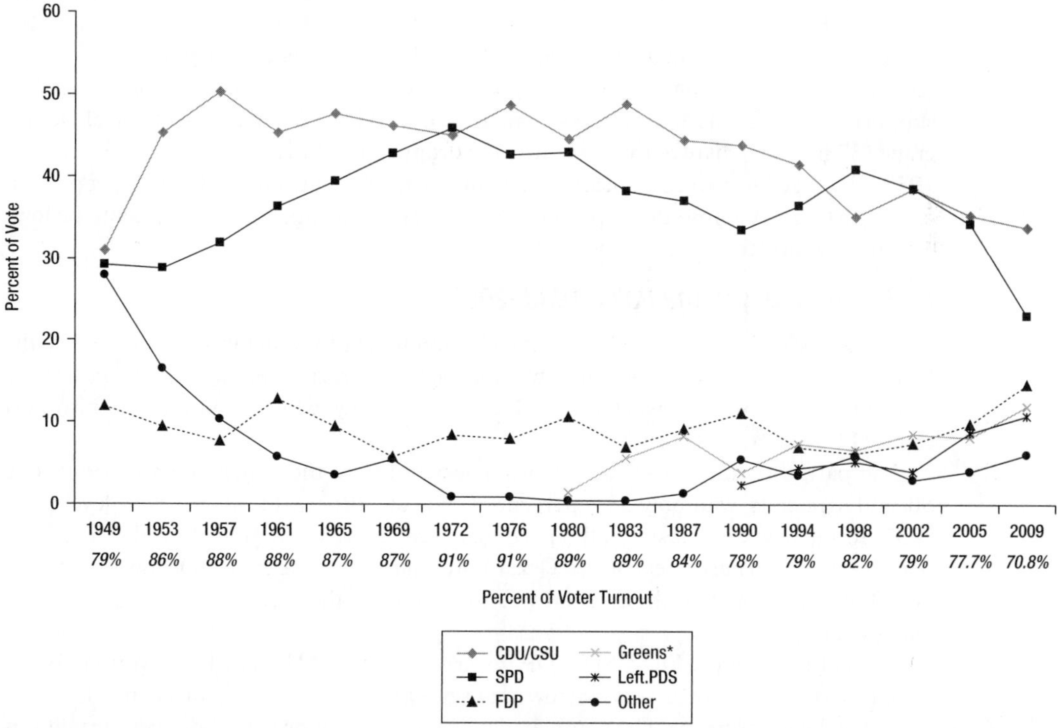

Source: Federal Statistical Office.

1957, rejected by the electorate. Campaigns of the 1950s focused on the performance of Adenauer's governments. CDU gains during this period were largely at the expense of the smaller parties. Most SPD advances between 1957 and 1972 were in the form of CDU/CSU voters and new voters, not those from the minor parties. The Free Democrats, depending on their coalition partner, attempted to appeal to CDU/CSU or SPD voters dissatisfied with their "regular" party. The FDP projected itself as a "liberal" corrective to the major parties: less conservative and less clerical than the CDU/CSU, but not as "radical" or "socialist" as the SPD. In election campaigns, the FDP, to some extent, had to campaign against its coalition partner.

In the 1983 election, voters solidly endorsed the CDU/CSU-FDP government of Helmut Kohl, which had governed since October 1982, when the SPD government fell. The Christian Democrats, with 48.8 percent of the vote, achieved their best result since 1957. The CDU/CSU gains came largely at the expense of the Social Democrats; almost 2 million 1980 SPD voters switched to the CDU. The major campaign issues were unemployment, security of the pension system, reduction in deficit spending, and price stability. In all these areas, the CDU/CSU was regarded as better qualified to deal with the problems than the SPD. In their campaign, the Social Democrats focused on the missile question, which was not nearly as important to the majority of voters as the bread-and-butter economic problems. The Free Democrats, with 7 percent of the vote, were able to gain the support of voters dissatisfied with the Christian Democrats, but who also wanted the coalition to remain in power. Nonetheless, the CDU's performance was its worst since 1969.

In 1987 voters returned the ruling CDU/CSU-FDP coalition to power, but with a reduced majority. For the first time in postwar electoral history, both major parties lost support in the same election. The combined CDU/CSU (44.3 percent) and Social Democratic (37 percent) share of the party-list vote dropped to 81 percent, the lowest level since 1953. The Free Democrats increased their vote to 9.1 percent, and the Greens' proportion of the party-list vote rose to 8.3 percent. Voting turnout dropped to 84.4 percent, the lowest since the first federal election in 1949.

Unified Germany at the Polls, 1990–2009

In the 1990 election, the first democratic election in all of Germany since the 1930s, the Kohl-led coalition was returned to power for the third straight time. Within the governing coalition, the big winner was the Free Democratic Party, which achieved the third-best result (11 percent) in its history.

The parties on the left of the political spectrum were the major losers in 1990. The Social Democrats, with only 33.5 percent of the vote, dropped to their lowest level since 1957. In the new eastern states, the party received less than one-fourth of the vote. This poor result was, in part, a reaction to Oskar Lafontaine's lukewarm attitude toward unification. The big surprise of the election was the failure of the western Greens to return to parliament.

In 1994 the ruling CDU/CSU-FDP government led by Helmut Kohl won its fourth straight election, but by a very narrow margin. Only about 48 percent of the electorate voted for the government. The complexities of the electoral process, however, turned this minority vote into a thin majority, 50.7 percent, of the seats.

In 1998 voters went to the polls for the fourteenth time since 1949, and for the first time they removed an entire incumbent government. In office since 1982, Chancellor Kohl's coalition government of Christian Democrats and Free Democrats was defeated soundly and replaced by a coalition of Social Democrats and Greens, nicknamed "Red-Green." The new government was headed by Gerhard Schröder, the chief executive of the state of Lower Saxony.

In 2002 the narrow government victory came largely as a result of a last-minute swing that can be traced to three discrete, unprecedented events: an August flood along the Elbe and Mulde rivers in the east, the emergence of American plans for a preemptive war against Iraq, and the televised one-on-one debates between Schröder and his challenger, Edmund Stoiber. Elections in Germany are usually not decided by last-minute developments, but in recent years, voters have been less attached to "their" parties and more likely to change their vote based on short-run factors such as candidate personality, media presentations, and events such as a flood or the Iraq war.

The 2005 election continued these trends. The major parties lost so many voters that neither of them could form a government with just one small partner as they had done since 1961. Unable to persuade two small parties to join in a government, they had no choice but to form a Grand Coalition, the first since 1966.[16] In 2005 the number of undecided and late-deciding voters reached record levels, as did the number of Germans splitting their ballots. Until hours before voting began, almost all of the usually accurate polling organizations predicted a victory for Angela Merkel's Christian Democrats and her preferred partner, the Free Democrats. At a minimum, the CDU/CSU was to receive about 41 percent of the vote. Apparently, however, between bedtime on election eve and the trip to the polls on Sunday, almost 2 million voters changed their minds.

In September 2009 at the seventeenth national election since the republic's founding and the fifth since unification, voters gave a majority of the parliamentary seats to the Christian Democrats and their old coalition partner, the Free Democrats, and replaced the Grand Coalition that had governed for four years. Chancellor Merkel remained in office, and the Social Democrats returned to the opposition for the first time since 1998. The Christian Democrats' new partner, the Free Democrats, returned to government after eleven years out of power. Many voters, however, stayed home, dropping the turnout rate to 70.8 percent, the lowest level in the history of the Federal Republic.[17]

The SPD ran a campaign in which it largely ignored the Agenda 2010 program of former chancellor Schröder that had so divided and weakened the party. Instead, it returned to the tried-and-true themes of social justice and unwavering support for the welfare state. It attempted to project itself as the guardian of social trust and an anchor in the world economic crisis. The CDU, its partner since 2005, was portrayed as the party of rich capitalists and managers, which would dismantle the welfare system that had given Germany social peace and prosperity for sixty years. Voters, however, did not buy this argument, and SPD support dropped from 34.2 percent to 23.0 percent, its worst performance in the history of the Federal Republic. Contributing to this defeat were heavy losses to the Christian Democrats and the low turnout.

Although Merkel's Christian Democrats won the election, they also saw their vote total decline, albeit far less than the Social Democrats. Nevertheless, the CDU's 33.8 percent was its worst performance since the Federal Republic's first election in 1949. This decline of the once dominant "major parties" indicates that many voters have lost their ties to these "elephants," as critics term the CDU and SPD, and are looking for new alternatives.

The big winner in 2009 was the Free Democratic Party, which received almost 15 percent of the vote, by far the best result in its history. The FDP's clear message of tax cuts and reduced government spending resonated well especially among younger middle-class voters. But the other "small" parties also did well. Both the Left Party and the Greens with 12 percent and 10.7 percent, respectively, achieved record highs in voter support.

Voting Behavior

The votes of most Germans can be explained by (1) the demographic characteristics of voters, especially social class and religion; (2) voters' attitudes toward major candidates; (3) the programs and policies of the political parties; (4) voters' attitudes toward the important policy issues facing the country; and (5) campaign events, especially those that attract widespread media attention.

Demographics Unionized manual workers still form the core of the Social Democratic electorate, whereas the middle-class and nonmanual occupations favor the Christian Democrats and the FDP. In 2005 unionized manual workers preferred the SPD over the other parties by about a ten-point margin. Among middle-class voters, support for the Christian Democrats and Free Democrats runs high. The religious factor also structures the party vote. The party preference of Catholics varies significantly according to their attachment to the church, as measured by church attendance. Most Catholics who regularly attend church are staunch supporters of the Christian Democrats, but Catholic voters who seldom or never go to church are far less likely to support that party. For nominal Catholics, social class, rather than religion, is a more important determinant of voting behavior. The SPD and FDP and the Greens receive disproportionate support from Protestants, especially those with a weak attachment to their church. The Greens also do well among voters who report no religious affiliation.

Although social class and religion remain important factors in voting behavior, their relative impact has declined since the early 1970s. The proportion of Germans in manual occupations dropped from 51 percent in 1950 to 33 percent in 2008, which leaves less of a "proletariat" on which the Social Democrats can draw. Similarly, the "old" middle-class component of the electorate—the small shopkeepers, farmers, and self-employed doctors and lawyers—declined from 28 percent in 1950 to only 10 percent by 2005. This reservoir of Christian Democratic–Free Democratic strength has become smaller as well.

The erosion of the social class cleavage is also evident in the religious division. A generation ago, conservative politicians characterized elections as a competition between Christian good and atheist evil, and such rhetoric succeeded in polarizing many voters along religious lines. But social change in the Federal Republic includes a strong secular trend. In the 1950s more than 40 percent of voters reported going to church on a weekly basis; by the 2009 election barely 20 percent attended church this regularly. Among Catholics, regular church attendance declined from 54 percent in 1953 to 16 percent in 2008.[18] Although church-going Catholics were about as likely to vote for the CDU/CSU in the twenty-first century as they were in the 1950s, their numbers and therefore the aggregate impact of religion on the vote have declined.[19]

These social changes have especially strong effects on young voters. They are the least likely to be tied to the old class and religious networks and the most likely to seek out new alternatives. In short, age is one demographic factor whose importance has increased, especially in explaining support for the Greens. In 2005 voters under forty-five years of age accounted for 57 percent of the Green vote. As Green voters age, this polarization should decline, but in the near future the generation gap will remain an important factor in voting behavior.[20]

Voters' Attitudes toward Candidates   Voters' perceptions of the major candidates, especially party leaders and those slated for the chancellorship or cabinet positions, are important influences on voting behavior. The incumbent chancellor generally has an advantage, or "bonus," over the challenger. As in other Western societies, the chief executive can to an extent make headlines by announcing tax cuts, spending hikes for social programs, and subsidies for various groups, all timed for the election.

A major factor in the landslide CDU/CSU victories in 1953 and 1957 was the personal popularity of Chancellor Konrad Adenauer. Indeed, more voters liked Adenauer than liked his party, and the SPD's chancellor candidates were less popular than their party. Likewise, the low popularity of the Christian Democratic candidate in 1980, Franz Josef Strauss, was an important factor in the victory of the SPD-FDP coalition. In 1990, after unification, Chancellor Helmut Kohl became more popular than his party. The narrow victory of Chancellor Gerhard Schröder in 2002 was greatly aided by his personal popularity advantage over his challenger. His performance in the TV debates yielded another increase in the polls for his party and government. In 2005 his near comeback from a fifteen-percentage-point deficit to a one-percentage-point loss was also attributable in part to his popularity advantage (53 percent to 39 percent) over Angela Merkel.[21]

In 2009 the Christian Democrats ran a campaign focused almost exclusively on Chancellor Merkel. From the beginning of her term in 2005, her personal popularity had been extraordinarily high, averaging about 75 percent over a four-year period. The great majority of Germans simply liked her even though they were far from enthusiastic about her party and some of her policies. Given this reality, the CDU campaign planners simply focused on her personality and said as little as possible about policy.

Party Programs and Policies   Through their policies and strategies, the parties also have played an independent role in shaping electoral outcomes. For example, by bringing down the Schmidt government in 1982, the Free Democrats lost many voters and were able to return to the parliament in 1983 only with the support of many CDU/CSU supporters who split their ballots. Indeed, the party narrowly escaped political extinction. The SPD's 1983 decision to all but ignore the unemployment issue and instead emphasize noneconomic issues such as the NATO missile decision cost the party sizable blue-collar support. In 1987 the Christian Democrats underestimated the extent of discontent among farmers, many of whom stayed home from the polls. In the 1987 election, the Social Democrats' decisions to seek an absolute majority and have their chancellor candidate conduct a U.S.-style campaign lacked credibility in the eyes of most voters. In 1990 the Social Democrats' division over the unification question was an important factor in the party's poor performance. And

Kohl's 1998 decision to try for a fifth straight win was probably a major mistake. Four years later, the Free Democrats' attempt in 2002 to run as if they were a major party was not taken seriously by many voters. In 2005 the CDU/CSU's strategic decision to run a "campaign of honesty" that promised tax increases and further cuts in social programs hurt the party's fortunes.

The SPD had a difficult task in 2009. It had to run against many of the policies it had enacted both in the 1998–2005 Schröder government and in the Grand Coalition. The cuts in social programs, the fusion of unemployment and welfare programs, the increase in the retirement age to sixty-seven from sixty-five were all done at the initiative of the Social Democrats. But in 2009 the party was railing against these programs and blaming everything on its "evil twin," the SPD in government.

Issues In most elections, the issues of prime concern to voters revolve around the economy and social stability. Some specific examples are inflation, unemployment, law and order (terrorism), and the viability of the social welfare system. Yet the bulk of the electorate does not want any major political or socioeconomic changes. In the 1994 election, the economy was the major issue, and the economic upturn that began in late 1993 was just in time and just enough to bring the Kohl government a narrow victory. In fact, Kohl became the first chancellor to escape unscathed from a recession. In 1998, however, record high unemployment worked against the incumbent government. In 2005 unemployment was again the voters' top concern. But many Germans were also worried about the security of their pensions and health care insurance system.

More specific issues, although perhaps not of concern to a great majority of the electorate, can be important in effecting the small voting shifts that may decide an election. In 1972 the SPD-FDP coalition was clearly helped by the issue of *Ostpolitik,* the government's policy of improving relations with the Soviet Union and Eastern Europe. Some voters, normally CDU/CSU, supported the government of Willy Brandt because of this issue; they saw the policy as a step toward a more lasting peace in Europe.

In the early 1980s noneconomic or "new politics" issues began to increase in importance. Chief among them was protection of the environment, specifically the problem of nuclear power plants. By 1990 almost 75 percent of voters considered the environment to be a "very important" issue, second only to unemployment. The 1986 nuclear disaster at Chernobyl in the Soviet Union struck Germany with special force, because citizens were told not to eat certain foods and to keep their children indoors. This crisis was soon followed by a series of chemical spills into the Rhine River. The ecological cries of the Greens were now being taken seriously by supporters of all political colors, and support for the Greens in public opinion polls soared. More than 40 percent of all voters considered the Greens to be the "most competent" party to deal with nuclear power issue—a percentage almost five times greater than the party's vote in the 1983 election. Other noneconomic issues whose importance increased in the 1980s and 1990s were women's rights, peace and disarmament, and the treatment of foreign minorities. In 2002 another noneconomic issue, the Iraq war and Germany's relationship with the United States, was an important factor in the Schröder government's come-from-behind win. But at the 2009 election, a major factor in the Free Democrats' success was their emphasis on tax cuts.

Thousands of Opel workers rally in Rüesselsheim, Germany, November 5, 2009, to protest General Motors's decision to abandon the unit's sale to new owners who the workers hoped would preserve jobs.

Source: AP Images/Michael Probst

Campaign Events In recent elections, as the traditional ties of class and religion have weakened, campaign events, as communicated by the media, have had an increasing influence on voting. In 2002 the first-ever American-style television debate between chancellor candidates Stoiber and Schröder apparently had a significant impact on the choice of many voters.[22] Schröder, the perceived winner, believed the debate helped his candidacy. In 2005 the televised debate between Merkel and Schröder again turned into an advantage for the incumbent, although it was not enough to keep him in office. Also during the 2005 campaign, Merkel's decision to name a professor of tax law as her potential finance minister proved to be a distinct negative for her cause. The professor had a mind of his own and did not stay on message. In his free-wheeling speeches, he suggested that the country needed a flat tax (Merkel disagreed) and that women should probably stay at home and raise children. Needless to say, after the election the professor's brief political career came to an end. In 2009 events related to the economic crisis played a major role. The SPD, behind in the polls and searching for another target in the Merkel camp, focused on her economics minister and his alleged refusal to help the Opel automobile company, a subsidiary of General Motors, and its 55,000 workers in the wake of the GM bankruptcy. His alleged indifference to the plight of the common worker, the Social Democrats argued, was symptomatic of the entire party and its ally, the probusiness Free Democrats.

NOTES

1. European Commission, *Eurobarometer,* no. 61, Brussels, February-March 2004, Question 7,09.
2. ALLBUS, 2004, Variables 846–847.
3. David P. Conradt, "The Christian Democrats in 1990: Saved by Unification?" in *The New Germany Votes,* ed. Russell J. Dalton (Providence, R.I., and Oxford: Berg Publishers, 1993), 59–75.
4. For a discussion of this point, see Gordon Smith, *Democracy in Western Germany* (New York: Holmes and Meier, 1979), 96ff.
5. Viola Neu, "FDP Bundesparteitag, Hannover, 15–17. Mai 2009," Parteienmonitoraktuell, Berlin: Konrad Adenauer Stiftung, 2009, 11.
6. Gerhard Lehmbruch, "Liberal Corporatism and Party Government," in *Trends toward Corporatist Intermediation,* ed. Philippe Schmitter and Gerhard Lehmbruch (Beverly Hills, Calif.: Sage Publications, 1979), 147–188.
7. Since 1999 white-collar workers have been organized in a United Service Sector Union, which is also part of the DGB. Indeed, it has replaced the metal workers as the largest component of the federation.
8. Nico Fickinger, "Deutsche Gewerkschaften suchen nach Antworten," *Frankfurter Allgemeine Zeitung,* April 30, 2005, 16; *Datenreport 2009,* Bonn: Bundeszentrale für politische Bildung, 2009, 234; DGB Web site: www.dgb.de/mitgliederzahlen.
9. *Das Parlament,* nos. 7–8, February 10–17, 1995, 7; Federal Statistical Office, *Datenreport 2002* (Bonn: Federal Center for Political Education, 2003), 602.
10. Michael Jungblut, "Die heimlichen Reichen," *Die Zeit,* November 10, 1978, 25.
11. Adalbert Zehnder, "Wo die 'Roten Barone' das Sagen haben," *Süddeutsche Zeitung,* September 26, 2000.
12. Kurt Sontheimer, "Die Bundesrepublik und ihre Bürger," in *Nach dreißig Jahren,* ed. Walter Scheel (Stuttgart: Klett-Cotta, 1979), 175–186.
13. Referendums are constitutionally possible in most states, and a little-known provision of the Basic Law allows local communities to be governed by citizen assemblies. Thus far, no locality has employed this form of governance.
14. In a July 2008 decision the Federal Constitutional Court ruled that parts of the current law are unconstitutional because in some cases all votes are not equally weighted and, indeed, a vote for a particular party can have a negative impact on its total number of seats; in other words, voting for a party can reduce its total number of seats. Although it was not specifically mentioned in the opinion, many observers consider the excess mandate provision to be a major factor contributing to the law's defects. The Court did not invalidate the 2005 election result; rather, it gave the parliament until June 30, 2011, to correct the current law or pass a new electoral law. The 2009 election, therefore, was conducted under the current law including the excess mandate clause. In short, in 2009 Germans went to the polls according to an electoral law that in 2008 its highest court had declared, in part, unconstitutional.
15. Two additional changes in the law were in effect only for the 1990 election, the first free all-German vote since 1932. First, largely as a concession to the East German parties, a party in 1990 was required to secure the 5 percent minimum in *either* the former West Germany or former East Germany. The PDS, the old Communist Party, and the East German Greens, which was allied with the East German citizen democracy movement, *Bündnis 90,* both won representation in the parliament, even though they only received 2.4 percent and 1.2 percent, respectively, of the national vote, but in the former East Germany they met the 5 percent minimum. Second, parties were allowed to combine their electoral lists—that is,

form alliances in the various states. This measure also was designed to help the new East German parties. Ironically, had the West German Greens formed such an alliance with their East German counterparts, they would have returned to parliament with about twenty-six seats.

16. The 1966 alignment was largely elite-driven. Both the CDU/CSU and the SPD could have formed a government with the Free Democrats, but important leaders in the major parties had other plans. The 2005 coalition was clearly driven by electoral realities.

17. Forschungsgruppe Wahlen, "Bundestagswahl. Eine Analyse der Wahl vom 27. September 2009," Berichte Nr. 138. Mannheim, 18–21. For an analysis of the 2009 election, see David P. Conradt, "The Shrinking Elephants," *German Politics and Society* 28, no. 3 (Fall 2010): 25–46.

18. ALLBUS, 2008, Variables 524–526.

19. Among Catholics who regularly attended services, support for the CDU/CSU in the 1950s averaged about 80 percent; at the 2005 election it was 72 percent; in 2009 it dropped to 67 percent. See David P. Conradt, "The Tipping Point: The 2005 Election and the De-Consolidation of the Party System?" *German Politics and Society* 24, no. 1 (Spring 2006): 11–26; for 2009, Forschungsgruppe Wahlen, "Bundestagswahl," 62.

20. Another party with strong support among young people, the Pirate Party, made its first appearance at the 2009 election. The Pirates trace their origins to Sweden, and they are identified with one issue: free, uncensored downloads of all Internet data. Although the party received only 2 percent of the vote, well short of the 5 percent minimum, it was supported by 7 percent of voters under twenty-five. Among first-time voters between the ages of eighteen and twenty-one, the Pirates vote reached double digits.

21. Forschungsgruppe Wahlen, "Bundestagswahl. Eine Analyse der Wahl vom 18. September 2005," Mannheim, 2005, 45. In 2002 Schröder had a twenty-three-percentage-point lead over his challenger, but support for the two major parties was about dead even at 39 percent.

22. Thorsten Faas and Jürgen Maier, "Chancellor-Candidates in the 2002 Televised Debates," *German Politics* 13, no. 2 (June 2004): 300–316.

How is Power Used?

THE FEDERAL REPUBLIC OF GERMANY HAS A COMPLEX POLITICAL system characterized by the presence of multiple power centers. Although the national executive with its control over the civil service initiates the broad outlines of policy, it cannot secure the approval of its policy proposals or their implementation without at least the tacit prior approval of other actors in the political system: major interest groups, extraparliamentary organizations of the governing parties, influential members of the parliament, the states, the courts, the leadership of the health and social security system (the semipublic institutions that are the subject of the next section), the Federal Labor Agency administration, and even the opposition parties through their chairmanship of several parliamentary committees and their delegates in the Bundesrat. Strong opposition by any of these actors will hinder the efforts of the government and chancellor to determine the "main guidelines" of policy.

Successful policymaking must be accomplished within the framework of the politico-economic consensus that has developed over the past six decades. The political system resists any efforts to introduce major innovations within a relatively short time frame. Change tends to be gradual and incremental, and rarely will it have a redistributive effect. The subsidies given to agriculture, the coal and steel industry, shipbuilding, and the construction trade have been a policy problem throughout much of the republic's history. Economic advisers, countless study commissions, and even the courts, in the case of the coal industry, have recommended that these subsidies be drastically reduced or eliminated. Most governments on entering office promise to tackle the problem, but regardless of their partisan composition the subsidies continue. Even the enormous financial demands of unification have not made a dent in programs that pay construction workers when the weather is bad, coal miners to produce coal for which there is no market, and farmers to grow crops that will be added to the stockpiles of the European Union (EU).

The federal structure of the republic, which gives the states extensive responsibilities in implementing national legislation, represents a further dispersion of political power and is yet another factor inhibiting major policy innovation.[1] The importance of the constituent states in the policy process has increased as the scope of their veto power in the Federal Council, or Bundesrat, has expanded. At present, more than half of all legislation is subject to a Bundesrat veto.

In addition, as discussed in Chapter 3.2, for most of the past forty years Germany has had the equivalent of "divided government"—that is, the governing coalition in the Federal Parliament (Bundestag) has differed from that in the Federal Council (Bundesrat). This situation has greatly reduced the capacity of a national government to use its power without extensive bargaining with the states. But even friendly states (those governed by the same coalition that rules in Berlin) can oppose, and indeed have opposed, national policy initiatives when they perceive a threat to state interests. The national government had to struggle for decades to change significantly the distribution of taxes between the national and state governments or to expand its influence in higher education, urban planning, and environmental protection legislation. In these areas, all the states have guarded their prerogatives, particularly when they are governed by parties not in power in the federal parliament (Bundestag). Many other reform initiatives during the past twenty years have been blocked by each of the major parties, depending on which one has held the majority in which chamber. During the Grand Coalition from 2005–2009, divided government ceased at least temporarily. The coalition of Social Democrats and Christian Democrats controlled more than 70 percent of the seats in the Bundestag and enjoyed a similar majority in the Bundesrat. The new government, elected in 2009, had a narrow majority in the Bundesrat for only a few months. In May 2010 both of the parties in Merkel's government lost seats at a state election and their short-lived majority in the Bundesrat.

Finally, the Federal Republic has transferred some important policymaking power to the institutions of the European Union. Agricultural policy is made largely in Brussels under the terms of the EU's Common Agricultural Policy. And since 1999 control over monetary policy has been in the hands of the European Central Bank, because Germany is a member of "Euroland," the sixteen nations that have adopted a common currency, the euro. As for defense, the Federal Republic's military is fully integrated into the command structure of the North Atlantic Treaty Organization (NATO), and Germany also participates fully in the EU's defense programs.

Semipublic Institutions

The use of political power in the Federal Republic is not restricted to the formal government institutions. Germany has an extensive network of semipublic institutions that play major roles in determining how power is to be used and how policy is to be implemented. Among the semipublic institutions, the social security and health systems, like the bureaucracy and courts, have survived the frequent and sudden regime changes of the past century. Both were established in the 1880s by the conservative chancellor Otto von Bismarck, who sought to ensure that the growing working class would support the existing monarchical regime and not the socialists. Through these social welfare programs, Bismarck tried, in effect, to buy workers' political support. The Federal Labor Agency (*Bundesagentur für Arbeit*), located in Nürnberg, administers a nationwide network of employment offices. This agency was established during the Weimar Republic and reemerged relatively intact after 1949. These institutions assume functions performed by national governments in centralized systems such as Great Britain and France. In Germany, they lessen the total political load carried by the national government, but they also reduce its strength.[2]

The Social Security and Health Systems

The German welfare state is one of the most generous and comprehensive in the world. Expenditures of the health, pension, industrial accident, child support, public housing, and veterans' programs account for about 40 percent of the national government's budget and provide citizens with more than one-fourth of their disposable income. Yet the administration of these huge programs is not carried out by either the national or state government, but by the more than eighteen hundred social security and health funds located throughout the country. The pension and health care programs are financed largely through equal employer and employee contributions. But the state pays for civil servant pensions and about 80 percent of the pension costs for farmers. The costs of other programs, such as child support, housing and rent subsidies, and welfare, are taken from general tax revenues. Employers must pay the costs of the accident insurance program. The health, or "sickness," funds cover about 90 percent of the population. They are organized by economic sector (business, agriculture, and the professions), occupational group, and geographic area. The social security (pension and accident) programs insure about 39 million adults.

Germany's social security and health programs have undergone extensive changes since the founding of the Federal Republic. The governing boards of all the funds are now based on the principle of parity representation for the various business, professional, and labor interests most concerned with the programs. After 1949, the left or labor wing of the ruling Christian Democratic Union (CDU), working with the trade unions and the opposition Social Democratic Party (SPD) and enjoying the support of Chancellor Konrad Adenauer, was able to convince business interests that the confrontational class politics of the Weimar Republic should be replaced with a new emphasis on "social partnership." This change of emphasis, however, required concessions from both business and labor. The trade unions gave up their majority control of the health funds, and employers did the same for the pension and accident insurance funds.

The administrative independence of these funds is limited by federal law. The size of pension payments and the taxes to pay for them are determined by the parliament. But the funds do have considerable power to set the fee structure for physicians, to oversee the construction and management of hospitals, and to monitor the investment of pension fund capital. The concept of social partnership extends to the state as well. Indeed, the health and pension system funds, according to one authority, are "political shock absorbers," connecting "state with society because they leave it to the major economic interest groups to mediate the state's administration of major social welfare programs."[3]

The postwar emphasis on consensus and social partnership was on view most clearly in the 1957 reform of the pension system. Previous pension legislation based the size of payments largely on the individual's contributions. The 1957 law, while retaining some elements of individual insurance, linked increases in pension payments, with some time lag, to increases in the overall national wage level. This dynamic feature enabled all pensioners, regardless of their individual contribution, to share directly in the expanding national economy.

In recent years, the combination of an aging population, a low birthrate, a weak economy, and the costs of unification has severely strained the postwar consensus on the welfare state. Contributions from employers and employees to the pension and health programs have not kept pace with expenditures. The resulting deficits have been covered from general tax revenues. In addition, high unemployment has put the unemployment insurance system into the red, adding further to the state deficit.

Since the 1980s a variety of cuts have been made in the welfare state. In 2001 Chancellor Gerhard Schröder's SPD-Green government passed a major overhaul of the pension system. Over the opposition of its core electoral clientele—blue-collar workers and the trade unions—the new system will effectively reduce pension payments from about 70 percent of a worker's prior income to 66 percent. This reform was accomplished by linking pension increases not to the average annual increase in wages, but rather to the increase in the cost of living. The "dynamic" in the dynamic pension system was gone.

To compensate for the lower payments, workers are being encouraged to establish their own retirement accounts. Up to 4 percent of annual income, capped at about $2,200 for singles and $4,400 for married couples, can be invested tax-free in an individual retirement account. In addition, as of 2010 the state will contribute an additional $400 annually as a premium to the individual accounts. For each child, an additional $200 will be contributed to the accounts. These funds will accumulate on a tax-deferred basis. Lower-income groups will also receive tax credits to encourage them to establish supplementary retirement accounts. But these measures may not be enough. Since 2005 the pension system has needed infusions of general revenue to remain solvent. Pensioners now receive increases which are not related to overall economic growth, sporadically, usually around elections.

Federal Labor Agency

The semipublic Federal Labor Agency has primary responsibility for organizing the labor market—that is, bringing jobs and job seekers together—and for administering the system of unemployment insurance. The agency also administers programs, financed from unemployment insurance revenues, that retrain workers and supplement the incomes of those people whose work hours have been cut back. In its programs, the agency gives special attention to the elderly, women, the handicapped, the long-term unemployed, and other special groups such as seasonal workers. Established in 1952, the agency is located in Nürnberg and is under the supervision, but not the direct control, of the Labor Ministry in Berlin. It is governed by a president, an executive committee, and a supervisory board, which includes representatives of trade unions, employers, and federal and state officials. The major guidelines determining labor policy are developed in Nürnberg and administered in hundreds of branch, local, and regional offices. Most of the unemployment compensation programs are financed by equal employer and employee contributions, which amount to about 3 percent of a worker's gross income. If the unemployment level is high, however, the federal government must subsidize the agency.

Since 1994 the government has permitted private commercial agencies to engage in job placement, thereby ending the near-monopoly of the Federal Labor Agency. These private agencies are now allowed to place employees in all available positions; previously, they were restricted to placing managers, artists, and models. Their fees, however, must be paid by the employer, not the job seeker.

In 2002 the Federal Labor Agency came under sharp criticism from the government's accounting office for overstating its record of securing jobs. The agency claimed that it was responsible for about 60 percent of all job placements in the country, but the accounting office said the actual figure was less than 20 percent. It turned out that the agency was taking credit for many job placements that were actually achieved by job seekers. The report undermined the credibility of the agency and damaged the Schröder government.

The agency's administrative structure also came under closer examination. Only about 10,000 of its 96,000 employees were directly involved in finding jobs for the unemployed. The remaining staff calculate unemployment benefits, direct retraining programs, issue labor permits, conduct economic research, or administer the organization.

In 2005, as part of the Agenda 2010 reform program, the agency, now under new leadership, was assigned a critical role in the new job placement plan. Its offices were extensively remodeled into "Job Centers" with state-of-the-art communications and computer facilities. So far, its record of job creation is mixed, and some political leaders of the CDU/Christian Social Union (CSU) and especially the Free Democratic Party (FDP) would like to abolish the agency and allow private firms to take over, with the government paying some of the costs.

The Use of Power in the Social-Liberal Era, 1969–1982

The basic pattern of incrementalism and a problem-solving, bargaining approach to politics that developed during the period of Christian Democratic control (1949–1969) continued unchanged under the social-liberal (SPD-FDP) coalition that governed from 1969 to 1982. The SPD achieved a gradual shift in distributive policies in the direction of greater benefits for lower- and lower-middle-status groups (tax, welfare, and education policies) and the germination of a possible shift in the distribution of power and influence within Germany's industrial enterprise (codetermination). The other major change associated with SPD rule from 1969 to 1982 was *Ostpolitik*, the normalization of relations among West Germany, the nations of Central Europe, and the Soviet Union. This change, however, did not represent any major challenge to the consensus. Instead, it drew on previous initiatives made during the mid- to late 1960s when the Christian Democrats were still the dominant party, so support for the "new policy" within the parliamentary opposition was considerable.

Conflicts between the two coalition partners arose more frequently over socioeconomic policy, and especially over questions of the organization of the economy, reform of vocational (apprenticeship) training, land use laws, inequality of capital resources (compulsory profit sharing), and tax reform. The Free Democrats generally opposed greater state intervention in the economy and greater worker participation in a company's decision-making process at the expense of capital and management. The FDP also opposed the leveling implied in the profit-sharing plans supported by the Social Democrats and their plans for increasingly progressive taxation. In short, when an issue involved the redistribution of economic resources and power—that is, increasing the resources of one group (workers) at the expense of another (the middle and upper classes)—there was extensive conflict within the coalition. In response, the Free Democrats were usually able to force a compromise that benefited its largely upper- and middle-class clientele. The Social Democrats, at least in this area, probably gave up more than their numerical strength required, and the Free Democrats exerted more influence than their size warranted.[4]

The coalition was more harmonious when problems were largely regulative and distributive in character. There was essentially little difference between Social Democrats and the Free Democrats in the areas of civil liberties, education, internal security, defense, and foreign policies. In fact, these issues dominated the legislative program of the first SPD-FDP government led by Willy Brandt (1969–1972).

How Power Was Used in the Kohl Era, 1982–1998

The Christian Democrats returned to power in 1982 promising a fundamental change (*Wende*) in the republic's policies and its "moral-cultural" climate. The era of free-spending, permissive socialism had, in the view of the Christian Democrats, had a corrupting effect on the West German community. Chancellor Helmut Kohl promised a return to traditional values: thrift, hard work, and discipline, as well as an end to the entitlement mentality of the SPD-FDP years. The victory of his government in the 1983 election, however, stemmed primarily from the recession of 1981–1983, Germany's worst since the Great Depression of the 1930s. Many voters associated this economic slump with the policies of the previous government. The Christian Democrats promised an economic upturn through a German version of supply-side economics: cuts in government spending, including most social programs; investment incentives for business; lower taxes; and reduced state deficits. Although these policies, when finally implemented, did not produce changes as drastic as those associated in the early 1980s with "Reaganomics" or "Thatcherism," they did represent a departure from the generous support given to social welfare programs during the SPD-FDP governments.

But the welfare state was by no means cut drastically during these years. Indeed, most analysts argue that most of the cutbacks in education, health, and pension spending lasted only until early 1984.[5] By 1985 the Kohl government was suffering from sharp losses in state elections to the Social Democrats, which dampened its enthusiasm for further cuts. Numerous surveys over the past thirty years have consistently shown that citizens are willing to accept marginal reductions during difficult economic times, but they still firmly support welfare programs and expect the state to assume fundamental responsibility for the health and well-being of the population. Spending for social programs dropped from 32.3 percent of the gross domestic product (GDP) in 1983 to 30 percent in 1986. Although budget deficits dropped from $30 billion in 1982 to $8 billion in 1987, by 1989 they had risen again to about $20 billion. In the 1987 election, there was little talk of a *Wende,* or of any further reductions in social programs by the Christian Democrats.

How Power Was Used in the Unification Process

The speed and effectiveness of the external dimension of unification belied the conventional wisdom that modern democracies cannot act in a timely and decisive manner. In less than eleven months after the opening of the Berlin Wall on November 9, 1989, the Kohl government concluded the following:

- Treaties with the four World War II powers that ended their occupation rights in Germany, including Berlin; reduced the German army by about half; and set the eastern borders of the unified country;

- a separate agreement with the Soviet Union in which Moscow agreed to withdraw its twenty-one Red Army divisions from East Germany by 1994 and to allow a unified Germany to remain in NATO in exchange for about $40 billion in aid; and

- major treaties with East Germany merging the countries' economic and social welfare systems (June 1990) and regulating the entrance of East Germany into West Germany's political, constitutional, and legal order (August 1990).

Also in less than eleven months, the Kohl government secured the support of all of Germany's neighbors and allies as well as its adversaries in the former communist bloc.

Even though Great Britain and France were initially opposed to unification, their influence was more than countered by the strong support of the United States.

Internal unification was a much more difficult process, requiring bargaining and compromise between and among the pivotal domestic political players. Some difficult unification-related issues such as abortion and property rights were not resolved in the unification treaties, but were left to the new parliament or the courts to resolve. The financing of unification is another example of incrementalism, influenced by political and electoral considerations.

In financing unification, the Kohl government proceeded with the usual political caution. Although some advisers in 1990 urged Chancellor Kohl to appeal to patriotic sentiments and call on West Germans to sacrifice and accept stiff tax increases to finance the rebuilding of the East, most public opinion polls found little support for such an approach. Instead, the government transferred about half of the costs to the pension, unemployment, and health care programs and financed the remainder of the $1.6 trillion through borrowing and a series of direct and indirect taxes.

It was also only *after* the 1990 election that taxpayers began to get the bills for unification. In spite of his campaign pledge of "no new taxes," Kohl announced in 1991 that the unexpectedly high costs of unification would necessitate a *temporary* increase in income taxes, specifically a 7.5 percent "solidarity" surtax. Additional revenues were raised by sharp hikes in gasoline taxes and social insurance premiums. Overall, since 1990, thirteen different tax increases have been imposed, usually in the manner just described.

The Use of Power by Schröder's Red-Green Coalition, 1998–2002

After their dramatic victory in 1998, the Social Democrats and the Greens assumed the reins of power with a full policy agenda. But few governments have ever gotten off to a worse start. Neither party had solid experience in governing at the national level. The Social Democrats had been out of power since 1982, and the Greens were in their first-ever national government. This lack of experience showed in the early months as confusing and conflicting policies were announced.

The SPD was divided between a traditionalist wing led by Finance Minister Oskar Lafontaine and the modernizers under Gerhard Schröder. Both were important in securing the 1998 election victory, with Lafontaine appealing to the party's historic working-class core and Schröder bringing in new voters from the center. But only one could eventually govern. Lafontaine wanted to stimulate consumer demand through tax cuts for lower- and middle-income groups and increases in spending for social programs. Schröder favored a probusiness policy of reductions in the costs of hiring new employees, tax breaks for investors, and reductions in welfare state spending. Lafontaine also advocated major changes in the international monetary system by returning to fixed exchange rates and limiting international capital movements. The conflict between the two men came to a head in early 1999 when Lafontaine resigned as finance minister and leader of the SPD. Schröder himself replaced Lafontaine as head of the party and appointed a new finance minister who would support his centrist policies.

The Schröder government chalked up a major policy achievement in 2000, when the chancellor skillfully guided a major tax reform package through both houses of the parliament. Under the new law, the most significant since World War II, the top corporate tax rate dropped from about 52 percent to 39 percent by 2005. Individual rates were also cut from a high of 51 percent to 42 percent, and the bottom rate went from 24 percent to 15 percent. The tax package was very similar to the one the Kohl government failed to pass in 1997.

Like Kohl, Schröder had a solid majority in the Bundestag, but his coalition held only a minority in the second chamber, the Bundesrat, which represents the states. To gain the Bundesrat's approval of the tax package, the Schröder government needed thirty-five votes. The five state governments governed either by the SPD alone or in coalition with the Greens were secure, but their vote total was only twenty-three. The six states governed either by the CDU, the CSU, or CDU-FDP coalitions had twenty-eight votes, but they opposed the tax package. Schröder needed to secure at least twelve of the seventeen remaining votes of the five states in which the SPD governed either in coalition with the CDU (Berlin, Bremen, Brandenburg), or with the FDP (Rhineland-Palatinate), or with the Party of Democratic Socialism, or PDS (Mecklenburg–West Pomerania). In the FDP and PDS states (seven votes), the SPD had a dominant position; among the Grand Coalition states it was the largest party in Bremen and Berlin.

Schröder and his finance minister had various sweeteners ready for the potential turncoats: Berlin received about $40 million to cover the extra security costs incurred by the influx of foreign dignitaries visiting the new/old national capital and to support the city's museums; the small and very poor state of Mecklenburg–West Pomerania received support for a new power plant. The smallest state, Bremen, was assured that the weighting system for state-to-state revenue sharing, which benefits the small states, would not change. This was pork-barrel politics German style. Late on the eve of the decisive vote, Schröder had his majority. The next day, he triumphantly proclaimed the end of slow growth and high unemployment; Germany was a competitive global economic player.

The CDU cried foul. "Never in my 30 years in politics," lamented one CDU state leader, "have I witnessed such an abuse of a constitutionally established institution. Behind the backs of elected state officials, new majorities were shamelessly put together." [6] Bavaria's Edmund Stoiber complained that the CDU states had been bought by the Schröder government—the CDU governments in Berlin and Bremen were traitors to the party, he claimed. The truth is that, irrespective of party, small states do not like to be dominated by the larger states, and Schröder was able to play on this fundamental principle of federalism. It did not hurt that, historically, there has been little love lost between Berliners (Prussians) and Bavarians. Indeed, the CDU mayor of Berlin essentially told his fellow Christian Democrat in Bavaria to mind his own business.

Schröder's Second Term, 2002–2005

After its narrow reelection in 2002, the Schröder government went into another free fall. Economic growth dropped to minuscule levels, and unemployment and state debt soared. New taxes and fees for health care further contributed to the government's low status in public opinion polls and, more important, in state elections, where it continued to lose votes. In March 2003, with his back to the wall, Schröder announced his Agenda 2010, calling it the most significant domestic policy change in the history of the Federal Republic. Ignoring his own party's history and the opinions of many of its members, he declared that "social welfare programs will be cut. Individual responsibility will be encouraged by government, which will also ask more of the individual in terms of financing social programs." [7]

In short, government would do less, and the individual would have to do more to sustain pensions, the health care program, and other social benefits. Unemployment compensation, welfare benefits, pensions, and health care programs were put on the chopping block. The government also would make it easier for employers to dismiss workers, thereby creating a more flexible labor market and a new low-wage sector.

Meanwhile, the savings from cuts in social programs and the elimination of some tax loopholes would be used to lower taxes and stimulate new investment and job growth. Tax breaks for new home buyers, a cherished program of the construction industry, would be phased out as well as the right of commuters to deduct the costs of traveling to their jobs. In the health care area, Schröder, with the consent of the CDU-controlled Bundesrat, introduced a copayment for office visits of about $12 and higher copayments for other medical procedures.

All of this was too much for many SPD supporters and the trade unions. Agenda 2010 was seen as a violation of the core principles of social democracy: social justice and a commitment to assist those in need. Thousands of people left the party, and the trade unions announced that they were reassessing their traditional support of the Social Democrats. Nevertheless, Schröder secured approval of this plan at a special party congress. With the help of the CDU in the Bundesrat, most of Agenda 2010 was passed in 2004 and began to take effect in 2005. Yet the program, which had heavy start-up costs, produced little immediate improvement in economic growth or job creation. One component of Agenda 2010—the lowering of some unemployment payments to the level previously paid to those on welfare—even provoked demonstrations through the country, especially in the eastern states. The change meant not only lower payments, but also means-testing the payments. Total family income, including the income from a spouse and savings, was to be considered in calculating the new welfare/unemployment benefit. In May 2005, with the economy still stagnant, unemployment at record levels, and his party deeply divided, Schröder, without consulting with his Green coalition partner, opted for new elections rather than continue this course. The seven-year Red-Green coalition was over.

How Power Was Used: Grand Coalition, 2005–2009

In November 2005, after almost two months of sometimes very difficult negotiations, the two largest parties—the Social Democrats and the Christian Democrats—entered into a Grand Coalition. The term *Grand* is used because the two parties together controlled almost three-fourths of the 614 parliamentary seats. In theory, then, there was little that this government could not do, if the two partners agreed.

The first task of this government was the economy. The new government was quick to continue the policies associated with Agenda 2010. And, as Table 3-8 shows, many of the reform measures passed by the Schröder government started to work under the Grand Coalition. From late 2005 until the final quarter of 2008, more than 1.5 million new jobs were created, many of them taken by older workers responding to the reduced unemployment benefits of Agenda 2010. The economy grew by 3 percent in 2006 and 2.5 percent in 2007 in spite of a steep increase in the national sales tax. Even in 2008 a modest growth rate of 1.3 percent was recorded, albeit most of it in the first nine months of the year. This solid economic performance also meant higher tax revenues and a sharp reduction in national debt. The finance minister predicted a balanced budget by 2011, if not earlier. By

Table 3-8 The Grand Coalition Economic Record, 2005–2009

Year	2005	2006	2007	2008	2009
Real GDP growth (percent)	0.8	3.0	2.5	1.3	−4.7
Employment (millions)	38.9	39.1	39.8	40.3	40.2
Unemployment (millions)	4.9	4.5	3.8	3.3	3.5
Unemployment (percent)	11.7	10.8	9.0	7.8	8.3
Inflation (consumer prices)	1.6	1.6	2.3	2.6	0.3
Federal deficit (€ billions)	74.2	38.1	4.7	3.3	−75.2
Federal deficit (percent GDP)	3.3	1.6	0.2	0.1	−3.1
Trade balance (percent GDP)	5.2	6.1	7.5	6.8	2.4

Sources: Deutsches Institut für Wirtschaftsforschung, *Wochenbericht*, no. 15-16, April 15, 2009, 250; and no. 42, October 12, 2009, 723; Federal Statistical Office, Press Release No. 293, August 24, 2010, 2.

2008 the federal deficit had dropped from € 74.2 billion to only € 3.3 billion. Alas, the worldwide economic crisis dramatically changed this outlook, and the 2009 deficit skyrocketed to over € 75 billion.

The worldwide financial and economic crisis, which began in 2008 and quickly became the deepest international recession since the Great Depression of the 1930s, was the greatest challenged faced by the Grand Coalition. In early October, less than three weeks after the collapse of the Lehman Brothers investment bank in New York, the Merkel government announced that all individual bank deposits, regardless of amount, would be guaranteed by the state. Previously this protection on individual accounts had been limited to about $27,000. A few days later both parliamentary chambers passed the largest bank bailout plan in the history of the republic. About $700 billion was made available to troubled banks.[8] By early November 2008, work was completed on an economic stimulus package that included tax cuts and a "cash for clunkers" program to stimulate auto sales and improve the fuel efficiency of the domestic fleet. Almost $7 billion dollars was provided to fund more than 2 million new car purchases. A second, even larger, stimulus package was introduced in late January 2009; it contained additional loans, bailouts, subsidies, and spending programs. These guarantees and bailouts were budget-busters, but still below the levels spent by governments in the United States and France in response to the crisis. By the second quarter of 2009, the economy began to stabilize and actually grew by a very small amount.

The current crisis is global and cannot be blamed on the specific acts of the government. Indeed, were it not for the reforms of Agenda 2010, which made the economy and labor markets leaner and more efficient, the economy would be in worse condition than it actually is. And in comparison to other large market economies, Germany is by no means a problem child. Even with record projected deficits in 2010, total debt as a percentage of GDP is estimated at about 5 percent as compared to 13 percent in the United States.

The Grand Coalition did have some other successes. In addition to the economic record discussed above, it maintained and extended Germany's position as a world leader in environmental protection and renewable energy. Thanks to high levels of private investment and government subsidies, by 2008, 15 percent of the country's electricity was produced from renewable sources, well above the Merkel government's target of 12.5 percent.

Demonstrators carry a banner featuring German chancellor Angela Merkel and Greek prime minister George Papandreou during a day of strikes in Greece in May 2010.

Source: Reuters/Pascal Rossignol

Moreover, almost 7 percent of Germany's total energy consumption by 2008 came from renewables. During the Grand Coalition, the number of "green" jobs also grew to almost 300,000. It now appears almost certain that by 2020 one-fifth of all electricity will be generated through renewable sources, a level unsurpassed by any other country of comparable size and development.[9]

On the negative side, the Grand Coalition did little to solve the problems of the country's health care system. A promised tax reform made little progress under the Merkel government. As we discuss in Chapter 3.5, two separate commissions charged with reforming the federal system to encourage more competition between the states produced few positive results. In spite of its lop-sided majority, the Grand Coalition was unable to reduce employer and employee contributions to the pension system, which actually rose to record levels (19.9 percent).

The Process of Policy Implementation

The process of implementing national legislation takes place largely through the administrative structures of the state (*Land*) governments, and the national government often must depend on the states if legislation is to have its intended effect. At first glance, this system would seem to allow the sixteen states, especially those governed by parties not in power in Berlin, to sabotage or undermine national legislation they oppose on ideological or partisan political grounds. In practice, however, such sabotage has not taken place.

One reason is that German federalism has some unifying or centralizing characteristics that make this implementation phase function remarkably well. First, state governments and their bureaucracies have extensive input into the national-level legislative process through their membership in the Bundesrat. They are well aware of what legislation will entail in terms of administrative machinery and resources. Second, the laws and rules of procedure for state bureaucracies are unified. Unlike under U.S. federalism, constituent states do not have different laws for divorces, bankruptcy, or criminal offenses. Also, the rules by which the civil service operates are the same for all states and the national government. Third, the constitution requires a "unity of living standards" throughout the republic. In practice, this "unity" means that richer states, such as Bavaria and Hesse, must pay, via grants and tax transfers, to bring the poorer states up to their levels of government services and standards.[10] Therefore, the expenditures of poorer states for public works or welfare are not drastically different from those of the more prosperous *Länder*. Differences between resources and expenditures are made up by this system of tax redistribution, or revenue sharing.

Differences between states do exist in policy areas in which the *Länder* have sole or major responsibilities—mainly education (especially primary and secondary) and internal security (police and law enforcement). Educational reform has proceeded differently in the various states. In states historically governed by the CDU/CSU such as Bavaria, there are relatively few comprehensive schools, whereas in the traditional SPD states, such as North Rhine–Westphalia, comprehensive schools are more numerous. Procedures for screening candidates for public employment also have varied, with CDU/CSU states taking a more hard-line position on this issue. Indeed, in CDU/CSU-governed states such as Bavaria and Baden-Württemberg some applications submitted by prospective school-teachers have been rejected for alleged radical political activity in SPD states. Until 1992 the abortion issue also divided the western states and the five new eastern regions. Although the abortion law applies to the whole country, it is easier for women to receive treatment in the Protestant states than in the Catholic regions. Implementation of the 2000 same-sex marriage law (Life Partnership Act) also has varied among the states. The more liberal states such as Hamburg and Berlin allow gay couples to register their union in a Registry Office (Standesamt) just like heterosexual couples (but none of the churches allows same-sex marriages). Conservative states such as Bavaria and Baden-Württemberg have denied same-sex couples the use of the Registry Office; they must go to the offices used to register "other" relationships and groups such as foreign residents. In some states, same-sex couples receive a marriage certificate, while others give only a "receipt" documenting their partnership. States opposed to such unions also charge same-sex couples two to three times the normal fee of about $30.[11]

NOTES

1. In June 1991 the parliament, in a close and dramatic vote, decided to relocate the government and parliament from Bonn to Berlin, which had been the national capital from 1871 to 1945. The decision was in part an attempt to demonstrate to East Germans that a unified Germany was more than a simple enlargement of the old Federal Republic. The narrow vote in parliament was preceded by a nationwide debate. Supporters and opponents of the

move were found in all the political parties. The 1990 unification treaty stated that Berlin was the capital, but left open whether the government and parliament would relocate. Supporters of Bonn contended that moving the government would weaken the postwar federal system. Bonn was associated with West Germany's postwar transformation into a stable democracy and a model member of the Western community of nations. For some, Berlin was a symbol of Germany's militaristic, authoritarian, and totalitarian past—the Prussian kaisers and Adolf Hitler all waged war from Berlin. The city's supporters countered that it was unfair to blame an entire city for the acts of a few individuals many years ago. They pointed to Berlin's steadfast commitment to Western values during the darkest days of the cold war. The vote was followed by more than eight years of planning and frequent postponements of the eventual move, which took place in summer 1999.

Although Berlin is the official political capital and the seat of the parliament and central government, not all major administrative units of the federal government have their central offices there, and the current practice is to disperse national offices throughout the country. None of the major federal courts is in Berlin; they are scattered about in Karlsruhe, Nürnberg, and elsewhere. The federal railways and federal bank are in Frankfurt; the airline has its administrative center in Cologne; the national archive is in Koblenz; and the Federal Criminal Office (the German version of the U.S. Federal Bureau of Investigation) is in Wiesbaden. This dispersion of administrative offices reflects the decentralized character of the Federal Republic and, perhaps more important, the fact that the states preceded the federal government after 1945. Indeed, many of these offices were the product of the occupation period. The five new states are receiving their share of federal offices. The Federal Administrative Court has moved from Berlin to Leipzig (Saxony), the national environmental protection office has moved from Berlin to Dessau (Saxony-Anhalt), and the Federal Labor Court has moved from the West German city of Kassel to Erfurt (Thuringia).

2. Peter J. Katzenstein, *Policy and Politics in West Germany* (Philadelphia: Temple University Press, 1987).

3. Ibid., 58.

4. Manfred G. Schmidt, "The Politics of Domestic Reform in the Federal Republic of Germany," *Politics and Society* 8, no. 2 (1978): 165–200.

5. Jens Alber, "Der Wohlfahrtstaat in der Wirtschaftskrise—Eine Bilanz der Sozialpolitik in der Bundesrepublik seit den frühen siebziger Jahren," *Politische Vierteljahresschrift* 27, no. 1 (March 1986): 28–60.

6. Cited in *Frankfurter Allgemeine Zeitung,* October 14, 2000, 2.

7. Cited in Matthias Geyer, Dirk Kurbjuweit, and Cordt Schnibben, *Operation Rot-Grün: Geschichte eines politischen Abenteuers* (Munich: Deutsche Verlagsanstalt, 2005), 260–261.

8. Katharina Schuler, "Ein historischer Tag in Berlin," *Die Zeit,* October 17, 2008, 1.

9. Spiegel Online, September 2, 2009, www.spiegel,de/politik/deutschland/0,1518.html.

10. By 2008 there were only four "rich states"(Bavaria, Baden-Württemberg, Hesse, and Hamburg) sharing revenue with the other twelve "poor" states. Obviously, the paying states would like this program changed. They argue that they are being penalized for their success and efficiency and must subsidize the spendthrift receiving states. In 2009 a constitutional amendment was passed requiring the states, with some exceptions, to balance their budgets. The amendment also places certain restrictions on the ability of the national government to borrow money.

11. David P. Conradt, *The German Polity,* 8th ed. (New York and London: Longman, 2005), 103.

What Is the Future of German Politics?

3.5

As the Federal Republic completes the first decade of the twenty-first century, it is faced with the most serious economic crisis in its history. Like its fellow developed democracies in Europe and North America, Germany since late 2008 has seen its economic growth decline, unemployment jump, and the public debt soar to new heights. The Federal Republic is not alone in the current crisis of market economies, but as the world's leading exporter of goods, it is particularly dependent on trade, and that requires healthy customers. When its trading partners sneeze, Germany catches a cold.

The worldwide economic recession hit Germany just as it appeared to be overcoming its own self-produced malaise. In following the stable, consensual, incremental approach to policy that has characterized the political process in the Federal Republic, governments smoothed over problems in such a way that no major group or interest ever lost. The decades of strong economic growth and a generous welfare state created a complex structure of vested interests with entitlements that were considered untouchable, regardless of whether the economic rationale that created them was still present.

Once undertaken, the numerous attempts at reform ended in a series of compromises that changed very little. As a result, Germany, once the economic powerhouse of Western Europe, had one of the continent's lowest growth rates. Its fabled welfare state, which ultimately must be financed through the economy, was deeply in the red.

As we discussed in Chapter 3.4, the strong medicine of the Schröder and Grand Coalition governments started a recovery process that began in late 2005 and continued until the recession began in late 2008. The downturn threatened to wipe out all the gains of the previous four years. Yet had these reforms not been implemented, the country would have been in a worse economic condition. Indeed, by the end of 2009 it appeared that Germany would be among the first group of countries to come out of the recession.

The uneven economic record since 2000 has also hindered the resolution of other major policy issues such as immigration and the treatment of foreign residents. To these problems—many of which are common to other developed democracies—must be added the continued challenge of unification. Twenty years after unification, the eastern regions still lag behind the "old" western states, and, perhaps more important, the eastern Germans' sense of second-class citizenship has not significantly declined. Unified Germany also must define its role in the international arena, especially its relationship to the postcommunist societies of Eastern Europe and the former Soviet Union. This chapter examines all these issues.

None of the republic's current tasks, however, should obscure its fundamental accomplishments since 1949: a consensus on liberal democracy has finally been achieved in a German political order. The Federal Republic has become a stable and legitimate democratic political system. The current challenges will be met within this democratic consensus. Although there is no lack of problems, few modern democracies have more resources to deal with these than the Federal Republic of Germany.

Institutional Gridlock and the Federal System

The political institutions and processes once considered major factors in the success of the Federal Republic are now viewed as major causes of its problems. The strong, stable party system that replaced the ineffective Weimar alignment and gave postwar governments reliable majorities was by the 1980s considered a liability. The parties treated the state as their prey, said one former president. They spent more time cooperating and insulating themselves from public scrutiny than they did competing for the support of the electorate. The heralded constitution with its strong commitment to basic civil liberties and many limitations on government (but also on direct populist influence) now seemed to be a negative veto machine. By contrast, the strong federal structure under which the constituent state governments were directly involved in national policymaking seemed inefficient and an unneeded check on centralized authority. Overall, the constitution, according to this view, now hinders the parliament, government, the states, and even the courts in their efforts to make innovative decisions within the context of a united Europe, a global economy, and the transnational challenges of inner security, terrorism, and immigration.

Would reform of the federal system help? Increasingly, state elections are not only influenced but also dominated by national issues. In May 2005, for example, widespread dissatisfaction with the Schröder government was the decisive factor in the Social Democrats' defeat in the state election in North Rhine–Westphalia, Germany's largest state. Voters used this and other state elections to vent their opposition to the national Red-Green

SPD leader Hannelore Kraft campaigns at the May 2010 state election in North Rhine–Westphalia, Germany's largest state (by population). After the election, Kraft's Social Democrats and the Greens formed a coalition government, replacing a CDU-FDP government and overturning Chancellor Merkel's majority in the Federal Council (Bundesrat).

Source: Volker Hartmann/AFP/Getty Images

government. One electoral reform proposal calls for scheduling all state elections midway through the term of the national government—that is, about two years after a national election. State elections would then become essentially midterm elections, thereby giving the national government time to pass and implement its program before the voters react. In short, the current system allows too many "veto players" into the policy process. Indeed, often the smallest state can veto an entire national program. This situation inhibits major reform and produces programs that are so compromised that their original purpose is difficult to identify in the final product

During the 2005–2009 Grand Coalition, a joint federal-state reform commission completed two major attempts at addressing these problems. The first reform, completed in 2006, gave the states almost complete autonomy in education policy and reduced the ability of the Federal Council (Bundesrat) to veto national legislation. The second reform in 2009 introduced debt limits on both the federal and state governments. Both reforms, but especially the first, required numerous constitutional amendments. But in the judgment of most experts, both fell short in addressing the more fundamental problems of revenue sharing and the distribution of taxes.[1]

The Economy

As discussed in Chapter 3.4, from 2006 until 2008 the Grand Coalition made substantial progress in dealing with the country's pressing economic problems. All of that ended when the world financial and economic crisis began to affect Germany during 2008. Discussions about reforming federalism or resolving the fiscal crisis of the welfare state would be far less urgent if the economy was growing at levels that created new jobs. Surprisingly, most economists agree on what policies are needed to turn the economy around. German wages, currently among the highest in Europe, need to be more competitive. Austria, for example, has a much stronger economy than its German neighbor, but its wage levels are about 20 percent lower. The problem is not so much the absolute level of the wage, but the *nonwage labor costs* incurred by the employer, such as those for health, accident, and unemployment insurance; pensions; sick pay; and holidays and vacations. Together, these costs add another 40 percent to the base cost of labor. The thrust of reform programs is to shift these costs from the worker and employer to the federal budget—that is, these programs would be financed through general revenue. Reform also would be directed at reducing the costs of these programs through more private insurance programs.

Job creation and economic growth would require further deregulation of labor markets. Because it is still so difficult to dismiss employees in Germany, employers are reluctant to hire, turning instead to technology and overseas labor markets. The traditional "one-size-fits-all" pattern of industry-wide collective bargaining so favored by trade unions could be liberalized to allow more local or plant-level bargaining between workers and management. Germany also needs to expand its entry-level, low-wage job sector that would enable less-qualified job seekers access to the labor market. And there is great potential for growth in the still undeveloped services sector of the economy.

Investments in education and infrastructure would stimulate long-term job creation and economic growth as well. The traditional three-track educational system described in Chapter 3.1 does not produce the quantity or quality of trained personnel needed in a competitive global economy. Although strong in traditional industrial fields such as machine tools, chemicals, and motor vehicles, Germany has lagged behind its major competitors in the high-tech fields of computers, telecommunications, and genetic engineering.

Such investments require reducing the soaring national debt and balancing the budget by reducing the costs of social programs. Since unification, the costs of social programs have increased by more than 30 percent. Pensions alone now consume 31 percent of the federal budget; interest on the debt eats up another 20 percent. Therefore, more than half of all federal spending goes to the "past." Since unification in 1990, the public debt has more than doubled, from $720 billion to $1.5 trillion. From 2005 until the last quarter of 2008, some progress was made in reducing this debt. With the onset of the current economic and financial crisis, and the bailouts and stimulus packages enacted, the total public debt has once again increased. Because of its heavy dependence on exports—40 percent of gross domestic product (GDP) as compared to 13 percent for the United States—Germany has been particularly hard hit by the global drop in demand, which began in late 2008. Investment goods such as heavy equipment (machines and machine tools), chemicals, and big-ticket items such as cars, trucks, and buses make up much of its exports.[2]

Putting Germany Back Together Again: The Continued Challenge of Rebuilding and Integrating the East

The 1990 unification added further burdens to an economy and society already in need of reform. It was not a merger of two independent sovereign states but a friendly takeover. East Germany was bankrupt; the communist regime had been discredited; and the great majority of easterners wanted unification—the security, prosperity, and freedom they associated with the west—as soon as possible. After the disappearance of their own state, however, East Germans discovered that many West Germans considered them an economic and political burden. Perhaps that is why surveys conducted from 1990 to 1999 found that more than 75 percent of easterners felt they were second-class citizens.[3] Today, they continue to resent the arrogance of some westerners and their colonialist attitudes, calling them *Besserwessis* ("know-it-all" westerners). Easterners also find westerners too materialistic and manipulative. Meanwhile, many easterners feel that their condition is just an accident of history. They have neither a sense of guilt nor a sense of responsibility for the forty years of communist dictatorship.[4] On the other side, since unification, westerners have realized that stiff tax increases and large deficits are the price for real unity, and many question why they should continue to sacrifice. Some westerners see the *Ossies* (easterners) as lazy, always expecting a handout: "They think they can live like we do without working for it." Political leaders continue to struggle with this "Berlin Wall in people's heads" or "inner unification."

Yet after almost twenty years of living together, Germans have made some progress toward breaching the psychological "Wall." When asked in 2004 whether they considered themselves to be the "winners" or "losers" in the unification process, about 60 percent of easterners saw themselves as winners, 20 percent as losers, and the remaining 20 percent somewhere between these two positions. Between 1993 and 2000, the proportion of winners rose from 32 percent to 55 percent. Younger, better-educated easterners were the most likely to feel they were winners. Since 2000, however, the level of confidence has declined in the east. In 2000, 67 percent of easterners stated that their hopes for unification had been completely or in large part fulfilled, but by 2008 this figure had declined to

56 percent. Likewise, in 2000 more than 80 percent of easterners considered the "living standard" to be the strength of the Federal Republic, but by 2004 this figure had dropped to 65 percent.[5] The weak national economy is taking its toll on inner unity.

The Economic and Environmental Reconstruction of the East

Unification revealed the full extent of the former East Germany's economic problems. Its economy was characterized by an outmoded, overstaffed industrial sector, an underdeveloped services sector, and a dilapidated infrastructure. Many of the region's industrial enterprises were largely incapable of competing in a market economy. Many East German products were obsolete, of poor quality, and, when priced in "hard" currency, more expensive than those of Western competitors. And many East Germans were underemployed; feather-bedding was widespread. By 1989 the average West German worker was producing almost four times as many goods and services as his or her East German counterpart—that is, the gross domestic product (GDP) produced by East Germany's 9.2 million workers equaled the GDP of only 2.4 million West Germans.

After unification, the economy of the former East Germany went into a free fall; hundreds of plants were closed, some for environmental reasons, and unemployment soared. Production in some areas dropped by as much as 70 percent. By the end of 1992, the region's workforce had declined by about 33 percent, from 9.2 million in October 1990 to 6.2 million in December 1992. One million were unemployed, an additional million and a half were on subsidized part-time work, and more than half a million had moved to western Germany.

These dislocations reflected in part West Germany's policy of privatizing the East German state-run economy as quickly as possible. After unification all state-owned property was put under the control of a Trusteeship Authority (Treuhandanstalt), which was tasked with cleaning up these companies and making them viable in a competitive market economy. The leadership of the authority quickly decided that the best way to clean up these enterprises was to privatize them, to sell them to private companies and individuals. Critics charged that the authority sold these properties, mainly to westerners, at bargain prices with huge job losses for East Germans. The Treuhand was denounced as a "job killer" and became a symbol for West German indifference to the feelings and accomplishments of easterners.

After almost twenty years, the economy in the region still remains partially dependent on transfer payments from the west. Between 1990 and 2010, total transfer payments to the east amounted to about $2 trillion (this figure does not include tax and other payments that then flowed back from the east to the west), or between 4 percent and 5 percent of the west's GDP. Because the western economy has not come close to growing by this amount, the eastern region represents a net drain on the total national economy. About 60 percent of the transfer payments have been used to supplement the east's social welfare programs—pensions, unemployment payments, health care—in order to bring them up to western standards. The remaining 40 percent have financed a variety of infrastructure investments such as transportation, telephone systems, and hospitals. Private sector investment during the 1990–2010 period totaled an additional $850 billion. These funds have been used mostly for new housing, commercial and industrial offices and plants, and equipment. Yet in the judgment of many analysts, the problems still outweigh the successes. The eastern region is still troubled by persistently higher unemployment levels, a weaker industrial base, and the continued outmigration of younger and well-trained people to the western states.

The transfers from western to eastern Germany have, however, had a major impact on the living standards of easterners since 1990. Their net monthly income increased from 55 percent of the western level in 1990 to about 88 percent by 1998. Pensioners in the east have fared even better. Under the communist regime, pensions were very low; in 1990 the core East German pension amounted to only 40 percent of the western level. By 1998 it had risen to about 87 percent. But this increase has come at the expense of the overall pension system, which has been in need of increasing subsidies from general revenue.

Easterners have used some of their additional income to acquire the services and durable goods long regarded as necessities in western Germany, but as scarce luxuries under communism. In 1990 only 18 percent of East Germans, largely the trusted party and state elite, had private telephones. By 1998 telephone service had reached the near-universal level of the west. A similar pattern was found for items such as computers, microwave ovens, and other household items. Private bathrooms and central heating were enjoyed by less than half of all East German households in 1990; by 1998 this figure had increased to 86 percent.

Overall, then, the economy of the eastern states has made progress in achieving parity with the western states (see Table 3-9). Between 1991 and 2009, the east German per capita GDP as a percentage of the western level rose from 43 percent to 73 percent. Wages and salaries grew from about half the western level to over 80 percent by 2009. The East-West productivity gap has also narrowed. By 2009 easterners were more than 80 percent as productive as their western cousins. Unit labor costs in the east in 2009 were about 103 percent of the costs in the west, but this figure is a substantial improvement over the situation in 1991 when labor costs were 144 percent of the western level. The key to increasing productivity was new investment in plants and equipment. But by 2004, after exceptionally high investment levels in the eastern states, their investment level had dipped below that of the west.

As discussed in Chapter 3.4, western taxpayers, present and future, are largely footing the bill for this economic and social reconstruction. The transfer payments have also come at the expense of the western economic base. The economic convergence of the once divided country is taking longer and is costing much more than was anticipated in the

Table 3-9 Catching Up, Eastern Germany versus Western Germany: Economic Indicators, Selected Years, 1991–2008 (eastern level as percentage of western level)

Indicator	1991	1994	1999	2004	2009
Gross domestic product per capita	43	57	61	64	73
Investment in plant and equipment	70	164	147	98	85
Wages and salaries	49	73	78	78	83
Productivity	41	65	69	72	81
Unit labor costs	144	113	114	108	103

Sources: 1991, 1994, 1999: Arbeitsgemeinschaft deutscher wirtschaftlicher Forschungsinstitute e.V, *Die Lage der Weltwirtschaft und der deutschen Wirtschaft im Herbst 2000,* Halle, 2000, 81; 2004: *Stand der deutschen Einheit 2005, Jahresbericht der Bundesregierung* (Berlin: Bundesverkehrsministerium, 2005), 7, 142–159; 2009: *Stand der deutschen Einheit 2010, Jahresbericht der Bundesregierung* (Berlin: *Bundesministerium des Innern,* 2010), Appendix, 1.

heady days after unification in 1990. The current special programs of eastern support, including the "solidarity" surtax on incomes, are scheduled to expire in 2019. Whether parity will be achieved by that time is still an open question.[6]

Cleaning Up the East

In addition to economic development, the eastern states had serious environmental problems. Water, ground, and air pollution levels were among the highest in Europe. Only 3 percent of the region's rivers and streams were ecologically intact, and only 1 percent of its lakes were free from pollution. Almost 80 percent of the area's water sources were either biologically dead or heavily polluted. The most important waterway in the east, the Elbe, was among the most polluted rivers in Europe.

Pollution was severest in the industrialized south and southwestern parts of the region. Outmoded industrial plants, many built before World War II, dumped millions of pounds of untreated industrial and chemical wastes into waterways or huge pits each year. The area's major source of energy, lignite or brown coal, was the chief cause of air pollution, including virtually nonstop smog during the fall and winter months. The sulfur dioxide emitted when lignite is burned affects the nose, throat, and lungs. Skin cancers and respiratory ailments were two to three times higher in this area than in the rest of the former East Germany.

Soil pollution was the most extensive in the uranium mine areas in the states of Saxony and Thuringia. From 1946 until 1990, more than 200,000 tons of uranium were shipped to weapons factories and power stations in the Soviet Union. Whole villages were evacuated and destroyed during the mining operations.

By 2009 most of the cleanup work had been completed. The strip mining of brown coal was reduced from 300 million tons in 1989 to 70 million in 2008, and the current operations are now consistent with international environmental protection standards. Indeed, eastern Germany now has the most modern brown coal–fired power plants in the world. The damaging carbon dioxide emissions have been reduced by almost 50 percent, which has helped Germany to achieve the target figures in the Kyoto Accords. The cleanup of old strip mining, chemical plant, and uranium mining operations is now largely finished. Most of these areas have been turned into nature preserves and parks with man-made lakes. The more than five hundred new sewage treatment plants have improved water quality in most rivers and streams. In the process, Germany has become a worldwide leader in the technology of complex environmental restoration.[7]

Minorities: Foreign Residents, Immigrants, and Right-Wing Violence

Because immigration has never been central to the German national identity, Germans have been slow to accept the reality that in an age of globalization they are becoming a multicultural society. Yet with Europe's largest economy, Germany is the chief target country for immigrants seeking a new life in Europe. Indeed, the condition of its more than 8 million foreign residents is the most complex social problem confronting the Federal Republic.[8] The economic miracle of the 1950s transformed Germany from an economy with a surplus of labor to one with an acute labor shortage. There were simply too many jobs available for the native workforce, especially in menial, low-paying positions. To remedy this problem and to maintain economic growth, the government, working closely with employers, recruited workers from Italy, Greece, Spain, Turkey, and other less-developed countries. Guest workers (*Gastarbeiter*), as they were euphemistically termed at the time, usually occupy the lowest rung on the jobs ladder—unskilled manual positions, sanitary and sewage workers, custodial and janitorial staff. They tend to be concentrated in large cities: Berlin, for example, has the third-largest Turkish population in the world.[9] Apart from their jobs, many foreign workers have little or no social contact with the native German population, and they have been subjected to discrimination in housing, which further isolates them.

The dependents of foreign workers, especially their children, have made immigration a potentially explosive issue. Many of these children have spent most or all of their lives in Germany, but their parents cling to the hope of someday returning to their home countries and want their children to retain their countries' languages and values. The result is that children grow up in a sort of twilight zone—they master neither their parents' language nor German. They invariably drop out of school and, urged on by the parents, attempt to secure employment to augment the family's finances and hasten its "return" to the homeland. The tighter job market, however, has made it difficult for young, half-literate, and untrained foreign people to find work. The result is a growing body of unemployed adolescents, especially in the large cities, involved in petty crime and the drug trade. More broadly, many foreign residents are living as a subculture, isolated from the mainstream. Because of native indifference, the cultural practices of some foreign groups—such as the subjugation of women, arranged marriages, child abuse, and honor codes, which clearly violate German law—are tolerated.

Discrimination, a lack of social mobility, and poor educational and job opportunities for their children are the result, in part, of the guest workers' lack of political influence. As non-Germans, they cannot vote, and the acquisition of citizenship is a difficult process even for those foreign residents who want to be naturalized. The political system has simply not responded to the needs of an unorganized, politically powerless minority, and as long as foreign workers do not have the vote, it is difficult to envision any major changes. In fact, the new restrictions on residency for foreign workers imposed by some local governments hinder their freedom of movement and decrease their prospects for upward social mobility.

Several proposals have been made to improve the status of guest workers and their families. One involves giving the franchise to foreign workers for local elections. Two states, Schleswig-Holstein and Hamburg, passed such legislation in 1989. This law would, it was argued, make local officials more responsive to guest workers' needs, especially in housing and education. In 1990, however, the Federal Constitutional Court declared the law unconstitutional. Since 1992, citizens from other member countries of the European Union (EU) have been able to vote in local elections.

In 1999, after years of debate, the Social Democratic–Green government passed legislation reforming the country's 1913 citizenship and naturalization laws. Based largely on the principle of lineage or blood, the old laws made it very difficult for foreign residents to become naturalized citizens. The new legislation grants automatic citizenship to anyone born in Germany if at least one parent has lived in the country for at least eight years. Dual citizenship is allowed until the age of twenty-three, when a choice must be made. The legislation also liberalized the naturalization process for foreign residents by reducing the required length of residency and the costs of the process. From 2000 to 2008, the first eight years after the law's passage, about a million, or roughly 12 percent, of the foreign population, acquired German citizenship. This figure represents substantial growth when compared with that under the old law.[10]

Immigration and Asylum

By the late 1980s the problem of foreign workers was compounded by the arrival of hundreds of thousands of "political" refugees from various developing countries and ethnic German resettlers from the Soviet Union and Eastern Europe. An antiforeigner backlash also developed among native Germans in some cities related to the successes of the radical right-wing Republican Party.

In 1991 and 1992, groups of skinheads and young neo-Nazis attacked some of the hostels and dormitories where many asylum seekers were housed. Resentment toward foreigners was especially strong in the former East Germany. Although political leaders and the great majority of the public condemned the violence, growing support for reducing the influx of foreigners prompted the government, with the support of the opposition, to amend the constitutional right to asylum in 1993.[11] The amendment sought to exclude persons who attempt to enter the country for largely economic reasons. By 1994 the number of asylum applications had declined by 60 percent. In 2004 a new immigration law was finally passed that attempts to limit further immigration by granting preferences to those with exceptional educational or technical skills. Germany, like many of its West European neighbors, now wants new immigrants only if they bring technical and scientific expertise in short supply among the native population.

Xenophobia and Right-Wing Violence

The new citizenship, asylum, and immigration laws have improved, but by no means solved, the problem of foreign residents and their integration into German society. Right-wing violence against foreigners, which began in the early 1990s, has not disappeared. A disproportionate amount of radical right-wing activity is found in the eastern regions. In 2008 there were about three violent acts per 100,000 of the population, as compared to only one in the western states. The range between individual states went from a high of 4.15 in the eastern state of Saxony-Anhalt to a low of 0.41 in Hesse, about a 10:1 ratio.[12] The relatively few foreigners in the eastern regions make them ideal targets for skinheads and other radical right-wing groups. Emigrants from Asia and Africa, whose skin color easily distinguishes them from Germans, are routinely insulted, harassed, and physically attacked by roving gangs of skinheads. Many native easterners have thus far been passive and indifferent, thereby giving some legitimacy to the violence.

Western Germany has not been immune from these xenophobic attacks. Since the end of the cold war, Germany's Jewish community has more than tripled, to about 300,000, largely through immigration from the former Soviet Union. Government support for Jewish immigration is based on the conviction that the Nazi past requires the country to be open to Jewish refugees. Among some ordinary Germans, however, there is a latent resentment about what is termed "Jewish blackmail."

In response, the Schröder government, joined by several states, proposed a ban on the radical rightist National Democratic Party (NPD), which many believe serves as a cover for the illegal neo-Nazi groups. Such a ban is permitted by the constitution, but the Federal Constitution Court must issue it. Critics of the ban argue that it will focus more attention on the party, which is electorally weak, and drive it underground.

The great majority of the public condemns the rightist violence. In November 2000, on the occasion of the fifty-second anniversary of *Kristallnacht* (Night of Broken Glass), when synagogues and Jewish businesses across Germany were attacked in a Nazi-orchestrated campaign and many Jews were sent to concentration camps, demonstrations were held throughout the country. In Berlin, 200,000 people, including Chancellor Schröder, marched through the capital in protest against right-wing violence. Meanwhile, the leaders of the Jewish community lashed out at conservative politicians for whipping up a national debate on immigration and suggesting that minorities had to adopt German culture.

Nevertheless, the issue of immigration and the role of foreign residents remain controversial. In 2010 a mainstream political figure from Berlin, Thilo Sarrazin, published a controversial book, *Germany Does Away With Itself,* in which he argued that immigrants were a drain on the economy and a threat to German culture and identity. His views were strongly criticized by all major parties as racist and xenophobic. In a television interview he also made reference to the unique genetic composition of Jews. His party, the Social Democrats, wants to expel him and he resigned from his post at the German national bank (Bundesbank). Yet his remarks about foreign residents and especially Muslims, struck a responsive chord among some sectors of the broader German public.

Germany's International Role

Like Japan, Germany has maintained a low profile in the international political arena since the end of World War II. Although it is an economic powerhouse, it has encouraged other Western nations, especially France, Great Britain, and the United States, to take the lead in dealing with international issues. During the 1991 Gulf War, it sent no combat troops to the Middle East, but it did make financial contributions amounting to billions of dollars to the effort. Yet because of its size and strength, Germany's allies and neighbors expect it to become a more important player in international politics in the future. Such a shift also means, however, that the Federal Republic will be a less compliant partner, particularly in its relations with the United States, than it has been in the postwar period.

Germany's more active role was on view in 1995 when the Federal Republic contributed four thousand troops to the UN Bosnian peace force. It was the largest single deployment of German soldiers since World War II. The German contingent was composed of medical, transport, and logistics units rather than combat troops. Mindful of Nazi atrocities against Serbs during the war, the Kohl government requested that German forces be stationed only in Croatia.

A new chapter in post–World War II foreign policy began in March 1999, when Luftwaffe jets took off from bases in Italy to participate in attacks on Serbia as part of the Kosovo operation of the North Atlantic Treaty Organization (NATO). It marked the first time since the 1940s that German military forces, once the most feared on the continent, had engaged in combat. The action was not without controversy. Several members of Schröder's Social Democratic Party (SPD)–Green government opposed the military deployment. It was one factor in the resignation of Oskar Lafontaine, the leader of the

SPD's left wing. At a stormy Green Party convention, Foreign Minister Joschka Fischer, who once advocated Germany's withdrawal from NATO and the country's unilateral disarmament, was pelted with bags of paint after he argued strongly that Germany had to take responsibility for stopping Serbian aggression in Kosovo. But while participating in the air war, the Schröder government steadfastly opposed the deployment of ground troops to drive out Serbian forces. The eventual cease-fire spared the government from an open conflict with the United States and Great Britain over this issue. In the meantime, Germany has contributed more than six thousand troops to the NATO peacekeeping force in the region.

Germany and the September 11 Attacks

After the September 11, 2001, terrorist attacks on the United States, Chancellor Schröder declared Germany's "unconditional solidarity" with the United States. Shortly thereafter, Schröder agreed to deploy up to 3,900 troops, including elite special forces units, to Afghanistan. Only the United States has more troops stationed in that country. Parliament approved this action in a narrow vote on November 16, 2001, which the chancellor also made a confidence vote on his government—that is, if the government had lost, it would have resigned. The Afghanistan deployment was continued and expanded during the 2005–2009 Grand Coalition. Public support for the Afghanistan mission, however, has declined.

Although it strongly supported the Afghanistan antiterror action and cooperated closely with the United States and its European allies in pursuing terrorists at home, the Schröder government adamantly refused in 2002 to support the planned American invasion of Iraq. Unlike the administration of President George W. Bush in the United States and the government of Prime Minister Tony Blair in Great Britain, the German government drew a sharp distinction between the antiterrorism campaign and Iraq. This antiwar position on Iraq tapped the latent pacifism of many Germans and the anti-Americanism of some elements of the SPD and the Green left. It also was supported among citizens in the eastern states who had no personal experiences with American support for Germany during the cold war and weaker attachments to NATO and other institutions of German and American cooperation. But it also expressed Berlin's increased sense of independence from Washington, which had been growing since unification.

The Iraq war decision was the first time in its history that the Federal Republic had openly opposed the United States on a major issue. Opposition to the war began during the 2002 election campaign when Schröder made Iraq a major campaign issue. In early 2003 Berlin took its opposition to the Bush administration Iraq policy a step further when it entered into an informal alliance with France and Russia in opposition to the war. At times, the relationship between Berlin and Washington became openly hostile and communication between President Bush and Chancellor Schröder broke down.[13] The 2005 Grand Coalition government considered the restoration of close U.S.-German ties to be a top foreign policy priority. Yet the Merkel government also made clear that it remains skeptical about military intervention.

The great majority of Germans in 2008 welcomed the election of Barack Obama as president of the United States. In a July 2009 national survey, more than 90 percent of respondents agreed that Obama will "do the right thing in world affairs." A year earlier, only 14 percent had the same attitude toward President Bush. Overall, the proportion of

Germans with a favorable view of the United States jumped from 31 percent in 2008 to 64 percent by 2009.[14]

Despite a showing of increased independence in the international arena, for a variety of reasons Germany is still reluctant to assume a leadership role. First, its elites and most of its citizens know that many of the country's neighbors still remember the Third Reich and what the Nazis did to Europe and the world. And they recognize that some neighbors still harbor a residual distrust of Germany stemming from this experience. Second, Germany's low political profile approach has been successful. Never before in history have so many Germans had so much peace and freedom as they have today. Third, Germans fear that expanded international leadership will eventually bring the country into a major military conflict somewhere in the world. The memories of the death and destruction caused by the world wars of the twentieth century are passed down from generation to generation and kept very much alive. There is a latent, yet pervasive, pacifism in the country that inhibits the actions of its political leadership. Fourth, the country will continue to struggle with unification, the common European currency, and the enlargement of the European Union for at least the next decade. Any international initiatives would be premature and not supported by public opinion. Finally, Germany hopes that its international responsibilities can be accommodated through its EU membership. It wants the EU to assume a stronger role, and it wants to act only with and through a united Europe.

Yet it is doubtful that these factors will be as important in Germany's future foreign policy as they have been in the past. With the collapse of the Soviet empire in Eastern Europe and of the Soviet Union itself, a vacuum developed. Germany has been in the process of assuming a leading economic and political role in this region. Hopes that this role can be carried out through the European Union have thus far been unfulfilled. For example, the EU failed its first foreign policy test when it was unable to stop the civil war in Yugoslavia.

As for its relationship with Russia, the Federal Republic has become Russia's major sponsor within the council of NATO and the European Union. Stressing the West's obligation to Russia, Germany has urged that NATO's expansion into Eastern Europe be accompanied by special partnership agreements between the alliance and Russia. Since the collapse of the communist bloc, German economic activity in Eastern Europe and the former Soviet satellites has skyrocketed. Russia has become the country's largest single supplier of oil and natural gas. With Europe's fastest-growing economy, Russia has become an important export market.[15]

The United States has encouraged Germany to send more forces to Afghanistan and to participate more extensively in combat operations. So far most of the Bundeswehr troops have been stationed in the more pacified northern regions of the country. In 2009 German forces, however, participated in the surge operations against the Taliban and were in some cases on the offensive. In September 2009, just weeks before the election, German forces were involved in a major combat operation, which became a source of friction between Berlin and Washington. German forces have generally been restricted to peacekeeping and reconstruction operations. But after Taliban forces hijacked two tanker trucks, the German commander, fearing they were part of an planned attack on German troops, called in a NATO airstrike, which killed about one hundred people, some of them civilians. The Afghan mission has become increasingly unpopular among the German public;

between 2002 and 2009 the proportion opposing the deployment more than doubled from 30 percent to almost 70 percent.[16] The United States and Germany also differ on how to deal with the international economic crisis. The United States prefers more government spending, but Germany, ever wary of inflation, supports more regulations of the economy and financial markets.

From 1945 to 1990, as a divided country protected against Soviet power by the nuclear shield of the Western alliance, Germany led a sheltered existence. Unification and the collapse of the Soviet empire will not only increase German influence, but also impose new responsibilities and challenges on the Federal Republic.

NOTES

1. Simone Burkhart, "Reforming Federalism in Germany: Incremental Changes Instead of the Big Deal," *Publius: The Journal of Federalism* 39 (June 2008): 341–365.
2. Anthony Faiola, "European Slump May Stall Global Rebound," *Washington Post,* May 23, 2009, 1.
3. David P. Conradt, "Political Culture and Identity: The Post-Unification Search for 'Inner Unity,'" in *Developments in German Politics,* ed. Stephen Padgett, William E. Paterson, and Gordon Smith (Basingstoke, UK: Palgrave Macmillan, 2003), 269–287.
4. EMNID surveys cited in *Der Spiegel,* July 22, 1991, 28; ALLBUS, 2008 Survey, Variables 503–504.
5. TNS Infratest surveys cited in *Der Spiegel,* September 20, 2004, 48, 49, 51.
6. When compared, however, not with western Germany, but rather to its eastern neighbors in the Czech Republic, Poland, and Hungary, the economic reconstruction of the eastern states is phenomenal. According to Federal Statistical Office figures, for example labor productivity in the Czech Republic in 2008 was only 41 percent of the eastern German level.
7. Bundestag, "Jahresbericht der Bundesregierung zum Stand der deutschen Einheit 2005," Berlin, 2005, 119–129.
8. There are probably an additional 1 million illegal foreign residents.
9. This also means that the religious and ethnic conflict in Turkey spilled over into Germany. As in their homeland, German Turks are divided into groups of Islamic fundamentalists, secularists, and Kurdish separatists. The radical left-wing Kurdish Workers Party (PKK) is believed responsible for much of the periodic violence against Turkish institutions in Germany.
10. Federal Statistical Office, "Einbürgerungen im Jahr 2008," press release, July 20, 2009.
11. Germany had the most liberal political asylum law in Western Europe, in part because many of the founders of the Federal Republic were themselves political refugees during the Third Reich. Germany contends, however, that many asylum seekers are not victims of political persecution but want access to the Federal Republic's prosperous economy and generous welfare state.
12. Federal Interior Ministry, *Verfassungsschutz Bericht 2008,* Berlin, 2008, 36; available at www.bmi.bund.de.
13. Although the government opposed the Iraq war, German military and intelligence authorities, according to reports leaked to the German and American press in early 2006, continued their normal cooperation with the United States. German military bases and facilities were used to transport American personnel and equipment into Iraq. After the evacuation of the German embassy in Baghdad, two German intelligence operatives remained behind

and relayed important information about Iraqi military deployments, including the Bagh-dad defense plan, to the approaching American forces. Officials in both the new (Merkel) and old (Schröder) governments have vehemently denied these reports. See "Liebesgrüsse nach Washington," *Der Spiegel,* January 16, 2006, 22–35, for the initial account of the alleged German-American military cooperation.

14. Pew Research Center, "Confidence in Obama Lifts U.S. Image Around the World," July 23, 2009, 1–2.
15. Marcus Walker, "Merkel Leads on Europe's Russia Policy," *Wall Street Journal,* August 21, 2008, A7.
16. Infratest DiMap surveys cited in *Der Spiegel,* July 6, 2009, 26.

FOR FURTHER READING

Ash, Timothy Garton. *In Europe's Name: Germany and the Divided Continent.* New York: Random House, 1993.

Botting, Douglas. *From the Ruins of the Reich: Germany, 1945–1949.* New York: Crown, 1985.

Bracher, Karl Dietrich. *The German Dictatorship.* New York: Praeger, 1970.

Breyman, Stephen. *Why Movements Fail: The West German Peace Movement, the SPD, and the INF Negotiations.* Boulder: Westview Press, 1994.

Brubaker, Rogers. *Citizenship and Nationhood in France and Germany.* Cambridge, Mass.: Harvard University Press, 1992.

Conradt, David P. *The German Polity.* 9th ed. New York and London: Houghton-Miflin, 2009.

———, et al., eds. *A Precarious Victory.* New York and Oxford: Berghahn Books, 2005.

Dettke, Dieter. *Germany Says No. The Iraq War and the Future of German Foreign and Security Policy.* Baltimore: Johns Hopkins University Press 2010.

Ferree, Myra Marx, et al. *Shaping Abortion Discourse. Democracy and the Public Sphere in Germany and the United States.* New York: Cambridge University Press, 2002.

Frankland, Gene E., and Donald Schoonmaker. *Between Protest and Power: The Green Party in Germany.* Boulder: Westview Press, 1992.

Fulbrook, Mary. *The People's State. East German Society from Hitler to Honecker.* New Haven: Yale University Press, 2005.

Goldhagen, Daniel Jonah. *Hitler's Willing Executioners.* New York: Knopf, 1996.

Green, Simon, and William E. Paterson, eds. *Governance in Contemporary Germany.* Cambridge and New York: Cambridge University Press, 2005.

Gunlicks, Arthur B. *Local Government in the German Federal System.* Durham, N.C.: Duke University Press, 1986.

Hamilton, Richard. *Who Voted for Hitler?* Princeton, N.J.: Princeton University Press, 1982.

Hancock, M. Donald, and Henry Krisch. *Politics in Germany.* Washington, D.C.: CQ Press, 2009.

Harrison, Hope M. *Driving the Soviets Up the Wall: Soviet-East German Relations, 1953–1961.* Princeton, N.J.: Princeton University Press, 2003.

Hough, Dan, et al. *The Left Party in Contemporary German Politics.* Basingstroke, UK: Palgrave Macmilllan, 2007.

Howard, Marc Morjé. "The Causes and Consequences of Germany's New Citizenship Law." *German Politics* 17, no. 1 (March 2008): 41–62.

Klein, Hans, ed. *The German Chancellors.* Chicago: EditionQ, 1996.

Kommers, Donald. *Constitutional Jurisprudence in the Federal Republic of Germany.* Durham, N.C.: Duke University Press, 1989.

Langenbacher, Erich, ed. *Launching the Grand Coalition.* New York: Berghahn Books, 2006.

Lees, Charles. *The Red-Green Coalition in Germany: Politics, Personality and Power.* Manchester and New York: Manchester University Press, 2000.

Naimark, Norman M. *The Russians in Germany: A History of the Soviet Zone of Occupation.* Cambridge: Harvard University Press, 1995.

Patton, David F. *Cold War Politics in Postwar Germany.* New York: St. Martin's Press, 2001.

Pond, Elizabeth. *After the Wall: American Policy toward Germany.* Washington, D.C.: Brookings, 1990.

Sarotte, Mary Elise. *1989: The Struggle to Create Post–Cold War Europe.* Princeton, N.J.: Princeton University Press, 2009.

Schneider, Peter. "The New Berlin Wall." *New York Times Magazine,* December 4, 2005.

Sinn, Gerlinde, and Hans-Werner Sinn. *Jumpstart: The Economic Unification of Germany.* Cambridge: MIT Press, 1993.

Smyser, W. R. *From Yalta to Berlin: The Cold War Struggle over Germany.* New York: St. Martin's Press, 1999.

Part 4

Italy

Raffaella Y. Nanetti

The Context of Italian Politics

4.1

AMONG THE LARGER INDUSTRIAL STATES OF EUROPE, ITALY POSSESSES certain striking characteristics. It is one of the world's seven leading industrial powers, yet the southern half of Italy is relatively underdeveloped and still lags behind the rest of the country and much of Europe in per capita income, levels of employment, and investments. Italy has achieved spectacular social and economic progress since World War II, and yet the Italian Communist Party—which in 1991 became the Democratic Party of the Left (PDS), in 1998 was renamed the Democrats of the Left (DS), and in 2008 merged with the reformist Catholics to form the Democratic Party (PD)—once was the strongest communist party in Western Europe. Although Italy has attained a high degree of modernization in its economic structures, it is burdened with an antiquated, inefficient central bureaucratic apparatus. At the same time, its reform of the national institutional structure—that is, the creation of regions in 1970 and the subsequent reinforcement of local governments—set the trend for state reform in most large and medium-size states in the European Union (EU).

In short, Italy presents a dramatic contrast between rapid economic and social change, on the one hand, and the survival of regional imbalances, political cleavages, and administrative deficiencies, on the other. Moreover, it became evident at the beginning of the 1990s that as long-rumored, corruption was permeating every level of the Italian political system. During the 1970s and 1980s, therefore, the Italian polity lagged behind the Italian economy, which during the same period was inventing "industrial districts" and experiencing an unprecedented expansion of small and medium enterprises (SMEs) in the northern and, especially, central parts of the country.[1] Then, between 1992 and 1994, the Italian political system underwent a swift but thorough and peaceful change of electoral rules, parties, and forms of democratic representation that was unprecedented in the rest of democratic Europe. Only after the collapse of the fascist military regimes in 1974 (Greece and Portugal) and 1976 (Spain) and the fall of the Berlin Wall in 1989 had similar peaceful transitions taken place elsewhere in Europe. Italy showed that it could renew its political party system and political class without placing at risk the country's political, economic, or social stability, or its role in Europe. What Italy demonstrated was that in the postwar period and within a new European context political change was possible without revolution or placing into question the country's economic or social order.

Italy covers only 116,341 square miles, compared with the 210,626 square miles that make up the domestic territory of France. In 2001 Italy's population (57.88 million) was almost as large as that of France (58.37 million).[2] Nevertheless, Italy's population density, while impressive by U.S. standards, is actually lower than that of Belgium, Great Britain, Germany, and the Netherlands. Moreover, Italy's birthrate of 8.18 births per 1,000 population (2010 estimate) is now one of the three lowest in Western Europe: only Germany and Austria have equivalent low birthrates. Due to significant inmigration, the population of the country rose to 60.225 million at the beginning of 2009, with 39.368 million residents in the center-north and 20.856 million in the south and islands.[3]

Thanks to its mountainous Alpine frontier, which clearly defines its northern boundary, Italy has an overwhelmingly Italian-speaking population. Ethnic minorities are relatively insignificant: 250,000–300,000 German-speaking people in the northeastern province of Bolzano, fewer than 100,000 French-speaking people in the northwestern Valle d'Aosta region, and a few thousand ethnic Slovenians near the border with Slovenia. The religious composition of Italy's population is also quite homogeneous. With the exception of about 75,000 Protestants and about 30,000 Jews, the population is at least nominally Catholic.

For all of their homogeneity, the people of Italy are divided by significant regional differences. These differences can be attributed partly to Italy's mountainous terrain. The Apennine mountain range divides central and southern Italy from the Po Valley in the north and impedes east-west transportation between the major cities of the south. Regional differences also stem from the many waves of invaders that have swept across the Italian peninsula, Sicily, and Sardinia. Phoenicians, Latins, Greeks, Etruscans, Celts, Germans, Huns, Moors, Normans, and Spaniards have settled and intermingled in various parts of Italy, producing a great variety of regional customs and dialects. Although the Italian language and its dialects are based on Latin, the transformations Latin has undergone reflect the ethnic background and composition of each region, so that the dialect of Piedmont in the northwest bears some resemblance to French, and Spanish surnames are common in Sicily. The Italian language, however, which derives from Tuscany, with Dante as its linguistic father, prevails in the schools and in the political and commercial life of the country.

Historical Context

Like Germany, Italy did not attain national unification until the latter half of the nineteenth century.[4] This long delay in the nation-building process stemmed from various reasons. For several centuries after the fall of the Roman Empire, northern Italy was under German political domination in the form of the Holy Roman Empire, and most of the south was under Byzantine or Moorish rule. Later, the south came under the control of the centralized, autocratic, but largely inefficient Kingdom of the Two Sicilies, and northern and central Italy was divided into prosperous but mutually antagonistic city-states. This internal division permitted foreign powers such as Spain, and later Austria, to dominate large portions of Italy. Not until the French Revolution of 1789–1793 and Napoleon Bonaparte's subsequent invasion of Italy did a sense of Italian nationality begin to gain ground among Italy's educated elites. Even so, after Napoleon's defeat in 1814–1815, Italy was still split into eight territorial units: the Kingdom of Sardinia (Piedmont) in the northwest; the Lombard and Venetian possessions of the Hapsburg Empire in the north and northeast; the duchies of Parma and Modena in north-central Italy; the duchy of Lucca, the Grand Duchy of Tuscany, the Papal State in central Italy, and the Kingdom of the Two Sicilies in the south.

Nationalist agitation in the nineteenth century culminated in 1848–1870 in a resurgence of nationalistic sentiment known as the Risorgimento. During that period, the Kingdom of Sardinia (Piedmont) led the drive for national unification after a republican movement headed by Giuseppe Mazzini and Giuseppe Garibaldi launched several unsuccessful uprisings against Austrian and papal rule. The Kingdom of Sardinia received military support from France in 1859 and from Prussia in 1866 and then exploited and took control of Garibaldi's unexpectedly successful invasion and occupation of the Kingdom of the Two Sicilies and by 1870 occupied the entire Italian peninsula. Backed mostly by an urban educated minority, the Risorgimento resulted in the creation of a unified Kingdom of Italy. The process of unification varied greatly from one area of the country to another. In the north, unification was cobbled together by the military victories of Piedmont. In the center, it was fueled by spontaneous revolts organized by educated elites at the grass roots. And in the south, unification was achieved through "a revolution from above" by means of Garibaldi's campaign of liberating the southern half of the peninsula from the Bourbon monarchy.

The newly established Kingdom of Italy was a constitutional democracy with a parliamentary form of government, but it faced a profound problem of legitimacy because of the way in which it had been created and consolidated. First, Italy had been unified by a series of military conquests, involving the elimination of several existing Italian states through their annexation by the Kingdom of Sardinia. Second, the fait accompli was ratified in the various Italian regions by plebiscites in which only the educated and propertied classes qualified as voters. Third, a rigidly centralized unitary system was erected, despite the considerable support for regional autonomy among the Risorgimento elites in several regions.[5] This extreme centralization followed the French model of a prefectoral unitary system (the German Second Reich was to move instead toward a federal system). Finally, by annexing the Papal State and storming Rome, the Kingdom of Italy provoked a conflict with the Catholic Church. As a result, devout Catholics abstained for almost half a century from playing an active role in Italian politics. They, and many other Italians, did not feel a moral obligation to obey the Italian government. When obedience is based mainly on expediency, a political system lacks full legitimacy.

In addition to its problem of legitimacy, the Kingdom of Italy faced the difficult task of achieving national integration—that is, of creating a sense of nationhood among Italians with diverse regional allegiances and ethnic origins. The elitist character of the Risorgimento had failed to give the peasant masses a feeling of participation in the nation-building process. It also tended to create certain contempt for majority rule among many Italian intellectuals, who were fully aware that the Risorgimento had been the work of an active minority. There was also a feeling among Italian elites that only new foreign conquests and foreign wars could create a sense of national allegiance among the common people of Italy. This sense of incomplete integration helps to explain the fight for the right to vote that was withheld from most industrial workers and peasants until 1912 and from women until 1946. It also helps to explain why Italy embarked on a series of colonial adventures in East Africa and Libya and why Italy intervened in World War I on the Allied side against the wishes of a neutralist parliamentary majority.

The Italian constitutional monarchy lasted less than a century, its last period shared with the Fascist regime. Italy's costly participation in World War I, in which more than 600,000 Italian soldiers died, brought the crises of legitimacy and integration to a head. The Italian masses—workers and peasants barred from the polls until 1912—voted mainly for the Socialist and Popular (Christian Democratic) Parties, both of which threatened to encroach on the rights of private property. Also, these parties had shown a marked reluctance to support Italy's entry into World War I in 1915. After the war, the rise of Benito

Mussolini's Fascist Party represented, to a considerable degree, a middle-class backlash against the redistributive and pacifist implications of the entry of the Italian masses into politics. With the aid of an armed militia financed by industrialists and large landowners, the Fascist Party unleashed between 1920 and 1922 a reign of terror against the Socialist and Popular Parties in local communities all over the nation. The army and police, like the Italian government itself, were unable or unwilling to intervene effectively against Fascist violence. Finally, in October 1922 Mussolini's militiamen (the "Blackshirts") marched on Rome. The king refused to sign a government decree to declare a state of emergency, the government resigned, and the king appointed Mussolini to be the next prime minister. Mussolini soon took advantage of his executive powers to establish a Fascist dictatorship under the guise of a constitutional monarchy—a regime that was to last until July 1943.

Mussolini's Fascist regime differed in some ways from Adolf Hitler's Nazi dictatorship. Italian fascism was far less totalitarian. Controls over Italian business and agriculture were nowhere near as thoroughgoing as those in Germany, although labor unions were suppressed and replaced by Fascist-sponsored organizations. Compared with Nazism, Italian fascism was more closely identified with propertied interests, and it did a much less effective job of mobilizing the economy for total war. In Italy, corruption and inefficiency reached almost incredible levels. Italian fascism never placed a primary emphasis on doctrines of racial supremacy, and the means it employed to suppress political opposition were less radical than those employed in Germany. In addition, it retained the king as nominal constitutional monarch, whereas Hitler assumed the position of chief of state as well as head of government after President Paul von Hindenburg's death in 1934. By keeping the monarchy, Italian fascism paved the way for its own legal demise. In July 1943, with the Allied armies newly landed in Sicily and Italian forces in full disarray, the king was persuaded by military and civilian notables to exercise his rarely used constitutional prerogative to remove the prime minister. He appointed Marshal Pietro Badoglio to replace Mussolini, and the Badoglio government signed an armistice with the Allies on September 8. This act was followed by the rapid German occupation of continental Italy and Mussolini's creation of the fascist Salo' Republic in the north—events that spawned the popular resistance movement of liberation (la Resistenza) led by partisan forces. Until May 1945, which marked the Allied victory over Nazi Germany, the Italian government exercised some limited authority only over the Allied-occupied areas of central and southern Italy, while in the north the resistance movement continued to engage the Germans and Italian Blackshirts in a protracted guerrilla campaign until the Allies moved north with their armies.[6]

The democratic parties that emerged in the liberated zones of Italy under the protection of the Western Allies did not forget the failure of the monarchy to support the legally elected government of Italy in 1922 during the march on Rome. After considerable discussion, an institutional referendum was held on June 2, 1946, on whether the monarchy should be retained. About 12 million Italians voted for a republic, and about 10 million voted to keep the monarchy, splitting the country along geographic lines. A majority in the north voted for the republic, and a majority in the south supported the monarchy. Following the referendum, the royal family went into exile, and Italy became a republic. An elected Constituent Assembly then drew up and ratified the new republican constitution, which went into effect in 1948.

The constitution of the Italian republic provided for a parliamentary system, but with some deviations from the classic parliamentary model. To be sure, it included the customary provisions for an elected parliament—a prime minister and cabinet responsible to that parliament—and an indirectly elected president to function as guarantor of the constitution. It also possessed features that differentiated it from most other parliamentary systems. First, both houses of the Italian parliament were to be popularly elected and were to be roughly equal in power, in contrast to the weaker, less representative upper houses in Great Britain, France, and Germany. Second, a constitutional court was to exercise the function of judicial review over parliamentary legislation. This was consistent with constitutional innovations in postwar Germany, but not with the British parliamentary system, characterized by parliamentary sovereignty, or with most other pre–World War II parliamentary systems. Third, there was an element of direct democracy in the form of provisions for the initiative and referendum. Finally, certain specified powers were entrusted to semiautonomous regions listed in the constitution. These regions were not to have as much power as states or provinces in a federal system, but they would enjoy a much higher status than did the subnational units of government in a unitary system such as the British or the French. In short, the Italian constitution established neither a unitary nor a federal system, but an intermediate form: regional devolution.

One flaw in the operationalization of the Italian constitution by the centrist coalitions that ruled the country during the first ten years of the republic was the slow pace at which the provisions just cited were implemented.[7] The Constitutional Court was not set up until 1955 and did not begin to function until 1956. Legislation to implement the referendum was not passed until 1970. As for the regions promised by the constitution, four "special regions" with special ethnic or separatist problems—Sardinia, Sicily, Trentino-Alto Adige, and Valle d'Aosta—were created shortly after World War II; the fifth special region, Friuli-Venezia Giulia, was established by the parliament in 1963. The fifteen "ordinary regions" listed in the constitution were not instituted until 1970.

The delays in implementing the constitution could be attributed to the unwillingness of the ruling Christian Democracy to share power with the opposition or to tolerate potentially crippling restraints on its power to govern Italy. Before 1948, when the Communists, Socialists, and Christian Democrats had governed together in a tripartite cabinet, the Christian Democrats had been staunch advocates of decentralization, judicial independence, and other checks on the executive. The Communists and Socialists, by contrast, had favored a strong parliament and cabinet and had opposed any checks on absolute majority rule, because they expected that a leftist government was just around the corner. After the 1948 parliamentary elections, which gave the Christian Democrats an absolute majority and made it clear that they would be the dominant force in Italian politics for many years to come, the roles were reversed. Now the Communists and Socialists demanded regional autonomy, judicial review, and similar checks on the government indicated by the constitution, and the Christian Democrats dragged their feet on implementing such measures.

The political history of postwar Italy can be divided into phases corresponding to the type of government formula that usually, but not invariably, prevailed. Between 1945 and 1947 the three major parties—the Christian Democrats, the Communists, and the Socialists—collaborated in cabinet coalitions, with the help of several minor parties of the center. This period of tripartite rule ended in 1947 when the Communists and their Socialist allies were ousted from the cabinet in response to a U.S. demand made of Prime Minister Alcide De Gasperi so that Italy could partake in the Marshall Plan for the reconstruction of Europe. From 1947 through 1962 Italy was usually governed by centrist coalitions that were always dominated by Christian Democracy. The minor center parties (Social Democrats, Republicans, and the business-oriented Liberals) were junior partners in these coalitions. Then, in 1962, the first center-left government came into existence: the Christian Democrats and the minor center parties formed a cabinet with the favorable abstention of the Socialist Party, which had gradually drifted away from its former close alliance with the Communists. After abstaining on confidence votes for a year and after sixteen years in opposition, the Socialist Party finally entered the cabinet in December 1963. The center-left formula simply subtracted the Liberals from, and added the Socialists to, the center coalitions of the 1947–1962 period.[8]

From 1962 until 1982, the center-left coalition was the dominant combination in Italian politics, although developments in the 1970s and early 1980s eroded this dominance. One development was the increasing moderation and therefore enhanced respectability of the Communist Party. The Communists were actually treated as part of the parliamentary majority between 1976 and 1979 when their surging electoral strength placed them right behind the Christian Democrats (although they were not granted any cabinet posts), and Italy seemed for a time to be on the verge of being governed by a grand coalition of all nonfascist parties. A second and related development was the declining strength of Christian Democracy.[9] This trend compelled the party to make greater concessions to its allies as the price for preserving the center-left formula. One concession was a willingness to relinquish the party's monopolistic stranglehold on the position of prime minister, so that in 1981 Italy had its first non–Christian Democratic prime minister in thirty-five years: Giovanni Spadolini, leader of the Republican Party. And in 1983 the Socialist leader, Bettino Craxi, was able to form a cabinet.

In 1982 a new phase was initiated. The moderate rightist Liberal Party was asked to share cabinet offices with the four center-left parties. For most of the period from 1982 to 1993, therefore, the center-left formula was replaced by an oversized five-party coalition ranging from the moderate left (Italian Socialist Party, or PSI) through the moderate right (Italian Liberal Party, or PLI). During the first nine months and the last four years of this period, the small centrist Republican Party chose to remain outside the coalition, thereby reducing the coalition membership to four.

In February 1992 corruption scandals began to emerge in Italy, and during the next two years they implicated a very large proportion of Italy's political elites. Meanwhile, the parliamentary elections of April 1992 and March 1994 produced an electoral earthquake. The result was that the traditional Italian coalition formulas began to undergo some startling changes. After the 1992 elections, the four-party coalition formula (Christian Democrats, Socialists, Social Democrats, and Liberals) was adopted once again, and again no Republicans. Its leader, however, was not a Christian Democrat but a Socialist, Giuliano Amato (Craxi's nomination was vetoed by the Christian Democrats). When Amato nominated a short-lived, reshuffled cabinet in February 1993, he included nonpolitical technocrats. These developments were accompanied by other signs of the Christian Democrats' political eclipse—the loss of twenty-eight seats in the Chamber of Deputies in 1992 and the growing strength of the fledgling and novel regional party the Lombard League (La Lega) in the north.

As the corruption scandals continued to unfold in 1993 and voter confidence in the traditional parties continued to decline, the Italian party system and the composition of Italian cabinets underwent truly fundamental changes. In April 1993 Carlo Azeglio Ciampi, director of the Bank of Italy, took over as prime minister. He was the first non-politician and nonparliamentarian to occupy that post. His cabinet included not only the four parties of the Amato coalition and nonpolitical technocrats but also three members of the PDS (the Democratic Party of the Left, the former Communist Party) and one Green Party member. Although the PDS members and the Green resigned less than twenty-four hours after their appointment in protest of the refusal of the Chamber of Deputies to lift Craxi's parliamentary immunity so he could face corruption charges, the fact remained that the former Communist Party, for the first time in forty-six years, had been invited to enter a cabinet.

The parliamentary elections of April 1994 fatally weakened the parties that had hitherto dominated Italian politics and brought some new parties to parliament. It was clear that the old coalition formulas were not merely going to be revised, but were going to be drastically transformed. The new cabinet, formed in May 1994, was headed by Silvio Berlusconi, a media magnate and leader of Forza Italia (Go, Italy), a new catchall party of the center-right that he had established and financed only a few months before the election. The other major parties in the coalition were the Northern League, an interregional and relatively new federalist and quasi-separatist party of the center-right, and the National Alliance, a party of former Fascists and monarchists whose central core was the MSI—the neo-Fascist Italian Social Movement. A few center-right cabinets had been formed in Italy since 1945, but never one that actually included a party dominated by former Fascists and that included some leaders who refused to renounce their Fascist past. For the first time since 1945, Italy veered sharply to the right, and former Fascists entered the corridors of power. Italian coalition politics had entered new and uncharted waters.

Yet the Berlusconi cabinet lasted only seven months—he was compelled to resign in December 1994 after serious disagreements split his center-right coalition. His successor was Lamberto Dini, a technocrat and top official of the Bank of Italy. Unlike the Ciampi cabinet of 1993–1994, which was partly composed of technocrats, the Dini caretaker cabinet of 1995 was all technocratic—another new development. Dini resigned on December 30, 1995, and the elections of March 1996 produced a center-left victory. Romano Prodi, a former Christian Democrat running under the party's new label, Olive Tree coalition (Ulivo), became prime minister. His cabinet coalition was center-left, but with one major difference from the earlier center-left coalitions: it included members of the Popular Party; the Italian Renewal (a new small party formed by Dini), the Democratic Union (a moderate party of the center-left), the Greens, and the PDS, which had become a more moderate center-left movement. Nevertheless, the admission of the former Communist Party to the cabinet as the dominant partner in the coalition marked a sharp break with the past.[10]

This break with the past was further confirmed in October 1998, when the Prodi cabinet resigned and Massimo D'Alema, leader of the PDS and then DS (Democrats of the Left), became the new prime minister. His cabinet, too, was largely center-left, but it included an extreme left element and a center-right element. They were, respectively, Armando Cossutta's small and newly formed Communist Party of Italy (a far cry from the old and much more powerful PCI of pre-1992 days) and the Democratic Union for the Republic (UDR), a center-right party of former Christian Democrats led by former president Francesco Cossiga and former labor minister Clemente Mastella in the first Berlusconi government. Cossiga and Mastella aspired to construct a vast centrist movement that would appeal to both Catholic and secular forces, as well as to those voters who were currently supporting Forza Italia. Cossiga saw Prodi, who was a member of the Catholic Popular Party, as an obstacle to his construction of such a movement, and a short time later Cossiga abandoned active politics. Mastella persevered and remained with the center-left bloc until 2008.[11] After the May 2001 elections, Berlusconi returned to office as head of a center-right coalition with an ambitious program to completely restructure Italy's social, economic, and political system.[12] But despite his promises, the period between 2001 and 2006 saw few of the reforms championed during the 2001 electoral campaign. The economy stagnated, and the main legislative innovations—decriminalizing accounting fraud, granting immunity from prosecution of the country's main political leaders, muzzling the judiciary, a new law on the media, and a constitutional reform that weakened the president and strengthened the prime minister—generated considerable controversy. Berlusconi's international initiatives also divided the country, especially his participation in the war in Iraq and the critical position he assumed toward the European Union.

The April 2006 parliamentary elections returned Romano Prodi to power in the closest election in Italian history. Taking advantage of the new electoral law passed by the Berlusconi government one month before the election, the Prodi coalition was able to translate a 0.5 percent majority in votes in the Chamber of Deputies into a 55 percent majority of seats, and in the Senate, despite having fewer votes (49.2 percent versus the 49.9 percent for the center-right), it was able to obtain a slim two-vote majority. The Senate majority eventually succumbed to the defections of a few members of the extreme left unhappy with Italy's continued engagement in the peacekeeping operations in Afghanistan and a small number of senators from Mastella's UDR. The Prodi government resigned in January 2008 and opened the way for a new round of parliamentary elections.

As expected, the electorate severely punished the parties of the former center-left coalition and brought Berlusconi's center-right coalition back to power in the April 2008 elections. Berlusconi's Partito della Libertà (PdL) won a resounding victory and elected solid majorities in both the House and Senate. Therefore, as the economic crisis rolled over Italy and the rest of Europe in 2008, the fourth Berlusconi government was called upon to respond to the fall in gross domestic product (GDP), employment, industrial production, and investments.[13]

Today, the far left and the far right have become relatively weak players on the Italian political stage. They have been replaced by institutionalized parties that have entered the mainstream of Italian politics. The PD is clearly no longer a party of the far left.[14] Instead, two small, avowedly communist parties, the Party of Communist Refoundation (PRC) and the Communist Party of Italy (PCd'I), and another small leftist but also libertarian party (Sinistra e Libertà) led by Niki Vendola, the president of the regional government of Puglia, are to its left on the political spectrum. As for the far right, Gianfranco Fini, former leader of the National Alliance and currently president of the Chamber of Deputies, has vigorously renounced the fascist past, particularly its racial excesses. With the merger of the National Alliance with Silvio Berlusconi's Forza Italia to form the PdL in 2008, Italy's center-right of the political spectrum is comparable to the Popular Alliance in Spain or the Conservative Party in the UK. The changes produced by the five elections in Italy since 1992 reveal that the country has clearly moved toward a bipolar system alternating between reformist left and moderate right ruling coalitions.[15]

Socioeconomic Context

Before World War I, the Italian economy was only partly industrialized, and most heavy industry was concentrated in the Milan-Genoa-Turin industrial triangle. Italy's total industrial production lagged far behind that of France, Germany, and Great Britain. The Fascist era was marked by a sluggish, stagnant economy, held back by the rigorously deflationary policies of the Fascist regime. World War II devastated Italian industry and transportation facilities alike. After an arduous period of postwar reconstruction, Italy managed to achieve what has been generally described as an "economic miracle." During the 1950s Italy's per capita income rose more than it had during the ninety-year span from 1861 to 1950.[16] The occupational composition of the labor force also underwent a remarkable transformation that both fueled and reflected economic expansion. When Italy was liberated in 1945, more than 40 percent of the Italian labor force was employed in agriculture; by 2005 only 3.9 percent was so employed, compared with 30.6 percent in industry and 65.4 percent in the services sector.[17]

The growth in per capita income and in industries and services at the expense of agriculture was accompanied by massive movements of people from rural areas to cities; from southern Italy, Sicily, and Sardinia to the northwest industrial triangle and from southern Italy to northern Europe. These migrations had far-reaching implications for the Italian economy and society. Overloaded social services in the cities, soil erosion and eventual flooding in depopulated mountainous rural areas, intolerance toward immigrants, and rising expectations were some of the less desirable side effects of the "economic miracle." Nevertheless, for most Italians the 1950s and 1960s were times of great economic progress and expanding cultural and social horizons. Rai, the national radio and television corporation, played an important role in bringing the country closer together through its programming. Italian cinema flourished, and film directors such as Luchino Visconti, Michelangelo Antonioni, Vittorio De Sica, Frederico Fellini, Pier Paolo Pasolini, and Roberto Rossellini became household names.

The spectacular economic growth depended on various favorable conditions. The war-shattered economy cried out for reconstruction and provided entrepreneurs with many investment opportunities. Marshall Plan aid from the United States furnished the necessary capital. A divided and weak labor movement was in no position to make major demands on Italian employers. Foreign raw material prices were conveniently low. And vigorous economic leadership was furnished by a free-spending public sector headed by giant public corporations that formed part of two industrial empires: the Institute for Industrial Reconstruction (IRI) and the National Hydrocarburants Corporation (ENI). The bold entrepreneurs who managed Italy's public corporations helped to create the climate of optimism and adventure that pervaded the growth-oriented Italian economy.

By the late 1960s, however, these favorable conditions were beginning to fade, and the 1970s brought a rude awakening to the Italian economy. A wave of unprecedented labor unrest during the "Hot Autumn" of 1969 sent a clear signal that Italian employers could no longer expect to deal with a docile, self-denying labor force. Employers had to grant far-reaching wage concessions, accept indexation arrangements that tied wages more closely to the cost of living, and relax discipline in the factories. Moreover, parliament passed legislation consolidating and extending the gains labor had achieved through collective bargaining. Italy's three labor confederations were impelled by these developments to work more closely together and to adopt a more militant posture. As a result, Italian labor costs rose sharply, not only in terms of wages but also in terms of social security benefits. The competitive advantage formerly enjoyed by Italian manufactured products became a thing of the past.

In the 1970s, further misfortunes befell the Italian economy, compounding the negative impact of the oil embargoes of 1973 and 1979 launched by the Organization of Petroleum Exporting Countries (OPEC) cartel countries against the industrialized economies. The increase in the prices of raw materials, particularly oil, seriously damaged Italy's balance of trade by raising the prices of imports and making Italian exports more expensive. Meanwhile, public corporations were engaging in financial speculation, empire building, currying favor with the major political parties, and allowing political considerations to influence their hiring and personnel policies. As a result, the public sector was running large deficits, keeping sick industries alive, and creating grave problems for the Italian economy. Italy's larger corporations, burdened with onerous health insurance and pension costs imposed by the unions as part of the wage package, were especially affected by this situation.

As large industries found it increasingly difficult to compete with the country's smaller producers and from more efficient European and international businesses, Italy underwent a second "economic miracle" with the rise of new production facilities outside of the country's traditional northwestern industrial triangle. New, smaller companies, making the shift from economies of scale realized within the firm (the traditionally organized vertical industries such as Fiat, Pirelli, and Olivetti are examples) to those realized outside the firm (industrial districts), began to gain market shares in the production of consumer goods such as appliances, textiles, clothing, furniture, leather goods, and musical instruments. These industrial districts surfaced in nontraditional industrial areas stretching from the Veneto and Friuli in the north to Umbria and Latium in the center, and, later, even into some of the southern regions such as Abruzzi, Puglia, Campania, and Basilicata. After the rise of small and medium enterprises and industrial districts, the traditional economic duality between the north (industrialized) and the south (agricultural) began to break down. The transformation of the country's industrial base was followed by a sustained restructuring of social classes and the diffusion of personal wealth. The class structure became much more open with the rise of new economic elites and extensive social mobilization.

In contrast to the first economic miracle of the 1950s, the second economic miracle of the late 1970s and 1980s was based largely on female labor. In part, this shift stemmed from the social services such as day care centers and full-time school programs being provided by the regional governments. It also stemmed from the rising levels of consumption, which were met by women entering the workforce in large numbers. Women also began to participate in political movements demanding equality of the sexes before the law, equal pay, and the freedom to choose on issues involving abortion and divorce. As a consequence, more women became lawyers, engineers, architects, and doctors and entered politics to advance the cause of women's rights.

From the changing conditions of the 1970s, the 1980s, and the early 1990s, new problems have emerged. One problem is unemployment, especially among young people seeking their first jobs. Facing high wage and social security costs and restricted in their ability to discharge surplus labor, many Italian employers have been reluctant to hire new personnel for what traditionally have been full-time jobs. Over the last decade, new kinds of labor contracts, the increasing use of part-time labor, and the appearance of private employment agencies have become the norm. As a result, Italy's unemployment rate went down significantly. Indeed, in 2007 unemployment fell to 5.9 percent as a result of the new employment schemes, but rose to 6.7 percent in 2008 and to 8.5 percent in 2009.

According to 2008 figures, 63.0 percent of the population between the ages of fifteen and sixty-four was either employed or actively seeking employment. Moreover, the differences between men and women were significant. The male employment rate (70.3 percent) has always been close to the European average, but what makes Italy different from the rest of the EU has been the employment rate for females (47.2 percent), the third-lowest level in all of the European Union after Hungary and Malta.[18]

A second problem has been the proliferation of a "submerged economy," consisting of a multitude of small employers scattered in the new industrialized areas in southern, central, and northern Italy. The submerged or "informal" economy often pays workers substandard wages, fails to pay social security and payroll taxes for its employees, and keeps economic operations a well-guarded secret from the prying eyes of the tax authorities. But it also has become a tool for injecting flexibility into economic activity by providing employers with the possibility of hiring employees on a part-time basis or seasonal schedule, creating apprenticeship programs, linking wages to output, and hiring immigrants for jobs not acceptable to native Italians.[19] These new forms of employment have become an important factor in raising employment levels in Italy (although not often captured in official statistics) and enticing new workers to join the labor force.

A third, related socioeconomic problem is posed by the growing gap between the relatively prosperous, traditionally employed workers, protected until very recently by indexation against economic vicissitudes, and the new workers in the flexible employment economy, where employment is based not on a traditional, full-time labor contract, but on the ability of the country's economy to produce jobs on a competitive basis. Italy has also witnessed the emergence of an extensive new class of entrepreneurs in industrial, service, and agricultural activities that have made self-employed workers the fastest-growing sector of the economy. At the same time, the country has continued to import labor from the non–European Union Central and Eastern European countries (CEECs) to the east and those to the south in northern and sub-Saharan Africa.

All of these changes would appear to call for the traditional remedy of higher levels of government intervention and spending. But it has become painfully and urgently evident in Italy that government spending has already reached excessively high levels, especially for social welfare programs and pensions that do not have the flexibility or capacity to meet the new social and economic challenges that vary greatly from one part of the country to another. By contrast, the regional and local authorities have increasingly taken on the role of providing incentives for industry and the creation of new businesses, because at the regional and local levels policies can be better earmarked for the local economy.[20]

By 1984 unsustainably high levels of government spending had brought the Italian national debt to 77.4 percent of Italy's GDP; by 1993 it had grown to 119.4 percent of GDP, and by 1996 to 122 percent of GDP. From 1996 to 1998 the Prodi government, under Minister of the Treasury Carlo Azeglio Ciampi, engaged in a sustained privatization program that used the proceeds from the sale of state assets to draw down the debt. By 2000 the debt was reduced to 111 percent of GDP, and it fell to 106 percent in 2003. Data for 2004 reveal the debt remained stable, a consequence of the indiscriminate tax cuts implemented by the Berlusconi government without cutting an equal amount of government spending. The debt began to decline once again under the guidance of Tommaso Padoa-Schioppa, Prodi's minister of the economy, but the economic crisis of 2008–2009 and the subsequent decline in tax revenues forced the debt-to-GDP ratio back up under the new Berlusconi government.

Budget deficits were also rising, reaching 12.3 percent of GDP by 1985. Strenuous economizing measures by post-1985 Italian governments (especially the post-1992 governments) managed to reduce the annual budget deficit to 9.5 percent of GDP in 1992 and 7.1 percent of GDP in 1996.[21] By 1997 the level of the annual budget deficit had dropped to 2.7 percent, and by 2001 it had been reduced to 1.4 percent through the series of spending cuts and tax increases introduced by the Prodi, D'Alema, and Amato center-left governments. Conversely, under the second center-right Berlusconi government, the annual deficit ran over the 3 percent maximum established by the EU's Stability and Growth Pact in both 2003 and 2004 and increased in 2005 and 2006 to 4.1 percent deficit levels, despite the sale of successive tranches of ENI and ENEL (the state electric power industry) stocks. In the early 1990s it was estimated that 95 percent of Italy's fiscal income was devoted to covering internal charges on the national debt.[22]

The introduction of the euro had a positive effect on the interest payments the country had to make on the money it borrowed to finance its debt. Before entering the Economic and Monetary Union (EMU), Italy had interest rates that were close to 10 percent, but after introduction of the euro, rates fell to 2.0–2.5 percent, and the interest that the country had to pay on government securities was cut by a half to two-thirds of past levels. The Prodi government was able to bring the annual deficit for 2007 down to 1.9 percent, and under the stewardship of the minister for the economy, the government's target was a zero annual deficit by 2010. These plans were rudely interrupted by the subsequent political crisis that forced Prodi to resign and new elections. But even more significant was the world financial crisis that hit Italy hard in 2008 and 2009. Italy's GDP declined by 4.7 percent in 2009, but it did not enter into the group of countries such as Greece, Ireland, Portugal, and Spain that ran the risk of default. Despite its economic woes, Italy remained comparatively immune from the collapse of its banks or of its real estate market.

Religion

The Catholic Church has traditionally played a major role in Italian politics. During the Middle Ages and the Renaissance, the Papal State, the temporal domain of the pope, resisted numerous attempts by the Germanic Holy Roman Empire to unite Italy. In the nineteenth century, the pope opposed Piedmont's bid to unify the Italian peninsula, and in fact the final event of the Risorgimento was the forcible seizure of Rome by Italian troops in 1870. From 1870 to 1913, the church hierarchy advised religious Italians to abstain from voting in Italian national elections. The Gentiloni Agreement of 1913, under which Italian Catholics began to give large-scale electoral support to candidates for parliament, brought this boycott of the Italian state to an end. In 1919 a Christian Democratic party—the Popular Party led by Don Luigi Sturzo—entered Italian national elections and openly campaigned for the support of religious voters. After Mussolini came to power, the Popular Party was disbanded, and in 1929 the church signed the Lateran Agreements with the Fascist state, signaling a complete reconciliation between church and state. One of these agreements, the Concordat of 1929, recognized the sovereignty of the pope over Vatican City, guaranteed religious education in Italian public schools, and declared Catholicism to be the official religion of the Italian state. The Catholic Church also was granted far-reaching privileges related to the holding of property and jurisdiction over marriage and divorce, among other things.

After the defeat of fascism, the church was able to strike a favorable bargain with the new Italian republic. The Lateran Agreements of 1929 were actually incorporated into the new constitution. Article 7 provided that the agreements could be modified only by mutual consent of both parties or by a constitutional amendment. The Communist delegates to the Constituent Assembly actually voted for Article 7 in 1947, possibly in an effort to conciliate their Christian Democratic coalition partners and avert the impending expulsion of the Communist Party from the Italian cabinet in light of Pope Pius XII's effective policy against that party.

During the 1940s and 1950s political Catholicism was an organized and pervasive force in Italian politics. With Christian Democracy dominant in the Italian political system, the church and its lay organizations enjoyed privileged access to national centers of decision making. Priests and bishops openly took sides in election campaigns, urging the faithful to support candidates sympathetic to the Catholic Church. Catholic Action, a church-sponsored lay organization, set up a network of civic committees to conduct canvassing and propaganda activities in behalf of Christian Democracy. Catholic interest groups representing labor, peasants, teachers, and others were directly affiliated with Christian Democracy, and they enjoyed a *parentela* relationship. Such groups had the right, as "members of the family," to be consulted on appointments to cabinet positions, nominations of candidates for parliament, and policy questions affecting their interests.[23] In short, the Italian Catholic Church was much more prominent on the political scene than its French counterpart.

Since the early 1960s, the political aggressiveness of Italian Catholicism has waned. Under Popes John XXIII (1958–1963) and Paul VI (1963–1978), the church assumed a lower profile in Italian politics and displayed less hostility toward leftist parties. The church itself, however, was by no means united. Some bishops continued to maintain a politically active stance and to oppose any alliances with leftist forces. Nevertheless, as the papacy abandoned in the early 1960s its antipathy to the idea of a center-left coalition government, most bishops reluctantly followed suit. Later, even the partial collaboration between Christian Democrats and Communists at the national level during 1976–1979 did not call down the anathema of the church.

Pope Benedict XVI, building on the legacy of Pope John Paul II, has continued to assert the resurgence of the Catholic Church as an important force in Italian politics.

Source: AP Images/Pier Paolo Cito

What underlay the more cautious line followed by the church was the growing secularization of Italian society. In the 1960s and 1970s church attendance declined, and larger numbers of Catholics, especially Catholic intellectuals, displayed independent attitudes in direct conflict with the dictates of the church hierarchy. Some Catholic associations loosened their ties with Christian Democracy. Also, the exodus from Catholic rural strongholds to the big cities, from agricultural occupations to industrial and service jobs, seriously undermined the influence of religious tradition.

Clear evidence of the weakening of religiosity in Italy was the passage of a divorce bill in 1970, despite the strong resistance of Christian Democracy and the Vatican. More striking still was the aftermath of the bill's passage. When militant Catholics pushed the issue to a referendum in an effort to achieve repeal of the divorce law, the result was a clear-cut victory for secularism. A 1974 referendum upheld the divorce law, with only 41 percent of voters casting their ballots for its repeal. Forces favoring divorce carried most of Italy, with the exception of the Catholic northeast and the continental south. Even Sicily, Sardinia, and Latium (the region that includes Rome) voted to retain divorce. The size of the vote against repeal clearly indicated that repeal lacked the support of a considerable number of Christian Democratic voters. In another referendum held in 1981 to decide whether a rather liberal abortion law should be repealed, 68 percent of Italians who took part in the balloting voted against repeal—a bigger majority than the pro-divorce majority of 1974. It is probably in recognition of its waning strength that the Catholic Church agreed in 1984 to accept a revision of the Concordat.

The church's influence rebounded in Italy during the papacy of John Paul II (1978–2005), and that trend is continuing under Benedict XVI. John Paul II's long reign was characterized by widespread popular support for his teaching against wars and in support of international development—teaching that helped to redefine popular attitudes toward the church. This support became abundantly clear in the unprecedented public response to the pope's attempted assassination in 1984 and death in 2005. The first five years of Benedict XVI's papacy have generated less popular enthusiasm than was the case with John Paul II, but the church has been able to reassert its doctrinal leadership on the future course of religious thought. The Catholic Church continues to wield a role in the media and political debate, but its direct influence is in question, particularly when it comes down to individual behavior or ethical values. In the 2008 election issues dear to the church were kept in the background and did not become issues for campaign debate.[24]

Education

The Italian educational system has undergone a major transformation since World War II. In the 1950s, 90 percent of the population had not attended school more than five years. Moreover, at the end of fifth grade, as was often the practice in Europe at the time, a child was assigned to either an academic junior high school or a terminal vocational school. Assigning a child to a secondary school on the basis of aptitude at such an early age meant that aptitude was all too frequently determined by family background and social class.

In the 1960s, with the entry of the Socialist Party into center-left cabinets, educational opportunities were broadened. A unified junior high school was established to replace the earlier two-track system and led to a significant increase in enrollments. By 2001, 96.3 percent of all children between the ages of six and fourteen, the age groups for which education is compulsory, were enrolled in elementary or lower secondary schools, without any significant differentiation in attendance figures between students attending elementary schools (ages six to ten) and lower secondary schools (ages eleven to fourteen) or between students living in the north and the south of the country.

These changes in turn led to a great increase in high school enrollment. They also brought about the lowering of standards to accommodate the incoming masses. Moreover, pressure for further democratization led to the adoption in 1970 of an open admissions policy for the universities, which became overcrowded and lost much of their elite status.

The initial results of these reforms were somewhat disappointing, producing unforeseen side effects. The great wave of student unrest that swept over Italian universities in the late 1960s and early 1970s, and that brought chronic indiscipline and frequent violence in its wake, was a direct outcome of the skyrocketing enrollments and the inability of the university system to make the necessary adjustments. The depressing working conditions that prevailed for the academic staff, the frustrated expectations of the students, and the protests that were gripping U.S. and French universities combined to foment student unrest. Indeed, many a young terrorist spent his formative years in the chaotic milieu of Italian higher education. In response to the growing problems, the Italian government sought to reorganize the university system by allowing universities to restore a selective admissions policy and granting universities greater autonomy in organizing their curricula.[25] In 2003 the Berlusconi government introduced other reforms of university education by creating short-term (three-year) bachelor's degrees, five-year graduate degrees, and, in selected disciplines, Ph.D programs. In the late 1990s and early 2000s, higher education in Italy moved from immobilization to rapid and revolutionary reform, although whether these changes will fully respond to the shortcomings of Italian higher education has yet to be assessed. In 2008 the subsequent Berlusconi government was forced to reduce funding for the university system as part of the need to cut overall government spending. The cuts have significantly impacted the funding for research and outreach programs to bring university education to smaller towns and cities.

Political Culture

In the six decades since Liberation, Italians have seen their country transformed by a pattern of drastic change—a remolding of the political, social, economic, religious, and educational landscapes. Inevitably, this metamorphosis has had a notable impact on political attitudes and culture.

But any examination of the changes that have taken place since the early 1960s must be prefaced with a look at the most significant attitudes that traditionally characterized Italian political culture. First, Italians tended to rank rather low in social trust—that is, they lacked faith in the motives and actions of their fellow citizens. Yet it was in Italy that the concept of "social capital" was born to explain the differentiation in the institutional performance of regional and local governments. High-performing governments were supported by a diffused level of social trust and the potential for community mobilization in the creation of common goods.[26] Second, Italians had a low degree of political trust—that is, they had little confidence in the efficiency and integrity of national government institutions and officials. They did believe that levels of government closer to the local community are more responsive to particular needs. Third, Italians who live in southern Italy tended to seek protection against a potentially hostile environment by joining informal but hierarchical groupings (cliques and clienteles) in which they could enjoy the protection of a powerful patron. In northern and central Italy clienteles were not as prominent. People relied more on organizations, groups, and associations to access social services or financial resources. Fourth, Italians finally acquired a sense of national identity after two world wars and a period of partisan resistance to the German occupation from 1943 to 1945, but they also maintained their regional and local identities and added a clearly expressed European identity. Fifth, Italians were politically active, voting much more regularly than citizens of other European countries or the United States. The turnout in national, local, and European elections regularly exceeded 70 percent to 75 percent of registered voters. Meanwhile, Italians were also not afraid to participate in mass demonstrations and marches demanding changes in government economic, domestic, or foreign policies.

The most important features of the Italian political culture are both its heterogeneity and its fragmentation. The attitudes just described were not universally shared. Instead, competing subcultures represented competing sets of values and attitudes. These divergent subcultures—elite or mass, northern or southern, liberal or clerical or Marxist—helped to shape Italy's party system and the tendency of Italian voters to think in left-right, clerical-anticlerical, north-south terms. They also accounted for the pre-1992 pattern of stable partisan preferences (voters frequently supported the same parties election after election) and the high degree of hostility that some parties aroused among voters at the other end of the political spectrum.

From 1965 to 1992, this set of attitudes underwent some significant changes. The balance of forces among competing subcultures shifted visibly, with Catholic (clerical) traditions losing popular support and suffering from a weakened organizational network. Partisan hostility diminished a great deal, especially that directed toward the former Communist Party, which gained considerable acceptance as a legitimate political force among Italian political elites. Among the more educated, influential Italians, there seemed to be a pronounced movement toward bridging the cleavages that had divided the subcultures. At the level of mass culture, however, much remained the same. Voters still tended to place themselves along a left-right spectrum, identifying themselves as left, center, or right. And although the Catholic tradition had declined, about 40 percent of Italian voters still supported repeal of the divorce law. As for attitudes toward the political system, they were still pronounced, despite the improved socioeconomic conditions experienced by most Italians.

In fact, evaluations of the political system, including the competence of politicians, were more negative in the 1990s than in the 1960s. The widespread political alienation and political distrust would help to explain the frequent direct confrontations between demonstrators—using a variety of provocative strategies—and public authorities. It also would help to explain the tendency of disaffected fringe groups to resort to acts of terrorism. Nevertheless, some scholars came to the conclusion that alienation and distrust did not represent a passionate rejection of the Italian style of democracy, but a sober and realistic recognition of the limited potentialities of any political system and the low level of responsiveness of Italian political elites at crucial stages in Italy's political history.[27]

In general, it seemed in 1990 that although Italian political elites were conducting their quarrels with more moderation and mutual forbearance, the potential for unrest and violent upheaval was still alive and well among noninfluentials. Yet the Italian political system had a record of great resiliency, and there were some very promising elements in the picture to offset the more negative features described here. Voters gave somewhat greater support than in the past to the middle-of-the-road minor parties, and parties on both the left and the right were significantly moderating their political stances and relations with their opponents. In Italy, terrorism was defeated not through draconian measures limiting civil liberties and torture, but through a sustained campaign of isolating the terrorists from the institutionalized social movements and organizations. The same can be said about the Mafia. After the 1992 murder of two judges and the 1993 bombings in Rome and Florence, the top Mafia leaders were rounded up and jailed under highly restrictive conditions. On the day after the April 2006 elections, Bernardo Provenzano, the "boss of bosses" of the Sicilian Mafia, was finally arrested outside of Corleone, his hometown, after more than forty years as a fugitive. Since then, other top leaders of the Mafia in Sicily and the Camorra in Naples have been arrested and brought to trial. These and other successes support the view that when the Italian justice system is allowed to function, it is able to resolve issues of law and order effectively and efficiently.

Secularization was visible in both the Catholic and Marxist camps, because Italian voters appeared to be rejecting extremist tendencies. In short, it was widely suggested that the Italian polity had once again survived the dangers to its democracy, as it had done so often in the past and will continue to do in the future. As Joseph LaPalombara has argued, democracy Italian style might not be pretty, but it has functioned well enough since the end of World War II to transform an authoritarian political culture into a vibrant democratic one in a peaceful and participatory manner.[28]

The corruption scandals of 1992–1994 did not undermine the basically optimistic prospectus. Because more than fifteen hundred political officeholders and businesspeople were swept up in an investigation of corruption and bribery in the awarding of government contracts, a sharp decline in the levels of social and political trust, and of political and administrative competence, was bound to take place. The growing sense of alienation had the effect of discrediting the previous political party system, or "first republic" (*prima repubblica*) as it is referred to now, because the Socialist and Christian Democratic Parties were those most deeply involved in the general pattern of corruption known as "Kickback City." But just like its response to the terrorist campaign, the Italian justice system carried out its function in an exemplary manner, identifying and prosecuting many perpetrators of the corruption regardless of their political and social positions and opening the way to the rise of new political parties and elites.

The victory of the center-right parties in 1994 made it clear that the electoral stability of partisan preferences was a thing of the past, as most of the parties that had dominated Italian politics since 1945 suffered enormous losses (if they participated in the elections at all), and many of them were denied representation in parliament. Meanwhile, new political parties and elites have come to the fore. It appeared in 1994 that the Italian political culture might be tilting to the right, because laissez-faire, authoritarian, and separatist tendencies were receiving spectacular support from the Italian masses. It soon became evident, however, that the victory of right-wing populism was to be short-lived. Berlusconi was ousted in late 1994, and the elections of 1996 brought the center-left to power. After five years in government, the center-left gave way to Berlusconi's center-right coalition in the next parliamentary elections. In 2001 in his electoral "contract with Italy" Berlusconi promised Italians lower taxes, higher spending on infrastructure, higher levels of economic development, more jobs, and higher wages. The terrorist attacks of September 11, 2001, on the United States and the resulting world economic downturn undermined the prime minister's rosy outlook. Italy went from a positive level of growth of 3.1 percent of GDP in 2000, the year before the election, to a full recession in 2004 and no recovery in 2005. During this time, the center-right coalition lost all of the major city, provincial, and regional elections. In the regional elections of 2005, the center-right parties lost six of their eight regional presidencies up for reconfirmation. The parties of the center-left were able to hold all seven of their previous regional presidencies, thereby giving the center-left victories in thirteen of the fifteen regional elections contested. Of the center-right parties, the one that suffered the greatest losses was Forza Italia, the party led by Berlusconi.

In the 2006 election, Forza Italia made a significant comeback, garnering 23.7 percent in the Chamber of Deputies, but the center-left opposition as a whole made a better showing. In 2001 the center-left had received 43.9 percent of the vote. Five years later, it reached 49.8 percent. Prodi's coalition won the election, because it had more appeal for Italy's younger voters, which was evident in the differentiation of the vote (the franchise is extended to eighteen-year-olds and up in elections for the Chamber of Deputies and twenty-five-year-olds and up in the Senate). In the elections for the Chamber of Deputies, the center-left gained 1,919,271 votes as opposed to the center-right's increase of 1,636,078 votes, thereby eliminating the center-right's numerical advantage (217,817 votes) among older voters in the Senate elections. In 2008 electoral sentiment returned to favor the center-right, with the PdL outperforming the center-left PD by 37.4 percent to 33.2 percent. For the time being, it appears that Italy's national government will continue to alternate between moderate center-left and moderate center-right coalitions. On the heels of the results of the 2008 elections, which were reaffirmed by the partial administrative elections of 2009 and by the elections for the European Parliament (see Table 4-4, page 372), the center-right is now clearly in the ascendancy. The center-left has been forced to return to the internal squabbling that pits one leadership group against another within the PD and has created a programmatic chasm between the moderate elements of the center-left and the more ideological components of the left.

NOTES

1. See Michael Piore and Charles Sable, *The Second Industrial Divide: Possibilities for Prosperity* (New York: Free Press, 1984).

2. See Istituto Nazionale di Statistica (ISTAT), *Censimento 2001* (Rome: ISTAT, 2004); and "France" and "Italy" in *The Europa World Year Book 1998* (London: Europa Publications, 1998), 1:1334–5, 1825.

3. SVIMEZ, *Rapporto SVIMEZ 2009* (Bologna: Il Mulino, 2009), 160; and ISTAT, Demografia in cifre, popolazione residente 2009.

4. For the period before 1970, see Raphael Zariski, *Italy: The Politics of Uneven Development* (Hinsdale, Ill.: Dryden Press, 1972), chap. 1.

5. See Filippo Sabetti, *The Search for Good Government: Understanding the Paradox of Italian Democracy* (Montreal: McGill-Queens University Press, 2000), 191–211.

6. For a detailed account of this period, see Charles Delzell, *Mussolini's Enemies: The Italian Anti-Fascist Movement* (Princeton, N.J.: Princeton University Press, 1961).

7. See Norman Kogan, *A Political History of Italy: The Postwar Years* (New York: Praeger, 1983), 104–106, 255–256.

8. For a detailed discussion of the political history of postwar Italy, see Paul Ginsborg, *A History of Contemporary Italy: Society and Politics, 1943–1988* (London: Penguin, 1990); and Ginsborg, *Italy and Its Discontents: Family, Civil Society, State, 1980–2001* (London: Penguin, 2001).

9. See Robert Leonardi and Douglas Wertman, *Italian Christian Democracy: The Politics of Dominance* (New York: St. Martin's Press, 1989).

10. For a discussion of the 1994, 1996, and 2001 elections, see Robert Leonardi and Raffaella Y. Nanetti, eds., *Italy: Politics and Policy*, vol. 1 (Aldershot, UK: Ashgate, 1996); and Robert Leonardi and Marcello Fedele, eds., *Italy: Politics and Policy*, vol. 2 (Aldershot, Hants, UK: Ashgate, 2003).

11. See Michele Simone, "Il Governo D'Alema inizia la sua navigazione," *La Civilta Cattolica* 149 (1998): 324–325. In 2006 Mastella was appointed minister of justice in the second Prodi government, and his resignation triggered the collapse of the Prodi coalition.

12. On the political phenomenon represented by Silvio Berlusconi, see Paul Ginsborg, *Silvio Berlusconi: Television, Power and Patrimony* (London and New York: Verso, 2004); and David Lane, *Berlusconi's Shadow: Crime, Justice and the Pursuit of Power* (London: Allen Lane, 2004).

13. See Michael Shin and John Agnew, *Berlusconi's Italy* (Philadelphia: Temple University Press, 2008; and James Newell, ed., *The Italian General Election of 2008: Berlusconi Strikes Back* (Basingstoke, UK: Palgrave Macmillan, 2009)

14. Marc Lazar, "The Birth of the Democratic Party," in *Italian Politics: Frustrated Aspirations for Change,* ed. Mark Donovan and Paolo Onofri (Oxford: Berghahn Books, 2008), 51–67.

15. See Vittorio Bufacchi, "The Coming of Age of Italian Democracy," *Government and Opposition* (1996): 322–346.

16. See Rosario Romeo, *Breve storia della grande industria in Italia* (Bologna: Capelli, 1967), 113–114.

17. See Istituto Nazionale di Statistica (ISTAT), first-quarter socioeconomic data, 2005, http://www.istat.it/.

18. ISTAT, "Noi Italia," www.istat.it. Emilia-Romagna is the region with the highest employment rate at 70.2 percent, and Campania (the region around Naples) has the lowest at 42.5 percent in 2008.

19. The estimates are that in 2007 undocumented workers accounted for 11.7 percent of the entire labor force. In the center-north of the country, the figure is estimated to be just above 10 percent, and in the south the estimate is double that amount. Calabria is estimated to have the highest level of undocumented workers (27.3 percent), and the use of undocumented workers is particularly acute in agriculture. Ibid.

20. For a discussion of the transfer of economic development policies to the local level, see Raffaella Y. Nanetti, *Growth and Territorial Policy* (London: Pinter Publishers, 1988).

21. Elisabetta Bertero, "An International Economic Perspective on the Results of the 2001 Italian Elections," in Leonardi and Fedele, *Italy: Politics and Policy*, 210–218.

22. Ibid., 212.

23. See Joseph La Palombara, *Interest Groups in Italian Politics* (Princeton, N.J.: Princeton University Press, 1964), chap. 9.

24. Luigi Ceccarini, "La fine della questione cattolica?" in Italian National Election Studies (ITANES), *Il ritorno di Berlusconi* (Bologna: Il Mulino, 2008), 123–136.

25. Giliberto Capano, "Higher Education Policy in Italy (1992–1997)," in Leonardi and Fedele, *Italy: Politics and Policy*, 86–107.

26. See Robert D. Putnam, with Robert Leonardi and Raffaella Y. Nanetti, *Making Democracy Work: Civic Traditions in Modern Italy* (Princeton, N.J.: Princeton University Press, 1993).

27. See Joseph LaPalombara, *Democracy Italian Style* (New Haven: Yale University Press, 1987), 152–155, 263–264.

28. Ibid.

Where Is the Power?

Ⓘ TALY, LIKE GREAT BRITAIN AND GERMANY, HAS A PARLIAMENTARY
system. Although in recent years some thought has been given to setting up a quasi-
presidential system on the French model, such institutional reform at the national level has
so far not generated sufficient support. Like Germany, Italy is a parliamentary republic
with a weak, indirectly elected president. Also, Italy is far more decentralized than most
parliamentary systems. It does not actually have a federal system like Germany; rather, it
has a form of regional devolution that differentiates it quite clearly from unitary systems
such as those of Great Britain, Greece, or Sweden.

The President: Guarantor of the Constitution and Ceremonial Chief of State

Unlike the hegemonic French president, the Italian president resembles the ceremonial
chief of state in other parliamentary republics (such as Germany). Yet at the same time the
president has the important function of guarantor of the constitution and the expression
of the country's national unity. The president's role in promulgating laws is to guarantee
that a proposed bill is not unconstitutional and that expenditure bills are covered by adequate resources. If not, the president would refuse to sign the bill and send it back to parliament for reconsideration and changes. Finally, like other ceremonial and representative
chief executives, Italy's president is expected to greet visiting dignitaries, dedicate major
public projects, visit disaster zones to comfort the populace, and perform other formal
duties as the symbolic head of the Italian state, such as during visits abroad.

Overall, the president's position is more powerful than that of a British monarch. First,
a strong, ambitious president may hold press conferences and discuss current issues or
may include controversial statements about public policy matters in a public address.
Second, the president may deliver a formal message to parliament and comment critically
on the state of the nation. Third, the president may return a bill to parliament for reconsideration, along with a message stating the reasons for doing so. Although such a suspensive veto may be overridden by a simple majority of those voting in each house of
parliament, the president's action would weigh heavily on the resolve of the members of
parliament (MPs). Fourth, because of the complex nature of Italy's multiparty system, the
president's formal function of appointing the prime minister carries with it a great deal of
potential influence. If no one party has a majority in parliament, the appointment of a new
prime minister is preceded by intricate negotiations among various parties and factions. In
the course of those negotiations, the president could seek to promote a candidate of his or
her own, as President Oscar Luigi Scalfaro did in 1993 and 1995, when he put forward
the names of Carlo Azeglio Ciampi and Lamberto Dini, respectively. Or the president
could ask a resigning prime minister to continue in office. Fifth, the president appoints five

of the fifteen judges on the Constitutional Court (of the other ten, five are elected by parliament and five are elected by the judges of the highest Italian courts), chairs the self-governing body of the judiciary (*consiglio superiore della magistratura*), and has the power to dissolve parliament if the government is defeated in a no-confidence vote and there is no possibility of forming a new majority.

Apart from the constitutional and customary restraints just cited, the power of the Italian president is politically limited by the manner of the presidential selection. The president is not directly elected by the people; instead, that official is "indirectly" elected by the Electoral Assembly, composed of members of the Chamber of Deputies (630), members of the Senate (322), three delegates from each of Italy's nineteen other regions, and a delegate from Valle d'Aosta.[1] Election is by secret ballot. On the first three ballots, a two-thirds majority of the members of the Electoral Assembly is needed to elect a president; from the fourth ballot on, an absolute majority suffices. Because of the secret ballot, party cohesion and party discipline are difficult to maintain. A party cannot really compel its members to support its officially designated candidate.

In the end, then, the nominee who emerges from this intricate procedure lacks the mandate to act as a popular tribune and to speak for the Italian nation over the head of its government. Indeed, this system of election, with its secret ballot procedures and resulting breakdowns in party discipline, often produces unforeseen results. It can turn out factional bosses capable of unpredictable adventures rather than leaders of broad vision. Some presidents have been quite distinguished: Luigi Einaudi (1948–1955), a prominent Liberal economist; Giuseppe Saragat (1964–1971), leader of the Social Democratic Party; Sandro Pertini (1978–1985), a venerable Socialist leader in the Resistance with a tendency to outspokenness; and Carlo Azeglio Ciampi (1999–2006), a former governor of the Bank of Italy, minister of the Treasury in various governments, and prime minister. Others have been Christian Democratic factional chieftains who have brought little credit to the office: Giovanni Gronchi (1955–1962), who appointed the notorious Fernando Tambroni to head a government that brought Italy to the brink of civil conflict; Antonio Segni (1962–1964), who was suspected by some journalists of having been involved in the preliminary planning for an abortive military coup; and Giovanni Leone (1971–1978), who was forced to resign six months before his term expired because of alleged complicity in several cases of tax fraud and bribery.

Francesco Cossiga, president from 1985 to 1992, was also a Christian Democrat. During the first five years of his term, he maintained a relatively low profile. After 1990, however, he became extremely outspoken, making numerous controversial and often intemperate statements on public issues and delivering blistering personal attacks on the competence and integrity of various Italian political leaders, even demanding the resignation of the chief justice of the Italian Constitutional Court. He was one of the chief advocates of a stronger presidency, and, on one occasion, he even claimed he might have the right to dissolve the parliament on his own, without the prime minister's consent. Indeed, in a break with precedent and with the letter of the constitution, Cossiga dissolved the parliament during his last six months in office—the so-called blank semester when a president is constitutionally barred from dissolving parliament. This action was apparently taken at the behest of the leaders of the various parties, because parliament's term had only two more months to run. In May 1992, in a surprise move, Cossiga resigned, two months before the end of his term.

Italy at a Glance

Type of Government
Republic

Capital
Rome

Administrative Divisions
Fifteen regions: Abruzzi, Apulia, Basilicata, Calabria, Campania, Emilia-Romagna, Latium, Liguria, Lombardy, Marches, Molise, Piedmont, Tuscany, Umbria, Veneto
Five autonomous regions: Friuli-Venezia Giulia, Sardinia, Sicily, Trentino-Alto Adige, Valle d'Aosta

Independence
March 17, 1861 (Kingdom of Italy proclaimed; Italy was not finally unified until 1870)

Constitution
Passed on December 11, 1947; became effective January 1, 1948; amended in 2000

Legal System
Based on civil law system; appeals treated as new trials; judicial review under certain conditions in Constitutional Court; has not accepted compulsory International Court of Justice jurisdiction. Subject to rulings by the European Court of Justice.

Suffrage
Eighteen years of age (except in senatorial elections in which minimum age is twenty-six); universal

Executive Branch
Chief of state: president
Head of government: prime minister (known in Italy as the president of the Council of Ministers)
Cabinet: Council of Ministers nominated by the prime minister and approved by the president
Elections: president elected by an electoral assembly consisting of both houses of parliament and fifty-eight regional representatives for a seven-year term; prime minister appointed by the president and confirmed by parliament

Legislative Branch
Bicameral parliament: Senate and Chamber of Deputies. Senate: 315 senators elected by popular vote, 309 by proportional representation, and 6 from overseas constituencies; 7 senators-for-life. Term: five years. Chamber of Deputies: 630 deputies, 612 elected by proportional representation, and 12 from overseas constituencies. Term: five years.

Judicial Branch
Constitutional Court composed of fifteen judges: one-third appointed by the president, one-third elected by parliament, and one-third elected by the ordinary and administrative Supreme Courts

Major Political Parties
Left: Party of Communist Refoundation (PRC); Communist Party of Italy (PCd'I); Greens; Center-Left Democratic Party (PD); Italy of Values (Di Pietro); Center: Union of Christian Democrats (UDC); Movement for Autonomy (MPA); South Tyrolese People's Party (SVP); Center-Right: Freedom Alliance (PdL); Northern League; Right: The Right; Social Movement Tricolored Flame (MFST).

Source: Ministry of the Interior, 2008 parliamentary election, and 2009 European Parliamentary election results.

The next president, Oscar Luigi Scalfaro, a Christian Democrat, a former Catholic partisan, and a member of the Constituent Assembly, was less controversial than his mercurial predecessor.[2] Yet in the turmoil after 1992 he, too, found it impossible to avoid making highly controversial decisions. When Prime Minister Silvio Berlusconi resigned in December 1994 and asked for the dissolution of parliament and new elections, President Scalfaro refused to comply with his request until the possibility of forming another cabinet had been fully explored. A cabinet was eventually formed in 1995 under an independent central bank official and former member of the outgoing cabinet, Lamberto Dini. But President Scalfaro was denounced and vilified by Berlusconi's supporters.

Neither Dini nor the prime minister appointed in 1993, Carlo Azeglio Ciampi, was a member of parliament; both were high officials of the Bank of Italy. By appointing non-MPs to head the cabinet, President Scalfaro was venturing where other presidents had feared to tread. He also established the informal custom of having prime ministers consult the president before making important decisions on cabinet appointments.

Scalfaro's successor, Ciampi, was forthright in his statements on public policy and Italy's role in Europe. It could be argued that as Prime Minister Berlusconi's political fortunes declined in 2004–2005, the visibility of the president increased, thereby providing a sense of stability and continuity to a troubled and at times chaotic governing party coalition. It remains to be seen whether future presidents will dare to magnify the president's role or to add to that office's prestige as Scalfaro and Ciampi have done.[3] President Ciampi, who was supported by both the Democratic Party of the Left (PDS) and Forza Italia because of his nonpartisan image, did not stir up controversy. Indeed, his personal style and ability to interact with different social strata made him one of Italy's most respected and beloved institutional figures. Two-thirds of the Electoral Assembly elected Ciampi president on the first ballot in May 1999, which was a major departure in Italian politics. In his first address to parliament later that month, Ciampi emphasized the need for constitutional and political reform.

In May 2006 a new president, Giorgio Napolitano, was elected on the fourth ballot and on the basis of a simple majority. He received 543 of the 1,010 votes in the Electoral Assembly. The center-left parties voted for him as a bloc, and only a few scattered votes came from the center-right. In 1992 Napolitano was leader of the reformist wing of the former Communist Party, but after 1992 he began to detach himself from the internal politics of the PDS and Democrats of the Left. During the 1994–1996 parliament, he served as president of the Chamber of Deputies, and in the first Prodi government (1996–1997) Napolitano was appointed minister of the interior. Between 1999 and 2004 he served in the European Parliament. As a European MP, he distinguished himself as a strong supporter of the draft European constitution and of further political integration. In his acceptance speech, he told the delegates of the Electoral Assembly that during his tenure he would emphasize his role as defender of the constitution and guarantor of national unity. Since his election, Napolitano has become a staunch advocate of Italian unity and of continued support of national policies to help stimulate growth in the less developed regions. His measured statements and bipartisan approach have also endeared him to the electorate and parties of the center-right. In Italy's fractured political system he continues to remain the political figure with the highest public approval.

The Prime Minister and the Cabinet

The Italian cabinet (officially the Council of Ministers) and the prime minister (whose official title is president of the Council of Ministers) together constitute the political wing of Italy's dual executive. They resemble the classic model of the political executive in a continental European parliamentary system. After an election or the resignation of a prime minister, the president consults with the parties in finalizing his choice of prime minister, and the prime minister, in turn, consults with the parties of his coalition in selecting the list of cabinet members. The cabinet—usually a coalition cabinet, composed of members of several parties—is selected from among the members of parliament and independent experts. The prime minister then discusses the composition of the cabinet with the president. Once agreement has been reached, the prime minister and his cabinet swear their allegiance to the constitution in the presence of the president. This section first describes the pre-1992 characteristics of the cabinet, and then touches on the major changes that have taken place in response to the upheavals of the 1990s.

The pre-1992 Italian cabinet was considerably larger than the British one; it included all the ministers in the government with the power to spend money and ministers without portfolio. Its size was attributable in large part to its representative function. Because Italy had a much more complex party system than France, Germany, or Great Britain, each party in the governing coalition had to receive adequate representation in the cabinet. In most cabinets, at least two parties were involved and had a right to their share of cabinet posts. Moreover, each Italian party had within its ranks highly organized factions that, too, demanded representation in the cabinet. A disgruntled intraparty faction was just as capable as a disaffected party of withdrawing its support from a coalition cabinet, thereby causing that cabinet to fall.

Also at that time, the prime minister did not really enjoy freedom of choice in selecting his cabinet. Before nominating members for appointment by the president, the prime minister had to consult the leaders of the various parties in his coalition, as well as some leaders of intraparty factions. Also, because he was more or less obligated to accept the recommendations of these party and factional leaders, his power of appointment was severely restricted. Moreover, the prime minister could not dismiss cabinet members (even if he could persuade them to resign, he would run the risk of alienating the parties or factions that had sponsored them).

Because each cabinet usually consisted of several parties and because even one-party cabinets were usually torn by interfactional strife, a cabinet could not and did not function as a united team. Its members, even when they belonged to the same party, regarded one another as political rivals. Consequently, they often failed to consult one another before initiating new legislation and frequently leaked to the press what took place in cabinet meetings. In addition to its heterogeneous partisan and factional character, the cabinet was split by some major functional cleavages. Most notably, financial and economic policy was divided among three separate ministries with overlapping functions: the Ministry of the Treasury, the Ministry of the Budget and Economic Planning, and the Ministry of Finance. The Ministry of the Treasury, primarily interested in a stable economy, usually prevailed over the expansion-minded Ministry of the Budget.

Unlike the French cabinet, the Italian cabinet had no residual or reserved powers to govern by decree in areas from which parliament had actually been excluded by the constitution. In this respect, the Italian cabinet was again in line with the classic parliamentary model in which legal sovereignty is vested in the parliament, as opposed to the French quasi-presidential system. The Italian cabinet could issue decrees under only two types of conditions. *Legislative decrees* could be enacted if parliament first passed an enabling act, with a time limit attached, that authorized the cabinet to legislate on specified subject matters in accordance with certain guidelines. *Decree laws* could be promulgated by the cabinet in an emergency, but they expired within sixty days of their publication unless converted into statutory law by parliament. In addition to these two types of decrees, the cabinet and individual ministries could issue administrative orders ("regulations") without prior authorization by parliament. These regulations were presumably more specialized in content and inferior in legal status to decrees.

Italian cabinets did not normally enjoy a long or peaceful existence. Their average lifespan was slightly less than a year, although some managed to survive for eighteen or even twenty-four months. The second Berlusconi government lasted a full five-year term with only slight, though important, changes in the ministers of foreign affairs, Treasury, and cultural affairs. Cabinets could be forced to resign in a variety of ways by either house of parliament. The legal procedure prescribed by the constitution stipulated that if 10 percent of the members of either of the two houses of parliament signed a motion of no confidence, and if a majority of those voting in that house supported the motion at least three days after it had been presented, then the cabinet had to resign. Numerous cabinets, however, resigned without waiting for this procedure to be employed. Some cabinets resigned after suffering a defeat on a government bill or after a party or faction announced that it no longer intended to support the cabinet. Even a hostile statement by a party secretary outside of parliament or an adverse resolution by a party congress or executive committee might precipitate a cabinet's resignation.

Yet what appeared on the surface to be extreme cabinet instability in Italy was accompanied by some features of continuity, until the massive changes that took place after 1992. From 1946 to 1992, with only two exceptions (Giovanni Spadolini of the Republican Party in 1981–1982 and Bettino Craxi of the Socialist Party in 1983–1987), all prime ministers were Christian Democrats. Some Christian Democratic leaders headed not one but several cabinets—more specifically, there were seven cabinets under Alcide De Gasperi, five under Aldo Moro, five under Mariano Rumor, and five under Amintore Fanfani. Some cabinet ministries—Interior and Treasury, for example—were continually or almost continually under the control of the same party from 1946 to 1992. And some ministers held the same position year after year, in successive cabinets. One, Emilio Colombo, was Treasury minister in no less than eleven cabinets. In 1992 this continuity was interrupted, and Christian Democratic hegemony became a thing of the past.

The fall of a cabinet usually produced not a complete turnover but a slight shift in the balance of power within the majority coalition. From 1946 to 1992 it was an unwritten rule of Italian parliamentary politics that Christian Democracy must form part of any majority coalition for the coalition to have enough votes to survive in parliament. The only two questions left open were which allies Christian Democracy would select and how cabinet positions were to be allocated among the various Christian Democratic factions and among the other parties in the cabinet. Otherwise, during this period relatively few general formulas were available for forming a cabinet. Those that were available included the tripartite formula, the center coalition, the center-right coalition, the center-left coalition, and a broader centrist coalition embracing five parties from the moderate left to the moderate right. When no decision could be reached among these formulas, an all–Christian Democratic caretaker cabinet would be set up for the purpose of buying time to reach an agreement on the establishment of one of the types of coalition cabinet.[4]

Two additional formulas were advocated in the 1970s, but they were never employed at the national level. The first was the *left alternative*—a Communist–Socialist–Social Democratic–Republican coalition cabinet that would seek the support of left-wing Christian Democrats. The Communist Party advocated this formula, but it was put into effect only at the regional and local levels, mainly in Italy's Red Belt area—that is, in the regions of Emilia-Romagna, Tuscany, and Umbria. The second formula was the *historic compromise*—a cabinet including Communists, Christian Democrats, Socialists, and all or almost all non-Fascist parties. This formula, which placed major emphasis on the Communist-Catholic alliance, was advocated by Communist Party leaders between 1976 and 1979, but was temporarily dropped by them in favor of the left alternative. It bore some resemblance to the tripartite formula of 1945–1947 and to the Grand Coalition that was tried out on occasion in Germany and Austria.

From 1993 through 2006, some interesting variations on past formulas were adopted:

- *A broadened center coalition with nonpolitical technocrats playing a major role.* The Ciampi cabinet in 1993–1994 was headed by a former central bank executive who was neither a member of parliament nor a politician.

- *A center-right coalition with a sharp tilt to the right:* the Berlusconi cabinet, appointed in 1994 and once again in 2001 and 2008.

- *An all-technocratic cabinet,* headed by a former central bank executive: the Dini cabinet of 1995.

- *A broader center-left coalition,* expanded to include the ex-Communists of the PDS or PD in leading roles: the Romano Prodi cabinet of 1996–1998.

- *A more inclusive center-left coalition,* headed by the PDS/Democrats of the Left (DS), but stretched to include a small, newly formed orthodox Communist Party (Armando Cossutta's Communist Party of Italy, or PCd'I) and a small center-right party of former Christian Democrats (Cossiga and Mastella's Democratic Union for the Republic, or UDR). This coalition made up the Massimo D'Alema cabinet, formed in October 1998, and the successor government headed by Giuliano Amato. It was repeated again in 2006 in the formation of the second Prodi cabinet.

Although before 1992 the cabinet was a loose-knit, motley body in which a great number of uncoordinated ministries often operated at cross-purposes, there was a growing trend in the 1970s and 1980s toward creation of a dominant position for the prime minister. Prime ministers were able to increase their influence by virtue of their ability to mediate differences among various power centers within and outside the cabinet and to give some measure of central direction to the government. They were able to assume this important role with the help of the Office of the Prime Minister, a staff agency that had grown remarkably since the 1950s and that by 1980 employed about eight hundred people. In the 1970s the Office of the Prime Minister acquired control over government spending, the expenditures of public corporations, supervision of relations with the regions, and some aspects of security and public order. The expansion of the prime minister's influence depended less on his formal powers than on his strategic location and his possession of a growing and skilled staff.[5]

In the years since 1992, the cabinet and the executive branch it controls have been further strengthened.[6] First, technocrats and ex–central bankers have played a dominant role in the economic ministries, and some have served as prime ministers. Several technocrats were in the reshuffled Amato cabinet of February 1993 and in the Ciampi cabinet of April 1993. In 1995 the Dini cabinet was again headed by a top official of the Bank of Italy and was composed entirely of technocrats. The Prodi cabinet of 1996–1998 was headed by a distinguished professor of economics, who had been at the helm of a giant public holding company (the Institute for Industrial Reconstruction, or IRI). It also included Ciampi as Treasury minister. In the D'Alema cabinet, appointed in October 1998, Ciampi was once again entrusted with the Treasury portfolio.

Second, the prime minister has more discretion in making appointments, particularly for the economic ministries. The party groups in parliament are still consulted, but they are no longer able to dominate the appointment process to the extent they did in the past. In fact, Prime Minister Ciampi did not bargain with the parties at all when he selected his cabinet.

Third, at times the executive has been given a free hand to deal with certain economic problems. The Amato cabinet was authorized to govern by decree in four policy areas considered to be the chief sources of budget deficits: health, pensions, public sector employment, and local government finance. Such delegations of authority were often justified by citing the need for Italy to conform to the economic and monetary guidelines laid down by the European Union (EU). In addition, the major reform of public finance has placed severe restrictions on parliament's power to modify the government's budgetary and financial proposals.

Fourth, some progress was made toward reducing the size of the cabinet and making it a less unwieldy body. Some ministries were actually abolished—some by law, some by referendum—despite the resistance of vested interests within the executive branch and in parliament.

Finally, both the Prodi cabinet (1996–1998) and the D'Alema cabinet (1998–2000) resolved the long-standing conflict between the expansion-minded Budget Ministry and the stability-biased Treasury Ministry by merging them into a single super ministry headed by the minister of the Treasury. In both cabinets, that minister was Ciampi, formerly director of the Bank of Italy. The hegemonic role of technocratic and banking interests in Italy and the concomitant dedication to economic stability were vividly symbolized in May 1999 by the election of Ciampi as president of the republic. In 2004, when Giulio Tremonti was ousted as minister of the Treasury because of his proclivity to make decisions without informing his cabinet colleagues, he was replaced by the administrative head of the ministry, Domenico Siniscalco, who served as a technocrat rather than a member of a particular party in the Berlusconi cabinet. In 2005 Siniscalco was ousted and replaced by Tremonti, because Siniscalco refused to turn a blind eye to a blatantly "electoral" budget that the cabinet insisted on passing in preparation for the 2006 parliamentary elections.

The Parliament

In its structure and mode of operation, the Italian parliament differs in some significant ways from most other Western European parliamentary bodies. First, it is truly bicameral. A bill must pass both houses—the Chamber of Deputies and the Senate—to become law. Moreover, the cabinet is equally responsible to both houses. This legal equality is reinforced by the fact that both houses are elected by popular vote. The main differences between the two elections are voting age and representation. The minimum voting age is eighteen for elections to the Chamber of Deputies and twenty-five for senatorial elections. At the end of 2005, the Berlusconi government did away with single-member districts for both the Chamber of Deputies and the Senate and replaced them with proportional representation (PR) list systems. For the Chamber of Deputies, the PR system operated at the national level in the distribution of seats; in the Senate the distribution of seats for the two coalitions was organized at the regional level. Because these differences are not very striking, the Senate can rightfully claim that it is hardly less representative than the Chamber of Deputies and is therefore entitled to equal legislative power.

Representing roughly similar electorates, the two houses do not differ sharply in their political makeup: the respective strength of the various parties is roughly the same in both chambers. Moreover, they tend to represent the Italian electorate at the same point in time. Although deputies originally served a five-year term and senators a six-year term, in practice the Senate was always dissolved simultaneously with the Chamber of Deputies. In 1963 the constitution was amended to establish a five-year term for both houses. Because of the similarity in the composition of the two houses, the Senate does not give special representation or protection to any specific minority interest (like the French Senate and the German Bundesrat). Bicameralism becomes little more than a device for delaying the passage of legislation.

A second, rather distinctive feature of the Italian parliament is the power possessed by its standing committees. They receive a bill just after first reading and may subject it to drastic changes before reporting it to the floor. The chair of a standing committee appears to be master of the committee's timetable and can expedite or slow down the progress of a bill without having to worry about pressure from the presiding officer (president) of the chamber. Most important, the committees have the power to pass certain bills. When the president of the chamber refers a bill to a standing committee, he or she decides whether the committee is to act *in sede referente* (report the bill back to the chamber with proposed amendments) or *in sede deliberante* (take final action on the bill—that is, pass it and send it on to the president of the republic or defeat it once and for all). Because most bills approved by the Italian parliament are enacted through the rather unique *in sede deliberante* procedure, the Italian standing committees literally act as miniature legislatures. Two limitations are placed on the use of *in sede deliberante*. First, certain kinds of important legislative proposals (constitutional amendments, electoral laws, delegations of legislative power, treaties, budgetary and spending bills) must be discussed on the floor after being considered in committee. Second, a bill being considered *in sede deliberante* must be brought to the floor of the chamber if so requested by the cabinet or by 10 percent of the members of the chamber or 20 percent of the members of the standing committee.

The Italian parliament has adopted several procedures that differentiate it from the parliaments of other Western European democracies. First, there is no effective limit on the number of private-member bills that can be introduced; the cabinet has far less control over the legislative agenda than is true in Great Britain and Germany. Second, there is no conference committee to iron out differences between Senate and Chamber of Deputies versions of a bill. Consequently, many bills shuttle between the two houses for years without ever achieving passage. Finally, there was until recently a requirement in the rules of the Chamber of Deputies that the final vote on a bill be taken by secret ballot. Such a procedure permitted recalcitrant Christian Democratic deputies ("snipers") to vote against measures supported by their party leadership. When a bill was defeated in a secret ballot, the cabinet could, however, ask for a formal vote of confidence, which required a roll call. Sniping was an embarrassing practice that lowered the prestige of cabinet members and occasionally impelled them to resign. The parliamentary secret ballot was recently weakened through the introduction of electronic voting, but it is still quite possible for parliamentarians to vote against their government or party without being detected.

In other respects, the Italian parliament resembles other Western European parliamentary systems (except that of France, which possesses both presidential and parliamentary features). It can pass any law that does not violate a provision of the constitution, and it can manage its own procedures and budget without being subject to external interference. Its powers are fairly conventional. It passes laws, delegates rule-making power to the cabinet, ratifies treaties, approves the budget, and conducts investigations. It meets in joint session to elect the president of Italy, to impeach the president for high treason or offenses against the constitution, and to elect one-third of the members of the Constitutional Court. It also may amend the constitution. An amendment must be approved twice by each chamber, and the two votes must be held at least three months apart. The first vote requires a simple majority of those voting. The second vote requires an absolute majority of each house. Unless at least two-thirds of the members of each house support the amendment on the second vote, it must be submitted to a popular referendum on the demand of one-third of the members of each house, or of 500,000 voters, or of five regional councils (legislatures).

The organization of the Italian parliament is also fairly orthodox. The two presiding officers, the president of the Senate and the president of the Chamber of Deputies, share control of the order of business with the Conference of Presidents (the heads of the various standing committees and parliamentary groups). The two officers have the power, subject to appeal, to assign bills to standing committees and to determine whether a bill should be passed in the committee itself *in sede deliberante* or reported to the floor *in sede referente*. They also appoint the members of select committees. Finally, the president of the Senate and then the president of the Chamber of Deputies are in line to succeed the president of the republic if the president were to die or become incapacitated in office. Unlike the Speaker of the British House of Commons, the presidents of the two chambers tend to be prominent partisans with ambitious plans for future advancement (to be president or prime minister). Yet, because of the loose power structure of the Italian parliament, the two presiding officers are quite limited in the power they can exercise.

In 1971 both houses of the Italian parliament adopted some major changes in their rules and procedures. One of the most ambitious of these changes gave formal recognition to the Conference of Presidents and assigned it the task of setting the legislative agenda, by unanimous agreement, for periods of from two to three months. The pious hope that long-term legislative planning by unanimous consent would somehow be possible has proved to be unjustified. What was supposed to be an organic plan for a long-term legislative program has turned out to be either an incoherent shopping list based on logrolling or a series of brief one- or two-week calendars for which unanimity is not required.[7]

In addition to a presiding officer who resembles the continental European model of an avowedly partisan Speaker and who has political clout and ambitions of his own, each house of the Italian parliament possesses another trait characteristic of a continental European parliamentary system: it is divided into parliamentary groups that are more or less cohesive and disciplined caucuses of the respective parties. These groups are responsible for assigning members to the standing committee positions that have been allocated to each group. They also advise the president of the chamber on the appointment of investigating committees and on filling vacancies on select committees.

The president of each parliamentary party group represents the group in the Conference of Presidents, which is supposed to reach agreement on the order of business for the chamber. The president of the republic also consults the parliamentary group leaders during a cabinet crisis or when a prime minister has resigned and a successor must be appointed. The parliamentary party group reaches binding decisions on how its members are to vote on pending legislation. But the parliamentary group can itself be subject to pressure from the party organization outside parliament. Some parliamentary groups have been more successful than others in maintaining a certain degree of autonomy against directives issued by extraparliamentary party organs. Yet overall, the party structure outside parliament has traditionally exercised more influence over legislative affairs in Italy than is true in either Great Britain or Germany.

That said, since 1992 party organizations outside parliament have lost much of their customary clout. Parties such as the Socialists and Christian Democrats first became weaker and more loosely organized, and then they literally disintegrated and others replaced them. New parties such as Forza Italia and the Northern League resemble U.S. parties in their emphasis on media-driven election campaigns and in their responsiveness to the political themes stressed by the party leader.

The executive domination of the parliament found in Great Britain and France has not really been present in the Italian parliamentary system. Rather, the multiparty, multifactional system that has prevailed in Italy has made the Italian parliament almost unmanageable, despite the existence of some degree of party cohesion (generally solid bloc voting by each parliamentary group) and party discipline (sanctions against individual legislators who stray from the party line). The power of dissolution has been rather ineffective, because elections rarely can be counted on to improve the government's mandate. What is the use of dissolving parliament when the percentage of the total vote polled by each party is subject only to relatively minor changes and proportional representation minimizes the impact of these changes? As a result, between 1948 and 1968 parliament was always allowed to serve out its full five-year term. After 1968, with the increasing volatility of the Italian electorate, elections were held at shorter intervals (four years, except in 1976–1979). The adoption in 1993 of a new election law providing for the election of most deputies and senators from single-member districts with election by plurality seemed to portend that the power of dissolution would be relied on more heavily in the future. And in fact, only two years after the election of 1992, parliament was again dissolved, and the process was repeated in 1996. Since 1996, however, the parliaments of 1996–2001 and 2001–2006 have been able to serve out their full terms despite the profound policy cleavages that separated the center-left coalition from the center-right coalition.

Some of the structural characteristics and procedures of the Italian parliament also have tended to protect it against executive dominance. These include the absence of any limit on private-member bills, the lack of tight cabinet control over the agenda, the power of standing committees to enact laws *in sede deliberante*, and the presence of a powerful popularly elected second chamber. And, lacking a secure majority, cabinets have come and gone. Parliament has been protected against dissolution by the party system and, until 1993, by the reluctance of governments to verify the level of popular support until forced to do so by the five-year electoral mandate.

One other basic characteristic of the pre-1992 Italian parliament also must be noted: its hybrid nature. On the one hand, it had relatively cohesive, disciplined parties acting through parliamentary groups in the tradition of European parliamentary systems. On the other, decision making was fragmented among the presidents of the two chambers, the standing committees and their chairs, and even private members, who played a far larger role in the Italian parliament than in other European legislative bodies. In these respects, the Italian parliament bore some vague resemblance to the U.S. Congress. This curious combination of "a fragmented but mostly stable and internally cohesive structure of parliamentary groups with parliamentary rules protecting individual and minority prerogatives" [8] made it difficult to neatly fit the Italian parliament into a category for classification purposes.

The post-1992 upheaval appears to have had a noticeable impact on parliament.[9] First, the executive managed to establish a more dominant position in relation to the parliament. The economic ministries, which are headed by or are highly responsive to technocrats, used their expertise and power of knowledge to issue and reissue executive decree laws. Meanwhile, the moral authority conferred on them by the general consensus that Italy should reduce its deficits to retain good standing in the Economic and Monetary Union (EMU) allowed these ministries to bypass many of the parliamentary barriers to policymaking. Parliament continues to service the demands of constituents, submit questions to the executive, and disseminate information. In fact, it performs these functions more vigorously than it did in the past. When it comes to general economic policy, however, the cabinet has increased its influence to a very marked degree.

A second and related point is that because a major party is no longer in permanent opposition in the Italian parliament, it is much easier to build a strong and reasonably coherent cabinet that enjoys a working majority. Before 1992, the Communist Party was barred by long-standing custom from entering the cabinet, as was the neo-Fascist Italian Social Movement (MSI). But these two parties at the extreme poles of the system controlled more than one-third of the seats in parliament. A cabinet could survive only with the support of over 50 percent of the members of parliament, which meant gaining the support of about three-fourths of the non-Communist, non-Fascist MPs. Currently, both the once Communist PDS/DS and the once Fascist National Alliance are regarded as within the mainstream. Over the long run, this situation has reduced the power of parliament to precipitate cabinet crises, and it has increased the frequency of elections. A defeat of the government in a vote of confidence in parliament produces a potentially "catastrophic" effect on the ruling coalition by possibly forcing it to resign and call new elections rather than taking the approach favored in the past when such crises were resolved through minor readjustments of cabinet posts within the ruling coalition.

The Bureaucracy

As of 2004, Italy had about 5.5 million state employees (Table 4-1). Of those, about 600,000 work in the national civil service. The rest are employed in regional, provincial, and local public administration jobs. According to Table 4-1, 22.5 percent of all employees (almost 24.5 million) are in the public sector, and this percentage has not changed much since 1990 (22.7 percent). The two decades between 1970 and 1990 witnessed the biggest increase in public employment, especially in the education, health services, and other public services sectors, because the Italian welfare state was being consolidated through, among other things, the move to full public education and the creation of the national health system. Not surprising, it was also the period during which annual deficits and the public debt rose exponentially.

The higher civil service (*carriera direttiva*) is staffed mostly on the basis of merit, although some patronage appointments and positions are filled without competitive examination by temporary appointees who eventually acquire permanent status. For those recruited by competitive examinations, either by direct entry from the universities or by promotion, the examinations tend to stress legal training rather than the broad social science background emphasized in France and Great Britain.

The recruitment system has resulted in the overrepresentation of the south in the higher civil service, because in the south, like other developing and economically backward areas, a higher percentage of the university population is attracted to the traditional professions (*professioni liberali*) such as law and medicine. Moreover, southerners are more apt to be attracted to the secure if rather humdrum careers provided by the bureaucracy; young people from economically stagnant regions more often than others lack the contacts and know-how to embark on a business career. Many southern recruits are apt to be of lower-middle-class origin, in sharp contrast to the upper-middle-class graduates of the Ecole

Table 4-1 Public Employment in Italy, 1970–2004 (thousands)

	1970	1980	1990	2000	2004
Public administration	1,129.80	1,299.80	1,484.10	1,389.60	1,341.00
Schools	817.4	1,390.30	1,670.80	1,603.40	1,655.40
Health and other social services	794.7	989.5	1,182.30	1,344.00	1,404.00
Other public services	538.4	517.1	793.3	1,002.60	1,110.20
Total public employment	3,280.30	4,196.70	5,130.50	5,339.70	5,510.60
Total employment	19,931.40	21,372.80	22,609.50	23,128.40	24,496.00
Public employment/ employment (percent)	16.5	19.6	22.7	23.1	22.5

Source: Istituto Nazionale di Statistica (ISTAT), Rome.

nationale d'administration (ENA) recruited into the French higher civil service. Italian higher civil servants therefore have been drawn disproportionately from the most under-developed, tradition-bound regions of Italy. This bureaucracy, which also receives a brief period of in-service training, tends to be cautious and negative in its attitude toward policy innovations.

Although exceptions to this tradition have increased, particularly since 1992 (the greater number of technocrats in political offices and European management require-ments have brought economists and other social scientists into higher ministerial posi-tions), there has been no thoroughgoing, coherent effort to reform the bureaucracy. Unlike public finance, which is under the control of the powerful Treasury Ministry, bureaucratic reform falls under the aegis of the minister of public administration, who is, in effect, a minister without portfolio dependent on the commitment and support of the prime min-ister, and prime ministers have not usually given this problem top priority. Rather, they have bowed to pressures to reform public finance to conform to EU expectations; there have been no such external pressures for broader bureaucratic reform.[10]

Two powerful innovations, however, have spurred the introduction over time of other changes into Italy's public administration. The first is the sustained devolution of policy—economic development, social concerns, health, urban and regional planning, tourism, and transport—since the 1970s from the national to the regional and local levels. The second major, and more recent, innovation is the Europeanization process, whereby policy sectors, such as monetary and market regulation policies as well as fiscal, foreign, defense, and justice policies, have been moved from the national to the European level as part of the consolidation of European integration. These two forms of policy transfers (upward and downward) have shifted the emphasis in the modus operandi of national bureaucrats from law and formal procedures to the policy-specific expertise and negotiation tech-niques needed to advance national priorities in the formulation of European policies, while maintaining a coordination function for the regions. Under such conditions, it has been easier to introduce a supplementary compensatory system based on merit and responsi-bilities assumed by the administrative elite at both the national and subnational levels.

Public Corporations and Semi-Independent Agencies

Another major source of policymaking in Italy has been the so-called parastate sector: public corporations and the semi-independent agencies that presided, until the late 1990s, over the Italian public sector and a variety of regulatory and welfare functions. These orga-nizations included holding companies such as the Institute for Industrial Reconstruction (IRI), the National Hydrocarbons Corporation (ENI), and the Corporation for Stock-holding and Financing of the Manufacturing Industry (EFIM), each of which supervised subsidiary companies that held controlling stock in a broad assortment of enterprises ranging from steel mills to oil refineries to motels. The parastate sector also included ENEL, the public corporation that runs the electric power industry (it was nationalized in 1962 and partially privatized through a series of public offerings of its stock under the Amato and Berlusconi governments). EFIM and GEPI (Management of State Industrial Enterprises), two financial agencies set up to help businesses in distress, were instead dis-solved during the 1990s, and the companies that remained viable from a market perspec-tive were sold off to Italian or foreign investors. Some social welfare and social insurance funds and a hodgepodge of miscellaneous agencies and companies were also part of the heterogeneous parastate sector, providing pensions or health care.

State control over the public sector has been uncoordinated and therefore ineffective. In the mid-1950s, both IRI and ENI were placed under the Ministry of State Share Holdings, but this cabinet department was unable to check the expansionist policies pursued by these giant holding companies and their subsidiaries. (In a referendum held in April 1993, 90.1 percent of voters elected to abolish this ministry.) More recently, the Ministry of the Economy (former Ministry of the Treasury) became the de jure holder of the stock of public corporations such as Telecom Italia, the national telephone company that was privatized in 1998, and the major stockholder in the country's major banks—the Bank of Rome, Bank of Naples, Bank of Sicily, and National Labor Bank—which were privatized during the same period. The other parastate agencies, ENEL and ENI, have been privatized, and the Italian government has reduced its holding of stock from a majority to a minority position. Alitalia Airlines, another major company that was part of IRI, was privatized in 2008; Tirrenia, a shipping company still under public control, is expected to be privatized by the end of 2010. The government therefore has mainly resorted to the privatization of state industrial and financial holdings to reduce the overall national debt. Under the center-left governments in place between 1996 and 2001, the level of debt was reduced from 119 percent of GDP to 106 percent. Under the center-right government of Silvio Berlusconi, the privatization of state assets slowed down, and the debt level has remained the same or increased.

In the 1950s and early 1960s, the public corporations, headed by adventurous entrepreneurs such as Enrico Mattei of ENI, were widely believed to be a major constructive force in Italy's economic recovery. By the 1970s, however, it had become all too evident that the public enterprises had contracted some serious economic maladies and developed some deplorable managerial and fiscal habits. Employing about 25 percent of the Italian labor force and producing about 25 percent of Italy's GDP, the Italian public sector became a serious drain on the country's economy.

Until the Ciampi government took office in mid-1993, little real progress had been made in selling off state assets. Some privatization had occurred, but it "represented little more than tinkering at the edges when taken in relation to the overall state holdings."[11] Lack of confidence in the government's willingness or ability to pay off the debts of public sector companies generally made private investors (especially foreign banks) somewhat reluctant to acquire state holdings when they were placed on the market. The technocratic Ciampi cabinet did, however, begin the process, and between mid-1993 and mid-1994 the Italian government sold off about $6 billion in state holdings.[12]

As minister for economic affairs (responsible for both the Treasury and the Budget Ministries) in the Prodi cabinet, Ciampi made additional progress on the privatization front. In 1997 he gave notice to the newly appointed director of IRI that the mammoth public holding company had to sell off its holdings within three years. He also moved toward privatizing the telephone industry and continued his efforts to hasten the sale of ENI's assets. Although all of these projects faced active and passive resistance from the trade unions, some top-ranking bureaucrats, the ex-Fascists, and the Party of Communist Refoundation, the need to reduce the country's overall deficit provided the political basis for the sale of government assets. Privatization also took place at the regional and local levels, where subnational governments were facing larger cuts in state transfers. In response to the reduction of state resources, regional and local governments had to increase local taxes to finance waste disposal, water, and energy services for their residents. They also turned to the private credit market to sell municipal and regional bonds to finance investment projects. But the attempt to liberalize or open to competition local services proved to be more difficult than expected. In 2007 Luigi Bersani, the minister for the economy in the Prodi government, tried to introduce greater choice in the delivery of local services, but his plan got bogged down in the internal squabbles within the government, and by 2008 it had completely come to a halt.[13]

The Judiciary

Like France and Germany, Italy has a legal system in the civil law tradition, which stems originally from Roman law. Judges are supposed to simply apply the law as stated in the relevant provisions of the legal code, not to analyze the facts of the case and explore the applicability of past judicial decisions, which is the practice in the British and American common law systems. Law, then, is not determined primarily by an accumulation of judicial opinions, but is found in statutes, executive decrees, legal codes, and the accepted interpretations of legal scholars. In short, the concept of judge-made law is foreign to the civil law tradition. The judge's function may appear to be somewhat mechanical, with little room for judicial discretion. Yet there are inevitable departures in any civil law country from this model of the civil law tradition. Since 1956 the Constitutional Court at the highest level of the system has been quite active in providing interpretations of the constitution and resolving conflict between different levels of government. Moreover, since 1958 the rulings of the European Court of Justice have had a significant impact on Constitutional Court rulings. The supreme example of this impact was the Costa v. ENEL case, which was referred through the Italian court system to the European level. The judges ruled that Italy's post-1958 legislation was subject to the provisions set out in the Rome Treaty. Therefore, national legislation (in this specific case the nationalization of the electrical industry) was subject to the provisions of that treaty. In essence, the ruling established the supremacy of European law (treaty provisions and regulations) vis-à-vis national law.

The Italian judicial system has some features in common with that of France. For one thing, there are two parallel judicial hierarchies: five tiers of ordinary law courts, culminating in the Court of Cassation, and a system of administrative courts in which the appeal process culminates in the Council of State and Court of Accounts. In addition, as in France, judges are recruited for a judicial career after graduation from law school, and they work their way up the judicial ladder in a series of promotions and transfers.

There are also some significant differences between the two systems. First, Italian judges on the lowest rung of the hierarchy receive much lower salaries than their French and German counterparts. Second, nothing in Italy corresponds to the National Center of Judicial Studies in France, which provides modern training for future magistrates; Italian judges enter the judicial corps with only the formalistic legal training they received in the universities. Third, promotion in Italy is less dependent on executive fiat than it is in France. It is generally agreed that the French executive branch has come to dominate the promotion process, but in Italy the Superior Council of the Judiciary has effective control over appointments, transfers, and promotions. From its inception, this council has been dominated by senior judges of the higher courts, who have tended to be somewhat conservative but who have been criticized by the center-right government as being too liberal. Italian judicial independence therefore has been threatened less by executive encroachment than by the financial penury that younger judges have had to endure and the domination senior judges of the higher courts have exercised over the promotion process. Reform measures in the 1960s and early 1970s eroded the hegemony of the senior judges by making promotion based on seniority virtually automatic and providing for guaranteed salary increases at periodic intervals. In the 1970s and 1980s, judicial power and prestige were greatly expanded as a result of the judiciary's role in the struggle against terrorism and organized crime.[14]

The administrative court system deviates from the French model to a still greater degree than the ordinary judicial system. There are two separate hierarchies of administrative courts, one headed by the Court of Accounts and the other by the Council of State. Italian administrative courts are less prestigious and self-assertive than their French counterparts, because at the lower levels they are staffed by civil servants rather than by full-time judges. Unlike the French administrative courts, which can hear suits by private citizens for damages against the state and suits challenging the legality of executive decrees, Italian administrative courts can consider only the question of legality. Damage suits must be introduced in the ordinary law courts. Finally, the Italian Council of State has been more cautious in challenging the executive than has the French Council of State, although recently it has taken a more independent course.

Despite the personal and political ties that many Italian judges have developed with the world of partisan and factional politics, the Italian judicial system enjoys a high degree of independence from executive control. This independence also applies to public prosecutors, who are considered part of the judiciary and are therefore responsible to the Superior Council of the Judiciary rather than to the Ministry of Justice. This de jure independence enabled a portion of the judiciary, especially in the Milan region, to initiate a series of investigations—"Operation Clean Hands"—of political corruption in 1992. The investigations, followed by a wave of prosecutions, were to some degree influenced and encouraged by some unprecedented events: heavy Christian Democratic losses and Northern League gains in the parliamentary elections of 1992 and in municipal and provincial elections and the rapidly declining electoral strength of the main political parties. At first, southern judges and prosecutors, more closely connected to the political parties than their Milanese counterparts, took a cautious stand, but the mushrooming of the corruption crisis resulted in a general weakening of the bonds between judges and politicians.[15]

The post-1992 investigations and prosecutions involving the network of bribery and corruption widely known as "Kickback City" resulted in the arrest of many national and local politicians, as well as business owners, industrial managers, and high-ranking bureaucrats. Thousands more were investigated. Prosecutors such as Antonio Di Pietro in Milan became national heroes in the eyes of large segments of the Italian public. Even those who came to power in 1994 were not immune from judicial scrutiny. The brother of Prime Minister Berlusconi, leader of the Forza Italia party, had to face trial on corruption charges, as did some senior executives of his Fininvest financial empire. Berlusconi himself has been the object of a series of trials related to his media empire, Mediaset, and some of his top collaborators—for example, Marcello Dell'Utri and Cesare Previti—engaged in the corruption of judges and tax evasion and had ties to the Mafia. Berlusconi was eventually indicted and convicted for bribery and fraud, but his control of the top political office in the country slowed down and sometimes stopped the three-stage appeals process that must be completed before a person is incarcerated. The leader of the Northern League, Umberto Bossi, also came under investigation for his involvement in the illegal financing of political parties and threats to judges investigating his party.

Such ongoing investigations highlight some of the less-appealing features of the Italian judicial system. Preventive detention may be used to subject a suspect to lengthy imprisonment while awaiting trial. Moreover, because of the unpleasant conditions prevailing in Italian prisons, the prospect of indefinite preventive detention may be employed to coerce a suspect into collaborating with the authorities. These possible abuses were cited by Prime Minister Berlusconi in July 1994, when his government issued a decree suspending the powers of the judiciary to order the preventive detention of corruption suspects. The decree aroused a major political uproar, however, spurring not only threats of resignation by several well-known public prosecutors and protests by the leaders of the opposition parties, but also vocal objections by Berlusconi's coalition partners, the Northern League and the National Alliance. As a result, the decree was rescinded.[16]

In one important respect, the Italian judicial system bears a strong resemblance to Germany's in that it has a Constitutional Court with powers of judicial review. Established by the constitution, this court was not actually set up by parliamentary law until 1956 because of the decade-long foot dragging of Christian Democracy, which saw the court as a threat to majority (that is, Christian Democratic) rule.

The Constitutional Court has fifteen members—five selected by the president of Italy, five elected by a three-fifths vote of a joint session of parliament, and five elected by judges of the highest Italian courts (the Court of Cassation, the Council of State, and the Court of Accounts). Members of the Constitutional Court serve a twelve-year term, which is not immediately renewable. The court has the power to determine the constitutionality of national and regional laws. Any case may be brought before the court on the appeal of an individual, a group, or a region. One serious obstacle to utilization of the appellate procedure is that the judge of the lower court from which an appeal to the Constitutional Court is being sought may block the appeal by issuing an interlocutory judgment to the effect that the appeal is patently unfounded. Because many Italian judges (especially in the Court of Cassation) resented the establishment of the Constitutional Court as a departure from the traditions of the Italian legal system and could not accept the concept of judicial review, such interlocutory judgments were not uncommon during the first years of the court's existence.

The Constitutional Court has had a major impact on the Italian political system. Among other things, it has struck down numerous provisions of the penal code adopted during the Fascist regime. In 1961, for example, it declared unconstitutional an old law that forbade any person to move from one locality to another without the guarantee of a job in the new locality. Various laws restricting freedom of expression have been invalidated. In controversies over divorce and abortion, the court has strengthened the cause of secularism. In 1970 it decided that a pending divorce bill would not require an amendment of the constitution, even though Article 7 of the constitution incorporated the Concordat of 1929, in which Italy agreed to make its rules on marriage and divorce conform to those of the Roman Catholic Church. Also in 1970 the court declared the Italian law forbidding adultery to be unconstitutionally discriminatory against women. In 1971 a law prohibiting the publication of birth control information and the sale of contraceptives was struck down. In 1975 the court declared unconstitutional some provisions of an antiabortion law of long standing.

Despite these rulings, many restrictions on civil liberties are still on the books, although the Constitutional Court has gone a long way toward extending individual freedom, while avoiding any major clash with the executive branch. In 2004 the Constitutional Court struck down the law passed by the second Berlusconi government suspending judicial proceedings against the country's top political leaders (prime minister, president of the republic, members of the Constitutional Court, and the presidents of the two chambers). Despite attacks by the center-right government, the courts have been successful in maintaining themselves free of encroachment by the executive.

Subnational Governments

The three main tiers of governmental authority below the national level are the regions, the provinces, and the communes. The regions—five "special regions" and fifteen "ordinary regions"—correspond in size to the twenty-two French regions and the fifteen German *Länder*. The 103 provinces are comparable to French *départements*. And the 8,078 communes are counterparts of the French communes, although they are far less numerous and fragmented than the French.

Before 1970 the French and Italian patterns of local government shared strong similarities. Both had elected local and departmental/provincial councils that, in turn, elected executive committees or juntas from their ranks. Both also had systems of appointed central officials—prefects—who were named by the minister of interior to supervise the departments/provinces and communes. The prefect for each department/province had the power to annul the decisions of the departmental/provincial or communal councils and to suspend local officials who were derelict in their duties. At the communal level, the executive committee or junta was headed by a mayor who supervised the executive organs of the commune and negotiated both with central government agencies and with the prefect.

The main difference between the two systems lay in the role of the prefect. The French prefect also acted as coordinator and supervisor of central government field agencies, whereas the Italian prefect was confined to controlling local government. Moreover, unlike the French prefect, the Italian prefect had to share this power of control with central government field services. In short, France had an integrated prefectoral system, and the Italian prefectoral system was unintegrated.[17]

With the ratification of the constitution of the Italian republic in 1947, Italy adopted a system that was neither unitary nor federal but possessed some quasi-federal features. Under a form of regional devolution, the Italian regions were granted extensive concurrent powers to share with the national government. As in a federal system, the powers of the regional governments are specified in the Italian constitution and may be formally repealed only by constitutional amendment, although the Constitutional Court may restrict or dilute those powers by judicial interpretation. Moreover, the regions were specifically named in the constitution, thereby protecting them against any ordinary parliamentary statute or executive decree reorganizing the boundaries and powers of subnational governments.

The Italian system of regional devolution contained, however, some definitely nonfederal restrictions on regional autonomy. First, the regions cannot exercise their concurrent powers until central government organs have issued the necessary enabling statutes and decrees. Second, the regions, which have received no original taxing power of their own, must depend on central legislation to authorize those taxes they were permitted to impose. Third, an appointed central government commissioner in each region has a suspensive veto over bills passed by the regional councils (legislatures). Finally, a bill passed once again by a regional council after such a veto can be blocked either by the Constitutional Court (which can rule on a bill's constitutionality before it goes into effect) or by the Italian parliament (which could declare that a bill was contrary to the national interest). Not only is national law supreme over regional law, but also regional law must give way to the national interest as defined by parliament.

Before 1970 the regional autonomy provided by the 1948 constitution remained largely a dead letter. Five "special regions" had been created because they contained special ethnic minorities or displayed marked separatist tendencies. These regions comprised three ethnic border zones—French-speaking Valle d'Aosta, partly German-speaking Trentino-Alto Adige, and partly Slovenian Friuli-Venezia Giulia—and the two big islands of Sicily and Sardinia. The powers granted to these five special regions broke with the general pattern just described. Sicily received the power of taxation and control over local government; Sardinia, Valle d'Aosta, and Trentino-Alto Adige received significant additional financial resources from the central government; and Friuli-Venezia Giulia was given substantial autonomy in policymaking and administration after the 1976 earthquake.

The other fifteen regions—the "ordinary regions"—remained regions only on paper, because no enabling legislation was passed until 1966 and 1970. Once again, just as it was for the Constitutional Court, the fault lay with the dominant Christian Democracy, which did not want to establish any institutional checks on majority rule even though the party was the major proponent of regionalization during the constitutional debate in 1947. By the late 1960s the situation was ripe for change. The centrist coalition cabinets of the 1950s gave way to a series of center-left cabinets that included the Italian Socialist Party, and the Socialists wanted to see the regions established at long last. Support for the regions was also strong among some of the more progressive factions of Christian Democracy, and the Communist Party was favorably inclined, because it expected to control several regional governments. Moreover, after the strikes and demonstrations of the "hot autumn" of 1969 it seemed advisable to deflect some popular grievances to the lower levels of government. Accordingly, enabling legislation was passed, and in 1970 the "ordinary regions" elected regional councils.

Nevertheless, the position of the regions remained quite precarious. The regional councils were up and running, and the regional juntas were assuming their executive duties, but few decision-making powers had been transferred to the regions. Not until 1975, when the left and particularly the Communists made remarkable gains in the second set of regional elections, was parliament motivated to authorize real progress toward regional devolution. A 1975 law directed the government to complete the transfer to the regions of all powers assigned to them by the constitution. In 1977 a set of decrees was issued carrying out many (but by no means all) of the transfers envisioned by the 1975 law and turning over to the regions approximately 25 percent of the national budget. With Law No. 382 (1975) and D.P.R. 616 (1977), the regions were finally in business.[18]

Since 1978 the regions have been engaged in an ongoing contest with the central government to defend and, if possible, extend the powers they have been granted, to obtain an adequate share of national revenues, to protect their policy turf against encroachment by the central government, and to clarify their role in relation to that of the central and local authorities. The regions believed their status left much to be desired.[19] The second Amato government in 2000–2001 undertook a significant devolution of power to the regions, and the transfer of power was ratified by a national referendum in 2001. First, the regions were empowered with exclusive responsibility for a whole series of "low politics" policy issues that extended from agriculture to transportation and from social policy to development policy issues. Second, regions were given co-policymaking roles in the budgetary process, which required extensive cooperation between the regions and the executive branch of government through the state-regional and the state-regional-city government commissions. Third, the central government still decides what revenues will be assigned to finance the national health system, but the regions and the government must agree on the size of the allocation. Fourth, the central government must coordinate with the regions the transposition of EU directives into national legislative provisions, because some of these directives involve both regional and national responsibilities. Fifth, the Constitutional Court has been empowered to rule on conflicts between the regions and national legislation. In recent years, the court has generally ruled on behalf of the regions in cases involving the encroachment of national legislation on regional powers. Finally, the national government has been forced to consult with the regions on initiatives taken at the European level in policy fields in which the regions have primary responsibility. As a result, the regions have been incorporated into the Office of the National Representative in Brussels and participate in meetings of the Council of Permanent Representatives.

The center-right government proposed strengthening the role of the regions in national policymaking even further by devolving to the regions exclusive responsibility in education, law enforcement, and health. But no provision was made to devolve to the regions greater responsibilities in generating their own resources through greater taxing powers. Critics have maintained that the center-right proposals threatened the viability of a national educational and health system because of the lower tax revenues collected by the southern regions. The reaction to the center-right's devolution proposal helped to fuel the across-the-board losses by the governing coalition in the 2005 regional and local elections, especially in southern Italy. In December 2005 the center-right government succeeded in passing the regional reform, but before it could come into force it had to be supported by a majority vote in the June 2006 referendum. In February 2006 the referendum on regional reform presented by fifteen regional councils was accepted by the Court of Cassation, and the referendum was scheduled for June 25–26, 2006. The voters overwhelmingly rejected the proposed constitutional reform: 52.3 percent of the electorate turned out to cast ballots, and 61.3 percent voted against the proposed change.

Still, the advances made in the regionalization of policymaking and implementation since the 1970s have served to change significantly the structure of the Italian state and its policymaking. In 2009 the Berlusconi government passed a constitutional amendment to introduce a system of *fiscal federalism* with the objective of allowing the regions to maintain a larger portion of taxes generated locally. The details of the proposal were not spelled out, however, and the time period foreseen for the implementation of the provision was five years.

Because the constitution gave provinces and cities an administrative role rather than a political role, the situation surrounding the local governments has been less problematic than it could have been. Despite the repeated introduction of abortive bills and numerous debates, it was not until the early 1990s that the Italian parliament finally got around to passing new legislation redefining the structure and powers of local governments and their relationship to the regions and the central government.

Yet even before the passage of Laws No. 142 (1990) and No. 81 (1992), some trends were discernible. The prefects were stripped of most of their supervisory powers over local governments, especially those involving prior surveillance of local government decisions. That function was now performed by a regional administrative tribunal, a majority of whose members were elected by the regional council. A second development was the delegation of certain powers to the local governments by both the national government and the regions.

Once passed, Laws No. 142 and 81 brought about significant changes,[20] and others are expected to occur. Law No. 142 granted statutory autonomy to the provinces and communes, permitting them to set up their own administrative structures and procedures instead of conforming to a national model imposed from above; stripped the regional administrative tribunals of most of their powers to exercise external controls over local decisions; strengthened the executive role of the junta and confined the functions of the elected council to legislative and oversight duties; introduced the German constructive vote of no confidence to make it impossible for a council to overthrow an executive junta and mayor, unless it simultaneously designates their successors; and charged the regional governments with the task of creating metropolitan authorities for nine of the largest cities in Italy.

Law No. 81 was even more far-reaching: it provided for the direct election by popular vote of the mayor and the president of the provincial junta (both had been elected by their respective councils) and replaced proportional representation with majority voting for the election of communal and provincial councils. Also, members of the executive were to be appointed directly by the mayor and were to be responsible to him or her, not to the separately elected communal council.

The years since 1993 have provided evidence of how these reforms have affected local and regional government. A new class of strong mayors with personal mandates from the electorate has emerged from the reform of local elections, and these mayors have been free to appoint nonpolitical experts to important executive posts in local government. Meanwhile, the stifling influence of the party machines over local and provincial administration has been greatly weakened. Moreover, the financial autonomy of local governments has been augmented by the creation of a local authority property tax with rates set by local governments.

The reforms at the local and regional levels have led to the emergence of regional presidents and city mayors who have benefited from a greater level of visibility and political importance. At the same time, the subnational executives have had to assume responsibility in choosing their cabinet members and ensuring that their governments respond to citizen demands. The mayors of major cities such as Milan, Rome, Naples, Bologna, Florence, Catania, Palermo, and Bari and the presidents of large regions (Campania, Emilia-Romagna, Latium, Lombardy, and Piedmont) are now treated by the media as important political leaders, and they certainly cannot be ignored by national politicians. Cooperation rather than unilateral dictation has become a strict necessity for the implementation of national policies at the subnational level.

NOTES

1. Valle d'Aosta is treated differently because of its size—it has a population of about 120,000—and because it has a French-speaking majority.
2. He was a member of the Constituent Assembly that set up the parliamentary system and then went out of existence once the constitution was ratified in 1947 and the first parliamentary elections were held in 1948. During its existence, this assembly provided a vote of confidence for the governments, but it could not legislate.
3. See David Hine and Emanuela Poli, "The Scalfaro Presidency in 1996: The Difficult Return to Normality," in *Italian Politics: The Center-Left in Power,* ed. Roberto D'Alimonte and David Nelken (Boulder: Westview Press, 1997), chap. 9.
4. On Italian cabinet formulas since 1946, see Alberto Marradi, "Italy: From 'Centrism' to Crisis of the Center-Left Coalitions," in *Government Coalitions in Western Democracies,* ed. Eric C. Browne and John Dreijmanis (New York: Longman, 1982), chap. 2, esp. 48–56; and Carol Mershon, "The Costs of Coalition: Coalition Theories and Italian Governments," *American Political Science Review* (September 1996): 534–554.
5. See Sabino Cassese, "Is There a Government in Italy? Politics and Administration at the Top," in *Presidents and Prime Ministers,* ed. Richard Rose and Ezra N. Suleiman (Washington, D.C.: American Enterprise Institute, 1980), 171–202.
6. See Vincent della Sala, "Hollowing Out and Hardening the State: European Integration and the Italian Economy," in *Crisis and Transition in Italian Politics,* ed. Martin Bull and Martin Rhodes (London: Frank Cass, 1997), 26, 30; Gianfranco Pasquino, "No Longer a 'Party State'? Institutions, Power and the Problem of Italian Reform," in Bull and Rhodes, *Crisis and Transition,* 48; Giacinto della Cananea, "The Reform of Finance and Administration in Italy: Contrasting Achievements," in Bull and Rhodes, *Crisis and Transition,* 196–202.
7. See Giuseppe Di Palma, "The Available State: Problems of Reform," in *Italy in Transition: Conflict and Consensus,* ed. Peter Lange and Sidney Tarrow (London: Frank Cass, 1980), 162–163; and Giacinto della Cananea, "Reforming the State: The Policy of Administrative Reform in Italy under the Ciampi Government," *West European Politics* (April 1996): 321–339.
8. Giuseppe Di Palma, *Surviving without Governing: The Italian Parties in Parliament* (Berkeley: University of California Press, 1977), 190.
9. See della Sala, "Hollowing Out and Hardening the State," 28, 30. Also see Vincent della Sala, "Italy: A Bridge Too Far?" *Parliamentary Affairs* 50 (July 1997): 398–406; and Luca Verzichelli, "The Majoritarian System, Act II: Parliament and Parliamentarians in 1996," in D'Alimonte and Nelken, *Italian Politics: The Center-Left in Power,* chap. 8.
10. See della Cananea, "Reform of Finance and Administration in Italy," 199–208.
11. See Peter Curwen, "Privatization, the Italian State and the State of Italy," *International Review of Administrative Sciences* 59 (1993): 469.

12. See Michael Brush, "Saving Italy's Economy," *Europe: Magazine of the European Union* 337 (June 1994): 11. Also see Fabrizio Galimberti and Luca Paolazzi, *Il volo del calabrone: Breve storia dell'economia Italian nel Novecento* (Forence: Lemonnier, 1998). For his own definition of the privatization model, see Romano Prodi, "Modello strategico per le privatizzazioni," *Il Mulino* 5 (1992): 851–862.

13. Andrea Boitani, "Liberalization Interrupted," in *Italian Politics: Frustrated Aspirations for Change,* ed. Mark Donovan and Paolo Onofri (Oxford: Berghahn Books, 2008), 157–178.

14. See Carlo Guarnieri, "The Judiciary in the Italian Political Crisis," in *Crisis and Transition in Italian Politics,* ed. Martin Bull and Martin Rhodes (London: Frank Cass, 1997), 159–164; Maria DeFranciscis and Rosella Zannini, "Judicial Policy-Making in Italy: The Constitutional Court," *West European Politics* 15, no. 3 (1993): 68–80; and Mary L. Volcansek, "Political Power and Judicial Review in Italy," *Comparative Political Studies* 26, no. 4 (1994): 492–511.

15. See Carlo Guarnieri, "The Italian Judiciary and the Crisis of the Political System," *Italian Journal* 7 (1993): 20–22; and Francesco Sidoti, "The Italian Political Class," *Government and Opposition* 28 (Summer 1993): 344–348.

16. See Patrick McCarthy, *The Crisis of the Italian State* (Basingstoke, UK: Macmillan, 1995), 188–191.

17. See Robert C. Fried, *The Italian Prefects: A Study in Administrative Politics* (New Haven: Yale University Press, 1963), 116–118, 249–295, 303–308.

18. Robert Leonardi, Raffaella Y. Nanetti, and Robert D. Putnam, "Devolution as a Political Process: The Case of Italy," *Publius* 11 (Winter 1981): 95–117; and *La pianta e le radici: l'Istituzionalizzazione delle regioni nel sistema politico italino* (Bologna: Il Mulino, 1985).

19. See "Editoriale," *Le Reqioni* 11 (January-April 1983): 1–4.

20. For the main highlights of the legislation reforming local government in Italy, see Marco Cammelli, "Eletto dal popolo: Il sindaco fra ruolo nuovo e vecchi poteri," *Il Mulino* 348 (July-August 1993): 1775–1784; and R. E. Spence, "Institutional Reform in Italy: The Case of Local Government," *Local Government Studies* 19 (Summer 1993): 226–241. For the impact and outcome of that legislation, see Bruno Dente, "Sub-National Governments in the Long Italian Transition," in Bull and Rhodes, *Crisis and Transition,* 176–193; and James Newell, "At the Start of a Journey: Steps on the Road to Decentralization," in *Italian Politics: Mapping the Future,* ed. Luciano Bardi and Martin Rhodes (Boulder: Westview Press, 1998), 149–167.

Who Has the Power?

IN THE ITALIAN POLITICAL SYSTEM, AS IN OTHERS, THE POWER RESIDES in political institutions. But who within these institutions makes the real decisions? In the past, the correct answer would have been, first, the political parties and, second, labor unions, professional organizations, cooperatives, banks, and interest groups such as Confindustria, a business lobby. But since 1992 other actors have joined the club, especially the individual leaders of the two contending coalitions. In Italy, as in other countries, political contests have become more personalized, and once in office the leaders of the winning coalition are in a position to exercise a considerable amount of personal power. Three of the four last parliamentary elections (1996, 2001, and 2006) were fought largely as a duel between the two personalities who have dominated Italian politics during the last decade, Silvio Berlusconi and Romano Prodi. The fourth in 2008 witnessed the clash between Berlusconi and the new leader of the Democratic Party (PD), Walter Veltroni. The nature of these two duels has highlighted the role of voters in the Italian political process. In the last analysis, it is the voters who have the final say on who wields power in their name and to achieve which objectives. This chapter looks at the changing nature of popular choices and the parties and interest groups that operate within the Italian political system.

Political Parties

Since 1992 the Italian party system has undergone a sweeping realignment. From 1946 to 1990, however, the party system appeared to be relatively stable, with few shifts in party identity, party strength, and voting behavior. A brief survey of some of the principal features of the traditional pre-1992 party system will help to put contemporary changes in perspective.

The Pre-1992 Italian Party System

The Italian multiparty system has been more complex than that of France or Germany.[1] In 1992 no fewer than nine national parties (parties that presented lists of candidates in all or most constituencies) were represented in the Italian parliament:

1. Democrats of the Left (DS)—a party known until 1991 as the Italian Communist Party (which was the strongest communist party in Western Europe) and later as the Democratic Party of the Left (PDS). The DS is usually referred to as the ex- (or post-) Communist Party.

2. Party of Communist Refoundation (PRC)—a party of orthodox Communists who objected to the moderate course and symbolic change of label adopted by the PDS in 1991.

3. Green Party—a party that tends to emphasize environmental and civil rights issues.

4. Italian Socialist Party (PSI)—a party once allied with the Communists, but after 1963 closer to the Christian Democrats.

5. Italian Social Democratic Party (PSDI)—a party even more cautious and moderate than its socialist cousin.

6. Italian Republican Party (PRI)—a party moderately left of center and very prestigious, despite its small size and voting strength.

7. Christian Democracy (DC)—a party that had played a dominant and usually hegemonic role in Italian politics since 1946.

8. Italian Liberal Party (PLI)—a party that was moderately conservative at the center-right.

9. Italian Social Movement (MSI)—a neo-Fascist party that was something of an outcast among the national political parties.

In addition to these national parties, various regional, ethnic, or splinter parties were represented in parliament: the newly powerful Northern League; the Venetian League; the South Tyrolese People's Party, a German-speaking party in Bolzano Province; the Valle d'Aosta List; the Network, representing an anti-Mafia movement in Sicily; the Pannella List, an assortment of former Radicals concerned with postmaterialist lifestyle issues; and the Party of Pensioners.

One set of characteristic features of the post–World War II Italian party system was the relative strength of the parties in the system. The dominant party—Christian Democracy—had headed every Italian cabinet between 1946 and 1981. The second-ranking party—the Communist Party (now the DS)—was the strongest communist party in Western Europe (and is now its strongest former communist party). The Italian Socialist Party had been split since 1947, with the exception of a brief interval from 1966 to 1969, so that Italian socialism was weaker than in most other Western European countries. Nowhere else in Western Europe except in France was there a neo-Fascist movement whose strength even remotely approached that of the Italian Social Movement. The MSI underwent a schism in 1972, but since then it has functioned as the main electoral home of far-right voters.

Of those scholars and others writing about Italy's party system, some, such as Giovanni Sartori, stressed the polarization of the system, which included powerful extremist parties (the Communists and the neo-Fascists) at its left and right poles.[2] Others referred to its remarkable stability.[3] Parties experienced only minor gains or suffered only minor losses in general elections, and voters rarely shifted far along the political spectrum, moving, perhaps, from extreme left to moderate left or from center to center-right. This stability was attributed in part to the high degree of party identification, in part to the existence of strong one-party regions such as the Catholic Veneto or Communist Emilia-Romagna, and in part to the remarkably large turnout that reduced the number of undecided voters to be mobilized. Finally, some authors pointed out that two of the parties in Italy's multiparty system tended to corner the lion's share of the vote.[4] Between them, the Communists and the Christian Democrats polled above 60 percent in every election from 1953 through 1987, reaching a high point of 73.1 percent in 1976 before their numbers began to ebb (see Table 4-2).[5] (The outcomes for party representation in the Chamber of Deputies are shown in Table 4-3.[6]) This situation led to the conclusion that Italy had an "imperfect two party system," with one of the two major parties permanently in the cabinet and the other permanently in the opposition.[7] The events of 1983–1992 cast considerable doubt on this thesis, however. The combined vote of the Communists and Christian Democrats dropped to 62.8 percent in 1983, 60.9 percent in 1987, and a startling 51.4 percent (counting the votes of both the PDS and Communist Refoundation) in 1992 (Table 4-2).

Another view of the Italian political system stressed the overall stability of the parties, but also the significant depolarization in the system of values, attitudes, and policy positions experienced by both the electorate and the party leaders.[8] The level of depolarization became evident as the old party structure collapsed and new parties emerged. Under the post-1992 party system, the ideological conflicts and differences that had characterized leftist versus rightist or government versus opposition parties quickly evaporated, revealing the substantial overlap in programs and policies shared by political elites after 1994.

Italian parties also possessed some organizational traits that endowed them with a distinctive character. They were highly centralized, and the central party organization did not hesitate to intervene in nominations at the local level. They also were cohesive: members of the party in parliament generally voted together as a solid bloc, with some deviations. And they were relatively disciplined: legislators who failed to follow the instructions of their party leaders and whips might be courting severe disciplinary sanctions, not excluding expulsion from the parliamentary party group. As for the party outside of parliament, it played an important role in its relationship with the parliamentary party. Many cabinet crises originated outside parliament by means of decisions reached by party secretaries or party directorates (executive committees). Yet the overlap between the parliamentary and extraparliamentary party organizations was extensive. The secretaries and members of party directorates were frequently themselves also members of parliament.

Perhaps the most interesting property of Italian political parties was the presence within their ranks of highly organized competing factions. These intraparty groupings reflected more than mere tendencies or currents of opinion. They had, in many cases, a well-defined organizational structure, press, and research organs to formulate and disseminate their views, their own sources of financing independent of the party organization, and their own leadership hierarchy. Factions vied with one another for control over the party organization and over patronage appointments, and they demanded appropriate representation when cabinets and regional and local juntas were being formed.[9] On numerous occasions, the formation of a cabinet or a regional or municipal junta was held up while negotiations proceeded to determine which Christian Democratic or Socialist factions were to be assigned which executive posts.

The Elections of 1992–2006

The 1990s proved to be a decade characterized by radical change and significant turmoil in the Italian political system. Between 1992 and 1994 traditional parties, such as the Christian Democrats, Socialists, and the communist parties, disappeared, and new parties

Table 4-2 Percentages of Total Vote Polled by Italian Parties in Elections for the Chamber of Deputies, 1948–2008

	1948	1953	1958	1963	1968	1972	1976	1979	1983	1987	1992	1994	1996	2001	2006	2008
PDUP	—	—	—	—	4.5	1.9	1.5	2.3	1.5	1.7	—	—	—	—	—	—
PRC	—	—	—	—	—	—	—	—	—	—	5.6	6.1	8.6	5.0	5.6	—
PCd'l	—	—	—	—	—	—	—	—	—	—	—	—	—	—	2.3	—
Rainbow Left	—	—	—	—	—	—	—	—	—	—	—	—	—	—	—	3.1
Radicals	—	—	—	—	—	—	1.1	3.5	2.2	2.6	—	—	—	—	2.6[i]	—
Greens	—	—	—	—	—	—	—	—	—	2.5	2.8	2.7	2.5	2.2	2.1	—
Di Pietro	—	—	—	—	—	—	—	—	—	—	—	—	—	—	2.3	4.4
PCI/PDS[a]	—	22.6	22.7	25.3	26.9	27.1	34.4	30.4	29.9	26.6	16.1	20.4	21.1	16.6	31.3[j]	—
PD	—	—	—	—	—	—	—	—	—	—	—	—	—	—	—	33.2
PSI/PSU[b]	31.0	12.7	14.2	13.8	14.5	9.6	9.6	9.8	11.4	14.3	13.6	2.2	—	—	—	—
PSDI	7.1	4.5	4.5	6.1	—	5.1	3.4	3.8	4.1	3.0	2.7	—	—	—	—	—
PRI	2.5	1.6	1.4	1.4	2.0	2.8	3.1	3.0	5.1	3.7	4.4	—	—	—	—	—
Prodi List[c]	—	—	—	—	—	—	—	—	—	—	—	—	6.8	—	—	—
Dini List[d]	—	—	—	—	—	—	—	—	—	—	—	—	4.3	—	—	—
DC/PPI/Marg.[e]	48.5	40.1	42.3	38.3	39.1	38.7	38.7	38.3	32.9	34.3	29.7	15.7	—	14.5	—	—
CCD/CDU[f]/UDC	—	—	—	—	—	—	—	—	—	—	—	—	—	3.2	6.8	5.6
UDEUR	—	—	—	—	—	—	—	—	—	—	—	—	—	—	1.4	—
MPA	—	—	—	—	—	—	—	—	—	—	—	—	—	—	—	1.1
PLI	3.8	3.0	3.5	7.0	5.8	3.9	1.3	1.9	2.9	2.1	2.8	—	—	—	—	—
LN	—	—	—	—	—	—	—	—	—	—	8.7	8.4	10.1	3.9	4.6	8.3
FI	—	—	—	—	—	—	—	—	—	—	—	21.0	20.6	29.4	23.7	—
PdL	—	—	—	—	—	—	—	—	—	—	—	—	—	—	—	37.4
PNM	2.8	6.8	4.8	1.7	1.3	—	—	—	—	—	—	—	—	—	—	—
MSI/DN/AN[g]	2.0	5.9	4.8	5.1	4.5	8.7	6.1	5.3	6.8	5.9	5.4	13.5	15.7	12.0	12.3	—

	1948	1953	1958	1963	1968	1972	1976	1979	1983	1987	1992	1994	1996	2001	2006	2008
Right	—	—	—	—	—	—	—	—	—	—	—	—	—	—	—	2.4
New PSI SI														0.9	0.7	1.0
Other[h]	2.3	2.9	1.7	1.3	1.4	2.1	0.7	1.7	3.2	3.3	8.2	14.7	4.5	6.7	3.2	3.5

Sources: 1948–2001 elections: Francesco Malgeri, ed., *Storia della Democrazia Cristiana,* vol. 5 (Rome: Edizioni Cinque Lune, 1989), 451–458; and issues of *Italian Politics,* 1994, 1996, 2001; 2006 elections: *La Repubblica,* April 10–12, 2006.

Note: "—" = no data. An empty cell indicates not applicable. PDUP = Democratic Party of Proletarian Unity; PRC = Party of Communist Refoundation; PCd'I = Communist Party of Italy; PCI/PDS = Italian Communist Party/Democratic Party of the Left; PSI/PSU = Italian Socialist Party/United Socialist Party; PSDI = Italian Social Democratic Party; PRI = Italian Republican Party; DC/PPI/Marg. = Christian Democracy/Italian Popular Party/Margherita List; CCD/CDU = Christian Democratic Center/United Christian Democrats; UDEUR = Union of the Democratic European Reformers; PLI = Italian Liberal Party; LN = Northern League; FI = Forza Italia (Go Italy); PNM = National Monarchist Party; MSI/DN/AN = Italian Social Movement/National Right/National Alliance.

[a] In 1948 the Communists and Socialists formed a single electoral bloc, the People's Democratic Front (FDP). The experiment was not repeated. In 1992 the Italian Communist Party (PCI) changed its name to the Democratic Party of the Left (PDS). An orthodox minority seceded to form the Party of Communist Refoundation (PRC).

[b] In 1968 the Socialists and Social Democrats ran as a unified party, the United Socialist Party (PSU). The party split in 1969.

[c] In the 1996 election, the Prodi List consisted of the Italian Popular Party (see note f), the South Tyrolese People's Party, the Republican Party, and the Democratic Union.

[d] The Dini List of candidates, which was headed by caretaker prime minister Lamberto Dini, sought support during the 1996 campaign from various moderate members of various right-wing parties. Also known as the Italian Renewal Party.

[e] In 2001 the Margherita List included the former PPI and the Prodi and Dini Lists.

[f] In 1994 the Christian Democracy (DC) disintegrated. It was replaced by two Christian Democratic parties: the Italian Popular Party (PPI) in the center and the much weaker Christian Democratic Center on the right. In the 1996 election, the PPI campaigned as part of the Prodi List of candidates.

[g] In December 1976, the Italian Social Movement (MSI) split, with about half of its deputies joining a new right-wing party, the National Right (DN). The DN failed to gain any representation in 1971. Between 1992 and 1994, Gianfranco Fini formed a broader National Alliance (AN). The AN included most of the old MSI (which was later dissolved as a party) and other right-wing factions. It claimed to have put the Fascist experience behind it and to be a mainstream conservative alternative, committed to the preservation of democracy, but it is actually neo-Fascist.

[h] The CCD formed part of Berlusconi's Forza Italia electoral slate in both the 1994 and 1996 elections. In 2006 "other" included 1.2 percent for the center-left—the South Tyrolese People's Party (SVP) plus other parties. In the center-right, it accounted for 1.6 percent of the vote. Only 0.4 percent of "other" represented parties not affiliated with either bloc. The breakdown for the twelve overseas constituencies is not included in this calculation of percentage votes for the parties.

[i] In 2006 the Rose in the Fist list included Radical and Italian Socialist voters.

[j] In 2006 the Democrats of the Left (DS) and the Margherita List ran together under the Ulivo (Olive Tree) list.

Table 4-3 Seats Won by Various Italian Parties in Elections for the Chamber of Deputies, 1948–2008

	1948	1953	1958	1963	1968	1972	1976	1979	1983	1987	1992	1994	1996	2001[a]	2006	2008
PDUP	—	—	—	—	23	0	6	6	7	8	—	—	—	—	—	—
PRC	—	—	—	—	—	—	—	—	—	—	35	39	35	11	41	—
PCd'l	—	—	—	—	—	—	—	—	—	—	—	—	—	10	16	—
Rainbow Left	—	—	—	—	—	—	—	—	—	—	—	—	—	—	—	0
Radicals	—	—	—	—	—	—	4	18	11	13	—	—	—	—	18[e]	—
Greens	—	—	—	—	—	—	—	—	—	13	16	—	16[c]	7	15	—
PCI/PDS/DS	131	143	140	166	177	179	227	201	198	177	107	174[b]	171[c]	136	220[f]	—
PD	—	—	—	—	—	—	—	—	—	—	—	—	—	—	—	217
PSI/PSU	52	75	84	87	91	61	57	62	73	94	92	—	—	—	—	—
SD	—	—	—	—	—	—	—	—	—	—	—	—	—	9	—	—
Di Pietro	—	—	—	—	—	—	—	—	—	—	—	—	—	—	16	29
New PSI	—	—	—	—	—	—	—	—	—	—	—	—	—	6	—	—
DC-PSI	—	—	—	—	—	—	—	—	—	—	—	—	—	—	4	—
PSDI	33	19	22	33	—	29	15	20	23	17	16	—	—	—	—	—
PRI	10	5	6	6	9	15	14	16	29	21	27	—	—	—	—	—
DC/PPI/Marg.	306	263	273	260	266	266	263	262	225	234	206	46	71	77	—	—
Dini List	—	—	—	—	—	—	—	—	—	—	—	—	26	—	—	—
CCD/UDC	—	—	—	—	—	—	—	—	—	—	—	33	30	30	39	36
UDEUR	—	—	—	—	—	—	—	—	—	—	—	—	—	8	10	—
MPA	—	—	—	—	—	—	—	—	—	—	—	—	—	—	—	8
PLI	15	13	17	39	31	20	5	9	16	11	17	—	—	—	—	—
LN	—	—	—	—	—	—	—	—	—	1	55	117	59	30	26	60
FI	—	—	—	—	—	—	—	—	—	—	—	107	123[d]	176	137	—
PdL	—	—	—	—	—	—	—	—	—	—	—	—	—	—	—	276
PNM	13	40	25	8	6	—	—	—	—	—	—	—	—	—	—	—
MSI/DN/AN	6	29	24	27	24	56	35	30	42	35	34	109	93	99	71	—
Right	—	—	—	—	—	—	—	—	—	—	—	—	—	—	—	0
Other	8	3	5	4	3	4	4	6	6	6	25	5	6	9	5	4
Total	574	590	596	630	630	630	630	630	630	630	630	630	630	617	630[g]	630

Sources: 1948–2001 elections: Francesco Malgeri, ed., Storia della Democrazia Cristiana, vol. 5 (Rome: Edizioni Cinque Lune, 1989), 452–458; and issues of Italian Politics, 1994, 1996, 2001; 2006 election: La Repubblica, April 10–12, 2006.

Note: "—" = no data. An empty cell indicates not applicable. PDUP = Democratic Party of Proletarian Unity; PRC = Party of Communist Refoundation; PCd'l = Communist Party of Italy; PCI/PDS/DS = Italian Communist Party/Democratic Party of the Left/Democrats of the Left; PSI/PSU = Italian Socialist Party/United Socialist Party; SD = Democratic Socialists; New PSI = party created by Gianni DeMichelis and Bobo Craxi for the 2001 election. In 2006 Bobo Craxi joined the Prodi coalition and DeMichelis joined up with a new DC to form the DC-PSI list; PSDI = Italian Social Democratic Party; PRI = Italian Republican Party; DC/PPI/Marg. = Christian Democracy/Italian Popular Party/Margherita List; CCD/UDC = Christian Democratic Center/Union of Christian Democrats; UDEUR = Union of the Democratic European Reformers; PLI = Italian Liberal Party; LN = Northern League; FI = Forza Italia (Go Italy); PNM = National Monarchist Party; MSI/DN/AN = Italian Social Movement/National Right/National Alliance. The Dini List is also known as the Italian Renewal Party.

a In 2001 thirteen seats were not attributed, because election officials could not decide whether they were votes for the government majority or the opposition.

b In 1994 the entire leftist bloc—that is, Progressive Bloc—included the PDS, Greens, and Socialists.

c The Olive Tree Alliance, made of the Democratic Party of the Left, the Greens, the Italian Popular Party/Prodi List, and the Dini List, polled 284 seats.

d The Freedom Pole Alliance, composed of Forza Italia, the Christian Democratic Center, and the National Alliance, polled 246 seats.

e In 2006 the Rose in the Fist list included Radical and Italian Socialist voters.

f In 2006 the Democrats of the Left and the Margherita List ran under the Ulivo (Olive Tree) list.

g In 2006 twelve deputies were elected from the four overseas constituencies: seven for the center-left, four for the center-right, and one independent.

appeared. What was even more striking was the substantial change in political elites and their replacement, in many cases, by a new brand of politicians who had not come up through the party ranks. A new link was therefore established between the voters and politicians and organized groups in civil society.

The Election of 1992   With the Italian parliamentary elections of 1992, some of the traditional features of the Italian party system seemed to be undergoing major and perhaps permanent alterations. For one thing, Christian Democracy appeared to be in serious danger of losing its hegemony over the Italian party system. It had already lost considerable ground in 1983 and 1987, but the 1992 election results were disastrous for the DC. With 29.7 percent of the total vote, it plumbed new depths of electoral failure, 3.2 percentage points below its 1983 all-time low (see Table 4-2).

The PDS (formerly the Italian Communist Party, or PCI) was still the second-ranking party on the Italian political scene. But the hitherto consistent forward progress of Italian communism had been halted as early as 1979, when the PCI captured only 30.4 percent of the vote as compared with its 1976 high-water mark of 34.4 percent (Table 4-2). This backsliding continued in the 1983 elections and, more sharply, in 1987, when the Communist Party received only 26.6 percent of the vote, its weakest showing since 1968. This was the "second most serious defeat in its history [as of that time]." [10] But the worst was yet to come.

In 1991, in response to an initiative launched by PCI secretary Achille Occhetto to dissociate the Italian left from the collapse of communism in Eastern Europe, the PCI split into the Democratic Party of the Left and the Party of Communist Refoundation. The Democratic Party of the Left, led by Occhetto and representing the bulk of the former Italian Communist Party, was committed to a moderate leftist posture. The Communist Refoundation was a party of diehards rebelling against the triumph of reformist tendencies in Italian communism. In the 1992 election, the Democratic Party of the Left received 16.1 percent of the vote, and the Communist Refoundation mustered only 5.6 percent. The combined total of 21.7 percent was 4.9 percentage points below the already deplorable 1987 mark of 26.6 percent and was the worst showing since 1946.

The socialist movement was still divided between Socialists (PSI) and the slightly more centrist-oriented Social Democrats (PSDI). Both parties were somewhat on the weak side, especially the PSDI, and their combined vote since 1968 had always oscillated between 12 percent and 18 percent of the total votes cast. In the 1987 election, after four years of relative stability under the commanding leadership of Socialist prime minister Bettino Craxi, the Italian electorate rewarded the PSI with 14.3 percent of the total vote—its highest percentage as an independent and distinctive party since 1946 (Table 4-2). In 1992, however, the PSI dropped back to 13.6 percent, undergoing its first loss of votes in relation to the previous election in twenty years. As for the PSDI, it steadily lost ground after 1983, receiving 3.0 percent in 1987 and 2.7 percent in 1992.

The other two minor center parties—the Republicans (PRI) and the Liberals (PLI)—chalked up very modest electoral achievements, with their combined vote since 1968 ranging from 4.4 percent to 8.0 percent of the votes cast (Table 4-2). In 1992 they again registered modest gains: the PRI rose to 4.4 percent and the PLI rose to 2.8 percent. As for the neo-Fascists of the Italian Social Movement, they had been in a state of decline since 1983, and despite the presence of Benito Mussolini's granddaughter on their ticket, in 1992 they polled only 5.4 percent of the total vote. The MSI, along with the centrist PRI and PLI, appeared to be facing a very unpromising electoral future.

After the 1992 election, Italy's "imperfect two-party system" seemed to be in critical condition. As noted, the combined Christian Democracy, Democratic Party of the Left, and Communist Refoundation vote dropped to 51.4 percent of the total vote (Table 4-2). By contrast, if the Socialist (PSI) vote is added to that of the three minor center parties (PSDI, PRI, and PLI), the bloc of secular democratic parties or the "lay bloc" won 23.5 percent of the vote in 1992. The "imperfect two-party system" was showing signs of unraveling, while the lay bloc seemed to be emerging as a powerful third force in Italian politics, reaching its highest levels in twenty years. It also appeared that the 8.7 percent of the vote garnered by the regionalist Northern League (dominated by the Lombard League) and the 5.6 percent captured by Communist Refoundation had been won at the expense of the Christian Democracy and the Democratic Party of the Left, not the lay bloc. Yet the apparent renaissance of the lay bloc was to prove a short-lived phenomenon.

The emergence of the Northern League, with 8.7 percent of the vote, as a major protagonist on the Italian political scene was one of the more striking outcomes of the 1992 election. With its clearly expressed antisouthern, anti-immigrant biases and with its demands that a federal Italy be created and that major functions and a significant share of national revenues be shifted from the central government to the regions, the Northern League represented a new and possibly centrifugal force in Italian politics. Like the split in Italian communism, the Northern League's appearance made it clear that the Italian party system of 1946–1991 was a thing of the past.

The 1992 election also called into question the stability so often ascribed to the Italian party system. Both of the factors that had contributed to this stability in the past—strong party identification and high voter turnout—seemed to be declining. In 1979 voter turnout dipped below 90 percent for the first time and never regained that level. Moreover, greater numbers of voters were casting blank and invalid ballots. Italian voting traditions seemed to be eroding under the impact of the social and cultural changes. One result was the remarkable downward dip in the Christian Democratic vote.

The Christian Democratic decline was foreshadowed in 1981 by the break in the Christian Democratic grip on the office of prime minister. In that year, the Republican leader, Giovanni Spadolini, became prime minister. Various factors facilitated Spadolini's takeover: a referendum vote to retain the relatively liberal abortion law, Christian Democratic implication in a scandal involving the political influence of a secret Masonic lodge, Christian Democratic losses in local elections that year, and Socialist demands that the office of prime minister be given to a Socialist or at least to a leading member of one of the center-left parties. Spadolini emerged as the compromise candidate, because the Christian Democrats were not yet ready to let the Socialist leader, Craxi, become prime minister. The visibility and credibility bestowed on the Republican Party by Spadolini's sixteen-month tenure as prime minister probably helped to explain Republican gains and Christian Democratic losses in 1983. Craxi's four-year span as prime minister (1983–1987) further weakened the Christian Democratic image as the perennial ruling party.

The Election of 1994 Between April 1992 and March 1994 the Italian party system underwent a series of massive transformations that altered the political map of Italy, decimated
the ranks of Italy's political elites, and brought a new cohort of political leaders to power.
The precipitating factor was the public's revulsion at the revelation that large segments
of the Italian governing class had accepted kickbacks from business firms in exchange for
government contracts and licenses or had cultivated and maintained illicit connections
with the Mafia and other criminal organizations. As a result of these scandals and the
ensuing prosecutions, many Christian Democratic and Socialist political leaders at the
national, regional, and local levels, including two former prime ministers, Socialist Bettino
Craxi and Christian Democrat Giulio Andreotti, came under criminal investigation. The
disgrace befalling the PSI and the DC led to the virtual disintegration of these parties
and the formation of successor rump parties under new leadership. Although fragments
of the PSI and DC did survive and soldier on, the Social Democrats, Republicans, and
Liberals virtually disappeared.[11]

The parties of the left, led by the Democratic Party of the Left, had hoped to win the
general election of March 27–28, 1994. After all, they had won against a divided right in a
majority of the mayoral elections held in November 1993, and they had not been implicated to a great extent in the kickback scandals that had overwhelmed the governing parties. Only four months later, however, the left alliance confronted a newly formed right
alliance, led by the charismatic media magnate Silvio Berlusconi, and a new center alliance
as well.

In the 1994 election, the Progressive Alliance, formed by the parties of the left, suffered
a clear-cut defeat. This alliance, designed to maximize the leftist probabilities of carrying
single-member districts by the necessary plurality, was made up of the Democratic Party
of the Left; the Communist Refoundation; the Greens; the moribund rump of the Italian
Socialist Party (which was disbanded shortly after the election); the anti-Mafia Network
Party, headed by Leoluca Orlando, mayor of Palermo; the Democratic Alliance, composed
mostly of former supporters of the minor center parties; the Christian Socialists; and one
or two additional splinter movements. The alliance received only 34.4 percent of the total
proportional representation vote.[12] Of this total, the PDS contributed 20.4 percent (compared with 16.1 percent in 1992); the Communist Refoundation 6.1 percent (5.6 percent
in 1992); the Greens 2.7 percent (2.8 percent in 1992); the Network 1.9 percent (no
change since 1992); the Democratic Alliance (which had not existed in 1992) 1.2 percent;
and the hapless Socialists, who had received 13.6 percent of the vote in 1992, a meager 2.2
percent (see Table 4-2).[13] The decline of the left as a whole from more than 40 percent
of the vote in 1992 to 34.4 percent of the vote in 1994 may be attributed almost entirely
to the collapse of the scandal-ridden Italian Socialist Party, some of whose supporters
migrated to the Democratic Party of the Left and others to Berlusconi's Forza Italia or to
the Northern League. In general, the Italian left suffered a severe defeat, but, within the
left, the PDS recovered from its debacle of 1992.

The four center parties—the PSDI, the PRI, the PLI, and the DC—had totaled 39.6
percent of the vote in 1992, but in 1994 they suffered a defeat of staggering proportions:
they went down to 15.7 percent of the vote. The minor center parties (the PSDI, PRI,
and PLI) simply disappeared, obliterated by the scandals and by the 4 percent threshold

imposed by the new election law as a precondition for receiving seats under proportional representation. The DC was replaced by two Christian Democratic parties: the Italian Popular Party in the center and the Christian Democratic Center (which formed part of Berlusconi's Forza Italia slates) on the right.

The centrist alliance in 1994, the Pact for Italy, was composed of two parties: the just-mentioned Popular Party and the Segni Pact headed by Mario Segni, a former Christian Democrat. Segni had led several successful referendum campaigns for electoral reform since 1991, including a drive to change and simplify the system of preferential voting and a movement to virtually eliminate the system of proportional representation in Senate elections. In 1994 the South Tyrolese People's Party received only 11.1 percent of the vote, and the Segni Pact, which contained former supporters of the minor center parties and some former Christian Democrats, received the other 4.6 percent for the total of 15.7 percent that went to the Catholic centrist bloc. Of the three major political alliances in Italy, the centrist alliance was the weakest.

The winner of the 1994 election was the rightist bloc, called the Freedom Pole in the north (where Forza Italia was allied with the Northern League) and the Pole of Good Government in the south (where Forza Italia was allied with the National Alliance). This curious binomial bloc consisted of three major political forces and two minor parties. The first major political force was Silvio Berlusconi's Forza Italia, a new center-right mass movement revolving around the charismatic business leader. Its electoral lists included candidates of a minor center-right Christian Democratic grouping called the Christian Democratic Center and of a centrist splinter movement called the Center Union. The second was Umberto Bossi's Northern League, particularly powerful in Lombardy. And the third was a self-styled post-Fascist party, the National Alliance, led by Gianfranco Fini, formerly the leader of the neo-Fascist Italian Social Movement. The Pole of Liberty and the Pole of Good Government amassed the largest number of votes: 42.9 percent of the total. Twenty-one percent of the electorate voted for the Forza Italia list (including about 3.5 percent for the Christian Democratic Center); 8.4 percent (compared with 8.7 percent in 1992) voted for Bossi's Northern League; and 13.5 percent (compared with only 5.4 percent in 1992) voted for Fini's National Alliance (see Table 4-2). The Northern League had barely held its own since 1992, but the National Alliance had more than doubled the strength of the neo-Fascist Italian Social Movement, and Forza Italia had carved out spectacular gains at the expense of the discredited old parties of the center and moderate right.

This election produced some striking results. First, the Pole of Liberty and the Pole of Good Government won a clear majority in the Chamber of Deputies (366 of 630 seats) and a near majority in the Senate (156 of 315 seats). Berlusconi was therefore able to form a cabinet composed of members from Forza Italia (nine), the Northern League (six), the National Alliance (six), the Center Union (two), and the Christian Democratic Center (one), plus three independents. Second, the complexion of parliament had changed remarkably since 1992. Of the nine national parties listed at the beginning of this chapter, the DC had vanished and was partially replaced by two weak successor parties; the PSI had been reduced to a mere fragment; the three minor center parties were no more; and the MSI had expanded into a watered-down post-Fascist movement whose leader preached moderation. On the right, the Northern League had become a major national actor rather than a regional protest movement, and Forza Italia had emerged as a new and possibly dominant protagonist on the national scene. Third, the composition of Italy's governing elite had undergone a bewildering metamorphosis. Of the 945 members elected to the two chambers of parliament, 645 were new—only 300 had prior service in parliament.[14] And most of the big political names that had dominated the headlines for so many years— Giulio Andreotti, Arnaldo Forlani, and Antonio Gava for the DC, Bettino Craxi and Gianni De Michelis for the PSI—vanished from the front pages and from parliament.

The results of the 1994 election were inconclusive and somewhat deceptive for two reasons. The first is that the election was conducted under a complex electoral system devised by the outgoing lame-duck parliament in 1993. The second and more compelling reason is that the center-right coalition that assumed power in the spring of 1994 proved to be fatally split by conflicting policies and personalities. In December 1994, under a hail of criticism, much of it coming from his coalition partners of the Northern League, Berlusconi felt compelled to resign as prime minister.

The Election of 1996 On April 21, 1996, after Berlusconi's 1994 victory had been dissipated by dissension among members of his center-right coalition and after Prime Minister Lamberto Dini's cabinet of technocrats had outlived its legitimacy and could no longer deal with a deadlocked parliament, new elections were called by President Oscar Luigi Scalfaro, even though parliament's term still had three years to run. Because no agreement could be reached on a new election law, the complex election law used in 1994 was retained. Impeded by the bewildering electoral alliances spawned by this law, the media were unable to report promptly on the exact distribution of seats in parliament.[15]

In the election, the Olive Tree coalition received a plurality of the vote (43.3 percent) and a bare majority of the seats in the Chamber of Deputies (319 of 630) and in the Senate. But one party in this alliance, the Communist Refoundation, which polled 8.6 percent of the vote and won thirty-five seats in the chamber, indicated that it would support Olive Tree initiatives only on a case-by-case basis and that its loyalty to the alliance would depend on the policies the alliance chose to adopt. The leading party in the alliance, the ex-communist Democratic Party of the Left, polled 21.1 percent of the vote, a gain of 0.7 percentag points since 1994, and the Communist Refoundation picked up 2.5 percentage points over its 1994 showing (Table 4-2). In terms of seats, the PDS far outnumbered the PRC: 172 seats to 35 (Table 4-3).

The other three parties in the Olive Tree coalition were the Greens, who won twenty-one seats with 2.5 percent of the vote compared with 2.7 percent in 1994; the Prodi List, led by the alliance's candidate for prime minister, Romano Prodi; and the Italian Renewal Party, led by the outgoing prime minister and former top official of the Bank of Italy, Lamberto Dini. Neither the Prodi List nor the Italian Renewal Party was on the ballot in 1994 (Tables 4-2 and 4-3). In 1996 the Italian Renewal Party received 4.3 percent of the total vote and twenty-four seats. The Prodi List, which received the support of the Popular Party of former Christian Democrats, the South Tyrolese People's Party, and the Republican Party, plus that of some even smaller splinter groupings, received 6.8 percent of the vote, compared with 11.1 percent polled by the Popular Party in 1994 (part of that vote had obviously been captured by Italian Renewal). Virtually all the seats won by the Prodi List went to the Popular Party, which picked up sixty-seven seats, while "Other" received five. Together, the Prodi List and Italian Renewal polled 11.1 percent of the vote, compared with the 15.7 percent received by the centrist alliance (Pact for Italy, composed of the Popular Party and the Segni Pact) in 1994.

The centrist alliance of 1994 had simply converged with the leftist Progressive Alliance of 1994 to form a center-left bloc, the Olive Tree coalition. The Olive Tree voting totals of 43.3 percent were actually less than the combined total polled by the leftist and centrist alliances, running separately in 1994 (50.1 percent).

Why, then, did the Olive Tree coalition win an electoral victory over the center-right? It won because the center-right alliance (the Freedom Pole) had lost one of its most electorally powerful members, the Northern League. The Northern League ran as an isolated list in 1996 and received 10.1 percent of the vote and fifty-nine seats, compared with 8.4 percent of the vote and 122 seats in 1994 (see Tables 4-2 and 4-3). As for the Freedom Pole, it racked up very respectable totals of 42.1 percent (42.9 percent in 1994). Of these voting percentages, 20.6 percent was accounted for by Forza Italia (21 percent in 1994), 15.7 percent by the ex-Fascist National Alliance (13.5 percent in 1994), and 5.8 percent by the Christian Democratic Center/United Christian Democrats (3.5 percent in 1994). Of the 246 seats won by the Freedom Pole, 123 went to Forza Italia, 93 to the National Alliance, and 30 to the CCD/CDU—a respectable showing. But the split with the federalist Northern League cost the Freedom Pole what would otherwise have been a popular majority and a probable majority in parliament.

In the Chamber of Deputies, with its total membership of 630, the 319 seats won by the Olive Tree coalition constituted a slender majority. But the orthodox communists of the Communist Refoundation had declared their independence. Subtracting their thirty-five seats would leave the Olive Tree coalition with only 284 seats, short of a majority. The Olive Tree coalition would therefore have to court the support of the Communist Refoundation or the Northern League (fifty-nine seats) to muster a majority on controversial legislation. But as noted earlier, the Olive Tree itself was a rather loose-jointed alliance of leftist and centrist parties, and its future cohesion was in doubt.

The Election of 2001 The Olive Tree coalition was indeed fragile, but it did manage to remain in office for the duration of its five-year term. Romano Prodi served as the first of the three Olive Tree prime ministers. He resigned in October 1998 after Communist Refoundation deputies rejected his government's austerity budget, and in March 1999 he was chosen president of the European Commission. His successor was Massimo D'Alema, a leader of the Democrats of the Left and Italy's first post-Communist head of government. D'Alema stepped down a year later after the Olive Tree coalition parties suffered losses to the center-right opposition in the regional elections in April 2000. Giuliano Amato reconstituted the Olive Tree coalition, but he failed to mobilize popular enthusiasm for either himself or the government's policies.

Silvio Berlusconi emerged early as the leading contender to wrest the premiership from the center-left in the campaign leading up to the national election in May 2001. He forged a more disciplined coalition between his own party, Forza Italia, and the Northern League and the National Alliance than had been the case in 1994, and he succeeded in casting himself (thanks in large part to his virtual monopoly ownership of private television in Italy) as a man of vision and action. Indeed, Berlusconi seized on his honorary title of *il Cavaliere* (the knight) to proclaim himself "the greatest politician in the world."

Campaigning jointly as the "Freedom House," the center-right parties relentlessly attacked the Olive Tree coalition for its internal dissension and alleged adherence to the status quo. Advocating radical changes in domestic policies through a much televised campaign that borrowed from the Republican Party in the United States with its promises made directly to the electorate and centered on a "contract with Italians," Berlusconi called for tax reform (including abolition of the inheritance tax), greater flexibility in the labor market, higher pensions, modernization of Italy's transportation and infrastructure system, and safer cities. Members of the Olive Tree coalition responded by nominating Francesco Rutelli, the popular mayor of Rome, to oppose Berlusconi in what became an electoral contest more between strong personalities than between competing ideologies. The center-left's criticism of *il Cavaliere* focused on the corruption charges that he faced but that had been dismissed because of the statute of limitations on the length of trials, and his collusion with the National Alliance and extreme right organizations such as Fiamma Tricolore, headed by Pino Rauti.

Berlusconi and his allies swept to a solid victory in both houses of parliament on May 13. The Freedom House parties won 42.5 percent of the popular vote and 366 seats in the Chamber of Deputies, compared with the Olive Tree's 38.7 percent and 242 seats. Had the Olive Tree coalition been allied with the Party of Communist Refoundation and Antonio Di Pietro, as it was in 1996, it would have easily defeated the center-right coalition in the Chamber of Deputies. Instead, Berlusconi was able to return as prime minister. The electoral outcome dismayed many Europeans, who were concerned about the rightist tilt of the winning coalition, but Italian president Carlo Azeglio Ciampi duly appointed Berlusconi premier in accordance with established democratic norms.

The Election of 2006   The April 9–10, 2006, election proved to be another hard-fought campaign between Italy's two most prominent political personalities of the last decade. Romano Prodi led the center-left coalition, made up of a variety of parties that in the past had been aligned or had run independent lists. In the Prodi coalition were the Democrats of the Left, the Daisy Coalition (headed by Francesco Rutelli), the Greens, the Communist Party of Italy (PCd'I), Antonio Di Pietro's Italy of Values party, the Rose in the Fist (made up of the Radicals and Italian Socialists), the Party of Communist Refoundation, and a variety of other minor parties (South Tyrolese People's Party, Valle d'Aosta party, Pensioners, European Republicans, and the Socialists, led by Bobo Craxi, Bettino Craxi's son). These parties were brought together for the purpose of defeating Berlusconi's coalition and ending what many considered the "Italian anomaly," in which Italy's wealthiest man was in a position to control national public policy and use public resources for his private benefit. The other major motivating factor behind the unity of the center-left coalition was the desire to reverse Italy's economic decline under the Berlusconi government. Italy was suffering zero growth, a fall in real income, a decline in competitiveness, and an increasingly precarious labor market. Internationally, what motivated the opposition was the desire to place Italy once again at the center of European integration and to disengage from Iraq in light of the unraveling political and security conditions there. Prodi promised to get Italy working again by investing in education, lowering the cost of labor, and reinforcing the system of health and social services.

The Berlusconi center-right coalition kept on board all the parties that had enjoyed ministerial posts during the previous five years. In addition to Berlusconi's Forza Italia party, the coalition was able to count on Gianfranco Fini's National Alliance, the Northern League, and the Union of Christian Democrats (UDC). Because the election was expected to be close, Berlusconi also succeeded in bringing into the coalition the remaining right-wing parties (Alessandra Mussolini's Social Alliance Party and Fiamma Tricolore's neo-fascists). The center-right campaigned mainly on three planks: (1) the center-left could not be trusted with power because it was a loose-knit coalition that would fall apart upon facing its first difficult measure and because Prodi's own political support within the coalition represented only a small minority; (2) the center-left coalition was dominated by extremist parties such as the Communist Refoundation and the Italian Communists, which were nostalgic for the past and would betray Italy's ties with the United States and Europe; and (3) "Italy had never had it so good" as under the Berlusconi government—employment was rising, and Italy had experienced an unprecedented period of consumer spending and national investments in infrastructure projects. In addition, Berlusconi promised to abolish the property taxes and other taxes levied by local governments.

A new electoral law, passed by the center-right government a month before the election, had a profound influence on the results. In anticipation that the center-right and center-left would run neck-and-neck in the elections for the Chamber of Deputies, the center-right had abolished the single-member districts and based the distribution of seats completely on proportional representation (PR). In the previous three elections, the center-left had always fared better in the single-member-district portion of the election used to distribute three-quarters of the seats based on the quality of its individual candidates, whereas the center-right did relatively better in the PR system used to distribute the remaining quarter of the seats. To prevent a deadlocked Chamber of Deputies, the new PR law provided the winning coalition (no matter how small the winning margin) with 55 percent (340) of the total of 630 seats. In the Senate, where the center-left was expected to do better, a national PR system was abandoned in favor of distributing votes according to the overall vote in Italy's twenty regions. Therefore, the coalition that received the most votes was awarded 55 percent of the seats. If a coalition gained more than 55 percent of the total vote, it would be allocated that portion of the seats. One final innovation introduced by the center-right was the creation of "overseas" electoral districts for Italians living abroad. In the Chamber of Deputies, twelve seats were allocated to these overseas districts, and in the Senate six. Of the six seats in the Senate, Prodi's coalition won four. Of the other two, one went to Forza Italia and the other to a Latin American independent. In the Chamber of Deputies, the center-left won seven of the overseas seats, Forza Italia won three, and one went to the independent list in Latin America and one to the National Alliance.

The new electoral law proved to be a godsend for the center-left (see Tables 4-2 and 4-3). In the Chamber of Deputies, the center-left won the national proportional representation competition with 49.8 percent of the vote, but picked up a solid 349-seat majority by putting together the 340-plus-one (Valle d'Aosta) seats allocated automatically by the electoral law to the winning coalition and 8 more seats from abroad (the 7 center-left seats and the 1 independent). By contrast, the center-right with 24,755 fewer votes and 49.7 percent of the total vote received only 277 seats within Italy and 4 more from the overseas constituencies for a total of 281 seats. An even clearer indication of how the center-right miscalculated the vote was provided by the result in the Senate. There, the center-right received 49.9 percent of the votes versus 49.2 percent for the center-left, but it received only a 1-seat majority, which was quickly overturned into a 3-seat minority once the overseas tally was factored in. In the Senate, the Prodi coalition garnered 154 seats within Italy and 4 overseas for a 158 majority compared with the 155 Italian seats and the 1 overseas seat, for 156 seats, allocated to the center-right. In the Senate, the seven "senators-for-life" are important in beefing up the center-left majority (most have historically been close to or had careers in the center-left). The center-right did not do as well in the distribution of the Senate seats, because the center-left votes were more evenly distributed throughout the country and it was able to draw from a much broader regional base of voters.

The first comments to emerge from the traumatic election results suggested that Prodi would find it very difficult to govern with such a thin majority, but the nature of his coalition suggested the existence of a strong base and the ability to mobilize his coalition in the coming years. In 1996 he had only a four-seat majority in the Chamber of Deputies with the Party for Communist Refoundation, which was not formally a part of his coalition and supported the government on a case-by-case basis. This time, the PRC was an integral part of the coalition, and the hope was that the strong attacks from the opposition would help to keep the coalition on track in implementing its electoral program. Once parliament was convened, the center-left coalition was able to elect the presidents of the Chamber of Deputies and Senate and then the president of the Republic, Giorgio Napolitano, in contests in which the center-right did not effectively wield either power or influence. The hope of keeping a stable majority was, however, short-lived. After a few months the Prodi government was in trouble. The bulk of the PRC remained loyal (even though in December 2007 Fausto Bertinotti, the charismatic leader of the PRC and president of the Chamber of Deputies, defined Prodi as "a great dead poet" of Italian politics), but a few (in fact, two) refused to follow the party's and the coalition's indication on voting. The result was that the days of the Prodi government were limited. The coalition's defeat was initiated by Clemente Mastella's withdrawal of UDEUR (Union of the Democratic European Reformers) support. Mastella took the pretext of what he termed less-than-enthusiastic support for his wife, who had been indicted in a scandal involving regional councilors in the Campania region where she was president of the regional assembly. On January 24, 2008, the bulk of the UDEUR voted against the government, inflicting a defeat in the vote of confidence in the Senate by 161 to 156. The second Prodi experience as prime minister was brought to an end due to internal dissension within the governing coalition.

The Election of 2008

The election of 2008 was conducted by rules set for the 2006 election because the parties of the governing coalition and the opposition were unable to agree on an alternative formula. Different from the 2006 contest, however, the 2008 election was not a contest between two broad catchall coalitions of the center-right and center-left: in the intervening two years, the leading political forces in both groupings had undergone significant change. On the center-left, the Democratic Party (Partito Democratico, PD) had been formed in October 2007 through the merger of the DS and Margherita parties that had run united slates in the 2004 European elections (Uniti per l'Ulivo) and 2005 regional elections. Walter Veltroni, the mayor of Rome, was the new party's leader. On the center-right, on November 18, 2007, Berlusconi and Fini merged Forza Italia and Alleanza Nazionale into one party called the People of Liberty (Popolo della Libertà, PdL). The two newly emerged parties shunned any alliance with parties too far from their centrist positions, aligning themselves, instead, with parties close to them from a programmatic perspective. The PD aligned itself with DiPietro's Italy of Values, and the PdL with the Northern League and Lombardo's MPA. The vote (see Table 4-4) produced an overwhelming victory on the part of the PdL and its allies with 46.8 percent of the vote in the Chamber of Deputies and 344 seats to the 37.6 percent for the PD and DiPietro grouping with 246 seats. In the Senate the alignment of forces was similar with a 174 to 132 majority on the part of the center-right. The new Berlusconi government was sworn into office on May 5, 2008.

Overall the center-left parties (PD and DiPietro) lost a considerable number of votes (more than 2 million) in addition to its overall political cohesion. The real losers, however, proved to be the "hard" left, with only 3.1 percent of the vote representing the Rainbow Coalition (Communist Refoundation, PDC, and Greens) that had triggered the crisis that ended the Prodi government. As a consequence, the hard left practically disappeared from the political scene. It no longer had political representation in parliament, and its role in the debate on national issues or issues of welfare and strategic economic choices was cancelled. The hard left's electoral woes continued into the 2009 elections for the European

Table 4-4 Comparison between the Election Results for the 2009 European Parliament and 2008 Chamber of Deputies

Party	European Parliament %	Chamber of Deputies %	Seats
Liberty Party (Berlusconi) PdL	35.3	37.4	276
Democratic Party PD	26.1	33.2	217
Northern League (Bossi) NL	10.2	8.3	60
IdV (DiPietro)	8.0	4.4	29
Union of the Center (Casini) UDC	6.5	5.6	36
Communist Refoundation PRC	3.4	3.1*	0
Left-Liberty (Vendola) S-L	3.1	—	
Bonino-Panella (Radicals)	2.4	—	
Autonomist (Lombardo) MPA	2.2	1.1	8
Socialist Party (Boselli) PS	—	1.0	0
The Right (Storace and Stantache`)	—	2.4	0
Others	2.8	3.5	4
Total	100.0	100.0	630

Source: 2009 results: www.europarl.curopa.eu/elections2009; 2008 results: Alessandro Chiaramonte, "Italian Voters: Berlusconi's Victory and the 'New' Italian Party System," in *The Italian General Election of 2008: Berlusconi Strikes Back*, ed. James Newell (Basingstoke, UK: Palgrave Macmillan, 2009), 201.

* In 2008 the leftist group was called the Left Rainbow Coalition, and it included the Communist Refoundation (PRC), the Communist Party of Italy (PDCdl), Greens, and opponents who left the PD after Veltroni's victory as party secretary.

Parliament, where it once again presented itself split into two electoral groups: Communist Refoundation, which received 3.4 percent of the vote, and a new group—Left and Liberty—organized around Niki Vendola, the president of the Puglia regional government. In 2008 Vendola had been narrowly defeated by Paolo Ferrero in the contest for the leadership of the party. The new party attempted to unify leftist objectives with those of environmentalist groups, and its overall result of 3.1 percent was only slightly less than that received by the PRC. The 2009 results confirmed Communist Refoundation's isolation in the political spectrum. Its leaders stated that they would be willing to coalesce in an electoral alliance with other leftist parties in an attempt to defeat the center-right in the 2010

President Giulio Napolitano (left) speaks with Prime Minister Silvio Berlusconi during their swearing-in ceremony at the Quirinal Palace in Rome, May 2008.

Source: Alessandra Benedetti/Corbis

regional and local elections, but they would not consider the prospect of joining governing coalitions, thereby relegating the center-left to a permanent minority status. If the center-left were to confirm its 2009 electoral results in the European parliamentary elections it would be destined to remain a minority party coalition. The center-right with 35.3 percent for the PdL and 10.2 percent for the Northern League continued to reflect the status as a majority of the electorate.

Just as in 2001, the new 2008 Berlusconi government was greeted in September of that year with the full force of a world financial crisis. As a result, economic activity melted away and with it government revenues. In 2006 the Prodi government had enjoyed larger then expected levels of tax revenue. In 2008 the opposite was true for Berlusconi. With declining economic activity (-1.0 percent fall in GDP in 2008 and -4.7 percent in 2009), the size of the annual deficit went from -1.5 percent in 2007 to -2.7 percent in 2008 and over 4 percent in 2009. A similar pattern emerged in the size of the overall debt, which went from 103.5 percent of GDP in 2007 to 105.8 percent in 2008. That the deficit and debt did not spiral out of control as in some other countries, such as Greece, served to cushion the negative consequences of Italy's position in the euro. Giulio Tremonti, the minister of the economy, was given the political support necessary to rein in spending and keep the nation's financial accounts under control.

The Changing Nature of Italy's Political Parties

Since the beginning of the Italian republic, the national organized parties have been the dominant political forces in Italy, although the names and leadership of the parties that have become the dominant forces on the left and right of the political spectrum have changed significantly. Since the early 1990s, the Italian political system has converged toward the center, with the result that election outcomes have depended on the ability of parties to occupy the center. It is also true that today political campaigns are contested by coalitions (center-right versus center-left) rather than by individual parties trying to stake out their own individual niche in the political spectrum.

The Ex-Communists and Orthodox Communists The Democratic Party of the Left (now known as the Left Democrats) was founded in February 1991, only thirty-two months after Achille Occhetto became secretary of the Italian Communist Party (PCI) in June 1988. Almost immediately after becoming party secretary, Occhetto, aided by a new generation of leaders of middle-class origin, began to campaign for radical changes in the structure and goals of the PCI. In doing so, he was continuing and accelerating the reformist course set by his predecessors, Enrico Berlinguer and Alessandro Natta. But Occhetto went further; he proposed breaking with the Marxist tradition, establishing close links with the West European socialist parties, democratizing the internal organization of the PCI, and, after the fall of the Berlin Wall in November 1989, changing the name of the PCI. At a special party conference held in March 1990, he won approval of his proposal for a party constituent assembly to debate and approve a statute for the new party he intended to create. Despite considerable internal opposition, his motion prevailed by an almost two-thirds majority. After much wrangling over the name, symbols, and goals of the new party, a party congress at Rimini in early 1991 voted to terminate the existence of the old PCI and to establish the new Democratic Party of the Left (PDS). A week or so later, many of Occhetto's opponents convened to found another new party, the Party of Communist Refoundation, or PRC. It pledged to continue the communist tradition.[16]

In one sense, the establishment of the PDS was not a complete break with the past in the history of Italian communism. Since 1956, when the PCI, responding to the invasion of Hungary by Soviet troops, had shifted from all-out opposition to constructive opposition within the system, the Communist Party had moved in the direction of greater moderation.[17] From 1973 to 1979, under Secretary Berlinguer, the Communist Party had proposed a "historic compromise" that would include all Italian parties willing to uphold the Italian constitution but would emphasize an alliance between the Communists and the Christian Democrats. It had also pledged to come to power through free elections, to maintain a multiparty system, to allow itself to be voted out of office; to enforce the constitution, to forego further nationalizations, and to crack down on both left-wing and right-wing terrorism. Its leaders had occasionally, albeit rather tentatively, spoken out for wage restraint and austerity. And in foreign affairs, the PCI had clearly and repeatedly asserted its independence from Soviet influence. Forcefully and almost prophetically, Berlinguer had raised the "moral question" in Italian politics, asking that his party conduct a sustained fight against systemic corruption and collusion, with organized crime as a top priority. This stance attracted the support of many leading intellectuals, who lent their support to the PCI, in the mode of Antonio Gramsci's "organic intellectuals." [18]

The PCI's independent and moderate stance had paid off in electoral terms as well. Practicing Gramsci's "politics of presence" by offering sensible pragmatic solutions to concrete problems in every area of Italian life, the PCI had won many positions in local, provincial, and regional government. Indeed, some of Italy's largest cities had Communist mayors. In national elections, the Communist voting percentages peaked in 1976, but as late as 1987, the PCI still commanded 26.6 percent of the Italian vote.

The PCI was, however, facing serious difficulties. Its moderate policies had somewhat dissipated the feelings of distrust that animated many Italians, but at the cost of arousing PCI rank-and-file discontent with its lack of militancy. Its collaboration with the Christian Democrats during 1976–1979 had laid it open to charges that it had joined the establishment and saddled the establishment with part of the blame for hard times. And if the PCI tried to halt the desertion of marginals and students on its left by making militant noises, it lost some moderate votes on its right.

When the PDS was founded in 1991, it did not escape the difficulties that had faced the old PCI. In fact, the secessionist diehards of the Communist Refoundation received 5.6 percent of the vote in 1992, compared with 16.1 percent for the PDS. The secession of the PRC therefore further weakened the already dwindling forces of Italian communism (Communist Refoundation) and the postcommunist movement (the PDS).

The disintegration of the PSI in 1992–1994 gave the PDS a new lease on life. It became, in effect, the standard-bearer for the moderate left. In the 1994 election campaign, the PDS advocated a program of economic austerity and privatization of state industries; supported reducing taxes and shifting control of tax revenues from the central to the regional and local governments; demanded that pensions be equalized; and called for further progress toward European integration and strengthening the North Atlantic Treaty Organization (NATO) as a force for peace. It also promised to back the outgoing prime minister, Carlo Azeglio Ciampi, a former director of the Bank of Italy and champion of austerity.[19] By contrast, the Communist Refoundation, its ally in the Progressive Alliance, favored a pump-priming program of decreasing work hours and increasing pensions, and it expressed opposition to NATO. Although its more radical ally cast some doubt on the credibility of the PDS, the Democratic Party of the Left nevertheless gained considerable ground in 1994.

At the end of 1994, after the resignation of Achille Occhetto and the rise to power of a new PDS leader, Massimo D'Alema, the PDS appeared to have taken over the moderate left area of the political spectrum once occupied by the PSI. In the 1996 election, it was the leading party in Prodi's Olive Tree coalition, and when Prodi became prime minister, it became a leading protagonist in the Prodi cabinet. After Prodi was forced to resign in October 1998, D'Alema formed a center-left cabinet that was broadened to include both the Communist Party of Italy (PCd'I), a new orthodox Communist Party that had seceded from the PRC to support the Olive Tree coalition, and the center-right Democratic Union for the Republic (UDR), headed by former president Francesco Cossiga.

The D'Alema government continued to pursue monetary stability, controlled public spending, and austerity to pave the way for Italian admission to the Euro Area in early 1999. The Party of Communist Refoundation, headed by Fausto Bertinotti, continued to demand heavier government spending (especially in the south), a thirty-five-hour workweek, the perpetuation of the existing cumbersome and expensive welfare structures, and opposition to NATO and the European Union. It was clear that the PDS and its leader faced a difficult balancing act, and that the policy cleavage between the PDS, on the one hand, and the PRC and PCd'I, on the other, posed a critical threat to the future of the Italian left.[20]

After heavy losses in the April 2000 regional elections to the center-right parties, D'Alema resigned and was succeeded by Treasury and Budget Minister Giuliano Amato. Amato reconstituted the center-left coalition, resisting opposition demands to call an early election. The party returned to a prominent position within the center-left in the 2001 and 2006 elections. Its position as the largest party in Prodi's Olive Tree coalition remained uncontested. But it also remained a supporter of center-left unity and recognized the need to find new organizational forms to unite the center-left. Under the leadership of Piero Fassino, who became secretary of the party in 2001, it continued to push tirelessly for the unity of Socialist parties within Italy and Europe and to extend the center-left coalition as much as possible by offering in 2001 a few of its safe seats under the previous single-member districts and offering in 2006 places on the party lists in the Chamber of Deputies and in the Olive Tree list in the Senate. The strategy of working in the direction of keeping the center-left unified paid off in May 2006 with the election of Giorgio Napolitano, the historic leader of the reformist wing of the former PCI, to the highest post in the country. In 2007 the drive to unite the moderate parties of the left found its point of arrival with the creation of the Democratic Party. After the experimentation with a unified party list in the 2004 European elections and 2005 regional elections, the leaders felt that the time was ripe to create a unified party. On October 14, 2007, a new leader of the party, Walter Veltroni, was elected overwhelmingly through a party primary with 75 percent of the vote on the part of 4 million party supporters.[21] As a consequence, the split with the dissenting voices in the old DS—the leftist minority led by Fabio Mussi and Cesare Salvi—and the Socialist aligned fringe led by Gavino Angius and Mauro Zani remained outside of the new party. Mussi and Salvi brought their dissenting leftist group into an electoral alliance with the PRC, PCd'I, and Greens in preparation for the 2008 elections and came away with a very disappointing 3.2 percent of the vote for the entire Left-Rainbow alliance. The other dissenters joined Boselli's Socialist SDI and stopped at 1.0 percent of the vote. The vast bulk of center-left voters backed the PD with 33.7 percent of the total vote.

The Death of the Socialist Party After the returns were in for the election of 1996, it was clear that the Italian Socialist Party, or PSI, was, to all effects and purposes, history. A tiny splinter group, the Italian Socialists (SI), had been allotted twelve single-member district candidacies under an electoral agreement with the predominantly ex–Christian Democratic Dini List. Thanks to the Dini List's support, it carried three of those twelve districts. But because more than three deputies are needed to form a parliamentary group, the three lonely Socialist deputies had to join a group of unaffiliated members of the Chamber of Deputies.

The demise of the PSI severely disappointed those who had hoped that this party would lead Italy to a brighter future. Its gradual disengagement from its 1946–1956 alliance with the Communist Party and its entry into a center-left cabinet with the Christian Democrats in 1963 had seemed to usher in a new and progressive era in Italian politics, but this "opening to the left" had a disillusioning outcome. The Socialist Party simply became a captive junior partner in Christian Democratic–dominated center-left cabinets. It proved unable to have much impact on government policy or to spur the Christian Democrats into speeding up progress toward social reform. By contrast, it proved very adept at obtaining its share of patronage. Just as the PSI's reputation had been seriously damaged by its earlier dependence on the Communist Party, similarly, its post-1963 alliance with the ruling Christian Democrats had overtones of dependency and opportunism. The result was electoral decline.

Efforts by the PSI to stem that electoral decline and establish a separate identity were partly successful in electoral terms, especially after Bettino Craxi took over as party leader in 1976. But the PSI's attempts to formulate attractive policies had a reactive quality to them.

It almost seemed as if the Socialist leaders were more interested in distinguishing their party from its giant neighbors on the political spectrum (the Italian Communist Party and the Christian Democracy) than in developing a coherent policy line of their own. This tactical opportunism seemed to pay off at the polls, especially after Craxi became prime minister and pursued moderate, pragmatic policies in the domestic and foreign spheres from 1983 to 1987. In 1987 the PSI polled an almost unprecedented 14.3 percent of the vote—its high-water mark since 1946 (Table 4-2). And in 1992 it dipped only slightly—to 13.6 percent.

By 1994 the PSI was reduced to the status of a discredited splinter party that desperately needed an alliance with the Democratic Party of the Left to pick up a handful of seats in parliament. After the 1994 election, the PSI, thoroughly disgraced by the scandals of "Kickback City," closed up shop. To avoid a prison sentence after a conviction for corruption, Craxi fled into exile to Tunisia, where he died of heart failure in January 2000.

Some new movements were founded to succeed the defunct PSI, but the election of 1996 seemed to indicate that the old PSI tradition, so thoroughly tainted by Craxian opportunism and corruption, could not be revived. If there was to be a renaissance of Italian socialism, it seemed more likely that it would be led by the PDS, which has staked a powerful and rather credible claim to the moderate left space on Italy's new political spectrum. In 2001 many of the old PSI leaders, such as Gianni De Michelis and Bobo Craxi (Bettino Craxi's son), who had fled to Berlusconi's Forza Italia party, came together to form the "New PSI," but in the proportional representation part of the ballot it garnered only 0.9 percent of the vote. In 2004 another attempt was made to extend the new PSI to include other parts of the Socialist diaspora (for example, Claudio Signorile) with greater leftist tendencies and a desire to assume an intermediate position between the two large coalitions, but the attempt was hijacked by De Michelis, who continued to support the center-right coalition in exchange for an undersecretary position in the Berlusconi government. Finally, during the 2005 regional elections the Signorile group of Socialists joined with autonomous Socialist forces and the SI socialists to create the foundation of a revised, leftist-leaning Socialist party that could be part of the new center-left coalition. In regions such as Puglia and Calabria, they were instrumental in bringing the center-left to victory. In the run-up to the 2006 parliamentary elections, Bobo Craxi and Signorile joined the center-left coalition (De Michelis remained allied with Berlusconi's center-right bloc) and put the center-left over the top with their 115,105 votes. Had Craxi and Signorile not shifted their allegiance to Prodi, the center-left would not have won the election. In 2007, even though the PD had as one of its main objectives the unity of social democratic forces in Italy, the official Socialist Party never became an integral part of the new political formation. Instead, it preferred to remain aloof. In 2008 it eventually succumbed to the dictates of the electoral law and disappeared from the Italian parliament along with the non-PD left. In the 2008 election the PD made a relatively good showing with 33.2 percent of the vote, but the rest of the left—extreme left (PRC and the Left-Rainbow Coalition) and moderate left (PS)—ceased to enjoy parliamentary representation and effectively disappeared from the national political debate.

The Successors to the Christian Democrats From 1992 to 1994 Christian Democracy suffered the same fate that had befallen the PSI. Both parties, along with their minor center allies, were irrevocably damaged by the series of judicial inquiries that revealed how corrupt, and in some cases how closely linked to organized crime, many of their more prominent leaders had been. The growing competition from the Northern League also played a role in shaking Christian Democratic morale. Heavy Socialist and Christian Democratic losses in the local elections of December 1993 revealed the extent of public disaffection and induced Christian Democracy to terminate its own existence. On January 18, 1994, the DC was officially dissolved, to be replaced by the Italian Popular Party (PPI), a title meant to conjure up memories of priest Don Luigi Sturzo's Popular Party, which had led a brief but relatively honorable existence from 1919 through most of 1926. The leader of the new party, Mino Martinazzoli, had not been one of the top DC hierarchs and was untainted by the "Kickback City" scandals. Under his leadership, the Popular Party steered a resolutely centrist course, rejecting overtures from both the left and the right alliances. Its only ally was also centrist: the Pact for National Renewal, led by Mario Segni, a former Christian Democrat. In 1994 the two parties polled only 15.7 percent of the total vote (Table 4-2). Another group of former DC members—the Christian Democratic Center (CCD)—rejected Martinazzoli's glorious isolation and chose to run candidates for parliament under Berlusconi's center-right Forza Italia.

The PPI and the Segni Pact center parties were able to poll a combined total of only 15.7 percent of the vote in the parliamentary election of 1994.[22] Their numbers were an unmistakable sign of the sharply reduced influence of the Catholic Church and the interest groups that used to revolve around the old Christian Democracy, such as those representing farmers, trade unions, shopkeepers, and artisans (these groups are described in more detail later in this chapter). To be sure, there were a few other splinter Catholic lists (the vote of the CCD could not be ascertained, because it formed part of the Berlusconi Forza Italia lists), but the total Catholic vote was well below 20 percent.

As a party, the DC was, first and foremost, heterogeneous and catchall in nature: it ranged across a large part of the Italian political spectrum, from moderate left to moderate right, and it included in its ranks supporters of virtually every type of alliance or cabinet combination. Among those who voted for the DC were industrialists, workers, small farmers, housewives, pensioners, the unemployed, and shopkeepers—a mixed bag, indeed.

The collapse and fragmentation of the DC constituted a revolutionary development in Italian politics. From 1946 through 1993, the DC had been the country's leading party. From 1946 to 1981, every Italian prime minister had been a Christian Democrat, and unlike the Communists and the Socialists, the Christian Democrats had formed a major part of every cabinet. But the question of what alliances the party should form had been a perpetual bone of contention and had helped to keep the DC divided into warring factions.

Not only was the DC faction-ridden, but also the factions were bewilderingly volatile. After the "historic compromise" of 1979, the factions quickly began to shed their ideological, social, and policy positions, and within the space of one or two years, a faction might have completely reversed its position on an issue involving party policies or party alliances. Party competition was then transferred from the ideological and programmatic arena to the accumulation of financial resources for the party organization and leadership through kickbacks on public contracts, but to the point that it became unsustainable on the part of small and medium-level contractors. In other words, the DC's system of corruption collapsed because of the need to generate increasing amounts of money for the party elites.

Once the judicial system began to investigate the corruption, the party was doomed to dissolution.[23] The impact was particularly devastating in northern Italy, where the Christian Democrats had mobilized support on the basis of Catholic social and moral values and the Socialists had done the same on the basis of their lay and reformist goals. Yet even before the investigation into the financial kickbacks collected by the party, Christian Democratic support had already begun to drain off in the north.

Policy matters also divided the DC, and more so than for other Italian parties. Party members included strong supporters of private enterprise and champions of the state sector, representatives of management and spokesmen for organized labor, diehard opponents of divorce and advocates of a more liberal set of moral codes for Italian society. In fact, the party had essentially tried to be all things to all people. As Christian Democrat Aldo Moro once put it in a revealing slip of the tongue, "The DC emphasizes everything."[24] Perhaps the one common denominator of the DC was its distributive approach to public policy. The party had built its strength, especially in the south, by judiciously allocating contracts, jobs, and public money among party supporters, but prior to 1979 it had not instituted a systematic kickback operation. The party was adequately supported by party members and financing from the state and parastate sectors.

The ambiguity and ambivalence of the DC had already taken their toll in election results. Even before the electoral debacles of 1983 and 1992, the DC had been unable, all through the 1960s and 1970s, to regain the 40 percent level it had once attained. In addition to voter reaction against its lack of a clear sense of purpose, the DC had suffered the inevitable erosion that affects any dominant party after an extended period in power. In the 1980s party leaders had tried to commit the party to a program of public austerity, to an abandonment of excessive reliance on the spoils system, and to an emphasis on productivity gains rather than purely distributive policies. But this initiative failed to be convincing in a system in which all of the governing parties had begun to use public contracts to systematically generate financial resources. One of the main causes of the collapse of the DC and the other parties of the five-party center-left coalition was the inability of the party elites to distance themselves from those accused and convicted of taking bribes. By 1994 the inability to purify the internal party apparatus had led to the disappearance of the Socialists, Social Democrats, Republicans, and Liberals (PSI, PSDI, PRI, and PLI) from the political scene. As for the DC, it led to schisms and the birth of new Catholic parties.[25]

The Catholic camp was still divided and weak in the 1996 election. The center-left Prodi List, Popular Party, Italian Renewal, and CCD/CDU polled together only 16.9 percent of the vote.[26] After the election the Catholic forces underwent a further repositioning. Francesco Cossiga, a former president of Italy, and Clemente Mastella, labor minister in the 1994 Berlusconi cabinet, formed a new party of ex–Christian Democrats called the Democratic Union for the Republic (UDR). This center-right party apparently received much of its support from legislators elected on the CCD/CDU party lists. In October 1998, of the 630 members of the Chamber of Deputies, 67 adhered to the Popular Party (same number as in 1996), 21 adhered to Dini's Italian Renewal (24 in 1996), and 31 identified with the UDR (the CDC/CDU had elected 30 in 1996, but it was not listed as a party group in October 1998). Apart from a few splinter deputies, the Catholic deputies totaled 119, or 18.9 percent of the membership.

Although the presence of political Catholicism in parliament was dramatically reduced by the electoral revolution of the 1990s, it is still a formidable force, despite its internal divisions. It remains to be seen whether the segments of the former Christian Democratic Party can ever reunite. In 2001 they continued to align themselves with the two opposing coalitions. The Union of Christian Democrats (UDC) that brought together the CCD of Pier Ferdinando Casini and the CDU of Rocco Buttiglione was placed under the organizational leadership of Marco Follini and continued to operate as a political ally of the center-right. In fact, after the 2001 election Casini was elected president of the Chamber of Deputies and Buttiglione was appointed minister for EU affairs and then, in 2004, minister of culture. After the debacle of the center-right in the 2005 regional elections, however, Follini and a part of the UDC began to openly criticize Berlusconi for continuing to insist on passing the regional devolution bill championed by the Northern League and the minister for administrative reform, Umberto Bossi. According to Follini, the collapse of support for Forza Italia and the National Alliance in the south was traceable to their support of Bossi's initiative, whereas the overall strength of the UDC lay in its criticism of the bill and its expected negative impact on the financial stability of southern regions and local governments. The reaction of Forza Italia and the Northern League encouraged the UDC to oust Follini as party secretary and replace him with Alberto Cesa, a member of the European Parliament supported by Casini. In the 2006 election, the UDC did quite well, garnering 6.8 percent of the vote in the Chamber of Deputies and thirty-nine seats versus the 3.2 percent it received five years earlier. In 2007 the UDC became increasingly critical of the radical opposition to the Prodi government encouraged by Berlusconi, and as a consequence in November of that year Casini rejected Berlusconi's offer to join the PdL. In the 2008 election the UDC was the only party not aligned with either the PD or the PdL to gain parliamentary representation. The party polled a respectable 5.6 percent in the Chamber of Deputies with thirty-six seats and 5.7 percent in the Senate with three seats. In the 2009 European parliamentary elections the party increased its support to 6.5 percent of the vote and in the 2010 regional elections promised to become the "kingmaker" by aligning itself with either the PD or PdL in a completely ad hoc manner based on expected electoral results.

The Minor Parties: A Forest of Shrubs Before 1994 the minor center parties included the Social Democrats (PSDI), whose commitment to social democracy appeared to focus on public works, social welfare measures, and a preoccupation with the interests of pensioners; the Republicans (PRI), a moderately left-of-center party committed to fiscal austerity and honesty in government, whose leader, Giovanni Spadolini, was the first non–Christian Democratic prime minister since 1945; and the Liberals (PLI), a party of the moderate right, competing with the Christian Democrats for the votes of business owners and large landowners. The one common strand connecting these three parties was their commitment to democracy and to a secular society. They tended to side with the DC on many issues but not on matters having to do with church-state relations.

In the years after 1946 the minor center parties registered very modest electoral performances: their combined share of the total vote was usually less than 10 percent. But the scandals of "Kickback City" and the new election law of 1993 sounded the death knell for these parties, which disappeared from the Italian parliament. They were replaced by a multitude of "shrubs"—a large number of splinter parties that allied themselves with major parties such as the PDS and Forza Italia in the hope of being allotted a few safe seats. Once such "shrubs" enter parliament, they join the group of unaffiliated deputies, because their respective splinter parties are not strong enough to be allowed to form parliamentary groups of their own.

In February 1999 former prime minister Romano Prodi formed yet another shrub party, the Democrats for the Olive Tree. Prodi was seeking to strengthen the center-left coalition, but critics feared that his initiative would further fragment the center-left. Once Prodi became president of the European Commission in March 1999, the Democrats joined with the Italian Popular Party and the Dini List to form the Margherita (daisy). This Catholic party did quite well in the 2001 election by becoming the third-largest party in the country and shifting the focus of the Catholic vote from the center-right to the center-left coalition. Party head Francesco Rutelli also became the prime minister–designate for the center-left coalition in the 2001 election. Despite his defeat by Berlusconi, Rutelli remained president of the Margherita and a major actor in center-left politics until Prodi, at the end of his presidency of the European Commission, returned as leader of the center-left and as prime minister–designate for the 2006 election. In the Chamber of Deputies, the Margherita joined the Democrats of the Left to form the Olive Tree coalition, which received 31.3 percent of the vote. In the Senate elections, however, the two parties ran separate lists, and the Margherita received 10.5 percent versus the DS's 17.5 percent, a level 3.3 percent below their Olive Tree total. In the 2008 elections the only parties that gained seats in the Chamber or Senate were the regionalist parties representing Trentino-Alto Adige (SVP), Valle d'Aosta, and Sicily (MPA). In the first two cases the seat allocation was not bound by the electoral rules applying in the rest of the country. In the case of the MPA, the party received two seats in the Senate and eight seats in the Chamber because it was allied with the PdL along with the Northern League. None of the other minor parties received parliamentary representation. The MPA presented itself in the 2009 European parliamentary elections allied with The Right of Storace and Santachè, but the result was much lower than what both parties received individually in the 2008 elections. The MPA electorate seemed to have remained solid, but the right-wing voters did not responded positively to this pragmatic electoral alliance.

The Northern League In the local and regional elections of 1990, a newcomer appeared on the Italian political scene: the Lombard League, which polled 19 percent of the vote in Lombardy (equivalent to 4.8 percent of the vote in Italy). Far outnumbering similar regional leagues elsewhere in northern Italy, the Lombard League stood for greater regional autonomy, restrictions on immigration from foreign countries, and an end to the "colonization" by southern Italians of the bureaucratic field services in northern Italy. It also demanded that the northern regions have greater control over their own revenue base instead of being taxed heavily by the central government to finance allegedly unproductive public investments in the south. In the election of 1992, the Lombard League formed an electoral bloc—the Northern League, in which it was the preponderant element—with several other regional leagues in northern and north-central Italy. Its showing in the election of 1992 was little short of spectacular for a new competitor in Italian party politics. With 8.7 percent of the vote in Italy as a whole (Table 4-2), the Northern League received more than 30 percent of the vote in Lombardy, allowing it to replace the DC as the leading party in some Lombard provinces. And it won no less than fifty-five seats in the Chamber of Deputies. In short, it had rapidly become the fourth-largest party in the Italian party system.

The Northern League made further progress at the local level when the PSI and the DC, hitherto dominant in Lombard local government, were brought to their knees by the wave of scandals and resulting indictments that captured public attention in 1992 and 1993. In local elections held in several Lombard provincial capitals in 1992, the Northern League outpolled both the DC and the PSI. In September 1993 Marco Formentini of the Northern League was elected mayor of Milan, a city in which the PSI had held sway for the previous twenty years.

In the 1994 election, after considerable vacillation, the volatile leader of the Northern League, Umberto Bossi, formed an electoral alliance in northern Italy with Berlusconi's Forza Italia and with the Christian Democratic Center. In the election of March 27–28, 1994, the Northern League polled not only 8.4 percent of the vote cast in Italy (Table 4-2) but also about 30 percent of the vote cast in northern Italy, where the great bulk of its strength was concentrated. Thanks to the Northern League's electoral alliance with Forza Italia, its candidates won far more single-member-district seats, 111, in the Chamber of Deputies than would have been possible under a system of proportional representation. By contrast, Forza Italia and its CCD allies won 139 seats, and the National Alliance won 109.

After the election, both the Northern League and the National Alliance of former neo-Fascists entered the Berlusconi cabinet. This center-right coalition, however, was internally divided from the start. Bossi disliked and distrusted both Berlusconi and the former neo-Fascists. He accused Berlusconi of not taking sufficiently bold steps toward a federal or quasi-federal Italy, of making some very questionable appointments to the regulatory boards charged with supervising the public sector in the field of mass communications, and of attempting to interfere with the way the judiciary was handling the investigations of corrupt practices by politicians and business leaders. As for the former neo-Fascists, Bossi claimed they were still untrustworthy because of their past connections with fascism. He also wanted privatization to be stepped up and was antagonized by the National Alliance's insistence that the public sector remain strong so that it might continue to transfer subsidies and public contracts to the south. As a result of Bossi's attitudes, the Berlusconi cabinet was paralyzed by internal conflicts, and in December 1994 Berlusconi resigned as prime minister, bitterly denouncing Bossi after he joined with the PPI in tabling a vote of no confidence against the government. With the creation of the Dini government, the Northern League continued to vote with the center-left, and it denounced Berlusconi for ties with the Mafia.

In 1996 the Northern League obtained 10.1 percent of the vote but only fifty-nine seats in the Chamber of Deputies (Tables 4-2 and 4-3). Its percentage of the total vote had risen from 8.4 percent, but it won far fewer seats (59 instead of 111) because it was no longer part of an alliance with other center-right parties. Consequently, its candidates in single-member districts could no longer count on the help and support of the center-right alliance. By late 1998 the Northern League had fifty-eight members in the Chamber of Deputies—less than half of its 1994–1996 delegation.[27]

During the campaign preceding the April 21, 1996, election, the Northern League adopted a more militant and dramatic posture. Instead of speaking of autonomy and a federal Italy, its leader, Bossi, spoke of the establishment of a northern state of Padania, which would secede from the rest of Italy and proclaim its independence. Lacking allies, the Northern League expected to lose many seats in parliament—as, in fact, it did. But it expected to play a balance of power role, because it believed that neither the center-left nor the center-right would be able to command a majority in a deadlocked parliament.

These hopes, however, were doomed to disappointment. Facing an unanticipated center-left majority in the new parliament, the Northern League launched a series of demonstrations along the entire length of the Po River. But mass participation in these demonstrations fell far short of expectations, and in the next few years the power and prestige of the Northern League visibly waned. It suffered losses in local and provincial elections, including the mayoralty election in Milan, and its strength was increasingly confined to the midsize cities and small towns of the Alpine foothills. Under these circumstances, Bossi had to modify his message. In early 1998 independence was abandoned as an immediate goal and presented as a long-range possibility, to be preceded by experimentation with a federal system under which the north would enjoy a high degree of fiscal autonomy.[28]

The waning electoral fortunes of the Northern League at the end of the 1990s forced the leadership to reconsider its go-it-alone strategy, and by the regional elections in 2000 it had decided to go back to the creation of an electoral bloc with the center-right parties. This shift in strategy helped the party to prepare for the 2001 election on the basis of a strong relationship with Berlusconi and guarantee of ministerial posts, but the move also disoriented a large number of followers who had supported the party in the past because of its antagonist position in relation to both electoral blocs. As a result, the party polled 3.9 percent in the 2001 election. Yet even though the party lost almost two-thirds of its previous electoral base, it was awarded powerful ministries in the new Berlusconi government. It is clear that the Berlusconi-Bossi relationship underpinned the center-right coalition; Berlusconi repeatedly demonstrated his reluctance to oppose policies and actions supported by Bossi, especially constitutional reform aimed at extreme federalism. The radical reform of the constitution championed by Bossi was finally passed in parliament at the end of 2005, but it was opposed by most regional governments in its proposal to devolve from the national to regional level powers over the provision of health services, education, and the police. What most disturbed the regions was that the reform transferred the responsibilities for the delivery of these services to the regional level, but without adding to the regions' revenue or taxing powers. The central state remained in control of the country's purse strings. During the spring of 2005 Bossi suffered a stroke that left him significantly incapacitated, and the control of the party passed to a group of leaders who vied for control. In 2006 the Northern League teamed up with the Autonomous League of southern Italy in the hopes of making major inroads, but the new alliance gained only 4.6 percent of the vote in the Chamber of Deputies, a slight increase from the Northern League's 3.9 percent in 2001. In 2008 the Northern League returned to political prominence with 8.3 percent of the vote in the Chamber, and with sixty seats in the Chamber and twenty-five seats in the Senate the party was able to dictate to a great extent the government's program on institutional reform and the economy during the following years. In essence, as a result of the 2008 election Berlusconi's majority was dependent on the votes of the Northern League in both houses of parliament.

Forza Italia Unlike the other parties discussed in this chapter, Forza Italia (Go Italy) was created only a few months before the 1994 election as the personal political vehicle of one man, Silvio Berlusconi, head of a vast private media, publishing, real estate, and retail merchandising empire held together by the giant holding company Fininvest and owner of the Milan soccer club. Alarmed by the victory in the municipal elections of December 1993 of the left bloc against a demoralized and discredited right-center that was all too often represented by neo-Fascist candidates, Berlusconi decided to launch his own party and pick up votes from former Christian Democrats and former Socialists. With the aid of his media properties, he created and funded a network of about twelve hundred Forza Italia clubs, which attracted about 1 million members.[29] These clubs were established to give Berlusconi a base of popular support and were not really designed to exercise policymaking or control functions or to practice internal democracy.

Unlike the uninspiring and rather pedestrian platform of the born-again moderate leftists of the Democratic Party of the Left, or PDS, Forza Italia presented the disillusioned Italian electorate with a series of right-wing populist appeals. It promised, not austerity, but a "new Italian miracle" in the form of tax cuts and a single income tax bracket at 33 percent, reductions in the deficit, privatization of health care and pensions resulting in lower costs and higher benefits, a million new jobs, and a quasi-presidential system resembling the French Fifth Republic. In short, it offered new vistas rather than the humdrum moderate formulas put forth by the PDS.[30] In the 1994 election, Forza Italia received 21.0 percent of the votes cast for proportional representation candidates in the Chamber of Deputies (including 3.5 percent cast for the Christian Democratic Center) and gained 111 seats (27 additional seats were allotted to the Christian Democratic Center candidates who were allowed to represent the Forza Italia slate in far more than their proportionate share of single-member districts). Because Forza Italia's 21.0 percent represented a plurality of the votes cast, Berlusconi was asked by President Scalfaro to form a cabinet.

The Berlusconi cabinet, like most Italian cabinets, was never a united team. Two of its most important component parties, the Northern League and the National Alliance, bickered constantly. And the Northern League's Umberto Bossi sniped continually at Berlusconi and his policies from a vantage point outside the cabinet. Berlusconi himself proved to be a disappointing and vacillating leader, unable to meet the far-reaching expectations he had raised during the election campaign of March 1994. Also, only a few months after taking office he came under judicial investigation for bribery and conflict of interest in relation to his vast private holdings of which he had failed to divest himself.

During Berlusconi's seven months in office, he attempted unsuccessfully to restrict the power of the judiciary to conduct investigations into political and business corruption and to place suspected culprits under preventive detention. Because the ongoing investigations were affecting his own Fininvest holding company and were implicating his own brother in a bribery scandal, Berlusconi's actions aroused a great deal of suspicion about his motives. His long-delayed budgetary proposals for deep cuts in health and pension benefits resulted in a storm of popular protest and had to be watered down. And he provoked widespread criticism for his efforts to intervene in the internal management of RAI, the state-owned broadcasting organization, and of the Bank of Italy.

The November 1994 municipal elections in various parts of Italy revealed a highly adverse voter reaction to the Berlusconi cabinet. In those elections, Forza Italia, which had polled 21.0 percent of the vote in the general election of March 1994 and had risen to 30.6 percent of the vote in the elections to the European Parliament in June 1994, dropped to a mere 8.4 percent. Under the pressure of judicial investigations, economic and political unrest, and constant bickering among members of his unwieldy coalition, Berlusconi finally resigned as prime minister in December 1994 once the Northern League joined the opposition in a vote of no confidence in the government. After the vote, President Scalfaro refused to accede to Berlusconi's request to dissolve parliament and call new elections. Instead, Lamberto Dini, an independent who had served as minister of the Treasury in the Berlusconi cabinet and second-ranking administrator of the Bank of Italy, was designated to form a cabinet. Dini was able to secure a parliamentary majority through the combined support of the left and center parties along with the Northern League.

The fall of the Berlusconi cabinet, and the strong possibility that Berlusconi might eventually be indicted and even convicted for corrupt practices, raised serious questions about the future of Forza Italia. The party had been compared to the Gaullist Party in France. But the Gaullists had been led by an incorruptible and untarnished military hero— a far cry from a business magnate like Berlusconi, whose actions and associations were far from immaculate. It appeared conceivable that the decline of the Christian Democracy in 1993–1994 might be followed by the similarly dramatic decline of Forza Italia.

The decline did arrive, but it was not as far-reaching or as sustained as many predicted. In the 1996 election, Forza Italia suffered a very slight setback. It garnered 20.6 percent of the vote, compared with 21.0 percent in 1994, and it won 123 seats in the Chamber of Deputies, compared with 112 in 1994. The gain in seats was illusory: it simply represented the number of single-member districts that had been allotted to Northern League candidates by the Pole of Liberty alliance in 1994 and were now allotted by the same alliance to Forza Italia candidates. But with the defection of the Northern League, the center-right alliance had suffered a clear-cut defeat, and the center-left came to power.

Yet Berlusconi remained the leader of Forza Italia, and he continued to survive both his legal problems stemming from his 1998 conviction on bribery and fraud charges and the increasing debts of his business empire, for which he frequently sought special privileges from the Italian state. But after Fininvest (or the holding company Mediaset) was floated on the Milan stock market and the stock rose quickly, Berlusconi's financial problems vanished.

Despite his faults and legal problems, Berlusconi retained the support of the middle-class masses that backed him in 1994 and 2001. The polls showed that about one-third of the electorate expressed hostility to him because of his fraudulent record, one-third felt he was unjustly accused, and one-third was neutral and believed that the judges may have gone too far. Whereas the Northern League is a populist middle-class party that appeals to the industrialized small towns and small business owners of the Alpine foothills, Berlusconi's Forza Italia is a populist middle-class party that appeals to the great metropolitan areas of the north. In 2001 it polled 29.4 percent of the vote and was by far the largest political party group in parliament with 176 seats in the Chamber of Deputies. In the 2004 European parliamentary elections and 2005 regional elections, its electoral fortunes waned, but it remained the top party and the leading force of the center-right coalition. In 2006 it bounced back to 23.6 percent of the vote on the heels of Berlusconi's media blitz during the electoral campaign. He appeared continually on news programs and on variety shows, and he called in to make his presence felt on the commentaries to the weekend soccer matches. Through his constant presence on television, he was able to keep the campaign focused on himself and his coalition as the champions of the middle class against the encroachments of the state and the privileges of the "power brokers." In his attacks against the judiciary and those who would impose "rules" on the country's entrepreneurs, he alienated a good part of the business establishment, organized labor, the cooperative movement, and artisans, but he still was able to retain in his coalition a good part of northern Italy (Lombardy, Veneto, Friuli-Venezia Giulia, and Piedmont) and slim margins in some of the southern regions such as Sicily and Puglia. In the rest of the country, the party was not able to return to its strong 2001 result and lost significant support in central and southern Italy. After the creation of the PdL in November 2007 and the collapse of the second Prodi government in January 2008, Berlusconi had the opportunity for making a significant electoral comeback. In the April 2008 election his unified party succeeded in gaining 37.4 percent of the vote, the most any single party had won since the 1979 election result for the DC. That result was repeated in the 2009 European parliamentary elections with 35.3 percent of the vote.

Despite all of the socioeconomic difficulties that have characterized Italy in 2008 and 2009, Berlusconi continues to enjoy widespread public support. His coalition has projected a solid front in both houses of parliament, and there is absolutely no doubt that Berlusconi is in charge of both his party and his government. With its hands tied by the overall level of government debt, Berlusconi's government has done little to stimulate the economy, nor has it undertaken to introduce serious changes in the system of welfare or education. In fact, most of the attention during his first years in office has been focused on his attempts to avoid appearing in court in cases dealing with the corruption of judges (SME trial), the diversion of funds abroad (the conviction of David Mills), and funding of his initial real estate investments by the Mafia (Dell'Utri and Spatuzza trials). When the first law shielding Berlusconi from appearing in court (Alfano law) was declared unconstitutional by the Constitutional Court, Berlusconi's majority introduced a new one to gain time and avoid damaging court appearances.

In the meantime, much public attention has been focused on Berlusconi's private life, including his affairs with call girls (Patrizia D'Addario), his friendship with a minor (Noemi Letizia), and the request of a divorce from his wife (Veronica Lario). During the last two years these stories have dominated the headlines and gossip columns. In Italy's male chauvinist culture such developments are not considered harmful to a politician's reputation but rather a confirmation of his virility and determination. Berlusconi has also been helped in riding out these scandals by the difficulties encountered by the center-left in remaining together and rallying behind a political leader with an equivalent level of charisma and boldness in seizing issues and using them for his own political gain. Berlusconi's ability to immediately use natural disasters (the Abruzzo earthquake), international meetings (G-7 and G-20 in 2008), and sporting events for his own purposes are legendary and have transformed him into a political leader with a huge and loyal following.[31]

The 'Post-Fascists': National Alliance From the late 1940s until 1994, the neo-Fascists of the Italian Social Movement, or MSI, were little more than a minor irritant on the right flank of Christian Democracy. They reached their peak in 1972 with 8.7 percent of the vote, whereas they usually polled between 5 percent and 7 percent (see Table 4-2). Their positions on public issues seemed conventionally ultraconservative. They opposed national economic planning and restrictions on free enterprise, favored repeal of the divorce law in the 1974 referendum campaign, and advocated heavy defense spending. Nevertheless, their commitment to a corporate state based on functional representation, as well as the undercurrent of violence that seemed to lurk behind their speeches and their party rituals, placed them under much suspicion. The other Italian parties generally treated them as untouchables, and their external backing for a coalition cabinet was considered tainted and unacceptable.

Between 1992 and 1994, under the leadership of Gianfranco Fini, a serious effort was made to transform the MSI into a mainstream conservative party, the National Alliance, committed to maintaining liberty and democracy. The party's fascist past was soft-pedaled. Although some diehards still uttered racist and fascist statements, Fini rejected anti-Semitism, said that fascism belonged to the past, and projected a moderate and reasonable image. His new party advocated a centralized Italy (rejecting Bossi's federalism in concept, although voting for all of the Bossi proposals in parliament); a unified national health service; a revamped pension system but with adequate safety nets to protect the neediest cases; a reformed policy of public investment in the south (again, contrary to the demands of the Northern League that such investment be drastically reduced); and retention of the big public corporations that have conducted investment programs in the south (disagreeing with both Bossi and Berlusconi on this score). As for Europe, Fini supported NATO and the European Union. But there was one note of nostalgia: the National Alliance favored renegotiating with Slovenia the status of the Istrian peninsula, which was annexed by Yugoslavia after World War II.[32]

With its new message, in 1994 the National Alliance was able to more than double the votes cast for the MSI in 1992. With the collapse of the patronage-nourished DC machine in the south, the National Alliance received in the 1994 election 13.5 percent of the vote and 109 seats in the Chamber of Deputies (versus 5.4 percent and 34 seats in 1992)—see Tables 4-2 and 4-3. It also was allotted six portfolios in the Berlusconi cabinet (the MSI had never been admitted to any cabinet). In the 1996 election, the National Alliance continued to advance in terms of votes, to 15.7 percent, but lost 16 seats because of the Northern League's defection from the Pole of Liberty electoral alliance.

Since 1996 Fini has steered an ever more moderate course. He worked closely with Massimo D'Alema on the bicameral commission for constitutional reform, which was instead sacked by Berlusconi; he has disavowed Mussolini and has edged the younger firebrands of fascist leanings out of the National Alliance; he now supports privatization and approves of Italy's entry into the Euro Area; he has softened his stand on immigration; and he has sought to identify with foreign conservative parties such as the Gaullists and the British Conservatives rather than with fascist parties such as Jean-Marie Le Pen's National Front in France.[33]

Fini's increasingly moderate stance is well illustrated by his tenure as minister of foreign affairs during 2004–2005, when he reemphasized all of Italy's traditional foreign policy positions in favor of Europe, the United States, and world peace. He was the first government official to distance himself from Italy's presence in the U.S.-led conflict in

Iraq, and he was an ardent supporter of the European constitution. In domestic politics, he supported two of the three June 2005 referenda on in vitro insemination (the Catholic Church was against all three) and was the first government minister to ask for the resignation of the director of the Bank of Italy, Antonio Fazio, when it was revealed that he personally favored and worked behind the scenes to help one of the consortia trying to gain control of the Antonveneta bank. In assuming these positions, Fini was not backed by the majority of his party. Indeed, when other party leaders were on the verge of organizing a coup, he exercised his prerogative as president of the party and sacked all of them. As a result, Fini has become one of the most respected leaders of the center-right in the country, eclipsing at the end of 2005 the popularity enjoyed by Silvio Berlusconi. Fini fully expected to participate on a par with Berlusconi in the 2006 electoral campaign, but the frenetic campaign unleashed by the former prime minister served to overshadow Fini as a potential alternative leader of the center-right coalition. With 12.2 percent of the vote in the Chamber of Deputies, the National Alliance remained stable in relation to its result in 2001, but fell behind its result in the 2004 European parliamentary elections and the 2005 regional elections. The merging with Silvio Berlusconi's Forza Italia in November 2007 has brought the National Alliance into the European democratic fold of center-right parties organized under the banner of the European Popular Party. In 2008 Gianfranco Fini was elected president of the Chamber of Deputies and has operated as a moderating force in managing potential conflicts between the Berlusconi government and the president of the republic. In this role he has raised his stature as both a supporter of the state institutions and a balancing force between the government and opposition blocs. On numerous occasions he has sought to differentiate his position from that of Berlusconi when he felt that the prime minister had gone too far in assuming a personal position that did not have widespread public support.[34]

The Voters: The Electoral System and Voting Behavior

Although Italy's major political parties hold the reins of government power, they are only as powerful as the support they receive from Italy's voters, another set of actors in the political process. As this section explains, elections in Italy are organized in ways that have important consequences for voters and the party system.

The Electoral System

Until 1994 members of the lower house of parliament, the Chamber of Deputies, were elected by a list system of proportional representation from multimember districts. The number of seats awarded to a party in an electoral district was determined by dividing that party's total vote by an electoral quotient (total number of seats plus two). The remainders resulting from this operation (if a party received no seats, its entire vote was treated as a remainder) were then sent to Rome to be totaled up for each party in the Single National College, which then proceeded to allocate several dozen additional seats on the basis of proportional representation.[35] A system of preferential voting gave the voters a chance not only to support their party list but also to express their preferences among the names on the party list. A more complex system, relying mostly but not entirely on proportional representation, was employed in electing members of the upper house, the Senate. By means of this electoral system, each party obtained a share of parliamentary seats roughly proportional to its share of the total vote. Moreover, under the distribution of remainders for the Chamber of Deputies by the Single National College, even a party with between 1 percent and 2 percent of the vote might be able to win a few seats.

The Italian electoral system had some important consequences for the party system. First, it favored the proliferation and survival of splinter parties with as little as 1 percent or 2 percent of the vote, because even such tiny parties were able to win a few seats. Second, the Italian electoral system prevented any landslide in parliamentary elections, and consequently made it all but impossible for one party to achieve a majority in parliament. Under proportional representation, small shifts in voting behavior only resulted in equally small shifts in legislative representation. Third, the system of preferential voting encouraged factionalism by giving minority factions in a party a chance to appeal to party voters over the heads of party leaders. It also encouraged corruption by compelling candidates on the same party lists to launch very expensive personal campaigns for preference votes and to solicit funds from private interests for that purpose.

In April 1993 Italian voters approved a referendum proposal to elect three-fourths of the members of the Senate from single-member districts by plurality vote (first-past-the-post). A parliamentary committee then prepared a bill to adopt a plurality system for both houses of parliament. The committee presented its proposal on August 5, 1993, and it was adopted by parliament later that year.

Under the law, about three-fourths of the members of each house were to be elected from small single-member constituencies by plurality—that is, the candidate with the largest number of votes would win the seat even if he or she did not gain an absolute majority of the votes. There was no provision for a second ballot. The remaining one-fourth of the members of each house would be elected from somewhat larger multimember districts on the basis of proportional representation. To be awarded any of the proportional representation seats set aside for the Chamber of Deputies, however, a party had to poll at least 4 percent of the total votes cast for the proportional representation lists nationwide.

The effect of the 1993 law, combined with the public revulsion engendered by "Kick-back City," was to eliminate the three minor center parties (Social Democrats, Republicans, and Liberals) that had played a supporting role in so many coalition cabinets. Even the Greens, the Network, the PSI, and the Democratic Alliance were unable to scale the 4 percent barrier. Nevertheless, they were able to win single-member seats by taking advantage of the law's provision for the formation of electoral alliances, which for them meant entering the Progressive Alliance led by the Democratic Party of the Left. Even the Communist Refoundation was able to carry twenty-nine single-member districts by representing the Progressive Alliance, while the PDS obligingly stood aside. Meanwhile, by entering into an electoral alliance (the Pole of Liberty) with Berlusconi's Forza Italia, the Northern League and the Christian Democratic Center were rewarded by being allowed to have their candidates run as the sole standard-bearers for the Pole of Liberty in some single-member districts. In this way, they were able to "win" more single-member districts than would have been possible had they contested those districts without allies. For this reason, the move to single-member districts with plurality voting did not result in a transition to a two-party system.[36]

How did the majoritarian electoral law affect the Italian party system? Not as much as was hoped. For example, the previous electoral law favored the proliferation of splinter parties, but under the majoritarian provision such parties could still gain entry to parliament by forming alliances with major parties. The previous proportional representation law prevented landslides in parliamentary elections and made it virtually impossible for a single party to win a parliamentary majority. The majoritarian law permitted landslides, but they were landslides for electoral alliances rather than single parties, and the parties in the Berlusconi alliance were soon at loggerheads and generating gridlock.

One major achievement of the first-past-the-post system was to eliminate preferential voting, which made it more difficult for minority factions to appeal to party voters over the heads of party leaders. Another achievement of the law was that it seemed, at first glance, to encourage a kind of moderate pluralism, with center-left and center-right alliances alternating in power—that is, a bipolar system. But the bargaining power of splinter parties was enhanced: their refusal to join an alliance could actually cost the alliance crucial single-member districts. In 1996 the extremist Social Movement Tricolored Flame (MFST), which polled only 0.9 percent of the vote, cost the Pole of Liberty several highly competitive seats simply by running its own separate candidates.

It was suggested that the majoritarian election law confers greater political weight prior to the election on smaller and midsize parties and offers a positive incentive for parties occupying the same part of the ideological spectrum to form an alliance. If small parties did not form alliances with the larger parties, it was highly improbable they would be able to overcome the 4 percent requirement to participate in the distribution of proportional seats (25 percent of the total). Both the center-right and center-left coalitions came to understand the need to partner with small parties prior to the election rather than fall prey to the whims of the electorate and iron-tight electoral rules after the vote. Such a shortcoming cost the center-right the 1996 election and the center-left the election in 2001. In the last analysis, then, the electoral law changed the nature of preelectoral party strategies and created the need for the broadest electoral coalitions, but it did not reduce the number of parties remaining in the system. As a result, the party system remained highly fragmented.[37]

Because the electoral law just described was generally regarded as unsatisfactory and provisional at the time of its passage in 1993, many observers speculated that a new election law would be enacted before very long. In fact, fearing that the previous rules would disproportionally favor the center-left, before the 2006 election the Berlusconi government changed the electoral rules back to proportional representation. Instead, the return to proportional representation based on national coalition lists in the Chamber of Deputies and regional coalition lists in the Senate served to favor the center-left. It allowed the center-left to transform its 23,000-vote majority in the Chamber of Deputies into a solid majority (349–281) and its minority status among voters in the Senate election into a majority of seats (159–156). In this result, the center-left was also helped by the allocation of 12 seats in the Chamber of Deputies and 6 in the Senate to Italians overseas.

The new electoral law did not help to reduce the number of political parties present in the Chamber of Deputies or Senate elections, but it did reduce the number of parties presenting themselves without an affiliation with either of the two major coalitions. In the Chamber elections of 2006, only 0.4 percent of the vote was represented by parties outside of the two main blocs, compared with 6.7 percent in 2001 and 4.5 percent in 1996.[38] Also, the new electoral law and the electrified nature of the national campaign helped to raise the level of voter participation. In 2006, 83.6 percent of the eligible electorate cast ballots versus 81.4 percent five years earlier, signaling a major increase in the number of voters between the ages of eighteen and twenty-five going to the polls. In 2001 a higher percentage of older voters turned out for the Senate elections (82.7 versus the 81.4 for the Chamber of Deputes). The percentage turnout for Chamber of Deputies and Senate elections in 2006 was practically the same (83.6 and 83.5 percent, respectively), and it was the center-left that disproportionally gained from the increase in young voters. In 2008, with the same electoral law but a different logic in the creation of the major party alliances, the number of parties succeeding in achieving parliamentary representation was severely reduced, as was the case for voter turnout, which declined by almost three percent. The parties that did not align themselves with the two major blocs—the Left Rainbow coalition bringing together the dissident DS group with the PRC, PDCdI, and Greens achieved only 3.1 percent of the vote in the Chamber; the Right (Destra) of Storace and Santachè polled 2.4 percent of the vote; and the Socialists won only 1.0 percent—were barred from the allocation of seats by the 4 percent ceiling dictated by the electoral law.

Voting Behavior

Voting patterns in Italy have been based to a considerable degree on the traditional social, economic, or religious cleavages. The prime example of a socioeconomic cleavage is social class. Before the political earthquake of the 1990s, the Communists had a plurality of the working-class vote, but substantial minorities were being polled by the Socialists and Christian Democrats. Among middle-class voters, a majority of shopkeepers and artisans and at least a plurality of business and professional people voted for the Christian Democrats, and the Liberals and neo-Fascists were their chief competitors. The Communists and Socialists had substantial success in penetrating one stratum of middle-class voters: white-collar workers and lower-level civil servants. Social class also served to divide the agricultural electorate, with large landowners mostly supporting Liberals and neo-Fascists, medium and small landowners voting overwhelmingly for the Christian Democrats, and sharecroppers and farm laborers backing the Communists and Socialists.

Other cleavages reduced the impact of social class. One such division was religious practice as opposed to anticlericalism. The Christian Democrats polled a substantial share of the working-class vote, especially in the devoutly Catholic areas in the northeast. Communist and Socialist successes among a substantial minority of middle-class voters in north-central Italy could be explained in part by the anticlericalism characteristic of regions such as Emilia-Romagna and Tuscany.

Region was another line of demarcation. Regional voting traditions cut across class lines in influencing voting behavior, but such regional traditions may have been simply expressing or reinforcing religious cleavages.

Finally, union membership may have been a more reliable factor than mere social class in predisposing voters to cast their ballots for leftist parties.

These traditional patterns of the 1950s and 1960s have been undergoing some major changes. For one thing, the rural exodus has uprooted great numbers of small landowners, sharecroppers, and farm laborers from their traditional political and social networks and often from their home regions as well. Second, the rise of the services sector has injected a new element of ambiguity into the Italian class structure. Third, families and social networks such as the Catholic Church and its lay organizations seem to be losing their ability to socialize young voters into traditional patterns of voting behavior. As a result, greater numbers of voters are making their choices less on the basis of traditional party identification (vote of *appartenenza* or belonging) and more on the basis of the parties' positions on the issues (vote of opinion). At the same time, the number and variety of voters who cast ballots on the basis of how happy or frustrated they are with how the incumbents are satisfying their personal needs (vote of exchange) are growing, especially now that the Christian Democrats have lost their monopoly over sources of patronage. Although the urban middle classes are most likely to cast a vote of opinion, the vote of exchange characterizes the precariously employed service workers of the urban subproletariat.[39]

Some early assessments of voting patterns in 1994 indicated more stability on the left than on the right. The PDS, like the PCI before it, continued to be the dominant party in the four regions of north-central Italy—Emilia-Romagna, Tuscany, Umbria, and the Marches—but the defection of most PSI voters reduced the strength of the left even in these historic strongholds. The PDS also showed a great deal of strength in parts of the south: Campania, Basilicata, and Calabria. The Northern League was particularly strong in Lombardy and the Veneto, but Forza Italia carried most of the north and also led in Sardinia and Sicily (where it was rumored to have Mafia support). In large parts of the continental south, especially Latium, Abruzzi, and Apulia, the National Alliance led the field. Therefore, the chief beneficiaries of the Socialist and Christian Democratic collapse have been the National Alliance and, to a lesser degree, the PDS in the south, and Forza Italia and, to a lesser degree, the Northern League in the north.[40]

After the 1996 election, some observers pointed out that the Northern League was becoming the dominant force in northeastern Italy, especially eastern Lombardy and the Veneto, which is an area of flourishing small and midsize industry and bustling small cities. In this area, which was once known as the "white" (that is, devoutly Catholic) northeast and in which Christian Democracy had once enjoyed hegemony, the Northern League's appeal grew with all classes and segments of the population. By contrast, Forza Italia was outstripping the Northern League in the big metropolitan centers of the north, which is a more competitive political milieu with many service workers. The old class alignments were losing their hold in the north.[41]

It is much too early to speak of a permanent party realignment or stable voting bases for the new parties. In fact, another political earthquake took place in 2005 when both Forza Italia and the Northern League lost substantial support in the regional and local elections in favor of the center-left. But the deeply rooted class and regional allegiances of the 1950s, 1960s, and early 1970s seem to have been seriously weakened in Italy and other parts of the Western world as the postindustrial age brings social and class redefinition in its wake. The regional distribution of the vote in 2006 demonstrated that the center-right led by Forza Italia remained the dominant political party in four northern regions (from Piedmont to Friuli-Venezia Giulia), but it was never able to break through in Valle d'Aosta and Trentino-Alto Adige. It also lost support in Liguria. In the south, both Forza Italia and National Alliance parties lost their previously dominant positions, with the exception of Sicily. In the rest of the south, Forza Italia has given way to the Olive Tree coalition. In 2008 the PdL made major gains throughout the country and especially in the south. In the 2009

European elections, however, the PdL lost important support in the south, especially in Sicily, due to its less-than-friendly stance on the effective allocation of regional development funds for southern infrastructure projects. The 2010 regional elections will represent a major test of the center-right's ability to bounce back as the dominant political force in the south.

Interest Groups

The changes in the party system in the 1990s were not paralleled by changes in the nature and structure of interest groups. What did change, however, was how interest groups interacted with the parties. Gone were the days when interest groups functioned as "conveyor belts," linking the political parties with civil society. Now through the media, political parties were in a position to speak directly with the voters, and interest groups became freer in choosing their preferred interlocutors for policy decisions that mattered to their members and leaders. In the past, interest groups such as trade unions, associations of shop owners, employers associations, artisan groups, farmers associations, pensioners groups, youth organizations, women's groups, environmental groups, cultural associations, cooperatives, and even sporting clubs had clear political affiliations and were part of the ideological subcultures that pervaded Italian society. But since the early 1990s these clear political affiliations have waned, and the policymaking process has been opened to some new actors and interests.

Postwar Italy's interest group system resembled the French system, but with some significant differences. Like France, Italy has had an ideologically divided labor movement that included a Communist-dominated labor confederation (the Italian General Confederation of Labor, or CGIL) that contained some Socialist members; a labor confederation (the Italian Union of Labor, or UIL) made up predominantly of Socialists and Republicans; and a Catholic-dominated labor confederation (the Italian Confederation of Workers' Unions, or CISL). The Italians and the French have also been somewhat more accepting of anomic group behavior (riots and demonstrations) than the citizens of Northern Europe.

There have also been some notable contrasts. Because the Italian parliament exerts greater influence on policymaking than does the parliament of the Fifth Republic, Italian interest groups have expended more effort in the legislative arena. They have found the powerful standing committees, which are able to enact minor bills directly into law, a most rewarding site for their endeavors. Many interest groups, going beyond mere lobbying, have tried to secure the election of their own officials to parliament on some party's list. These so-called *parentela* (kinship) groups have had close official ties with a political party and have acted openly as organized factions within that party in parliament. By contrast, the *clientela* (customers) groups have been regarded by government agencies as the sole official representatives of a given set of interests. An example of a past *clientela* group was the Italian General Confederation of Industry (Confindustria), and an example of a *parentela* group was Catholic Action in Christian Democracy. With the disappearance of the formerly dominant mass parties, such as the Christian Democracy and the Italian Communist Party, the *parentela* groups have been able to strike out on their own. The rest of this section describes the interest groups representing various sectors of the Italian economy and organized religion.

Agricultural Interest Groups

Because Italian family farms have tended to be much smaller than French or German family farms, the Italian General Confederation of Agriculture (Confagricoltura), which speaks for medium and large landowners, represents only a minority of Italian agricultural proprietors. The more powerful farm organization is the National Confederation of Direct Cultivators (Coldiretti), whose members live mostly on smaller farms. Coldiretti used to be a *parentela* group directly affiliated with the Christian Democrats. By virtue of its control over the Federation of Agricultural Consortiums (Federconsorzi), a quasi-public organization that furnished credits, subsidies, storage facilities, and other services to farmers, Coldiretti was once one of Italy's most powerful pressure groups. With the disappearance of Christian Democracy, Coldiretti has had to reposition itself in the political spectrum and redefine its role as a representative institution. This need has led Coldiretti to join with what in the past were farm organizations affiliated with other parts of the ideological spectrum and become more visible to their members and the general public in championing certain causes, such as organic farming, and policies.

Since the 1980s Italian agricultural pressure groups have become remarkably weaker. This trend is understandable in view of the steady movement of agricultural workers to cities and towns. With the farm population rapidly diminishing, groups such as Coldiretti have suffered a loss of clout. Indeed, farm organizations are still powerful, but the curve plotting their influence definitely slopes downward. One of the difficulties faced by farm organizations has been the shift of the policymaking from the national to the European level. The past dominance of the DC allowed farm organizations to remain influential at the national level and depend on the government linkages provided by the Ministry of Agriculture to represent the organization at the European level. After the implosion of the DC and the old party system, however, organizations such as Coldiretti had to forge their own autonomous links to Europe and build at the national level alliances across party lines with other agricultural organizations. The strategy seems to have worked, because during the last few years many Italian agricultural products, from Sicilian blood oranges to Parmigiano Reggiano cheese, have received the EU's "protected designation of origin" label, thereby shielding local products from imitations from other parts of Europe or abroad.

Labor Interest Groups

Italian organized labor has been weakened in the past by its division into the three politically affiliated organizations. Italian unions also have been chronically weak in recruiting members, collecting dues, and amassing the economic resources needed to support possible strikes. Lack of leadership at the plant level has been another disability. Heavy unemployment in the post–World War II era weakened the bargaining power of Italian unions and resulted in persistently low wages for Italian workers. But it also resulted, it must be admitted, in lower prices and other competitive advantages for Italian exports, thereby encouraging expansion of the Italian economy.

After 1968, new tendencies developed within the Italian labor movement. First, the three labor confederations manifested greater independence from their respective parties and showed a marked tendency to cooperate with each other on many issues. Second, the unions no longer allowed their officials to hold a parliamentary seat and a trade union office simultaneously. Third, in the 1970s labor became more powerful, and the CGIL, CISL, and UIL confederations were much more militant in pushing their demands. In fact, at times, particularly in 1976–1979 when the Communist Party was supporting austerity, the Catholic unions made more far-reaching demands than the Communist unions. Labor's greater intransigence reflected pressure from newly employed southern migrants and semiskilled workers, who demanded rapid progress to make up for past deprivations.

Developments in the trade union field were by no means marked by linear progression, however. After greater expansion, intransigence, and decentralization of authority to the plant level in 1968–1972, trade union memberships began to decline, union authority was recentralized at the national level, and unions began to pursue a more cooperative relationship with employers and with the state during the 1980s. Meanwhile, the problem of selling Italian products in increasingly competitive export markets, the impact of free collective bargaining on improving the lot of skilled workers while raising economic hurdles against the employment of marginal workers, and the rising burden of inflation greatly weakened the unions and persuaded union leaders to moderate their demands. The January 1983 agreement by the non-Communist unions to accept a slight downward modification of the system of wage indexation (the so-called *scala mobile,* or escalator, that ties wages to the price index) was a straw in the wind. The failure of the Communist attempt to challenge the government's settlement with the non-Communist unions by appealing to the voters in a referendum was a clear indication of labor's diminished influence. In July 1992 the Amato cabinet was able to reach an agreement with the three principal labor confederations and the representatives of organized business to abolish the system of wage indexation altogether. This achievement marked the beginning of a new and more positive decade in labor-government relations.

What seemed in the late 1980s to be dismal prospects for organized labor improved considerably in the 1990s. In 1992–1993 the Amato and Ciampi cabinets, in which nonpolitical technocrats were prominent, showed a new willingness to bring the unions into the decision-making process as equal partners. The ongoing disintegration of the major political parties made this kind of close cooperation more feasible, because neither the labor confederations nor the cabinet could be viewed any longer as mere mouthpieces of the party machines. The improved climate in government-labor relations was temporarily interrupted in 1994 during the short-lived Berlusconi cabinet. When Berlusconi attempted to push through pension reform without eliciting sufficient input from the labor confederations, the unions launched a wave of massive protest demonstrations that helped to bring down the government. When the Dini cabinet took office in early 1995, the unions showed their willingness to collaborate closely with Dini, another nonpolitical figure, in drawing up a plan for pension reform.

The position of organized labor in Italy, therefore, has improved substantially. The three labor confederations, frequently referred to as the Triple Alliance, are more inclined to cooperate with each other now that they are no longer party-dominated. Their moderation, and their willingness to accept industrial, economic, and social change as long as they are given a major voice in shaping that change, has made the government willing to use them as virtual coalition partners. Their greater readiness to consult their rank and file at the plant level through a newly established system of works councils has made it easier for them to obtain rank-and-file support for whatever bargains they strike with the government. Their new authority and credibility have induced the center-left government to use them as unofficial coalition partners to counterbalance the extreme demands of the Party of Communist Refoundation. The trade unions have remained powerful among socioeconomic organizations in Italy, because they have carved out an important role as public rather than membership-based social service organizations. Through their *Patronati,* or social service offices, the trade unions help Italian and immigrant workers, and their families when the laws apply to them, to do their taxes, apply for pensions, determine eligibility for unemployment compensation, and access home health care and other social services made available by Italy's welfare system. Therefore, Italy's trade unions are important not only in organizing workers to deal with industrial relations and wage demands but also in acting as a preferred channel by many to navigate the waters of Italy's welfare state.

Business Interest Groups

In the first few decades after World War II, Italian business was characterized by a higher degree of concentration and less distrust of big business than business in France. Also, small business lacked the autonomy and self-assertiveness of the big firms of the Genoa-Milan-Turin industrial triangle. Confindustria, representing the great majority of industrial firms, tended to speak for big-business interests. During the 1980s and 1990s that relationship changed, and small and midsize enterprises began to have more influence in shaping the relationship between business and trade unions and participation in the design of government policies.

Confindustria had a classic lobbying relationship with the Christian Democracy. Its efforts to transform this *clientela* relationship into a *parentela* bond, however, were not successful. It was also unsuccessful in preserving a united front among Italian employers. Some industrial giants such as Fiat preferred to pursue their own policies, independent of Confindustria guidance. Far more important was the position taken by the public corporations, which had their own employers association, Intersind. Although Confindustria tended to be allied with the Liberals and with the right wing of the Christian Democrats, Intersind seemed more inclined toward a kind of Italian New Deal, based on welfare capitalism and social reforms. In this, it had much in common with the Socialists and with the left-wing Christian Democrats.

Recent developments have changed this picture, however. First, the public sector enterprises were discredited by their partisan connections and by the gross inefficiency that increasingly reigned in their factories. By the 1970s they had lost the aura of infallibility they had acquired in the 1960s. With the disintegration of the Christian Democratic and Socialist Parties in the early 1990s, public sector enterprises were deprived of their principal political allies. Their current situation has changed considerably through the government's privatization campaign, which has significantly taken the state out of the role of entrepreneur and owner of the country's major industrial assets. Second, Confindustria staged something of a comeback in Italian public opinion in the 1970s, profiting from the backlash against the "Hot Autumn" of 1968–1969. Third, small business owners are playing a more decisive role in Confindustria. This development reflects the economic slump that hit the traditional heavy industry of the northwest triangle, while small and medium enterprises (SMEs) brought great prosperity to the central Italian regions of Emilia-Romagna, Tuscany, Umbria, Latium, and beyond. And finally, Confindustria has become larger and more heterogeneous; indeed, it has virtually absorbed Intersind. The other business organizations representing SMEs and the artisan sector, such as the Confederation of Small Firms, the Artisan Confederation, and the National Confederation of Artisans, have become quite important in determining national wage levels and industrial relations. For example, Antonio D'Amato served as president of Confindustria from 2000 to 2004. During his tenure, D'Amato, who had close ties with Berlusconi, took positions that increased the conflict between business and the trade unions. But the SME and artisan trade associations did not agree with Confindustria's hard stance against the unions and went ahead and signed a labor agreement with them. Eventually, Confindustria had to back down from its position. Luca di Montezemolo, the head of Ferrari and Fiat who took over Confindustria from D'Amato in 2004, quickly abandoned his predecessor's policy by detaching himself and his organization from the Berlusconi government. He reestablished a good working relationship with the SME and artisan organizations and began to cooperate with the trade unions in pushing the government to formulate policies spawning investments in a variety of innovative sectors from technologically advanced industries to sustainable tourism.

During the 2008 election campaign Berlusconi succeeded in alienating most of the organized interest groups from Confindustria to the labor unions and agricultural interests. In his vitriolic attacks against the "establishment" and organized interests, he claimed that they were attempting to block the entry of new actors in the economy and social system. Berlusconi has always seen himself as a "new man" fighting the establishment, while his predecessor, Romano Prodi, presented himself as one able to work with organized interests in seeking common solutions. The election on March 13 of Emma Mercegaglia as the first female president of Confindustria helped to heal the rift between the employers organization and the Berlusconi government. Confindustria was particularly concerned about the need for concerted government action in response to the mounting economic crisis that had drastically cut production and exports. The government, however, could only repeat that because of the size of the overall public debt, it was restricted in undertaking any bold action other than providing unemployment compensation to laid-off workers. In retrospect, the economic crisis proved to have a silver lining in that Italian business and financial institutions were able to make significant inroads into markets where they had previously been absent. The best example of this outcome was the case of Fiat and the bailout of Chrysler in the United States and the repositioning of Fiat as an important European and global actor in the automobile industry.

Catholic Interest Groups: The Church and Its Lay Organizations

The Catholic Church and the various associations of Catholic laypeople have always been active in Italy's interest group system. Heavily influential throughout Italian public life by means of the Concordat of 1929 (which has constitutional status and can be altered only by a bilateral agreement between church and state or by a formal constitutional amendment), the Catholic Church intervened openly in Italian domestic politics for two decades after World War II. But its intervention grew less pronounced in the 1960s and 1970s under Popes John XXIII and Paul VI. Under Popes John Paul II and Benedict XVI, the church has begun to reestablish closer ties with the state. It has become more assertive in asking for public resources in support of Catholic schools; limitations on gay marriage, in vitro fertilization, and adoption policies; and maintenance of Catholic religious instruction in the state's elementary schools.

The principal church-sponsored lay organization is Catholic Action, which at its peak had 3 million members. Its separate groups or branches include the Union of Men, the Union of Women, Italian Catholic Action Youth, and the Federation of Italian Catholic University Students. The president of Catholic Action and the presidents of its component branches are appointed by individual bishops at the diocesan level. Other Catholic associations, not under the tutelage of the hierarchy, pursue specialized nonreligious goals. They include Coldiretti, the Italian Association of Catholic Schoolteachers, and the Christian Association of Italian Workers (ACLI). These organizations have acted as economic and social pressure groups and have not behaved primarily as spokespersons for the church.

Since the late 1960s, the influence of the church and its lay organizations has been greatly diminished. The failure of a referendum campaign in 1974 to repeal the divorce law and in 1981 to repeal an abortion law, as well as the revision of the Concordat, are all indicative of waning clerical influence. Some Catholic lay organizations, such as the Confederation of Catholic University Students, came out in favor of the divorce law. Meanwhile, associations such as the ACLI have been steering a more autonomous course: even before the political upheaval of the 1990s, ACLI cut its formal ties with both Catholic Action and Christian Democracy, although it still maintained a dialogue with the church.

Perhaps one reason for the increasingly independent stance adopted by Catholic organizations was their greatly reduced strength, which was itself a symptom of the growing secularization of Italian society. Catholic Action, which had 3 million members at its peak in the 1950s, was down to 600,000 by the late 1970s. ACLI, which had about a million members in the 1950s, had only 400,000 in the late 1970s.[42] Clearly, Catholic organizations are no longer the dominant, hegemonic force they were in the immediate postwar decades. And there is no longer a single mass Catholic Party to unite and energize these organizations. Nor is such a party being encouraged by the dominant elements in the church, which seem to favor something like the German Christian Democratic Union—a large center party composed of both Catholics and center-right liberals.[43]

Catholic groups assumed a more vocal stance in the summer of 2009 as the scandal involving the prime minister and his use of paid escorts became public. The Catholic groups, especially the newspaper *Avvenire* and the magazine *Familia Cristiana*, argued that public figures should assume a more sober life style and not pretend that personal behavior does not have an impact in the framing of public morality. In late 2009 the editor of *Avvenire* was forced to resign due to alleged pedophile tendencies. Those accusations by a newspaper run by Berlusconi's brother have proved to be false, and now the whole nature of church-government relations is up for scrutiny by an inquiry ordered by the pope. Whatever this investigation turns up, it is clear that the relations between the church hierarchy and the prime minister's office will never be as close as they were in the past.

Current Trends: The Advent of Fragmented Pluralism and the Rise of NGOs

According to some observers, the Italian interest group system seems to be moving in the direction of fragmented pluralism—that is, toward the weakening of old established interest groups speaking for business or labor as a whole and toward the rise of a multiplicity of new groups, such as nongovernmental organizations (NGOs), each expressing a narrow range of interests and concerns. These Italian lobbies, like U.S. lobbies, serve the specific social and economic interests of their members.[44] For example, social service delivery organizations have emerged in response to the increased decentralization of social services by the regional, provincial, and city governments. Communion and Liberation, a conservative Catholic movement founded by Don Giussani, has been particularly active in the provision of services in Lombardy and other regions in the north. This growing Catholic movement has made its mark in center-right politics by fielding candidates for political office such as Roberto Formigoni, the powerful president of the Lombardy region.

NGOs have greatly benefited from the trend toward the privatization of service delivery in areas such as school lunch programs, drug rehabilitation centers, management of hospitals, and programs for seniors and the handicapped. In this respect, it is not surprising that in the more leftist regions, where regional and local governments have always pioneered innovations in social and economic development policies and yielded high performance, NGOs have made their strong presence felt. There, the NGO phenomenon has taken the form of tremendous growth in the personal services cooperatives tied to the leftist cooperative movement, together with producer and consumer cooperatives that have made great strides in capturing a significant part of the market in food distribution through supermarket chains.

NOTES

1. See Raphael Zariski, "Italy," in *Western European Party Systems: Trends and Prospects,* ed. Peter H. Merkl (New York: Free Press, 1980), 122–152.
2. Giovanni Sartori, "European Political Parties: The Case of Polarized Pluralism," in *Political Parties and Political Development,* ed. Joseph LaPalombara and Martin Weiner (Princeton, N.J.: Princeton University Press, 1966). See the response by Robert Leonardi, "Polarizzazione o convergenza nel sistema politico italiano," in *La politica nell'Italia che cambia,* ed. Alberto Martinelli and Gianfranco Pasquino (Milan: Feltrinelli, 1978), 299–319.
3. See Joseph LaPalombara, *Democracy Italian Style* (New Haven: Yale University Press, 1987); and Samuel H. Barnes, *Representation in Italy: Institutional Tradition and Electoral Choice* (Chicago: University of Chicago Press, 1977).
4. Robert Leonardi and Douglas A. Wertman, *Italian Christian Democracy: The Politics of Dominance* (New York: St. Martin's Press, 1989); and Donald Sassoon, *The Strategy of the Italian Communist Party: From the Resistance to the Historic Compromise* (London: Frances Pinter, 1981).
5. Leonardi and Wertman, *Italian Christian Democracy,* 130; and "The New Parliament," *News from Italy* (published by the Fondazione Giovanni Agnelli) 10 (July 1983): 11. Also see Robert H. Evans, "The Italian Election of June 1987," *Italian Journal* 1, nos. 2 and 3 (1987): 15.

6. See Zariski, "Italy," 131, and "New Parliament," 11. Also see "A Comprehensive Report on the 1987 Political Elections: Nine Tables of Statistical Data," *Italian Journal* 1, nos. 2 and 3 (1987): 24.

7. See Giorgio Galli, *Il bipartitismo imperfetto* (Bologna: Il Mulino, 1966).

8. See Robert Leonardi, "Polarizzazione o convergenza nel sistema politico italiano?" in *La politica nell'Italia che cambia*, ed. G. Martinelli and Gianfranco Pasquino (Milan: Feltrinelli, 1978), 299–319.

9. On factions within the DC, see Leonardi and Wertman, *Italian Christian Democracy*, 90–124.

10. See Evans, "Italian Election," 12.

11. For the disastrous effects of the corruption scandals and the Mafia connections on the DC, the PSI, and the minor center parties, see Mario Caciagli, "Italie 1993: Vers la Seconde Republique?" *Revue française de science politique* (April 1993): 229–256.

12. Under the new election law of 1993, three-fourths of the seats in the Chamber of Deputies were allocated to single-member districts that could be won by the candidate of a party (or alliance of parties) if he or she obtained a plurality of the votes cast. The other one-fourth was to be distributed on the basis of proportional representation. Because several parties did not run candidates in every single-member district, party voting performance was calculated on the basis of each party's share of the proportional representation vote.

13. For the results of the 1994 election, see Edmondo Berselli, "Solution on the Right: The Evolving Political Scenario," *Italian Journal* 8 (1994): 13–21; Robert H. Evans, "Italy . . . Quo Vadis?" *Italian Journal* 8 (1994): 4–12; Michael Gallagher, Michael Laver, and Peter Mair, *Representative Government in Western Europe*, 2nd ed. (New York: McGraw-Hill, 1995), 168–169; Mark Gilbert, "Italy Turns Rightwards," *Contemporary Review* 265 (July 1994): 4–10; and Francesco Sidoti, "The Significance of the Italian Elections," *Parliamentary Affairs* 47 (July 1994): 333–347.

14. *La Repubblica*, March 31, 1994, 13.

15. For the results of the 1996 elections, see James L. Newell and Martin Bull, "Party Organizations and Alliances in Italy in the 1990s: A Revolution of Sorts," in *Crisis and Transition in Italian Politics*, ed. Martin Bull and Martin Rhodes (London: Frank Cass, 1997), 104.

16. For an analytical account of the process that led to the demise of the PCI and the formation of the PDS, see Leonard Weinberg, *The Transformation of Italian Communism* (New Brunswick, N.J.: Transaction, 1995).

17. See Donald L. M. Blackmer, "Continuity and Change in Postwar Italian Communism," in *Communism in Italy and France*, ed. Donald L. M. Blackmer and Sidney Tarrow (Princeton, N.J.: Princeton University Press, 1975), 21–68.

18. Antonio Gramsci was one of the founders of the Italian Communist Party. He was jailed by the Fascists on November 8, 1926, and died on April 27, 1937, after eleven years in prison. During his imprisonment, Gramsci wrote a series of notebooks, which provided the intellectual foundation for the transformation of the Italian Communist Party from a sectarian splinter group of Italian Marxism to the largest mass party in Western Europe. Antonio Gramsci, *The Modern Prince and Other Writings* (New York: International Publishers, 1957).

19. On the PDS program in 1994, see Evans, "Italy . . . Quo Vadis?" 10; and Sidoti, "Significance of the Italian Elections," 336–337.

20. On the PDS conflict with the PRC, see Stephen Hellmann, "The Italian Left after the 1996 Elections," in *Italian Politics: The Center-Left in Power*, ed. Roberto D'Alimonte and David Nelken (Boulder: Westview Press, 1997), 83–101.

21. Marc Lazar, "The Birth of the Democratic Party," in *Italian Politics: Frustrated Aspirations for Change*, ed. Mark Donovan and Paolo Onofri (Oxford: Berghahn Books, 2008), 51–67.

22. In retrospect, the 15.7 percent garnered by the PPI and Segni electoral bloc in 1994 represented a respectable showing in relation to the votes they attracted in subsequent elections. See Robert Leonardi and Paolo Alberti, "From Dominance to Doom? Christian Democracy in Italy," in *Christian Democratic Parties in Europe since the End of the Cold War,* ed. Steven Van Hecke and Emmanuel Gerard (Leuven, Belgium: Leuven University Press, 2004), 105–132.

23. See Vittorio Buffachi, "The Success of Mani Pulite: Luck or Skill?" in *Italy: Politics and Policy,* vol. 1, ed. Robert Leonardi and Raffaella Y. Nanetti (Aldershot, UK: Ashgate, 1996), 189–210.

24. "Centro sinistra e politica locale," *Il Mulino* 12 (March 1963): 240.

25. See Leonardi and Alberti, "From Dominance to Doom?" 105–132.

26. See Newell and Bull, "Party Organizations and Alliances," 104.

27. For some early discussions of the Northern League, see, for example, Tom Gallagher, "The Regional Dimension in Italy's Political Upheaval: Role of the Northern League, 1984–1993," *Government and Opposition* 29 (Summer 1994): 456–468; and Dwayne Woods, "The Crisis of the Italian Party-State and the Rise of the Lombard League," *Telos* 93 (Fall 1992): 111–126.

28. For a discussion of the Northern League's political program, see Carlo Ruzza and Stefano Fella, *Re-inventing the Italian Right* (London: Routledge, 2009), 85–88.

29. See Adrian Lyttelton, "Italy: The Triumph of TV," *New York Review of Books,* August 11, 1994, 27; and Vincent R. Tortora, "Italy's Second Republic," *New Leader,* May 9–23, 1994, 6.

30. See Evans, "Italy . . . Quo Vadis?" 10–11; and Sidoti, "Significance of the Italian Elections," 339–340.

31. For an analysis of Berlusconi's territorial support, see Michael Shin and John Agnew, *Berlusconi's Italy* (Philadelphia: Temple University Press, 2008).

32. See Sidoti, "Significance of the Italian Elections," 342–344.

33. See "Gianfranco Fini: A Nearly Respectable Post-Fascist," *Economist,* February 21, 1998, 56.

34. A new political group, Future and Liberty (FLI), was created by Gianfranco Fini in September 2010 within the PDL.

35. For a fuller discussion of the Italian electoral system under the pre-1993 electoral law, see Raphael Zariski, *Italy: The Politics of Uneven Development* (Hinsdale, Ill.: Dryden Press, 1972).

36. On the 1993 election law and its effects, see Evans, "Italy . . . Quo Vadis?" 6–8; and Gallagher, Laver, and Mair, *Representative Government in Western Europe,* 168–189.

37. See Stefano Bartolini and Roberto D'Alimonte, "Majoritarian Miracles and the Question of Party System Change," *European Journal of Political Research* 34 (1998): 151–169, esp. 151–157 and 162–168.

38. In 2008 that level was back up to 3.6 percent.

39. See Arturo Parisi and Gianfranco Pasquino, "Changes in Italian Electoral Behavior: The Relationship between Parties and Voters," in *Italy in Transition: Conflict and Consensus,* ed. Peter Lange and Sidney Tarrow (London: Frank Cass, 1980), 6–30.

40. See Evans, "Italy . . . Quo Vadis?" 11–12.

41. See Ilvo Diamanti, "The *Lega Nord:* From Federalism to Secession," in D'Alimonte and Nelken, *Italian Politics: The Center-Left in Power,* 68–72; Roberto Biorcio, "La Lega Nord e la transizione italiana," *Rivista italiana di Scienza Politica* 29 (April 1998): 55–85; and Patrizia Messina, "Opposition in Italy in the 1990s: Local Political Cultures and the Northern League," *Government and Opposition* 33 (Autumn 1998): 462–478.

42. See Gianfranco Pasquino, "Italian Christian Democracy: A Party for All Seasons?" in *Italy in Transition: Conflict and Consensus,* ed. Peter Lange and Sidney Tarrow (London: Frank Cass, 1980), 92–93.

43. See Sandro Magister, "The Church and the End of the Catholic Party," in *Italian Politics: The Stalled Transition,* ed. Mario Caciagli and David I. Kertzer (Boulder: Westview Press, 1996), 223–240.

44. See Raphael Zariski, "Italy: The Fragmentation of Power and Its Consequences," in *First World Interest Groups: A Comparative Perspective,* ed. Clive S. Thomas (Westport, Conn.: Greenwood Press, 1993), 127–138.

How Is Power Used?

CHAPTER 4.3 DESCRIBED THE SHARP DIVISIONS OF POWER THAT EXISTED within the Italian decision-making system before 1992: coalition cabinets were split, not only by competing parties but also by competing intraparty factions; parliament was not really under the unifying tutelage of any cohesive leadership structure or ruling committee; public corporations enjoyed a high degree of de facto autonomy. These cleavages within the decision-making apparatus made it difficult to ascertain who, if anyone, was in charge. Reflecting these internal divisions, the policymaking process itself was fragmented. Although inefficiency and lack of central direction can be found in any policymaking system, including the much-touted British and American models, Italy seemed to constitute a particularly acute case of poor coordination and lack of harmony. This chapter both describes and analyzes the policymaking and policy implementation processes in place in Italy before the 1990s and then points to some important changes that took place after 1992. The chapter also looks at the important changes that have taken place in terms of specific policy outputs related to immigration and the flexibility of labor and wages in Italy.

Policy Formulation

The process of policy formulation begins with proposals. In any democratic country, policy proposals are brought to the attention of policymakers by parties, pressure (interest) groups, higher civil servants in the bureaucracy, and individual legislators.

Policymaking Up to the 1990s

In Italy, before the changes introduced in the 1990s, individual members of parliament were given a comparatively strong voice in the process of policy initiation. Italy, in fact, was one of the few Western democracies that placed no restrictions on the introduction of private-member bills in parliament. Even though a majority of the bills *introduced* in parliament were private-member bills, only a minority of bills *passed* by parliament were initiated by individual deputies and senators without some sort of executive sponsorship. Therefore, once the phase of proposal initiation was completed, the executive still emerged as wielding more weight than the legislature in the process of policy formulation.

Of those bills originating from the executive, there was strong reason to suspect that parties and pressure groups played a more important part in initiating legislation than did the bureaucracy. Indeed, it is well known that Italian civil servants tend to be conservative and legalistic in their attitudes and to show little interest in policy innovations. Unlike French higher civil servants who are known for their creative involvement in the policymaking process, Italian civil servants are unlikely to search for new and controversial solutions to socioeconomic problems.

The political parties affected the initiation of policy proposals in various ways. Although they did not bother with the great number of *leggine* ("little laws"—that is, private or minor bills) initiated by government agencies and individual members of parliament, they did stimulate the introduction of broader bills of general application.[1] Also, in a broad sense, they sometimes replaced the cabinet as the source of general policy decisions. Between 1976 and 1979, when the Communist Party was part of the ruling coalition without actually holding ministerial positions, the cabinet committed itself to applying a program agreed on by the parties that supported the ruling coalition. Because these parties included some (such as the Communist Party) that were not represented in the cabinet, a particular procedure was followed. The government program was drawn up outside of parliament by leaders of the parties committed to supporting the cabinet. The cabinet then adopted the program. In effect, then, the cabinet was simply ratifying decisions adopted by an extra-parliamentary conference of party leaders.[2]

Parties also had a major impact on detailed and specific policy initiatives, even if they did not as *parties* introduce vast numbers of proposed *leggine* in parliament. Especially after the opening to the left in the early 1960s, a tendency emerged toward allocating policymaking positions in various executive and administrative agencies to the political parties supporting the cabinet. Before the 1960s the Christian Democrats almost invariably were those receiving patronage in the form of such decisional posts.[3] After the opening to the left, Socialists and the other allies of the Christian Democracy became more successful in obtaining a significant share of strategic jobs. The distributive spending decisions made by such government agencies were, for all intents and purposes, made by the political parties that participated in managing the agencies. In effect, then, the Christian Democratic–dominated spoils system was broadened to include other parties, with pieces of the action distributed on a quota basis.[4]

In addition to political parties, Italian pressure groups initiated proposals that ministries adopted as their own. One reason for the accentuated role of pressure groups was that the Italian bureaucracy was not able to generate many proposals on its own—in part because of the inadequacy of the research facilities available to the bureaucracy and to parliament and in part because of the quick rotation of ministers and their administrative staff. As a result, both the bureaucracy and parliament were unusually dependent on pressure groups (interest groups and parties) for information and expertise.

Once a proposal was initiated, the ministry involved engaged in a long process of consultation with affected interests. Each ministry had an advisory council representing the various *clientela* groups with which the ministry dealt. Moreover, an intricate system of cabinet committees was supposed to keep ministers informed about what their colleagues were doing or planning to do. But there were gaps in this consultation process, and very often interested groups and agencies were not kept informed and ministries were unaware of each other's projects.

One complaint often voiced was that there was no adequate coordination of the various policy proposals initiated by government agencies. The great number of cabinet committees made for a functional decentralization of policy. Each cabinet committee had its own restricted sphere of public policy in which it all too often acted as final arbiter; the cabinet, supposedly the supreme organ of policy coordination, was too large and too internally divided to perform this function. As a result, many bills came before the cabinet without adequate notice and caught ministers by surprise; meetings were called suddenly with much the same effect; minutes were sketchy and incomplete; and there was no regular exchange of information among cabinet members. In short, the cabinet did not maintain adequate control over policy formulation.[5]

In the absence of effective cabinet surveillance, there were few real limitations on the activities of Italy's various executive agencies and public corporations. Many of their decisions involved awarding grants or contracts or loans and required no action by the legislature. The Office of the Prime Minister exercised some oversight over policy formulation, but it was in no position to block initiatives of which it disapproved. Some checks on excessive spending could be imposed by the Ministry of the Treasury and the governor of the Bank of Italy by regulating the cash reserves required of Italian banks, thereby encouraging or curtailing borrowing or lending. But the Bank of Italy, for all the technocratic expertise of its governor, was not as independent as many observers assumed, nor could it intervene in the political decisions taken by a government. The Administrative Council of the bank, which chose the new governor, was made up of the incumbent governor and fifteen members, twelve of whom were nominated by an assembly of banks and credit agencies that held Bank of Italy stock. The governor was responsible, then, to Italian banking interests, but these interests, in turn, were partly under the influence of Christian Democratic–controlled public corporations such as the Institute of Industrial Reconstruction.[6] In 1991, when the Bank of Italy became independent of government control, any leverage that it had over day-to-day policymaking vanished.

Apart from the credit and monetary restraints imposed by the Ministry of the Treasury and the Bank of Italy, there was no effective check within the executive branch on the process of policy formulation. As noted, the cabinet did not serve as a reliable gatekeeper, preventing the introduction of bills that did not enjoy general support within the executive branch. Indeed, the executive branch did not speak with one voice. In its divisiveness and lack of coherence, it bore more resemblance to the U.S. executive branch than to the executive branch of a model parliamentary system. Some executive and administrative agencies had more clout than others (just as a feudal system has greater and lesser feudal lords), but no single committee or institution was clearly in charge.[7]

Numerous policy proposals—such as those involving investments, grants, and loans undertaken by public corporations and other government agencies—did not need approval by parliament. These corporations and agencies merely secured the approval of the relevant supervisory ministry (often the Ministry of State Holdings, which was abolished in the early 1990s) or of the entire cabinet, and that approval usually was forthcoming. The president of the Chamber of Deputies or the president of the Senate assigned policy proposals that did go the parliamentary route in the form of bills to a standing committee. The committee would be instructed to report the bill back to the floor *in sede referente*, with its recommendations, or to enact the bill into law *in sede deliberante*. Whichever path was chosen, the committee stage was the crucial stage in the life of a bill. Many controversial bills never emerged from committee. In fact, the standing committees, by preventing bills from reaching the floor for a vote, spared the executive branch much embarrassment by sidetracking measures the executive organs did not support wholeheartedly but were afraid not to sponsor.

If the *in sede referente* procedure was followed and if the bill was reported to the floor, the Conference of Presidents (heads of parliamentary party groups) decided the bill's place on the legislative calendar. The bill was then discussed in the chamber, first on a general motion for approval and then article by article. In this second and more detailed discussion, amendments could be introduced and voted on. After the amendment stage, the entire house voted on the final version of the bill. If it passed, it went on to the other chamber, which followed the same lengthy and cumbersome procedure. The bill had to pass both chambers in the same form to become law, which meant shuttling the bill between the chambers so that discrepancies could be ironed out.

Most laws were adopted in committee through the *in sede referente* procedure. This procedure was used mostly for *leggine*, the incremental bills of minor importance that affected relatively small segments of society. Such bills were often introduced by the government as an alternative to an executive decree, which might be blocked by the Court of Accounts, or they originated with private members seeking to curry favor with some constituents. Under the *in sede deliberante* procedure, 10 percent of the members of parliament or 20 percent of the members of a standing committee could prevent passage of a bill by insisting that it be brought to the floor for plenary debate. The Communist Party always had enough votes to prevent the procedure from being used, and yet it did not usually employ this power to obstruct legislation, even in the 1950s and 1960s when it was still considered an antisystem party. Such outcomes suggest that within the Italian parliament there were strong incentives for parties to "parliamentarize" themselves—that is, become constructive members of the legislative process so that they would be in a better position to bargain with the governing parties to get their proposals through parliament. Evidently, then, there were many compromises with the Christian Democratic regime within the standing committees before the 1970s.

Executive orders (legislative decrees, decree laws, and regulations) had to jump through many hoops before approval. For one thing, numerous consultations were required by law or by administrative practice. If a cabinet measure was involved—not just a minor regulation of interest to only a single ministry—the measure had to be considered by a cabinet committee before receiving the consent of the cabinet as a whole. The cabinet committee stage was crucial in most cases. The Council of State also had to be consulted in its advisory capacity. And then there was always the chance that the Court of Accounts would refuse to register the executive order. Finally, the president of Italy had the right (exercised only occasionally) to refuse to authorize the issuance of a cabinet decree or the introduction of a government bill in parliament.

One device for redressing the apparent weakness of the executive branch in relation to parliament, the parties, and the pressure groups was the use of decree laws to obtain quick, temporary action and bypass the normal legislative procedures. Although decree laws expired within sixty days unless approved by parliament, at least some kind of action had been taken. Moreover, if parliament, during the sixty days, rejected or drastically modified a decree law, the cabinet did not feel obligated to resign.[8]

Changes in Policymaking Introduced in the 1990s

In the 1990s some major changes were made in the Italian policymaking process—changes that were accelerated by the political cataclysm of the early 1990s, but were already under way in the late 1980s. First, the political parties began to play a smaller role in initiating policy proposals, because many of the parties had become more patronage-oriented. In fact, their heavy reliance on patronage and subsidies to a wide variety of beneficiaries began to pile up an unsustainable burden of debt and injure Italy's ability to compete in world markets. With the passage of the Maastricht Treaty in 1992 and the gearing up to create the Economic and Monetary Union (EMU), the Italian system had to focus on austerity and stability rather than on satisfying pressures for patronage. In fact, after the precipitous fall of the lira on the foreign exchange markets in September 1992, the Amato government introduced a severe cut in government spending that crippled the Christian Democracy and Socialist Party patronage machines and contributed to the collapse of the regime.[9]

Second, technocrats and academic experts assumed the central role in initiating major economic and financial policies. Officials from the Bank of Italy, the technocrats at the helm of the Treasury Ministry, the professors of economics at the head of the Ministry of Finance, and the financial and economic advisers in the prime minister's office replaced the career politicians who used to dominate the economic and financial ministries. The ministerial cabinets that provide ministers with crucial advice on economic and financial policy matters are staffed by technocrats and social scientists rather than legalistically inclined high civil servants. And think tanks, such as the Europe Research Center, Institute of Social Research, and Rosselli Foundation, serve as forums for the discussion of economic and financial policy and help to shape the prevalent elite consensus on the desirability of maintaining economic stability, cutting deficits, and reducing spending.[10] Moreover, with increasing frequency, ministries are strengthening their own technical capacity by creating special research units within their ranks, such as the evaluation unit in the Ministry of the Economy that is responsible for both assessing the economic impact of the European structural funds and offering the ministry strategic input to formulate effective policy decisions.

Third, the executive branch gained strength. It exercises greater control over the budget-making process, particularly in setting forth the main objectives, controlling the timetable, and rejecting amendments by the Chamber of Deputies to the government's financial proposals. In addition, the cabinet relies more frequently on decree laws to bypass potential resistance in parliament, and is not reluctant to reissue those decree laws again and again when parliament fails to approve them within the sixty-day time limit.[11]

Fourth, the government is making use of the referendum as a device for overcoming parliamentary resistance to a controversial policy proposal. The legalization of divorce and abortion and the establishment of a plurality system for the election of three-fourths of the members of the Chamber of Deputies were goals ratified by the Italian public in referendums. One result has been a significant voter backlash against what is seen as overuse and abuse of the referendum. This backlash seems to be confirmed by the low turnout in referendum votes.[12] In the spring of 1999 a referendum proposal to scrap the rule whereby 25 percent of the seats in parliament are assigned by proportional representation was approved by a comfortable margin of those voting. But the turnout was too low for the referendum to be legally binding. A similar problem arose in the spring of 2005, when the referendum called by lay and leftist forces against restrictive legislation on human fertilization and genetic research issues—a referendum strongly opposed by the church—failed for lack of a quorum. Finally, in June 2009 the referendum on the abolition of the current electoral law drew a turnout of only 23 percent of the voters, in comparison to those who voted on the same day for the second round of provincial (46 percent) or communal (61 percent) elections.

Fifth, since 1992 and the launch of the Single Market at the European level and the implementation of the convergence criteria for the realization of EMU, Italy has experienced even greater "Europeanization" of policymaking in the areas of monetary policy, market regulation, competition, and regional policy. Like other European Union (EU) countries, Italy has often found itself in a position of accepting directly into its legislation European regulations and transposing into law European directives that were the product of European-level rather than national decision-making procedures. These changes, affecting important "high politics" policy areas, have introduced a more complex two-level decision-making process. This process involves the interaction of domestic and European politics, as well as separate institutions at the European level (Council of Ministers, European Commission, and European Parliament) that no longer adhere to the kinds of policy linkages in place before 1992. Such changes have forced interest groups to mobilize their lobbying efforts at multiple levels and have challenged administrative structures to manage issues successfully at both the national and European levels.

Finally, in the 1990s the Italian decision-making process introduced a further complicating factor that was tied to the active devolution of "low politics": socioeconomic policies were gradually transferred to the regional and local levels for management. Ministries were no longer in a position to decide on their own the course of such policies, but had to agree to policy choices and contents in conjunction with an increasing number of relevant actors at the subnational level. It is this evolving context, in which government officials must coordinate at the European level the choice of basic policies and agree with the regions and local governments on how to implement specific socioeconomic policies, that has served to change the structure of decision making in the Italian political system from a single-level to a multi-level process. Now, the important centers of decision making are represented by the Conference of Regional Presidents, which formulates the position of the regions and subsequently the State and Regional Conference, which assumes the final decision on policies requiring the coordination of national and regional policymaking initiatives. The same process is the case where the state and local governments share joint decision-making powers.

Policy Implementation

The responsibility for implementing policies that emerged from the policy formulation process lay originally with the Italian national bureaucracy.

Policy Implementation Up to the 1990s

In the decades leading up to the changes of the 1990s, Italian civil servants tended to be obsessed with the primacy of the law and with the need to find a legal justification for every action. As a result, policy implementation proceeded with agonizing slowness and indecision. Each step in the implementation of a law or decree had to be subjected to a series of controls and procedures: approval by a subsidiary branch of the General Accounting Office, registration by the Court of Accounts, consultation with the Council of State for all contracts above a certain sum, and so on. At any one of numerous way stations, a file might be sent back to the point of origin because of some minor irregularity or might even be mislaid. Implementation, then, could take years, even when no particularly controversial problem was involved.

Overcentralization also slowed down the policy implementation process. Local authorities and regional authorities were subject to a variety of central controls. National field services of ministries in Rome were compelled to refer a great number of relatively minor decisions to the capital for the signature of the director general of a bureau. In fact, even when the rules did not so specify, minor officials often preferred to pass the buck to their superiors in the hierarchy. This centralizing tendency had deep roots in Italian political culture.

Other factors impeding effective policy implementation were overstaffing and corruption. The expansion of the bureaucracy since World War II had contributed to the sluggishness of bureaucratic procedures. The introduction of more modern methods would mean a reduction in staff; yet the imposition of an additional set of checks or controls might serve to justify an individual's salary. As for corruption, favoritism, often based on family or friendship ties, was a favorite subject of the media to a greater degree than in other Western democracies. In a civil service recruited from a traditionalist region such as the Italian south, family loyalty was bound to have a serious effect on behavior.

One glaring example of the inefficiency of the policy implementation process was the growing importance of so-called *residui passivi* (unspent residuals) in Italy. These were funds that were allocated to an agency in a given budgetary period to be invested in projects but that remained unspent. Unspent residuals were growing in size, which helps to explain why so many reform measures represented only paper promises because of the bureaucratic controls that stood in the way of transforming words into deeds.[13] It is also clear that some political forces were not interested in administrative change and therefore never undertook to introduce the measures that would have made a significant difference in the way policies were made and implemented.

Changes in Policy Implementation Introduced since the late 1980s

Since the late 1980s, a thoroughgoing, coordinated reform of Italian public finance and administrative structures has been under way. In addition to the modernization of procedures and the increased professionalization of administrative elites, Italy has been undergoing a three-part de facto restructuring of the Italian state apparatus through the Europeanization of certain policy areas, the devolution of policy to the regional and local levels, and the privatization of large firms and banks.

The *Europeanization* of policy has taken the form of moving certain policy areas from individual to collective decision-making processes that are no longer subject to the exclusive influence of party politics or interest group interactions at the national level.

The *devolution* of policy has taken the form of effectively regionalizing and localizing many other policy issues through strengthening subnational government based on putting the dictates of the Italian constitution into operation. With the transfer of policy areas to the regional and local governments, local parties, as well as the local branches of interest groups, have been reinforced. Another contributing factor to the devolution of policy has been the greater visibility and clout of regional and local executives. With the direct election of regional presidents and mayors, the decision-making process has been simplified and no longer has to go through a complex process of mediation among the governing parties.

The policy of *privatization* pursued by successive governments during the 1990s and continuing into the 2000s has removed some important policy problems associated with the distribution of financial resources from the public sphere. As a result, it is more difficult for political considerations to affect the decisions of the large industrial firms or banks that must compete in the market or must adhere to European rules and procedures. The effects of these changes are readily evident in the balance sheets of the businesses and banks involved. Before 1992 the ENEL (electrical energy) and the ENI (petroleum and gas) produced more losses than gains even though they enjoyed monopolies in Italy's energy sector. Since privatization, they have become among the most profitable companies in Europe. The same is true in Italy's banking sector. Before privatization, all of Italy's major banks were owned and controlled by the state, and they were lucky if they broke even at the end of the year. Now, after a considerable reorganization of the sector, the Italian banking system became one the most profitable in Europe and therefore attracted the attention of German, Spanish, and Dutch firms that entered the Italian market.

The combined effect of these three forces has significantly changed the nature of Italian decision making and implementation. Gone are the days when national political leaders had a stranglehold on policy matters and when decisions could be made behind the scenes without public knowledge or without the scrutiny of other levels in the governance structure. Today, the policy process in Italy is more transparent and more accessible to different institutional and socioeconomic actors. It is still unclear whether this change has brought about an overall improvement in policies, but it has certainly decreased the level of manipulation exercised by the political parties and national administrative elites.

Policy Outputs

In discussions about policy, there may be confusion about the differences between policy outputs (which may include passing legislation, spending government budgets, implementing sectoral policies, and enforcing the laws) and policy outcomes, which could include growth rate of the gross domestic product, unemployment, activity rates, inflation rates, interest rates, trade balances, levels of foreign direct investment, and rate of domestic investments. The policy outcomes in Italy during the postwar period have already been described in some detail in the previous chapters, and more will be said in Chapter 4.5 about the future of Italy. This section, therefore, focuses on Italy's policies in two areas: immigration and labor flexibility.

Immigration

Until the beginning of the 1990s immigration had never been an acute problem in Italy. Indeed, to the contrary, Italy has traditionally suffered from the problem of the outmigration (or emigration) of Italians to other parts of Europe and beyond. Up until the mid-1960s, Italy consistently exported its excess labor to other parts of the world, while undergoing significant shifts of population from the southern part of the country to the north. It was only with the restructuring of large industry during the 1970s and the diffusion of small and medium-size industry in the center and south that significant population flows stopped within the country and Italians began to return to the country and to their regions of origin in small numbers.

Around the same time the signs of an influx of foreign nationals began to appear. By 1977 an estimated 300,000–400,000 foreigners were present in Italy, and the numbers continued to rise.[14] By 1985 the official number of foreign-born residents in Italy was 423,000. Six years later, that number had doubled to 896,000.[15] By 2004 the total was about 1.5 million. Expressed differently, the number of immigrants has steadily climbed, from about 0.6 percent of Italy's population in 1991 to 3.4 percent in 2004 (see Table 4-5).[16] In 2003 the largest contingent of immigrants was from Europe. Southern Europeans represent half of the European total. Of these, most were from the Balkans—Albania (187,162), Macedonia (26,210), and Yugoslavia (40,237), but a surprising number came from the older EU member states such as France (26,274), Germany (36,320), Spain (20,930), and the United Kingdom (24,491). Many emigrated from the new EU member states—such as Poland (34,980) and Romania (94,818). Of those emigrating from the Americas, the majority came from Latin America (96,685, of which large numbers were from Argentina, Brazil, and Peru), and the United States (45,642 in 2003).

The first major bill to confront the problem of immigration was passed in 1986 (Law No. 943). It permitted foreign workers to be granted the same rights as Italian workers and permitted foreigners who had been in the country for a period of time to be granted residence status. Union support was crucial for passage of the 1986 bill, because the unions were afraid that undocumented workers would inevitably drive down wages and because about two-thirds of the immigrants were in the workforce. The pressure was strong to "regularize" workers—that is, to give them access to the status of resident and to grant them the benefits of unionization and the services provided by the Italian welfare state.[17] Three years later, a legislative decree (Decree Law No. 416 of December 30, 1989, popularly known as the Martelli law) set out to codify the existing practices of allowing nationals from non–European Community countries to enter for purposes of tourism, education, health, or work; to codify expulsion procedures; and to establish the grounds for a second amnesty campaign. The Martelli decree was the first legal provision to set out the procedure through which non-European refugees could be protected. In 1990 the Martelli decree was converted into law, along with Italy's signature of the Schengen Agreement on the free circulation of people among the signatory countries of the European Union. At the same time that these steps toward liberalization were being taken, there was an upsurge in immigration from across the Adriatic.

Until 1990 the Italian government did not have a specific policy to attract immigrants to the country or to block immigrants from arriving. All of this changed in 1991 because of exogenous factors linked to the collapse of the Soviet Union, the growing interethnic conflict in the former Yugoslavia, and the collapse of the pyramid schemes in Albania.[18] In 1992 Italy experienced its first significant wave of immigrants from the eastern part of the Adriatic, who reached Italy either by boat or by walking across its border with Slovenia and Croatia. After the initial wave of immigrants from the Balkans, people began arriving from Africa (both from the north and the sub-Saharan region), Eastern Europe (Poland, Russia, Ukraine, and Moldova), and Asia (China, the Philippines, and Sri Lanka). Most immigrants initially entered the country illegally (that is, without papers) or on temporary tourist or education visas. Once the visas expired, they awaited the subsequent amnesty. Nevertheless, the demand for foreign workers continued to outstrip the supply produced by the official immigration procedures created by Law No. 943 and the Martelli law, because undocumented workers play an important role in the economy by filling the jobs that Italians prefer not to take. Foreigners tend to fill many of the jobs in the steel and iron foundries in the north and take on the heavy work in the fields in southern Italy. Another growing sector for foreign female workers is the care of the elderly in the home. In the past,

Table 4-5 Migration into Italy, 1990–2003

	1990	1991	1992	1993	1994	1995	1996
Africa	203,813	237,821	227,531	180,446	190,799	189,802	205,947
Americas	90,655	106,010	94,298	90,934	95,172	95,267	104,117
Asia	80,612	110,512	120,798	102,551	107,642	112,271	123,481
Europe	175,377	238,287	202,799	212,257	252,267	274,409	292,566
Oceania	—	—	2,612	2,475	2,427	2,242	2,244
Stateless	—	—	897	794	795	800	814
Total	550,457	692,630	648,935	589,457	649,102	674,791	729,169
Percent of total population	—	—	—	1.0	1.1	1.2	1.3

Source: Migration Information Source, http://www.migrationinformation.org/GlobalData/countrydata/data.cfm Originally published by the MPI Data Hub, a project of the Washington, D.C.-based Migration Policy Institute, an independent, nonpartisan, nonprofit think tank dedicated to the study of movement of people worldwide.

Note: The total number of immigrants in 2004 represented 3.4 percent of the population.

Immigrants line up at the post office in Siena to apply for work permits and the chance to become permanent residents of Italy.

Source: AP Images/Fabio Muzzi

the close-knit Italian family usually looked after the elderly without relying on outside help. But that pattern changed as more women entered the workforce and Italian families found themselves with more income at their disposal to pay for care-givers. As for the distribution of legal immigrants, the vast majority settled in the north (more than half) and center (one-third) of the country, and only a small number reside permanently in the south.

The increase in the demand for foreign workers forced the Dini government in 1995 and the Prodi government in 1998 to pass two more amnesty laws, but they, too, represented temporary solutions to the problems of regularizing the vast number of undocumented workers present in the country. The goal of 1998 law (No. 40), sponsored by the minister of the interior, Giorgio Napolitano, and the minister of social affairs, Livia Turco, was to stem illegal migration by reinforcing border controls and permitting the expulsion of those immigrants who became involved in crime and the exploitation of other immigrants. Moreover, for the first time the Turco-Napolitano law separated the issue of refugees from immigration and set up a procedure for granting refugee status to those fleeing persecution in their own countries. It also instituted a system of quotas for immigration.

	1997	1998	1999	2000	2001	2002	2003
Africa	301,305	310,748	316,434	389,532	388,327	401,927	401,442
Americas	129,625	133,461	138,726	161,237	162,790	170,343	177,852
Asia	186,947	197,365	213,167	263,055	271,593	287,084	288,135
Europe	365,265	378,423	419,546	523,794	554,035	585,915	632,562
Oceania	2,201	2,225	2,282	2,420	2,430	2,547	2,680
Stateless	677	674	665	617	574	576	615
Total	986,020	1,022,896	1,090,820	1,340,655	1,379,749	1,448,392	1,503,286
Percent of total population	1.5	1.7	1.9	2.2	2.5	—	2.7

Even though expulsions increased dramatically and greater control was achieved over the illegal flow of refugees, immigration became an important issue in the 2001 parliamentary campaign. The center-right insisted that illegal entry into the country should be turned into a criminal offence and that non-EU immigrants should be barred from gaining permanent residence. Spearheading the attack on the Turco-Napolitano law were the parties led by Gianfranco Fini of the National Alliance and Umberto Bossi of the Northern League. Once the center-right came to power, the two leaders presented a bill that became Law No. 189 on July 30, 2002. The center-right proposal on immigration began as an attempt to undermine the fundamental elements of the Turco-Napolitano law, but as the proposal passed through parliament, the restrictive measures foreseen in the initial proposal were gradually softened to the point that a general amnesty of illegal immigrants already living in Italy was introduced on September 9. This law therefore repeated the attempts of previous governments to find a temporary solution to the presence of thousands of undocumented workers on Italian soil. The Northern League insisted that the amnesty would be limited to foreigners assisting in the care of the elderly, but the pressures brought by the employers' association (Confindustria) and Catholic groups succeeded in extending the amnesty to all other types of workers. Finally, just before the 2006 election the center-right proposed a new decree to introduce an amnesty for foreign workers *after the election* as a means of responding to those voters who were heavily dependent on non-Italian workers to fill positions in manufacturing and agriculture as well as for domestic care.

Since 1991 it has become evident that legislation will not stem the tide of immigration, nor will it solve the demand for foreign labor generated by the Italian economy. Italy's geographic position in the middle of the Mediterranean and its long and mostly unpatrolled 4,720-mile coastline make it an ideal transit point for the illegal traffic of immigrants.[19] Italy needs, in fact, a radical reform of its approach to immigration within a European rather than a strictly national perspective. Italy's exposed borders call for a clear and enforceable *European* policy on immigration that can treat the problem at its source rather than at its point of arrival. The European Union should establish a clear policy of entry and regulation of flows with the countries in the Balkans and the southern Mediterranean. In addition, Europe should devise a recruitment policy for skilled workers, who are now in short supply in Europe. Only by operating at the national and European level can Italy or other countries along the southern frontier of Europe resolve their immigration problems and meet the challenge of falling birthrates. An agreement aimed at stemming some of the flow of immigrants through Libya was reached with Muammar Gaddafi, who promised to take back all immigrants using Libyan ports who are intercepted in the Mediterranean. Many protested this agreement because it failed to protect people fleeing political persecution in Libya. The current economic crisis has slowed the flow of immigrants as unskilled employment disappears and greater competition for existing jobs increases from unemployed Italian workers.[20]

Labor Flexibility

The flexibility of the Italian labor market has been an important component of the ongoing debate on the competitiveness of the Italian economy since the Workers' Statute came into effect in 1970 (Law No. 300). On the heels of the workers' mobilization of 1969, the trade unions made significant strides in institutionalizing the rights of workers through the courts. One of the main features of the 1970 statute was Article 18, which permitted workers to go to court to contest their dismissal without just cause by an employer. This article applied only to businesses with more than fifteen employees—not smaller companies. The impact of the provisions of Article 18 was cited as one of the reasons why Italian industry remained small and why companies preferred to remain below the fifteen-worker mark. During the 1980s and the 1990s the employers' organization Confindustria periodically emphasized the need to eliminate Article 18 and bring greater flexibility to the Italian labor market. In 2002 Antonio Fazio, the governor of the Bank of Italy, cited the results of a comparative study by the Organisation for Economic Co-operation and Development (OECD) on labor mobility to argue that Italy's labor laws were far more restrictive than their counterparts in the rest of the OECD: "Italian legislation on individual dismissal from work is one of those where the degree of workers' protection in the case of unfair dismissal is particularly high. This is due to both the considerable number of cases where the law provides for the workers' reinstatement, and to the costs involved."[21]

The perceived wisdom was that the rigidity of the Italian labor market was contributing to the sluggish growth of the economy and its inability to respond to foreign competition.[22] The goal of having a free hand in the hiring and firing of workers was particularly important to Confindustria, and in April 2001 Prime Minister Silvio Berlusconi appeared at the organization's annual meeting to suggest that his party's electoral manifesto was close to that of the employers' confederation when it came to reform of the labor laws.

With the victory of the center-right in the 2001 election, Article 18 of the Workers' Statute and the desire to open up the Italian labor market came to the forefront. In suggesting some solutions to the problem, the center-right government built on some developments before 2001. First, in 1998 the Treu law (named after Minister of Labor Tiziano Treu in the Prodi government) had introduced a series of new labor contracts for beginning workers (temporary, part-time, and training contracts) to encourage more young workers to enter the labor market. The Treu Law left untouched the status of workers who already were employed. Second, in 2000 the Radical Party launched a referendum to abolish Article 18 and to dismantle the trade union movement's presence in the *Patronati* (agencies to help laid-off workers receive compensation and apply for pensions). The results of the referendum were nullified by the failure to reach the required number of votes (50 percent plus one of voters). Nevertheless, Confindustria, under the leadership of Antonio D'Amato, took up the banner of abolishing Article 18 and placed pressure on the government to fulfill its electoral pledge.[23]

The new Berlusconi government responded with a "White Paper on the Italian Labor Market" that sought to restructure employment relations, reconsider existing labor laws, and open up the job market by eliminating the government's role in the stipulation of national contracts and by emphasizing the need to move toward regionally based negotiations between employers and labor.[24] Trade unions responded in a muted fashion. Although the unions did not denounce the contents of the government's white paper, they had little enthusiasm for it. Even the trade unions closest to the center-right—that is, the Italian Confederation of Workers' Unions, or CISL (National Alliance), and the Labor General Union, or UGL (Forza Italia)—remained silent. As the implications of the government's white paper began to sink it, however, opposition began to mount. The Italian General Confederation of Labor, or CGIL (the largest and most leftist trade union), denounced the government's intention to refuse to enter into tripartite agreements with employers and unions in regard to national labor contracts. The other two unions—the Italian Confederation of Workers' Unions, or CISL (Catholic), and the Italian Union of Labor, or UIL (moderate Socialists)—initially attempted to work with the government. In July 2002 they signed an agreement, the Pact for Italy, with the government on the need to increase the flexibility of Italian labor markets. When the CGIL refused to join the pact, it appeared that the Italian labor movement had been outmaneuvered by the government. But the government hesitated to introduce its proposed legislative initiatives in the hope that the labor movement would become permanently split between the more radical CGIL and the more moderate CISL and UIL.

This hope began to crumble in 2003 as the relationship between the trade unions and Confindustria began to evolve. At the beginning of 2003, a new referendum on Article 18 proposed by Fausto Bertinotti, leader of the Party of Communist Refoundation, to extend coverage to small companies with fewer than fifteen workers was accepted by the Constitutional Court as valid. Therefore, the referendum could be put to a vote. Bertinotti had initiated the collection of signatures in support of the referendum in an attempt to split the Democrats of the Left (DS) and throw the center-left into turmoil, but the result was quite different. First of all, the trade unions assumed a lukewarm attitude toward the referendum and did not become actively involved in the campaign. Even the CGIL preferred to abstain, as did the main leaders of the center-left such as Piero Fassino and Francesco Rutelli. On June 15, 2003, only a quarter of voters bothered to participate in the referendum, thereby nullifying the proposal. Three days later, the trade unions signed an agreement with Confindustria to work together to spur investment in the south and in new technologies, and they pledged to return to the bargaining table to work out mutually acceptable solutions to working conditions and salaries. By late June the trade unions and Confindustria had put to rest the controversy over Article 18 and were able to focus their attention on the issue of labor market flexibility. Another casualty of the June 2003 referendum was the Pact for Italy.

The conflict generated during 2001–2002 by the leaders of Confindustria and the government in their single-minded drive to suspend the provisions of Article 18 led to the rise of internal dissent within Confindustria—between small and large industries and between the leaders closest to the center-right and those who wanted the confederation to maintain a neutral response. In April 2003 D'Amato was replaced at the helm of Confindustria by Luca di Montezemolo, the head of Ferrari and Fiat, who campaigned on a more open approach toward the unions and for a less dogmatic position on Article 18.

Despite the growing rapprochement between Confindustria and the trade unions, in October 2003 the government passed Law No. 30 (the Maroni law) and introduced a greater variety of work contracts. According to Lucio Baccaro and Marco Simoni, the new law "introduced a wide range of new contractural frameworks (from on-call jobs to new forms of apprenticeship) with the aim of bringing together the various productive needs that might emerge in the Italian economy." [25] The expectations were that the new law would build on the job creation schemes introduced by the previous Treu law, which by 2001 had given rise to the emergence of new "atypical" jobs on the basis of part-time, flexible time, and temporary contracts. In 2001 more than 20 percent of the jobs in industry and services were based on "atypical" contracts, and this sector of the labor force was booming.

The center-right government was not so lucky. Two years after the introduction of its labor law, the boom in job creation petered out. During the third quarter of 2005, the Italian labor market continued to exceed the previous year's figures by 57,000 jobs, but in the meantime more than 294,000 people stopped looking for work.[26] The dropout rate from the labor market particularly affected female workers and young people in southern Italy.

The fate of the two different legislative initiatives of the center-left government in 1998 and the center-right government in 2003 illustrate the point made at the beginning of the chapter: policy outputs should not be confused with policy outcomes. For the Treu law, the Italian economy was already in the midst of an upward surge in new jobs that began in 1995. Between 1995 and 2002, the labor market increased by 1.2 percent each year, but as economic growth started to lag under the Berlusconi government, so did the rate at which new jobs were created. It is undeniable that one of the factors accounting for the growth in jobs, aside from the increase in "atypical" employment, is the regularization of immigrant workers. In 2005 the new jobs created were those filled almost exclusively by immigrants in light of the 0.7 percent increase in the gross domestic product (GDP). Job creation continued for two more years as GDP began to grow again and the employment rate stabilized at 59.7 percent of the labor force in 2007 and 2008; the unemployment rate hit a low of 6.1 percent in 2007 but rose to 8.5 percent in 2009. In retrospect, the Treu law appears to have had great success in generating new jobs and opening up the Italian job market to new forms of employment contracts, whereas the Maroni law proved to be less successful because the job market and economic conditions had, in the meantime, worsened. Italy's economic indicators for 2008 and 2009 document the worsening economic situation characteristic of all of Europe and the United States. In Italy the fall in GDP and rise of the deficit indicate that the country is to a great extent limited in the choice of policies that it can make in response to the crisis and is, to a great extent, dependent on the policy choices made by others in lifting the country's economy back to growth.

Table 4-6 illustrates the fate of the Italian economy under Silvio Berlusconi and Romano Prodi. When Berlusconi came to power in 2001, he was preceded by the best performance

Table 4-6 Italian Economic Indicators, 2000–2009 (percent)

Indicator	2000	2001	2002	2003	2004	2005	2006	2007	2008	2009
Change in gross domestic product (GDP)	3.7	1.8	0.5	0	1.5	0.7	2	1.6	−1.3	−5.0
Employment rate	53.7	54.8	55.5	56.1	57.6	57.6	58.4	58.7	58.7	57.2
Unemployment rate	10.1	9.1	8.6	8.4	8	7.6		6.1	6.7	8.5
Deficit/GDP	−0.6	−3.2	−2.7	−3.2	−3.2	−4.3	−3.3	−1.5	−2.7	−5.6

Source: Eurostat, February 8, 2010.

of the Italian economy in a decade. Soon thereafter the terrorist attacks of September 11, 2001, on the United States and the general economic downturn in Europe undermined Italy's economic prospects. Growth rates declined precipitously, and so did the prospects of internal investments and the financing of an ambitious program of public infrastructure. All of the attempts by the government and Minister of the Economy Giulio Tremonti to prime the economy through deficit spending (the annual deficit immediately climbed back over 3 percent in violation of the provisions of the EU's Stability Pact) proved unable to change the performance of the economy. When Prodi returned to power in 2006, he was able to bring the deficit back below 3 percent for 2007 and 2008. Meanwhile, the flexibility of the labor market lost its aura; it was unable to help pull the country out of its economic malaise in the face of a government that was incapable of providing the investment policies needed to stimulate the economy so that in 2004 and 2005 it could join in the general upswing in the European economy. In 2006 and 2007 the economy began to revive only to be hit by the impact of the world economic crisis in 2008 and 2009. But as subsequent events would show, the lack of previous dynamism in the economy helped to shield it from the full brunt of the economic downturn. The Italian economy lost jobs and output, but its financial system was not brought to the brink of collapse as was the case in other Southern European countries.

NOTES

1. Giuseppe Di Palma, *Surviving with Governing* (Berkeley: University of California Press, 1977).
2. See Stefano Bartolini, "The Politics of Institutional Reform in Italy," *West European Politics* 5 (July 1982): 207–208.
3. The actual nature and depth of this penetration are discussed by Robert Leonardi in "Political Party Linkages in Italy: The Nature of the Christian Democratic Party Organization," in *Political Parties and Linkages: A Comparative Perspective,* ed. Kay Lawson (New Haven: Yale University Press, 1980), 243–265.
4. See Carlo Donolo, "Social Change and Transformation of the State in Italy," in *The State in Western Europe,* ed. Richard Scase (London: Croom Helm, 1980), 195–196; and Giuseppe Di Palma, "The Available State: Problems of Reform," in *Italy in Transition: Conflict and Consensus,* ed. Peter Lange and Sidney Tarrow (London: Frank Cass, 1980), 153–157.
5. See Sabino Cassese, "Is There a Government in Italy? Politics and Administration at the Top," in *Presidents and Prime Ministers,* ed. Richard Rose and Ezra N. Suleiman (Washington, D.C.: American Enterprise Institute, 1980), 175, 201–202.

6. See Alan R. Posner, "Italy: Dependence and Political Fragmentation," in *Between Power and Plenty: Foreign Economic Policies of Advanced Industrial States,* ed. Peter J. Katzenstein (Madison: University of Wisconsin Press, 1978), 234–235.

7. See Donolo, "Social Change and Transformation," 172–175.

8. See Bartolini, "Politics of Institutional Reform in Italy," 208.

9. See Martin Bull and Martin Rhodes, "Between Crisis and Transition: Italian Politics in the 1990s," in *Crisis and Transition in Italian Politics,* ed. Bull and Rhodes (London: Frank Cass, 1998), 4–8.

10. See Claudio M. Radaelli, "How Does Europeanization Produce Domestic Policy Change? Corporate Tax Policy in Italy and the United Kingdom," *Comparative Political Studies* 30 (October 1997): 557–561; and Claudio M. Radaelli, "Networks of Expertise and Policy Change in Italy," *South European Society and Politics* 3 (Autumn 1998): 4–18. Also see the special issue of the *Journal of European Public Policy,* "The Europeanisation of the Italian Political System: Politics and Policy" (November 2004).

11. See Vincent della Sala, "Hollowing Out and Hardening the State: European Integration and the Italian Economy," in Bull and Rhodes, *Crisis and Transition in Italian Politics,* 29–30; Giacinto della Cananea, "The Reform of Finance and Administration in Italy: Contrasting Achievements," in Bull and Rhodes, *Crisis and Transition in Italian Politics,* 196–197; and Vincent della Sala, "Italy: A Bridge Too Far?" *Parliamentary Affairs* 50 (July 1997): 399–400.

12. See "Referendum in Italy: Take It to the People," *Economist,* February 6, 1999, 52.

13. See Donolo, "Social Change and Transformation," 182.

14. John Veugelers, "Recent Immigration Politics in Italy: A Short Story," *West European Politics* 17 (April 1994): 33–49.

15. Kimberly Hamilton, "Italy's Southern Exposure," Country Profiles, Migration Information Source, 2003, http://www.migrationinformation.org/Profiles.

16. The figures for 2004 do not appear in Table 4-5 because geographic breakdowns are not available.

17. Italy has very restrictive provisions for obtaining Italian citizenship: an immigrant must have resided in the country for at least ten years and have been gainfully employed during that period. As a result, about 85 percent of naturalizations are based on marriage to an Italian citizen. See Hamilton, "Italy's Southern Exposure."

18. See Asher Colombo and Giuseppe Sciortino, "The Bossi-Fini Law: Explicit Fanaticism, Implicit Moderation, and Poisoned Fruits," in *Italian Politics: The Second Berlusconi Government,* ed. Jean Blondel and Paolo Segatti (Oxford: Berghahn Books, 2003), 162–179.

19. Christopher Hein, "Italy: Gateway to Europe, but Not the Gatekeeper," in *Kosovo's Refugees in the European Union,* ed. Joanne van Selm (London: Pinter Publishers, 2000), 139–161.

20. Demetrios Papademetriou, Madeline Sumption, and Will Somerville, "Migration and the Economic Downturn: What to Expect in the European Union," Migration Policy Institute, January 2009, www.migrationpolicy.org/transatlantic/EU_Recession_backgrounder.pdf.

21. Organisation for Economic Co-operation and Development, *International Mobility of the Highly Skilled* (Paris: OECD, 2002), 135–136.

22. See Edmund S. Phelps, *Enterprise and Inclusion in Italy* (Norwell, Mass.: Kluwer Academic Publishers, 2002), 155–186; and Roberto Schiattarella and Paolo Piacentini, "Old and New Dualisms in the Italian Labour Market," in *The Italian Economy at the Dawn of the 21st Century,* ed. Massimo Di Matteo and Paolo Piacentini (Aldershot, UK: Ashgate, 2003), 81–99.

23. Aris Accornero and Eliana Como, "The (Failed) Reform of Article 18," in Blondel and Segatti, *Italian Politics: The Second Berlusconi Government,* 199–220.

24. The coordinator of the team that drafted the white paper was Marco Biagi, one of Italy's leading labor lawyers, who was assassinated by the Red Brigades in March 2002.
25. Lucio Baccaro and Marco Simoni, "Article 18 and Labor Market Flexibility," in *Italian Politics: Italy between Europeanization and Domestic Politics,* ed. Sergio Fabbrini and Vincent della Sala (Oxford: Berghahn Books, 2004), 177.
26. Istituto Nazionale di Statistica (ISTAT), "Rilevazione sulle forze di lavoro," December 20, 2005.

What Is the Future of Italian Politics?

THIS TREATMENT OF THE ITALIAN POLITICAL SYSTEM HAS FOCUSED more on its weaknesses and imperfections than on its substantial accomplishments. Indeed, serious problems have faced the Italian economy and Italian society: the disruptive effects of rapid modernization; the survival of widespread political alienation at the level of the mass culture; the lack of unified, coherent political leadership; the absence of effective coordination of the institutions responsible for policy formulation and policy implementation; and the ubiquity of patronage and corruption. Yet, until the upheavals of the 1990s, the Italian political system had endured for more than forty years and produced a significant modernization of Italian society and economy despite all of its imperfections.

This final appraisal begins with a brief discussion of the positive features of the pre-1992 Italian political system—features that have enabled the system to survive since the end of World War II and to weather various fundamental crises. It also deals briefly with the catalytic factors that helped to bring about—after so many false alarms—the political earthquake of 1992–1996 and the institutional change in the late 1990s. It then turns to some of the more difficult problems that Italy must still confront.

Elements of Strength and Seeds of Crisis in the Italian Political System

Some contemporary observers of Italian politics have pointed to a number of the possible reasons why the Italian republic, before 1992, was able to endure despite all its travails.[1] This section first describes the political and socioeconomic factors at work before 1992 and then takes a harder look at the response of the Italian economy to the enlarged European market.

Pre-1992 Political and Socioeconomic Factors

One factor that has contributed to the survival of Italy's political system is the relatively moderate nature of its political parties. The Communist Party—representing the extreme left over most of the past six decades—was generally a temperate and constructive force in parliament, in subnational government, and in its socioeconomic organizations. In other words, it was well rooted in Italian society and engaged from the very beginning in working within the Italian political system. Moreover, until 1994 Italy lacked a strong party on the extreme right. The country did not become engaged in protracted foreign wars or colonial adventures (as part of the post–World War II peace agreement, Italy was stripped of its former colonies), which could have sapped public morale and resources or politicized the Italian armed forces. And, until the 1990s, no ethnic or regional minority had called into question the continued existence of the Italian state. In short, there were no irreconcilable conflicts to overload the Italian polity.

Five other political factors have contributed to system survival as well. First, the party Christian Democracy (DC), for all its faults, managed to bridge the divisions among social classes by virtue of its catchall nature, to strengthen small and medium enterprises (SMEs), and to give invaluable transfusions to backward regions, all while keeping the Catholic middle class committed to democratic institutions and democratic methods. Second, the Italian political elites—with all their inefficiency and seemingly unprincipled opportunism— showed resourcefulness, empathy, imagination, and an ability to take remedial action in various crises. In fact, they were far more united and willing to cooperate than they appeared. Third, subcultural differences began to narrow as the secularization of Italian society and the increasing moderation of the Communist Party brought the Catholic and Marxist subcultures closer together. In the 1980s the rising generations of party activists appeared to be less ideologically committed than their fathers had been. Fourth, the parties of the left— including the Communists—had acquired a stake in the system. They were by no means excluded from the politics of patronage practiced by the Christian Democratic–dominated regime. To the contrary, their share of the action was increasing. Finally, the political compromise represented by the 1948 constitution was, in the last analysis, underwritten by all of the main parties in the political system, and the proportional representation electoral law adopted in 1948 made it easy for political parties to win seats in parliament or other elected offices with a minimal amount of support. All types of parties, big and small, were included in the system. The barriers to entry into the system were purposely kept low to favor political inclusion and the parliamentarization of parties.

Certain socioeconomic factors also contributed to the resilience and underlying strength of Italian democracy. Living standards had risen enormously since the late 1940s when movies such as *Bitter Rice, Umberto D.,* and *Bicycle Thief* dramatized the plight of the Italian masses. Indicators of this trend included the decline in both the birthrate and the death rate, the growing per capita consumption of meat and dairy products, and the rise in consumer purchases of automobiles and household appliances.[2] Urbanization, too, undermined the traditional allegiances that had divided Italy into regions committed to different political families. Although the regional differences in voting behavior remained, they no longer seemed to reflect fundamental cleavages in values and political orientations. Meanwhile, some Italian regions had a solid presence of social capital that facilitated the mobilization of citizens in support of government policies to build roads, railroads, hospitals, day-care centers, and other public policy outputs necessary for a better quality of life and economic development. The rise of the services sector did much to reduce the intensity of class conflict. And the advent of mass education fostered national integration, reduced the differences among regional subcultures, and perhaps contributed to the more pragmatic attitudes displayed by Italian voters. The "vote of *appartenenza*"—based on pure party identification—was to some degree being replaced by the "vote of opinion" and the "vote of exchange." Although the Italian economy and Italian society were suffering from major weaknesses, many of them were weaknesses that are beginning to surface throughout the Western industrial world. It was, therefore, no longer possible simply to dismiss Italy as the sick man of Europe. In fact, the experience of other Southern European political systems in making the transition from authoritarianism to democracy highlighted how Italy blazed

Ferrari and the other carmakers in the Modena-Reggio sports car industrial district represent the competitiveness of Italian products in top-of-the-line consumer goods.

Source: Reuters/Max Rossi.

the trail toward parliamentary democracy after the fall of fascism. Italy set the standard and became the model of how a peaceful transition to democracy could take place without major socioeconomic dislocation or acute political conflict. This track record was important for the transition to democracy of countries in Southern, Central, and Eastern Europe.[3]

Some profound long-term economic trends were, however, quietly transforming these structural political and cultural tendencies.[4] First, the need to compete in world markets and in the European Union (EU) had led to a restructuring of Italian industry, and especially the big industries of the northwest industrial triangle. The changes in the northwest were accompanied by the emergence of a new form of industrial organization, the industrial district, in the northeastern and central parts of the country. Because of the flexibility and innovation introduced through the organization of SMEs into industrial districts, Italian companies were able to penetrate European and international markets in a variety of top-of-the-line consumer goods. These changes not only weakened class consciousness and spread wealth around the country, but also they increased the demand for employment and, in the last analysis, created the basis to import labor from abroad. Italy's greater dependence on immigrant labor, especially in the low-skilled jobs, served to awaken the country to an historical change: during the 1990s Italy became a net importer of labor, thereby putting an end to more than a century of experience in exporting its excess labor supply to other parts of Europe, North America, South America, and Australia.[5]

Second, the new social programs and heavy spending of the early 1970s had not only created a full-fledged welfare state, but also increased the annual deficit from 3.7 percent of the gross domestic product (GDP) in 1970 to 11.6 percent in 1975. Efforts to trim the deficit after 1975 were not very successful. In 1981 it still stood at 11.4 percent of GDP, and in 1991 at 10.2 percent. But far more intolerable was the growth in the public debt:

38 percent of GDP in 1970, 57.6 percent in 1975, 59.9 percent in 1981, and a staggering 101.4 percent in 1991. It reached a peak of 122.9 percent in 1995. Two years later, the country undertook a significant U-turn and began running budgetary surpluses at the level of 3.5 percent to 5 percent of annual accounts so that it could reduce its annual deficit to under 3 percent and bring its overall public debt back down to a little over 100 percent of GDP. This dramatic turn in the level of the Italian deficit and overall debt illustrates two important points. First, when change needs to take place, it often does. Italian political elites have been willing to sacrifice their clienteles and patronage structures to meet the standards necessary to maintain a healthy economy. Second, Italy is determined to remain a central actor at the European level, rejecting the anti-European position of the Northern League. Any threat to that position, such as the anti-euro declarations by Northern League politicians in the spring of 2005, immediately receives a strong response among all types of political, economic, and cultural elites of various ideological persuasion. In other words, Italy possesses a large enough positive consensus on European integration that the country is willing to make domestic sacrifices to maintain that position.

The Italian Economy: Competitiveness in an Enlarged European Market

One of the chief problems facing Italy is the same one that confronts every modern industrial society: how to maintain an expanding economy with a low rate of unemployment while avoiding excessive inflation and an unstable currency and keeping exports competitive in world markets. This problem became acute in the "Hot Autumn" of 1969, when Italian labor abandoned its postwar behavior pattern of relatively docile industriousness, and in the fall of 1973, when skyrocketing oil prices began to affect the economy. Since that time, the Italian economy has undergone some dramatic changes that have reinforced its competitive position in international markets.

Strong measures taken by the governments of Bettino Craxi (1983–1987), Giuliano Amato (1992–1993), and Carlo Azeglio Ciampi (1993–1994) succeeded in lowering the rate of inflation to less than 5 percent (3.7 percent in mid-1994). The rest was completed under the Romano Prodi, Massimo D'Alema, and the second Amato governments as Italy hitched its monetary wagon to the Economic and Monetary Union. Interest rates and inflation came down, and Italy was protected from the speculative attacks on its currency that had occurred periodically until 1994. With the introduction of both the Single Market in 1993 and the euro in 2001, the Italian economy did not suffer in terms of competitiveness, exports, and market shares as many feared.

But after the advent of the Berlusconi government in 2001, Italy's economic performance began to decline. Whether the decline stemmed primarily from the inadequacy of government policies or from the combined effect of world recession and globalization, together with the emergence of China as a major exporter of low-priced textile and commercial products, is difficult to determine. What is clear is that Italy's economic performance has lagged under the center-right government. The combination of politically driven spending, such as the bailout of Alitalia in 2008 and the abolition of local property taxes, and the difficulty in generating existing tax revenues has hobbled the center-right in maintaining its projected public investment promises. This less-than-brilliant economic performance during periods of sustained growth in other countries, however, has served to shield the Italian economy from the worst aspects of the economic downturn. In 2004 the country registered the EU's lowest level of growth. The data for 2005 (0.7 percent) and the loss of 100,000 jobs since the previous year suggested that the country's economy had not yet turned the corner, whereas Germany and France demonstrated strong signs of recovery. Italy's growth rate turned upward during the following two years. What is evident from the data is that government spending had to be reduced and government revenues needed to rise if Italy wanted to maintain its welfare state and increase economic growth. Under Berlusconi, the annual deficit rose to 4.3 percent and the overall debt rose by two percentage points in a year to 108.5 percent of GDP in 2005. Under the second Amato government, the annual deficit was below 2 percent and the overall debt was expected to fall below 100 percent of GDP. The rising level of indebtedness of the country led Standard and Poor's in February 2006 to lower the country's credit rating from AA to AA-. During the two years of the Prodi government, there was a concerted government effort to lower the debt once again. In 2007 the level had returned to 103.5 percent of national GDP, but the process was once again reversed in 2009 under the Berlusconi government; the debt rose to 116 percent of GDP. Expectations were that the annual deficit and the overall debt would rise much faster, but the restricted spending policy of Giulio Tremonti served to keep the negative economic indicators under control. As expected, in 2010 the Italian economy expanded once again, this time by a timid but positive 0.7 percent.[6]

Despite the recurrent ebbs and flows of Italy's economic trends, there is a basic consensus that the country needs to maintain public spending within the parameters of Maastricht.[7] How did this degree of consensus develop? The economic factors that precipitated the political crisis of 1992–1996 have already been noted. Also important was the globalization of the world economy: with protection against foreign competition becoming a thing of the past, the old free-spending ways would have to be jettisoned. And, finally, Italy's desire to enter the Economic and Monetary Union and the Euro Area was a crucial factor. After the Maastricht Treaty was signed in 1992, a growing consensus developed among central bankers, the executives of large companies and the associations representing SMEs and exporters, and the members of think tanks. The central theme of this consensus was the perceived need for Italy to adjust its economy and its public finance to the goals set by the Maastricht Treaty. This adjustment would require ensuring sound money, controlling inflation, maintaining the independence of the Bank of Italy from the executive branch, and restraining government spending. By the mid-1990s, this point of view was shared by the vast majority of the policy-oriented intellectuals who were beginning to influence the Italian economic decision-making process.[8]

Italy and the European Union

Italy was one of the original six members of the European Union. When it was first established in 1958 by the Treaty of Rome, the group of nations was known as the European Economic Community (EEC). In 1969 the EEC was renamed the European Community (EC), but with the ratification of the Maastricht Treaty in 1994 it became known as the European Union. After the first few years of Italy's membership in the EEC, Italians shed the apathy with which many of them had greeted the decision to enter the Common Market and reached a general consensus in favor of continuing this link with France, West Germany, and the Benelux countries. The European connection was thought to stimulate and challenge Italy's already burgeoning industrial economy and offer wider markets for Italian products. It also provided employment opportunities for Italian workers in Northern Europe and eased Italy's labor surplus and unemployment problem. In addition, the predecessor to the EEC, the European Coal and Steel Community, had proven a success in guaranteeing steady policy decision making and efficiency in this crucial sector of industrial development for postwar Europe, including Italy. Finally, Italy's poorer regions (the south and the islands) were able to obtain assistance from the European Investment Bank through low-cost loans to develop needed infrastructure and to create new businesses. The European Social Fund also helped Italians migrating to northern cities to adjust to their new workplace environments.

Many Italians, especially those who wanted to modernize and reform their country, also had powerful and compelling political reasons for giving solid support to the ambitious programs being formulated in Brussels. And these political motives have become paramount now that Italy has attained prosperity and no longer needs economic assistance to the same degree as in the past. First, membership in the EU gives Italian policymakers a sense of belonging to a larger and more powerful entity and of playing a vital role in the building of a new Europe. International recognition and prestige enhance their status. Second, many Italians feel that the EU is a force for peace and prosperity in the world, offering a model of development that is based less on the neoliberal principles of free trade and minimal regulations and more on the principles of social and economic cohesion and planning to lessen the gaps in development across Europe's regions. Third, many Italians see membership in a united Europe as an ideal goal to compensate for the perceived limitations of their own political and administrative systems. Finally (and this factor has become increasingly salient), EU obligations furnish Italian political leaders with convenient leverage for demanding domestic reforms and rigorous stabilization measures to enable Italy to fulfill its duties as a member of the EU.[9]

The Italian government loyally accepted some of the more onerous side effects of EC obligations in the past and continues to do so with the EU today. EC policies hurt southern agriculture and compelled the shutdown of some unprofitable steel mills, both of which the Italian public sector was enjoined from subsidizing any longer. The Italian government sponsored the enlargement of the EC, which admitted Italy's Southern European competitors such as Greece in 1981 and Spain and Portugal in 1986. Italy thereby showed itself to be a constructive and public-spirited member of the EC, always ready to sacrifice its own short-term interests for the greater good of Western Europe as a whole and its long-term interest in widening the European market.

Yet, even though the Italian government displayed a very cooperative attitude on major issues, it was somewhat laggard in following through on its ambitious commitments, in implementing EC regulations, and in enacting legislation to fulfill the terms of EC directives. These legal and administrative difficulties were tied to the archaic character of Italian administrative institutions, but Italy was able to surmount these problems with legislative innovations. One such was the 1994 LaPergola law, which provided for the immediate applicability of European directives to Italy's legal system while waiting for parliament to transpose the directives into national legislation. Italy's current record on adopting EU directives is no worse and no better than that of other major players at the European level. Internal reforms within parliament and the executive branch have raised the profile of the legislative sessions dedicated to European directives and have made the transposition of directives faster than before.

The Single European Act of 1986, the Maastricht Treaty of 1992, and the EU's decision to move toward the adoption of a common monetary policy and currency once again presented Italy with some weighty tasks. Certain convergence criteria were laid down by the protocols attached to the Maastricht Treaty. To adopt the single EU currency, the euro, a member state was required to have an annual public deficit approaching 3 percent or less of GDP, a national debt approaching 60 percent or less of GDP, and an inflation rate below certain clearly defined limits. In addition, the central bank of the member state had to be independent of direct government control. The performance of member states in meeting their obligations under the Maastricht Treaty was monitored by the European Commission on an annual basis, and noncompliance was publicized. To meet these convergence criteria, and to continue to meet them in the future, the Italian government had to sacrifice its ability to devaluate its way out of its uncompetitive position in relation to producers in other countries.[10] Italy, therefore, had to relinquish its ability to devalue its currency to the ability to guarantee the stability of the new currency.

The Prodi cabinet of 1996–1998 accepted the mission of making significant progress toward meeting the convergence criteria. By mid-1998 Prodi had succeeded in his goal: several of the convergence criteria had been met, including the prescribed reduction of the annual deficit, and moderate but satisfactory progress had been made toward reducing the national debt. As a result, Italy was admitted to participation in the Economic and Monetary Union along with Belgium, Portugal, and Spain, which also had problems in fully meeting the Maastricht criteria. To obtain the support he needed from the extreme leftist PRC, however, Prodi had to rely on tax increases to pay for most of the cost of conforming to the convergence criteria: he did not feel prepared to defy the PRC by tackling welfare or pension reform. Indeed, to appease his leftist allies, he was compelled to incur the displeasure of the center-right—especially the Northern League, but also, to a lesser degree, Forza Italia (Go Italy).[11]

Once again, then, the Italian government successfully played the European card. It dragooned the Italian economy and the Italian body politic into greater progress by conjuring up an external threat: Italian exclusion from the inner circle of the EU. Both the D'Alema and Amato cabinets committed themselves to continuing Prodi's policies of conforming to EU guidelines. With Prodi serving as the newly designated president of the European Commission and with Mario Monti, a highly regarded economist from a leading Italian university, serving as the commissioner responsible for competition, Italy's status in Europe was secured.

In 2004, however, chinks began to appear in Italy's European armor. Italy took over the EU presidency during the second half of 2003. On July 1 Prime Minister Silvio Berlusconi presented the program of the Italian presidency to the European Parliament. The main objectives of the program, which was ambitious, were ratifying a draft European constitution, redefining the EU's relationship (that is, its neighborhood policy) with the Mediterranean countries and those bordering the EU to the east, and bringing EU expansion to fruition through the entry of ten new member states, in addition to expanding the list of candidate countries. During the question period that followed his presentation, Berlusconi stopped referring to his prepared text and began responding to the questions of a representative of Germany's Social Democratic Party (SPD) about the conflict of interest between his dual role as Italy's media magnate and prime minister. In an unprecedented intemperate exchange with the SPD member, Berlusconi effectively lost his and the country's momentum during the remaining six months.

After July 2003 the achievements of the Italian presidency were overshadowed by the breakdown of relations between the German SPD and the European Parliament, on one side, and the Italian government, on the other. Another blow to Italy's European status was dealt by the Northern League's rabid opposition to a measure passed by the European Parliament—the European arrest warrant. This measure was supported by member states as a means of preventing criminals and terrorists from moving easily from one country to another to avoid arrest. The final episode occurred in 2004 during the appointment of the new European Commission on the heels of the European parliamentary elections. The Italian government's appointee, Rocco Buttiglione, who was designated to fill the post of commissioner for justice, was rejected in the confirmation hearing by the European Parliament because of his open stance against homosexuals. As a result, the entry into office of the new European Commission headed by José Manuel Barroso of Portugal was delayed by one month so that Buttiglione could be replaced with an acceptable candidate. That candidate was Italy's minister of foreign affairs, Franco Frattini. The Buttiglione snafu also delayed Prodi's return to the leadership of the center-left by one month. His five-year term as Commission president, however, gave him greater visibility in his attempt to topple Berlusconi in the next round of parliamentary elections.

Under the Berlusconi government of 2008, the mistakes made during the previous center-right cabinet were avoided. Franco Frattini was able to provide guidance from the beginning as minister of foreign affairs. The overall balanced guidance provided to Italy's position in the EU was reaffirmed during the June 2009 summit as well as during the G7 summit in Aquila. Italy's stance on the Lisbon Treaty did not waiver at all during the final run-up to its ratification on the heels of the successful second Irish referendum, even though ratification of the treaty will oblige the country to undertake significant reforms of its internal institutional structure.

The Question of Institutional Reform

The results of the 2006 and 2008 parliamentary elections placed the question of institutional reform back on center stage. In 2006 the Prodi government faced the issue of the referendum on institutional reform—that is, devolution—passed by the previous Berlusconi government against the strenuous objections of the opposition and the majority of Italy's regions and cities. It also had to disentangle the issue of the relationship between the two executives—president of the republic and prime minister—and whether the two should be merged or whether the remaining autonomous powers of the president (dissolution of parliament, selection of the prime minister, swearing-in of the cabinet, and promulgation of laws) should be transferred to the prime minister. Finally, the government had to clarify whether Italy could maintain its unitary welfare state structure or whether that structure should be regionalized, which would mean that wealthy regions will be able to offer a wider variety of public services and poorer regions would have to cut back on the services and benefits offered to their citizens. After the 2006 election, the Prodi government took a clear stance on the institutional referendum. It would not support the changes undertaken by the Berlusconi government. Nor would it undertake an undermining of the existing welfare system.

Many Italian politicians have raised the question of whether Italy's political institutions should be changed to enable the government to develop a more coherent set of policies based on a firm mandate. The question always has been: if a government were more stable, would it be in a position to produce better policy outputs? Most have felt that the answer to the question is yes, but after five years of the Berlusconi government between 2001 and 2006 many began to seriously doubt the correlation between the stability of the government and its ability to produce significant polices.

Yet proposals have been offered. One such proposal calls for emulating the French quasi-presidential system. A popularly elected chief executive might be better able to dominate parliament and coordinate his own cabinet. An electoral law based on single-member districts with election by absolute majority, or a runoff election if the threshold was not reached, might force the major parties to combine their forces (as in France) and might bring about firm parliamentary majorities such as those attained by the Gaullists in the 1960s or by the Socialists in 1981. This type of proposal (generally championed by Berlusconi and the center-right) has aroused considerable opposition from the center-left. It is feared that because of Italian political traditions, the system might produce an Italian reincarnation of Benito Mussolini rather than an Italian Charles de Gaulle or an Italian François Mitterrand. The idea of adopting a French-style system of single-member districts with runoff elections has been resisted by the small and medium-size parties, because they feared that larger parties such as the Democratic Party and PdL might dominate the electoral alliances promoted by a French-type runoff system. There is no assurance, then, that the adoption of certain French constitutional procedures would result in a duplication of the positive result achieved in France: the establishment of a strong, stable, democratic executive with a popular mandate and (usually) a firm majority in parliament. The election results of 2001 and 2008 have assured the center-right governments with stable majorities. Where this has not occurred is in center-left governments, which have been chronically weak because of internal dissent and usually razor-thin majorities in at least one chamber in parliament.

Other critics have proposed to reform the present parliamentary system by bolstering the power of the prime minister and the cabinet. Supporters of this goal are often attracted by those features of the German system that would strengthen the prime minister and the cabinet and reinforce the dominant party at the expense of the smaller parties in the system. Some would like to adopt the German constructive vote of no confidence, which would make it impossible for parliament to overthrow a cabinet except by a resolution approved by an absolute majority of the members of either chamber—a resolution that would specifically designate the outgoing prime minister's successor. Some have also suggested reducing the number of parties in the Italian parliament by adopting something similar to the German 5 percent rule, which permits a party to benefit from proportional representation in Bundestag elections only if it carries three single-member districts or polls 5 percent of the total vote. A rule applied in Italy by the 1993 electoral law governing elections to the Chamber of Deputies required a party to obtain 4 percent of the votes to obtain a proportional share of the seats reserved for party lists elected by proportional representation (about one-fourth of the seats in the Chamber of Deputies were covered by this provision). It did reduce somewhat the number of parties in parliament, but its effect was diluted by the formation of interparty alliances for the capture of single-member districts—alliances in which some splinter parties were allotted a quota of seats by their more powerful allies.

Just before the 2006 election, the center-right reintroduced a proportional representation electoral system in hopes of diminishing the center-left's margin of victory. The result was that the new law *prevented* the center-right from winning the elections and gave the center-left a slim majority in the Senate and a comfortable one in the Chamber of Deputies. The new electoral rules and they way they were applied by the major political parties (Forza Italia and DS) did not, however, reduce the number of parties. They continued to multiply, especially those in the center-left coalition. The new law also eliminated the need for parties to meet a percentage threshold in the Chamber of Deputies elections to achieve representation in parliament. Because a threshold of 3 percent was maintained in the Senate, the Rose in the Fist list did not receive any seats despite having gained 2.4 percent of the votes (see Table 4-3, page 362). Two years later, when the two main parties (in this case, PD and PdL) decided not to bring under their wing the minor parties, the result was completely different. A majority of the small parties on both the left and right failed to go above the 4 percent threshold and lost parliamentary representation. Currently, the two major parties enjoy an unprecedented concentration of political support (77.9 percent in the Chamber and 82.3 percent in the Senate). Therefore, an electoral system based on proportional representation and maintaining a 4 percent threshold for representation can reduce the number of parties in the system, and the wining coalition can be stable, if the margin of seats in parliament is sufficient to beat back minor defections and if the leadership and program of the government are clear and effective.

As for reform of the constitution in relation to regional devolution, under Berlusconi the center-right supported the approach championed by the Northern League of devolving powers over health, education, and law enforcement to the regions. It also proposed granting the prime minister the power to dissolve parliament, thereby effectively overshadowing the president's role as head of state. The bill was adopted during the last days of the Berlusconi government, but fifteen regions had already asked the Constitutional Court for a referendum for ratification. That request was granted, and the referendum was scheduled for June 2006. All indications were that the referendum would be rejected, because the proposal was not supported by a majority of the regions (especially the southern ones), nor was it supported by the Prodi government. The reform also did not have the support of much of the public, which was wary of giving added powers to the national government to the detriment of the president of the republic. But the new Berlusconi government that came to power in 2008 immediately set out to pass a reform initiative proposed by the Northern League: fiscal federalism. Under this proposal the regions will have to make do mostly with the tax revenues generated locally rather than depending on constant transfer payments from the central government. The exact nature of the formula and how it will affect public expenditures in the southern regions—that is, whether there will be a national compensatory instrument to take into account levels of wealth and overall tax revenues—still have to be spelled out, but it is clear that Italy is heading toward a new era of center-periphery relations in which the outcomes are not clear.

An Uncertain Future

In the first decade of the new millennium, the future of the Italian polity has been clarified to a great extent. Indeed, some of the fundamental questions about the political system have been answered. First, the rules of the game of electoral competition have been respected. No matter the margin of victory, there has been a smooth transfer of powers from government to opposition, from center-right to center-left and back again, just as in all elections since 1994. In effect, then, Italy has become a "normal" democracy in which power is transferred from one group to another in a peaceful and legal fashion. Sergio Fabbrini and Leonardi Morlino have argued that Italy has moved from a "consensus" to a "competitive" democratic system[12] where parties and political leaders alternate in power.

Second, the roles of the various institutions—that is, the presidency, the courts, parliament, and government—have been respected and kept within their constitutional limits. Third, despite all of the evidence presented in surveys of how dissatisfied voters are with national government, electoral campaigns can still mobilize extensive participation from the Italian electorate. In 2006 more than 83 percent of the electorate went to the polls, and two years later when the result was already clear, 80.5 percent turned out. This level of participation represents one of the highest in all of Europe and in the Western world. In Italy, politics matter to the ordinary citizen.

Yet unanswered questions remain about some of the fundamental aspects of the country's political system. Will Italy become a federal state, or will it continue to be an example of strong regionalism within a unitary design? Will Italy regain its central role in providing intellectual and political guidance to a larger and more cohesive Europe, or will it become one of the more marginal members of the EU? Will Italy gain control of its immigration problem and begin to integrate those who arrive into its political and socioeconomic system, or will it be overwhelmed by the successive waves of desperate immigrants trying to escape the poverty and hunger so prevalent outside of Europe? These issues are not unique to Italy. They are the burning issues in other political systems in Europe, and in Italy they are part of the debate that animates national as well as European and local politics.

More than sixty years of democracy have helped the country to overcome problems that seemed insurmountable. Since the first parliamentary elections in 1948, Italy has undergone a transformation from a predominantly rural, agricultural society to an urban, industrial, and postindustrial society. Elections have taken place in an uninterrupted and peaceful manner. New parties have come and gone, and some have been able to scale successfully the heights of political power. The institutional structure has undergone dramatic changes through the introduction of a Constitutional Court and an independent judiciary. The political and social culture that was once dominated by machismo now guarantees equality of the sexes and equal opportunity. Finally, the role of the Catholic Church in politics has changed from wielder of raw power to the moral conscience of the nation.

From an international perspective, the country has changed profoundly. For three decades, Italy was treated as "the sick man of Europe" because of the size of its Communist Party, the depth of its socioeconomic cleavages, and the backwardness of its economy. The Italy of the new millennium is cast in a completely different light. Its former Communist Party has been brought into the mainstream of the political process—its leaders have served in the cabinet and have held the office of prime minister, and its successor parties have joined the European Socialist Party federation as one of its leading elements. In retrospect, Italy was never "the sick man of Europe"; rather, it was engaged in the process of becoming a solid parliamentary regime that set the standard for future democratic states in Southern and Eastern Europe when they emerged from dictatorship. Italy has also been an outlier in its struggle to defeat internal terrorism from both the left and the right and to reduce the presence of organized crime without introducing draconian measures that would have limited civil and individual rights. In fact, the Italian state responded to these two types of threats by enhancing the role of the judiciary, rather than that of the police or the army, in internal affairs. It has chosen to respond to attacks against the state and civil society with the rule of law and accepted judicial procedures.

It must also be remembered that Italy has to a great extent been in the vanguard of the European integration movement. While other countries have at times been lukewarm about European integration, Italy's leaders have always expressed a clear vision of where Italy and Europe were heading—toward the creation of a European federation of nation-states in which national governments maintain their central role of coordination but in which power is allocated to other levels of government—European and regional—in the search of policy efficiency and efficacy.[13] Such was the vision enunciated by Altiero Spinelli (adviser to Alcide De Gasperi and member of the High Authority on Coal and Steel)[14] and carried forward by three generations of political leaders—Alcide DeGasperi to Giuliano Amato and Romano Prodi to Silvio Berlusconi.

It is highly likely, then, that the recourse to law, the judiciary, and representative institutions will continue to be the usual Italian response to socioeconomic crises and challenges to its institutions, and especially so as the country becomes increasingly integrated into an expanding European economy and reinforced institutional structure. Indeed, it could be argued that from the beginning Europe was an Italian idea, that its basis in law, language, culture, and religion sprang from Italian roots.

NOTES

1. See, for example, Sidney Tarrow, "Italy: Crisis, Crises, or Transition?" in *Italy in Transition: Conflict and Consensus,* ed. Peter Lange and Sidney Tarrow (London: Frank Cass, 1980), 166–185. Also see Norman Kogan, *A Political History of Italy: The Postwar Years* (New York: Praeger, 1983), chap. 22.
2. Kogan, *Political History of Italy,* 329. By 1979 there was one automobile in Italy for every 3.4 people.
3. See Laurence Whithead, "Democracy by Convergence and Southern Europe: A Comparative Politics Perspective," in *Encouraging Democracy: The International Context of Regime Transition in Southern Europe,* ed. Geoffrey Pridham (London: Lyden Press, 1991), 45–61.
4. See Vincent della Sala, "Hollowing Out and Hardening the State: European Integration and the Italian Economy," in *Crisis and Transition in Italian Politics,* ed. Martin Bull and Martin Rhodes (London: Frank Cass, 1997), 22–27; Maurizio Ferrera, "The Uncertain Future of the Italian Welfare State," in Bull and Rhodes, *Crisis and Transition in Italian Politics,* 243–247; and Dermot McCann, "European Integration and Explanations of Regime Change in Italy," *Mediterranean Politics* 3 (Autumn 1998): 79–85.
5. This change in migration flows took place in stages. During the 1960s Italian labor largely stopped moving abroad, but continued to move north. The 1970s and 1980s were marked by the return of Italians who had initially immigrated to other parts of Europe, as well as by

the first small numbers of immigrants from abroad. It was during the 1990s that Italy began importing large contingents of labor from outside of the European Union. In 2004 that presence was estimated at 2.0 million workers from outside of the EU.

6. Michele Capriati, "The Economic Context," in *The Italian General Election of 2008: Berlusconi Strikes Back,* ed. James Newell (Basingstoke, UK: Palgrave Macmillan, 2009), 43–61.

7. In fact, the criticism aimed at the two main political blocs was that their economic programs seemed to be photocopies of their opponent's program. See ITANES, *Il ritorno di Berlusconi:* (Bologna: Il Mulino, 2008), 179–180.

8. See Claudio M. Radaelli, "Networks of Expertise and Policy Change in Italy," *South European Society and Politics* 3 (Autumn 1998): 5–8.

9. See Raffaella Y. Nanetti, "Adding Value to City Planning: The European Union's Urban Programs in Naples," *South European Society and Politics* 6 (Winter 2001): 33–57; and Giovanna Antonia Fois, "The EU and International Contexts," in Newell, *The Italian General Election of 2008,* 62–84.

10. See della Sala, "Hollowing Out and Hardening the State," 20–21.

11. See James I. Walsh, "The Uncertain Path to Monetary Union," in *Italian Politics: Mapping the Future,* ed. Luciano Bardi and Martin Rhodes (Boulder: Westview Press, 1998), 93–110;. Leila S. Talani, *Betting for and Against EMU* (Aldershot, UK: Ash Press, 2000); and Talani, *European Political Economy: Political Science Perspectives* (Aldershot, UK: Ashgate, 2004).

12. "The consensual model is characterized by the disaggregated representation of social interests, by multi-party systems and by the absence of alternation in government between alternative groupings. . . ." and "The competitive model, in contrast, is characterized by the aggregated representation of interests, by two-party or bipolar party systems and by the presumption of alternation in government between alternative line-ups . . . ." Sergio Fabbrini, "The Transformation of Italian Democracy," *Bulletin of Italian Politics* 1, no. 1 (2009): 30. See also Leonardo Morlino, "Transition from Democracy to Democracy: Is It Possible in Italy?" *Bulletin of Italian Politics* 1, no. 1 (2009): 7–27.

13. Sergio Fabbrini and Mario Brunazzo, "Federalizing Italy: The Convergent Effects of Europeanization and Domestic Mobilization," *Regional and Federal Studies* 13 (Spring 2003): 100–120.

14. Michael Burgess, "Introduction: Federalism and Building the European Union," *Publius* 26 (Fall 1996): 1–16.

FOR FURTHER READING

Aberbach, Joel D., Robert D. Putnam, and Bert A. Rockman. *Bureaucrats and Politicians in Western Democracies.* Cambridge: Harvard University Press, 1981.

Allum, P. A. *Italy: Republic without Government?* New York: Norton, 1973.

Bardi, Luciano, and Martin Rhodes, eds. *Italian Politics: Mapping the Future.* Boulder: Westview Press, 1998.

Belloni, Frank P., and Dennis C. Beller, eds. *Faction Politics: Political Parties in Comparative Perspective.* Santa Barbara, Calif.: ABC-Clio Press, 1978.

Blackmer, Donald L. M., and Sidney G. Tarrow, eds. *Communism in Italy and France.* Princeton, N.J.: Princeton University Press, 1975.

Bull, Martin, and Martin Rhodes, eds. *Crisis and Transition in Italian Politics.* London: Frank Cass, 1997.

Burnett, Stanton H., and Luca Mantovani. *The Italian Guillotine: Operation Clean Hands and the Overthrow of Italy's First Republic.* Lanham, Md.: Rowman and Littlefield, 1998.

Caciagli, Mario, and David I. Kertzer, eds. *Italian Politics: The Stalled Transition.* Boulder: Westview Press, 1996.

Cassese, Sabino. "Is There a Government in Italy? Politics and Administration at the Top." In *Presidents and Prime Ministers,* edited by Richard Rose and Ezra N. Suleiman. Washington, D.C.: American Enterprise Institute, 1980.

D'Alimonte, Roberto, and David Nelken, eds. *Italian Politics: The Center-Left in Power.* Boulder: Westview Press, 1997.

Diani, Mario. *Green Networks: A Structural Analysis of the Italian Environmental Movement.* Edinburgh: Edinburgh University Press, 1995.

Di Palma, Giuseppe. *Surviving without Governing: The Italian Parties in Parliament.* Berkeley: University of California Press, 1976.

Donovan, Mark, and Paolo Onofri, eds. *Italian Politics: Frustrated Aspirations for Change.* Oxford: Berghahn Books, 2008.

Grew, Raymond. "Italy." In *Crises of Political Development in Europe and the United States,* edited by Raymond Grew. Princeton, N.J.: Princeton University Press, 1978.

Kogan, Norman. *A Political History of Italy: The Postwar Years.* New York: Praeger, 1983.

Lange, Peter, and Sidney Tarrow, eds. *Italy in Transition: Conflict and Consensus.* London: Frank Cass, 1980.

LaPalombara, Joseph. *Democracy Italian Style.* New Haven: Yale University Press, 1987.

———. *Interest Groups in Italian Politics.* Princeton, N.J.: Princeton University Press, 1964.

Leonardi, Robert. *Convergence, Cohesion and Integration in the European Union.* New York: St. Martin's Press, 1995.

Leonardi, Robert, and Raffaella Y. Nanetti, eds. *Regional Development in a Modern European Economy: The Case of Tuscany.* London: Pinter Publishers, 1994.

Low-Beer, John R. *Protest and Participation: The New Working Class in Italy.* Cambridge: Cambridge University Press, 1978.

Newell, James R. *The Italian General Election of 2008: Berlusconi Strikes Back.* Basingstoke, UK: Palgrave Macmillan, 2009.

Pasquino, Gianfranco, and Patrick McCarthy, eds. *The End of Postwar Politics in Italy: The Landmark 1992 Elections.* Boulder: Westview Press, 1993.

Putnam, Robert D. *Making Democracy Work: Civic Traditions in Modern Italy.* Princeton, N.J.: Princeton University Press, 1993.

Ranney, Austin, and Giovanni Sartori, eds. *Eurocommunism: The Italian Case.* Washington, D.C.: American Enterprise Institute, 1978.

Ruzza, Carlo, and Stefano Fella, eds. *Re-inventing the Italian Right.* London: Routledge, 2009.

Sani, Giacomo. "The Political Culture of Italy: Continuity and Change." In *The Civic Culture Revisited,* edited by Gabriel A. Almond and Sidney Verba. Boston: Little, Brown, 1980.

Shin, Michael, and John Agnew. *Berlusconi's Italy: Mapping Contemporary Italian Politics.* Philadelphia: Temple University Press, 2008.

Tarrow, Sidney. *Between Center and Periphery: Grassroots Politicians in Italy and France.* New Haven: Yale University Press, 1977.

Vannicelli, Primo. *Italy, NATO, and the European Community.* Cambridge: Center for International Affairs, Harvard University, 1974.

Weinberg, Leonard. *The Transformation of Italian Communism.* New Brunswick, N.J.: Transaction Publishers, 1995.

Willis, F. Roy. *Italy Chooses Europe.* New York: Oxford University Press, 1971.

Zariski, Raphael. *Italy: The Politics of Uneven Development.* Hinsdale, Ill.: Dryden Press, 1972.

Zuckerman, Alan S. *The Politics of Faction: Christian Democratic Rule in Italy.* New Haven: Yale University Press, 1979.

Part 5

Sweden

M. Donald Hancock

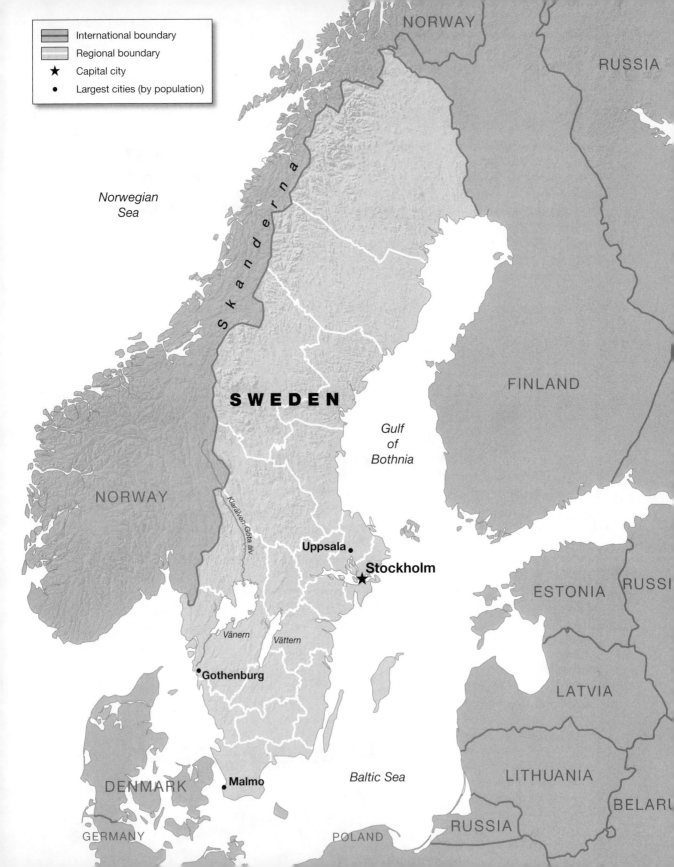

International boundary
Regional boundary
★ Capital city
● Largest cities (by population)

Norwegian Sea

NORWAY

RUSSIA

S k a n d e r n a

SWEDEN

FINLAND

Gulf of Bothnia

NORWAY

Klarälven-Göta älv

● Uppsala

Stockholm ★

ESTONIA

RUSSI

Vänern

Vättern

LATVIA

● **Gothenburg**

RUSSI

LITHUANIA

DENMARK

● **Malmo**

Baltic Sea

BELARU

GERMANY

POLAND

RUSSIA

The Context of
Swedish Politics

For DECADES SWEDEN HAS FASCINATED MANY OUTSIDE OBSERVERS. Some commentators have enthusiastically praised Sweden's economic and social achievements as a "middle way" between competitive capitalism and state socialism and as a "model for the world."[1] Others, ranging from skeptical conservatives to radical socialists, have criticized the centralization of political and economic power in the hands of public officials, unions, and an alleged governing class made up of a small group of wealthy capitalists, respectively.[2] For decades, these diametrically opposed assessments underscored Sweden's singularity in comparison with more familiar capitalist democracies such as France, Germany, Great Britain, and the United States. More recently, national elections in September 2010 yielded a new source of ideological conflict when the anti-immigrant Sweden Democrats Party succeeded in gaining entry to the Swedish parliament, thereby confounding the traditional left-right political cleavage.

Sweden has undeniably attained one of the world's highest standards of living and most fully developed welfare systems. At the same time, twentieth-century economic and social reforms resulted in an extraordinarily high rate of taxation and pervasive tendencies toward bureaucratization. Sweden's political parties and organized interest groups have responded with different strategies of policy modification and system change. The result is an ongoing struggle to redefine fundamental tenets of the "Swedish model" of advanced industrial society.

This chapter and those that follow describe the basic historical, contextual, institutional, party, and group characteristics of modern Sweden. Analytically, the principal objective is to assess Sweden's status with respect to the distinction that policy specialist Lawrence D. Brown draws between breakthrough politics and a more restrictive form of rationalizing politics. Breakthrough politics, according to Brown, means government initiatives to expand the scope of public commitment in response to socioeconomic need. By contrast, rationalizing politics refers to attempts by public officials "to solve evident problems of existing government programs."

Breakthrough politics therefore implies a strategy of active system change, whereas rationalizing politics constitutes less ambitious government measures to make public policies "more rational, that is, problem free."[3] The latter approach, Brown contends, has characterized phases of postwar American politics and, by implication, policy choices by Thatcherite Conservatives in the United Kingdom, Christian Democrats in Germany, and "nonpartisan" government experts in Italy as well.

The empirical test of these contrasting approaches to economic and social management in contemporary Sweden involves a long-term process of system adaptation to domestic and international changes. Historical traditions of breakthrough reforms confront external factors of globalization and Europeanization in the continuing redefinition of the Swedish model.

Geography, Resources, and Population

Sweden is geographically part of the northwestern European landmass known as Scandinavia, or Norden, located on approximately the same latitude as Alaska and northern Siberia. Other Nordic states are neighboring Denmark, Finland, and Norway, as well as more remote Iceland in the North Atlantic.[4] Sweden is the largest of the Scandinavian countries, with an area of 420,295 square kilometers (somewhat greater than that of California). It shares a long, largely mountainous boundary with Norway to the west and a considerably shorter border with Finland to the northeast. The rest of Sweden is surrounded by water: the Gulf of Bothnia to the east, the Baltic Sea to the east and south, and a narrow passageway known as the Kattegat, which separates Sweden from Denmark to the southwest.

Sweden is a land of rugged beauty. Much of the country is covered by forests and lakes, with the hills of central and northern Sweden yielding gradually to majestic peaks along the northwestern border. Approximately 10 percent of the land is arable. The richest soil is located in the southernmost province of Skåne, although highly productive farms also surround Lakes Vättern and Vänern in the south-central lowlands. A relatively mild climate, attributed to warming winds from the Atlantic and the indirect effects of the Gulf Stream, permits good harvests despite a short growing season. Rivers crisscross the country, providing transportation links and indispensable sources of natural energy. Two large islands guard the Baltic approaches to Sweden: Gotland, with its ancient fortress city of Visby, and Öland, now connected by a modern causeway to the mainland.

Various natural resources serve as the mainstay of Sweden's economy. Among them are large deposits of some of the world's highest-grade iron ore, timber and timber by-products, and abundant fish in the coastal waters. Partially compensating for the absence of domestic supplies of coal and oil are numerous rivers and waterfalls that serve as a plentiful and cheap source of hydroelectric power. The other principal sources of energy are imported oil and ten nuclear energy plants. (By comparison, in 2010 the United States had 104 nuclear plants, France 59, Japan 55, the United Kingdom 24, and Germany 22.)

Sweden's population of 9.2 million inhabitants (2008) is unevenly distributed. Fully 85 percent of Swedes live in the southern half of the country, where most industry, services, and agriculture are concentrated. The remainder of the populace is scattered throughout the various provinces that make up the forested and mining regions of Norrland. Stockholm, Sweden's capital, is the largest city, with a population of nearly 2 million (including surrounding suburbs). Göteborg, on the west coast, is second with 906,691. Third in size is Malmö, which is located in Skåne directly across the sound from Copenhagen, with 635,224 inhabitants. Other important cities are Uppsala, the site of Scandinavia's oldest university, founded in 1477; Västerås, Örebro, Norrköping, and Helsingborg, all of which are centers of industry, shipping, or both; and the mining town of Kiruna in the far north.[5]

Similar to the other Scandinavian countries but in contrast to the United Kingdom and most of continental Europe, Sweden is a highly homogeneous nation. Ethnically, most Swedes are descendants of the ancient Germanic tribes that settled the region beginning in 7,000–5,000 BCE. The native exceptions are the some forty thousand Finnish-speaking

Swedes, most of whom live along the Finnish border, and the approximately seventy thousand Samis (Lapps) in the northern provinces. Traditionally, many of the latter were nomads, moving with their herds of reindeer across northern Scandinavia in search of pasture with the annual change of seasons. In recent decades, however, more and more Samis have settled in permanent residences. In August 1998 a cabinet official formally apologized to the Sami people for centuries of economic and social discrimination by mainstream society.

Like France, Germany, and Great Britain, Sweden also claims a sizable contingent of immigrants. In 2008 they numbered more than 1.1 million (an increase of 64,000 since 2002) and made up nearly 14 percent of the total population. Approximately half a million are Muslims. Most immigrants occupy the lower-paying jobs in industry and services. By far the largest group, native Finns (who constitute 14 percent of foreign nationals) are followed in descending order by Serbs, Poles, Iranians, Bosnians, Danes, and Norwegians. Because of their close linguistic, ethnic, and other affinities with the Swedes, the Norwegians and Danes are virtually invisible within the majority culture. By contrast, many Finns and especially the immigrants from the Middle East, southeastern Europe, and Asia are less well integrated.

Most foreign workers and their families interact socially far more with members of their own subculture than with the majority Swedes. The murder of a young Kurdish woman in 2002 by her father because of her refusal to enter into an arranged marriage with a stranger from her native country prompted government officials to invest more heavily in crisis centers and support groups for both native and foreign victims of domestic violence. In addition, the government maintains long-standing policies to provide quality housing for immigrants and facilitate instruction in Swedish for the adults during working hours and bilingual education for their children at school.[6]

Religion and language reinforce national cohesiveness. An overwhelming majority of Swedes (87 percent) are nominal Lutherans. The remainder are either members of dissenting Protestant sects, Catholic, or non-Christian. In addition, virtually all citizens speak Swedish as their common language, albeit with regional variations in pronunciation, especially among Finno-Swedes and in Skåne, which until the seventeenth century belonged to Denmark.

Although Sweden's ethnic and cultural homogeneity strikes some foreign observers as monotonous in comparison with more colorfully diverse societies elsewhere in Europe, the absence of significant social cleavages has proved to be an important factor contributing to distinctive national political traits. Among them is Sweden's largely peaceful transition from an agrarian society governed by a traditional monarchy to today's advanced industrial democracy.

Early Political Development

Swedish political development is a product of both regional and domestic factors of system change. From the appearance of the first hunters and fishermen in prehistoric times until the beginning of the Viking era in the ninth century CE, Swedish history was virtually indistinguishable from that of the Scandinavian region as a whole. Gradually, however, separate Danish, Norwegian, and Swedish kingdoms began to evolve on the basis of rudimentary legal codes, recognized political authority in the form of elected monarchs,

Premodern Swedish political, cultural, and religious history can be read in carved inscriptions on some two thousand rune stones scattered about the country. Many date from the 4th century.

Source: Richard T. Nowitz/CORBIS

a sense of national identity shaped by language and an oral tradition of heroic sagas, and warfare with other Europeans. The advent of Christianity in the ninth century helped to domesticate Viking impulses of pillage and conquest and facilitated the incorporation of the Scandinavian kingdoms into the larger fabric of Western civilization. Christianization also encouraged incipient processes of modernization within the region as members of the clergy introduced literacy and codified the legal basis of state authority.

Through conquest, Sweden absorbed present-day Finland in the thirteenth century. Domestically, feudal estates similar to those elsewhere in Europe—that is, they consisted of a landed aristocracy, the clergy, and farmers—gradually evolved. By the fifteenth century, a fourth estate of urban "burghers" (borgare) had emerged as well. Unlike later developments in Russia and even neighboring Denmark, the independence of farmers, which was rooted in their ownership of land, prevented the emergence of serfdom in Sweden, and each estate retained its corporate autonomy.

The three Scandinavian kingdoms were united temporarily under Danish dominance in 1397, but eventually the more numerous Swedes became resentful of their Danish rulers. Representatives of the nobility and the borgare undertook an early move toward Swedish independence when they convened Sweden's first parliament (Riksdag) in 1435 to select a military commander. Full rebellion ensued in 1521 when peasants, miners, and nobles joined in an armed uprising in response to some punitive acts by the Danes. Their efforts succeeded, and in 1523 the Riksdag unanimously elected the leader of the rebellion, Gustav Vasa, Sweden's king. As Gustavus I, the youthful monarch centralized political and administrative authority in Stockholm and proclaimed Sweden's break with Catholicism in support of the Protestant Reformation in 1540.

During the sixteenth and seventeenth centuries, successive kings and their armies wrested sovereignty over Skåne and other southwestern provinces from Denmark and established a formidable Baltic empire. The most important of Sweden's heroic monarchs was Gustav II Adolf, who reigned from 1611 to 1632. Under his energetic leadership, Sweden extended its boundaries eastward and southward at the expense of both Russia and Poland and intervened decisively in the Thirty Years' War (1618–1648). To pursue Sweden's wartime exploits more effectively, Gustav Adolf and his advisers further centralized state authority by reorganizing the Riksdag as a four-estate parliament formally representing the nobility, clergy, borgare, and farmers. Through a series of taxation and financial reforms, the government also encouraged economic development and the growth of Stockholm, Göteborg, and other urban centers.

Sweden's defeat at the hands of Russia in 1709 marked the beginning of an extended period of territorial retrenchment that culminated in Russia's annexation of Finland in 1808–1809. The victorious anti-Napoleonic coalition that had opposed Emperor Napoleon Bonaparte's efforts to establish hegemony throughout Europe from 1805 to 1815 sought to compensate Sweden for the loss of Finland by transferring control over Norway from Denmark to Swedish authorities in 1814. Norway's peaceful bid for independence in 1905 reduced Sweden to its present boundaries.

Democratization and Industrialization

From independence through the Napoleonic Wars, Sweden experienced successive constitutional cycles that oscillated between extremes of monarchical versus parliamentary supremacy. Defeat by Russia prompted a palace coup against the last of the despotic monarchs in 1809, resulting in the adoption of a new constitution that institutionalized shared authority between the king and the four-estate Riksdag. The outcome was a broadly based elite consensus on constitutional arrangements comparable to the Glorious Revolution in England in 1688. Members of parliament elected Jean-Baptiste Bernadotte, a French marshal, regent in 1810. He served as king from 1818 until his death in 1844. An unanticipated consequence of Bernadotte's foreign birth was the devolution of monarchical authority to French-speaking parliamentarians who served as his principal advisers.

The diffusion of liberal political doctrines during the first half of the nineteenth century, coupled with the spread of industry and the advent of social democracy during the second half, brought about Sweden's piecemeal democratization. Liberal demands to transform the archaic four-estate parliament into a more modern representative body resulted in the introduction of a bicameral Riksdag in 1865–1866. Popular agitation for more sweeping political reforms followed in the wake of industrialization, which began in the 1850s and reached "takeoff" proportions in the 1890s.

Out of industrialization arose an organized labor movement and the Swedish Social Democratic Workers' Party (SAP), founded in 1889. Together, the Liberals and the Social Democrats advocated an extension of the right to vote and the introduction of a parliamentary form of government. Conservative leaders at first resisted, but, acknowledging the inevitable, they conceded manhood suffrage in exchange for the introduction of proportional representation in the Great Compromise of 1907–1909. This agreement codified a new elite consensus on fundamental political principles comparable to the constitutional settlement of 1809.

The Liberals and the Social Democrats formally established a parliamentary form of government, based on the British model, when they formed a majority coalition in 1917. The coalition partners proceeded to introduce universal suffrage in 1918, which was ratified by constitutional amendments in 1919–1921, as the final major step in Sweden's democratization. Subsequent constitutional revisions have refined but not substantially modified the historic achievements of 1907–1921.

Political Culture: Constants and Change

Sweden's evolutionary process of system change during the nineteenth and twentieth centuries is both cause and effect of a political culture that affirms traditional values and simultaneously endorses efforts at political creativity. Linking these attributes is a historic willingness among political actors to seek compromise solutions to partisan disagreements.

The most important traditional element inherent in Swedish political culture is a deeply ingrained respect for constitutionalism and law. Among Sweden's oldest historical documents are legal codes that served to limit kingly power and prescribe procedures for settling private disputes. Indeed, as political scientist Dankwart A. Rustow observes, an ancient Swedish adage proclaims *Land skall med lag byggas* ("The country shall be built with law").[7] Shared respect for orderly legal procedures among legislative, administrative, and military officials underlay the restoration of constitutional government in 1809 and has served as a powerful stimulus for regulating conflict within the political system and the labor market in the intervening years.

Associated with diffuse support for government by law is elite-mass veneration of established political institutions. The Riksdag dates from the fifteenth century and the monarchy from the sixteenth. As they do in British custom, important monarchical occasions serve as unifying symbols of national identity and pride. These occasions range from the annual ceremonies opening the Riksdag and honoring Nobel Prize recipients to intermittent royal marriages, births, and funerals. Other institutions that have proven their worth over time are similarly valued, including the office of the parliamentary ombudsman, a form of legislative watchdog, and Sweden's decentralized form of public administration (both are discussed in the next chapter).

Respect for law and traditional institutions by no means translates into resistance to system change. On the contrary, receptivity to institutional reform and policy innovation stands out as a third basic tenet of Swedish political culture. Legal codes have been continually revised to meet changing political, economic, and social conditions, just as both the Riksdag and the monarchy have undergone profound transformation in the course of democratization. In each instance, reforms were products of group demands to revise existing structures and government policies advanced variously by Liberals, Conservatives, farmers, Social Democrats, and others.

That reform aspirations did not spark violent social confrontations comparable to events in France, Germany, and Russia reflects shared values of moderation and pragmatism. These attributes of Sweden's acclaimed "politics of compromise" are rooted in diverse factors. Among them are cultural-ethnic-religious homogeneity; a historical pattern of collaboration among members of the medieval estates; the absence of oppressive government measures directed against the advocates of reform; and responsible behavior on the part of Liberal, Social Democratic, and trade union officials. A willingness among influential political and economic actors to seek compromise solutions to partisan disputes significantly facilitated the constitutional settlements of 1809, 1865–1866, and 1907–1909, as recounted above. In more recent decades, party and interest group leaders have similarly acted on traditional values of moderation and pragmatism to achieve consensus on successive economic, social, and constitutional initiatives.

A modern facet of Sweden's political culture is public-private affirmation of greater citizen equality. An extension of women's social entitlements is associated with the expansion of the welfare state in the twentieth century (see the last section in this chapter) and Social Democratic policy initiatives during the 1970s. Two-thirds of women are employed, which is one of the highest levels in the world, and during the 2006–2010 legislative period fully 47 percent of members of parliament were female—a percentage exceeded only by Rwanda.[8] In a 2006 survey, the World Economic Forum declared that Sweden stood out "as the most advanced in the world, having closed over 80 percent of its gender gap, followed closely by Norway (2), Finland (3), Iceland (4) and Denmark (8)."[9] As discussed later in this chapter and in those that follow, however, "greater" equality does not translate into "perfect" equality. Many women remain discontent with the wage gaps between men and women and other domestic issues.

Swedish authorities, like those throughout the rest of Scandinavia and much of Western Europe, have legally sanctioned same-sex civil unions. In October 2005 delegates to the national assembly of the Church of Sweden voted to establish a religious blessing for same-sex unions to the consternation of some conservative churches elsewhere in Europe (notably Russia).

Sweden's penchant for political compromise has not precluded recurrent class or political conflict. Employers and public officials linked forces to disperse striking workers in a major local dispute in 1879 and on a national scale in 1909. More recently, nonsocialist spokesmen vehemently opposed postwar Social Democratic initiatives to establish supplementary pensions, extend worker rights, and introduce a compulsory system of wage-earner funds. Nevertheless, a willingness among political and economic elites to accept reforms (at least ultimately) rather than sabotage them through obstructionist tactics remains a central hallmark of Swedish political culture.

Nor have prevailing traditions of moderation and restraint precluded individual acts of violence, as tragically demonstrated by the assassination in February 1986 of Prime Minister Olof Palme. Chair of the Social Democratic Party and head of government from 1969 to 1976 and again after the September 1982 election, Palme was gunned down by an assailant late one evening on a street in Stockholm as he and his wife were returning home by foot from a movie. In late 1988 police arrested a native Swede previously convicted of murder as a suspect in the slaying. He was later tried and acquitted for lack of evidence.

Another victim of assassination was Foreign Minister Anna Lindh, who died from severe internal injuries in September 2003 after being repeatedly stabbed a day earlier in a Stockholm department store. Several weeks later, Swedish police arrested a Serbian-born Swedish citizen, who claimed to have had no personal malice against the foreign minister but "heard voices in his head" prompting the attack. In March 2004 a Stockholm court sentenced him to life imprisonment for his "reckless and ruthless brutality."

Neutrality and Internationalism

An important example of political consensus in Sweden is the elite-mass endorsement of the country's foreign policy of neutrality. Since 1814 Sweden has successfully avoided involvement in European wars. National attempts to escape invasion during World War II failed in Denmark, Finland, and Norway, but not in Sweden. As a result, Swedish leaders resolved to maintain a voluntary policy of nonalignment during the postwar period despite decisions by Denmark, Iceland, and Norway to join the North Atlantic Treaty Organization. Finland, too, remains nonaligned within the Nordic region, albeit on the basis of a state treaty with the former Soviet Union that bound the country not to undertake measures detrimental to the Soviets.

Sweden enforces its neutrality by maintaining a strong national defense. In 2007 Sweden spent 1.4 percent of its gross national product on military expenditures, with a principal emphasis on air and naval defense. This percentage was lower than that of the United States (4.0 percent) and the United Kingdom (2.4 percent), but it was on a par with that in most other advanced industrial democracies. Sweden's per capita defense expenditures in 2008 were $578, compared with $1,785 in the United States, $1,035 in Norway, $961 in the United Kingdom, $873 in France, $554 in Italy, $451 in Germany, and $475 in Canada.[10]

Government officials further underscored Sweden's neutrality by carefully circumscribing economic cooperation with other European nations. In 1960 Sweden joined the European Free Trade Association (EFTA), which is strictly an intergovernmental organization designed to promote industrial free trade among its member states.[11] But in the early 1970s Sweden studiously refused to follow Denmark, Great Britain, Ireland, and Norway in applying for membership in the more ambitious European Economic Community (EEC). However attractive the economic advantages of tariff-free access to the EEC market were for the country's industrial and agricultural exporters, cabinet spokesmen declared that EEC membership would undermine the international credibility of Sweden's policy of neutrality by potentially restricting the government's freedom of action in the event of war. Sweden in 1972 negotiated a more restricted industrial free trade agreement that did not formally bind the nation to political or economic decisions by the EEC. Norway negotiated a similar agreement after a narrow majority of voters rejected a proposed membership treaty in a popular referendum. The next year, Denmark, Great Britain, and Ireland formally joined the European Community (EC).

Later, however, the demise of communism in Eastern and Central Europe and the end of the cold war prompted national leaders to reconsider Sweden's relations with the European Community. After a majority of the members of parliament voted in December 1990 to endorse full membership in the EC, the cabinet submitted Sweden's application in 1991. The European Commission issued a favorable position on the Swedish application (along with parallel applications by Austria, Finland, and Norway) in 1992, and government officials negotiated a treaty of accession the next year. A majority (52.2 percent) of Swedish voters endorsed the membership treaty in a national referendum on November 13, 1994, and Sweden officially joined the European Union (EU) on January 1, 1995.[12] While affirming Sweden's right to decide for itself whether to engage in military action, government leaders have joined in the EU's Common Foreign and Security Policy and have contributed small but politically significant military missions to help maintain regional peace in southeastern Europe.

Sweden couples its policy of nonalignment with strong support for the United Nations and other international organizations such as the International Monetary Fund, the Organisation for Economic Co-operation and Development, and the World Trade Organization.

Politically, Swedes and other Scandinavians have affirmed collective security and principles of international economic and social cooperation since the founding of the League of Nations in the 1920s. In the post–World War II period, all Scandinavian states have contributed troops and materiel to a variety of UN peacekeeping operations in Africa and the Middle East. Dag Hammarskjöld, a distinguished civil servant whose father was Swedish prime minister during World War I, served as secretary-general of the United Nations from 1953 until his untimely death in a plane crash in Africa in 1961.

The material basis for Sweden's internationalism rests in economic self-interest. Sweden is highly dependent on world trade for continued economic growth and affluence. Exports and imports account for the bulk of Sweden's gross domestic product (GDP). Trade as a percentage of GDP increased from 58.8 percent in 1990 to 86.4 percent in 2000 and 97.2 percent in 2007.[13] In 2008 Sweden's global share of merchandise exports and imports was 1.14 percent and 1.02 percent, respectively (ranking eighteenth in the world). Its share of global commercial trade was 1.9 percent of exports and 1.56 percent of imports (ranking twenty-fourth in the world). Sweden's principal trading partners are fellow member states of the EU (60 percent in 2009), followed by Norway (10 percent), the United States (7 percent), Russia (2 percent), and China (2 percent).[14]

Development of the Welfare State

An object of both widespread support and partisan dissent in Sweden is the nation's vast array of welfare services. The development of the Swedish welfare state is primarily associated with the Social Democrats. With the support of the Agrarians and occasionally the Liberals, they sponsored legislation from the mid-1930s on that provided for a voluntary program of unemployment insurance, an improved national pension system, school lunch subsidies, and public assistance to individuals and families in need. World War II interrupted the social reform movement, but by the late 1940s the Social Democrats had resumed their efforts to provide minimum standards of collective social security. Postwar legislation included the introduction of compulsory health insurance (1947), improved basic retirement benefits (1948), a new system of supplementary pensions based on individual earnings (1959), and the Law on Social Help (1956), which consolidated and extended a variety of welfare benefits. Among the latter are government-financed maternity care, quarterly cash allowances to single parents or families with children, and rent subsidies to those in need.

The cumulative effect of these measures is that all citizens and registered aliens (including foreign workers) enjoy an extraordinary degree of social security. Swedes pay relatively little out-of-pocket for health care and education and are guaranteed generous pensions upon retirement. Because workers and families whose income falls below minimum standards receive a variety of government payments to help defray rent and other expenses, a strikingly visible consequence of Sweden's comprehensive welfare system is the virtual absence of urban slums comparable to those in most metropolitan areas in North America and elsewhere in Western Europe.

To finance their extensive welfare provisions, Swedes pay some of the highest taxes in the world (although the tax rate has marginally declined in recent years). As indicated in Table 5-1, the per capita tax contribution in 2007 in Sweden was the equivalent of $23,938. This amount was lower than in Denmark and Norway but higher than in other advanced

Table 5-1 Comparative Tax Payments, 2007

Country	Annual per capita tax payment (U.S. dollars)	As percentage of gross domestic product (GDP)
Norway	36,031	43.6
Denmark	27,638	48.7
Sweden	23,938	48.3
Finland	19,995	43.0
France	17,646	42.5
Italy	15,478	43.5
Germany	14,581	36.2
United Kingdom	16,635	36.1
United States	12,871	28.3
Canada	14,585	33.3
OECD total	14,896	35.8
Europe 15	18,429	39.8

Source: Organisation for Economic Co-operation and Development, *Revenue Statistics 1965–2008* (Paris: OECD, 2009), 78, 94. Data based on OECD (2009), *Revenue Statistics 2009,* OECD Publishing, http://dx.doi.org/10.1787/rev_stats-2009-en-fr.

capitalist democracies. As a percentage of GDP, Sweden's tax rate was 48.3 percent (down from 50.2 percent in 2002).

A majority of the electorate repeatedly honored the Social Democrats for their social policy achievements. During the 1930s and 1940s the Social Democrats steadily increased their share of the popular vote and over the years achieved an absolute majority on five occasions (see Table 5-2 in Chapter 5.3). Since the end of World War II, their electoral strength has fluctuated between a high of 50.5 percent in 1968 and a low of 30.9 percent in 2010, for a postwar average of 41.2 percent in national elections. Because of their majority status in parliament, the Social Democrats were able to retain control of the national executive from 1932 to 1976 with virtually no interruption. Since then, the Social Democrats have alternated in power with various nonsocialist governments. They remain Sweden's largest political party.

Yet the welfare state is not without its critics. Conservatives and other nonsocialists have repeatedly attacked both the nation's high rate of taxation and bureaucratizing tendencies within the public sector. On the left, radical socialists earlier condemned the Social Democrats for their failure to achieve a socialist society and, more recently, criticized the majority party for cutbacks in welfare state provisions. Feminists decry the lingering inequalities in incomes. These opposing views, combined with a counteroffensive initiated by the Social Democrats in the 1970s to extend workers' and union rights, helped to set the stage for an intense public debate about Sweden's political and economic future.

NOTES

1. See, for example, Marquis W. Childs, *Sweden: The Middle Way*, rev. ed. (New Haven: Yale University Press, 1947); and Hudson Strode, *Sweden: Model for a World* (New York: Harcourt, Brace, 1949). Childs updated and marginally revised his optimistic assessment in *Sweden: The Middle Way on Trial* (New Haven: Yale University Press, 1980).

2. For contrasting right versus left critiques, see Roland Huntford, *Sweden: The New Totalitarians* (New York: Stein and Day, 1972); and Jan Myrdal, *Confessions of a Disloyal European* (New York: Pantheon, 1968).

3. Lawrence D. Brown, *New Policies, New Politics: Government's Response to Government's Growth* (Washington, D.C.: Brookings, 1983), 7.

4. Greenland, a self-governing county of Denmark located off the North Atlantic coast of Canada, is also culturally and politically a part of Scandinavia.

5. Population data (including the number of immigrants) are from Statistiska centralbyrån [Statistics Sweden], *Statistisk årsbok för Sverige 2010* (Stockholm: Statistiska centralbyrån, 2010).

6. Government policies in neighboring Denmark are more restrictive toward immigrants. Under a center-right government elected in November 2001, authorities have acted to make it more difficult for foreigners to enter the country to join their spouses (even native Danes). "Immigrants in Sweden and Denmark. The Worries and the Welcomes," *Economist*, January 31, 2002, http://www.economist.com/displaystory.cfm?story_id=E1_JGGTPD.

7. Dankwart A. Rustow, *The Politics of Compromise* (New Haven: Yale University Press, 1957), 236–237.

8. "Kvinnor i riksdagen," Sveriges Riksdag, http://www.riksdagen.se/templates/R_Page____ 11567.aspx, and "Swedish Politics: A Spoil-the-Men's Party," *Economist*, April 14, 2005, http://www.economist.com/research;subje4ct=Sweden.

9. World Economic Forum, "The Global Gender Gap. Report 2006," 3. The report notes that Germany, the United Kingdom, and Ireland also number among the top ten nations with significantly reduced gender gaps. Canada ranks fourteenth, the United States twenty-second, Russia forty-ninth, and Italy seventy-seventh. See http://www.weforum.org/pdf/gendergap/report2006.pdf.

10. Calculated from data reported in Statistiska centralbyrån, *Statistisk årsbok för Sverige 2010*, 662.

11. The other founding members included Austria, Denmark, Norway, Portugal, Switzerland, and the United Kingdom. Finland and Iceland later joined the EFTA. Most of the original member-states have now joined the European Union, leaving EFTA's membership in 2010 limited to Iceland, Liechtenstein, Norway, and Switzerland.

12. An even greater majority (57 percent) similarly endorsed membership in a national referendum in Finland the same month, but 52.4 percent of Norwegian voters rejected membership in a referendum in November.

13. World Bank, *World Development Indicators 2009* (Washington, D.C.: World Bank, 2009).

14. World Trade Organization Statistics Database, http://stat.wto.org/.

Where Is the Power?

SWEDEN'S CONTEMPORARY INSTITUTIONAL ARRANGEMENTS ARE THE product of two centuries of evolutionary political and constitutional change. The constitution of 1809 provided for a division of power between the king and parliament. Over the course of the nineteenth century, the Riksdag gradually grew in competence as various categories of law became subject to joint rather than royal jurisdiction. In parallel fashion, members of the king's advisory council (the cabinet) gradually displaced the monarch as the effective center of executive authority. The prime minister and members of the cabinet later became politically accountable to the Riksdag as Sweden advanced toward democratization between 1907 and 1921. Sweden's contemporary status as a parliamentary democracy was formally ratified with the adoption of a series of constitutional amendments in 1968–1969 and a wholly new constitution in 1973–1974.

In Sweden, therefore, the cabinet and the Riksdag are the principal sites of policy initiative and ratification, and the role of the monarch has been reduced to ceremonial and symbolic functions. Because Sweden is a unitary rather than a federal state, national and local institutions that are constitutionally subordinate to parliament and the central government exercise other political functions.

The Riksdag

From 1866 to 1970 the Riksdag consisted of two houses: a popularly elected "second chamber" equivalent to the British House of Commons and a smaller, indirectly elected "first chamber" whose members were chosen by Sweden's twenty-four provincial assemblies. Constitutional reforms ratified in 1968–1969 and implemented in 1970 abolished the bicameral system and established in its place a unicameral parliament similar to the national legislatures in Denmark and Finland. Further changes were incorporated with the adoption of the new Instrument of Government and the Riksdag Act in 1973–1974, which went into effect in 1975. These documents define executive and legislative functions and the organization of the Riksdag, respectively. The two acts can be amended only by majority vote by two successive sessions of parliament with an intervening election.[1]

The preamble to the Instrument of Government defines the principles of Swedish parliamentary democracy as follows: "All public power in Sweden emanates from the people. The Swedish democracy is founded on freedom of opinion and on universal and equal suffrage and shall be realized through a representative and parliamentary polity and through local self-government. Public power shall be exercised under the laws." The first of these principles is institutionalized in the form of free, competitive elections to the Riksdag and to the nation's city and county representative assemblies. Full rights of suffrage are accorded citizens eighteen years of age and older. Registered aliens also have the right to vote, but only in local elections. Until the abolition of the previous bicameral parliament, national and city-county elections were held at staggered four-year intervals. Accompanying the advent of unicameralism in 1970 were constitutional provisions for simultaneous national and local elections every three years. The constitution was then amended in 1994 to reestablish a four-year electoral cycle. Parliamentary elections are held on the third Sunday in September, unless a dissolution election intervenes. In the latter event, Riksdag deputies merely serve out the remainder of the legislative term rather than constitute a new parliament as is the practice elsewhere in Europe. The result is that dissolution elections are extremely rare in Sweden; since the advent of parliamentarianism, the Riksdag has been dissolved only once—in 1958.

Sweden employs a proportional electoral system, dating from the constitutional reforms of 1907–1909, which utilizes a modified version of the St. Lague method for distributing seats among contending parties.[2] The nation's twenty-nine regional constituencies vote in the election of the Riksdag's 349 deputies. Most of the seats (310) are allocated among the constituencies on the basis of the number of eligible voters and the relative strength of the parties competing for support in each of them. The remaining thirty-nine "adjustment seats" are distributed among the parties according to their aggregate percentage of votes within the country as a whole. The purpose of the latter provision is to compensate the largest party or parties for the possible loss of seats in individual constituencies and thereby ensure strict proportionality. To be represented in the Riksdag, a party must receive a minimum of either 4 percent of the national vote or 12 percent of the vote in a single constituency.

The Riksdag provides the legislative basis for cabinet formation and tenure and serves as Sweden's principal lawmaking body. In its capacity of forming the cabinet, the Riksdag elects the prime minister (*statsminister*) after each general election. If a government resigns, which occurred in 1978 and 1981, the Riksdag elects a successor prime minister. The Instrument of Government does not require that a candidate receive an absolute majority (as is true under normal circumstances in Germany). Instead, a prime minister is elected if not more than half of the members of the Riksdag vote against him or her. This feature of Swedish constitutionalism makes possible the formation of minority governments in the absence of a majority by a single party or coalition of parties.

Since 1970 the Riksdag has also been empowered to move a vote of no confidence against an incumbent prime minister and individual cabinet officials. Such a motion must be signed by a tenth of the deputies and approved by an absolute majority. In such an event, a prime minister or cabinet member would be compelled to resign. To date, however, there have been no votes of no confidence in Sweden.

As in other parliamentary systems, one of the most important functions of the Riksdag is to hold the government accountable for its actions and omissions on a day-to-day basis. In doing so, Riksdag deputies rely on written as well as oral questions, which are addressed to cabinet ministers during a public question period, and the right of general debate. Although party discipline has thus far ensured the survival of even minority cabinets in the face of parliamentary queries and criticism, the various control devices usefully serve as a means of extracting information on and official justifications of government policy. The number of written questions (known as interpellations) averaged 515 a year between 1996 and 2009, and the annual number of written questions averaged 1,494 during the same period.[3]

Sweden at a Glance

Type of Government
Constitutional monarchy

Capital
Stockholm

Administrative Divisions
Twenty-one counties: Blekinge, Dalarna, Gävleborg, Gotland, Halland, Jämtland, Jönköping, Kalmar, Krono-berg, Norrbotten, Örebro, Östergötland, Skåne, Södermanland, Stockholm, Uppsala, Värmland, Västerbotten, Västernorrland, Västmanland, Västra Götaland

Independence
June 6, 1523 (Gustav Vasa elected king)

Constitution
January 1, 1975

Legal System
Civil law system influenced by customary law; accepts compulsory International Court of Justice jurisdiction, with reservations

Suffrage
Eighteen years of age; universal

Executive Branch
Chief of state: reigning monarch
Head of government: prime minister
Cabinet: appointed by the prime minister
Elections: prime minister elected by the parliament after legislative elections

Legislative Branch
Unicameral parliament (Riksdag): 349 members elected by popular vote on a proportional representation basis. Term: four years.

Judicial Branch
The court system consists of ninety-four judicial districts, each served by a district court, six courts of appeal, and a Supreme Court *(Högsta Domstolen)* whose members are appointed by the prime minister and the cabinet. The system includes a Labor Court, twenty-three County Administrative Courts, four Administrative Courts of Appeal, and a Supreme Administrative Court.

Major Political Parties
Left Party (V, postcommunist); Environmentalist Party–the Greens (MP); Social Democratic Party (SAP); People's Party (FP, Liberals); Center Party (C); Moderate Unity Party (M, liberal conservatives); Christian Democratic Union (KDS); and Sweden Democrats (SD, anti-immigrant).

Sources: U.S. Central Intelligence Agency, *The World Factbook,* https://www.cia.gov/library/publications/the-world-factbook/ and LLRX (Law and Technology), "Features: A Guide to the Swedish Legal System," November 2000.

The Riksdag's legislative powers include the exclusive right of taxation and appropriation. In addition, the parliament shares authority with the cabinet to propose constitutional amendments, initiate changes in civil and criminal law, and schedule advisory referendums on major political issues. National referendums were held five times in the twentieth century on the following legislative proposals: prohibition in 1922, which failed; a switch from left-hand to right-hand traffic in 1955, which also failed but was nevertheless implemented by the Riksdag in 1977 based on public opinion polls indicating a majority in favor; supplementary pensions in 1957; nuclear energy in 1980; and Swedish membership in the European Union (EU) in 1994. The first referendum of the twenty-first century was held on September 14, 2003, when a majority (56.1 percent) of voters rejected adoption of the EU's common currency, the euro, in favor of retaining Sweden's national currency, the krona (some of these measures are discussed in more detail in Chapter 5.4).

For deliberative purposes, the Riksdag is divided into seventeen standing committees whose powers of scrutiny and amendment are broadly comparable to those of committees in the U.S. Congress or the German Bundestag. They include committees on finance, taxation, environment and agriculture, justice, foreign affairs, defense, social insurance, health and welfare, the labor market, civil affairs, the constitution, industry and trade, education, cultural affairs, and transport and communication. A principal purpose of the constitution committee is to examine the minutes of cabinet meetings to determine whether any member of the government has violated the law. If a member has done so, the committee is authorized to bring legal charges against the offending official before a special court of impeachment. In practice, the committee has not initiated formal charges against a cabinet member since 1854.

Riksdag officers include a Speaker and three Deputy Speakers, all of whom are elected by majority vote. (In practice, the positions are distributed among the major parties represented in parliament.) The Speaker and Deputy Speakers exercise legislative power by presiding over parliamentary deliberations and determining, in consultation with the chairs of the standing committees and four other elected members of parliament, the order in which bills and committee reports are considered on the floor of the Riksdag. In addition, the Speaker is empowered under the 1975 constitution to nominate a prime minister for election by parliament.

The Prime Minister and the Cabinet

The significance of the Riksdag and the cabinet in Sweden's policymaking process varies according to the strength of the government's parliamentary backing. During the 1920s, when no party or coalition commanded a stable majority, the Riksdag was the dominant partner. The advent of "majority parliamentarianism" under Social Democratic–Agrarian aegis in 1932–1933 marked the beginning of a long-term shift in the balance of power in favor of the prime minister and the cabinet. During the 1970s and early 1980s, periods of minority rule under the Social Democrats and later the nonsocialists resulted in a reassertion of parliamentary influence. Because of its direct access to administrative structures and organized interest groups, however, the cabinet remains the central source of policy initiative and coordination.

Since 1932 most Swedish prime ministers have been selected because of their status as chairs of either the largest party in parliament (the Social Democrats) or the largest party within a nonsocialist coalition (as was true in 1976–1978, 1980–1981, 1991–1994, and 2006–2010). Recent exceptions include nonsocialist leaders who held office as prime ministers in minority cabinets in 1978–1979, 1981–1983, and after the September 2010 election. Until the constitutional reforms of 1973–1974, the king appointed the prime minister on the advice of party leaders in parliament. Since 1975, as previously noted, the Riksdag has elected the prime minister.

The prime minister is *primus inter pares* (first among equals) of the seventeen or so persons who make up the cabinet. (The actual number varies from government to government.) The prime minister chairs cabinet sessions and is primarily responsible for determining the broad outlines of government policy. He or she is also the chief spokesperson for cabinet policy both within and outside parliament. The prime minister is assisted by a deputy with cabinet rank who coordinates and plans government activities and a staff of political advisers and professional civil servants who make up the royal chancery.

The prime minister selects the members of the cabinet. They may be dismissed by the prime minister or through a vote of no confidence by parliament. Ministerial positions, which largely correspond to the standing committees in the Riksdag, include finance, budgetary affairs, foreign policy, defense, the European Union, justice, social policy, communications, education, agriculture, labor market, housing, industry, and interior. The deputy prime minister and three to five ministers without portfolio serve as policy generalists with rotating responsibilities.

Each of the designated ministers heads an administrative "department" that is responsible primarily for policy formation (including preparation of the annual budget). Unlike the national ministries in other Western democracies, Swedish departments are small. Typically, they consist of an administrative assistant to the minister (a "state secretary," who usually is a high-level civil servant rather than a political appointee), an office manager, a legal adviser, and a relatively small number of civil servants who handle departmental planning, budgetary proposals, and policy coordination. The actual implementation of policy is delegated to a decentralized network of administrative agencies (described later in this chapter).

The Monarch

The reigning monarch of Sweden is Carl XVI Gustaf, who was crowned king in September 1973 after the death of his grandfather, King Gustaf VI Adolf. King Gustaf performed residual executive functions dating from the nineteenth century in his constitutional role as chair of formal cabinet sessions, but even this monarchical prerogative was abolished with the adoption of the present constitution in 1973–1974. One reason was lingering Social Democratic resentment of efforts by King Gustaf V, who had reigned from 1907 to 1950, to influence cabinet policy in Germany's favor during both world wars. Since 1975 the monarch's role has been restricted largely to ceremonial acts, such as presiding over the annual opening of parliament and conferring Nobel Prizes on academic and literary dignitaries.

King Carl XVI Gustaf helped to ensure the survival of the monarchy through his marriage in 1976 to an attractive German "commoner" from Bavaria. As Queen Silvia, she has charmed even many erstwhile republicans within Social Democratic ranks. First in line of succession to the king is Princess Victoria Ingrid Alice Desiree, born in 1978

Crown Princess Victoria, thirty-two, wed her former personal trainer, Daniel Westling, thirty-six (who now bears the title Duke of Västergöt-land), in a tradition-rich ceremony at Stockholm Cathedral in June 2010. Nearly a thousand guests attended, including much of European royalty. Princess Victoria is heir apparent to the Swedish throne. Her father, Carl XVI Gustaf, has been king since 1973.

Source: Stephane Cardinale/People Avenue/Corbis

and the eldest of the royal couple's two daughters and one son. The constitution was amended in 1979–1981 to permit Crown Princess Victoria, as the first-born, to succeed her father as future Swedish monarch. Previously, the constitution had permitted succession only by male offspring. In June 2010 Princess Victoria married her former trainer in an elaborate royal ceremony in Stockholm; his formal title is now Prince Daniel, Duke of Västergötland.

Other Institutional Actors

Although policymaking authority in Sweden is concentrated in the hands of the cabinet and parliament, the powers of implementation and enforcement are functionally dispersed among a variety of institutions. They include public administrative bodies, county and local government units, state-owned enterprises, the court system, and four ombudsmen.

The Public Administration

Responsible for most policy implementation in Sweden is a decentralized network of central administrative boards (*centrala ämbetsverk*) and a dual system of county and municipal government. At the national level, the administrative boards number approximately eighty. Among the most significant are the National Board of Health and Welfare, the National Industrial Board, the Labor Market Board, the National Nuclear Energy Inspection Board, and the Central Office of Statistics. Other important administrative agencies include the national railways, the postal service, telecommunications, civil defense, and the court system. Many administrative agencies, especially those dealing with economic and social policy, maintain regional offices at the level of county government.[4]

Alongside the central administrative boards are several legislative agencies that perform important policy tasks as well. They include the Bank of Sweden, which issues currency and controls the nation's money supply, and the National Debt Office, which is empowered to borrow money in the name of the government and is responsible for administering the national debt.

In contrast to the hierarchical structure of public administration in Great Britain and on the continent, Sweden's administrative boards and agencies are legally autonomous from the cabinet and the parliament. The present system, which dates from the seventeenth century, was established to maximize the rational implementation of public policy. As political scientist Thomas J. Anton observes: "Administrative power was . . . a function of Swedish insistence that 'political' and 'administrative' decisions were clearly distinct and that the latter could be made simply by applying law to the facts of a particular case. The administrative boards . . . were designed to provide such legal judgments, and officials were assigned full authority to make those judgments, free from 'political interference.'"[5]

Despite their legal autonomy, Sweden's administrative agencies are nevertheless subordinate to the central government and the Riksdag for authoritative policy directives. Moreover, in recent decades cabinet officials have relied increasingly on detailed budgetary guidelines as a means of overseeing and coordinating day-to-day administration.

Regional and Local Governments

Regional and local governments consist of partially overlapping structures made up of appointive county administrative boards and elective county and municipal councils. Heading the administrative boards in each of Sweden's twenty-one counties is a county governor appointed by, and therefore responsible to, the cabinet. The elected members of the parallel county councils designate the fourteen other members of the administrative boards. The appointive administrative boards supervise regional planning, county employment offices, worker retraining programs, environmental protection, and the administration of justice.

Sweden's twenty-one elected county councils and 284 subordinate rural and municipal assemblies are responsible for implementing medical and health care; social welfare; education; housing policy; land use; ambulance service; fire protection; and cultural, youth, and athletic policies. The regional administrative agencies, appointive county administrative boards, and elective councils work closely together in coordinating and implementing their designated policy assignments.

Growth of the Public Sector

Sweden's public sector has grown significantly in both size and economic importance. From fewer than 45,000 civil servants at the beginning of the twentieth century, the number of public officials had increased by 2008 to nearly 1.3 million, or 38 percent of the country's workforce of 3.5 million. Private enterprise accounts for the lion's share (72 percent in 2007) of the gross domestic product, and the public sector contributes approximately 29 percent of the total.[6]

Contrary to the postwar policies of the British Labour Party and the French Socialists, Sweden's Social Democrats have nationalized very little industry.[7] The Swedish state administers fifty-five industrial enterprises and financial institutions; it is the sole owner of forty-two of these and partial owner of the remaining thirteen. Although state-owned firms constitute less than 10 percent of Sweden's overwhelmingly private economy, they give the national government varying degrees of control over investments, production, and sales in designated economic sectors. The major economic sectors in which the government is sole owner or majority shareholder are various banks and insurance companies, forestry, home mortgages, the nation's waterworks and canals, and Systembolat (a monopoly controlling the distribution and sale of wine, liquor, and strong beer).[8]

Courts and the Administration of Justice

The Swedish court system dates from legislation originally passed in 1734. Three levels define its basic structural hierarchy: some ninety-four district courts of first instance (*tingsrätter*), six intermediate courts of appeal (*hovrätter*), and a Supreme Court (*Högsta Domstolen*). Jurisdiction extends at each level to both civil and criminal law.

By far the most cases are settled in the courts of first instance. In 2008 the district courts heard 83,037 criminal cases and 72,446 civil disputes. The courts of appeal, by contrast, reviewed 9,030 criminal cases and 2,752 civil appeals. That same year, the Supreme Court passed judgment in only 138 cases, rejecting or postponing some 5,282 appeals.[9]

Judges, who must have university degrees in legal studies, are appointed by the cabinet. They are assisted in all criminal and most civil cases on the local level by panels (*nämnd*) of lay judges who are elected for six-year terms by the county councils. Unlike Anglo-American juries, the *nämnd* not only hear evidence and help to reach a verdict but also confer with the judge on points of law.

The Riksdag has also established various specialized courts to deal with conflicts that arise outside normal civil and criminal jurisdiction. They include the fiscal courts of appeal, the supreme administrative court, the labor court, and the market court. The purpose of the market court is to help enforce the Competition Act of 1982, which the Riksdag implemented to prohibit restrictive business practices.

The Ombudsmen

A distinctive Swedish institution that serves as an important legislative control device over administrative behavior is the parliamentary ombudsman (Justitieombudsman, or JO for short). The office was created under the constitution of 1809 as a means of preventing the abuse of executive-administrative power, as had occurred under the deposed absolutist monarch. Elected for a four-year term by the Riksdag, the JO has the legal autonomy to investigate the internal records of all state agencies (including the central administrative boards, courts, the military, and county and local governments) in an effort to determine whether public officials are guilty of violating constitutional or statutory law. Ombudsmen may undertake such investigations either on their own initiative or in response to complaints by individual citizens.

Through the years, the JO's caseload has increased so much that the office has been steadily expanded. In 1915 a military ombudsman was added. In 1968 the two positions were merged and three ombudsmen were established in their place, each with equal legal competence. A fourth parliamentary ombudsman was added in 1976. Their collective case load has increased from 5,226 in 2002–2003 to 6,918 in 2008–2009.[10] Only a handful of cases ultimately result in a formal reprimand or prosecution through the courts.

Additional ombudsmen offices have been established under the authority of the national government to enforce citizen rights: one for consumer protection, a second to safeguard the rights of children and young adults, and a third to promote equality. The latter office consists in turn of officials with specialized assignments to investigate charges of discrimination against ethnic groups, handicapped persons, and sexual orientation.[11]

A Consensual Democracy

Sweden's institutional pluralism facilitates a type of polity—characteristic of Scandinavia as a whole—that political scientists Neil Elder and colleagues have termed "consensual democracy."[12] In contrast to the adversarial model of democracy characteristic of alternating periods of partisan party government in Great Britain and periods of polarized politics between the Republicans and Democrats in the United States, consensual democracies such as Sweden "disperse and constrain power. Indeed, the laws make electoral majorities rare and tentative."[13] Contributing factors to Sweden's mode of consensual democracy include the moderating influence of political culture, discussed in Chapter 5.1, and proportional representation, which ensures parliamentary representation of all major political parties.

NOTES

1. Four documents make up the composite Swedish constitution: the Instrument of Government, the Act of Succession, the Freedom of the Press Act, and the Fundamental Law on Freedom of Expression. They are compiled in English translation in the Swedish Riksdag, *Constitutional Documents of Sweden* (Stockholm: Norstedts Tryckeri, 1975).
2. Under the St. Lague method of proportional representation, which was adopted in 1952, the total of the votes for each party in a given electoral district is divided by a succession of uneven numbers (1.4, 3, 5, etc.), and seats are awarded to the highest quotients obtained among the various parties. For a detailed discussion of Swedish electoral law, see Dankwart A. Rustow, *The Politics of Compromise* (Princeton, N.J.: Princeton University Press, 1955), 123–128.
3. Statistiska centralbyrån [Statistics Sweden], *Statistisk årsbok för Sverige 2010* (Stockholm: Statistiska centralbyrån, 2010), 576.
4. Statistiska centralbyrån, *Statliga förvaltningsmydigheter 2010*, http://www.myndighetsregis tret.scb.se/Myndighet.aspx.
5. Thomas J. Anton, *Administered Politics: Elite Political Culture in Sweden* (Boston/The Hague/London: Martinus Nijhoff, 1980), 5.
6. Statistiska centralbyrån, *Statistisk årsbok för Sverige 2010,* 274 and 360–361.
7. Instead, the SAP has relied more heavily on a combination of fiscal, monetary, and active labor market policies to achieve its economic objectives of continued growth and full employment. In ironic contrast, the nonsocialist parties nationalized the shipbuilding industry while they were in office from 1976 to 1982 in an attempt to salvage the branch in the face of increased international competition (see Chapter 5.4).
8. *Regeringskansli, The state as a company owner* (with links to annual reports on state-owned companies from 1999 to 2007), http://www.sweden.gov.se/sb/d/2106/a/197929.
9. Statistiska centralbyrån, *Statistisk årsbook för Sverige 2010,* 493.
10. Ibid, 494.
11. In 2008–2009 these offices investigated 22,524 consumer cases, 1,345 cases involving children, and 4,931 cases of alleged equality abuses.
12. Neil Elder, A. H. Thomas, and D. Arter, *The Consensual Democracies? The Governments and Politics of the Scandinavian States* (Oxford, UK: Martin Robinson, 1982).
13. Eric Einhorn and John Logue, *Modern Welfare States: Scandinavian Politics and Policy in the Global Age,* 2nd ed. (Westport, Conn., and London: Praeger, 2003), 66.

Who Has the Power?

T HE CAPACITY TO PARTICIPATE IN POLICY DECISIONS IN SWEDEN IS shared by political parties, organized interest groups, and administrative officials. Of these diverse political actors, parties and interest groups play the central role in initiating systemic reforms as well as basic policy decisions, including political democratization, the rise of the welfare state, the extension of workers' rights, and ongoing changes in the political management of the economy. Administrative elites, by contrast, play significant roles in policy refinement, continuity, and implementation.

Political Parties

From the early part of the twentieth century through most of the 1980s, Sweden sustained a multiparty system consisting of five major parties: a small Left Party (formerly the Communists), the far larger Swedish Social Democratic Workers' Party, the People's Party (Liberals), the agrarian-based Center Party, and the Moderate Party (Conservatives). A sixth political movement, known as the "Environmentalist Party—the Greens," became in September 1988 the first new party to enter the Riksdag in seventy years. In the September 1991 election, two other minor parties succeeded in gaining representation in the Riksdag: the conservative Christian Democratic Union and New Democracy, the latter a "new right" movement advocating substantial tax cuts and other radical reforms. New Democracy later disappeared from the political landscape, but two new parties—an anti-European Union (EU) party and a feminist party—competed in the 2006 parliamentary election but failed to secure enough votes to win seats in parliament. A maverick Pirate Party, espousing libertarian principles, won seats in elections to the European Parliament in June 2009 but has not been able to replicate that success on the national level. The newest splinter group to enter the Riksdag are the anti-immigrant Sweden Democrats, who won 5.7 percent of the vote in the September 2010 election. (See the section on "Newer Parties" below.)

Party fragmentation in Sweden has not meant political stalemate or an immobile parliament, as was true in the final years of the Weimar Republic of Germany and frequently in postwar Italy and the Third and Fourth Republics of France. Instead, Sweden's multiparty system has proved capable of sustaining stable governments and adapting to changing economic and social conditions. The principal explanation lies in the persistence of loosely united socialist and nonsocialist blocs that partially blunt the parliamentary effects of party fragmentation. The Social Democrats and Left Party are popularly identified as the socialist bloc because they usually vote together on most legislative matters; the Liberals, the Center, the Moderates, and the Christian Democrats make up the nonsocialist bloc. During the 1989–1991 legislative session and again after September 1994, the Greens were officially unaligned but generally sided with the Social Democrats, just as New

Democracy tacitly supported the other nonsocialist parties in the Riksdag during the 1991–1994 legislative session. The existence of opposing socialist and nonsocialist alignments therefore facilitates both cabinet stability and legislative cooperation across party lines (see Table 5-3, page 470).

The Social Democrats

The Swedish Social Democratic Workers' Party (Sveriges socialdemokratiska arbetareparti, or SAP) was founded in 1889 and is Sweden's oldest political party and, since 1917, its largest. The party was originally established to represent working-class political and economic interests in efforts to reform suffrage, introduce parliamentarianism, and improve working conditions and social services. With time, the party extended its appeal to middle-class voters as well. Thanks to the success of its economic and social policies after 1932, the SAP increased its popular support from 38 percent in the 1920s to an average of nearly 47 percent during the 1930s and 1940s (see Table 5-2). From 1948 through 1994 the party averaged 45 percent of the popular vote in successive national elections. Its postwar peak came in 1968 when the SAP mobilized 50.1 percent of the vote. Electoral support has averaged 41.2 percent in thirteen subsequent elections, reaching its lowest level since 1928 of 30.9 percent in 2010. Recent electoral fluctuations have primarily involved trading votes with the Greens and the more radical Left Party. In the 2010 parliamentary election, the party drew most of its support evenly divided among men and women aged thirty to sixty-four.[1]

Historically, the SAP's principal ideological commitment—comparable to that of other Western European democratic socialist parties—has been to collective measures designed to enhance individual economic and social security and equality of opportunity. Social Democratic leaders have pursued these objectives through economic policies aimed at promoting material growth and full employment, parliamentary action (in the form of welfare legislation, educational reforms, and the extension of workers' rights), and trade union negotiations with employers' associations on the labor market. In recent decades, the Social Democrats have modified their programmatic principles to embrace a neo-liberal approach to economic management—primarily in response to the external influence of policies pursued by the European Union. (See chapters 5.4 and 5.5.) A distinctive feature of Swedish social democracy is that the movement emerged simultaneously with organized liberalism during the latter part of the nineteenth century. Because both parties were intent on achieving similar political objectives, they were able to cooperate during the formative decades of industrialization and democratization rather than engage in fratricidal conflict, which characterized relations between competing liberal and social democratic parties in much of continental Europe. This historical legacy has contributed to the emergence of Sweden's largely consensual political culture.

The SAP is also distinguished by a tradition of stable leadership. Since the party was founded, six men and currently one woman have served as party chair: Hjalmar Branting (1889–1926), Per Albin Hansson (1926–1946), Tage Erlander (1946–1969), Olof Palme (1969–1986), Ingvar Carlsson (1986–1995), Göran Persson (1996–2007), and Mona Sahlin (2007–). Each leader has been an able parliamentarian and adept at forging unity among diverse party factions, thereby enhancing the party's claim to long-term executive competence.

Table 5-2 Election Results: Sweden, 1932–2010

Type of election		Political party								
Year		V	MP	SAP	FP	C	M	KDS	NYD	SD
1932	R	8.3		41.7	11.7	14.1	23.5			
1934	C	6.8		42.1	12.5	13.3	24.2			
1936	R	7.7		45.9	12.9	14.3	17.6			
1938	C	5.7		50.4	12.2	12.6	17.8			
1940	N	4.2		53.8	12.0	12.0	18.0			
1942	C	5.9		50.3	12.4	13.2	17.6			
1944	R	10.3		46.7	12.9	13.6	15.9			
1946	C	11.2		44.4	15.6	13.6	14.9			
1948	R	6.3		46.2	22.8	12.4	12.3			
1950	C	4.9		48.6	21.7	12.3	12.3			
1952	R	4.3		46.1	24.4	10.7	14.4			
1954	C	4.8		47.4	21.7	10.3	15.7			
1956	R	5.0		44.6	23.8	9.4	17.1			
1958	R	3.4		46.2	18.2	12.7	19.5			
1958	C	4.0		46.8	15.6	13.1	20.4			
1960	R	4.5		47.8	17.5	13.6	16.5			
1962	C	3.8		50.5	17.1	13.1	15.5			
1964	R	5.2		47.3	17.0	13.2	13.7			
1966	C	6.4		42.2	16.7	13.7	14.7			
1968	R	3.0		50.1	14.3	15.7	12.9			
1970	R	4.8		45.3	16.2	19.9	11.5			
1973	R	5.3		43.6	9.4	25.1	14.3			
1976	R	4.8		42.7	11.1	24.1	15.6	1.4		
1979	R	5.6		43.2	10.6	18.1	20.3	1.4		
1982	R	5.6		45.6	5.9	15.5	23.6	1.9		
1985	R	5.4		44.7	14.2	12.4	21.3			
1988	R	5.8	5.5	43.2	12.2	11.3	18.3	2.9		
1991	R	4.5	3.4	37.7	9.1	8.5	21.9	7.1	6.7	
1994	R	6.2	4.1	45.3	7.2	7.7	22.4	4.1	1.2	
1998	R	12.0	4.5	36.4	4.7	5.1	22.9	11.7	—	
2002	R	8.4	4.6	39.9	13.4	6.2	15.3	9.2	—	
2006	R	5.8	5.2	35.0	7.5	7.9	26.2	6.6	—	
2010	R	5.6	7.2	30.9	7.1	6.6	30.0	5.6	—	5.7

Source: Statistiska centralbyrån [Statistics Sweden], *Statistiskårsbok för Sverige* (Stockholm: Statistiska centralbyrån, various issues).

Note: R = Riksdag (parliamentary) elections; C = communal (county and municipal) elections; N = national elections; V = Left Party (postcommunists); MP = Environmentalist Party—the Greens; SAP = Swedish Social Democratic Workers' Party; FP = People's Party (Liberals); C = Center Party; M = Moderate Unity Party (Conservatives); KDS = Christian Democratic Union; NYD = New Democracy; SD = Sweden Democrats.

A major strength of the Social Democratic Party is its close organizational link with the National Federation of Trade Unions (LO). Because union members make up a significant part of the SAP's Executive Committee and the party itself, the LO contributes important policy initiatives as well as the bulk of the SAP's electoral support. Unions also provide a major share of SAP's financial contributions.

The Left Party

Similar to other European communist movements, the Swedish Communist Party was formed in the aftermath of the Bolshevik revolution of 1917 as a leftist offshoot of the Social Democrats. Unlike most of their continental counterparts, Sweden's Communists maintained a tradition of ideological independence of the former Soviet Union rooted in their country's historical antipathy toward Russia and prevailing political cultural values of moderation and pragmatism. A Stalinist faction exists within the party, but it is overshadowed by a revisionist majority that affirms Western-style parliamentary democracy and individual civil liberties. A small group of hard-core Stalinists broke with the party to form a separate Swedish Communist Party in 1977, but thus far they have failed to attract appreciable electoral support.

Party leaders adopted the name of Left Party–Communists (Vänsterpartiet-kommunisterna) and a new party program in 1967 in an effort to affirm their allegiance to democratic norms. Left Party activists define themselves as a radical alternative to the SAP through their ideological critique of capitalism; their advocacy of state ownership of major industries, banks, and insurance companies; and their strong support for welfare provisions. In 1990 party leaders dropped the designation "Communist" altogether and shortened the official party name to Left Party (Vänsterpartiet, or V) in an effort to distance themselves from discredited Marxist-Leninist regimes in East and Central Europe. In 1996 the Left Party added feminism to its core ideological advocacy, proclaiming its opposition to discrimination against women in all spheres of private and public life.[2] The party drew a majority of its support in the 2010 election from voters aged fifty to sixty-four, a majority of them women.[3]

The Left draws most of its electoral support from industrial workers and intellectuals. During the cold war era, the Left's share of the popular vote fluctuated between a high of 6.3 percent (1948) and a low of 3.4 percent (1958) for an average of nearly 5.0 percent (see Table 5-2). The Left Party expanded its electoral support to 12 percent in the 1998 election, primarily by positioning itself as a defender of Sweden's welfare state at a time when the governing SAP was adopting stringent fiscal policies to facilitate neoliberal economic policies and more vigorous economic performance (see Chapter 5.4). Four years later, in 2002, party strength declined to 8.4 percent as the SAP regained support at the Left's expense. Contributing to the party's loss was the forced ouster in 2003 of the party's chair, Gudrun Schyman, because of personal issues and a tax scandal. Schyman went on to found a new feminist party, described later in this chapter. Electoral support declined still further to 5.8 percent in 2006 and 5.6 percent in 2010.

Because of its minuscule size, the Left's only hope of affecting policy outcomes is through a tactical alliance with the Social Democrats in the Riksdag. Party deputies usually support SAP parliamentary initiatives (or at least abstain in crucial votes) and thereby have helped to ensure the continuance of Social Democratic governance at recurrent intervals during the postwar era.

The Environmentalist Party–the Greens

The Environmentalists-Greens are also identified as a "left" party, but with a much less clearly defined ideological profile than either the Left Party or the Social Democrats. Officially, the movement calls itself the Environmentalist Party–the Greens (Miljöpartiet De Gröna, or MP). The movement was founded during the early 1980s in emulation of similar parties in Germany, Finland, and Denmark. By mid-decade the Greens had succeeded in winning seats on more than half of Sweden's city and county councils, and in September 1988 they made their first entrance into parliament with 5.5 percent of the popular vote. Its electoral appeal is overwhelmingly to voters eighteen to forty-nine years of age (53 percent in the 2010 election).[4]

Similar to their counterparts in other West European countries, the Greens stress measures to protect the natural environment and promote the socioeconomic interests of less privileged groups. Accordingly, they advocate an end to the use of nuclear energy, the introduction of new taxes on energy use and factory and automobile emissions, and tax cuts for lower-income workers. They also urge a ban on new highway construction in favor of greater reliance on the nation's extensive railway system and more strenuous national and international efforts to combat climate change.

The Greens are a highly heterogeneous movement that attracts most of its members and voters from among younger, better-educated urban citizens. The party is led by a committee made up of rotating members, with no officially designated leader. Twenty Green deputies served in the Riksdag from September 1988 until the September 1991 election, when the Greens received only 3.4 percent of the vote, which was not sufficient to remain in parliament. The Greens reentered the Riksdag in 1994 after winning 4.1 percent of the popular vote, and marginally increased their support in three subsequent elections. In 2010 they received 7.2 percent of the national vote (see Table 5-2).

The Nonsocialist Bloc

The fragmentation of Sweden's nonsocialist forces historically inhibited the emergence of a cohesive alternative to Social Democracy comparable to the Conservatives in Great Britain or the Christian Democrats in Germany. Beginning in the mid-1960s, leaders of the Liberal, Center, and Moderate Unity Parties forged a limited form of bourgeois unity that enabled them to displace the Social Democrats in cabinet office from 1976 to 1982. The nonsocialist parties once again won a parliamentary majority in 1991 and governed jointly until the September 1994 election when the Social Democrats returned to power. In 2006 they campaigned jointly with the Christian Democrats as the "Alliance for Sweden," winning a combined total of 48.2 percent of the national vote and a parliamentary majority of 178 seats to form a renewed nonsocialist governing coalition under Moderate Unity leadership. Aggregate support for the four parties increased to 49.3 percent in the 2010 election, but the entrance of the radical right Sweden Democrats into parliament deprived the nonsocialist bloc of a governing majority. Hence, they formed a minority government, with the Moderates once again claiming the prime ministership.

The Liberals The Liberals were the smallest bourgeois party from 1968 until the parliamentary election of September 1985 when they scored 14.2 percent of the popular vote to become the second-largest nonsocialist party. In later elections, Liberal support steadily dwindled to about a third of that level, but rebounded to 13.4 percent in 2002 only to fall to 7.5 percent in 2006 and 7.1 percent in 2010 (see Table 5-2). In 2010 the Liberals drew a majority of their support from voters aged thirty to forty-nine.[5]

The Liberals' formal name, Folkpartiet (People's Party, or FP), suggests their simultaneous strength and weakness. As a broad-based movement appealing variously to businesspeople, workers, intellectuals, prohibitionists, and free thinkers, the Liberals have at times been Sweden's largest nonsocialist party. They peaked at 40 percent of the popular vote in 1911, trailed Conservatives during the 1930s and early 1940s, and then resumed their dominant status among the nonsocialist parties from 1948 until 1958. At the same time, the very diversity of the Liberals' popular support makes them highly vulnerable to electoral shifts within the nonsocialist bloc. From 1958 through the mid-1980s, the Liberals lost votes to both the Center and the Moderates, declining to 5.9 percent in 1982. Their temporary resurgence in 1985 was, in turn, primarily at the expense of the other two nonsocialist parties. Electoral support for the Liberals subsequently declined in the next three elections to a postwar low of 4.7 in 1998.

The Liberals' support of suffrage reform and parliamentarianism enabled them to play an important role, through cooperation with the Social Democrats, in achieving Sweden's democratization. They lost votes to the left during the 1920s and 1930s because of their opposition to government activism in the economy and society. But under new leadership the Liberals dramatically increased their electoral support in the late 1940s by endorsing the Social Democrats' social program and simultaneously advocating greater individual economic freedom. Their recovery was halted in 1958 when they proposed a compromise solution to a controversy over supplementary pensions that failed to satisfy either the left or the right.

Liberals have contributed significantly to the nonsocialist critique of centralizing tendencies within government and the economy, even though the party itself suffered recurrent electoral losses during the 1990s and later elections. In an attempt to ensure the party's survival in the light of the 4 percent minimum threshold for parliamentary representation, Liberal deputies elected a new chair in October 1983—Bengt Westerberg, a former state secretary in the Department of Finance and an acknowledged party moderate. Westerberg's factual and pragmatic style of leadership contributed to the Liberals' advance during the mid-1980s. The Liberals' current chair is Jan Björklund, a long-time party activist and a former military officer whose policy priority is education. The party's electoral fortunes waned in the 2006 and 2010 elections, although the Liberals have succeeded in displacing the Center as Sweden's second-largest nonsocialist party.

The Center Party The Center Party (Centerpartiet, or C) is more solidly anchored than the Liberal People's Party in terms of core socioeconomic support. Yet, like the Liberals, the Center is vulnerable to recurrent electoral shifts. Founded in 1921 as the Farmers' Party (a successor organization to several nineteenth-century ruralist movements), the Center adopted its present name in 1959 along with a broader-based program emphasizing the need for economic decentralization and a more humane urban environment. The party's transformation coincided with increased public concern about ecological issues as symbolically expressed by the advent of a popularly based *gröna vågen* (green wave). The result was an increase in electoral support, primarily at the expense of the Liberals. Center strength rose from 9.4 percent in 1956 to an average of almost 14 percent during the 1960s and a peak of 25.1 percent in 1973 (see Table 5-2). Most of the increase reflected the party's strategic success in expanding its appeal from farmers, who still contribute a quarter of the party's support, to blue- and white-collar workers, who together make up 42 percent of Center voters. The Center later lost support, first to the Moderates and more recently to the Liberals. Party strength began to decline in 1976; by 1998 it had fallen to 5.1 percent. The Center marginally increased its support in the next two elections and with 7.9 percent of the vote in 2006 once again became the second-largest nonsocialist party after the Moderates. It lost this status to the Liberals in the 2010 election. The Center appeals predominantly to men aged thirty to forty-nine.[6]

Recent fluctuations in the Center's electoral fortunes reflect the party's stand on policy issues. Increased Center support in the 1976 election was attributed primarily to the party chair's (Thorbjörn Fälldin) opposition to an expansion of Sweden's nuclear energy program—opposition that served as a central plank in the party's pro-ecological stance. Conversely, the party's electoral declines in 1979 and 1982 were related to an interim resolution of the nuclear energy conflict in 1980 (see Chapter 5.4) and the Center's subsequent failure to identify new policy issues as a basis for mobilizing continued popular support.

Largely in response to the party's electoral decline, Fälldin resigned under pressure as Center chair in 1986. He was succeeded by Karin Söder, former foreign minister and the first woman to head a major Swedish political party. Söder stepped down a year later because of ill health. She was succeeded by Olof Johansson, party secretary and a specialist in economics. In 2001 Maud Olofsson, a party activist in northern Sweden who had never served in the national government, was unanimously elected chair at a special party congress. She claims impeccable credentials as a party loyalist: her father is a Centrist and a close friend of former chair Fälldin; both her brothers are members of the party; and she is married to a Centrist. Olofsson was elected to the Riksdag for the first time in 2002.

The Moderate Unity Party Since 1979 the largest of Sweden's nonsocialist parties, the Moderate Unity Party (Moderaterna samlingsparti, or M), has consistently offered clear policy alternatives to those of the Social Democrats. Among its chief demands are tax reductions, deregulation of private enterprise, and the partial privatization of education and childcare services. During the 1970s and 1980s the Moderates strongly opposed measures supported by the LO and the SAP to extend the collective economic influence of organized labor.

Sweden's nineteenth-century bureaucratic-economic Conservatives initially opposed democratization but endorsed the introduction of manhood suffrage in the Great Compromise of 1907–1909 in exchange for proportional representation as a means to ensure their political survival. Separate conservative party organizations, which were established in the former upper and lower houses of parliament in 1912, were known as the National Party and the Ruralist and Citizens' Party, respectively. The two factions merged in 1935 as "the Right" (*Högern*), a term used throughout Scandinavia from the mid-nineteenth century onward to designate conservatives.

From the 1930s through the 1950s, the right distinguished itself primarily by its opposition to the Social Democrats' activist economic and social policies. As a consequence, the party steadily lost popular support. Its share of the national vote fell from 29.4 percent in 1928 to an average of 20.6 percent during the 1930s and 15.4 percent in the 1940s (see Table 5-2).

Conservative strength rose marginally during the 1950s under the articulate leadership of a new party chair, Gunnar Heckscher, a political scientist at the University of Stockholm, who sought to establish a more positive party profile. His successors pursued a similar strategy, and the adoption of the party's present name as the Moderates and a progressive program in 1969 signaled a determined effort by conservative spokesmen to adjust the party's image and ideology to changing economic and social conditions. The Moderates have embraced a more positive view toward government intervention in the economy and society while defending principles of private ownership and political decentralization. The party draws most of its core support from affluent white-collar workers in the private sector.

The Moderates' ideological affirmation of individual "freedom, independence, and security" rooted in an ethical tradition of humanism[7] facilitated the party's electoral recovery. Its strength increased from 11.5 percent in 1970 to 14.3 percent in 1973 and continued to climb through the 1982 election. The party lost support in 1985 and 1988, but reversed its decline through the 1998 election. In 2002 Moderate support dropped dramatically to 15.3 percent, in part because some party workers expressed anti-immigrant attitudes in secretly recorded conversations with an undercover television journalist.[8]

The Moderates have had three leaders since the mid-1980s. The best known is Carl Bildt, who was elected chair in 1986. From 1991 to September 1994 he served as Sweden's first conservative prime minister in sixty years. One of his achievements was signing Sweden's accession treaty in 1994 to join the European Union. Bildt resigned as chair in 1999 to assume a prestigious international assignment as the UN secretary general's special envoy for the Balkans; in 2006 he returned to national politics as foreign minister in a nonsocialist coalition government.

Bildt was succeeded as party chair by Bo Lundgren, a former minister of finance, who stepped down after the party's loss in the 2002 election. Fredrik Reinfeldt, a former leader of the Moderate youth organization and a parliamentary expert on legal issues, was elected party chair in October 2003. Reinfeldt promptly signaled his determination to steer the Moderates toward a more centrist position in domestic politics, a strategy that helped garner the party its highest share of popular support in history with 26.2 percent of the vote in 2006 among white-collar workers, especially senior salaried employees.[9] In 2010 party strength advanced still further to 30.0 percent.

Sweden's Newer Parties

A number of splinter parties have emerged in recent decades to challenge the hegemony of Sweden's long-established five-party system, although most have quickly disappeared from the political scene. Two small center-right political parties—the Christian Democratic Union (Kristlig demokratisk samling, or KDS) and New Democracy (Ny Demokrati, or NYD) gained entry to the Riksdag in 1991, but only the KDS survived later national elections.

The Christian Democrats established themselves as a national political party in the 1960s using the model of the Christian People's Parties in Denmark and Norway. Their sober affirmation of traditional values of family and Christian morality appealed to fundamentalist voters, but their organizational weakness and lack of a solid socioeconomic basis restricted their initial electoral advances to local and provincial assemblies. The Christian Democrats sought to legitimize their claim to national office through a tactical electoral alliance in 1985 and 1988 with the Center, and in September 1991 they finally managed to surpass the minimum threshold for representation in the Riksdag when the party won 7.1 percent of the vote, primarily at the expense of the Center and the Liberals (see Table 5-2). Contributing to its electoral success was widespread public confidence in the party chair, Alf Svensson, a strong supporter of European integration. Svensson resigned in 2006 to pursue a career in European Union politics and was succeeded by a party protégée, Göran Hägglund, who had previously been active in the Christian Democratic youth movement. Popular support for the KDS fell to 4.1 percent in 1994 but rebounded to 11.7 percent four years later. In 2002 party strength dropped to 9.2 percent and declined still further to 6.6 percent in 2006 and 5.6 percent four years later.

New Democracy was a self-proclaimed maverick in Swedish politics. The party was founded in late 1990 by two antiestablishment cultural figures: Bert Karlsson, an amusement park owner and publisher of popular music, and Ian Wachtmeister, a satirist and industrialist who is a member of Sweden's nearly extinct aristocracy. Both leaders claimed to speak for an emergent "new populism" that reflected a growing popular distrust of state bureaucrats and the high cost of government. In addition to its attacks on the state and demands for steep tax cuts, New Democracy demanded stiffer penalties for criminals and restrictions on rights of immigration. Ideologically, the party therefore corresponded closely with other "new right" parties in Europe, including the Progress Parties in Denmark and Norway, the National Front in France, and the Republikaner in Germany. New Democracy became an overnight success in the September 1991 election by attracting the support of 6.7 percent of the electorate. The party later lost political credibility, in part because of public bickering between its two leaders. In September 1994 it received only 1.2 percent of the popular vote and is no longer represented in the Riksdag.

Two additional parties tested their mettle in the September 2006 parliamentary election: the June List, an anti-EU party that mobilized 14.5 percent of the popular vote in a 2003 referendum on whether Sweden should adopt the EU's common currency (see Chapter 5.4), and the Feminists. Gudrun Schyman, former leader of the Left Party, established the Feminist Party in 2004 to protest remaining wage and other inequalities between the sexes. She positioned herself as a rhetorical radical outside the mainstream of majority political culture, accusing Swedish men of being "no better than the Taliban."[10] At its founding congress in October 2005, the party called for the abolition of marriage and the creation of "gender-neutral" names.[11] Because of the Feminists' tilt toward leftist radicalism, in-fighting among party leaders, and criticism from Social Democrats and the media, the party failed to mobilize the minimum threshold of 4 percent needed to gain entrance to the Riksdag.

The Pirate Party (Piratparti) abruptly emerged in 2006 as a libertarian movement critical of all forms of government and private power. The Pirates gained overnight domestic and international attention because of their strong defense of personal privacy on the Internet, in banking, and everyday life. Additional demands include the decriminalization of shared music files and the abolition of monopolies such as patents on pharmaceuticals and computer software.[12] The Pirates garnered 7.1 percent of votes in the June 2009 election to the European Parliament, which translated into a win of two seats. Their ideological stance has inspired the creation of equivalent Pirate organizations in Denmark, Finland, Germany, and a number of other European countries. Together, the various parties formed an international umbrella organization, the Pirate Parties International (with headquarters in Belgium) in 2009.

The newest—and most controversial—splinter group are the Sweden Democrats (Sverigedemokraterna), an anti-immigrant party with neo-Nazi roots. Confounding the democratic sentiments of an overwhelming majority of citizens, the Sweden Democrats mobilized 5.7 percent of the vote in the September 2010 election to win twenty seats in the Riksdag. Their success was attributed primarily to widespread resentment especially among young urban males directed toward Sweden's immigrant Muslim population of 500,000 at a time of stubbornly high unemployment, approximately 10 percent on the eve of the election. In addition, the charismatic qualities of the Democrats' leader, Jimmie Åkesson, helped crystallize the party's appeal. A youthful (at age thirty-one) and forceful speaker, Åkesson depicted "Muslim population growth as the greatest foreign threat to the country since World War II" and called for a 90 percent reduction in immigration.[13]

The immediate effect of the Democrats' entry into parliament was to deprive the four-party nonsocialist coalition of a parliamentary majority, thereby compelling Prime Minister Reinfeldt to form a minority government. Their longer-term prospects remain uncertain. Although the Sweden Democrats resemble other right-wing movements in Europe—including Progressive Parties in Denmark and Norway and the National Front in France—their strident nationalist rhetoric is discordant with Sweden's pragmatic and consensual political culture. Accordingly, they may well suffer the same political irrelevance and eventual disappearance as New Democracy experienced a decade and a half earlier.

Interest Groups

Alongside Sweden's national parties, three organized interest associations stand out as major centers of political power: the National Federation of Trade Unions (LO), the Confederation of Swedish Enterprise, and the Central Organization of Salaried Employees (TCO). Also important, but less influential than these groups, are the Swedish Central Organization of University Graduates (SACO-SR), the National Association of Farmers (LRF), and the Swedish Cooperative Association (KF).

The political significance of Sweden's principal organized interest groups lies primarily in their affiliation or alignment with important political parties and their participation in the legislative consultative process. In addition, the LO, the SAF, and their constituent organizations influence economic and social outcomes through their direct negotiations with each other on the labor market. Employer groups and organized labor also participate in the formation and implementation of labor market policy through their membership (along with government officials) in the National Labor Market Board (AMS), which is discussed in Chapter 5.4.

National Federation of Trade Unions (LO)

The most important labor association is the LO (Landsorganisationen), which was founded in 1898 as a federation of local and regional craft (later, industrial) unions. Since then, the federation has grown to encompass fifteen national trade unions that together claimed as members 41 percent of Sweden's total labor force in 2008 (1.6 million out of 4.2 million employees). The LO's largest constituent units are the Association of Local Government Workers with 513,284 members and the Metal Workers' Union with 391,004 members (2008).[14]

As noted above, the National Federation of Trade Unions is closely linked with the SAP. The LO's affiliation with the SAP has enabled LO leaders to initiate some significant legislative measures in recent decades. As Chapter 5.4 discusses, these measures have primarily involved extensions of the rights of individual workers and unions in the workplace.

In its simultaneous role as Sweden's principal bargaining agent in behalf of higher wages and improved working conditions, the LO negotiated directly with the Swedish Association of Employers to establish annual framework agreements covering all its member unions. This practice, which was instigated in the 1950s, was abandoned in 1983 when the Metal Workers' Union negotiated its own wage pact. The LO remains responsible for coordinating the overall negotiation process, but actual agreements are now reached on an industry-by-industry basis. Union leaders and employers have welcomed the return to a more decentralized system of wage negotiations on the grounds that it permits greater flexibility.

Since the 1950s the LO and its member unions have pursued a largely cooperative strategy in their relations with the SAF. As a result, Sweden has maintained one of the world's lowest levels of industrial conflicts. A major exception was a protracted dispute over wages in 1980 that resulted in a national lockout by the SAF and a retaliatory strike by the LO affecting nearly a million workers. The country was virtually paralyzed for three days before the two labor market partners agreed on a compromise solution. Since then, organized labor and employers have succeeded in reaching wage agreements with a minimum of open strife.

The pattern of peaceful labor relations is rooted in two important historical accords: (1) the Collective Agreements Act of 1918, which prohibited strikes and lockouts over the interpretation of wage contracts and required that they be settled instead by a newly created Labor Court; and (2) the Saltsjöbaden Agreement of 1938, which was negotiated by the SAF and the LO and established a consensual framework governing wage negotiation and grievance procedures.

Central Organization of Salaried Employees (TCO)

Sweden's second most important labor organization is the TCO (Tjänstemännens Centralorganisation). Representing primarily white-collar workers, the TCO consists of sixteen national unions that together claim nearly 1.2 million members (2008). Slightly more than half of its membership is employed in the public sector at either the national or regional and local levels of government; the remainder work for private firms.[15]

Because the TCO has a more heterogeneous clientele than the LO, its leaders studiously pursue an official strategy of "neutrality" in their relations with the principal political parties. The TCO cooperates closely with the LO in promoting bread-and-butter economic issues such as annual wage increments on behalf of its members. As a result, the TCO leadership is inclined, on balance, to endorse SAP legislative initiatives more than those of the nonsocialist parties.

Confederation of Swedish Enterprise (SN)

The Confederation of Swedish Enterprise (Svenskt Näringsliv/Arbetsgivarförbund) (formerly known as the Swedish Employers Association (Svenska Arbetsgivareföreningen, or SAF) was founded in 1902 as a counterpart employers' organization to the LO. Similar to both the LO and the TCO, the SN is a national group made up of the branch associations of industrial and service firms. In 2008 its membership consisted of 59,917 companies represented in the national organization through fifty branch associations. The largest corporate members are those involved in manufacturing, commerce, and forestry.[16]

Like the LO, the employers' association has a dual identity. On the one hand, the SN and its branch associations are responsible for negotiating wage and related agreements with organized labor. On the other hand, politically the SN is closely aligned with the nonsocialist bloc, especially the Moderates. Through a combination of research and publication activities, publicity campaigns, participation in government commissions and a consultative role in the legislative process (see Chapter 5.4), and lobbying of the cabinet and parliament, the SN seeks to maximize employer influence in policy outcomes. In recent decades, the SN has concentrated on tax reform, wage restraint, and a campaign to impede Social Democratic–LO initiatives to extend the power of unions in economic decisions.

Administrative Elites

High-level civil servants—that is, the administrative elites who manage the planning and budgetary processes within the various cabinet-level departments—are also instrumental actors in Sweden's policy process. Unlike leaders of the various parties and interest groups, they are not politically accountable to the public at large or organizational members. Instead, they exercise power on the basis of their academic qualifications, institutional status, and bureaucratic skills. As such, Sweden's departmental bureaucrats are a principal source of empirical information, technical expertise, and long-range reform perspectives.

As American political scientist Thomas J. Anton observes in his assessment of the elite political culture in Sweden, the administrative elites who constitute the ministerial departments in Stockholm are distinctive compared with those in other countries primarily because of their close personal interaction "in a world that is small, comfortable, well-understood, and highly specialized"; their social skills, coupled with a pragmatic orientation toward people and problem solving; and their formal participation alongside politicians and interest group representatives in Sweden's myriad state commissions.[17] Together, these personal and institutional attributes of the administrative elites contribute significantly to Sweden's highly deliberative and rational mode of policymaking.

Elections

Electoral outcomes determine whether socialists or nonsocialists—and therefore indirectly which organized interest groups—dominate the legislative agenda. Between elections, the composition of the cabinet and interparty as well as intergroup bargaining determine the specific content of policy choice.

Sweden is the only country among the seven nations presented in this volume that held competitive elections on schedule throughout the twentieth century. Even the onset of World Wars I and II did not spur political leaders to postpone national elections. From democratization through 1968, Riksdag elections were held every four years, except for a special dissolution election in 1958. Elections to county and city assemblies were also conducted at four-year intervals, albeit midway through each legislative session. Swedes therefore voted every two years, alternating between Riksdag and county and local elections. The election dates were merged through the constitutional reforms of 1968–1969 (effective in 1970) that reduced the terms of national and regional office from four to three years. Legislative terms were extended once again to four years beginning with the 1994 election.

Electoral outcomes are associated with three stages of Swedish parliamentary development. The first was one of "minority parliamentarianism" (1920–1932) and was characterized by the absence of stable legislative majorities by a single party or governing coalition. The Social Democrats' advance in the 1932 election inaugurated a second stage, "majority parliamentarianism," which brought forty-four years of informal and formal coalitions between the SAP and other parties alternating with periods of a Social Democratic legislative majority. In the third stage, which began in 1976, Sweden has experienced more indeterminate electoral results resulting in the formation of successive majority and minority cabinets and an alternation of executive power between the Social Democrats and nonsocialist parties.

The strength of the Social Democratic Party, Sweden's largest party since 1917, peaked during two electoral cycles in the twentieth century: in the late 1930s and early 1940s and for a shorter period in the 1960s. The nonsocialist bloc has seen considerable electoral fluctuations over time. The Liberals relinquished their dominant status to the Conservatives in the aftermath of World War II, but regained it from the mid-1940s through the mid-1960s. From then through the early 1980s, the Center and the Moderates vied for leadership among the nonsocialist forces. The Liberals subsequently displaced the Center as the second largest nonsocialist party from 1985 until 1994, when the Center reclaimed that position. In subsequent elections the Liberals and the Center have periodically alternated as Sweden's second-largest nonsocialist party (except in 1989 when the Christian Democrats were second).

The emergence of a shared sense of nonsocialist identity among the Liberal, Center, and Moderate Parties during the 1960s effectively transformed the conditions of electoral competition. Henceforth, blocs rather than merely party outcomes became decisive in determining government formation and the thrust of policy decisions. An increase in aggregate nonsocialist strength, beginning in 1970, as indicated in Table 5-3, enhanced bloc competitiveness between the socialist and nonsocialist parties and presaged later shifts in executive leadership. Electoral advances by the Christian Democrats and New Democracy contributed to a discernible increase in aggregate nonsocialist strength in 1991.

Table 5-3 Bloc Alignments in National Elections, 1958–2014

Legislative Period	Socialist parties[a]	Nonsocialist parties[b]	Right-wing
1964–1968	52.5	43.9	
1968–1970	53.1	42.9	
1970–1973	50.1	47.6	
1973–1976	48.9	50.4	
1976–1979	47.5	50.2	
1979–1982	48.8	50.4	
1982–1985	51.9	46.9	
1985–1988	51.6	47.9	
1988–1991	54.5	44.7	
1991–1994	45.6	46.6	6.7[c]
1994–1998	55.6	41.4	1.2[c]
1998–2002	52.9	45.5	
2002–2006	52.9	44.0	
2006–2010	46.0	48.2	
2010–2014	43.7	49.3	5.7[d]

Source: Statistiska centralbyrån [Statistics Sweden], *Statistiskårsbok för Sverige* (Stockholm: Statistiska centralbyrån, various issues).

[a] Combined support for the Social Democratic Party, the Left Party, and the Greens.

[b] Combined support for the Liberals, the Center Party, the Moderates, and (after 1991) the Christian Democratic Union (KDS). In 1985 and 1988 the Center Party and the KDS formed an electoral alliance.

[c] New Democracy (radical populist).

[d] Sweden Democrats (anti-immigrant).

Continuity and change characterize recent electoral behavior. Each party retains an identifiable core of supporters. Both the Social Democrats and the Left Party draw most of their support from among workers and lower-level salaried employees; the Liberals recruit broadly among all major occupational groups; the Center draws most of its support from among farmers, workers, and civil servants; and the Moderates attract the bulk of their voters among businesspeople and high- and mid-level civil servants.

At the same time, new political issues have motivated many voters (especially the young) to abandon their occupational or class identities to vote across party or bloc lines. These voters are concerned about nuclear energy, the environment, economic and social policy, personal privacy, and immigration. Increased electoral volatility has contributed, in turn, to discontinuities in executive leadership from the mid-1970s onward. Reinforcing electoral volatility is a decline in party membership. The percentage of citizens who belong to a political party fell from 13.8 percent in 1980–1981 to 5.3 percent in 2006–2007.[18] Electoral participation declined from a peak of 91.8 percent in 1973 to 80.0 percent in 2002 but rose marginally to 82 percent in 2006 and 2010.

Governments and Opposition

From 1932 through the 2010–2014 legislative session, eighteen coalitions or single-party governments will have held executive office (see Table 5-4). The Social Democrats controlled the cabinet, either alone or in coalition with one or more of the nonsocialist parties, between 1932 and 1976. A succession of nonsocialist cabinets governed from 1976 to

Table 5-4 Swedish Governments, 1932–2014

Years	Composition	Prime minister and party
1932–1936	SAP	Hansson (SAP)
1936-1939	C	Pehrsson i Bramstorp (C)
1936–1939	SAP-C	Hansson (SAP)
1939–1945	SAP-C-FP-M	Hansson (SAP)
1945–1951	SAP	Hansson/Erlander (SAP)
1951–1957	SAP-C	Erlander (SAP)
1957–1976	SAP	Erlander/Palme (1969) (SAP)
1976–1978	C-FP-M	Fälldin (C)
1978–1979	FP	Ullsten (FP)
1979–1981	C-FP-M	Fälldin (C)
1981–1982	C-FP	Fälldin (C)
1982–1991	SAP	Palme/Carlsson (SAP)
1991–1994	M-FP-C-KDS	Bildt (M)
1994–1998	SAP	Carlsson/Persson (SAP)
1998–2002	SAP	Persson (SAP)
2002–2006	SAP	Persson (SAP)
2006–2010	M-FP-C-KDS	Reinfeldt (M)
2010–	M-FP-C-KDS	Reinfeldt (M)

Note: The Social Democrats (SAP) generally governed with the indirect parliamentary support of the postcommunist Left Party (V) and the Environmentalist Party–the Greens (MP). Explanation of other party abbreviations: FP = People's Party (Liberals); C = Center Party; M = Moderate Unity Party (Conservatives); KDS = Christian Democratic Union.

1982: first, a three-party coalition led by the Center, followed successively by a Liberal minority cabinet, a restored three-party coalition, and a Center-Liberal minority coalition. The Social Democrats resumed executive leadership after the 1982 parliamentary elections. They lacked an absolute majority, but they could rely, depending on the policy issue at stake, on either the Left, the Greens (after 1988), or one or more of the nonsocialist parties to enact their legislative agenda.

In October 1991 a four-party coalition was formed consisting of the Moderates, the Liberals, the Center, and the Christian Democrats that was tacitly supported by New Democracy. The nonsocialists governed until the September 1994 election when Ingvar Carlsson resumed the prime ministership as head of a minority SAP cabinet supported by the Left Party, the Greens, and tactically by some members of the bourgeois bloc. The SAP retained executive office after the September 1998 and 2002 elections but yielded power to a nonsocialist majority in 2006. Prime Minister Reinfeldt formed a four-party coalition consisting of his own Moderate Unity Party, the Christian Democrats, the Center, and the Liberals. The coalition partners narrowly lost their parliamentary majority in the 2010 election—thanks to gains by the far right—but remained in office as a minority government (see Chapter 5.5).

Long-term Social Democratic governance, interrupted by nonsocialist interregnums in 1976–1982, 1991–1994, and after 2006, therefore distinguishes Swedish politics from that of other advanced industrial democracies. The SAP utilized its executive status to pursue a succession of transforming—and often controversial—policy initiatives that constitute a long-term pattern of breakthrough politics followed by a shift toward neoliberalism similar to policies pursued by Great Britain's "New Labour" Party under Tony Blair and Gordon Brown (1997–2010) and Germany's Gerhard Schroeder (1998–2006) and Angela Merkel (2006–). Perceived shortcomings of these strategies have prompted spirited public debate and recurrent electoral realignments.

NOTES

1. Val myndigheten (Electoral Central Office), *Val till riksdagen—Ålder och kön,* www.val.se/val/val2010/statistisk/R/rike/alderkon.html. The survey of party preferences by age and gender was conducted in September 2010.
2. "Welcome to Vänsterpartiet!" http://www.vansterpartiet.se/.
3. Val myndigheten, *Val till riksdagen—Ålder och kön.*
4. Ibid.
5. Ibid.
6. Ibid.
7. Moderata samlingsparti, "Moderat grundsyn" [Moderate principles], adopted at the 1993 party congress, http://www.moderat.se.
8. John T. S. Madeley, "The Swedish Model Is Dead! Long Live the Swedish Model!" *West European Politics* 26 (April 2003): Electronic Collection A103473794, 5.
9. "Press Release: General elections, election study 2006: White collar workers elected the New Moderates," *Statistisk årsbok,* January 31, 2008.
10. "Swedish Politics: A Spoil-the-Men's Party," *Economist,* April 14, 2005, http://www.economist.com/research;subje4ct=Sweden.
11. "Swedish Feminism Put to the Test," *International Herald Tribune,* October 20, 2005.
12. "Pirate Party Declaration of Principles 3.2," http://docs.piratpartiet.se/Principles%203.2.pdf.
13. "Swedish Anti-Immigration Party Claims Seats," *New York Times* reprints, September 19, 2010, NYTimes.com.
14. Statistiska centralbyrån [Statistics Sweden], *Statistisk årsbok för Sverige 2010,* (Stockholm: Statistiska centralbyrån, 2010), 292.
15. Ibid.
16. Ibid., 291.
17. Thomas J. Anton, *Administered Politics: Elite Political Culture in Sweden* (Boston/The Hague/London: Martinus Nijhoff, 1980), esp. 129–157.
18. Statistiska centralbyrån, *Statistisk årsbok för Sverige 2010,* 567.

How Is Power Used?

THE USE OF POWER IN ALL POLITICAL SYSTEMS INVOLVES A COMBINATION of policy process and outcomes. In Sweden, power as process corresponds to political scientist Stein Rokkan's concept of a "two-tiered system of decision-making," which he used in the mid-1960s to describe his own country, Norway.[1] The first tier consists of popularly elected members of the parliament and the county and municipal assemblies, who are responsible for formulating and ratifying government policy. The second tier of decision makers is made up of the representatives of the principal organized interest groups and the public administration, who receive a recognized policy role through their participation in state commissions and various consultative procedures. A third tier of participants—not included in Rokkan's analysis—are the voters, who are given a consultative voice in important policy decisions via the referendum procedure.

The sum of these arrangements is the form of democratic corporatism defined in the introduction to this volume: institutionalized consultative arrangements that permit public officials, representatives of the nation's principal interest associations, and citizens to confer jointly about pending policy issues. Coupled with the strength of the Swedish Social Democratic Workers' Party (SAP) and organized labor, democratic corporatism facilitated efforts by political and group leaders to sustain a pattern of active systemic change throughout much of the postwar era.

Policy Process

Thanks in large measure to its executive authority over the various departments and administrative agencies (see Chapter 5.2), the cabinet plays the central role in Sweden's formal policymaking process. Riksdag deputies by no means hesitate to propose their own legislative initiatives (3,961 motions in 2008–2009), but most private members' bills are dismissed in committee. By contrast, most government proposals, which numbered 232 in 2008–2009, are duly enacted into law.[2]

All bills, whether submitted by the cabinet or by backbench members of parliament, are referred to the relevant committee for deliberation. Unlike U.S. congressional practice, Swedish committees may not pigeonhole (and thereby kill) legislation, but must report all bills back to parliament. The committees' recommendations almost invariably serve as the basis of legislative enactment.

The cabinet's authority to mobilize the resources of Sweden's powerful organized interest groups in the prelegislative stage of parliamentary decisions further enhances its policymaking role. Since the nineteenth century, Swedish cabinets have regularly appointed "state commissions" (*statsutredningar,* commonly mistranslated as royal commissions) to gather facts and advise the government on pending legislation. On major questions, such commissions characteristically consist of experts representing the important interest groups, political parties, and relevant administrative agencies. Commission members are usually very thorough in their work, and their final recommendations frequently serve as the basis of the cabinet's legislative proposal on the issue.

Interest group viewpoints are also solicited through a consultative process known as *remiss;* ministerial departments invite organized groups and administrative agencies to comment on pending legislation. A government proposal to the Riksdag contains a summary of the state commission's report and *remiss* replies, along with the government's own recommendation for action.

Together, the state commissions and the *remiss* procedures constitute the formal core of Sweden's version of democratic corporatism. By serving as channels for initiating and reviewing important legislative initiatives, the commissions and the practice of *remiss* give organized interest groups a more direct means of influencing policy outcomes than is true in most Western democracies.

In addition to casting their votes in national and other elections, citizens also participate in the political decision process through periodic consultative referendums. Six referendums have been held so far, the first in 1922 and the most recent in 2003 (these referendums are listed in Chapter 5.2, and the referendums of 1957, 1980, 1994, and 2003 are described in more detail below). Constitutionally, the referendums are not legally binding on the executive or parliament, but the government has largely accepted the results as the basis for authoritative decisions. As noted in Chapter 5.2, the one exception was the decision in the 1960s to introduce right-hand traffic despite a negative vote in the 1955 referendum. The cabinet and parliament based their decision on subsequent public opinion polls that indicated public support for the change.

Policy Outcomes

Swedes' pragmatism and willingness to seek compromise solutions to partisan differences have facilitated a largely consensual approach to many aspects of both domestic and foreign policy. The leaders of the major political parties, the Confederation of Swedish Enterprise (SN), the National Federation of Trade Unions (LO), and other organized interest groups have jointly affirmed not only the constitutional reforms that modernized Swedish parliamentarianism in the 1970s but also the need to sustain neutrality, an active labor market policy, and material growth based on cooperation among the SN, LO, and Central Organization of Salaried Employees (TCO). Within this broad consensus on the fundamental principles of Swedish politics and economics, however, the socialist and nonsocialist blocs have simultaneously promoted competing ideological visions of systemic change. In short, power is used by Sweden's political parties and organized interest groups in behalf of both shared and divergent socioeconomic objectives.

Among Sweden's most important political actors, the Social Democrats and the LO have decisively influenced policy outcomes because of their numerical and organizational strength, the SAP's long-term parliamentary majority, and the earlier fragmentation of the nonsocialist opposition. During their decades of executive leadership from the early 1930s onward, the Social Democrats undertook major policy initiatives and systemic reforms that culminated in today's comprehensive welfare state. Many of the attributes associated with the Swedish model are products of the SAP-LO's strategic commitment to active systemic change, including the "historic compromise" between private capital and organized labor codified in the Saltsjöbaden Agreement of 1938 and an overarching commitment to full employment and great citizen equality.

The nonsocialist parties, the SN, and other organized groups have endorsed many of the SAP-LO's innovations, but on important occasions they also have resisted Social Democratic initiatives. With the maturation of the Swedish model during the 1960s and 1970s, the result was a mixed record of economic and social performance accompanied by recurrent political conflict.

Economic Performance

Economic factors significantly enhanced the SAP's long-term claim to cabinet office. By introducing expansionist fiscal policies along Keynesian lines when they first came to power in 1932, the Social Democrats helped to engineer Sweden's recovery from the devastating effects of the Great Depression. The advent of World War II led to a sharp reduction in trade and the introduction of rationing, as well as numerous economic controls that resulted in a temporary decline in the nation's standard of living. But from the late 1940s onward, Sweden, like most of Western Europe, North America, and Japan, experienced an unprecedented rate of economic growth and national prosperity. The upshot is that today Sweden claims a per capita income that ranks among the highest in the world's industrial democracies.

Much of Sweden's postwar economic expansion resulted from external factors. Among them were American loans and grants to Sweden and other Western European countries under the Marshall Plan (initiated in 1947), a rapid expansion of world trade beginning in the early 1950s, and the success of the European integration movement in stimulating growth throughout Western Europe as a whole. Yet international economic trends alone do not account for other, more distinctive Swedish patterns of economic performance. Among them are one of the lowest unemployment rates among the industrial democracies and a long-term pattern of labor peace.

After World War II, Sweden sustained virtually full employment until the early 1990s. The unemployment rate fluctuated between a high of 3.5 percent in 1983, when unemployment climbed to record postwar levels in much of Europe and North America, and a low of 1.5 percent in 1989. Equally noteworthy, Sweden experienced comparatively little labor-management conflict. During the 1960s workers went on strike an average of only eighteen times a year, compared with an annual average of 166 times in Germany, 1,943 in France, 2,446 in Great Britain, and 4,107 times in the United States. The number of strikes in Sweden increased during the 1970s to an annual average of eighty-seven. Yet even this figure is significantly lower than the annual averages during the same decade in other industrial democracies: 2,604 in Great Britain, 3,258 in France, and 5,249 in the United States.[3] During the 1980s only Germany among the countries surveyed in this volume maintained a lower level of industrial conflict.[4]

Sweden's low levels of unemployment and industrial conflict have not been accidental. First, the SAP's executive leadership from 1932 to 1976 and again from 1982 to 1991 facilitated long-term efforts to fine-tune the nation's economic performance through a combination of indicative economic planning, short-term adjustments in fiscal and monetary policies, and government measures designed to encourage economic rationalization.[5] As a result, Sweden was spared abrupt changes in macroeconomic policymaking associated with periodic shifts in power between conservative and socialist parties in post-war Great Britain and during the 1980s in France.

Second, the Social Democrats used their executive status to promote an active labor market policy in collaboration with their LO allies and the SN. The concept of such a policy was originally formulated by several prominent LO economists during the 1950s and was formally implemented by the Social Democrats in response to an economic slow-down during the late 1960s. In contrast to Keynesian theory and practice, which empha-size reliance on fiscal measures to combat unemployment, advocates of an active labor market policy urged collaborative actions by administrative officials, unions, and employ-ers to maintain or create jobs at the level of individual firms. A basic instrument for this purpose is the National Labor Market Board (AMS), which is composed of government, union, and employer representatives. The AMS coordinates public and private efforts to promote employment through a combination of training and retraining programs, the relocation of workers displaced when companies are forced to shut down, and temporary relief work. The government supplements the activities of the AMS and its decentralized network of county and local employment agencies by providing cash subsidies to compa-nies willing to hire workers who might otherwise not be able to find a job, among them many young people and the handicapped. An important consequence of the active labor market policy is that in Sweden far fewer people are "on welfare" than traditionally has been true in the United States.

Another political factor that has contributed specifically to labor peace is the numerical strength of the LO and its member unions. That strength has permitted organized labor to bargain effectively with employers' groups to secure higher wages and improved working conditions, thereby lessening potential causes of employee dissatisfaction.

And yet another political factor is the pattern of institutionalized collaboration between employers and unions that has governed SAF-LO relations since their Saltsjöbaden Agree-ment of 1938. The decision by leaders of both associations to resolve differences with minimal government interference and, during the 1960s and 1970s, to negotiate nation-wide collective wage agreements, significantly facilitated labor-management cooperation. But this cooperation does not mean that labor disputes do not occur in Sweden. As noted earlier, a major wave of strikes and a national lockout by employers took place in May 1980, but the conflict proved shorter and less disruptive than comparable labor-manage-ment confrontations in most other industrial democracies.

The Welfare State: Achievements and Dissent

A crucial adjunct of the Social Democrats' emphasis on active economic management is their successive extension of welfare services (see Chapter 5.1). Postwar SAP reform ini-tiatives have included improved unemployment and retirement benefits, a national health insurance program, and a variety of individual and family cash allowances. As a prominent LO economist has observed, the result of these measures is that "public services and pay-ments are provided, under specific rules, to everyone who is entitled to them, regardless of means-tested need. Good examples are children's allowances and pensions, which are sent automatically to millionaires and the unemployed alike."[6]

With varying degrees of enthusiasm, nonsocialist leaders endorsed most of the SAP's early postwar reform initiatives. A dramatic exception occurred in the mid-1950s, however, when the LO and the Social Democrats moved to introduce a new system of supplementary pensions (ATP). The basic purpose of the ATP was to give individual workers additional retirement benefits amounting to an average of 60 percent of their taxable income during their fifteen best-paid years of employment. In addition, for Social Democrats the reform was a means of generating collective savings that could be used for government-sponsored economic objectives such as the construction of new apartments to relieve recurrent housing shortages. All three nonsocialist parties, as well as the national employers' association, opposed the compulsory features of the SAP-LO proposal. In fact, dissent was so intense that the Center Party withdrew from the government coalition with the Social Democrats in 1957. A national referendum, held that same year, and a dissolution election, conducted in 1958, were required to settle the issue.

The Social Democrats obtained a relative majority of votes in both the referendum (45.8 percent) and the dissolution election (46.2 percent). The Center and the Moderates, which had rejected the mandatory pension legislation, gained in electoral support, while the Liberals, who had advocated a "positive compromise solution" that would enable individual workers to opt out of a collective system of supplementary pensions, lost heavily (see Table 5-2, page 459). The Social Democrats interpreted their electoral advance as a mandate to proceed with implementing their version of supplementary benefits. The ATP proposal was endorsed by a single-vote parliamentary majority in May 1959.

Since then, Swedish welfare provisions have become among the most comprehensive in the world. Sweden's current government disbursements, including the purchase of goods and services as well as transfer payments, are among the highest in the world, and its annual rate of infant mortality is one of the lowest. In parallel fashion, postwar Social Democratic legislative initiatives to enhance educational opportunities for lower-middle-class and working-class youth have led to more public investment in education than in most other advanced democracies. In 2008 the government spent 14.6 percent of the national budget on illness and disability security, 8.8 percent in support of families and children, and 6.9 percent on health care, medical care, and social services.[7] As noted in Chapter 5.2, Sweden draws on a correspondingly high rate of taxation to finance its extensive social programs and other government services.

Dealignment and Erosion of the Swedish Model: A Chronology

In response to the postwar growth of the welfare state, critics on the right and left joined in attacking the concentration of power and the high cost of public services in Sweden while advocating specific partisan remedies. Nonsocialist leaders criticized bureaucratization and "excessive" government expenditures and repeatedly denounced Sweden's high tax rate as a disincentive to private initiative and savings. From the opposite end of the political spectrum, the Left Party and other left socialists attacked the Social Democrats for their failure to socialize industry and thereby mitigate the concentration of private economic power in the hands of wealthy shareholders. The cumulative effect of left and right criticism of Social Democratic governance set off the continuing pattern of dealignment in electoral behavior and the gradual erosion of the central tenets of the Swedish model. These developments are described in the sections that follow.

The Nonsocialist Interlude

The joint left-right criticism of the Social Democrats resulted in a sharp decline in SAP electoral strength in the 1966 county and municipal elections. The SAP recovered in the 1968 parliamentary election but gradually lost support during the 1970s as the nonsocialist parties succeeded in projecting an image of bloc unity in behalf of an alternative program of government decentralization and tax reduction. The outcome was a nonsocialist electoral victory in 1976 and the formation of a Center-Liberal-Moderate coalition that displaced the Social Democrats after forty-four years of executive leadership.

Once in power, however, the coalition proved incapable of maintaining interparty unity on important policy issues. The first conflict involved nuclear energy. During the 1976 campaign, Center Party leaders had strenuously opposed SAP plans to increase Sweden's nuclear energy plants from six to thirteen by the mid-1980s. Liberal and Moderate officials, by contrast, endorsed the measure. After the election, the Liberals and Moderates compelled Prime Minister Thorbjörn Fälldin to reverse his Center Party's campaign stance and agree that a seventh plant could begin operations.

The Center Party later held firm in its resolve to oppose any further development of nuclear energy. A government crisis ensued in October 1978 when the Moderates and Liberals endorsed a recommendation of the National Nuclear Energy Inspection Board to activate two additional nuclear energy plants. Fälldin and his fellow Centrists promptly resigned from the cabinet in protest. The Liberals then formed a minority government in place of the previous three-party coalition.

The nuclear energy impasse was resolved in March 1980 when a majority of the Swedish electorate voted in a national referendum in favor of temporary expansion of the country's nuclear energy program to include a maximum of twelve plants. Eventually, the Liberals and Social Democrats concurred on a joint government-opposition decision to phase out all twelve plants by the early part of the twenty-first century in tandem with a policy of stringent conservation and the development of alternative sources of energy such as solar and fusion.

Despite their interbloc disagreement on the nuclear energy issue, the nonsocialist parties won a one-seat majority in the September 1979 Riksdag election. Accordingly, they reconstituted a three-party coalition government under Center leadership.

Ultimately, however, the nonsocialists failed once again to sustain executive unity. Ironically, the second divisive issue proved to be taxation policy. In spring 1981 the Center and Liberals acted to honor an earlier agreement with the Social Democrats to reduce the marginal tax rates in exchange for a simultaneous cut in the tax deduction allowable for interest paid on home mortgages. In response, Moderates, who were opposed to the trade-off on ideological grounds, angrily withdrew from the government coalition. As a result, the Center and the Liberals formed a minority government in May 1981 and governed jointly until September 1982, when the Social Democrats resumed power with the indirect support of the Left Party.

The Quest for Economic Democracy

Intense partisan disagreements over nuclear energy and tax policy during the late 1970s and early 1980s revealed a deepening conflict between nonsocialist forces and the Social

Democrats over long-term economic policy and strategies of systemic change. Similar to other advanced industrial nations, Sweden had experienced a slowdown in economic growth since the mid-1970s. The causes were rooted primarily in global factors, including successive oil price increases in 1973–1974 and 1978–1979 and greater international trade competition from Asia in industries such as steel production and shipbuilding.

With the onset of "stagflation" internationally, Sweden's average annual growth rate fell from 4.4 percent during the 1960s to 2 percent or less from 1970 through the early 1980s. Accompanying the decline in economic growth were increases in the rate of inflation, which jumped from an annual average rate of 4.3 percent during the 1960s to 9.3 percent in the 1970s, and unemployment, which rose from an annual average of 1.8 percent in 1956–1978 to more than 3 percent by the summer of 1982. A spiraling budgetary deficit and a negative trade balance further exacerbated Sweden's bleak economic situation.

During their time in office, nonsocialist leaders sought to restore domestic growth through a combination of measures. Among them were the Liberal-Center-SAP accord in 1981 to reduce marginal taxes, the introduction of tax-sheltered savings and equity programs designed to stimulate the growth of investment capital, the socialization of Sweden's ailing shipbuilding industry, and government subsidies to encourage higher employment among the young. To pay for these expansionary measures, the nonsocialists resorted to heavy borrowing from international capital markets and raised the value-added tax (VAT), which is a form of national sales tax, from 17.65 to 23.46 percent. In addition, in 1982 the Center-Liberal minority government reduced health care benefits marginally in an effort to decrease public expenditures and thereby limit the growing budgetary deficit.

The Social Democrats attacked the nonsocialists' economic strategy from both an immediate and a longer-term perspective. In the short run, the SAP and the LO criticized the nonsocialists on the grounds that their fiscal policies were inadequate to achieve the economic recovery that presumably all Swedes desired. Above all, the SAP cited the unprecedented postwar jump in the unemployment rate after 1976 as evidence of the inadequacy of the nonsocialist response to the prevailing international conditions of stagflation. As an alternative approach, the Social Democrats called for even greater government economic activism to be financed by yet another increase in the VAT.

Far more controversial was the SAP-LO's ideological commitment to a "breakthrough" strategy of industrial and economic democracy. LO and SAP leaders had jointly launched a series of important legislative reforms during the mid-1970s that considerably strengthened the status of individual workers and unions in relation to private management. Among these reforms, the Employment Security Act of 1974 restricted the right of employers to dismiss workers; the Work Environment Act of 1974 gave floor-level safety stewards sweeping powers to enforce strict health and safety standards; and the Employee Participation Act of 1976 transformed the traditional right of managers to "direct and allocate work" into an object of collective bargaining.[8] In 1976 the LO formally urged that these increments in the collective power of organized labor be augmented through the introduction of a national system of wage-earner funds.

The LO's proposal emerged from a study group appointed by the LO in 1970 to investigate steps to create a profit-sharing arrangement that would tap the "excess" profits in private industry to the collective advantage of organized labor.[9] Five years later, the study group, which was headed by Rudolf Meidner, a leading LO economist, submitted a report recommending a collective system of employee funds that would be financed through a tax on company profits. The funds would be empowered to purchase company shares on the domestic stock market, and in time, the funds could acquire majority ownership of individual companies. That prospect outraged employers' groups and the nonsocialist parties and caused even many rank-and-file Social Democrats to question the wisdom of the Meidner plan. The resulting controversy over the LO proposal proved to be a major factor in the SAP's electoral defeat in 1976.

Although in opposition, the LO and the SAP refined the original Meidner concept to include provisions for a decentralized system of funds and the transfer of dividend income into the ATP system as a means of safeguarding future individual retirement benefits. From 1977 onward, the Social Democrats also stressed the importance of the wage-earner funds as a source of domestic investment capital. These revisions were endorsed by overwhelming majorities at LO and SAP congresses held in the early fall of 1981.

The Social Democrats therefore conducted their 1982 campaign against the Moderates, the Center, and the Liberals on the dual basis of short-term charges of economic mismanagement and longer-term advocacy of enhanced economic democracy. The SAP victory in September 1982 enabled the Social Democrats to proceed with new initiatives on both fronts.

The Social Democrats Back in Office

Prime Minister Olof Palme and members of his cabinet proceeded cautiously but with a clear sense of direction when they resumed office in 1982. They began by honoring the SAP's campaign promises to restore nonsocialist-sponsored reductions in health care and increase government expenditures in behalf of job creation (both of which were financed by a higher VAT rate). They also moved to stimulate renewed economic growth by devaluing the Swedish krona (crown) by 16 percent in an effort to reduce the cost of Swedish exports and encourage an export-led recovery from the economic doldrums of the early 1980s. The cabinet simultaneously enacted an austere budgetary policy designed to push the government's deficit below levels projected by the previous Center-Liberal coalition. In the process, Social Democratic leaders incurred the temporary wrath of some trade unionists and rank-and-file activists who demanded a more expansionist economic policy even at the cost of a greater budget deficit.

Early in their renewed term of office, the Social Democrats also acted to implement the controversial system of wage-earner funds. Despite nonsocialist criticism and the absence of a popular majority in support of the concept (as measured by successive public opinion surveys), the SAP formally proposed during the summer of 1983 the creation of five regional funds to be financed through a combination of a 20 percent tax on company profits and a 0.2 percent increase in employee contributions to the ATP retirement system. The funds would be governed by appointive boards dominated by trade union officials. The government sought to diffuse nonsocialist fears that the wage-earner funds could eventually acquire majority ownership of specific companies by restricting both the funds' total capitalization (to a maximum of 17.5 billion Swedish krona by 1990) and the percentage of shares that each of the funds could purchase in a single enterprise (8 percent per fund for a hypothetical total of 40 percent shared by the five funds). Moreover, the Social Democrats stipulated that the wage-earner funds would remain in place only through 1990. The cabinet believed this seven-year period would suffice to facilitate the necessary structural transformation of the Swedish economy with the assistance of the investment capital generated by the five funds.

The Riksdag endorsed the government's proposal in December 1983. The Social Democrats voted solidly in favor of the bill, the Left Party abstained to ensure the bill's passage, and the three nonsocialist parties voted against it. The bill went into effect on January 1, 1984.

Tactically, the SAP legislative initiative on the wage-earner fund issue was dictated by both the timing of parliamentary elections and the party's calculation of foreseeable international economic trends. The Riksdag's approval of the government's proposal in late 1983 ensured that the funds would be operative prior to the September 1985 election. If the domestic economy improved noticeably by then, the Social Democrats could reasonably expect an electoral plurality and therefore a renewed parliamentary mandate. To help ensure that outcome, the LO and its constituent unions negotiated—as an explicit tradeoff for the introduction of the wage-earner fund system—wage settlements averaging a modest 5 percent or less in both 1982–1983 and 1983–1984. The LO's policy of wage restraint was intended to curtail domestic inflationary pressures and thereby facilitate Sweden's economic recovery from the doldrums that prevailed at the beginning of the decade.

The diluted version of the wage-earner fund system enacted in 1983 was not designed to achieve outright nationalization or "trade unionization" of industry (to the consternation of some left Social Democrats), because the legislation explicitly restricted the total percentage of company shares that the regional funds were permitted to purchase. Nevertheless, SAP and LO leaders anticipated that the extension of collective ownership of company stock—in combination with the various workplace reforms implemented during the 1970s—would encourage managers to be more responsive to union demands about employment, investments, and production. At a minimum, then, the funds would increase managerial awareness of the social consequences of microeconomic decisions and indirectly strengthen workplace democracy.

Precisely because the wage-earner fund system involved central issues of share ownership and managerial prerogatives, the nonsocialist parties, the SAF, and other private interests remained adamantly opposed to the concept of collective ownership and control of the funds as a potentially important source of investment capital. Accordingly, nonsocialist leaders repeatedly announced their determination to abolish the funds when they returned to power.

Economically, the Social Democratic policies met with greater interim success. The SAP's return to power coincided with the beginning of a general improvement in international economic conditions. The renewed growth of world trade and a decline in the world oil prices by the mid-1980s helped to stimulate renewed domestic growth. From -2.3 percent in 1981, Sweden experienced a steady increase in its real gross national product through 1984, when the rate peaked at 4 percent. Accompanying the restoration of growth was a decline in the unemployment rate, which fell from 4.5 percent in 1993 to less than 3 percent by the end of the decade. Other positive signs were a substantial increase in exports and the attainment of a slight budget surplus in 1987. These solid achievements contributed to a Social Democratic victory in the September 1985 election and the extension of the SAP's executive mandate into the early 1990s.

In a major departure from their ideological principles, however, the Social Democrats signaled through their actions that the era of social reform was at an end. They were determined to maintain the existing welfare state, but because of severe budgetary constraints, they in effect announced that no additional benefits would be forthcoming. In addition, party leaders yielded to long-standing nonsocialist claims that Sweden's taxation rate was too high. In 1988 the SAP initiated negotiations with the Liberals and other opposition parties to reduce taxes, thereby bringing them closer in line with the prevailing rates of their principal trading partners. The declared purpose of tax reform was to encourage greater private investment at home and, in the process, discourage a damaging drain of investment capital abroad, primarily to European Community countries and the United States.

The principal architect of Sweden's new "politics of austerity" was Kjell-Olof Feldt, a moderate Social Democrat whom Prime Minister Palme appointed minister of finance when the SAP resumed power in 1982. Economically conservative and distrustful of LO demands to transform property relations via the wage-earner fund system, Feldt sought to impose financial discipline on the nation by urging unions to practice self-restraint in their negotiations with employers over annual wage increases. His most compelling argument was that wage increases in excess of government guidelines of 3 percent or less had contributed to a higher inflation rate in Sweden than in other industrial democracies. When union leaders balked at his demands, Feldt persuaded the cabinet to adopt a stringent anti-inflationary program in February 1990 that prescribed a freeze on prices, wages, and rents and prohibited strikes by unions.

The cabinet's restrictive economic proposals and attempt to curtail trade union activity sparked immediate outrage from organized labor, the Left Party, many rank-and-file Social Democrats, and the nonsocialist parties. After a heated debate, an overwhelming majority of Riksdag deputies rejected the government's package in February 1990. The cabinet then resigned, and Prime Minister Ingvar Carlsson (who became prime minister after Palme was assassinated on February 28, 1986) formed a new Social Democratic government when nonsocialist leaders rejected an offer from the Speaker of the Riksdag to form a minority coalition. Feldt thereupon resigned from the cabinet.

Electoral and Political Flux

Although the Social Democrats survived the government crisis of February 1990, they remained on the political defensive. They clearly confronted a policy and ideological crisis from which they could not readily recover. Growing LO and rank-and-file worker dissatisfaction with SAP economic and financial policies coincided with an incipient electoral dealignment at the expense of the Social Democrats. The Social Democrats had confronted an earlier decline in support during the late 1940s and 1950s as the number of industrial workers—their traditional core of supporters—dwindled in the wake of postindustrialization, but they managed to recoup their losses during the 1960s by extending their appeal to salaried employees. Beginning in the early 1970s, however, the party experienced a renewed erosion of support (except for periodic fluctuations during the early 1980s) as more and more citizens switched partisan allegiances or abstained from voting altogether. By the spring and summer of 1991, opinion polls indicated a clear realignment in favor of the nonsocialist bloc, with the Christian Democrats and New

Democracy emerging as the principal beneficiaries. Explanations for the electoral shift include voter protests against short-term Social Democratic economic policies, disappointment on both the left and right over tax reform, discontent among women over wage inequalities, and the diffusion of "postmaterialist" values among many younger citizens, who were critical of the conformist norms and bureaucratic constraints associated with the existing welfare state.[10]

Diverse international and domestic factors converged in 1991 to spell another interim disruption in Social Democratic governance. The SAP lost heavily in the September election—falling to its lowest point since the early 1930s—while the nonsocialist bloc garnered 53.3 percent of the popular vote (see Table 5-2, page 459). The election revealed a pattern of continued electoral volatility, accompanied by a decline in the importance of party as a determinant of voter choice. Voter participation (86.7 percent) marginally increased compared to the 1988 election (86.0 percent) but was still lower than the 96.6 percent turnout recorded in 1976. At the same time, the number of voters who did not know which party they would support a week prior to a given election rose steadily, from 6 percent in 1985 to 9.1 percent in 1988 to 13.4 percent in 1991. Only 7 percent of Swedish voters switched party allegiances between elections during the late 1950s, but fully 20.2 percent changed loyalties in 1988. In the September 1991 election, voters deserted not only the Social Democrats but also the Liberals, the Center, and the Greens. New Democracy benefited most dramatically from the decline of voter loyalty, drawing support from both the traditional nonsocialist parties and especially the Social Democrats. Indeed, exit polls revealed that a majority of New Democracy adherents were trade unionists.

After the election, Prime Minister Carlsson submitted his resignation, and in early October Carl Bildt formed a nonsocialist coalition made up of the Moderates, Liberals, Center Party, and Christian Democrats. To achieve its declared determination to bring Sweden's "age of collectivism" to an end, the Moderate-led cabinet announced the following policy objectives: a reduction in public expenditures, economic deregulation, additional tax reforms designed to encourage private savings and strengthen small business firms, the partial privatization of education and social services, and a reaffirmation of Swedish membership in the European Community.

From the outset, the nonsocialist coalition confronted several formidable obstacles to its capacity to enact a coherent agenda of policy innovation. One was its minority status in parliament. Although the four parties together commanded 170 out of 349 seats in the Riksdag, they lacked nine votes for a majority in their own right. Therefore, to remain in office, the coalition was indirectly dependent on the support of New Democracy's twenty-five deputies. This dependency not only posed the ever-present risk of a government crisis, but also gave the New Democrats a disproportionate policy influence despite strong antipathy among traditional nonsocialist leaders, especially the Liberals, toward the New Democrats' populist ideological demands.

An even more daunting obstacle was Sweden's continuing economic malaise. In the face of sluggish growth, rising inflation, and a surge in the unemployment rate from 3.0 percent in 1991 to 8.2 percent in 1993, the nonsocialist cabinet assigned highest policy priority to reducing government expenditures to encourage private investments and curtail Sweden's worsening public deficit as means of stimulating economic recovery. This strategy entailed a succession of budget cuts beginning in January 1992, primarily at the expense of established welfare entitlements, including unemployment and retirement benefits, sick pay, and housing subsidies. Simultaneously, the nonsocialists eliminated taxes on electricity and fuel for industrial use and declared their intention to lower the nation's high VAT rate.

Both of these obstacles—minority status in parliament and the economic malaise—ultimately thwarted nonsocialist aspirations to achieve fundamental changes in Sweden's political economy and its welfare state. New Democracy repeatedly held the minority government hostage to specific policy demands (including a successful effort in 1992 to earmark a portion of the wage-earner funds as risk capital accessible to small businesses) even as leaders of the maverick party discredited themselves in the eyes of the electorate through an extended public feud. Members of the New Democracy legislative faction voted against cabinet bills twice in 1993, including the proposed budget for 1993–1994, but abstained in a crucial no-confidence vote to ensure the government's survival.

Meanwhile, economic imperatives loomed even larger. In their efforts to trim public expenditures and welfare entitlements, the nonsocialists confronted Sweden's worst economic crisis since the 1930s. In tandem with recessionary international economic trends in 1992–1993 and an accompanying European currency crisis, which triggered intense pressure on Swedish banks and a de facto devaluation of the krona by 9 percent, the nation's growth rate stagnated. The annual rate of inflation fell from 10.2 percent to 2.4 percent by the end of 1992, but unemployment spiraled relentlessly upward, from 5.3 percent in 1992 to 8.0 percent in 1994. In addition, Sweden's economic doldrums, combined with the government's tax cuts, caused the public debt to jump from 7.3 percent of the gross domestic product (GDP) in 1992 to 13.5 percent a year later.

Return of the Social Democrats to Power

Swedish voters responded to the worsening economic conditions and the nonsocialist cuts in social entitlements by restoring the Social Democrats to power in the September 1994 election. Voter participation fell marginally, to 86.3 percent, but the SAP dramatically reversed its earlier decline by mobilizing 45.3 percent of the national vote. The Left Party increased its share to 6.2 percent, and the Environmentalists-Greens returned to parliament with 4.1 percent of the vote. The Moderates increased their share slightly, to 22.4 percent, but the Liberals, the Center, and the Christian Democrats lost support (see Table 5-2, page 459). New Democracy effectively disappeared from the political scene with only 1.2 percent.

After Carl Bildt's resignation as leader of the nonsocialist coalition, Ingvar Carlsson was once again sworn in as Social Democratic prime minister. The Social Democrats introduced an austerity budget of their own that prescribed further reductions in some public expenditures, but it also included an increase in taxes and restoration of the previous government's curtailment of unemployment and health benefits. To deal with a looming crisis in the banking sector, the government established two state-owned banks in 1993 to take over bad credit risks from private banks and manage them until they could be sold for a profit. After successfully fulfilling this mandate, both banks closed shop in 1997.

Prime Minister Carlsson declared that the SAP's principal policy objective would be to reduce the nation's high unemployment rate (8 percent) through economic growth. As a means to that end, the Social Democrats successfully led the campaign to ratify Sweden's accession treaty with the European Union (EU) in November 1994. Carlsson also declared that the Social Democrats would seek to reduce the government deficit (which peaked under nonsocialist governance at 13 percent of GDP in 1993) to 3 percent by the end of 1997; "improve conditions for enterprise" as a means of encouraging job growth in small and medium-size firms; encourage new forms of social and political cooperation; and promote "lifelong learning" by integrating school, preschool, and leisure center activities and expanding postsecondary educational opportunities. "Sweden will be competing [in the world market] with high qualifications," Carlsson declared, "not low wages."[11]

Prime Minister Carlsson's policy declaration contained echoes of traditional Social Democratic values—for example, his emphasis on "the equal value of all persons"—but in essence it affirmed a neoliberal reorientation of public policy in conformity with EU norms. Indeed, the government's fiscal and economic objectives were explicitly formulated to meet the "convergence criteria" required for eventual membership in the EU's Economic and Monetary Union (see Chapters 8.1 and 8.4). Carlsson announced his decision to retire as party chair and prime minister in November 1995. He was succeeded by Göran Persson, a moderate Social Democrat and former minister of finance who was elected prime minister by the Riksdag in March 1996. Persson's election heralded the next phase in the continuing redefinition of the Swedish model. Under his leadership, the Social Democrats used executive power to modify public policy in accordance with EU norms while confronting the paradoxical consequences of electoral backlash and economic revitalization.

Sweden and the European Union

Also constraining traditional Social Democratic policy preferences for an expansive public sector and a regulated economy were Sweden's close ties with the European Community (EC).[12] Recognizing that the country's economic fortunes were inexorably linked with the EC by virtue of expanding trade with its continental neighbors, the Swedish cabinet had issued a policy paper in December 1987 outlining a strategy to promote intensified cooperation between Sweden and the EC.[13] The proposal entailed extensive coordination of Swedish monetary, fiscal, and industrial policies with those of the EC; elimination of existing restrictions on the free flow of investment capital; and deregulation of agriculture, including a gradual reduction in government subsidies to farmers. In this way, the government hoped to encourage the "increased movement of goods, services, people, and capital in Western Europe as well as the maintenance of full employment and social security."[14]

With the fall of the Berlin Wall less than two years later, symbolizing the collapse of Soviet-style communism in Central and Eastern Europe, Swedish leaders concluded that neutrality no longer precluded formal collaboration with the EC. Accordingly, Carlsson submitted a bid for membership in June 1991. Sweden negotiated an accession treaty with the European Union in 1993 that a majority of voters affirmed in a national referendum in November 1994 (see Chapter 5.2), and Sweden formally joined the EU on January 1, 1995.

Swedish membership in the EU coincided with stabilizing economic trends associated with expanding trade, government measures to encourage entrepreneurial initiatives through tax incentives and deregulation, and what the Organisation for Economic Co-operation and Development (OECD) has praised as a "sound macroeconomic policy approach" characterized by fiscal restraint and "solid public finances"[15] From 2004 through 2007 Sweden's average annual growth rate of 3.5 percent exceeded the Euro

Table 5-5 Swedish Referendum on the Introduction of the Euro, September 14, 2003

Options	Participation as percentage of eligible voters	Number of votes	Percentage of votes
	82.6	5,840,313	100.0
Yes to the euro		2,453,899	42.0
No to the euro		3,265,341	55.9
Blank ballots		121,073	2.1

Source: Statistiska centralbyrån [Statistics Sweden], *Statistisk årsbok för Sverige 2005* (Stockholm: Statistiska centralbyrån, 2005), 642.

Note: 3,475 ballots were declared void.

Area's annual average of 2.4 percent. (The Euro Area refers to the twelve member states of the EU that adopted the euro as a common currency beginning in January 1999.) During the same period, Sweden's average annual rate of inflation of 1.1 percent was half that of the Euro Area's 2.2 percent, while Sweden's average unemployment rate from 2004 through 2007 of 7.2 percent was under the Euro Area's rate of 8.4 percent.[16]

Paradoxically, Sweden's robust economic performance into the first decade of the twenty-first century proved a factor in the electorate's rejection of Swedish adoption of the euro by a resounding margin of 55.9 percent in a national referendum held on September 14, 2003 (see Table 5-5). Many voters were more impressed by their own country's economic performance than the Euro Area's desultory record of higher rates of inflation and unemployment (particularly in the larger member states of France, Germany, and Italy) and therefore preferred remaining outside the Economic and Monetary Union. Even more important as an impetus for the "no" vote were political considerations. Despite exhortations by the governing Social Democrats, Moderates, and Liberals that Swedish exclusion from the Euro Area would diminish the country's influence at EU headquarters in Brussels, most voters expressed concern about a loss of national sovereignty and "an unfocused sense that their welfare state is threatened by the EU."[17]

The anti-EU June List Party capitalized on such fears by mobilizing the third-highest vote total in the June 2004 election to the European Parliament after the Social Democrats and Moderates. June List candidates gained votes partly at the expense of the Left Party and the Greens (see Table 5-6). Support for the June List plummeted in the 2009 European

Table 5-6 Swedish Elections to the European Parliament, 1995–2009 (percentage distribution of party support)

Year	June List	Left Party	Greens	Pirate Party	Social Democratic Party	People's Party (Liberals)	Center Party	Moderate Party	Christian Democratic Union	Other
1995		12.9	17.2		28.1	4.8	7.2	23.2	3.9	1.9
1999		15.8	9.5		26.0	13.9	6.0	20.7	7.6	0.5
2004	14.5	12.8	6.0		24.6	9.9	6.3	18.2	5.7	1.7
2009	3.6	5.7	11.0	7.1	24.4	13.6	5.5	18.8	4,7	11.4[a]

[a] The total includes 5.7 percent votes cast for the European United Left and 2.2 percent for the Feminist Initiative.

Source: Statistiska centralbyrån [Statistics Sweden], www.scb.se/statistik/_publikationer/LE0001_2009K02_TI_02_A05TI0902.pdf

parliamentary election, while another new party, the Pirates—campaigning on a libertarian platform advocating citizen rights—won 7.1 percent of the national vote and two seats in the European Parliament. Despite ambivalence among many voters toward the EU, a majority of Swedish citizens affirm continued membership in the EU. For compelling economic reasons exit is not a viable option.

The 2006 Election, Nonsocialist Governance, and the International Economic Crisis

In the run-up to the September 2006 Riksdag elections, the Social Democrats had overseen an impressive average annual growth rate of nearly 3 percent but failed in their efforts to reduce a stubbornly high unemployment rate. More important, the SAP's historical legacy as a party of reform had clearly waned by then as a consequence of the government's embrace of neoliberal regulatory and monetary policies emanating from Brussels and the European Central Bank in Frankfurt.[18] Under these circumstances, Sweden's four nonsocialist parties—dominated by the resurgent Moderates under the energetic leadership of their new chair, Fredrik Reinfeldt—presented a credible electoral alternative. Campaigning under the joint banner of an "Alliance for Sweden" on a program of proposed tax cuts intended to benefit lower-income and middle-class voters, the nonsocialist bloc swept to a convincing victory with 48.2 percent of the popular vote (compared to 46.0 percent for the Social Democrats and their allies) and a majority of 178 seats in the Riksdag. Persson promptly stepped down as prime minister, and Reinfeldt was elected in his place as leader of a four-party nonsocialist coalition more united than ever.

The initial years of nonsocialist governance were characterized by a number of positive results. Exports of goods and services increased from 46.3 percent of GDP (2004) to 52.4 percent (2007), and Sweden's annual growth rate rose from 3.3 percent (2005) to 4.09 percent a year later. The unemployment rate fell from 8.0 percent (2005) to 7.0 percent in 2006 and to 6.0 percent in 2007.[19] In its 2007 assessment of the Swedish economy, the authoritative OECD praised the long-term effects of regulatory reforms introduced by the Social Democrats in the early 1990s in helping generate "excellent macroeconomic performance." It added that the "new government . . . has renewed the commitment to sound macroeconomic framework conditions."[20]

True to its campaign pledge, the nonsocialist coalition sponsored legislation in January 2007 to reduce income taxes for most wage earners over a two-year period. In a partial reversal of previous Social Democratic policies, the government also introduced tighter administrative rules governing the payment of disability pensions and health insurance benefits. The immediate result, the OECD noted in its 2007 report, was a perceptible decline in the number of sickness absences incurred by employees. A significant departure from previous policy was a sharp reduction in expenditures earmarked for active labor market policies from 8.2 percent of the 2006 budget to a minuscule 0.7 percent in 2008.[21]

The onset of the international financial and economic crisis in 2008 cast a pall over Sweden, as it did throughout the rest of Europe. Thanks to reforms instigated during the early 1990s by the Social Democrats,[22] the banking sector escaped the massive credit crunch and failures that afflicted banks in Britain, Iceland, the United States, and other industrialized nations, but leading economic indicators signaled a reversal of the OECD's initial optimistic prognosis. The annual growth rate plummeted to -0.4 percent by 2008,

New foreign investors have acquired ownership of both of Sweden's prestigious automobile firms, Volvo and Saab. In March 2010 the Ford Motor Company sold Volvo—whose assembly line in Torslanda, near Gothenburg on the western coast, is shown here—to Geely, one of China's largest automotive conglomerates. Earlier in the year, General Motors sold Saab to Spyker, a small Dutch company that specializes in the manufacture of sports cars.

Source: AFP/Getty Images

and unemployment was projected to rise to 10.7 percent by the end of 2010 as major companies laid off thousands of workers.

One of the potential candidates for liquidation was the automobile company Saab, which Sweden's leading airplane manufacturer had launched on the domestic market in 1949. Saab had become a prestigious niche export to the United States and northern Europe by the 1960s, and General Motors purchased the company in 1989 as part of its strategy to expand global manufacturing and marketing. GM's bankruptcy in 2009, however, compelled the company to suspend production at Saab's assembly lines and seek a new investor. In January 2010 GM announced that—with the help of the Swedish government—it had found a buyer in Spyker Cars, a small Dutch manufacturer of quality sports cars. The sale by no means guaranteed Saab's ultimate survival, but for the short term it preserved some 34,000 jobs.

In a parallel move, Ford Motor Company sold Sweden's largest automotive company, Volvo, in March 2010 to Zehjian Geely Auto in China. Volvo—the manufacturer of a prestige line of cars as well as heavy-duty trucks, buses, and numerous other products—was established in 1927 on the foundations of a ball-bearing company. It became a dominant force on the domestic market and emerged after World War II as one of the Sweden's leading exporters, with Western Europe and North America its principal markets. Ford purchased the Volvo car division in 1999 as part of a globalization strategy, but after sales faltered in the United States Ford decided to divest itself of the company. Volvo's new owner, Geely, is one of China's largest automotive conglomerates. Geely executives announced they would maintain Volvo as an autonomous enterprise with two assembly plants in Sweden, one in Belgium, and one in China.[23]

Partially mitigating the cumulative effect of negative economic trends was Sweden's management of the rotating presidency of the European Union during the second half of 2009. Prime Minister Reinfeldt displayed political finesse while chairing summit meetings of the European Council, as did fellow members of his cabinet at sessions of the Council of Ministers. Swedish officials emphasized collaborative efforts to combat the economic crisis and climate change as policy priorities during their EU presidency, but their greatest achievement was using discrete diplomacy to help promote the ratification and implementation of the Lisbon Treaty as the EU's new legal framework.[24] "We did our best," Carl Bildt, Sweden's foreign minister during the presidency, declared when Sweden handed over the office to Spain in January 2010.[25]

The 2010 Election: Swedish Politics under Duress

Sweden's sluggish economic performance mid-way through Prime Minister Reinfeldt's term initially portended an electoral threat comparable to those that befell previous cabinets, whether Social Democrat or nonsocialist. Cuts in social benefits enacted by the government at a time of increased unemployment helped the Social Democrats to post an eleven-point lead in voter preference over the Reinfeldt coalition in January 2010.[26]

A resumption in the rate of economic growth (from -4.7 percent in 2009 to a projected rate of 2.0 percent[27]), coupled with a lackluster campaign on the part of the Social Democrats, benefited the nonsocialists in the weeks leading up to the September election. While the three junior coalition partners all lost support compared to the 2006 results, the Moderates gained ten seats to enable the coalition to retain a majority over the socialist bloc (172 seats to 157). Sweden Democrats were the spoilers in the election, however—gaining twenty seats to deprive the nonsocialists of an absolute governing majority. Nevertheless, Prime Minister Reinfeldt reconstituted the nonsocialist cabinet as a minority government that will likely count on tactical support by members of the socialist opposition on specific legislative votes.

Swedish politics therefore has become more volatile in the face of recurrent economic flux, continuing electoral dealignment, and new social conflicts over issues such as immigration and individual rights. While Sweden remains distinctive with respect to a largely consensual form of democracy and extensive welfare entitlements, it has come to resemble more closely political norms associated with its European neighbors.

Like Britain, other fellow EU member states, and the United States, Sweden has become vulnerable to homegrown acts of terrorism, as graphically demonstrated by the abortive suicide bombing attack on a crowded Stockholm street in December 2010. In the event, only the bomber himself (a neutralized Swedish citizen of Iraqi parentage) was killed when his strapped-on explosives detonated prematurely.

NOTES

1. Stein Rokkan, "Norway: Numerical Democracy and Corporate Pluralism," in *Political Oppositions in Western Democracies,* ed. Robert Dahl (New Haven: Yale University Press, 1966), 107.

2. Statistiska centralbyrån [Statistics Sweden], *Statistisk årsbok för Sverige 2010* (Stockholm: Statistiska centralbyrån, 2010), 576. Swedish scholars reported that during a single legislative session, 1980–1981, the cabinet initiated fully 26,220 executive actions. They included 203 government bills, 4,434 budgetary and other decrees, 8,690 appeals, and 7,560 miscellaneous measures, including administrative appointments. Bengt Owe Birgersson and Jörgen Westerståhl, *Den svenska folkstyrelsen* (Stockholm: Liber Förlag, 1982), 171.

3. The averages are tabulated on the basis of annual data published in International Labour Office, *Year Book of Labour Statistics* (Geneva: ILO, 1950 to the present).

4. During the 1980s the number of working days lost in Sweden as a result of strikes and lockouts ranged from none in 1982 to 1.06 days per civilian worker in 1980. In Germany, the only statistically relevant year of conflict during the decade was 1984, when twenty-one working days per worker were lost.

5. A useful, though decidedly apolitical, account of postwar Swedish fiscal and monetary policy is Assar Lindbeck's *Swedish Economic Policy* (Berkeley and Los Angeles: University of California Press, 1974). A central component of the government's effort to facilitate structural and technological modernization on the part of Swedish industry and services has been greater public spending on research and development as part of an active industrial policy. See the chapter "Industrial Policies in the United Kingdom, Sweden, and Germany: A Study in Contrasts and Convergence," in *Managing Modern Capitalism: Industrial Renewal and Workplace Reform in the United States and Western Europe,* ed. M. Donald Hancock, John Logue, and Bernt Schiller (Westport, Conn.: Greenwood-Praeger, 1991).

6. Gösta Rehn, "The Wages of Success," *Daedalus* (Spring 1984): 142.

7. Statistiska centralbyrån, *Statistisk årsbook för Sverige 2010,* 379.

8. These reforms are described and assessed in greater detail in M. Donald Hancock and John Logue, "Sweden: The Quest for Economic Democracy," *Polity* (Fall/Winter 1984). Also see Bernt Schiller's chapter, "The Swedish Model Reconstituted," in Hancock, Logue, and Schiller, *Managing Modern Capitalism.*

9. According to the LO, "excess profits" were the additional profits gained by individual firms attributable to wage restraint exercised by the trade unions.

10. An excellent assessment of citizens' demands for new forms of political participation in Sweden is Olof Petersson's "Democracy and Power in Sweden," *Scandinavian Political Studies* 14 (1991): 173–191. Diane Sainsbury discusses efforts by the Social Democrats to respond to domestic economic and social change in "Swedish Social Democracy in Transition: The Party's Record in the 1980s and the Challenge of the 1990s," *West European Politics* 14 (1991): 31–57. The diffusion of postmaterialist values in Western democracies is explored in Ronald Inglehart, *The Silent Revolution: Changing Values and Political Styles among Western Publics* (Princeton, N.J.: Princeton University Press, 1977); and Inglehart, *Culture Shift in Advanced Industrial Democracies* (Princeton, N.J.: Princeton University Press, 1990).

11. Sweden, Ministry for Foreign Affairs, Press Section, "Statement of Government Policy Presented by the Prime Minister to Parliament, Friday 22 March 1996" (unofficial translation), Stockholm, 1996.

12. European Community (EC) officials declared their intention to eliminate the remaining restrictions on free trade and the movement of capital and labor within the EC with the

adoption of the Solemn Declaration on European Union in 1983 and the Single European Act in 1986. The Swedish cabinet coupled Sweden's affirmation of closer ties with the EC with a renewed declaration that prospective membership in the Community would be incompatible with the nation's traditional foreign policy of neutrality.

13. "Ökat samarbete utan medlemskap är Sveriges linje mot EG," *Från Riksdag & Departementet,* January 15, 1988, 13.

14. Sweden, Ministry for Foreign Affairs, Press Section, "Statement of Government Policy," Stockholm, December 1987.

15. Organisation for Economic Co-operation and Development, *OECD Economic Surveys, Sweden, 2004* (Paris: OECD, March 2004), 9.

16. Organisation for Economic Co-operation and Development, *Economic Outlook* 86, November 2009, 271, 283, 288. Throughout the first part of the decade, the Euro Area included Austria, Belgium, Finland, France, Germany, Greece, Ireland, Italy, Luxembourg, the Netherlands, Portugal, and Spain. Malta, Slovakia, and Slovenia subsequently joined, and Estonia will become a member in January 2011.

17. "Why Sweden Said No to the Euro," *Economist,* September 18, 2003, http://www.econo mist.com/research/articlesBySubject/displayStory.cfm?story_ID=2072849&subject= Sweden.

18. American political scientist John Logue has argued that the twin forces of globalization and Europeanization have severely diminished the capacity of the nation-state—in Sweden as elsewhere—to serve as "the appropriate unit for . . . economic and social policy-making." Logue, "Small Frogs, Big Pond. Can the Scandinavian Social Democratic Welfare States Adopt to Globalization?" paper presented at the conference on the Swedish EU Presidency and the Nordic Countries in the 21st Century, U.S. Department of State, Washington, D.C., January 22, 2001, 3, 14.

19. World Bank, *World Development Indicators,* http://ddp-ext.worldbank.org.

20. Organisation for Economic Co-Operation and Development, *Economic Surveys, Sweden, 2007* (Paris: OECD, 2007).

21. Statistiska centralbyrån, *Statistisk årsbok för Sverige 2010,* 379.

22. "Swedish crisis advice: Bite the bullet on banks," *International Herald Tribune,* January 23, 2009.

23. "Chinese Company Geely to Buy Volvo," *New York Times,* March 28, 2010.

24. See "Part 8: European Union" in this volume for details of the Lisbon Treaty.

25. An unforeseen consequence of the international economic crisis was increased public support for Sweden joining the Euro Zone and thereby adopting the euro in place of its own currency (the krona). According to a party preference survey conducted by Statistics Sweden in November 2009, a narrow plurality of voters would favor such a step: 43.8 in favor, 42.0 percent opposed, and 14.2 percent uncertain. "EMU/Euro preferences in Sweden 1997–2009. Party Preference Survey (PSU)," Statistiska centralbyrån, November 2009.

26. "Trouble at home. Sweden leans left again," *Economist,* January 21, 2010.

27. OECD, *Economic Outlook* 86.

What Is the Future of Swedish Politics?

5.5

INTERNATIONAL AND DOMESTIC TRENDS HAVE GRADUALLY TRANSFORMED the Swedish political model. In addition to the effects of globalization and Europeanization on domestic macroeconomic and social choices, Sweden has experienced an erosion in solidarity within the ranks of the Social Democrats and organized labor. At stake in the redefinition of the Swedish model is the continuing tension between the "breakthrough politics" of reform and the "rationalizing politics" of retrenchment.

Transforming Trends

An early trend contributing to the redefinition of the Swedish model was the abandonment of centralized wage negotiations on the labor market between the National Federation of Trade Unions (LO) and the Swedish Association of Employers (SAF). Simultaneous pressure by individual trade unions (notably in the engineering industries) and employer associations within the SAF to pursue direct bargaining over wages and other terms of employment yielded during the 1980s a more decentralized mode of industrial relations. Although direct negotiations have facilitated more flexible responses to changing labor market conditions, including labor shortages in manufacturing and construction, an unintended consequence was to undermine worker solidarity. The result was increased trade union "egoism" and heightened discord between public and private sector employees. Empirical measures of weakened solidarity among LO and Central Organization of Salaried Employees (TCO) members included an increase in strike activity during the latter part of the 1990s and resistance by the unions to Minister of Finance Kjell-Olof Feldt's ill-fated attempt to impose greater trade union discipline through legislation in February 1990.

A further change was heralded by the intermittent conflict between the LO and the Swedish Social Democratic Workers' Party (SAP) over important political issues. Incipient discord was already apparent during the 1970s when the LO promoted, more aggressively than the party itself, the introduction of wage-earner funds. LO leaders were partially mollified when the Social Democrats proceeded to introduce a version of the system in 1983, but the regional wage-earner funds were restricted in their capitalization and capacity to purchase majority shares in individual firms, which curtailed their effectiveness as a direct instrument of economic democratization. Instead, with the maturation of the wage-earner funds in 1990, the Social Democrats proposed that they be merged with existing national pension funds to create a series of five "superfunds" with capital assets totaling 430 billion kronor that would be used for investment purposes. The result was the demise of the wage-earner fund system as an instrument to promote economic democracy.

In the late 1980s tensions heightened between the Social Democrats and the LO over the government's austere budgetary policies and its agreement with the nonsocialist parties in 1988 to proceed with an overhaul of the tax system designed to benefit middle- and upper-income citizens. LO leaders charged that the reform would prove disadvantageous to lower-income workers and successfully pressed the SAP to grant marginal concessions. Despite continued LO misgivings, the tax reform was implemented on January 1, 1990.

Each of these outcomes reveals a gradual weakening of the LO in relation to other economic and political actors. Much like Tony Blair's "New Labour" in Great Britain, the SAP has marginally distanced itself from organized labor in its embrace of an EU-inspired neoliberal approach to economic and social management.

A social trend that threatens to undermine the long-term vitality of Sweden's welfare state is a gradual decline in employees' identification with the disciplined work ethic of earlier generations of workers. An empirical measure is the high number of Swedes who call in sick. Only 1.9 percent of employees within the European Union (EU) as a whole are ill for a week or more, but in 2002 nearly 10 percent of Swedish employees fell into that category.[1] Authorities attribute this extraordinarily high rate of absenteeism to Sweden's generous sick pay benefits, which, according to government officials and employer representatives, invite abuse of the system. As Eric S. Einhorn and John Logue have observed, "By transferring responsibility for dealing with all social ills to the society (the state), the welfare state diminishes the reciprocal responsibility of each individual for his or her family, neighbors, and workmates. It atomizes society, destroying a significant portion of the social fabric simply by making it unnecessary."[2] Recognizing the seriousness and high costs of absenteeism, the Persson government created a new ministerial post to deal with the issue and increased public funding for rehabilitation and improvements in the workplace.[3] Whether these measures will prove effective remains to be seen.

A Work in Progress

The transformation of the Swedish model remains a work in progress, characterized by multiple economic and political changes. While in office from 1991 to 1994 and again in 2006, the nonsocialist parties implemented some policy changes designed to trim the national budget deficit that proved to be highly unpopular. The nation's sluggish economic performance in the early 1990s, however, undermined the credibility of the nonsocialists to offer a viable set of policy alternatives to those of the Social Democrats. The cumulative effect of all this discontent was a convincing SAP victory in the 1994 national election. The same pattern may repeat itself in future elections.

Substantively, the Social Democrats have continued many of the policies initiated by the nonsocialists, particularly those directed at budgetary austerity and marginal reductions in welfare benefits. Under the leadership of former prime minister Göran Persson, who assumed office in 1996, the government simultaneously adjusted national policy principles in response to EU precepts. A primary example was "the transition to a credible inflation targeting regime, from the highly inflationary environment during the 1970s and 1980s, which embodied a cycle of excessive wage growth and exchange rate adjustment."[4] The government also gave the Central Bank greater independence and proclaimed price stability to be "the explicit objective of monetary policy," targeting an

Carl Bildt, former Moderate party chair and prime minister who was appointed foreign minister in 2006, is the international face of nonsocialist efforts to define a new "Swedish model" characterized by neo-liberal economic principles and greater social choice by individual citizens.

Source: Kamal Akray/epa/Corbis

annual inflation rate of 2 percent.[5] A central feature of the government's embrace of a neoliberal approach to economic management was deregulation in accordance with the EU's Single European Act directives of 1985 (see Chapter 8.3). According to the Organisation for Economic Co-operation and Development, "Sweden embraced rapidly all the directives under the internal-market programme of the European Union. . . . Sweden has gone farther than most countries in exposing the former public monopolies to competition."[6]

'Breakthrough' versus 'Rationalizing' Politics

Policy enactments by both the nonsocialists and Social Democrats represent a retreat in Sweden from the distinction policy specialist Lawrence D. Brown draws between "breakthrough politics" and a more restrictive style of "rationalizing politics" (see Chapter 5.1).[7] From their rise to power in 1932 through most of the postwar period, the Social Democrats sponsored successive breakthrough initiatives that had the cumulative effect of achieving a distinctive model of advanced industrial society: implementation of a coordinated approach to economic management, extension of welfare benefits, introduction of a supplementary pension system (which not only provided individualized retirement benefits but also gave the state significant sources of investment capital), legislation during the 1970s that extended workers' rights, and creation of the wage-earner fund system.

By the early 1980s, however, the Social Democrats had embarked on a strategy of ideological retrenchment when they began to embrace a market approach to economic management and suspended the march toward economic democracy as well as further social reforms. The welfare state remains largely intact, but in practice the Social Democrats have acted in concert with nonsocialist government officials to harmonize Swedish policies with those of the EU. In the process, both the SAP and the nonsocialists have shifted course toward a "rationalizing" approach to public policy. An important consequence, in the view of Swedish co-authors of a critical analysis of Swedish democracy, is "the fall of the strong state," which is characterized by weakened linkages between elections and policy.[8] Nonsocialist leaders have celebrated these changes as the basis for a new "Swedish model" of decentralized power and greater citizen autonomy. Whether Sweden's contemporary era of rationalizing politics will necessarily make politics "more problem-free," as Brown suggests, is another question.

NOTES

1. "Not Healthy: Too Many Employees Are Off 'Sick,'" *Economist,* October 24, 2002, 1.
2. Eric S. Einhorn and John Logue, *Modern Welfare States: Scandinavian Politics and Policy in the Global Age,* 2nd ed. (New York: Praeger, 2003), 310.
3. "Not Healthy," 2.
4. Organisation for Economic Co-Operation and Development, *OECD Economic Surveys, Sweden, 1998–1999* (Paris: OECD, 1999), 10.
5. Ibid., 11–12.
6. Ibid., 15.
7. Lawrence D. Brown, *New Policies, New Politics: Government's Response to Government's Growth* (Washington, D.C.: Brookings, 1983).
8. Johannes Lindvall and Bo Rothstein, "Sweden: The Fall of the Strong State," *Scandinavian Political Studies* 29 (2006): 47–63.

FOR FURTHER READING

Adler-Karlson, G. *Functional Socialism: A Swedish Theory for Democratic Socialism.* Stockholm: Prisma, 1969.

Anton, Thomas J. *Administered Politics: Elite Political Culture in Sweden.* The Hague/London/Boston: Martinus Nijhoff, 1980.

Aspalter, Christian. *The Importance of Christian and Social Democratic Movements in Welfare Politics: With Special Reference to Germany, Austria and Sweden.* New York: Nova Science Publishers, 2001.

Castles, Francis. *The Social Democratic Image of Society: A Study of the Achievements and Origins of Scandinavian Social Democracy in a Comparative Perspective.* Boston: Routledge and Kegan Paul, 1978.

Childs, Marquis W. *Sweden: The Middle Way on Trial.* New Haven: Yale University Press, 1980.

Daedalus, "Nordic Voices" (Spring 1984); and "The Nordic Enigma" (Winter 1984).

Einhorn, Eric S., and John Logue. *Modern Welfare States: Scandinavian Politics and Policy in the Global Age.* 2nd ed. New York: Praeger, 2003.

Esping-Andersen, Gøsta. *Politics against Markets: The Social Democratic Road to Power.* Princeton, N.J.: Princeton University Press, 1985.

———. *Social Foundations of Postindustrial Economics.* Oxford and New York: Oxford University Press, 1999.

Freeman, Richard B., Robert Topen, and Birgitta Swedenborg. *The Welfare State in Transition: Reforming the Swedish Model.* Chicago: University of Chicago Press, 1997.

Freeman, Ruth. *Death of a Statesman. The Solution to the Murder of Olof Palme.* London: Robert Hale, 1989.

Furniss, Norman, ed. *Futures for the Welfare State.* Bloomington: Indiana University Press, 1986.

Furniss, Norman, and Timothy Tilton. *The Case for the Welfare State.* Bloomington: Indiana University Press, 1977.

Geyer, Robert, Christine Ingebritsen, and Jonathan Moses, eds. *Globalization, Europeanization and the End of Scandinavian Social Democracy?* Basingstoke and London: Macmillan; New York: St. Martin's Press, 2000.

Giddens, Anthony. *The Third Way and Its Critics.* Cambridge, UK: Polity Press, 2000.

Hancock, M. Donald. *Sweden: The Politics of Postindustrial Change.* Hinsdale, Ill.: Dryden Press, 1972.

Hancock, M. Donald, and John Logue. "Sweden: The Quest for Economic Democracy." *Polity* 16 (Winter 1984): 248–270.

Hancock, M. Donald, John Logue, and Bernt Schiller, eds. *Managing Modern Capitalism: Industrial Renewal and Workplace Democracy in the United States and Western Europe.* New York and Westport, Conn.: Greenwood Press, 1991.

Heckscher, Gunnar. *The Welfare State and Beyond: Success and Problems in Scandinavia.* Minneapolis: University of Minnesota Press, 1984.

Heclo, Hugh. *Modern Social Politics in Britain and Sweden.* New Haven: Yale University Press, 1974.

Heclo, Hugh, and Henrik Madsen. *Policy and Politics in Sweden: Principled Pragmatism.* Philadelphia: Temple University Press, 1987.

Heidenheimer, Arnold J., Hugh Heclo, and Carolyn Teich Adams. *Comparative Public Policy: The Politics of Social Choice in Europe and America.* 3rd ed. New York: St. Martin's Press, 1990.

Katzenstein, Peter. *Small States in World Markets.* Ithaca, N.Y.: Cornell University Press, 1985.

Koblik, Steven, ed. *Sweden's Development from Poverty to Affluence, 1750–1970.* Minneapolis: University of Minnesota Press, 1975.

Korpi, Walter. *The Democratic Class Struggle.* London: Routledge and Kegan Paul, 1983.

———. *The Working Class in Welfare Capitalism: Work, Unions and Politics in Sweden.* London: Routledge and Kegan Paul, 1981.

Lewin, Leif. *Ideology and Strategy: A Century of Swedish Politics.* New York: Cambridge University Press, 1988.

Lindbeck, Assar. *Swedish Economic Policy.* Berkeley: University of California Press, 1974.

———. *The Swedish Experiment.* Stockholm: SNS Förlag, 1997.

Lindvall, Johannes and Bo Rothstein, "Sweden: The Fall of the Strong State." *Scandinavian Political Studies* 29 (2006): 47–63.

Meidner, Rudolf. *Employee Investment Funds: An Approach to Collective Capital Formation.* London: Allen and Unwin, 1978.

Milner, Henry. *Sweden: Social Democracy in Practice.* New York: Oxford University Press, 1989.

Misgeld, Klaus, Karl Molin, and Klas Åmark, eds. *Creating Social Democracy. A Century of the Social Democratic Labor Party in Sweden.* University Park: Pennsylvania State University Press, 1992.

Olsen, Gregg M. *The Struggle for Economic Democracy in Sweden.* Aldershot, UK: Ashgate, 1992.

Petersson, Olof. *The Government and Politics of the Nordic Countries.* Stockholm: Fritzes, 1994.

Ponusson, Jones. *The Limits of Social Democracy: Investment Politics in Sweden.* Ithaca, N.Y.: Cornell University Press, 1992.

Rothstein, Bo. *The Social Democratic State: The Swedish Model and the Bureaucratic Problem of Social Reforms.* Pittsburgh: University of Pittsburgh Press, 1996.

Rustow, Dankwart A. *The Politics of Compromise: A Study of Parties and Cabinet Government in Sweden.* Princeton, N.J.: Princeton University Press, 1955.

Sahr, Robert C. *The Politics of Energy Policy Change in Sweden.* Ann Arbor: University of Michigan Press, 1985.

Sainsbury, Diane. "Swedish Social Democracy in Transition: The Party's Record in the 1980s and the Challenge of the 1990s." *West European Politics* 14 (1991): 31–57.

Schiller, Bernt, et al. *The Future of the Nordic Model of Labour Relations: Three Reports on Internationalization and Industrial Relations.* Copenhagen: Nordic Council of Ministers, 1993.

Scott, Franklin D. *Sweden: The Nation's History.* Minneapolis: University of Minnesota Press, 1977.

Sullivan, Michael. *The Politics of Social Policy.* Herts, UK: Harvester Wheatsheaf, 1992.

Tilton, Timothy. *The Political Theory of Swedish Social Democracy: Through the Welfare State to Socialism.* New York: Oxford University Press, 1990.

Tomasson, Richard F. *Sweden: Prototype of Modern Society.* New York: Random House, 1970.

Wheeler, Christopher. *White-Collar Power: Changing Patterns of Interest Group Behavior in Sweden.* Urbana: University of Illinois Press, 1975.

Whyman, Philip. *An Analysis of the Economic Democracy Reforms in Sweden.* Lewiston, UK: Edwin Mellen Press, 2004.

Part 6

Russia

Stephen White

The Context of Russian Politics

WINSTON CHURCHILL ONCE COMPLAINED THAT RUSSIA WAS A "RIDDLE in a mystery wrapped inside an enigma." A nineteenth-century Russian poet, Fedor Tiuchev, went even further: Russia, he insisted, could not be understood, it could "only be believed in." Modern social scientists are understandably less willing to explain the politics of the world's largest state by referring to the complexities of the Slavic soul. Like everywhere else, its resources are limited, and their allocation is determined by the competition of organized interests within a structured framework. But if Russia is not unique, it certainly is distinctive: in its territorial expanse, its encompassing of Europe and Asia, its centuries-long experience of authoritarian rule. Its distinctive characteristics, in turn, have helped to shape a political system that combines the formal institutions of Western democracy with a strong emphasis on central leadership of a kind that has not always attached the same importance to the rights of ordinary citizens.

A Continent More than a Country

Of all the forces that make Russia what it is today, geography is arguably the most important. Every Russian government, whatever its political complexion, has to reckon with the fact that this is the world's largest state (more than 17 million square kilometers, or about a seventh of the world's land surface) with an extraordinary variety of human and physical features. Such is its size and variety that it is better described as a continent than as a country. Its land area stretches over 9,000 kilometers across Europe and Asia, from the Atlantic to the Pacific, embracing eleven different time zones, and over some 4,000 kilometers from north to south. It shares the world's longest land frontier with China and has the world's longest (mostly frozen) coastline. And it borders sixteen other states, from Norway and Finland in the west to Mongolia and North Korea in the Far East, and then to sea borders with Japan and the United States. Many of these borders, since the collapse of the Union of Soviet Socialist Republics (USSR) and the emergence of an independent Russian state at the end of 1991, are still undemarcated, and some border areas—such as the Kurile Islands, claimed by Japan—are in dispute.

The great extent and variety of the Russian landmass have always made it difficult for central governments in the Kremlin to impose their authority on outlying areas, especially in earlier centuries when communications were few and imperfect. Russia's great size presents major difficulties for the national railway and air transport systems, which operate on Moscow time to avoid total confusion. Similar difficulties face Russian radio and television, which have to rebroadcast their programs at different times in different time zones. Russia's vast open boundaries have subjected it to frequent invasions, from the east as well as the west. But its enormous size has meant that this country is almost impossible to conquer, as warlords from the Tatars, Poles, and Swedes to Napoleon in the early nine-teenth century to Hitler's armies during World War II all discovered to their cost.

The climate makes a difference as well, with its wide variations from place to place and from season to season, largely because few parts of Russia are close to the moderating influence of the sea. In fact, unlike most of the world's other industrial powers, the whole of Russia lies in the northern latitudes. Its northernmost point is just a few hundred miles south of the North Pole, and 40 percent of its surface area consists of permafrost—land that is permanently frozen. The southernmost parts of the Russian landmass, by contrast, are in the subtropical regions that border on the Black and Caspian Seas, and farther south is desert. Moscow, the capital, is about as far north as Newfoundland in Canada, but it is much colder in January (when the average temperature is −9°C) and rather warmer in summer (the average temperature in July is 18°C). St. Petersburg, the former capital, is nearly as far north as Anchorage, Alaska; the average temperature in St. Petersburg is −8°C in January and 17°C in July.

Elsewhere in the country the range of climate variation is far greater. Yakutsk, in eastern Siberia, has an average January temperature of −44°C. Temperatures there are as low as anywhere in the inhabited world, but in summer they are as high as in most parts of west-ern Europe (an average of 19°C in July). This wide range of climatic variation makes agriculture difficult in all but the most temperate parts of the country, hinders transport, and makes construction slow and much more expensive (at such low temperatures metal becomes brittle and oil rapidly solidifies). Some observers have even speculated that the variation in climate may help to explain the Russian character, with its characteristic swings between sorrow and joy, apathy and enthusiasm, and sobriety and drunkenness.

Climate, in turn, has implications for settlement. Population densities across the country as a whole are relatively low at just 8.7 persons per square kilometer, which is half the level of the United States and just a seventeenth of the population density of the European Union. What matters more is that settlement is unevenly distributed, with nearly 80 percent of the population concentrated in the European part of the country, which accounts for no more than a quarter of the total land area. The far north, by con-trast, with about 70 percent of the country's land area, has only 8 percent of its entire population. There is a similar mismatch between the distribution of population and of natural resources. More than three-quarters of Russian industry is in European Russia, to the west of the Urals. But 90 percent of the country's coal reserves lie in Siberia and the Far East, as do most of its oil and gas and two-thirds of its hydroelectric power potential. That potential is enormous: Russia accounts for more than a third of the world's known reserves of gas and for between 12 percent and 13 percent of its oil. There is even a mismatch in the water supply, with only 16 percent of Russia's river water flowing across its central and southern regions, and most of its 120,000 rivers emptying them-selves uselessly into the Arctic Ocean.[1]

A Slavic People

Russia is equally varied in its ethnic composition, although Russians and other Slavs account for the overwhelming majority (see Table 6-1). Russia, in fact, has never been more "Russian" than it is today: the population of the Russian Empire in 1897 was just 43 percent ethnically Russian, and in the Soviet period Russians were just over half the

Table 6-1 Some Characteristics of Russia's Population

Total population (January 2010)	**141,904,000**
Gender composition (percent)	
Male	46
Female	54
Geographical distribution (percent)	
Urban	73
Rural	27
Ethnic composition (2002 census, percent)	
Russian	79.8
Tatar	3.8
Ukrainian	2.0
Bashkir	1.2
Chuvash	1.1
Other	12.1

Source: Compiled by the author from official statistics.

total. Altogether, contemporary Russia is made up of at least a hundred recognized nationalities, who speak 155 languages, of which 80 are also written and about 100 are sustained by substantial indigenous communities. Russian, for obvious reasons, is the most widely spoken language (at the time of the 2002 census more than 98 percent of the population claimed to speak it fluently, in most cases as a native language). Perhaps surprising, English is the second most widely spoken language (nearly 7 million claimed to speak it fluently), followed by Tatar (5.3 million), German (2.9 million), and Ukrainian (1.8 million). Russian is recognized as the official state language (other languages may have official status at lower levels of government), and it operates as the medium through which the country's different nationalities most easily communicate with each other.

Because many Russians lived outside their own republic during the Soviet years, at the end of 1991, when the Soviet Union broke up, they found themselves in newly independent and foreign states. At the time of the last Soviet census in 1989, nearly 83 percent of all Russians lived within the Russian Federation, and nearly 82 percent of the population of the Russian Federation consisted of Russians. More than 25 million Russians lived in other Soviet republics—more than 11 million lived in Ukraine and more than 6 million lived in Kazakhstan—often constituting a large proportion of the population of the state in which they resided: more than a fifth of the population of newly independent Ukraine and about a third of the populations of Kazakhstan, Latvia, and Estonia. Understandably, the fate of these fellow nationals has been a central concern of Russian foreign policy makers, particularly in the Baltic States, where Russian nationals have been denied citizenship and the right to vote unless they satisfy various linguistic and other requirements.

Russians are united by their religion, as well as by their language and territory. Historically, they are a Christian people, members of the Russian Orthodox Church, which is a branch of Eastern Christianity. Although all confessions suffered from a variety of forms of direct and indirect repression during the Soviet period, at least half of the Russian population—according to survey evidence—claims to be believers. Yet few attend church with the regularity that is a feature of many Western countries. About 8 percent of the adult population attended a service at least once a month in the early 2000s, compared with 19 percent in the United Kingdom and 48 percent (an unusually high figure in comparative terms) in the United States.[2] Although Russians are often prepared to identify themselves as Orthodox and as believers, they also appear to be unsure of many of the essentials of their faith. Atheists, for their part, are often positive toward the role of Orthodoxy in their society, attend church services on a regular basis, and want their children to have a religious upbringing. These loose and amorphous patterns have helped to ensure that there are few clear divisions between believers and others in their political attitudes or party support, although frequent church attendees (like those in other countries) are somewhat more inclined to support "conservative" positions on questions related to censorship, the role of women, or the rights of sexual minorities.

Patterns of History

Russia today is a product of its history as well as of its geography, and some features of its past still figure prominently in attempts to understand present-day Russian policies and attitudes.[3] One of the most important of these legacies is the tradition of autocratic rule, a pattern established in early medieval times and virtually unbroken up to the present. Scandinavian traders—the records suggest—established the first Russian state, founded in the ninth century in the city republics of Novgorod and Kiev, of which Kiev quickly became the cultural capital. It was under one of the first rulers of this Kievan state, Vladimir, that Russia embraced Christianity as its official religion and later began to establish its own codes of law. But an enduring pattern was soon established of disputed successions and local rivalries, and this pattern made it less easy to defend the new state against outside invaders. Profiting from these divisions, Mongol armies led by the grandson of Genghis Khan overran the country in the thirteenth century, taking Kiev and the other major cities and imposing a pattern of subordination, tribute, and military service. The patronage of the Mongols helped the city of Moscow to establish a dominant position among the Russian principalities, and that position, in turn, allowed the city to assemble a military force and lead it to victory over the Mongols at the battle of Kulikovo Field in 1380 and to the final overthrow of the "Mongol yoke" in the next century.

Under a succession of skillful leaders, Moscow extended its rule over other Russian cities and established itself as the core of a revived and independent Russian state. Ivan the Terrible, the first to be known as tsar, began Russia's territorial expansion to the east, annexing the Kazan khanate in 1552 as the Mongol empire began to collapse. Russia's territorial boundaries expanded rapidly in the seventeenth and eighteenth centuries, and relations became closer with the rest of Europe, particularly under the modernizing leadership of Peter the Great (1682–1725). A large part of Poland and Lithuania was annexed under Catherine the Great in the late eighteenth century, together with the northern shores of the Black Sea. In the nineteenth century Russia advanced into Central Asia and the Far East, in a pattern that was reminiscent of the colonial expansion that other European powers were conducting in their overseas dominions. It was an empire built on conquest and occupation, and any resistance was mercilessly suppressed. Poland, which rose several times in resistance, was eventually incorporated as a Russian province and its people subjected to a campaign of Russification.

Russian rule was autocratic—not just in its territorial acquisitions but also within the lands that formed the historic core of the state itself. Tsars and emperors ruled with a firm hand; their subjects had little influence on the decisions of government; and the rights and liberties of subjects were poorly respected even by the standards of the time. Under the laws of the empire, the tsar was an absolute ruler, subordinate only to God. The nobility were scarcely a check on his authority, because their position was defined by state service; the commercial and professional classes were few in number and weak in political influence. Considerable changes did take place in the later tsarist period, particularly after 1905 when a constitutional reform allowed an elected parliamentary body (the State Duma) to come into existence. But its electoral base was narrow and its powers were limited: it had no direct influence on the composition of government or on two-thirds of state expenditure. A limited freedom of the press was also permitted after 1905, and bodies such as trade unions and political parties were given some legal standing. In 1917 the Provisional Government extended these freedoms further. But even the most generous interpretation makes it clear that this move represented a short break in a tradition of authoritarianism that arguably survives to the present day.

Russians, in addition, were accustomed to a state that was prominent in economic and social life, as owner and manager and not simply as custodian of the public interest. Before 1917, as well as after, the state owned a considerable proportion of the country's productive resources, including coal, oil, and gold, and most of the railway system. By the time serfdom was abolished in 1861, more peasants were in the hands of the state than in the hands of private landlords. The state had a large measure of control over the other parts of the economy through the banking system, and particularly through the State Bank, which was the largest in the world in the assets it controlled and a central agency of economic management. In addition, the state decided appointments and regulated what was taught at all levels of education, and it exercised a strict system of censorship over all forms of publication. One of its decisions was to allow the publication of Karl Marx's *Kapital* on the grounds that it was far too complicated to influence an ordinary worker, but Bolshevik newspapers had to be smuggled into the country in false-bottomed suitcases, and all Western publications were carefully scrutinized at the border.

The rule of law was limited. Despite the significant reforms of the 1860s, including a declaration that judges were independent of government, there was no trial by jury in political cases, and a system of special courts introduced in 1881 allowed the governors in each region to arrest or exile any citizen, to ban any meeting, and to close any newspaper or journal. Large numbers of citizens were held in prison camps in various parts of the country or were exiled to remote places for extended periods. Vladimir Lenin's brother lost his life for his part in a conspiracy to assassinate the tsar, and the Soviet leader himself spent three years in Siberia. The state also exercised a considerable degree of influence over organized religion. The Russian Orthodox Church, as the national church, was given a series of privileges as well as financial support, and other denominations were subject to various forms of discrimination (this was most obviously true in the case of Jews, who were allowed to live only in certain parts of the country—the Pale of Settlement—and were admitted to higher education in deliberately restricted numbers).

Government control was admittedly far less effective outside the towns, and the great majority of citizens who still lived in the countryside were normally able to get on with their lives with little external interference. Villagers were generally part of a peasant commune, the *mir,* and their social world revolved around it. The *mir* made its decisions collectively, and usually unanimously, based on the participation of the heads of all the households concerned. It was responsible for most of the economic activities of the community and for administrative matters such as taxation and military service, and it took a close interest in the beliefs and behavior of its members as well. Although the *mir* was beginning to break up in the years before World War I, in part because of government support for individual farming, it was the way in which the social world of the great majority of Russians was organized until comparatively recent times. It would be surprising, in turn, if adoption of the *mir* did not have at least something to do with the apparent acceptability to many Russians in Soviet and more recent times of forms of government that are authoritarian and collectivist, but which also include some genuine concern for the public welfare.

The Impact of Communist Rule

There was strong support for a change from tsarist rule in 1917, although not necessarily for a Bolshevik dictatorship. The old regime had provided incompetent leadership during the war; the court itself was compromised by the German nationality of the empress and by the unsavory intrigues that circulated around Rasputin, the semiliterate Siberian monk who established a hold over the tsarina and who was eventually put to death by patriotic noblemen in 1916. Tsarist rule was ended by the February Revolution of 1917, which led to the abdication of Nicholas II and the formation of a Provisional Government headed by Alexander Kerensky, a moderate socialist. But the new government failed to provide decisive leadership, above all by its refusal to withdraw from an increasingly disastrous war, and in October (or, by the Western calendar, early November) it was replaced by a Soviet government headed by Vladimir Ilich Ulyanov, more widely known by the name he used in revolutionary politics, Lenin. In the elections to a constituent assembly that took place over the following weeks, Lenin's Bolshevik Party took about a quarter of the vote, but it had a majority in the bigger cities. About two-thirds of the vote went to socialist parties that were committed in various ways to a republic that would give a wider range of rights to ordinary people.

Lenin had not expected a Soviet government to be able to remain in power in an isolated country. Russia, after all, was one of Europe's most backward regions, far from the developed capitalism that Marx had suggested was the natural precursor to a socialist society. By itself, all Russia could do was to set off a wider European and then a worldwide revolution, taking advantage of the fact that the major capitalist countries were interconnected and that Russia was their "weakest link." In the event, it took some time for the Soviet government to establish authority within its own territory after a civil war and foreign intervention failed to dislodge it. After the early 1920s, there was no serious domestic challenge to the Soviet government, and over the seventy years or more in which it was in power the new regime pushed through a series of policies that were designed to reshape all aspects of the society it had inherited.

One of the most important features of the new regime was political monopoly. The early Soviet government was a coalition, but after the summer of 1918 the Bolsheviks ruled by themselves, acting in the name of a "dictatorship of the proletariat." Detailed censorship was imposed on a "temporary" basis that lasted until the end of the 1980s.

Opposition parties were marginalized and then closed down. Elections became increasingly formalistic, and elected institutions became passive instruments of the ruling party. Within the party itself, internal opposition and differing opinions of any kind were gradually eliminated. The party leadership became a source of unchallengeable authority, and within it the general secretary (Joseph Stalin from 1922 until his death) became the central figure. Lenin died in 1924, and by the end of the decade Stalin had succeeded in establishing his dominance. Under Stalin's leadership authoritarianism became a full-fledged terror. The lowest point was in the late 1930s, when a series of show trials were staged at which former members of the leadership confessed to the most ridiculous of "crimes," such as plotting to assassinate Lenin. No agreement exists on the number of victims of the purges, which swept across the whole of the society and not simply the political elite, but it is clear that at least 600,000 death sentences were handed out for what were essentially political offenses between the late 1930s and 1953.[4] In addition to executions, the population suffered prison sentences, periods of exile, and other forms of repression.

During the years of Stalinist rule, a full-scale offensive was launched to industrialize and collectivize the still-backward society. Industrialization involved eliminating what remained

Joseph Stalin (1878–1953) speaks to a meeting on agricultural collectivization in 1935. Stalin was already the dominant figure in Soviet politics, but he had not yet launched the full-scale repression that was associated with the purge trials of his political opponents.

Source: AP Images

of private ownership and expanding production at a rate that was without historical precedent. Industrialization was promoted by a series of five-year plans, the first of which was introduced in 1928 and pronounced achieved "ahead of time" in 1932. The plans, which emphasized heavy industry and defense rather than consumer goods, recorded impressive achievements. In 1928 Soviet industrial output was just 7 percent of the corresponding U.S. figure; by 1938 it was up to 45 percent. To many inside the Soviet Union and even outside it, the country appeared to have discovered the secret of rapid and continuing economic growth at a time when the West was suffering from depression and mass unemployment. Indeed, "the plan" became a rallying point, and the whole country began to be organized around its continuous fulfillment. Reflecting the popular enthusiasm, parents and others began to call children "Tractor," "Five-Year Plan," or even "Ninel" (Lenin spelled backward).

The collectivization of agriculture was launched a year after the conclusion of the first five-year plan, in 1929. By then only 4 percent of rural homesteads had been "collectivized" or grouped into rural cooperatives. By 1938 more than 93 percent fell into this category. The collectivization campaign focused particularly on *kulaks,* who were defined as rich and exploiting farmers but who were often simply more efficient. Stalin called for their "liquidation as a class." The campaign, however, extended much further as the regime consolidated its control over the countryside and brought the entire society within its ambit. As many as 6 million citizens died in one of the largest and most brutal social changes ever attempted.

The modern Soviet Union emerged from these harsh processes of change. It was also shaped by the impact of war, when German leader Adolf Hitler broke off the Nazi-Soviet Pact of 1939 and ordered an invasion of the Soviet Union in 1941. The German army blockaded Leningrad and reached the outskirts of Moscow, but the resistance was determined, and the harsh winter conditions took their toll on the enemy. A turning point in the conflict was the Battle of Stalingrad in 1943, when Field Marshal Friedrich Paulus and his huge army were forced to surrender. The Red Army was able to launch a counteroffensive and in 1945 it was the first to reach Berlin and plant its flag on the Reichstag. But the losses suffered in the war were enormous: at least 27 million dead (half of them civilians or prisoners), 25 million left homeless, and transport and industry devastated. The war had other effects as well: it helped to legitimate Communist Party rule (it had led the resistance, and 3 million of its own members had died), and it increased the determination of Soviet leaders to ensure that at the Yalta conference in 1945 they established firm control over Eastern Europe.

Communist rule began to liberalize after the war, reflecting a society that was itself maturing. The single most important development was the Communist Party's 20th Congress in 1956, at which party first secretary Nikita Khrushchev accused his predecessor, Stalin, of a "whole series of exceedingly serious and grave perversions of party principles, of party democracy and of revolutionary legality." Over the years that followed, there was a gradual attempt to establish at least a limited rule of law, or "socialist legality." There was greater freedom in the arts, even to the point that Alexander Solzhenitsyn was allowed to publish his harrowing account of a Stalinist prison camp, *One Day in the Life of Ivan Denisovich* (1962). Internationally, the Soviet Union established closer relations with India, Egypt, and other developing countries. Khrushchev also made the first-ever visit by a Soviet leader to the United States, where he got into an argument with President Richard Nixon and banged his shoe on the podium at the United Nations. The momentum of reform slowed down under Khrushchev's successor, Leonid Brezhnev, party leader from 1964 up to 1982, but it speeded up again under Yuri Andropov (1982–1984) and then acquired an entirely new scope and purpose under Mikhail Gorbachev (1985–1991), when it became known as *perestroika,* or "restructuring."

Political Development and Democratization

It proved much easier to dismantle communist rule than to construct a democratic political system in its place. The Soviet system, after all, had lasted more than two generations. By the time of the 1989 census, more than 70 percent of the population had been born since World War II, and very few had any personal experience of another form of society. More positively, it was a system that had "won the war," with Communist Party members in the front line. It had eliminated illiteracy (or at least it claimed to have done so—the 1989 census found that more than 4 million, mostly elderly, were still unable to read and write). It had pioneered the exploration of outer space. The circulation of daily newspapers, another indicator of "modernity," was among the highest in the world. Almost everyone also had a television by 1989, although less than half of the population had a telephone. There were more professionals, and more tourists in both directions. It was, indeed, one of the explanations for the end of communist rule that it had been outgrown by the complexity of Soviet society as a result of the changes that the Communist Party itself had sponsored.

Clearly, the passage of time could be no guarantee of regime survival. But in the Soviet case, the regime lacked a model to follow. It could not return to Russia's precommunist past. There was no precommunist constitution, as there had been in each of the Baltic republics, and there were no traditions of competitive elections, as there had been in most of East Central Europe. Equally, almost all of the members of the governing group had acquired their political experience in the Soviet system, and usually within the senior ranks of the Communist Party. The dissidents who had led mass movements to power in Eastern Europe did not exist inside Russia. Boris Yeltsin, Russia's first president, had been a party member for thirty years, and about three-quarters of the leadership as a whole had their origins in the communist *nomenklatura* (as leading officials were known). Indeed, in some respects communist rule continued after the Soviet Union dissolved: the Communist Party of the Russian Federation took a large share of the vote at successive elections, and it controlled a series of local assemblies and governorships.

Other, longer-term continuities went back further than seventy years. One of these was the relative powerlessness of the ordinary citizen. The new constitution guaranteed multi-party politics, but political parties were weakly developed, and electoral contests were weighted heavily in favor of the Kremlin and the parties and candidates it had chosen to support. The rule of law scarcely existed, and the state could not stop the steadily rising tide of crime and corruption. There was a wide diversity of opinion in the press, but readership had dropped to low levels, and the state had established effective control over all the national television channels in a way that, for some, was very Soviet. By the early 2000s, Russia was no longer a communist system; but it fell some distance short of the accountable relationship between rulers and ruled, within a framework of law and human rights, that is central to most definitions of democracy.

Gorbachev and Perestroika

A very different atmosphere had prevailed in March 1985 when a vigorous, stocky Politburo member from the south of Russia became the leader of what was still a united and ruling party. Mikhail Gorbachev, according to his wife, Raisa, had not expected the nomination and spent some time deciding whether to accept it. All that was clear was that (in a phrase that later became famous) "we just can't go on like this." The advent of a new general secretary had made a considerable difference in the past to the direction of public policy, although any change took some time to establish itself as the new leader marginalized his opponents and promoted his supporters to positions within the leadership. Gorbachev, however, told the Politburo members who agreed to nominate him that there was "no need to change [their] policies."[5] He gave little indication at the outset that he was likely to advance what eventually became a comprehensive reform program. Indeed, little was known about his thinking. The new general secretary had not addressed a party congress, had no published collection of writings to his name, and had made just two official visits to other countries—Canada and the United Kingdom—on both occasions as the head of a delegation of Soviet parliamentarians. Only a few important speeches—in particular, an address to an ideology conference in December 1984 and an electoral address in February 1985 that mentioned *glasnost,* social justice, and participation—gave some indication of his personal priorities.[6]

It was some time, in fact, before a new policy agenda began to take shape. In his acceptance speech, Gorbachev paid the customary tribute to his immediate predecessors, Yuri Andropov and Konstantin Chernenko (who served briefly from 1984 to 1985), and pledged to continue their policy of "acceleration of socio-economic development and the perfection of all aspects of social life," which was the political language of the Brezhnev era. In April 1985, at the first Central Committee he addressed as leader, he spoke in a fairly orthodox manner about the need for a "qualitatively new state of society," including modernization of the economy and extension of socialist democracy. The central issue in these early months was the acceleration of economic growth. Such acceleration was quite feasible, Gorbachev thought, if the "human factor" was called more fully into play and if the reserves throughout the economy were properly utilized. This progress, in turn, would require a greater degree of decentralization, including cost accounting at the enterprise level and a closer connection between the work people did and the payment they received. But he did not mention "radical reform," let alone a "market." In the months that followed, however, he gradually assembled a leadership team that could direct these changes and the further extension of what was still a very limited mandate for change.[7]

Of all the policies that were promoted by the Gorbachev leadership, *glasnost* was perhaps the most distinctive and the one that had been pressed furthest by the end of communist rule. *Glasnost,* usually translated as openness or transparency, was not the same as freedom of the press or the right to information. Nor was it original to Gorbachev: it figured in the constitution adopted in 1977 under Leonid Brezhnev. It did, however, reflect the new general secretary's belief that without a greater awareness of the real state of affairs and of the considerations that had led to particular decisions, the Soviet people would be unwilling to commit themselves to his program of *perestroika* or reconstruction. The existing policies were, in any case, ineffectual and counterproductive. In November 1985 the newspaper *Sovetskaya Rossiya* reported the case of Mr. Polyakov of Kaluga, a well-read man who followed the central and local press and never missed the evening news. He knew a lot about what was happening in various African countries, Polyakov complained, but had "only a very rough idea what was happening in his own city."[8] In late 1985 another reader complained about media coverage of a major earthquake in Tajikistan in Soviet Central Asia: no details were revealed other than that "lives had been lost." At about the same time, an earthquake in Mexico and a volcanic eruption in Colombia had been covered extensively with on-the-spot reports and full details of the casualties. Was Tajikistan really farther from Moscow than Latin America?[9]

Influenced by considerations such as these, the Gorbachev leadership made steady and sometimes dramatic progress in removing taboos from the discussion of public affairs and exposing both the Soviet past and present to critical scrutiny. The Brezhnev era was one of the earliest targets. It had been a time, Gorbachev told the 27th Party Congress in 1986, when a "curious psychology—how to change things without really

The Gorbachev Reforms: Some Key Terms

Democratization	A term used, especially from 1987 onward, to refer to a series of changes in political life, including a more competitive electoral system, an effective parliament, and a society in which citizens would take a more active part in public life. The aim of democratization, as the specially convened 19th Party Conference put it in the summer of 1988, was to "open up maximum scope for the self-government of society and create conditions for the full development of the initiative of citizens, representative bodies of power, party and public organisations, and labor collectives."
Glasnost	A term usually translated as openness or transparency and understood to refer to the widening of the boundaries of permitted public debate in the Gorbachev period. Gorbachev explained at the 28th Party Congress in 1986 that *glasnost* was "a question of principle": "Without *glasnost* there is not and cannot be democratism, political creativity by the mass population, or their participation in management. It is, if you wish, a guarantee of a state whose relationship with tens of millions of workers, collective farms and intellectuals is animated by a feeling of responsibility, and is the point of departure of the psychological *perestroika* of our officials."[1]
New political thinking	A term used to refer to the rather different conceptualization of international relations that was developed by the Gorbachev administration and that often alluded to the overriding danger represented by nuclear weapons. Gorbachev appears to have first referred to "new political thinking" in a declaration of January 1986 that called for the elimination of such weapons by the year 2000. He also referred to it in his television address on May 14, 1986, on the Chernobyl nuclear explosion, explaining that "the nuclear age demands new political thinking and new politics."
Perestroika	A term usually translated as "restructuring" and the most general designation of the Gorbachev reforms. In the summer of 1986, Gorbachev was asked what was this *perestroika* he had been talking about? "The present *perestroika*," he replied, "covers not only the economy but also all other aspects of social life: social relations, the political system, the spiritual and ideological sphere, the style and methods of party work, of all the work of our officials. *Perestroika* is a capacious word. I would equate the words *perestroika* and revolution."[2]

1. M. S. Gorbachev, *Izbrannye rechi i stat'i* [Selected Speeches and Articles], vol. 3 (Moscow: Izdatel'stvo politicheskoi literatury, 1987), 241.
2. Ibid., 4:37.

changing anything"—had been dominant. Some of its leading representatives had been openly corrupt, and some, such as Brezhnev's son-in-law, Yuri Churbanov, had been brought to trial and imprisoned for serious state crimes. More generally, it had been a period of "stagnation," of wasted opportunities, when party and government leaders had lagged behind the needs of the times. The Stalin question was a still more fundamental one. To begin with, Gorbachev was reluctant even to concede there was a question. Stalinism, he told the French press in 1986, was a "notion made up by enemies of communism"[10]—after all, the 20th Party Congress in 1956 had condemned Stalin's "cult of personality" and drawn the necessary conclusions. By early 1987, however, Gorbachev was insisting that there must be "no forgotten names, no blank spots" in Soviet literature and history, and by November of that year, when he addressed the seventieth anniversary of the February Revolution of 1917, he was ready to condemn the "wanton repressive measures" of the 1930s, "real crimes" in which "many thousands of people inside and outside the party" had suffered.

In the course of this speech, Gorbachev announced that a Politburo commission had been set up to investigate the repression of the Stalinist years. This step led, beginning in 1988, to the rehabilitation of many prominent figures from the party's past (and thousands of others). The most important figure to be restored to full respectability in this way was the former *Pravda* editor Nikolai Bukharin, whose sentence was posthumously quashed in February 1988. Because Bolshevik politician and Marxist theorist Leon Trotsky had not been sentenced by a Soviet court, no judgment was reconsidered. But the Soviet press began to recognize his personal qualities, and from 1989 onward his writings began to appear in mass-circulation as well as scholarly journals. Meanwhile, scholars and others debated the numbers that Stalin had condemned to death: the estimates ranged from about 1 million to 12 million, according to historian and commentator Roy Medvedev, with another 38 million repressed in other ways.[11] About the same time, some of the mass graves of the Stalin period began to be uncovered, the most extensive of which were in the Kuropaty Forest near Minsk. The victims, as many as forty thousand (it became apparent later that the numbers were much larger than this), had been shot between 1937 and 1941. These graves, and the others that were still being discovered in the early 1990s, were a more powerful indictment of Stalinism than anything the historians could hope to muster.

Glasnost led to further changes in the quality of Soviet public life, from literature and the arts to a wide-ranging debate about the future of Soviet socialism and the availability of accurate statistics. The public became better informed through the publication of new figures on abortion, suicide, and infant mortality and the extensive coverage of subjects that had been taboo during the Brezhnev years, including violent crime, drugs, and prostitution. Many events of the past, such as the nuclear accident that had taken place in the Urals in 1957, were belatedly acknowledged. Figures for defense spending and foreign debt were revealed to the newly elected parliament, the Congress of People's Deputies, when it met in 1989; figures for capital punishment followed in 1991. The proceedings of the Congress itself were televised in full and followed avidly throughout the Soviet Union; so, too, were the plenary meetings of the Communist Party Central Committee. Still more remarkable, the Soviet media were opened up to foreign journalists and politicians, and even to a few open opponents of Soviet socialism. The first "spacebridges" were instituted as well, linking studio audiences in the Soviet Union and Western nations (the first linked Leningrad and Seattle). Opinion polls suggested that *glasnost,* for all its limitations, was the change in Soviet life that was most apparent to ordinary people and the one they most valued.

The "democratization" of Soviet political life was an associated change, and it was similarly intended to release the human energies that, for Gorbachev, had been choked off by the bureaucratic centralism of the Stalin and Brezhnev years. The Soviet Union, he told a specially convened party conference in the summer of 1988, had pioneered the idea of a workers' state and of workers' control and of the right to work and equality of rights for women and all national groups. The political system established by the October Revolution of 1917, however, had undergone "serious deformations," leading to the development of a "command-administrative system" that had extinguished the democratic potential of the elected soviets (government councils). Party and state officialdom had increased out of all proportion, and this "bloated administrative apparatus" had begun to dictate its will in political and economic matters. Nearly a third of the adult population was regularly elected to the soviets, but most of them had little influence over the conduct of government. Social life as a whole had become unduly politicized, and ordinary working people had become "alienated" from the system that was supposed to represent their interests. This "ossified system of government, with its command-and-pressure mechanism," was now the main obstacle to *perestroika.*

The party conference agreed to undertake a radical reform of the political system. That decision led to a series of constitutional and other changes from 1988 onward aimed at developing a model of socialism that would recover what reformers believed to be its democratic nature. An entirely new electoral law, approved in December 1988, broke new ground in providing for a choice of candidate in elections to local and national-level authorities. A new state structure was established, incorporating a smaller working parliament for the first time in modern Soviet history and (from 1990) a powerful executive presidency. A constitutional review committee, similar to a constitutional court, was set up as part of a move to what Gorbachev called a "socialist system of checks and balances." Judges were to be elected for longer periods of time and given greater independence in their work. And the Communist Party of the Soviet Union (CPSU) itself was to be "democratized," although the changes were less far-reaching than in other parts of the political system and in the end were not sufficient to preserve the party's authority or the confidence of its individual members. Leading officials, it was agreed, should be elected by competitive ballot for a maximum of two consecutive terms; members of the Central Committee should be involved more directly in the work of the leadership; and more information should be made available about all aspects of the party's work, from its finances to the operation of its decision-making bodies.

Gorbachev also sought radical reform of the Soviet economy. Levels of growth had been declining since at least the 1950s (see Table 6-2). In the late 1970s they reached the lowest levels in Soviet peacetime history, and there was no growth at all once the increase in population was taken into account. Indeed, as Gorbachev explained in early 1988, if the sale of alcoholic drink and of Soviet oil on foreign markets were excluded, there had been no increase in national wealth for at least the previous fifteen years. But for many reformers growth could not be an end in itself. What was important was the satisfaction of real social needs, not "the plan for the sake of the plan." It was equally apparent that without some improvement in living standards there would be no popular commitment to *perestroika* and no prospect that socialism would recover its appeal to other nations as a means by which ordinary working people could live their lives in dignity and sufficiency. There was indeed a real danger, in the view of reforming economists such as Nikolai Shmelev, that without radical reform the Soviet Union would enter the twenty-first century a "backward, stagnating state and an example to the rest of the world how not to conduct its economic affairs."[12]

Table 6-2 Soviet Economic Growth, 1951–1991 (percent)

	1951– 1955	1956– 1960	1961– 1965	1966– 1970	1971– 1975	1976– 1980	1981– 1985	1986– 1990	1991
Official data	11.4	9.2	6.5	7.8	5.7	4.3	3.2	1.4	−15
Western data	5.3	3.8	4.0	5.2	4.1	0.9	1.6	0.5	−6.3

Sources: Adapted from the Soviet statistical yearbook *Narodnoe khozyaistvo,* various years, showing average annual percentage changes in produced national income, and the gross domestic product (GDP) figures (in U.S. dollars) reported in Angus Maddison, *The World Economy: Historical Statistics* (Paris: Organisation for Economic Co-operation and Development, 2003), 98–99.

Radical reform, as Gorbachev explained to the 27th Party Congress and to a Central Committee meeting in the summer of 1987, involved a set of related measures. One of the most important was a greater degree of decentralization of economic decision making, leaving broad guidance of the economy in the hands of the State Planning Committee (Gosplan), but giving factories and farms throughout the Soviet Union more freedom to determine their own priorities. They should be guided in making such decisions by a wide range of "market" indicators, including the orders they received from other enterprises and the profits they made on their production. Retail and wholesale prices would have to reflect costs of production more closely, so that enterprises could be guided by "economic" rather than "administrative" regulators and the massive subsidies that held down the cost of basic foodstuffs could be reduced and if possible eliminated. Factories that persistently failed to pay their way could be liquidated; the state sector, more generally, should be reduced in size; and cooperative or even private economic activity should be expanded in its place. Gorbachev described these changes, which were gradually brought into effect beginning in 1987, as the most radical to take place in Soviet economic life since the adoption in the early 1920s of the New Economic Policy, which had allowed some private trading and a wider range of political freedoms.

But there was one still larger objective, discussed by academics and commentators as well as the political leadership: the elaboration of a "humane and democratic socialism" that would build on Soviet achievements but combine them with the experience of other nations and schools of thought, including environmentalism and feminism. Khrushchev had promised in the party program adopted under his leadership in 1961 that the Soviet Union would construct a communist society "in the main" by 1980. His successors dropped that commitment and began to describe the Soviet Union, from the early 1970s, as a "developed socialist society" whose evolution into a fully communist society was a matter for the distant future. Brezhnev's successors, in turn, made it clear that the Soviet Union was at the very beginning of developed socialism and that its further development would require a "whole historical epoch." Gorbachev, for his part, avoided the term "developed socialism" and opted instead for "developing socialism," which was, in effect, a postponement into the still more distant future of the attainment of a fully communist society. Later still, in 1990, the objective became "humane, democratic socialism." In 1991 the revised version of the party program was entitled "Socialism, Democracy, Progress," with communism mentioned only in passing.

Yet it remained unclear, these generalities aside, how a socialist society of this kind was to be constructed. Gorbachev resisted calls to set out the way ahead in any detail: did they really want a new "Short Course," he asked the Party Congress in 1990, referring to the discredited Marxist primer that had been produced under Stalin's auspices in 1938? And what was the point of programs structured like railway timetables, with objectives to be achieved by particular dates. Wasn't socialism supposed to be the achievement of ordinary people, not something they were directed toward by others? Gorbachev's objectives emerged as a set of fairly general propositions: a humane and democratic socialism would assume a variety of forms of property and would not necessarily exclude small-scale capitalism; it would be ruled by a broad coalition of "progressive" forces, not just by communists; it would guarantee freedom of conscience and other liberties; and it would cooperate with other states in an "interconnected, in many ways interdependent" world. But however adequate as an expression of general principle, this prescription could scarcely offer practical guidance to party members and the broader public in their daily lives. Nor did it carry conviction at a time of economic difficulty, nationalist discontent, and the acknowledgment of public policy mistakes for which the party that had monopolized political power for seventy years could hardly avoid responsibility.

In the end, the search for a "third way" that would combine Western-style democracy with a Soviet commitment to equality and social justice turned out to be a delusion. More open elections led, not to the return of committed reformers, but to the success of nationalist movements in the non-Russian republics and to the election of anticommunist mayors in Moscow and Leningrad, which once again became St. Petersburg. The opportunity to organize outside the CPSU led to "informal" movements and then to political parties that were openly hostile to communist rule. Demonstrations were organized, not in support of a humane and democratic socialism, but (in early 1990) calling for the removal of the party's political monopoly from the constitution. Writers, protected by *glasnost,* moved toward an explicit critique of Lenin as the founder of what they described as a "totalitarian" system, and they launched a more general attack on revolutions as progenitors of violence and repression. The Soviet Union as such was still very popular: 76 percent voted in favor of its retention as a "reformed federation" when the matter was put to a referendum in March 1991, and surveys in the early years of the new century showed that the principle of a larger union of some kind had lost none of its appeal. But belief in communist rule had fallen to a very low level by the end of 1991, after the failure of an attempted coup by hardliners that accelerated the disintegration of a state they had sought to preserve. There was little support for a return to a system that had clearly failed, but there was even less consensus about the form of government that should take its place.

Constructing Postcommunism

The Soviet Union was formally dissolved at the end of 1991, and its fifteen constituent republics, one of which was Russia, became independent states. But what kind of state was this newly independent Russia? Formally at least, there was no doubt about the commitment to certain liberal principles. Under the new constitution that was adopted by popular vote in December 1993, the state was to have "ideological diversity" but no official belief system of any kind. The constitution also called for "political diversity" and multiparty politics (Art. 13). The state was secular, but there was freedom of conscience, including the right to practice and to "disseminate religious and other views and act according to them" (Art. 28). The rights and freedoms of citizens were declared inalienable, and they were based on internationally recognized norms and principles (Art. 17). Finally, the constitution provided for equality before the law (Art. 19), the inviolability of private life and the home (Arts. 23 and 25), and freedoms of movement (Art. 27), speech (Art. 29), association (Art. 30), and peaceful assembly (Art. 31).

Several further rights related to ownership and economic activity had particular significance in a formerly communist system. The right to private property was protected by law, including the right to hold and to dispose of property and to pass it on to heirs (Art. 35). The basis for the right to private property in the form of land was to be established by subsequent legislation (Art. 36). And there was protection for the right to engage in entrepreneurial activity (Art. 34). Many of these rights—including the right to practice a religion or to engage in entrepreneurial activity—were "entrenched" in that they could not be limited even by the declaration of a state of emergency (Art. 56). The entire chapter on rights and freedoms, moreover, could not be modified by the Federal Assembly, but only by a constitutional conference or a referendum (Art. 135). Many of the provisions of the new constitution were modeled on those of its Western counterparts (it even began "We, the multinational people"). Indeed, the new constitution took the rights of citizens further than those in many other countries, such as in the requirement that official bodies allow access to the information they were holding on citizens that was relevant to those citizens' rights and freedoms (this requirement was close to the "freedom of information" legislation that existed in the United States, but not in most of Western Europe).

At the same time, however, many had serious doubts about the constitution as a political and legal basis for a new and consolidating Russian democracy. For a start, although it was meant to be the "basic law," questions arose about the legality of its adoption. Under the much-amended Russian constitution of 1978 that was in effect at the time of the new constitution's adoption, it should have been submitted to a referendum, not (as it was described) a "national vote." But it was submitted to a national vote, because the president had no power to call a referendum on his own authority. That power belonged to the Russian parliament, originally elected in 1990 and dominated by President Boris Yeltsin's political opponents. The rules that applied to the national vote were different from those applied to a referendum. Under the law that applied at the time, a referendum was carried if a majority of the electorate voted in favor of the proposition. Yeltsin, however, decreed that his national vote would be carried if it secured the support of a majority of those who actually voted, whether or not they constituted a particular proportion of the entire electorate. As for the requirement that at least half of the electorate take part in the exercise, there was continuing controversy about whether this requirement had actually been satisfied, although it was reported officially that 54.8 percent of the electorate had taken part.

More important, the new constitution imposed a strongly presidential system for which there was no national consensus and which raised political and constitutional difficulties of its own. Support was widespread for the provisions included on civil rights, many of which codified existing legislation, but there was no corresponding agreement on the adoption of what the Russian newspaper *Izvestiya* described as a "superpresidential republic."[13] It clearly reflected the president's own preferences (what else would you expect, Yeltsin asked an interviewer, "in a country that is used to tsars and strong leaders?"[14]). His successor, Vladimir Putin, showed no more inclination to share his extensive powers, and indeed began to strengthen the "executive vertical." A superpresidential system of this kind, however, depended heavily on the judgment and good health of the incumbent (which could not be taken for granted under Yeltsin), and it tended in any case to weaken the institutions that might otherwise have balanced presidential authority, such as the legislature, the media, and the courts of law. One reason that political parties were so slow to develop in Russia was that it made little difference whether they won a substantial share of the seats in the Russian parliament, because the government was not accountable to the parliament but to the president.

Russians themselves had rather mixed views when they were asked to characterize their new system and to judge the one they had left behind. According to the survey evidence, Russians were very clear that they had more religious freedom than in the Soviet period (86 percent), more freedom to express their views (78 percent), and more freedom to join an organization (78 percent).[15] But ordinary Russians were less persuaded that they were better protected against the risk of improper arrest (45 percent thought their position had improved, but 14 percent thought it had worsened), and they thought there had been no change at all in their influence on government (25 percent thought their influence had increased, but 25 percent thought it was less than in the Soviet period). Remarkably, only 17 percent thought they were more likely to be treated fairly and equally by government than in the Soviet years; 34 percent took the opposite view. On the whole, personal liberties were better protected than in the Soviet past (or at least, ordinary Russians thought they were better protected), but the relationship between citizens and government had shown no real improvement, and in some respects it was worsening.

Surveys have also asked what ordinary Russians make of the Soviet system they have left behind, and what they think were its positive or negative features (see Table 6-3). Generally, Russians thought that the Soviet system gave them a wide range of social and economic benefits. Everyone had a job; there was no ethnic conflict (or very little); there was more equality between the various social groups; and public order was maintained. The most general criticism of the Soviet system was that economic growth had slowed down and public life was heavily bureaucratized. Some were concerned about the lack of human rights. But it was notable that relatively few (11 percent) cited human rights as their primary reservation about the Soviet system, and just as many thought it had no bad features at all. These results suggested a strong commitment to what some described as

Table 6-3 Looking Back at Communist Rule: Results of a Survey, 2010

Good features	Percentage of respondents in agreement	Bad features	Percentage of respondents in agreement
Guaranteed employment	28	Economic stagnation	28
Kept peace between nationalities	17	Bureaucracy	21
More equality	17	Corruption	12
Economic stability	16	Lack of human rights	10
Maintained public order	13	No bad features	9
No good features	2	Environmental pollution	6

Source: National representative survey conducted for the author and associates by Russian Research; fieldwork conducted from February 12 to March 1, 2010; n = 2,000.

a "socialism that worked"—that is, a political system that was capable of sustaining a high level of public welfare, and yet one that allowed a wider range of opinion than had been possible during the communist period.

NOTES

1. See A. P. Gorkina et al., *Rossiya: entsiklopedicheskii spravochnik* [Russia: Encyclopedic Dictionary] (Moscow: Drofa, 1998), 5. Several good modern geographies are available, including that by Denis J. B. Shaw, *Russia in the Modern World: A New Geography* (Oxford, UK: Blackwell, 1998).

2. The Russian figure derives from a 2008 survey conducted for the author and others by Russian Research (n = 2,000); the discussion otherwise draws on Stephen White, Bill Miller, Sarah Oates, and Ase Grodeland, "Religion and Political Action in Postcommunist Europe," *Political Studies* 48, no. 4 (September 2000): 681–705.

3. Numerous modern histories of Russia, from the earliest times to the postcommunist years, have been published. See, for example, Geoffrey Hosking, *Russia and the Russians: From Earliest Times to 2001* (Cambridge: Harvard University Press, 2001); Catherine Evtukhov, David Goldfrank, Lindsey Hughes, and Richard Stites, *A History of Russia: People, Legends, Events, Forces* (Boston and New York: Houghton Mifflin, 2004); and Nicholas V. Riasanovsky and Mark Steinberg, *A History of Russia,* 7th ed. (New York: Oxford University Press, 2005).

4. This is the estimate presented in Gregory L. Freeze, ed., *Russia: A History* (New York: Oxford University Press, 1997), 315. There is a fuller discussion of the contentious issues involved in J. Arch Getty and Roberta T. Manning, eds., *Stalinist Terror: New Perspectives* (Cambridge and New York: Cambridge University Press, 1993).

5. Party archives, reprinted in *Istochnik* [Source], no. 0 [trial issue] (1993): 66–75.

6. Here and elsewhere references to Gorbachev's speeches and statements are taken from M. S. Gorbachev, *Izbrannye rechi i stat'i* [Selected speeches and articles], 7 vols. (Moscow: Politizdat, 1987–1990).

7. Several more detailed accounts of Gorbachev and the reforms that took place under his leadership are available. See, for example, Richard Sakwa, *Gorbachev and His Reforms, 1985–1990* (Hemel Hempstead, UK: Philip Allan, 1990); Stephen White, *After Gorbachev,* rev. ed. (Cambridge and New York: Cambridge University Press, 1994); Archie Brown, *The Gorbachev Factor* (Oxford: Oxford University Press, 1996); and Jerry F. Hough, *Democratization and Revolution in the USSR, 1985–1991* (Washington, D.C.: Brookings, 1997).

8. *Sovetskaya Rossiya,* November 24, 1985, 1.

9. *Sovetskaya Rossiya,* January 5, 1986, 3.

10. Gorbachev, *Izbrannye rechi i stat'i,* vol. 3, 162.

11. *Moscow News,* no. 48, 1988, 8–9.

12. Nikolai Shmelev, "Ekonomika i zdravyi smysl" [Economics and Common Sense], *Znamya* (July 1988): 179–184, at 179.

13. *Izvestiya,* October 12, 1994, 4.

14. *Izvestiya,* November 15, 1993, 4.

15. What follows draws on a national representative survey conducted between December 21, 2003, and January 16, 2004, by Russian Research for this author and associates. Two thousand people were interviewed in their homes using the agency's normal sampling procedures, and their responses were then weighted in accordance with the sex, age, and education in each region.

Where Is the Power?

IN THE SOVIET PERIOD, THERE WAS NO DOUBT WHERE POLITICAL POWER was located. The Communist Party enjoyed a monopoly of political authority, enshrined after 1977 in a constitution that declared it the "leading and guiding force of Soviet society and the nucleus of its political system, of all state bodies and public organizations." Within the party, the leadership was exceptionally powerful, helped by a principle of "democratic centralism" that required each lower level of the party organization to accept its instructions. Within the leadership itself, the first secretary or (as he was more often known) general secretary was clearly the person who mattered most. His judgments were the most authoritative; his statements were the ones that were quoted most often in *Pravda* editorials; and his picture was the one that appeared most frequently on its front page. His six-hour speech was the one that, by convention, opened the party congress, and it was the one that was applauded the most enthusiastically. When Leonid Brezhnev spoke in 1981 at his last party congress, his address was interrupted seventy-eight times by "applause," forty times by "prolonged applause," and eight times by "stormy, prolonged applause." There were shouts of "hurrah" a few days later when it was announced that he had been unanimously reelected to head the new Politburo.[1]

Central control of this detailed kind was already breaking down in the last years of Soviet rule. The party leadership had steadily evolved into a collective based on discussion and consensus and representing the most important interests in Soviet life—the army, the ministerial bureaucracies, and the largest cities and regions. Meanwhile, a diversity of opinion began to emerge in public life, reflecting an increase in the numbers of highly educated professionals and the increasing complexity of policy choices. The media began to pursue a wider variety of stories, especially after Mikhail Gorbachev started promoting his policy of *glasnost* in the mid-1980s. The rule of law began to strengthen at the same time, encouraged by legislative changes that gave more independence to the courts and to those who worked within them. Electorally, beginning in 1989 elections were largely competitive, and there was a new working parliament. Meanwhile, the Communist Party began to share its authority with other parties and movements, particularly after March 1990 when its guaranteed political monopoly was removed from the constitution. This was still a Soviet system, but it was already one in which a considerable degree of political pluralism had been institutionalized.

Communist rule came to an end in December 1991. The Soviet Union broke into fifteen constituent republics, and political power moved into the hands of a strongly anti-communist president, Boris Yeltsin. But the end of communist rule was clearly not the same as the establishment of a liberal democracy. Nearly two decades after its "transition," political power in Russia remains highly centralized, with a concentration of power in the hands of an enormously powerful president and his administration. There is a choice of political parties at elections, but few that have a substantial and committed following. There is a choice of newspapers and television channels, but few that are prepared to offer a continuing and independent critique of government policy. The courts, meanwhile, offer little protection against the abuse of office or to wealthy businesspeople with political ambitions such as Mikhail Khodorkovsky, who was arrested in October 2003 and sentenced to nine years' imprisonment in June 2005. Some observers, such as economist Grigorii Yavlinsky, have called this a "criminal oligarchy with a monopolistic state"; others have described it as a "*nomenklatura* democracy" that has left ordinary people with no more influence over those who rule them than they enjoyed in the last years of Soviet rule.[2]

The Russian Presidency

However its political system was classified, the central institution in postcommunist Russia was clearly the powerful presidency established in the spring of 1991. Mikhail Gorbachev had established a Soviet presidency the year before, and over the months that followed, almost all of the Soviet republics moved toward a fully presidential system. Russians voted overwhelmingly in favor of an elected executive presidency in the referendum of March 1991; at the same time a referendum was held on the future of the Soviet Union itself. In June 1991 Boris Yeltsin was elected to the newly established office with 57 percent of the vote in a six-way contest. Russia was still, up to the end of that year, one of the republics of the Soviet Union, but there was already no doubt that the dominant figure in its political life was its first-ever directly elected president, not the Soviet president to whom he was nominally subordinate. When the Soviet Union itself collapsed at the end of 1991, the authority of the Soviet president passed naturally to the newly elected Russian president, and Russia itself assumed the position that the Soviet Union had occupied in the international community.

Yeltsin owed much of his authority to his direct election by the people, unlike the Soviet president who had been elected by the national parliament. Yeltsin had won additional respect when he faced down an attempted coup in August 1991 at some risk to his own life; the whole world saw him standing on a tank in front of the Russian parliament, reading out his denunciation of the attempt to depose Gorbachev and demanding the immediate release of the Soviet president whom the rebels had confined in Crimea. Yeltsin's public standing was never higher than in the immediate aftermath of the thwarted coup, and he became the dominant figure in the negotiations among the republics that led eventually to the collapse of the Soviet Union and its replacement by the Commonwealth of Independent States. At the same time, he had to govern through a parliament that had also been elected (in 1990) and that could also claim to represent the popular will. The parliament had originally been supportive of Yeltsin and had elected him as its own first chair. But as the Yeltsin government pushed through a package of economic reforms that left millions of Russians in destitution, there was understandably some resistance from their elected representatives.

Yeltsin, speaking to the parliament in December 1992, complained that it was creating "intolerable working conditions for the government and the president," attempting to turn deputies into the "absolute rulers of Russia" and aiming in the last resort at the "restoration of the totalitarian Soviet-communist system." It had become "impossible" to go on working with such a parliament, he told the deputies, and he demanded a referendum to resolve the

Russia at a Glance

Type of Government
Federation

Capital
Moscow

Administrative Divisions (2010)
Forty-six regions (oblasts), twenty-one republics, four autonomous areas (okrugs), nine federal territories (krais), one autonomous oblast, and two federal cities.

Declaration of Sovereignty
June 12, 1990

Constitution
Adopted December 12, 1993

Legal System
Based on civil law system; judicial review of legislative acts

Suffrage
Eighteen years of age; universal

Executive Branch
Chief of state: president
Head of government: premier
Cabinet: premier and deputy premiers, ministers, and selected other individuals; all appointed by the president
Note: A presidential administration provides staff and policy support to the president, drafts presidential decrees, and coordinates policy among government agencies. A Security Council also reports directly to the president.
Elections: president elected by popular vote for a six-year term (from 2012 onwards); no vice president. If the president cannot exercise his powers because of ill health, impeachment, resignation, or death in office, the premier serves as acting president until a new presidential election is held, which must be within three months. Premier is appointed by the president with the approval of the Duma.

Legislative Branch
Bicameral federal assembly: Federation Council and State Duma. Federation Council: 166 members chosen by the executive head and legislature in each of the eighty-three (as of 2010) federal administrative units. Term: four years. State Duma: 450 members, popularly elected from 2007 onwards by proportional representation from party lists winning at least 7 percent of the vote. Term: four (from 2011, five) years.

Judicial Branch
Constitutional Court; Supreme Court; Superior Court of Arbitration. Judges for all courts are appointed for life by Federation Council on recommendation of president.

Major Political Parties
A Just Russia; Communist Party of the Russian Federation (CPRF); Liberal Democratic Party of Russia (LDPR); Right Cause; United Russia; Yabloko.

Source: U.S. Central Intelligence Agency, *The World Factbook: 2005,* http://www.cia.gov/cia/publications/factbook/geos/rs.html; http://www.russianembassy.org/RUSSIA/GEOGRAF.HTM; author's data.

tension between "two irreconcilable positions."[3] The referendum, when it took place in April 1993, suggested that most Russians supported the president and his policies in this confrontation. The result encouraged the presidential camp to press ahead with the preparation of a new constitution that would resolve the continuing impasse in favor of the president.

The parliamentarians had a rather different view, and they raised a rather different issue: Should government be accountable, not just elected, and should a broadly representative parliament be allowed to act as a counterbalance to what would otherwise be an overly powerful executive? For Ruslan Khasbulatov, the parliamentary Speaker, the state in Russia had always been identified with the power of an autocratic ruler, and in the communist years the party leader had become "almost a tsar." Parliament, in these circumstances, had a vital role: it could represent the society as a whole, and it could help to limit the power of the executive in matters such as public spending and the composition of government. A parliamentary system was particularly important in postcommunist Russia, Khasbulatov argued, because it needed to reconcile the differences that still remained and to build a supportive consensus.

These differences, which would have been recognized by most constitutional theorists, were at the center of a series of discussions that took place between parliamentarians and the executive during 1992 and with a view toward securing an agreed and workable compromise. In the end, however, the differences that remained were resolved by military force. In late September 1993 the Russian parliament was suspended by a presidential decree, and then in early October it was shelled and taken over by the Russian army after it voted for Yeltsin's impeachment and after a popular demonstration encouraged army leaders to believe they were about to take power. Khasbulatov and the other leaders of this "parliamentary insurrection" were taken into custody; some parties and publications were banned; and another referendum was held in December that allowed Yeltsin to secure approval of a new version of the draft constitution that incorporated a more strongly presidential form of executive authority.[4]

Presidential Power in Postcommunist Russia

Under the 1993 Russian constitution, the president is head of state and guarantor of the constitution itself, to which he swears an oath of allegiance. The president represents the Russian Federation at home and abroad and defines the "basic directions of the domestic and foreign policy of the state" (Art. 80). He prepares an "annual address on the situation in the country," clearly modeled on the U.S. president's State of the Union address, which he delivers to both houses of parliament at the start of each year (Art. 84). The president also has extensive powers of appointment. He appoints the premier "with the consent of the State Duma," the lower house of parliament, and can preside over meetings of the government. He also nominates candidates to head the State Bank, appoints and dismisses deputy premiers and ministers, and nominates candidates to the Constitutional Court, the Supreme Court, and the Procuracy, the agency responsible for the administration of judicial oversight and for criminal investigations—a holdover from the Soviet days. Finally, the president forms and heads the Security Council—the small group of high-ranking officials who take overall responsibility for defense matters—and appoints and dismisses his representatives in the Russian regions as well as the high command of the armed forces and diplomatic representatives (Art. 83).

The Russian president, in addition, can initiate legislation (Art. 84), and he has the right to dissolve the Duma in specified circumstances: if the Duma refuses his nomination for premier three times in a row or if it passes votes of no confidence in the government twice within three months (Arts. 111 and 117). The Russian president also enjoys the right to issue his own decrees, which have the force of law throughout the federation (Art. 90). Formally, any decrees of this kind are supposed to be consistent with the constitution and with existing legislation, but in practice they have often exceeded such limits. The decree that suspended the parliament in September 1993 was in clear violation of the constitution that prevailed at the time; and the president also broke new ground in the decree in December 1994 that began the war with Chechnya and in some of his decrees on privatization. Finally, the president heads the armed forces and can declare a state of war as well as a state of emergency (Arts. 87 and 88).

There are, in fact, few limits on the powers of a Russian president. He can be impeached, but less easily than in the constitution that prevailed before 1993: the Duma must first vote in favor of impeachment proceedings by a two-thirds majority on the initiative of at least a third of the deputies after a special commission of deputies has decided the president is guilty of treason or a crime of similar gravity. The Supreme Court must then rule that there are grounds for such an accusation, and the Constitutional Court must confirm that the proper procedures have been followed. The Federation Council, the upper house of the Russian parliament, must then vote in favor of the president's removal from office by a two-thirds majority no less than three months after the original charges were presented (Art. 93). It is unlikely, in view of this elaborate procedure, that any Russian president will be forced out of office on this basis, although attempts have periodically been made to initiate proceedings. A more serious restriction on the powers of the presidency is the ability of the Russian parliament to override a presidential veto by a two-thirds majority vote in both houses (Art. 107).

Unlike its predecessor, the 1993 constitution does not forbid the president to dissolve the Russian parliament or suspend its operation (Yeltsin's decree of September 1993 was in effect a constitutional coup). The constitution also allows the president to approve the military doctrine of the Russian Federation (Art. 83), which is a constitutional novelty, and the president, not the parliament, calls a referendum once the necessary procedures have been completed.

The constitution mentions that the president forms an "administration" (Art. 83), but it gives little indication of its role in government. The presidential administration has served, in practice, as a sort of supergovernment, headed by the president's closest advisers and with a substantial staff. It is reminiscent in many ways of the central party bureaucracy of the Soviet period—indeed, it is housed in the same buildings. The head of the presidential administration has always ranked among the most influential figures in Russian political life, although this position is not an elective one. The administration is, in effect, the presidential "court," with its favorites and its gossip, intrigue, and, as it became clear in the late 1990s, greed and corruption.

Electing the Russian President: 2000, 2004, and 2008

Under the constitution, the Russian president is elected directly by the adult population for four (from 2012 onwards, six) years and cannot hold office for more than two consecutive terms (Art. 81). Unlike his U.S. counterpart, a former president can, in theory, be reelected to the presidency at a later time. A Russian president must be at least thirty-five years old and must have lived in the Russian Federation for at least ten years (Art. 81). This provision was presumably intended to rule out émigré candidates like those who had emerged in some East European countries in the postcommunist period, in some cases with remarkable success.[5] The 1993 constitution specifies a lower age limit for a candidate for the Russian presidency, but no upper age limit, presumably because Boris Yeltsin would have passed the age of sixty-five before his first term came to an end. No provision is made for a vice president who could help to ensure continuity if the president dies or becomes incapacitated; in this event, the prime minister temporarily assumes the president's responsibilities.

Yeltsin had first been elected president of Russia in 1991 when it was one of the constituent republics of the Soviet Union, and was reelected on the second round in 1996. The Constitutional Court ruled that this earlier election must count as a first election to the post, and so he had no alternative but to stand down in the next election, scheduled for June 2000. At the end of December 1999, Yeltsin took the political world by surprise when he resigned, allowing Premier Vladimir Putin to take over as acting president. Yeltsin had already identified Putin as his chosen successor when he nominated him to the premiership in August 1999. With his early resignation, the presidential election was brought forward to March 26, 2000, which gave Putin, already the incumbent, a substantial advantage. Putin's success, however, owed even more to the campaign against "terrorism" in Chechnya. The conflict with Chechnya appalled international opinion because of apparent violations of human rights, but it appeared to have persuaded Russians themselves that at last they had found a vigorous leader who could ensure their physical security. Putin's approval rating, only 2 percent when he became premier, had reached 62 percent by mid-January 2000, and the only real question at the start of the campaign was whether he would win on the first ballot.

Putin refused to campaign directly or to use the public funds he had been allocated for publicity, and he did not issue a preelection manifesto. He did, however, publish an "Open Letter to Russian Voters," and in early March 2000 he published a series of interviews with journalists entitled *First Person*.[6] In the interviews, Putin gave two themes particular attention: the need for a strong state and the need for a properly functioning market economy. The stronger the state, Putin suggested, the stronger the individual. Nor was there any conflict between a strong state and a market economy: the state was needed to protect property rights, encourage entrepreneurs, and collect taxes. Putin emphasized the dangers of a "second Yugoslavia" in Russia if fundamentalist Islam were allowed to spread from Chechnya to the middle Volga, and, more generally, he promised to restore Russia's place as a great and respected power. His campaign was greatly assisted by the attention he automatically attracted as premier and acting president. He made a further contribution by undertaking a series of energetic stunts, such as piloting an air force jet between two of his engagements, which underscored the difference between him and his ailing predecessor.

In the end, Putin won narrowly on the first ballot (see Table 6-4). The runner-up was Communist Party leader Gennadii Zyuganov, with a more respectable vote than many had expected. Yabloko Party leader Grigorii Yavlinsky came third, but with a smaller share

Table 6-4 Russian Presidential Elections, 2000, 2004, and 2008

Candidate	Number of votes	Percentage of total
Election of March 26, 2000		
Vladimir Putin (independent)	39,740,434	59.94
Gennadii Zyuganov (Communist)	21,928,471	29.21
Grigorii Yavlinsky (Yabloko)	4,351,452	5.80
Aman-Geldy Tuleev (independent)	2,217,361	2.95
Vladimir Zhirinovsky (Liberal Democratic Party)	2,026,513	2.70
Konstantin Titov (independent)	1,107,269	1.47
Ella Pamfilova (independent)	758,966	1.01
Stanislav Govorukhin (independent)	328,723	0.44
Yuri Skuratov (independent)	319,263	0.43
Aleksei Podberezkin (independent)	98,175	0.13
Umar Dzhabrailov (independent)	74,898	0.10
Against all	1,414,648	1.88
Election of March 14, 2004		
Vladimir Putin (independent)	49,565,238	71.31
Nikolai Kharitonov (Communist)	9,513,313	13.69
Sergei Glazev (independent)	2,850,063	4.10
Irina Khakamada (independent)	2,671,313	3.84
Oleg Malyshkin (Liberal Democratic Party)	1,405,315	2.02
Sergei Mironov (Russian Party of Life)	524,324	0.75
Against all	2,396,219	3.45
Election of March 2, 2008		
Dmitri Medvedev (United Russia)	52,530,712	70.28
Gennadii Zyuganov (Communist)	13,243,550	17.72
Vladimir Zhirinovsky (Liberal Democratic Party)	6,988,510	9.35
Andrei Bogdanov (independent)	968,344	1.30

Source: Central Electoral Commission.

Note: Turnout (ballots cast as a percentage of eligible voters) was 68.74 percent in 2000, 69.58 in 2004, and 69.71 in 2008. "Against all" votes could no longer be cast in 2008.

of the vote than he had secured in 1996. None of the other candidates secured more than 3 percent, which meant that they would be obliged to return the state funds that had been made available for their campaigns. The turnout, at 68.7 percent, was very close to the turnout recorded in the first round of the 1996 presidential campaign. Putin's decisive victory took him beyond the margin of victory that might have been attributed to his manipulation of the airwaves. It was equally clear that he had enjoyed all the advantages of office, including the de facto support of the state machine, and that he had received quite a disproportionate degree of attention from the mass media (more than a third of the television coverage given to all candidates and about half of the entire news and current affairs output). He won an even more decisive victory, with more than 71 percent of the vote, in the March 2004 election, but had to stand down in 2008 when his second term came to an end. He would, however, be eligible to stand again at a future presidential election at which the successful candidate would receive a six-year mandate.

There had been speculation about the "2008 problem" that would arise when Putin reached the end of his second term, and some thought the constitution might be changed to allow him to continue for a third term or even longer. Putin, however, made it known in the course of the Duma election campaign that he would be happy to take on the premiership if there was a new president with whom he could establish a working relationship, and in December 2007 he announced the nomination of first deputy prime minister Dmitri Medvedev to the position. Medvedev faced no serious challenge and, indeed, scarcely campaigned at all; but his activities as first deputy premier were covered extensively in the official media, and he made clear that he would be continuing Putin's policies if he was successful. He won a majority that was almost as decisive as Putin's in 2004 (see Table 6-4). He was inaugurated on May 7, and the following day nominated Putin to the premiership, to which he was confirmed by a record majority. The new arrangement was what Russians called a "tandem," with Medvedev as president and Putin as prime minister, but Putin remained the dominant figure according to surveys of expert as well as of mass opinion, and he was widely expected to return to the presidency at the 2012 election, if not before.

Putin and Medvedev

In a political system that invests the president with so much power and has few of the informal constraints on executive authority that have developed in Western countries, the personal qualities of the Russian president make a real difference. This was true of Boris Yeltsin, the bulky Siberian who was Russia's first postcommunist president, and it was also true of Vladimir Putin, a former member of the Committee for State Security, known more familiarly as the KGB, who took over as acting president at the end of 1999 and was then elected to the office in March 2000. Putin was much younger than Yeltsin and had a black belt in judo; there was certainly no reason to think his health or public behavior would be uncertain. His policy priorities, however, remained somewhat opaque, apart from bringing the "antiterrorist operation" in breakaway Chechnya to a successful conclusion. Putin, born in Leningrad in 1952, graduated from Leningrad University's law faculty in 1975. He went to work in the foreign intelligence administration of the KGB and spent a long time in East Germany, where he became fluent in the language and drank (he thought) too much beer. He returned to Leningrad in 1991 and worked in the city administration. There, he became closely associated with its reform-minded mayor. In 1996 Putin moved to Moscow, where he worked in Yeltsin's administration as deputy head of the president's business office. In July 1998 he became director of the Federal Security Bureau, the successor to the KGB, and then moved up to the premiership in August 1999.

Some of Putin's objectives became a little clearer in an address he issued at the end of 1999 when he became acting president upon Yeltsin's early retirement.[7] Even though he recognized its considerable achievements, Putin rejected a return to the totalitarian past. At the same time, he rejected the "abstract models and schemes taken from foreign textbooks" that had been applied during the free-market experiments of the 1990s. He appeared to recognize the importance of universal values such as freedom of expression and freedom to travel abroad, but he placed more emphasis on traditional Russian

ВМЕСТЕ ПОБЕДИМ!

2 МАРТА ВЫБОРЫ ПРЕЗИДЕНТА РОССИИ

Vladimir Putin (left) and Dmitri Medvedev (right) appear together in a billboard campaign advertisement before the March 2008 presidential elections, under the slogan "We'll win together!"

Source: Stephen White

principles of government, such as patriotism and the greatness of the nation itself. Russia, Putin insisted, was and always would remain a great power in economic and cultural, if not necessarily in military, terms. "Statism" was another traditional virtue: the state and its institutions had always been strong in Russia, and there was no immediate or even long-term prospect that Russia would become a "second edition of, say, the United States or Great Britain in which liberal values have deep historic traditions." Social solidarity was also important, with its emphasis on cooperation rather than individualism. Clearly, this view of the Russian future was one that would respect liberal freedoms, but also would emphasize the need for a strong and protective state in line with rather longer-standing national traditions.

Putin's successor as president, Dmitri Medvedev, is also from Leningrad and also a law graduate of the city's university, where he taught for some years in the 1990s. He was not particularly engaged in the political activism of the *perestroika* years (during the attempted coup of August 1991 he was hospitalized with a broken leg), but being more than a decade younger than Putin—he was born in 1965—his experience of the Soviet system was considerably less than that of Putin, and he was never a member (or known to have been a member) of the Communist Party. He moved to Moscow in 1999 to a position in the government and then the presidential administration, becoming Putin's chief of staff in 2003. He moved on to the federal government in November 2005 as first deputy prime minister, taking particular responsibility for the ambitious "national projects" that were launched in health, agriculture, education, and housing. Interviews began to fill in something of his personal background: his particular passion was the vinyl records of the 1970s and 1980s and hard rock groups such as Deep Purple and Black Sabbath, but he was also interested in yoga and could already stand on his head. The most distinctive feature of his presidential campaign was his emphasis on "legal nihilism" (or disregard of rule of law), and once he had assumed office, he gave particular attention to the struggle against corruption.

The Premier and Government

The daily business of Russian government is in the hands of the premier and his colleagues under the overall authority of the president. (The arrangement is not very different from the Soviet practice by which the party ruled and the government carried its decisions into effect.) Under the constitution, the president, with the consent of the State Duma, appoints the premier; the entire government submits its resignation to the new president (Art. 116), and the president, in turn, has to submit his premiership nomination within two weeks of taking office (Art. 111). But unlike in other parliamentary systems, there is no question of the premier submitting his resignation to a newly elected Duma and securing the support of deputies in order to continue. Indeed, Viktor Chernomyrdin, who was premier at the time of the December 1995 Duma election, went out of his way to insist that there would be no change of policy or personnel, even though the party he had led into the election—Our Home Is Russia—had secured no more than 10 percent of the popular vote. Conversely, the succession of changes in the premiership that took place in 1998 and 1999 had nothing to do with an election, a Duma resolution, or a change in public attitudes.

The Duma does have some influence over the choice of premier, but it is a power of last resort. The Duma has a week to vote on any nomination to the premiership. If it rejects three nominations in a row, the president is obliged (and not simply empowered) to dissolve the Duma and call a new election (Art. 111). The Duma also has another power of last resort, which is its right to call for a vote of no confidence in the government as a whole. If it does so twice within three months, the president must either announce the resignation of the government or dissolve the Duma. The government can also decide to offer its own resignation, which the president can either accept or reject (Art. 117). Both of these powers are unlikely to be used in normal circumstances, however, because they would normally precipitate a constitutional crisis.

In carrying out the ordinary business of government, the premier and his colleagues make proposals to the president on the structure of the government as a whole and on who should serve as deputy premiers and ministers (Art. 112). More generally, he is supposed to identify the "basic guidelines" of government activity and to "organize its work" (Art. 113). It is the government that submits an annual budget to the Duma and reports on its fulfillment. The government also takes charge of finance, credit, and currency matters, and it conducts a "uniform state policy" in culture, education, science, health, social security, and the environment. The government is responsible as well for state property, public order, and foreign policy (Art. 114), and it can issue resolutions and directives to put its decisions into effect (Art. 115).

At the start of 2010 the Russian government was headed by Premier Putin, two first deputy premiers, and four deputy premiers, one of them the finance minister and another the head of the government bureaucracy. The government further consisted of eighteen ministers with responsibility for agriculture, civil defense and emergency situations, culture and mass communications, defense, economic development and trade, education and science, finance, foreign affairs, health and social development, industry and energy, information technology and communications, internal affairs, justice, natural resources, regional development, and transport. A smaller "Presidium" of ministers meets weekly. The ministries direct a larger system of services and agencies, which carry out more specialized functions. In addition are independent services and agencies that are the equivalent of ministries. One of them is the Federal Security Bureau, the successor to the KGB.

The Duma and the Legislative Process

Just as its elections lacked any element of choice until the late Gorbachev years, so, too, did the Soviet system lack any element of parliamentarianism. The elected soviets (or councils) were meant to be very different from the representative institutions that existed in capitalist countries. There was no separation of powers, for a start, because working people were supposed to have a common interest that made it unnecessary for an artificial division between making laws and adjudicating on their application. The Soviet parliament, the Soviet Union Supreme Soviet, met for only two or three days at a time twice a year, and its votes were normally unanimous. So predictable were its proceedings that parliamentary correspondents could file their reports the previous day. Deputies were part-timers, so they could combine their representative duties with their regular employment, and a high proportion were replaced from election to election, which gave others a chance to run. In practice, ministers were immune from criticism, and ordinary people had little confidence in the institution through which their interests were supposedly being represented.

Fundamental changes were made in this system in the Gorbachev years as part of the new party leader's program of "democratization." For one thing, the first working parliament in modern Soviet history was established in 1989, and its deputies carried out their responsibilities on a full-time basis. Ministers were chosen in competitive elections, and their terms were limited. A still larger change took place with the adoption of the new constitution in December 1993. An entirely new Federal Assembly was established, with a lower house, the State Duma, made up of deputies elected either by individual constituencies or by a competition between party lists. The upper house, the Federation Council, was made up of 178 representatives, 2 each from the (then) eighty-nine republics and regions. It considered issues that related to the federation as a whole: it approved boundary changes, the introduction of martial law, and the deployment of Russian troops in foreign countries. But because its members had full-time positions in the regions from which they came, it met irregularly, just one week in three.

Most parliamentary activity took place in the lower house, or State Duma. The Duma had to approve nominations to the premiership. It also appointed and dismissed the chair of the State Bank (and the chair of the Accounting Chamber), who scrutinized the use of public funds. Above all, the Duma was a legislative body. Between 1993 and 1995 the first Duma alone adopted more than four hundred laws, many of which were designed to consolidate the postcommunist state system. Much of the work of the Duma was conducted through its twenty-nine committees, whose chairs were often figures of some political authority. The Duma's legislative decisions had to be approved by the upper house, but the Duma could override a veto by confirming its original decision with a two-thirds majority. The president could refuse to sign a bill that had gone through both houses, but a two-thirds majority in both houses could override a veto.

The conduct of the Duma and its members did not always encourage respect for their positions. One nationalist deputy who was a deputy chair of the committee on women, families, and youth lived openly with three women and proposed a bill to legalize polygamy—because, he explained, there were not enough men to go around. "The majority of Russian men are too poor to support one family, let alone several," he told reporters. "I have the money and energy to keep all my women fully satisfied, materially and physically."[8] A session convened in September 1995 to discuss the North Atlantic Treaty Organization bombings in Bosnia was particularly remarkable. A far-right deputy, Nikolai Lysenko, took the opportunity to physically attack one of his opponents, Orthodox priest Gleb Yakunin, as he was returning to his seat. Another deputy tried to separate them but became involved in the melee; so did two women deputies. At this point, the leader of the Liberal Democratic Party of Russia, Vladimir Zhirinovsky, waded in, elbowing one of the women out of the way (she suffered a concussion) and seizing the other in an arm lock. A bloodied Yakunin later announced that he would be taking legal action against Lysenko for the theft of his cross, banditry, and offending the sensibilities of believers.

The standing of the Duma may have owed something to the occasionally outrageous behavior of its members; it owed rather more to its subordinate position in political and constitutional terms. Once the ruling party, United Russia, had established an overall majority, it was unlikely to challenge any proposals that were placed before it. The Russian government, for the same reason, had no need to defend its policies in front of elected representatives, and often operated by means of informal agreements that were reached behind the scenes and sometimes before the relevant legislation had been introduced. There was some talk during the Putin presidency of a "government of the parliamentary majority" that would take account of the distribution of opinion in the legislature. But the idea was later abandoned, and both Putin and Medvedev made clear that they had no intention of departing from a strongly presidential constitution in favor of a more parliamentary system. This meant that government would continue to depend on the support of the president of the day, rather than the confidence of elected deputies. It also meant that political parties had no real incentive to compete for the votes of the mass electorate if party representatives would have no opportunity to form a new government or to influence the policies it might choose to adopt. This arrangement was clearly satisfactory to those who held political authority—indeed, it was almost Soviet—and for this reason it was unlikely to change as long as they remained dominant.

NOTES

1. Iu. K. Aksyutin, ed., *L. I. Brezhnev: Materialy k biografii* [Brezhnev: Materials for a Biography] (Moscow: Politizdat, 1991), 276.
2. Quoted respectively in *Sotsiologicheskie issledovaniya* 4 (1997): 73; and *Izvestiya,* June 1, 1994, 1, 7.

3. Cited in Stephen White, *Russia's New Politics* (Cambridge and New York: Cambridge University Press, 2000), 80.

4. The text of the Russian constitution was published in *Rossiiskaya gazeta,* December 25, 1993, 3–6. For a convenient edition, see Vladimir V. Belyakov and Walter J. Raymond, eds., *Constitution of the Russian Federation* (Lawrenceville, Va.: Brunswick, 1994).

5. A Canadian businessman of Polish origin had come an astonishing second in the Polish presidential election of 1990, and a Lithuanian American who had retired from the U.S. Environmental Protection Agency won the Lithuanian presidential election of early 1998. Latvians elected an émigré Canadian psychology professor to their own presidency in 1999, but by a parliamentary rather than a popular vote.

6. Vladimir Putin, with Nataliya Gevorkyan, Natalya Timakova, and Andrei Kolesnikov, *First Person: An Astonishingly Frank Self-Portrait by Russia's President Vladimir Putin,* trans. Catherine A. Fitzpatrick (New York: Public Affairs, 2000).

7. Vladimir Putin, "Russia at the Turn of the Millennium," *Rossiiskaya gazeta,* December 31, 1999. A complete translation is provided as an appendix to Putin's *First Person,* 209–219.

8. Masha Gessen, "Cross Purposes," *New Statesman and Society,* September 22, 1995, 22–23.

Who Has the Power?

6.3

THE SOVIET SYSTEM, UP TO ALMOST ITS END, ALLOWED NO CHOICE of party or even candidate in its periodic elections. Only a single candidate appeared on the ballot paper, and to vote in favor of that candidate a voter merely had to drop the ballot, unmarked and possibly unread, into the box. A vote against was rather less easy: a screened-off booth for this purpose was placed inside the polling station, but if voters went off to use it their intentions could hardly be secret. The results were so predictable that newspapers could prepare their front pages with pictures of the successful candidates the day before the election took place. The Politburo, as late as the 1980s, could approve the report of the central electoral commission two days before the polls opened.

The 1987 local elections saw the first partial break with these arrangements: a small number of combined districts were allowed to nominate more candidates than seats available. Then in 1988, as "democratization" developed further, a new election law was adopted that provided for the first elements of genuine competition. There was no limit on the number of candidates who could be nominated (formally this was not a change, but now it was going to be more than an empty provision). More important, ordinary citizens who had collected five hundred or more signatures could nominate candidates—not just those in the Communist Party and other approved organizations. Also for the first time, candidates had to put forward their own manifestos, even if they had to stay within the bounds of the constitution and legal system, and they had campaign staff to assist them, paid from public funds. The results, in March 1989, were a sensation, because nearly forty officials, including a member of the ruling Politburo, went down to defeat, and Boris Yeltsin romped home in Moscow with a majority so large it went straight into the *Guinness Book of Records*. The Politburo's leading conservative, Yegor Ligachev, called the whole exercise "political shock therapy."[1]

Nearly two decades into postcommunist Russia, it was far less clear that the institution of free elections had handed power back to ordinary citizens in a way that made it possible to speak of Russia as a democracy. Certainly, regular multiparty elections took place, but the government was accountable to the president, not to elected representatives. Elections, when they occurred, were heavily influenced by national television, which reflected the views of the state. In many of the republics and regions, the political process was even more strongly dominated by executive authority, with Soviet-style majorities for single candidates and a press that was entirely in the pocket of the local administration. In the early postcommunist elections, international monitors were very supportive of the attempt being made to organize competitive elections in what was still a "young democracy." By the end of the 1990s, however, opinions were more qualified, and the verdict of the largest monitoring organization on the March 2004 presidential contest was that it "did not adequately reflect principles necessary for a healthy democratic election."[2] In 2007 and 2008 the largest monitoring organization, the Organization for Security and Cooperation in Europe, was not represented at all, and further changes in the law meant that elections provided even less opportunity to select the kind of deputies who might be able to hold a dominant leadership to account on behalf of the citizens who had elected them.

Toward Competitive Politics

Although the Communist Party of the Soviet Union (CPSU) was mentioned in earlier versions, the constitution adopted under the guidance of Leonid Brezhnev in 1977 had converted the party's effective dominance into a formal political monopoly. In March 1990 Article 6 of the constitution was amended to refer to the CPSU and "other political parties, as well as trade union, youth, and other public organizations and mass movements." A legal basis for multiparty politics was established the following October, when a new law on public organizations was adopted, covering the formation of trade unions, sporting clubs, women's and veterans' associations, and political parties; the law also set out a procedure for them to register with the Ministry of Justice. The new constitution, adopted in December 1993, made it clear that postcommunist Russia was firmly committed to "political diversity and a multiparty system," subject only to a requirement that parties and associations refrain from a forcible challenge to the state and from incitement to social, ethnic, or religious strife. And there would be, under this constitution, no state or compulsory ideology (Art. 13).

The first test of this emerging but still weakly formed party system was the election of December 1993, called the same day as a referendum to approve the new constitution. The election was held less than three months after President Yeltsin, in late September, issued a decree suspending the Russian parliament and after he ordered the Russian army, two weeks later, to seize the parliament building when substantial numbers of deputies refused to accept the legitimacy of his action. Some newspapers were banned; several of Yeltsin's leading opponents were taken out of the parliament building with their hands in the air; and sixteen parties or movements were suspended on the grounds that they had been involved in the "events" of early October. All of this created a rather unusual and inhospitable environment for the conduct of Russia's first-ever multiparty election. In the end, thirteen parties or movements appeared on the party-list ballot, and another 1,567 independent or party-sponsored candidates were nominated in one or another of the 225 single-member constituencies, which accounted for the other half of the new legislature.[3]

The results of the election were a considerable shock, not just to Yeltsin and his colleagues, but also to the Western governments that had backed his attack on an elected parliament. Most successful of all were the independents, who won 141 of the 225 constituency seats; that outcome gave them nearly a third of all the seats in the new Duma. The most successful of the parties was Russia's Choice, led by former premier Yegor Gaidar, with a total of 67 seats. But there was a sensational result in the party-list contest, which was won by the Liberal Democratic Party led by right-wing nationalist Vladimir Zhirinovsky, with the Communists in third place (see Table 6-5). Television coverage was suspended in the early morning because of "technical difficulties," and U.S. vice president Al Gore, invited to witness the birth of a new Russian democracy, had to leave in some embarrassment. Gaidar acknowledged that reformers had suffered a "bitter defeat"; the

Table 6-5 Elections to the Russian State Duma, 1993–2003

	1993				1995				1999				2003			
	List %	List seats	SMC seats	Total seats	List %	List seats	SMC seats	Total seats	List %	List seats	SMC seats	Total seats	List %	List seats	SMC seats	Total seats
LDPR	22.9	59	5	64	11.2	50	1	51	6.0	17	0	17	11.5	36	0	36
RC	15.5	40	27	67	3.9	0	9	9	—	—	—	—	—	—	—	—
CPRF	12.4	32	16	48	22.3	99	58	157	24.3	67	46	113	12.6	40	12	52
WR	8.1	21	2	23	4.6	0	3	3	2.0	0	0	0	—	—	—	—
AP	8.0	21	11	33	3.8	0	20	20	—	—	—	—	3.6	0	2	2
Yabloko	7.9	20	6	26	6.9	31	14	45	5.9	16	4	20	4.3	0	4	4
PRUC	6.7	18	1	19	0.4	0	1	1	—	—	—	—	—	—	—	—
DPR	5.5	14	1	15	—	—	—	—	—	—	—	—	0.2	0	0	0
OHR	—	—	—	—	10.1	45	10	55	1.2	0	7	7	—	—	—	—
Unity	—	—	—	—	—	—	—	—	23.3	64	9	73	—	—	—	—
FAR	—	—	—	—	—	—	—	—	13.3	37	31	68	—	—	—	—
URF	—	—	—	—	—	—	—	—	8.5	24	5	29	4.0	0	3	3
UR	—	—	—	—	—	—	—	—	—	—	—	—	37.6	120	103	223
Rodina	—	—	—	—	—	—	—	—	—	—	—	—	9.0	29	8	37
Other	8.7	0	8	8	34.0	0	32	32	12.2	0	9	9	17.2	0	23	23
Independents	—	—	141	141	—	—	77	77	—	—	105	105	—	—	67	67
Against all	4.2	—	—	—	2.8	—	—	—	3.3	—	—	—	4.7	—	—	—

Source: Central Electoral Commission.

Note: SMC = single-member constituency; LDPR = Liberal Democratic Party of Russia; RC = Russia's Democratic Choice);
CPRF = Communist Party of the Russian Federation; WR = Women of Russia; AP = Agrarian Party; PRUC = Party of Russian Unity and Concord; DPR = Democratic Party of Russia; OHR = Our Home Is Russia;
FAR = Fatherland–All Russia; URF = Union of Right Forces; UR = United Russia.

Moscow evening paper, more dramatically, warned that Russians had "woken up in a new state" after the "Communo-Fascists' success."

The 1993 Duma, however, was a transitional one that held office for only two years. The elections that followed in December 1995 were far more important, as they had the potential to shape Russian party politics for the next four years or even longer. This time, parties or movements were required to collect 200,000 signatures, no more than 7 percent of which could be drawn from any single republic or region. Forty-three eventually satisfied this requirement, more than three times as many as in 1993, and 2,267 independent or party-sponsored candidates competed for the 225 single-member constituencies.[4] With so many parties competing for seats, it was clear that very few would reach the 5 percent threshold needed to take part in the allocation of party-list seats, and in the end only four did so, led by the Communist Party of the Russian Federation (CPRF). These four accounted for just over half the total party-list vote, which meant that just under half of the vote had been "wasted," or cast for parties that had secured no representation. It also meant that the parties that reached the threshold had twice as many seats in the new Duma as their share of the vote would otherwise have obtained for them. There was no precedent anywhere in the world for this degree of disproportionality.

The 1999, 2003, and 2007 Duma Elections

The election law that led to this skewed result came under increasing criticism over the years that followed, and attempts were made to have the results themselves declared unconstitutional. In the end, no fundamental changes were made to the law that was approved in June 1999 and which then governed the elections that took place the following December. As before, the new Duma would be divided into two halves, one of 225 party-list seats and the other of 225 single-member seats. But the law now provided that if the parties or movements that reached the 5 percent threshold secured less than half the party-list vote among them, other parties that had won at least 3 percent would be added, starting with the one closest to the threshold, until their combined total reached at least half of the entire party-list vote. Similarly, if a single party won more than half the total party-list vote and no other party reached the threshold, a second party would be added to the allocation of seats. This was a "floating" rather than a fixed threshold.

The results of the voting took some time to emerge, but from early on it was clear that pro-Kremlin parties—and particularly the recently formed party called Unity—had performed much better than expected. The winner, as in 1995, was the Communist Party, with a larger share of the party-list vote. But Unity followed closely and secured almost as many party-list seats in the new Duma. An anti-Kremlin coalition, Fatherland–All Russia, came in third, but with a smaller share of the vote than the polls had predicted, and the Union of Right Forces (URF) did rather better than expected, helped (it was thought) by an energetic and imaginative campaign as well as by the implicit support of Prime Minister Vladimir Putin. Zhirinovsky's Liberal Democrats came in fifth with scarcely more than half of their 1995 vote, but they were still above the threshold. Yabloko failed to achieve the breakthrough it had hoped for, but it was the sixth of the parties that secured representation in their own right. The parties that had reached the threshold accounted for 81 percent of the party-list vote, a result that gave few grounds for challenging the representativeness of the result. Turnout, at 63 percent, was slightly below the level achieved in 1995, and in eight single-member constituencies—for the first time—the vote was declared invalid, because the number of ballots cast "against all" the candidates had exceeded the number cast in favor of the most successful candidate.

The December 2003 Duma election was dominated by United Russia, a party formed by a merger of the pro-Kremlin Unity Party and its main noncommunist rival in the previous election, Fatherland–All Russia. United Russia's success was a clear demonstration of the influence that the Kremlin had come to play itself in the establishment and operation of the entire range of political forces in postcommunist Russia: it could provide jobs, funding, publicity, and guidance on strategy, and also make life rather difficult for its opponents. The immediate question was the share of the party-list vote that would be taken by United Russia, using the advantages of Kremlin support. In the end, it took nearly 38 percent, rather more than expected and enough to allow it to assume the chairs of all the Duma's newly formed committees. At the same time, there was a substantial decline in Communist support and a strong result for the left-nationalist Rodina Party, which had evidently enjoyed Kremlin support in order to take votes away from the Communists. Turnout was lower than ever before, 56 percent, and three seats had to be left vacant because more had voted "against all" than for any of the candidates in the single-member districts.

The December 2007 election was even more overwhelmingly dominated by United Russia than the previous contest. One reason was the adoption of a new electoral law in 2005 that eliminated the single-member districts entirely and allocated all 450 seats to the national party-list contest. Only registered political parties were allowed to contest these seats, and they had to secure more than 7 percent (previously 5 percent) of the vote to be represented (see Table 6-6). All of this strengthened the hand of the Kremlin authorities. At the same time, United Russia presented itself as a party that was defined by its support for President Putin and aimed to implement "Putin's plan," and in this way it hoped to attract the support of those who had helped the outgoing president to achieve

Table 6-6 The Russian Duma Election, December 2, 2007

Name of party	Votes cast	Share of vote (%)	Seats
United Russia	44,714,241	64.30	315
Communist Party of the Russian Federation	8,046,886	11.57	57
Liberal-Democratic Party of Russia	5,660,823	8.14	40
A Just Russia: <u>Rodina</u>/Pensioners/Life	5,383,639	7.74	38
[Under the 7 percent threshold]			
Agrarian Party of Russia	1,600,234	2.30	—
Yabloko	1,108,985	1.59	—
Civic Force	733,604	1.05	—
Union of Right Forces	669,444	0.96	—
Patriots of Russia	615,417	0.89	—
Party of Social Justice	154,083	0.22	—
Democratic Party of Russia	89,780	0.13	—
Invalid votes	759,929	1.09	—

Source: Central Electoral Commission.

Gennadii Zyuganov, leader of Russia's Communist Party and presidential candidate, casts his ballot in a polling station in Moscow.

Source: Reuters/Shamil Zhumatov

his exceptionally high approval ratings. Putin, indeed, agreed to stand as the top candidate on the United Russia list, although he was not (and did not become) a member of the party itself. The outcome was a massive vote for the United Russia list, and a new Duma that was wholly subservient to the Kremlin. Putin expressed some satisfaction that the parties that had reached the threshold accounted for more than 90 percent of the vote among them, and there was more general satisfaction that the level of turnout, at nearly 64 percent, was somewhat higher than it had been four years earlier.

The Political Parties

Of the four parties that reached the representation threshold in the 2007 Duma election, the closest to a political party of the conventional kind was the Communist Party of the Russian Federation (CPRF). It was the successor to the Communist Party of the Soviet Union and, much earlier, the Russian Social Democratic Workers' Party, which was formed in 1898 and later led the October Revolution.[5] The CPRF had a substantial grassroots membership and a functioning national structure, both largely inherited from Soviet times. And it had the best-established party press: three national newspapers (including *Pravda*) and two oppositional papers that were broadly supportive. Its leader was Gennadii Zyuganov, a party official from the late Soviet period, whose booming voice and regular media appearances ensured his nationwide recognition. He had been the party's standard-bearer in the 1996 presidential election, when he took Boris Yeltsin to a second round, but he was less successful in 2000 when Putin won on the first round, and he did not compete in 2004; he stood again in 2008, coming a distant second.

The party program, in its successive versions, reflected nationalist as well as socialist priorities. It took issue with the "barbaric and primitive" form of capitalism that had been established in Russia after 1991 rather than with private property as such, and it warned of the dangers that this form of capitalism implied for "Russian civilization" as well as for the living standards of ordinary people. The party's more specific aims were "people's power," expressed through the elected soviets; social justice, including guaranteed employment and social benefits; equality, based on the elimination of exploitation and the primacy of state ownership; patriotism; the responsibility of individuals to society; a renewed form of socialism; and communism as the "historic future of humanity." Internationally, the party suggested, the choice lay between a divided world in which a few rich countries dominated an impoverished periphery, and a rather different world that emphasized the stable and equitable development of all of its members on the basis of their own circumstances and historical experience.[6]

The Communists, in spite of these ambitious objectives, were losing ground in the early 2000s. Part of the problem was an aging and dwindling membership. Another was their ambiguous attitude toward Vladimir Putin—they supported the Russian president (and his successor) insofar as he was a "patriot," but they could hardly approve of his moves toward private ownership of land and reduction of state subsidies for housing, transport, and other public services. A more immediate problem was fragmentation. Leading members found themselves tempted to retain their positions in the Duma even if the party instructed them to do otherwise, and entire parties were encouraged by the Kremlin to compete for a share of the vote that might otherwise have gone to their best-organized opponents. The Kremlin had enormous resources to commit to such purposes, including its ability to offer public employment and to control access to state television. In addition, it could draw on the advice of its own pollsters and "election technologists" to design and carry out its strategy.

The "center" was occupied by United Russia, which was, as President Putin told television interviewers in November 2003, the "political force that [he had] relied upon throughout these four years." Putin was not a member of this or any other party, but he lost no opportunity to make clear his personal commitment to United Russia, which, in turn, virtually defined itself by its support of the Russian president. He attended United Russia's party congress in September 2003 so that he could "signal his gratitude," and the list of candidates that went forward in December 2003 and again in December 2007 was heavy with governors and other representatives of the administration. It was also representative of the country's largest companies, not just so they could exercise influence in the new Duma, but also so they could demonstrate their political loyalty. United Russia won 223 seats in the December 2003 election, but had 300 by the time the Duma convened as independents and candidates of other parties transferred their loyalties to the winning side, and won even more in 2007. With a majority of this size, United Russia could guarantee the adoption of any legislation that required a "qualified" or two-thirds majority, and its leader, Interior Minister Boris Gryzlov, became Speaker of the entire assembly.

It was less clear what the new party stood for, other than support for the president and his policies. Gryzlov told the party's preelection congress in September 2003 that the party's ideology was "common sense"; government should simply "do what is good for the majority of citizens." A more elaborate manifesto, "The Path of National Success," was adopted at about the same time in an attempt to map out a coherent and distinctive strategy. The manifesto called for a "new nationwide recovery," based on an "ideology of success" that could bring together all sections of the society. One step toward this end was a "new level of internal unity," minimizing the differences between rich and poor, young and old, and among state, business, and society. The economy should at the same time combine state regulation and market freedoms, with the benefits of further growth distributed for the most part to the less fortunate. The party rejected left-wing and right-wing ideologies in favor of a "political centrism" that could unite all sections of society and one that was expressed in the policies of President Putin, whose reforms were "vital for Russia." For Russians, the best way to describe a party of this kind was as a "party of power"—that is, a party heavily composed of state officials whose sole purpose was to maintain them in their positions of influence.[7] A Just Russia, based on a merger that took place in 2007 and included Rodina (Motherland), was also centrist and strongly pro-Kremlin.

The more ideological liberal or pro-market "right" suffered a heavy defeat in the December 2003 election, and neither of its two main representatives, Yabloko or the Union of Right Forces, was able to reach the 5 percent threshold and take part in the allocation of party-list seats (although they both won single-member constituencies). They were even less successful in December 2007. Yabloko, formed as an electoral bloc in late 1993, was one of the oldest of the new Russian parties. It was led up to 2008 by economist Grigorii Yavlinsky; indeed, it incorporated the first two letters of his surname, as well as letters from the surnames of the other two founders. Yabloko identified itself as "democratic," or broadly supportive of the political and economic changes that had taken place since 1991. But it was strongly critical of the "corrupt oligarchy" that had taken power and outspoken in its defense of all who depended on the state for their employment or social support. Yabloko rejected the communist system that had "brought the country to a dead end," but it also rejected the "vulgar economic policies" of the postcommunist years, which had led to a decline in living standards, deepening social divisions, and a crisis in education, health care, and science. Meanwhile, business and government had become so closely associated that corruption was endemic, and a bureaucratic and authoritarian system had established itself that served the interests of a small minority.[8]

Yabloko's proposals were broadly social democratic—indeed, its entire strategy was modeled on the values of Russia's European neighbors. The party aimed to establish a stable democratic order, including a state based on the rule of law, a socially oriented market economy, a civil society, a modern system of security, and a postindustrial strategy within what it described as the European path of development. More generally, it favored a "society of equal opportunities, based on the principles of social justice and social solidarity of the strong and the weak." Private initiative was important, but the market was not an end in itself; it had to be associated with a set of measures that would protect all sections of society. Yabloko, alone among the major parties, referred not only to the need to combat terrorism but also to the need to do so by engaging in political dialogue in Chechnya, as elsewhere. Russia, Yabloko believed, was a "European country in its historical destiny, its cultural traditions, [and] its geographical situation," with a potential that could only be realized by "making creative use of the values of European civilization." Yabloko was, accordingly, a supporter of Russian membership in the European Union (although, admittedly, it was not an immediate prospect) and in other European organizations.

539

Yabloko's companion on the liberal margins of the political spectrum was the Union of Right Forces, formed in August 1999 shortly before the Duma election of that year. Its leaders were former prime minister Sergei Kirienko, former deputy premier Boris Nemtsov, and entrepreneur Irina Khakamada. The party program, as modified in 2001, committed the party to "liberal values," including freedom of speech and association, separation of powers, decentralization, the rule of law, democratic control of society over the state, private property, equality of rights and opportunities for all citizens, and tolerance of diversity. Only a liberal market economy, in the party's view, would be able to ensure the accumulation and proper distribution of the national wealth. The party placed less emphasis than Yabloko on redistribution and more on cutting taxes and respecting the rights of private property.[9] The Union of Right Forces, however, was even less successful than Yabloko in the December 2003 Duma election. Its three leaders resigned their positions, and although Khakamada ran in the 2004 presidential election, she did so without the party's official backing and later withdrew from politics entirely. At the end of 2008, following another bad result in the December 2007 election, the Union of Right Forces merged with two other parties to form a new probusiness grouping, Right Cause, that appeared to have better electoral prospects, although it had been formed with the approval of the Kremlin and was expected to represent a "constructive" rather than uncompromising opposition in a new Duma.

The oldest of the new parties was the Liberal Democratic Party of Russia (LDPR), led by its outspoken chair Vladimir Zhirinovsky. The party, despite its name, was usually seen as right-wing nationalist or even fascist. It had been the surprise winner of the party-list contest in 1993, and it took party-list seats again in 1995, 1999, 2003, and 2007—the only party, apart from the Communists, to do so. The Liberal Democrats were closely identified with their leader, an effective media performer who had himself run for the presidency. Zhirinovsky supported the attempted coup of 1991, and he opposed the agreement that brought the Soviet Union to an end later that year. He was particularly successful in identifying the problems of ordinary Russians and suggesting simple remedies, such as shooting the leaders of organized crime or forcing all the Chechens over the border and then closing it. Despite the LDPR's oppositional rhetoric, it was broadly pro-government in its voting behavior in the Duma, and the Kremlin appeared to offer the party its covert support to ensure that it regularly reached the party-list threshold.

The LDPR's program aimed squarely at Russia's revival as a great power. It called for the restoration of a unitary Russian state and for a simplification of the federal system into a smaller number of provinces, each of which would be headed by an appointed governor, who would, in turn, appoint subordinates at lower levels. The LDPR opposed communism, but also the "wild capitalism" that was constructed over the postcommunist period. It favored a society of social justice in which there would be no hungry, homeless, or unemployed. The LDPR was also concerned about "anti-Russian and amoral" programs on television, and it opposed the presence of nontraditional sects in Russia, whose activities were "as a rule" directed by the espionage services of foreign states that wanted to undermine Russian power and stability. The LDPR favored a mixed economy with a variety of forms of ownership, but the state should be responsible for the management of the economy as a whole, and it should maintain a substantial manufacturing sector of its own. The state should also control the sale of tobacco, sugar, and alcohol, and land should be left in the hands of those who cultivated it.[10]

Parties and Politics in Postcommunist Russia

So far, there is little evidence that Russia's parties have engaged the loyalties of the Russian people. In part, this situation simply reflects the high level of turnover in the parties themselves. In all, more than eighty parties or blocs contested at least one of the Duma elections between 1993 and 2007, but only three (Communists, Liberal Democrats, and Yabloko) contested all five of them, and only two (Communists and Liberal Democrats) won party-list seats in each of them. To put it another way, all the parties or movements that contested the 1993 party-list election, taken together, won no more than 32 percent of the party-list vote in 2003. Conversely, more than half the parties that competed in December 2003 had not fought a previous election, and nearly two-thirds of the party-list vote was won by parties or blocs that had not contested a single previous election. The latter included two of the four parties that reached the 5 percent threshold, Rodina (Motherland) and United Russia.

A more direct measure of party legitimacy is the extent to which respondents are willing to "trust" political parties compared with other institutions. Russia's national public opinion research center has asked questions of this kind since the early 1990s. Consistently, the church and the armed forces enjoy the highest levels of confidence. The presidency, after a bad patch in the later Yeltsin years, overtook both in the early 2000s and sustained its leading position under Putin and Dmitri Medvedev. Local government is normally more widely respected than central government, and the media are more widely respected than the agencies of law enforcement, which are more often associated with corruption and maltreatment than with the administration of justice. Political parties, however, consistently appear at the bottom of the list, below even the parliament in which they are represented. In fact, it appears that political parties are not the least trusted civic institution only when respondents are asked to express confidence in a list that includes the investment funds that (for the most part) defrauded ordinary citizens of the vouchers they obtained as a result of the privatization of state property.[11]

A distinctive feature of Russian parties has been the extent to which they are identified with their leaders. Yabloko was all but synonymous with its leader Grigorii Yavlinsky, and the Liberal Democrats with their flamboyant standard-bearer Vladimir Zhirinovsky. Some of the parties that took part in the 1995 election were known simply as the "bloc" of a particular leader, and the same was true in 1999. There was the Zhirinovsky Bloc, formed when difficulties arose with the registration of the Liberal Democrats as a party, and the Bloc of General Andrei Nikolaev and academician Svyatoslav Fedorov. Only the Communist Party enjoyed a substantial individual membership, of about 134,000 when it was re-registered in 2006, although United Russia quickly claimed even larger numbers, more than 943,000 as of the same date. Over the country as a whole, no more than 2 percent of the population was estimated to belong to one or another of the parties, and no more than 22 percent identified themselves as committed supporters, compared with about 87 percent in the United States and 92 percent in the United Kingdom.[12] Indeed, many of the new parties avoided the word *party* altogether, reflecting the long period of Soviet rule when the single ruling organization was generally thought to have abused its position.

The weakness of Russian parties stemmed from a lack of the kinds of organized interests—of labor or of capital—that might have helped to sustain them. And it stemmed from the political system itself. The electoral system certainly gave parties a real advantage in that they were allocated half the seats in the Duma in addition to the seats they could hope to win in the single-member districts; from 2007, as we have seen, they were allocated all the seats as the Duma election became a competition of party lists. But there were few incentives to put forward a coherent or responsible program, because even a majority party would not necessarily play any part in government, and changes in government— like the replacement of Mikhail Kasyanov by Mikhail Fradkov as prime minister in March 2004, or of Fradkov himself by Viktor Zubkov in September 2007—had nothing directly to do with changes in the distribution of seats. In these circumstances, parties were less a means of attempting to "win power" and rather more a device through which prospective presidential candidates could obtain media exposure in the Duma election and in this way strengthen their positions in the contest that really mattered.

It is no surprise that ordinary people tend to think that their views have not been sufficiently considered by the government that rules in their name. In the United States, about 42 percent of those who are asked think "people like me have no say" in the making of government decisions; in the United Kingdom, the figure is about 54 percent. In Russia, according to a 2005 survey, only 3 percent think that ordinary people have a "significant" influence; 14 percent believe they have "some" influence on government; 23 percent think they have an "insignificant" influence on government; and 58 percent think they have "no influence at all." In other responses, an overwhelming 88 percent think it is "difficult" or "very difficult" for ordinary people to secure the rights with which they have supposedly been endowed; 38 percent think "most" and 42 percent think "almost all" public officials are corrupt; and 89 percent think public officials "not very often" or "not at all" treat individual citizens equally.[13] Similar results are shown in Table 6–7. It is certainly a paradox that the introduction of the institutions of liberal democracy—separation of powers, rule of law, and multiparty politics—is associated with an electorate who feel themselves no nearer to—in some cases further away from—a real degree of influence over the society in which they live.

Table 6-7 Russians and the Political Process: Results of a Survey, 2003

Form of activity	Percentage of respondents who think it is effective	Percentage of respondents who employed it in past year
Working through political parties	5	1
Providing monetary inducements	10	6
Working through trade unions	11	4
Taking part in strikes and demonstrations	13	3
Appeals to government or the media	19	4
Use of personal contacts	19	8
Appeals through the courts	20	5
See no effective forms of influence/ have employed none	46	78

Source: Adapted from a representative national survey in June 2003 as reported in *Mirovaya ekonomika i mezhdunarodnye otnosheniya* [World economy and International Relations], no. 8 (2004): 28. Percentages have been rounded.

NOTES

1. Yegor K. Ligachev, *Zagadka Gorbacheva* [The Gorbachev Puzzle] (Novosibirsk: Interbuk, 1992), 75.

2. The fullest reports on successive Russian elections have been those prepared by the Office for Democratic Institutions and Human Rights of the Organization for Security and Cooperation in Europe (OSCE), available for consultation at http://www.osce.org/odihr/. Their report on the March 2004 presidential election, *Russian Federation: Presidential Election 14 March 2004. OSCE/ODIHR Election Observation Mission Report* (Warsaw: ODIHR, June 2004), is quoted at p. 1.

3. For book-length treatments, see Peter Lentini, ed., *Elections and Political Order in Russia* (Budapest: Central European University Press, 1995); and Jerry F. Hough and Timothy J. Colton, eds., *Growing Pains: The 1993 Russian Duma Election* (Washington, D.C.: Brookings, 1998).

4. For a fuller discussion of the 1995 Duma election, see Stephen White, Richard Rose, and Ian McAllister, *How Russia Votes* (Chatham, N.J.: Chatham House, 1997), chaps. 9–11.

5. At least two book-length studies are available in English of Russia's Communists: Joan Barth Urban and Valerii D. Solovei, *Russia's Communists at the Crossroads* (Boulder: Westview Press, 1997); and Luke March, *The Communist Party in Post-Soviet Russia* (Manchester: Manchester University Press, 2002).

6. "Programma" [Program], in *Kommunisticheskaya partiya Rossiiskoi Federatsii v rezolyutsiyakh i resheniyakh sezdov, konferentsii i plenumov TsK (1999–2001)* [Communist Party of the Russian Federation in Resolutions and Decisions of Congresses, Conferences and Central Committee Plenums (1999–2001)] (Moscow: Izdatel'stvo ITRK, 2001), 4–21.

7. Full documentation is available on the party's Web site, http://www.edinros.ru.

8. Yabloko's policies are quoted unless otherwise stated from its Web site, http://www.yabloko.ru. A full English language study of this party is available: David White, *The Russian Democratic Party Yabloko* (Aldershot, UK: Ashgate, 2006).

9. Party documents are quoted from its Web site, http://www.sps.ru.

10. The party's program can be found on its Web site, http://www.ldpr.ru.

11. There is a brief discussion of Russian polling and its interpretation in Stephen White, *Russia's New Politics* (Cambridge and New York: Cambridge University Press, 2000), 182–194. A fuller study is Matthew Wyman, *Public Opinion in Postcommunist Russia* (London: Macmillan, 1997). A wide variety of findings may be consulted on the home pages of the survey organizations themselves. See, for example, the home page of the Public Opinion Foundation (an English version is available at http://english.fom.ru) and of the Levada Center (http://www.levada.ru), much of which is available in English at http://www.russiavotes.org.

12. See White, Rose, and McAllister, *How Russia Votes*, 135. The estimate of party membership levels nationally is from *Argumenty i fakty*, September 8, 1999, 24.

13. The U.S. figure is drawn from the 2004 National Election Study, question V045202 M2b, consulted at http://www.umich.edu/~nes; the UK figure from the British Election Study, post-2001 election survey, question BQ65a, consulted at http://www.essex.ac.uk/bes; and the Russian figures are from a nationwide survey conducted for the author and associates by Russian Research in 2005 with two thousand respondents who were interviewed face-to-face in their own homes.

How Is Power Used?

IN THE COMMUNIST PERIOD, THE TASK OF POLICY IMPLEMENTATION was relatively simple. There was, in principle, a "correct" position, based on the official ideology. It was the job of the ruling party to express that position and of the government to carry it into effect. The party dominated all important positions and supervised the government in its work. The parliament was effectively appointed, and so were the leading officials at lower levels of government. Soviet citizens were not given any opportunity, in practice, to challenge official policies through the courts or to mobilize opposition to them on the streets. And they were not given any opportunity to criticize official policies, directly at least, in the mass media, because the editors of the media were party appointees and the contents of the media were censored.

The Soviet policy process was rather more complicated. The leadership, for a start, was often divided in its loyalties—by region or by the sector of the economy with which its individual members were most closely associated. And the differences grew wider between hard-liners committed to central planning and a "class approach" and their more moderate colleagues, who were prepared to allow a greater element of private ownership in the economy and a wider range of opinion in public life. The mass public could criticize the performance of leading officials, if not the principles on which they operated. And if all else failed, citizens had other ways of making their views known, such as by getting in touch with their elected representatives or sending letters to government bodies and the press.

The postcommunist system, in principle, was a very different one. The political parties and presidential candidates competed openly. Implementation was a matter of government decision, enforced where necessary by the rule of law. Decisions that violated the law or constitution could be contested in the courts. Indeed, on occasion even the president was overruled, such as when Boris Yeltsin tried to merge the Interior Ministry with the security service in the mid-1990s. And every aspect of policy could, in theory, be challenged by newly independent media. In practice, however, much remained the same. The ruling group was largely made up of the same people as before, particularly in the regions; the parliament was still peripheral; the broadcast media—the only ones with real influence—were mostly in the hands of government itself; and the rule of law was very limited in cases in which the authorities themselves took an interest. In these circumstances, policy advanced—if it did at all—through a series of one-off deals between the Kremlin and the larger organized interests, although this deal making was often concealed behind the outward appearance of an all-powerful president who did not hesitate to use the powers of his office to maintain central authority.

Privatizing the Economy

The central challenge for Russia's postcommunist leadership was to replace a failing command economy with a capitalist market.[1] "We must," Yeltsin declared in October 1991, "provide economic freedom, lift all barriers to the freedom of enterprises and of entrepreneurship, and give people the opportunity to work and to receive as much as they can earn, throwing off all bureaucratic constraints." Presidential decrees later in the year abolished limits on earnings, liberalized foreign economic relations, and commercialized shops and services. Most dramatically of all, prices were "freed" on January 2, 1992. Within a month, they were three-and-a-half times higher, and by the end of the year they were twenty-six times higher. Price reform, Yeltsin acknowledged, was a "painful measure," but it was the path the "whole civilized world" had been obliged to follow.[2]

A program for the next stages of reform was adopted in July 1992. It set out a series of objectives, including deregulation, a balanced budget, privatization, structural change (such as demilitarization), and the creation of a competitive market economy. The main outline of a privatization program had already been approved by the Russian parliament in July 1991, and a committee for the management of state property had been appointed to supervise the entire exercise. All citizens, it was agreed in the summer of 1992, would receive "privatization checks" or vouchers for 10,000 rubles (about US$30 at the time), which was the nominal value of all property that belonged to the state divided by the population. Vouchers could be used to buy shares in one's own workplace or shares at an auction where other enterprises were being sold, or they could be placed in investment funds. The first vouchers were distributed in October 1992, and they had to be used by the end of 1993. "The more property owners and business people there are in Russia," Yeltsin declared in a television address, "the sooner Russia [will] be prosperous and the sooner its future [will] be in safe hands."[3] By the time voucher privatization came to an end in June 1994, approximately 100,000 enterprises had changed their forms of ownership, and more than 40 million citizens had nominally become property owners—indeed, at this time Russia had more private shareholders than either Great Britain or the United States.

A second stage of privatization began in 1994, involving the sale of large enterprises at auction, and a third stage, involving smaller individual projects, began in 1996. By then, the pace of privatization was slowing, but already 63 percent of all Russian enterprises had moved from the state into private hands, accounting for about a quarter of total output because relatively few were in large-scale, heavy industry; many more were in retail trade and catering. At least for Western advisers, the whole exercise had been an "extraordinary achievement."[4]

Privatization of agriculture had not progressed as far by the late 1990s, even though private ownership of land had been incorporated into the Russian constitution in 1990 and had then formed part of the new constitution adopted in 1993. A presidential decree of March 1992 and another decree in June had provided for the sale of private plots of land. A more far-reaching decree of October 1993, hailed as a historic step, established that it was legal for those who owned land to buy, sell, lease, and exchange it, although any change in ownership had to take into account the "rational organization of land areas." Changes in ownership, for this and other reasons, advanced slowly: the number of commercial farms increased but then fell again, and by the end of the 1990s they accounted for no more than 2 percent of the value of all agricultural output (they were most important for their production of sunflower seeds).

The larger problem, apart from the regulations themselves, was that Russia's farms were mostly unprofitable, which provided little incentive to take over their ownership. By the late 1990s, more than 80 percent of collective and state farms were running at a loss. There was strong political opposition in any case to the "speculation" that might result from a free market in land. The Russian parliament pushed in these circumstances for lifetime leasing rather than outright ownership, and there was little willingness to legislate for private ownership in the Russian regions. Meanwhile, agricultural output fell steadily from year to year, livestock numbers collapsed, and farmers who continued to produce slipped even deeper into a debt abyss.

The privatization of industry produced mixed results as well. The change in ownership had little effect on investment or enterprise behavior, and labor productivity actually fell. Output became even more highly concentrated in a small number of factories than it was before the move to private ownership, and energy costs per unit of output rose rather than fell. Meanwhile, there were few signs of a revolution in managerial attitudes. On the contrary, managers were just as keen as their Soviet predecessors to retain state subsidies, cheap credit, and protection from foreign competition. And although there was an investment crisis of "astounding proportions," managers as well as workers were opposed to the sale of shares in their enterprise even if a new owner was likely to bring them the resources they needed to expand and modernize.[5]

Why was privatization being carried out at all? More for political reasons than for economic ones, it appeared. Once a substantial share of property had been placed in private hands, there would be a powerful group with a vested interest in the postcommunist order. It was less important who the new owners were or how the property itself had been acquired; capitalism in the West had, after all, established itself by violence and robbery as well as by thrift and innovation. But once a new class of owners had been formed, they would, it was assumed, find it in their interests to establish more civilized procedures. The new owners, in fact, found it easier and quicker to make money by exploiting their control of the state to secure public assets at prices that were below historic costs, and safer to invest their money in foreign bank accounts than in the future of their own society. They were committed to public order, but not necessarily to the rule of law (which might mean submitting to an investigation of their own fortunes) or to democracy (which might mean losing influence over their government, and possibly their liberty). Communists and nationalists had been skeptical from the outset, and they were scathing about the results. *Pravda* spoke of an "enormous swindle" in which a "narrow stratum of 'new Russians' feeding off the budget and raw material exports had got richer and richer," and a former minister spoke similarly about an exercise in which "under the guise of 'reforms' the most substantial property in world history [had] come into the hands of a criminal community."[6]

A liberalized economy was meant to achieve its purposes by, among other things, attracting foreign direct investment. As part of this process, Russia became a member of the World Bank and the International Monetary Fund during 1992, and the Group of Seven of the

Table 6-8 Russian Economic Performance, 1992–2009 (percentage change year on year)

	1992	1993	1994	1995	1996	1997	1998	1999	2000
GDP	86	91	87	96	97	101	95	103	110
Index (1990 = 100)	81	74	65	62	60	60	57	59	65
Industrial output	82	86	79	97	96	102	85	108	120
Agricultural output	91	96	88	92	95	101	88	104	108
Investment	60	88	76	90	82	95	93	106	121

Source: Compiled by the author from official statistics.

major industrial nations eventually became the Group of Eight, although Russia was clearly in a rather different position than the other members. Meanwhile, a series of agreements brought Western funds to the assistance of the Russian economy, starting with a ruble stabilization fund in 1992 of $24 billion. Yet foreign assistance was unlikely to bring about the transformation widely expected. It took some time to materialize; it came with strings attached; and it cost more and more to finance, swallowing up resources that might otherwise have been devoted to domestic investment as well as to social programs of various kinds. At the same time, Russian capital was moving abroad more quickly than foreign assistance was arriving; an estimated $50 billion was leaving every year in the late 1990s, much of it used to acquire property. In Nice alone, at least fifty villas valued at $850,000 or more were being sold to Russians every year in the late 1990s. In the spa town of Carlsbad in the Czech Republic, a "ruble mafia" had bought up most of the hotels, and locals concluded it had become a " 'zone of peace' for Russian godfathers seeking a break from life at home and a convenient place to launder their profits."[7]

Meanwhile, foreign investment remained at a low level—lower, for example, than in Peru. Why were foreign investors so reluctant to entrust their resources to a newly democratic Russia, but happy to do so in communist-ruled China? Some of them confided their reservations to the weekly paper *Argumenty i fakty*.[8] A French electronics entrepreneur found that the new Russian business owners were simply too vulgar: they threw money around in the casino, while he read Tolstoy and Dostoevsky and tried to develop his company so that it could employ more workers in the future. Others were worried by the level of serious crime and the threat of political instability. Still others were discouraged by the bribes they found they had to pay. Russia was one of the most corrupt countries in the world, according to the figures produced annually by Transparency International.[9] "How to make a million in the former Soviet Union?" asked one exasperated American investor. "Bring two million and it will soon be down to one."[10]

Ten years or more after economic reforms had been launched, therefore, they had produced a decidedly mixed record. Growth, for a start, had failed to materialize; living standards had fallen, public services had been starved of resources, and essential infrastructure had not been renewed. The Soviet economy had certainly contracted in its final years: by 4 percent in 1990 and by 15 percent in 1991 as the state itself fell apart. The decline continued throughout the Yeltsin administration, with a minor upturn in 1997 but a still more dramatic downturn in August 1998 as Russia defaulted on its foreign obligations and the ruble collapsed on the foreign exchanges. By the end of the decade, the Russian economy had contracted to about half of its size at the end of the period of communist rule—a steeper fall than the West experienced during the Great Depression—although there was some sign of recovery in the early 2000s, assisted by high world oil prices (see Table 6-8).

	2001	2002	2003	2004	2005	2006	2007	2008	2009
GDP	105	105	107	107	106	108	108	106	92
Index (1990 = 100)	68	71	76	81	86	93	100	106	98
Industrial output	105	104	107	106	104	107	108	101	85
Agricultural output	108	102	101	102	102	104	103	109	100
Investment	112	109	108	111	111	117	121	110	84

Elderly shoppers buy cottage cheese and other milk products at an open-air market in Moscow in 1999, a few months after the collapse of the ruble. The economy has recovered strongly in recent years on the back of high oil prices, but social differences have widened, and many older Russians still do their shopping in markets of this kind, where prices are normally lower than in the stores.

Source: AP Images/Mikhail Metzel

Economic observers and others had widely expected that after a short period of adjustment, growth would resume. They also anticipated that the output of heavy industrial goods for which there was no longer a demand would fall and that the economy would bounce back leaner and fitter.[11] The sharpest falls, however, were in the output of modern consumer goods, including electronics. Oil, steel, and gas fell by a third or more, but the output of personal computers was down by 60 percent, of cameras and watches by more than 80 percent, and of color televisions by more than 90 percent. Meanwhile, investment fell every year, to just a quarter of its 1990 level, and foreign trade was even more overwhelmingly dependent on raw materials, including oil and gas, rather than manufactured products incorporating added value. At least for critics of the government's strategy, this situation represented deindustrialization rather than regeneration, and it carried the risk that Russia would become a colonial appendage of the Western countries, exporting its natural resources and importing a few luxuries, while taking over some of the low-tech and environmentally detrimental production that Western countries had no wish to retain.

These rates of decline had obvious implications for Russia's economic place among the nations. In 1990 Russia's gross domestic product (GDP) was about a third that of the United States; by the end of the decade it was barely a fifth. The Russian economy was still, in absolute terms, one of the largest in the world, but by the early years of the new century it had fallen behind those of Brazil, China, and South Korea, as well as those of the major Western democracies. In terms of population, Russia was well below the global average, behind Latin American countries such as Costa Rica and Ecuador, and African countries such as Gabon and Namibia.[12] For a nationalist like Alexander Solzhenitsyn, what was taking place was nothing less than the "destruction" of the Russian economy rather than the rapid turnaround that Western advisers had rashly predicted. Others went even further, speaking of "genocide."[13]

In the short run, certainly, economic reform had led to a sharp fall in living standards, with a widening gap between rich and poor, higher unemployment, and the degradation of public services. It was hardly surprising that Russians were looking for another way forward in the new century, one that was neither a return to the past nor the continuation of a liberal experiment that appeared to have failed even more comprehensively. And it was hardly surprising that they supported "Putin's Plan," if it meant an economy that was once again expanding and living standards that were once again improving—even if the economy was more heavily reliant on the state itself and even more dependent on the world price of oil and gas than it had been in the Soviet period.

Foreign and Security Policy

Foreign policy had already begun to change in the late Soviet years.[14] The term "new thinking" was apparently inspired by a book, *New Hopes for a Changing World,* written by British philosopher Bertrand Russell some years earlier.[15] As conceived by Mikhail Gorbachev and his colleagues in the leadership, the term meant a reconsideration of almost all aspects of the Soviet relationship with the outside world. The fragility of the world described by Gorbachev lay in the underlying threat of a nuclear war in which there would be no winners; global challenges, such as pollution and depletion of the world's natural resources, for which neither capitalism nor socialism had all the answers; and the difficulties facing the developing nations.[16]

These views departed radically from earlier Soviet orthodoxy and from Marxism-Leninism itself, which placed its primary emphasis on class forces. They led, in turn, to a series of departures in foreign and security policy that brought about the end of the cold war. The Soviet Union ended its costly presence in Afghanistan, following international negotiations, in 1989. It then "de-ideologized" its relations with Cuba and opened or restored relations with Israel, the Vatican, and the Arab monarchies. In 1987 the Soviets reached an agreement with the United States that eliminated an entire class of nuclear weapons, land-based intermediate and shorter-range missiles. That agreement was followed by the Strategic Arms Reduction Talks (START) agreement in 1991, which made the first substantial cuts in the weapons available to each side. An even more far-reaching change affected Soviet relations with Eastern Europe, where the "Sinatra doctrine" ("I'll do it my way") replaced the Brezhnev doctrine that was imposed after the brutal suppression of Prague Spring in 1968.

Russia's new president, Boris Yeltsin, had little experience in foreign affairs when he assumed the leadership of the Soviet Union's largest republic and then of an independent state at the end of 1991. But he lost no time in signaling the change that had taken place. In January 1992 he announced that Russian nuclear weapons would no longer be directed against targets in the United States, and he went on to announce a series of unilateral cuts in nuclear and conventional arms. In an address to the UN Security Council the same month, Yeltsin insisted that he saw the Western powers "not just as partners, but as allies." While Yeltsin was in North America for the UN speech, he met President George H. W. Bush, who announced that they were meeting "not as adversaries, but as friends" and presented Yeltsin with a pair of cowboy boots (the boots turned out to be too small, but the Russian president kept them anyway). The "Camp David declaration" that was issued at the end of their talks confirmed that relations between the two countries were now based on "friendship and partnership" and that both presidents would personally seek to "eliminate the remains of the hostile period of the 'Cold War.'"[17]

In the first U.S.-Russian summit, held in the summer of 1992, both sides spoke of a still closer "democratic partnership." At a January 1993 summit, an ambitious arms reduction treaty, START II, was concluded, under which each side undertook to dismantle two-thirds of its strategic nuclear warheads. It was, Yeltsin suggested, the most important agreement ever reached in the history of disarmament (and yet its ratification by the Russian parliament took almost a decade). Yeltsin met President Bill Clinton three months later in Vancouver, British Columbia, where both presidents committed themselves to a "dynamic and effective Russo-American partnership." A new Russian military doctrine, adopted at the end of the year, underscored the change in attitudes that had occurred. No country would be regarded as an adversary of the new Russia, and there would be no use of military force unless Russia was itself attacked. The primary purpose of the armed forces under these new and rather different circumstances would be domestic peacekeeping.

Past rivalries, however, soon began to make themselves apparent. For a start, Russian diplomats were firmly opposed to the eastward expansion of the North Atlantic Treaty Organization (NATO), which incorporated the Czech Republic, Hungary, and Poland in 1999, and four other former communist-ruled countries—Bulgaria, Romania, Slovakia, and Slovenia—together with the three Baltic republics that had been part of the Soviet Union—Estonia, Latvia, and Lithuania—in 2004. Yeltsin, addressing the UN in 1995, called for a more general framework of European security rather than the expansion of existing alliances and a "new confrontation." But the communist presence was much larger in the new Duma, elected at the end of that year, and therefore less domestic support for the pro-Western policies that had characterized the first years of the postcommunist administration. Yeltsin's first foreign minister, Andrei Kozyrev, found himself under increasing attack (critics claimed he had been representing the interests of the West and not those of his own country), and so in early 1996 he was replaced by Yevgenii Primakov, a career Arabist who had served in the Politburo of the Communist Party of the Soviet Union and who took a much more skeptical view of Western actions. Russia, Primakov insisted, was still a great power, and it had not "lost" the cold war but instead shared in common victory. Accordingly, Russia would be looking for an "equal partnership" with the United States—one in which relations with the West as a whole were less important than before and a greater emphasis would be placed on the former Soviet republics and China.

The accession of Vladimir Putin to the Russian presidency appeared to mark a change in Russian attitudes, at least in the direction of greater predictability, and after the September 11, 2001, attacks on the United States, a common front began to develop in the "war on terrorism." The West began to take a more indulgent view of Russian behavior in the breakaway Chechen republic, which, Russia insisted, was in the front line of a common struggle against Islamic fundamentalism. Russia, for its part, began to cooperate in military and intelligence matters with its Western counterparts, and reluctantly accepted the U.S.-led military action against Iraq. On March 20, 2003, shortly after fighting erupted, however, Putin issued an official statement in which he called the action a "major political mistake," not only in humanitarian terms but also in the threat it represented to the international order.[18] If some states felt able to impose their will on others without regard to their sovereign status, not a single state anywhere in the world could feel secure. Russia called for an early end to the hostilities and for resolution of the conflict to be entrusted to the UN Security Council.

A more nuanced approach emerged several weeks later when Putin met with a group of journalists. "For political and economic reasons," Putin told them on April 3 in remarks that were broadcast on national television, "Russia does not have an interest in a US defeat. Our interest is in shifting efforts to resolve this problem to the floor of the United Nations."[19] It was not, commentators remarked, a popular position—public opinion would have preferred more forthright support of a long-standing Soviet and Russian ally. But neither had Putin accepted the new U.S. doctrine of preemptive war. Rather, Putin's statement reflected a pragmatic calculus. It was clear that the U.S. government would be the dominant influence in any decisions made after the war about the allocation of rights to Iraqi oilfields, and Russia, which was owed substantial sums by the former regime, had no interest in being excluded. Russians, however, like many Europeans, demonstrated against the war. The demonstration in Moscow, which attracted about twenty thousand participants, was the largest ever held anywhere in the country since the end of Soviet rule.[20] The Iraq war suggested that East and West could cooperate in certain situations, but it was less clear that a fundamental unity of interests and values had replaced the divisions and hostility of the cold war.

East and West were still geopolitical rivals in the former republics of the Soviet Union, particularly in Georgia and Ukraine, where pro-Western leaders came to power, after civil disturbances, in early 2003 and in late 2004. Would their countries be allowed to join NATO and maintain NATO bases on what had formerly been Soviet territory? Relations were no easier with the European Union. It accounted for more than half of Russia's foreign trade after the three Baltic republics joined it in 2004, but Europeans were seriously concerned about a "values gap" in relation to matters such as freedom of the press, the rule of law, and violations of human rights in Chechnya. The fate of the Kaliningrad exclave was a particular difficulty. There was no problem when Russia and the other Soviet republics were all part of a larger union, but once the Baltic republics regained their independence in 1991, Kaliningrad (formerly the city of Königsberg) found itself separated from the rest of the Russian Federation by Poland and Lithuania, which became EU member states in 2004. Would Russians now be obliged to obtain international visas to visit another part of their own country? In 2002 a compromise was achieved after some difficult negotiations. It allowed Russians to travel through Lithuania on the basis of a transit document that would be issued free of charge, but would require travelers to present a recognized passport.[21]

Underlying these various disagreements was a rather different view of the kind of international order that should replace cold war divisions. For Russians, it must at all costs not be a unipolar world dominated by the United States. Accordingly, in its foreign policy concept of 2000 (and in a revised version that appeared in 2008), the Russian government emphasized the importance of a multipolar world and condemned any form of "hegemonism." It was very skeptical about humanitarian intervention in countries such as the former Yugoslavia, claiming to see such intervention as a hypocritical cover for the imposition of Western domination. But there was not much that Russia could do about such situations because of the weak Russian economy—at least in the 1990s—and the understandable desire of many of the countries that had once been part of the Soviet sphere of influence, or indeed of the Soviet Union itself, to secure a reliable guarantee of their long-term independence. It was, then, not surprising that Russian policymakers placed so much emphasis on international law—which normally rules out any form of interference in the internal affairs of other countries—and on the United Nations, where Russia had a seat in the Security Council and could exercise a veto.

The CIS and the East

Relations were easier with the other states that were once part of the Soviet Union and with the Asian states that had enjoyed a close relationship with the Soviets—particularly India and China. The new framework within which relations were conducted with the former Soviet republics was the Commonwealth of Independent States (CIS), which was founded in December 1991 as the Soviet Union collapsed into its constituent republics. The CIS was not a state or a supranational structure of any kind; it had no capital, only a headquarters. Least of all was it an attempt to revive the old Soviet Union. It did, however, provide a mechanism by which a group of states once closely integrated could consider their common purposes. In practice, those purposes were to promote trade and maintain public order through the deployment of peacekeeping forces to trouble spots throughout the territories of its member states, such as the civil war in Tajikistan. The CIS conducted its affairs through a council of heads of state, which served as its "supreme organ." There were other forms of coordination at the ministerial level and an interparliamentary assembly. But according to its own executive secretary, the CIS was a "mechanism for reconciling interests, nothing more,"[22] and relations among its member countries reflected quite distinct sets of considerations.

Among the CIS member countries, Russia had particularly close relations with neighboring Belarus, where Alexander Lukashenko had won an overwhelming victory in the presidential election of 1994. The following year, Lukashenko and Yeltsin signed a treaty of friendship and cooperation during a visit by the Russian president to what he described as "Russia's closest partner." In 1996 the two countries established a "deeply integrated Community" that had a common foreign policy, a common power grid, and eventually a common currency. They also shared military infrastructure. An agreement of April 1997 converted the community into a union that would involve a common legislative space and a single citizenship. These agreements, however, stopped well short of a loss of sovereignty by either side, and the momentum slowed considerably when Putin succeeded Yeltsin as Russian president and a much more pragmatic attitude began to assert itself on the Russian side. Russia was still Belarus's biggest trading partner; the two countries spoke (more or less) the same language; and they were a human community as well, with large numbers of family members on either side of the border. But there was no immediate prospect of a confederation.

Reviewing Russia's pattern of relations with the other CIS states at the end of the 1990s, *Izvestiya* noted that they spanned a wide spectrum. Russia had "almost model" relations with Belarus, but "uncertain" relations with Ukraine in spite of "encouraging tendencies." Relations became still more uncertain at the end of 2004 when a pro-Western liberal, Viktor Yushchenko, won the rerun of a contested presidential election in what became known as the "Orange Revolution." There was "no convergence" in Russia's relations with Georgia; indeed, matters reached the point of open warfare in August 2008 after Georgia had sought to assert its authority over two breakaway enclaves, Abkhazia and South Ossetia, which Russia subsequently recognized as independent states. Neighboring Armenia was "almost an ally," and the Moldovans were "well-disposed partners." In Central Asia, Uzbekistan was "demonstratively independent" and "pragmatic," whereas relations were "contradictory" with Tajikistan and characterized by "less and less understanding" with Turkmenistan, but "more clarity and consistency" with Kazakhstan. Kyrgyzstan was a "loyal and well-disposed partner."[23] Popular attitudes reflected the desire of most people to have closer relations with the other Slavic states. In foreign trade, the largest flows of imports and exports linked Russia with Ukraine, Belarus, and Kazakhstan. Perhaps not coincidentally, these were three of the four republics with the largest numbers of Russians living within their boundaries.

The Soviet Union's relationship with Asia was dominated by its relationship with the still-communist China—the two countries shared the world's longest land boundary as well as a system of government. The Chinese authorities were clearly distressed by the gradual relaxation of communist control in the Soviet Union and Eastern Europe, but both sides agreed to preserve normal relations and to accept differences in their "ways and means of pursuing reforms within the framework of the socialist choice." With the collapse of the Soviet Union in late 1991, the two countries no longer shared their ideology, but other forces helped to unite them: both favored a multipolar world in which the United States was not allowed to dictate its will; both insisted that their domestic affairs, including Tibet and Chechnya, were of no proper concern to the outside world; and both had every reason to favor an increase in trade, particularly (on the Chinese side) in armaments.

By the late 1990s, with Russian foreign policy becoming more assertive in relation to the West, there was a further shift of emphasis toward the larger Asian powers. In particular, during Yeltsin's visit to Beijing in 1996 the two countries established what they agreed to describe as "relations of equal partnership, based on trust, that [were] aimed at strategic cooperation in the twenty-first century." In their joint communiqué, Yeltsin committed Russia once again to China's positions on Taiwan and Tibet, and the Chinese endorsed Russia's policy toward Chechnya (an internal affair of Russia) and toward NATO expansion.[24] The following year, the two countries spelled out an elaborate declaration on a "multipolar world and the formation of a new world order."[25] Later the same year they announced that almost all issues that related to their common boundary had been regulated.[26] But even though both sides could agree to deplore the "hegemonism" of a single power, the Chinese remained reluctant to underwrite Russian plans for a joint system of Asian security, and bilateral trade remained at a disappointing level. By December 1999, when Yeltsin (against his doctor's advice) made yet another visit to the Chinese capital, the Russian press had concluded that a "political alliance—or at least the basis for forging one"—was already in place.[27] Under Putin and Medvedev, the larger Shanghai Cooperation Organization began to acquire importance, uniting Russia and China with Kazakhstan, Kyrgyzstan, and Uzbekistan in what looked to some like an eastern counterpart to NATO.

Overall, there were striking signs throughout the postcommunist years that foreign and domestic policies were connected and that Russian foreign policy in particular was becoming part of the wider patterns of a globalizing world. In the past, the Soviet Union had maintained an official exchange rate for its ruble, which insulated it from the vicissitudes of the international economy and from speculative pressures, but now the ruble was bought and sold both inside and outside of the country, and more Russians held their assets in dollars than in the national currency to protect themselves against inflation. The Soviet Union had regulated movement across its frontiers and jammed the foreign broadcasts that it regarded as hostile. Now there were no serious restrictions on foreign travel (rather, it was the Western countries, worried about Russian godfathers extending their criminal empires, that were seeking to exert controls), and the Russian authorities themselves pressed for the introduction of a visa-free regime with the rest of Europe. The Gorbachev leadership had begun a partial reintegration of Russia into the international economy, liberalizing foreign investment and moving toward a convertible ruble. Postcommunist Russia then became part of the global economy, but a weak and vulnerable part, apart from its mineral wealth, with a productive base that was uncompetitive and a domestic environment that did not encourage investment in the future.

Russian policymakers, by the early 2000s, had a difficult hand to play. They had to stand up to the West to show they were independent, but at the same time cooperate with the West against the threat of Islamic fundamentalism. They could demonstrate power by cutting off gas supplies (as they did with Ukraine in 2005–2006 and Belarus in early 2007), but that scarcely made them a more attractive partner, and in the long run it encouraged a search for alternative suppliers. They pressed for a share in the resolution of regional and global issues, but without the geopolitical weight that would have ensured it. They had to take account of the interests of Russians in other countries, particularly in the Baltic republics, but without appearing to question their sovereignty. And they had to act as if they represented a great power, but one with a per capita purchasing power that was less than half the average of what the World Bank described as "high income" countries, and with a population that was in apparently terminal decline. It was hardly surprising in the circumstances that Russian policy was often contradictory or ambiguous, or that those who helped to shape it sometimes appeared to have conflicting objectives.

NOTES

1. For a fuller review, see, for example, Thane Gustafson, *Capitalism Russian-Style* (New York: Cambridge University Press, 1999); and Marshall Goldman, *The Piratization of Russia: Russian Reform Goes Awry* (London: Routledge, 2003).
2. *Rossiiskaya gazeta,* January 17, 1992, 1.
3. *Izvestiya,* August 20, 1992, 2.
4. See, for example, Anders Aslund, *How Russia Became a Market Economy* (Washington, D.C.: Brookings, 1995), 223, 266. Similarly, see Brigitte Granville, *The Success of Russian Economic Reforms* (London: RIIA, 1995); and Richard Layard and John Parker, *The Coming Russian Boom* (New York: Free Press, 1996).
5. Joseph R. Blasi, Maya Kroumova, and Douglas Kruse, *Kremlin Capitalism: The Privatization of the Russian Economy* (Ithaca, N.Y.: Cornell University Press, 1997), 179, 180–181.
6. *Pravda,* September 27, 1997; Sergei Glazev, *Genotsid: Rossiya i novyi mirovoi poryadok* [Genocide: Russia and the New World Order] (Moscow: Astra sem, 1997), 29.
7. *Izvestiya,* May 22, 1998; *Sunday Telegraph* (London), September 20, 1998.
8. "Akuly starogo biznesa boyatsya 'novykh russkikh'" [The Sharks of Old Business Are Scared of the "New Russians"], *Argumenty i fakty,* April 26, 1995, 6.

9. *Izvestiya,* May 29, 1998, 1.

10. Quoted in Jerrold L. Schecter, *Russian Negotiating Behavior: Continuity and Transition* (Washington, D.C.: U.S. Institute of Peace Press, 1998), 146.

11. See, for example, Glanville, *Success of Russian Economic Reforms;* and Layard and Parker, *Coming Russian Boom.*

12. Figures of this kind are conveniently available from the World Bank's annual *World Development Report,* http://www.worldbank.org/wdr.

13. Solzhenitsyn is quoted from his interview, "Zheltoe koleso" [Yellow Circle], in *Argumenty i fakty,* January 18, 1995, 5; Glazev, *Genotsid.*

14. Fuller discussions of late Soviet and Russian foreign policy are available in several studies, including Robert H. Donaldson and Joseph L. Nogee, *The Foreign Policy of Russia: Changing Systems, Enduring Interests,* 4th ed. (Armonk, N.Y.: M. E. Sharpe, 2009; Jeffrey Mankoff, *Russian Foreign Policy: The Return of Great Power Politics* (Lanham, Md.: Rowman and Littlefield, 2009); and Andrei P. Tsygankov, *Russia's Foreign Policy: Change and Continuity in National Identity,* 2nd ed. (Lanham Md.: Rowman and Littlefield, 2010).

15. Bertrand Russell, *New Hopes for a Changing World* (London: Allen and Unwin, 1951). The book was derived from a series of radio broadcasts for the British Broadcasting Corporation.

16. Gorbachev set out this thinking in his address to the 27th Party Congress in 1986 and in his best-selling *Perestroika: New Thinking for Our Country and the World* (New York: Harper and Row, 1987).

17. *Diplomaticheskii vestnik,* no. 4–5, 1992, 12.

18. *Rossiiskaya gazeta,* March 21, 2003, 2.

19. *Izvestiya,* April 4, 2003, 1.

20. For a fuller discussion, see Stephen White, "Russia: Diminished Power," in *The Iraq War: Causes and Consequences,* ed. Rick Fawn and Raymond Hinnebusch (Boulder: Lynne Rienner, 2006).

21. For a fuller discussion, see Roy Allison, Stephen White, and Margot Light, *Vladimir Putin and a Wider Europe* (London: Routledge, 2006).

22. *Izvestiya,* September 17, 1998. On the CIS itself, see, for example, Martha Brill Olcott, Anders Aslund, and Sherman W. Garnett, *Getting It Wrong: Regional Cooperation and the Commonwealth of Independent States* (Washington, D.C.: Carnegie Endowment for International Peace, 1999).

23. *Izvestiya,* April 29, 1998.

24. *Diplomaticheskii vestnik,* no. 5, 1996, 18.

25. *Diplomaticheskii vestnik,* no. 5, 1997, 19–21.

26. *Diplomaticheskii vestnik,* no. 12, 1997, 9–10.

27. *Nezavisimaya gazeta,* December 11, 1999.

What Is the Future of Russian Politics?

Iᴛ ɪs ᴀʟᴡᴀʏs ᴅɪꜰꜰɪᴄᴜʟᴛ ᴛᴏ ᴍᴀᴋᴇ ᴘʀᴇᴅɪᴄᴛɪᴏɴs, Oꜱᴄᴀʀ Wɪʟᴅᴇ ᴏɴᴄᴇ remarked, especially about the future. Predictions about the future of Soviet and now of Russian politics have been particularly wide off the mark. In its early days, few observers expected the Bolshevik government to last, not least because it seemed to have turned economic science on its head. "No sane man would give them as much as a month to live," the London *Daily Telegraph* pronounced on January 5, 1918. The *New York Times* gave its readers a similar impression. In America, two young journalists, Charles Merz and Walter Lippmann, made their name in 1920 with a careful investigation of U.S. newspaper reports about the Soviet Union. During the first two years of Soviet rule, they found, its demise had been announced at least ninety-one times. It was twice reported that Vladimir Lenin was planning retirement, three times reported that he had been imprisoned, and once reported that he had been killed. Four times the *Times* had told its readers that Lenin and Leon Trotsky were planning to flee and three times that they had already left the Kremlin. Following the rigors of war, when communism had been replaced by the New Economic Policy, equally confident assurances appeared that the communist experiment had been officially abandoned.[1]

Scholars did little better when it came to predicting the end of the Soviet Union. The Soviet system was well understood to have systemic weaknesses, and the falling rate of growth was there for all to see. But it had survived so long that it had, some thought, become taken for granted. The Soviet Union had survived a civil war, World War II, and the cold war, and it appeared to have forged a sort of bargain with its population based on authoritarian forms of political control in exchange for full employment and low prices. Mikhail Gorbachev's difficulties, wrote one respected scholar as late as 1990, had been "grossly exaggerated"; the real story of that year was the "further consolidation of Gorbachev's political position," and he was "almost certain to remain in power at least until the 1995 presidential election." The Communist Party itself, according to an article by the same author that was published in 1991, was likely to become the "dominant electoral party . . . [for] the rest of the century."[2] Meanwhile, the U.S. ambassador to Russia, a long-standing student of Soviet affairs, was telling his government that Gorbachev was likely to remain in power "for at least five (possibly ten) years."[3]

A decade or more after its establishment, Russia's postcommunist system appeared to be more securely established. There was still substantial support for communist rule, and more Russians subscribed to a broadly communist ideology than to any other. But even more were not committed to any philosophy at all, and few of them were willing to accept the social costs of another transition. Nor was there substantial support for other forms of rule, such as a monarchy or military rule—only 3 percent strongly supported either alternative at the start of the new century, although somewhat more, 11 percent, favored a dictatorship.[4] The questions that remained dealt with internal matters: What would be the balance of authority between the federal government and the Russian regions as President Vladimir Putin strengthened the "executive vertical"? Would the Russian media offer a variety of viewpoints in spite of the government's increasingly effective control of the major television channels? Perhaps the biggest question was whether Russia would move, however slowly, toward a state in which the rule of law had some significance, or whether it would move in a Latin American direction, with elections that allowed some degree of choice but within a society that had wide divisions between rich and poor, a ruling group that was privileged and often corrupt, and a political system that gave ordinary people few effective means of resisting those in power.

An Incomplete Democracy

Formally, at least, the new constitution of December 1993 marked a step forward. It was a constitution that committed the new state to ideological pluralism, political diversity, and a multiparty electorate. In a clear break with the past, there could be no state or compulsory ideology. Indeed, a whole section dealt with the rights and freedoms of the individual, including equality before the law and equal rights for men and women. And there were guarantees of personal inviolability and privacy; freedom of information, under which citizens would receive access to any documentation held about them by an official body unless security considerations were involved; freedom of movement across and within national boundaries; freedom of conscience, of thought and speech, of association and assembly, and of the press; and freedom from censorship.

Yet Russia's new constitutional design possessed grave weaknesses. For a start, it was unilaterally imposed after the parliament had been bombed into submission. This made it "Yeltsin's constitution," not a document that reflected a broader national consensus. It was, moreover, a seriously unbalanced constitution. Formally, it called for a separation of powers: the president had powers in relation to the Duma, and the Duma had powers in relation to the president, and both of them were protected in the exercise of their powers by an independent judiciary. But in theory and practice the president's powers were much greater—in particular, his power to sack the government, which President Boris Yeltsin did four times in 1998 and 1999 without reference to parliamentary or public opinion and which President Putin did again in 2004. The parliament enjoyed a direct popular mandate, but its influence over the president was limited. Its "consent" was needed for the appointment of a new prime minister, but if that consent was withheld it ran the risk of dissolution. And there was no serious prospect that the president could be impeached, which was the parliament's ultimate sanction.

Meanwhile, countervailing forces of all kinds were weak. Among the many political parties, only one—the Communist Party of the Russian Federation—had achieved the degree of institutionalization needed to make it comparable with parties in the liberal democracies; United Russia was more an extension of the Kremlin itself than a conventional party. And yet how else were Russian voters to be given an organized choice of political alternatives? The trade unions repeatedly pointed out that they could bring millions into the streets on "days of action," but there was little point in striking, because the employers, and sometimes entire regional administrations, were bankrupt themselves. The press was vigorous and often oppositional, but it had increasingly become the plaything of rich financiers, and newspaper circulations had fallen dramatically—by more than half during the 1990s. Judges, in accordance with the constitution, were "independent" and "inviolable," but the Constitutional Court, which was supposed to regulate the behavior of the highest levels of government, was appointed on the recommendation of the president (it had previously been elected by the parliament) and was not in the last resort a guarantee of the rule of law.

Human Rights

These departures from fully democratic norms were reflected in a human rights performance that worried the Western organizations that regularly survey such matters. Amnesty International repeatedly expressed concern about the physical abuse of conscripts and the deportation of asylum seekers. Conditions in pretrial prisons, it found, were "appalling," characterized by overcrowding, inadequate diets, lack of medicines, and even oxygen starvation. Thousands died awaiting trial, and those who survived had often been tortured or otherwise maltreated. In Chechnya, where a guerrilla war had been under way for at least a decade, there were indiscriminate killings, detention without trial, torture, and extrajudicial executions. Several outrages reached the attention of the Western press. In April 1995 in Samashki, on the border between Chechnya and Ingushetia, about 250 civilians, including women and children, were reportedly killed by troops who were burning down houses and throwing grenades into the shelters where local people were taking cover. Other atrocities were reported after the war resumed in 1999, including well-documented cases of torture and indiscriminate killings. Meanwhile, the number of prisoners was the highest in the world per capita (the United States followed closely behind).[5]

Human Rights Watch had a wider range of concerns, including freedom of thought and expression as well as the physical abuse of prisoners. It drew particular attention to the Russian provinces, which had degenerated into "fiefdoms that engage[d] in civil and political rights violations with impunity from Moscow." In what was apparently a quid pro quo for support of its policies, the central government turned a blind eye to corruption by regional leaders and refused to investigate the human rights violations for which they were clearly responsible. Regional leaders, for their own part, made every effort to extend their control over local newspapers and radio stations. Such efforts usually presented few difficulties because newspapers and radio stations typically ran at a loss, but in some cases local leaders were prepared to sanction beatings and even murders to achieve their ends. The editor of an opposition paper in the primarily Buddhist republic of Kalmykia was stabbed to death in the summer of 1998 in what Human Rights Watch described as "by far the most convincing case of government collusion in the death of a journalist."[6] Many more attacks against the media occurred, the most widely reported of which was the murder of investigative journalist Anna Politkovskaya in 2006. In this, as in other cases, the guilty parties remained unpunished.

The Russian judicial system was another cause for concern. According to Human Rights Watch, it was moving further away from Council of Europe standards as well as those that were appropriate to a democracy. Their investigators found that corruption and abuse were the "rule rather than the exception" and that torture while in police custody had reached "epidemic proportions."[7] Criminal justice officials solicited and accepted bribes, and crime-solving statistics were "improbably high, due in part to torture." Torture, it emerged, was most likely to occur in the early hours of detention when police isolated suspects from their families and lawyers; confessions were then extracted using beatings, asphyxiation, electric shock, and other forms of physical and psychological torture. Requests for legal assistance were routinely refused and "often resulted in more violence." A shortage of judges slowed down the trials themselves, and acquittal rates were below 1 percent, "reminiscent of the Soviet era."[8]

What was the broad trajectory of change over this period? Amnesty International and Human Rights Watch choose not to attach figures to the human rights performances with which they are concerned. Freedom House, by contrast, produces ratings that students of comparative politics regularly use. The Freedom House "annual evaluation of political rights and civil liberties everywhere in the world" is expressed in a seven-point scale, which, in turn, yields a threefold classification: a regime is "free" if it scores between 1 and 3, "partly free" if it scores between 3 and 5.5, and "not free" if it scores between 5.5 and 7. At the beginning of the 2000s, 44 percent of the world's independent states were rated "free," 31 percent were rated "partly free," and 25 percent (but with 36 percent of the world's population) were rated "not free."[9]

Based on this evidence, Russia has seen no dramatic improvement in civil and political rights since the end of communist rule. The Soviet Union in the Brezhnev years had been "unfree"; by the beginning of 1991, while still under communist rule, it was rated "partly free." Freedom House took the view that the new union treaty under consideration at the time was based on human rights and the creation of a democratic state that was founded on the principle of popular representation and the rule of law. All fifteen republics had declared some form of sovereignty; reformers had been successful in local elections in many parts of the country; Gorbachev's directives were being routinely disregarded; and by 1990 the Soviet parliament had adopted laws guaranteeing freedom of the press and freedom of religion.[10]

At first, postcommunist Russia was placed in a much higher category than its Soviet predecessor, but still only "partly free." In early 2005, in a controversial judgment, Freedom House announced that Russia had slipped into the ranks of the "not free," and it remained there over the years that followed (see Table 6-9). The judgment reflected dissatisfaction with the elections of 2003 and 2004, with the consolidation of state domination of the media, and with the "many political measures that [had] significantly narrowed the freedom enjoyed by opposition parties and groups." All of this was the culmination of a "growing trend under President Vladimir Putin toward the centralization of authority, media restrictions, and politicization of the law-enforcement system."[11] Russia, on this basis, was about as "democratic" as Afghanistan, Egypt, or Pakistan. Among the former Soviet republics, it was above Belarus and the Central Asian states, but below Armenia, Georgia, Moldova, and Ukraine (which were "partly free") and still further below the Baltic states, all of which were "free." The Russian media, in a separate exercise, were judged "unfree" because of libel laws, harassment, violence against journalists, and the disproportionate influence of financial and industrial interests connected to the government.[12]

Table 6-9 Freedom House Scores, 1980s–2010

	1980s	1990	1990s	2010
"Free"	United States United Kingdom Germany	United States United Kingdom Germany	United States United Kingdom Germany	United States United Kingdom Germany
"Partly free"		Gorbachev's Soviet Union	Yeltsin's Russia	
"Not free"	Brezhnev's Soviet Union			Putin's Russia

Source: Adapted from http://www.freedomhouse.org

Yet few of the former Soviet republics had the kinds of freedoms achieved in the former communist countries of Central and Eastern Europe. Countries such as Hungary, Poland, and Yugoslavia had all accommodated a more pluralistic form of communist rule. Poland and Yugoslavia had retained private agriculture and handicrafts; Hungary had a burgeoning "second economy"; and all three allowed the publication of authors such as George Orwell and Alexander Solzhenitsyn, who would have been banned elsewhere in the region. After communist rule, all of them were regarded as "free." But long-standing cultural differences made themselves apparent in the contrast between the former communist countries in Europe and the former Soviet republics of Central Asia. One of the former Soviet republics, Tajikistan, was among the world's eight most oppressive countries, according to Freedom House; the three Baltic republics were at the other extreme, with Estonia as "free" as the United States.

Why had democratic practices been restored in Central and Eastern Europe and in post-Soviet Estonia, Latvia, and Lithuania, but not in Russia? Clearly, at least a part of the explanation stemmed from the external influence. German investment made more of a difference in the Czech Republic—a smaller country, with a common border—than it could possibly do in Russia. In spring 1999 the Czech Republic, Hungary, and Poland became members of the North Atlantic Treaty Organization, which bound them politically as well as militarily to the West. Seven more countries in the region—Bulgaria, Estonia, Latvia, Lithuania, Romania, Slovakia, and Slovenia—joined them in May 2004. The three Baltic countries, as well as the Czech Republic, Hungary, Poland, Slovakia, and Slovenia, joined the European Union (EU) the same year, and Bulgaria and Romania followed them in 2007. All of the new EU member countries had to accept the "Copenhagen criteria" before they could be considered for admission, including minority rights and the rule of law. Indeed, even before they had entered the EU, their domestic structures were beginning to adapt to these new requirements.

There was no prospect of Russia joining the Western alliances, nor could the mechanisms of democratic compliance work in the same way. Russia's future politics depended much more on domestic processes, and they, in turn, reflected a culture and practice that pointed more firmly toward a form of nationalist authoritarianism than liberal democracy.

In an influential study of Italian civic traditions, Robert D. Putnam suggested that Palermo might be the "future of Moscow," essentially because of Russia's lack of the "networks of civil engagement" that had been built up in Italy since the Middle Ages and that under-pinned its democracy in more recent times.[13] This observation suggested, in turn, that the construction of democratic institutions in the former Soviet republics would take longer—and might not take place at all—than in the former communist countries that had shared in the Western experience of cooperation and self-government within the framework of the rule of law. In Russia and in the other Soviet republics, little of this tradition was available to be restored; it had to be "democracy from scratch."

The changes taking place in postcommunist Russia also were often unhelpful to a democratic outcome. The institution of an overly powerful presidency weakened the parliament and inhibited the development of political parties. The collapse in living standards that took place under the Yeltsin government was on a scale that had undermined the state itself in other countries; living standards improved under Putin, but it was not until the end of his second presidential term that the Russian economy returned to the level it had achieved at the end of the Soviet period. Nor was it just a matter of statistics: life expectancies fell throughout the 1990s; the population had been declining continuously since 1992; and social divisions were much wider than they had been during the compulsory egali-tarianism of the communist period. Some of the richest Russians were indeed among the richest people in the entire world, according to the annual report in *Forbes* magazine, although they suffered more heavily than others in the international financial crisis that began to affect the entire society in late 2008.

Initially, both Putin and Dmitri Medvedev were inclined to explain the crisis as an external development that stemmed from ill-considered bank lending in the United States and would have no significant effects in Russia. But Russian banks began to experience difficulties and had to be rescued. Credit became more difficult to obtain and, if obtainable at all, more expensive. That put pressure on individual companies, many of which were the sole or at least the most important single employer in their towns. The ruble began to slip against the dollar and had to be supported. Share values fell sharply; unemployment increased rapidly; and forecasts of economic growth had to be revised downward. Indeed, the World Bank predicted a fall of 8 percent in GDP in 2009 and did not foresee a recovery until 2012. This exposed some of the weaknesses in an economy that depended so heavily on the export of natural resources; and it placed some pressure on a political leadership that had been able to increase public spending for almost a decade, and in almost every category.

Certainly, some forces were pulling Russia toward more pluralist forms of politics in the 2000s. Many new freedoms were securely established, including religious liberty and a freedom that was peculiarly important in a formerly communist society—the freedom not to play a part in political life. Almost anything could be published, albeit at some risk to journalists. A large part of the economy was outside the direct control of the state. And large numbers of citizens had a higher education. But there were enduring weaknesses in terms of popular control over government action and an increasing disposition on the part of the Kremlin leadership to seek to resolve the country's problems by the reimposition of a Soviet-style discipline. Clearly, there was no inevitability about "democratization": a few of the former Soviet republics had established market economies and liberal democracies, but others had regressed to forms of dictatorial rule that were often more authoritarian than the later years of communism. Russia, entering a new century, seemed likely to retain its basic freedoms, but its political system was more likely to emphasize the Russian tradition of executive authority than the Western tradition of limited and accountable government within a framework regulated by law.

NOTES

1. See S. J. Taylor, *Stalin's Apologist* (New York: Oxford University Press, 1990), 96, 113. For some of these later assurances, see, for example, Peter Filene, *Americans and the Soviet Experience* (Cambridge: Harvard University Press, 1967).
2. See, respectively, Jerry F. Hough, "Gorbachev's Endgame," *World Policy Journal* 7 (Fall 1990): 642, 669; Hough, "Understanding Gorbachev: The Importance of Politics," *Soviet Economy* 7 (April-June 1991): 106. Wider issues of interpretation are considered in Michael Cox, ed., *Rethinking the Soviet Collapse: Sovietology, the Death of Communism and the New Russia* (London: Pinter, 1999).
3. Quoted in *Novaya i noveishaya istoriya* [Modern and Contemporary History] 1 (1996): 113, in a telegram of February 1989.
4. These data are drawn from the New Russia Barometer 8, fielded in January 2000 (N = 1,940) and available at http://www.russiavotes.org.
5. *Izvestiya,* March 13, 1999, 1, and more generally the annual reports of Amnesty International.
6. This discussion is based on the relevant sections of *Human Rights Watch World Report 1999* (New York: Human Rights Watch, 1999).
7. *Guardian* (London), November 11, 1999, 19.
8. *Human Rights Watch World Report 1999,* 283–286.
9. *Journal of Democracy* 11 (January 2000): 189–190.
10. *Freedom Review* 22 (January-February 1991): 8.
11. Arch Puddington and Aili Piano, "Worrisome Signs, Modest Shifts," *Journal of Democracy* 16 (January 2005): 105.
12. *Freedom Review* 27 (January-February 1996): 10; and Adrian Karatnycky, ed., *Nations in Transit: Civil Society, Democracy and Markets in East Central Europe and the Newly Independent States* (New Brunswick, N.J.: Transaction Books, 1997), 439.
13. Robert D. Putnam, *Making Democracy Work* (Princeton, N.J.: Princeton University Press, 1993), 173, 183.

FOR FURTHER READING

Barany, Zoltan, and Robert G. Moser, eds. *Russian Politics: Challenges of Democratization.* Cambridge and New York: Cambridge University Press, 2001.

Bremmer, Ian, and Ray Taras, eds. *New States, New Politics: Building the Post-Soviet Nations.* 2nd ed. Cambridge and New York: Cambridge University Press, 1996.

Brown, Archie. *The Gorbachev Factor.* Oxford and New York: Oxford University Press, 1996.

———, ed. *Contemporary Russian Politics: A Reader.* Oxford and New York: Oxford University Press, 2001.

Cohen, Stephen F. *Failed Crusade: America and the Tragedy of Post-Communist Russia.* New York: Norton, 2000.

Colton, Timothy J. *Transitional Citizens.* Cambridge, Mass., and London: Harvard University Press, 2000.

Donaldson, Robert H., and Joseph L. Nogee. *The Foreign Policy of Russia: Changing Systems, Enduring Interests.* 4th ed. Armonk, N.Y., and London: M. E. Sharpe, 2009.

Dunlop, John B. *The Rise of Russia and the Fall of the Soviet Empire.* Princeton, N.J.: Princeton University Press, 1993.

Gill, Graeme, and Roger D. Markwick. *Russia's Stillborn Democracy? From Gorbachev to Yeltsin.* Oxford and New York: Oxford University Press, 2000.

Gorbachev, Mikhail. *On My Country and the World.* New York: Columbia University Press, 1999.

———. *Perestroika: New Thinking for Our Country and the World.* London: Collins; New York: Harper and Row, 1987.

Gustafson, Thane. *Capitalism Russian-Style.* Cambridge and New York: Cambridge University Press, 1999.

Hough, Jerry F. *Democratization and Revolution in the USSR, 1985–1991.* Washington, D.C.: Brookings, 1997.

———. *The Logic of Economic Reform in Russia.* Washington, D.C.: Brookings, 2000.

Huskey, Eugene. *Presidential Power in Russia.* Armonk, N.Y., and London: M. E. Sharpe, 1999.

Mankoff, Jeffrey. *Russian Foreign Policy: The Return of Great Power Politics.* Lanham, Md.: Rowman and Littlefield, 2009.

Mawdsley, Evan, and Stephen White. *The Soviet Elite from Lenin to Gorbachev.* Oxford and New York: Oxford University Press, 2000.

McFaul, Michael, Nikolai Petrov, and Andrei Ryabov. *Between Dictatorship and Democracy: Russian Post-Communist Political Reform.* Washington, D.C.: Carnegie Endowment for International Peace, 2004.

Mickiewicz, Ellen. *Changing Channels: Television and the Struggle for Power in Russia.* Rev. ed. Durham, N.C.: Duke University Press, 1999.

Miller, William L., Stephen White, and Paul Heywood. *Values and Political Change in Postcommunist Europe.* London: Macmillan; New York: St. Martin's Press, 1998.

Putin, Vladimir. *First Person: An Astonishingly Frank Self-Portrait by Russia's President Vladimir Putin.* New York: Random House; London: Hutchinson, 2000.

Reddaway, Peter, and Dmitri Glinski. *The Tragedy of Russia's Reforms: Market Bolshevism against Democracy.* Washington, D.C.: U.S. Institute of Peace Press, 2001.

Remington, Thomas F. *The Russian Parliament: Institutional Evolution in a Transitional Regime, 1989–1999.* New Haven: Yale University Press, 2001.

Sakwa, Richard. *Russian Politics and Society.* 4th ed. London: Routledge, 2008.

Shevtsova, Lilia. *Russia Lost in Transition: The Yeltsin and Putin Legacies.* Washington, D.C.: Carnegie Endowment for International Peace, 2007.

Tsygankov, Andrei P. *Russia's Foreign Policy: Change and Continuity in National Identity.* 2nd ed. Lanham Md.: Rowman and Littlefield, 2010.

Urban, Michael E. *The Rebirth of Politics in Russia.* Cambridge and New York: Cambridge University Press, 1997.

White, Stephen. *After Gorbachev.* 4th ed. Cambridge and New York: Cambridge University Press, 1994.

———. *Understanding Russian Politics.* Cambridge and New York: Cambridge University Press, 2011.

White, Stephen, Richard Rose, and Ian McAllister. *How Russia Votes.* Chatham, N.J.: Chatham House, 1997.

White, Stephen, Richard Sakwa, and Henry Hale, eds. *Developments in Russian Politics 7.* Basingstoke: Palgrave; Durham, N.C.: Duke University Press, 2010.

Wyman, Matthew. *Public Opinion in Postcommunist Russia.* London: Macmillan; New York: St. Martin's Press, 1997.

Part 7

Poland

Marjorie Castle

The Context of Polish Politics

I N 2009 POLAND CELEBRATED BOTH THE TWENTIETH ANNIVERSARY OF the fall of communist rule and the fifth anniversary of its entry into the European Union. With two decades of an unblemished record of alternations of power (if anything, too much alternation) determined by free and fair elections Poland is undeniably democratic—more than that, Poland may be called a consolidated democracy. As for its identity as an integral part of Europe, as an EU member in excellent standing, Poles can point to the July 2009 selection of former Polish prime minister Jerzy Buzek to be president of the European Parliament, the first from Central and Eastern Europe to hold that office. But huge questions remained about this democratic and European Poland. Would this largely Roman Catholic country eventually resemble the senior EU members as a modern secular democracy, or would it emerge as something more traditional and more religious, a new-old kind of European democracy? On the economic front, would it manage to catch up with its European neighbors, or would it remain forever in a second tier, with its return to Europe never quite completed?

The transformations Poland experienced during the twentieth century bring up equally important questions. What would be the long-term impact of the several decades of communist rule on Poles' political culture, on their economic potential, and on the divisions among them? How would the mode of transition from communist rule to market democracy affect these same factors? How well does this still-young Polish democracy serve its citizens, their preferences, and their interests? Has democratization made a difference—a positive difference—in the lives of Poles?

Geographic and Historical Context

The country that confronts these questions is one of the largest in Europe. With a surface area of 312,685 square kilometers, Poland is smaller than Germany but a little larger than Italy. Like Germany, most of Poland consists of the low plains of central Europe, with no natural borders to the west or east. The Baltic Sea borders Poland to the north, and mountain ranges create something of a natural boundary in the south. Poland's location has long been a cross it has had to bear. Currently, it possesses what might seem to be an excess of neighbors—Belarus, the Czech Republic, Germany, Lithuania, Russia, Slovakia, and Ukraine. But the classic problem for Poland has been its location between Germany and Russia. In view of the last few centuries of European history, no more difficult location can be imagined.

Depending on how one counts the years, Poland is one of the oldest countries in Europe. A Polish state had already emerged by the tenth century, and any Pole would tell you that the Polish nation has existed since 966, when Mieszko I converted to Christianity and became Poland's first king. Poland at that time and for centuries afterward would not qualify as a nation by modern standards, because the "national" community consisted solely of its nobility or gentry. The people who worked on their lands or traded in their towns—that is, the peasants and merchants with their several languages, religions, and ethnic traditions—were not included. Nevertheless, the 829 years that the kingdom of Poland existed created a powerful and lasting national myth that endures today. Poles have a strong sense of nation, unalloyed by the more local loyalties and identities that characterize nations founded more recently.

Mieszko I's descendants, the Piast dynasty, ruled Poland for four hundred years, expanding Poland from a relatively small principality to a large and important sovereign state, with access to the Baltic Sea. Some characteristics of this era have had lasting effects. The direct relationship between Rome and the Polish state began with Mieszko's decision to accept conversion from Rome rather than through the German church. Poland's bond with Catholicism was complemented by the preference of Piast rulers for Western models and influences. Indeed, although Poles shared a linguistic family and an ethnic heritage with eastern Slavic nations, including Russia, their orientation, like that of other western Slavs, was toward the West. Their rulers encouraged Jews and Germans to immigrate to Poland, bringing their skills with them, and the Polish gentry developed ties with France and Italy.

The Rise and Fall of the Commonwealth of Two Nations

The founding of the Jagiełłonian dynasty in 1386 brought huge changes to Poland. For one thing, it meant the union of Poland with the Grand Duchy of Lithuania, thereby creating the Commonwealth of Two Nations, which was one of the leading powers in Europe for three centuries. The Commonwealth, which ruled over a multinational population but was increasingly characterized by Polish culture and language, had history-changing military successes: in 1410 it defeated the Teutonic knights at the battle of Grunwald, and in 1683 it defeated the Turks outside of Vienna. The battle against the Turks confirmed Poles' views that they were serving as Roman Catholicism's easternmost bulwark, confronting not just the Orthodox Christians to the east but also the forces of Islam.

Another crucial aspect of the origins of the Jagiełłonian dynasty was that Jagiełło, the grand duke of Lithuania, was given the Polish crown (and a Polish-Hungarian queen) by the choice of the Polish nobility. From this point on, each Polish king would be subject to confirmation by a vote of Polish nobles. Although absolutism waxed elsewhere in Europe, in the Commonwealth the parliament of nobles, called the Sejm, gained power and the monarchy grew weaker. In fact, the Polish nobility—a large sector, making up 7 percent to 10 percent of the population—may have been the most powerful class of its kind in Europe. Its members enjoyed an impressive set of civil liberties, including the right to form a "confederation" to mobilize for redress of grievances. Over time the Sejm acquired greater powers, eventually gaining the exclusive right to pass laws.

When the Jagiełłonian dynasty died out in 1572 and the choice of king became a more contentious matter, the power of the nobles increased even more, with Poland becoming effectively a republic, whose throne was occupied by a succession of relatively powerless and indifferent foreigners. Unfortunately for Poland, its institutions increasingly failed to provide effective government—a serious necessity in sixteenth- and seventeenth-century Europe as new military powers arose and the Commonwealth turned out to be over-extended, attempting to control territories that were too numerous and too diverse.

Eventually, the right to form a confederation turned into the right to launch insurrection and—most important—the liberum (free) veto emerged. Under this principle, the most notorious aspect of the Commonwealth, any member of the Sejm could veto any act. By the second half of the 1700s, this veto had paralyzed the government process.

But in eighteenth-century Europe, as now, a country did not have to be a major military power or even have an effective government to survive. Poland, however, had powerful and expansionist neighbors, especially Russia and Prussia. Meanwhile, the Commonwealth's weaknesses were intensified by its failure to integrate any of the ethnically diverse peasant and merchant classes into the national community, forcing it to rely on the nobility, many of whom were willing to be bought by foreign powers, most notoriously at Targowica in 1792. There, several nobles used an institution originally intended to protect the Commonwealth from a monarch's autocratic rule and formed a confederation, which then condemned the new liberal constitution of 1791 and invited Russian troops in to put down rebellion. Because Poland had neither the strength nor the will to resist foreign pressures, in a series of partitions its lands were shortly divided up by Russia, Prussia, and Austria in 1772, 1793, and 1795. The final partition in 1795 eliminated the Polish state from the map of Europe.

Poland under Partition: A Nation without a State

As a result of partition, the Polish nation was without a state for 123 years—years that would shape the nation in three crucial ways. First, during this period the sense of Polish nationhood was preserved and even strengthened in the absence of a Polish state. The existing state, whether Russian, Prussian (later German), or Austrian, was an alien entity that did not serve the interests of the nation, and rarely served individual interests. The disappearance of Poland as a country had the effect, then, of making the Polish national identity, together with the history it embodied, especially precious. The one institution that might define and promote this identity was the Catholic Church.

Second, the many decades of foreign rule fostered two kinds of political strategy, each of which became a tradition in its own right. One tradition was insurrection, with its occasional armed rebellions and its continuing clandestine political activity. Each uprising would go down in the annals of Polish political history, but none would accomplish anything other than provoking reprisals and greater repression. The failure of these rebellions, together with the costs of those failures, led some Poles to adopt a contrasting approach called "organic work." This philosophy emphasized strengthening Polish society independently of the state through education and economic development.

Third, during partition Poles lived under three separate empires, each of which had its own approach to the management of its subjects. Although the period of partition apparently had little impact on the identities of Poles—who upon the rebirth of Poland did not distinguish themselves as Austrians, Germans, or Russians—it created distinct patterns that would result in geographically defined differences of culture and economic development. Russia was the most oppressive of the three empires, at least by the 1820s, and so faced the most insurrections from Poles—a mutually reinforcing relationship. Both Russia and Germany eventually tried to assimilate Poles by restricting their use of Polish and other forms of cultural expression. In addition, both Orthodox Russia and Protestant-ruled Germany conducted official campaigns against the Catholic Church. At the same time, the Russians and Germans oversaw considerable economic development—with the resulting urbanization—in their respective territories, as mining and manufacturing took off. Catholic Austria had no problem with the church. Because it tended to rule its multi-national empire through relative tolerance and by granting a good deal of autonomy to loyal subject nations, it gave Poles a very different experience. Poles living in the Austro-Hungarian Empire could participate in representative government, and Polish culture could flourish in centers such as Cracow and Lvov.

Independence Regained: The Second Republic

The rebirth of Poland took place as a side effect of a major crisis in world history—World War I. After four years of carnage, much of it taking place on former Polish territory, and after the loss of 450,000 Polish troops, the peace of 1918 arrived in a very different Europe. Germany was defeated, the Austro-Hungarian Empire had collapsed, and the Bolsheviks had temporarily withdrawn Russia from European politics. Not only were the obstacles to Polish independence at least temporarily removed, but President Woodrow Wilson of the newly involved United States was a fervent advocate of national self-determination. November 1918 saw the reconstitution of an independent Polish state, led by provisional president Józef Piłsudski, a Polish Socialist Party leader who had led Polish troops against the Russians.

The Second Polish Republic faced serious challenges, beginning with its international environment. Sandwiched between a resentful Germany and a gradually more ambitious and aggressive Soviet Russia, Poland had no friends in its immediate vicinity (territorial disputes kept Czechoslovakia and Poland at odds), and its closest ally was distant France. The reintegration of the three parts of Poland, with their distinct and disconnected economic infrastructures, was in itself a huge policy problem, and the worldwide economic depression did not make things easier. Minority issues created another set of difficulties. At a time when nationalism was increasingly important—for Poles and for other Central and East European peoples—the Second Republic was only 70 percent Polish. The rest of the population included Ukrainians, Jews, Belarussians, Lithuanians, and Germans, many of whom had serious doubts about the Polish national project and how it might affect their own interests.

In the face of all this, the institutions of Poland's first real democracy proved inadequate. After protracted wrangling, the political parties elected to the Constituent Sejm in 1919 produced in the March constitution of 1921 a parliamentary system with a weak president. The parliamentary elections of 1922, conducted under a proportional representation system, resulted in a highly fragmented Sejm of roughly thirty parties, in which no political bloc held a majority of the seats. Stable government proved unattainable. In 1926 Piłsudski carried out a coup d'état, unseating the fifth government in less than four years. He then set up an authoritarian regime that would use rigged but contested elections together with harassment and even internment of opponents to remain in power. Yet it did allow considerable freedom of speech and assembly.

The Impact of World War II

All of Poland's internal problems were rendered moot by the rise of Nazi Party leader Adolf Hitler in Germany, who had an openly expansionist policy toward the east. When the German Third Reich and the Soviet Union concluded the Hitler-Stalin Pact (also called the Molotov-Ribbentrop Pact) in August 1939, Poland's immediate fate was sealed once again—it was to be divided between Germany and Russia. Poland's quick defeat was followed by very costly occupations in human terms. More than 6 million Polish citizens (3 million of them Jews) lost their lives during World War II. Although all Poles suffered, facing massacres, confiscations, and forced resettlement, both the Soviet and German occupation policies hit the middle and upper classes especially hard. For the Soviets, these groups were class enemies, to be forcibly resettled and retrained or simply killed (such as the fifteen thousand Polish military officers at Katyń). For the Nazis, who planned to use Slavs as the manual labor force of Central Europe, they were an inconvenient obstacle to be gradually eliminated through measures such as forbidding education beyond the elementary level and executing any particularly troublesome individuals.

From 1939 to 1944 the Polish nation therefore was not only once again stateless, but also confronted a serious threat to its very existence. At first, the divisions of the interwar period largely disappeared, because all noncommunist forces united under the London government in exile, supporting its resistance arm, the Home Army, while the communists participated in the Soviet-supported People's Guard to resist the German occupiers. Although the Home Army later split into two and then three distinct factions, the Polish resistance continued to be probably the most effective of all resistance movements facing the Nazis. It maintained the partition-era tradition of clandestine activity, carrying out thousands of successful attacks on occupation forces and providing underground cultural, social, and educational services for Polish citizens. Like partition, Nazi occupation seemed to only strengthen Polish national identity. Indeed, seventy years after the German invasion nearly three-fourths of Poles still considered World War II to be a vital part of Polish history that must be remembered.[1]

The end of World War II brought only nominal independence for Poland. It was the Red Army, entering Warsaw on January 17, 1945, that liberated Poland from the Nazis, and, as a result of the superpowers' postwar division of spheres of influence, it was the Soviet Union that determined Poland's future for the next several decades. Poland would officially be a sovereign state, but Soviet leaders would be the ultimate decision makers. Soviet leader Joseph Stalin ensured the outcome by installing a regime ruled by the Communist Party—that is, the People's Republic of Poland, which largely followed the Soviet model.

One other consequence of the postwar settlement was highly important for Poland. Politically speaking, Poland may have been placed firmly in the east, but physically it was moved several hundred miles to the west. On its eastern side, it lost about 180,000 square kilometers to the Soviet Union, but on its western side it gained 103,000 square kilometers from Germany, including Pomerania, Silesia, and half of East Prussia. Millions of Poles from the eastern lands were moved to the former German territories, which would take on a distinct regional character shaped by the dynamics of resettlement, the heritage of the eastern lands, and the economic resources and infrastructure left by the Germans. As a result of these territorial transfers and population resettlements, postwar Poland became much more homogeneous—well over 95 percent of its population was ethnic Poles.

The People's Republic of Poland and Its Legacies

By 1948 the Polish United Workers' Party had complete control of the Polish state, which it used to take over almost all sectors of the Polish economy and many aspects of Polish society, including most forms of social organization. Politically, the Communist Party's domination was total, at least in the public sphere; for example, all media were subject to censorship. A handful of other parties were allowed to exist and were even allocated seats in the Sejm, but these parties were completely under the control of the Communist Party. The range of political variation allowed, even in puppet form, was limited. Right-wing parties were totally proscribed, and any intellectual activities based on right-wing and nationalist currents of the Polish tradition were undertaken only with extreme difficulty. To be involved in public policy—indeed, to accomplish almost anything in public life—required joining or at the very least closely cooperating with the Communist Party. For those who chose not to make that compromise, the Soviet-based state remained nearly as alien an entity as it had been during partition or occupation.

The communist regime followed the Soviet economic model, taking over almost all means of production and distribution and instituting central planning. The growth of heavy industry was a top priority. Eventually, Soviet-style development transformed the Polish economy: within a few decades the proportion of the population employed in agriculture had been cut in half, and women had become an integral part of the workforce. Nevertheless, this pattern of development had significant costs in terms of environmental damage, institutionalization of inefficiencies, and investment in outmoded production methods.

Despite their similarities, Polish-style communism diverged in some crucial ways from the Soviet model. Private agriculture in the form of small, peasant-owned farms was allowed to persist, although much agricultural land—especially in the new western territories—was collectivized. Even more important, one very important social actor retained its autonomy—the Polish Catholic Church was the only major independent institution operating in a communist system. After the regime's attempts to either subvert the church or repress it (by imprisoning several high church officials, including Stefan Cardinal Wyszyński) failed, by the 1970s church and state reached a compromise. Church interests were then furthered through private negotiations between representatives of the church hierarchy and members of the communist leadership, with the result that the church remained a sanctuary and a resource base for independent forms of social organization—a factor that would figure importantly in opposition movements. The church's symbolic impact was equally great. With the communist-ruled state viewed as illegitimate by many Poles, the church filled the vacuum, playing the roles of repository and guardian of the national identity. In 1978 the elevation of Cardinal Karol Wojtyła to the papacy intensified this phenomenon—the installation of a Polish pope was viewed as an extraordinary moral victory for the Polish nation.

Not surprisingly, of the countries under communist domination Poland was one of the unruliest. The history of the People's Republic of Poland was a series of crises—in 1956, 1968, 1970, 1976, 1980–1981—in which one or more social groups challenged the regime. In all of these crises, the Soviet factor played a crucial role, with the Kremlin setting limits beyond which Poland could not go—that is, limits to the compromises that Poland's leaders might make.

One important aspect of these crises was the emergence of workers as a major political force in Poland. Because workers were symbolically privileged in the communist ideology, their protests—strikes—were particularly powerful. Moreover, it was relatively easier to

Electrician (and later Nobel Peace Prize winner and president of Poland) Lech Wałęsa speaks at the shipyard strikes in Gdansk in August 1980. These strikes resulted in the founding of the independent trade union Solidarity, an unprecedented event that would eventually lead to the collapse of the communist bloc.

Source: Reuters/Erazm Ciolek/Landov

protest as workers, carrying out occupation strikes in the factories rather than simply marching in the streets. In fact, the Polish opposition eventually centered on worker mobilization. Intellectuals played a major role, defining goals, suggesting tactics and strategy, and running the underground press, but organizing and mobilizing efforts were focused on and in large part carried out by workers. The culmination of this effort was the creation in 1980 of the Solidarity trade union—the first and only free trade union in the communist bloc. By the end of 1981, Solidarity had grown far beyond a mere trade union to a nationwide social movement. Out of a total workforce of 16 million, nearly 11 million belonged to Solidarity or to Rural Solidarity, its affiliate organization for farmers.

But there were still fundamental limits on political possibilities in Poland, and when Solidarity challenged the regime too abruptly, the limits were crossed. At the end of 1981, the communist regime declared martial law and outlawed Solidarity, thereby ushering in several years of political stagnation and half-hearted, unsuccessful economic reforms.

By the late 1980s, the Polish ruling elite still appeared to control all the important power resources. But this elite, like the party leaderships in other countries of the Soviet bloc, had sources of power that differed greatly from those controlled by elites in most noncommunist authoritarian regimes. The Polish ruling elites were, above all, *political* rulers; their authority and power were derived not from the support of an independent and privileged military or from capital ownership but from their positions within the political system. For Polish communists, the one political resource independent of the domestic political system had been Soviet support. But when Soviet leader Mikhail Gorbachev decided that maintaining the Soviet Union's Central and East European empire was too costly, this crucial support was withdrawn. This withdrawal would not only remove a major power resource from play but also change the relative importance of other potential resources.

Transition from Communist Rule to the Third Republic

The result was that the 1989 transition from communist rule was a comedy of errors that would have lasting but unexpected consequences for subsequent Polish politics. For the communist regime, economic reforms that required social sacrifices were unavoidable, but it realized that it was incapable of implementing such reforms without the cooperation and support of the Solidarity-led opposition. The opposition believed itself equally incapable of a unilateral solution to Poland's problems because of the powerful cards the communist regime was believed to hold, including the assumed Soviet veto of systemic change. The two sides met in roundtable negotiations and concluded a pact that was expected to result in a slow, controlled (and perhaps even reversible) political transition. Once the transition process began, however, all the participants quickly realized that they had overestimated the ruling coalition's strength and became aware that the Soviet Union was no longer setting limits on Polish possibilities. Consequently, the pact produced a flawed but real transfer of power. The communists suffered a humiliating defeat in the June 1989 elections and lost control of the government, but they retained their guaranteed Sejm seats until 1991 and occupied the presidency until 1990.

The transitional pact had some specific institutional consequences, particularly the restoration of the presidency and the restoration of the Senat. Yet it delayed full democratization for two years—years in which completely free elections took place in other former communist countries, as the entire bloc realized that Soviet limitations were no longer in place. Although this delay did not preserve communist power, it did tend to discredit the Polish transition process, thereby making the legitimation of the new institutions and the consolidation of democracy more difficult. There would be no single dramatic break between the communist past and the democratic present in the Polish transition.

In fact, the pact and its aftermath discredited compromise itself. An agreed-upon peaceful transition might be expected to heal historical wounds and reduce the intensity of conflict-induced cleavages. In Spain's transition to democracy after the death of dictator Francisco Franco, for example, the 1978 Moncloa pact symbolized reconciliation among the opposing parties. Making pacts and compromising became virtues. But the Spanish pact was a conscious compromise; the mistakes of the Polish transition, with its unexpected outcomes, led to so many recriminations between and within the opposing sides that compromise came to be seen as either—at best—a self-delusion or—at worst—a deceit. Democratic politics, especially in the parliamentary arena, requires compromise, and the leading parties have learned how to make deals. But when compromise itself is disgraced, these deals tend to be ad hoc and implicit rather than contracted and explicit. Structured and lasting compromises have thus far proved impossible across certain cleavages, which the pact-supported transition deepened rather than lessened.

Another legacy of the transition was, therefore, a deep cleavage between anticommunist forces and the former communists. This cleavage, which has long obstructed political compromise and cooperation, took the form of one side believing that the other did not have the moral right to participate in Polish politics. Each still views the other side's victories as dangerous for Poland and its future.

The pact may also have created or at least deepened an additional division—one within the former opposition camp. This schism divided those who participated in the roundtable process and believed it to have been valuable for Poland and those who rejected its compromises, ascribed present problems to the pact's flaws, and even saw the pact as a conscious betrayal of the Polish nation. The secular groups that undertook the pact with the communists were condemned by Catholic and nationalist groups, who expressed disgust with the agreement.

Certainly, the communist camp had equal reason for mutual recriminations because of the power position its leaders had bargained away in 1989. Why did the bitterness and criticism not make it difficult for the former communists to operate as a unified and effective political force? Perhaps the answer is in the failure of the communists to ensure firm and fast institutional guarantees for themselves. Their vulnerability meant that the only effective protection was to be found in unity and mutual support—that is, in maintaining and strengthening political organizations to represent their interests. This recognition of the need for unity, together with their 1989 electoral humiliation and the first Solidarity government's failure to challenge the party's rights to its own organizational assets, left the communists in a surprisingly advantageous position as the democratic game began.

An interesting contrast, however, was the position of the Catholic Church. It appeared to be triumphant—it had consistently backed the now victorious opposition forces, and it no longer faced an explicitly atheist regime. It seemed likely, then, that the church would play an even greater role in politics and policy. But just like the other political players, the church would have to adapt its tactics and resources to the new democratic political arena.

Present-Day Cleavages

Out of the transition to democracy, several questions have emerged. For one thing, how has this history affected Polish society, and, in particular, how has it affected divisions among Poles? How do Poles differ from one another in interests, ideologies, and identities? Do these cleavages result only in differing policy preferences—the raw material of democratic politics—or are they fault lines along which Polish society might fracture? Finally, which of these cleavages dominate and thus limit the possibilities with which Polish politicians must work?

One striking consequence of Poland's tumultuous twentieth century is the lack of ethnic divisions among its citizens. Indeed, territorial shifts and population resettlements, together with the horrendous consequences of Nazi Germany's policy of exterminating Jews and Gypsies, have today produced a population of which no more than 2 percent declares a nationality or ethnicity other than Polish. In fact, in a 2005 Public Opinion Research Center survey only 27 percent of respondents stated that they knew anyone who was not of Polish ethnicity.[2]

Although removal of the ethnic factor would seem to simplify Polish politics, serious cleavages remain. Some affect how Poles see one another as political beings, sometimes even to the point of creating barriers between them and delegitimizing political action by the "other." These barriers include class, religiosity, and the distinction between former communists and anticommunists. Other barriers—region, age, and gender—although not as divisive, are still reflected in voting patterns and therefore shape politicians' choices. Some of these cleavages can be usefully understood as the division between winners and losers in the huge transformations which Poland has undergone. Sizable percentages of Poles view themselves and their families as having profited or lost by these changes. Significantly, the number of self-perceived losers has been cut in half since 1997, while the number of self-perceived winners has tripled; still, these divisions remain.[3] Who are the winners and who are the losers in contemporary Polish society?

Socioeconomic Differences

The forty-odd years of communist rule in Poland, with the ideological goal of a classless society, might have been expected to eliminate class as a factor in Polish politics. Instead, it created a distinctive kind of class structure. The official favor shown industrial workers produced a strong class identity, with certain sectors—especially miners—constituting a kind of proletarian elite. Meanwhile, the size of the urban working class grew considerably under communism, and the living standards of former peasants improved considerably. Those agricultural workers who still worked on small, family-owned farms found themselves far outside the mainstream of communist society, as did a tiny sector of private businesspeople who owned small workshops and retail outlets. The intelligentsia was somewhat diversified, because the children of workers and peasants found greater opportunity for university education in the first decades of the People's Republic. Although not officially favored, members of this class enjoyed the possibility of serious advancement through careers in the Communist Party. At the top were the communist functionaries and their families.

Since Poland's transition to a capitalist market economy, the size and role of these classes have changed dramatically. The working class has shrunk in both size and prestige. Sectors that were favored in the past—much of heavy industry and particularly coal mining—have turned out to be comparatively inefficient and thus unprofitable. As a result, industrial workers now constitute only 25 percent of the labor force.[4] Although most workers were once employed in large, state-owned firms, many now find themselves working in small or medium-size private firms. Employment in the services has grown to 11 percent. Like the working class, the intelligentsia finds itself increasingly divided, as the fates of those who have turned entrepreneur or found well-paid positions in high-growth sectors diverge from those who remain in poorly paid jobs in fields such as education. In any case, higher education is now viewed as essential to advancement. University enrollments have exploded, with corresponding increases in the numbers of institutions of higher education.

Peasants—whether working on small farms or former state agricultural cooperatives—make up the most distinctive socioeconomic class, marked by low income and low education levels. About one-fourth of the labor force is still employed in agriculture, a huge percentage in view of the fact that agriculture constitutes a relatively low share of the Polish economy—a share that can be attributed both to the small size and inefficiency of the traditional family farm and to long-term neglect of investment in agriculture. The 2002 census revealed that 38 percent of Poles live in rural areas.

Economic inequality has grown considerably with marketization, although the exact extent of this inequality is hard to measure because of the communist system's lack of transparency. Several factors have contributed to income disparities. The salaries of management and of public officials have increased dramatically, while the wages of manual and pink-collar (female) workers have stagnated. Certain sectors—including finance and telecommunications—have taken off, but others, such as health care, are characterized by low salaries. Poverty is widespread in the agricultural sector, with the notable exception of a very small group of owners of large agricultural enterprises. Although unemployment has decreased in recent years, a significant number of Poles remain unable to find jobs. The official unemployment rate (12.8 percent in January 2010) does not, however, give a full picture because many of the long-term unemployed are no longer registered. These trends contribute to a social structure characterized by a very large low-income sector, a significant (and growing) high-income sector, and not that much in the middle. Poland is increasingly divided between those who are succeeding (or have a chance of success) in the market economy and those who are very aware they have been left behind.

Religiosity

At first glance, it does not seem likely that religion would be a dividing line among Poles. After all, 95 percent of Poles identify themselves as Catholics. Of the others, only 1 percent specify another religion or denomination, and the remainder define themselves as either atheist or generically Christian. Yet a deep and politically significant religious cleavage exists in Polish society—the division between devout and regularly practicing Catholics and those in whose lives the church and religious practice are less important. The latter group includes people with a family heritage of secularism (derived from nineteenth- and twentieth-century leftist traditions), as well as those for whom religion now plays a smaller role, perhaps as a result of disincentives under the communist regime. A good statistical indicator of the size of these groups is the proportion of Poles who attend church regularly or who consider themselves to be good observant Catholics. According to surveys carried out in 2009, 54 percent of Poles attend church at least once a week; similarly, 53 percent define themselves as following the dictates of the church. Important subsets here are the 5 percent of the total who attend church more than once a week and the 13 percent who describe themselves as "deeply religious" rather than merely "religious"—largely overlapping groups.[5]

Not all regular churchgoers adhere strictly to church teachings in sociocultural areas such as abortion and birth control. Nevertheless, there is a very strong relationship between religious practice and belief, on the one hand, and the desire to see state policy reflect religious values, on the other. Polish sociologists have found that religion appears to play a much larger role than any other socioeconomic factor in determining whether a person identifies himself or herself as right-wing or left-wing.

Indeed, the largest single gap in left–right self-identification is between those who describe themselves as deeply religious and everyone else. This finding suggests that although the politically pertinent cleavage might lie between the majority constituted by regular churchgoers and the rest of society, it might just as well lie between the deeply religious minority and the rest—depending on the issue and on elites' mobilization efforts.[6]

Former Communists versus Anticommunists

Although the cleavage between those who supported the communist regime and those who opposed it may seem increasingly irrelevant over time, issues deriving from the communist past do play a role in contemporary Polish politics and, in turn, in political identification today. Research has shown that both those who participated in Communist Party structures and those who did not but still look back fondly on communism tend to identify themselves as left-wing. Conversely, those who participated in the anticommunist opposition as well as those who simply condemn the communist past tend to identify themselves as right-wing.[7] In a 2009 survey 36 percent of Poles over the age of thirty-four asserted that they had considered themselves opponents of the communist regime, and 20 percent claimed they had participated in strikes or other anticommunist protests.[8] This cleavage may decline with generational change, but it is also possible that these traditions will be passed on within families, especially because the religious cleavage tends to reinforce the communist-anticommunist cleavage.

Region, Age, and Gender

Differences by region in Poland derive from the history and socioeconomic divisions described earlier. Although family farms continued to dominate agriculture in most of Poland, the territories acquired after World War II were subject to collectivization, and now tend to have large agricultural properties rather than small farms. Although these territories suffered higher rates of social pathologies such as crime and alcoholism stemming from the difficulties of resettlement, their reknit social fabric was more amenable to communist social engineering. Today, the Polish political left tends to receive more of its votes from these areas than from the traditionally Polish regions. One additional angle complicates politics in Silesia: Poland's unproductive coal mines and related industries are located in this former German region, and therefore it has a high concentration of dissatisfied industrial workers. The source of other differences can be found further back in the history of partition. The highest rates of voter turnout are found in Galicia, long ruled by the Austro-Hungarian Empire, and the provinces east of Warsaw, which were under Russian rule, have the lowest turnout.

The dramatic political and economic changes that Poland underwent at the end of the twentieth century make generational differences potentially important. One division lies between those who have been able to adapt to the new economic system (together with those growing up in it) and those who were too old to successfully make their own transition. Much of the latter group now consists of retirees and persons receiving disability benefits. At more than one-quarter of the Polish population, this sector constitutes an important part of the electorate and has been politically active in defense of its interests. At the other end of the spectrum, the youngest members of the labor force also face a difficult situation. Unemployment rates for people under age twenty-five are more than twice the national average. Nevertheless, the younger generations (ages eighteen to thirty-four) declare much higher rates of satisfaction with their lives than do their elders.[9]

Unemployment has also affected women disproportionately. Hardest hit by the economic transition were the sectors dominated by female labor: light industry, health care, education, and the state administration. Employers have targeted men for new jobs using discriminatory recruitment practices. As a result, many women have left the labor force and are no longer actively seeking employment. For that reason, the official female unemployment rate, which runs only slightly higher than the male rate, may not be a useful indicator. In 2008 only 52.4 percent females aged fifteen to sixty-four were employed, while 66.3 percent of males of the same age were employed. Although this disparity could reflect personal choices and traditional family patterns, what is striking is that this gender gap had widened considerably since 2003, from 10.5 percent to 13.9 percent. The gender gap among older workers (aged 55–64) increased even more dramatically, from 15.4 to 23.4 percent. When the Polish economy prospers, as it has in recent years, it is males who have higher rates of employment.[10] Another gender difference that affects Polish politics is religiosity. Women tend to attend church more regularly and describe themselves more frequently as "deeply religious," although the difference between the genders is declining among urban dwellers.[11]

Political Culture

Several features of Polish history might be expected to work against the development of a democratic political culture. First, most of the last two centuries passed without a state effectively controlled by Poles, and the state itself was an alien entity. Second, Poland experienced more than four decades of communist rule with its propaganda, incentives, and sanctions aimed at encouraging submission. And, third, Poland had fewer than ten years of experience with democracy before 1990. Conversely, one might hope that the strong sense of Polish nationhood, together with experiences of independent organization under partition, under World War II occupation, and under communist rule, might provide important cultural resources.

Surveys of public opinion reveal a mixed picture. In comparison with West European nations, Poles appear less committed to democracy. In a 2009 survey only 50 percent of Polish respondents agreed that it was "very important" to them to live in a democracy, in contrast to roughly 80 percent of British, French, and German respondents. Nevertheless, this result is several times higher than the 16 percent of Russians who answered similarly; and when respondents who answered "somewhat important" are added in, it appears that 88 percent of Poles put at least some importance on democracy.[12]

That roughly 40 percent to 70 percent of survey respondents have regularly declared themselves dissatisfied with Polish democracy is not in itself evidence of undemocratic attitudes. As the following chapters show, Poles have many reasons to be dissatisfied. More telling is that in surveys a growing number of Poles have chosen the statement "democracy is, above all, disorder and chaos" over the statement "democracy is, above all, human freedom." As of 2005 a majority of 60 percent still chose to equate democracy with freedom, while 31 percent chose disorder and chaos, and yet the respective proportions were 72 percent and 19 percent ten years earlier. In the same 2005 survey, a large majority (77 percent) agreed with the statement that there is too much indecision and talk in democracy; nearly as many (73 percent) agreed that democracy does a poor job of maintaining order. While in 2005 the largest percentage ever in the postcommunist Polish democracy (40 percent) agreed with the statement that a strong man in power could be better than democratic governments, by 2008 this number had fallen to 24 percent. Since 1992 Polish survey respondents have been regularly asked whether some nondemocratic governments could be preferable to democratic governments. The number agreeing in 2009 was almost identical to the number agreeing in 1992 (36 percent and 35 percent), but the number disagreeing had noticeably increased, from 26 percent to 40 percent.[13]

Surveys reveal evidence of healthy and even growing participatory attitudes among Poles. As of 2006, 63 percent of Poles surveyed (versus 50 percent in 2002) declared that people such as themselves working together with others could help to serve the needy or to resolve problems in their neighborhoods or cities. Fifty-six percent asserted that they had done just that at least once. Another relevant indicator is the proportion of Poles who state that they participate in at least one civic organization—since 1998 this number has hovered at about 23 percent.[14]

It is not surprising in view of their history that Poles tend to see themselves as more patriotic than their neighbors. Since 1992 well over 70 percent of Poles have chosen the word *patriotic* to describe the typical Pole, while 52 percent or fewer have described the typical European in such a way.[15] In 2004 the typical Pole was characterized as religious by 90 percent of Polish respondents, while only 34 percent would have used that word to describe Europeans. What is interesting is that only 47 percent of respondents described the typical Pole as honest, and 56 percent described the typical European in such terms. Even more striking were the percentages who declared the typical Pole dishonest (34 percent) and the typical European dishonest (18 percent).

The same series of surveys provides even more information about Poles' self-images. One of the most striking differences between how Poles see themselves and how they see Europeans is seen in answers to whether the typical representative of either group "strives for success in his/her life" or "above all else wants peace in his/her life." (The word translated here as peace, *spokój*, could also be understood as "lack of stress.") In 2004, 77 percent of respondents saw the typical European as striving for success, and 57 percent saw Poles as success-driven; likewise, 35 percent saw Poles as preferring lack of stress (and 12 percent saw Europeans as similarly unambitious). Poles and their neighbors have long held stereotypes of Poles as poor workers, but Poles' answers to questions about the work ethic have been changing. In 2004 most Poles still considered the typical Pole as valuing family over work (61 percent to 25 percent) and the typical European as valuing work over family (52 percent to 25 percent), but since 1992 this difference has steadily declined. The percentage of respondents declaring that Poles respect work increased from 50 percent in 1992 to 75 percent in 2004, and the percentage declaring that Poles work well increased from 47 percent to 76 percent.

Given these patterns it is interesting to examine the results of a survey that asked—after five years of membership in the European Union—whether Poles considered themselves to be only Polish, Polish and European, European and Polish, or only European. Only a negligible number of respondents chose "only European," and only 3 percent chose "European and Polish." Nevertheless, nearly as many (42 percent) chose "Polish and European" as chose "only Polish" (52 percent).[16]

How do Poles evaluate the huge political, economic, and social transformations Poland has undergone since 1989? Poles' views of the old socialist system did not change perceptibly from 1994 to 2009. Throughout this period, roughly one-third of respondents asserted that the socialist system had brought more benefits than costs to the majority of Poles; another third declared that the costs were greater than the benefits; and yet another third considered that the benefits and costs roughly balanced each other out; meanwhile the percentage with no opinion on the matter has slowly increased. Answers to a similar question about the impact of the post-1989 changes varied more widely. The number declaring that the benefits outweighed the costs was 45 percent in 2004, but increased to 80 percent in 2009. In spite of this cost-benefit calculus, larger numbers of these same respondents (never less than a majority) have declared that changing the system in 1989 was worthwhile.[17] Although some of these results may appear contradictory, one clear picture emerges. The young, students, the educated, those who hold managerial positions, those with higher incomes, and those who live in large cities tend to see the post-1989 changes as for the best. Older citizens, the retired, the unemployed, those living in rural areas or small towns, peasants, and manual workers view the same changes negatively. The same groups, respectively, tend to approve or disapprove of the functioning of Polish democracy and tend to hold prodemocratic or antidemocratic attitudes. The 33 percent who in 2009 agreed with the statement that "for people like me it doesn't really matter whether the government is democratic or nondemocratic" were disproportionately old, retired, poorly educated, or simply poor.[18] Their judgments were based on what had happened to them in the fifteen years since the communist regime had fallen, and although their numbers had significantly declined since the early 1990s. they still constituted one-third of Polish society. Thus, this examination of postcommunist Polish political culture has revealed a country divided into winners and losers, with each group drawing understandable conclusions from their experiences.

NOTES

1. Centrum Badania Opinii Społecznej, "Siedemdziesiąt lat od wybuchu II wojny światowej," August 2009.
2. Centrum Badania Opinii Społecznej, "Tożsamość narodowa Polaków oraz postrzeganie mniejszości narodowych i etnicznych w Polsce," May 2005.
3. Centrum Badania Opinii Społecznej, "Polacy o minionym dwudziestoleciu," February 2009.
4. All employment statistics are from the 2002 National Census, Główny Urząd Statystyczny.
5. Centrum Badania Opinii Społecznej, "Co ła czy Polako'w z parafia ?" March 2005; Centrum Badania Opinii Społecznej, "Wiara i religijnos'c' Polako'w dwadzies'cia lat po rozpocze ciu przemian ustrojowych," March 2009; and Centrum Badania Opinii Spolecynej, "Dwie dekady przemian religijnos'ci w Polsce," September 2009.
6. See, for example, Mirosława Grabowska, "Boskie i cesarskie: Religijność oraz stosunki między państwem a Kościołem a postawy i zachowanie polityczne," in *Wybory parlamentarne 1997: System partyjny, postawy polityczne, zachowanie wyborcze*, ed. Radosław Markowski (Warsaw: Instytut Studiów Politycznych Polskiej Akademii Nauk, 1999), 167–202.
7. Centrum Badania Opinii Społecznej, "Dwie dekady przemian religijności w Polsce," September 2009.
8. Centrum Badania Opinii Społecznej, "Niektóre opozycyjne doświadczenia Polaków przed rokiem 1989," February 2009.
9. Centrum Badania Opinii Społecznej, "Polacy o swoim zadowoleniu z życia," January 2010.
10. Commission Staff Working Document, accompanying document to the Report from the Commission to the Council, the European Parliament, the European Economic and Social

Committee, and the Committee of the Regions: Equality between Women and Men—2010, European Commission, Brussels, December 18, 2009.

11. Centrum Badania Opinii Społecznej, "Dwie dekady przemian religijności w Polsce," September 2009.

12. Centrum Badania Opinii Społecznej, "Światowa opinia publiczna o demokracji," October 2009.

13. Centrum Badania Opinii Społecznej, "Stosunek Polaków do demokracji," December 2005.

14. Centrum Badania Opinii Społecznej, "Stan społeczeństwa obywatelskiego w latach 1998–2006," January 2006.

15. All data comparing images of typical Poles and typical Europeans are taken from Centrum Badania Opinii Społecznej, "Typowy Polak i Europejczyk—podobieństwa i różnicy," April 2004.

16. Centrum Badania Opinii Społecznej, "Dylematy związane z funkcjonowaniem Unii Europejskiej," July 2009.

17. Centrum Badania Opinii Społecznej, "Polacy o minionym dwudziestoleciu," February 2009; and "Oceny I rozliczenia okresu PRL w opinii publicznej," June 2009.

18. Centrum Badania Opinii Społecznej, "Opinie o funkcjonowaniu demokracji w Polsce," February 2009.

Where Is the Power?

7.2

FOR THE ENTIRE NINETEENTH CENTURY AND FOR DECADES INTO THE twentieth century, power lay outside Poland, with Polish lands controlled by foreign empires. For nearly half of the twentieth century, power lay in the hands of the leaders of Poland's Communist Party and their Soviet supervisors—the constitution of the People's Republic of Poland was a fiction. Now, political power is held by democratically elected representatives of Polish citizens, with constitutional rules at least shaping, if not determining precisely, where power lies.

Politics by Trial and Error: Changing Rules with Uncertain Implications

Although the Communist Party lost its monopoly on political power in 1989 and democratic presidential elections were held in 1990, a new constitution was not enacted until 1997. While other former communist countries were putting new constitutions into effect (Bulgaria and Romania in 1991, Slovakia in 1992, and the Czech Republic in 1993), Polish politicians were debating at length (and usually futilely) in constitutional committees and revising the existing rules one by one when politically or practically necessary. The slow pace meant that the first eight years of democratic politics in postcommunist Poland were subject to changing and often ambiguous rules of the game. The process, although messy and at times even frightening, allowed the eventual constitution to be informed by democratic political practice.

Differing Degrees of Legitimacy

From summer 1989 until fall 1991, Poles were governed by a mix of politicians, some of whom were put in office by democratic elections and others who gained office because of their position and allegiance under the communist regime. At the beginning, only the newly re-created Senat, with its limited powers, was the product of completely free elections. The Sejm's legitimacy was tainted by the fact that 65 percent of seats had been filled in races limited to candidates from parties of the former ruling coalition. Meanwhile, it was derogatorily referred to as the contract Sejm, because of its origins in the Roundtable Pact. President Wojciech Jaruzelski's legitimacy was even weaker. He had been elected by the National Assembly, composed of the 100-seat Senat and the 460-seat Sejm, in which representatives holding guaranteed party seats held a majority. Even more important, the choice to make the first secretary of the Communist Party the new president was dictated by how Poles saw their situation in the summer of 1989. Choosing anyone other than a communist leader as president appeared far too risky, potentially provoking Soviet displeasure and threatening the loyalty and discipline of the communist-dominated military and internal security forces. The problem of the president's legitimacy was resolved by a fully democratic election in 1990, which placed Solidarity's most famous leader, Lech

Wałęsa, in office. Only after new Sejm and Senat elections in October 1991 were all these institutions controlled by democratically elected officeholders.

Therefore, for those first twenty-odd months, issues of democratic legitimacy shaped power relations as much as constitutional rules. The negotiated revisions to the 1952 Stalin-era constitution gave the new office of president (conceived as a guarantee to the old regime) considerable powers, including a veto that could be overturned only by a two-thirds vote in the Sejm, sole power to nominate a prime minister (subject to the Sejm's confirmation or rejection), important responsibilities in security and foreign affairs, and the power to dissolve the Sejm if it failed to pass a budget or confirm a government in a timely fashion or if it interfered with the president's "constitutional responsibilities." But Jaruzelski, aware of his politically weak position, was hesitant to use these powers. He had no democratic mandate and soon not even a practical rationale for his power: within a few months the collapse of other communist regimes in Eastern and Central Europe revealed that the fears on which his presidency was based were groundless. By January 1990 President Jaruzelski seemed at best an anachronism. He therefore cooperated consistently with the Solidarity-led government, which, because it was based largely on the 35 percent freely elected portion of the Sejm, had a greater claim to legitimacy. Conversely, when Wałęsa was sworn into the office of president in December 1990 his prestige far outweighed his power. He had an undisputed mandate as the popularly elected president, clearly trumping the mandate of any government based on the contract Sejm, which necessarily relied at least in part on the votes of deputies holding party-guaranteed seats.

Flawed Parliaments

The free and fair elections to the Sejm and Senat held in 1991 could have been expected to contribute to a more predictable and rule-driven political arena, but both this Sejm and the one that succeeded it in 1993 were weakened by a combination of flawed electoral rules and mistaken political strategies. The 1991 Sejm elections took place under an electoral ordinance that was extremely proportional and so was very favorable to small parties and that appeared to serve not only the self-interest of deputies in the contract Sejm—who were uncertain of their parties' chances and anxious to assure themselves at least a foothold in the new legislature—but also the goal of including all significant political forces and thereby discouraging antisystem activity. The result was a parliament composed of twenty-nine parties, in which the largest party held only 13 percent of the seats. The support of at least five parties was needed to form a majority coalition, and, in fact, because the second-largest party, the former Communist Party, was an unacceptable coalition partner for many, any actual majority coalition had to contain at least six parties. The inevitable result of this extreme fragmentation was unstable, weak governments and frequent legislative gridlock. Moreover, in spite of its legitimacy, this Sejm did not prove to be an effective counterbalance to President Wałęsa.

To avoid such a result in the future, the electoral ordinance was revised to make the system less proportional. District sizes were decreased, and the formula for calculating seats was changed to favor larger parties. Most important, thresholds were instituted. To be assigned any seats, a party had to win at least 5 percent of the nationwide vote; an official coalition of parties had to win at least 8 percent. In 1993 a government crisis resulted in the dissolution of the Sejm and gave the country an opportunity to try out the new rules.

Poland at a Glance

Type of Government
Republic

Capital
Warsaw

Administrative Divisions
Sixteen provinces: Dolnośląskie, Kujawsko-Pomorskie, Łódzkie, Lubelskie, Lubuskie, Małopolskie, Mazowieckie, Opolskie, Podkarpackie, Podlaskie, Pomorskie, Śląskie, Świętokrzyskie, Warmińsko-Mazurskie, Wielkopolskie, Zachodniopomorskie

Independence
November 11, 1918 (independent republic proclaimed)

Constitution
Adopted by the National Assembly on April 2, 1997; passed by national referendum on May 25, 1997; effective October 17, 1997

Legal System
Mixture of continental (Napoleonic) civil law and holdover communist legal theory; changes being gradually introduced as part of broader democratization process; limited judicial review of legislative acts, but rulings of the Constitutional Tribunal are final; court decisions can be appealed to the European Court of Justice in Strasbourg

Suffrage
Eighteen years of age; universal

Executive Branch
Chief of state: president
Head of government: prime minister
Cabinet: Council of Ministers responsible to the prime minister and the Sejm; prime minister proposes, president appoints, and Sejm approves the Council of Ministers
Elections: president elected by popular vote for a five-year term; prime minister and deputy prime ministers appointed by the president and confirmed by the Sejm

Legislative Branch
Bicameral legislature: Senat and Sejm. Senat: one hundred seats; members are elected by a majority vote on a provincial basis for four-year terms. Sejm: 460 seats; members are elected under a complex system of proportional representation for four-year terms. The designation of National Assembly (Zgromadzenie Narodowe) is used only on those rare occasions when the two houses meet jointly.
Note: Two seats are assigned to ethnic minority parties in the Sejm only.

Judicial Branch
Supreme Court (judges are appointed by the president on the recommendation of the National Judicial Council for an indefinite period); Constitutional Tribunal (judges are chosen by the Sejm for a single nine-year term).

Major Political Parties
Law and Justice (PiS); Civic Platform (PO); Self-Defense (Samoobrona); Alliance of the Democratic Left (SLD); League of Polish Families (LPR); Polish Peasant Party (PSL); Social Democracy of Poland (SdPl); Democratic Party (PD)

Source: U.S. Central Intelligence Agency, *The World Factbook 2010,* http://www.cia.gov/cia/publications/factbook/geos/pl.html.

The former Communist Party competed as a single bloc, and the Polish Peasant Party—previously a mainstay of the communist regime—also remained united, but former oppositionists campaigned in as many as ten different parties or coalitions. The result was the polar opposite of that in 1991. Only six parties (plus a handful of representatives of the German minority) won seats in the Sejm. Two of these parties, the former Communist Party and the Polish Peasant Party, controlled nearly two-thirds of the seats, although they had won only 36 percent of the votes. Nearly 35 percent of the votes had gone to parties that were shut out of the Sejm by the electoral thresholds, including one grouping that chose to register as a coalition rather than a party and won 6.4 percent of the vote—not enough to reach the threshold for coalitions. The 1993 Sejm could easily form stable governments capable of passing coherent legislative programs, but it suffered from a certain lack of legitimacy because important political forces were not represented—most of the unsuccessful votes (25 percent of the total) were for post-Solidarity right-wing or center-right parties.

The President as Loose Cannon

From the end of 1990 through 1995, these flawed Sejms and the five successive governments based on them confronted a president who exhibited erratic behavior and exercised ambiguous powers. The lessons drawn from this experience shaped later institutional choices. It has been suggested that Wałęsa found the office of president of Poland to be a comedown. As leader of the Solidarity movement since 1980 and winner of the Nobel Peace Prize, he had already served for nearly ten years as the embodiment of the Polish nation in the eyes of many Poles and much of the world. Now this larger-than-life persona had to be squeezed into the relatively narrow confines of a constitutionally regulated presidency. The solution Wałęsa chose, naturally, was to try to expand the powers of his office—through constitutional revisions if possible, through highly imaginative exploitation of ambiguous rules if necessary, and potentially through even less formal means. Unpredictability was his hallmark; he appeared to use the presidential veto almost randomly, sometimes vetoing nearly every bill passed in a month, but no policy program seemed to underlay his vetoes.

Three of the governments Wałęsa faced were headed by comrades from the former opposition; two were made up of former communists and their allies. Nevertheless, he managed to have sharp confrontations with governments from both camps. His first serious conflict occurred in 1992 with the government led by former oppositionist Jan Olszewski. Wałęsa publicly clashed with Olszewski's defense minister over personnel policies in the military, amid accusations that the subject of coup d'état had come up in discussions between members of Wałęsa's staff and military officers. Barely weeks later, the Olszewski government fell in a perfectly constitutional vote of no confidence in response to a scandal in which the minister of internal affairs illegally publicized the names of certain alleged secret police informers. Wałęsa, who found himself on that list, played a major role in instigating the government's demise.

The Little Constitution and Its Limitations

By this point it was clear that even though progress on a new constitution was stalled in committees arguing over the roles of God, church, and nation in possible preambles, the lines of constitutional authority, and especially the relationship between the president and the parliament, desperately needed to be clarified. Consensus among political elites on this need produced a provisional document, the Little Constitution, passed by the Sejm with the necessary two-thirds majority in November 1992. Most analysts agree that this document made the powers and responsibilities of the president and the parliament clearer, but did not alter the basic balance of power between the two institutions. The president's special responsibilities in foreign affairs and security matters were backed up by concrete powers: the prime minister had to ask for and respect the president's opinion in the nomination of the ministers of foreign affairs, internal affairs, and defense. The president also was to have specific input into the personnel policies of those ministries. The presidential power to dissolve the Sejm for the vaguely worded "interference" with his own constitutional duties was eliminated, although the president retained the power to dissolve the Sejm if it failed in its own duties to form a government or to pass a budget.

The Little Constitution did not, however, bring an end to the conflicts between Wałęsa and the parliamentary government. With the 1993 elections and the domination of the Sejm by former communists and their ally, the Peasant Party, cohabitation between a president of one camp and a government of another became necessary. Wałęsa, to put it mildly, was not happy. He began to make outrageous political threats, suggesting that the Polish people might demand that he play the role of dictator and that he would not refuse. He used his special powers related to the military and the internal security apparatus to court their support. At a 1994 lunch with senior military commanders he encouraged them to speak out against the defense minister and asked them to vote on the minister's record. They voted overwhelmingly against the minister, and so Wałęsa then asked that minister to resign—a move that both the Sejm and government protested vociferously. Meanwhile, the minister complained of a creeping mutiny, with generals persistently refusing to carry out ministerial instructions. Wałęsa also seemed to be using his control of nominations at the Ministry of Internal Affairs to gain the loyalty of pivotal figures there, often dismissing former oppositionists and rehiring communist-era secret police officers. In the end, because of disagreements between Wałęsa and the prime minister, the positions of minister of defense and minister of foreign affairs were difficult to fill after the resignations of the incumbents.

In these and other policy spheres, Wałęsa delayed legislation by first vetoing bills, and then—after the Sejm routinely overturned his veto with the necessary two-thirds vote—referring them to the Constitutional Tribunal for a ruling on their constitutionality. Finding a constitutional pretext for dissolving a Sejm in which two allied parties held more than 65 percent of the seats would have seemed almost impossible under the rules of the Little Constitution, yet Wałęsa nearly discovered a way. First he vetoed the 1995 budget, and then threatened to dissolve the Sejm for its failure to pass a budget within three months—a move of doubtful legality with the potential for dire consequences. Wałęsa's defeat by former communist Aleksander Kwaśniewski in the second round of the 1995 presidential election ended this precarious period of Polish politics.

Clearly, then, Polish democracy got off to a rocky start. Under unclear rules of uncertain import, the outcomes often represented neither the politicians' nor the voters' intentions, and the system's legitimacy was questioned more than once. Nevertheless, the Third Republic survived its difficult first years, and its eventual constitution was shaped by those lessons.

The Institutions of Power

The new constitution went into effect in October 1997, after acceptance by the bicameral National Assembly (consisting of the Sejm and the Senat), approval by the president, and a national referendum.[1] With only minor revisions, its rules continue to shape the political arena today. But its legitimacy was questioned from the start, because it was formulated and approved by the 1993 Sejm representing only 65 percent of Polish voters and a body from which the right wing of the political spectrum was missing. Efforts were made to correct this problem by building a larger-than-necessary consensus within the parliament, including two post-Solidarity parties, and especially through consultation with the extra-parliamentary parties, the Catholic Church, and the Solidarity trade union. But the resulting compromises proved insufficient to win wider approval. In the May 1997 referendum campaign, the constitution was opposed by Solidarity, by several right and center-right parties (including the coalition that five months later would win 44 percent of seats in the parliamentary elections and lead the new government), by significant parts of the church, and by former president Wałęsa. In the end, then, only 53 percent of voters approved the constitution, and 46 percent voted against it. The turnout was a disappointing 43 percent.

The major complaints concerned not the political institutions but the role of religious values and identity in the constitutional order. In fact, whatever its legitimacy, the 1997 constitution has since proved to be a workable institutional structure for democratic politics, resulting in greater predictability and more stable and effective government. The institutions are basically the same as those that structured Polish politics from 1990 to 1997; their powers and relationships are only somewhat altered and certainly refined. The presidency was undoubtedly weakened, but this was accomplished through incremental reductions in the powers of that office, together with the elimination of hazy areas in which presidential and prime ministerial authority appeared to overlap.

The President

Wałęsa and his supporters had wanted to strengthen the Polish presidency, turning it into an office with the power to direct the state through the serious challenges of the economic, social, and geopolitical transition. In fact, Wałęsa had a greater impact than anyone else on the eventual shape of this institution; his actions during his single presidential term demonstrated both the potential danger of a powerful president and the probable harm of ambiguous lines of authority between president and parliament. As a result, the Polish presidency is not nearly as strong as that in France, which many Poles saw as a model, and it has distinct and clearly delineated powers and responsibilities. The limited power of the Polish presidency may be seen in how well Poland weathered the deaths of President Lech Kaczyński and more than a dozen of his appointees and staff in a plane crash in April 2010.

The president continues to command a symbolic mandate, because he (or perhaps she someday) is elected directly by the national electorate. If no candidate wins a majority in the first round, the top two vote-getters compete in a second round two weeks later. The president serves a five-year term and may not serve more than two terms. In the event of his death, incapacity, or impeachment for serious offenses, the president is replaced by the Speaker of the Sejm (there is no vice president) and a new election is called. The popular mandate gives the president the authority to speak and be heard on matters of importance for Poland; indeed, the mandate is a powerful if informal political instrument. Benefiting from a constitutionally defined term of office, the president is able to play an independent role, without the need to court a political base. After Wojciech Jaruzelski resigned from the Communist Party in 1989 upon becoming president, the practice developed that the president shall not belong to any political party, although party support is crucial for winning election in the first place, as well as reelection. Nevertheless, the first two post-Wałęsa presidents were closely identified with a major political party that they previously helped found—Aleksander Kwaśniewski (1995–2005) with the Alliance of the Democratic Left, and Kaczyński (2005–2010) with Law and Justice, headed by his twin brother, Jarosław. Under the constitution, as "supreme representative of the Republic of Poland," the president is head of state, but not head of government. He is "guarantor of the continuity of State authority" and must "ensure observance of the Constitution, [and] safeguard the sovereignty and security of the State as well as the inviolability and integrity of its territory." These are weighty responsibilities, which might justify a wide variety of actions, but, significantly, the president exercises those duties "within the scope of and in accordance with the principles specified in the Constitution and statutes" (Art. 126). This formulation means that the president's responsibilities cannot be construed to imply additional powers beyond those specified by law.

The president continues to have the right to present legislative projects to the Sejm for its consideration. The presidential veto power has been retained but weakened—a vote of at least three-fifths (60 percent), rather than two-thirds, is now required to overturn a presidential veto. Furthermore, the president is expressly prohibited from referring a bill whose veto was overturned to the Constitutional Tribunal. A president can veto a bill or question its constitutionality, but he cannot stall legislation excessively by doing both. Nor can he veto the government's budget. Many of the legal acts the president may take (except measures such as the veto) require the countersignature of the prime minister.

The presidential chancellery, which is made up of the official administrative staff, helps presidents to carry out their duties and provides them with expertise. Although this body is constitutionally defined and is filled with ministers or secretaries of state appointed by the president, its officials have influence only through the advice they give the president and wield no legal authority.

The president's input into how the government is formed has been somewhat reduced as well. He still has the right and responsibility to nominate a prime minister, but if the Sejm refuses to grant this candidate a vote of confidence, the right to nominate a prime minister passes to the Sejm. The president's powers to dissolve parliament are specific and limited: he can dissolve the Sejm and Senat (thereby calling new elections) for failure either to form a government or to pass a budget in a timely fashion. But the president now lacks any power to obstruct these processes himself, because his budgetary veto was eliminated. He still commands the power to declare martial law or a state of emergency, but the exercise of this power requires the cooperation of the prime minister's government and the Sejm.

In the areas of foreign affairs and internal security, most of the president's previous special powers and responsibilities have been eliminated. He has no input into the selection of any minister, including the foreign minister, the minister of internal affairs, and the defense minister. The president continues to represent the state in foreign affairs and to appoint members of the diplomatic service, but he is constitutionally obliged to cooperate with the prime minister and the cabinet in matters of foreign policy, which is primarily the cabinet's responsibility. The president remains the supreme commander of the armed forces and appoints top military officials, subject to the approval of the prime minister.

Because the president's term is five years and the parliamentary term is four years (or less) and because control of parliament has alternated between opposing political camps, this system nearly guarantees that each president will experience at least some time working with a government of the same political camp and at least some in cohabitation, facing a government of the opposing political camp. The Polish record with cohabitation has been mixed. President Wałęsa found himself in conflict with prime ministers of either camp, but his successor, Kwaśniewski, managed to avoid acrimony and even to work well with each of his prime ministers. Indeed, when a governing coalition from the opposing camp came to power in 1997, Kwaśniewski endorsed it and emphasized the importance of cooperation and consensus building. He played by the rules and even used restraint in exercising his constitutionally granted powers, vetoing some but not all of the bills with which he disagreed. For ten years, this approach earned Kwaśniewski the highest public opinion ratings of any Polish politician since the fall of communism.

In 2005 President Kaczyński came to power at the same time as a minority government controlled by his twin. To no one's surprise the Kaczyński brothers worked smoothly together during the two years their party, Law and Justice, led the government, but new elections in 2007, followed by the creation of a cabinet composed of the centrist Civic Platform and the Polish Peasant Party, created a new situation. The president was openly critical of many of the policies of Civic Platform's Prime Minister Donald Tusk and used his veto on several legislative projects that Tusk's government considered of essential importance. He also delayed the implementation of several bills by referring them to the Constitutional Tribunal. The most absurd instance of problems with cohabitation, however, came in the weeks leading up to the European Union summit in Brussels in October 2008 and Tusk and Kaczyński could not agree on which of them should represent Poland. Tusk insisted that the issues to be discussed at the meeting, the global financial crisis and energy questions, fell within his sphere of authority, and he flew to Brussels, leaving no official plane for Kaczyński's travel. The president, who insisted on being present to discuss strategic issues involving Georgia, chartered a plane and took his seat in the Polish delegation.

A subsequent plane trip ended in tragedy. On April 10, 2010—a new date to be entered into the Polish historical calendar—President Kaczyński's plane crashed while attempting to land at the airport in Smolensk, Russia. A large Polish delegation including the president, the first lady, several presidential ministers and advisers, the military chiefs of staff, and a dozen other prominent politicians representing all the major parties had intended to commemorate the seventieth anniversary of the Katyń massacre. All ninety-seven on board perished. Ironically, it was Kaczyński's likely rival in the upcoming presidential race, Bronisław Komorowski, who as Speaker of the Sejm was his constitutionally designated successor. Placed in an awkward position, Komorowski played a caretaker role until his July electoral victory over the late president's twin. In spite of all this, with government power firmly in the hands of the prime minister and his cabinet, Polish affairs proceeded without a blip, and investors maintained their confidence in the Polish economy.

The Sejm and Senat

As the main legislative body and the chamber from which the government derives its support and to which it must answer, the 460-seat Sejm is at the heart of the Polish political system. In the 1990s problems with fragmentation and legitimacy weakened the Sejm, and the political process was plagued with instability and uncertainty. Because of Poland's multiparty system and proportional representation election rules, no party has so far won a majority in the Sejm; after the 2005 election six parties held seats in that body. This multiplicity of parties, together with a frequent lack of party discipline, produces a lively body in which the major issues are debated intensely and few legislative outcomes are predetermined.

Although Poland's legislative system is bicameral, the Sejm is by far the dominant body. All legislation must first be passed by the Sejm, although the govern-

A few short hours after the Smolensk plane crash, Polish prime minister Donald Tusk kneels by pieces of the wreckage, while Russian prime minister Vladimir Putin looks on. The deaths of President Lech Kaczyński and ninety-six other Poles were a horrible tragedy, but caused no interruption in the day-to-day functioning of Poland's predominantly prime-ministerial government.

Source: RIA Novosti/Reuters/Corbis

ment, the president, and the Senat share with individual Sejm deputies the right to introduce legislative projects to the Sejm. All bills passed by the Sejm must go to the Senat for its approval and possible amendment, but any Senat rejection or amendment can be overturned by a simple majority vote in the Sejm, less than the three-fifths required for overturning a presidential veto. The constitution can be amended by two-thirds of Sejm deputies if supported by a majority in the Senat. The Sejm can also call a referendum by a simple majority vote. Finally, the Sejm has an active committee structure, and chairmanship of an important committee is a route for political advancement.

The Sejm not only can grant or withhold a vote of confidence in a new government (and not every candidate for prime minister in the history of the Third Republic has succeeded in forming a government), but also it can vote no confidence in a particular minister, thereby forcing him or her out of office. The 1997 constitution specifies, however, that the Sejm cannot pass a simple vote of no confidence in the government and force it out of office; it must simultaneously name a replacement. This system is known as a constructive vote of no confidence, modeled on the German example.

The Senat began impressively in 1989 as the one freely elected body in Poland, but it has not been able to build on that initial legitimacy to expand its powers. Its veto can be easily overturned, and it possesses no special powers or responsibilities. But because its one hundred senators constituted nearly 18 percent of the National Assembly that enacted the controversial 1997 constitution, and because a majority of senators must approve any new constitutional amendments, it has endured and probably will remain part of the political system.

Elections to the Sejm and the Senat are held every four years—or earlier if the president dissolves the Sejm under the now precisely defined conditions or if two-thirds of the Sejm votes for its own dissolution. Under the current constitution, elections to the Sejm produce proportional representation, and the current electoral ordinance retains the 5 percent and 8 percent thresholds. Five parties won seats in the Sejm in 1997, six in 2001 and 2005, and four in 2007. (In addition, Poland's German minority has regularly elected one or two representatives to the Sejm.) The Senat is elected under a first-past-the-post system. Both senators and Sejm deputies enjoy immunity from criminal prosecution during their terms, a constitutional rule that has had notorious implications.

The Prime Minister and Government

The Council of Ministers, the Polish government in the parliamentary sense of the word, consists of the prime minister and the cabinet. The constitution entrusts this body with almost all executive powers: it is responsible for both "internal affairs and foreign policy"; it manages "the government administration"; and it commands all the powers not explicitly reserved for other state organs or local governments (Art. 146). The cabinet also drafts the budget and supervises its implementation, and in certain instances can issue decrees without the need to seek legislative approval. The government may have gained few powers in the 1997 constitution, but it was freed from presidential interference in important policy areas. Each Council of Ministers owes its legal authority to the Sejm's vote of confidence that put it into office, and each can be removed if the Sejm passes a constructive vote of no confidence designating a prime ministerial candidate to form a new government. During the first eight years after the communist regime fell, Poland had seven different governments, but since 1997 there have been only six. Whether a result of constitutional changes or of the consolidation of the party system or both, the increase in government stability has brought about more coherent policymaking and greater political predictability.

Even though the president has greater prestige, the prime minister holds the single most powerful office in Poland. He or she selects the government's ministers (and can fire them if need be) and coordinates and supervises their work. Even some of the president's powers cannot be exercised without the express consent of the prime minister, whose countersignature is necessary for many presidential acts. But the practical political power of the person in the prime minister's office is a different matter.

In carrying out their duties, prime ministers are dependent on the continued support of the parties in the governing coalition. Achieving this support is not simply a matter of procuring the loyalty of a junior coalition partner (or of silent supporters such as those sought by the minority government that took power in 2005). Of the six prime ministers since 1997, only three—Leszek Miller (2001–2004), Jarosław Kaczyński (2006–2007), and Donald Tusk (2007–)—were the leaders of the majority party. Jerzy Buzek (1997–2001) was an important figure in the Solidarity Election Action (AWS) coalition, but Marian Krzaklewski, leader of both the Solidarity trade union and the political coalition, remained the power behind the throne. Economist and former member of the Alliance of the Democratic Left (SLD) Marek Belka (2004–2005) had served as minister in earlier SLD-led governments, but had never been a member of the party's leadership. Jarosław Kaczyński, leader of the Law and Justice Party (PiS), finally appeared ready to take on the prime ministership in 2005, but instead turned it over to a relative unknown, Kazimierz Marcinkiewicz, when Kaczyński's twin brother, Lech, won the presidency. Regardless of official title, no one doubted that from 1997 to 2001 Krzaklewski was one of the two or three most powerful people in Poland, and later Jarosław Kaczyński would be still more powerful, even before he took over the premiership from Marcinkiewicz in July 2006.

This practice of the most powerful political figure—that is, the one who may have chosen the prime minister—remaining behind the scenes began with Wałęsa's selection of Tadeusz Mazowiecki (1989–1990) as prime minister, while Wałęsa himself remained free of political responsibility for a few more months. Hanna Suchocka (1992–1993) was not the leader of her party, Democratic Union, and Waldemar Pawlak (1993–1995) was leader of the Peasant Party, the junior coalition party in his government. Clearly, this practice worked well earlier for Jarosław Kaczyński. When the first party he founded and led, the Center Accord (PC), formed a government, he let Jan Olszewski (1991–1992) become prime minister. The scandal in which Olszewski's government fell left Kaczyński untouched, and he still plays a larger role in Polish politics than any of the politicians who served as prime minister in the 1990s. Nevertheless, this practice may be declining since Prime Minster Tusk has led both his party and the government successfully since 2007 and apparently finds these positions sufficiently powerful to outweigh any attractions of the presidency. Polish political analysts speculate that combining the roles of prime minister and party leader may give an individual the clout necessary to combat his party comrades' tendencies to enrich themselves through corruption—if indeed he is so inclined.

Other Institutions

The judiciary is a constitutionally separate branch, independent of the legislative and the executive. The main judicial system, which deals with ordinary criminal, civil, family, and labor law cases, rarely plays a political role. Judges on its highest level, the Supreme Court, are appointed by the president, but the president's choices are made on the recommendation of the National Judicial Council. These judges serve life terms and cannot be removed. A separate system of administrative courts, headed by the Chief Administrative Court, oversees the performance of the state administration. Administrative judges are also appointed by the president on the recommendation of the National Judicial Council.

Two separate judicial bodies—the Constitutional Tribunal and the Tribunal of State—play a much greater political role. The Constitutional Tribunal is responsible for judicial review, including ruling on whether laws conform to the constitution, delimiting the jurisdiction of other state organs, and issuing binding interpretations of laws. Its fifteen judges are elected by the Sejm for a single term of nine years. Various state officials, including the president, the Speakers of the Sejm and the Senat, and the prime minister, may refer a case to the Constitutional Tribunal; any group of fifty Sejm deputies or thirty senators also has that right. The performance of the Constitutional Tribunal since the democratization of Poland has earned it respect and credibility from many. It has even, on occasion, gone against the will of the parliament.

The Constitutional Tribunal has played its most notable role on the issue of lustration—exposing and/or sanctioning those who collaborated with the communist regime. In 1992 it declared the first law on this topic unconstitutional, resulting in major revisions that took several years to be worked out. Fifteen years later the Tribunal again addressed this topic, rejecting major articles of a new lustration law that would have required people in fifty-three different occupations, including in the private sector, to be lustrated by the Institute of National Remembrance, exposing any evidence of collaboration with the communist-era secret police. This issue would have played out very differently in Poland were it not for the Constitutional Tribunal and its independence from parliament and the executive.

The Tribunal of State has a different responsibility: the leaders of national institutions (including the president, members of the Council of Ministers, and other senior state officials) must answer to this court. If the Tribunal of State finds that they have violated the constitution or committed other offenses, it can remove them from office, revoke their political rights and any awards or privileges, or apply criminal penalties. The Sejm selects the members of the Tribunal, who serve only during the term of that Sejm. This court has also shown its independence.

Local government in Poland has been in flux since the fall of communism. Self-government on the local level was viewed as an important part of Poland's democratizing political transformation, but the task required the decentralization of decision making to levels that had never borne such a responsibility before. In 1999 a comprehensive legislative act drastically revised territorial administration. The previous forty-nine provinces were compressed into sixteen provinces, representing a return to the more historical, precommunist regions of Poland. Each province has a locally elected government, which must work with a prefect (*wojewoda*) appointed by the national government. Beneath the provincial level are the county and town levels, with their own elected bodies, and beneath them is the district or village level with elected bodies of its own. These and earlier reforms were intended to make local government bodies autonomous and effective. Obstacles have included lack of political will among central decision makers and resistance among the interest groups and state bureaucracies affected by these reforms. Nevertheless, the popularity of local government, especially on the lowest level, demonstrates considerable progress.

NOTE

1. Polish Constitution of 2 April 1997 (Konstytucja Rzeczypospolitej Polskiej z dnia 2 kwietnia 1997 r.).

Who Has the Power?

T HE ADVENT OF DEMOCRATIC POLITICS IN POLAND MEANT A SEA change in the nature and number of political actors. In the communist era, politics had been viewed either as a war of "them versus us" ("them" understood to be the communists and "us" the Polish people, a subset that somehow did not include the communists) or as a game of factional politics among the communist elite. If the picture was ever so simple, now it is much more complex, with a wide array of political parties vying for power, while interest groups seek to influence power holders.

Parties and the Party System

For more than ten years after democratization, the Polish party system was visibly in flux. In the 2001 elections, six parties made it into the Sejm. Only two of these parties had ever held seats before; three had been formed less than a year earlier; and the two parties that had formed the outgoing government coalition failed to win any seats. By contrast, the 2005 parliamentary election results suggested a level of party system stability unprecedented for Poland—the same six parties, and only those six parties, won seats again. The 2007 results suggested downright party system consolidation, with only four parties or electoral alliances making it into the parliament (the smallest number ever)—all of them parties (or alliances based on parties) that had been in the previous Sejm. But postcommunist Polish politics is still best understood in terms of camps rather than parties. Camps are groupings defined not by organizational lines but by patterns of association, similar worldviews, or shared policy orientations. In the Polish case, one can distinguish camps of the left, the right, and the center, as well as a subset of peasant-based parties that fits into neither the camp scheme nor any version of the left-right spectrum.

In Poland, the terms *left* and *right* have very specific meanings. This distinction is based not on the classic economic policy preferences—to the frustration of observers and of many politicians themselves—but rather on a deep historical-cultural cleavage. The cleavages within Polish society described in Chapter 7.1 are echoed among political elites. According to sociologist Mirosława Grabowska, these elites come from two separate worlds: on the one hand, a world of devout Catholics with a Solidarity past and, on the other hand, a world of nonreligious people with a communist past.[1] Religion and history reinforce each other: indeed, studies have shown that political elites with roots in the anticommunist opposition, who dominate in the right camp, tend to go to church at least once a week, and those with roots in the communist regime and its allied organizations do not, and this group dominates in the left camp.[2] These differences not only have dictated party membership, but also have shaped politicians' attitudes toward each other and constrained political possibilities. The strongest antipathies in postcommunist Polish politics have been between former communists and former oppositionists. Until 2001 no electoral alliance or democratically formed government coalition cut across this cleavage.

The Left

Even though the left is dominated by politicians from the former communist side of the historical-cultural cleavage and their younger colleagues, rightist politicians also occasionally refer to former oppositionist colleagues who oppose strict decommunization policies as leftist. For many Poles, the left, by definition, consists of the former communists and perhaps those who are willing to work with them or at least not reject their participation in the public sphere.

The history of the left in contemporary Poland is the story of the seemingly inexorable rise of the communist successor party, currently called the Alliance of the Democratic Left (SLD), followed by its humiliating crash in 2004–2005. Until 2005 the SLD had increased its vote in every free parliamentary election—from 12 percent in 1991, to 21 percent in 1993, to 27 percent in 1997, to 41 percent (for its electoral coalition with a small junior partner) in 2001. Then in 2005 it earned its lowest share ever, less than 12 percent, which it increased only marginally, to 13 percent, in 2007. Why was the SLD so successful for well over a decade? And why did it then perform so abysmally after ten years of a popular president from the SLD and after an SLD government triumphantly led Poland into the European Union (EU) and into the North Atlantic Treaty Organization (NATO)?

The answer to the first question lies in the extraordinary pragmatism of the SLD, and the answer to the second question may be related. Both sociological research and political observation suggest that the SLD is remarkably pragmatic. When party activists are surveyed, those from the postcommunist left are most likely to assert that their party should strive for electoral support that is as broad as possible. They are also the most likely to agree that their party may need to abandon some of its campaign pledges once in office.[3]

This pragmatic approach to politics, clearly shared by the SLD leadership, has been increasingly apparent in economic policy, foreign policy, and sociocultural issues since the early 1990s, which perhaps explains the increase in votes for the SLD through 2001. In view of its origins in a Marxist-Leninist party that created and ran a centrally planned economy, the SLD has been surprisingly moderate in economic policy in both propaganda and practice. Every time it has campaigned against a rightist incumbent government, it has pledged not to abandon market-oriented economic reforms, but instead to execute them more effectively and to take care of those hurt worst by the reforms. When in government, the SLD has made no major changes of direction in economic policy. The ease with which the SLD turned away from socialist economic ideology is not surprising because of the visible bankruptcy of the command economy in its final decades. Nevertheless, the broad spectrum of economic orientations present in the SLD still extends all the way from neoliberalism to nostalgia for socialism. Such breadth does not in and of itself guarantee moderation: politics would be far too easy if one could simply average out a variety of opinions and go with the arithmetic mean. Yet these differences have never developed into the crippling public schisms that have characterized the right side of the Polish political spectrum.

SLD foreign policy also has been remarkably pragmatic. Most important, the SLD turned its orientation from the east (the Soviet Union and now Russia) to the west (Western Europe and the United States). Heir to the Communist Party that kept Poland in the Soviet-dominated Warsaw Pact and viewed NATO as its sworn enemy, the SLD shifted to supporting Poland's entry into NATO and now points with pride to the positive role that

President Aleksander Kwaśniewski played in this process. Similarly, the SLD was one of the strongest supporters of Poland's entry into the EU, and it considers Poland's membership perhaps the most important achievement of the 2001–2004 SLD-led government. Such a dramatic turnaround in policy positions might have torn a different party apart.

Pragmatism in sociocultural issues should have been harder for the SLD. Its activists share a set of policy preferences directly derived from their shared secular leftist heritage, reinforced by their daily lives and never invalidated by geopolitical changes or discredited in the way socialist economic values were discredited by the failings of the socialist economy. These activists differ dramatically from the vast majority of Poles in their church-going habits and in their preferences about issues such as religion in schools. Yet the SLD has managed to convince significant percentages of church-going Poles to vote for its parliamentary and presidential candidates by moderating its stance in matters of church-state relations and religious values in policy. After a "cold war" with the Catholic Church in the early 1990s, SLD leaders gradually adopted a strategy of compromise, giving up their goal of removing religious education from public schools and choosing not to reverse restrictive abortion laws when in power. Swearing off anticlerical slogans and policies, the SLD has effectively relegated its own activists' secular values—not religious values—to the private realm.

This pragmatism has allowed the SLD to mold its image and program to the voters' wishes and to make macroeconomic and foreign policy choices that meet with the approval of international organizations and important foreign states. It also has made possible an impressive degree of cohesion and party discipline. The unity of the postcommunist left— with no fissures resulting in a loss of significant resources until 2004—would be impressive in any new democracy, but against the chaos of mutual recriminations, accusations, schisms, fractures, and defections characterizing the rest of the Polish political scene, it appears miraculous. When the former ruling party, the Polish United Workers' Party, dissolved itself in January 1990, its final congress was immediately transformed into the founding congress of the Social Democracy of the Republic of Poland (SdRP). The SdRP soon brought together smaller parties, trade unions, other organizations, and independents to create a lasting coalition, the SLD. This coalition, which was dominated by the SdRP, proved more cohesive and coherent than almost any Polish party.

Indeed, in 1999 it transformed itself into a political party, taking over the role of the SdRP but dispensing with the stigma of being the official successor to the Communist Party. Until 2004 the SLD, like the SdRP before it, avoided visible intraparty struggles. Leadership continuity within the party was remarkable—that is, by Polish standards. At the SdRP founding congress in 1990, delegates had elected as their chair former communist junior minister Aleksander Kwaśniewski, who would serve until his election as president of the Republic in 1995. The secretary-general elected at the same congress, Leszek Miller, was a former Central Committee secretary supported by the Communist Party apparatus, who would later lead the SLD to its 2001 victory and serve as prime minister from 2001 to 2004. Neither this continuity nor the lack of dramatic internal struggles should, however, be interpreted to mean that there were no serious differences of opinion or personal rivalries among party leaders. Instead, SLD politicians managed to keep the public expression of such differences to a minimum—with few exceptions, their conflicts took place behind closed doors.

All of this worked together to create an image of the SLD as competent and professional. The Polish electorate distrusts ideology, associating it with conflict and inefficiency, and has a strong preference for practical and pragmatic politicians. Social psychologist Mirosława Marody put it this way: "The average voter sees it like this: 'All politicians are swine, but there are amateur swine and professional swine. Of the two evils I prefer the latter.'" The SLD were the professional swine, the ones whose competence if not their honesty could be trusted, the ones who would not let ideology get in the way of running the country and pleasing the voters.[4]

What then happened to the professional swine, the SLD, in 2004 and 2005? To put it simply, the SLD's swinishness went too far. Corruption has been a major feature of democratic politics in Poland. By the mid-1990s, it was already clear to Poles that government contracts, licenses, hiring, and many of the other types of decisions that benefit particular interests in the private sector were an economic bonanza to those who controlled them—whether the payoff took a quasi-legal form such as jobs or investment opportunities for the officeholder's relatives or the traditional cash-filled envelope. Although no one would claim that this phenomenon was unique to SLD-led governments, it is significant that in 2001, when Miller's SLD-led government took power, Poland's ranking on Transparency International's Corruption Perceptions Index (CPI) was forty-fourth out of the 158 countries on the index, and in 2004—when that government fell—Poland's CPI ranking was sixty-seventh, giving it one of the most corrupt images in Central and Eastern Europe.

During Miller's premiership, Polish public opinion was affected by several major scandals involving SLD politicians. On top of the numerous financial scandals that implicated regional SLD leaders, two major scandals at the national level ("Rywingate" and "Orlengate"), together with the subsequent parliamentary investigations, tarnished the images of important SLD figures irrevocably and revealed to the public a private world in which incompetent and cynical politicians served their own self-interest with no regard for law. The public opinion ratings of Miller's government and the SLD plummeted in early 2004, and for the first time serious ruptures appeared in the unity of the postcommunist left. Sejm marshal Marek Borowski and several other SLD deputies then formed a new party, the Social Democracy of Poland (SdPl), and other SLD activists defected to the newly formed centrist Democratic Party. More important than any resources Borowski and others took with them was that the left was no longer united; rather, it was now subject to the same intense fraternal mudslinging as the center and the right. Miller's government soon fell: in a survey held a few days after Miller's resignation, 51 percent of respondents evaluated his performance as poor or very poor; only 8 percent evaluated it as good, and 39 percent felt his government had achieved nothing. The only success that a significant proportion of respondents (33 percent) associated with Miller was Poland's entry into the EU. When asked about the greatest flaws of the Miller government, the largest share—42 percent—mentioned corruption or scandals.[5] Five months later, in the 2005 Sejm elections, only die-hard leftist loyalists voted for the SLD or the SdPl—and the 4 percent of the electorate who chose the SdPl saw their votes wasted when the party failed to reach the 5 percent threshold. The SLD returned to the Sejm, but with only fifty-five seats—seats that seemed relatively useless because of the unwillingness of most of the other parliamentary parties to ally with the former communists.

In the 2006 local elections and the 2007 Sejm elections, the pragmatism of the Polish left reasserted itself. The SLD, the SdPL, and two very small post-Solidarity leftist and center-leftist parties formed an electoral alliance: the Left and Democrats (LiD). Nevertheless, this latest incarnation of the Polish left failed to accomplish its usual comeback, and in fact garnered fewer votes in 2007 than the SLD and SdPL had won separately in 2005. The scandals of the Miller government may have been too fresh in the voters' minds. The left's reputation for competence had been tarnished, and the voters finally had an attractive alternative between the discredited left and the discredited right in the form of an apparently new center.

The Right

The Polish right, whether defined as the post-opposition camp or as those parties and political elites that emphasize traditional and religious values, has been less effective than the Polish left and remains so. It has proved less able than the left at two crucial political tasks: consistently mobilizing the support of its political core to achieve political power (or at least parliamentary seats) and winning over centrist and undecided voters. Therefore, the political impact of the right has not reflected the distribution of right-left preferences in Polish society.

What is wrong with the Polish right? Three flaws stand out: (1) the right is much more divided than the left—even after the SLD debacle of 2004–2005; (2) it is much more ideologically bound; and (3) it may be equally corrupt as the left.

Unity remains an unattainable goal for the Polish right. The most notorious example of the right's inability to unite even in the face of dire political necessity occurred in the 1993 parliamentary elections, when Polish parties first faced thresholds for representation—5 percent for parties and 8 percent for coalitions. In spite of these new rules, the right and the center-right chose to compete in seven separate political groupings, of which only two made it into the Sejm, together commanding 12 percent of the seats. The other rightist parties, which won a total of more than 30 percent of the vote, failed to meet the threshold. As a result, the SLD, with an undivided 20 percent of the vote, easily formed a governing coalition with the Polish Peasant Party.

The 1993 results are the most glaring example of the cost of disunity for the right, but there are other examples as well. Voters went to the polls in 1993—less than two years after the previous Sejm elections—only because of defections in a center-right coalition; four months earlier, Solidarity deputies had voted against the government they had previously supported. The center-right government before that had fallen as a result of a controversy about lustration—the process of opening up secret police files to identify former collaborators in contemporary public life. Certain rightist elites accused others of having been informers during the communist era, while other rightist elites accused the accusers of misusing these files for private political gain. If the strongest antipathies in Polish politics have been between former communists and former oppositionists, hostilities among former oppositionists have run a close second.

The 1995 presidential election took place while most right and center-right parties continued to be shut out of the Sejm, but these parties still failed to agree on a single candidate for president. They presented their electorate with four candidates, and it is highly unlikely that all the voters who supported other rightist candidates turned out to vote for LechWałęsa in the second round, which he narrowly lost to former communist Kwaśniewski.

Not surprisingly, empirical data together with political practice reveal that this divided right is much more ideological than any other part of the Polish political spectrum, including centrist and peasant parties as well as the left. The lack of organizational continuity on the right—with new parties forming, splintering, merging, and splintering again (with emphasis on the splintering)—has made it hard for social scientists to identify particular rightist parties for long-term research projects. The exception has been the Christian-National Union (ZChN), which was founded in 1989. It stubbornly persisted for more than fifteen years and supported the Kaczyńskis in 2005, with some former ZChN members joining the minority Law and Justice government after the election. According to research on the ZChN, its elites were consistently more ideological than those of the leftist and centrist parties. Sixty-eight percent of the ZChN party congress delegates surveyed said that the party should stick to all of its campaign promises. More than twice as many ZChN delegates as delegates to other party congresses claimed that they joined the party in order to achieve its goals. Survey research on other rightist party leaderships suggests that they share at least some of the attitudes associated with ideological dogmatism. For example, Krzysztof Jasiecki found that a significant proportion of rightist elites look askance at political consensus and compromise. Although this attitude was not present among all rightist politicians surveyed, it was conspicuously absent in other Polish political groupings. Rightists used phrases such as "giving up your principles to win political office" and "political prostitution" to describe political consensus. Jasiecki ascribes this attitude at least in part to negative evaluations of the 1989 Roundtable Pact and its aftermath; for some, it appears, political compromise was forever discredited by this historical agreement between communists and oppositionists.[6]

These two related characteristics of the Polish right—its tendency to splinter rather than unite and the emphasis on ideology—have made it impossible for rightist politicians to emulate the SLD and unify their camp into a single disciplined and effective party. Instead, the most recent rightist governments have been based on two distinct strategies, each with varying degrees of success. The first strategy is to form a catchall organization based on a large and relatively loose coalition of parties. The second is to forge a disciplined, ideologically coherent party with a significant but limited appeal.

The formation of Solidarity Election Action (AWS) in 1996 represents the first approach. More than twenty rightist parties united around the Solidarity trade union and its leader, Marian Krzaklewski, who was credited with reconciling the irreconcilable. Party and union leaders signed a common charter, attracted still more parties and organizations to join them, and soon were running neck and neck with the governing SLD in public opinion polls. The AWS won a plurality (34 percent of the vote) in the 1997 parliamentary elections and formed a government with the relatively compatible Union of Freedom (UW) as junior partner. But victory did not strengthen the bonds holding the AWS together. It was plagued by internal disputes during all four of its years in government. Ominously, these disputes intensified as the next election approached; its member parties squabbled about policy, personnel, and principles—and they made a point of doing so publicly. To the surprise of all observers, the various components of the AWS ended up fighting the 2001 election campaign in only two separate incarnations—a smaller catchall coalition, the AWS-Right, and a new political party, Law and Justice (PiS). Another new rightist party, the League of Polish Families (LPR), included at least one politician formerly from the AWS.

The failure of the AWS-Right to pass the 5 percent threshold in 2001 and the relative success of PiS (10 percent) and the LPR (8 percent) indicated that the right's future might lie in the alternative strategy of more ideologically coherent parties. (PiS was originally united by its law-and-order concerns, while the LPR consists of devoutly Catholic Euro-skeptics.) That these young parties won seats not only in the 2001 Sejm but again in the 2005 Sejm, when PiS increased its vote share to a plurality of 27 percent, supported this idea. Both PiS and the LPR have distinct ideological profiles. The results of a 2005 survey revealed that the LPR had the clearest profile of any Polish party. From 73 percent to 92 percent of Poles could easily identify its stand on major sociocultural issues such as church-state relations, abortion, and decommunization, as well as on crucial economic issues. Although the profile of PiS is not nearly as clear to Poles, especially on economic issues, roughly 75 percent of Poles could distinguish its positions on abortion and decommunization.[7]

PiS has been a disciplined and effective party, which allowed it upon its founding in 2001 to rapidly become a major political actor. Launched on the basis of the popularity achieved by Lech Kaczyński as a hard-hitting minister of justice in the AWS-led government, it brought together rightist activists from within and out of the AWS, especially those who had participated in Center Accord (PC), a conservative party founded by the Kaczyński brothers in 1990. Less than four months after its official formation, PiS fought an effective parliamentary campaign, winning a respectable forty-four Sejm seats. The following year, its candidate, Lech Kaczyński, won an intensely competitive race for mayor of Warsaw. After coming in third in Poland's first elections to the European Parliament in 2004, PiS proved victorious in both the presidential and parliamentary elections of 2005. In a field of seven serious candidates, the right side of the political spectrum had for once only one real candidate: Kaczyński. This was an extraordinary political accomplishment. Support from the LPR and especially from its ally, the ultra-Catholic station Radio Maryja, proved decisive in mobilizing conservative voters in the second round, when Kaczyński won 54 percent of the vote.

The 2005 results, however, revealed both the potential and the limitations of the strategy chosen by PiS leaders. One month before winning such a solid majority in the presidential election, PiS was able to garner only 34 percent of seats in the parliamentary elections, with their different dynamics and political logic. This very respectable share, in the absence of any rival alternative coalition, proved sufficient to form a minority government. But without coalition partners willing to carry out large parts of PiS's political program, the party was condemned either to ineffectiveness as a weak government failing to command a majority in the Sejm or to a coalition with apparently incompatible partners. When PiS chose the latter strategy in May 2006, it found itself allied with two parties whose leaders it had previously condemned as irresponsible and even dangerous. The result was a government characterized by tension and conflict so apparent that within a year after its formation half of Poles surveyed characterized cooperation within the coalition as somewhat bad and another 11 percent called it very bad.[8] Ideological coherence and party discipline have borne similar fruit for the LPR. Although it was able to enter the

PIS-led government in 2006, gaining a deputy premiership for its leader and several cabinet posts, the likelihood of it ever widening its appeal enough to dominate a government was extremely low, and in 2007 it failed to even pass the threshold for parliamentary representation.

The final fatal flaw of the right is that it has also shown itself to be extremely corruptible. The post-opposition governments of the early 1990s had already shown such tendencies; it was not without reason that critics termed them the "republic of buddies." Nevertheless, the practices of patronage and corruption implied by this term were further developed under the 1993–1997 SLD governments, which allowed the AWS to present itself as the morally superior alternative—that is, the people who would clean up the Augean stables left by the postcommunist left and their allies. But the center-right government that took power in 1997 continued the same practices that had been quasi-institutionalized under the previous governments. Scandal followed scandal, and although many government ministers and party leaders appeared irreproachable in their conduct, they had plenty of colleagues who more or less explicitly subscribed to what was commonly called the "TKM" philosophy—short for a Polish phrase best translated as "f★★★, it's our turn now!"

In its first years PiS managed the Herculean task of disassociating itself from this phenomenon in the public eye, campaigning from the start on slogans of law and order and battling corruption. This image helped it considerably in the 2005 campaigns that came on the heels of the huge SLD scandals. Once in power, however, PiS made it clear that this government intended to practice patronage politics whenever possible, putting its own people and their friends and relatives into sensitive and important positions. Moreover, many PiS politicians quickly demonstrated that they had not lost their taste for private enrichment at public expense, while some of their coalition partners, particularly from Self-Defense (discussed below), were greedy enough to make both PiS and the left look like comparative angels. Thus the Polish public was

Jarosław Kaczyński (left), Law and Justice's candidate and surviving twin of late Polish president Lech Kaczyński, and Bronisław Komorowski, Civic Platform's candidate, cast their votes in the 2010 presidential election. Although Kaczyński did better than expected, Komorowski won in the second round, 53 percent to 47 percent.

Source: Reuters/Kacper Pempel/Pawel Kopczynski

treated to the edifying spectacle of an anticorruption government torn apart by competing accusations of corruption.

When the collapse of the coalition led to early elections in October 2007, PiS increased its vote share, as befitted a party presiding over an economy with a high growth rate and falling unemployment, but only from 27 percent (its 2005 share) to 32 percent. Unfortunately for PiS it gained these votes mainly at the expense of its erstwhile allies, neither of which crossed the threshold for parliamentary representation, and therefore it found itself in the Sejm with the second-largest share of seats and no potential coalition partner. Furthermore, once out of power PiS no longer appeared to be immune to the Polish right's tendency towards fragmentation. By January 2010, eight of its Sejm deputies, including some prominent figures, had left PiS and formed a new parliamentary club, Poland Plus; they criticized PiS and Jarosław Kaczyński for moving too far towards the center.

The Center and Others

Until 2001 the center of the Polish political spectrum was relatively cohesive and characterized by organizational continuity. In the first years of democratic politics, it was represented by two post-opposition parties, the Democratic Union (UD) and the Liberal-Democratic Party (KLD). In 1994 the two came together to form the Union of Freedom (UW), a party that constituted the center of the political spectrum until Civic Platform emerged to deal it a lethal blow in the 2001 parliamentary elections.

The UW and its predecessors had limited electoral appeal, never winning more than 15 percent of the vote. Nevertheless, these parties and their leaders played crucial roles in the first years of postcommunist Poland. Politicians who were or who became leaders of these parties began the economic transformation and carried out pivotal stages of it. Government ministers from or supported by these parties crafted much of the new democracy's foreign policy and many of its important institutional reforms.

These parties' positions on the historical-cultural cleavage were, however, always ambiguous, which may have contributed to their weakness. Although both the UW and the UD were strongly associated with the anticommunist opposition, many rightists criticized the roles played by their most prominent former oppositionists (as well as the past membership of several of them in the Communist Party). Because these centrists had helped to craft Poland's historic compromise, the Roundtable Pact, and had shaped the moderate and conciliatory policies of the first noncommunist government, they were condemned by much of the right.

On both sociocultural and historical issues, the UW and its predecessors tended to take positions precisely in the center—in between the former communists and the right, which made the center appear to be consciously noncommittal on such issues and to concentrate instead on economic policy. Here the UW's position was not at all centrist. As the neoliberal party, the party of fiscal restraint and rapid economic transformation, the UW stood at one end of the economic policy spectrum, and the left and the right stood together at the other end. The UW was defined by a specific economic approach, and it remained vague on sociocultural issues, while both the left and the right spanned a broad range of economic views, but were also defined by their preferences on sociocultural and historical issues.

For more than ten years, the center's approach to politics allowed it to have an impact on government policy far greater than the electoral strength of its parties. The center parties could be fairly described as policy seekers rather than vote seekers—that is, they made many decisions on the basis of a vision of what was best for the country (or at least for its economy and the business climate) rather than what would win votes. Whether the policies pursued by these centrist parties were in Poland's best interests is a question best left to the economists or better yet to historians: what is certain is that many of these policy choices were very costly for the UW. In a dramatic defeat in 2001, the UW failed to meet the 5 percent threshold for Sejm seats.

When in 2001 Civic Platform, or PO, replaced the UW in the center of the Polish political spectrum, the role of the center fundamentally changed. Although PO proclaimed a neoliberal economic orientation, which gained it the support of significant business interests as well as of many small entrepreneurs, its first prominent policy position was its opposition to state subsidies for political parties. Oddly, even though former UW activists and former AWS activists played major roles in founding PO, its strongest rhetoric was directed against parties and politicians. This antiparty strategy succeeded. Less than nine months after its founding, PO won nearly 13 percent in the Sejm elections—almost exactly the same as the percentage received by the UW in 1997.

And PO has continued to prove a more skilled player of the electoral game than its centrist predecessors, while clearly inheriting their cohesiveness. In 2005 it nearly doubled its share of the Sejm vote, garnering more than 24 percent and therefore 29 percent of the seats. The vote that its leader, Donald Tusk, received in the second round of the presidential election was even more impressive—46 percent. PO chalked up these achievements while maintaining its neoliberal position on economic issues, such as advocating a flat income tax during the 2005 campaign, but moving to the right on sociocultural issues. It used its years in opposition to the PiS-led government to establish itself as the party of normality and of the future. Voters saw PO as even more pro-European than the SLD, whose leaders had presided over Poland's entry into the European Union. It would be simplistic to call PO the party of Poland's "winners," yet 49 percent of PO's supporters describe themselves as having benefited from Poland's transformation, while only 31 percent of PiS's supporters and 27 percent of SLD's supporters describe themselves similarly.[9]

In the short election campaign of 2007, urbane and cosmopolitan Tusk appeared the perfect antithesis to PiS prime minister Kaczyński's confrontational style with hints of xenophobia, especially in a decisive televised debate. PO went on to win 42 percent of the vote, entering the Sejm with 45 percent of seats and—a crucial asset—the ability to work with two of the other three parliamentary parties, excepting only PiS, its new arch-rival. Tusk's PO-led government managed to maintain relatively good approval ratings for its first few years, in spite of the global economic crisis; these ratings suffered a qualitative drop only after the outbreak of a scandal over gambling legislation and the casino industry. Several high-level PO officials resigned and a parliamentary investigation got under way; PO had shown itself susceptible to the chronic disease of Polish political parties: corruption while in power.

As long as there have been political parties in Poland—from partition, through interwar independence, through the communist period, and to the present—there has been a subset of parties that simply do not fit into any version of the left-right spectrum: the agrarian parties. In a country in which the rural population is well over a third of the electorate, these parties are a force to be reckoned with. In postcommunist Polish politics, rural interests have been represented by two competing organizations, the Polish Peasant Party (PSL) and Self-Defense, both of which aspire to represent a broader array of Polish society, based on various combinations of traditional values, patriotism, and populism.

The PSL contains elements of the historical Peasant Party (the interwar PSL), but in terms of organization, personnel, and resources, it is primarily a successor to the United Peasant Party (ZSL), a satellite of the ruling party in the communist era. This relationship is reflected in its large membership, its nationwide organizational structure, and its wealth—most of its income is derived from valuable real estate inherited from the ZSL. Its position within the Polish party system has also been an asset; the PSL has been the largest party willing to work with and form coalitions with the SLD, but that distinction becomes much less valuable when the SLD is in decline. Although the PSL has held onto its material resources, the party's electoral clout has declined considerably. It received more than 15 percent of the Sejm vote in 1993 and formed an important part of the 1993–1997 governing coalition (led by its own prime minister for two years), but in the 2005 elections it earned its lowest-ever share, not quite 7 percent. The 2007 elections somewhat restored the PSL's fortunes: it won almost 9 percent of the vote and proved an appropriate coalition partner for the victorious PO.

At one point it appeared that the PSL might lose its lock on the core of the peasant vote to Andrzej Lepper's Self-Defense. Self-Defense emerged in 1991 as a populist agrarian movement and became notorious for organizing illegal and sometimes violent protests. Its early electoral attempts were failures—3 percent in the 1993 Sejm elections and 1 percent for Lepper in the 1995 presidential elections, but its leaders, particularly Lepper, demonstrated skill at presenting themselves to the public as advocates of the most discontent. Advocating Euro-skepticism and state intervention in the economy, the party won more than 10 percent of the vote in the 2001 Sejm elections and more than 11 percent in 2005, drawing most of its support from rural areas. Lepper's support for Kaczyński in the second round of the 2005 presidential election was seen as an important factor in his victory. Self-Defense then entered the government for the first time in May 2006 in a coalition with PiS and the LPR, but soon disgraced itself with scandals involving not only corruption but also sexual harassment; it won barely 1.5 percent of the vote in the subsequent elections and is currently an extraparliamentary party. Many political observers have expressed doubts about the commitment of Self-Defense to the democratic political game. The average Self-Defense supporters are the least likely among Poles to believe that democracy is the best form of government. Indeed, in a 2006 survey, during a period in which their party was gaining greater influence on the government (and would enter the government just three months later), only 51 percent of Self-Defense supporters agreed that democracy was the best form of government; 26 percent asserted that it was not. The closest party on the scale was PiS: 65 percent of members supported democracy, and 16 percent said it was not the best. Even Poles who did not intend to vote for any party looked more favorably on democracy than did Self-Defense supporters.[10]

Other Political Forces at Work

Although parties are the competitors for political office in Poland's democratic system, other organized actors have interests that can be affected by government policies, and so they attempt to influence those decisions. Some of the most important of these actors, the church and the trade unions, also operated under the communist regime and have had to adapt to the democratic game.

The Catholic Church

To the surprise of many, the Catholic Church in Poland at first floundered in the new environment of democratic politics after 1989. In the communist era, after initial difficulties (including the imprisonment of Stefan Cardinal Wyszyński), the church eventually adapted effectively to operating within a communist-ruled system. The church had its sphere, the Communist Party and the state had theirs, and any disagreements were worked out in private by elites from both sides. In spite of maintaining such a cooperative relationship with communist leaders, the church also provided moral and practical support for moderate opposition to the regime. Through this delicate balancing act, the church managed to pursue its own interests while preserving its own moral authority, and all surveys showed it to be by far the most respected institution in Poland.

But democratic politics proved to be an entirely new ballgame. The church saw an opportunity to use the political process to achieve many of its goals—such as outlawing abortion and requiring religious education in schools—but at first it tried to play too direct a role. Its initial approach of extending direct support to church-allied parties and calling openly for various policy changes was largely unsuccessful, thereby lowering public respect for the church and strengthening an anticlerical backlash. The 1995 attempt of one well-meaning priest at St. Catherine's Church in Warsaw to bring together rightist parties to nominate a single presidential candidate ended in utter failure and became a symbol of what is wrong with the Polish right. Meanwhile, the church has not been able to solve the problem of disunity within the right.

A more successful strategy for the church has been maintaining and even strengthening its moral authority among a large proportion of Polish society and developing the capability to influence opinion through its own mass media. In fact, political disunity rather than unified top-down action has resulted in a greater impact for the church on politics, even if the consequences may not always be to the liking of the church hierarchy. The station Radio Maryja, created and run by Catholic fundamentalists, is a political powerhouse, commanding the allegiance of a significant portion of the extremely devout, even while not appealing to a majority of Catholics. Its support, whether directed to the LPR or to PiS, has proved very valuable. Attempts by the hierarchy to rein in Radio Maryja have been unsuccessful.

Trade Unions and Business Interest Groups

As was true of the church, the Solidarity trade union also played a more powerful and more straightforward role in Polish politics during the communist era. Whether legal (1980–1981, 1989) or illegal (1982–1988), it was the opposition plain and simple, opposed to all the communist regime stood for but willing to work for what it could achieve within the perceived geopolitical limits. As democratic politics began and many Solidarity activists and advisers formed new political movements and parties, Solidarity had to become a true trade union rather than a national political movement. It could not maintain its 1981 membership level of nearly 10 million; its current membership is less than 1.5 million.

Solidarity's greatest success in post-1989 politics was the formation of the AWS and, to a lesser extent, the AWS-led government. Union leader Marian Krzaklewski used the group's resources—not least of which was the very power of its name—to bring together major rightist parties under the trade union's umbrella, and Krzaklewski remained leader of the AWS, while not entering the government. Nevertheless, the period of AWS government was not viewed as a major achievement for Solidarity; the union and its members were not satisfied with the policies carried out.

Solidarity's trade union rival, the All-Poland Alliance of Trade Unions (OPZZ), has about the same number of members, and in many ways it appears to be Solidarity's mirror image. OPZZ was created in 1984 as the communist-sponsored alternative to Solidarity, and, naturally, it enjoyed a privileged position until the communist regime fell. Until 2001 OPZZ was an important part of the SLD coalition, and it still maintains close and friendly relations with the SLD, and it has been able to exercise significant influence during periods of SLD-led government.

Because these two unions constitute the lion's share of Polish organized labor—the smaller union organizations have a total membership of about half a million—Polish state-labor relations have been shaped by the unions' political affiliations. Neither is merely the creature of the parties with which it is affiliated, and yet each finds itself operating according to the alternation of power—that is, one set of possibilities and tactics when its camp is in power and a completely different set when the opposing camp is in power.

Business interests in Poland follow a completely different logic. Many organizations exist to represent business interests, which include large umbrella organizations as well as those representing owners of small and medium-size enterprises or executives of state-owned companies. Yet business has its greatest impact on politics through the lobbying conducted by individuals and individual firms. Polish sociological studies have consistently shown that informal personal contacts between businesspeople and politicians are pervasive and are believed by the participants to have a significant influence on policy. This situation confirms the impression of the average Polish citizen not involved in these processes—that individual businesses and businesspeople, if not the business sector as a whole, have a disproportionate impact on political outcomes in Poland.

NOTES

1. Mirosława Grabowska, "Partie polityczne jako działający aktorzy: Partyjne organizacje—programy—elity," in *Budowanie demokracji: Podziały społeczne, partie polityczne, i społeczeństwo obywatelskie w postkomunistycznej Polsce,* ed. Mirosława Grabowska and Tadeusz Szawiel (Warsaw: Wydawnictwo Naukowe PWN, 2001), 363.

2. Jacek Wasilewski, "Normatywna integracja Polskiej elity potransformacyjnej," in *Jak żyją Polacy,* ed. Henryk Domański, Antonina Ostrowska, and Andrzej Rychard (Warsaw: Wydawnictwo IFiS PAN, 2000), 94; and Wasilewski, "The Crystallization of the Post-Communist and Post-Solidarity Political Elite," in *After Communism: A Multidisciplinary Approach to Radical Social Change,* ed. Edward Wnuk-Lipiński (Warsaw: Institute of Political Studies, Polish Academy of Sciences, 1995), 127.

3. Grabowska, "Partie polityczne jako działający aktorzy," 347.

4. Mirosława Marody, interviewed by Agata Nowakowska, *Gazeta Wyborcza,* April 4, 2001.

5. Centrum Badania Opinii Społecznej, "Jakim premierem był Leszek Miller? Opinie o sukcesach i porażkach jego rządu," May 2004.

6. Krzysztof Jasiecki, "Konsens i konflikt w poglądach elity politycznej," in *Polityka i Sejm: Formowanie się elity politycznej,* ed. Włodzimierz Wesołowski and Barbara Post (Warsaw: Wydawnictwo Sejmowe, 1998), 63–64.

7. Centrum Badania Opinii Społecznej, "Percepja stanowisk partii politycznych w wybranych kwestiach społecznych, politycznych, i gospodarczych," August 2005.

8. Centrum Badania Opinii Społecznej, "Opinii o koalicji PiS-Samoobrona-LPR po roku sprawowania władzy," October 2009.

9. Centrum Badania Opinii Społecznej, "Polacy o minionym dwudziestoleciu," February 2009.

10. Centrum Badania Opinii Społecznej, "Blaskie i cienie demokracji w Polsce," April 2006.

How Is Power Used?

7.4

DELINEATING THE ACTORS AND THE INSTITUTIONS WITHIN WHICH they operate is not sufficient to answer the question of how postcommunist Polish democracy is performing for Poles themselves. The answer requires a closer look at how power is actually used in Poland. Different criteria can be employed to examine the use of power in Poland and to evaluate the performance of this political system. Here, we rely on electoral accountability and policy responsiveness.

Two Criteria: Electoral Accountability and Policy Responsiveness

Electoral accountability can be understood very simply as the answer to this question: Can the electorate "kick the rascals out" when dissatisfied with their performance? In Poland, it most certainly can, and the sequence of Polish governments since the fall of communism clearly demonstrates this fact. After the first completely free parliamentary elections in 1991, the four successive governments (some quite brief) were controlled by multiparty coalitions composed of post-opposition parties. The next elections, in 1993, produced coalition governments by two parties of the opposing camp, postcommunist parties. The 1997 elections resulted in government by post-opposition parties, and the 2001 elections in governments led by postcommunist/post-opposition parties. The 2005 elections brought to power a post-opposition party that declared itself the bitter enemy of the most recent pair of governing parties. Thus, until 2007 each set of parliamentary elections resulted in alternation of power between the two major political camps; the 2007 election produced an alternation of a different kind, from a rightist government to a centrist government. The presidential elections show a similar pattern, with the exception of the 2000 reelection of popular president Aleksander Kwaśniewski.

These electoral results reflect voter dissatisfaction with the performance of these governments. Even though no Polish government is thought to have performed well in terms of public opinion, two of the three most recent sets of governments (1997–2001 and 2001–2005) hit all-time lows, with approval ratings barely in the teens. Such regular turnovers indicate that the Polish system has performed relatively well in terms of accountability, especially when compared with its Russian and Ukrainian neighbors. When the governments perform badly (which eventually all have done so far), the rascals are thrown out and replaced by their worst enemies.

But electoral accountability does not necessarily imply policy responsiveness. Are Polish voters' preferences articulated in public policy? Do the preferences of the majority, or at least of the plurality, of voters have a discernible impact on major policy areas? It is striking that economic policies in postcommunist Poland have been made largely without reference to popular concerns or regard for the short-term well-being of the general populace. Since 1989 economic policies have been more or less consistently neoliberal. These policies, which are those that affect voters' lives most directly and that voters see as most important, have not been changed by these alternating governments.

Explaining Political Performance

A likely explanation for Poland's performance on these two criteria can be found in the pattern of political cleavages that characterized nearly the first two decades of democratic politics in Poland. In fact, it may derive from a single aspect of this pattern—that political actors have been divided more decisively and effectively by historical-cultural differences than by socioeconomic orientations, such as preference for the free market or for state intervention, despite the enormous economic challenges Poland has faced. But the fact that this cleavage dominates in politics does not necessarily mean that it dominates in Polish society. Parties and their alliances are not a direct reflection of popular preferences or of society-wide cleavages. Rather, in the Polish case, the cleavage that has shaped politics—that is, alliance patterns and choices offered to the voters—and political outcomes is expressed very distinctly within the political elite, but not necessarily as strongly in society as a whole.

The Historical-Cultural Cleavage

The two postcommunist and post-opposition camps have defined and limited Polish political possibilities. The primacy of the political past becomes evident when one looks more closely at how political elites view parties other than their own. Here the most striking feature is the antipathy that has been shown to the former communists of the SLD by elites from all post-opposition parties. This antipathy has been manifested in public and private remarks, legislative initiatives, and reporting and commentary by media allied with those parties. As a matter of course, many politicians from these parties refer to their counterparts in the Alliance of the Democratic Left (SLD) as Reds, postcommunists, and communists. They frequently "slip" and use the initials PZPR (Polish United Workers' Party) rather than SdRP (Social Democracy of the Republic of Poland) or SLD. The long-lasting debate over decommunization was particularly intense. Many politicians favored a legal ban—as long as ten years—on placing former communists (or former communist officials of a certain rank) in political or administrative positions. It should not be at all surprising that when pollsters asked party elites about their levels of sympathy toward various other parties, the SLD came in dead last. Who then did SLD politicians dislike intensely, disregarding any similarity in their policy positions? The answer is the only political competitor at that time using the name Solidarity—that is, the Solidarity trade union's electoral list.

This antipathy also affects the parties' behavior toward electoral alliances or governing coalitions at the national or local level and therefore directly shapes and limits political possibilities. As the overview of government turnover in Poland suggests, no national governing coalition has been able to cut across the divide between former communists and former oppositionists, even though coalition government has been the rule, with no one party ever winning enough seats to govern by itself.

This pattern of government formation has not been just a matter of chance, of how the political dice (or rather the numbers of seats) fell each time a government was to be formed. A multinational team of political scientists who examined the responses of party elites to a survey question on possible coalition partners could find only one pair of Polish parties—the SLD and the Union of Labor (UP)—in which most party elites were willing to cooperate with each other across this fundamental divide.[1] But even this apparent exception—the participation of the UP, a party with some post-Solidarity roots, in the 2001–2004 SLD-led government—proves the rule. Whether to cooperate closely with the former communists of the SLD tore the UP apart. The issue was resolved only by the departure of those post-oppositionists who had rejected such cooperation.

The Economic Policy Cleavage

This profound cleavage based primarily on the political past is not necessarily the most important division among Polish elites. For example, consistent patterns of differing economic policy orientations among elites could play an equal or larger role in shaping the party system (and therefore the electorate's options). Indeed, since 1989 Polish political elites have had different opinions about the economic policy issues confronting Poland, such as whether to privatize slowly or quickly or whether to fight unemployment through public works programs or lower taxes. Certainly, Polish elites disagree on important aspects of how to deal with Poland's economic challenges. In spite of a near consensus on the benefits of a market economy and capitalism, individual politicians and groups of politicians can be distinguished by how large a role they see for the state in the economy, as well as the costs the young, the old, and the unemployed should be expected to pay for a healthy and efficient economy.

But these disagreements find only partial expression in the party system itself. Economic policy orientations vary not only from party to party (although some surprising pairs of parties have similar profiles on economic issues), but also widely within parties. The 1997 parliamentary elections were primarily a battle between the two major electoral blocs, the SLD and Solidarity Election Action (AWS), each of which represented a roughly similar wide range of opinion on economic policy. Their campaigns, however, were dominated by cultural and historical issues, such as the role of the church and decommunization, and barely touched on economic problems. Moral-historical issues were not so important in the 2001 campaign, and yet the two sides still did not face off on economic policy. The eventual winners, the postcommunists, made no campaign promises to reverse existing government economic policies, even going so far as to emphasize in their party conventions that they must not make too many promises to the voters.

Cleavages and the Party System

Although important differences in economic policy preferences exist among Polish elites, these policy differences do not define the elites, nor do they determine the fundamental dynamics of elite politics. Instead, it is the historical-cultural cleavage that has structured the party system, shaping elite choices to form new parties or to become involved in a particular party, as well as limiting the possibilities of cooperation between parties. This factor has been one of the major reasons for the regular government turnovers in Poland, and it has enabled the existence of two clear and nonoverlapping camps. If parties from one camp fail in government—indeed, even if the immediate outcomes of their policies disappoint the electorate—they can be punished by replacement with any parties from the other camp. And so it is the depth of this cleavage, which does not allow any governing coalition to cross ideological lines, together with the simplicity of the cleavage pattern, in which one point of view is so important that other differences do not shape the party system or alliance patterns, that has facilitated the Polish version of accountability. The political camps are very clear, and one can always be replaced by the other.

The importance of this cleavage also explains how relatively consistent economic policy requiring regular sacrifices from a good portion of the electorate has emerged out of the intensely competitive Polish political fray. The opponents of neoliberal economic policy have had no way in which to unite. Those with a communist past found themselves, because of the deep moral-historical cleavage, with their only political haven in the postcommunist SLD. They had nowhere else to go. But the SLD has been dominated since its founding by market-oriented leaders, with decided sympathies for neoliberal approaches. If the cleavage were not so deep, competitive electoral pressures might well have brought the more "leftist" leftists to power in the SLD. But for the first fifteen years of democratic politics, the SLD did not have to rely on its economic policy stances to win over voters. Its core voters stuck with it because they saw no other choice—the SLD was the only party that could protect them and guarantee at least some respect for the achievements of the former communist regime. The party has tended to win the rest of its voters through its image as a band of competent, pragmatic professionals, better suited to governing Poland than anyone else. Even though the image of the SLD as competent and professional was deeply tarnished by the disgraces of the Miller government, this party may be committed (by its past achievements) to a pro–European Union stance, which means effectively that it is committed to a pro–market approach. By contrast, the opponents of neoliberal economic policy among the former oppositionists and the more religious part of the political elite have found themselves cut off from many of their natural allies by this historical-cultural divide.

As a result, the major political debates and the election campaigns have revolved not around economic policy preferences, but around historical or cultural issues—or often around the simple issue of how badly the incumbents screwed up and whether the challengers can do any better. The historical-cultural divide has determined what parties exist and the parties with whom they can work. Thus when going to the polls, the voters have not been afforded choices that would allow them to express their economic preferences. As Polish parliamentarian Bogdan Pęk put it during a July 2, 1999, debate, this polarization over noneconomic issues had led over and over again to a situation in which, regardless of whether the left or the right wins, the finances of the state are managed by "the basic party organization of SGPiS"—that is, the former School of Economic Planning and Statistics, now the Warsaw School of Economics, dominated by neoliberals. This pattern, characterizing a society increasingly divided between winners and losers, between those who are succeeding in the market economy and those who are left behind, has brought up serious questions about policy responsiveness and, indeed, about the quality of Polish democracy.

NOTE

1. Herbert Kitschelt, Zdenka Mansfeldova, Radoslaw Markowski, and Gabor Toka, *Post-Communist Party Systems: Competition, Representation, and Inter-Party Cooperation* (Cambridge and New York: Cambridge University Press, 1999).

What Is the Future of Polish Politics?

THE HISTORICAL-CULTURAL CLEAVAGE AMONG POLITICAL ELITES HAS shaped the political possibilities and outcomes of postcommunist Polish politics since 1989. Will it endure and continue to shape Polish politics? One would expect this cleavage, based as it is on a specific historical experience—the communist period—to disappear over time, and indeed it should already be fading. After all, a generation of twenty-somethings is now entering politics with no adult memories of life under communist rule. Yet research on much older democracies has shown that cleavages deriving from particular societal conflicts can endure long after the experiences that gave rise to them. If partisan alignments are rooted in sociodemographic traits, if the corresponding values are passed down from generation to generation, and if patterns of association are structured around the cleavage, the cleavage can last for a long time.

These conditions appear to be present in Poland. The historical-cultural cleavage is strongly associated with a person's level of religiosity—a sociodemographic trait; related political traditions have been passed down from generation to generation in Poland for well over a century; and the cleavage is articulated in associations such as political parties. Eventually, new generations may become bored with evaluating the communist regime's achievements or determining who was to blame for communist-era crimes—but at present surveys show that one-fifth of Poles continue to believe lustration to be one of the most urgent issues facing their country. If and when these issues finally disappear, they may be replaced by new cultural controversies based on religious and moral values, with the warring sides still taking up their positions along the old fault line.

Political Realignment

Although the historical-cultural cleavage may not ever fade away, it may be losing its dominant position in Polish politics and so would no longer prevent other cleavages and interests from being expressed. The hardest battles in both the 2005 and the 2007 elections were fought between two parties with post-opposition roots, Civic Platform (PO) and Law and Justice (PiS). Because PO had moved closer to PiS on issues of church-state relations, the two parties were distinguished primarily by their positions on economic issues. PO remained a fervent proponent of the free market, advocating a flat income tax, budgetary restraint, and faster deregulation and privatization. By contrast, PiS took a statist rather than a liberal approach to economic issues, and it emphasized what the state should do for the neediest of its citizens. Its leader accused PO of proposing to continue policies "in which the economically weaker part of society would finance the privileges of the richer part of society." [1] Polish voters took note of these differences in the two parties' platforms. Analysis of the second round of the 2005 presidential election showed that, overwhelmingly, it was the economic "losers"—older people, rural residents, and the less educated—who voted for the PiS's Lech Kaczyński, while the economic "winners" or potential winners—the young, students, urban dwellers, and the better-off—voted for PO's Donald Tusk. The deepest cleavage in Polish society had finally been articulated both in an election campaign and in electoral results. As Kaczyński's victory with 54 percent of the vote demonstrated, in 2005 the economic losers were more numerous than the winners.

Significantly, this division was now reflected both in partisan alignments and in the formation of the government. When faced with only PiS and PO candidates in the second round, the electorates of the League of Polish Families (LPR), Self-Defense, and the Polish Peasant Party (PSL) chose PiS's Kaczyński, who had been endorsed by those parties' leaders. The common element in all these parties was certainly not an oppositionist background; after all, the PSL had roots in the loyal Peasant Party partner to the Communist Party, and many prominent activists in Self-Defense had communist backgrounds. Instead, these parties shared a populist approach to economic issues. Meanwhile, well over 70 percent of supporters of both the postcommunist Alliance of the Democratic Left (SLD) and the party that had recently split off from it voted for former oppositionist and PO candidate Tusk.[2] After the 2005 parliamentary election, in spite of preelection promises of a PiS-PO coalition, this same division shaped formation of the government. Coalition talks between PiS and PO—parties that were led by men who had fought on the same side against the communist regime and that included many prominent activists who had worked together in various parties and alliances since 1989—proved fruitless. A minority PiS government limped along for more than half a year until Self-Defense and the LPR joined PiS in a governing coalition. What is remarkable is that a rematch between PiS and PO barely two years later brought about the highest voter turnout in a parliamentary election in the history of the Third Republic—54 percent—after 2005's record low, 41 percent. Polling stations ran out of ballots, causing the election to be extended two hours as additional ballots were rushed to the polls. Perhaps voters cared more about the outcome when the battle lines were drawn over Poland's future—traditional and insular or modern and European—rather than over Poland's past.

The key to this political realignment, as well as to the previous political configuration, might be in the fortunes of the SLD. For as long as the postcommunists remained the most united and powerful force in Polish politics, the division between them and former oppositionists would be the defining feature of the political landscape. But in the vacuum left by the SLD's 2004–2005 collapse, all bets were off, and the socioeconomic cleavage could finally be articulated in political terms. It remains to be seen whether the SLD can recover anything close to its previous strength. Paradoxically, a political environment no longer dominated by the historical-cultural cleavage may prove more challenging for the SLD, because a greater variety of political opportunities would be available to its activists as well as its electorate.

Policy Challenges for Poland's Realigned Political Parties

As Poland began its third decade of postcommunist democracy, its major political parties were fewer and in a qualitatively different configuration, facing a different set of archrivals and potential allies, which according to the analysis above might make them more responsive to voter concerns. But they face many of the same issues that have come up again and again during the Third Republic, as well as some new types of challenges.

The one issue that could be fading from the political scene is lustration. Large majorities of Poles appear to consider continuing lustration not a crucial or pressing policy issue. In fact, many believe it has become nothing but a convenient weapon in the political game—an easy means of discrediting one's political opponent or a useful scare tactic. The Constitutional Tribunal's 2007 rejection of much of the latest lustration legislation met with understanding and

Corruption scandals alleging match-fixing and other crimes have involved Polish football (soccer), the country's most popular sport. Here Polish fans cheer on their national team during a 2008 match against Croatia. Investigations beginning in 2005 have resulted in the arrests of more than two hundred people, including referees, coaches, players, and league officials.

Source: Janek Skarzynski/AFP/Getty Images

even relief from many Poles. Only one significant political player, PiS, still remains ready to play the lustration card, a position that meets with approval from its hardcore electorate but seems unlikely to win it any more adherents. In these circumstances, lustration seems on its way to becoming a dead issue—unless new secret police files implicating major political figures come to light.[3]

Corruption, another perennial and characteristic issue of the first two decades of postcommunist Poland, persists. In Transparency International's 2009 Corruption Perceptions Index, Poland earned its best score ever, finally making it to the halfway point on the 10-point scale. But this meant that Poland was still perceived as much more corrupt than fellow EU members such as Ireland or Germany. The perceptions of Poles themselves bear this out—in the same year 89 percent of Poles surveyed asserted that corruption was a very big (40 percent) or somewhat big (49 percent) problem. Although businesspeople and other experts surveyed by Transparency International saw improvement, Poles perceived the situation to be worsening.[4] As for the complexity of this problem, Polish voters have found it easy enough to identify which party is the most corrupt; they know it is, without exception, whichever party is currently in power. Parties in opposition have found it equally easy to deal with this issue—attack the governing parties for their outrageous corruption and their unwillingness to rein in corruption in government bureaucracies and public services. Governing parties have faced more of a dilemma— how to control their own members in office and how to combat the pervasive corruption throughout the public sector while still running a government and observing the rule of law. In the eyes of many of its critics, the PiS government chose to compromise the rule of law as well as to elevate the battle against corruption over most other government business; the effectiveness of this strategy is debatable, but in any case it alienated a good portion of the Polish electorate. The PO-led government has chosen a more moderate approach and has been challenged by the 2009–2010 casino policy scandal implicating some of its own members.

During the first years of the Third Republic the management of Poland's foreign affairs was characterized by a relative consensus, on both the elite and the popular levels. Skilled diplomacy under postcommunist Poland's first foreign affairs minister, Krzysztof Skubiszewski, and his successors took advantage of Poland's political and economic transformation to establish good relations on a new foundation with most of Poland's neighbors as well as regional and world powers. A crucial part of foreign policy is the integration of Poland into regional multilateral structures, including NATO in 1999 and the European Union in 2004.

Preparation for and eventual membership in the EU had a major impact on Polish politics, opening up a new dimension of political discord by dividing Euro-skeptics and Europhiles. Although the slogan of a "Return to Europe" resonated strongly with Poles, fears emerged about the possible implications of such far-reaching integration into a supranational body. Worries about the overall economic implications were amorphous, but Polish peasants had specific reasons for concern, given that the generous EU agricultural subsidies had not customarily been directed to small farms. Another set of doubts concerned the impact of Europeanization on the Polish identity—a crucial question in a country with Poland's history—and on its traditional norms and Catholicism. These worries and doubts provided a base for the Euro-skeptic parties, PiS, the LPR, and Self-Defense. These fears proved at least temporarily unfounded—with EU membership and the accompanying subsides providing significant benefits for the Polish economy while no major conflicts between European and Polish values have yet emerged. With 65 percent of Poles seeing EU integration as bringing Poland more benefits than costs, and only 13 percent seeing more costs than benefits, the base for Euro-skepticism has shrunk.[5] Not surprisingly, the LPR and Self-Defense are now insignificant extraparliamentary parties, and PiS is moderating its position on Europe. Further integration questions, such as entry into the euro-zone, will doubtlessly bring up new points of disagreement and may afford a new life for Polish Euro-skepticism.

One fundamental disagreement on how to manage Poland's foreign affairs has arisen: the question is whether Poland is best served by a confrontational approach, emphasizing aggressive defense of Polish interests in both bilateral and multilateral relations, or by a more moderate approach, emphasizing traditional diplomacy and compromise. The PiS-led government opted for confrontational statements in relations with Germany's Christian-Democratic government and with Russia, as well as in multilateral structures. Since its creation in 2007 the PO-led government has chosen the traditional route. It remains to be seen which approach works better, especially in crucial areas such as trans-Atlantic relations or the EU's Eastern Policy, where Poland has a special interest in strengthening Europe's relations with Belarus, Georgia, Moldova, and Ukraine, while maintaining good relations with Russia. After two years of Tusk's government, 57 percent of Poles surveyed saw Poland's international situation as good, but roughly the same number held that view in the last months of the PiS-led government. On the other hand, Poles did perceive improvements specifically in relations with both Russia and Germany—no small matters.[6]

Finally, the economy has presented a huge set of challenges for each successive Polish government. More than that, it may have constituted each government's Achilles' heel, the reason why, as of 2010, no governing party had yet won a subsequent parliamentary election. The transition from a planned economy to a market economy has progressed relatively smoothly—with Poland being one of the most successful and thorough of the former communist systems in this regard. Not all Poles approve, but as of 2009, 59 percent agreed with the statement that a capitalist economy based on private enterprise is the best economic system for Poland.[7] One of the most troublesome aspects of changing the economy has been privatization—a process that is still under way after more than twenty years (it began already under the communist regime) and that has become associated in the public's mind with unemployment, corruption, and outright theft—for good reason.

Nevertheless, the Polish economy weathered the onset of the global financial crisis remarkably well—arguably better than any of the other twenty-six EU members. Poland reported the only positive growth rate in the EU for 2009, a low but respectable 1.7 percent. European analysts attributed this outcome to the Polish government's conservative fiscal and monetary policies, as well as to reforms in the pension system. No doubt, the considerable influx of EU subsidies and credits helped, but Poland was not the only new EU member at the receiving end of these funds. On the other hand, billions more euros are scheduled to flow into Poland well past the latest possible date for new parliamentary elections—2011. The governing PO has a chance of associating itself with economic success rather than hardship and thereby breaking previous governments' electoral jinx. What this might do to the Polish political scene is uncertain, but it would likely involve a strengthening of the current centripetal tendency, in which all political actors seem to be racing to the center to emulate the centrist PO. In Polish society itself the winners appear to be doing better than ever, while the losers find their numbers gradually declining and their political clout fading even faster.

NOTES

1. Polska Agencja Prasowa, September 18, 2005.
2. Maciej Kochanowicz, *Gazeta Wyborcza*, October 23, 2005.
3. Centrum Badanii Opinii Społecznej, "O lustracji i sposobie ujawniania materiałow zgromadzonych w IPN," June 2007.
4. Centrum Badanii Opinii Społecznej, "Opinii społecznej o korupcji w Polsce," April 2009.
5. Centrum Badanii Opinii Społecznej, "Bilans pięciu lat członkowstwa Polski w Unii Europejskiej," April 2009.
6. Centrum Badania Opinii Społecznej, "Bezpieczeństwo Polski na arenie międzynarodowej," July 2009; and "Stosunki polsko-rosyjskie i polsko-niemieckie z historią w tle," September 2009.
7. Centrum Badanii Opinii Społecznej, "Polacy wierzą w gospodarkę wolnorynkową," March 2009.

FOR FURTHER READING

Aberg, Martin, and Mikael Sandberg. *Social Capital and Democratisation: Roots of Trust in Post-Communist Poland and Ukraine*. Aldershot, UK; Burlington, Vt.: Ashgate, 2003.

Ascherson, Neil. *The Polish August: The Self-Limiting Revolution*. Harmondsworth, UK: Penguin, 1981.

Balcerowicz, Leszek. *Socialism, Capitalism, Transformation.* Budapest: Central European University Press, 1995.

Bernhard, Michael H. *The Origins of Democratization in Poland: Workers, Intellectuals, and Oppositional Politics, 1976–1980.* New York: Columbia University Press, 1993.

Bernhard, Michael H., and Henryk Szlajfer. *From the Polish Underground: Selections from Krytyka, 1978–1993.* University Park: Pennsylvania State University Press, 1995.

Blazyca, George, and Ryszard Rapacki, eds. *Poland into the 1990s: Economy and Society in Transition.* New York: St. Martin's Press, 1991.

Castle, Marjorie. *Triggering Communism's Collapse: Perceptions and Power in Poland's Transition.* Lanham, Md.: Rowman and Littlefield, 2003.

Castle, Marjorie, and Ray Taras. *Democracy in Poland.* Boulder: Westview Press, 2002.

Chodakiewicz, Marek J., John Radzilowski, and Dariusz Tolczyk, eds. *Poland's Transformation: A Work in Progress.* Charlottesville, Va.: Leopolis Press, 2003.

Cirtautas, Arista Maria. *Polish Solidarity Movement: Revolution, Democracy and Natural Rights.* London; New York: Routledge, 1997.

Connor, Walter D., and Piotr Ploszajski. *The Polish Road from Socialism: The Economics, Sociology, and Politics of Transition.* Armonk, N.Y.: M. E. Sharpe, 1992.

Curry, Jane L. *Poland's Journalists: Professionalism and Politics.* Cambridge and New York: Cambridge University Press, 1990.

Curry, Jane L., and Luba Fajfer, eds. *Poland's Permanent Revolution: People Versus Elites, 1956 to the Present.* Washington, D.C.: American University Press, 1996.

Davies, Norman. *God's Playground: A History of Poland.* Vols. 1–2. New York: Columbia University Press, 2004.

Dunn, Elizabeth C., Bruce Grant, and Nancy Ries, eds. *Privatizing Poland: Baby Food, Big Business, and the Remaking of Labor.* Ithaca, N.Y.: Cornell University Press, 2004.

Ekiert, Grzegorz, and Jan Kubik. *Rebellious Civil Society: Popular Protest and Democratic Control in Poland, 1989–1993.* Ann Arbor: University of Michigan Press, 1999.

Garton Ash, Timothy. *The Polish Revolution: Solidarity.* New Haven: Yale University Press, 2002.

Goodwyn, Lawrence. *Breaking the Barrier: The Rise of Solidarity in Poland.* New York and Oxford: Oxford University Press, 1991.

Hicks, Barbara E. *Environmental Politics in Poland: A Social Movement between Regime and Opposition.* New York: Columbia University Press, 1996.

Jackson, John E., Jacek Klich, and Krystyna Poznanska. *The Political Economy of Poland's Transition: New Firms and Reform Governments.* Cambridge and New York: Cambridge University Press, 2005.

Kaminski, Bartlomiej. *The Collapse of State Socialism: The Case of Poland.* Princeton, N.J.: Princeton University Press, 1991.

Kennedy, Michael D. *Professionals, Power, and Solidarity in Poland: A Critical Sociology of Soviet-type Society.* Cambridge and New York: Cambridge University Press, 1991.

Longhurst, Derry. *The New Atlanticist: Poland's Foreign and Security Priorities.* Oxford: Blackwell, 2005.

Michnik, Adam. *Letters from Freedom: Post–Cold War Realities and Perspectives.* Berkeley: University of California Press, 1998.

Michta, Andrew. *The Soldier-Citizen: The Politics of the Polish Army after Communism.* New York: St. Martin's Press, 1997.

Millard, Frances. *Polish Politics and Society.* London: Routledge, 1999.

Osa, Maryjane. *Solidarity and Contention: Networks of Polish Opposition.* Minneapolis: University of Minnesota Press, 2003.

Ost, David. *The Defeat of Solidarity: Anger and Politics in Postcommunist Europe*. Ithaca, N.Y.: Cornell University Press, 2005.

———. *Solidarity and the Politics of Anti-politics: Opposition and Reform in Poland since 1968*. Philadelphia: Temple University Press, 1990.

Paczkowski, Andrzej. *The Spring Will Be Ours: Poland and the Poles from Occupation to Freedom*. University Park: Pennsylvania State University Press, 2003.

Penn, Shana. *Solidarity's Secret: The Women Who Defeated Communism in Poland*. Ann Arbor: University of Michigan Press, 2005.

Perdue, William Dan. *Paradox of Change: The Rise and Fall of Solidarity in the New Poland*. Westport, Conn.: Praeger, 1995.

Sachs, Jeffrey. *Poland's Jump to the Market Economy*. Cambridge, Mass.: MIT Press, 1994.

Sanford, George. *Democratic Government in Poland: Constitutional Politics since 1989*. Harmondsworth, UK: Palgrave Macmillan, 2004.

Simon, Jeffrey. *Poland and NATO: A Study in Civil-Military Relations*. Lanham, Md.: Rowman and Littlefield, 2003.

Slay, Ben. *The Polish Economy: Crisis, Reform, and Transformation*. Princeton, N.J.: Princeton University Press, 1994.

Staar, Richard F., ed. *Transition to Democracy in Poland*. New York: St. Martin's Press, 1993.

Staniszkis, Jadwiga. *The Dynamics of the Breakthrough in Eastern Europe: The Polish Experience*. Berkeley: University of California Press, 1991.

Szczerbiak, Aleks. *Poles Together? The Emergence and Development of Political Parties in Post-Communist Poland*. Budapest: Central European University Press, 2001.

Taras, Ray. *Ideology in a Socialist State: Poland, 1956–83*. Cambridge and New York: Cambridge University Press, 1984.

Toranska, Teresa. *Them: Stalin's Polish Puppets*. New York: HarperCollins, 1987.

Tworzecki, Hubert. *Parties and Politics in Post-1989 Poland*. Boulder: Westview Press, 1996.

Weschler, Lawrence. *Solidarity: Poland in the Season of Its Passion*. New York: Simon and Schuster, 1982.

Wydra, Harald. *Continuities in Poland's Permanent Transition*. Harmondsworth, UK: Palgrave-Macmillan, 2001.

Zuzowski, Robert. *Political Dissent and Opposition in Poland: The Workers' Defense Committee "KOR."* Westport, Conn.: Praeger, 1992.

Part 8

European Union

**M. Donald Hancock
and B. Guy Peters**

European Union:
Member
Non-member
Candidate
⦿ Government seat

Government Branch:
Brussels:
European Parliament
Council of the European Union
European Commission

Luxembourg:
Court of Justice
European Parliament
Council of the European Union

Strasbourg:
European Parliament

Norwegian Sea

SWEDEN

FINLAND

ESTONIA

LATVIA

LITHUANIA

North Sea

Baltic Sea

DENMARK

IRELAND

UNITED KINGDOM

NETHERLANDS

GERMANY

POLAND

BELGIUM
⦿ Brussels

ATLANTIC OCEAN

LUX.
Luxembourg ⦿

CZECH REP.

SLOVAKIA

Strasbourg ⦿

AUSTRIA

HUNGARY

ROMANIA

Black Sea

FRANCE

SLOVENIA
CROATIA

Adriatic Sea

BULGARIA

MACEDONIA

TURKEY

MONACO

ITALY

GREECE

PORTUGAL

SPAIN

Mediterranean Sea

CYPRUS

The Context of
European Union Politics

FOLLOWING DELAYED RATIFICATION BY SEVERAL RECALCITRANT MEMBER states, the Treaty of Lisbon—signed in December 2007 and implemented in December 2009—significantly streamlines and strengthens the European Union (EU) as a sui generis regional political-economic system. Since its origins as a coal and steel community founded by six West European countries in 1951–1952, the EU has expanded to include twenty-seven European countries (with several candidate nations waiting in the wings to join). The significance of the EU lies not only in its economic status as the world's largest trading bloc but also in its dual attainment during the 1990s of a single regional market and an economic and monetary union, accompanied by the introduction of a common currency, the euro, among more than half its members. Major provisions of the Lisbon Treaty underscore efforts to enhance institutional coherence and democratic procedures and extend foreign and security cooperation as a means to enable the EU to play a more assertive role in world affairs.

The European integration movement that began in the early 1950s has resulted in the transfer of significant degrees of domestic regulatory powers, economic sovereignty, and budgetary allocations to the combination of supranational and intergovernmental institutions that make up today's EU. The EU's supranational component consists of decision-making structures that possess the legal authority to make rules that are binding on the member states. Principal institutional examples include the European Commission, the European Court of Justice, the European Central Bank, and (to a lesser extent) the European Parliament. Intergovernmental authority, by contrast, is exercised by member states acting as autonomous national actors exercising weighted votes and sometimes the right of veto in the Council of Ministers, which is made up of national government cabinet members, and the European Council, composed of the heads of state or government of the member states. The Council of Ministers, in various guises, is responsible for day-to-day decisions governing the EU, whereas the European Council constitutes more of a "summit" decision-making institution governing new directions in policy, new treaties, and the admission of new member states to the EU. All of these structures and their powers are explained in greater detail in the following chapters.

Parallel processes of "deepening" (extending institutionalized cooperation to a greater range of policy areas) and "widening" (adding new member states through successive waves of enlargement) have characterized the integration process from the outset. The pace of integration has proceeded through alternating cycles of acceleration and slowdown, punctuated by recurrent political and economic crises that have challenged the confidence of even the most ardent Europeanists. Recent examples include the rejection by a majority of French and Dutch voters in May 2005 of a proposed constitutional treaty and a prolonged delay in the ratification of the Lisbon Treaty in 2007–2009.

A Comparative Overview

Today's European Union consists of the original six founding members (France, Germany, Italy, and the three Benelux countries) and twenty-one other countries in northern, southern, and East-Central Europe that joined the EU from the early 1970s to 2007. Its territory stretches from the Atlantic Ocean in the west to the Baltic Sea in the northeast, the Mediterranean and Aegean seas in the south, and the Black Sea in the southeast. Germany claims the largest population within the EU, followed in descending order by France, the United Kingdom, Italy, Spain, and Poland. Geographically, the largest country is France, followed by Spain, Sweden, Germany, Poland, Finland, and Italy. The smallest member state, measured in terms of both population and territory, is Malta (see Table 8-1).

Table 8-1 Population and Area of Twenty-seven EU Member States (2008)

	Population (in millions)	Area (in square kilometers)
Germany	82.1	357,000
France	62.0	550,754
United Kingdom	61.4	245,273
Italy	59.9	301,300
Spain	45.6	504,782
Poland	38.1	312,685
Romania	21.5	238,391
Netherlands	16.4	41,526
Greece	11.2	131,957
Portugal	10.6	92,000
Belgium	10.7	30,528
Czech Republic	10.4	78,866
Hungary	10.0	93,030
Sweden	9.2	449,792
Austria	8.3	84,000
Bulgaria	7.6	110,879
Denmark	5.5	43,000
Slovakia	5.4	48,845
Finland	5.3	304,593
Ireland	3.2	70,000
Lithuania	3.4	65,200
Latvia	2.3	64,589
Slovenia	2.0	20,273
Estonia	1.3	45,226
Cyprus	0.8	9,251
Luxembourg	0.5	2,596
Malta	0.4	316

Source: WDI Online, *World Development Indicators,* http://ddp-ext.worldbank.org, 2010; and U.S. Central Intelligence Agency, *The World Fact Book, 2010,* www.cia.gov

Table 8-2 Per Capita Gross Domestic Product of EU Member States, United States, and Canada (2009 current U.S. dollars, purchasing power parity)

Luxembourg	$105,044
Denmark	55,992
Ireland	51,049
Netherlands	47,917
Austria	45,562
Finland	44,581
Belgium	43,671
Sweden	43,654
France	41,051
Germany	40,670
United Kingdom	35,165
Italy	35,084
Spain	31,774
Cyprus	31,410
Greece	29,240
Slovenia	23,726
Portugal	21,903
Malta	18,209
Czech Republic	18,139
Slovakia	16,176
Estonia	14,238
Hungary	12,868
Latvia	11,616
Poland	11,273
Lithuania	11,141
Romania	7,500
Bulgaria	6,423
European Union	31,900
United States	45,989
Canada	39,599

Source: WDI Online, *World Development Indicators,* http://data.worldbank.org, 2010; and U.S. Central Intelligence Agency, *The World Fact Book, 2010,* www.cia.gov. Data for Cyprus are from 2008 and for Malta from 2007.

Despite its small size, Luxembourg has the highest per capita gross domestic product (GDP) among the twenty-seven member states. A majority of EU members similarly count among the most affluent nations in the world, while Romania and Bulgaria are the least well off (see Table 8-2). Closely associated with differences in national wealth are contrasting levels of national economic development. Luxembourg, the United Kingdom, Denmark, Belgium, France, Malta, the Netherlands, and Sweden rank as the most "postindustrial" member states, as measured by the percentage of workers engaged in public and private services as opposed to workers employed in agriculture (see Table 8-3). The least developed countries, as measured by the percentage of those employed in agriculture, are Lithuania, Poland, and Romania. (Table 8-3).

Geographically, the EU as a whole at 4,324,782 square kilometers is nearly half the size of the United States (9,632,420 square kilometers) and Canada (9,984,679 square kilometers), but its population of more than 492 million is significantly larger than that of both the United States (310 million) and Canada (34.1 million). The EU's estimated per capita GDP in 2008 ($33,700) nearly equaled that of the United States ($35,445). (See Table 8-2.) Together, the EU member states dominate world trade with 37.6 percent of global imports and 36.5 percent of exports. In descending order, Germany, France, the United Kingdom, Italy and the Netherlands are the largest trading partners. The United States, in comparison, claims 13.5 percent of world imports and 8.2 percent of exports. China exports more than the United States with 9.0 percent of global exports while importing 7.1 percent. (See Table 8-4, page 626.)

Table 8-3 Levels of Economic Development of EU Member States, 2005–2008 (est.)

	Percentage of employees in public and private services	Percentage of employees in agriculture
Luxembourg	80.6	2.2
United Kingdom	80.4	1.4
Netherlands	80.0	2.0
Belgium	73.0	2.0
Denmark	72.7	2.9
France	71.8	3.8
Sweden	70.7	1.1
Cyprus	71.0	8.5
Finland	69.9	4.5
Spain	69.5	4.0
Malta	68.5	2.3
Germany	67.8	2.4
Austria	67.0	5.5
Ireland	67.0	6.0
Italy	65.1	4.2
Greece	65.1	12.4
Hungary	62.6	5.0
Latvia	61.8	3.1
Estonia	61.6	4.7
Slovenia	61.5	2.5
Portugal	60.0	10.0
Slovakia	56.9	4.0
Czech Republic	56.2	3.6
Bulgaria	57.0	7.5
Lithuania	56.9	14.0
Poland	53.4	17.4
Romania	47.1	29.7
European Union	66.7	5.6
United States	76.8	.6
Canada	76.0	2.0

Source: U.S. Central Intelligence Agency, The World Factbook, 2010, http://www.cia.gov

Table 8-4 Imports and Exports by Region and Country, 2008 (in constant U.S. dollars and percentages, as indicated)

Region/Country	Imports (in dollars)	Exports (in dollars)	Percentage of World Imports	Percentage of World Exports
World	160,111,892	15,826,004		
European Union (EU)	6,023,110	5,781,920	37.6	36.5
EU members				
Germany	1,205,522	1,467,244	7.5	9.3
France	696,957	596,081	4.3	3.8
United Kingdom	622,329	436,414	3.9	2.8
Italy	558,544	548,955	3.5	3.5
Netherlands	489,171	541,433	3.0	3.4
Non-EU countries				
United States	2,165,980	1,301,110	13.5	8.2
Canada	407,170	452,175	2.5	2.9
Russia	267,084	467,907	1.7	3.0
China	1,131,620	1,428,660	7.1	9.0

Source: Calculated by the author from United Nations, *2008 International Merchandise Trade Statistics, Vol. I, Trade by Country,* http.// comtrade.un.org/pb. Data not available for Cyprus.

From the ECSC to the European Community

In its present form, the European Union is the institutional culmination of early postwar initiatives by West European governments, which were inspired by a combination of idealism, national self-interest, and political and economic pragmatism. These initiatives were directed at transcending the historical factors of national rivalry and hostility that had contributed to the outbreak of the Franco-Prussian war in the nineteenth century and World Wars I and II in the twentieth century.[1] Prominent early architects of the integration movement included Jean Monnet, head of the General Planning Commission in the first postwar government of France, who proposed the initial blueprint for West European economic integration; Robert Schuman, who as French foreign minister formally submitted the plan in 1950 for what became the European Coal and Steel Community; Konrad Adenauer, who served from 1949 to 1963 as West Germany's first federal chancellor; and Alcide De Gasperi, founder of the Italian Christian Democratic Party and prime minister in eight coalition governments between 1945 and 1953. All four statesmen were ardent Europeanists and advocates of a trans-Atlantic political and military alliance with the United States.

Political leaders from France, West Germany, Italy, Belgium, the Netherlands, and Luxembourg established the European Coal and Steel Community (ECSC) in 1951–1952 as a first step toward regional economic and political integration. The purpose of the ECSC was to eliminate customs duties on iron, coal, and steel products among the six member countries and simultaneously to erect a common external tariff, thereby creating a limited customs union. The executive and legislative powers of the new organization were divided between a Council of Ministers, representing the six governments, and an appointive High Authority with supranational executive authority to initiate common decisions and oversee their execution. Largely symbolic consultative authority was vested in a European Assembly, whose deputies were appointed by the national parliaments of the six member states. In addition, a European Court of Justice was established to adjudicate disputes over the interpretation and implementation of the ECSC treaty. The signatories agreed that the Council of Ministers and High Authority would meet in Brussels, the Assembly would conduct its plenary sessions in Strasbourg, and the Court of Justice would hear its cases in Luxembourg.

The success of the ECSC in promoting regional economic growth encouraged the same six nations to create the more ambitious European Economic Community (EEC) in 1957. "Determined to lay the foundations of an ever closer union among the peoples of Europe [and] resolved to ensure the economic and social progress of their countries by common action to eliminate the barriers which divide Europe," France, Germany, Italy, and the Benelux countries pledged to achieve economic integration as a crucial move toward ultimate political union.[2] Alongside the ECSC and the EEC, the six signatories also established a third regional organization known as Euratom, which was designed to promote intergovernmental cooperation

Jean Monnet is generally considered the "father" of the postwar European integration movement. Monnet served as head of the French General Planning Commission after World War II and wrote the blueprint for the creation of the European Coal and Steel Community (ECSC). Because it was Foreign Minister Robert Schuman who submitted the proposal to the French parliament in 1950, it is known as the Schuman Plan. The ECSC was established a year later and became the forerunner of today's European Union.

Source: Time & Life Pictures/Getty Images

in the development of peaceful uses of nuclear energy.[3] The Treaty of Rome, which provided the legal foundations for the new EEC, called for the gradual elimination of customs duties on all industrial and agricultural products, the establishment of a common external tariff, the free movement of labor and capital, and the implementation of common policies in areas such as agriculture, transport, and competition. Executive-legislative structures parallel to those of the ECSC were established in the form of an intergovernmental Council of Ministers and a supranational European Commission. Serving both regional organizations were the European Assembly and the European Court of Justice.

The United Kingdom, which had refused to join in the negotiations leading to the creation of the ECSC and the EEC because British officials and most citizens objected to relinquishing national sovereignty to supranational bodies such as the High Authority and the European Commission, led a regional counteroffensive to establish a strictly intergovernmental economic organization that would restrict itself to the elimination of tariffs on industrial products among its members. British efforts resulted in the creation of the European Free Trade Association (EFTA) in 1960. In addition to Great Britain, founding members of EFTA were Austria, Denmark, Norway, Portugal, Sweden, and Switzerland. Institutional authority was vested in an EFTA Council, in which each member country was represented by a single delegate with the power to veto any collective decision. Finland, Iceland, and Liechtenstein later joined EFTA.

Rapid economic expansion within the EEC during the 1950s and early 1960s prompted Great Britain to abandon its commitment to EFTA and apply for membership in the EEC in 1961. French president Charles de Gaulle publicly vetoed the British initiative at a press conference in January 1963, but his successors proved more responsive to expanding the boundaries of the EEC to include Great Britain and other European democracies. The United Kingdom, Denmark, and Ireland joined the EEC in 1973; they were followed in 1981 by Greece and in 1986 by Spain and Portugal. On January 1, 1995, Austria, Finland, and Sweden became members as well. Ten additional countries (eight of them postcommunist regimes in Central and Eastern Europe) joined on May 1, 2004: the Czech Republic, Estonia, Hungary, Latvia, Lithuania, Poland, Slovakia, and Slovenia, as well as Cyprus and Malta in the Mediterranean. Bulgaria and Romania became members on January 1, 2007. Norway twice negotiated treaties of accession with the EEC (in 1972 and 1993), but both times a majority of Norwegians rejected membership in popular referendums. Candidate countries include Croatia, Iceland, and Turkey. (Their status and prospects for membership are discussed in Chapter 8.5. Turkey is an especially problematic case.)

In October 1991 the EEC negotiated an agreement with the remaining EFTA nations to establish a joint European Economic Area (EEA) for the free flow of capital, goods, services, and people among eighteen of the nations that made up the two regional blocs. Only Switzerland refused to join the EEA when a majority of Swiss voters rejected the treaty in a referendum in December 1992. The EEA treaty was implemented on January 1, 1994.

The demonstrated advantages of regional economic integration, as measured by the EEC countries' steady expansion of industrial and agricultural production and foreign trade, inspired French, German, Italian, and other European leaders to broaden the EEC's policy responsibilities and give it greater institutional autonomy. In 1962 they agreed on the implementation of a Common Agricultural Policy (CAP) designed to stabilize prices and guarantee a higher standard of living for farmers through a system of subsidies; they achieved the completion of a customs union in 1968 (eighteen months ahead of schedule); and they gave the EEC financial autonomy in 1970 by agreeing to allocate to it all customs duties on imported industrial and agricultural goods and a percentage of the value-added tax (VAT) collected by each of the member countries. Simultaneously, the EEC members acted to strengthen the EEC's institutions. In 1965 they concluded a treaty to combine the ECSC, the EEC, and Euratom as the European Communities (EC), effective 1967. The two councils then became a single council, and the High Authority and the European Commission merged to form a unified commission.

A decade later, in 1974–1975, the Council of Ministers agreed to allow the direct election of delegates to the renamed European Parliament. This move, which was accompanied by an enlargement of the Parliament and an increase in its budgetary powers, significantly enhanced its authority in relation to other EC institutions by giving it greater legitimacy in the eyes of national electorates.

The integration movement experienced a serious setback in December 1965. The Treaty of Rome for the EEC stipulated that majority voting in the Council of Ministers was to take effect in 1966. Fearing a reduction in France's influence in the Council of Ministers and encroachments on French national sovereignty, President de Gaulle ordered French officials to boycott EC activities in protest against the scheduled introduction of majority voting.[4] Seven months later, in June 1966, EC officials resolved the crisis by negotiating an agreement known as the "Luxembourg compromise," which in effect retained the original rule of unanimity in Council decisions in issues deemed of "vital interest" to an individual member.[5] Mollified, de Gaulle ordered a resumption of French participation in EC affairs.

From the EEC to the EU

Under de Gaulle, the French had been consistently mistrustful of the value of European integration for the French economy. Official French skepticism about the scope and pace of European integration abated, however, after de Gaulle's resignation from the presidency in 1969. Under his successors, Presidents Georges Pompidou, Valéry Giscard d'Estaing, François Mitterrand, Jacques Chirac, and Nicholas Sarkozy, France has linked forces above all with Germany in promoting not only a territorial enlargement of the EEC but also an expansion of its policy responsibilities. In successive moves, the EC implemented common measures on regional policy, research and development, the free movement of labor, workers' rights, vocational training, the environment, energy, and fisheries. In 1978–1979 the EC undertook an important qualitative step toward further "deepening" when its members agreed to establish a common European Monetary System (EMS) as a means of promoting economic stability and growth in response to the international crisis of "stagflation" during the early 1970s. Major components of the EMS included a new European Currency Unit (the ECU) for accounting and budgetary purposes, provisions for exchanging information about economic conditions, provisions for stable currency exchange rates via an Exchange Rate Mechanism (ERM), and greater convergence of economic policies among the member countries.[6]

To improve high-level policy consultation and coordination, the Council of Ministers inaugurated regular meetings of the foreign ministers of the member states in 1970. At a summit meeting in 1974 in Paris, the heads of government and the French head of state concurred that they, too, should personally convene several times a year as the European Council. Together, these moves created highly visible and effective mechanisms for the EC to extend its role from regional economic and social policy to foreign policy as well.

A Conservative Party electoral victory in 1979 in Great Britain and the formation of an assertive new government under Margaret Thatcher set the stage for confrontation between Great Britain and other members of the EC on the pace and scope of European integration. Voicing reservations about the expansion of EEC policy responsibilities and concern about the costs of membership, Prime Minister Thatcher and her cabinet strenuously

advocated changes in the Common Agricultural Policy and a reduction in British contributions to the annual EC budget. The other EEC countries reluctantly acceded to both
demands, agreeing at successive Council meetings in 1984 to curb agricultural surpluses
and grant the United Kingdom monetary compensation for what the British considered to
be excessive budgetary payments (the Thatcher cabinet depicted these payments as subsidies to less efficient agricultural markets on the Continent). In September 1988 Thatcher
criticized EC aspirations to achieve economic and political union in a widely publicized
speech in Bruges, Belgium, and she adamantly refused at a meeting of the European Council in 1989 to join the other eleven members of the EC in affirming a common social
charter (Charter of the Fundamental Social Rights of Workers) designed to protect workers' rights. Thatcher and her partisan supporters viewed her actions not as a repudiation of
the European idea, but instead as an affirmation of legitimate national self-interests and a
commitment to a form of internationalism that included but was not restricted to the EC.[7]

Several factors converged during the 1980s to add increased momentum to the integration movement despite British misgivings. The first was a second international economic
crisis in 1979–1980, which had prolonged effects. That crisis compelled European leaders
to intensify their attempts to coordinate policies in an effort to combat inflation and revive
growth. The second was the appointment of Jacques Delors as president of the European
Commission in 1985. Delors, a former minister of finance in the French government,
proved to be a visionary policy activist. He repeatedly used his institutional authority to
mobilize support in favor of expanding the responsibilities and power of the EC. The third
factor was that influential members of the elective European Parliament demanded a
renewed commitment to European political integration. Their demands culminated in the
adoption by the Parliament in 1984 of a draft Treaty on European Union.

Under Delors's leadership, in June 1985 the European Commission submitted to the
European Council a White Paper that outlined a comprehensive strategy for transforming
the European Communities from a customs union and free trade area into a fully integrated regional market. As the Commission declared, "Europe stands at the crossroads. We
either go ahead—with resolution and determination—or we drop back into mediocrity." [8]
Emphatically favoring the former approach as consistent with the Treaty of Rome's vision
of eventual European union, the Commission put forth nearly three hundred measures to
eliminate technical and other barriers to the attainment of an integrated regional market
by the end of 1992. The measures, which required the approval of the member countries
to be fully implemented, ranged from the abolition of frontier controls and technical
restraints on the free movement of goods to technological standardization, the mutual
recognition of professional qualifications, the attainment of a common market for services,
and the harmonization of financial and fiscal policies within the EC.[9]

The initiatives of the European Parliament and the European Commission resulted in
the formation of an intergovernmental conference that drafted the Single European Act, a
treaty signed by members of the European Council in Luxembourg on February 17, 1986.
The agreement endorsed the goal of an integrated single market envisioned in the commission's White Paper of 1985, including the free movement of goods, services, people,
and capital, and it called on the member countries to cooperate to ensure policy convergence in these important areas. To facilitate this process, the Single European Act substi-
tuted the earlier unanimity rule with a new "qualified majority voting" procedure for

decisions of the Council of Ministers governing the implementation of the internal market, research and development, economic and social cohesion, and improved working conditions. Under the new procedure, France, Germany, Italy, and the United Kingdom were each given ten votes; Spain eight; Belgium, Greece, the Netherlands, and Portugal five each; Denmark and Ireland three votes; and Luxembourg two. Fifty-four votes constituted a "qualified majority," which meant that at least seven states had to concur in a Council decision. Under this system, then, neither the large countries as a bloc nor a coalition of small ones could prevail over each other, which placed a premium on compromise and joint decisions in Council deliberations. The arithmetic of qualified majority voting in Council decisions changed marginally with the accession of Austria, Finland, and Sweden as new member states on January 1, 1995, and has been modified yet again under subsequent European Union treaties (see Chapter 8.2).

In addition, the Single European Act established a new "cooperation procedure" involving an expanded role by the European Parliament in Council of Ministers decisions that were subject to qualified majority voting. Henceforth, the Council was required to consider parliamentary opinions on proposed legislation (including possible amendments and rejection) in a second reading of a proposed decision. The agreement also granted the Parliament the right of joint decision making in the accession of new members and agreements of association and cooperation with nonmember countries. The Single European Act was merged into the Treaty of Rome in the form of amended and new articles.

In a crucial summit meeting held in Hannover, Germany, in June 1988, the European Council appointed a committee headed by European Commission president Delors and composed primarily of the governors of the central banks in the twelve member countries to study and propose concrete stages that would lead to an economic and monetary union (EMU). The Delors committee published its report in June 1989. Its central provisions called for progress toward an EMU through successive stages of implementation: an initial preparatory stage; a second stage consisting of the attainment of a monetary union encompassing ever closer cooperation among the central banks in the member states, the attainment of permanently fixed foreign currency exchange rates, and the creation of a European system of central banks as a precursor to a central European bank; and a third stage characterized by economic union, which would encompass "effective competition policy, common policies for structural change, and macroeconomic policy coordination."[10] The European Council endorsed the Delors report that same month in Madrid and declared that the first stage leading to economic and monetary union would begin on July 1, 1990.

At a summit meeting in Dublin in June 1990, members of the European Council resolved to formulate a concrete integration agenda by convening parallel intergovernmental conferences on economic, monetary, and political union. European commissioners and high-level diplomats from each of the twelve member states labored for the next year and a half to produce successive drafts of such a treaty. Thatcher and her Conservative Party successor, Prime Minister John Major, restated British opposition to major features of the envisioned union, but all parties to the deliberations concurred on the basic objective to "deepen" institutionalized economic and political cooperation within the EC. The work of the intergovernmental conferences culminated in a historic accord at a European Council meeting in early December 1991 in Maastricht, the Netherlands, in which the EC heads of government, foreign ministers, and finance ministers signed separate draft treaties on political union and economic and monetary union. The two treaties were then merged into the single Treaty on European Union. Its implementation would signal a historic transition of the established European Communities into the European Union.

Important provisions of the Maastricht agreement included an enhanced role of the European Parliament in EU decisions; a commitment to a common foreign and security policy; and the attainment of an economic and monetary union through successive stages of institutionalized policy coordination, beginning with implementation of the second stage of the Delors plan and establishment of the European Monetary Institute (EMI) on January 1, 1994. The stated purposes of the EMI were to "strengthen cooperation between the national central banks; strengthen the coordination of the monetary policies of the Member States, with the aim of ensuring price stability; . . . [and] monitor the functioning of the European Monetary System." [11] The Treaty on European Union also established a three-pillar system of governance: Pillar I encompassed the supranational powers of the EEC, the ECSC, and Euratom; Pillar II consisted of largely intergovernmental decision-making authority assigned to the EU's common foreign and security policy; and Pillar III was devoted to judicial and police cooperation among the member states.

The decisive next stage in the movement toward an economic and monetary union entailed the creation of a common currency and a central European bank. To join in this stage, the treaty requires the member states to meet four stringent convergence criteria: (1) a high degree of price stability as measured by "an average rate of inflation . . . that does not exceed by more than 1 1/2 percentage points that of, at most, the three best performing Member States"; (2) the absence of "excessive" budgetary deficits; (3) the maintenance of currency exchange rate stability within "the normal fluctuation margins provided for by the exchange-rate mechanism of the European Monetary System"; and (4) an average long-term interest rate "that does not exceed by more than two percentage points that of, at most, the three best performing Member States in terms of price stability." [12] The Treaty on European Union stipulated further that the European Council could decide by a two-thirds vote to implement the third stage as early as 1997 if at least seven member states met these criteria. If the Council did not make such a decision, the third stage would begin automatically on January 1, 1999.

Great Britain joined the other eleven members of the EC in affirming the Maastricht Treaty's basic intent to establish "an ever closer Union of the peoples of Europe" as well as most of its specific provisions, but the Major government reserved the right to "opt out" of the commitment to establishing a common currency and refused to endorse the accompanying "Agreement on Social Policy" that committed the member states to promoting various economic and social objectives within the European Union as a whole. [13] The separate treaties on the economic and monetary union and political union were later merged into the single Treaty on European Union, which was formally signed by the twelve governments on February 7, 1992.

Political euphoria over the Maastricht accord quickly dissipated in the face of domestic and international events that unexpectedly delayed the treaty's ratification and implementation. Ratification was subject only to a majority vote in the parliaments of most of the member states, but the ratification process became highly politicized in those countries whose constitutions either required or permitted national referendums on important political decisions. Populist concerns about the centralization of bureaucratic power in Brussels and fears of potential dominance by the larger states in the proposed European Union resulted in the treaty's rejection by a narrow majority of 50.7 percent of Danish voters in a referendum on June 2, 1992. A domestic conflict over abortion initially clouded the prospective outcome of a referendum in Ireland as well, although 69 percent of the electorate endorsed the Treaty on European Union when the vote was held on June 16.[14] In response to the negative outcome of the Danish referendum, President Mitterrand hastily announced that he would schedule a referendum in France to restore European confidence in the ratification process. Although opinion polls initially indicated strong French support for the treaty, opponents mobilized an effective campaign during the summer against its ambitious objectives. In the end, only 51.05 percent of French voters endorsed the accord in the September referendum.

France's lukewarm "*petit oui*" to the Maastricht Treaty coincided with a European currency crisis, which was triggered by heavy international speculation in favor of the strong German mark at the expense of weaker currencies. As a consequence, both Great Britain and Italy suspended participation in the Exchange Rate Mechanism, and the Italian lira was effectively devalued by 3.5 percent. Moreover, this first major realignment of the European Monetary System since its inception was accompanied by a deepening recession during 1992, which was marked by a decline in national growth rates and a precipitous jump in unemployment throughout Europe. In a dual effort to assuage domestic opponents and sustain the ratification process under increasingly difficult international economic conditions, the Danish government submitted a White Paper in early October 1992 that would allow Denmark to opt out of the proposed currency union and common defense arrangements envisaged by the Maastricht Treaty. EC leaders met in a special session of the European Council in Birmingham, England, in mid-October to affirm their support for ratification of the treaty "without renegotiation," but at a second summit in Edinburgh, Scotland, in December they accepted the Danish conditions. In a second national referendum held on May 18, 1993, 56.8 percent of Danish voters endorsed the "amended" Treaty on European Union.[15]

Facing intense opposition to prospective economic and political union among both his fellow Conservatives and some members of the opposition Labour Party, British prime minister John Major delayed a final decision on the Maastricht Treaty until after the second Danish referendum. The British Parliament then ratified the accord in July. Once Germany's Federal Constitutional Court dismissed a domestic legal challenge to the treaty in October 1993, EC leaders reconvened in Brussels to proclaim the "completion of the ratification process." The Treaty on European Union was formally enacted on November 1, 1993. With this step, the European Communities became the European Union.

Despite domestic controversies surrounding the Maastricht accord and recurrent economic crises, movement toward an economic and monetary union within the European Union continued through the 1990s, albeit at a slower pace than optimists had originally anticipated. Ninety percent of the directives contained in the White Paper of 1985 were implemented by June 1992, and at the beginning of January 1993 the Single Market became a reality. A second currency crisis in August 1993 temporarily strained Franco-German political relations—the German Bundesbank refused to lower its discount rate, prompting intense speculative pressure against the franc. The crisis eased, however, when the EU financial ministers agreed to allow the exchange value of European currencies to fluctuate more broadly on both sides of the central ERM rate. Gradually improving economic conditions accompanied the implementation of the second stage of economic and monetary union on January 1, 1994, in accordance with the timetable stipulated in the Treaty on European Union. As noted, a central feature of the second stage was the creation of the European Monetary Institute, with its headquarters in Frankfurt.

Determined efforts by the governments of the member states to meet the "convergence criteria" required for EMU membership proved successful in a majority of cases. The EMI certified in April 1998 that eleven countries had qualified for inclusion in the EMU: Austria, the three Benelux nations, Ireland, Finland, France, Germany, Italy, Spain, and Portugal. The United Kingdom and Denmark acted on their treaty right to opt out of membership, at least for the time being, as did Sweden (the latter for domestic political reasons). Greece succeeded in lowering its initially high budgetary deficit and inflation rate to qualify for membership on January 1, 2001. The newest members of the Euro Area to meet the treaty's convergence criteria include Slovenia (2007), Cyprus (2008), and Malta (2008).

The European Central Bank (ECB) was duly established in Frankfurt in July 1998. The third and decisive stage of the now formal Economic and Monetary Union was implemented on January 1, 1999, although it excluded Great Britain, Denmark, Sweden, and Greece. After meeting the requisite economic criteria, Greece joined the EMU as its twelfth member in January 2001. The ECB assumed responsibility for macroeconomic and monetary policy among the states participating in the EMU, and the euro became their common currency for transaction purposes. Euro bills and coins began to circulate in January 2002 in place of the more familiar francs, marks, lira, and other national currencies.

The Amsterdam and Nice Treaties

Accompanying the EU's progress toward the Economic and Monetary Union were successive steps toward further "deepening" and the eastward enlargement of the EU. At the behest of the European Council, an intergovernmental conference was convened in 1996 to review the EU's institutional arrangements and policy competence. Preliminary assessments by both the European Commission and the Council of Ministers concurred on the need to revise the Treaty on European Union to simplify decision-making procedures, enhance the role of the European Parliament, and provide a more effective basis for the conduct of a common foreign and security policy.[16] Most of these proposals (along with French-inspired provisions on employment and economic growth) were subsequently incorporated in the Treaty of Amsterdam, which the European Council endorsed in June 1997. After ratification by the member states, the treaty was implemented in 1999.

Despite its achievements, the Amsterdam Treaty was conspicuous for its omissions. Among them was the failure of the EU member states to agree on proposed changes in the composition of the European Commission and in the weight of individual country votes in qualified majority voting. An intergovernmental conference convened in early 2000 to address these issues in preparation for a new treaty by the end of the year. The deadline was urgent, given the important implications for institutional dynamics and community finances of the EU's scheduled enlargement of ten new member states in 2004.

Intense intergovernmental negotiations culminated in a compromise treaty, which the European Council endorsed at a summit meeting in Nice, France, in February 2001. An early disagreement between Germany and France over a German proposal to increase its share of votes in qualified majority voting (QMV) to reflect its larger population was resolved through personal diplomacy on the part of Chancellor Gerhard Schröder and French president Jacques Chirac when both leaders agreed to maintain the existing parity of votes between the two countries. Principal provisions of the Treaty of Nice included agreements to cap the future number of commissioners and the size of the European Parliament following enlargement, extend the QMV to a greater range of policy areas, and simplify decision-making cooperation between the Council and Parliament. In addition, an annex to the treaty, the Declaration on the Future of Europe, called for "a deeper and wider debate about the future of the European Union." The annex specified that this process should address fundamental institutional reforms, a simplification of the existing treaties "with a view to making them clearer and better understood without changing their meaning, . . ." and the incorporation of a Charter of Fundamental [citizen] Rights.[17]

Ratification of the Treaty of Nice proceeded smoothly in all member states except Ireland, where a majority of voters rejected the document in a national referendum in June 2001. A principal reason was public apprehension that the treaty would compromise Irish neutrality in the conduct of a common European defense policy. To assuage this concern, the European Council adopted a resolution in June 2002 that recognized Ireland's right to submit any such decisions to both cabinet and parliamentary approval. Subsequently, 60 percent of voters approved the treaty in a second referendum held in October 2002. It entered into force the following February.

From Nice to Lisbon

The European Council acted on the Declaration on the Future of Europe at a summit meeting in December 2001. The Council endorsed a resolution calling for the creation of an intergovernmental conference to draft a constitutional treaty that would address legal competences between the member states and the EU, simplify institutional arrangements and decision-making processes, and other important issues.[18] The convention consisted of former French president Giscard D'Estaing as chair and 104 other members representing the governments of the member states (plus the candidate states), the national parliaments, the European Parliament, and the European Commission. Convention deliberations extended for seventeen months in a succession of open plenary sessions and smaller working groups[19] and culminated in the publication of a draft constitution treaty in July 2003. Senior representatives of the EU member states signed the treaty in Rome on October 29, 2004.

Sweeping in its scope, the constitutional treaty called for the elimination of the three-pillar system of governance in favor of a multitiered system of shared and exclusive legal policy between the member states and the EU, provided for the creation of an indirectly elected European president and an appointive Union Minister for Foreign Affairs, an extension of QMV to more policy areas, and an eventual reduction in the size of the European Commission from twenty-seven members to eighteen. The treaty also incorporated a document, the Charter of Fundamental Rights of the Union, which contains fifty-four articles affirming fundamental principles of human dignity and democratic freedoms. Among them were the right to individual liberty and security; freedom of expression, thought, religion, assembly and association; and legal equality. "Positive" rights, many of them associated with twentieth-century European constitutionalism and political reform, ranged from workers' rights to information and consultation in enterprises to the right of collective bargaining and action, universal access to heath care, and environmental and consumer protection.[20]

As with the Treaty of Nice and previous treaty enactments, the constitutional treaty required the unanimous approval of all the EU member states before it could be implemented. A majority of national parliaments eventually endorsed the treaty, but it suffered a stunning defeat at the hands of a majority of voters in national referendums held in May 2005 in France and the Netherlands. Multiple reasons account for the rejection, including the sheer complexity of the document, an electoral backlash against an increasingly unpopular President Chirac in France, and citizen unease in Holland over national and EU immigration policies. In the aftermath of the treaty's demise, EU government leaders called for a "period of reflection" before undertaking further action. To many Euroskeptics, this move seemed to portend the end of a European constitution.

When Germany assumed the rotating European Council presidency during the first half of 2007, Chancellor Angela Merkel initiated a renewed drive to achieve the equivalent of a constitutional treaty. Declaring that the period of reflection had come to an end, the European Council endorsed the Berlin Declaration on May 25, 2007 (the fiftieth anniversary of the signing of the Treaty of Rome that had created the EEC), in which member states affirmed: "With European unification a dream of earlier generations has become a reality. Our history reminds us that we must protect this for the good of future generations. For that reason we must also renew the political shape of Europe in keeping with the times. That is why today . . . we are united in our aim of placing the European Union on a renewed common basis before the European Parliament elections in 2009." [21]

The Berlin Declaration prompted the creation of an intergovernmental conference whose mandate was to draft a less ambitious substitute for the failed constitutional treaty. The culmination was the Treaty of Lisbon, which Council members endorsed during the Portuguese presidency in October 2007. Without referring to itself as a "constitution for Europe," the treaty nevertheless contained many of the major provisions of the earlier document—including a simplification of decision-making rules, the extension of QMV, increased empowerment of the European Parliament, the creation of an indirectly elected president and—instead of a Union Minister for Foreign Affairs—a less grandiose sounding High Representative for Foreign Affairs and Security Policy. The treaty omitted the text of the Charter of Fundamental Rights of the Union but referred to the document as legally binding on the member states. In addition, the Lisbon Treaty reaffirmed the EU's goal of reducing the number of commissioners in the interest of great institutional efficiency, but accorded the Council to right to determine the final number.

During the subsequent ratification process, the French and Dutch governments decided to forego national referendums on the proposed treaty in fear of a second electoral backlash, but Ireland was politically committed to holding one. All other governments submitted the treaty to their national parliaments for approval. Due partly to domestic opposition to the proposed reduction in the number of commissioners, which would inevitably be at the cost of smaller member states such as Ireland, a majority of voters rejected the treaty by 53.4 percent to 46.6 percent in June 2008. Determined to allay Irish concerns in the interest of the common good, Council members agreed to retain the number of commissioners at twenty-seven. Intense international and domestic lobbying by protreaty advocates—combined with the onset of a debilitating global economic crisis in 2008—prompted a change of heart on the part of Irish voters. In a second referendum held on October 3, 2009, 67.1 percent of voters endorsed the treaty.

Despite the reversal of electoral fortunes in Ireland, the ratification process was further delayed by personal opposition to the treaty by the Polish and Czech presidents, both of whom expressed reservations about it. The Polish president delayed his signature to annoy cabinet officials for partisan reasons, whereas the Czech president expressed his resistance to the perceived emergence of the EU as a "nascent superstate."[22] But in the end, both heads of state relented and signed off on the treaty: the Polish president in October 2009, the Czech president in November. The Treaty of Lisbon took effect on December 1, 2009.

With its implementation, the Treaty of Lisbon was merged with the amended Treaty on European Union to create a consolidated version designated in official Brussels language as "the Treaties." Together, they provide the basis for the EU's stated objectives, its legal competence, institutions, decision processes, and policies. These are the subjects of the chapters that follow.

NOTES

1. The concept of European regional integration had deep philosophical and historical roots, but it did not begin to take concrete form until shortly after the end of World War II. Important milestones included a widely publicized speech by wartime British prime minister Winston Churchill in Zurich in 1946, in which Churchill advocated the creation of a United States of Europe; the formation of a privately supported "European Movement" later that same year; U.S. encouragement of European economic cooperation with the proclamation of the Marshall Plan aid program in 1947; the formation of the Organization for European Economic Cooperation in 1948 to promote the reduction of financial and tariff barriers to free trade throughout the region; and the creation of the Council of Europe in 1949. These initiatives, which many idealistic adherents hoped would culminate in a federal political system, coincided with the formation of partially overlapping military security systems in the form of the Western European Union (1948) and the North Atlantic Treaty Organization in 1949. A comprehensive account of postwar integration efforts can be found in Derek W. Unwin, *The Community of Europe: A History of European Integration since 1945* (New York: Longman, 1991).

2. Quoted from the preamble to the Treaty of Rome, published by the Office for Official Publications of the European Communities, *Treaties Establishing the European Communities* (Brussels and Luxembourg: ECSC-EEC-EAFC, 1987), 217.

3. In contrast to the ECSC and the EEC, Euratom proved relatively moribund as a regional organization.

4. Prior to this scheduled change in voting procedures, all Council decisions required unanimous consent among the member countries. De Gaulle was also strongly opposed to efforts by the other member countries to grant the EEC financial autonomy.

5. The agreement is named after the city where it was reached.

6. The ECU served as a unit for calculating EC revenues and expenditures and in accounting for intergovernmental transactions among member states. Its value "derive[d] from a weighted average of the value of the different Community currencies, with each currency given an influence to reflect its relative economic importance." House of Lords, Select Committee on the European Communities, *The Delors Report. With Evidence* (London: Her

Majesty's Stationery Office, 1989), 5. The ECU did not physically exist in the form of banknotes and coins, but it was the basis for the introduction of the euro. Meanwhile, the ERM promoted currency exchange rate stability within Western Europe by establishing a central parity for each national currency against the currencies of the other member states. With the introduction of the Economic and Monetary Union in January 1999, currency exchange rates among the participating states became fixed in relation to the euro.

7. Such commitments include British membership in the North Atlantic Treaty Organization and the United Nations and its leadership role in the Commonwealth of Nations. See Stephen George, *Britain and European Integration since 1945* (Cambridge, Mass., and Oxford, UK: Blackwell, 1991). A more recent and excellent analysis of Britain's relations with its continental neighbors is David Gowland, Arthur Turner, and Alex Wright, *Britain and European Integration Since 1945: On the Sidelines* (London and New York: Routledge, 2010.)

8. Commission of the European Communities, "Completing the Internal Market," *White Paper from the Commission to the European Council,* Brussels, June 1985, 55.

9. Ibid.

10. House of Lords, Select Committee on the European Communities, *Delors Report,* 7.

11. Council of the European Communities and Commission of the European Communities, *Treaty on European Union* (Brussels and Luxembourg: ECSCC-EEC-EAEC, 1992), 41.

12. Ibid., 41 and 183–184.

13. The social objectives included "the promotion of employment, improved living and working conditions, proper social protection, dialogue between management and labor, the development of human resources with a view to lasting high employment and the combating of exclusion." Ibid., 197.

14. The controversy involved a legal and moral conflict between the Republic of Ireland's constitutional ban on abortion and EC law permitting the free movement of persons to EC countries where abortions were permitted.

15. Consistent with the declaration by members of the European Council at the Birmingham summit, the treaty was not formally renegotiated; instead, the Danish conditions were appended to the treaty in a special protocol.

16. Commission of the European Communities, "Report on the Operation of the Treaty on European Union," Brussels, 1995; and Council of the European Communities, "Draft Report of the Council on the Functioning of the Treaty on European Union," Brussels, 1995.

17. "Declaration on the future of the Union," The Treaty of Nice amending the Treaty on European Union, http://www.eurotreaties.com/nicefinalact.pdf.

18. The declaration is known as the Laeken Declaration, named after the site of the December 2001 European Council meeting.

19. The European Convention, the Secretariat, *Report from the Convention Presidency to the President of the European Council,* Brussels, July 18, 2003; http://european-convention.eu.int/docs/Treat/cv00851.en03.pdf.

20. The European Convention, the Secretariat, *Draft Treaty Establishing a Constitution for Europe,* Brussels, July 18, 2003.

21. *Declaration on the occasion of the fiftieth anniversary of the signature of the Treaties of Rome,* http://www.eu2007.de/de/News/download_docs/Maerz/0324-RAA/English.pdf.

22. "Poles, Czechs and the Lisbon treaty; The awkward squad; Why the Polish and Czech presidents drag their feet over the Lisbon treaty," *Economist,* July 23, 2009.

Where Is the Power?

DESPITE RESERVATIONS EXPRESSED DURING THE RATIFICATION PROCESS by the Czech president, the European Union is not a superstate. Instead, the EU remains a hybrid political system consisting of a mix of supranational, intergovernmental, and subnational components. Through successive phases of institutional and policy "deepening" since the creation of the European Coal and Steel Community in 1951, the EU has become what David Gowland and colleagues depict as "an organization still delicately poised between a confederation of states and a federal state. . . . Yet the EU still falls far short of possessing the competence of a state. . . . It has no independent powers to tax its citizens. Furthermore, it has neither the right nor the resources to exercise the legitimate use of force within and beyond its borders."[1] Nevertheless, through its stated objectives, legal competence, hybrid decision-making structures, and multifaceted policies, the EU exercises considerable power over its member states and their citizens.

Objectives and Levels of Union Competence

- Restating the objectives of European cooperation contained in the amended Treaty of Rome, EU leaders affirm in the preamble to the consolidated version of the Treaty on the Functioning of the European Union their joint determination to, among other goals: "lay the foundation of an ever closer union among the peoples of Europe,

- "ensure the economic and social progress of their States by common action to eliminate the barriers which divide Europe,"

- affirm "as the essential objective of their efforts the constant improvements of the living and working conditions of their peoples,"

- remove "existing obstacles . . . to guarantee steady expansion, balanced trade and fair competition,"

- "contribute, by means of a common commercial policy, to the progressive abolition of restrictions on international trade,

- "strengthen the unity of their economies and to ensure their harmonious development by reducing the differences existing between the various regions and the backwardness of the less favoured regions,

- "preserve and strengthen peace and liberty, and calling upon the other peoples of Europe who share their ideal to join in their efforts, [and]

- "promote the development of the highest possible level of knowledge for their peoples through a wide access to education and through its continuous updating."[2]

In pursuit of these objectives, the treaties incorporate a federal-like system of exclusive and shared jurisdiction that replaces the earlier three-pillar system. The EU, which the treaties refer to as the Union, is assigned authority to coordinate economic and employment policies "within arrangements as determined by this Treaty" and "to define and implement a common foreign and security policy, including the progressive framing of a common defence policy." It is also accorded exclusive competence in the following areas: "customs union, the establishing of the competition rules necessary for the functioning of the internal market, monetary policy for the Member States whose currency is the euro, the conservation of marine biological resources under the common fisheries policy, [and] common commercial policy. The treaties also confer on the Union the exclusive right to negotiate international agreements that are "provided for in a legislative act of the Union or [are] necessary to enable the Union to exercise its internal competence, or in so far as [their] conclusion may affect common rules or alter their scope."[3]

Alongside these areas of exclusive jurisdiction, the Treaties assign a number of policies to shared jurisdiction between the Union and the member states. These include the "internal market; social policy for the aspects defined in this Treaty; economic, social and territorial cohesion; agriculture and fisheries . . . ; environment; consumer protection; transport; trans-European networks; energy; area of freedom, security and justice; [and] common safety concerns in pubic health matters, for the aspects defined in this Treaty." While member states are assigned primary responsibility for coordinating their economic policies, the Union is empowered to adopt "broad guidelines for these policies." Similarly, the Union may undertake measures to encourage the coordination of employment policies and social policies of the member states.[4]

The member states are accorded authority to govern pubic health, industry, culture, tourism, education, civil protection, vocational training, youth, and sport. Yet even in these policy areas, the treaties acknowledge Union competence "to support, coordinate or supplement the actions of the Member States."[5]

Union Institutions

The most important EU executive-legislative institutions are the European Council, the Council of Ministers, the European Commission, and the elective European Parliament. Other central institutions include an appointive Court of Justice, the European Central Bank, the European Bank for Reconstruction and Development, the Economic and Social Committee, the Committee of the Regions, and a Court of Auditors. Institutional authority is geographically dispersed among a number of locations: meetings of the Council of Ministers, most of those of the European Council, and committees of the European Parliament are held in Brussels, which is considered the capital of the EU; the European Parliament holds most of its plenary sessions in Strasbourg, France, but has a secondary location in Brussels; the European Commission has its headquarters in Brussels; the Court of Justice convenes in Luxembourg; the European Central Bank is located in Frankfurt, Germany; the Economic and Social Committee and the Committee of the Regions meet in Brussels; and the Court of Auditors is situated in Luxembourg.

The European Council and the Council of Ministers

Both the European Council and the Council of Ministers consist of high-level government officials representing the twenty-seven member states of the European Union. As such,

European Union at a Glance

Political Structure
A hybrid intergovernmental and supranational organization

Capital
Brussels, Belgium
Note: The European Council meets in Brussels and other European cities; the Council of Ministers meets in Brussels; the European Commission meets in Brussels; the European Parliament meets in Strasbourg, France, and Brussels; the European Court of Justice convenes in Luxembourg; and the European Central Bank has its headquarters in Frankfurt, Germany.

Member States
Twenty-seven countries: Austria, Belgium, Bulgaria, Cyprus, Czech Republic, Denmark, Estonia, Finland, France, Germany, Greece, Hungary, Ireland, Italy, Latvia, Lithuania, Luxembourg, Malta, Netherlands, Poland, Portugal, Romania, Slovakia, Slovenia, Spain, Sweden, United Kingdom. Candidate countries: Croatia, Iceland, Macedonia, Turkey. Potential candidates: Albania, Bosnia and Herzegovina, Montenegro, Serbia, Kosovo.

Independence
February 7, 1992: Treaty on European Union signed establishing the EU; November 1, 1993: Treaty on European Union entered into force. The EU is an outgrowth of earlier agreements establishing a European Coal and Steel Community (1951) and the European Economic Community (1957).

Constitution
Based on a series of treaties: Treaty of Paris, which set up the European Coal and Steel Community (ESCS) in 1951; Treaties of Rome, which set up the European Economic Community (EEC) and the European Atomic Energy Community (Euratom) in 1957; the Single European Act in 1986; Treaty on European Union (Maastricht) in 1992; Treaty of Amsterdam in 1997; Treaty of Nice in 2001; and Treaty of Lisbon in 2009.

Suffrage
Eighteen years of age, universal, for elections to the European Parliament

Executive Branch
President of the European Union
High Representative of the European Union for Foreign Affairs and Security Policy (de facto foreign minister)
President of the European Commission
Chief policy-initiating institution: European Commission, composed of twenty-seven members, one from each member state; each commissioner is responsible for one or more policy areas.
Elections: President of the European Union is elected by members of the European Council for a two-and-a-half-year term (renewable once); High Representative for Foreign Affairs, President of the European Commission, and other commissioners are appointed by the European Council subject to approval by the European Parliament.
Note: The European Council is made up of the President of the European Union, heads of government or presidents of the twenty-seven member states, and President of the European Commission. The High Representative for Foreign Affairs and Security Policy attends most meetings. The European Council usually meets four times a year. The Council's chief function is to provide the impetus for the major political issues related

(Continued)

(Continued)

to European integration (including new treaties and the admission of additional member states, the latter subject to co-decision by the European Parliament) and to issue general policy guidelines.

Legislative Branch

Council of Ministers, composed of twenty-seven member state ministers who have, among them, 321 votes (the number of votes is roughly proportional to the member states' populations). The Council acts on proposals submitted to it by the European Commission. Important decisions require a qualified majority of 255 votes representing two thirds of the member states. The Council now shares most decision-making power with the European Parliament.

European Parliament: 736 seats allocated among member states in proportion to their populations. Members are elected by direct universal suffrage for a five-year term.

Judicial Branch

Court of Justice of the European Union: composed of twenty-seven judges appointed for staggered six-year renewable terms by the European Council. The Court of Justice ensures that the treaties are interpreted and applied correctly (that is, according to European treaties and other legal documents).

General Court (formerly the Court of First Instance): composed of twenty-seven judges appointed for staggered six-year renewable terms by the European Court. The General Court hears and decides most judicial cases involving direct actions initiated by individuals or member states. Appeals are submitted to the Court of Justice.

Major Political Groups

European People's Party (EPP), Christian Democrats; Socialists and Democrats (S&D); Alliance of Liberals and Democrats for Europe (ALDE); Greens/European Free Alliance (Greens/EFA); European Conservatives and Reformists (ECR), anti-federalist Euroskeptics; European United Left/Nordic Green Left (GUE/NGL); Europe of Freedom and Democracy (EFD), right-wing Euroskeptics; Independents.

Sources: Europa, *Gateway to the European Union,* http://europa.eu/index_en.htm; Europa, *Treaty of Lisbon,* http://europa.eu/lisbon_treaty/full_text/index_en.htm; U.S. Central Intelligence Agency, *The World Factbook, 2010,* https://www.cia.gov/library/publications/the-world-factbook/index.html; author's compilations.

the councils constitute the EU's principal intergovernmental components, interacting with other executive, legislative, regulatory, judicial, and advisory institutions to shape and oversee central Union policies. Under terms of the consolidated treaties, each is chaired differently and has a different political mandate.

The European Council

Today, the European Council straddles the political apex of the EU. It consists of the heads of government or heads of state of the twenty-seven member states plus a Council president and the president of the European Commission. The High Representative of the Union for Foreign Affairs and Security Policy also participates in its deliberations. The consolidated treaties stipulate that the central purpose of the European Council is to "provide the Union with the necessary impetus for its development and [to] define the general political directions and priorities thereof."[6] In effect, this means that the Council is charged with macropolicy initiatives and directives, including the approval of new treaties and the admission of new member states. (The latter authority is shared with the European Parliament.)

Another crucial prerogative of the European Council is that of nomination and appointment of important institutional actors. On the basis of a qualified majority vote of its members, the Council nominates the president of the European Commission and, in consultation with the president-designate, the remaining commissioners. The European Council also nominates the High Representative who serves as a vice president of the Council. A majority of members of the European Parliament must concur in the nominations, after which the Council appoints the Commission president, the High Representative and other commissioners on the basis of a qualified majority vote. In addition, the European Council has the authority to ratify nominations submitted by the European Commission for membership on the EU's Economic and Social Committee and the Committee of the Regions. The Council shares powers of legislation and budgetary approval with the European Parliament, as explained below.

Until the implementation of the Lisbon Treaty, a representative of a member state government served as president of the European Council on a rotating six-month basis. Under the consolidated treaties, the Council is now chaired by a president who is elected "by a qualified majority, for a term of two and a half years, renewable once. In the event of an impediment or serious misconduct, the European Council can end the President's term of office in accordance with the same procedure." [7] The president is charged with chairing Council meetings, preparing the Council's agenda, promoting "cohesion and consensus within the European Council," and submitting a report to the European Parliament after each meeting. [8]

During initial speculations among national politicians and in the media, former British prime minister Tony Blair was viewed as a possible first choice for the EU presidency because of his political experience and charisma. Ultimately, however, his candidacy floundered primarily because of opposition in Britain and on the Continent to his interventionist stance during the Iraq war. Instead, EU leaders opted in favor of a lesser-known and therefore less-controversial choice in the person of Herman Van Rompuy, who until then had served as Belgian prime minister for less than a year. France and Germany both supported Rompuy's nomination allegedly on the grounds that he is "a modest conservative from a small country who would chair EU summits without overshadowing them." [9]

An office of a High Representative of the Union for Common and Security Policy was established with the implementation of the Amsterdam Treaty in 1999. Javier Solana, a Spanish socialist and former secretary-general of NATO, occupied the office from 1999 to 2009. The Lisbon Treaty expanded the authority of the High Representative to include a European Commission vice presidency and chairmanship of the important Foreign Affairs Council (a specialized version of the Council of Ministers—see below). As foreign minister in all but name, the High Representative interacts closely with the president and other members of the European Council and with the European Commission in formulating and conducting the EU's common foreign and security policies. As Solana's successor, the European Council nominated Catherine Ashton of Great Britain as the first High Representative with these expanded powers. Lady Ashton previously served as a junior minister in the Labour government under Tony Blair and as EU commissioner in charge of trade in 2008–2009.

The European Council is directed to meet twice every six months; it may also convene in special sessions at the behest of the president or the High Representative. Depending on the issue at hand, the Council may invite a government minister or member of the Commission to join in its deliberations. Council decisions have the weight of EU law. In ordinary matters, the Council is expected to reach decisions on the basis of consensus. Unanimity is required for weightier issues such as the adoption of a new treaty, the admission of new member states, and major institutional appointments. The Council may also issue regulations that are binding on the member states but require national legislation to take effect.

Council of Ministers

The European Council meets only a few times a year in what are often highly visible summits, but the Council of Ministers exercises quieter day-to-day legislative and budgetary functions on behalf of the Union. The Council of Ministers is made up of cabinet-level officials representing each of the twenty-seven member states of the Union, plus one representative of the European Commission whose assignment is to propose and defend policies and represent the interests of the EU as a whole. In the language of the consolidated treaties: "It shall carry out policy-making and coordinating functions as laid down in the Treaties." [10] Specifically, these functions include the power to make Community law (in cooperation with the European Parliament), coordinate economic policies among the member states, negotiate international agreements on behalf of the EU, and define common foreign and security policies under guidelines established by the European Council. In addition, the Council of Ministers shares budget-making authority with Parliament and determines policies affecting common police and judicial measures affecting the member states. The Council of Ministers cannot initiate policies on its own, but instead acts of recommendations or proposals submitted by the European Commission. The Council does have the authority to request studies by the European Commission that, in time, may become the basis of Community legislation. Informally, individual members of the Council may suggest policy initiatives to the Commission as well.

The Council of Ministers is not a single body; rather, it assumes a variety of configurations, consisting of different cabinet members from the member states, depending on the policy issue being considered. The most important are the Foreign Affairs Council, Ecofin (the economics council), and the Council of Agriculture Ministers. Other councils include Justice and Home Affairs; Employment, Social Policy, Health, and Consumer Affairs; the Internal Market; Environment; Transport, Telecommunications and Energy; and Education, Youth, and Culture. An informal Council exists in the form of the Eurogroup, which is made up of representatives of states that belong to the euro zone.

Unlike the European Council, the Council of Ministers is not chaired by an elected president. Instead, the presidency rotates among the EU's member states on a six-month basis. The president, any of the Council's members, and/or the Commission is authorized to request a meeting. Contrasting decision modes characterize proceedings of the Council of Ministers: simple majorities in the case of procedural issues, and a qualified majority (QMV) in most substantive policy issues.

Council members are assisted by the Committee of Permanent Representatives (Coreper), which is composed of ambassadors and their deputies representing each of the member countries. Coreper's task is to help in the preparation and management of the work of the Council. The Committee is organized in two bodies: Coreper I, which deals with most economic and social policies, and Coreper II, which manages external relations, budgetary issues, and justice and home affairs. Coreper is chaired by the member state holding the rotating Council presidency. Assisting Coreper is a secretary-general who oversees the activities of several thousand professional civil servants making up the Committee's secretariat.

Qualified Majority Voting

Under prevailing treaty rules dating from the Treaty of Nice, qualified majority voting in both the European Council and the Council of Ministers is based on a sliding scale of votes accorded each of the member states depending on the approximate size of its population. The number of votes ranges from twenty-nine for each of the four largest West European members (France, Germany, Italy, and the United Kingdom) to twenty-seven for Spain and Poland down to three for Malta, which has the smallest population (see Table 8-5). Proposals submitted from the European Commission require at least 255 favorable votes representing a majority of the member states; in other cases, "decisions shall be adopted if there are at least 255 votes in favour representing at least two thirds of the members." A member state may ask for confirmation that the votes in favor represent at least 62 percent of the total population of the EU. If this is not the case, the decision will not be adopted.[11]

Table 8-5 Distribution of Votes under Qualified Majority Voting (until 2014)

France	29
Germany	29
Italy	29
United Kingdom	29
Poland	27
Spain	27
Netherlands	13
Belgium	12
Czech Republic	12
Greece	12
Hungary	12
Portugal	12
Austria	10
Sweden	10
Denmark	7
Finland	7
Ireland	7
Lithuania	7
Slovakia	7
Cyprus	4
Estonia	4
Latvia	4
Luxembourg	4
Slovenia	4
Malta	3
Total	**321**

Source: *Official Journal of the European Union*, Protocol 36, Title II, Provisions Concerning the Qualified Majority, Article 3.

Rules governing qualified majority voting are scheduled to change on November 1, 2014. From that date onward, "a qualified majority shall be defined as at least 55% of the members of the Council, comprising at least fifteen of them and representing Member States comprising at least 65% of the population of the Union. A blocking minority must include at least four Council members, failing which the qualified majority shall be deemed attained."[12]

Although the larger members of the EU are clearly more powerful than the smaller states, the requirement that a qualified majority must consist of 255 votes out of a total of 321 prevents the larger countries from dictating policy to the smaller. The same decision-making rule simultaneously protects the larger countries from attempts by the smaller countries to impose policies the larger countries oppose or that may require more from their greater economic contributions to the EU budget. Decision making within the European Union therefore emphasizes the formation of coalitions rather than relying on national vetoes for protection. This central feature of decision making at the Council level distinguishes the EU as an example of "fragmented pluralism" (as opposed to "majoritarian pluralism"), as discussed in the introduction to this volume.

The European Commission

A powerful third EU institution is the European Commission, a supranational body that has been a major driving force in the long-term process of EU deepening. With the accession of new member states from the early 1970s to 2007, the Commission has been gradually expanded to include twenty-seven members. Effective November 1, 2014, the number of commissioners will be reduced to correspond to two-thirds of the number of member states ("unless the European Council, acting unanimously, decides to alter this number"). The Consolidated Version of the Treaty on European Union stipulates that the "members of the Commission shall be chosen from among the nationals of the Member States on the basis of a system of strictly equal rotation, . . . reflecting the demographic and geographical range of all the Member States." [13] The intent of streamlining the size of the Commission is to facilitate decision making and to make policy coordination more efficient.

Currently, each member state is represented by a single commissioner. (Previously, France, Germany, Italy, the United Kingdom, and Spain were allocated two commissioners apiece, but their representation was reduced to one under the Treaty of Nice because of pending EU expansion.) After each European parliamentary election, the European Council submits the names of a Commission president and other commissioner-designates to the European Parliament for its consideration. Following parliamentary approval, the European Council then formally appoints the Commission members by a qualified majority vote for a term of five years. Once appointed to office, commissioners are bound by treaty to act independently and therefore accept no instructions "from any Government or other institution, body, office or entity." [14] Similar to a vote of no confidence in national parliamentary systems, the European Parliament has the treaty authority to compel the Commission to resign as a body through a vote of censure. A two-thirds majority is required "representing a majority of the component members of the European Parliament." [15]

The commission exercises extensive powers in its treaty mandate to "promote the general interest of the Union and take appropriate initiatives to that end." [16] These powers include the authority to:

- Propose legislation to the Council of Ministers;

- Ensure the application of the treaties and policy regulations;

- Oversee the "application of European law under the control of the Court of Justice" (the Court of Justice is discussed below);

- Administer the EU's budget;

- Exercise various executive and management functions, for example, with respect to provisions of the original European Coal and Steel Community; and

- Represent the Union in external relations—with the important exception of common foreign and security policy.

The commissioners oversee the administrative activities of some 2,500 senior civil servants and 10,000 additional staff members who collectively make up the aggregate European Commission as a bureaucratic entity. Senior-level officials are typically recruited from the member states, whereas the vast majority of their subordinates are EU civil servants. The principal task of this veritable army of "Eurocrats" is to assist the commissioners in drafting and enforcing Union legislation and regulations. The sheer size and anonymity of the Commission bureaucracy have proven a continuing source of government and citizen discontent with the EU.

Table 8-6 European Commissioners by Portfolio Assignments and Nationalities, 2010–2014

President: José Manuel Barroso (Portugal)

Vice President and High Representative for Foreign Affairs and Security: Catherine Ashton (United Kingdom)

Vice President, Justice, Fundamental Rights and Citizenship: Viviane Reding (Luxembourg)

Vice President, Competition: Joaquin Almnía (Spain)

Vice President, Transport: Siim Kallag (Estonia)

Vice President, Digital Agenda: Neelie Kroes (Netherlands)

Vice President, Industry and Entrepreneurship, Antonio Tajani (Italy)

Vice President, Inter-Institutional Relations and Administration: Maros Šefčovič (Slovakia)

Environment: Janez Potočnik (Slovenia)

Economic and Monetary Affairs: Olli Rehn (Finland)

Development: Andris Piebalgs (Latvia)

International Market and Services: Michel Barnier (France)

Education, Culture, Multilingualism, and Youth: Androulla Vissiliou (Cyprus)

Taxation and Customs Union, Audit, and Anti-Fraud: Algirdas Šemeta (Lithuania)

Trade: Karel De Gucht (Belgium)

Health and Consumer Policy: John Dalli (Malta)

Research, Innovation, and Science: Máire Geoghegan-Quinn (Ireland)

Financial Programming and Budget: Janusz Lewandowski (Poland)

Maritime Affairs and Fisheries: Maria Damanaki (Greece)

International Cooperation, Humanitarian Aid, and Crisis Response: Kristalina Georgieva (Bulgaria)

Energy: Günther Oettinger (Germany)

Regional Policy: Johannes Hahn (Austria)

Climate Action: Connie Hedegaard (Denmark)

Enlargement and European Neighborhood Policy: Štefan Füle (Czech Republic)

Employment, Social Affairs, and Inclusion: László Andor (Hungary)

Home Affairs: Cecilia Malmström (Sweden)

Agriculture and Rural Development: Dacian Cioloş (Romania)

Source: Europa: European Commission: The Commissioners (2010–2014), http://ec.europa.eu/commission_2010-2014/index_en.htm.

The Commission is divided into multiple directorates-general (DGs), which correspond to specific functional or policy tasks. Each DG is headed by a director-general, who serves under the supervision of a commissioner and a cabinet of no more than six personal advisers. As a result of reforms initiated by the European Commission in 1999, cabinet members must be recruited from at least three different nationalities. President Barroso, who serves without portfolio, is assisted by seven vice presidents and nineteen additional commissioners whose portfolios numbered thirty-three. (See Table 8-6.) Nine of the commissioners serving in 2010–2014 are women.

The European Parliament

The fourth major political institution of the European Union is the European Parliament (EP). Originally made up of representatives delegated from the national parliaments of the member states of the European Coal and Steel Community and later the European Economic Community (EEC), the Parliament in its early years was little more than a forum for debate on European issues with little real power. As such, the EP epitomized a serious "democratic deficit" within the EEC, because Community law was decided behind the closed doors of the Council of Ministers with little effective parliamentary input. In an effort to correct this deficiency and bring the EP closer to the citizens, EEC leaders amended the Treaty of Rome to provide for direct elections. The first direct elections to the European Parliament were held in 1979; subsequent elections have been held in 1984, 1989, 1994, 1999, 2004, and 2009.

Membership in the European Parliament was increased from 518 deputies to 567 deputies prior to the June 1994 election, primarily to take into account the growth in the German population after unification in 1990. In January 1995 the EP was expanded once again to allow for the inclusion of additional deputies from Austria, Finland, and Sweden. After the EU's enlargement to include ten additional members in 2004 and two in 2007, the EP's size was increased to 736. Member countries are allocated seats in the Parliament according to the size of their populations (see Table 8-7).

From 1979 through 1985 deputies were chosen in the continental member states according to national variations of proportional representation, and delegates from the United Kingdom and Ireland were elected on the basis of each country's plurality electoral system. The European Parliament later established a Community-wide electoral system of proportional representation, beginning with the June 1999 election. Once elected, deputies are formally designated members of the European Parliament (MEPs). They choose from their ranks a president and fourteen vice presidents to preside over the day-to-day parliamentary proceedings. An important organizational component of the EP is its complex structure of standing committees, which number twenty. Each corresponds to one of the EU's policy areas and affords MEPs an opportunity to review pending legislation and prepare reports submitted to parliament as a whole. Most plenary sessions of the EP are held in Strasbourg, although a second parliamentary building has been erected in Brussels. Committee meetings are conducted in Brussels to facilitate closer scrutiny by MEPs of Council proceedings.

As previously noted, elections to the European Parliament are conducted every five years. Candidates are nominated by political parties organized on a European-wide basis or by parties that campaign in several countries. Once elected, MEPs sit by party, not by nation. Seven party groups (plus a nonattached group) are currently represented in the European Parliament. The largest group is the European People's Party, a center-right faction that includes mainly Christian Democrats. Next in size are the Socialists (Social Democrats), followed by the Liberals and Greens (see Table 8-8). Elections address Europe-wide themes: economic growth, unemployment, inflation, and purchasing power dominated the 2009 campaign,[17] as well as national issues such as voter confidence in or discontent with governing parties. For example, in the June 2009 election, Germany's Christian Democrats handily outpolled their principal rivals, the Social Democrats, in what proved to be a harbinger of a change in government in September; Britain's Labour Party under Gordon Brown suffered a scathing defeat to the Conservative Party and a Euro-skeptic U.K. Independent Party; and Greek voters reacted angrily to a series of domestic scandals and the ongoing global economic crisis by according the opposition Socialist Party an electoral victory over the governing conservatives.

Under the Treaty of Rome, the power of the European Parliament was initially limited to its right to approve the Community's budget, censure the European Commission and therefore force its resignation (which it never exercised), and debate Community issues and the Commission's annual general report. The Council of Ministers could consult the EP on pending legislation, but was not obligated to amend bills in response to parliamentary objections.

The relative powerlessness of the European Parliament became a matter of increased concern among European leaders in response to parliamentary and citizen complaints about the Community's democratic deficiencies, as illustrated by its lack of decision-making transparency. Accordingly, the powers of the European Parliament have been steadily expanded through treaty enactment. An important first step was the adoption of the Single European

Table 8-7 Allocation of Seats per Member State in the European Parliament, 2009–2014

Germany	99
France	72
Italy	72
United Kingdom	72
Poland	50
Spain	50
Romania	33
Netherlands	25
Belgium	22
Czech Republic	22
Greece	22
Hungary	22
Portugal	22
Sweden	18
Bulgaria	17
Austria	17
Denmark	13
Finland	13
Slovakia	13
Ireland	12
Lithuania	12
Latvia	8
Slovenia	7
Cyprus	6
Estonia	6
Luxembourg	6
Malta	5
Total	736

Source: http://europa.eu/institutions/inst/parliament/index_en.htm.

Table 8-8 Allocation of Seats by Party Group in the European Parliament, 2009–2014

Party group	Number of MEPs
European People's Party-European Democrats (EPP-ED)	265
Socialist Group (PES)	184
Alliance of Liberals and Democrats for Europe (ALDE)	84
Greens/European Free Alliance (Greens/EFA)	55
European Conservatives and Reformists Group (ECR)	54
Confederal Group of the European United Left/Nordic Green Left (GUE/NGL)	35
Europe of Freedom and Democracy Group (EFD)	31
Nonattached (NA)	28
Total	736

Source: http://europa.eu/institutions/inst/parliament/index_en.htm.

Act in 1986, which introduced a new cooperation procedure allowing for parliamentary approval of—and proposed amendments to—pending Council of Ministers decisions governing social policy, regional policy, research, and the creation of the Single Market. The Treaty on European Union, which was implemented in 1994, further strengthened parliamentary prerogatives. First, it required EP approval of the European Council's nomination of the president and other members of the European Commission and all accession and association agreements with other states. Second, it authorized EP members (at least a fourth of the membership is required) to request the appointment of temporary committees of inquiry "to investigate . . . alleged contraventions or misadministration in the implementation of Community law" (Art. 193 [ex 138c]). In addition, the treaty empowered the Parliament to appoint an investigatory ombudsman who is "empowered to receive complaints from any citizen of the Union" (Art. 195 [ex 138e]).

The Treaty on European Union and the Amsterdam Treaty expanded the legislative role of the European Parliament by according it new "co-decision" powers with the Council of Ministers. These powers allow Parliament the right to formally approve a Council proposal (in which case the Council shall "definitively enact" the bill and it becomes law) or decide, by majority vote, to reject or amend a Council proposal. In the case of rejection, the Council may convene a conciliation committee composed of a representative of the Commission and an equal number of members of the Council or their deputies and members of the European Parliament in an effort to reconcile the differences. After such deliberations, the EP has the option of once again rejecting the proposal by an absolute majority (in which case it fails) or of proposing amendments to the act in question. The Council may decide within three months to accept such amendments, either by a qualified majority if the Commission concurs in them or unanimously if the Commission rejects the amendments. In either event, the proposal becomes law.

In practice, the co-decision procedure became the norm for most legislative decisions in the early 2000s and largely displaced the weaker consultation and cooperation procedures. This shift toward enhanced power in the hands of the European Parliament is codified in the Treaty of Lisbon, which extends co-decision rules to more than forty new policy areas—including agriculture, energy, immigration, justice and home affairs, health, and EU funds. In addition, the EP is now entitled to decide the entire EU budget in concert with the Council of Ministers, approve international trade agreements negotiated by the Council, and propose treaty changes.

The Court of Justice of the European Union

Established as a component of the European Coal and Steel Community during the initial take-off phase of the integration movement, the European Court of Justice (ECJ) has evolved into an increasingly potent instrument of supranational authority. The central purpose of the ECJ, in the language of the consolidated treaties, is to "ensure that in the interpretation and application of the Treaties the law is observed."[18] In performing this vital task, the ECJ complements the activities of the European Court of Human Rights, located in Strasbourg, which enforces provisions of the European Convention on Human Rights drawn up by the Council for Europe in 1950.[19] Decisions by both courts have contributed, perhaps even more than the "high politics" at the level of the ministerial councils and the European Parliament, to a growing sense of a "European" identity among ordinary citizens.

The ECJ consists of twenty-seven justices, one representing each EU member state. They are appointed "by common accord of the governments of the Member States" for staggered six-year terms, which are frequently renewed. The justices are assisted by eight advocates-general, five from the larger EU member states and three from the smaller countries, who serve on a rotating basis. The assigned duty of the advocates-general is "to make, in open court, reasoned submissions on cases brought before the Court of Justice, in order to assist the Court in the performance of the task assigned to it." The consolidated treaties stipulate that both the ECJ justices and the advocates-general "shall be chosen from persons whose independence is beyond doubt and who possess the qualifications required for appointment to the highest judicial offices in their respective countries."[20] These provisions ensure both continuity and periodic renewal of incumbents as well as high levels of legal competence.

The ECJ meets in Luxembourg, either in plenary sessions attended by all of its members or in smaller chambers consisting of three or five justices. Court decisions are based on majority votes. No specific provision is made for the justices to publish dissenting opinions comparable to the well-established practice of their counterparts on the U.S. Supreme Court.

As legal guardian of EU institutions and rules, the ECJ exercises authority under the amended treaties in three principal areas:

1. *The power to enforce conformity to EU rules among the member states.* The consolidated treaties affirm the power of the ECJ to "rule on actions brought by a Member State, an institution or a natural or legal person."[21] If the Court concurs in formal charges brought by the European Commission or a member state that a member state has failed to fulfill a treaty obligation, it is empowered to require the country in question "to take the necessary measures to comply." In such a case, the Court can impose, at the behest of the Commission, a "lump sum or penalty payment" on the offending government.[22]

2. *The power of judicial review.* Several provisions of the consolidated treaties give the ECJ the right to determine whether EU policies and institutional behavior conform to treaty provisions. Article 263 allows the Court to "review the legality of legislative acts adopted by the Council, the Commission, the European Central Bank." The treaty continues: "If the action is well founded, the Court of Justice shall declare the act concerned to be void."[23]

3. *The power to intervene in domestic judicial disputes.* Article 267 allows the ECJ to rule on the validity and interpretation of issues raised in courts in the member states if national courts or tribunals request such a ruling.

Over time, the European Court of Justice has evolved from a weak judiciary with no authority to enforce compliance with its rulings to a much more activist and powerful institution. An important milestone in this process was the creation in 1989 of the Court of First Instance of the European Communities (now officially entitled the General Court), which relieved the ECJ of the responsibility for dealing with most cases involving individual challenges to domestic or Community law. The ECJ is therefore able to concentrate more of its energy on selective cases involving macro issues such as legal integration and the supremacy of EU law. In addition, its authority under Article 267 allows the Court to extend Union law directly to the member states. A binding precedent was a 1991 ruling in which "the ECJ won for the EC legal system the right to provide remedies for some violations of European law, declaring that national courts could require compensation by the national government for individuals hurt by a failure of a national government to implement EC directives punctually and properly (*Francovich v. Italy*)."[24] The long-term consequence, as Simon Hix observes, has been "a high penetration of EU law into the national legal system. . . . [By] enabling national courts to enforce ECJ judgements, the preliminary references procedure has the effect of making national courts the lower tier of an integrated EU court system, and the ECJ the quasi-supreme court at its pinnacle."[25]

Moreover, subsequent rulings by the ECJ have reinforced growing appreciation of the importance of European law at the citizen level of politics. In January 2000 the ECJ declared a German military law that forbade a female recruit from bearing arms to be unconstitutional because it violated EU guidelines governing equal rights of men and women in the workplace. After the ruling, the woman who had pressed her case through the German courts to the ECJ in Luxembourg declared: "It was an absolute discovery, and a very good discovery, the existence of this European court. I used to think of myself as German. Now I feel a little European, too."[26] The German parliament later amended the country's constitution to permit women to take on combat roles in the armed forces.

The European Central Bank and the European Bank for Reconstruction and Development

An EU institution that has commanded a high European and international profile since its inception in 1998 is the European Central Bank (ECB), which has its headquarters in Frankfurt, Germany. The ECB serves as the executive arm of the European System of Central Banks (ESCB), which represents the national central banks of the nations belonging to the EU's Economic and Monetary Union (EMU).

With the implementation of the third stage of the Economic and Monetary Union on January 1, 1999, the ECB assumed supranational responsibility for macroeconomic policy on behalf of the member states belonging to the euro zone. Its task is to promote the basic objectives of the EMU as contained in the original Treaty on European Union: "the adoption of an economic policy that is based on the close coordination of the Member States' economic policies, on the internal market and on the definition of common objectives, and conducted in accordance with the principles of an open market economy with free competition." Means to these ends include "the irrevocable fixing of exchange rates leading to the introduction of a single currency, . . . and the definition and conduct of a single monetary policy and exchange rate policy the primary objective of both of which shall be to maintain price stability and . . . to support the general economic policies of the Community" (Art. 4 [ex 3a]).

The ECB is empowered to define and implement monetary policy, conduct foreign exchange operations, and hold and manage the official foreign reserves of the member states (Art.105). It is also authorized to fix interest rates and issue the euro as a common currency. Its institutional authority is distributed among four decision-making bodies: the General Assembly, which is made up of the governors of the national banks in all the EU member states; a smaller Eurosystem, consisting of the bank governors of the countries belonging to the euro zone; an executive board of six officials; and the Governing Council, which includes the members of the Executive Committee and the Governing Council. The executive board consists of a president, a vice president, and four other members. They are appointed for nonrenewable eight-year terms by unanimous consent by the European Council. Serving on the board in 2010 were Jean-Claude Trichet (a former governor of the Bank of France who has served since November 2003), a Greek as vice president, an Austrian, a Belgian, a Spaniard, and a German—all of whom were highly trained and experienced economists. The consolidated treaties grant the ECB complete independence from "Community institutions and bodies, from any government of a Member State or from any other body" (Art. 130).

A second EU financial institution is the European Bank for Reconstruction and Development (EBRD), which the European Council authorized in December 1990 in response to an initiative by former French president François Mitterrand. The EBRD was established with an initial capitalization of $12 billion to disburse loans for technical assistance, equity investment, and security offerings in the emerging postcommunist regimes in Central Europe. Its declared purpose was "to foster a transition toward open-market economies and to promote private and entrepreneurial initiatives in the Central and East European countries committed to and applying the principles of multiparty democracy, pluralism, and market economics." [27] After the collapse of the Soviet Union in 1991, the Russian Federation and other successor states became eligible for EBRD loans as well. EU member states collectively own a majority of shares in the bank, but the United States is the largest single shareholder. In deference to France, the first two EBRD presidents were French officials.[28]

Other Institutions

Other EU institutions include the European Economic and Social Committee, the Committee of the Regions, and the European Court of Auditors. Both the European Economic and Social Committee (EESC) and the Committee of the Regions (CoR) serve as advisory bodies to the Council of Ministers and the European Parliament and give "voice" to constituencies that are not otherwise represented in the EU. The EESC, which dates from the creation of the European Economic Community, represents employers, trade unions, professional associations, farmers, and consumers. Its 344 members are apportioned among the member states according to the relative size of their population (Table 8-9). Delegates are nominated by their national governments and appointed by the Council of the European Union, acting unanimously, for four-year terms. The consolidated treaties stipulate that the Council of Ministers and the Commission must consult with members of the EESC on specified policy matters and in other cases "in which they consider it appropriate" (Art. 262 [ex 198]). Opinions of the EESC, however, are not binding on actions by either the Council or the Commission.

The Committee of the Regions was established under the Treaty on European Union to represent regional and local bodies within the member states. CoR is also composed of 344 members, distributed on the same basis as members of the EESC. They are appointed for four-year terms by the Council of Ministers. Although they are nominated by their home governments, once in office members of the committee "may not be bound by any

Table 8-9 Allocation of Seats per Member State of the European Economic and Social Committee and the Committee of Regions

France	24
Germany	24
Italy	24
United Kingdom	24
Poland	21
Spain	21
Romania	15
Austria	12
Belgium	12
Bulgaria	12
Czech Republic	12
Greece	12
Hungary	12
Netherlands	12
Portugal	12
Sweden	12
Denmark	9
Ireland	9
Lithuania	9
Slovakia	9
Finland	9
Estonia	7
Latvia	7
Slovenia	7
Cyprus	6
Luxembourg	6
Malta	5
Total	**344**

Source: Europa: Gateway to the European Union, http://europa.eu/about-eu/institutions-bodies/index_en.htm.

mandatory instructions. They shall be completely independent in the performance of their duties, in the general interest of the Community" (Art. 263 [ex 198a] of the Treaty of Rome). Like the EESC, the Committee of the Regions performs strictly advisory functions in relation to the Council of the European Union and the Commission. In practice, CoR has demonstrated that it more effectively represents regional interests in member states that have functioning state or regional political structures—notably, Germany, Great Britain, Italy, and Spain—than in unitary states such as France.

The Court of Auditors serves as an independent "watchdog" agency. It was established as an independent oversight body in 1975 to allay parliamentary concerns about the proper monitoring of Union finances. The Court has twelve members who are appointed for six-year terms by the European Council subject to parliamentary approval. Their assignment is to "examine the accounts of all revenue and expenditure of the Community" and to "provide the European Parliament and the Council with a statement of assurance as to the reliability of the accounts and the legality and regularity of the underlying transactions" (Art. 248 [ex 188c] of the Treaty of Rome). In addition, the Court assists the European Parliament and the Council in exercising their budgetary control functions.

Citizens

European citizens are an important indirect source of power as voters in national and European elections and, in some states, in national referendums. (This role is discussed in the following chapter.) Citizens also have the right to submit written criticisms about alleged EU administrative abuses—such as unfairness, discrimination, and unnecessary delays—to the European Ombudsman for investigation. The office, which was introduced by the Treaty on European Union as a corollary of European citizenship, is modeled after a Swedish constitutional precedent dating from the early nineteenth century that was created to guard against the abuse of administrative authority following a prolonged period of political despotism; a number of European countries have subsequently established an equivalent institution of their own.

The European Ombudsman is appointed by the European Parliament for a five-year term and is granted full investigatory independence. The office is charged with informing the targeted EU institution or body of the complaint and, if necessary, recommending steps to redress a grievance. In 2004 the European Ombudsman received 3,536 citizen petitions; of these, the office pursued an official inquiry in 343 cases (approximately 10 percent of the total). In his annual report to the European Parliament for 2005, the ombudsman noted: "These figures should not lead to underestimate the fact that, in addition to the enquiries opened, the Ombudsman gave complainants advice (in 2117 cases), recommending that they turn to a national or regional ombudsman (906 cases), address a petition to the European Parliament (179 complainants), or contact the European Commission (359 cases).[29]

The Lisbon Treaty introduced another, potentially more powerful instrument of grassroots power in the form of a direct democracy procedure known as the European Citizens' Initiative. This procedure will permit citizens to place an item on the legislative agenda of the European Commission if they garner a million signatures (about 0.2 percent of the EU population) in support. The full meaning of the new provision remains unclear and must await public consultations and the adoption of an enabling regulation by the European Parliament and the Council of Ministers before it can take effect.[30]

NOTES

1. David Gowland, Arthur Turner, and Alex Wright, *Britain and European Integration Since 1945: On the Sidelines* (London and New York: Routledge, 2010), 13.
2. The amended treaty texts, including provisions of the Lisbon Treaty, are available in *Official Journal of the European Union,* Consolidated Version of the Treaty on European Union, and Consolidated Version of the Treaty on the Functioning of the European Union, 2010/C 83/01, 49, http://eur-lex.europa.eu/LexUriServ/LexUriServ.do?uri=OJ:C:2010:083:FULL:EN:PDF. Citations in this and subsequent chapters refer by name to one or both consolidated treaty documents with appropriate article numbers. The provisions cited in this note are from the Consolidated Treaty on the Functioning of the European Union, Preamble, 49.
3. Ibid., 51.
4. Ibid.
5. Ibid., 52–53.
6. Article 14, Consolidated Version of the Treaty on European Union, 23.
7. Article 15, ibid. 23.
8. Ibid.
9. "How the European Union's horse-trading over top jobs reflects murky coalition-building," *Economist,* November 26, 2009.
10. Article 16, Consolidated Version of the Treaty on European Union, Title III, Provisions on the Institutions, 24.
11. Europa Glossary, Qualified majority, http://europa.eu/scadplus/glossary/qualified_majority_en.htm.
12. Article 16, Consolidated Version of Treaty on European Union, 24.
13. Article 17, ibid., 25.
14. Title III, Provisions on the Institutions, Article 17, ibid., 25.
15. Article 234, ibid., 152.
16. Article 17, ibid.
17. Eurobarometer, *The 2009 European Elections,* December 2008, 10.
18. Article 19, Consolidated Version of the Treaty on European Union, 27.
19. The European Convention on Human Rights, whose declared purpose is to enforce individual rights contained in the United Nations Universal Declaration of Human Rights of 1948, was enacted in 1953. The Court of Human Rights was established in 1959 and currently exercises jurisdiction in forty-one European nations.
20. Article 19, Consolidated Version of the Treaty on European Union, and Article 252, Consolidated Version of the Treaty on Functioning of the European Union, 158.
21. Article 260, Consolidated Version of the Treaty on Functioning of the European Union, 161.

22. Ibid.,

23. Article 264, ibid.

24. Karen J. Alter, "European Court of Justice (ECJ)," in *Encyclopedia of the European Union,* ed. Desmond Dinan (Boulder and London: Lynne Rienner, 1998), 190.

25. Simon Hix, *The Political System of the European Union,* 2nd ed. (New York: Palgrave Macmillan, 2005), 107.

26. "A European Identity: Nation-State Losing Ground," *New York Times,* January 14, 2000.

27. Bernt Schiller and M. Donald Hancock, "The International Context of Economic and Political Transitions," in *Transitions to Capitalism and Democracy in Russia and Central Europe,* ed. M. Donald Hancock and John Logue (Westport, Conn., and London: Praeger, 2000), 317.

28. "European Bank for Reconstruction and Development (EBRD)," *Encyclopedia of the European Union,* ed. Desmond Dinan (Boulder and London: Lynne Rienner, 1998), 178.

29. "Petition to the European Parliament and complaint to the Ombudsman," Europa, *General Report on the Activities on the Activities of the European Union, Chapter XIII: Area of freedom, security, and justice, Union citizenship,* http://ec.europa.eu/justice_home/fsj/citizenship.

30. A skeptical op-ed commentary about the Citizens' Initiative is Charlemagne's "Allons, citoyens de l'Europe," *Economist,* January 16, 2010. The author notes: "It could get messy, in short. But then democracy is messy."

Who Has the Power?

THE EUROPEAN UNION (EU) IS DEEPLY EMBEDDED IN THE POLITICAL and socioeconomic fabric of its member states, while simultaneously manifesting a high degree of institutional and political autonomy in its own right. Political power in the EU is thus distributed among multiple domestic, intergovernmental, supranational, group, and individual actors that interact in making EU policy and shepherding the course of European integration. Therefore, addressing the question "Who has the power in the EU?" requires multilevel analysis.

The most important instruments of European Union power are national governments, the Council of Ministers and the European Council, the European Commission, the European Parliament, the European Court of Justice, and the European Central Bank. Other players include political parties and private interest groups (notably, industrial firms, employer associations, and organized labor). European citizens also affect EU actions, sometimes in a forceful fashion.

National Governments as Actors

Since the inception of the European Coal and Steel Community (ECSC) in the early 1950s, national governments have embodied the intergovernmental principle of the European integration movement. They are represented on the basis of member state equality in two of the EU's central legislative-executive institutions: the Council of Ministers and the European Council. Until the advent of qualified majority voting (QMV) under the Single European Act, important Community decisions were based on the unanimity principle. This practice allowed each member state to exercise a veto over Community initiatives, which had the effect of postponing (sometimes indefinitely) Council decisions. Since the mid-1980s, QMV has significantly facilitated joint decision making and therefore accelerated the EU's deepening process, but it does not diminish the central fact that national governments continue to exercise authority over treaty revisions and the initiation of new policies. National governments also exercise executive oversight over EU policies, including the Economic and Monetary Union (EMU) as well as common foreign and defense policies, and they share power with the European Parliament in determining the content of EU legislation and the admission of new member states. Moreover, national governments—acting through the European Council on the basis of prior agreement among themselves—formally appoint leading EU officials, such as members of the European Commission and the European Court of Justice.

Domestic political considerations determine to a significant degree the behavior of member states in the various councils. Among these considerations are the contrasting degrees of national commitment to European integration based on subjective calculations of costs and benefits, the partisan composition of governments, and coalition strategy within the EU. Leaders of some of the smaller member states—notably the Benelux countries—have traditionally been among the most ardent supporters of the European idea as a means of promoting their political and economic interests vis-à-vis their larger and more powerful neighbors. Nations on the southern, western, and northeastern and central European peripheries of the EU—including Greece, Ireland, Poland, Portugal, Spain, and the Baltic republics—are positive players with the expectation of EU financial assistance in the form of agricultural subsidies and regional development funds.

By contrast, some member states have expressed serious reservations about further integration. An early example was French president Charles de Gaulle's veto of Great Britain's application to join the European Economic Community (EEC) in 1963 on the grounds that British membership would diminish French influence within the Community. Another is Britain's and Denmark's resolve in 1991 to opt out of automatic membership in the EMU under terms of the Treaty on European Union to avoid subordinating their macroeconomic policies to supranational control. In 2005 the French and Dutch rejections of the draft constitutional treaty expressed deeply rooted elite and citizen ambivalence toward further EU deepening. In 2009 Polish and Czech leaders delayed ratification of the Lisbon Treaty for either domestic political reasons or because of their resistance to increased EU power under the treaty.

Scandinavian members of the EU have been divided in their views of the EU. For reasons similar to Great Britain's reservations about supranationalism, both Denmark and Sweden chose to postpone joining the EMU. A majority of Danish and Swedish citizens later voted against full EMU membership, at least for the foreseeable future, in national referendums in 2000 and 2003. By contrast, Finland has ardently embraced the full responsibilities and consequences of EU membership (including the EMU) as a means of enhancing its national security and economic ties with the West.

Who governs in individual countries affects national policy toward the EU as well. Georges Pompidou, who became the president of France in 1969, reversed de Gaulle's negative stance toward British membership in the EEC when he agreed with German chancellor Willy Brandt and other heads of government to expand the Community. Nearly thirty years later, New Labour's electoral victory under Tony Blair led to more positive British engagement in EU affairs than had been evident under Conservative leaders Margaret Thatcher and John Major. Newly elected Conservative prime minister David Cameron signaled renewed British reservations at a European Council meeting in October 2010 when he rejected a 6 percent increase in the 2011 Union budget proposed by the European Parliament. He and fellow members of the European Council subsequently compromised on a 2.9 percent increase.

Germany is a special case. During the early postwar years in West Germany, the two major parties—the Christian Democrats and the Social Democrats—were divided in their attitudes toward European and trans-Atlantic relations. The Christian Democrats, under the leadership of Konrad Adenauer, proved to be ardent advocates of both economic and military cooperation within Europe and the broader North Atlantic community, but the Social Democrats were skeptical of any steps that might deepen Germany's division. That the Christian Democrats dominated the national executive office when the formative decisions were reached to launch the ECSC and later the EEC made an enormous difference in Germany's commitment to the integration movement. Only later, with the adoption of a new pro-Western and a more moderate ideological program in 1959, did the Social Democrats unequivocally embrace European integration as well. Changes of government since then have had little substantive impact on Germany's involvement in European affairs.

National governments also affect Community actions—and therefore the course of the integration movement—through coalition strategies with other member states. The most important and durable coalition is a strategic alliance between France and Germany. This alliance is rooted in a mutual recognition among postwar leaders in both countries of the imperative of political reconciliation after three disastrous wars in less than a century. It was deepened by the close personal friendship between de Gaulle, the first president of the Fifth Republic, and Adenauer, the first chancellor of the Federal Republic of Germany. In January 1963 the two leaders signed the historic Treaty of Friendship and Cooperation, which institutionalized Franco-German reconciliation and established the foundation for long-term policy rapport between the two countries.[1] Their mutual support was decisive in achieving important milestones in the EU's parallel processes of widening and deepening. In a speech in June 2000 to members of the German parliament in Berlin, French president Jacques Chirac publicly affirmed Franco-German cooperation as the "motor" driving European integration.[2]

Alongside the two councils, another instrument for the exercise of national power within the EU is the intergovernmental conference (IGC), a diplomatic forum in which representatives of the member governments consider the adoption of new European treaties or treaty amendments. The first IGC spanned the negotiations among the six founding members of the European Coal and Steel Community to establish the EEC and Euratom in 1957. Important IGCs since then include those leading to the Single European Act, the Treaty on European Union, the Treaty of Amsterdam, the Treaty of Nice, and the Lisbon Treaty. In 2000 another IGC deliberated proposed treaty changes governing qualified majority voting and the composition of both the European Commission and the European Parliament in anticipation of the eastward expansion of the EU. Partisan divisions among the member states initially clouded the prospects of agreement on the requisite treaty amendments. The protracted disagreement underscored the power exercised by the national governments within the EU, straining even the cohesiveness of the Franco-German alliance as a crucial force driving the European integration movement.[3]

Another manifestation of national power within the EU was a decision made by fourteen member states (the total at the time was fifteen) to impose a bilateral freeze on high-level political contacts with Austria after the right-wing Freedom Party joined the conservative People's Party in a national coalition in February 2000. Leaders of the fourteen countries were motivated by their displeasure with the neo-Nazi sympathies expressed by a leader of the Freedom Party. The sanctions, although not formally an action by the EU, resulted in strained relations within the Community that were eased only when they were lifted toward the end of the year.

The Councils as Actors

Despite national autonomy in bilateral relations and important aspects of EU affairs, successive treaties—from the Single European Act to the Lisbon Treaty—have diminished the intergovernmental character of the various EU councils. Each of these treaties has

The first two executive officers to serve under the new Treaty of Lisbon are former Belgian prime minister Herman Van Rompuy (left) who was elected president of the European Council by fellow members of the Council, and Catherine Ashton, who was chosen the High Representative of the European Union for Foreign Affairs and Security Policy (the EU's de facto foreign minister) by members of the Council and affirmed by majority vote in the European Parliament.

Source: Thierry Tronnel/Corbis

significantly deepened European cooperation, giving the councils and other EU institutions, including the European Commission and the European Parliament, new collective powers and policy responsibility.

Although national governments retain the right of veto over some executive and legislative matters, the dynamics of the QMV have transformed the Council of Ministers and the European Council into quasi-supranational bodies. Peer pressure, combined with the arithmetical imperative of the QMV for member states seeking to enter into policy coalitions in Council deliberations, discourages obstructionist behavior by national actors. On occasion, when a member government decides it cannot endorse a collective action, it chooses to "opt out" of the decision rather than unilaterally veto it. One example is the Thatcher government's 1989 decision not to endorse the Social Charter. The right of member states to "constructive abstentions" from Council decisions is explicitly recognized in treaty provisions governing the EU's Common Foreign and Security Policy (CFSP), as explained in Chapter 8.4.[4]

The long-term trend toward increased supranationalism in the legislative-executive functions at the Council level has been reinforced by the inclusion of the president of the European Commission in meetings of the European Council and the elevation of the more powerful High Representative of the Union as a vice president of the European Commission.

The European Commission and 'Bureaucratic Politics'

The EU's overtly supranational institutions are also important instruments of power and decision making. Most visible among them is the European Commission. In contrast to the "high politics" characteristic of Council decisions, the European Commission, with its extensive staff of professional civil servants, embodies a less visible level of "bureaucratic politics" that is highly significant in the day-to-day activities of the EU. The bureaucratic level of policymaking—and therefore of politics—has been characterized by an accretion of common policies and standards produced by the European bureaucracy (and its masters within the Commission). The process of bureaucratic rulemaking is facilitated by the powers given the Commission to initiate rules and the regulatory nature of much of the emerging European political system.

Policymaking at the bureaucratic level appears fragmented into relatively narrow, specialized fields of competence. This fragmentation and the now more numerous linkages between components of the Commission and components of national bureaucracies are a crucial aspect of decision making within the EU. For that reason, much of the politics of the European Union can best be understood as bureaucratic politics.[5] The tendency of bureaucratic decision making to occur within policy communities (especially those of a technical nature) has had the effect of depoliticizing what could have been highly divisive issues. As a result, the less overt politics of the EU has been able to force, or perhaps cajole, integration along.

European Parliament as Legislator and Watchdog

A supranational institution from the outset, the European Parliament has steadily increased its power in relation to the various councils. Expanded powers of joint decision making in Union legislation significantly augment the EP's established authority with respect to most facets of EU governance.

Within the Parliament, power is concentrated in the various party factions whose members are elected at five-year intervals. The moderate European People's Party (EPP) and the Socialist Group (PES) dominate legislative procedures because of their sheer size. Since 1952 these two groups have alternated at regular intervals in claiming the presidency of the European Parliament, except for a brief interlude from 1979 to 1982 when a Liberal held the office. Because neither the PPE nor the PES can claim an absolute majority of seats in its own right, both parties have been compelled to cooperate in asserting parliamentary authority in relation to the councils and the Commission. Facilitating the strategic alliance between the two groups is their common support for a more assertive role of the European Parliament in Community affairs and especially their agreement on social issues.

Meanwhile, institutional authority is dispersed among the EP's presiding officials, including the president and fourteen vice presidents, and its intricate committee structure. The presiding officials play a decisive role in determining the parliamentary agenda and overseeing daily proceedings, and the EP's twenty standing committees are responsible for most preparatory work and the drafting of parliamentary reports and resolutions.

A dramatic exercise of parliamentary power occurred in January 1999 when members of the European Parliament exercised their authority under Article 201 (ex 144) of the Treaty of Rome (renumbered Article 226 in the consolidated treaties) to create the Committee of Inquiry to investigate allegations of fraud among members of the European Commission. (An earlier motion to censure the Commission failed to receive the requisite two-thirds majority.) The committee's findings that individual commissioners were indeed guilty of favoritism and financial mismanagement prompted the voluntary resignation in March of the Commission led by Jacques Santer of Luxembourg. The commissioners continued their work in a lame-duck capacity until Romano Prodi and a new set of officials took office in May.

Together with the authoritative rulings of the European Court of Justice on issues such as job discrimination (see Chapter 8.2), the activities of the European Parliament come closest to addressing the EU's persistent "democratic deficit." The direct election of its members, its expansive legislative functions, and its watchdog functions are an important link with a European citizenry familiar with the prerogatives and functions of national parliaments. Yet the European Parliament will not fully resemble a parliamentary regime until future treaty revisions give it the right to initiate legislation and the ability to more closely scrutinize the behavior of individual members of the European Commission.

Private Interests

Even though the national governments and the EU's own institutions are the pivotal instruments of power within the Community, trans-European interest groups also exercise varying degrees of influence. According to informed estimates, some three thousand groups maintain offices in Brussels with the unadorned purpose of lobbying the EU on behalf of special interests. The most important of these groups are industrial firms and employer associations, followed at a distance by organized labor. Together, representatives of private capital and labor are recognized as "social partners," who play an important role in the "low politics" of economic and social legislation.[6]

Industrial firms are represented in Brussels by two major groups: the European Round Table of Industrialists (ERT) and Business Europe, which was founded in 2007 as a successor organization to the Union of Industrial and Employers' Confederations of Europe (UNICE). ERT is made up of the chief executives of some of Europe's leading multinational companies—among them, Phillips, Royal Dutch Shell, Siemens, Fiat, Renault, Nokia, and Volvo. Created in 1985, ERT formulated the original vision of a single European market that was later transformed through the Commission and the European Council into the Single European Act.[7] Business Europe, larger and more bureaucratized than ERT, was established in 1958 to advise EU institutions on pending legislation of interest to business associations.[8] Business Europe represents forty member federations from thirty-four countries (its most prominent non-EU member states include Croatia, Norway, Switzerland, and Turkey). Institutionally, the association consists of a Council of Presidents, made up of the presidents of the national federations; a Committee of Permanent Delegates, consisting of "ambassadors" of the federations; policy committees that have functional responsibilities for economic and financial affairs, external relations, social affairs, industrial affairs, and company affairs; and a professional secretariat that coordinates the work of the policy committees and disseminates association views at both the Union and national levels. The shared policy priorities of the ERT and Business Europe include market liberalization and deregulation, which they promote through multiple informal and formal contacts primarily with Commission officials. Business Europe also uses its membership on the advisory European Economic and Social Committee for similar purposes.

Organized labor's counterpart organization is the European Trade Union Confederation (ETUC). Union leaders were initially highly skeptical of the integration movement because it seemed to benefit private business more than ordinary workers, but the economic realities of a deepening Community prompted representatives of national trade union federations in the member states to establish ETUC in 1973. It currently consists of eighty-two national trade union confederations spanning thirty-six European countries representing a combined membership of 60 million workers. ETUC gives organized labor an institutional voice on the European Economic and Social Committee and in Commission deliberations, albeit one that is not as strong as those of the better financed and more powerful ERT and Business Europe. Because of ETUC's weaker status, the Commission "has consistently bolstered ETUC in order to provide a counterweight on the labor side to UNICE on the management side." [9]

The European Commission has expressly encouraged a "social dialogue" among Business Europe, ETUC, and other labor market partners to augment the material dimensions of European integration, particularly since the advent of the Single Market in the 1980s. Their collaboration has frequently been fruitful, although the social partners have differed in their attitudes toward the Social Charter and the Social Protocol attached to the Treaty on European Union (ETUC was strongly supportive, whereas Business Europe officials were far more reserved). In recent years, both ETUC and Business Europe have constructively contributed to Commission efforts to devise strategies to promote Community-wide economic growth and reduce unemployment—especially in response to the international economic and financial crisis that began in 2008.

Citizen Inputs

Even though European citizens lack direct access to executive instruments of power in Brussels, they are able to affect Community activities in many ways. Most important, they determine the composition of national governments and the European Parliament through the electoral process. The integration movement is primarily elite-driven, but the executive bodies in the member states—and through them central EU institutions—are ultimately dependent on the general support, or electoral sanctions, of the voting public.

In addition to determining the outcome of national and European elections, voters in some of the member states exercise the right of referendum to decide the fate of crucial EU initiatives. Nowhere is this more important than in Ireland, where legal precedents require referendums on constitutional amendments and therefore on pending Union treaties. As previously recounted, a majority of Irish voters initially rejected both the Treaty of Nice and the Lisbon Treaty, only to reverse themselves in subsequent referendums. Other dramatic instances of citizen-level distrust of the EU occurred in 2005 when French and Dutch voters rejected the proposed EU constitutional treaty, thereby spelling its demise. In both cases, voter discontent over domestic political issues and leadership played a more pivotal role in the treaty's rejection than opposition to the European Union per se.

Referendums have also been common in Scandinavia. Norway has twice rejected membership in the Community through national referendums (1972 and 1994). In Denmark, six referendums have been held on the EU. In the first, in 1972, 63 percent of the electorate voted in favor of joining the EEC. A narrower majority approved the Single European Act in 1986, but in June 1992 Denmark stunned its fellow member states when 50.7 percent of voters rejected the initial version of the Treaty on European Union. Only after the European Council agreed to add a "Danish protocol" allowing the nation to opt out of the economic and monetary union did a majority of Danish voters approve the treaty in May 1993.[10] Denmark once again proved a naysayer to the EU in September 2000, when 53.1 percent of voters rejected joining the EMU and adopting the euro. In the fall of 1994, national referendums were also held in neighboring Sweden and Finland on accession to the EU, with positive outcomes in each case. In September 2003, however, a majority of 55.5 percent of Swedish voters followed the earlier Danish lead by rejecting their country's membership in the euro zone.

The linkage between public opinion and election outcomes and the European Union is meaningful, if sometimes fitful and disruptive. Recurrent voter skepticism toward the integration process reflects both citizen unease about the EU's "democratic deficit" and widespread concerns that the further harmonization of fiscal and social policies on the European level constitutes a potential threat to domestic political systems. Specifically, most of the British seem loath to cede further slices of national sovereignty to central decision-making institutions on the Continent, just as many Danes and Swedes are reluctant to relinquish distinctive features of their well-established welfare states.

Influential Individuals

Alongside collective actors such as governments, EU institutions, private interest groups, and voters, certain individuals have wielded significant influence in Community affairs. Foremost among them are the "founding fathers" of the integration process: Jean Monnet and Robert Schuman of France, Konrad Adenauer of Germany, Paul-Henri Spaak of Belgium, and Alcide De Gasperi of Italy. Together, these statesmen forged an unprecedented degree of European elite unity that was a necessary condition for launching the ECSC and EEC in the 1950s. In contrast to their more nationalist predecessors in executive office, they shared a commitment to international cooperation rooted in their individual origins as "borderland" Europeans and their shared humanistic religious values.[11] Willy Brandt, chancellor of West Germany from 1969 to 1974, similarly proved to be an effective architect of both deeper and wider European union based in his wartime exile submersion in the internationalist traditions of Norwegian and Swedish social democracy.

Activist presidents of the European Commission have also advanced the European idea. Among them are Walter Hallstein of Germany, who served as the first president of the Commission from 1958 to 1967; Roy Jenkins of the United Kingdom (1977–1981); and especially Jacques Delors of France (1985–1995). Hallstein helped to institutionalize the fledgling EEC; Jenkins skillfully managed the Community's second round of enlargement and the introduction of the European Monetary System; and Delors was a principal architect of both the Single European Act and the Economic and Monetary Union.

Romano Prodi assumed the Commission presidency in September 1999 intent on following in Delors's footsteps. His would-be activism, however, was curtailed by a more assertive European Council toward the Commission as a whole. Prodi's eclipse suggests that the autonomous authority of Commission presidents is subject to the assent of the national government officials making up the Council. This constraint has characterized the presidency of Prodi's successor, José Manuel Barraso, as well.

NOTES

1. See Haig Simonian, *The Privileged Partnership: Franco-German Relations in the European Community 1969–1984* (Oxford, UK: Clarendon Press, 1985).
2. "French Leader, in Berlin, Urges a Fast Track to Unity in Europe," *New York Times,* June 28, 2000.

3. "The Franco-German Axis Creaks," *Economist,* November 18, 2000.

4. Article 31 of the Consolidated Treaties. These provisions apply to abstentions only by one or at most a small number of EU members. If abstentions constitute a third or more of a Council vote, "the decision shall not be adopted."

5. Jerel Rosati, "Developing a Systematic Decision-Making Framework: Bureaucratic Politics in Perspective," *World Politics* 10 (1981): 234–252.

6. A third social partner is the European Center of Public Enterprises (CEEP), which represents civil servants.

7. Maria Green Cowles, "Setting the Agenda for a New Europe: The European Round Table of Industrialists and EC 1992," *Journal of Common Market Studies* 33 (December 1995): 501–526.

8. "Union of Industrial and Employers' Confederation of Europe (UNICE)," in *Encyclopedia of the European Union,* ed. Desmond Dinan (Boulder and London: Lynne Rienner, 1998), 220.

9. Desmond Dinan, *Ever Closer Union? An Introduction to European Integration,* 3rd ed. (Boulder and London: Lynne Rienner, 2005), 451.

10. They did so by a margin of 65.7 percent to 43.3 percent. In a fifth referendum on the EU in May 1998, 55.1 percent of Danish voters endorsed the Treaty of Amsterdam.

11. Monnet was active before World War I in international business in Canada and served as an international economic adviser in China and Romania during the interwar years. Schuman was born in Luxembourg, grew up in France, and studied at German universities in Bonn, Munich, and Berlin. Adenauer was a native of the Rhineland in western Germany, and so he was physically closer and personally more sympathetic to neighboring France, Luxembourg, and Belgium than to "Prussian" Berlin to the east. Similar to Chancellor Willy Brandt's experience, Spaak learned to think in global terms while in wartime exile in London. De Gasperi had served as a deputy in the Austrian parliament before becoming an Italian citizen in 1919. All were Roman Catholics.

How Is Power Used?

MULTIPLE INSTITUTIONAL, NATIONAL, AND OTHER PLAYERS INTERACT to make European Union policies—or at least try to influence them. Outside powers also play a role in helping shape Community initiatives and its use of power, beginning with the United States from the early stages of the integration process onward and including Russia, other neighboring European nonmember states, countries in the Middle East, and China.

The European Union exercises power in myriad ways and contexts. Its principal achievements have been in the realm of economics, but it has also contributed to political development through its support for democratization and market reforms on its southern and eastern peripheries and international peacekeeping through its common foreign and security policies. Its chief policy instruments include money, regulations, political example, and diplomacy.

This chapter explores the central arenas of EU policymaking and implementation—beginning with the budgetary process and continuing through economic management and expenditures, regional policies, the "Lisbon Strategy," the Single Market, rules of competition and state aids, social and environmental policies, the economic and monetary policy within the Euro Area, and foreign relations. Although the EU is not the superstate that some of its critics decry, its policies have a significant effect on European economic performance, politics, and society at large.

The Budgetary Process

European Union expenditures account for just over 1 percent of its member states' gross domestic product (GDP), but despite their comparatively small magnitude, they matter a great deal, especially with respect to economic management and regional development. The budget for 2009 totaled €133.8 billion (the equivalent of approximately $188.5 billion). The EU lacks the power to tax the member states' citizens directly, but instead draws on a variety of direct and national revenue sources to finance its operations.

Agreement on the annual budget involves complex negotiations among the European Commission, the Council of Ministers, and the European Parliament. On September 1 of each year, the European Commission submits a draft budget to the Council and Parliament based on estimates drawn up by the various EU bodies, with the exception of the European Central Bank, which manages its own finances. The consolidated treaties stipulate that revenues and expenditures must be "in balance."[1] The Commission's proposal is then debated among members of both institutions. It is at this point that national and supranational interests have sometimes clashed. The European Parliament has twice rejected the budget until compromise agreements could be negotiated with the Council and postponed its approval of the budget in 2005 in a dispute over agricultural subsidies.

Table 8-10 European Union Appropriations, 2009–2010

Source of Revenue	Budget 2010 (in billions of euros)	Budget 2010 (in rounded percentages)	Budget 2009 (in billions of euros	Change (%)
Net amount from custom duties	14.43	11.74	14.58	−2.59
VAT-based own resource at the uniform rate	13.95	11.35	13.67	+2.07
National contributions based on gross national income (GNI)	93.32	75.9	81.99	+13.86
Miscellaneous revenue	1.43	1.2	2.4	−40.10
Surplus available from the preceding financial year	—		1.8	—
Total Revenue	122.94		113.04	+8.76

Source: Part A: Introduction and Financing of the General Budget, http://eur-lex.europa.eu/budget/data/LBL2010_Vol1/EN/Vol1.pdf.

After reaching a preliminary decision, the Council submits its version of the budget to the European Parliament. Parliament then has the option of either approving or not opposing the budget, in which case it is adopted. Conversely, a majority of Parliament members may propose amendments, in which case the budget is sent back to the Commission and the Council for further consideration. The Council may then accept the amendments, which is tantamount to budgetary approval, or it may convene a meeting of a conciliation committee (made up of an equal number of members representing the Council and Parliament) to resolve differences. In that case, final approval is subject to a qualified majority among members of the Council and a majority vote in the European Parliament.[2] Once both the Council and the Parliament have approved the budget, the Commission is assigned responsibility for its execution and program management.[3]

The Union draws most of its revenue from three major sources: (1) custom duties on industrial and agricultural imports, which are collected at the point of entry and automatically transferred to Brussels; (2) a percentage of the base used to calculate value-added taxes in each member state; and (3) national contributions based on a capped rate of the annual gross national income generated in each member state. Far smaller amounts include surpluses carried over from the previous year and miscellaneous income such as interest on deposits and payments from non-EU organizations. As Table 8-10 indicates, national contributions are overwhelmingly the largest source of revenue, followed at a considerable distance by custom duties and VAT-based resources.

The largest contributors to EU revenue, in declining order, are Germany, France, Italy, and the United Kingdom. Given its diminutive population, Malta is predictably the smallest contributor. (See Table 8-11.) These disparities in budgetary contributions have periodically prompted sharp national criticism of alleged unfairness, resulting in a reluctant agreement by other Community member states to grant the United Kingdom an annual rebate in 1984 (as recounted in Chapter 8.1) but an unsuccessful attempt by Germany at a EU summit in 2000 to adjust the amount of its annual contribution.

Table 8-11 Four Largest and Four Smallest National Contributors to the 2010 Budget

Country	Total national contributions (in millions of euros)	Percentage of total national contributions
Germany	21,016	19.59
France	19,318	18.00
Italy	14,884	13.87
United Kingdom	11,173	10.41
Latvia	175	.16
Cyprus	176	.16
Estonia	135	.12
Malta	58	.05

Source: Part A: Introduction and Financing of the General Budget, http://eur-lex.europa.eu/budget/data/LBL2010_Vol1/EN/Vol1.pdf.

Economic Management and Expenditures

The EU budget breaks expenditures down into five general categories. As indicated in Table 8-12, until 2009 the largest of its appropriations was allocated to the preservation and management of natural resources, most of which is spent on the Common Agricultural Policy (CAP). Since then (and projected into the immediate future), the largest category has been sustainable growth—which includes various regional development funds. Beginning in the 2011 budget, appropriations earmarked for foreign policy activities displaced administrative expenses as the third-largest category. The smallest appropriation is apportioned to citizenship, freedom, security, and justice.

Each of these expenditure categories (with the exception of administrative salaries and related expenses) is discussed in turn, beginning with the preservation and management of natural resources by virtue of CAP's venerable status as "one of the oldest and most controversial Community policy." [4]

Preservation and Management of Natural Resources: CAP and Rural Development

Natural resource management includes the Common Agricultural Policy and support for rural development. CAP's principles were enshrined in the Treaty of Rome in 1957, and for decades CAP proved the Union's single greatest expenditure. Over the decades, CAP has been subject to repeated efforts to decrease its cost, increase its efficiency, and add new policy requirements.

As reaffirmed in the consolidated treaties,[5] the purpose of CAP is:

- "to increase agricultural productivity by promoting technical progress and by ensuring the rational development of agricultural production and the optimum utilisation of the factors of production, in particular labour;

- "thus to ensure a fair standard of living for the agricultural community, in particular by increasing the individual earnings of persons engaged in agriculture;

- "to stabilise markets;

- "to assure the availability of supplies;

- "to ensure that supplies reach consumers at reasonable prices."

Ministerial officials concluded an agreement in 1962 to promote these objectives through the creation of a unified market for the free movement of agricultural products among member states of the European Economic Community (EEC). The market was engineered to favor goods produced within the Community and protected by a common external tariff, regulated prices, the creation of a central funding mechanism financed by

Table 8-12   EU Appropriations by Category, 2007–2013 (in millions of euros and percentages of total appropriations)

Category	2007	2008	2009	2010	2011	2012	2013	Total 2007–2013
Preservation and Management of Natural Resources (including Common Agricultural Policy)	55,143	59,193	56,333	59,955	60,338	60,810	61,289	413,061
Percentage	44.0	44.4	42.0	42.6	42.0	41.5	40.1	42.4
Sustainable Growth (including Cohesion Funds)	53,979	57,653	61,696	63,555	63,638	66,628	69,621	436,770
Percentage	43.8	43.6	45.9	45.4	44.8	45.6	46.1	44.8
Foreign Policy	6,578	7,002	7,440	7,893	8,430	8,997	9,595	55,935
Percentage	5.3	5.3	5.5	5.6	5.9	6.1	6.3	5.7
Citizenship, Freedom, Security, Justice	1,273	1,362	1,518	1,693	1,889	2,105	2,376	12,216
Percentage	1.0	1.1	1.1	1.2	1.3	1.4	1.6	1.2
Administration	7,039	7,380	7,525	7,882	8,334	8,670	9,095	55,925
Percentage	6.0	5.7	5.7	5.6	5.8	5.9	6.0	5.7
Total	124,457	132,797	134,722	141,273	142,629	147,210	151,976	974,769

Source: European Commission, Financial Programming and Budget, *Budget in Figures, General Budget of the European Union for the Financial Year 2010,* http://ec.europa.eu/budget/documents/2010_en.htm?go=t1_0#table-1_0. Percentage allocations calculated by the author. The percentages for 2007–2013 represent averages.

levies on industrial and agricultural imports to be administered by the European Commission, internal subsidies to encourage production (to ensure an equitable standard of living for farmers), and export subsidies designed to make European products competitive on the world market. These provisions were implemented by 1968.

In subsequent years, CAP succeeded in achieving its declared treaty objectives of increased production, market stabilization, a plentiful and diverse food supply, and higher incomes for farmers. At the same time, CAP generated a host of unforeseen problems. Guaranteed prices led to over-production of a number of products (including milk, butter, and wine) and costly storage arrangements at the expense of the EEC; moreover, subsidies to farmers in a noncompetitive market resulted in high prices for consumers. Financing the system became steadily more expensive, so that by the 1960s CAP's share of the annual EEC budget exceeded 50 percent. In addition, the system yielded unfair advantages to larger farmers over smaller ones and to some member states over others. France, with its strong agrarian lobby, in particular enjoyed a proportionally higher level of agrarian subsidies than its neighbors.

These shortcomings prompted a series of reform measures by the Council of Ministers. The first initiative was the Mansholt Plan of 1968 (named after the commissioner of agriculture at the time). The plan entailed the introduction during the 1980s of a "co-responsibility" levy on dairy farmers to help cover the cost of storage of milk and cheese products, the introduction of milk production quotas, and a cap on future CAP spending. An even more radical policy shift followed in 1992 with the MacSherry Plan (also named after an agricultural commissioner), which called for price cuts for certain products, including beef and grain; subsidies to farmers to withdraw land from production and to practice better environmental protection measures; and a partial shift from price supports to direct income payments to farmers.

The European Council endorsed the next major reform at a summit in Berlin in 1999 in anticipation of the then-pending enlargement of the Union into Central and Eastern Europe. With its adoption of a comprehensive political agreement known as *Agenda 2000*, the Council mandated that CAP should promote greater EU competition on the world market through a reduction in the price of agrarian products. This goal would be achieved by cutting production subsidies for grain, milk and milk products, and beef and veal. Direct income payments would compensate farmers for their loss of subsidies. The reform also called for a new system of national financial allocations that would allow member states to distribute agricultural aid "according to their own priorities, subject to certain Community criteria to prevent distortions of competition."[6] In addition, *Agenda 2000* introduced a new dimension of agrarian policy in the form of financial support for rural development to be financed in part through regional funds (discussed below). Its declared purpose—as outlined in a detailed plan spanning 2007–2013—is to encourage diversification of the rural economy, improve the environment and the countryside, and improve the competitiveness of the agricultural and forestry sectors.[7] Since 2000 the EU has allocated nearly €4.4 million (approximately $6.2 million) a year to these objectives.[8]

Changes envisaged in *Agenda 2000* were codified in a mid-term review of CAP submitted by the European Commission in July 2002. The Commission's policy recommendations included provisions to decouple direct aid and production, simplify the system of direct payments to farmers, and reduce intervention prices in various agrarian sectors. The European Council endorsed the Commission's proposals the following January. In November 2008 the EU's agricultural ministers agreed to further measures to decouple direct aid from production and allow for greater flexibility in allocating funds to sectors with special problems, such as those involving environmental measures or "improving the quality and marketing of products in that sector." The commissioner's decision also calls for phasing out of milk quotas by April 2015, an increase in support for rural development, and provisions for investment aid to young farmers.[9]

CAP was augmented with the creation in 2000 of the European Agricultural Guidance and Guarantee Fund. Its purpose was to promote sustainable rural development through measures to modernize and diversify agricultural investments and encourage younger farmers to stay on the land. This fund was superseded by the European Agricultural Fund for Rural Development, which was established in 2006 with the same general objectives. The Council approved funding of €5 billion (nearly $7 billion) for 2009–2010 for investment in biodiversity, water management, dairy restructuring, renewable energy programs, and the development of rural broadband infrastructure.[10]

The cumulative effect of these policy reforms has been to reduce CAP expenditures, promote market flexibility in place of centralized bureaucratic management, introduce greater self-discipline among farmers, and encourage rural development. The reforms have also increased EU bargaining leverage in international negotiations to reduce global barriers to freer world trade. In the view of European critics, even bolder measures are warranted. In November 2007 former agricultural minister Mariann Fischer Boel from Denmark called for the elimination of agrarian subsidies altogether—a radical proposal that met with tepid response from her colleagues but might prove feasible in future CAP reforms.

Sustainable Growth and Regional Policies

The member states of the European Union represent enormous variety in levels of economic development, national income, and employment prospects. Observers often speak of discernible "north-south," "east-west," and "core-periphery" divisions between the richer and poorer regions. Exacerbating this problem has been the successive enlargement of the EC/EU to include, first, Spain, Portugal, and Greece on the southern periphery, and, second, ten post-communist governments to the east. Discernible regional differences also exist within individual member states. Northern Italy is far more industrialized and wealthier than southern Italy; the reverse is true of regional contrasts between northern and southern England and western and eastern parts of Germany.

To address material and social differences between and within the member states, the European Union has adopted an active regional policy to promote economic cohesion within the Community by reducing economic disparities. The beginnings of a regional policy can be traced back to the Treaty of Rome, and major new financial commitments to development and economic-social cohesion within the Community were initiated under the Delors Commission, coinciding with the implementation of the Single Market program and the Single European Act. The admission of twelve new member states since 2004 has further underscored the importance of activist regional development measures.

Regional policy is channeled through various structural funds designed to promote economic development and greater social cohesion within the Community. These include:

1. The European Social Fund (ESF), which was created in 1958 to promote employment and vocational training. The ESF will distribute some €75 billion (approximately $104.5 billion) to member states for these purposes during the period 2007–2013.[11]

2. The European Regional Development Fund (ERDF), established in 1975. Its assigned purpose is to cofinance investments with national and subnational governments to promote the creation or maintenance of jobs, strengthen regional infrastructure, and encourage local development initiatives spearheaded by small and medium-size enterprises.[12] In pursuing these objectives, the ERDF focuses on the following missions:

   - Objective 1: Eligible regions are those in which the per capita GDP is below 75 percent of the Community average. These currently include most of Central and Eastern Europe, southern Italy; much of Greece, Portugal, and Spain; parts of the United Kingdom and eastern Germany; and the thinly populated areas of Sweden and Finland. Nearly 156 million EU inhabitants are affected.

   - Objective 2: regions experiencing an unemployment rate higher than the Community average caused by laggard performance in the industrial and service

Pictured is a prototype of one of Poland's super-fast PKP Intercity railway trains, which will be in service in time for Euro 2012, the 14th European Championship. The train will be modeled after France's TGV. The European Union is providing 50 percent of the funds to pay for the railroad modernization project.

Source: Pitchal Frederic/Corbis Sygma

sectors, a decline in traditional sectors in rural areas, and difficulties facing the fishing industry. Targeted regions include much of northern England; most of Spain not covered by Objective 1 assistance; much of central France and central Italy; parts of Austria, southern Finland, and the Baltic states; and most of Cyprus. The European Commission reports that 15 percent of the total population of the EU is affected by Objective 2 aid.

- Interregional cooperation designed to strengthen economic and social cohesion across national boundaries and between remote regions and more developed areas. Examples include the Atlantic area, the Baltic Sea region, and southwestern Europe.[13]

3. The European Investment Bank (EIB), which was founded in 1958 with the purpose of making long-term loans for capital investment projects. The bank is owned by the member states and operates wholly outside of the EU budget. The EIB provides loans to public and private bodies and enterprises for up to 50 percent of the investment costs of a project, technical assistance, and venture capital to small and medium-size enterprises.[14] Projects funded by the EIB must promote EU objectives—including economic and social cohesion and convergence, innovation

aimed at fostering the development of a knowledge-based economy, the development of trans-European networks in the areas of transport and energy supplies, and improvements in the urban environment. According to its 2007 annual report, the EIB invested €41.4 billion (approximately $57.8 billion) in the member states and European Free Trade Association countries and €6.4 billion ($8.9 billion) in neighboring nonmember countries.[15]

4. The Cohesion Fund, implemented in May 1994. Its stated objective is to help member states stabilize economic development and reduce social disparities. To this end, the fund finances up to 85 percent "of eligible expenditure of major projects involving the environment and transport infrastructure." Eligible recipient nations are those whose per capita GNP is less than 90 percent of the EU average. In 2005–2006 the Cohesion Fund invested €28.2 billion ($39.3 billion) in these countries. The European Commission determined that after 2006 the activities of the Cohesion Fund would be more closely integrated with the EU's other structural funds.[16]

The Lisbon Strategy

Augmenting the Union's regional development policies is a broad initiative launched by the European Council in March 2000 during the Portuguese presidency, appropriately named the Lisbon Strategy. Its ambitious purpose was to make the Community more internationally competitive and achieve full employment by 2010 (the latter goal has proven wholly unrealistic in light of subsequent financial and economic upheavals throughout the world). The Lisbon Strategy spelled out a ten-year action and development plan that called for the transition to a more dynamic knowledge-based economy and the "modernization" of human resources through increased investments in education and means to promote greater labor mobility. An environmental component added in 2001 at a European Council meeting in Sweden would "draw attention to the fact that economic growth must be decoupled from the use of natural resources."[17] From the outset, members of the European Council decreed that the implementation of the Lisbon Strategy would depend heavily on supportive measures by member state governments.

The Lisbon Strategy failed to achieve the European Council's early anticipated results. As an adviser to the European Commission on the effects of pending EU enlargement, Dutch prime minister Wim Kok conducted a review of the Lisbon process in 2002 in which he concluded that the EU must redouble its efforts to promote growth and job creation. The Commission acted on Kok's assessment in February 2005 by proposing that the Lisbon Strategy be streamlined through a clear division of policy responsibilities between the Community and member state governments. The latter were required to submit detailed three-year national reform programs containing specific information on implementation and results in their country. The first of the reports were submitted in 2006, prompting the Council to issue a salutary report in 2008 welcoming results achieved during the initial three-year cycle. At the same time, Council members soberly acknowledged that further structural reforms throughout the Union "are now particularly important against a backdrop of a slowdown of the economy, higher oil and commodity prices, and ongoing turbulence on financial markets."[18]

The Single Market

One of the most important uses of regulatory power to deepen European integration and promote economic growth is the attainment of a Single Market for the free movement of goods, finances, services, and people within the Community. As recounted in Chapter 8.1, the blueprint for the Single Market was laid out in the White Paper of 1985, which was drawn up by the European Commission during the early tenure of Jacques Delors as president and promptly endorsed by the European Council. The impetus for moving beyond the established common market came from a combination of business interests, Commission personnel, and members of the European Parliament with a shared interest in making the Community more prosperous and internationally more competitive. Its essence, as spelled out in 282 directives contained in the White Paper—which obligated the member states to enact appropriate enabling legislation—was the elimination of technical, physical, and fiscal barriers that impeded economic union. The Commission and the Council set December 1982 as the deadline for implementing the Single Market.

The principal features of the White Paper included:

- The abolition of most physical controls on the transport of goods across national frontiers within the Community.

- The elimination of "barriers created by different national product regulations and standards" through the introduction of a mutual recognition principle that would allow the free entry of "goods lawfully manufactured and marketed in one Member State . . . into other Member States."

- The removal of fiscal barriers and the harmonization of national value-added tax (VAT) systems, which involved the introduction of a standard Community-wide VAT rate of 15 percent (with permissible national exceptions for such items as food, medicines, and books that would qualify for a lower rate) and the elimination of border controls for VAT.

- Community-wide liberalization of public procurement in construction and services.

- The free movement of self-employed workers and professionals through a general system of mutual recognition of the comparability of university studies, degrees, and diplomas. As a corollary to this principle, the Commission declared its intention "to increase its support for cooperation programmes between [higher] education establishments in different Member States with a view to promoting the mobility of students, facilitating the academic recognition of degrees and thus diplomas, and helping young people, in whose hands the future of the Community's economy lies, to think in European terms."

- The liberalization and harmonization of financial services and "financial products" such as insurance policies, savings contracts, and consumer credit.[19]

Alongside requisite national legislation to implement the directives mandated by the White Paper, the Single European Act of 1987 enhanced Community capacity to govern the Single Market by extending administrative powers of the European Commission in areas of social policy, research, and the environment. In addition, the act introduced the important principle of qualified majority voting in decisions by both the European Council and Council of Ministers.

An important adjunct to the Single Market was the abolition of frontier passport controls among most of the member states. This goal was achieved through the progressive implementation of the Schengen Agreement, named after the location in Luxembourg where it was signed in 1985 by France, Germany, and the Benelux countries. After Greece, Italy, Portugal, and Spain came on board, the Schengen accord became operational in 1992. The agreement guarantees the free movement of persons and established common rules governing visa requirements, asylum requests, and border controls. It also created a framework for transnational cooperation between police services and judicial authorities. A core component is the Schengen Information System, which links national data base systems to facilitate information exchange concerning missing persons, arrest warrants, and false passports.[20]

The Schengen accord was incorporated into the EU's legal and institutional system under the Treaty of Amsterdam and is an integral part of today's consolidated treaties. Thirty states are currently members of the Schengen area, including three non-EU countries: Iceland, Norway, and Switzerland. Ten Central and East European member states joined in December 2008. Border controls remain in place in Bulgaria, Cyprus, and Romania, pending a decision to eliminate them by the European Council. The United Kingdom and Ireland remain outside the Schengen area, although they have the right of consultation and cooperation with participating members.

Rules on Competition and State Aids

Much of the construction of the Single Market involves what economists call "negative integration," or the elimination of discriminatory barriers to freedom of movement across national borders. Accompanying these measures are complementary forms of "positive integration," which A. M. El-Agraa defines as "the modification of exiting instruments and institutions and, more importantly, the creation of new ones so as to enable the market of the integrated area to function properly and effectively and also to promote other broader policy aims of the union." [21] An important instrument of positive integration is the delegation of national political authority by the member states to the European Commission to enforce common rules on competition and state aids.

Jean Monnet and other founding leaders of the European integration movement were inspired by the American precedent of antitrust legislation and the dismantling of cartels in occupied Germany after World War II to assign regulatory policies to the fledgling EEC. Council directives and decisions by the European Court of Justice during the 1960s expanded the regulatory power of the Commission and the ascendancy of European law in enforcing competition policies. The Treaty on European Union elaborated common rules governing competition and state aids, which have been retained in the consolidated treaties. Article 102 in Title VII of the Treaty on the Functioning of the European Union expressly proclaims: "Any abuse by one or more undertakings of a dominant position within the internal market or in a substantial part of it shall be prohibited as incompatible with the internal market in so far as it may affect trade between

Member States." Examples of such abuse include price fixing and "limiting production, markets or technical development to the prejudice of consumers."

The European Commission is assigned responsibility for enforcing these provisions, including authorizing member state governments to undertake remedial measures. It is specifically authorized to monitor restrictive practices and abuse of dominant positions and to pre-approve company mergers with EU-wide dimensions. In July 2009 the Commission exercised its antitrust powers by fining major German and French energy cartels $1.53 billion because they had maintained a market-sharing agreement not to sell imported Russian gas on each other's markets despite the liberalization of European gas markets.[22]

The consolidated treaties are similarly firm with respect to government subsidies or tax breaks that unduly benefit national enterprises or services. Article 107 states in seemingly unequivocal language: "any aid granted by a Member State or through State resources in any form whatsoever which distorts or threatens to distort competition by favouring certain undertakings or the production of certain goods shall, in so far as it affects trade between Member States, be incompatible with the internal market." The treaty allows permissible—if potentially disingenuous—exceptions to this general rule with respect to government measures to promote economic development in areas "where the standard of living is abnormally low or where there is serious underemployment," aid of a "social character" granted to individual consumers, and "aid to make good the damage caused by natural disasters or exceptional occurrences."

On balance, the Commission has been relatively more successful in enforcing antitrust rules than in curbing state aid. It succeeded in blocking a proposed merger of General Electric and Honeywell in 2001, and compelled the Microsoft Corporation—under threat of a lawsuit—to agree in 2009 to distribute browsers of European software companies through its Windows operating system. In May 2009 the Commission levied a $1.45 billion fine for antitrust violations against Intel on charges that the company had illegally used its dominance in the European market to discriminate against competitors. (Intel promptly announced it would appeal the decision.) Google has also been targeted by the European Commission and individual member state governments on charges of alleged invasions of privacy on its site.

In contrast, a number of governments in the EU have resisted Commission efforts to curtail state aid to designated industries or sectors. Among them are France, Italy, and Spain, all of which maintain traditions of "state intervention and 'indicative' [economic] planning."[23] The German government has pursued a more subtle form of resistance, mainly because economic and social dislocations in the wake of national unification in 1990 have compelled extensive public investment in the eastern states. Despite occasional conflicts between the European Commission and individual member states, state aid as a percentage of GDP has declined as a result of the economic and monetary union among a majority of EU states and the diffusion of neoliberal attitudes toward economic management. Brian Ardy reports that the percentage has fallen from 3 percent during the first half of the 1980s to 0.6 percent in 2004.[24]

Social Policy and the Environment

In addition to the implementation of the Single Market and the extension of the Commission's regulatory authority to enforce rules of competition, the Union is committed to promoting a "social dimension" to augment the material effects of economic integration. This commitment has taken the form of an ambitious Social Charter, which eleven of the then-twelve members of the European Council endorsed in 1989,[25] and the adoption by the European Commission of a "renewed social agenda" in 2008. Both documents are largely rhetorical affirmations of the need for greater social and economic cohesion, expanded investments in vocational training and job creation, and greater gender equality. Few resources are available to EU officials for pursuing these objectives. Instead, the Union relies primarily on the member states for the implementation of social policy. They, rather than the EU, are primarily responsible for administering and funding basic social services such as health care and unemployment benefits.

The European Union is relatively more successful in pursuing an activist environmental policy than its social policy. In collaboration with its member states, the EU has utilized the Commission's regulatory powers to aggressively promote environmental health and comprehensive "green" standards for recycling, air quality, water purity, sustainable energy technologies, and the use of pesticides in agriculture. In 2002 the Council of Ministers and the European Parliament adopted an action program for 2002–2012 that emphasizes continued efforts to sustain high environmental standards in these and other areas such as climate change.[26] Some EU environmental policies—such as the Commission's strict regulation of imports of genetically modified food—have generated trade disputes, especially with the United States.

The EU and other international participants failed in their efforts to achieve agreement on an international treaty limiting greenhouse gas emissions at the December 2009 Copenhagen climate conference, but the European Council promptly reaffirmed a conditional offer by the Community "to move to a 30% reduction by 2020 compared to 1990 levels, provided that other developed countries commit themselves to comparable emission reductions and that developing countries contribute adequately according to their responsibilities and respective capabilities." In the same statement, the EU and its member states signaled their willingness to contribute €2.4 billion ($3.25 billion) to implement the agreement.[27] The EU is the world's first group of nations to offer such an incentive to help developing countries.

The Euro Area: Achievements and Crisis

An important corollary area of positive integration is the EU's implementation of the Economic and Monetary Union (EMU) in 1999 and the introduction of the euro as a common currency among qualified and willing member states on January 1, 2001. By 2009 seventeen countries belonged to the euro zone: Austria, Belgium, Cyprus, Denmark, Finland, France, Germany, Greece, Ireland, Italy, Luxembourg, Malta, the Netherlands, Slovakia, Slovenia, Spain, and Portugal. Several "mini-states" have also adopted the euro as their currency: Monaco, San Marino, and Vatican City, although they do not formally belong to the EMU. As previously noted, the United Kingdom, Denmark, and Sweden have so far opted out of membership even though they qualify according to the economic convergence criteria contained in the Treaty on European Union. Prospects for Polish membership in the euro zone were clouded in 2010 because of domestic conflicts between opposing political blocs and personalities over implementing the requisite economic reforms to qualify.[28] Estonia joined at the beginning of 2011.

As recounted in Chapter 8.2, the European Central Bank (ECB) administers the EMU on behalf of the Union. The Treaty on European Union, which established the legal basis for the EMU, accords the ECB complete independence from governments and other EU bodies, although events have demonstrated that it is not wholly immune from politics. An early indication was French pressure to appoint a French banker as first president of the powerful executive board. After elaborate negotiations, member states named a Dutch national, but in a compromise political gesture he agreed to serve only the first half of his term before relinquishing it to a French banker. His successor, Jean-Claude Trichet, a former governor of the Bank of France, has served since 2003, and his term expires in 2011.

The ECB is empowered to make and administer monetary policy in the Euro Area, which has important indirect effects on the monetary policies of nonmember states as well. Alongside its responsibility to issue euro bills and coins, the primary treaty-assigned task of the ECB is to promote price stability. The principal means to this end is the bank's control of the supply of money in circulation, which it manages through its power to set interest rates. The ECB is also charged with holding and managing the foreign reserves of the member states and conducting foreign exchange operations.

From the outset, a hallmark of ECB policy has been its determination to contain inflation through a strict monetarist policy—reminiscent of the earlier policies of the German Federal Bank after which the ECB is modeled. From 2000 through the summer of 2008, the bank doggedly maintained an average interest rate of 4.5 percent despite recurrent pressure from some governments and enterprises to lower it to facilitate cheaper borrowing. Its policies succeeded to the extent that the average monthly inflation rate in the euro zone from 2006 through 2008 was 2.5 percent. Only in response to the international financial crisis triggered in 2007 did the Governing Board reduce the rate to an unprecedented 1.0 percent in July 2008. Because of falling demand triggered by recession, the Euro Area's monthly inflation rate averaged only 0.7 percent through 2009.[29]

In response to the worsening global economic crisis, national governments and various EU institutions undertook multiple initiatives to encourage the restoration of financial confidence within member states and the Community at large. These included government measures to increase deposit guarantees at banks and the declaration of a Commission commitment "to promote transparency and responsibility in the financial sector and support the development of the internal market." The European Parliament chimed in with demands for legislation "to improve the framework for the supervision of hedge funds and private equity and . . . new rules to provide greater transparency in hedge fund and private equity policies."[30] EU officials met repeatedly in various venues—including sessions of the European Council, the Eurogroup, and the euro zone's largest industrial members—to discuss coordinated measures to strengthen the financial systems.

In April 2009 leaders of France, Germany, Italy, Spain, and the United Kingdom conferred with the government heads of fifteen major industrial and developing nations at a Group of Twenty (G-20) summit in London. Collectively, the participants agreed to provide $1.1 trillion to help restore international confidence, growth, and jobs, but the deliberations revealed a deep policy chasm between Anglo-American support for expansive government-sponsored stimulus packages to help jump-start stalled economies and a preference by France, Germany, and Italy for tighter regulation of financial markets and reliance on their countries' established social safety networks to ease the effects of increased unemployment. These differences were papered over in a final communiqué that affirmed the need for joint action to monitor more closely the international financial system but was short on specific enforcement mechanisms and a coordinated program of stimulus measures.[31]

For the rest of the year and into 2010, the economic record was mixed. The EU's two strongest economies—Germany and France—were able to achieve a modest restoration of growth by emphasizing job retention and environmental innovation.[32] In disturbing contrast, however, member states on the EU's southern periphery experienced continuing recession and deepening budget deficits caused by profligate government spending during times of easy credit. Whereas growth rates in both France and Germany (as well as Poland) exceeded the performance level forecast for the Euro Area as a whole, Greece, Italy, Portugal, and Spain all performed below the projected average.[33]

In an urgent attempt to stave off a potential collapse of the Greek economy due to a staggering national debt exceeding 12.7 percent of its GNP, in March 2010 EU member states and the IMF reluctantly agreed to a financial rescue package—accompanied by a firm deadline for repayment—totaling the equivalent of $146 billion. In return, Greek officials announced draconian budget cuts designed to reduce the country's deficit to less than 3 percent by 2012.[34] The cost of the bailout proved immensely unpopular in much of northern Europe, especially in Germany, where voters dealt the governing Christian Democrats a stunning electoral defeat in state elections in North Rhine–Westphalia in May. In Greece, thousands of citizens took to the streets to protest the cuts.

The crisis in Greece underscored anew the fundamental contradiction between the ECB's power to regulate monetary policy within the euro zone, on the one hand, and continued national political autonomy to conduct fiscal policy (including taxation, borrowing, and government spending), on the other. Whether member states would ever be willing to countenance an extension of Community power over national fiscal policies is a highly controversial idea. A more likely response is ad hoc intervention by the more affluent member states, similar to the aid package to Greece, to shore up weaknesses elsewhere in the euro zone. The alternative—a collapse of the euro system—is theoretically conceivable but unlikely because of the enormous economic and political costs it would entail. To help avert such a calamity, members of the European Council established a rescue fund of €750 billion—the equivalent of about $1 trillion—in May 2010 to help other troubled Euro Zone members. (German Chancellor Angela Merkel has resisted initiatives by ministers in other EU governments and the International Monetary Fund to increase the size of the fund.) In addition, the European Council agreed at a summit meeting in October 2010 to endorse recommendations of a Task Force on Economic Governance calling on member states to increase fiscal discipline, deepen policy coordination, and establish a new institutional framework for crisis management.

The EU as a Global Player

The external outreach of EU power touches on the entire global community, with particular significance accorded its relations with the United States, Russia, and China. The Union also has vested foreign policy interests in non-member European countries, the Middle East, and world trade negotiations. Its policies embrace an array of bilateral and multilateral instruments.

Relations with the United States

The United States commands a special relationship with the European Union by virtue of history, politics, and economics. In addition to deeply rooted ethnic and cultural ties based on centuries of immigration and a shared civilization, Europe and the United States have together experienced two world wars and post–World War II initiatives to create a security community free of the threat of armed conflict within the North Atlantic region. The institutionalization of that community through the parallel creation of NATO and the Western European Union for collective defense purposes coincided with early moves to launch the European integration movement. From the outset, the United States has been a vital participant in the economic and political reconstruction of Europe and the evolution of the European Union out of the initial impetus of the Marshall Plan aid program and successive stages in the expansion of a transnational community.

Diplomatic relations were established between the United States and the European Coal and Steel Community in 1953. Ambassadorial status was accorded the European Economic Community's delegation to the United States (in Washington, D.C.) in 1971. The two sides institutionalized regular high-level political consultations with the Transatlantic Declaration in 1990, which established the machinery for biannual meetings between the U.S. president and presidents of the European Council and the European Parliament. In 1995 the United States and the EU adopted a joint action plan that committed both partners to intensified cooperation in promoting international peace, stability, democratization, and economic development. Bilateral diplomatic relations are augmented by extensive academic, educational, scientific, and cultural exchanges and cooperation.

Economics is a core pillar of the North Atlantic partnership. The EU and the United States are each other's principal trading partners. Together they account for 60 percent of global GDP, 30 percent of world trade in goods, and 42 percent of world trade in services. In 2007 EU countries exported €260 billion in goods to the United States ($354.8 billion) and imported €180 billion ($245.6 billion) in goods. Trade in services included EU exports of €139.0 billion ($189.68 billion) to the United States and imports from the United States totaling €127.9 billion ($174.5 billion). U.S. direct investments in EU countries amounted to €144.5 billion ($197.2 billion); investments from member states in the U.S. economy totaled €112.6 billion ($153.6 billion).[35] Regular economic policy consultations are conducted through organized business, legislative, and consumer "dialogues."[36] Trade disputes occasionally flare up between the EU and the United States, mainly over charges of discriminatory import regulations and food safety, but according to Commission calculations, they impact only about 2 percent of trans-Atlantic trade.[37]

Military security is a second major foundation block of partnership between the United States and the EU. Ten West European countries joined with the United States and Canada in establishing NATO in 1949; the alliance expanded in tandem with the escalation of the cold war during the 1950s and 1960s to include other strategic European players such as West Germany, Greece, Spain, and Turkey. Today, twenty-one EU member states belong to NATO, including ten former communist countries that have joined since 1999. Five nonaligned EU states (Austria, Finland, Ireland, Malta, and Sweden) are members of NATO's Partnership for Peace, a nonmilitary program launched in 1994 to promote cooperation with non-NATO countries (including the Russian Federation and various former communist republics in Eastern Europe).

Security issues commonly involve greater reliance on bilateral negotiations between the United States and individual European countries than is characteristic of economic relations within the North Atlantic area, as evidenced by recent American initiatives to bypass the EU in negotiating directly with the governments of Poland, the Czech Republic, and Romania about stationing components of a new antimissile defensive shield on their territory.

The Russian Bear

Daunting historical legacies, expansive economic and political ties in the postcommunist era, and intermittent conflicts characterize relations between individual European countries and the EU as a whole and its towering neighbor to the east: Russia. Successive military invasions from the West dating from Swedish expansion in the seventeenth century continued through the Napoleonic wars in the early nineteenth century, Imperial Germany's defeat of the Czarist empire in World War I, and Nazi Germany's savage onslaught during World War II. The Soviet Union's defeat of Germany on the eastern front and its occupation of much of Central and Eastern Europe helped create the postwar division of Europe into hostile communist and democratic-capitalist camps. Soviet bellicosity during the cold war strengthened West European resolve to forge a military alliance with the United States and initiate the regional integration process. Stalin and his successors viewed the European Coal and Steel Community and the European Economic Community with deep suspicion as integral features of an alleged capitalist encirclement. Accordingly, the Soviet leaders refused to accord diplomatic relations to the European Community and to cultivate meaningful economic relations. This policy of self-imposed isolation began to change only after Mikhail Gorbachev's rise to power in the mid-1980s and his determination to improve ties with the West as a means to facilitate far-reaching reforms at home.

The subsequent implosion of communism throughout Central and Eastern Europe—including the Soviet Union itself—set the stage for a fundamental reorientation of EU-Russian relations. Building on principles of economic assistance already in place in Poland, Hungary, and other former communist regimes, the European Commission extended technical aid to the Russian Federation in 1991 to help the government pursue its dual transitions to democracy and a market economy. Within a scant two years, assistance to Russia spiraled from $254 million to $9.7 billion. The level of assistance declined through the remainder of the decade in tandem with the incipient success of market reforms and the infusion of direct investments from the West.[38]

The EEC's early initiative has been expanded under the EU into more extensive links with the Russian Federation. The 1991 economic assistance program—designated TACIS (Technical Aid to the Commonwealth of Independent States)—was supplanted in 1994 by a Partnership and Cooperation Agreement. The partnership agreement, which was extended in 1997, calls for closer EU-Russian economic integration, a relaxation of mutual visa requirements, joint efforts to combat terrorism, and an expansion of educational exchange and joint research endeavors. Most of the same objectives are incorporated in a parallel European Neighbourhood and Partnership Instrument with various successor states to the former Soviet Union and other countries. The Partnership and Cooperation Agreement has been augmented by an EU pledge to provide €60 million ($82.6 million) annually to pursue these objectives plus additional funds to promote nuclear safely in the Russian Federation.[39] Supplementing the network of intergovernmental linkages is the growing importance of trade, dominated by Russian exports of oil and gas. Russia currently ranks as the EU's third-largest trading partner after the United States and China.

681

Despite these positive achievements, various conflicts have clouded European-Russian relations. One is Russia's intermittent disruption of gas exports through Ukraine to a number of European countries. On three occasions (in 2005, 2008, and 2009) the Russian state-run gas monopoly, Gasprom, temporarily cut off or reduced gas exports because of commercial disputes (albeit with political overtones) over the price of gas and Ukrainian charges for pipeline transit. A second energy dispute erupted in 2008 when Gasprom announced it would construct a pipeline—with German financial backing—under the Baltic Sea. Known as Nord Stream, the pipeline will bypass both the Ukraine and Poland to allow the direct export of gas from Russia to Germany and West European markets beyond. Polish officials promptly objected to the project on political grounds, alleging that their government was not sufficiently consulted about the agreement and hinting that it would make Germany too energy dependent on a potentially volatile Russia. Representatives of other EU countries bordering on the Baltic—notably Denmark, Estonia, Finland, and Sweden—were initially skeptical for environmental reasons, fearing that construction of the pipeline could damage the Baltic seabed. After receiving assurances from Russia and Germany that the environment would be sufficiently protected, they approved the project in 2009. The completion date was set for 2012. In 2007 Russia had already announced plans to construct a southern pipeline that would cross Bulgaria (with a branch going into Turkey) and pass through Italy to France. Known as South Stream, the second pipeline is also due for completion in 2012.

Nationalism has fueled more vitriolic confrontations. A decision by Estonian officials in April 2007 to move a Soviet-era bronze soldier memorial from the center of the country's capital to a location on its outskirts provoked a massive cyber attack against Estonian ministries, parliament, political parties, banks, and other offices, which caused a breakdown in public and private communications and prompted widespread concern within NATO ranks about the threat of cyber warfare to national security in all Western societies. The Estonian foreign minister and other officials attributed the attacks to Russian authorities, which the Russian government denied; several pro-Kremlin youth groups later claimed responsibility. No one has been officially charged.

An armed conflict between Russia and a neighboring European country erupted in August 2008 when Russian and Georgian forces clashed over opposing territorial claims to two disputed Georgian provinces on Russia's border. The republic of Georgia, which had declared its independence from the former Soviet Union in 1991, claimed jurisdiction over the provinces, even though they had effectively broken away from Georgian control in the early 1990s under de facto Russian protectorship. When Georgian troops attempted to wrest military control of the provinces, Russia counterattacked and invaded parts of Georgia itself. The Bush administration offered rhetorical support to Georgia, which it had designated a potential member of NATO, but relinquished political initiative for responding to the conflict to the European Union. EU government officials promptly closed ranks and agreed at an emergency meeting of the European Council at the beginning of September to suspend further talks on a new partnership agreement with Russia until the Russian government agreed to withdraw troops from Georgian territory. French president Nicolas Sarkozy then brokered a ceasefire between Russia and Georgia, which was enforced by some three hundred unarmed peace monitors recruited from EU member states and dispatched to regions bordering on the disputed provinces. Over Western objections, Russia subsequently recognized the two provinces as independent states. International tensions gradually abated as both sides recognized that the conflict involved a very limited war that did not significantly change the strategic balance between West and East.[40] The EU has resumed policy consultations with Russia in a series of high-level meetings devoted to trade, energy, and environmental issues.

China

The European Union's relations with China are driven primarily by trade. Diplomatic relations were established in 1975, and a decade later the two systems concluded a Trade and Cooperation Agreement that was subsequently broadened into a Partnership and Cooperation Agreement. In recent years China has become the EU's second most important trading partner after the United States, and in 2009 China displaced Germany as the world's largest exporting nation. The trade balance is heavily skewed in favor of China, which in 2008 exported €247.6 billion (approximately $337.4 billion) worth of primarily industrial goods to the EU compared to imports from the EU of €78.4 billion ($106.8 billion). Direct investments by EU firms in China that year totaled €4.5 billion ($6.1 billion)) in contrast to Chinese investments in the EU of a scant €1 billion ($136 million).[41]

The EU strongly endorsed Chinese membership in the World Trade Organization, which it joined in 2001, on the grounds "that a WTO without China was not truly universal in scope."[42] Despite this conciliatory stance, trade relations between the two partners have been a source of recurrent conflict. The European Commission imposed antidumping duties on Chinese shoe imports in 2006, which it extended in 2009. These steps prompted the Chinese government to file an unfair trade case with the WTO against the EU, arguing that the EU's actions "caused damage to the legitimate rights and interests of Chinese exporters." China complained again to the WTO in early 2010. The Commission spokesman for trade issues responded by saying, "Anti-dumping measures are not about protectionism, they're about fighting unfair trade. Our decision was taken on the basis of clear evidence that dumping of Chinese products has taken place and that this is harming the otherwise competitive E.U. [shoe] industry."[43]

Human rights issues are also an object of EU-Chinese contention. The General Affairs and External Relations Council joined the British government in strongly condemning the execution in late 2009 of a Pakistan-born British businessman who was sentenced to death on charges of importing several kilos of heroin in his baggage aboard an airline. In early 2010 Catherine Ashton, the EU's new High Representative for Foreign Affairs and Security Policy, protested the unexplained disappearance of a prominent Chinese human rights activist from his home as well as the conviction of Liu Xiaobo, another human rights activist, on charges of "inciting subversion of state power" when, in the official view of the EU, he had been exercising the legitimate right of free speech.[44] In October 2010 the imprisoned Liu Xiaobo was awarded the Nobel Peace Prize in recognition of his role in promoting democratic rights in China.

European Neighborhood Policy, Iraq, and Iran

The EU draws on its economic and diplomatic resources to pursue active foreign policies toward a number of regions and countries in addition to those discussed above. Similar to its partnership agreement with Russia, the EU has concluded a series of action programs with sixteen countries in Eastern Europe and the Middle East. Established in 2004 under the aegis of the European Neighborhood Policy (ENP), the action programs were implemented to promote closer economic relations and strengthen shared political values with nearby countries.[45] The European Commission depicts the ENP as "a privileged relationship, building upon a mutual commitment to common values (democracy and human rights, rule of law, good governance, market economy principles and sustainable development. The ENP goes beyond existing relationships to offer a deeper political relationship and economic integration." The EU has allocated €12 billion ($16.4 billion) to the ENP for the 2007–2013 budgetary period to help support economic and political reforms in the targeted nations.[46]

Two Middle Eastern countries that are conspicuously absent from the list of ENP recipients are Iraq and Iran. The EU has helped monitor national, provincial, and regional elections in Iraq and has announced its intention to negotiate a Partnership and Cooperation Agreement, but remains wary about Iraq's arduous process of democratization and its continuing crisis of refugees and displaced persons. At the same time, Union officials have signaled their willingness to cooperate with Iraq on energy. The EU and the Iraqi government signed a "memorandum of understanding" in January 2010 that calls for cooperative measures to enhance the safety of Iraqi pipelines for the export of gas and oil to the Community while the EU helps develop Iraq's electrical system and expand its supplies of renewable energy.[47]

Iran remains a special case of concern because of its potential development of a nuclear weapons capability, which both the EU and most of the international community view as a serious threat to regional security. In protest against the Iranian government's proclaimed uranium enrichment strategy, the EU foreign ministers imposed in 2008 a total arms embargo and a partial travel ban against persons involved in Iran's nuclear program. Three EU member states—the United Kingdom, France, and Germany—joined with the United States and other members of the United Nations Security Council in negotiating a tentative diplomatic agreement with the Iranian government in October 2009 that called for Iran to export most of its enriched uranium for processing in the West. If implemented, this would effectively postpone the development of nuclear weapons. Conservative Iranian hawks promptly forced the government to rescind the deal out of fear the West would not return the uranium. In early 2010 Iran escalated international tensions by announcing that scientists had begun enriching uranium, ostensibly for use in medical isotopes, in a process that could rapidly yield the potential to produce weapons-grade uranium.[48] EU foreign policy officials initially deferred a response to the Security Council, but declared their determination to impose financial and energy sanctions of their own if the UN fails to act.

Common Foreign and Security Policy

Parallel with their pursuit of a wide range of regional economic and social issues and their conduct of foreign relations with nonmember countries, European Union leaders have undertaken significant moves to implement a Common Foreign and Security Policy (CFSP) in their quest for a more viable collective role in broader European and world affairs. This quest involves a delicate process of balancing national self-interests and foreign policy traditions with the creation of new institutional and enforcement mechanisms under Community control. An important factor in the Union's pursuit of a CFSP is the looming edifice of NATO as the alliance confronts its own imperative to redefine its mission and strategies in the post–cold war era.

The original six members of the EEC established a preliminary framework for forging a common foreign policy when they launched a consultative procedure known as European Political Cooperation (EPC) in 1969 and agreed to convene regular meetings of the European Council, beginning in 1974. This framework for foreign policy consultations was partially institutionalized in the form of a Political Committee, which served common administrative purposes, and a Group of Correspondents, which monitored EPC activities, to keep each of the member countries informed. The linkage between the Community and EPC was deepened when the European Council adopted a "Solemn Declaration on European Union" in Stuttgart in June 1983 that committed the member states to "intensified consultations with a view to permitting timely joint action on all major foreign policies." [49] The relationship between the Community and the EPC became more formalized with the adoption of the Single European Act in 1987, which mandated consultation and policy consistency between the two entities. The Persian Gulf crisis of 1991 and the outbreak of civil war that same year in what is now the former Yugoslavia provided additional impetus for Community leaders to intensify efforts to coordinate their foreign policy strategies.

This resolve was codified in the Treaty on European Union (TEU) of 1991, which called on the member states to define a Common Foreign and Security Policy (CFSP) through new institutional channels of consultation and implementation and the creation of the office of High Representative of the Union for Foreign Affairs and Security Policy through the Treaty of Amsterdam of 1997. The underlying principle of CFSP was intergovernmental collaboration and decision making rather than supranationalism.

The preamble of the Lisbon Treaty affirms the joint determination of the EU member states "to implement a common foreign and security policy including the progressive framing of a common defense policy, which might lead to a common defence. . . ." Building on the language contained in the Amsterdam Treaty, the treaty specifies that the general objectives of CFSP are to:

- safeguard [the Union's] values, fundamental interests, security, independence and integrity;

- consolidate and support democracy, the rule of law, human rights and the principles of international law;

- preserve peace, prevent conflicts and strengthen international security, in accordance with the purposes and principles of the United Nations Charter . . . ;

- foster the sustainable economic, social and environmental development of developing countries with the primary aim of eradicating poverty;

- encourage the integration of all countries into the world economy, including through the progressive abolition of restrictions on international trade;

- help develop international measures to preserve and improve the quality of the environment and the sustainable management of global natural resources, in order to ensure sustainable development;

- assist populations, countries and regions confronting natural or man-made disasters; and

- promote an international system based on stronger multilateral cooperation and good global governance.[50]

The Union is assigned exclusive authority to make decisions governing common foreign policy actions, positions, and implementation (Art. 25 of the Consolidated Treaty). The Union's power to do so is dispersed among the European Council, the Council of Ministers, and the High Representative for Foreign Affairs and Security Policy. The European Council is responsible for defining "the Union's strategic interests," objectives, and general CFSP guidelines (Art. 25). The Council of Ministers, meanwhile, is charged with framing specific common foreign and security policies and taking decisions to implement them "on the basis of the general guidelines and strategic lines defined by the European Council" (Art. 26). The High Representative—who, as previously noted, serves as chair of the Foreign Affairs Council and a vice president of the European Commission—is responsible for implementing CFSP decisions (Art. 26). He or she may submit policy proposals to the Foreign Affairs Council and the European Council (as may any member state). The High Representative also represents the Union to third parties and international organizations and at international conferences (Art. 27).

Complex rules govern the CFSP decision process. The European Council is required to act unanimously on recommendations submitted to it by the Council of Ministers. Once a vote is taken, member states are obligated to honor the decision. The treaty does allow for member states to abstain from voting, however. In such a case the member state "shall not be obliged to apply the decision, but shall accept that the decision commits the Union. In a spirit of mutual solidarity, the Member State concerned shall refrain from any action likely to conflict with or impede Union action based on that decision." A decision is not adopted, however, if a third of the member states representing at least a third of the population of the Union abstain (Art. 31).

Although unanimity—qualified by the option of constructive abstentions—is the norm in CFSP decision making, the treaty allows the Council of Ministers to make some decisions by a qualified majority. This is the case (in the convoluted language of the treaty) when the ministers adopt a decision "defining a Union action or position on the basis of a decision of the European Council . . . [and] when adopting a decision defining a Union action or position, on a proposal which the High Representative for the Union for Foreign Affairs and Security Policy has presented following a specific request from the European Council" (Art. 31).

In addition to providing an institutional basis and rules for common foreign policy positions, the consolidated treaty reaffirms established provisions governing operational (or enforcement) measures under a parallel European Security and Defence Policy (ESDP). Such measures are officially defined as "missions outside the Union for peacekeeping, conflict prevention and strengthening international security. . . . The performance of these tasks shall be undertaken using [civilian and military] capabilities provided by the Member States," and typically take the form of multinational units. The European Council is required to base operational decisions on the unanimous consent of its members.

In recognition that not all member states belong to NATO, the treaty explicitly declares that operational decisions "shall not prejudice the specific character of the security and defence policy of [individual] Member States" (Art. 42).

Successive Council agreements and new treaty provisions have affirmed the autonomous capacity of the EU to undertake joint measures in security and defense. In 1999 British prime minister Tony Blair acted to resolve an earlier dispute among member states about whether military aspects of the CFSP should be subordinated to NATO or the Western European Union (WEU) by advocating the institutional integration of WEU and the EU.[51] The European Council affirmed the merger of both organizations at a summit in Berlin in March 1999, declaring that EU armed forces would be subordinate to the WEU in peacetime but to NATO in the event of war. The Treaty of Nice later provided an institutional basis for future military action by authorizing the creation of a political and security committee, a military committee, and a military staff within the EU to address potential European crises in close consultation with NATO. As France declared at the conclusion of the Nice summit in December 2000, "Consultations and cooperation between the two organizations will be developed in matters of security, defence and crisis management of common interest in order to make possible the most appropriate military response to a given crisis and ensure effective crisis management, while fully respecting the decision-making autonomy of NATO and the EU." [52]

The EU's Common Foreign and Security Policy remains contingent on intergovernmental cooperation. When consensus prevails, the member states are able to act together. Early initiatives included dispatching EU peacekeeping forces to Macedonia and the Democratic Republic of the Congo in 2003. By 2007 the EU had established fifteen Battlegroups, each consisting of fifteen hundred or more troops recruited from the member states, as contingency ESDP units for rapid deployment where needed.[53] After President Sarkozy mediated an end to the Russian-Georgian military conflict in 2008, EU member states dispatched some two hundred peace monitors to help enforce the cease-fire in the disputed territories. They returned to their home countries by the end of 2009.

In contrast, divergent national interests have provoked several intense policy disputes within the Union. A dramatic example was the inability of the EU to forge a common response to the American-led invasion of Iraq in 2003.[54] Great Britain and several other EU member states joined in supporting actions by the Bush administration, while France and Germany adamantly opposed armed intervention. Sweden, Greece, and other EU countries adopted a more diplomatic stance, advocating reliance on collective security measures under the aegis of the United Nations.

EU states and many of their citizens are similarly divided in their degree of support for NATO military operations against Taliban insurgents in Afghanistan. At the beginning of 2010, twenty-six European members of NATO had troops stationed in Afghanistan alongside American and Canadian forces. The largest European contingents were from the United Kingdom and Germany. Four nonaligned EU members, Austria, Finland, Ireland, and Sweden, also contributed a small military presence. Opposition to involvement in the war was especially strong in Germany and in the Netherlands, which announced after a government crisis over the issue in February 2010 that it would withdraw its troops from the conflict.

Citizenship, Freedom, Security, and Justice

The scant 1.2 percent of appropriations that the EU committed to Citizenship, Freedom, Security and Justice (see Table 8-12) for the 2007–2013 period understates the significance of the Union's role in helping to administer this diverse range of regional policies. Most direct expenditures are borne by the member states, but the Union performs important—if sometimes desultory—responsibilities in policy coordination and implementation.

Citizenship, freedom, security, and justice policies can be divided into humanistic and societal security components. The humanistic component encompasses a range of educational and cultural activities. The flagship venture is the Erasmus higher education and training program, which has enabled some 2.2 million university students to study and work abroad since its inception in 1987.[55] Parallel educational activities include the Leonardo da Vinci program of vocational training, which emphasizes job placement for younger workers; Grundtvig, which funds transnational adult education programs among the member states; and Comenius, which sponsors secondary school partnerships aimed at developing promising pedagogical practices and curricula.[56] A broader cooperative effort, which was launched in 1999 and extends beyond the EU, is the "Bologna Process" of institutional cooperation among universities in some forty-seven European countries that seeks to develop a European Higher Education Area aimed at facilitating occupational mobility by students in today's knowledge society.[57]

Another important example of humanistic policies is the EU's designation of a succession of cities as "European capitals of culture" because of their historical contributions as philosophical, architectural, and literary centers of cultural creativity. Beginning in 1985 with the European Commission's selection of Athens as the initial European capital of culture, the honorific title has been bequeathed in turn to Florence, Amsterdam, Paris, Glasgow, Stockholm, Weimar, Vilnius, Istanbul, and other cities of renown. The purpose of these humanistic measures is to promote a stronger sense of "neo-national" European citizenship based on personal educational experience and mutual cultural appreciation.[58]

Societal security, in contrast, involves the use of regulatory and enforcement powers by multiple levels of government, intelligence agencies, and police units to promote law and order and thereby minimize physical and other threats to individuals and society at large. Such measures correspond to a core Union objective to provide "an area of freedom, security and justice" to all its citizens.[59] At the same time, the amended EU treaties explicitly acknowledge that national security constitutes an "essential State function" that "remains [alongside the defense of territorial integrity] the sole responsibility of each Member State."[60] Therein lies a persisting tension between Union and member state responsibilities.

Asylum and Immigration Policies

In the official parlance of the European Commission, asylum can be defined as "a form of protection given by a State on its territory based on the principle of . . . internationally or nationally recognized refugee rights. It is granted to a person who is unable to seek protection in his/her country of citizenship and/or residence in particular for fear of being persecuted for reasons of race, religion, nationality, membership of a particular social group or political opinion." [61] EU asylum policy is based on an intergovernmental agreement negotiated by twelve member states in 1997 governing rights of asylum within the Community. Known as the Dublin Convention, the accord (which has subsequently been broadened to include additional member states and incorporated into Community law) stipulates that asylum-seekers must submit their application for asylum in the first EU country they enter. The purpose of this provision is to eliminate an earlier pattern of "asylum shopping" from one EU member state to another and to set firm conditions for processing individual requests. Persons who are denied asylum must return to their home country rather than being allowed to seek asylum in another EU member state.[62]

The EU statistical office reports that nearly 240,000 asylum applicants were registered in 2008 throughout the Union. Their principal countries of origin were Iraq (12 percent of the total), Russia (9 percent), Somalia (6 percent), Serbia (6 percent), and Afghanistan (5 percent). The highest number of applicants were registered in France, followed in descending order by the United Kingdom, Germany, Sweden, Greece, Belgium, and the Netherlands.[63] Given the enormous differences in national legislation and bureaucratic procedures governing asylum, the European Commission and the European Council have sought to achieve greater intergovernmental coordination in the asylum process—but with limited success. The Consolidated Treaty on the Functioning of the European Union calls on the member states to formulate a common policy on asylum but provides no specific criteria.[64] Members of the European Council have conceded that "further advances are necessary."[65]

EU immigration policies are somewhat less problematic. The principle of labor mobility, which was enshrined in the Treaty of Rome establishing the EEC and augmented during the 1960s by a network of bilateral agreements between individual member states (notably West Germany) and nonmember countries such as Turkey, was extended to include white-collar workers through the implementation of the Single Market program. Beginning in the mid-1990s, however, immigration (including waves of illegal immigrants) became a major political issue in many of the member countries. The Organisation for Economic Co-Operation and Development reports that France and Austria witnessed net increases of 18.2 percent and 13.4 percent, respectively, in the influx of immigrants in 2001, while the Czech Republic, Finland, and Ireland experienced immigration rates of approximately 15 percent that same year. The comparable rate in Germany—which in 1993 constitutionally limited what had previously been a virtually unrestricted right of entry—was 6 percent.[66]

Despite restrictive national immigration policies and tighter border controls, the number of legal and illegal immigrants continued to increase. In January 2008, 19.5 million foreign citizens lived in the twenty-seven member states of the EU: 6.0 million from non-EU European countries, 4.7 million from Africa, 3.7 million from Asia, and 3.2 million from the Americas. The largest number of foreign citizens resided in Germany (7.3 million), followed by Spain (5.3 million), the United Kingdom (4.0 million), France (3.7 million), and Italy (3.4 million).[67] In response to the growing numbers, government officials agreed at a European Council meeting in Tampere, Finland, in 1999 on principles of a common EU immigration policy. The Tampere agenda called for joint agreements among the member states "on a comprehensive approach to the management of migratory flows so as to find a balance between humanitarian and economic admission . . . and the development of partnerships with countries of origin including policies of co-development."

Over the next two years, the European Commission submitted a series of proposals to the Council and the European Parliament to facilitate the formation and implementation of a common immigration policy. These proposals served as the basis for a succession of Council directives in 2003–2005 that codified terms of family reunification and long-term EU resident status, which are legally binding on all member states (except Britain, Denmark, and Ireland, which maintain autonomous immigration policies in accordance with their "op-out" treaty provisions). In a parallel move, the Council of Ministers adopted punitive measures to combat illegal immigration and the trafficking of human beings for prostitution and other nefarious purposes.[68]

Measures Against Organized Crime

In addition to calling for a common EU immigration policy, government leaders also agreed at the Tampere summit in 1999 to create a judicial unit (Eurojust) as an institutional mechanism to consolidate and streamline efforts to combat cross-national crime. A provisional body composed of national prosecutors was established in Brussels in 2000; Eurojust then moved to its permanent facilities at The Hague in 2003. Composed of prosecutors, magistrates, and police officers recruited from the twenty-seven member states, Eurojust is the EU's principal instrument for negotiating cooperation agreements with law enforcement agencies and nonmember countries to allow "the exchange of judicial information and personal data." They include Europol, the EU's criminal intelligence unit with headquarters at The Hague;[69] CEPOL, the European Police College, based in Britain; OLAF, a European anti-fraud office; and Croatia, Iceland, Macedonia, Norway, Switzerland, and the United States.

The European Council voted to strengthen the operational capabilities of Eurojust and expand its cooperative links with intelligence and enforcement organizations in 2008.[70] The implementation of the Lisbon Treaty in December 2009 reaffirmed the Union's resolve to promote "a high level of security through measures to prevent and combat crime, racism and xenophobia, and through measures for coordination and cooperation between police and judicial authorities and other competent authorities." [71]

Anti-Terrorist Policies

Closely related to judicial and intelligence cooperation between the EU and its member states is the Union's antiterrorist strategy, which targets Islamic extremists, violence-prone separatists, religious fundamentalists, and antisystem ideological factions. Although terrorist attacks have taken place on European soil for decades (notably in Germany, Ireland, Spain, and the United Kingdom), the attacks of September 11, 2001, on the United States and subsequent bombings in Madrid and London in 2005 prompted the EU and its member states to intensify efforts to combat international terrorism. An important first step was Council agreement in September 2001 to establish a European arrest warrant, which is valid throughout the territory of the EU and replaces earlier cumbersome country-to-country extradition procedures. A European arrest warrant may be issued by a court in one member state against a person charged with a crime who resides in another state. Judicial authorities in the second country are charged with arresting and returning such a person as quickly as possible. The new procedure, which entered into force in January 2004, significantly expedites the surrender process. In the authoritative view of the European Commission, the European arrest warrant "also means that Member States can no longer refuse to surrender to another Member State their own citizens who have committed a serious crime, or who are suspected of having committed such a crime in another country, on the grounds that they are nationals." [72]

The implementation of the new law had immediate consequences. By September 2004, 2,600 arrest warrants had been issued, resulting in the arrest of 653 persons and the surrender of 104. According to the European Commission, the average time to execute a warrant has been reduced from nine months to forty-three days. Despite these successes, some member states—which were unnamed in the Commission report—have resisted or delayed executing the warrants to protect their nationals against trial in another country.[73]

Other antiterrorist measures include the adoption of the Action Plan against Terrorism in 2001 and the European Council Framework Decision on Combating Terrorism in 2002 (amended in 2007). These documents call on the member states to undertake coordinated measures to reduce terrorists' access to financial and economic resources, expand intergovernmental and interagency cooperation in an effort to prevent future terrorist attacks, establish a more effective system of border controls, and harmonize national antiterrorist legislation. In November 2007 the Commission augmented the objectives of the 2001 Action Plan with a series of regulations that criminalize terrorist training, recruitment, "public provocation to commit terrorist offenses," and the use of explosives by terrorists. The Commission's regulations also allow for "the use of airline passenger information in law enforcement investigation." [74]

The Action Plan and Council Framework on the EU level have significantly enhanced intelligence exchange and cooperation among governments and law enforcement agencies on the basis of more explicit criminal legal provisions. Anecdotal evidence is illustrative of initial successes in the implementation of antiterrorist measures by national authorities. In 2001 French and Belgian police arrested a group of conspirators who were charged with an al Qaeda plot to destroy the American Embassy in Paris and a munitions dump in Belgium. In Germany, public authorities had initiated 195 proceedings against alleged fundamentalist terrorists by the end of 2004. In 2007 the police arrested three suspects belonging to a German cell of the terrorist group, "Islamic Jihad Union," who were charged with preparing a "horrific" car bomb attack against U.S. military facilities.[75] After the London bombings of 2005, the British government initiated legislation criminalizing the "glorification of terrorism." By year's end, some sixty persons charged with planning terrorist acts were awaiting trial.[76] An example of cross-national policy cooperation between an EU and a non-EU state was the arrest in July 2010 of three suspected terrorists with ties to al Qaeda operatives in Pakistan: one in Germany and two in Norway.[77]

In aggregate terms, the number of terrorist attacks in the larger West European members of the EU declined in the immediate three-year period after 9/11, compared to the decade as a whole. Since 2006, however, the number has once again risen in tandem with a global increase in incidents of terrorism. (See Table 8-13; data on Russia, the United States, and Canada are included for comparative purposes.) EU member states experiencing the fewest number of terrorist attacks after 9/11 include the Scandinavian countries, the three Baltic republics, Austria, Belgium, Bulgaria, the Netherlands, Portugal, Slovakia, and Slovenia. Greece recorded a total of 378 attacks from 2002 through 2009, most of them instigated by ideological militants.[78]

Table 8-13 Domestic and Global Terrorist Attacks, 2002–2009

Country	2002–2005		2006–2009		2002–2009	
	Attacks	Victims	Attacks	Victims	Attacks	Victims
EU member						
France	125	29	158	30	283	59
Germany	2	2	8	1	10	3
Italy	30	5	12	26	42	31
Spain	112	2,163	225	174	337	2,337
United Kingdom	88	915	77	109	165	1,024
Non-EU countries						
Russia	416	3,320	1,311	2,694	1,727	6,014
United States	10	0	13	73	23	73
Canada	1	0	7	1	8	1
Global Totals	14,277	105,397	51,602	259,267	65,879	364,664

Source: National Counterterrorism Center, Worldwide Incidents Tracking System database. Under reports, select "Grouped by country" and then filter by the desired date range.

EU Policy Assessment

How power is used in the European Union underscores the hybrid nature of the organization as a confederal political system combining supranational and intergovernmental components. The EU is most powerful in its conduct of redistributive policies involving regional development programs and the Common Agricultural Policy, which are financed primarily by its own economic resources. Through the implementation of successive Council directives (including the White Paper of 1985) and especially new treaty provisions, the EU has also gained institutional authority in supranational decision making, the conduct of foreign policy, and the pursuit of common humanistic endeavors. Yet, as the preceding discussion of societal security illustrates, national actors retain important reservoirs of political and bureaucratic power as both autonomous actors and as instruments of EU policy.

NOTES

1. Title II, Article 310, Consolidated Version of the Treaty on Functioning of the European Union.
2. Article 314, ibid.
3. Article 17, Consolidated Version of the Treaty on European Union.
4. Desmond Dinan, *Ever Close Union? An Introduction to the European Community,* 3rd ed. (Boulder: Lynne Rienner, 2005), 354.
5. Article 39, Consolidated Version of the Treaty on Functioning of the European Union.
6. Agenda 2000—A CAP for the Future, http://ec.europa.eu/agriculture/publ/review99/08_09_en.pdf.
7. Agriculture and Rural Development, http://ec.europa.eu/agriculture/rurdev/index_en.htm.
8. Reform of the Common Agricultural Policy, http://europa.eu/legislation_summaries/agriculture/general_framework/160002_en.htm.

9. European Commission, Agriculture and Rural Development, "Health Check of the Common Agricultural Policy," http://ec.europa.eu/agriculture/healthcheck/index_en.htm.

10. "Rural development: €5 billion in total injected into rural development programmes," http://europa.eu/rapid/pressReleasesAction.do?reference=IP/10/102&format=HTML&aged=0&language=EN&guiLanguage=en.

11. European Commission, "SF—European Social Fund," http://ec.europa.eu/social/main.jsp?langId=en&catId=325.

12. European Regional Development Fund, http://ec.europa.eu/regional_policy/funds/prord/prord_en.htm.

13. Ibid.

14. European Investment Bank, http://www.eib.org/.

15. European Investment Bank, *Annual Report 2007*, http://www.eib.org/attachments/general/reports/fr2007en.pdf.

16. European Commission, Regional Policy, "The Cohesion Fund at a Glance," http://ec.europa.eu/regional_policy/funds/procf/cf_en.htm.

17. Europa, Summaries of EU legislation: Lisbon Strategy, http://europa.eu/legislation_summaries/glossary/lisbon_strategy_en.htm.

18. European Commission, Lisbon Strategy for Growth and Jobs, "Towards a green and innovative economy," http://ec.europa.eu/growthandjobs/faqs/developments/index_en.htm#faq01.

19. Commission of the European Communities, *Completing the Internal Market* (Brussels, June 14, 1985), http://europa.eu/documents/comm/white_papers/pdf/com1985_0310_f_en.pdf.

20. Europa, *The Schengen area and cooperation*, http://europa.eu/legislation_summaries/justice_freedom_security/free_movement_of_persons_asylum_immigration/l33020_en.htm.

21. A. M. El-Agraa, ed., *The Economics of the European Community*, 4th ed. (London: Harvester Wheatsheaf, 1994), 2.

22. "E.U. Issues Big Antitrust Fines to E.ON, GDF Suez," *New York Times*, July 9, 2009.

23. Brian Ardy, "Industrial Policy and the Lisbon Strategy," in El-Agraa, *The Economics of the European Community*, 269.

24. Ibid., 268.

25. The United Kingdom abstained from voting on the Charter because the Thatcher government objected to its regulatory character.

26. EU Business, "The Sixth Environmental Action Programme of the European Community 2002–2012," http://www.eubusiness.com/topics/environ/6th-eap.

27. Council of the European Union, "Presidency conclusion on COP 15—Copenhagen climate conference," December 2009, http://www.consilium.europa.eu/uedocs/cms_data/docs/pressdata/en/envir/112067.pdf.

28. "Euro Membership and Higher Pension Age Embroil Polish Politics," *New York Times*, December 8, 2009.

29. Global Economics Research, Trading Economics, Euro Area Inflation Rate, http://www.tradingeconomics.com/Economics/Inflation-CPI.aspx?Symbol=EUR.

30. Europa, *General Report 2008*, http://europa.eu/generalreport/en/2008/rg15.htm.

31. "World Leaders Pledge $1.1 Trillion for Crisis," *New York Times*, April 2, 2009.

32. "The euro-area economy: Growing apart?" *Economist*, August 20, 2009; and "In a Recession, Europe's Focus on Saving Jobs Pays Off," *New York Times*, February 4, 2010.

33. These projections were compiled by the Economist Intelligence Unit and published in "Economic and financial indicators," *Economist*, February 6, 2010.

34. "Europe Lays Plans for How to Bail Out Greece," *New York Times*, January 29, 2010; and "European Union Sets Deadline for Greece to Make Cuts," *New York Times*, February 17, 2010.

35. European Commission, "Trade: Bilateral Relations: USA," http://ec.europa.eu/trade/creating-opportunities/bilateral-relations/countries/united-states/.

36. See ibid. for links to these venues.

37. Ibid.

38. Organisation for Economic Co-Operation and Development, *Geographical Distribution of Financial Flows to Aid Recipients 1992–1996* (Paris: OECD, 1998).

39. European Commission, "*External Relations: Russia: Financial-cooperation,*" http://ec.europa.eu/external_relations/russia/financial_cooperation_en.htm.

40. Ekaterina Stepanova, "South Ossetia and Abkhazia: Placing the Conflict in Context," SIPRI Policy Brief, November 2008, http://books.sipri.org/files/misc/SIPRIPB0811.pdf. SIPRI is an independent international institute located in Stockholm that is dedicated to research into conflict, armaments, arms control, and disarmament. For further information, consult the SIPRI home page: http://www.sipri.org/.

41. European Commission, "Trade: China," http://ec.europa.eu/trade/creating-opportunities/bilateral-relations/countries/china/index_en.htm.

42. Ibid.

43. "Breaking News," *New York Times*, February 4, 2010.

44. Statements by HR Catherine Ashton on human rights in China, February 9 and February 12, 2010, http://www.consilium.europa.eu/.

45. They include Armenia, Azerbaijan, Belarus, Georgia, Moldova, and the Ukraine in Eastern Europe, and Algeria, Egypt, Israel, Jordan, Lebanon, Libya, Morocco, the Palestinian territory, Syria, and Tunisia in the Middle East.

46. "EU in the World: European Neighbourhood Policy: The Policy: What is the European Neighbourhood Policy?" http://ec.europa.eu/world/enp/policy_en.htm.

47. Europa, Press Release, "EU and Iraq sign a Strategic Energy Partnership Memorandum of Understanding," Brussels, January 18, 2010, http://europa.eu/rapid/pressReleasesAction.do?reference=IP/10/29.

48. "Iran's Nuclear Program," *New York Times*, February 14, 2010, http://www.nytimes.com/info/iran-nuclear-program/?inline=nyt-classifier.

49. Federal Republic of Germany, *European Political Co-operation (EPC)*, 5th ed. (Bonn: Press and Information Office, 1988), 75–76.

50. Title V: General Provisions of the Union's External Action and Specific Provisions on the Common Foreign and Security Policy, Article 21, Consolidated Version TEU.

51. The Western European Union was founded in 1955 as a successor military alliance to the Brussels Treaty Organization, established in 1948. The WEU serves as an institutional voice for European views on regional security and coordinated EU defense policy within the EU. It currently has ten full members (Belgium, France, Germany, Greece, Italy, Luxembourg, the Netherlands, Portugal, Spain, and the United Kingdom); six associate members (Czech Republic, Hungary, Iceland, Norway, Poland, and Turkey); and seven associate partners (Bulgaria, Estonia, Latvia, Lithuania, Romania, Slovakia, and Slovenia). Denmark and the four neutral members of the EU (Austria, Finland, Ireland, and Sweden) have observer status within the organization.

52. "Presidency Report on the European Security and Defence Policy," press release no. 14056/2/00, Brussels, December 12, 2000.

53. Some Battlegroups consist of soldiers from only one country—including France, Italy, Spain, and Britain—but most are multinational in composition. Examples include a German-Czech-Austrian Battlegroup, a Nordic Battlegroup, and a Czech-Slovak Battlegroup.

54. Philip H. Gordon and Jeremy Shapiro, *Allies at War: America, Europe, and the Crisis over Iraq* (New York and London: McGraw Hill, 2004). Also see Donald Hancock and Brandon Valeriano, "Western Europe," in *The Bush Doctrine and the War on Terrorism: Global Responses, Global Consequences,* ed. Mary Buckley and Robert Singh (London and New York: Routledge, 2006).

55. European Commission Education and Training, "The Erasmus Programme," ec.europa .eu/education/lifelong-learning-programme/doc80_en.htm.

56. European Commission, "Education, Training, Youth," http://europa.eu/pol/educ/index_ en.htm.

57. European Higher Education Area, "Budapest-Vienna Declaration on the European Higher Education Area, March 12, 2010." See also Hans Pechar, "'The Bologna Process': A European Response to Global Competition in Higher Education," *Canadian Journal of Higher Education* 37 (2007): 109–125.

58. Elizabeth Meehan provides a useful discussion of various dimensions of European citizenship in "Citizenship," in *Encyclopedia of the European Union,* ed. Desmond Dinan (Boulder and London: Lynne Rienner Publishers, 1998), 42–44.

59. Consolidated Version, Article 3, paragraph 2.

60. Ibid.

61. European Commission, "The European Union Policy towards a Common European Asylum System," http://ec.europa.eu/justice_home/fsj/asylum/fsj_asylum_intro_en.htm.

62. Irish Refugee Council, "Fact Sheet on the Dublin Convention," http://www.irishrefu geecouncil.ie/factsheets/dublinconvention4.html.

63. Eurostat, *eurostat news release,* "Asylum in the EU in 2008," 66/2009, May 2009, http://epp. eurostat.ec.europa.eu/cache/ITY_PUBLIC/3–08052009-AP/EN/3–08052009-AP-EN .PDF.

64. Article 67, paragraph 2, Consolidated Treaty on the Functioning of the European Union.

65. European Council, "European Pact on Immigration and Asylum," http://register.consil-ium.europa.eu/pdf/en/08/st13/st13440.en08.pdf.

66. OECD, *Trends in International Migration, Annual Report 2003 Edition* (Paris: OECD, 2004), 25.

67. Eurostat, *eurostat news release,* "Population of foreign citizens in the EU27 in 2008," 184/2009, December 16, 2009, http://epp.eurostat.ec.europa.eu/cache/ITY_PUBLIC/3– 16122009-BP/EN/3–16122009-BP-EN.PDF.

68. European Commission, "Towards a common European Union immigration policy," http:// ec.europa.eu/home-affairs/policies/immigration/immigration_intro_en.htm.

69. Europol's declared purpose is to improve "the effectiveness and cooperation of the competent authorities in the Member States in preventing and combating terrorism, unlawful drug trafficking and other serious forms of organized crime." Europol, http://www.europol. europa.eu/.

70. The European Union's Judicial Cooperation Unit, http://www.eurojust.europa.eu/about. htm. Because of the classified nature of most intelligence work, no empirical data are readily available on the activities of Eurojust or its associated agencies.

71. Consolidated Treaty on the Functioning of the European Union, "Title V: Area of Freedom Security and Justice," Article 67.

72. European Commission, "European arrest warrant replaces extradition between EU Member States," http://ec.europa.eu/justice_home/fsj/criminal/extradition/fsj_criminal_extradi tion_en.htm.

73. Ibid.

74. European Commission, "The EU fights against the scourge of terrorism," http://ec.europa.eu/justice_home/fsj/terrorism/fsj_terrorism_intro_en.htm.

75. "Islamist Terrorists Planned Massive Attacks in Germany," *Spiegel Online International,* September 5, 2007, www.spiegel.de/international/germany/0,1518,504037,00.html.

76. Cafebabel.com, *The European Magazine,* http://www.cafebabel.co.uk/article/2013/escalating-threats-and-anti-terrorist-measures.html.

77. *New York Times,* July 9, 2010.

78. National Counterterrorism Center, Worldwide Incidents Tracking System database.

What Is the Future of European Union Politics?

T HE IMPLEMENTATION OF THE LISBON TREATY IN 2009 REESTABLISHED the European Union on a firmer legal basis, thereby eliminating much of the political uncertainty that had characterized the Community after the failure of the constitutional treaty in 2005. The EU remains a distinctive political system embracing both intergovernmental and supranational institutional arrangements and policy actors. It embodies a system of dual sovereignty that contains the potential—though by no means the certainty—of developing into a federal European government. The Lisbon Treaty advances that goal by establishing a presidency of the European Council and expanding the authority of the High Representative for Foreign Affairs and Security Policy as well as the powers of the European Parliament. At the same time, the treaty's implementation has been accompanied by unanticipated controversies and policy conflicts, some of which date from earlier years. Union leaders must confront these issues among their first priorities in seeking to maximize the Community's continued viability as a political-economic system.

Institutional and Policy Imperatives

Institutional tensions characterized relations between the European Council presidency and the rotating presidency of the Council of Ministers during the initial phase of the Lisbon Treaty's implementation. These tensions were due in part to the uncertainty until well into 2009 concerning whether and when the treaty would be finally ratified, which left the Spanish presidency of the Council of Ministers unprepared about how to share executive power. Exacerbating relations between the two offices were the low-key political profiles of the first presidential incumbent, former Belgian prime minister Herman van Rompuy, and the EU's new foreign policy chief, Catherine Ashton.[1] Early tensions between these executive institutions and personalities may only have reflected an awkward transitional phase of structural innovation, but they must be resolved to avoid potential institutional deadlock in the future. Overcoming this problem will require political resolve and administrative backing by the EU's member states, especially France and Germany.

France and Germany also bear a major responsibility for managing economic and monetary cohesion within the euro zone. As principal architects of the Economic and Monetary Union (EMU), the two countries shared a common interest in eliminating the destabilizing effects of currency fluctuations and institutionalizing supranational decision-making procedures within the European Central Bank through the adoption of the Treaty on European Union. Their joint obligation in the wake of the international financial and economic crisis of 2008–2010 and Greece's near default on an array of government bonds and loans, a subsequent bailout in Ireland, and potential crises in other member states such as Spain and Portugal is to reconcile their differences over whether EMU should primarily serve monetary stability (which is Germany's policy priority) or as an instrument of EU economic governance (which is the French goal). Whether that is possible will be a crucial test of the Franco-German partnership and the future of economic union itself.

The anonymous author of an op-ed article in the *Economist* is not sanguine about such a prospect: "When today's German politicians talk about euro-zone harmonization, they mean extending fiscal rigour to all. French politicians, as usual, want more intervention; by harmonization they mean the abolition of economic tools in other EU countries, like lower tax rates or weaker labour laws, that can undermine intervention in the French economy. . . . What next? . . . Expect talk about Europe's politicians demonstrating that they are stronger than markets, and lots of bluster about the wickedness of Anglo-Saxon 'speculators.'" [2] As the chief economist at London's Center for European Reform has observed: "The crisis should lead to political unity, but it could just as easily lead to a divided Europe" [3] That prospect was potentially heightened when President Nicholas Sarkozy of France and Chancellor Angela Merkel of Germany, meeting at a summit in October 2010, proposed negotiating new treaty provisions that would restrict voting rights by member states that do not exercise sufficient fiscal discipline. It is likely that a number of EU governments will resist such draconian measures.

The Lisbon Treaty has also complicated aspects of EU foreign policy. Shortly after its implementation, turf wars broke out among the European Commission, the High Representative's office, and national governments over EU diplomatic representation abroad. A case in point was the controversy in early 2010 over the appointment of a close aid to Commission president Barrosso as head of the EU delegation in Washington, D.C. Some European critics characterized the move as a "pre-emptive strike" by the Commission. [4]

The European Parliament caused a more serious diplomatic rift when it used its expanded powers of co-decision to reject an agreement between the United States and the EU to allow access by American authorities to financial transfers by Union citizens suspected of terrorist-related activities. [5] The action by Parliament may have contributed to President Barack Obama's decision not to attend a scheduled summit meeting with EU leaders in May 2010. Similar disputes are likely to occur in the future as an inevitable expression of increased institutional assertiveness and rivalry under the Lisbon Treaty, but are not necessarily evidence of an endemic crisis in foreign relations.

Pending Enlargement of the EU

Future widening to include additional member states is another important item on the EU's agenda. The European Commission has opened negotiations with four applicant countries to determine their eligibility on the basis of the Copenhagen criteria for accession: Croatia, Iceland, Macedonia, and Turkey. Another five countries are potential candidates for admission: Albania, Bosnia and Herzegovina, Montenegro, Serbia, and Kosovo.

Among the applicant nations, Turkey has had the longest—and most controversial—relationship with the European Community. Straddling Europe and the Middle East, Turkey is a Eurasian country and as such is not considered by many officials and citizens to be fully European. Turkey is an Islamic state with a turbulent political history that spans its ascendancy in the Ottoman Empire and its rebirth as an independent nation after the demise of the Ottoman Empire during World War I. In the interwar years, Turkey, under the leadership of Mustafa Atatürk, became a secular, Western-oriented nation after declaring its independence in 1923. Turkey cooperated with the Allies in the military-political struggle against European fascism in World War II and later joined NATO as a territorial and military bulwark against the Soviet Union and its allied states. Turkey's postwar history has been characterized by recurrent cycles of political democracy and military dictatorship. In an effort to encourage its political and economic integration with Western Europe, the European Economic Community (EEC) signed an association agreement with Turkey in 1963 and established a customs union in 1995. Accession negotiations began in October 2005, but have proven inconclusive.

If Turkey were to join the EU, it would be by far the largest member state geographically: 780,580 square kilometers compared with France's 550,754 and Spain's 504,782. And it would have the second-largest population after Germany: 76.8 million compared with 82.3 million. Turkey's large population is reason enough for many Europeans to be concerned about Turkish membership because of its implications for Turkey's prospective share of votes in qualified majority voting in the Council of the European Union. In addition, nearly 30 percent of Turkey's population is employed in agriculture, and its per capita gross domestic product (GDP) was just $11,200 in 2009—below that of most current EU member states (see Table 8-2). These factors indicate that Turkey would potentially pose serious financial problems for the EU's Common Agricultural Policy and its regional development policies. Other pressing concerns are Turkey's overwhelmingly Muslim population—which contrasts with Europe's majority Christian denominations—and its violation of human rights, especially against its sizable Kurdish population.

Croatia became a candidate nation for accession in June 2004. With Catholics making up 89.6 percent of the population and its close geopolitical ties with the rest of Europe, Croatia enjoys a better prospect of EU membership than Turkey. Croatia declared its independence from the former Yugoslavia in 1991 and after a bitter ethnic civil war between the majority Croats and minority Serbs achieved political stability four years later. Croatia joined NATO in April 2009.

The European Council accorded Macedonia candidate status in 2005, but negotiations with the European Commission on eligibility had not yet begun during the first half of 2010. Like Croatia, Macedonia is a remnant state of the former Yugoslavia. After declaring independence in 1991, it became embroiled in a diplomatic dispute with neighboring Greece over its name (which Greek officials consider "too Hellenic"). Macedonia has also been beset by ethnic conflicts, in its case with a vocal Albanian minority.

Most of the remaining potential candidates for accession (Albania, Bosnia and Herzegovina, Serbia, and Kosovo) are farther down the EU's list of likely members, at least for the foreseeable future. A common problem confronting all four countries is a widespread sense of "enlargement fatigue" among the core West European members of the Community. The financial and political costs of absorbing even the twelve newest members since 2004 weigh heavily on domestic politicians and their voting publics.

An exception might apply to the newest candidate for EU membership: Iceland, a North Atlantic island country with a population of only 306,693. Iceland is culturally and politically an integral part of the Nordic region and was constitutionally joined with Denmark until it achieved independence during World War II. Heavily dependent on the fishing industry, manufacturing, and a mix of public and private services, Iceland sustained

European Commission president José Manuel Barroso (right) and visiting Macedonian president Gjorge Ivanov field questions during a press conference at the European Union headquarters in Brussels. Macedonia is one of four applicant nations, along with Croatia, Iceland, and Turkey, seeking membership in an expanded EU.

Source: Wu Wei/Xinhua Press/Corbis

a high degree of prosperity accompanied by rapid growth and low unemployment until its economy was abruptly jolted by the onset of the international financial crisis in 2008. Its annual growth rate plummeted to near zero percent, and its external debt surged to five times its GDP. An especially debilitating blow came with the collapse of its three largest banks, which resulted in a freeze on accounts held by private foreign investors—principally British and Dutch—and brought the government to the brink of bankruptcy. That worst-case scenario was averted by an emergency $2.2 billion loan from the International Monetary Fund secured in November 2008, but political fallout from the crisis forced the Icelandic prime minister to resign in January 2009.

Scrambling to find a long-term solution to the financial crisis by joining the euro zone, Icelandic leaders applied for EU membership in July 2009. The country already maintains close ties with the Community through a bilateral free trade arrangement, negotiated in 1972, and its participation in the European Economic Area, the Schengen accord, and a range of Community policies. Full membership would be a logical next step. In June 2010 the European Council agreed to open membership negotiations on the condition that Iceland resolve its dispute with Britain and the Netherlands over monetary compensation to depositors who had lost money in the Icelandic bank collapse. The Council declared that the pace of negotiations "will depend on Iceland's progress." [6]

The Future Is Now

Both conceptually and empirically, one of the most perceptive assessments of the European Union's contemporary status is Robert Cooper's *The Breaking of Nations.*[7] Cooper, a former adviser to British prime minister Tony Blair and later a director-general of external and politico-military affairs for the Council of the European Union, distinguishes among three kinds of worlds in today's international system:

1. The premodern world, consisting of "pre-state, post-imperial chaos. Examples of this are Somalia, Afghanistan, and Liberia. The state no longer fulfils Max Weber's criterion for having the legitimate monopoly on the use of force."

2. The modern world, which Cooper characterizes as being "linked to that great engine of modernization, the nation-state." In this world, "the ultimate guarantor of security is force." Leading examples include the United States, the Russian Federation, and China.

3. The postmodern world (best exemplified by the EU), which Cooper contends "does not rely on balance, nor does it emphasize sovereignty or the separation of domestic and foreign affairs. The European Union is a highly developed system for mutual interference in each other's domestic affairs, right down to beer and sausages. Its principal foundations include the Treaty of Rome (as amended and expanded through subsequent treaties) and the Treaty on Conventional Forces in Europe (the CFE Treaty): this was born of the failures, wastes and absurdities of the Cold War."[8]

Whether other states or regions join the postmodern world remains to be seen, but for much of the policymaking and institutional cooperation within the EU, that future is now. Admittedly, it remains a work in progress. As the preceding chapters have shown, postmodernity within the European Union is far advanced in terms of regulatory policies and economic integration. Yet at the same time, member states frequently scrap over budgetary, agricultural, and other issues. A particularly serious gap concerns the EU's Common Foreign and Security Policy (CFSP). The member states are committed to foreign policy coordination and have undertaken important treaty revisions expanding the scope of the CFSP and assigning it actual leadership with the creation of the office of the High Representative for the CFSP. Yet as events have proved (particularly in the case of the Iraq war), the intergovernmental basis of decision making limits its effectiveness when there is no consensus on which policy to embrace. This is a serious liability for the EU in the competition for leadership with more determined and assertive modern states both within Europe and across the globe.

The European integration movement has succeeded far beyond the most hopeful expectations of its founders in creating what the eminent Czech-American political scientist Karl Deutsch termed a "security community" based on the premise that interstate conflicts are settled peaceably rather than through resort to war or other forms of violence.[9] From the outset, European integration was elite-driven, with political leaders such as Jean Monnet, Robert Schuman, Konrad Adenauer, and Alcide De Gasperi acting in concert during the formative 1950s to lay the foundation for the original European Coal and Steel Community and its legal and institutional progeny, the European Economic Community.

Their transforming initiatives inspired later generations of leaders to advance still further the depth and scope of the integration project, culminating in today's European Union. Notable among them were Jacques Delors, the proactive president of the European Commission from 1985 to 1995; German chancellors Willy Brandt and Helmut Kohl; and French presidents Charles de Gaulle (in his own contrary way) and François Mitterrand. An economic powerhouse, the EU is still seeking to define a corresponding international political role. Only time will tell whether future leaders will succeed in this enterprise.

For much of the course of the integration movement, average European citizens have experienced the EEC-EU as subjects rather than as political participants, despite provisions since 1979 for the direct election of members of the European Parliament and more recent treaty provisions designed to make decision making and institutional accountability more transparent. Although a majority of citizens are optimistic about the future of the EU,[10] many Europeans remain not just ambivalent about the Union, but downright hostile, as reflected in the votes cast against proposed treaty provisions in national referendums held at different times in Denmark, France, Ireland, and the Netherlands. The ultimate challenge of European integration is to create and sustain a shared sense of social and political community that complements national identities.

NOTES

1. "Lisbon Pact Failing to Lift the E.U. on Global Stage," *New York Times,* February 22, 2010.
2. See Charlemagne, "A Grimm tale of euro-integration," *Economist,* February 20, 2010.
3. Simon Tilford, quoted in "Contemplating the Future of the European Union," *New York Times,* February 12, 2010.
4. "Lisbon Pact Fails to Lift the E.U. on Global Stage."
5. Four countries, Austria, Germany, Greece, and Hungary, had abstained in the November 2009 vote by members of the Council of Ministers on the agreement because of their fear that private data might be passed on to third parties. It became apparent that this concern was also shared by a majority of European Parliament members.
6. "Estonia Given Clearance to Adopt Europe," *New York Times,* June 17, 2010.
7. Robert Cooper, *The Breaking of Nations: Order and Chaos in the Twenty-First Century* (New York: Atlantic Monthly Press, 2003).
8. Ibid., 16, 22, 27.
9. Karl Deutsch, *Political Community and the North Atlantic Area: International Organization in the Light of Historical Experience* (Princeton, N.J.: Princeton University Press, 1957).
10. "First Results," *Eurobarometer 72. Public Opinion in the European Union* (Brussels: European Commission, December 2009). According to the survey, 66 percent of EU residents are optimistic about the future of the European Union, while 27 percent are pessimistic. Even most British citizens—traditionally the most pronounced Euroskeptics—have positive views (50 percent), although their level of support is eclipsed by the 79 percent of respondents in Denmark and the Netherlands who are (somewhat paradoxically) optimistic.

FOR FURTHER READING

Andersen, Svein S., and Kjell A. Eliassen, eds. *Making Policy in Europe.* 2nd ed. London: Sage, 2001.

Avery, Graham, and Fraser Cameron. *The Enlargement of the European Union.* Sheffield, UK: Sheffield Academic Press, 1998.

Bache, Ian. *The Politics of European Union Regional Policy: Multi-Level Governance or Flexible Gatekeeping?* Sheffield, UK: Sheffield Academic Press, 1998.

Born, Hans and Heiner Hänggi, eds. *The 'Double Democratic Deficit': Parliamentary Accountability and the Use of Force Under International Auspices.* Aldershot, UK: Ashgate Publishing Limited, 2004.

Burgess, Michael. *Federalism and European Union.* London: Routledge, 1989.

Cooper, Robert. *The Breaking of Nations: Order and Chaos in the Twenty-First Century.* New York: Atlantic Monthly Press, 2003.

Corbett, Richard, Francis Jacobs, and Michael Shackleton. *The European Parliament.* 7th ed. London: John Harper, 2007.

Cowles, Maria Green, and Michael Smith, eds. *The State of the European Union.* Vol. 5. Oxford: Oxford University Press, 2000.

Deckmyn, Veerle, and Ian Thomson, eds. *Openness and Transparency in the European Union.* Maastricht, Netherlands: European Institute of Public Administration, 1998.

Dinan, Desmond. *Europe Recast. A History of European Union.* Boulder: Lynne Rienner, 2004.

———. *Ever Closer Union? An Introduction to the European Community.* 3rd ed. Boulder: Lynne Rienner, 2005.

———, ed. *Encyclopedia of the European Union.* Updated edition. Boulder: Lynne Rienner, 2000.

El-Agraa, A. M., ed. *The Economics of the European Community.* 4th ed. London: Harvester Wheatsheaf, 1994.

Ginsberg, Roy. *Demystifying the European Union: The Enduring Logic of Regional Integration.* Lanham, Md.: Rowman and Littlefield, 2007.

———. *The European Union in International Politics. Baptism by Fire.* Lanham, Md.: Rowman and Littlefield, 2001.

Greer, Alan J. *Agricultural Policy in Europe.* Manchester, UK, and New York: Manchester University Press, 2005.

Haas, Ernst B. *Beyond the Nation State: Functionalism and International Organization.* Stanford, Calif.: Stanford University Press, 1964.

———. *The Uniting of Europe: Political, Social, and Economic Forces, 1950–1957.* Stanford, Calif.: Stanford University Press, 1958.

Heisenberg, Dorothee. *The Mark of the Bundesbank: Germany's Role in European Monetary Cooperation.* Boulder: Lynne Rienner, 1999.

Henderson, Karen, ed. *Back to Europe: Central and Eastern Europe and the European Union.* London: UCL Press, 1999.

Hervey, Tamara, and Jeff Kenner, eds. *Economic and Social Rights under the EU Charter of Fundamental Rights—A Legal Perspective.* Oxford and Portland, Ore.: Hart Publishing, 2003.

Hix, Simon. *The Political System of the European Union.* 2nd ed. New York: Palgrave Macmillan, 2005.

Hix, Simon, Abdul G. Nourny, and Gerard Roland, *Democratic Politics in the European Parliament.* Cambridge and New York: Cambridge University Press, 2007.

Ifestos, P. *European Political Cooperation: Towards a Framework of Supranational Diplomacy.* Aldershot, UK: Avebury, 1987.

Jones, Robert A. *The Politics and Economics of the European Union: An Introductory Text.* Cheltenham, UK, and Brookfield, Vt.: Edward Elgar, 1996.

Judt, Tony. *Postwar: A History of Europe since 1945.* New York: Penguin Press, 2005.

Kapteyn, Paul. *The Stateless Market: The European Dilemma of Integration and Civilization.* London and New York: Routledge, 1996.

Kay, Adrian. *The Reform of the Common Agricultural Policy: The Case of the MacSherry Reforms.* Wallingford, UK: CAB International, 1998.

Knudsen, Ann-Christina L. *Farmers on Welfare. The Making of Europe's Common Agricultural Policy.* Ithaca, N.Y.: Cornell University Press, 2009.

Lindberg, Leon, and Stuart Scheingold. *Europe's Would-Be Polity: Patterns of Change in the European Community.* Englewood Cliffs, N.J.: Prentice Hall, 1970.

Lieven, Anatol, and Dmitri Trenin, eds. *Ambivalent Neighbors. The EU, NATO and the Price of Membership.* Washington, D.C: Carnegie Endowment for International Peace, 2003.

Lodge, Juliet, ed. *The European Community and the Challenge of the Future.* 2nd ed. New York: St. Martin's Press, 1993.

McCormick, John. *The European Union: Politics and Policies.* 2nd ed. Boulder: Westview Press, 1999.

Michta, Andrew A. *The Limits of Alliance. The United States, NATO, and the EU in North and Central Europe.* Lanham-Boulder-New York-Toronto-Oxford: Rowman and Littlefield, 2006.

Milward, Alan S. *The European Rescue of the Nation-State.* 2nd ed. London and New York: Routledge, 2000.

Morgan, Roger, and Caroline Bray. *Partners and Rivals in Western Europe: Britain, France, and Germany.* Aldershot, UK, and Brookfield, Vt.: Gower, 1986.

Nugent, Neill. *The Government and Politics of the European Community.* 4th ed. Durham, N.C.: Duke University Press, 1999.

Page, Edward C. *People Who Run Europe.* Oxford, UK: Clarendon Press, 1997.

Pentland, Charles. *International Theory and European Integration.* New York: Free Press, 1973.

Peterson, John, and Elizabeth Bomberg. *Decision-Making in the European Union.* New York: St. Martin's Press, 1999.

Rae, Gavin. *Poland's Return to Capitalism. From the Socialist Bloc to the European Union.* London and New York: Tauris Academic Studies, 2008.

Pridham, Geoffrey, and Pippa Pridham. *Towards Transnational Parties in the European Community.* London: Policy Studies Institute, 1979.

Rifkin, Jeremy. *The European Dream. How Europe's Vision of the Future Is Quietly Eclipsing the American Dream.* New York: Jeremy P. Tarcher/Penguin, 2005.

Rosamond, Ben. *Theories of European Integration.* New York: St. Martin's Press, 2000.

Ross, George. *Jacques Delors and European Integration.* New York: Oxford University Press, 1995.

Sbragia, Alberta M., ed. *Euro-Politics: Institutions in the "New" European Community.* Washington, D.C.: Brookings, 1992.

Scherpereel, John A. *Governing the Czech Republic and Slovakia. Between State Socialism and the European Union.* Boulder and London: First Forum Press, 2009.

Schmitter, Philippe C. *How to Democratize the European Union . . . And Why Bother?* London: Rowman and Littlefield, 2000.

Seidentopf, Heinrich, and Jacques Ziller. *Making European Policies Work: The Implementation of Community Legislation in the Member States.* London: Sage, 1987.

Simonian, Haig. *The Privileged Partnership: Franco-German Relations in the European Community, 1969–1984.* Oxford, UK: Clarendon Press, 1985.

Smith, Karen. *The Making of EU Foreign Policy: The Case of Eastern Europe.* London: Macmillan, 1999.

Söderbaum, Fredrick, and Patrik Stålgren, eds. *The European Union and the Global South.* Boulder and London: Lynne Rienner, 2010.

Spaak, Paul-Henri. *The Continuing Battle: Memoirs of a European, 1936–1966.* Translated by Henry Fox. Boston: Little, Brown, 1971.

Springer, Beverly. *The Social Dimension of 1992: Europe Faces a New EC.* New York: Praeger, 1992.

Symes, Valerie. *Unemployment and Employment Policies in the EU.* London: Kogan Page, 1998.

Tang, Helena, ed. *Winners and Losers of EU Integration. Policy Issues for Central and Eastern Europe.* Washington, D.C.: World Bank, 2000.

Tömmel, Ingeborg, and Amy Verdun, eds. *Innovative Governance in the European Union. The Politics of Multilevel Policymaking.* Boulder and London: Lynne Rienner, 2009.

Urwin, Derek W. *The Community of Europe: A History of European Integration since 1945.* New York: Longman, 1991.

Wallace, Helen, ed. *Interlocking Dimensions of European Integration.* Basingstroke, UK; New York: Palgrave, 2001.

Wallace, Helen, and William Wallace, eds. *Policy-Making in the European Community.* 4th ed. Oxford: Oxford University Press, 2000.

Wood, David, and Briol A. Yesilada. *The Emerging European Union.* White Plains, N.Y.: Longman, 1996.

Young, John W. *Britain and European Union, 1945–1999.* 2nd ed. New York: St. Martin's Press, 2000.

Appendix

Table A-1 Per Capita Gross National Product (GNP), 1997–2008 (constant 2000 U.S. dollars)

	1997	1998	1999	2000	2001	2002
France	19,977	20,603	21,194	21,914	22,202	22,271
Germany	21,553	21,998	22,429	23,114	23,366	23,316
Italy	18,079	18,227	18,592	19,269	19,608	19,636
Poland	3,874	4,065	4,250	4,454	4,532	4,600
Russian Federation	1,591	1,511	1,614	1,775	1,870	1,968
Sweden	24,479	15,406	26,557	27,689	27,903	28,480
United Kingdom	22,744	23,495	24,231	25,089	25,613	26,054
United States	31,716	32,671	33,748	34,606	34,513	34,738
Canada	20,911	21,580	22,586	23,560	23,739	24,215
	2003	**2004**	**2005**	**2006**	**2007**	**2008**
France	22,300	22,707	22,998	23,321	23,636	26,605
Germany	23,256	23,544	23,740	24,470	25,106	25,473
Italy	19,481	19,585	19,568	19,853	20,017	19,657
Poland	4,781	5,039	5,224	5,552	5,932	6,222
Russian Federation	2,122	2,286	2,444	2,644	2,866	3,030
Sweden	28,921	29,994	30,873	31,984	32,560	32,258
United Kingdom	26,679	27,273	27,674	28,281	28,945	28,955
United States	35,304	36,253	37,003	37,674	38,063	37,867
Canada	24,426	24,937	25,402	25,922	26,361	26,200

Source: World Bank, *World Development Indicators* database, 2010.

Table A-2 Average Annual Growth Rate of Gross Domestic Product (GDP), 1985–2011

	1985–1995	1996	1997	1998	1999	2000	2001	2002
France	2.2	1.0	2.2	3.5	3.2	4.1	1.8	1.1
Germany	2.7	1.0	1.9	1.8	1.9	3.5	1.4	0.0
Italy	2.2	1.0	1.9	1.3	1.4	3.9	1.7	0.5
Poland	na	6.2	7.1	5.0	4.5	4.3	1.2	1.4
Russia								
Sweden	1.6	1.5	2.7	3.7	4.3	4.5	1.2	2.4
United Kingdom	2.5	2.9	3.3	3.6	3.5	3.9	2.5	2.1
Euro Area	2.5	1.5	2.6	2.8	2.8	4.0	1.9	0.9
United States	2.9	3.7	4.5	4.4	4.8	4.1	1.1	108
Canada	2.3	1.6	4.2	4.1	5.5	5.2	1.8	2.9
	2003	**2004**	**2005**	**2006**	**2007**	**2008**	**2009**	**2010**	**2011**
France	1.1	2.3	1.9	2.4	2.3	0.3	−2.3	1.4	1.7
Germany	−0.2	0.7	0.9	3.4	2.6	1.0	−4.9	1.4	1.9
Italy	0.1	1.4	0.8	2.1	1.5	−1.0	−4.8	1.1	1.5
Poland	3.9	5.3	3.6	6.2	6.8	5.0	1.4	2.5	3.1
Russia			6.4	7.4	8.1	5.6	−7.9	NA	NA
Sweden	2.0	3.5	3.3	4.5	2.7	−0.4	−4.7	2.0	3.0
United Kingdom	2.8	3.0	2.2	2.9	2.6	0.6	−4.7	1.2	2.2
Euro Area	0.8	1.9	1.8	3.1	2.7	0.5	−4.0	0.9	1.7
United States	2.5	3.6	3.1	2.7	2.1	0.4	−2.5	2.5	2.8
Canada	1.9	3.1	3.0	2.9	2.5	0.4	−2.7	2.0	3.0

Sources: Organisation for Economic Co-operation and Development, *OECD Economic Outlook* No. 86 (Paris: OECD, December 2009); *Russian Statistical Yearbook, 2009*, www.gks.ru, 2010; *Russia in Figures, 2009*.

Table A-3 Consumer Prices, 1985–2011 (percentage change from previous year)

	1985–1995	1996	1997	1998	1999	2000	2001	2002
France	–	2.1	1.3	0.7	0.6	1.8	1.8	1.9
Germany	–	1.2	1.5	0.6	0.6	1.4	1.9	1.4
Italy	–	4.0	1.9	2.0	1.7	2.6	2.3	2.6
Poland	–	19.8	14.9	11.6	7.2	9.9	5.4	1.9
Russia		21.8	11.0	84.4	36.5	20.2	18.6	15.1
Sweden	5.2	0.5	0.7	+0.3	0.5	0.9	2.4	2.2
United Kingdom	–	2.5	1.8	1.6	1.3	0.8	1.2	1.3
Euro Area	–	2.3	1.7	1.2	1.2	2.2	2.4	2.3
United States	3.5	2.9	2.3	1.5	2.2	3.4	2.8	1.6
Canada	3.3	1.6	1.6	1.0	1.7	2.7	2.5	2.3

	2003	2004	2005	2006	2007	2008	2009	2010	2011
France	2.2	2.3	1.9	1.9	1.6	3.2	0.1	1.0	0.6
Germany	1.0	1.8	1.9	1.8	2.3	2.8	0.2	1.0	0.8
Italy	2.8	2.3	2.2	2.2	2.0	3.5	0.7	0.9	0.8
Poland	0.7	3.4	2.2	1.3	2.5	4.2	3.5	2.2	1.9
Russia	12.0	11.7	10.9	9.7	9.0	14.1	11.7	NA	NA
Sweden	1.9	0.4	0.5	1.4	2.2	3.4	−0.3	1.4	3.2
United Kingdom	1.4	1.3	2.0	2.3	2.3	3.6	2.1	1.7	0.5
Euro Area	2.1	2.2	2.2	2.2	2.1	3.3	0.2	0.9	0.7
United States	2.3	2.7	3.4	3.2	2.9	3.8	−0.4	1.7	1.3
Canada	2.8	1.9	2.2	2.0	2.1	2.4	0.4	1.3	1.0

Sources: Organisation for Economic Co-operation and Development, *OECD Economic Outlook* No. 86 (Paris: OECD, December 2009); *Russian Statistical Yearbook, 2009,* www.gks.ru, 2010; *Russia in Figures, 2009.*

Table A-4 Annual Unemployment Rates, 1992–2008 (percent)

	1992	1993	1994	1995	1996	1997	1998	1999	2000
France	9.8	11.0	11.6	11.0	11.5	11.4	11.0	10.4	9.0
Germany	6.3	7.6	8.2	8.0	8.7	9.4	9.1	8.3	7.5
Italy	8.8	9.8	10.6	11.2	11.2	11.2	11.4	11.0	10.1
Poland	–	14.0	14.4	13.3	12.4	10.9	10.2	13.4	16.2
Russian Federation									
Sweden	5.6	9.0	9.3	8.8	9.5	9.9	8.2	6.7	5.6
United Kingdom	9.8	10.2	9.3	8.5	7.9	6.8	6.1	5.9	5.4
Euro Area	8.5	10.0	10.7	10.4	10.6	10.6	10.1	9.3	8.5
United States	7.5	6.9	6.1	5.6	5.4	4.9	4.5	4.2	4.0
Canada	11.2	11.4	10.4	9.5	9.6	9.1	8.3	7.6	6.8

	2001	2002	2003	2004	2005	2006	2007	2008
France	8.3	8.6	9.0	9.3	9.3	9.3	8.3	7.8
Germany	7.6	8.4	9.3	9.8	10.6	9.8	8.4	7.3
Italy	9.1	8.7	8.5	8.0	7.7	6.8	6.1	6.8
Poland	18.3	20.0	19.7	19.0	17.8	13.9	9.6	7.2
Russian Federation					7.1	7.2	6.1	6.3
Sweden	4.9	4.9	5.6	6.3	7.3	7.0	6.2	6.1
United Kingdom	5.0	5.1	5.0	4.7	4.6	5.4	5.3	5.6
Euro Area	8.0	8.4	8.8	9.0	9.0	8.3	7.5	7.6
United States	4.7	5.8	6.0	5.5	5.1	4.6	4.6	5.8
Canada	7.2	7.7	7.6	7.2	6.8	6.3	6.0	6.1

Sources: Organisation for Economic Co-operation and Development, *OECD Economic Outlook* No. 86 (Paris: OECD, December 2009); *Russian Statistical Yearbook, 2009,* www.gks.ru, 2010; *Russia in Figures, 2009.*

Table A-5 General Government Total Outlays as Percentage of Nominal GDP, 1995–2011

	1995	1996	1997	1998	1999	2000	2001	2002	2003
France	54.4	54.5	54.1	52.7	52.6	51.6	51.6	52.6	53.2
Germany	54.8	49.3	48.3	48.1	48.2	45.1	47.5	48.0	48.4
Italy	52.5	52.5	50.2	49.3	48.2	46.1	48.0	47.2	48.3
Poland	47.5	51.0	46.4	44.3	42.7	41.1	43.8	44.2	44.6
Russian Federation	34.0	30.4	35.8	32.0	26.1	33.7	34.6	37.1	35.7
United Kingdom	44.1	42.2	40.6	39.5	38.8	36.6	39.9	40.9	42.4
Euro Area	53.2	50.7	49.4	48.6	48.2	46.3	47.3	47.6	48.0
United States	37.1	36.6	35.4	34.6	32.2	33.9	35.0	35.9	36.3
Canada	48.5	46.6	44.3	44.8	42.7	41.1	42.0	41.2	41.2

	2004	2005	2006	2007	2008	2009	2010	2011
France	53.3	53.4	52.7	52.3	52.7	55.5	55.4	54.8
Germany	47.3	46.9	45.3	43.6	43.8	47.7	48.4	47.6
Italy	47.8	48.1	46.7	47.9	48.8	51.7	51.2	50.6
Poland	42.6	43.4	43.9	42.2	43.3	43.8	44.0	42.1
Russian Federation	33.6	31.5	31.2	33.0	33.9	40.6	NA	NA
United Kingdom	43.1	44.1	44.1	44.1	47.5	52.1	53.4	53.2
Euro Area	47.6	47.4	46.6	46.0	46.9	50.7	51.0	50.4
United States	36.0	36.2	36.0	36.8	38.8	41.5	41.5	40.9
Canada	39.9	39.3	39.4	39.1	39.7	43.6	43.5	42.9

Sources: Organisation for Economic Co-operation and Development, *OECD Economic Outlook* No. 86 (Paris: OECD, December 2009); *Russian Statistical Yearbook, 2009,* www.gks.ru, 2010; *Russia in Figures, 2009.*

Table A-6 General Government Total Tax and Nontax Receipts as Percentage of Nominal GDP, 1995–2011

	1995	1996	1997	1998	1999	2000	2001	2002	2003
France	48.9	50.4	50.8	50.1	50.8	50.1	50.0	49.4	49.1
Germany	45.1	46.0	45.7	45.9	46.7	46.4	44.7	44.4	44.4
Italy	45.1	45.5	47.6	46.2	46.5	45.3	44.9	44.4	44.7
Poland	43.3	46.1	41.8	40.1	40.4	38.1	38.6	39.2	38.4
Russian Federation	30.6	26.0	30.4	26.1	25.2	28.7	30.0	32.5	31.4
United Kingdom	38.2	38.0	38.4	39.4	39.8	40.3	40.6	39.0	38.7
Euro Area	45.6	46.4	46.7	46.2	46.7	46.2	45.4	45.0	44.9
United States	33.8	34.3	34.6	34.9	34.9	35.4	34.4	31.9	31.3
Canada	43.2	43.8	44.5	44.9	44.3	44.1	42.6	41.1	41.1

	2004	2005	2006	2007	2008	2009	2010	2011
France	49.6	50.5	50.3	49.6	49.3	47.3	46.7	46.8
Germany	43.5	43.6	43.7	43.8	43.8	44.5	43.1	42.9
Italy	44.2	43.8	45.3	46.4	46.0	46.2	45.8	45.5
Poland	36.9	39.4	40.2	40.3	39.6	37.4	36.2	35.3
Russian Federation	32.3	39.6	39.6	38.1	38.8	34.4	NA	NA
United Kingdom	39.6	40.8	41.4	41.4	42.2	39.5	40.1	40.7
Euro Area	44.6	44.8	45.3	45.4	44.9	44.6	44.2	44.2
United States	31.6	33.0	33.8	34.0	32.3	30.3	30.8	31.5
Canada	40.7	40.8	41.0	40.7	39.8	38.8	38.3	38.4

Sources: Organisation for Economic Co-operation and Development, *OECD Economic Outlook* No. 86 (Paris: OECD, December 2009); *Russian Statistical Yearbook, 2009,* www.gks.ru, 2010; *Russia in Figures, 2009.*

Table A-7 Trade Balances for Goods and Services, 1995–2011 (billions of U.S. dollars)

	1995	1996	1997	1998	1999	2000	2001	2002	2003
France	19.7	23.3	40.9	37.8	30.9	12.7	15.1	25.1	17.2
Germany	11.8	22.0	27.0	29.6	18.0	7.0	38.4	93.4	98.2
Italy	43.2	58.5	46.3	37.1	22.1	10.5	15.3	11.6	9.0
Poland	3.0	−2.2	−6.1	−8.3	−9.9	−11.0	−7.0	−6.9	−5.8
Russian Federation	19.8	19.8	14.6	14.8	34.9	60.1	48.1	46.3	59.9
United Kingdom	−1.4	1.0	7.3	−11.3	−21.9	−27.2	−34.6	−42.7	−42.7
Euro Area	108.1	132.2	148.8	130.4	92.3	42.3	91.1	173.8	172.7
United States	−90.7	−96.3	−101.4	−161.8	−262.1	−382.1	−371.0	−427.2	−504.1
Canada	18.9	24.7	12.6	12.3	24.2	41.6	41.2	32.4	32.5

	2004	2005	2006	2007	2008	2009	2010	2011
France	2.9	−17.9	−29.8	−49.5	−72.4	−45.1	−50.8	−53.3
Germany	137.9	147.0	167.4	237.9	228.7	119.9	136.8	161.5
Italy	11.4	−0.9	−15.0	−5.1	−11.8	−5.6	−3.1	−2.0
Poland	−5.9	−2.2	−6.2	−12.3	−21.5	−2.9	−4.9	−5.0
Russian Federation	87.1	118.5	139.2	132.0	179.7	112.1	NA	NA
United Kingdom	−59.5	−77.7	−76.7	−90.1	−70.3	−48.5	−37.1	−28.8
Euro Area	196.8	151.3	125.7	197.0	151.6	150.7	199.1	246.6
United States	−618.7	−722.7	−769.3	−713.8	−707.8	−378.6	−440.1	−495.9
Canada	42.7	42.5	32.2	27.3	25.3	−25.8	−34.6	−35.5

Sources: Organisation for Economic Co-operation and Development, *OECD Economic Outlook* No. 86 (Paris: OECD, December 2009); *Russian Statistical Yearbook, 2009,* www.gks.ru, 2010; *Russia in Figures, 2009.*

Table A-8 Infant Mortality Rates, 1990–2010 (per 1,000 live births)

Country	1990–1995	1995–2000	2005–2010
France	7	5	4
Germany	5	4	4
Italy	6	4	4
Poland	10	7	7
Russian Federation	21	17	12
Sweden	5	3	3
United Kingdom	8	6	5
United States	8	7	6

Source: United Nations, Department of Economic and Social Affairs, Population Division, *World Population Prospects: The 2008 Revision,* June 2009 update, UN data, http://data.un.org.

Table A-9 Life Expectancy at Birth, 2006

Country	Male	Female
France	77	84
Germany	77	82
Italy	78	84
Poland	71	80
Russian Federation	60	73
Sweden	79	83
United Kingdom	77	81
United States	78	80
Canada	78	83

Source: United Nations, Department of Economic and Social Affairs, Population Division, *World Population Prospects: The 2008 Revision,* June 2009 update, UN data, http://data.un.org.

Table A-10 Religious Affiliation and Nonaffiliation (percent)

Country	Catholic	Protestant	Greek/Russian Orthodox	Jewish	Muslim	Others	Unspecified	Unaffiliated
France	83.0–88.0	2.0		1.0	5.0–10.0			4.0
Germany	34.0	34.0			3.7			28.3
Italy	90.0					10.0		
Poland	89.9	0.3	1.3				8.3	
Russian Federation			15.0–20.0		10.0–15.0	2.0		
Sweden		87.0				13.0		
United Kingdom	9.6 in England and Wales; 14.0 in Scotland; and 43.8 in Northern Ireland	71.6 (including 53.1 in Northern Ireland)		1.0	3.0	2.6		10.0
United States	23.9	51.3		1.7	0.6	4.4		4.0
Canada	42.6	23.3			1.9	11.8		16.0

Sources: Central Intelligence Agency, *The World Factbook, 2010,* www.cia.gov; for the percentage of Catholics in England, Wales, and Scotland, Reuters, *Factbox: Catholicism in Britain,* September 2010, http://www.reuters.com/article/idUSTRE68C1R420100913; and for Catholics and Protestants in Northern Ireland, Cain Web Service, *Background Information in Northern Ireland Society–Population and Vital Statistics,* http://cain.ulst.ac.uk/ni/popul.htm.

Note: In Italy "Others" include Protestants, Jews, and Muslims; in Sweden "Others" include Roman Catholics, Orthodox, Baptists, Muslims, Jews, and Buddhists; and in the United Kingdom they include primarily Hindus.

Table A-11 European Parliamentary Elections, June 2009

Party group	Number of deputies
European People's Party (EPP)	265
Progressive Alliance of Socialists and Democrats (S&D)	184
Alliance of Liberals and Democrats for Europe (ALDE)	84
Group of Greens/European Free Alliance (EFA)	55
European Conservatives and Reformists Group (ECR)	54
Confederal Group of the European United Left-Nordic Green Group (GUE-NGL)	35
Europe of Freedom and Democracy Group (EFD)	32
Nonaligned	27

Source: http://europa.edu/institutions/inst/parliament/index_en.htm.

Table A-12 Four Largest National Contributors to the EU Budget, 2010 Budget

Country	Millions of Euros	Percentage of Total National Contributions
Germany	21,016	19.59
France	19,318	18.0
Italy	14,884	13.87
United Kingdom	11,173	10.41

Source: http://ec.europa.eu/budget/budget-detail/current-year-en.htm.

Table A-13 Percentage of EU Appropriations by Category, 2010 Budget

Expenditure Category	Billions of Euros	Percentage of Budgetary Allocation
Sustainable growth (including regional development)	64.3	45.4
Preservation and management of natural resources (includes Common Agricultural Policy)	59.5	42.0
Administration	7.9	5.5
EU as a global player	8.1	5.7
Citizenship, freedom, security, and justice	1.7	1.2
Total	141.5	100.0

Source: http://ec.europa.eu/budget/budget-detail/current-year-en.htm.

Figure A-1 Population 2008 (in millions)

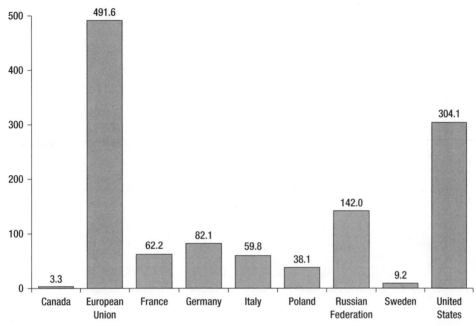

Sources: World Bank, *World Development Indicators* database, 2010, for individual countries; Central Intelligence Agency, *The World Factbook, 2010,* for the European Union.

Figure A-2 Population Density (per square kilometer)

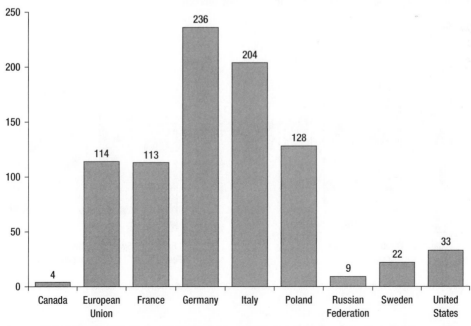

Sources: World Bank, *World Development Indicators* database, 2010, for individual countries; Central Intelligence Agency, *The World Factbook, 2010,* for the European Union.

Figure A-3 International Immigrants, 1990–2010 (average of estimated migrants at mid-year, in millions)

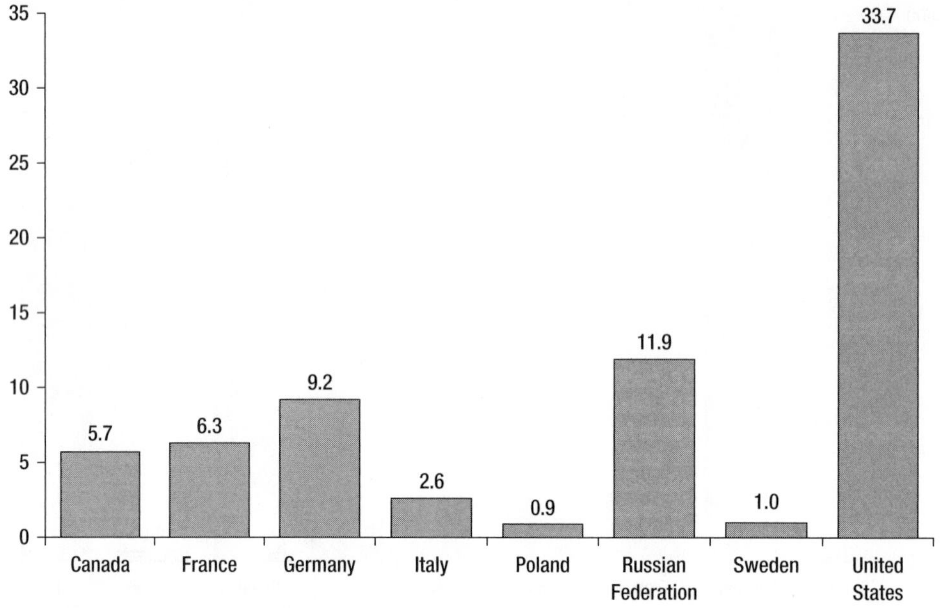

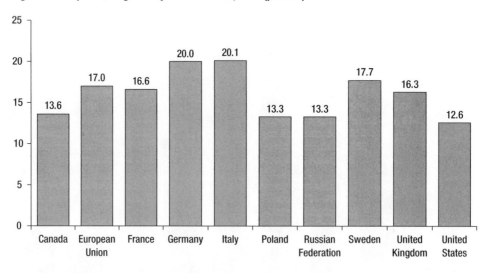

Source: United Nations, Population Division, *International Migrant Stock: The 2008 Revision*, http://esa.un.org/migration.

Note: Comparable European Union data are not available.

Figure A-4 Population Aged Sixty-five and Older, 2008 (percent)

Sources: World Bank, *World Development Indicators* database, 2010; European Commission, Eurostat database, 2010.

Figure A-5 Gross Domestic Product (GDP) per Capita, 2009 (current U.S. dollars)

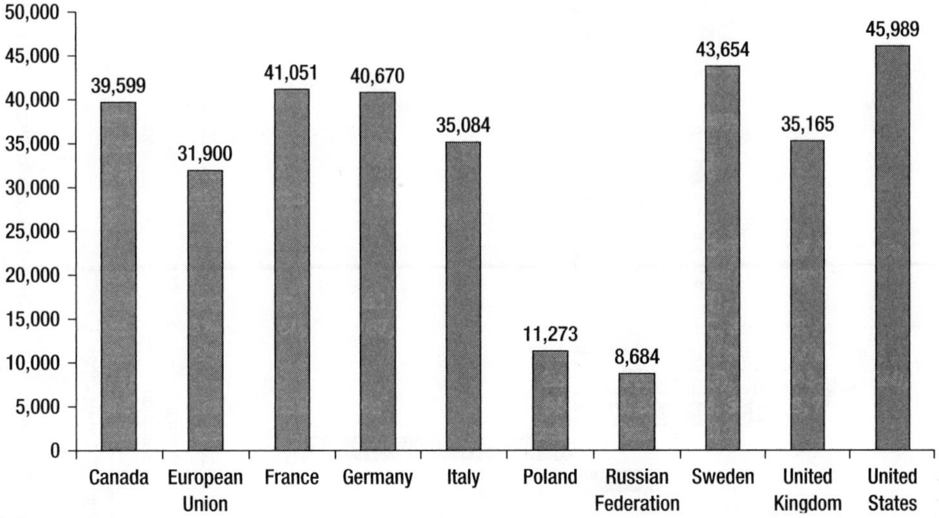

Sources: World Bank, *World Development Indicators* database, 2010; Central Intelligence Agency, *The World Factbook, 2010,* for the European Union (2009 estimate).

Figure A-6 Average Annual Growth Rate of GDP, 1981-2007 (percent)

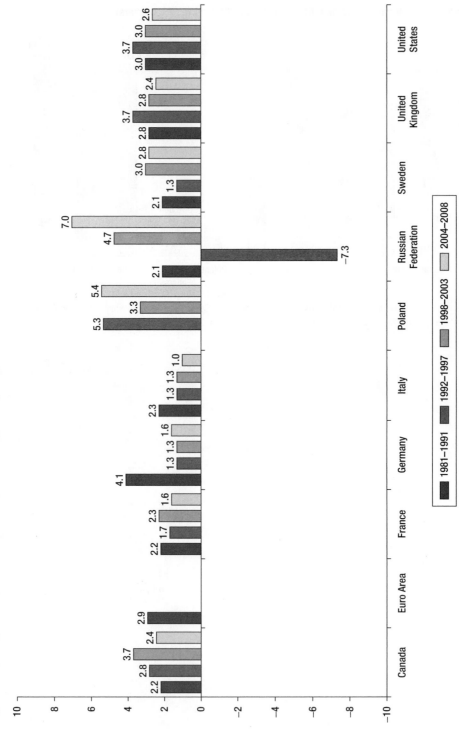

Sources: Organisation for Economic Co-operation and Development, *OECD Economic Outlook* No. 78 (Paris: OECD, December 2005), for 1981–1991 data for Western Europe; *Russian Statistical Yearbook, 2005* (Moscow: Federal State Statistics Service, 2005); *Russia in Figures, 2000* (Moscow: Information and Publishing Centre, "Statistics of Russia," 2000), for 1981–1991 data for the Russian Federation; World Bank, *World Development Indicators* database, 2010, for 1992–2008 data for all countries.

Figure A-7 Average Annual Inflation Rate, 1981–2008 (percent)

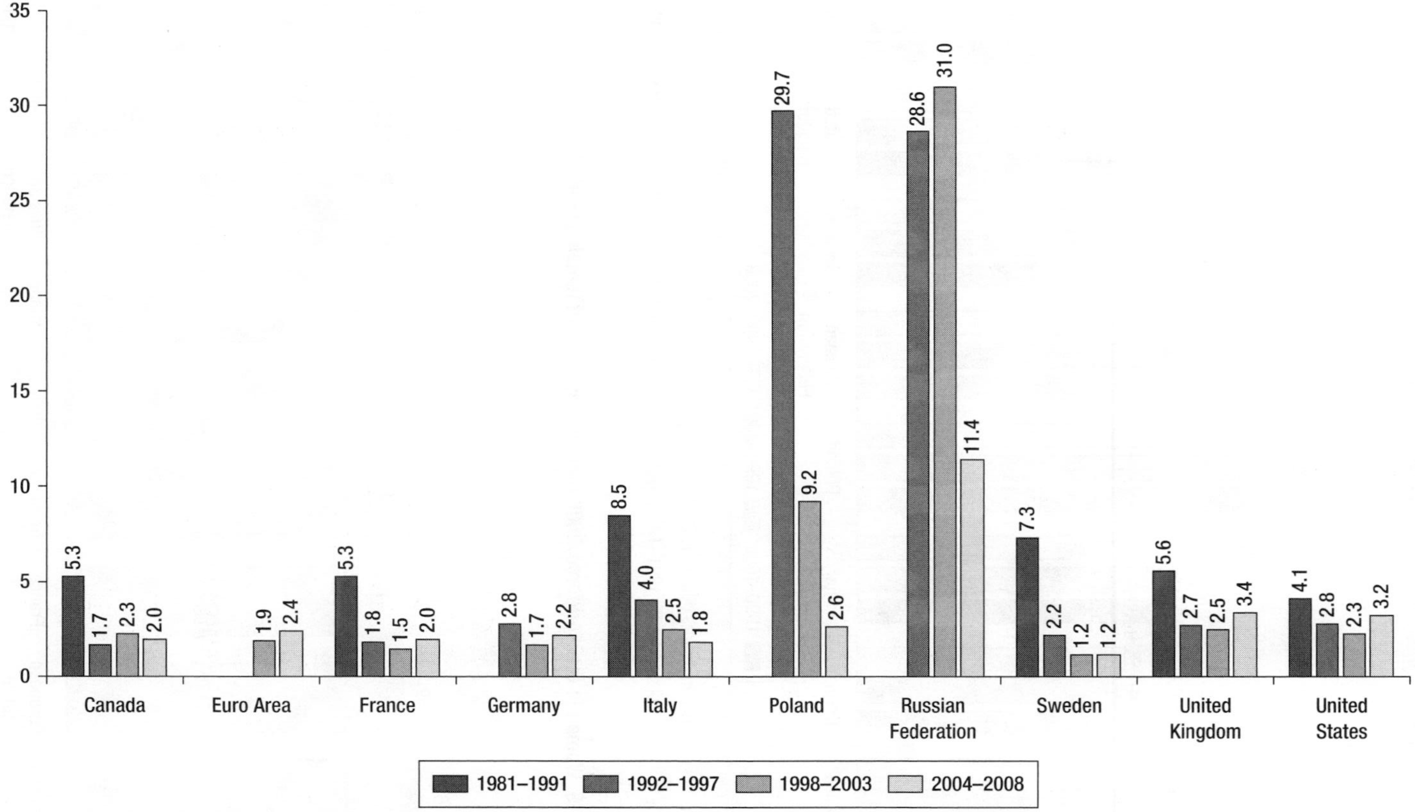

Legend: 1981–1991 | 1992–1997 | 1998–2003 | 2004–2008

Country	1981–1991	1992–1997	1998–2003	2004–2008
Canada	5.3	1.7	2.3	2.0
Euro Area			1.9	2.4
France	5.3	1.8	1.5	2.0
Germany	2.8	1.7	2.2	
Italy	8.5	4.0	2.5	1.8
Poland	29.7	9.2	2.6	
Russian Federation	28.6	31.0	11.4	
Sweden	7.3	2.2	1.2	1.2
United Kingdom	5.6	2.7	2.5	3.4
United States	4.1	2.8	2.3	3.2

Sources: Organisation for Economic Co-operation and Development, *OECD Economic Outlook* No. 78 (Paris: OECD, December 2005), for 1981–1991 data for Western Europe; *Russian Statistical Yearbook, 2005* (Moscow: Federal State Statistics Service, 2005); *Russia in Figures, 2000* (Moscow: Information and Publishing Centre, "Statistics of Russia," 2000), for 1981–1991 data for the Russian Federation; World Bank, *World Development Indicators* database, 2010, for 1992–2008 data for all countries.

Figure A-8 Average Annual Unemployment Rate, 1990–2008 (percent)

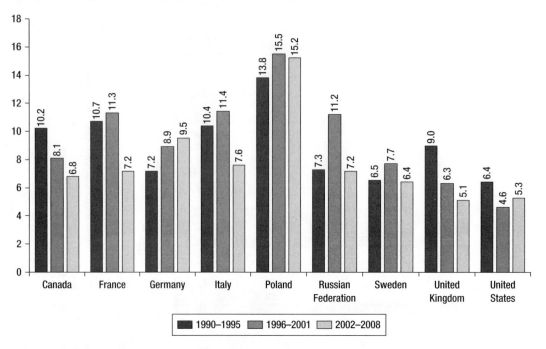

Sources: World Bank, *World Development Indicators* database, 2010.

Note: Averages for Germany in the first column are for 1991–1995; averages for Poland and Russia in the first column are for 1992–1995.

Figure A-9 Women in the Workforce, 2008 (percentage of adult female population)

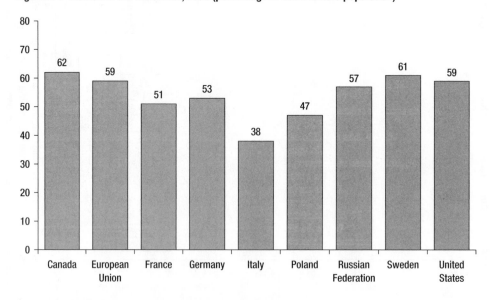

Sources: World Bank, *World Development Indicators* database, 2010.

Figure A-10 Average Annual Balance of Trade, 1993–2011 (billions of U.S. dollars)

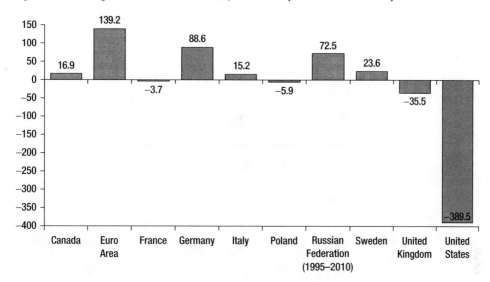

Sources: Organisation for Economic Co-operation and Development, *OECD Economic Outlook* No. 86 (Paris: OECD, December 2009); *Russian Statistical Yearbook, 2009* (gks.ru, 2010); *Russia in Figures, 2009.*

Figure A-11 Average Annual Export of Goods and Services as Percentage of GDP, 2005–2009

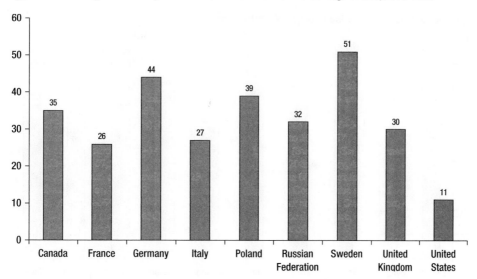

Sources: World Bank, *World Development Indicators* database, 2010.

Figure A-12 Imports of Goods and Services as Percentage of GDP, 2005–2009

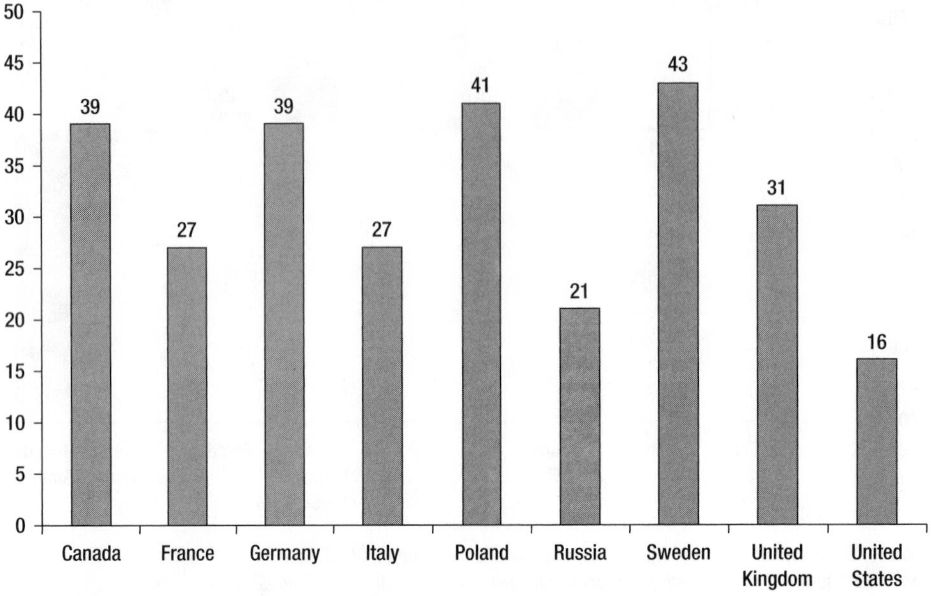

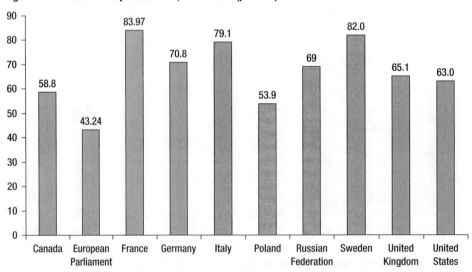

Source: The World Bank, *World Development Indicators* database, December 2010, http://data.worldbank.org/indicator/NE.IMP.GNFS.ZS.

Figure A-13 Voter Participation Rates, 2006–2010 (percent)

Sources: Percentages compiled on the basis of published election results and national statistical yearbooks.

Notes: All turnout figures are for parliamentary elections, 2006–2010, except for the United States, which is for the 2008 presidential election. Participation rates for France are for the second round of the 2007 parliamentary and presidential elections, respectively.

Figure A-14 Vote for Radical Left Parties in Most Recent National Election (percent)

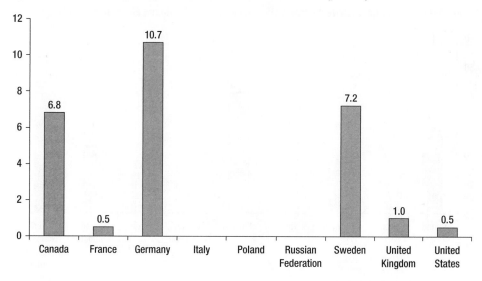

Sources: Percentages compiled on the basis of published election results and national statistical yearbooks.

Figure A-15 Vote for Green Parties in Most Recent National Election (percent)

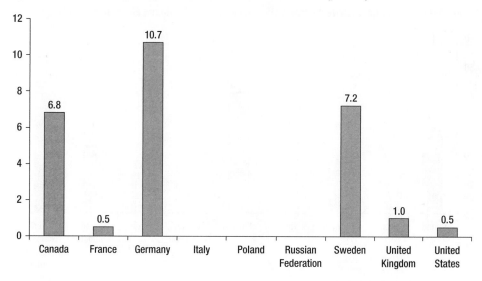

Sources: Percentages compiled on the basis of published election results and national statistical yearbooks.

Figure A-16 Vote for Social Democratic/Labor Parties in Most Recent Legislative Election (percent)

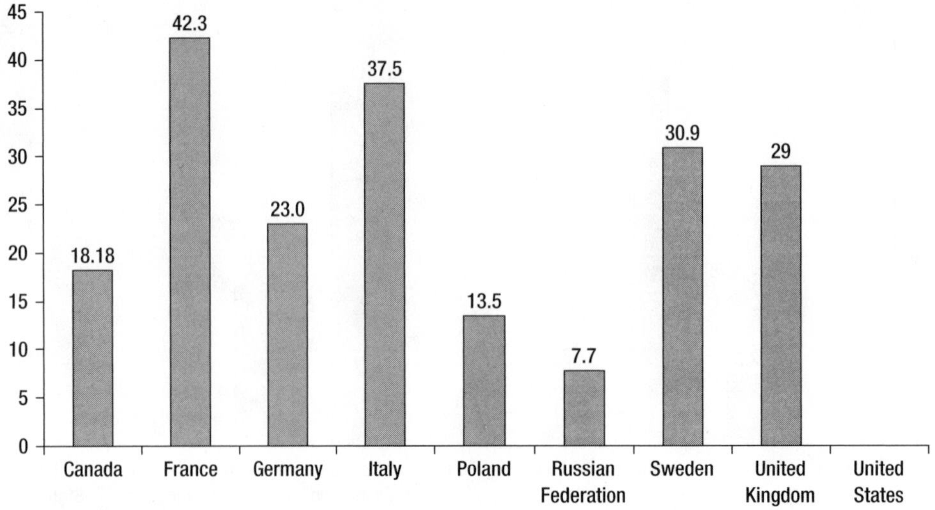

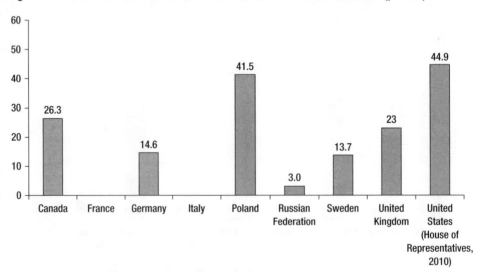

Sources: Percentages compiled on the basis of published election results and national statistical yearbooks.

Note: No Social Democratic (moderate left-center) parties competed in the Russian election.

Figure A-17 Vote for Centrist/Neoliberal Parties in Most Recent National Election (percent)

Sources: Percentages compiled on the basis of published election results and national statistical yearbooks.

Figure A-18 Vote for Conservative Parties/Coalitions in Most Recent National Election (percent)

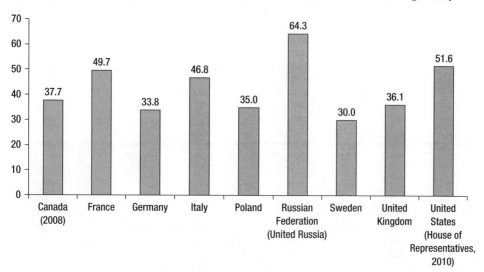

Sources: Percentages compiled on the basis of published election results and national statistical yearbooks.

Note: "Conservative parties" refer to center-right parties (not extremists).

Figure A-19 Vote for Radical Right/Anti-Immigration Parties

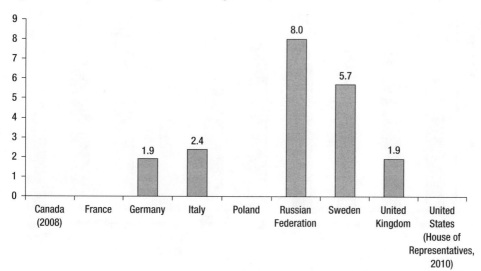

Sources: Percentages compiled on the basis of published election results and national statistical yearbooks.

Figure A-20 Number of Post–World War II/Postcommunist Governments

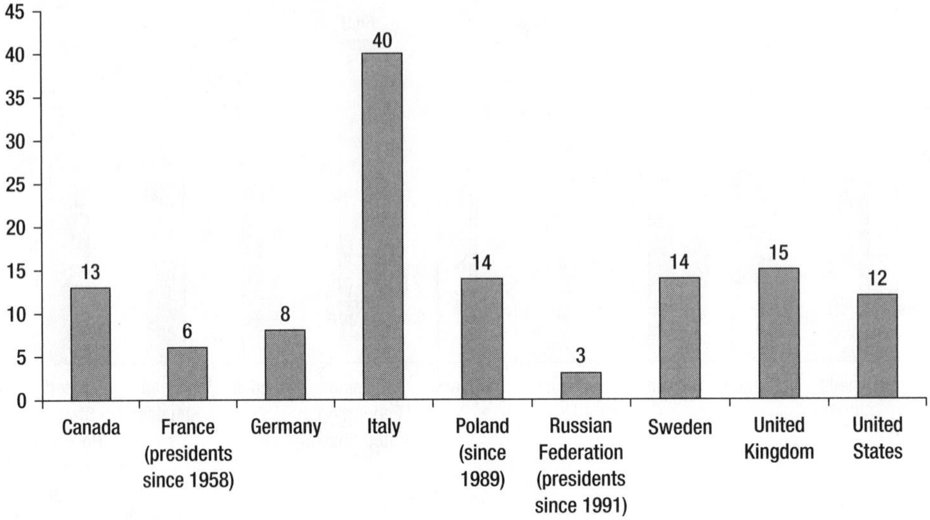

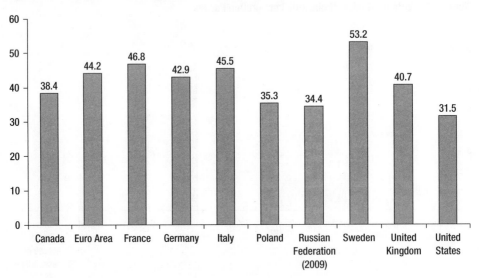

Sources: Percentages compiled on the basis of published election results and national statistical yearbooks.

Figure A-21 Comparative Tax Payments as a Percentage of GDP, 2011

Sources: Organisation for Economic Co-operation and Development, *OECD Economic Outlook* No. 86 (Paris: OECD, December 2009); *Russian Statistical Yearbook, 2009* (www.gks.ru, 2010); *Russia in Figures, 2009.*

Figure A-22 Total Government Expenditures as a Percentage of Nominal GDP, 1992–2011

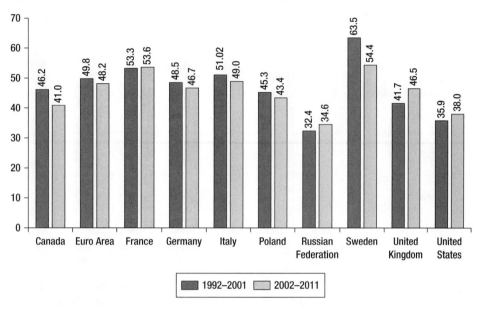

Sources: Organisation for Economic Co-operation and Development, *OECD Economic Outlook* No. 86 (Paris: OECD, December 2009); *Russian Statistical Yearbook, 2009* (www.gks.ru, 2010), *Russia in Figures, 2009.*

Note: Data for Poland in the first column are for the years 1995–2009. Data for Russia are for 1995–2001 in the first column and 2002–2009 in the second column.

Figure A-23 Defense Expenditures as a Percentage of GDP, 2007

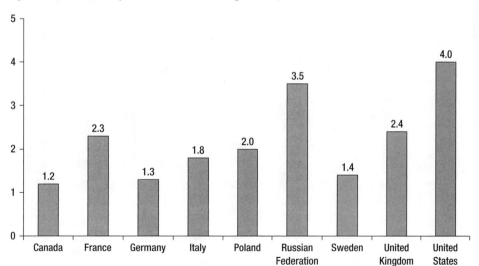

Sources: SIPRI (Stockholm International Peace Research Institute) 2009 database, www.sipri.org/databases/milex.

Figure A-24 Gini Inequality Index

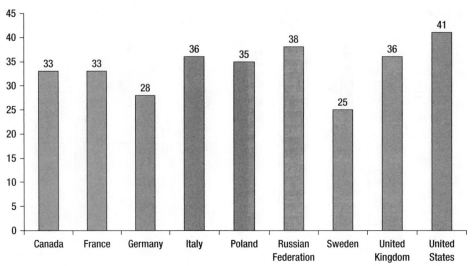

Sources: World Bank, *World Development Indicators* database, 2010. Country data range from 1995 for France; 1999 for the United Kingdom; 2000 for Germany, Italy, Sweden, the United States, and Canada; to 2005 for Poland and Russia.

Note: The Gini inequality index is a measure of the extent to which income distribution departs from perfect equality. The lower the number, the more equal is the distribution. The Gini coefficient is a measure of statistical dispersion developed by the Italian statistician Corrado Gini and published in his 1912 paper "Variability and Mutability" (*Variabilità e mutabilità*).

Figure A-25 Health Expenditures as Percentage of GDP (2006)

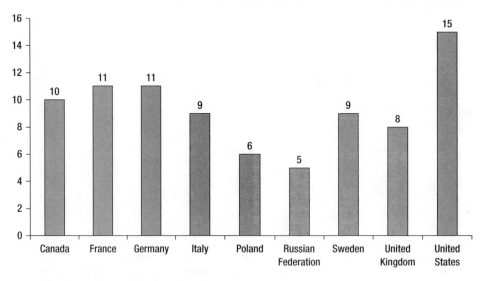

Sources: World Bank, *World Development Indicators* database, 2010.

Figure A-26 Internet Users per One Hundred People, 1995–2007

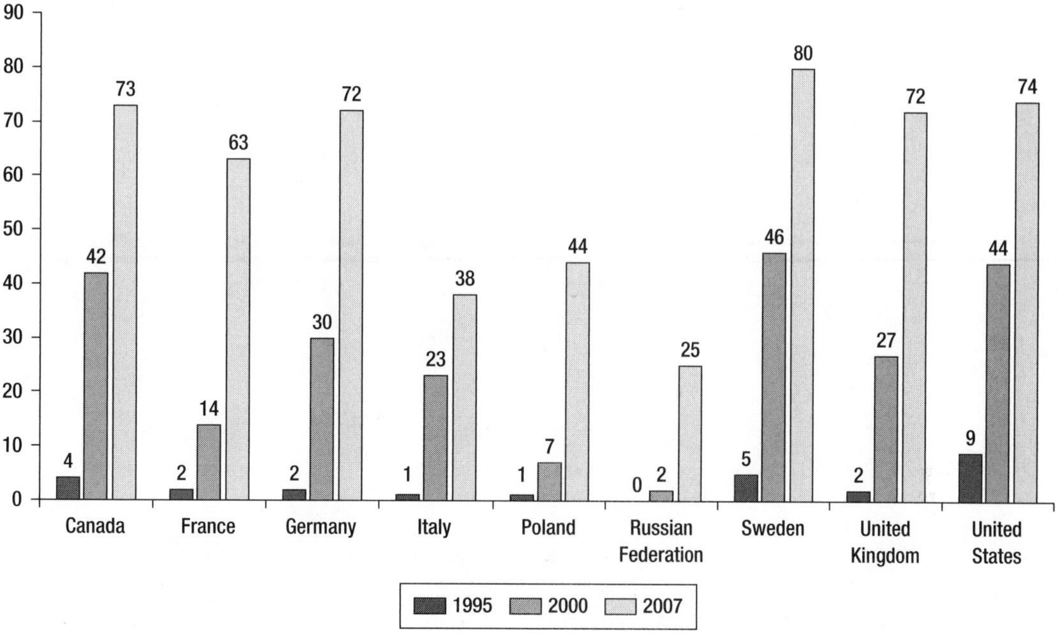

Sources: World Bank, *World Development Indicators* database, 2010.

Index

Figures and tables are indicated with f and t following the page number.